3RD EDITION

The Economics of Developing Countries

E. WAYNE NAFZIGER
Kansas State University

Prentice Hall, Upper Saddle River, NJ 07458

To Dad (in memoriam), Mother, Elfrieda, Brian, and Kevin

Executive Editor: Leah Jewell
Associate Editor: Gladys Soto
Editorial Assistant: Kristen Kaiser
Editor-in-Chief: James Boyd
Marketing Manager: Susan McLaughlin
Production Editor: Maureen Wilson
Production Coordinator: David Cotugno
Managing Editor: Carol Burgett
Manufacturing Buyer: Kenneth J. Clinton
Manufacturing Supervisor: Arnold Vila
Manufacturing Manager: Vincent Scelta
Design Director: Patricia Wosczyk
Composition: Impressions Book and Journal Services, Inc.
Cover Art: SuperStock, Inc.

The author and publisher kindly acknowledge permission to reprint from the East-West Center for table from E. Wayne Nafziger, *Class, Caste, and Entrepreneurship,* University Press of Hawaii. Copyright © 1978.

Library of Congress Cataloging-in-Publication Data

Nafziger, E. Wayne.
    The economics of developing countries / E. Wayne Nafziger. — 3rd ed.
      p. cm.
    Includes index.
    ISBN 0-13-339995-8
    1. Developing countries—Economic conditions. 2. Income distribution—Developing countries. 3. Economic development.
    I. Title.
HC59.7.N23 1997
330.9172'4—dc20
                                          96-22745
                                             CIP

Prentice-Hall International (UK) Limited, London
Prentice-Hall of Australia Pty. Limited, Sydney
Prentice-Hall Canada, Inc., Toronto
Prentice-Hall Hispanoamericana, S.A., Mexico
Prentice-Hall of India Private Limited, New Delhi
Prentice-Hall of Japan, Inc., Tokyo
Simon & Schuster Asia Pte. Ltd., Singapore
Editora Prentice-Hall do Brasil, Ltda., Rio de Janeiro

Printed in the United States of America

10 9 8 7 6 5 4 3 2 1

Contents

Preface

The growth in real income per person in the third-world nations of Latin America, Asia, and Africa, about twofold since 1950, is a mixed record. On the one hand, the growth warrants optimism, particularly in Taiwan, South Korea, Singapore, Malaysia, Thailand, Indonesia, China, other fast-growing Pacific Rim countries, and Brazil. The tragedy however is that sub-Saharan Africa, encountering growing misery and degradation from 1965 to 1996, has not shared in these gains. The sub-Sahara is not only vulnerable to external price shocks and debt crises that destabilized the global economy in the 1970s, 1980s, and 1990s, but also plagued by increasing food deficits, growing rural poverty, urban congestion, and falling real wages, difficulties that represent an inadequate response to adjustment, reform, and liberalization, often imposed by the International Monetary Fund (IMF) or World Bank as a last resort. The problems of Bangladesh, Nepal, Afghanistan, Myanmar (Burma), Cambodia, and Haiti are as severe as Africa's.

This edition expands on a previous emphasis, an analysis of China and other countries that were socialist during most of the post-World War II period. The major upheaval in the field since early 1989 has been the collapse of state socialism in Eastern Europe and the former Soviet Union and economists' downward revisions of estimates of their average economic welfare. Since the late 1980s and early 1990s, post-socialist European countries, like other developing countries, have undertaken structural adjustment and market reforms, generally under IMF or World Bank auspices. Yet, with rare exceptions, these liberalizing post-socialist economies have still not attained their pre-1989 peak in economic welfare. This edition reflects this reality by increasing examples from such countries as Russia, Poland, Hungary, and other transitional economies in a textbook concentrating on middle-income and low-income countries.

Yet I have not allowed the problems of Eastern Europe and the former Soviet Union, important as they are, to overshadow the primary emphasis of the book on Asia, Africa, and Latin America. The major focus is on their real world problems—from those of newly industrializing countries, such as Taiwan and South Korea, to those of the slow-growing sub-Sahara—rather than abstract growth models. The response by reviewers, instructors, students, and practitioners in the United States, Canada, Europe, Japan, Australia, New Zealand, and the developing world to this stress in the book's second edition is gratifying. This revision continues previous themes, such as the origins of modern growth, problems measuring growth, and the origin and resolution of the debt crisis, and integrates social, political, and economic issues, and emphasizes poverty, inequality, and unemployment in the discussion of economic policies and planning discussed throughout the book.

In the face of the increased difficulties that post-socialist and other developing countries have had attaining both internal (growth and price stability) and external balances, I have put more emphasis on adjustment and stabilization programs throughout the book. A new chapter, Chapter 20, includes a discussion of whether adjustment, stabilization, and reform programs, including decontrol of prices, devaluation, curtailed government budget deficits, and privatization, can reduce the international goods, services, and income deficit while accelerating economic growth, decreasing unemployment, and attaining price stability.

The edition's other major changes reflect recent literature or readers' suggestions. I have revised the box in Chapter 2 with a more recent example that reflects the World Bank's present procedure of applying the developing country's GNP price deflator to GNP in local currency. In the same chapter, I add new United Nations indicators, the human development index (HDI), and gender-related development index (GDI) to the less used physical quality of life index (PQLI); include a section on the use of early or late weights in price indexes; and reorganize and clarify the discussion of purchasing-power adjustment. In Chapter 3, I add sections on: the Korean-Taiwanese development model; the effect of productivity growth in the last 150 years on living standards in the United States, Canada, and other developed countries; and the convergence controversy.

My revision of Chapter 5's discussion of development theory exemplifies the current emphasis on neoclassical theories of development and growth. I also include a synopsis of the new (endogenous) growth theory, which criticizes the neoclassical approach; subsequent chapters also examine neoclassical economics. Moreover, I have moved the model of W. Arthur Lewis from the chapter on employment to Chapter 5's survey of theory, and have added the related Fei-Ranis model. Other models in the chapter include the heterodox models of Karl Marx, Paul Baran, and dependency theorists (Celso Furtado and Andre Gunder Frank); and the institutionalist models of Walter W. Rostow, vicious circle theory, and balanced and unbalanced growth. The appendix to Chapter 5 analyzes the Harrod-Domar growth model.

Chapters 6 and 7 expand the emphasis on malnutrition, interlinked with poverty. Chapter 6 updates figures on poverty and income distribution, while purging some sources in light of evidence by Terrence Moll, "Mickey Mouse Numbers and Inequality Research in Developing Countries," of the substantial unreliable statistics of the World Bank and United Nations on income distribution. The chapter incorporates the recent literature on concepts and measures of poverty, while adding discussions of Amartya Sen's concepts of head-count and income-gap approaches and the measurement capabilities, the elasticity of the poverty gap with regard to the Gini index, measures of global economic disparities, new country comparative studies of income distribution, income inequality between men and women within a household, the cumulative distribution function, workfare, targeting aid, the inclusion of social safety nets in economic adjustment programs, and group lending, such as the Grameen Bank, as a vehicle for providing credit for the poor. Chapter 7, on rural poverty and agricultural transformation, has new sections on the growth in food demand, the decline of fish harvesting, and a table on rural poverty in less-developed countries (LDCs).

I have revised and changed the order of Chapters 8–13 on factors of growth. The initial chapter in this section, Chapter 8, is on population and development. This placement will accommodate the instructors who integrate the discussion of population with basic concepts of economic development and income distributions. Chapter 8's analysis of population confronts the evidence that global foodgrain production per person began declining in the late 1980s, asking whether this is transitory or whether this means, as neo-Malthusians believe, the reaching of a limit in the earth's carrying capacity. The chapter also adds discussion of the concept of negative externalities in childbearing and China's "one couple, one child" policy. Chapter 9, the chapter on employment, introduces the production function. This chapter also examines the removal of capital cost distortions in adjustment programs and the effect of stabilization and adjustment on wages. In Chapter 10, the analysis of economic returns to education relies on recent empirical work on marginal rates of return to education that changes substantially conclusions about the relative rates of return to different levels of education. In addition, Chapter 10 discusses the effect of AIDS on LDC productivity and growth and an example of how to reduce the isolation and low productivity of LDC scientists. The new chapter, 13, on natural resources, the environment, and sustainable development, combines material on natural resources similar to that in the previous edition with new analyses of the impact of poverty on the environment, the market imperfections that contribute to environmental degradation, pollution and economic growth, the decision-making rule for abating pollution, how to place a monetary value on pollution discharges, the economics of biological diversity, the economics of "global warming," policy issues related to green taxes, the adjustment of economic welfare for resource depletion and environmental damage, and altering investment criteria for the effect of environmental degradation on future generations.

Chapter 15 on "Monetary, Fiscal, and Incomes Policy, and Inflation" places more emphasis on stabilization, especially incomes policy, during high inflation, as in some Latin America countries in the 1980s or 1990s, and Russia and Eastern European countries in the 1990s. The analysis of inflation adds sections on monetary inflation, incomes policies and external stabilization, and the dynamics of high inflation, and includes the value-added tax in the section on the goals of tax policy. The chapter also has a discussion of the differential effect of financial liberalization on individual firms. In addition, in the section on Islamic banking, the chapter includes a synopsis of Timur Kuran's careful analysis of economic Islamization.

Chapter 17 on the LDC external debt crisis is reorganized to focus on the origins of the debt problem before discussing the effects of the crisis. This chapter also expands the section on proposals to resolve the debt crisis and includes a discussion of the International Monetary Fund, World Bank, rich-country governments, and commercial banks as a policy cartel. Chapter 18, on international trade, separates the analysis of shifts in the terms of trade from arguments for tariffs. The chapter includes a discussion of the Uruguay Round negotiations for the General Agreements on Tariffs and Trade/World Trade Organization, the Asian and North American borderless economies, the North American Free Trade Agreement (NAFTA), arguments by rich countries in favor of protecting goods that embody cheap labor or use polluting processes, intellectual property rights, the trade of services, protection in agriculture, illegal transactions and black markets, the liberal concept of the international economic order, and the impossible trinity of exchange-rate stability, free capital movement, and monetary autonomy.

This edition includes the perspectives of Ronald Coase and Oliver Williamson that the choice between organization within the firms or by the market depends on the transactions costs of using the price system. The transactions-cost approach applies to the discussion in Chapter 12 of LDC entrepreneurs as gap-fillers, who make up for market deficiencies. Coase's theorem about property rights affects the debate about policies to reduce negative externalities associated with the environment, discussed in Chapter 13. But perhaps most importantly, Coase and Williamson's views of the costs of the plan and market as separate ways of coordinating transactions influence the changing emphases on development planning, discussed in Chapter 19.

Chapter 20, the concluding chapter, reflects the emphasis of international agencies since 1980 on stabilization, adjustment, and reform relative to development. This chapter adds an assessment and critique of World Bank and International Monetary Fund adjustment programs in LDCs, an analysis of the goals of internal and external balances, and the sequence of trade, exchange-rate, and capital market reforms, as well as an analysis of the collapse of state socialism and problems with economic reform in Russia, the transition from socialism to the market in Poland, and the transition to the socialist market economy in China. These sections are integrated with revised material previously included in the last chapter of the second edition, that on public enterprises and their performance, privatization, and the problems of the Chinese industrial reforms. The concluding section of the chapter asks what lessons LDCs can learn from Russian, Polish, and Chinese transitions to the market.

This text incorporates substantial new material to reflect the rapidly changing field of development economics. Furthermore, I have updated tables, figures, and chapter-end questions to discuss and guides to readings.

I am indebted to numerous colleagues and students in the developed and developing world for helping shape my ideas about development economics. I especially benefited from the comments and criticisms of Professors John Adams, Edgar S. Bagley, Maurice Ballabon, Thomas W. Bonsor, Antonio Bos, Martin Bronfenbrenner, Robert L. Curry, Jr., Wayne Davis, Lloyd J. Dumas, David Edmonds, Patrick J. Gormely, Roy Grohs, Margaret Grosh, Nancy Hammerle, Ichirou Inukai, Philip G. King, Paul Koch, Bertram Levin, Elliott Parker, Harvey Paul, James Ragan, James Rhodes, Alan Richards, Gordon Smith, Howard Stein, Shanti Tangri, Roger Trenary, Rodney Wilson and Mahmood Yousefi. L. Naiken from the Food and Agriculture Organization of the United Nations was kind enough to compile Table 7-1 for the book. Leah Jewell, Kristen Kaiser, and others at Prentice Hall contributed their professionalism to the book. Elfrieda, Brian, and Kevin Nafziger not only assisted in the project, but tolerated inconveniences and assumed responsibilities to leave me more time for writing. Although I am grateful to all who helped, I am solely responsible for any errors.

I am also grateful to the following for permission to reproduce copyrighted materials: the American Economic Association for graph from Paul M. Romer, "The Origins of Endogenous Growth," *Journal of Economic Perspectives* 5 (Winter 1994); Basil Blackwell Ltd. for table from David Morawetz, "Employment Implications of Industry in Developing Countries," *Economic Journal* 84 (September 1974); the International Food Policy Research Institute for table from Leonardo A. Paulino, *Food in the Third World: Past Trends and Projections to 2000*, Research Report 52, Washington, D.C., June 1986; Prentice Hall for quotation from Rudiger Dornbusch, *Stabilization, Debt, and Reform: Policy Analysis for Developing Countries*; Redefining Progress for tabular material from Clifford Cobb and Ted Halstead, *The Genuine Progress Indicator: Summary of Data and Methodology*; Joginder S. Uppal for table from *Economic Development in South Asia*, St. Martin's Press; the Population Council for figure from Tim Dyson, "Population Growth and Food Production: Recent Global and Regional Trends," *Population Development Review* 20 (June 1994); the *Economic Record* for table from M.L. Parker, "An Interindustry Approach to Planning in Papua New Guinea," September 1974; Routledge for material from Maurice Dobb, *Capitalist Enterprise and Social Progress*; the United Nations Development Programme for tables, figures, and other materials from the 1992, 1993 and 1994 Human Development Reports (New York: Oxford University Press); the United Nations for table from *National Accounts Statistics: Main Aggregates and Detailed Tables, 1992* (New York, 1992); the United Nations for ECA for quotes from "ECA and Africa's Development, 1983–2008," Addis Ababa, 1983, and *African Alternative Framework to Structural Adjustment Programmes for Socio-Economic Recovery and Transformation (AAF-SAP)*, Addis Ababa, April 10, 1989; the United Nations for the Department of Economic and Social Information and Policy Analysis for table from *World Urbanization Prospects: The 1992 Revisions—Estimates and Projections of Urban and Rural Population and of Urban Agglomerations*; the United Nations for Inter-Agency Task Force, for a quote from *Khartoum Conference on Human Dimensions of Africa's Economic Recovery and Development* (Khartoum, March 1988); the United Nations for UNCTAD for a table from *World Investment Report, 1994: Transnational Corporations, Employment and the Workplace*; Population Reference Bureau, Inc. for graphs from Thomas W. Merrick, "World Population in Transition," *Population Bulletin*, Vol. 41, No. 2 (April 1986); Arthur Haupt and Thomas T. Kane, *Population Handbook: International Edition* (Washington, D.C.: Population Reference Bureau, 1991); and Madgda McHale and John McHale, "World of Children," *Population Bulletin*, Vol. 33, No. 6 (January 1979).

I acknowledge material from a table and box on official development assistance from OECD DAC countries in 1993. © OECD, 1995, *Development Cooperation 1994 Report—Efforts and Policies of the Members of Development Assistance Committee*. Reproduced by permission of the OECD. I am grateful to Cambridge University Press for a table from Celso Furtado, *Economic Development in Latin America*. Reprinted with the permission of Cambridge University Press. I am also grateful to Johns Hopkins Press for figure from E. Wayne Nafziger, *The Debt Crisis in Africa*. Copyright © 1993. Reprinted by permission of the Johns Hopkins University Press. The material on the functions of the entrepreneur is reprinted with permission of the publisher from Chapter 1 of *Entrepreneurship and Economic Development*, Peter Kilby, Editor. Copyright © 1971 by The Free Press, an imprint of Simon & Schuster. I have made every effort to trace copyright owners, but in a few cases this was impossible. I apologize to any author or publisher on whose rights I may have unwittingly infringed. Finally, Figure 7-2 was reprinted from *Who Will Feed China?* by Lester R. Brown with permission of Worldwatch Institute, Washington D.C., copyright 1995.

PART I: PRINCIPLES AND CONCEPTS OF DEVELOPMENT

CHAPTER 1 Introduction

Nature and Scope of the Text

This book is an introduction to the economics of less developed countries of Asia, Africa, Latin America, and Eastern Europe. It is suitable for students who have taken principles of economics.

The book differs from many other development textbooks:

1. Unlike most texts, it discusses why modern economic growth originated in the West; gives reasons for Japanese growth; and explains different growth rates among developing countries, including the success of the newly industrialized countries—especially South Korea and Taiwan.

2. The book illustrates concepts from all major third-world regions (Latin America, Asia, Africa, and Eastern Europe), with an emphasis on sub-Saharan Africa's food and economic crisis.

3. I provide a more detailed and balanced discussion of economic adjustment (structural or sectoral adjustment, macroeconomic stabilization, or economic reform) in developing countries, including former socialist economies, such as China, Russia, Ukraine, Poland, the Czech Republic, and Hungary, making the transition to a market economy. The text also analyzes the roles of rich nations, the International Monetary Fund (IMF), and the World Bank in supplying external resources and setting domestic and international economic conditions for adjustment. Moreover, the book examines the lessons learned during the reaction against reforms imposed by the IMF and other external lenders on Africa and Latin American in the 1980s and 1990s, and on such countries as Russia, Ukraine, Poland, and Hungary in the 1990s. Although the material is scattered throughout the book, I present a comprehensive treatment of adjustment programs in Chapter 20.

4. The case studies I discuss—Russia-Soviet Union, Japan, South Korea, Taiwan, China, the Philippines, Thailand, Indonesia, Malaysia, Bangladesh, India, Nigeria, Zaïre, South Africa, Argentina, Brazil, and Mexico—are not isolated at the ends of chapters, but are integrated into the discussion of major concepts in the chapters.

5. Instead of stressing abstract models of aggregate economic growth, the text emphasizes poverty, inequality, unemployment, and deficiencies in food, clothing, housing, education, and health of people in less developed countries.

6. Rather than being isolated in a separate chapter, employment and income distribution are discussed along with development throughout the book.

7. Problems of measuring economic growth are stressed along with adjusting income for purchasing power.

8. Social and political factors are discussed throughout instead of limited to one or two chapters.

9. Economic performance is explained in the context of both domestic and global economies, and international interdependence is stressed. Three chapters are devoted to the balance of payments, aid, foreign investment, technical transfer, the external debt crisis, international trade, exchange-rate policies, and regional economic integration. We discuss a subject little noted by other economists—how the Asian, European, North American, and Asian-Pacific borderless economies, a phenomena since the mid-1980s, have increased international competition and reduced production costs.

10. The text analyzes views opposed to prevailing Western economic thought. Two of these views are the dependency theory, which explains the underdevelopment of the third world in terms of the economic and political domination of the industrialized world; and Neo-Marxism, which sees international class conflict as a struggle by workers and peasants in the developing world against their own political elite, who are in alliance with the elite of the developed world. Only by carefully considering these perspectives can a reader understand third-world economic ideologies and political discontent. Indeed, most Neo-Marxists put more emphasis on criticizing the prevailing system, especially capitalism, than on prescribing socialism. I try to present a balanced view of Neo-Marxism and the dependence theory—neither attributing these views to a "devil theory of history" nor using them to explain the distributional effects of international trade as unequivocally unfavorable to developing countries.

11. The discussion on planning and the market is integrated with other chapters, emphasizing that antipoverty programs, family planning, agricultural research and extension, employment policies, education, local technology, savings, investment project analysis, monetary and fiscal policies, entrepreneurial development programs, and international trade and capital flows are included in planning. I analyze the *dirigiste* debate (largely on the role of government) and discuss the liberalizing process in the new chapter on adjustment programs.

Organization of the Text

The book is organized into six parts. The first five chapters focus on principles and concepts of economic development. Chapters 6–7 examine income distribution, including a discussion of the distribution between urban and rural areas and the process of agricultural transformation. Chapters 8–13 analyze the role of population, production factors, and technology in economic development, with special emphasis in Chapter 13 on the environment and natural resources. Chapters 14 and 15 discuss policies to mobilize domestic resources, while Chapters 16–18 include the international economics of development. Chapter 19 looks at planning for economic development, and Chapter 20 analyzes stabilization, adjustment, reform, and privatization.

Sections presenting terms to review, questions to discuss, and guides to readings can be found at the end of each chapter. Highlighted terms are defined or identified on pages designated in boldface in the Subject Index. While the guides to readings provide bibliographical help for each chapter's topic, the Name and Author Index indicates in boldface the page on which each bibliographical item is first cited in full.

How the Other Two-Thirds Live

Development economics focuses primarily on the poorest two-thirds of the world's population. These poor are the vast majority, but not all, of the population of developing countries. Many of them are inadequately fed and housed, in poor health, and illiterate. A careful estimate of international protein and calorie distribution indicates that about 1.4 billion of the world's 5.8 billion people are undernourished.[1] Most Americans and Canadians have never seen poverty like that in most of Africa, Asia, and Latin America.

If you have an average income in the United States and Canada, you are among the richest 10 percent of the world's population. The economic concerns of this 10 percent are in stark contrast to those of the majority of people on this planet. The majority see the American with average income as incredibly rich, perhaps as an average American views the Mellons or Rockefellers. Income inequality is even greater for the world as a whole than for countries having high income concentration, such as South Africa and Honduras. To see these contrasts more clearly, let us briefly compare living conditions in one low-income country to those in the United States and Canada.

An average intact family in the United States and Canada, the Smiths, a family of four, has an annual income of $40,000 to $45,000. They live in a comfortable apartment or suburban home with three bedrooms, a living room, kitchen, and numerous electrical appliances and consumer goods. Their three meals a day include coffee from Brazil, tinned fruit from the Philippines, and bananas from Ecuador.

The Smith children are in good health and have an average life expectancy of 76 years. Both parents received a secondary education, and the children can be expected to finish high school and possibly go to a university. Their jobs, even where these require physical work, will probably be relieved by modern machinery and technology. But though the Smiths seem to have a reasonably good life, they may experience stress, frustration, boredom, insecurity, and a lack of meaning and control over their lives. Their air may be dirty, water polluted, and roads congested. Some of these problems may even result from economic progress. Nevertheless millions of less fortunate people throughout the world would be happy with even a portion of the Smiths' material affluence.

The family of Balayya, a farm laborer in India, has a life far different from the Smiths'. Though work, family structure, food, housing, clothing, and recreational patterns vary widely in the developing world, Balayya's family illustrates the relative poverty of a majority of the world's population. Balayya, his wife, Kamani, and their four children, ranging in age from 3 to 12 years, have a combined annual income of $600 to $800, most of which consists of goods produced rather than money earned. Under a complex division of labor, the family receives consumption shares from the patron (or landlord) in return for agricultural work—plowing, transplanting, threshing, stacking, and so on.

---

[1]This figure is based on World Bank, *World Development Report, 1992: Development and the Environment* (New York: Oxford University Press, 1992), p. 30; and other sources cited in Chapter 7.

The rice-based daily meal, the one-room mud house thatched with palm leaves, and the crudely stitched clothing are produced locally. The house has no electricity, clean water, or latrine. Kamani fetches the day's water supply from the village well, a kilometer (three-fifths of a mile) away. Although there is much illness, the nearest doctor, nurse, or midwife is 50 kilometers away, serving affluent city dwellers. Average life expectancy is 57 years. Few villagers can afford the bus that twice daily connects a neighboring village to the city, 40 kilometers away. The family's world is circumscribed by the distance a person can walk in a day.

Neither Balayya nor Kamani can read or write. One of their children attended school regularly for 3 years but dropped out before completing primary school. The child will probably not return to school.

Despite inadequate food, Balayya and the two sons over 7 years old toil hard under the blazing sun, aided by only a few simple tools. During the peak season of planting, transplanting, and harvesting, the work is from sunrise to sunset. Kamani, with help from a 6-year-old daughter, spends most of her long working day in the courtyard near the house. Games, visiting, gossip, storytelling, music, dancing, plays, worship, religious fairs and festivals, weddings, and funerals provide respite from the daily struggle for survival.

Balayya has no savings. Like his father before him, he will be perpetually in debt to the landlord for expenditures, not only for occasional emergencies, but also for the proper marriages of daughters in the family.

The common stereotype is that peasant, agricultural societies have populations with roughly uniform poverty, a generally false view. Although many third-world villagers are poor, a number are better off. A tiny middle and upper class even exists. Accordingly, Sridhar, Balayya's landlord, together with his extended family—his wife, two unmarried children, two married sons, their wives, and their children—is relatively prosperous. The family, whose annual income is $4,000, lives in a five- to six-room, brick house with a tile roof and a large courtyard. Their two daily meals consist of a variety of meats as well as seasonal fruits and vegetables.[2] Machine-stitched clothes are acquired from the local tailor, the village bazaar (open-air marketplace), or on monthly bus trips to the city. The house has electric lights and fans. Servants shop for food, cook, clean, carry water, and tend the lawn and garden. Sridhar and his sons and grandchildren have completed primary school. Some of the grandsons, and occasionally a granddaughter, will complete secondary school, or even graduate from the university.

In the large Indian cities, there are few proper footpaths for pedestrians or separation of fast moving vehicles from slower ones; the flow of traffic consists of the juxtaposition of buses, automobiles, trucks, jeeps, bicycles, human-drawn and motorized rickshaws, oxcarts, handcarts, cattle, dogs, and pedestrians walking or carrying head loads. Congestion, squalor, destitution, and insecurity characterize the lives of the unemployed, underemployed, and marginally employed in cities such as Calcutta, Bombay, and Delhi—more so than for the rural, landless worker. In the central city, people literally live in the street, where they eat, wash, defecate, and sleep on or near the pavement.[3] During the monsoon season, they huddle under the overhanging roofs of nearby commercial establishments. Others with menial jobs live in crowded, blighted huts and tenement houses that make up

---

[2]Some Indian castes prohibit eating meat for religious reasons.

[3]See N. Vijay Jagannathan and Animsesh Halder, "Income-Housing Linkages: A Case Study of Pavement Dwellers in Calcutta," *Economic and Political Weekly* 23 (June 4, 1988): 1175–78.

urban shantytowns. In contrast, the family whose major income earner is steadily employed as an assembly line worker in a large company or as a government clerk may live in a small house or apartment. Upper-income professionals, civil servants, and business people usually live in large houses of five to six rooms. Although they have fewer electrical appliances than the Smiths, they achieve some of the same material comfort by hiring servants.

Social institutions and lifestyles vary greatly among third-world countries. Nevertheless, most low-income countries have income inequality and poverty rates as high as India's. Even the poorest Americans and Canadians are better off than most of the people in India and other low-income countries.

Yet both Indians and North Americans are living in worlds affected by domestic economic change and greater integration into the global economy. Increasingly, families such as the Smiths are falling from the middle class from job loss or rising to higher incomes. In India, the gains from economic growth and reform, while bypassing some, mean rising commercial farm income for the families of Sridhar and Balayya and increased business and employment opportunities in the cities.

Critical Questions in Development Economics

An introduction to development economics should help you gain a better understanding of a number of critical questions relating to the economics of the developing world. The following list is a sample of 20 such questions. Each is numbered to correspond to the chapter where it is primarily discussed.

1. How do the poorest two-thirds of the world live?
2. What is the meaning of economic development and economic growth?
3. How have developing countries performed economically since World War II?
4. What are the major characteristics of developing countries?
5. What are the major theories of economic development?
6. Has economic growth in the third world improved the living conditions of its poor?
7. How can poverty be reduced in the rural areas of low-income countries?
8. What effect does population growth have on economic development and income equality?
9. Why is there so much unemployment in developing countries?
10. What factors affect labor skills in the third world?
11. What criteria should be used to allocate capital between alternative projects?
12. What factors contribute to successful entrepreneurial activity in developing countries?
13. Are humankind's economic policies sustainable over the next few centuries?
14. How can a country increase its rate of capital formation?
15. What monetary and fiscal policies should a country use to achieve economic development with price stability?
16. How can less-developed countries (LDCs) export more and import less?
17. What policies can ease the debt crisis in many developing countries?
18. What trade strategies should developing countries use?

19. Should developing countries rely on market decisions or state planning in allocating resources?
20. Does price and exchange-rate decontrol, financial liberalization, deregulation, and privatization improve LDC performance?

Limitations of Standard Economic Theory

These questions are only some of those to be explored. The answers may be more complex than you think. When analyzing the developing countries, rigid adherence to standard economic theory creates problems. Unlike developed countries, developing economies frequently do *not* have a mobile and highly educated labor force, commercial farmers with sizable land holdings, large numbers of responsive entrepreneurs, a favorable climate for enterprise, a high level of technical knowledge, local ownership of industry, heavy reliance on direct taxes for revenue, a large number of export commodities, an average income substantially above subsistence, a well-developed capital market, and a high level of capital goods. The problems of developing economies are often unique. You may have to unlearn much when studying their economies. As a leading development economist, Dudley Seers, suggests, "The abler the student has been in absorbing the current doctrine, the more difficult the process of adaptation" to a study of the third world.[4] Although this is probably overstated, you must set aside your preconceptions and keep your mind open to other approaches and concepts in analyzing a world different, in many ways, from the United States, Canada, and Western Europe.

Questions to Discuss

1. What do you hope to gain from a course in economic development (besides a good grade)?
2. Why is studying economics so central to understanding the problems of developing countries?
3. What impact might rapid economic development have on the lifestyle of Balayya's family? Calcutta's marginally employed?
4. Would you expect the development goal for the Indian poor to be a lifestyle like that of the Smiths?
5. Why are economic theories about developing countries different from those based on Western experience? What assumptions are involved in each case?
6. Give an example of how rigid adherence to Western economic theory may hinder understanding the developing world.

Guide to Readings

H. W. Arndt, *Economic Development: the History of an Idea* (Chicago: University of Chicago Press, 1987), traces the history of thought about economic devel-

---

[4]Dudley Seers, "The Limitations of the Special Case," *Bulletin of the Oxford Institute of Economics and Statistics* 25 (May 1963): 77–98.

opment as a policy objective. Gerald M. Meier and Dudley Seers, *Pioneers in Development* (New York: Oxford University Press, 1984) use biography to examine the history of the field. Development surveys include John Eatwell, Murray Milgate, and Peter Newman, eds., *The New Palgrave: Economic Development* (New York: Norton, 1989); Nicholas Stern, "The Economics of Development: A Survey," *Economic Journal* 99 (September 1989): 597–685; and Norman Gemmell, ed., *Surveys in Development Economics* (Oxford: Blackwell, 1987). For professional economists, Hollis Chenery and T.N. Srinivasan, eds., *Handbook of Development Economics*, vols. 1 and 2 (Amsterdam: North-Holland, 1988 and 1989), survey economic development, with bibliographies. Seers (note 4) is the focus of discussion by Kurt Martin and John Knapp, eds., *The Teaching of Development Economics* (Chicago: Aldine, 1967), the proceedings of a conference on teaching and learning development economics. In *International Development Review* 11 (December 1969): 1–16, Seers examines "The Meaning of Development," reprinted in David Lehmann, ed., *Development Theory: Four Critical Studies* (London: Frank Cass, 1979), with critical essays on development theory by Seers, E. Wayne Nafziger, Donal Cruise O'Brien, and Henry Bernstein. Deepak Lal, *The Poverty of "Development Economics"* (Cambridge, Mass.: Harvard University Press, 1985), criticizes Seers's emphasis on government involvement in LDCs (see Chapter 19).

The February 1986 issue of *World Development* 14 is devoted to a review of the methodology of development economics. Paul Streeten discusses development theories in "A Problem to Every Solution," *Finance and Development* 22 (June 1985): 16–21.

Nobel laureate Gunnar Myrdal discusses the role of values and biases in development economics in *The Challenge of World Poverty: a World Antipoverty Program in Outline* (New York: Vintage Books, 1970), pp. 3–29.

Jagannathan's and Halder's survey (note 3) of the life and work of pavement dwellers in Calcutta is excellent.

The instructor and student should find the following journals useful. The most widely cited development journals include the *Journal of Development Economics* (JDE), a journal from North-Holland which requires more theoretical and mathematical rigor; *Economic Development and Cultural Change* (EDCC), from the University of Chicago Press; the *Journal of Development Studies* (JDS), from Frank Cass in London; *World Development* (WD), a source on development policy from Pergamon Press in Britain; and *Developing Economies*, a Japanese journal in English, published in Tokyo. *Development and Change*, a theoretical journal from the World Bank and International Monetary Fund, *Finance and Development*, a monthly journal dealing with policy issues from the Bank and Fund; the *World Bank Research Observer*, which discusses issues of development policy and theory of interest to the World Bank; the *IMF Staff Papers*, an international trade and monetary journal; and the *IMF Survey* and *World Bank's News*, weekly newsletters with up-to-date reports, are other useful sources. Other development journals include the *Journal of Development Planning*, a United Nations journal; the

Journal of Developing Areas, an interdisciplinary development journal from Western Illinois State University; the *IDS Bulletin*, from a leading British development institute, the Institute for Development Studies at Sussex University, Brighton; the *International Development Review*, the policy-oriented journal of the Society for International Development; the *Journal of International Development*; *International Economic Insights*, from the Institute for International Economics, Washington, D.C.; and the *Third World Quarterly*, an interdisciplinary journal. *Population and Development* and the *Population Bulletin* are major journals discussing population, labor force growth, and economic development. In addition, the *Journal of Economic Literature* frequently has excellent surveys in development economics; other general economics journals sometimes have articles on development. Each of the major LDC regions—Asia, the Middle East, Africa, and Latin America—have major development journals, as do the United Nations regional agencies. An excellent popular source, the weekly London *Economist*, frequently has articles on development. Undergraduates with a strong interest in development economies should investigate *WD*, *Finance and Development*, *EDCC*, *JDS*, the *IDS Bulletin*, and regional journals.

CHAPTER 2

The Meaning and Measurement of Economic Development

Scope of the Chapter

This chapter introduces and evaluates terms and measures needed to discuss international differences in material well-being. The purpose is to help LDCs in assessing their attainment of development goals. We include the following:

1. The meaning of economic growth and economic development.
2. The calculation of economic growth.
3. Basic indicators of development and growth in more than 140 countries.
4. The classification of rich and poor countries.
5. The price-index problem.
6. The distortion in comparing income per head between rich and poor countries.
7. Adjustments to income figures for purchasing power.
8. Alternative measures and concepts of the level of economic development besides income per head.
9. The problems of alternative measures.
10. The costs and benefits of economic development.

Growth and Development

A major goal of poor countries is economic development or economic growth. The two terms are not identical. Growth may be necessary but not sufficient for development. **Economic growth** refers to increases in a country's production or income

9

per capita (Box 2–1). Production is usually measured by **gross national product (GNP)**, an economy's total output of goods and services. **Economic development** refers to economic growth accompanied by changes in output distribution and economic structure. These changes may include an improvement in the material well-being of the poorer half of the population; a decline in agriculture's share of GNP and a corresponding increase in the GNP share of industry and services; an increase in the education and skills of the labor force; and substantial technical advances originating within the country. As with children, growth involves a stress on quantitative measures (height or GNP), whereas development draws attention to changes in capacities (such as physical coordination and learning ability, or the economy's ability to adapt to shifts in tastes and technology).

The pendulum has swung between growth and development.[1] A major shift came near the end of the United Nations' first development decade (1960–70), which had stressed economic growth in poor countries. Because the benefits of growth did not often spread to the poorer half of the population, disillusionment with the decade's progress was widespread, even though economic growth exceeded the U.N. target. In 1969, Dudley Seers signaled this shift by asking the following questions about a country's development:

What has been happening to poverty? What has been happening to unemployment? What has been happening to inequality? If all three of these have become less severe, then beyond doubt this has been a period of development for the country concerned. If one or two of these central problems have been growing

---

BOX 2-1

Computing Growth Rates

Assume that in 1995, GNP for India is Rs. (rupees) 11,098.45 billion and its population 935 million, so that **GNP per capita** is Rs. 11,870. The GNP in 1996, Rs. 12,868.625 billion, must be divided by the **GNP price deflator**, 1.10 (corresponding to an annual inflation rate of 10 percent) to give a GNP of Rs. 11,698.75 billion at constant (1995) prices. This figure, divided by the population in 1996, 955 million, nets a GNP per capita of Rs. 12,250. **Real economic growth** (growth in GNP per capita) from 1995 to 1996 is (if expressed in 1995 constant prices)

$$\frac{12,250 - 11,870}{11,870} = 3.2 \text{ percent}$$

This growth rate is used by such organizations as the World Bank for average annual growth rate, 1995–96. At a 1996 exchange rate of Rs. 35=$1, India's GNP per capita is $350 (at 1996 prices), used by the World Bank as GNP per capita.

---

[1]Immediately after World War II, scholars and third-world governments were concerned with wider objectives than simply growth. However, Nobel laureate W. Arthur Lewis set the tone for the late 1950s and 1960s when he noted that "our subject matter is growth, and not distribution." *The Theory of Economic Growth* (Homewood, Ill.: Richard D. Irwin, 1955), p. 9.

worse, especially if all three have, it would be strange to call the result "development," even if per capita income has soared.[2]

In 1972, Robert McNamara, then World Bank president, declared that despite the relatively rapid economic growth of developing countries, the world remains one

> in which hundreds of millions of people are not only poor in statistical terms but are faced with day-to-day privations that degrade human dignity to levels which no statistics can adequately describe. . . . Two-thirds of the children [who live beyond five years of age] have their physical and mental growth stunted by malnutrition. There are 100 million more adult illiterates than there were twenty years ago. Education and employment are scarce, squalor and stagnation common.[3]

Despite past growth, the Economic Commission for Africa's (ECA's) 1983 twenty-fifth anniversary projection of past trends to 2008 envisions the following nightmare of explosive population growth pressing on physical resources and social services:

> The socio-economic conditions would be characterized by a degradation of the very essence of human dignity. The rural population, which would have to survive on intolerable toil, will face an almost disastrous situation of land scarcity whereby whole families would have to subsist on a mere hectare of land. Poverty would reach unimaginable dimensions, since rural incomes would become almost negligible relative to the cost of physical goods and services.
>
> The conditions in the urban centers would also worsen with more shanty towns, more congested roads, more beggars and more delinquents. The level of the unemployed searching desperately for the means to survive would imply increased crime rates and misery. But, alongside the misery, there would continue to be those very few who, unashamedly, would demonstrate an even higher degree of conspicuous consumption. These very few would continue to demand that the national department stores be filled with imports of luxury goods even if spare parts for essential production units cannot be procured for lack of foreign exchange.[4]

The *Khartoum Declaration*, expressing the views of the U.N. Inter-Agency Task Force and numerous African ministers, high-ranking officials, and senior experts from government, stated in 1988:

> Regrettably, over the past decade the human condition of most Africans has deteriorated calamitously. Real incomes of almost all households and families declined sharply. Malnutrition has risen massively, food production has fallen relative to population, the quality and quantity of health and education services have made tens of millions of human beings refugees and displaced persons. In many cases, the slow decline of infant mortality and of death from preventable, epidemic diseases has been reversed. Meanwhile, the unemployment and underemployment situation has worsened markedly.[5]

---

[2]Dudley Seers, "The Meaning of Development," *International Development Review* 11 (December 1969): 3–4.

[3]Robert S. McNamara, address to the U.N. Conference on Trade and Development, Santiago, Chile, April 14, 1972 (Washington, D.C.: World Bank, 1972), pp.2–3.

[4]Economic Commission for Africa, "ECA and Africa's Development, 1983–2008," Addis Ababa, 1983, pp. 93–94.

[5]U.N. Inter-Agency Task Force, *Khartoum Conference on the Human Dimensions of Africa's Economic Recovery and Development* (Khartoum, March 1988).

The ECA described Africa's economic situation in 1984 as the worst since the Great Depression, and Africa as "the very sick child of the international economy." Recognizing this, the United Nations devoted its thirteenth special session in 1986 to develop a strategy to safeguard Africa's economic survival.[6] Growth (1960 to 1996) took place without development.

Economic development can refer not only to the *rate* of change in economic well-being, but also to its *level*. Between 1870 and 1995, Japan had a rapid rate of economic development. Its real (inflation-adjusted) growth rate in GNP per capita was about 3.5 percent per year, and there was substantial technical innovation, improved income distribution, and a decline in the share of the labor force in agriculture. On the other hand, Japan has a high level of economic development—its 1993 per capita GNP, $31,490, placed it among the two richest countries in the world (Table 2–1). Other measures indicate most Japanese are well fed and housed, in good health, and well educated. Only a relative few are poor. This book will use both meanings of economic development.

Classification of Countries

When the serious study of development economics began in the late 1940s and early 1950s, it was common to think of rich and poor countries as separated by a wide gulf. The rich included Western Europe, the United States, Canada, Australia, New Zealand, and Japan; and the poor, Asia, Africa, and Latin America.

The boundary between rich and poor countries, overly simple then, has become even more blurred in the 1990s. Today an increasing number of the high- and upper-middle-income countries are non-Western, and the fastest-growing countries are not necessarily the ones with the highest per capita GNP. Those countries considered poor in 1950 grew at about the same rate as rich countries during the subsequent three decades (see Chapter 3). A few of the poor countries in 1950, such as Brazil, Taiwan, Turkey, South Korea, Malaysia, Thailand, and major oil exporter Saudi Arabia, grew so much more rapidly than some higher-income countries in 1950 (Ireland and New Zealand, for example) that the GNP per capita of the countries of the world now forms a continuum rather than a dichotomy.[7]

---

[6]Economic Commission for Africa, *Survey of Economic and Social Conditions in Africa, 1983–1984*, E/ECA/CM 11/16, Addis Ababa, 1985, p. 3; and U.N. General Assembly, *Program of Action for African Economic Recovery and Development, 1986–1990* (New York, 1986).

[7]Graduating from developing to developed country is not merely of academic interest, since the United States Agency for International Development (and other aid agencies) withdrew the GSP (generalized system of tariff preferences discussed in Chapter 8) to several graduates in the late 1980s. The GSP had accounted for more than 10 percent of U.S. exports to prosperous LDCs such as South Korea, Taiwan, Hong Kong, and Singapore; as much as 5 to 10 percent of these countries' exports may have been diverted to other countries as a result of the loss of the United States' GSP. Additionally, the General Agreements of Tariffs and Trade/World Trade Organization (GATT/WTO), that sets rules for international trade, had expected reciprocity among developed countries in trade agreements but extended preferential treatment to developing countries. K.A. Koekkoek, "The Integration of Developing Countries in the GATT System," *World Development* (August 1988): 947–57. However, under the GATT Uruguay Round (1986–94), DCs expect tariff reciprocity among LDCs.

In 1995, the World Bank announced that South Korea became the first country to graduate from a borrowing country to a contributor to the Bank's loan funds for LDCs. "World Bank Reports Successful Year," *Kansas City Star* (September 25, 1995): p. B-6.

TABLE 2-1   Selected Indicators of Development

Country	Population (millions) mid-1996	GNP per Capita 1993 ($)	Annual Growth Rate of GNP per Capita 1960–1980 (percent)	Average Annual Growth Rate of GNP per Capita 1980–1992 (percent)	Average Annual Growth Rate of GNP per Capita 1960–1992 (percent)[a]	Life Expectancy at Birth 1992 (years)	Infant Mortality per 1,000 Live Births 1992	Adult Literacy Rate 1992 (percent)	HDI[b]	Consumption per Capita (kilograms of oil equivalent) 1992
Low-income economies	3413.9	380	1.2[c]	3.9		62	73	60		338
Low-income economies (excluding China & India)	1254.7	300	1.0	1.2		56	91	55		151
*Mozambique	16.7	90	–0.1	–3.6	–1.4	46	148	34	.252	32
*Tanzania[d]	31.9	90	1.9	0.0	1.2	51	103	—	.306	30
*Ethiopia (and Eritrea)	58.7	100	1.4	–1.9	0.1	46	123	—	.249	21
*Sierra Leone	4.9	150	—	–1.4	—	42	144	24	.209	73
Vietnam	76.5	170				66	41	88	.514	77
*Burundi	6.4	180	2.5	1.3	2.0	48	106	52	.276	24
*Uganda	21.0	180	–0.7	—	—	43	104	51	.272	24
*Bhutan	0.8	180	–0.1	6.3	2.3	48	131	—	.247	15
*Nepal	23.2	190	0.2	2.0	0.9	53	100	27	.289	20
*Malawi	10.0	200	2.9	–0.1	–0.1	45	143	—	.260	40
*Chad	6.8	210	–1.8	3.4	0.1	47	123	33	.212	16
*Rwanda	8.1	210	1.5	–0.6	0.7	46	111	52	.274	28
*Bangladesh	122.3	220		1.8		52	109	37	.309	59
*Madagascar	14.4	220	–0.5	–2.4	–1.2	55	110	81	.396	38
*Guinea-Bissau	1.1	240		1.6		43	141	—	.224	37
Kenya	28.8	270	2.7	0.2	1.8	59	67	71	.434	92
*Mali	9.7	270	1.4	–2.7	–0.2	45	160	36	.214	22
*Niger	9.4	270	–1.6	–4.3	–2.6	46	125	31	.209	39
*Lao PDR	5.0	280	—	—	—	50	98	—	.385	41
*Burkina Faso	10.7	300	0.1	1.0	0.3	48	118	20	.203	16
India	955.9	300	1.4	3.1	2.0	60	89	50	.382	235
Nigeria	104.3	300	4.1	–0.4	2.4	52	97	52	.348	128
Albania	3.5	340	—	—	—	73	17	85	.714	455
Nicaragua	4.6	340	0.9	–5.3	–1.5	65	53	78	.583	253
*Togo	4.6	340	3.0	–1.8	1.2	54	86	45	.311	46
*Gambia, The	1.2	350				45	130	27	.215	57
*Zambia	9.6	380	0.2	—	—	46	84	75	.352	158
Mongolia	2.5	390	—	—	—	63	61	—	.607	1082
*Central African Republic	3.3	400	0.9	–1.5	0.0	47	105	40	.249	29
*Benin	5.6	430	0.4	–0.7	0.0	46	88	25	.261	19
Ghana	17.9	430	–1.0	–0.1	1.1	55	82	63	.382	96
Pakistan	133.6	430	2.8	3.1	2.9	58	99	36	.393	223
Tajikistan[e]	6.2	470		—		70	49	97	.629	—

TABLE 2-1   Continued

Country	Population (millions) mid-1996	GNP per Capita 1993 ($)	Annual Growth Rate of GNP per Capita 1960–1980 (percent)	Average Annual Growth Rate of GNP per Capita 1980–1992 (percent)	Average Annual Growth Rate of GNP per Capita 1960–1992 (percent)[a]	Life Expectancy at Birth 1992 (years)	Infant Mortality per 1,000 Live Births 1992	Adult Literacy Rate 1992 (percent)	HDI[b]	Consumption per Capita (kilograms of oil equivalent) 1992
China	1218.4	490	3.7	7.6	5.1	70	27	73	.644	600
*Guinea	6.7	500	0.3	—	—	44	135	27	.191	67
*Mauritania	2.4	500	1.6	−0.8	0.7	47	118	34	.254	108
Zimbabwe	11.9	520	0.7	−0.9	0.1	56	59	69	.474	450
Georgia[e]	5.6	580		—		73	19	99	.747	891
Honduras	5.6	600	1.1	−0.3	0.6	65	61	75	.524	175
Sri Lanka	18.4	600	2.4	2.6	2.5	71	24	89	.665	101
Ivory Coast	14.9	630	2.5	−4.7	−0.3	52	91	56	.370	125
*Lesotho	2.0	650	6.1	−0.5	3.6	56	59	69	.476	—
Armenia[e]	3.8	660		—		72	21	99	.801	1092
Egypt, Arab Rep.	61.6	660	3.4	1.8	2.8	61	58	50	.551	586
*Myanmar (Burma)	47.1	—	1.2	—	—	57	83	82	.406	42
*Yemen, Rep.	13.8	—		—		52	107	38	.323	241
*Somalia	10.4	—	—	—	—	46	123	27	.217	7
*Sudan	30.0	—	−0.2	—	—	51	100	28	.276	69
Middle-income economies	1505.8	2480	3.8[c]	−0.1		68	43	73		1812
Azerbaijan[e]	7.7	730		—		71	32	96	.730	—
Indonesia	206.1	740	4.0	4.0	4.0	62	66	84	.586	303
Senegal	8.7	750	−0.3	0.1	−0.2	49	81	40	.322	111
Bolivia	8.7	680	2.1	−1.5	0.7	61	86	79	.530	255
Cameroon	13.9	820	2.6	−1.5	1.0	55	64	57	.447	77
Macedonia, FYR	2.1	820				72	26			
Kyrgyz Republic[e]	4.7	850		—		68	37	97	.689	1148
Philippines	72.0	850	2.8	−1.0	1.4	65	40	90	.621	302
Congo	2.5	950	0.8	−0.8	0.2	52	83	59	.461	131
Uzbekistan[e]	23.3	970		—		69	42	97	.664	—
Morocco	29.9	1040	2.5	1.4	2.1	62	70	52	.549	278
Moldava[e]	4.5	1060		—		69	23	96	.714	1600
Guatemala	10.9	1100	2.8	−1.5	1.2	64	49	56	.564	161
Papua New Guinea	4.2	1130	2.8	0.0	1.7	55	54	65	.408	235
Bulgaria	8.4	1140	5.6	1.2	3.9	72	16	94	.815	2422
Romania	22.7	1140	8.6	−1.1	4.9	69	23	97	.729	1958
Jordan[f]	4.5	1190	5.7	−5.4	1.4	67	37	82	.628	813
Ecuador	11.1	1200	4.5	−0.3	2.7	66	58	87	.718	524
Dominican Republic	8.1	1230	3.4	-0.5	1.9	67	57	84	.638	347
El Salvador	5.5	1320	1.6	0.0	1.0	65	46	75	.543	225
Lithuania[e]	3.7	1320		−1.0		73	16	98	.868	—
Colombia	37.0	1400	3.0	1.4	2.4	69	30	87	.813	670

TABLE 2-1 Continued

Country	Population (millions) mid-1996	GNP per Capita 1993 ($)	Annual Growth Rate of GNP per Capita 1960–1980 (percent)	Average Annual Growth Rate of GNP per Capita 1980–1992 (percent)	Average Annual Growth Rate of GNP per Capita 1960–1992 (percent)[a]	Life Expectancy at Birth 1992 (years)	Infant Mortality per 1,000 Live Births 1992	Adult Literacy Rate 1992 (percent)	HDI[b]	Consumption per Capita (kilograms of oil equivalent) 1992
Jamaica	2.6	1440	0.6	0.2	0.4	73	14	98	.749	1075
Peru	23.8	1490	1.1	−2.8	−0.4	64	77	86	.642	330
Paraguay	5.1	1510	3.2	−0.7	1.7	67	47	91	.679	209
Kazakstan[e]	17.5	1560		—		69	31	80	.778	4722
Tunisia	9.0	1720	4.8	1.3	3.5	67	44	68	.690	567
Algeria	29.3	1780	3.2	−0.5	1.8	66	62	61	.553	988
Namibia	1.7	1820		−1.0		58	71	—	.425	—
Slovak Republic	5.3	1950		—		71	13	—	.872	3202
Latvia[e]	2.5	2010		0.2		71	17	99	.865	—
Thailand	61.1	2110	4.7	6.0	5.2	69	26	94	.798	177
Costa Rica	3.3	2150	3.2	0.8	2.3	76	14	93	.848	506
Ukraine[e]	51.3	2210		—		70	18	95	.823	3885
Poland	38.8	2260	5.3	0.1	3.3	72	14	99	.815	2494
Russian Federation[e]	147.2	2340		—		70	20	99	.858	5665
Panama	2.6	2600	3.3	−1.2	1.6	72	21	90	.816	520
Czech Republic	10.3	2710		—		72	10	99	.872	3873
*Botswana	1.5	2790		6.1		60	61	75	.670	395
Venezuela	22.4	2840	2.6	−0.8	1.3	70	33	89	.820	2296
Belarus[e]	10.3	2870		—		71	15	98	.847	4154
Brazil	160.6	2930	5.1	0.4	3.3	66	57	82	.756	681
Turkey	64.5	2970	3.6	2.9	3.3	67	57	82	.739	948
South Africa	43.4	2980	2.3	0.1	1.5	62	53	—	.650	2487
Iran, Islamic Rep.[g]	65.7	3010	—	−1.4	—	67	41	56	.672	1256
Mauritius	1.1	3030		5.6		70	18	80	.778	385
Estonia[e]	1.5	3080		−2.3		71	13	99	.867	—
Malaysia	20.4	3140	4.3	3.2	3.9	70	14	80	.794	1445
Chile	14.5	3170	1.6	3.7	2.4	72	17	94	.848	837
Hungary	10.2	3350	4.5	0.2	2.9	70	15	99	.863	2392
Mexico	95.9	3610	2.6	−0.2	1.5	70	36	89	.804	1525
Trinidad and Tobago	1.3	3830	3.0	−2.6	0.9	71	18	96	.855	4910
Uruguay	3.3	3830	1.4	−1.0	0.5	72	20	97	.859	642
Oman	2.1	4850		4.1		69	30	35	.654	3070
Gabon	1.2	4960		−3.7		53	95	62	.525	784
Slovenia	2.0	6490		—		73	8	—	—	—
Puerto Rico	3.7	7000		0.9		74	13	—	—	2018
Argentina	34.8	7220	2.2	−0.9	1.0	71	29	96	.853	1351
Greece	10.4	7390	5.8	1.0	4.0	77	8	94	.874	2173
Saudi Arabia	19.2	7510	8.1	−3.3	3.7	69	31	64	.742	4463

TABLE 2–1   Continued

Country	Population (millions) mid-1996	GNP per Capita 1993 ($)	Annual Growth Rate of GNP per Capita 1960–1980 (percent)	Average Annual Growth Rate of GNP per Capita 1980–1992 (percent)	Average Annual Growth Rate of GNP per Capita 1960–1992 (percent)[a]	Life Expectancy at Birth 1992 (years)	Infant Mortality per 1,000 Live Births 1992	Adult Literacy Rate 1992 (percent)	HDI[b]	Consumption per Capita (kilograms of oil equivalent) 1992
Korea Rep.	45.4	7660	7.0	8.5	7.6	70	21	97	.859	2569
Taiwan[g]	22.0	8480	8.0	6.7	7.5	74	6	95		
Portugal	9.9	9130	5.0	3.1	4.3	74	9	86	.838	1816
Turkmenistan	4.3	—		—		66	54	98	.697	—
Syrian Arab Republic	15.0	—	3.7	—	—	66	40	67	.727	823
High-income economies	844.8	23090	3.6[c]	2.3		77	7	99		5101
New Zealand	3.6	12600	1.8	0.6	1.3	75	7	99	.907	4284
Ireland	3.6	13000	3.1	3.4	3.2	75	5	99	.892	2881
Spain	39.3	13590	4.5	2.9	3.9	77	8	98	.888	2409
Israel	5.6	13920	3.8	1.9	3.1	76	9	95	.900	2367
Australia	18.1	17500	2.7	1.6	2.3	77	7	99	.926	5263
Hong Kong[h]	5.9	18060	6.8	5.5	6.3	77	6	90	.875	1946
United Kingdom	58.6	18060	2.2	2.4	2.3	76	7	99	.919	3743
Finland	5.1	19300	4.0	2.0	3.2	75	6	99	.911	5560
Kuwait	1.4	19360		−4.3		75	17	73	.821	4217
Italy	57.2	19840	3.6	2.2	3.1	77	8	98	.891	2755
Singapore	3.0	19850	7.5	5.3	6.7	74	8	92	.836	4399
Canada	29.5	19970	3.3	1.8	2.7	77	7	99	.932	7912
Netherlands	15.5	20950	3.2	1.7	2.6	77	6	99	.923	4560
United Arab Emirates	1.8	21430	4.3	−4.3	1.0	71	23	65	.771	14631
Belgium	10.1	21650	3.8	2.0	3.1	76	9	99	.916	5100
France	58.5	22490	3.9	1.7	3.1	77	7	99	.927	4034
Austria	8.0	22510	4.1	2.0	3.3	76	7	99	.917	3266
Germany[j]	81.0	22560	3.3	2.4	3.0	76	6	99	.918	4358
Sweden	8.9	24740	2.3	1.5	2.0	78	5	99	.928	5395
United States	264.5	24740	2.3	1.7	2.1	76	9	99	.925	7662
Norway	4.3	25970	3.5	2.2	3.0	77	6	99	.928	4925
Denmark	5.2	26730	3.3	2.1	2.8	75	7	99	.912	3729
Japan	125.8	31490	7.1	3.6	5.8	79	5	99	.929	3586
Switzerland	7.0	35760	1.9	1.4	1.7	78	6	99	.931	3694
South and Southeast Asia	1270.0	310		3.0		60	85	45		209
Sub-Saharan Africa	606.4	520		-0.8		52	99	50		258
East Asia and Pacific (excluding Japan)	1771.3	820		6.1		68	39	76		593

TABLE 2–1 Continued

Country	Population (millions) mid-1996	GNP per Capita 1993 ($)	Annual Growth Rate of GNP per Capita 1960–1980 (percent)	Average Annual Growth Rate of GNP per Capita 1980–1992 (percent)	Average Annual Growth Rate of GNP per Capita 1960–1992 (percent)[a]	Life Expec- tancy at Birth 1992 (years)	Infant Mor- tality per 1,000 Live Births 1992	Adult Literacy Rate 1992 (percent) HDI[b]	Con- sumption per Capita (kilograms of oil equiv- alent) 1992
Middle East and North Africa (LDCs)	278.8	1950		–2.3		64	58	55	1109
Developing Europe and Central Asia	504.5	2450		—		70	30	—	3179
Latin America and Caribbean	482.9	2950		–0.2		68	44	85	923
Developing countries[c]	4912.3	1090	2.1	0.9		64	65	64	790
Developed countries[c]	844.8	23090	3.6	2.3		77	7	99	5101
World[k]	5757.1	4420	2.4	1.2		66	60	65	1447

Note: Blank cell refers to countries not listed by the sources. Countries may not be listed because they are too small (Guinea-Bissau and Botswana in 1980), because they lacked data (Afghanistan, Cambodia, Cuba, Haiti, Iraq, Liberia, North Korea, and Zaïre in 1993), or because they did not yet exist (for example, Georgia and Armenia in 1980).

A dash (—) refers to a lack of information for countries listed by the sources.

East Asia does not include Japan or Hong Kong. South and Southeast Asia do not include Singapore. The Middle East and North Africa do not include Israel.

[a]Growth rates are rough approximations, subject to price-index number and subsistence valuation problems discussed below in this chapter.

[b]HDI (Human Development Index) is a composite based on three indicators—life expectancy at birth, education (adult literacy rate and mean years of schooling for persons over 25 years of age), and living standards (real per capita GDP in purchasing power parity dollars, with a progressively increasing discount of income in excess of that needed to attain a minimal nutritional level (see below).

[c]Countries designated as low-income, middle-income, and high-income economies changed from the 1960–80 to 1980–92 periods. As indicated in Chapter 3, selecting countries as low income, middle income, or high income in 1992 can bias the relative growth rates of the three income classifications.

[d]Data cover mainland Tanzania only.

[e]Estimates for economies of the former Soviet Union are very preliminary and subject to more than the usual range of uncertainty.

[f]Data for Jordan cover the East Bank only.

[g]Author's estimates for Iran and Taiwan.

[h]Refers to figures before unification with China in 1997.

[i]Growth rates refer to the Federal Republic of Germany before unification.

[j]Includes few of the socialist countries, 1960–80, and few current economies in transition, 1980–92.

*=least-developed countries

Sources: Population Reference Bureau, *1994 World Population Data Sheet* (Washington, D.C., 1994); World Bank, *World Development Report, 1995* (New York: Oxford University Press, 1995), pp. 162–63; World Bank, *World Development Report, 1994* (New York: Oxford University Press, 1994), pp. 162–63, 170–71, 210–11, 214–15; World Bank, *World Development Report, 1982* (New York: Oxford University Press, 1982), pp. 110–11; and United Nations Development Program, *Human Development Report, 1994* (New York: Oxford University Press, 1994), pp. 129–31, 136–37.

Several GNP per capita rankings shifted substantially between 1950 and 1992. Among present-day Asian, African, and Latin American LDCs listed in both GNP per capita rankings for 1950 in a World Bank study and for 1993 in Table 2–1, Venezuela fell from first to fifteenth, Uruguay from second to sixth, Argentina from third to fourth, Chile from fifth to ninth, Peru from eleventh to twenty-third, and Bolivia from thirty-first to thirty-fifth, being overpassed by war-affected Japan, Taiwan (which rose from thirty-fifth to first), and South Korea, which vaulted from forty-fifth to second. In Africa, Morocco, engaged in conflict with Algeria over the Spanish Sahara and with local labor unions over social policy, declined from seventeenth to thirty-first; Zambia, with rapidly falling relative world copper export prices after the mid-1970s, fell from twenty-second to fifty-third; and Ghana, with chronic cedi overvaluation and low farm prices that discouraged export expansion until the 1980s, dropped from a two-way tie for fifteenth and sixteenth to forty-ninth. During this period, Ghana was leapfrogged by Korea, Taiwan, Cameroon, the Ivory Coast, Malaysia, Turkey, Colombia, and Indonesia, as well as Thailand, which rose from forty-ninth to eighteenth."[8]

One classification of development levels used by the World Bank divides countries into three groups on the basis of per capita GNP. In 1993, these categories were low-income countries (less than $700), middle-income countries ($700–12,000), and high-income countries (more than $12,000) (see Table 2–1). Each year the boundary between categories rises with inflation, but few countries shifted categories between 1974 and 1993.

Sometimes the high-income countries are designated as developed countries (DCs) or the North, and middle- and low-income countries as developing, underdeveloped, or less-developed countries, or the South. *Underdeveloped* was the term commonly used in the 1950s and 1960s, but it has since lost favor. Perhaps all countries are underdeveloped relative to their maximum potential. However, the term *underdeveloped*, like *less developed*, has declined in use recently, not because it is inaccurate, but because officials in international agencies consider it offensive. And the term *developing countries* appears to be a euphemism when applied to parts of sub-Saharan Africa that grew (and developed) very little, if at all, from the 1960s through the 1990s. Nevertheless, this book uses the latter term as it is widely understood within the world community to refer to countries with low and middle GNP per capita.

The 127 Asian, African, and Latin American members of the **United Nations Conference on Trade and Development (UNCTAD)** are often referred to as the **third world,** a term originating in the early post–World War II decade.[9] By refusing to ally themselves with either the United States or the Soviet Union, nonaligned nations forged a third political unit in the United Nations.[10] Today the term has lost its original meaning, no longer connoting nonalignment but distinguishing UNCTAD countries from the **first world,** or capitalist countries, where capital and land are owned by individuals; and the second world socialist, or cen-

---

[8]Rankings from 1950 were computed from David Morawetz, *Twenty-five Years of Economic Development, 1950 to 1975* (Baltimore: Johns Hopkins University Press for the World Bank, 1977), pp. 77–79.

[9]The purpose of UNCTAD, a permanent organization first convened in 1964, is to enhance the position of LDCs in the world economy.

[10]Leslie Wolf-Phillips discusses "Why 'Third World'?: Origin, Definition and Usage," in *Third World Quarterly* 9 (October 1987): 1311–27.

trally directed countries, where the government owns the means of production. (Contrary to Western usage, the second world described its economic system as **socialism** rather than communism. In Marxian terminology, communism refers to a later stage of development when distribution is according to needs, money is absent, and the state withers away.) Even a mixed economy, such as that of Great Britain, having government economic planning and limited public ownership of industry (especially under Labour party control), or welfare states, such as Sweden, are classified in the first world.

The term second world is rarely used now, especially since 1989–91, when Eastern Europe, the former Soviet Union, Mongolia, China, and Vietnam have been moving, albeit haltingly, toward the market and (sometimes) private ownership. From 1989 to 1993, income per capita fell about one-third to one-half in the former Soviet Union, and about one-fourth in Eastern Europe, while the rise in unemployment ranged from 14 percent of the labor force in Poland to a lower, but unknown, percentage in Russia. Among former socialist European and Eurasian countries, Poland reversed its output collapse in 1992 and Albania and the Czech Republic in 1993.[11] The London *Economist* estimates that much of Eastern Europe will achieve their 1989 level of GNP per person in 1996, but that Bulgaria, Romania, and the former Yugoslavia will not attain 1989 levels by the end of the twentieth century.[12] Russia and other states of the former Soviet Union are not expected to attain 1989 levels before the end of the century. With the widespread overestimation of the pre-1989 output of the former European and Soviet socialist countries, and the collapse of their output since 1989, these countries are now included among developing (mostly middle-income) countries.

The South Commission, chaired by Julius K. Nyerere, an articulate spokesperson for the poor who was head of government in Tanzania from 1961 to 1985, declares that "The primary bond that links the countries and peoples of the South is their desire to escape from poverty and underdevelopment and secure a better life for their citizens."[13] Yet economic interests still vary substantially between and within the following types of developing countries: (1) the 26 **economies in transition** (the new grouping for Eastern Europe and the former Soviet Union), recognized as separate by the South Commission;[14] (2) the three **newly industrializing countries (NICs)**; (3) the eight members of the **Organization of Petroleum Exporting Countries**, or **OPEC** (not including high-income Kuwait and the United Arab Emirates); (4) the 46 poorest countries, designated as **least developed countries** and starred in Table 2–1; and (5) 108 other developing countries. (Fifteen of the less populous or data-poor least developed countries and 63 other developing countries are *not* included in Table 2–1.)

The label economies of transition (implying a passage to the market) may be the DCs' euphemism. Many transitional political economies are in flux. Some citizens experiencing immediate falling standards of living fear destitution before they arrive at the promised land of long-run equilibrium. Indeed, by 1995, in Russia,

---

[11]United Nations, Department of Economic and Social Information and Policy Analysis, *World Economic Survey, 1993/94: Student Edition* (New York, 1993), pp. 7–9; International Monetary Fund, World Economic Outlook, October 1993 (Washington, D.C., 1993), pp. 84–85.

[12]"Survey: Business in Eastern Europe," *Economist* (September 21, 1991), p. S4.

[13]South Commission (Julius K. Nyerere, Chairman), *The Challenge to the South: The Report of the South Commission* (Oxford: Oxford University Press, 1990), p. 1.

[14]Ibid., pp. 3–4.

Ukraine, Lithuania, Poland, Hungary, Romania, Bulgaria, and Slovakia, the former ruling Communist Party (reincarnated as a socialist or social democratic Party and opposed to central planning) had won a parliamentary plurality back from transient ruling parties or cliques committed to rapid economic reform and liberalization. These political swings make it difficult to project these countries' strategies in 2000.

South Korea, Taiwan (China-Taipei), and Singapore (and Hong Kong, the largest investor in and a major recipient of investment from China, and a part of China beginning in 1997), and sometimes Mexico, Brazil, and others, are included among the NICs. These relatively advanced LDCs have been growing rapidly and are industrially diversified.[15]

The upper- and upper-middle-income oil exporters are Kuwait, Libya, Saudi Arabia, Venezuela, the United Arab Emirates, and Gabon. Iran and Iraq dropped from upper-middle to lower-middle income status after the oil output disruptions during the 1979 Iranian revolution, the 1980–88 Iraqi-Iranian war, and the U.N.-imposed trade ban after August 1990. Indonesia, newly graduated to lower-middle-income status, and low-income Nigeria, each with populations more than 90 million, spend most foreign exchange on basic import requirements, such as machinery, equipment, food, and raw materials.

In 1971, the United Nations designated 25 countries with a low per capita income, low share of manufacturing in gross product, and low adult literacy rates as least developed. A number of countries asked to be so designated, hoping to obtain economic assistance, especially from the United Nations. Since then, the United Nations has added other criteria, including low levels of human development (on indicators such as life expectancy, per capita calorie supplies, and primary and secondary school enrollment rates), natural handicaps (such as a small population, severe climatic risks, landlockedness, and geographical isolation), and low economic diversification. The list of countries has grown to 46 (including Afghanistan, Bangladesh, Burkina Faso, Burundi, Cambodia, Ethiopia, Haiti, Liberia, Malawi, Mali, Mozambique, Myanmar or Burma, Nepal, Niger, Rwanda, Somalia, Sudan, Tanzania, Uganda, Yemen, Zaïre, and Zambia), overlapping greatly with the low-income countries in Table 2–1. Most least developed countries, however, are small. Most U.N. supporters of this program feared that DCs would treat the proposal seriously only if the number of countries were clearly limited. Thus populous countries, such as India, Pakistan, Vietnam, and Nigeria, were not included.[16]

During the mid- and late 1970s, major aid recipients, such as Bangladesh and Zaïre, were interested in the expansion of official loan facilities, especially to finance increased oil prices. Their attempts to improve financing were directed at OPEC countries in Africa and Asia. The NICs, on the other hand, which rely heavily on manufactured exports, have been more interested in reduced DC trade bar-

---

[15]John W. Sewell, Stuart K. Tucker, and contributors, *Growth, Exports, and Jobs in a Changing World Economy: Agenda, 1988* (New Brunswick, N.J.: Transaction Books, 1988), p. 204, also include Argentina, India, China, Portugal, South Africa, and Turkey.

[16]Udo E. Simonis, "Least Developed Countries—Newly Defined," *Intereconomics* 26 (September/October 1991): 230–35; and Michael P. Blackwell, "From G-5 to G-77: International Forums for Discussion of Economic Issues," *Finance and Development* 23 (September 1986): 40–41.

For criticism of the U.N. method of identifying least developed countries, see Perry Selwyn, "The Least-Developed Countries as a Special Case," *World Development* 2, nos. 4 and 5 (April-May 1974): 35–42.

riers against manufacturers than in the primary commodity stabilization agreements sought by Uganda, Malawi, Sri Lanka, and Honduras.

Nevertheless, OPEC countries have maintained an alliance with oil-importing, developing countries on a broad range of economic and political issues in international forums. In the 1980s, many OPEC countries and oil-importing LDCs shared a concern with debt relief and reorganization. Additionally, most OPEC countries, despite their high per capita GNP, face problems common to most of the developing world—high illiteracy, high infant mortality, and dependence on imported technology.

Thus in 1974 to 1975, OPEC countries joined with other members of UNCTAD in the successful adoption by the U.N. General Assembly of a declaration on principles and programs to reduce the adverse impact of the **international economic order** on LDC development. This order includes all economic relations and institutions, both formal and informal, that link people living in different nations. These economic institutions include international agencies that lend capital, provide short-term credit, and administer international trade rules. Economic relations include bilateral and multilateral trade, aid, banking services, currency rates, capital movements, and technological transfers.

Problems with Using GNP to Make Comparisons Over Time

Economists use national-income data to compare a given country's GNP over time. Table 2.1 shows the economic growth of 207 countries. For example, Malaysia's growth in GNP per capita was 5.7 percent yearly and its overall GNP growth, 8.0 percent, 1985–92. On the basis of a simple calculation, you might state: "This means that Malaysia's GNP in 1992 was 71 percent larger than it was in 1985." Yet a statement such as this, based on official growth figures, is subject to serious question as to accuracy.

Students know that the GNP price deflator affects government and World Bank figures for GNP and its growth. Whether the price deflator is 112.5, 125, 150, or another figure depends on which weighted price index is used. A number of countries, especially in Africa and Eastern Europe, have not changed the quantity weighting of commodity prices since before 1972, despite substantial output structural change. Economic development changes prices with shifts in supply and demand. A newly modernizing country may find that a good, such as steel, which is of little importance in the output mix in the premodern era, looms large during the process of modernization. Whether the country uses early or late (sometimes premodern or modern) weights in devising a price index makes a substantial difference in determining how large the price deflator will be in adjusting GNP growth.

Let us use Malaysia to illustrate the price-index problem. In showing how Malaysia calculates its GNP price deflator, assume that Malaysia produces only two goods, electronic calculators and rubber boots. Suppose Malaysia produces 20 million electronic calculators at R400 apiece (with R the Malaysian currency ringgit) and 200 million pairs of rubber boots at R100 per ton in 1985, and 100 million calculators at 100 ringgit apiece and 400 million pairs of rubber boots at 200 ringgit per ton in 1992. The output of boots grew steadily as prices doubled, while the output of calculators increased fivefold and prices were cut substantially, as the industry benefitted from large-scale economies and a rapidly-improving technology.

Malaysia may use the **Laspeyres price index**, applying base-period or 1985 (*not* late-year or 1992) quantities to weight prices. The aggregate price index

$$P = \frac{\sum p_n q_0}{\sum p_0 q_0} \tag{2-1}$$

where p is the price of the commodity produced, q the quantity of the commodity produced, 0 the base year (here 1985), and n the given year (1992).

$$P = \frac{\left(20 \text{ m. calculators} \times R100\right) + \left(200 \text{ m. units of boots} \times R200\right)}{\left(20 \text{ m. calculators} \times R400\right) + \left(200 \text{ m. units of boots} \times R100\right)}$$

$$= \frac{R42,000 \text{ million}}{R28,000 \text{ million}} = 1.5$$

The World Bank's method for computing real growth (Box 2.1) uses current price weights, similar to the **Paasche price index**, which applies terminal-year (1992) outputs for weighting prices, so that price index

$$P = \frac{\sum p_n q_n}{\sum p_0 q_n} \tag{2-2}$$

In Malaysia, then

$$P = \frac{\left(100 \text{ m. calculators} \times R100\right) + \left(400 \text{ m. units of boots} \times R200\right)}{\left(100 \text{ m. calculators} \times R400\right) + \left(400 \text{ m. units of boots} \times R100\right)}$$

$$= \frac{R90,000 \text{ million}}{R80,000 \text{ million}} = 1.125$$

In Malaysia, the GNP price deflator using the Laspeyres index, 1.5, exceeds that using the Paasche index, 1.125. To the extent that industries with more rapid growth, such as the electronic calculator industry, show relatively less rapid increases (or here even reductions) in price, a Laspeyres index, which uses base-period weights, will show higher values than Paasche-type indexes, which use weights from a current period.[17] The Laspeyres index is biased upward and the Paasche index biased downward. While the **Fisher ideal index**, a geometric average of the Laspeyres and Paasche indices, removes bias, it is not used much because of its complexity.

Problems in Comparing Developed and Developing Countries' GNP

International agencies generally do not regularly collect primary data themselves. These agencies almost always base their statistical publications on data gathered

---

[17]A useful mnemonic device for remembering Laspeyres is "long time ago" and Paasche is "present."

by national statistical agencies, which often use different concepts and methods of data collection. The United Nations has not yet successfully standardized these concepts and methodologies.[18] But aside from these problems, there are other incomparabilities, especially between the GNPs of rich and poor countries.

According to Table 2–1, per capita GNP varies greatly between countries. For example, compare the GNP per capita of India and the United States. The 1993 U.S. GNP per capita of $24,740 is over eighty-two times that of India's $300. Could an Indian actually survive for one year on less than the weekly income of an average American? In reality income differences between developed and developing countries are very much overstated.

One difference is that developed countries are located in predominantly temperate zones, and LDCs are primarily in the tropics. In temperate areas like the northern United States, heating, insulation, and warmer clothing merely offset the disadvantages of cold weather and add to GNP without increasing satisfaction.

Apart from this discrepancy, *the major sources of error and imprecision in comparing GNP figures for developed and developing countries are as follows:*

1. GNP is understated for developing countries, since a greater proportion of their goods and services are produced within the home by family members for their own use, rather than for sale in the marketplace. Much of the productive activity of the peasant is considered an integral part of family and village life, not an economic transaction. The economic contribution of the housewife who grinds the flour, bakes the bread, and cares for the clothes may not be measured in GNP in poor countries, but the same services *when purchased* are included in a rich country's GNP. In addition, subsistence farmer investments in soil improvements and the cultivation of virgin land are invariably understated in national income accounts. Although a shift from subsistence to commercial production may be slow enough to be dismissed in a country's GNP for 3 to 5 years, it is an important distortion for longer run or intercountry comparisons.[19]

   In some ways, distortions in income differences between the poor country and rich country are analogous to those between the United States in the nineteenth and twentieth centuries. Although estimates indicate U.S. real per capita income for 1860 was one-eleventh what it was in 1993, adjustments would indicate a figure closer to one-fifth. Great-great-great-grandfather grew his fruits and vegetables, raised dairy cattle for milk and sheep for wool, and gathered and chopped firewood. Great-great-great-grandmother processed the food, prepared the meals, and sewed quilts and clothes for the family. But few of these activities added to national product. Today their great-great-great-grandchild purchases milk, fruits, and vegetables at the supermarket, buys meals at restaurants, and pays heating bills—all items that contribute to national product. Moreover, our great-great-great-grandparents' grain output, when estimated, was valued at farm-gate price, excluding the family's food processing. Statistics show U.S. cereal product consumption increased by 24 percent from 1889 to 1919, even though it decreased 33.5 percent if you impute the value of economic processes at home,

---

[18]T.N. Srinivasan, "Data Base for Development Analysis: An Overview," *Journal of Development Economics* 44 (June 1994): 3–27.

[19]Alan Heston, "National Accounts: A Brief Review of Some Problems in Using National Accounts Data in Level of Output Comparisons and Growth Studies," *Journal of Development Economics* 44 (June 1994): 39, estimates that, in 1975 in LDCs, the mean share of the subsistence sector in GDP was 15 percent, but does not estimate what the corresponding margin of error for GDP was.

like milling, grinding, and baking.[20] Part of today's increased GNP per capita (over that of our great-great-great-grandparents) occurs because a larger percentage of consumption enters the market and is measured in national income.

2. GNP may be overstated for developed countries, since a number of items included in their national incomes are intermediate goods, reflecting the costs of producing or guarding income.[21] The Western executive's business suits and commuting costs should probably be considered means of increasing production rather than final consumer goods and services, just as expenditures on smog eradication and water purification that add to national income are really costs of urbanization and economic growth. Furthermore, part of defense spending is a cost of guarding higher incomes, and not for national power and prestige.[22]

3. The exchange rate used to convert GNP in local currency units into U.S. dollars, if market clearing, is based on the relative prices of internationally traded goods (and not on purchasing power—see below). *However, GNP is understated for developing countries because many of their cheap, labor-intensive, unstandardized goods and services have no impact on the exchange rate, since they are not traded.* Many of the necessities of life are very low priced in dollar terms. In 1993, for example, rice—the staple in the diet of an Indian villager—cost 3 rupees (about 10 U.S. cents) per capita per day.[23] Also services in India tend to be inexpensive. Thus 1993 annual salaries for elementary teachers were about one-tenth as high as those in the United States—a case that surely overstates differences in the quality of instruction.

4. GNP is overstated for countries (usually developing and socialist countries) where the price of foreign exchange is less than a market-clearing price. This overstatement can result from import barriers, restrictions on access to foreign currency, export subsidies, or state trading. Suppose that in 1993 India's central bank had allowed the exchange rate to reach its free market rate, Rs. 50 = $1, rather than the official, controlled rate of Rs. 30 = $1. Then the GNP per capita figure of Rs. 9,000 would have been $180 (9,000 divided by 50) rather than $300 (9,000 divided by 30). On balance other adjustments outweigh this effect, so that income differences between rich and poor countries tend to be overstated.[24]

---

[20]Dan Usher, *The Price Mechanism and the Meaning of National Income Statistics* (Oxford: Clarendon Press, 1968), p. 15; and Simon S. Kuznets, *Economic Growth of Nations: Total Output and Production Structure* (Cambridge, Mass.: Harvard University Press, 1971), pp. 10–14.

[21]This statement is somewhat speculative, since intermediate-good output is difficult to measure. In addition, as LDCs become more affluent and urbanized, the percentage of their output devoted to intermediate goods has increased.

[22]When we use GNP as a measure of welfare, we do not inquire about the composition of output between civilian and military goods, between milk and cigarettes, or between pornographic literature and Shakespeare. Most economists assume, for example, that military spending, when it adds to national prestige and power, increases the satisfaction of its citizens. Yet countries such as Benin, which spend only $6 per person on the military, have more resources available for civilian goods and services than Pakistan, which spends $27 per person on the military. United Nations Development Program, *Human Development Report, 1994* (New York: Oxford University Press, 1994), pp. 170–71; and World Bank, *World Development Report, 1994* (New York: Oxford University Press, 1994), pp. 162–63.

[23]Amartya Sen, *Inequality Reexamined* (Cambridge, Mass.: Harvard University Press, 1992), p. 115, argues that "money buys less of some types of commodities in the richer countries." For example, in most U.S. localities, money cannot buy repairs for toasters or staplers, or the mending of shirts and sweaters.

[24]Simon S. Kuznets, *Population, Capital and Growth* (London: Norton, 1974), pp. 333–36, argues that nonagricultural prices divided by agricultural prices are overstated in LDCs relative to DCs, thus exaggerating the importance of the fastest growing industrial sectors and the size of recent LDC growth. However, the finding of Angus Maddison, "A Comparison of the Levels of GDP Per Capita in Developed and Developing Countries, 1700–1980," *Journal of Economic History* 43 (March 1983): 27–41, is the reverse of Kuznets' contention, indicating that, if anything, the nonagricultural sector's weight is understated in developing countries relative to that in developed countries.

Comparison Resistant Services

Comparison resistant services, like health care, education, and government administration, which comprise more than 10 percent of most countries' expenditure, distort cross-national, but not necessarily DC–LDC, GNP comparisons. People do not buy a clearly defined quantity of university education, crime prevention, health maintenance, and forest management as they do food and clothing. The usual ways of measuring service output are unsatisfactory: by labor input cost or to use productivity differences for a standardized service (for example, a tonsillectomy) as representative of general differences (for example, in medicine).[25]

Confidence Intervals for Growth Rates

Derek Blades estimates that, given the errors of population growth and price weights used to aggregate output indicators, the confidence interval for the economic growth of LDCs may be as much as 2 to 3 percent. For Africa, Blades suggests an estimated growth of -1 percent in GNP per capita yearly together with a confidence interval of 3 percent means an estimated growth rate that is likely to be between -4 percent and 2 percent.[26]

Additionally, there may be problems in estimates of sectoral aggregate output that distort GNP figures. In many LDCs, production estimates for domestic food crops, often the largest sector in the economy, are based on informal estimates agricultural officers make about whether output increased or decreased. Here even small errors may be of major importance. Assume GNP in 1996 is $10,000 million. If GNP in 1997 is $10,300 million, with a 5-percent margin, much

[25]Irving Kravis, "Comparative Studies of National Income and Prices," *Journal of Economic Literature* 22 (March 1984): 1–57; and Robert Summers and Alan Heston, "The Penn World Table (Mark 5): An Expanded Set of International Comparisons, 1950–1988," *Quarterly Journal of Economics* 106 (May 1991): 330–31.

There are additional distortions in using GNP to measure welfare that affect comparisons, but not those between DCs and LDCs. Per capita GNP figures do not consider differences in average work week and average leisure between two countries. In addition GNP measures all activity generated through the market whether the activity is productive, unproductive, or destructive. An outbreak of influenza leading to greater drug sales increases GNP, although absence of the disease, by decreasing pharmaceutical consumption, reduces GNP. Likewise durable buildings decrease future GNP because they reduce future construction demand. Wars or earthquakes may increase GNP, since they lead to reconstruction. Furthermore during war, as tanks and bombers go up in smoke, the effective demand for new production may increase. Kimon Valaskakis and Iris Martin, "Economic Indicators and the GPID: an Attempt to Bring Economics Back into the Church without Losing the Faith" (Tokyo: United Nations University, 1980).

Another distortion is the black market, which is not adequately covered in official data. The black market originates in the process of evading or avoiding the fiscal or legal system (of prices or exchange rates). T.N. Srinivasan, "Data Base for Development Analysis: An Overview," *Journal of Development Economics* 44 (June 1994): 8–9, estimates that black-market income comprised 18 to 21 percent of official GDP in India in 1980–81. While this share of GDP is probably larger than black-market income shares in U.S. GDP, how the relative share of black-market income varies generally between DCs and LDCs is not certain.

[26]I have adjusted Blades's statement to apply to 1980–92 growth rates shown in Table 2–1. Derek Blades, "What do we Know about Levels and Growth of Output in Developing Countries? A Critical Analysis with Special Reference to Africa," in R.C.O. Mathews, ed., *Economic Growth and Resources: Proceedings of the Fifth World Congress, International Economic Association, Tokyo*, vol. 2, *Trends and Factors* (New York: St. Martin's Press, 1980), 71–72; and Alan Heston, "National Accounts: A Brief Review of Some Problems in Using National Accounts Data in Level of Output Comparisons and Growth Studies," *Journal of Development Economics* 44 (June 1994): 48–49.

from agriculture, the range is between $9,785 million (representing a 2.15-percent decrease in GNP) and $10,815 million (an 8.15 percent increase).

Purchasing-Power Parity (PPP)

Earlier we pointed out that exchange rates omit nontraded goods, and that the relative prices of nontraded goods to traded goods are lower in developing than in developed countries. The International Comparison Project of the United Nations Statistical Office and the University of Pennsylvania converts a country's GDP from its own currency into international dollars (I$) by measuring the country's purchasing power relative to all other countries rather than using the exchange rate. (**GDP** or **gross domestic product** is income earned within a country's boundaries instead of gross national product, income accruing to a country's residents.) Penn researchers Robert Summers and Alan Heston compute **(P) the price level of GDP** as the ratio of the **purchasing power parity (PPP)** exchange rate to the actual (or market) exchange rate, where both exchange rates are measured as the domestic-currency price of the U.S. dollar.

The PPP exchange rate is that at which the goods and services comprising gross domestic product cost the same in both countries. Thus the London *Economist*, assuming only one good, the Big Mac, calculates the Big Mac PPP, the exchange rate at which this McDonald's hamburger would cost the same in both countries. In 1992, a Big Mac price of Peso 3.30 in Argentina and $2.19 in the United States meant a PPP of Peso 1.51 = $1 compared to the actual exchange rate of Peso 0.99 = $1, so that P was 152.5 percent and the peso was overvalued. Similarly, the Chinese Big Mac price of Yuan 6.30 indicates a PPP of Yuan 2.88 = $1 compared to an exchange rate of Yuan 5.44 = $1, with P 52.9 percent, indicating hamburgers were cheap in China.[27] In the real world, while the purchasing power of Rs. 13.25 = $1, the exchange rate is Rs. 35 = $1, so that India's P is 37.9 percent of that of the United States. The nominal GDP per capita for 1992, $310, divided by P, 37.9 percent, equals I$818 or real GDP per capita.

The Penn economists use a series of simultaneous equations to solve the PPP for 81 (60 in the mid-1980s and 34 in the 1970s) benchmark and quasi-benchmark countries and world average prices for 400 to 700 commodities and services, specified in detail for quantity and quality. The averaging, which uses a specialized multiple regression, is designed to consider the fact that not every country prices every item. If a country fails to price an item (for example, the rental of an apartment in a 20-year old multistoried building, of 120 square meters, with central heating, and one bathroom), researchers calculate the cost of making appropriate quality adjustments to a substitute item that is directly observable. Indeed the Penn researchers describe their basic procedure as the potato-is-a-potato rule. "A potato with given physical characteristics was treated not only as the same pro-

---

[27]"Big MacCurrencies," *Economist* (April 18, 1992): p. 81.

Should MacDonald's open a franchise in India, it would probably not serve Big Macs, as many Indians refrain from eating beef for religious reasons.

John Williamson, ed., *Estimating Equilibrium Exchange Rates* (Washington, D.C.: Institute for International Economics, 1994), p. 13, is not amused by Big Mac PPPs. He rightly indicates that the effort of the *Economist*, which interprets PPP in terms of the classic contention that the nominal exchange rate should reflect the purchasing power of one currency against another, is a "misconceived endeavor." Moreover, Williamson points out a major discrepancy between the Big Mac and Burger King Whopper index.

duce but also as the same quantity, whether it was purchased in the country or in the city, in January or in June, by the piece or by the bushel, and whether it was purchased at a retail market or consumed out of own production."[28] For 57 non-benchmark countries, the economists use a shortcut estimating equation where PPP is a function of nominal GNP per capita, steel production per capita, telephone use, motor vehicles, and other variables.[29]

The U.N.-Penn estimates indicate a *P* of 44.8 percent for Africa, 67.4 percent for Asia, 44.1 percent for Latin America, and 116.5 percent for Europe. The figure for Africa means that its purchasing-power adjusted (I$) GDP is 2.322 (1/.448) times its GDP converted into U.S. dollars at the existing exchange rate.

How much must an average-income earner in India have to earn in U.S. dollars to attain the same living standard (that is, same basket of goods) in the United States that the earner does in India? How does this dollar amount compare with the average income earned in the United States?

P_{GNP} (or the price level of GNP), 37.5 percent (*P*, which applies to GDP, is 37.9 percent) for India, indicates that United States' per capita GNP is not 75 times but 28 (75 × .375) times that of India.[30] The U.S. per capita expenditure on food is almost 11 times what it is in India, but only 6 times with adjustments in purchasing power. For such staples as bread, rice, and cereals, U.S. per capita consumption is twice that of India, but only 1.5 times as much with the adjustment.[31]

Yet these comparisons do not provide answers to these two questions. You need to determine the dollar price of India's basket of goods and services (wheat cakes, mangos, papayas, rice, sitars, brass tables, and so forth) in the United States and then compare this figure to the dollar price of U.S. average income. While we cannot indicate the ratio of the dollar price of GNP per capita in the United States to that in India, the ratio is clearly less than 28. If Indians need to replicate their goods, and cannot substitute wheat bread for wheat cakes, oranges for mangos, potatoes for rice, violins for sitars, or wooden for brass tables, the ratio might be very low; indeed it might cost the U.S. per capita income to replicate these goods in the United States. How detailed the goods are specified determines how high the ratio is and how well off India appears.

---

[28]Irving Kravis, Alan Heston, and Robert Summers, *World Product and Income: International Comparisons of Real Gross Product* (Baltimore: Johns Hopkins University Press, 1983), p. 31.

[29]Robert Summers and Alan Heston, "The Penn World Table (Mark 5): An Expanded Set of International Comparisons, 1950–1988," *Quarterly Journal of Economics* 106 (May 1991): 327–68, and the computer diskette that provides the expanded Penn World Table 5.

[30]The percentage of GNP to GDP is from the computer diskette that provides the expanded Penn World Table 5 version of Robert Summers and Alan Heston, "The Penn World Table (Mark 5): An Expanded Set of International Comparisons, 1950–1988," *Quarterly Journal of Economics* 106 (May 1991): 327–68.

[31]Irving Kravis, "Comparative Studies of National Income and Prices," *Journal of Economic Literature* 22 (March 1984), 1–57; Robert Summers and Alan Heston, "A New Set of International Comparisons of Real Product and Price Levels Estimates for 130 Countries, 1950–1985," *Review of Income and Wealth* 34 (March 1988): 1–25; Robert Summers and Alan Heston, "Improved International Comparisons of Real Product and its Composition: 1950–1980," *Review of Income and Wealth* 30 (June 1984): 207–62; Irving B. Kravis, "The Three Faces of the International Comparison Project," *World Bank Research Observer* 1 (January 1986): 3–26; Irving Kravis, Alan Heston, and Robert Summers, *United Nations International Comparison Project: Phase II; International Comparisons of Real Product and Purchasing Power* (Baltimore: Johns Hopkins University Press, 1978); and Irving Kravis, Alan Heston, and Robert Summers, "Real GDP per Capita for More than One Hundred Countries, *Economic Journal* 88 (June 1978): 215–42; Irving Kravis, Alan Heston, and Robert Summers, *World Product and Income: International Comparisons of Real Gross Product* (Baltimore: John Hopkins University Press, 1983); and Robert Summers and Alan Heston, "The Penn World Table (Mark 5): An Expanded Set of International Comparisons, 1950–1988," *Quarterly Journal of Economics* 106 (May 1991): 327–68.

Put the shoe on the other foot. How much must an average income earner in the United States earn in rupees to secure the same living standard in India that the person acquires in the U.S.? The rupee price of an average U.S. basket of goods (including milkshakes, hamburgers, computers, automobiles, rock-and-roll compact disks, and so forth) would be substantially more than 28 times the average Indian basket. The U.S. consumption basket would be more costly relative to the Indian basket the more Americans refuse, for example, to consume yogurt and vegetables instead of milkshakes and hamburgers.

Dan Usher suggests that you can compare income per capita more directly if you calculate the geometric average of (1) the ratio of the U.S. to Indian output of per capita goods and services in relative prices in dollars, and (2) the ratio of the U.S. to Indian output of per capita goods and services in relative prices in rupees. We might expect this geometric average to correspond roughly to ICP results. Both analyses, however, assume no substitution in consumption resulting from changes in prices.[32]

Penn-ICP GDP figures, expressed in international dollars, are the best available for adjusting for purchasing power, and are relatively easy to interpret. However, ICP calculations, with their detailed prices for a large number of commodities, require much extra time and effort to obtain figures that are several years behind the most current figures, those of the World Bank's *World Development Report*, which are themselves 2 years old. Moreover, a majority of the 138 countries are either nonbenchmark countries (and thus based on an estimating equation) or quasi-benchmark countries, with substantial missing variables for commodities or services. The problems are even more serious when you require a reliable time series. The quality of data for former socialist countries is especially suspect.[33] T.N. Srinivasan contends that Summers and Heston "use problematic procedures of extrapolation from data for a few years and countries to many more."[34]

By and large, the greater the difference in per capita income between two countries, the greater the correction for purchasing power. Chapter 6 indicates that worldwide income inequality is reduced considerably when the gross product in developing countries is adjusted for purchasing power.

ICP figures do not alter the *rankings* of countries greatly from conventional per capita income figures. Thus this book, in an effort to be current, most frequently uses income data based on conversions between currencies by means of exchange rates rather than PPPs. However, you should remember that these data exaggerate per capita income differentials.

A Better Measure of Economic Development?

But even with the more precise U.N.–Penn figures, using income as a measure of development is a weak tool, and efforts have been made to replace GNP per capita

---

[32]Dan Usher, *The Price Mechanism and the Meaning of National Income Statistics* (Oxford: Clarendon Press, 1968).

[33]For example, as Chapter 20 indicates, Chinese growth rates are overstated as they are heavily based on growth in physical output rather than deflated expenditures. For further discussion, see Nicholas R. Lardy, *Foreign Trade and Economic Reform in China, 1978–1990* (Cambridge: Cambridge University Press, 1992), pp. 150–55.

[34]T.N. Srinivasan, "Human Development: A New Paradigm or Reinvention of the Wheel," *American Economic Review* 84 (May 1994): 241.

with a more reliable measure—usually an index of several economic and social variables.

THE PHYSICAL QUALITY OF LIFE INDEX (PQLI)

One alternative measure of welfare is the **PQLI**, which combines three indicators—infant mortality (the annual number of deaths of infants under 1 year of age per 1,000 live births), life expectancy (at age 1, to not overlap with infant mortality), and adult literacy rate (in percentage). The first two variables represent the effects of nutrition, public health, income, and the general environment. For example, infant mortality reflects the availability of clean water, the condition of the home environment, and the mother's health. Literacy is a measure of well-being as well as a requirement for a country's economic development.[35]

Critics of this measure stress a close correlation between the three PQLI indicators and the composite index and GNP per capita. Nevertheless, figures on PQLI (between the most unfavorable performance in 1950, valued at 0, and the most favorable figure, 100, expected by the year 2000) reveal exceptions to the correlation (see Table 2–1). For instance, China's life expectancy and infant mortality rates, matching those of the United States in 1940, were achieved at a per capita income of $490. On the other hand, a relatively high per capita does not necessarily reflect widespread well-being, as in the case of such affluent oil countries as Saudi Arabia and Oman.

However, PQLI indicators are of limited use in distinguishing levels of development beyond middle-income countries. All three PQLI variables—life expectancy, literacy, and infant mortality—are highly related to per capita income *until* nutrition, health, and education reach certain high levels, then the value of the variables levels off. These indicators have asymptotic limits reflecting biological and physical maxima.[36] Thus, except for city-states Hong Kong and Singapore and affluent oil exporters Kuwait and the United Arab Emirates, all high-income countries have infant mortality rates below 10 per 1,000, literacy rates of 98 percent or above (except for Israel with 95 percent), and a life expectancy of 75–79 years (see Table 2–1).

There are difficulties with PQLI not encountered with standard per capita GNP data. Scaling and weighting a composite index, as with PQLI, present a problem, since rescaling raw data to a 0–1 range is somewhat arbitrary and there is no clear conceptual rationale for giving the core indicators equal weights. Moreover, 87 of 117 LDCs with PQLI figures have not compiled reliable data on life expectancy since 1980, and 60 LDCs lack data on adult literacy since 1980.[37] In addition, as scholars changed their estimates of the most favorable figures for components by 2000, the maxima and scaling for PQLI indicators have had to be changed. Furthermore, economists question the meaning of the PQLI growth rate, called the **disparity reduction rate**, not only because of the unreliable time-series data but also because most high-income countries are pressing near the practical

---

[35]Martin M. McLaughlin and the Staff of the Overseas Development Council, *The United States and World Development: Agenda, 1979* (New York: Praeger, 1979), pp.129–33.

[36]Norman L. Hicks and Paul Streeten, "Indicators of Development: The Search for a Basic Needs Yardstick," *World Development* 7 (June 1979): 572–75.

[37]T.N. Srinivasan, "Human Development: A New Paradigm or Reinvention of the Wheel," *American Economic Review* 84 (May 1994): 238–43; and T.N. Srinivasan, "Introduction," *Journal of Development Economics* 44 (June 1994): 1–2.

maximum (99 percent for adult literacy, for example) for some indicators, giving little scope for growth.

THE HUMAN DEVELOPMENT INDEX (HDI)

The United Nations Development Program (UNDP) defines human development as "a process of enlarging people's choices. The most critical ones are to lead a long and healthy life, to be educated and enjoy a decent standard of living."[38] In the face of widespread assessment that the 1980s was a "lost decade" for developing countries, UNDP has argued that human development disparities between DCs and LDCs are much less than disparities in income per capita, that human development narrowed considerably between DCs and LDCs while income gaps were widening, and that LDCs (including least developed countries such as Afghanistan, Burkina Faso, and Somalia) have made tremendous progress in human development.[39] In its effort to measure human development, UNDP has constructed another alternative measure of welfare, the **Human Development Index**.

The **HDI** summarizes a great deal of social performance in a single composite index combining three indicators—longevity (a proxy for health and nutrition), education, and living standards. Educational attainment is a composite of two variables, a two-thirds weight based on the adult literacy rate (in percentage), and a one-third weight on the mean years of schooling for persons over 25 years of age. Longevity is measured by average life expectancy (in years) at birth, computed by assuming that babies born in a given year will experience the current death rate of each age cohort (the first year, second year, third year, and so forth through the nth year) throughout their lifetime. The indicator for living standards is real per capita GDP in purchasing power parity (PPP) dollars, with no discount up to a global poverty level based on the income needed to attain a minimal nutritional level (I$4,829 in 1990), and a progressively increasing discount as income rises, reflecting a diminishing marginal utility of income.

To construct a composite index, you determine the maximum and minimum values for each of the three variables—life expectancy, education, and adjusted real GDP per capita. You normalize the observed value for each of the three variables into a 0–1 scale. Then you measure the deprivation that a country suffers in each of the three variables, averaging the three deprivation rates to arrive at HDI. HDI can assume values from 0 to 1.

Here is how India computes the percentage deprivation for each of three indicators to calculate its 1990 HDI from the *Human Development Report, 1993*.[40]

Maximum life expectancy = 78.6 (for Japan)	India's life expectancy deprivation $= (78.6 - 59.1)/(78.6 - 42.0)$ $= 19.5/36.6 = 0.533$
Minimum life expectancy = 42.0 (for Sierre Leone)	

[38]United Nations Development Program, *Human Development Report, 1990* (New York: Oxford University Press, 1990), p. 10.

[39]United Nations Development Program, *Human Development Report, 1991* (New York: Oxford University Press, 1991), pp. 16–18.

[40]United Nations Development Program, *Human Development Report, 1993* (New York: Oxford University Press, 1993), pp. 100–07, 135–37.

Maximum adult literacy rate =
   99.0% (19 countries)
Minimum adult literacy rate =
   18.2% (for Djibouti)
India's adult literacy rate =
   48.2%

India's adult literacy rate
   deprivation = (99.0 – 48.2)/(99.0 – 18.2)
   = 50.8/80.8 = 0.629

Maximum mean years of
   schooling = 12.3 (USA)
Minimum mean years of
   schooling = 0.1 (Niger and
   Burkina Faso)
India's mean years of
   schooling = 2.4

India's mean years of schooling
   deprivation = (12.3 – 2.4)/(12.3 – 0.1)
   = 9.9/12.2 = 0.811

India's educational attainment deprivation = 2/3 × adult literacy rate deprivation
   (0.629) + 1/3 × mean years of schooling (0.811) = 0.419 + 0.270 = 0.689

Maximum adjusted real GDP per
   capita (I$), with
   progressively increasing
   discount as income rises =
   5,075 (for the USA)
Minimum adjusted real GDP per
   capita (I$) = 367 (for Zaïre)
India's adjusted real GDP per
   capita (I$) = 1,072, the same
   as real GDP per capita in I$
   in India, since it is below
   the global poverty level

India's adjusted real GDP per
   capita deprivation
   (5075 – 1072)/(5075 – 367)
   = 4003/4708 = 0.850

India's average deprivation = 0.533 + 0.689 + 0.850/ 3 = 0.691
India's human development index = 1 – 0.691 = 0.309

Some critics argue that development problems are essentially economic problems, a matter of stimulating economic growth. R. Reichel finds that per capita income at purchasing power parity explains a large proportion of other HDI components. The proportion of variation explained, or R^2, is 0.783 for life expectancy and 0.535 for literacy rate. He concludes that we do not need to measure human development separately from average income. However, most development experts and international agencies reject Reichel's position, arguing that income measures still neglect many important aspects of the development process, leaving much of human development unexplained.[41]

One example of a substantial divergence between HDI and income rankings is that of South Africa, which ranked fifty-seventh in GNP per capita but only eighty-fifth among 173 countries in HDI.[42] Despite the introduction of a universal adult ballot in South Africa in 1994, the country's social indicators still reflect the

---

[41]R. Reichel, "Der 'Human Development Index'—ein sinnvoller Entwicklungsindikator?" *Zeitschrift fur Wirtschaftspolitik* 40(1): 57–67; and Harald Trabold-Nubler, "The Human Development Index—A New Development Indicator?" *Intereconomics* 26 (September-October 1991): 236–43.

[42]United Nations Development Program, *Human Development Report, 1993* (New York: Oxford University Press, 1993), pp. 135–37.

legacy of decades of a white-ruled **apartheid** (racially separate and discriminatory) economy. South Africa is explained more adequately by HDI (0.650) and its
components than GDP per capita, comparable to that of Venezuela and Malaysia,
with HDIs of 0.820 and 0.794, respectively. The purchasing-power adjusted GDP
per capita of black, Asian, and mixed-race South Africa (1992) was I\$1,710, about
the same as Senegal's I\$1,680, and in excess of the I\$1,116 for Africa as a whole. Yet
this low income for 36.1 million nonwhite South Africans stands in stark contrast
to that of 7.3 million white South Africans, I\$14,920 income per capita, a figure
higher than New Zealand's I\$13,970. Life expectancy, an indicator of health, was
62 in South Africa compared to 71 in Malaysia and 70 in Venezuela. But life expectancy was only 52 for black South Africans, 62 for Asians and mixed races, and
74 for whites, 54 for Africa generally, and 77 for DCs, while the adult literacy rate
was 67 percent for nonwhites and 85 percent for whites.[43]

HDI, when disaggregated regionally, can vary widely within a country. Kerala, a south Indian state with one of the lowest incomes per capita in the country
but with a more favorable policy on female education and property ownership,
communal medical care, and old-age pensions, surpasses the Indian average in
the following categories: a life expectancy at birth of 72 years compared to 59
years, an infant mortality rate of 18 compared to 90 per 1,000, an adult literacy rate
of 91 percent compared to 52 percent, a female literacy rate of 87 percent to 39 percent, and an HDI of 0.532 compared to 0.309.

In 1994 in Chiapas state, the Zapatista army, representing Indian smallholders and landless workers or *campesinos*, rebelled against Mexico's ruling party,
which they believed was responsible for their poverty and distress. In the state,
GDP per capita (PPP\$) was 43 percent below and adult literacy 24 percent below
the national average. At the same time, North-East Brazil lagged behind Southern
Brazil 69 to 52 years in life expectancy, 91 percent to 58 percent in adult literacy
rate, and 40 percent in real GDP per capita, disparities larger than those in Mexico.[44]

HDI does not capture the adverse effect of gender disparities on social
progress. In 1995, the United Nations Development Program measured the **gender-
related development index (GDI)**, or HDI adjusted for gender inequality. GDI
concentrates on the same variables as HDI, but notes inequality in achievement
between men and women, imposing a penalty for such inequality. The GDI is
based on female shares of earned income, the life expectancy of women relative to
men (allowing for the biological edge that women enjoy in living longer than

---

[43] E. Wayne Nafziger, *Inequality in Africa: Political Elites, Proletariat, Peasants, and the Poor* (Cambridge:
Cambridge University Press, 1988), p. 18; Jacques Lecaillon, Felix Paukert, Christian Morrisson, and
Dimitri Germidis, *Income Distribution and Economic Development* (Geneva: International Labor Office,
1984), p. 46, both sources updated to the present; United Nations Development Program, *Human Development Report, 1993* (New York: Oxford University Press, 1993), pp. 27, 136; and United Nations Development Program, *Human Development Report, 1994* (New York: Oxford University Press, 1994), pp.
14–17, 98, 130–31.

    The last source cited shows that South Africa's HDI ranking, life expectancy, adult literacy rate,
and infant mortality rate are substantially less favorable than the same indicators for two countries
with about the same average income levels, Chile and Malaysia, but more favorable than for Iraq, with
roughly the same per capita income.

[44]World Bank, *World Development Report, 1993* (New York: Oxford University Press, 1993), pp. 238–304;
United Nations Development Program, *Human Development Report, 1993* (New York: Oxford University Press, 1993), pp. 19, 135–37; United Nations Development Program, *Human Development Report,
1994* (New York: Oxford University Press, 1994), pp. 98–99; and Amartya Sen, *Inequality Reexamined*
(Cambridge, Mass.: Harvard University Press, 1992), pp. 126–27.

men), and a weighted average of female literacy and schooling relative to those of males. However, GDI does not include variables not easily measured such as women's participation in community life and decision-making, their access to professional opportunities, consumption of resources within the family, dignity, and personal security. Because gender inequality exists in every country, the GDI is always lower than the HDI. The four top-ranking countries in GDI are Scandinavian countries—Sweden, Finland, Norway, and Denmark, in that order, but Eastern European countries, Hong Kong, Singapore, Uruguay, and Thailand also have GDI rankings substantially higher than HDI rankings. The bottom five places, in ascending order for GDI, include Afghanistan, Sierre Leone, Mali, Niger, and Burkina Faso, where women face a double deprivation—low human development achievement and women's achievement lower than men.[45]

Many who agree that human development needs separate attention are critical of HDI. HDI has similar problems to those of PQLI—problems of scaling and weighting a composite index, the lack of rationale for equal weights for the core indicators, and the lack of reliable data since 1980. Additionally, school enrollment figures are not internationally comparable, since school quality, drop-out rates, and length of school year vary substantially between and within countries. Moreover, before its 1994 revisions, the United Nations Development Program shifted the goal posts for HDI each year, not allowing economists to measure growth over time; thus, a country's HDI could fall with no change or even an increase in all components if maximum and minimum values rose over time. On the other hand, the scaling of life expectancy, for example, meant that even if developing countries increased their minimum values from 42 to 75 years, while the maximum continued to be 78.6 years, the transformed values would still range from 0 to 1 and would not reflect this large leap in human development.[46]

The base for the GDP per capita component (in I$) rises and falls on the validity of PPP calculations. In addition, many economists are critical of the UNDP's adjustment to Penn-ICP figures, in which income above the poverty level or income above average GDP per capita in PPP$ beginning in 1994, only a slight upward revision, contributes only marginally to human development.[47] Thus, the

[45]United Nations Development Program, *Human Development Report, 1995* (New York: Oxford University Press, 1995), pp. 72–79.

[46]Joseph Chamie, "Population Databases in Development Analysis," *Journal of Development Economics* 44 (June 1994): 131–46; Jere Behrman and Mark Rosenzweig, "Labour Force: Caveat Emptor: Cross-Country Data on Education and the Labor Force," *Journal of Development Economics* 44 (June 1994): 147–71; T.N. Srinivasan, "Human Development: A New Paradigm or Reinvention of the Wheel," *American Economic Review* 84 (May 1994): 238–43; T.N. Srinivasan, "Introduction," Journal of Development Economics 44 (June 1994): 1–2; and United Nations Development Program, *Human Development Report, 1994* (New York: Oxford University Press, 1994), pp. 90–96.

[47] Patrick J. Gormely, "The Human Development Index in 1994: Impact of Income on Country Rank," *Journal of Economic and Social Measurement* 21 (January 1995): 1–15, who contends "that the UNDP's method of 'adjusting' a country's real per-capita GDP causes a country's income above the threshold level to contribute practically nothing to development" (p. 6), suggests no or only a modest discount of increases of income above the threshold. No discount means several changes in 1994 HDI rankings (which use 1991 income figures). Nations with a low HDI relative to GDP per capita rise, including the United States from eighth to second, Singapore from forty-third to twenty-fifth, North Korea from one-hundred-first to seventy-fifth, and Vietnam from one-hundred-sixteenth to ninety-eighth. Countries with a low GDP per capita relative to HDI fall, including Sweden from fifth to eighth, Argentina from thirty-seventh to forty-sixth, Ukraine from forty-fifth to fifty-eighth, Colombia from fiftieth to sixty-third, Turkey from sixty-eighth to ninety-third, and Syria from seventy-third to one-hundredth. Switzerland still remains first regardless of the adjustment used.

United States, with the highest real GDP per capita in 1990, I$21,449, had an adjusted real GDP per capita of only 5,075, only 74 in excess of that of Saudi Arabia, which had an I$10,989 GDP per capita and 5,001 adjusted GDP per capita, and only 180 more than Mexico, with I$5,918 GDP per capita and 4,895 adjusted real GDP per capita.[48]

The concept of human development is much richer and more multifarious than what we can capture in one index or indicator. Yet HDI is useful in focusing attention on qualitative aspects of development, and may influence countries with relatively low HDI scores to examine their policies regarding nutrition, health, and education.

Weighted Indices for GNP Growth

Another reason why the growth rate of GNP can be a misleading indicator of development is because GNP growth is heavily weighted by the income shares of the rich. A given growth rate for the rich has much more impact on total growth than the same growth rate for the poor. In Thailand, a country with moderate income inequality, the upper 50 percent of income recipients receive about 80 percent ($80 billion) and the lower 50 percent about 20 percent ($20 billion) of the GNP of $100 million. A growth of 10 percent ($8 billion) in income for the top-half results in 8-percent total growth, but a 10-percent income growth for the bottom-half ($2 billion) is only 2-percent aggregate growth. Yet the 10-percent growth for the lower-half does far more to reduce poverty than the same growth for the upper-half.

We can illustrate the superior weight of the rich in output growth two ways: (1) as above, the same growth for the rich as the poor has much more effect on total growth; and (2) a given dollar increase in GNP raises the income of the poor by a higher percentage than for the rich.

When GNP growth is the index of performance, it is assumed that an $8 billion additional income has the same effect on social welfare regardless of the recipients' income class. But in Thailand, you can increase GNP by $8 billion (a 8-percent overall growth on $80 billion) either through a 10-percent growth for the top 50 percent or a 40-percent increase for the bottom 50 percent.

One alternative to this measure of GNP growth is to give equal weight to a 1-percent increase in income for any member of society. In the previous example, the 10-percent income growth for the lower 50 percent, although a smaller absolute increase, would be given greater weight than the same rate for the upper 50 percent, since the former growth affects a poorer segment of the population. Another alternative is a **poverty-weighted index** in which a higher weight is given a 1-percent income growth for low-income groups than for high-income groups.

Table 2–2 shows the difference in annual growth in welfare based on three different weighting systems: (1) GNP weights for each income quintile (top, second, third, fourth, and bottom 20 percent of the population); (2) equal weights for each quintile; and (3) poverty weights of 0.6 for the lowest 40 percent, 0.3 for the next 40 percent, and 0.1 for the top 20 percent. In Panama, Brazil, Mexico, and Venezuela, where income distribution worsened, performance is worse when

---

[48]United Nations Development Program, *Human Development Report, 1993* (New York: Oxford University Press, 1993), pp. 135–37; with criticisms by Harald Trabold-Nubler, "The Human Development Index—A New Development Indicator?" *Intereconomics* 26 (September-October 1991): 236–43.

TABLE 2-2   Income Equality and Growth

Country	Period	I. Income Growth			II. Annual Increase in Welfare		
		Upper 20 Percent	Middle 40 Percent	Lowest 40 Percent	(A) GNP Weights	(B) Equal Weights	(C) Poverty Weights
Korea	1964–70	10.6	7.8	9.3	9.3	9.0	9.0
Panama	1960–69	8.8	9.2	3.2	8.2	6.7	5.6
Brazil	1960–70	8.4	4.8	5.2	6.9	5.7	5.4
Mexico	1963–69	8.0	7.0	6.6	7.6	7.0	6.9
Taiwan	1953–61	4.5	9.1	12.1	6.8	9.4	10.4
Venezuela	1962–70	7.9	4.1	3.7	6.4	4.7	4.2
Colombia	1964–70	5.6	7.3	7.0	6.2	6.8	7.0
El Salvador	1961–69	4.1	10.5	5.3	6.2	7.1	6.7
Philippines	1961–71	4.9	6.4	5.0	5.4	5.5	5.4
Peru	1961–71	4.7	7.5	3.2	5.4	5.2	4.6
Sri Lanka	1963–70	3.1	6.2	8.3	5.0	6.4	7.2
Yugoslavia	1963–68	4.9	5.0	4.3	4.8	4.7	4.6
India	1954–64	5.1	3.9	3.9	4.5	4.1	4.0

Note: Equal weights imply a weight of 0.2 for the upper 20 percent, 0.4 for the middle 40 percent, and 0.4 for the lowest 40 percent, while poverty weights are calculated giving weights of 0.1, 0.3, and 0.6, respectively.

Source: Hollis Chenery, Montek S. Ahluwalia, C. L. G. Bell, John H. Duloy, and Richard Jolly, eds., *Redistribution with Growth* (London: Oxford University Press, 1974), p. 42.

measured by weighted indices than by GNP growth. In Colombia, El Salvador, Sri Lanka, and Taiwan, where income distribution improved, the weighted indices are higher than GNP growth. In Korea, the Philippines, Yugoslavia, Peru, and India, where income distribution remained largely unchanged, weighted indices do not alter GNP growth greatly.[49]

Is poverty-weighted growth superior to GNP-weighted growth in assessing development attainment? Maximizing poverty-weighted growth may generate too little saving, as in Sri Lanka of the 1960s, since the rich have a higher propensity to save than the poor (Chapter 15).

Although the different weighting systems reflect different value premises, economists usually choose GNP weights because of convenience and easy interpretation. Given present data, it is easier to discuss poverty reduction by using both GNP per capita and income distribution data than to calculate poverty-weighted growth.

"Basic-Needs" Attainment

During the late 1960s, many economists were frustrated that economic growth seemingly had only a limited effect in reducing third-world poverty. Partly in reaction, in the 1970s, there was widespread disillusionment with the emphasis on per capita GNP growth in the late 1970s. Strategies that rely on raising productivity in

[49]Montek S. Ahluwalia and Hollis Chenery, "The Economic Framework," in Hollis Chenery, Montek S. Ahluwalia, C. L. G. Bell, John H. Duloy, and Richard Jolly, eds., *Redistribution with Growth* (London: Oxford University Press, 1974), pp. 38–42.

developing countries are thought to be inadequate *without* programs that directly focus on meeting the basic needs of the poorest 40–50 percent of the population— the **basic-needs approach.** This direct attack is needed, it is argued, because of the continuing serious maldistribution of incomes; because consumers, lacking knowledge about health and nutrition, often make inefficient or unwise choices in this area; because public services must meet many basic needs, such as sanitation and water supplies; and because it is difficult to find investments and policies that uniformly increase the incomes of the poor.

MEASURES

The basic-needs approach shifts attention from maximizing output to minimizing poverty. The stress is not only on *how much* is being produced, but also on *what* is being produced, in *what ways*, for *whom*, and *with what impact*.

Basic needs include adequate nutrition, primary education, health, sanitation, water supply, and housing. What are possible indicators of these basic needs? Two economic consultants with the World Bank identify the following as a preliminary set of indicators:[50]

- Food: Calorie supply per head, or calorie supply as a percent of requirements; protein
- Education: Literacy rates, primary enrollment (as a percent of the population aged 5–14)
- Health: Life expectancy at birth
- Sanitation: Infant mortality (per thousand births), percent of the population with access to sanitation facilities
- Water supply: Infant mortality (per thousand births), percent of the population with access to potable water
- Housing: None (since existing measures, such as people per room, do not satisfactorily indicate the quality of housing)

Each of these indicators (such as calorie supply) should be supplemented by data on distribution by income class.

Infant mortality is a good indication of the availability of sanitation and clean water facilities, since infants are susceptible to waterborne diseases. Furthermore, data on infant mortality are generally more readily available than data on access to water.

GROWTH AND "BASIC NEEDS"

High basic-needs attainment is positively related to the rate of growth of per capita GNP, since increased life expectancy and literacy, together with reduced infant mortality, are associated with greater worker health and productivity. Fur-

[50]Norman L. Hicks and Paul Streeten, "Indicators of Development: The Search for a Basic Needs Yardstick," *World Development* 7 (June 1979): 567–80.

thermore, rapid output growth usually reduces poverty.[51] Thus GNP per head remains an important figure. But we must also look at some indicators of the composition and beneficiaries of GNP. Basic-needs data supplement GNP data but do not replace them. And as the earlier South African example indicates, we must go beyond national averages to get basic-needs measures by income class, ethnic group, region, and other subgroups (see Chapter 6 for a discussion of inequality).

IS THE SATISFACTION OF BASIC NEEDS A HUMAN RIGHT?

The U.S. founders, shaped by the scientific and intellectual activity of the Enlightenment, wrote in the Declaration of Independence: "We hold these truths to be self-evident, that all men are created equal; that they are endowed by their Creator with certain unalienable rights." The U.N. Universal Declaration of Human Rights goes beyond such civil and political rights as a fair trial, universal adult vote, and freedom from torture to include the rights of employment, minimum wages, collective bargaining, social security, health and medical care, free primary education, and other socioeconomic rights. In fact, for many in the third world, the fulfillment of economic needs precedes a concern with political liberties. In Africa there is a saying, "Human rights begin with breakfast"; and a beggar in one of Bertolt Brecht's operas sings, "First we must eat, then comes morality."

Some LDCs may have to reallocate resources from consumer goods for the well-off to basic necessities for the whole population. However, even with substantial redistribution, resources are too scarce to attain these social and economic rights for the masses in most low-income countries. Consider the right of free primary education. Most LDCs have less than one-twentieth the per capita GNP of the United States, 1.5 times the population share aged 5–15 (see Chapter 8), and greater shortages of qualified teachers, all of which means a much greater share of GNP would have to be devoted to education to attain the same primary enrollment rates as in the United States. Far less income would be left over for achieving other objectives, such as adequate nutrition, housing, and sanitation. Furthermore, primary school graduates in Africa and Asia migrate to the towns, adding to the unemployed and the disaffected. A carefully selective and phased educational program, including adult literacy programs, can often be more economical, and do more for basic needs, than an immediate attempt at universal primary education.

Setting up Western labor standards and minimum wages in labor-abundant LDCs is not always sensible. With a labor force growth of 2–3 percent per year, imitating labor standards from rich countries in LDCs may create a relatively privileged, regularly employed labor force and aggravate social inequality,

---

[51]Norman L. Hicks, "Growth versus Basic Needs: Is There a Trade-Off?" *World Development* 7 (November/December 1979): 985–94.

The International Fund for Agricultural Development measures basic needs through a basic needs index (BNI), which consists of an education index (adult literacy rate and primary school enrollment rate) and health index (number of physicians per head of the population, infant mortality, and access to health care, safe water, and sanitation). Idriss Jazairy, Mohiuddin Alamgir, and Theresa Panuccio, *The State of World Rural Poverty: an Inquiry into its Causes and Consequences*, Published for the International Fund for Agricultural Development (New York: New York University Press, 1992), pp. 28–29, 41–44, 392–99. The BNI especially focuses on indicators of interest to the very poor. Still, the BNI is subject to problems of scaling and weighting similar to indicators such as the PQLI and HDI.

unemployment, and poverty. Economic rights must consider the scarcity of available resources and the necessity of choice.[52]

Liberation Versus Development

In the 1970s, some leftists, including Latin American Roman Catholic radicals, French Marxists, and scholars sympathetic to China's Cultural Revolution (1966–76), rejected economic growth tied to dependence on Western-type techniques, capital, institutions, and elite consumer goods. These scholars believed that the LDCs should control their own economic and political destiny and free themselves from domination by Western capitalist countries and their elitist allies in the third world. According to them, the models for genuine development are not such countries as South Korea, Taiwan, and Brazil, but Tanzania, Cuba, and Maoist China. The latter three countries were viewed as stressing indigenous economic and political autonomy, the holistic development of human beings, the fulfillment of human creativity, and selfless serving of the masses rather than individual incentives and the production of material goods.[53]

Since Mao Zedong's death in 1976, the Chinese government has repudiated much of the Cultural Revolution's emphasis on national self-sufficiency, non-economic (moral) incentives, and central price fixing and is stressing household and management responsibility, limited price reform, and assistance from capitalist countries. After 1982, Presidents Nyerere and Ali Hassan Mwinyi agreed that peasant resettlement into planned rural village communities had been spoiled by corrupt and ineffective government and party officials and the influence of rich peasants. Although Cuba, in the decade following the victory of Fidel Castro's revolution in 1959, provided greater economic security and met most of the basic needs of the bulk of the population, average consumption levels have been low and declining since the 1980s. Consumption standards especially fell after the Soviet Union ceased its international aid, trade subsidies, and debt writedowns just before the Soviet collapse of 1991.

The Liberationists were not really criticizing development but rather growth policies disguised as development. Including income distribution and local economic control in the definition of development would be a better approach than abandoning the concept of development. For in the 1980s and 1990s, the leaders of China, Tanzania, and Cuba seem to have replaced the language of liberation with that of development, specifically self-directed development.

For the South Commission: "Development is based on self-reliance and is self-directed; without these characteristics there can be no genuine development. . . . The South cannot count on a significant improvement in the international economic environment for its development in the 1990s. . . . The countries of the South will have to rely increasingly on their own exertions, both individual and collective, and to reorient their development strategies, which must benefit from the lessons of past experience."[54] Dragoslav Avramovic argues: "Adjustment

---

[52]Paul Streeten, "Basic Needs and Human Rights," *World Development* 8 (February 1980): 107–11.

[53]Denis Goulet, " 'Development' . . . or Liberation," *International Development Review* 13, no. 3 (September 1971): 6–10; and John W. Gurley, "Maoist Economic Development: The New Man in the New China," *Review of Radical Political Economics* 2, no. 4 (Winter 1970): 26–38. For a somewhat different emphasis, see Gustavo Gutierrez, *A Theology of Liberation: History, Politics and Salvation* (Maryknoll, N.Y.: Orbis, 1973).

[54]South Commission, *The Challenge to the South: The Report of the South Commission* (Oxford: Oxford University Press, 1990), pp. 11, 79.

and development programmes should be prepared, and seen to be prepared, by national authorities of [Latin American, Asian, and] African countries rather than by foreign advisors and international organizations. Otherwise commitment will be lacking."[55] Many nations, especially in Africa, lack experience in directing their own economic plans and technical adaptation and progress.

Self-reliance does not mean isolation from the global economy. Perhaps the most successful developing country, early modern Japan, received no foreign aid and virtually no foreign direct investment, but was liberal in foreign trade and exchange and the world champion borrower of foreign technology. Japan, in the late nineteenth and early twentieth centuries, directed its development planning, the creation of financial institutions, the officials and business people sent to learn from abroad, the foreigners hired to transfer technology to government and business, the modification of foreign technology (especially in improving the engineering of traditional artisans), and the capturing of technological gains domestically from learning by doing[56] (see Chapter 3). In a similar fashion, today's developing countries, when receiving funds and assistance from DCs and international agencies, should be in charge of their planning and development so they can benefit from learning through experience.

Small Is Beautiful

Mahatma Gandhi, nonviolent politician and leader of India's nationalist movement for 25 years prior to its independence in 1947, was an early advocate of small-scale development in the third world. He emphasized that harmony with nature, reduction of material wants, village economic development, handicraft production, decentralized decision making, and labor-intensive, indigenous technology were not just more efficient, but more humane. For him, humane *means* for development were as important as appropriate *ends*.

Gandhi's vision has inspired many followers, including the late E. F. Schumacher, ironically an economist who was head of planning for the nationalized coal industry in Britain. His goal was to develop methods and machines cheap enough to be accessible to virtually everyone and to leave ample room for human creativity. For him, there was no place for machines that concentrate power in a few hands and contribute to soul-destroying, meaningless, monotonous work.

Schumacher believed that productive activity needs to be judged holistically, including its social, aesthetic, moral, or political meanings as well as its economic ends. The primary functions of work are to give people a chance to use their faculties, join with other people in a common task, and produce essential goods and services.[57]

---

[55]Dragoslav Avramovic, "Africa's Debts and Economic Recovery," North-South Roundtable, Abidjan, Ivory Coast, July 8–9, 1991, p. ii.

[56]E. Wayne Nafziger, *Learning from the Japanese: Japan's Pre-War Development and the Third World* (Armonk, N.Y.: M.E. Sharpe, 1995).

[57]E. F. Schumacher, *Small Is Beautiful—Economics as If People Mattered* (New York: Harper & Row, 1973).
  United Nations Economic and Social Commission for Asia and the Pacific, *Human Resources Development: Intersectoral Coordination and Other Issues* (New York, 1992), p. 1, argues that an integrated approach to development recognizes that "people are both a 'means' and an 'end' of development."

Schumacher stressed that LDCs need techniques appropriate to their culture, abundant labor, and scarce capital and these might frequently involve simple labor-intensive production methods that have become economically unfeasible to DCs. These technologies are intermediate between Western capital-intensive processes and the LDCs' traditional instruments. Yet intermediate technology may not be suitable where (1) an industry requires virtually unalterable factor proportions; (2) modifying existing technologies is expensive; (3) capital-intensive technology reduces skilled labor requirements; and (4) factor prices are distorted (see Chapter 9).

Are Economic Growth and Development Worthwhile?

Economic development and growth have their costs and benefits.[58] Economic growth widens the range of human choice, but this may not necessarily increase happiness. Both Gandhi and Schumacher stress that happiness is dependent on the relationship between wants and resources. You may become more satisfied, not only by having more wants met, but perhaps also by renouncing certain material goods. Wealth may make you less happy if it increases wants more than resources. Furthermore, acquisitive and achievement-oriented societies may be more likely to give rise to individual frustration and mental anguish. Moreover, the mobility and fluidity frequently associated with rapidly growing economies may be accompanied by rootlessness and alienation.

BENEFITS

What distinguishes people from animals is people's greater control over their environment and greater freedom of choice, not that they are happier. Control over one's environment is arguably as important a goal as happiness, and in order to achieve it, economic growth is greatly to be desired. Growth decreases famine, starvation, infant mortality, and death; gives us greater leisure; can enhance art, music, and philosophy; and gives us the resources to be humanitarian. Economic growth may be especially beneficial to societies where political aspirations exceed resources, since it may forestall what might otherwise prove to be unbearable social tension. Without growth the desires of one group can be met only at the expense of others. Finally, economic growth can assist newly independent countries in mobilizing resources to increase national power.

COSTS

Growth has its price. One cost may be the acquisitiveness, materialism, and dissatisfaction with one's present state associated with a society's economic struggles. Second, the mobility, impersonality, and emphasis on self-reliance associated with economic growth may destabilize the extended family system, indeed the prevailing social structure. Third, economic growth, with its dependence on rationalism and the scientific method for innovation and technical change, is frequently a threat to religious and social authority. Fourth, economic growth usually requires greater job specialization, which may be accompanied by greater imper-

---

[58]Much of the material in this section is from W. Arthur Lewis, *The Theory of Economic Growth* (Homewood, Ill.: Richard D. Irwin, 1955), pp. 420–35.

sonality, more drab and monotonous tasks, more discipline, and a loss of crafts-manship. Fifth, as such critics as Herbert Marcuse charge, in an advanced indus-trial society, all institutions and individuals, including artists, tend to be shaped to the needs of economic growth.[59]

Additionally, the larger organizational units concomitant with economic growth are more likely to lead to bureaucratization, impersonality, communica-tion problems, and the use of force to keep people in line. Economic growth and the growth of large-scale organization are associated with an increased demand for manufactured products and services and the growth of towns, which may be accompanied by rootlessness, environmental blight, and unhealthy living condi-tions. Even though the change in values and social structure may eventually lead to a new, dynamic equilibrium considered superior to the old static equilibrium, the transition may produce some very painful problems. Moreover, the political transformation necessary for rapid economic growth may lead to greater central-ization, authoritarianism, and coercion, and greater social disruption.

Thus, even if a population is seriously committed to economic growth, its at-tainment is not likely to be pursued at all costs. All societies have to consider other goals that conflict with the maximization of economic growth. For example, be-cause it wants its own citizens in high-level positions, a developing country may promote local control of manufacturing that reduces growth in the short run. The question is, What will be the tradeoff between the goal of rapid economic growth and such noneconomic goals as achieving an orderly and stable society, preserv-ing traditional values and culture, and promoting political autonomy?

RISING EXPECTATIONS

Increasingly as literacy rates rise, the previously inarticulate and unorganized masses are demanding that the political elite make a serious commitment to a bet-ter way of life for all. These demands in some cases have proved embarrassing and threatening to the elite, since the broad economic growth the lower classes ex-pect requires much political and economic transformation.

In the face of increasing expectations, few societies choose stagnation or re-tardation. Increasingly the LDC poor are aware of the opulent lifestyle of rich countries and the elite. They have noticed the automobiles, houses, and dinner parties of the affluent; they have seen the way the elite escape the drudgery of backbreaking work and the uncertain existence of a life of poverty; they have been exposed to new ideas and values; and they are restless to attain a part of the wealth they observe.

So most LDC populations want economic growth, despite some costs. And LDCs also want better measures of growth and development. The central focus of this book is to discuss how LDCs can achieve and assess their development goals.

Summary

1. Economic growth is an increase in a country's per capita output. Economic de-velopment is economic growth leading to an improvement in the economic wel-fare of the poorest segment of the population, a decrease in agriculture's share of

[59]Herbert Marcuse, *One-Dimensional Man* (Boston: Beacon Press, 1966).

output, an increase in the educational level of the labor force, and indigenous technological change.

2. Even though it is common to classify countries as high-income (developed countries), middle-, and low-income countries (developing countries), rankings by measures of the level of economic welfare form a continuum rather than a dichotomy.

3. The third world of Africa, Asia, and Latin America is very diverse, ranging from the least developed countries with a low per capita income and little industrialization to newly industrializing countries like South Korea, Taiwan, and Singapore.

4. Figures for economic growth depend on what kind of GNP price deflator is used. When industries with more rapid growth, such as computers, show relatively less rapid increases in price, a Laspeyres index, which uses base-period weights, will indicate higher growth than Paasche-type indexes, which use weights from a current period.

5. The GNP of the LDCs is understated relative to that of the West because LDCs have a higher portion of output sold outside the marketplace, a smaller share of intermediate goods in their GNP, and a large percentage of labor-intensive, unstandardized goods having no impact on the exchange rate.

6. The per capita GNP of LDCs *relative* to the United States increases by one and one-half to four times when adjustments are made for purchasing power.

7. Per capita GNP is an imperfect measure of average economic welfare in a country. For example, social indicators suggest that Malaysia has done better in meeting the basic needs of the majority of its people than South Africa, which has roughly the same average income level.

8. Disadvantages of the PQLI as an alternative measure of average material well-being are its insufficient conceptual rationale for scaling and weighting, the extra time and expense required for its formulation, the lack of current figures, and difficulty in interpreting it. The Human Development Index (HDI) has similar problems, including the fact that income above poverty levels contributed only marginally to the index.

9. Since GNP is heavily weighted by the income shares of the rich, its growth can be a misleading indicator of development. Alternative measures of growth are those giving equal weights to a 1-percent increase in income for any member of society, or those giving higher weights to a 1-percent income growth for lower income groups than for higher income groups.

10. Economists who emphasize basic needs stress providing food, housing, health, sanitation, water, and basic education in LDCs, especially for low-income groups. However, despite the view that these needs are rights, resources may be too limited in LDCs to guarantee their fulfillment.

11. Some leftists wish to substitute the goal of liberation, or freedom from external economic and political control, for that of economic development, which they understand as implying economic growth dependent on Western techniques, capital, institutions, and consumer goods. However, the countries they choose as examples (Tanzania, Cuba, and Maoist China) fall far short of the model of liberation they espouse. Furthermore, the Liberationists are not really criticizing development but growth policies disguised as development.

12. Is economic growth worthwhile? People increase their happiness, not only by having more wants met, but also by renouncing certain material goods. How-

ever, economic growth gives us more control over our environment and greater freedom of choice. Yet the LDCs, faced with rising expectations, may not have the option of a no-growth society.

Terms to Review

- economic growth
- GDP
- GNP
- economic development
- GNP per capita
- GNP price deflator
- real economic growth
- first world
- third world
- socialism
- newly industrializing countries (NICs)
- economies in transition
- least developed countries
- United Nations Conference on Trade and Development (UNCTAD)
- Organization of Petroleum Exporting Countries (OPEC)

- international economic order
- Laspeyres price index
- Paasche price index
- Fisher ideal index
- comparison-resistant services
- Purchasing Power Parity (PPP)
- International Comparison Project
- (P) the price level of GDP
- Physical Quality of Life Index (PQLI)
- disparity reduction rate
- the Human Development Index (HDI)
- the Gender-related Development Index (GDI)
- poverty-weighted index
- basic needs approach
- apartheid

Questions to Discuss

1. Is economic growth possible without economic development? Economic development without economic growth?

2. What do you consider the most urgent goal for LDCs to attain by the year 2025? Why is this goal important? What policy changes should LDCs undertake to increase the probability of attaining this goal?

3. Give an example of an LDC that you think has had an especially good (poor) development record in the past two to three decades. Why did you choose this LDC?

4. List three or four countries that have moved significantly upward or downward in the GNP per capita rankings in the last two decades. What factors have contributed to their movements?

5. How useful are generalizations about the third or developing world? Indicate ways of subclassifying the third world.

6. Discuss the price-index problem that LDCs face in measuring economic growth.

7. According to the *World Bank Atlas, 1994*, Canada's 1992 GNP per capita ($20,710) was about sixty-seven times higher than Kenya (with $310). Can we surmise that the average economic well-being in Canada was about sixty-seven times the average economic well-being in Kenya?

8. Nigeria's 1992 GNP per capita was $320, about three times that of Tanzania's $110. What other assessments of socioeconomic welfare (other than GNP per

capita in U.S. dollars at the prevailing exchange rates) could be used in comparing Nigeria and Tanzania? What are the advantages and disadvantages of these alternative assessments?

9. Compare basic needs attainment, HDI, PQLI, and the International Comparison Project's Purchasing Power Parity to GNP per capita in U.S. dollars at existing exchange rates as measures of economic well-being.

10. In what ways might conventional basic-needs measures be inadequate in assessing the material welfare of the poorest 20 percent of a developing country's population?

11. Are economic welfare and political freedom complementary or competing goals?

12. Choose a country, for example, your own or one you know well. What have been the major costs and benefits of economic growth in this country?

Guide to Readings

The annual *World Development Report* by the World Bank (see the sources to Table 2–1) is not only the best up-to-date source for basic economic data on LDCs, but also contains a good discussion of current development issues. The World Bank's annual *World Bank Atlas* has similar data, but less discussion of current issues. The United Nations' annual *Human Development Report* (notes to Table 2–1) has basic economic and social data. The United Nations Development Program, *Human Development Report (HDR), 1991* (New York: Oxford University Press, 1991), p. 20, ranks countries on a human freedom index (HFI) on civil and legal rights, freedom from torture and censorship, electoral and religious freedom, ethnic and gender egalitarianism, independent media, courts, and trade unions, and related indicators. The authors rank Sweden and Denmark first, the United States thirteenth, and China, Ethiopia, Romania, Libya, and Iraq at the bottom of eighty-eight countries. The United Nations Development Program, *Human Development Report (HDR), 1994* (New York: Oxford University Press, 1994), pp. 30–31, ranks DCs by various indices of human distress; one example indicates that the homicide rate in the United States is six times the rate of most DCs and twelve times that of Japan. Other useful economic data sources are the annual *World Economic Survey* by the Department of International Economic and Social Affairs of the United Nations, the annual *World Economic Outlook* by the International Monetary Fund, the World Bank's annual *Trends in Developing Countries* (data by country) and *Global Economic Prospects and the Developing Countries* (Washington, D.C.) various publications of the Overseas Development Council, such as *U.S. Foreign Policy and Developing Countries: Discourse and Data, 1991* (Washington, D.C.: Overseas Development Council, 1991), and U.N. regional economic commissions, such as the ECA (notes 4 and 6).

The *HDR, 1991*, pp. 1–11 and subsequent HDRs explain the human development index (HDI) and Srinivasan (note 25); Paul Streeten, "Human Development: Means and Ends," *American Economic Review* 84 (May 1994): pp. 232–37; and Harsha Aturupane, Paul Glewwe, and Paul Isenman, "Poverty, Human Development, and Growth: An Emerging Consensus," ibid., pp. 244–54 criticize HDI.

T.N. Srinivasan, "Data Base for Development Analysis: An Overview," *Journal of Development Economics* 44 (June 1994): 3–27; Alan Heston, "National Accounts: A Brief Review of Some Problems in Using National Accounts Data in Level of Output Comparisons and Growth Studies," *Journal of Development Economics* 44 (June 1994): 29–52; and Richard Ruggles, "Issues Relating to the United Nations System of National Accounts and Developing Countries," *Journal of Development Economics* 44 (June 1994): 77–85; discuss the flaws in crossnational data used by international agencies. Usher's and Kuznets' books (note 25) have good discussions of errors in crossnational income comparisons. Sources on adjusting national product for purchasing power are Summers and Heston (note 25) and Kravis (note 31); Srinivasan (note 34) criticizes work on purchasing-power parity. Weighted indices for GNP growth are discussed in Hollis Chenery, Montek S. Ahluwalia, C.L.G. Bell, John H. Duloy, and Richard Jolly, eds., *Redistribution with Growth* (London: Oxford University Press, 1974).

Hollis Chenery and T.N. Srinivasan, eds., *Handbook of Development Economics*, vols. 1 and 2 (Amsterdam: North-Holland, 1988 and 1989), include essays by Amartya Sen, "The Concept of Development," vol. 1, pp. 9–26, and Lance Taylor and Persio Arida, "Long-run Income Distribution," vol. 1, pp. 161–94.

Goulet (note 53) discusses replacing the concept of development with that of liberation. The classic discussion of the costs and benefits of economic growth appears in the appendix of Lewis's *Theory of Economic Growth* (note 58). On basic needs see Hicks and Streeten (note 50), Hicks (note 51), and Streeten (note 52).

3

Economic Development in Historical Perspective

Scope of the Chapter

To analyze the economics of developing countries, we need some basic facts about their growth and development. First, it is essential to understand the origins of modern economic growth and why, prior to this century, it was largely confined to the West. Second, we must examine two non-Western growth models, those of Japan and today's newly industrializing countries, especially South Korea and Taiwan. Third, we look at another non-Western development model, that of the Soviet Union-Russia, and the reasons for its earlier success and its eventual collapse. Fourth, we must look at the recent economic growth of developing countries, comparing their development in the years before and after World War II. Fifth, we sketch in the diverse economic performance among LDCs by comparing fast- and slow-growing countries, low- and middle-income countries, and different regions of the world.

Sixth, the U.N. General Assembly perceives today's major international problem as the widening income gap between rich and poor countries. Has income indeed widened, and is narrowing the gap an important goal? A later section draws on earlier sections of this chapter to ask whether income levels between DCs and LDCs is converging or diverging.

Beginnings of Sustained Economic Growth

Historians hesitate to name a threshold period in history when economic growth took off. Although there were periods of economic growth during ancient and medieval times, rapid, sustained growth was rare. Living standards remained at a subsistence level for the majority of the world's population. The rapid, sustained increase in per capita GNP characteristic of **modern economic growth** began in the West (Western Europe, the United States, Canada, Australia, and New Zealand) one to two centuries ago. Industrialization and sustained economic growth had begun in Great Britain by the last half of the eighteenth century; in the United States and France in the first half of the nineteenth century; in Germany, the Netherlands, and Belgium by the middle of that century; and in Scandinavia, Canada, Japan (a non-Western country), Italy, and perhaps Russia, by the last half of the century.

The West and Afro-Asia: The Nineteenth Century and Today

GNP per capita for developed countries in Europe in the early 1990s was roughly 15 to 20 times that of Afro-Asian less-developed countries. The gap was not so great 130 to 150 years ago, since people could not have survived on one-fifteenth the per capita income of European DCs in the nineteenth century. Nobel laureate Simon Kuznets estimates a gap of 5:1 then. Updating a rough assessment by Kuznets indicates that at that time Western Europe, the United States, Canada, and Australia had an average real income higher than that of most African and Asian countries today. The DC economic growth has been much more rapid during the past century, and of course the DCs are adding to an already substantial economic base.[1]

Capitalism and Modern Western Economic Development

Why did sustained economic growth begin in the West? A major reason is the rise of **capitalism,** the economic system dominant there since the breakup of feudalism from the fifteenth to the eighteenth centuries. Fundamental to capitalism are the relations between private owners and workers. The means of production—land, mines, factories, and other forms of capital—are privately held; and legally free but capital–less workers sell their labor to employers. Under capitalism, production decisions are made by private individuals operating for profit.

Capitalist institutions had antecedents in the ancient world, and pockets of capitalism flourished in the late medieval period. For example, a capitalist woolen industry existed in thirteenth-century Flanders and fourteenth-century Florence, but it died out because of revolutionary conflict between the workers and capitalists. Thus the continuous development of the capitalist system dates only from the sixteenth century.

Especially after the eleventh century, the growing long-distance trade between capitalist centers contributed to the collapse of the medieval economy. As European trade activity expanded during the next few centuries, certain institutions facilitated the growth of modern capitalism. Among them were private property, deposit banking, formal contracts, craft guilds, merchant associations, joint stock companies (the precursor of the corporation), insurance, international financial markets, naval protection of trade vessels, and government support in opening markets and granting monopoly privileges for inventions.

---

[1]This is based on an updating of Simon Kuznets, *Economic Growth of Nations—Total Output and Production Structure* (Cambridge, Mass.: Harvard University Press, 1971), pp. 23–28.

At the same time, burgeoning industrialization and urbanization further weakened the feudal economy, an agricultural system based on serfs bound to their lord's land. Ultimately these changes in trade, industry, and agriculture transformed the medieval economy into a new society fueled by capitalistic endeavors.

Before the twentieth century, only capitalist economies were successful in large capital accumulation and in generating and applying a vast scientific and technical knowledge to production. Why was capitalism first successful in the West?

1. The breakdown of the authority of the medieval Roman Catholic Church, together with the Protestant Reformation of the sixteenth and seventeenth centuries, stimulated a new economic order. Although Protestantism, like Catholicism, was ascetic, manifesting itself in the systematic regulation of the whole conduct of the Christian, economic historian Max Weber contended that the new **Protestant ethic** translated its "inner-worldly" asceticism into a vigorous activity in a secular vocation, or *calling* (in contrast to the "other-worldly" asceticism of the Catholic monastery). The Protestant ethic fostered hard work, frugality, sobriety, and efficiency, virtues coinciding with the spirit essential for capitalist development.[2] Acceptance of the Protestant idea of a calling led to the systematic organization of free labor and gave a religious justification for unstinting work even at low wages in the service of God (and incidentally the employer).[3]

   Chapter 12 questions Weber's thesis, suggesting that Protestantism's secularization or accommodation may better explain any association between Protestantism and capitalism. Still most economic historians would agree that the decline of the church's all-encompassing power in political, economic, and ideological realms was necessary to free the spirit of capitalist development.

2. Between the sixteenth and nineteenth centuries, Western Europe witnessed the rise of strong national states that created the conditions essential for rapid and cumulative growth under capitalism. The nation-state established a domestic market free of trade barriers, a uniform monetary system, contract and property law, police and militia protection against internal violence, defense against external attack, and basic transportation and communication facilities—all of which fostered capitalism. Initially absolute monarchs wrested power from feudal lords and town authorities and consolidated territory into large political and economic units—the nation-state. The nation-state was necessary for the larger markets and economies of scale of capitalist expansion. Eventually monarchy ceded power to the **bourgeoisie,** the capitalist and middle classes. Where an absolute monarch existed, the capitalist class, who enjoyed only a precarious existence under autocratic authority, ultimately stripped the monarch of power and installed representatives more favorable to their economic interests.

3. The declining influence of the church coincided with the Enlightenment, a period of great intellectual activity in seventeenth- and eighteenth-century Europe that led to the scientific discoveries of electricity, oxygen, calculus, and so on. These discoveries found practical application in agriculture, industry, trade, and transport and resulted in extended markets, increased efficiency of large-scale production, and enhanced profits associated with capital concentration. Further-

[2]Max Weber, *The Protestant Ethic and the Spirit of Capitalism* (New York: Charles Scribner's Sons, 1930). The first German edition was in 1904–1905.
[3]See Chapter 12.

more the rationalism permeating the new science and technology meshed with the spirit of capitalist enterprise.

4. Protestantism's spiritual individualism (the "priesthood of all believers"), coupled with the philosophical rationalism and humanism of the Enlightenment, emphasized freedom from arbitrary authority. In the economic sphere, this liberalism advocated a self-regulating market unrestricted by political intervention or state monopoly. These views were tailor-made for the bourgeoisie in its struggle to overthrow the old order.

5. Intellectual and economic changes led to political revolutions in England, Holland, and France in the seventeenth and eighteenth centuries that reduced the power of the church and landed aristocracy. The bourgeoisie took over much of this power. Economic modernization in Europe would probably not have been possible without these revolutions.[4]

6. Modern capitalism is distinguished from earlier economic systems by a prodigious rate of capital accumulation. During the early capitalism of the sixteenth and seventeenth centuries, the great flow of gold and silver from the Americas to Europe inflated prices and profits and speeded up this accumulation. Inflation redistributed income from landlords and wage laborers, whose real earnings declined, to merchants, manufacturers, and commercial farmers, who were more likely to invest in new and productive enterprises.[5]

Capitalism, as an engine for rapid economic growth, spread beyond Europe to the outposts of Western civilization—the United States, Canada, Australia, and New Zealand. Indeed, during most of the twentieth century, capitalism has been more successful in the United States than in other Western economies.

However, modern industrial capitalism was established in the West at great human costs. Physical violence, brutality, and exploitation shaped its early course. In England and Belgium, wages dropped and poverty increased markedly during the accelerated industrial growth of the latter eighteenth and early nineteenth centuries. In both countries, it took a half-century before the absolute incomes of the poor reached pre–Industrial Revolution levels.[6] Perhaps Charles Dickens best portrays the starvation, destitution, overcrowding, and death among the mid–nineteenth century unemployed and working class. The lives fictionalized in *Nicholas Nickleby, A Christmas Carol,* and *Oliver Twist* were grim indeed. Dickens's

---

[4]Even though capitalism originated in the modern West, much of what contributed to its rise originated in other civilizations. For example, much of its scientific and technical content came from the Middle East and India, the philosophical from ancient Greece, and the legal and political from ancient Greece and Rome.

[5]Much of this section is from Dudley Dillard, *Economic Development of the North Atlantic Community: Historical Introduction to Modern Economics* (Englewood Cliffs, N.J.: Prentice Hall, 1967), pp. 72–149; Dudley Dillard, "Capitalism," in Charles K. Wilber, ed., *The Political Economy of Development and Underdevelopment* (New York: Random House, 1979), pp. 69–76; and Douglass C. North and Robert Paul Thomas, "An Economic Theory of the Growth of the Western World," *Economic History Review* 23 (April 1970): 1–17.

Neo-Marxists and dependency theorists (discussed in Chapter 5) argue that Western capitalism, through informal imperialism and late nineteenth- and early twentieth-century colonialism, developed at the expense of Latin America, Asia, and Africa, capturing their **surplus** (output above wages, depreciation, and purchases from other firms) through policies controlling their raw materials, markets, international trade, and planning. Most Western mainstream economists would not add imperialism as a contributor to Western capitalist success.

[6]Irma Adelman and Cynthia Taft Morris, "Growth and Impoverishment in the Middle of the Nineteenth Century," *World Development* 6 (March 1978): 245–73.

novels are an accurate portrayal of not only the English working class but of other Western workers during this time.[7] Although these human costs may not be inevitable, similar problems have not been avoided by newly industrializing countries in subsequent periods. But despite these costs, even the late Marxist Maurice Dobb conceded that capitalism has improved the level of living for a large proportion of the Western population since the early nineteenth century.[8]

Economic Modernization in the Non-Western World

Capitalism led to modern economic growth in only a few non-Western countries. Chapter 5 discusses the relative importance of barriers to capitalism extant in traditional societies, as well as the effects of colonialism and other forms of Western political domination on the slow development of non-Western economies. Irrespective of the cause, it is clear that most non-Western countries lacked the strong indigenous capitalists and the effective bureaucratic and political leadership essential for rapid economic modernization.

THE JAPANESE DEVELOPMENT MODEL[9]

One notable exception was Japan, one of the five non-Western countries that escaped Western colonialism. Despite unequal treaties with the West from 1858 to 1899, Japan had substantial autonomy in economic affairs compared to other Afro-Asian countries.

Japan's level of economic development was much lower than Western countries in the middle to latter nineteenth century. However, since 1867, when Japan abolished feudal property relationships, its economic growth has been the most rapid in the world.

Japan's "guided capitalism" under the Meiji emperor, 1868 to 1912, relied on state initiative for large investments in **infrastructure**—telegraphs, postal service, water supply, coastal shipping, ports, harbors, bridges, lighthouses, river improvements, railways, electricity, gas, and technical research; for helping domestic business find export opportunities, exhibit products and borrow abroad, establish trading companies, and set marketing standards; for importing machines sold on lenient credit terms to private entrepreneurs; for laws encouraging freedom of enterprise and corporate organization; for organizing a banking system (with the central Bank of Japan); for sending students and government officials for training and education abroad; and (in the absence of foreign aid) for hiring thousands of foreigners to adapt and improve technology under local government or business direction.

---

[7]However, as Ben Polak and Jeffrey G. Williamson, "Poverty, Policy, and Industrialization in the Past," in Michael Lipton and Jacques van der Gaag, *Including the Poor: Proceedings of a Symposium Organized by the World Bank and the International Food Policy Research Institute* (Washington, D.C.: World Bank, 1993), pp. 229–30, indicate, rural poverty rates were higher than urban poverty rates in both England and France during the industrial revolution.

[8]Maurice Dobb, *Capitalist Enterprise and Social Progress* (London: Routledge, 1926).

[9]This section is based on E. Wayne Nafziger, *Learning from the Japanese: Japan's Prewar Development and the Third World* (Armonk, N.Y.: M.E. Sharpe, 1995); and E. Wayne Nafziger,"The Japanese Development Model: Its Implications for Developing Countries," *Bulletin of the Graduate School of International Relations, International University of Japan* no. 5 (July 1986): pp. 1–26.

In the late nineteenth century, government initiated about half the investment outside agriculture but sold most industrial properties, often at bargain prices, to private business people. Additionally government aided private industry through a low-wage labor policy, low taxes on business enterprise and high incomes, a favorable legal climate, destruction of economic barriers between fiefs, lucrative purchase contracts, tax rebates, loans, and subsidies. Japan acquired funds for industrial investment and assistance by squeezing agriculture, relying primarily on a land tax for government revenue. From the state-assisted entrepreneurs came the financial cliques or combines **(zaibatsu)** that dominated industry and banking through World War II.

Nevertheless, unlike the contemporary Indian government, the Meiji government retained small industry, compelling the zaibatsu to provide technical advice, scarce inputs, and credit, and encouraging small firms to take cooperative action. Creating small industry from scratch is not so effective as the Japanese approach of maintaining and upgrading workshop, handicraft, and cottage industry from an earlier stage of development.

Meiji Japan did not stress large leaps to the most advanced state of industrial technology available, but step-by-step improvements in technology and capital as government departments, regions, firms, and work units learned by doing. In the 1870s, this meant technical and management assistance and credit facilities to improve and increase the scale of crafts and small industry from the feudal period, causing less social disruption, since small industry's environment was not alien.

Regarding Japan's technology acquisition, Lawrence G. Franko contends that

> The Japanese are without doubt the world's champion importers of 'other people's' technology. Unlike other industrial nations which may have forgotten how much of their technological development was in fact based on seeking out, stumbling upon, or helping themselves to foreign discoveries and innovations, Japan has continuously sent its sons to be educated abroad and then to live or travel abroad to search out ways of catching up with or surpassing the West.[10]

The fact that today Japan probably has the highest mass standards for primary and secondary schools in the world, and shares underlying national values, is no accident. Japan's rulers laid the foundation in the late feudal period, when Japan's primary enrollment rate was higher than the British, and in 1872, when a national system of universal education stressing scientific and technological education was established.

Moreover, from 1868 to World War II, the Japanese had a policy (first forced and later chosen) of multilateral, nondiscriminatory foreign trade outside their empire (1904–45). Unlike today's LDCs, Japan did not discriminate against exports. The increased tariff protection in the first quarter of the twentieth century, which reduced the price of foreign exchange, was offset by government export promotion, which brought the exchange rate close to a market-clearing rate (see Chapter 18 on foreign exchange rates). From 1868 to 1897, the Japanese yen, on a silver standard that declined relative to gold, chronically depreciated vis-à-vis the U.S. dollar.

---

[10]Lawrence G. Franko, *The Threat of Japanese Multinationals—How the West Can Respond* (Chichester, U.K.: Wiley, 1983), p. 23.

Today's international economic conditions are not so favorable to LDC export expansion. The most rapidly expanding LDC manufactured exports during the 1970s through the early 1990s were textiles, clothing, footwear, and simple consumer goods requiring widely available labor-intensive technology. But competition from other aspiring newly industrial exporting countries is more severe than it was for Meiji Japan. Still LDCs could benefit from the Japanese approach of using international competition and market-clearing exchange rates to spur exports.

While a contemporary LDC can learn useful lessons from the Japanese model, these lessons are limited because of Meiji Japan's historically specific conditions and because aspects of the Japanese approach also contributed to pathologies in growth, such as zaibatsu concentration, income inequality, labor union repression, militarism, and imperialism. These pathologies were not reduced until military defeat in 1945 was followed by land, educational, demilitarization, labor union, anti-monopoly, monetary stabilization, constitutional, and other reforms undertaken by the U.S. occupational government, supported by the revolutionary momentum of the Japanese populace. This series of events associated with military devastation is not to be recommended nor likely to accelerate economic development and democratize the political economy in LDCs as it did in Japan.

THE KOREAN-TAIWANESE MODEL

The fastest growing developing countries are the **Asian tigers** or newly industrializing countries (NICs) of East and Southeast Asia—South Korea, Taiwan, and Singapore, and Hong Kong, a part of China after 1997. Both Singapore and Hong Kong have been prosperous city-states, providing trade and financial links for their hinterlands, for other parts of Asia, and between Asia and the external world. As city-states, however, they are not likely to serve as models for more populous nation-states. Thus, we concentrate here on the two remaining Asian tigers, Taiwan and Korea, which have both enjoyed a real per capita growth rate of more than 7 percent since 1960 and are poised to graduate to developed economies by the turn of the twenty-first century.

The model of Korea and Taiwan is similar to that of Japan, perhaps unsurprisingly for two countries that were also a part of greater Chinese civilization for centuries and that were Japanese colonies from about the turn of the twentieth century through World War II. Similar to Japan, the governments of Korea and Taiwan systematically intervened to further economic development, building infrastructure, providing tax incentives and subsidized credit for export manufacturing and other selected industries, investing heavily in primary education and other human capital, and maintaining macroeconomic stability during external shocks (for example, from oil price increases in 1973–74 and 1979–80 and American dollar depreciation in the late 1980s), thus restraining inflation and avoiding external debt crises.[11]

---

[11]World Bank, *The East Asian Miracle: Economic Growth and Public Policy* (New York: Oxford University Press, 1993); Alice H. Amsden, "Why Isn't the Whole World Experimenting with the East Asian Model to Develop?: Review of the *East Asian Miracle*," *World Development* 22 (April 1994): 627–33; Jene Kwon, "The East Asia Challenge to Neoclassical Orthodoxy," *World Development* 22 (April 1994): 635–44; Sanjaya Lall, "*The East Asian Miracle*: Does the Bell Toll for Industrial Strategy?" *World Development* 22 (April 1994): 645–54; Toru Yanagihara, "Anything New in the *Miracle* Report? Yes and No," *World Development* 22 (April 1994): 663–70.

Korea and Taiwan, also like Japan, have had a high quality of economic management provided by the civil service, with merit-based recruitment and promotion, compensation competitive with the private sector, and economic policy making largely insulated from political pressures. Both Asian tigers have combined creating **contested markets**, where potential competition keeps prices equal or close to average price, with business-business and government-business cooperation. In Korea, this had meant inter-firm and public-private sharing of information alongside competition by a few, but usually evenly matched, firms in economic performance, especially in exports. The World Bank uses the following metaphor: Just as adults may prefer to organize party games to letting children do as they please, so running the economy as the Japanese, Koreans, and Taiwanese do as contests with substantial rewards, clear, well-enforced rules, and impartial referees (such as central banks and ministries of finance) may be preferable to **laissez-faire** (government noninterference).[12]

Both countries have pursued a dual-industrial strategy of protecting **import substitutes** (domestic production replacing imports) and promoting labor-intensive manufactures in exports, although since the 1960s, they have facilitated a shift in the division of labor to more capital- and technology-intensive exports.[13] Yet Korea established a timetable for international competitiveness that provided performance standards for each industry assisted. Moreover, the Koreans and Taiwanese did not cling to a given nominal exchange rate in the face of continuing inflation, as many African and Latin American countries did, but depreciated when necessary. Additionally, like early twentieth-century Japan, the two tigers subsidized exports to offset tariff protection. All in all, Korea and Taiwan avoided the excessive real currency appreciation of many other LDCs, so that like early Japan, they did not discriminate against exports.[14]

During the first twenty-five years after World War II, industrialization in Korea and Taiwan benefitted from United States aid, capital inflows, and rapidly growing demand for manufactured goods in Asia. Yet aid as a percentage of GDP in early post-World War II Taiwan (6 percent in 1951–61) was even lower than the same percentage in Africa recently (8 percent in 1987).[15] Since the 1970s, the two tigers have been closely linked economically and geographically to Japan and other high-performing Asian economies, facilitating trade and investment flows. Beginning in late 1985, when the U.S. dollar began devaluing relative to the Japanese yen, Japanese companies have tried to retain their international price competitiveness in manufacturing by organizing the **Asian borderless economy**. This

---

[12]World Bank, *The East Asian Miracle: Economic Growth and Public Policy* (New York: Oxford University Press, 1993), pp. 93–95.

[13]Koichi Ohno and Hideki Imaoka, "The Experience of Dual-Industrial Growth: Korea and Taiwan," *Developing Economies* 25 (December 1987): 310–23; and Colin I. Bradford, Jr., "Trade and Structural Change: NICs and Next Tier NICs as Transitional Economies," *World Development* 15 (March 1987): 299–316.

[14]World Bank, *The East Asian Miracle: Economic Growth and Public Policy* (New York: Oxford University Press, 1993), pp. 21–22, 113–15.

[15]Deborah Brautigam, "What can Africa Learn from Taiwan? Political Economy, Industrial Policy, and Adjustment," *Journal of Modern African Studies* 32 (March 1994): 111–38.

Korea probably received more aid as a proportion of GNP than Taiwan during this period. Over 80 percent of Korea's imports in the 1950s were financed by U.S. assistance. Idriss Jazairy, Mohiuddin Alamgir, and Theresa Panuccio, *The State of World Rural Poverty: An Inquiry into Its Causes and Consequences*, Published for the International Fund for Agricultural Development (New York: New York University Press, 1992), p. 11.

Japanese-led system, which encompasses a new international division of knowledge and function, selected more sophisticated activities including research and development-intensive and technology-intensive industries for the four tigers, while assigning the less sophisticated production and assembly, which use more standardized and obsolescent technologies, to China and three members (Indonesia, Malaysia, and Thailand) of the regional economic group, the Association of South East Asian Nations (ASEAN).[16]

In both countries, government owned and controlled financial institutions provided cheap investment funds for the private sector. Korea and Taiwan established long-term development banks and other credit institutions to direct development, applying commercial criteria to select and monitor projects. The countries also kept interest rates low, especially for exporters, providing capital from the high-saving households (much from postal savings) to firms at subsidized rates.[17]

The Koreans and Taiwanese, like the Japanese, borrowed substantial technology from abroad, often increasing productivity while learning to meet foreign standards for manufactured exports. The two NICs overcame imperfections in the market for knowledge through the purchase of new equipment to acquire technology, information transmitted by exacting customers, technology licensing, knowledge from returning nationals educated overseas, domestic research to improve exports and reduce the costs of protection, the transfer of nonproprietary technology from engineering publications, trade literature, and independent consultants, and foreign direct investment (although, like Japan, this was restricted or closed for varying periods). This transfer was expedited by the high domestic educational investments and standards (Koreans have the longest primary and secondary school year in the world) and the large number of nationals attending universities and graduate schools. Many of these specialized in science and engineering and a substantial percentage received their higher education overseas. For example, *all* the postgraduates employed in Taiwanese industry are foreign-educated nationals.[18]

In 1949–52, Korea and Taiwan, with American assistance, undertook redistribution that reduced substantially the inequality of land holdings from colonialism but also supported the former landed class in investing in trade and industry.[19] The two countries, similar to Meiji Japan, subordinated agriculture to industry, using a state **monopsony** (or single buyer) to keep farm prices low, transferring many of the revenues captured to aid industry. But beginning in the 1960s, as the United States reduced its subsidized Public Law 480 surplus grain sales to both countries, both countries reversed their anti-farm bias, subsidizing and protecting agriculture and increasing the procurement price for grain, thus partly reducing the gap between the city and the countryside.[20] Other policies supporting agricul-

[16]Tokunaga Shojiro, "Japan's FDI-Promoting Systems and Intra-Asia Networks: New Investment and Trade Systems Created by the Borderless Economy," in Tokunaga Shojiro, ed., *Japan's Foreign Investment and Asian Economic Interdependence* (Tokyo: University of Tokyo Press, 1992), pp. 11–37. The Asian borderless economy and product-cycle model are discussed further in Chapter 18.

[17]World Bank, *The East Asian Miracle: Economic Growth and Public Policy* (New York: Oxford University Press, 1993), pp. 16–20, 42–43, 133–34, 220–21).

[18]World Bank, *The East Asian Miracle: Economic Growth and Public Policy* (New York: Oxford University Press, 1993), pp. 301–02, 317–20.

[19]Clive Hamilton, "Class, State and Industrialisation in South Korea," *IDS Bulletin* 15 (April 1984): 38–43.

[20]Mick Moore, "Agriculture in Taiwan and South Korea: The Minimalist State?" *IDS Bulletin* 15 (April 1984): 57–64.

ture were agricultural research and extension services to speed diffusion of the high-yielding varieties of grain of the **Green Revolution** and exchange rates close to market-clearing rates to spur farm exports.[21]

Both countries achieved widely shared improvements in economic welfare, which brought legitimacy to government policy. These wealth-sharing programs included not only the postwar reform which distributed land to the tiller, but also emphases on labor-intensive development (which also included small- and medium-scale industries programs in Taiwan), family-planning programs (the success of which is correlated with income egalitarianism—see Chapter 8), and public-supported mass primary education, which reached the poor, children in rural areas, and girls. In the 1950s, South Korea invested heavily in expanding primary and secondary education. By the early 1960s, the literacy rate of Korea was 80 percent, a high level for a country that was then at such a low level of development.[22]

The experiences of Korea and Taiwan since 1945 reinforce many of the lessons of the Japanese development model: the importance of guided capitalism, infrastructure investment, technological borrowing and learning, universal primary education, high educational standards, and market-clearing prices of foreign exchange. The two tigers relied on authoritarian governments and repressed labor unions, as Japan did in their early modernization, but, unlike Japan, were successful in achieving low income inequality before undertaking political democratization. Korea and Taiwan's rapid economic growth and relative economic egalitarianism have facilitated efforts in the late 1980s and early 1990s to evolve toward greater democratic government.

DCs such as the United States have begun treating Taiwan and Korea as rich countries, withdrawing preferences they received when they were developing countries and demanding that they adhere to more liberal trade and exchange-rate policies. In addition, the two countries have faced increasing pollution and congestion that have derived, in part, from their growing affluence. Yet despite problems, the two countries' economic development can provide lessons for today's low-income and lower-middle-income countries.

A 1993 World Bank study entitled *The East Asian Miracle* identifies eight high-performing Asian economies: in addition to Japan, these include the four tigers—Taiwan, South Korea, Hong Kong, and Singapore; and the ASEAN three—Malaysia, Thailand, and Indonesia.[23] Indonesia, which just graduated from a low- to a middle-income country in 1995, is not yet ready to be a model. But Thailand's 6.0-percent growth rate, 1980–92, is the fastest among lower-middle-income economies and Malaysia graduated to the upper-middle-income category in the early 1990s (see Table 2–1). The *Economist* asks: Who are the next newly industrializing countries or NICs? Their answer: Malaysia, whose secondary schools and universities, however, are mediocre, and Thailand, whose educational system is weak in science and engineering and whose enrollment in secondary school as a

---

[21]World Bank, *The East Asian Miracle: Economic Growth and Public Policy* (New York: Oxford University Press, 1993), pp. 32–35.

[22]Danny M. Leipziger, "Editor's Introduction: Korea's Transition to Maturity," *World Development* 16 (January 1988): 1–5; Kihwan Kim, "Korea in the 1990s: Making the Transition to a Developed Economy," *World Development* 16 (January 1988): 7–18; and World Bank, *The East Asian Miracle: Economic Growth and Public Policy* (New York: Oxford University Press, 1993), pp. 47, 52–53, 160.

[23]World Bank, *The East Asian Miracle: Economic Growth and Public Policy* (New York: Oxford University Press, 1993).

percentage of children 12–17 years old was only 33 percent compared to 98 percent in South Korea in 1991.[24] Moreover, as indicated in Chapter 18, Malaysia and Thailand, while enjoying limited prosperity, have paid relatively little attention to bottom-up development of indigenous technology generation and industrial innovation, sacrificing their economic autonomy to less-sophisticated, labor-intensive, low-value-added production in the Japanese-organized division of labor. And slower growth in global income and trade after the early 1970s may inhibit Malaysia and Thailand emulating the earlier experience of the NICs.

THE RUSSIAN-SOVIET DEVELOPMENT MODEL

The Stalinist Development Model.   The 1917 Communist revolution in Russia provided an alternative road to economic modernization, an approach usually associated with Soviet leader Joseph Stalin from 1924 to 1953. The main features of Soviet socialism, beginning with the first 5-year plan in 1928, were replacing consumer preferences with planners' preferences, the Communist party dictating these preferences to planners, state control of capital and land, collectivization of agriculture, the virtual elimination of private trade, plan fulfillment monitored by the state banks, state monopoly trading with the outside world, and (unlike the Japanese) a low ratio of foreign trade to GNP. In a few decades, the Soviet Union was quickly transformed into a major industrial power. Indeed the share of industry in net national product (NNP) increased from 28 percent to 45 percent, and its share of the labor force from 18 percent to 29 percent, from 1928 to 1940, while agriculture's share in NNP declined from 49 percent to 29 percent and the labor force share dropped from 71 percent to 51 percent over the same period—an output shift that took 60 to 70 years,[25] and a labor force shift that took 30 to 50 years in the West and Japan. Moreover, a 60-percent illiteracy rate, an average life expectancy of about 40 years, and widespread poverty before the revolution gave way to universal literacy, a life expectancy of 70 years, and economic security.

The Soviets diverted savings from agriculture (at great human cost, as Chapter 7 points out) to industry (especially metallurgy, engineering, and other heavy industry). They did not use a direct tax like the Japanese, but collectivized farming (1928–38), enabling the state to capture a large share of the difference between state monopsony procurement at below-market prices (sometimes below cost) and a sales price closer to market price.[26]

Russia's tsarist economic performance in the decades before 1917 is a matter of controversy. Walter W. Rostow dates Russia's takeoff into sustained growth, 1890–1914, when industrial growth was rapid, though discontinuous. Even so, growth in agriculture and other sectors lagged behind industry's. And surely the autocracy and social rigidity existing under the tsars would not have been consis-

---

[24]"Who's Nicst?" *Economist* (August 13, 1994): pp. 31–32; World Bank, *World Development Report, 1994* (New York: Oxford University Press, 1994), pp. 216–17.

[25]Chapter 20 discusses the reasons for Russia's fall in life expectancy from 70 years in 1978–92 to 64 years in 1994.

[26]Paul R. Gregory and Robert C. Stuart, *Soviet and Post-Soviet Economic Structure and Performance* (New York: HarperCollins, 1994), pp. 1–144; and Simon Kuznets, "A Comparative Appraisal," in Abram Bergson and Simon Kuznets, eds., *Economic Trends in the Soviet Union* (Cambridge: Harvard University Press, 1963), pp. 345–47.

tent with the investment in education and capital equipment needed for economic modernization.[27]

Many economists and policymakers thought that Soviet-style central planning had transformed the economy from economic lethargy before the revolution to fast economic growth and improvement in material living standards during the four decades after 1928. The Stalinist economic model was not only emulated by Eastern European Communist governments in the Soviet sphere of influence, but also provided an inspiration (and sometimes a prototype) for many leaders in Asia, Africa, and Latin America. During the 1950s, under Chairman Mao Zedong, with centralized material-balance planning, expanded heavy industry investment, and the development of communes (collective farms), and heavy dependence on Soviet aid, China emphasized the slogan, "Learn from the Soviet Union."[28]

The Fel'dman-Stalin Investment Strategy. China and India used the Soviet priority on investment in the capital goods industry as the centerpiece of planning in the 1950s. One of the most creative periods for debate on investment choice was from 1924 to 1928, a time of acute capital shortage in the Soviet Union. During this period, Stalin, who was consolidating his power as successor to revolutionary leader Vladimir Ilich Lenin as head of the Communist party, was not so rigid in his approach to economic policy as he was after 1929. The Soviet industrialization dispute during this period anticipated many current controversies on development strategies, including those of balanced versus unbalanced growth (see Chapter 5).

The driving force in G. A. Fel'dman's unbalanced growth model, developed for the Soviet planning commission in 1928, was rapid increase in investment in machines to make machines. Long-run economic growth was a function of the fraction of investment in the capital goods industry (λ_1).

The **Fel'dman model** implies not merely sacrificing current consumption for current investment, but also cutting the fraction of investment in the consumer goods industry (λ_2) to attain a high λ_1. A high λ_1 sacrifices the short-run growth of consumer goods capacity to yield high long-run growth rates for capital goods capacity and consumption. A low λ_1 (or high λ_2) yields a relatively high short-term rate and relatively low long-term growth rate in consumption.

Soviet investment and growth patterns bear a close resemblance to the Fel'dman model. Between 1928 and 1937, heavy manufacturing's share of the net product of total manufacturing increased from 31 percent to 63 percent, whereas light manufacturing's share fell from 68 percent to 36 percent. During this same period, gross capital investment grew at an annual rate of 14 percent, and the ratio of gross investment to GNP doubled from 13 percent to 26 percent. However, household consumption scarcely increased (0.8 percent per year during the period), while the share of consumption in GNP (in 1937 prices) declined from 80 percent to 53 percent. Over the period from 1928 to the present, the Soviet Union's unbalanced approach to investment not only contributed to its greatest economic successes—

[27]Paul R. Gregory and Robert C. Stuart, *Soviet and Post-Soviet Economic Structure and Performance* (New York: HarperCollins, 1994), pp. 13–43; and Walter W. Rostow, *The Stages of Economic Growth: A Non-Communist Manifesto* (Cambridge: Cambridge University Press, 1971), pp. 65–67.

[28]E. L. Wheelwright and Bruce McFarland, *The Chinese Road to Socialism: Economics of the Cultural Revolution* (New York: Monthly Review Press, 1970), pp. 13–65; and Carl Riskin, *China's Political Economy: The Quest for Development since 1949* (Oxford: Oxford University Press, 1987), pp. 53–113.

rapid economic growth and industrialization—but also to its chief failure: an average consumption level lower than almost all of Western Europe.

Indian Adaptation of the Soviet Investment Model.   For India's second 5-year plan (1955/56–1960/61), Jawaharlal Nehru, India's first prime minister, and Professor P. C. Mahalanobis, a statistician who headed the Indian planning commission, tried to combine the Fel'dman–Stalin investment strategy with democratic socialism to reduce capital shortages. The Mahalanobis planning model, like that of Fel'dman, stressed expanding the investment share in steel and capital goods. Eventually even agriculture was supposed to benefit from this emphasis, since the production of inputs, such as fertilizer and farm machinery, was to increase.

The actual investment pattern differed from the plan. Setting a fraction of investment in the capital goods industry as a target had little practical effect on investment decisions. To begin with, planning in India does not represent a binding commitment by a public department to spend funds. Moreover, it was extremely difficult to identify capital and consumer goods sectors in the industrial statistics at any reasonable level of disaggregation (or subdivision). The division between capital and consumer goods completely ignored intermediate goods, which comprise the bulk of manufacturing output in most economies. Furthermore, most industries produce at least two types of goods. For example, the automotive industry produces automobiles (consumer goods), trucks (capital goods), and replacement parts (intermediate goods). In practice the Mahalanobis model left investment choice in a number of enterprises and industries virtually unaffected.

Additionally new investments in heavy industry occurred more slowly than had been planned because of technical and managerial problems, and the increased output from each unit of investment was lower than expected. Yet heavy industry still had high rates of surplus capacity because of a lack of demand. Not only had planners miscalculated the demand for consumer and capital goods as a result of unreliable figures on population growth, income distribution, and demand elasticities; more fundamentally, they had failed to consider that there were not enough investors ready to buy the capital goods produced. In contrast in the Soviet Union, where planning was comprehensive and industry was state-owned, the government provided the market for capital goods from other industries producing capital goods and armaments.

During India's second 5-year plan, real GNP grew by only 3.7 percent per year compared to the 5.5-percent annual target, and the 2.5-percent annual growth rate in the early 1960s was even further below the 5.4-percent third-plan target. Slow growth in agricultural and capital goods sectors, as well as balance of payments crises from rapidly growing food and capital imports, convinced the Indian government to abandon the Mahalanobis approach by the late 1960s.[29]

Lessons from the Soviet Investment Model in LDCs.   The Chinese revoked their emphasis on the Soviet investment strategy in 1960, in part because the So-

---

[29]Lance Taylor, *Macro Models for Developing Countries* (New York: McGraw-Hill, 1979), pp. 119–27; Paul R. Gregory and Robert C. Stuart, *Soviet Economic Structure and Performance* (New York: Harper & Row, 1981), pp. 63–92, 327–96; Angus Maddison, *Class Structure and Economic Growth: India and Pakistan since the Moghuls* (New York: Norton, 1971), pp. 111–15; and India, Planning Commission, *Fourth Five-Year Plan, 1969–74* (Delhi, 1969).

viet aid agency, offended by Chinese missionary activity against Soviet Premier Nikita Khrushchev's revisionist criticisms of Stalinism, ceased credits for Chinese purchases, canceled contracts for the delivery of plant and equipment, withdrew their scientists, engineers, and technicians, and took the blueprints for projects, such as the half-completed 3-kilometer (2-mile) bridge in Beijing.[30] But Chinese officials also noted that some major weaknesses of a Soviet-type unbalanced economy have been undue emphasis on accumulation while overlooking consumption, too much investment in heavy industry and too little in light industry and agriculture, and the consequent lopsided development of the economic structure. One of the aims of current economic readjustment is to balance the branches of the economy which are seriously out of proportion, and reduce the overconcentration on heavy industry so that the process of production, distribution, circulation, and consumption can be speeded up to produce better economic results. To realize this change, the production of consumer goods will be given an important position. Indeed, these officials surmised that heavy-industry "construction can only be carried out after proper arrangements have been made for the people's livelihood."[31]

Thus, past experience unbalanced investment in the capital goods industry suggests several lessons: (1) a larger investment share in this industry is likely to increase economic growth if there is sufficient demand for capital goods; (2) the squeeze on current consumption implied by the unbalanced investment pattern may be at least as long as a generation; and (3) planners in capitalist and mixed economies may have too limited a control over total investment to implement a Fel'dman investment strategy.

Perestroika and the Soviet Collapse.   Mikhail Gorbachev became increasingly aware that the Soviet economy, without reform, would succumb to some of the major economic weaknesses that became apparent in the 1970s and early 1980s (retrospective data indicate that **total factor productivity**, or output per combined factor inputs, fell by almost 1 percent yearly, 1971–85).[32] The **perestroika** (economic restructuring) of Gorbachev, head of government from 1985 to 1991, recognized that the Soviets could no longer rely on major sources of past growth—substantial *increases* in **labor participation rates** (ratio of the labor force to population), rates of investment, and educational enrollment rates. Continued growth requires increased productivity per worker through agricultural decollectivization, more decentralized decisionmaking, a reduced bureaucracy, greater management and worker rewards for increased enterprise profitability, more incentives for technological innovation, and more price reform. Yet ironically, the destruction of old institutions before replacing them with new ones contributed to rising economic distress, which contributed to the attempted coup against Gorbachev, the end of the Communist party's monopoly, the breakup of the Soviet Union into numerous states, and the replacement of Gorbachev by Russia's President Boris Yeltsin in 1991. (Chapter 20 discusses reasons for the collapse of Russia's state socialism and problems associated with economic reform.)

---

[30]Carl Riskin, *China's Political Economy: The Quest for Development since 1949* (Oxford: Oxford University Press, 1987), pp. 74–76, 138–44.

[31]China, Government of, *Economic Readjustment and Reform* (Beijing: Beijing Review, 1982), p. 15.

[32]Paul R. Gregory and Robert C. Stuart, *Soviet and Post-Soviet Economic Structure and Performance* (New York: HarperCollins, 1994), p. 243.

LESSONS FROM NON-WESTERN MODELS

Since the collapse of Soviet communism, only a few countries, such as Cuba and North Korea, still adhere to the Russian model. But it would be inadvisable to accept the Japanese or Korean-Taiwanese models without modification. The Meiji Japanese and pre-1980 Koreans and Taiwanese were not democratic, spent heavily on the military, and repressed labor organizations, while early Japan's development was highly unequal and imperialistic, while Japan and Korea both had high industrial concentration rates. Still LDCs can selectively learn from these East Asian countries: some major ingredients of their successes included high homogenous standards (especially in science) of primary and secondary education, able government officials that planned policies to improve private-sector productivity, substantial technological borrowing and modification, exchange-rate policies that lacked discrimination against exports, and (in Japan and Taiwan) emphases on improving the skills of small- and medium-scale industrialists.

Growth in the Last 100 To 150 Years

For the last 130 years or so, average annual growth rates of real GNP per capita in Japan, Sweden, Germany, and Canada have been at least 2 percent, a rate that multiplies income sevenfold in 100 years. Of course, these growth rates, subject to serious price-index number and subsistence valuation problems, are only rough approximations. Japan's growth of 3.5 percent per year since the mid-nineteenth century has been the most rapid in the world (Table 3–1), doubling income in 20 years,[33] and increasing at a rate of 31 times per century. This long period of growth in the West and Japan is unparalleled in world history.[34] It is much more rapid than that of the developing countries, whose growth (with a few exceptions, such as Brazil, Argentina, Mexico, and Malaysia) for the same period was only a fraction of 1 percent per year.[35]

---

[33]A quick and fairly accurate method for computing doubling time is 70 divided by the percentage rate of growth. To illustrate, the Japanese growth of 3.5 percent yearly means income doubles in 70/3.5 or 20 years, and the Canadian growth of 2.0 percent annually indicates doubling in 35 years.

[34]What explains the United Kingdom's and the United States' slow and Japan's and Germany's accelerated growth since World War II? Lester Thurow, *The Zero-Sum Solution: Building a World-Class American Economy* (New York: Simon and Schuster, 1985), attributes Japan's superior performance to that of the United States to higher savings rates, higher primary and secondary educational standards, more emphasis on technical and applied science education, a higher propensity to import technology, the scientific and technological background of top managers, their longer time horizons, and the "leaner" management bureaucracy.

Mancur Olson, *The Rise and Decline of Nations: Economic Growth, Stagflation, and Social Rigidities* (New Haven: Yale University Press, 1982), argues that the growth of special interests in developed countries with long periods of stability (without invasion or upheaval), such as Britain and the United States, reduces efficiency and growth. Thus the Allied powers' defeat and occupation of Japan and Germany in the late 1940s abolished special interests that slowed economic growth, while encouraging the establishment of highly encompassing interests. Yet four decades is long enough for encrusted interests to form in Japan and Germany, perhaps thus contributing to recent deceleration in the two countries' growth rates.

Paul Kennedy, *The Rise and Fall of the Great Powers: Economic Change and Military Conflict from 1500 to 2000* (New York: Random House, 1987), contends that great powers emerge because of a strong economic base but decline (for example, Britain in the mid-twentieth century and the United States in the late twentieth century) from military overcommitment obstructing economic growth.

[35]Based on an update of David Morawetz, *Twenty-five Years of Economic Development, 1950 to 1975* (Baltimore: Johns Hopkins University Press for the World Bank, 1977), p. 14.

TABLE 3-1   Annual Rate of Growth of Real GNP per Capita (percent)

Annual Growth Rates, columns (1)-(5)

Country	(1) 1860 or 1870 to 1910	(2) 1910 to 1950	(3) 1950 to 1975	(4) 1975 to 1986	(5) (Long period) 1860 or 1870 to 1986	Multiplication of 1860 GNP per capita in 1986
Japan	2.9	1.8	7.6	3.4	3.5	76[e]
Sweden	2.4	2.6	2.6	2.4	2.5	23
Germany[a]	2.0	0.7	4.5	2.4	2.1	14
Canada	2.2	1.3	2.4	2.2	2.0	11
Denmark	1.8	1.3	2.9	2.5	1.9	11
France[b]	1.5	0.9	3.8	2.3	1.9	11[c]
United States	2.5	1.1	2.0	2.0	1.9	11
Russia-USSR[d]	1.0	2.0	2.7	1.9	1.8	9[c]
Ireland	1.7	1.4	2.6	1.9	1.8	9
Italy	0.8	1.3	4.3	2.2	1.8	9
United Kingdom	1.2	1.2	2.2	1.8	1.4	6

[a] Since World War II, West Germany.

[b] Figures for period 1 and the long period begin in 1840.

[c] Multiplication for period 1860–1986 at same annual growth rate as that in column 5.

[d] The periods are: (1) 1870–1913 and (2) 1913–1950.

[e] This multiple is probably overstated. Growth rates and corresponding multiples are rough approximations (see text).

Sources: Simon Kuznets, "Levels and Variations of Rates of Growth," *Economic Development and Cultural Change* 5 (October 1956): 13; David Morawetz, *Twenty-five Years of Economic Development, 1950 to 1975* (Baltimore: Johns Hopkins University Press for the World Bank, 1977), p. 80; Gur Ofer, "Soviet Economic Growth: 1928–1985," *Journal of Economic Literature* 25 (December 1987): 1778. The 1975 to 1986 rates (except for the USSR) are estimates based on World Bank, *World Bank Atlas, 1987* (Washington, D.C., 1987), pp. 6–9.

The Power of Exponential Growth—
The United States and Canada:
The Late Nineteenth Century and Today

A real growth in GNP per capita (or productivity per person) of 2 percent yearly multiplies income sevenfold over a century and nineteenfold for one and one-half centuries. We can get a better sense of what this has meant by describing the living conditions of some North American families in the late nineteenth century, and comparing them to twentieth-century conditions. In 1885, a family of a rural Pennsylvania mechanic and farmer, who had no horse and wagon or public transport, lived 11 kilometers (or 7 miles) from the nearest village, built its house and dug its well by hand, made most of its own tools, raised wheat, corn, fruit, pigs, chickens, and a garden, and shot game birds, squirrels, and deer on 6.5

hectares (16 acres).[36] The children walked 8 kilometers (or 5 miles) to a one-room school, while the father walked to the nearest village to pay his taxes. They borrowed a horse to plow the field, and used a handmade spade, hoe, clod-breaker, and wheelbarrow, a hand-pulled sled, and a hand-pushed tiller for farm work. Their house had no indoor plumbing, so water had to be pumped, carried by a bucket for use and disposal, and heated on a stove and poured in a basin for washing. Their few changes of clothes (mostly handmade except for men's suits and work clothes) lay in handmade chests or hung on wall pegs, as there were no closets. They scrubbed their clothes with a washboard, and ironed with flatirons heated on a stove. In winter, they chopped down a tree in a nearby forest, dragged it on a hand-pulled sled, chopped it into stove lengths, staked it, and carried it into the house for a wood stove, which heated one room, in which they worked, ate, cooked, and sat; the family slept in other rooms which were cold in the winter. They raised most of their food—potatoes, turnips, beets, other vegetables, and fruits—which they spent many hours preserving or kept in a root cellar over the winter. They dug dandelions, ground their roots for coffee, cooked wintercress and wild mustard greens, and made tea from the dried leaves of wild plants. The daughters stopped school after the eighth grade to reduce spending for the fees and board of the town public school. Although family members could read, they had little reading material available.

Although people who lived in rural areas worked hard and faced a difficult life, their comfort probably was higher than a factory worker's family, who lacked outdoor space, healthful environment, a varied and adequate diet, and control over time and effort. Cities, with their wretched housing conditions or crowded tenements for the majority, were unsanitary, crowded places that provided no privacy and few basic amenities, and were breeding grounds for disease. Nutrition, public health, and medical care were appalling, so that epidemics of deadly diseases were common, life expectancy was only 40 years, and infant mortality was 170 per 1,000 births.

In the 1850s, a typical Atlantic-coast worker's family spent 45 percent of its income, estimated at $550–600 yearly in today's dollars, on food, and 95 percent on food, clothing, and shelter, leaving little for medical care, entertainment, and so on. Travelers in North America during this time lamented the ubiquity of the one-pot stew, which was, however, an improvement over most of Western Europe during good harvests then and for centuries before. The alternative to this stew for most people was a minimal amount of nutritionally inferior foods, such as potatoes, lard, cornmeal, and salt pork, restricted by local weather conditions, crop cycles, no refrigeration, and limited transport. Housing during the mid-nineteenth century varied from a single 3-by-3.5 meters (10-by-12-foot) room for six persons in a New York City tenement to a small house of logs or loosely boarded frame construction (usually without glass windows) for most rural people to better housing for the few in the more prosperous towns and cities. Obviously, no homes had electricity, few had gas, fewer still had hot running water, less than 2 percent had indoor toilets and cold running water, and baths were a luxury. Furthermore, the typical workweek (6 days) was 66–70 hours in 1850 and 57 hours in 1900. Vacations or retirement for the elderly was unknown, except for the very rich.

---

[36]This section is from William J. Baumol, Sue Anne Batey Blackman, and Edward N. Wolff, *Productivity and American Leadership: The Long View* (Cambridge, Mass.: MIT Press, 1989), pp. 30–64. Among other sources, the authors cite Peggy Heim, "Living Conditions of a Mechanic's Family in Rural Pennsylvania, 1885 to the Early Twentieth Century," mimeo, 1985, for material on the farmer-mechanic; and the 1980 U.S. Census of Housing.

In contrast, in the late 1970s or early 1980s, an urban middle-income family spent 25 percent of its income on food (including fresh fruits and vegetables transported across the continent year-round, freeze-dried, frozen, and canned produce, and other items packaged for safety and nutrition), and 54 percent on food, clothing, and shelter. According to the 1980 U.S. Census of Housing, only 2.2 percent of American housing units lacked complete plumbing (defined as hot and cold piped water, a flush toilet, *and* a bathtub or shower for the exclusive use of the housing unit) and only 4.5 percent were occupied by more than one person per room. And 99.9 percent of U.S. households owned an electric vacuum cleaner, toaster, radio, iron, coffeemaker, and television, 99.8 percent had electric refrigerators, and 77 percent had electric washing machines. The adult literacy rate was 99 percent (compared to 80 percent in 1870), life expectancy was 74 years, and infant mortality was 12 per 1,000. Most North Americans spent a substantial portion of their evenings, weekends, and vacations in television viewing, cultural events, sports, and other recreational and leisure activities.

For the Japanese, the contrast from the nineteenth to twentieth centuries is even greater than for North America. Asians, Africans, and Latin Americans aspire to at least 2-to-3 percent annual real growth, expecting this growth to affect their material levels of living as radically as it affected North Americans, Western Europeans, and Japanese in the past.

Economic Growth in Europe and Japan After World War II

Europe and Japan were devastated economically during the war. In the late 1940s and early 1950s, the reorganization of the international trade and financial system coupled with U.S. technical and economic assistance (such as the Marshall Plan) provided the basis for the rapid recovery of war-torn economies, including the economic miracle in West Germany and Japan. Many expected the same jump start with capital and technological expertise to create similar economic miracles in underdeveloped countries. But this did not occur. Countries with cultures vastly different from those of the West, with undeveloped industrial complexes, low literacy, and few technical skills, were simply not able to use the capital fully.

It became obvious that the remarkable growth in Germany and Japan occurred because technical knowledge and human capital were still intact, even though factories, railroads, bridges, harbors, and other physical capital lay in ruins. Starting growth in an underdeveloped economy was far different from rebuilding a war-torn economy.[37]

Recent Economic Growth in Developing Countries

Economic growth in developing countries was much more rapid after World War II than before. Data before this war are generally poor or lacking altogether. From the start of the twentieth century until independence in 1947, real growth in India, the LDC with the best estimates, was no more than 0.2 percent per year, compared

[37]With this awareness, scholars began thinking seriously in the 1950s about the economic development of Asia, Africa, and Latin America as a field of inquiry separate from the economics of the West. By the last part of the decade, several courses on the economic development of underdeveloped countries were introduced into U.S. universities.

to an annual 1.9-percent growth from 1950 to 1992. World Bank studies indicate real growth rates for developing countries as a whole from 1870 to 1950 to be less than 1 percent a year compared to growth from 1950 to 1992 of about 2.5 percent per year and a doubling time of 28 years, a rough approximation, subject to price-index number and subsistence valuation problems discussed in Chapter 2.

This rate has been more rapid than earlier predictions and targets would indicate; at least this is true of growth in the 1960s and early 1970s. Forecasts in the 1960s by three prominent economists, Paul Rosenstein–Rodan, Hollis Chenery, and Alan Strout, underestimated the growth of LDCs in the 1960s and 1970s. Furthermore, growth in the GNP of developing countries during the United Nation's first development decade of the 1960s exceeded the target.[38]

The annual growth rate of 2.5 percent was faster than the median long-term growth (1.9 percent per year; see Table 3–1) since 1860 or 1870 for developed countries on which there are data. Yet this comparatively favorable record does not satisfy developing countries. Many of them made systematic planning efforts to condense into a few decades development that took the West more than a century. Furthermore, LDC annual growth, only 1.6 percent since 1950 and 1.2 annually since 1975, had plummeted enormously, adding to third-world discontent.[39]

RAPID AND SLOW GROWERS

Such rapid growth masks a wide diversity of performance among the 4.5 billion people in the developing world. About 16 of the developing countries, with 43 percent of LDC population in 1996 (1.9 billion), grew at an average annual rate of 3.0 percent or more from 1960 to 1992 (Table 3–2), a rate which increased GNP per capita eightfold during the 32 years. More than three-fifths of this population is from China, which, despite incentives for provincial officials to overstate economic performance, still had fast growth under socialism, and even faster growth during market reforms after 1978. Other fast growers included the high-performing Asian economies discussed before, South Korea, Taiwan, Thailand, Malaysia, and Indonesia (the other three high performers—Japan, Singapore, and Hong Kong—are high-income economies). Brazil, despite an annual inflation rate of 107 percent, 1960–1992 (Table 15–3), and a debt overhang in the 1980s and early 1990s that slowed import and overall growth, was the only Latin American country experiencing fast growth. Turkey and Portugal gained from increasing integration into an affluent Europe. Neighboring rivals, mixed-economy Greece and socialist Bulgaria, both achieved rapid growth during the period.

[38]David Morawetz, *Twenty-five Years of Economic Development, 1950 to 1975* (Baltimore: Johns Hopkins University Press for the World Bank, 1977), pp. 16–22; Paul Rosenstein-Rodan, "International Aid for Underdeveloped Countries," *Review of Economics and Statistics* 43, no. 2 (May 1961): 107–38; and Hollis Chenery and Alan Strout, "Foreign Assistance and Economic Development," *American Economic Review* 56, no. 4 (September 1966): 679–733.

[39]David Morawetz, *Twenty-five Years of Economic Development, 1950 to 1975* (Baltimore: Johns Hopkins University Press for the World Bank, 1977), pp. 12–14; Alan Heston and Robert Summers, "Comparative Indian Economic Growth: 1870–1970," *American Economic Review* 70, no. 2 (May 1980): 96–101; World Bank, *World Development Report, 1988* (New York: Oxford University Press, 1988), p. 187; World Bank, *World Bank Atlas: 1988 Update* (Washington, D.C., 1988), pp. 6–9; Jogindar S. Uppal, *Economic Development in South Asia* (New York: St. Martin's Press, 1977), pp. 15–17; World Bank, *The World Bank Atlas, 1994* (Washington, D.C.:, 1993), p. 18; World Bank, Global Economic Prospects and the Developing Countries (Washington, D.C., 1994); and Ruddar Datt and K.P.M. Sundharam, *Indian Economy* (New Delhi: S.Chand & Co., 1993), p. 13.

TABLE 3-2   GNP per Capita and Its Annual Growth Rate, Developing Countries, 1960–92

Country	Population 1996 (millions)	GNP per Capita 1992 U.S. Dollars 1960	GNP per Capita 1992 U.S. Dollars 1992	Annual Growth Rate 1960–92 (percent)
Fifteen most populous countries				
China	1218.4	96	470	5.1
India	955.9	164	310	2.0
Indonesia	206.1	191	670	4.0
Brazil	160.6	980	2770	3.3
Russian Federation	147.2	..	2510	..
Pakistan	133.6	168	420	2.9
Bangladesh	122.3	..	220	..
Nigeria	104.3	150	320	2.4
Mexico	95.9	2155	3470	1.5
Vietnam	76.5	..	..	..
Philippines	72.0	493	770	1.4
Iran, Islamic Rep.	65.7	..	2200	..
Turkey	64.5	701	1980	3.3
Egypt	61.6	264	640	2.8
Thailand	61.1	363	1840	5.2
Eighteen fastest growing countries				
Korea, Rep.	45.4	632	6590	7.6
Taiwan	22.0	743	7520	7.5
Thailand	61.1	363	1840	5.2
China	1218.4	96	470	5.1
Romania	22.7	244	1130	4.9
Portugal	9.9	1937	7450	4.3
Indonesia	206.1	191	670	4.0
Greece	10.4	2078	7290	4.0
Malaysia	20.4	820	2790	3.9
Bulgaria	8.4	391	1330	3.9
Saudi Arabia	19.2	2348	7510	3.7
Lesotho	2.0	190	590	3.6
Tunisia	9.0	572	1720	3.5
Brazil	160.6	980	2770	3.3
Turkey	64.5	701	1980	3.3
Poland	38.8	676	1910	3.3
Pakistan	133.6	168	420	2.9
Hungary	10.2	1190	2970	2.9
Sixteen slowest growing countries				
Niger	9.4	650	280	−2.6
Nicaragua	4.6	551	340	−1.5
Mozambique	16.7	94	60	−1.4
Madagascar	14.4	338	230	−1.2
Peru	23.8	1080	950	−0.4
Ivory Coast	14.9	737	670	−0.3
Mali	9.7	331	310	−0.2
Senegal	8.7	832	780	−0.2

TABLE 3-2   Continued

| Country | Population 1996 (millions) | GNP per Capita | | Annual Growth Rate 1960–92 (percent) |
| | | 1992 U.S. Dollars | | |
		1960	1992	
Ghana	17.9	465	450	-0.1
Malawi	10.0	217	210	-0.1
Benin	5.6	410	410	0.0
Central African Republic	3.3	410	410	0.0
Ethiopia (and Eritrea)	58.7	106	110	0.1
Zimbabwe	11.9	552	570	0.1
Chad	6.8	213	220	0.1
Congo	2.5	966	1030	0.2

Note: Two dots (..) refer to a lack of information.

Sources: Population Reference Bureau, *1994 World Population Data Sheet* (Washington, D.C., 1994); World Bank, *World Development Report, 1994* (New York: Oxford University Press, 1994), pp. 162–63, 170–71, 210–11, 214–15; and World Bank, *World Development Report, 1982* (New York: Oxford University Press, 1982), pp. 110–11.

Hungary (just below 3-percent growth) and Poland grew fast while at the forefront of Eastern European reform socialism during the 1970s and 1980s and avoided the severe economic collapse that other Eastern European countries suffered when regional trade patterns were curtailed during the early 1990s. Other top performers were Saudi Arabia, the world's largest petroleum exporter; Tunisia, whose exports to Arab oil producers grew rapidly; and Lesotho, an enclave within South Africa, whose exports to and workers' remittances from the country grew rapidly.

On the other hand, 25 of the less-developed countries, with 6 percent of the LDC population (0.3 billion) grew by less than 1 percent per year, 1960–92. However, adding low-income economies without growth figures (in Table 2–1) and Vietnam, Zaïre, North Korea, Iraq, Afghanistan, Cambodia, and Haiti (not listed in Table 2–1), which lacked data, totals 43 slow-growing countries with 0.8 billion or 16 percent of the LDC population. Slow growers consisted of 36 of the 46 sub-Saharan countries, and Peru, Bolivia, Uruguay, Honduras, Nicaragua, Jamaica, and Nepal.

The contrast is instructive between Thailand and the Philippines, presently members of the Association of South East Asian Nations (ASEAN) and both with a population of 41 million and a GNP per capita of $310–330 in 1968 (in 1968 U.S. dollars), according to the World Bank.[40] However, there was a considerable discrepancy between the income distribution in the two countries during the late 1960s and 1970s. The top 10 percent of the population in the Philippines was significantly richer than the same group in Thailand, but the bottom 20 percent was more than twice as well-off in Thailand. One indicator of the greater egalitarianism in Thailand was its superior progress in rural electrification, especially among

---

[40]World Bank, *World Bank Atlas, 1970: Population, Per Capita Product and Growth Rates* (Washington, D.C.: International Bank for Reconstruction and Development, 1970).

the poor, to that in the Philippines. Furthermore, from 1968 to 1992, the annual real growth per capita was 4.8 percent for Thailand compared to 2.2 percent for the Philippines.

There are several reasons for Thailand's better economic performance. In contrast to the Philippines, Thai banks have been more likely to be privately owned and to exercise independent authority over lending. Moreover, in its credit policies, the government of Thailand targeted small- and medium-scale agriculture and industry, unlike the Philippines, which was more oriented toward large enterprises.

Since World War II, Thailand has had lower import barriers than the Philippines, even during Thailand's emphasis on import-substitution emphasis during the 1970s. Thailand stressed exports of natural resources in the 1960s, shifting in the 1980s to exports of labor-intensive manufacturing and assembly, much of which were a part of the Japanese-directed borderless economy. In the 1990s, Thailand attracted a larger share of foreign investment in capital- and knowledge-intensive export sectors. Because of corruption, trade and exchange-rate restrictions, and political instability, the Philippines attracted much less investment than Thailand.

Thailand had greater success than the Philippines avoiding inflation during the oil price increases in 1973–74 and 1979–81, using macroeconomic policies to restrict spending in contrast to large budget deficits and monetary expansion in the Philippines. Furthermore, a real devaluation of the Thai bhat, 1984–88, together with Japanese and Taiwanese investment in labor-intensive manufacturing, spurred exports, while helping the country avoid both international and domestic imbalances during the late 1980s and early 1990s. In comparison, the Philippines' currency appreciated in real terms as the currency remained fixed in the face of inflation faster than the rest of the world.[41]

Thailand's population in 1996 was 61.1 million compared to the Philippines' 72.0 million (Table 2–1). Indeed, Thailand experienced a marked decline in crude birth rate from 1970, when the rate was slightly higher than that of the Philippines, to 1992, when the birth rate was 2.0 percent of the population in Thailand compared to 3.2 percent in the Philippines.[42] Moreover, Thailand's fall in fertility reduced the percentage of children aged less than 15 years to 29 percent of the population, while the Philippines' percentage remained high at 39 percent,[43] thus increasing the share of spending on food, health, and education for the dependent population. The fact that the poorest segment of the Thai population was substantially better off than the Filipino population helped explain why Thailand's fertility rate is lower than the Philippines. More people had reached a socioeconomic level in Thailand that promoted birth control (see Chapter 8). A further benefit from Thailand's rapid fertility decline was the deceleration in annual labor-force growth, from 2.8 percent (1970–80) to 2.2 percent (1980–92) to 1.5 percent (1992–2000), while the Philippines' annual growth remained virtually static, with 2.4 percent (1970–80), 2.5 percent (1980–92), and 2.3 percent (1992–2000).[44]

[41]World Bank, *The East Asian Miracle: Economic Growth and Public Policy* (New York: Oxford University Press, 1993).

[42]World Bank, *World Development Report, 1994* (New York: Oxford University Press, 1994), pp. 212–13.

[43]Population Reference Bureau, *1994 World Population Data Sheet* (Washington, D.C., 1994).

[44]World Bank, *World Development Report, 1994* (New York: Oxford University Press, 1994), pp. 210–11.

REGIONS OF THE WORLD

As argued in the next section, figures in Table 2–1 cannot reveal whether the DCs or LDCs have been growing faster since 1960. Yet several LDC regions have experienced stagnation or even negative growth since the slowdown of the world economy after the collapse of the post-1945 **Bretton Woods international monetary system** of fixed exchange rates and the increased prices of oil and other raw materials in the early 1970s. Sub-Saharan Africa, Latin America, and the Middle East have suffered mutually reinforcing, negative growth and severe debt crises since 1980. On the other hand, East Asia, with the newly industrializing countries and China, has grown at a rate in excess of 6 percent yearly since 1980. Still, because of earlier development, Latin America appears to have the highest GNP per capita of the LDC regions and, because of widespread sluggish growth in the early post-World War II period, South and Southeast Asia appears to have the lowest average GNP among LDC regions (Table 2–1). Regional figures, however, are fraught with a high degree of uncertainty. Many experienced economists contend that, despite the figures, Sub-Saharan Africa is the poorest world region. If this is not yet true, it may soon be true if existing trends continue.

THE CONVERGENCE CONTROVERSY

In 1969, a commission on international development chaired by Lester Pearson (former Canadian prime minister) contended that "the widening gap between the developed and developing countries" is one of the central issues of our time.[45] Are rich countries getting richer and poor countries poorer? One measure, real per capita income, indicates that since World War II both developed and developing countries are better off. Is the gap widening? the answer is complex, since it depends on the definition of the gap, the time period used, how we define a rich country and a poor one, and whether or not we view a country at the beginning or the end of the time period.

A key question is whether poor countries grow faster than rich ones, so that income per capita is **converging**. Convergence concurs with the predominant neoclassical growth model (discussed in Chapter 5), which presumes diminishing returns to capital as an economy develops, and similar technology from one economy to another. Robert J. Barro and Xavier Sala-i-Martin show that in the United States, low-income states have narrowed the relative economic gap vis-à-vis high-income states from 1840 to 1988.[46] Does this finding apply to countries? William J. Baumol's answer is "yes," arguing that growth among 16 DCs converged from 1870 to 1970.[47] However, Baumol demonstrates selection bias, by choosing, after the fact, a sample of countries that have successfully developed and are now among the richest countries in the world. He could have avoided selection bias if

---

[45]Lester Pearson et al., *Partners in Development: Report of the Commission on International Development* (New York: Praeger, 1969), p. 1.

[46]Robert J. Barro and Xavier Sala-i-Martin, "Convergence," *Journal of Political Economy* 100 (April 1992): 223–51.

[47]William J. Baumol, "Productivity Growth, Convergence, and Welfare: What the Long-Run Data Show," *American Economic Review* 76 (December 1986): 1072–85.

FIGURE 3–1 Testing for Convergence

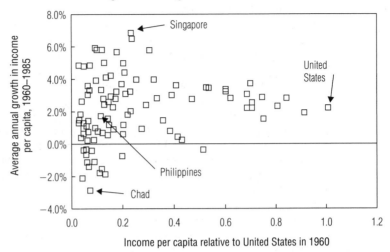

Source: Paul M. Romer, "The Origins of Endogenous Growth," *Journal of Economic Perspectives* 5 (Winter 1994): 5.

he had tested convergence, as other scholars did, by examining the subsequent growth rates of the richest countries in 1870.[48] Figure 3–1 indicates that from 1960 to 1985, poor countries grew at about the same rate as rich countries, so that income per capita of the developed countries is neither growing faster than (**diverging** with) nor growing slower than (converging with) income per capita of the developing countries.[49]

Summary

1. In the last one to one and one-half centuries, sustained economic growth occurred primarily in the capitalist countries of the West and Japan. During this period, the economic growth rate of a number of these countries was over 1.5 percent per

---

[48]J. Bradford de Long, "Productivity Growth, Convergence, and Welfare: Comment," *American Economic Review* 78 (December 1988): 1138–54. See also Moses Abramovitz, "Catching Up, Forging Ahead, and Falling Behind," *Journal of Economic History* 46 (June 1986): 394.

    Even so, Baumol would not have found convergence if he had compared the United States to other Western countries from 1870 through the immediate period after World War II. As Abramovitz, *Journal of Economic History* 46: 391–97, points out, the United States widened its lead because: (1) of rapid advance in general and technical education, (2) technological change during that period was heavily scale dependent but biased in labor-saving but capital- and resource-saving directions, where America enjoyed great advantages, and (3) World Wars I and II were serious setbacks for Europe but stimuli to growth in the United States.

    The World Bank, *World Development Report, 1990* (New York: Oxford University Press, 1990), p. 10, in asserting that the performance of LDCs diverged in the 1980s, is also guilty of selection bias. After the fact, fast-growing countries tend to have higher per capita incomes than slow-growing countries, just as fast-growing teenagers are generally taller than slow-growing teens.

[49]Paul M. Romer, "The Origins of Endogenous Growth," *Journal of Economic Perspectives* 5 (Winter 1994): 3–22.

year. Thus the gap between these countries and the developing countries of Afro-Asia has increased greatly.

2. The rise of capitalism in the West can be traced to the decline of feudalism, the breakdown of church authority, strong nation–states supporting free trade, a liberal ideology tailor-made for the bourgeoisie, a price revolution that speeded capital accumulation, advances in science and technology, and a spirit of rationalism from the fifteenth to eighteenth centuries.

3. During the late nineteenth century, the Japanese government helped individuals and organizations acquire foreign technology, established a banking system, assisted private business people (including selling factories to them), aided technical improvement in small industry, implemented universal education, and kept foreign exchange rates close to market-clearing rates. However, the lessons contemporary LDCs can learn from early modern Japan are limited because of her historically specific conditions.

4. The South Korean and Taiwanese approaches have been similar to those of Japan. Moreover, the Korean-Taiwanese model stressed government-business cooperation alongside government creation of contested markets among businesses.

5. The 1917 Communist revolution in Russia provided an alternative to capitalism as a road to economic modernization. The state took control of economic planning and capital accumulation. In only a few decades, Soviet centralized socialism transformed Russia. Yet the major sources for this rapid growth, increased capital formation and increased labor participation rates, were exhausted in the decade or two before the collapse of communism in 1991.

6. The rapid growth of the United States in the past century corresponds to remarkable improvements in the average living standard.

7. The economic growth of developing countries since World War II has been much more rapid than before the war. Yet the postwar growth of developing countries has been no faster than the growth of developed countries, suggesting no tendency toward convergence between rich and poor countries.

8. Moreover, this growth masks a wide diversity of performance among the developing countries. From 1960 to 1992, almost half the LDC population lived in countries growing at an annual rate of 3 percent or better, but about one-fourth of this population grew by no more than 1 percent yearly. Since 1980, East Asia has grown the fastest and sub-Saharan Africa the slowest among world regions.

Terms to Review

- modern economic growth
- capitalism
- bourgeoisie
- surplus
- Protestant ethic
- Japanese development model
- zaibatsu
- infrastructure
- Asian tigers
- Korean-Taiwanese development model
- contested markets
- laissez-faire
- import substitutes
- Asian borderless economy
- monopsony
- Green Revolution
- Stalinist development model

- perestroika
- Fel'dman-Stalin investment Strategy
- total factor productivity
- labor participation rate
- Bretton Woods international monetary system

- real domestic currency depreciation
- real domestic currency appreciation
- terms of trade
- convergence
- divergence

Questions to Discuss

1. What are the characteristics of modern economic growth? Why was modern economic growth largely confined to the West (Western Europe, the United States, and Canada) before the twentieth century?
2. How important were noneconomic factors in contributing to modern capitalist development in the West?
3. How does the *relative* gap between the West and Afro-Asian LDCs today compare to the gap a century and a quarter or half ago? How do we explain this difference?
4. Which countries outside the West have had the most development success in the last century? Are these non-Western development models useful for today's LDCs?
5. Evaluate Russia-the Soviet Union as a model for today's LDCs.
6. Compare the economic growth of today's LDCs before and after World War II.
7. Indicate in some detail how sustained economic growth in North America has changed the material level of living from about 100 to 150 years ago to today.
8. Has average income in the rich and poor countries converged since 1960? In the past 100 to 150 years?

Guide to Readings

Simon Kuznets's *Economic Growth of Nations* (note 1) and *Modern Economic Growth: Rate, Structure, and Spread* (New Haven: Yale University Press, 1966) analyze the origin of modern economic growth. Initially modern growth meant capitalist growth as Dillard indicates in a book and article (note 5). For criticisms of Weber's thesis (note 2) on the Protestant ethic and capitalist development, see Chapter 12; R. H. Tawney, *Religion and the Rise of Capitalism* (New York: Harcourt, Brace, and Co., 1926); Kurt Samuelsson, *Religion and Economic Action: A Critique of Max Weber* (New York: Harper & Row, 1957); and H. M. Robertson, *Aspects of the Rise of Economic Individualism: A Criticism of Max Weber and His School* (New York: Kelley and Millman, 1959).

The annual *World Development Report* by the World Bank is the best of several sources on recent economic growth of LDCs and DCs (see the bibliographical note in Chapter 2). Morawetz's book (note to Table 3–1) has an excellent analysis of major trends in the economic growth of LDCs from World War II to 1975. The books by Kuznets noted above, although somewhat dated, are the best sources on long-run economic growth. Paul Bairoch's careful statistical work in *The Economic Development of the Third World since 1900*, trans. Cynthia Postan (Berkeley and Los Angeles: University of California Press, 1975); "Europe's Gross National Product: 1800–1975," *Journal of European Economic History* 5 (Fall 1976): 273–340; and "International Industrialization Levels from 1750 to 1980," *Journal of European Economic History* 11 (Fall 1982): 269–333; is worth perusing, although I think Bairoch, unlike Kuznets, underestimates nineteenth-century differences between GNP per capita in the DCs and the third world. Baumol et al. (note 36) have detailed comparisons showing how rapid economic growth changed the welfare and lifestyle of Americans since the nineteenth century. Gregory and Stuart's book (note 26) on Russian-Soviet economic development and Riskin's book on Chinese development (note 28) are excellent.

Kazushi Ohkawa and Gustav Ranis, eds., *Japan and the Developing Countries* (Oxford: Basil Blackwell, 1985); Kunio Yoshihara, *Japanese Economic Development* (Oxford: Oxford University Press, 1994); and Nafziger (note 9), with useful references, examine implications of the Japanese development experience for LDCs. Takatoshi Ito, *The Japanese Economy* (Cambridge, Mass.: MIT Press, 1992) and Kunio Yoshihara, *Japanese Economic Development* (New York: Oxford University Press, 1994) are excellent sources on the contemporary Japanese economy.

For students interested in the high-performing Asian economies, see the World Bank, *The East Asian Miracle* (note 11), and a series of articles assessing that monograph in *World Development*, April 1994 (also see note 11). *World Development* 16 (January 1988), has a special issue devoted to South Korea (see note 22).

Paul Krugman dissents from the prevailing view in "The Myth of Asia's Miracle," *Foreign Affairs* 73 (November/December 1994): 62-78.

Tessa Morris–Suzuki examines *The Technological Transformation of Japan: From the Seventeenth to the Twenty–First Century* (New York: Cambridge University Press, 1994).

Profile of Developing Countries

Scope of the Chapter

This chapter surveys the characteristics of developing countries. It looks at income distribution, political framework, family system, relative size of agriculture, technical and capital levels, saving rates, dualism, international trade dependence, export patterns, population growth, labor force growth, literacy, and skill levels. Subsequent chapters will expand on the economic pattern of development.

Varying Income Inequality

As economic development proceeds, income inequality frequently follows an **inverted U-shaped curve,** first increasing (from low- to middle-income countries), and then decreasing (from middle- to high-income countries). Even so, the proportion of the population in poverty drops as per capita income increases (see Chapter 6).

Political Framework

VARYING POLITICAL SYSTEMS

Only about 36 of the LDCs are political democracies; that is, a system enjoying wide competition between organized groups and elections that are regularly and fairly conducted.[1] Since democracies include populous India, they comprise more than one-third of the total population of LDCs.

---

[1]This definition is from *Africa Demōs: A Bulletin of the African Governance Program, the Carter Center* 3 (March 1995): 35.

A SMALL POLITICAL ELITE

Unlike Western democracies, political control in LDCs tends to be held by a relatively small **political elite.** This group includes not only individuals who directly or indirectly play a considerable part in government—political leaders, traditional princes and chiefs, high-ranking military officers, senior civil servants and administrators, and executives in public corporations—but also large landowners, major business people, and leading professionals. Even an authoritarian leader cannot rule without some consensus among this influential elite unless he or she uses police and military repression, perhaps with the support of a strong foreign power.

LOW POLITICAL INSTITUTIONALIZATION

For the political elite, economic modernization often poses a dilemma. Although achieving modernity breeds stability, the process of modernization breeds instability. Certainly modernization enhances the ability of a governing group to maintain order, resolve disputes, select leaders, and promote political community. But urbanization, industrialization, educational expansion, and so on, eventually involve previously inactive ethnic, religious, regional, or economic groups in politics. According to Samuel Huntington, the explosion of mass participation in politics relative to institutional capacity to absorb new participants leads to political instability.[2] (Of course civil conflict is not confined to newly modernizing countries. Currently ethnic, religious, and regional conflicts exist in Canada, Belgium, and Spain.)

EXPERIENCE OF WESTERN DOMINATION

Except for Japan, in the past 200 years—and especially in the first half of the twentieth century—most of Africa and Asia were Western-dominated colonies. Even such countries as Afghanistan and Thailand, which were never Western colonies, experienced Western penetration and hegemony. And although most of Latin America became independent in the nineteenth century, it has been subject to British and U.S. economic and political suzerainty since then. Thus during the century or two of rapid economic growth in the Western countries, most LDCs have not had the political independence essential for economic modernization.

An Extended Family

The **extended family,** including two or more nuclear families of parent(s) and children, is a common institution in developing countries. Although some scholars regard the extended family as an obstacle to economic development, I disagree. To be sure, if one family member earns a higher income and saves, others may demand the savings be shared, which hinders development, since funds are diverted from capital formation. However, if family members attend secondary school or university, acquire training, seek urban employment, or start a new business, the larger family unit may pool risks to support them financially and so contribute to economic development.

---

[2]Samuel P. Huntington, *Political Order in Changing Societies* (New Haven: Yale University Press, 1968).

Peasant Agricultural Societies

Most low-income countries are predominantly peasant agricultural societies. **Peasants** are rural cultivators. They do not run a business enterprise as do farmers in the United States, but rather a household whose main concern is survival. Although patterns of land ownership, tenure, and concentration vary considerably, most of the land in these societies is worked by landless laborers, sharecroppers, renters, or smallholders rather than large commercial farmers. In Afro-Asia the average farm is usually less than 5 hectares or 12 acres in size (see Chapter 7).

A High Proportion of the Labor Force in Agriculture

In low-income countries, 50–75 percent of the labor force is in agriculture, forestry, hunting, and fishing; 5–20 percent in industry (manufacturing, mining, construction, and public utilities); and 20–40 percent in services (see Table 4–1). In contrast high-income countries tend to have less than 10 percent of the labor force in agriculture; 30–40 percent in industry; and 50–65 percent in services. (A generation or two ago, the share of the labor force in agriculture in low-income countries may have been 90 percent, about the same as that of the United States in 1776.)

In low-income countries, the average agricultural family produces a surplus large enough only to supply a small nonagricultural population. In these countries, two-thirds of the labor force produce food, one-twenty-fifth do so in the United States. Obviously agricultural productivity in low-income countries is much lower than in the United States and other developed countries.

A High Proportion of Output in Agriculture

Figure 4–1 indicates that as countries develop, the output and labor force share in agriculture declines, and that in industry and services increases. The least developed and low-income countries of Asia and Africa are now in the early part of the labor force change, while the middle-income states of Latin America, East Asia, and the Middle East are in the later part. In high-income countries, the rising output and labor force share of services leads to stability and then an eventual decline in the share of industry.

Typically the shift in labor force shares from agriculture to industry lags behind the shift in production shares. One reason is the unprecedented growth of the labor force since the 1950s; it has far exceeded industry's capacity to absorb labor (see Chapter 9). In addition, partly because of advanced technology and greater capital intensity, industry's labor productivity is higher than agriculture's. Thus the output percentage in agriculture for low-income countries, 25–35 percent, is lower than the labor force percentage and higher in industry, 20–40 percent. (Note the range of figures in Table 4–1.) Figure 4–1 indicates that although industry and agriculture account for equal shares of output at an income level of just under $700 per capita (in 1977 U.S. dollars), parity in labor force shares is not reached until income is more than twice that level. In high-income countries, less than 10 percent of production is in agriculture, 30–40 percent in industry, and more than half in services.

TABLE 4-1 Industrial Structure in Developing and Developed Countries

	Percent of Labor Force in		Percent of Gross Domestic Product (GDP) in	
	Agriculture (1990–92)	*Industry (1990–92)*	*Agriculture (1992)*	*Industry (1992)*
Categories of countries				
Least developed	73	8	37	20
Low-income countries	66	10	29	31
Middle-income countries	46	25	12	37
All developing countries	58	15	17	36
Developed countries	9	33	4	37
Countries				
Bangladesh	59	13	34	17
India	62	11	32	27
Pakistan	47	20	27	27
Philippines	45	16	22	33
China	73	14	27	34
Tanzania	85	5	61	12
Kenya	81	7	27	19
Nigeria	48	7	37	38
Indonesia	56	14	19	40
Egypt	42	21	18	30
Syria	23	29	30	23
Colombia	10	24	16	35
Brazil	25	25	11	37
Mexico	23	29	8	28
Argentina	19	26	6	31
South Korea	43	30	8	45
U.S.	3	25	2	29
Canada	5	23		
Germany	3	39	2	39
Japan	7	34	2	42

Blank cells indicate no information available.

Sources: United Nations Development Program, *Human Development Report, 1994* (New York: Oxford University Press, 1994), pp. 162–63, 180–81, 194, 205; World Bank, *World Development Report, 1994* (New York: Oxford University Press, 1994), pp. 166–67; and World Bank, *World Development Report, 1992* (New York: Oxford University Press, 1992), pp. 222–23. U.S. figures on GDP shares, which are for 1989, are from the World Bank, *World Development Report, 1991* (New York: Oxford University Press, 1991), p. 209.

Although the relative size of the nonagricultural sector is positively related to per capita income, this relationship does not mean industrialization creates prosperity; instead industrialization may be a consequence of shifts in the composition of aggregate demand caused by higher per capita incomes. At the lowest levels of per capita income, almost one-half of total demand is for food, and relatively large shares are for shelter and clothing. However as average income increases, the percentage spent on food and other necessities falls (Table 4–2, line 3b), and the percentage spent on manufactured consumer goods and consumer services rises.

FIGURE 4–1   Economic Development and Structural Change

As GNP per capita increases, the output and labor force share in agriculture decreases, while that in industry and services increases.

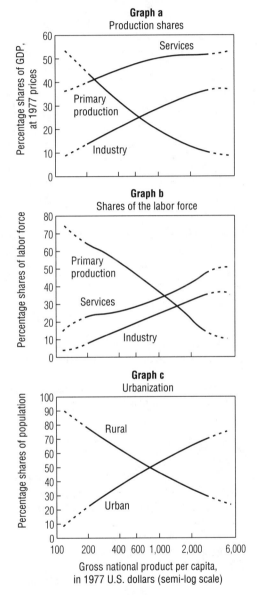

Graph a
Production shares

Graph b
Shares of the labor force

Graph c
Urbanization

Gross national product per capita, in 1977 U.S. dollars (semi-log scale)

Source: World Bank, *World Development Report, 1979* (Washington, D.C., 1979), p. 44.

TABLE 4–2   Normal Variation in Economic Structure with Level of Development

| | Predicted Values at Different Income Levels (stated in 1964 prices) | | | | | | | | | |
| | Mean[a] Under $100 | $100 | $200 | $300 | $400 | $500 | $800 | $1,000 | Mean[b] Over $1,000 | Change |
Process										
1. Tax revenue	0.106	0.129	0.153	0.173	0.189	0.203	0.236	0.254	0.282	0.176
2. Education expenditure	0.026	0.033	0.033	0.034	0.035	0.037	0.041	0.043	0.039	0.013
3. Structure of domestic demand										
a. Government consumption	0.119	0.137	0.134	0.135	0.136	0.138	0.144	0.148	0.141	0.022
b. Food consumption	0.414	0.392	0.315	0.275	0.248	0.229	0.191	0.175	0.167	−0.247
4. Structure of trade										
a. Exports	0.172	0.195	0.218	0.230	0.238	0.244	0.255	0.260	0.249	0.077
b. Primary exports	0.130	0.137	0.136	0.131	0.125	0.120	0.105	0.096	0.058	−0.072
c. Manufactured exports	0.011	0.019	0.034	0.046	0.056	0.065	0.086	0.097	0.131	0.120
d. Service exports	0.028	0.031	0.042	0.048	0.051	0.053	0.056	0.057	0.059	0.031
e. Imports	0.205	0.218	0.234	0.243	0.249	0.254	0.263	0.267	0.250	0.045

[a]Approximately $70. Mean value of countries with per capita GNP under $100 vary slightly according to composition of the sample.

[b]Approximately $1,500. Mean values of countries with per capita GNP over $1,000 vary slightly according to composition of the sample.

Source: Hollis B. Chenery and Moises Syrquin. *Patterns of Development, 1950–1970* (New York: Oxford University Press, 1975), pp. 20–21.

The correlation of increased shares of industry and services in output and employment with economic growth is closely related to shifts in economic activity from rural to urban areas (Graph c, Figure 4–1). Modern, nonagricultural activities benefit greatly from economies of location. As these activities increase their shares in output and employment, they spur the growth of urban centers.[3]

Inadequate Technology and Capital

Output per worker in LDCs is low compared to developed countries because capital per worker is low. Lack of equipment, machinery, and other such capital and low levels of technology, at least throughout most of the economy, hinder production. Although output per unit of capital in LDCs compares favorably to that of rich countries, it is spread over many more workers.

Production methods in most sectors are traditional. Many agricultural techniques, especially in low-income countries, date from biblical times. Wooden plows are used. Seed is sown by hand. Oxen thresh the grain by walking over it. Water is carried in jugs on the head, and the wind is used to separate wheat from straw.

Generally most manufacturing employment, although not output, is in the **informal sector.** These may be one-person enterprises, or at most, units with less

---

[3]World Bank, *World Development Report, 1979* (Washington, D.C., 1979), pp. 44–45.

than 10 workers, many of whom are apprentices or family workers. Production is labor-intensive. Simple tools are used, and there is no mechanical power.

Low Saving Rates

Gross domestic savings as a percentage of GDP (1992) is 18 percent for low-income countries (excluding China and India) compared to 23 percent for middle-income countries and 22 percent for high-income countries. Capital inflows from abroad (in the form of equity investment, loans, and grants) increase the gross investment rate to 22 percent for low-income countries, while gross investment rates in middle-income and high-income countries are the same as gross savings rates.[4]

A country's **capital stock** is the sum total of previous gross investments minus capital consumptions (or depreciations). During the 1960s and 1970s, saving rates for low-income countries were 10–15 percent of gross domestic product. Although figures on depreciation are rough, it was perhaps 6–9 percent of GDP. Accordingly, net saving rates for these countries probably averaged 6–9 percent per year. With capital inflows, their net investment rates were probably not much more than 10–12 percent a year, an amount that approximated the 1980s' *net* rates. Thus overall levels of capital stock in low-income countries remain low.

A Dual Economy

Even though in the aggregate low-income countries have inadequate technology and capital, this is not true in all sectors. Virtually all low-income countries and many middle-income countries are **dual economies.** These economies have a traditional, peasant, agricultural sector, producing primarily for family or village subsistence. This sector has little or no reproducible capital, uses technologies handed down for generations, and has low marginal productivity of labor (that is, output produced from an extra hour of labor is less than the subsistence wage).

In the midst of this labor-intensive, subsistence, peasant agriculture (together with semisubsistence agriculture, petty trade, and cottage industry) sits a capital-intensive enclave consisting of modern manufacturing and processing operations, mineral extraction, and plantation agriculture. This modern sector produces for the market, uses reproducible capital and new technology, and hires labor commercially (where marginal productivity is at least as much as the wage). According to the Lewis model (Chapter 5), the dual economy grows only when the modern sector increases its output share relative to the traditional sector.[5]

In the 1950s and 1960s, this modern sector tended to be foreign owned and managed. Today it is increasingly owned domestically, by either government or private capitalists, and sometimes jointly with foreign capital. Despite local majority ownership, operation of the modern sector often still depends on importing inputs, purchasing or leasing foreign patents and technology, and hiring foreign managers and technicians.

---

[4]World Bank, *World Development Report, 1994* (New York: Oxford University Press, 1994), pp. 178–79; and World Bank, *World Development Report, 1992* (New York: Oxford University Press, 1992), pp. 234–35.

[5]W. Arthur Lewis, "Economic Development with Unlimited Supplies of Labour," *Manchester School* 22 (May 1954): 139–91.

Varying Dependence on International Trade

The ratio of international trade to GNP varies with population size but not income per capita. Thus the United States and India have low ratios and the Netherlands and Jamaica high ratios.

Even so many developing countries are highly dependent on international trade and subject to volatile export earnings. Small countries especially depend a great deal on a few commodities or countries for export sales. For example, in 1992, **export primary commodity concentration ratios,** the three leading **primary products** (food, raw materials, minerals, and organic oils and fats) as a percentage of the *total* merchandise exports, were high for low-income sub-Saharan Africa, Central America, and a few other LDCs. Percentages included Nigeria (crude petroleum and petroleum products, cocoa), 96; Iran (crude petroleum, petroleum products, miscellaneous fruits), 94; Ethiopia (coffee; undressed hides, skins and furs; and crude vegetable materials), 87; Saudi Arabia (crude petroleum, fin fish, shellfish), 87; Venezuela (crude petroleum, petroleum products, gas), 81; Ecuador (crude petroleum, bananas, shellfish), 81; Zambia (copper, cotton, unmanufactured tobacco), 80; Uganda (coffee, cotton, undressed hides, skins, and furs), 79; Togo (natural phosphates, cotton, cocoa), 75; Papua New Guinea (copper, timber, coffee), 71; Cameroon (crude petroleum, cocoa, timber), 68; Myanmar or Burma (timber, vegetables, shellfish), 67; Honduras (bananas, coffee, shellfish), 64; Trinidad and Tobago (petroleum products, crude petroleum, gas), 64; Paraguay (cotton, soybeans, vegetable meal), 61; Panama (bananas, shellfish, sugar), 60; the Ivory Coast (cocoa, timber, coffee), 59; Chile (copper, timber, animal feeds), 55; Bolivia (zinc, gas, tin ore), 53; Nicaragua (coffee, beef and cattle, cotton), 52; Kenya (tea, coffee, dried preserved fruit), 52; Madagascar (spices, shellfish, coffee), 52; Central African Republic (coffee, timber, cotton), 52; and Syria (crude petroleum, petroleum products, shellfish), 51. But more diversified and industrially oriented South Korea had a percentage of 4, China 6, India 8, Turkey 10, the Philippines 11, Brazil 14, Thailand 14, and Pakistan 15. In 1985, six primary products accounted for more than 70 percent of sub-Saharan Africa's export earnings.[6]

Furthermore, although 79 percent of the exports of developed countries is to other DCs and only 21 percent with LDCs; 76 percent of LDC trade is with DCs and only 24 percent with other LDCs (Table 4–3). Some trade between rich and poor states—very important to developing countries—is not nearly so essential to developed countries. For example, one-third of Ghana's exports is cocoa to Britain, corresponding to only a fraction of 1 percent of its imports. And one-third of 1 percent of an English firm's sales comprise all the machinery bought by Ghana's largest shoe manufacturer.

A High Proportion of Primary Product Exports

Among LDCs primary products comprise 47 percent of exports and 27 percent of imports. In developed countries, primary products are 18 percent of exports and 25 percent of imports. Developing countries supply 38 percent of the world's exports of primary products but only 17 percent of manufactured exports. Price in-

---

[6]World Bank, *Global Economic Prospects and the Developing Countries, 1994* (Washington, D.C., 1994), pp. 82–83; and E. Wayne Nafziger, *Inequality in Africa: Political Elites, Proletariat, Peasants, and the Poor* (Cambridge: Cambridge University Press, 1988), p. 55.

TABLE 4-3 Patterns of Trade between Developed and Developing Countries, 1992 (percentage of total exports)

	Exports to	
Exports from	Developed Countries	Developing Countries
Developed countries	79	21
Developing countries	76	24
All countries	78	22

Source: World Bank, *Global Economic Prospects and the Developing Countries, 1994* (Washington, D.C., 1994), p. 80.

stability is common for primary commodities, whose demand and supply tend to be inelastic (that is, the relative change in quantity is less than the relative change in price). The average deviation of world market prices of all 14 major agricultural products from the price trend exceeded 14 percent from 1964 to 1984, while the deviation of manufactured products averaged less than 10 percent.

Yet the trend is changing. Primary product exports declined from 78 percent of total exports in 1965 to 47 percent in 1986 and 1992, and the share of manufactures rose from 22 percent in 1965 to 53 percent in 1986 and 1992. And the three newly industrializing countries (NICs)—Taiwan, South Korea, and Singapore—plus Hong Kong, which constitute 1.5 percent of the LDC population, comprise 34 percent of 1992 LDC manufactured exports. Exports of these four countries grew 11.0 percent yearly from 1980 to 1992; all LDC exports increased 2.6 percent annually during the same period.[7]

Rapid Population Growth

About 4.9 billion people, or 85 percent of the world's 5.8 billion people in 1996, live in developing countries. Developing countries have a population density of 519 per cultivated square kilometer (54 per square kilometer or 140 per square mile) compared to 184 per cultivated square kilometer (22 per square kilometer) in the developed world. These figures contribute to a common myth that third-world people jostle each other for space. However, India, with 489 inhabitants per cultivated square kilometer, while more densely populated than Canada (56), the United States (132), and the Soviet Union (125), is less densely populated than Britain (800) and Germany (813). Moreover China (1,095) and Bangladesh (1,164) are not so dense as the Netherlands (1,622) and Japan (2,657).[8]

---

[7]I added Singapore and Hong Kong to the LDC population for purposes of this calculation.

World Bank, *World Development Report, 1994* (New York: Oxford University Press, 1994), pp. 162–91; World Bank, *Global Economic Prospects and the Developing Countries, 1994* (Washington, D.C., 1994), p. 81; World Bank, *World Development Report, 1988* (New York: Oxford University Press, 1988), pp. 242–47; and World Bank, *World Development Report, 1986* (New York: Oxford University Press, 1986), pp. 86–87.

[8]Computed from *United Nations Development Report, 1994* (New York: Oxford University Press, 1994), pp. 174–175, 202; and *Geographical Digest* (London: George Philip, 1986), pp. 30–31.

The problem in LDCs is not population density but low productivity (low levels of technology and capital per worker) combined with rapid population growth. Between 1945 and 1995, death rates in developing countries were cut more than half by better public health, preventive medicine, and nutrition. Additionally, improved transport and communication made food shortages less likely. While the population growth rate in industrialized countries was 0.3 percent in 1994, LDC birth rates remained at high levels, resulting in an explosive annual growth of 1.9 percent (a rate doubling population in 36 years). High fertility means a high percentage of the population in dependent ages, 0–14, and the diversion of resources to food, shelter, and education for a large nonworking population (see Chapter 8).

This rapid population is contributing to a LDC labor force growth estimated at 2.0 percent per year between 1992 and 2000—a much faster labor force growth than that of industrialized Europe in the nineteenth century (which grew at less than 1 percent a year). Industrial employment's demand growth lags behind this labor force growth, so that unemployment continues to rise in developing countries, especially in urban areas (Chapter 9).

Low Literacy and School Enrollment Rates

When compared to developed countries, literacy and written communication are low in developing countries. Low-income countries have an adult literacy rate of 60 percent; middle-income countries, 73 percent; and high-income countries, 99 percent. Among world regions, South and Southeast Asia has a literacy rate of 45 percent; sub-Saharan Africa, 50 percent; East Asia, 76 percent; the Middle East, 55 percent; and Latin America, 85 percent (Table 2–1). While LDC literacy rates are low compared to those of DCs, LDC rates have increased steadily since 1950 when a majority of third-world adults were illiterate, and substantially since 1900.

Recently a number of low-income countries made primary education free or compulsory, so that LDC primary enrollment rates (taken as a percentage of children aged 6–11) doubled from 1960 to 1980 (except in East Asia and Latin America, where 1960 rates were more than 60 percent). Enrollment was 88 percent in low-income countries, 90 percent in middle-income countries, 46 percent in sub-Saharan Africa, 67 percent in South and Southeast Asia, 89 percent in the Middle East, 87 percent in Latin America, and virtually 100 percent in East Asia and DCs. Secondary enrollment rates (children aged 12–17) were 41 percent in low-income countries, 55 percent in middle-income countries, 18 percent in sub-Saharan Africa, 39 percent in South and Southeast Asia, 50 percent in East Asia, 56 percent in the Middle East, 47 percent in Latin America, and 93 percent for high-income countries.[9]

It is difficult to determine if education is a cause or effect of economic development. A well-educated citizenry contributes to higher income and productivity, which in turn lead to a greater investment in primary education and adult literacy programs. In any case, literacy and enrollment rates are *not* so highly correlated to GNP per head as might be expected. First, there is little correlation at upper-income levels. Most countries have attained nearly 100 percent literacy by the time

---

[9]World Bank, *World Development Report, 1994* (New York: Oxford University Press, 1994), pp. 216–17; and World Bank, *World Development Report, 1989* (New York: Oxford University Press, 1989), p. 220.

average yearly income reaches $8,000 and virtually universal primary education before $8,000. Second, such places as Kerala (in southwestern India), Sri Lanka, and Nicaragua, which have tried to meet basic educational and other needs for even the poorest portion of the population, have higher literacy rates (91 percent, 89 percent, and 78 percent, respectively) than would be expected from a per capita GNP of $400 a year or less. Third, adult literacy rates in countries like Saudi Arabia, the United Arab Emirates, Iran, Iraq, and Oman, all with no more than 65 percent, lagged behind income levels, which were elevated by the sudden oil-created affluence of the 1970s.[10]

Most LDCs continue to place a premium on education and employment opportunities for men. Literacy rates for women in low-income countries tend to be three-fourths, and enrollment rates 80 to 90 percent, the rates for men.[11]

An Unskilled Labor Force

Production patterns and low literacy rates in LDCs correspond to a relatively unskilled labor force. In 1960, 12 percent of the labor force in low-income countries (under $700 per capita GNP) were in white-collar jobs (professional, technical administrative, executive, managerial, clerical, and sales) compared to 21 percent in middle-income countries ($700 to $1,500 per capita GNP), and 31 percent in high-income countries (over $1,500 per capita GNP). In developing countries, a large share of the labor force is unskilled and the population lower class (mostly peasants and manual workers); in developed countries, the reverse is true.

As economic development occurs, the structure of the work force changes. Capital and skilled labor are substituted for unskilled labor. Thus from 1960 to 1980, LDC white-collar worker shares increased by more than one-third. Moreover in the United States, the number of white-collar workers rose from 17 percent in 1900 to 45 percent in 1960, while the share of manual laborers declined sharply from 71 percent to 45 percent.[12]

Another characteristic of low-income countries is a small middle class of business people, professionals, and civil servants. As economic development takes place and the social structure becomes more fluid, the size of this middle class increases.

Summary

1. Income inequality tends to increase from low- to middle-income countries and decrease from middle- to high-income countries (an inverted U-shaped curve). Poverty, on the other hand, drops as income rises.

2. The explosion of mass participation in politics relative to institutional capacity to absorb new participants may result in increased political instability.

---

[10]Norman Hicks and Paul Streeten, "Indicators of Development: The Search for a Basic Needs Yardstick," *World Development* 7 (June 1979): 572–73.

[11]World Bank, *World Development Report, 1994* (New York: Oxford University Press, 1994), pp. 162, 216.

[12]Lyn Squire, *Employment Policy in Developing Countries: A Survey of Issues and Evidence* (New York: Oxford University Press, 1981), pp. 49–53; and Simon Kuznets, *Modern Economic Growth: Rate, Structure, and Spread* (New Haven: Yale University Press, 1966), pp. 191–92.

3. Almost all LDCs experienced Western colonialism or political domination in the past 200 years.

4. Most low-income countries are predominantly peasant agricultural societies. Sixty to 70 percent of the labor force in these countries is in agriculture, compared to less than 10 percent in high-income countries. Only 10 percent of the labor force in low-income countries is in industry compared to 30–35 percent in high-income countries. Because labor's productivity is higher in industry than in agriculture, the share of output in industry for low-income countries is higher, and the share of output in agriculture lower, than labor force shares.

5. Most low-income countries are dual economies. They have a capital-intensive enclave consisting of modern manufacturing and mining operations and plantation agriculture, and a traditional labor-intensive sector. Despite this modern sector, saving rates, capital per worker, and levels of technology are generally low in these countries.

6. The overwhelming majority of DC exports are manufacturing goods, and a disproportionate share of LDC exports are primary products. However, the share of manufactures in LDC exports has been growing steadily, especially among middle-income countries.

7. The population density of LDCs is two to three times that of DCs. Moreover population growth in LDCs is 1.9 percent per year compared to 0.3 in DCs. This rapid growth has contributed to a rapid growth in the labor force and increasing urban unemployment in LDCs.

8. Adult literacy rates are 60 percent in low-income countries and 73 percent in middle-income countries. These rates are expected to rise, particularly in low income countries, because of the expansion in primary enrollment rates.

9. As economic development takes place, the share of white-collar workers in the labor force increases and that of blue-collar workers declines.

Terms to Review

- inverted U-shaped curve
- political elite
- extended family
- peasants
- informal sector
- capital stock
- dual economy
- primary products
- export commodity concentration ratio

Questions to Discuss

1. What are some common characteristics of LDCs? Which of these characteristics are causes and which accompaniments of underdevelopment?
2. How might today's LDCs differ from those of the 1950s?
3. How might a list of common characteristics of low-income countries vary from that of LDCs as a whole?
4. What is a dual economy? Are all LDCs characterized by economic dualism?
5. Will the skill composition of the labor force change as rapidly in LDCs as it did in the past in DCs?

Guide to Readings

Statistical sources that present data on the characteristics of LDCs include the World Bank's annual *World Tables* and the annual *World Development Report* and *World Economic Survey* (guide to readings, Chapter 2). Even though parts of Chenery and Syrquin (note to Table 4–2) and Kuznets (note 1, Chapter 3) are out of date, they contain useful data on growth patterns. Hollis Chenery, Sherman Robinson, Moshe Syrquin, *Industrialization and Growth: a Comparative Study*, (New York: Oxford University Press, 1986), and Moshe Syrquin, "Patterns of Structural Change," in Hollis Chenery and T.N. Srinivasan, eds., *Handbook of Development Economics*, vol. 1, *Economic Development: Concepts and Approaches* (Amsterdam: North-Holland, 1988), 203–73, discuss structural change.

The best-known model of the dual economy is that of W. Arthur Lewis (note 5), discussed in Chapter 5.

Huntington's book (note 2), although somewhat dated, is a standard work on the politics of LDCs. Critics of Huntington's approach are Donal Cruise O'Brien, "Modernization, Order, and the Erosion of a Democratic Ideal: American Political Science, 1960–1970," *Journal of Development Studies* 8 (July 1972): 353–80; and Terry Nardin, "Violence and the State: A Critique of Empirical Political Theory," Sage Professional Papers in Comparative Politics Series Number 01–020 (Beverly Hills, Calif.: Sage Publications, 1971).

CHAPTER **Theories of Economic Development**

To many people, a theory is a contention that is impractical or has no factual support. Someone who says that free migration to the United States may be all right in theory, but not in practice implies that despite the merit of the idea, it would be impractical. Likewise the statement that the idea of lower wealth taxes in India stimulating economic growth is just a theory indicates an unverified hypothesis.

For the economist, however, a **theory** is a systematic explanation of interrelationships among economic variables, and its purpose is to explain causal relationships among these variables. Usually a theory is used not only to understand the world better, but also to provide a basis for policy. In any event, theorists cannot consider all the factors influencing economic growth in a single theory. They must determine which variables are crucial and which are irrelevant. However, reality is so complicated that a simple model may omit critical variables in the real world.[1] And although complex mathematical models can handle a large number of variables, they have not been very successful in explaining economic development, especially in the third world.

Scope of the Chapter

This chapter discusses a few of the major theories of economic development, reserving for subsequent chapters less comprehensive theories dealing with specific economic questions. In the 1970s, scholars paid less attention to grand theories of development than they did in the 1950s and 1960s. However, in the 1980s, many economists stressed an all-encompassing theory of development, neoclassicism.

The first two models of economic development discussed—that of the English classical economists, and of their foremost critic, Karl Marx—were developed more than a century ago, at the time of early capitalist development in Western Europe and the United States. Despite this focus on DC growth, the theories have some application today in LDCs.

---

[1]Charles P. Kindleberger and Bruce Herrick, *Economic Development* (New York: McGraw-Hill, 1977), p. 40.

The next theories presented in this chapter, largely formulated since World War II, concentrate on the experience of developing countries. Walter Rostow's model, written as an alternative to Marx's theory of modern history, sets forth five stages of economic growth for LDCs, based on the experience of the industrialized countries. The vicious circle theory, which focuses on the reasons for low saving rates in poor countries, was widely accepted in the early 1950s. The theoretical debate on balanced versus unbalanced growth has clarified important issues concerning the "big push" and economies of scale. The Lewis-Fei-Ranis model views the accumulation of capital by profits from the industrial capitalist sector hiring an unlimited supply of surplus labor from agriculture as the impetus to economic growth in LDCs. Paul Baran's coalitions model draws on Marx's historical dynamics and Lenin's theory of imperialism to analyze economic backwardness in Asia, Africa, and Latin America. Finally dependency theory, which borrows from Baran's approach, argues that underdevelopment in third-world countries results from their participation in the international capitalist system.

During the 1980s and early 1990s, a period of economic conservative governments in much of the West and Japan, a leading approach among development economists was **neoclassicism**, an economic theory and policy that stressed freedom from the state's economic restraint. Neoclassical economists dominate the two most powerful international financial agencies in developing countries, the World Bank and International Monetary Fund. Neoclassicism also includes a formal growth theory, which emphasizes the importance of capital formation for economic growth. The fact that the neoclassical growth theory assumed perfect competition and had no explanation for the level of technology within the model motivated other economists to propose an endogenous growth theory where technical progress, the chief source of growth, was explained within the model.

The Classical Theory of Economic Stagnation

MODEL

The **classical theory,** based on the work of nineteenth-century English economist David Ricardo, *Principles of Political Economy and Taxation* (1817), was pessimistic about the possibility of sustained economic growth. For Ricardo, who assumed little continuing technical progress, growth was limited by land scarcity.

The classical economists—Adam Smith, Thomas R. Malthus, Ricardo, and John Stuart Mill—were influenced by Newtonian physics. Just as Newton posited that activities in the universe were not random but subject to some grand design, these men believed that the same natural order determined prices, rent, and economic affairs.

In the late eighteenth century, Smith argued that in a competitive economy, with no collusion or monopoly, each individual, by acting in his or her own interest, promoted the public interest. A producer who charges more than others will not find buyers, a worker who asks more than the going wage will not find work, and an employer who pays less than competitors will not find anyone to work. It was as if an **invisible hand** were behind the self-interest of capitalists, merchants, landlords, and workers, directing their actions toward maximum economic growth.[2] Smith advocated a **laissez-faire** (governmental noninterference) and

---

[2]Adam Smith, *An Inquiry into the Nature and Causes of the Wealth of Nations,* Cannan edition (New York: The Modern Library, 1937). First published 1776.

free-trade policy except where labor, capital, and product markets are monopolistic, a proviso some present-day disciples of Smith overlook.

The classical model also took into account (1) the use of paper money, (2) the development of institutions to supply it in appropriate quantities, (3) capital accumulation based on output in excess of wages, and (4) division of labor (limited primarily by the size of the market). A major tenet of Ricardo was the **law of diminishing returns,** referring to successively lower extra outputs from adding an equal extra input to fixed land. For him diminishing returns from population growth and a constant amount of land threatened economic growth. Since Ricardo believed technological change or improved production techniques could only temporarily check diminishing returns, increasing capital was seen as the only way of offsetting this long-run threat.

His reasoning took the following path. In the long run, the natural wage is at subsistence—the cost of perpetuating the labor force (or population, which increases at the same rate). The wage may deviate but eventually returns to a natural rate at subsistence. On the one hand, if the wage rises, food production exceeds what is essential for maintaining the population. Extra food means fewer deaths, and the population increases. More people need food and the average wage falls. Population growth continues to reduce wages until they reach the subsistence level once again. On the other hand, a wage below subsistence increases deaths and eventually contributes to a labor shortage, which raises the wage. Population decline increases wages once again to the subsistence level. In both instances, the tendency is for the wage to return to the natural subsistence rate.

With this **iron law of wages,** total wages increase in proportion to the labor force. Output increases with population, but other things being equal, output per worker declines with diminishing returns on fixed land. Thus the surplus value (output minus wages) per person declines with increased population. At the same time, land rents per acre increase with population growth, since land becomes more scarce relative to other factors.

The only way of offsetting diminishing returns is by accumulating increased capital per person. However, capitalists require minimum profits and interest payments to maintain or increase capital stock. Yet since profits and interest per person declines and rents increase with population growth, there is a diminishing **surplus** (profits, interest, and rent) available for the capitalists' accumulation. Ricardo feared that this declining surplus reduces the inducement to accumulate capital. Labor force expansion leads to a decline in capital per worker or a decrease in worker productivity and income per capita. Thus the Ricardian model indicates eventual economic stagnation or decline.

CRITIQUE

Paradoxically the stagnation theory of Ricardo was formulated amid numerous scientific discoveries and technical changes that multiplied output. Clearly he underestimated the impact of technological advance in offsetting diminishing returns. Before he wrote, the steam engine (1769), the spinning jenny (1770), the Arkwright water frame (1771), the puddling process for making wrought iron (1784), the power loom (1785), the cotton gin (1793), interchangeable parts (1798), improved soil tillage and improved breeds of livestock (around 1800), the steamboat (1807), the water mill for powering factories (1813), and the three-piece iron plow (1814) were all developed. Since Ricardo's time, rapid technological progress contributed to unprecedented economic growth.[3] Furthermore the iron law of wages did not foresee the extent to which population growth could be limited, at least in the West, through voluntary birth control.

Moreover it did not occur to Ricardo that private ownership of land and capital is not an economic necessity. Land and capital would still be used even if rents and interest were not paid, as in state ownership of these means of production. Ironically Ricardian stagnation might result in a Marxian scenario, where wages and investment would be maintained only if property were confiscated by society and payments to private capitalists and landlords stopped.[4]

As discussed later in the chapter, contemporary neoclassical economists take the classical stress on savings, free trade, and freedom from government restriction, and add an emphasis on technological change as an important component of economic growth. These ideas are major features of the neoclassical theory of growth, a dominant present-day theory of economic growth.

Marx's Historical Materialism

Karl Marx's views were shaped by radical changes in Western Europe: the French Revolution; the rise of industrial, capitalist production; political and labor revolts; and a growing secular rationalism. Marx (1818–83) opposed the prevailing philosophy and political economy, especially the views of utopian socialists and classical economists, in favor of a world view called **historical materialism.**

THEORY

Marx wanted to replace the unhistorical approach of the classicists with a historical dialectic. Marxists consider classical and later orthodox economic analysis as a still photograph, which describes reality at a certain time. In contrast, the dialectical approach, analogous to a moving picture, looks at a social phenomenon by examining where it was and is going and its process of change. History moves from one stage to another, say, from feudalism to capitalism to socialism, on the basis of changes in ruling and oppressed classes and their relationship to each other. Conflict between the forces of production (the state of science and technology, the organization of production, and the development of human skills) and the existing relations of production (the appropriation and distribution of output as well as a society's way of thinking, its ideology, and world view) provide the dynamic movement in the materialist interpretation of history. The interaction between forces and relations of production shapes politics, law, morality, religion, culture, and ideas.

Accordingly, feudalism is undercut by (1) the migration of serfs to the town, (2) factory competition with handicraft and manorial production, (3) expanded transport, trade, discovery, and new international markets on behalf of the new business class, and (4) the accompanying rise of nation-states. The new class, the

---

[3]Some contemporary economists, culminating with James E. Meade, *A Neoclassical Theory of Economic Growth* (New York: Oxford University Press, 1963), have added a variable reflecting technical progress while retaining most of the classical premises.

[4]Stephen Enke has a detailed discussion of the classical model in *Economics for Development* (Englewood Cliffs, N.J.: Prentice Hall, 1963), pp. 70–90.

proletariat or working class, created by this next stage, capitalism, is the seed for the destruction of capitalism and the transformation into the next stage, socialism. Capitalism faces repeated crises because the market, dependent largely on worker consumption, expands more slowly than productive capacity. Moreover, this unutilized capacity creates, in Marx's phrase, a **reserve army of the unemployed,** a cheap labor source that expands and contracts with the boom and bust of business cycles. Furthermore, with the growth of monopoly, many small business people, artisans, and farmers become propertyless workers who no longer have control over their workplaces. Eventually, the proletariat revolts, takes control of capital, and establishes socialism. In time socialism is succeeded by communism, and the state withers away.

Marx's ideas were popularized by his collaborator, Friedrich Engels, especially from 1883 to 1895, when he finished Marx's uncompleted manuscripts, interpreted Marxism, and provided its intellectual and organizational leadership.

CRITIQUE

Marx's main analysis was of capitalism, but his discussions of socialism and communism were not well developed. Even his analysis of capitalism, and the transition to socialism, had a number of flaws. He had theorized worker revolt in the industrialized West, but the revolution occurred first in Russia, one of the least developed capitalistic countries in Europe.

Marxists suggest several reasons why Western workers have yet to overthrow capitalism. Having realized the dangers of a rebellious working class at home, the capitalists have developed a tactic of divide and rule that depends on exploitation of workers outside the West. Furthermore, the news media, educational institutions, and churches create a false consciousness supporting ruling-class ideologies. And the capitalist state has powerful legal, police, military, and administrative machinery to quell potential resistance.

Marx also overlooked the possibility that the interests of workers and capitalists might not conflict. Thus workers in the West may have supported capitalism because they gained more in the long run by receiving a relatively constant share of a rapidly growing output than by trying to acquire a larger share of what might have been a more slowly growing output under an alternative system.

Regardless of how we view Marxism, it remains a rallying point for discontented people. The irony is that nationalist groups that overthrow their rulers in the name of Marxism are frequently threatened by class antagonisms from those they rule. Almost no other socialist government is willing to go as far as the late Chairman Mao Zedong of China, who recognized the existence of classes under socialism, and called for a continuing revolution to oppose the encrusted, socialist, upper classes. Other theorists have revised or added to Marxism, including Paul Baran and the dependency theorists. We consider these views in succeeding sections of this chapter.

Rostow's Stages of Economic Growth

People existed for centuries with little change in their economic life. When major changes occurred, as in the last 500 years or so, they often took place abruptly. In *The Stages of Economic Growth* (1961), Walter W. Rostow, an eminent economic historian, sets forth a new historical synthesis about the beginnings of modern economic growth on six continents.

FIVE STAGES

Rostow's economic stages are (1) the traditional society, (2) the preconditions for takeoff, (3) the takeoff, (4) the drive to maturity, and (5) the age of high mass consumption.

Rostow has little to say about the concept of traditional society except to indicate that it is based on attitudes and technology prominent before the turn of the eighteenth century. The work of Isaac Newton ushered in change. He formulated the law of gravity and the elements of differential calculus. After Newton, people widely believed "that the external world was subject to a few knowable laws, and was systematically capable of productive manipulation."[5]

PRECONDITIONS STAGE

Rostow's **preconditions stage** for sustained industrialization includes radical changes in three nonindustrial sectors: (1) increased transport investment to enlarge the market and production specialization; (2) a revolution in agriculture, so that a growing urban population can be fed; and (3) an expansion of imports, including capital, financed perhaps by exporting some natural resources. These changes, including increased capital formation, require a political elite interested in economic development. This interest may be instigated by a nationalist reaction against foreign domination or the desire to have a higher standard of living.

TAKEOFF

Rostow's central historical stage is the **takeoff,** a decisive expansion occurring over 20 to 30 years, which radically transforms a country's economy and society. During this stage, barriers to steady growth are finally overcome, while forces making for widespread economic progress dominate the society, so that growth becomes the normal condition. The takeoff period is a dramatic moment in history, corresponding to the beginning of the Industrial Revolution in late eighteenth-century Britain; pre–Civil War railroad and manufacturing development in the United States; the period after the 1848 revolution in Germany; the years just after the 1868 Meiji restoration in Japan; the rapid growth of the railroad, coal, iron, and heavy-engineering industries in the quarter-century before the 1917 Russian Revolution; and a period starting within a decade of India's independence (1947) and the Communist victory in China (1949).

Rostow indicates that three conditions must be satisfied for takeoff.

1. Net investment as a percentage of net national product (NNP) increases sharply—from 5 percent or less to over 10 percent. If an investment of 3.5 percent of NNP leads to a growth of 1 percent per year, then 10.5 percent of NNP is needed for a

---

[5]Walter W. Rostow, *The Stages of Economic Growth: A Non-Communist Manifesto* (Cambridge: Cambridge University Press, 1961), p. 4.

3-percent growth (or a 2-percent per capita increase if population grows at 1 percent).

2. At least one substantial manufacturing sector grows rapidly. The growth of a leading manufacturing sector spreads to its input suppliers expanding to meet its increased demand and to its buyers benefiting from its larger output. In the last three decades of the 1700s, for example, the cotton textile industry in Britain expanded rapidly because of the use of the spinning jenny, water frame, and mule in textiles and the increased demand for cotton clothing. The development of textile manufactures, and their exports, had wide direct and indirect effects on the demand for coal, iron, machinery, and transport. In the United States, France, Germany, Canada, and Russia, the growth of the railroad, by widening markets, was a powerful stimulus in the coal, iron, and engineering industries, which in turn fueled the takeoff.

3. A political, social, and institutional framework quickly emerges to exploit expansion in the modern sectors. This condition implies mobilizing capital through retained earnings from rapidly expanding sectors; an improved system to tax high-income groups, especially in agriculture; developing banks and capital markets; and in most instances, foreign investment. Furthermore, where state initiative is lacking, the culture must support a new class of entrepreneurs prepared to take the risk of innovating.

DRIVE TO MATURITY

After takeoff there follows the drive to maturity, a period of growth that is regular, expected, and self-sustained. This stage is characterized by a labor force that is predominantly urban, increasingly skilled, less individualistic, and more bureaucratic and looks increasingly to the state to provide economic security.

AGE OF HIGH MASS CONSUMPTION

The symbols of this last stage, reached in the United States in the 1920s and in Western Europe in the 1950s, are the automobile, suburbanization, and innumerable durable consumer goods and gadgets. In Rostow's view, other societies may choose a welfare state or international military and political power.

CRITIQUE

Rostow's theory was the vogue among many U.S. government officials in the 1960s, especially in the international aid agencies, since it promised hope for sustained growth in LDCs after substantial initial infusions of foreign assistance. But among scholars, Rostow's work met with, at best, mixed reviews. Rostow is accused of overambition. Ian Drummond complains that "probably no theory has been so widely circulated from so slight a base of organized fact and careful analysis."[6]

Another economic historian, A. K. Cairncross, argues that one can believe in an abrupt takeoff, or industrial revolution, only if one's knowledge of history is flimsy and out of date. Cairncross argues that many of Rostow's conditions are de-

---

[6]Ian Drummond, review of *The Stages of Economic Growth*, in *Canadian Journal of Economics and Political Science* 13 (February 1961): 112–13.

fined so vaguely that they stretch to cover any case and he seems only too willing to admit exceptions when takeoff occurs at a time other than his theory suggests.[7]

Indeed, Rostow's stages, imprecisely defined, are difficult to test scientifically. For a theory to be meaningful, it must be possible to prove it wrong. If the stages are to explain how economic development is caused, the relationships cannot be circular. The stages must be defined in terms other than economic development, the variable the theory is trying to explain. For example, the concepts of *traditional society* and *high mass consumption society* define rather than explain reasons for the level of economic development. Furthermore, past economies—primitive, ancient, medieval, and those of the presently developed countries of a century or two ago—are all grouped with presently underdeveloped countries in a single category, the traditional society.

The designation of traditional societies as pre-Newtonian neglects the dualism of many present-day LDCs. Much of the large manufacturing, plantation, and mining sectors of India, Indonesia, Nigeria, and Pakistan use modern methods and techniques and cannot be considered traditional in Rostow's sense.

Much of Rostow's thesis about conditions for takeoff is contradicted by empirical data. Increases in investment rates and growth do not occur in the 20- to 30-year span Rostow designates for takeoff. Growth in investment rates and net national product in Great Britain, Germany, Sweden, and Japan indicate a slow and relatively steady acceleration rather than an abrupt takeoff.

Frequently the characteristics of one of Rostow's stages are not unique to it. Why would the agricultural revolution, capital imports, and social overhead investment of the preconditions stage not be consistent with the abrupt increase in investment rates during the takeoff stage? Why could the development of leading sectors or the emergence of an institutional framework exploiting growth not take place in the preconditions stage as well as the takeoff stage? Why would the abrupt increase in growth and investment rates during takeoff not continue through the drive to maturity?

Unlike Marx's dialectical materialism, Rostow's approach does not show how the characteristics and processes of one stage move a society to the next stage. How do we explain the relatively effortless self-sustained growth after takeoff? Presumably some obstacles to growth have been removed. What are they, and how does his theory explain their removal?

Rostow's premise that economic modernization implies a change from an underdeveloped economy to one similar to those in North America and Western Europe today poses another problem. Rostow compares LDCs at independence to the formation of nation–states in the West. He assumes that the development of underdeveloped countries will parallel earlier stages of today's advanced countries, but he neglects the relationship of contemporary underdeveloped countries with developed countries as well as each LDC's highly individual history.

Rostow is ethnocentric when he chooses high mass consumption society, characterized by automobiles, suburbanization, and consumer gadgets, as the culminating stage of economic growth. For him today's modernized societies, the archetype of which is the United States, are an image of the future of traditional societies. Surely the study of comparative history should alert us to the danger of using the experience of the United States (or any other country) as a model for countries with very different cultural and political backgrounds to emulate.

---

[7]A. K. Cairncross, "Essays in Bibliography and Criticism, XLV: The Stages of Economic Growth," *Economic History Review* 14 (April 1961): 454.

Vicious Circle Theory

The **vicious circle** theory indicates that poverty perpetuates itself in mutually reinforcing vicious circles on both the supply and demand sides.

SUPPLY SIDE

Because incomes are low, consumption cannot be diverted to saving for capital formation. Lack of capital results in low productivity per person, which perpetuates low levels of income. Thus the circle is complete. A country *is* poor because it *was previously* too poor to save and invest.

Japan's high savings rates during periods of rapid economic growth during the 1950s, 1960s, and 1970s, and the high savings rates of the Asian tigers, Malaysia, and Thailand imply the other side of the coin of the vicious circle. As countries grow richer, they save more, creating a **virtuous circle** where high savings rates lead to faster growth.[8]

DEMAND SIDE

Furthermore, because incomes are low, market size (for consumer goods, such as shoes, electric bulbs, and textiles) is too small to encourage potential investors. Lack of investment means low productivity and continued low income. A country *is* poor because it *was previously* too poor to provide the market to spur investment.

INSUFFICIENT SAVING: A CRITIQUE

The vicious circle theory seems plausible to those Westerners who imagine that the *entire* population of the third world is poor and hungry. They are surprised that anyone in the LDCs saves. But you can probably identify some flaws in these views. Westerners may be judging the saving potential in LDCs on the basis of Western standards of living. Of course most of us find it difficult to imagine saving on the $7,000 annual salary received by a middle manager in India. But remember the relative position that $7,000 represents in India. There is reason for believing that low-income countries can save substantially more than they do. The highest income groups in low-income LDCs live far above subsistence levels. A study by World Bank economist Shail Jain indicates that their richest 5 percent receives about 15 to 35 percent of the income, an amount per head 8 to 20 times that of the poorest 10 percent of the people.[9] Since evidence indicates that consumption levels are determined less by absolute levels of income than by relative income (income in comparison to neighbors and members of the community), the higher income classes in LDCs could save considerably if they were sufficiently motivated. One reason they may not do so is because of the **demonstration effect** of consumption levels in the West and of elites in the LDCs. That is, people may spend beyond their income in order to keep up with the Joneses, the Sridhars, or the Abdullahis.

---

[8]Sebastian Edwards, "Why are Savings Rates So Different Across Countries? An International Comparative Analysis," Cambridge, Mass., National Bureau of Economic Research Paper No. 5097, April 1995; and "Politics, Pensions, and Piggy Banks," *Economist* (July 1, 1995): 72.

[9]Shail Jain, *Size Distribution of Income* (Washington, D.C.: World Bank, 1975).

You should also keep in mind that personal saving is usually a small proportion of total saving in a LDC. Corporate saving, government saving, public enterprise profits, social security contributions, life insurance premiums, and provident and pension fund reserves may be other sources for saving (see Chapter 14).

If we look at saving from this broader viewpoint, there are additional arguments to suggest that poor countries have a substantial capacity to save. Throughout history few societies have been too poor to wage war. Yet any war requires a share of the country's resources that would be sufficient for a significant rate of capital formation. The Overseas Development Council indicates that more than 3 percent of the GNP of nineteen low-income countries goes for military expenditures.[10] Perhaps if countries mobilized for economic development as they did for war, they could increase saving.

Furthermore, some poor societies have been able to build magnificent monuments. As A. K. Cairncross argues, "Anyone who looks at the pyramids, cathedrals, and pagodas that civilizations have bequeathed, can hardly regard the construction of railways, dams, and power stations as imposing an unprecedented burden on a poor community."[11]

SMALL MARKETS: A CRITIQUE

Everett E. Hagen contends that the market is ample for using modern production methods effectively for products commonly consumed by low-income people—sugar, milled rice, milled flour, soap, sandals, textiles, clothing, cigarettes, matches, and candies. He argues that even a fairly small improvement in productivity for any of these commodities would capture a sizable market.[12]

Moreover, large establishments require not only large markets but, more importantly, complex machinery and processes, which demand entrepreneurial, managerial, and technical skills and experience that are frequently scarce in developing countries. Hla Myint argues that cost advantages from early entry, or "economies of experience," are more important for large-scale production than economies of scale from increased market size.[13]

Balanced Versus Unbalanced Growth

A major development debate from the 1940s through the 1960s concerned **balanced growth** versus **unbalanced growth.** Some of the debate was semantic, since the meaning of *balance* can vary from the absurd requirement that all sectors grow at the same rate to the more sensible plea that some attention be given to all major sectors—industry, agriculture, and services. However, absurdities aside, the discussion raised some important issues. What are the relative merits of strategies of

---

[10]Roger D. Hansen and contributors to the Overseas Development Council, *U.S. Foreign Policy and the Third World: Agenda, 1982* (New York: Praeger, 1982), pp. 218–19. The *IDS Bulletin*, 16 (October 1985), has an entire issue devoted to disarmament and development.

[11]A. K. Cairncross, "Capital Formation in the Take-off," in Walter W. Rostow, ed., *The Economics of Take-off into Sustained Growth* (London: Macmillan, 1963).

[12]Everett E. Hagen, *On the Theory of Social Change: How Economic Growth Begins* (Homewood, Ill.: Dorsey Press, 1962), pp. 42–43.

[13]Hla Myint, "An Interpretation of Economic Backwardness," *Oxford Economic Papers, New Series* 6 (June 1954): 132–63.

gradualism versus a big push? Is capital or entrepreneurship the major limitation to growth?

BALANCED GROWTH

The synchronized application of capital to a wide range of different industries is called balanced growth by its advocates. Ragnar Nurkse considers this strategy the only way of escaping from the vicious circle of poverty. He does not consider the expansion of exports promising, since the **price elasticity of demand** (minus percentage change in quantity demanded divided by percentage change in price) for the LDCs' predominantly primary exports is less than one, thus reducing export earnings with increased volume, other things being equal.[14]

BIG PUSH THESIS

Those advocating this synchronized application of capital to all major sectors support the **big push thesis,** arguing that a strategy of gradualism is doomed to failure. A substantial effort is essential to overcome the inertia inherent in a stagnant economy. The situation is analogous to a car being stuck in the snow: It will not move with a gradually increasing push; it needs a big push.

For Paul N. Rosenstein-Rodan, the factors that contribute to economic growth, like demand and investment in infrastructure, do not increase smoothly but are subject to sizable jumps or **indivisibilities.**[15] These indivisibilities result from flaws created in the investment market by **external economies,** that is, cost advantages rendered free by one producer to another. These benefits spill over to society as a whole, or to some member of it, rather than to the investor concerned. As an example, the increased production, decreased average costs, and labor training and experience that result from additional investment in the steel industry will benefit other industries as well. Greater output stimulates the demand for iron, coal, and transport. Lower costs may make vehicles and aluminum cheaper. In addition other industries may benefit later by hiring laborers who acquired industrial skills in the steel mills. Thus the social profitability of this investment exceeds its private profitability. Moreover, unless government intervenes, total private investment will be too low.

Indivisibility in Infrastructure.   For Rosenstein–Rodan a major indivisibility is in infrastructure, such as power, transport, and communications. This basic social capital reduces costs to other industries. To illustrate, the railroad from Kanpur to the Calcutta docks increases the competitiveness of India's wool textiles domestically and abroad. However, the investment for the 950–kilometer, Kanpur-Calcutta rail line is virtually indivisible in that a line a fraction as long is of little value. Building the Aswan Dam or the Monterrey-Mexico City telegraph line is subject to similar discontinuities.

Indivisibility in Demand.   This indivisibility arises from the interdependence of investment decisions; that is, a prospective investor is uncertain whether the

---

[14]Ragnar Nurkse, *Problems of Capital Formation in Underdeveloped Countries* (New York: Oxford University Press, 1953).

[15]Paul N. Rosenstein-Rodan, "Problems of Industrialization of Eastern and Southeastern Europe," *Economic Journal* 53 (June-September 1943): 202–11.

output from his or her investment project will find a market. Rosenstein-Rodan uses the example of an economy closed to international trade to illustrate this indivisibility. He assumes that there are numerous subsistence agricultural laborers whose work adds nothing to total output (that is, the marginal productivity of their labor equals zero). If 100 of these farm workers were hired in a shoe factory, their wages would increase income.

> If the newly employed workers spend all of their additional income on shoes they produce the shoe factory will find a market and would succeed. In fact, however, they will not spend all of their additional income on shoes. There is no "easy" solution of creating an additional market in this way. The risk of not finding a market reduces the incentive to invest, and the shoe factory investment project will probably be abandoned.[16]

However, instead let us put 10,000 workers in 100 factories (and farms) that among them will produce the bulk of consumer goods on which the newly employed workers will spend their wages. What was not true of the shoe factory is true for the complementary system of 100 enterprises. The new producers are each others' customers and create additional markets through increased incomes. Complementary demand reduces the risk of not finding a market. Reducing interdependent risks increases the incentive to invest.

CRITIQUE OF BALANCED GROWTH

Advocates of balanced growth emphasize a varied package of industrial investment at the expense of investment in agriculture, especially exports. But Chapter 18 shows that a country cannot grow rapidly if it fails to specialize where production is most efficient. Recent experience indicates that LDCs cannot neglect agricultural investment if they are to feed their population, supply industrial inputs, and earn foreign currency. Chapter 15 points out that the recent demand for primary product exports increased so that their value grew as fast as GNP.

Furthermore, infrastructure is not so indivisible as Rosenstein-Rodan implies. Roads, rivers, canals, or air traffic can substitute for railroads. Roads may be dirt, graveled, blacktopped, or paved and of various widths. Power plants can differ greatly in size, and telegram and telephone systems can be small, large, or intermediate. Large infrastructure facilities, though perhaps economical at high levels of economic development, are not essential for LDC growth.[17]

Some critics argue that the resources required for carrying out a policy of balanced growth are so vast that a country that could invest the required capital would not, in fact, be underdeveloped. In fact farm workers with zero marginal labor productivity are not available (Chapter 9). In any case, where will a LDC obtain the capital, skilled labor, and materials needed for such wide industrial expansion? We cannot forget that although new industries may be complementary on the demand side, they are competitors for limited resources on the supply side.

Advocates of balanced growth assume LDCs start from scratch. In reality every developing country starts from a position that reflects previous investment

---

[16]Paul N. Rosenstein-Rodan, "Notes on the Theory of the Big Push," in Howard S. Ellis, ed., *Economic Development for Latin America* (London: Macmillan, 1951), p. 62.

[17]Everett E. Hagen, *The Economics of Development* (Homewood, Ill.: Irwin, 1980), pp. 89–90.

decisions. Thus at any time, there are highly desirable investment programs not balanced in themselves but well integrated with existing capital imbalances.[18]

But perhaps the major discreditor of the balanced growth strategy was the widespread evidence in the 1960s and 1970s that LDCs were growing rapidly—without any attempt at the massive investments in the wide range of industries that advocates of the strategy considered essential.

HIRSCHMAN'S STRATEGY OF UNBALANCE

Albert O. Hirschman develops the idea of unbalanced investment to complement existing imbalances.[19] He contends that deliberately unbalancing the economy, in line with a predesigned strategy, is the best path for economic growth. He argues that the big push thesis may make interesting reading for economists, but it is gloomy news for the LDCs: They do not have the skills needed to launch such a massive effort. The major shortage in LDCs is not the supply of savings, but the decision to invest by entrepreneurs, the risktakers and decision makers. The ability to invest is dependent on the amount and nature of existing investments. Hirschman believes poor countries need a development strategy that spurs investment decisions.

He suggests that since resources and abilities are limited, a big push is sensible only in strategically selected industries within the economy. Growth then spreads from one sector to another (similar to Rostow's concept of leading and following sectors).

However, investment should not be left solely to individual entrepreneurs in the market, since the profitability of different investment projects may depend on the order in which they are undertaken. For example, assume investment in a truck factory yields a return of 10 percent per year; in a steel factory, 8 percent, with the interest rate 9 percent. If left to the market, a private investor will invest in the truck factory. Later on as a result of this initial investment, returns on a steel investment increase to 10 percent, so then the investor invests in steel.

Assume, however, that establishing a steel factory would increase the returns in the truck factory in the next period from 10 to 16 percent. Society would be better off investing in the steel factory first, and the truck enterprise second, rather than making independent decisions based on the market. Planners need to consider the interdependence of one investment project with another so that they maximize overall *social* profitability. They need to make the investment that spurs the greatest amount of new investment decisions. Investments should occur in industries that have the greatest linkages, including **backward linkages** to enterprises that sell inputs to the industry, and **forward linkages** to units that buy output from the industry. The steel industry, having backward linkages to coal and iron production, and forward linkages to the construction and truck industries, has good investment potential, according to Hirschman.

Even a government that limits its major role to providing infrastructure can time its investment projects to spur private investments. Government investment

---

[18]Hans Singer, "The Concept of Balanced Growth and Economic Development Theory and Facts," University of Texas Conference on Economic Development, April 1958, as cited in Benjamin Higgins, *Economic Development: Problems, Principles, and Policies* (New York: Norton, 1968), pp. 333–35; and Marcus Fleming, "External Economies and the Doctrine of Balanced Growth," *Economic Journal* 65 (June 1955): 241–56.

[19]Albert O. Hirschman, *The Strategy of Economic Development* (New Haven: Yale University Press, 1958).

in transport and power will increase productivity and thus encourage investment in other activities.

Initially planners trying to maximize linkages will not want to hamper imports too much, since doing so will deprive the country of forward linkages to domestic industries using imports. In fact officials may encourage imports until they reach a threshold in order to create these forward linkages. Once these linkages have been developed, protective tariffs will provide a strong inducement for domestic entrepreneurs to replace imports with domestically produced goods.

CRITIQUE OF UNBALANCED GROWTH

Hirschman fails to stress the importance of agricultural investments. According to him, agriculture does not stimulate linkage formation so directly as other industries. However, empirical studies indicate agriculture has substantial linkages to other sectors; moreover, agricultural growth makes vital contributions to the nonagricultural sector through increased food supplies, added foreign exchange, labor supply, capital transfer, and larger markets.[20]

What constitutes the proper investment balance among sectors requires careful analysis. In some instances, imbalances may be essential for compensating for existing imbalances. On the other hand, Hirschman's unbalanced growth should have some kind of balance as an ultimate aim. Generally the concepts of balance and imbalance are of limited value. To be helpful, their meanings need to be defined carefully in specific decision-making contexts.

The Lewis-Fei-Ranis Model

The purpose of the Lewis and Fei-Ranis models is to explain how economic growth gets started in a less developed country with a traditional agricultural sector and an industrial capitalist sector. In the Lewis-Fei-Ranis model, economic growth occurs because of the increase in the size of the industrial sector, which accumulates capital, relative to the subsistence agricultural sectors, which amasses no capital at all. The source of capital in the industrial sector is profits from the low wages paid an unlimited supply of surplus labor from traditional agriculture.

THE LEWIS MODEL

Urban industrialists increase their labor supply by attracting workers from agriculture who migrate to urban areas when wages there exceed rural agricultural wages. Sir W. Arthur Lewis elaborates on this explanation in his explanation of labor transfer from agriculture to industry in a newly industrializing country. In contrast to those economists writing since the early 1970s, who have been concerned about overurbanization, Lewis, writing in 1954, is concerned about possible labor shortages in the expanding industrial sector.

Lewis believes in zero (or negligible) marginal productivity of labor in subsistence agriculture, a sector virtually without capital and technological progress. Yet he contends that the wage (w) in agriculture is positive at subsistence (s): w_s (see Figure 5–1). For this to be true, it is essential only that the *average* product of

---

[20]Bruce F. Johnston and John W. Mellor, "The Role of Agriculture in Economic Development," *American Economic Review* 51 (September 1961): 571–81.

FIGURE 5-1   Industrial Expansion in the Lewis Model
An unlimited supply of labor available to the industrial
sector facilitates capital accumulation and economic
growth.

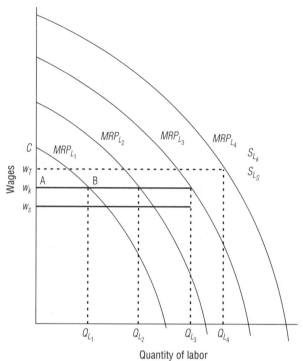

Source: Based on W. Arthur Lewis, "Economic Development with Unlimited Supplies of Labor," *Manchester
School* 22 (May 1954): 146.

labor be at a subsistence level, since agricultural workers divide the produce
equally among themselves until food availability is above subsistence. Lewis feels
equilibrium wages in agriculture stay at w_s through the classical mechanism of the
iron law of wages, in which higher wages are brought down by population
growth, and lower wages raised as output spread over a smaller population is reduced by an increased mortality rate.

For the more capital-intensive urban industrial sector to attract labor from
the rural area, it is essential to pay w_s plus a 30-percent inducement, or w_k (the capitalist wage). This higher wage compensates for the higher cost of living as well as
the psychological cost of moving to a more regimented environment. At w_k the
urban employer can attract an unlimited supply of unskilled rural labor. The employer will hire this labor up to the point Q_{Q1}, where the value of its extra product
(or the left marginal revenue product curve MRP_{L1}) equals the wage w_k. The total
wages of the workers are equal to OQ_{L1}, the quantity of labor, multiplied by w_k,
the wage (that is, rectangle OQ_{L1} BA). The capitalist earns the surplus (*ABC* in Figure 5–1), the amount between the wage and that part of the marginal product
curve above the wage.

Lewis assumes that the capitalist saves all the surplus (profits, interest, and rent) and the worker saves nothing. Further he suggests that all the surplus is re-invested, increasing the amount of capital per worker and thus the marginal product of labor to MRP_{L2}, so that more labor Q_{L2} can be hired at wage rate w_k. This process enlarges the surplus, adds to capital formation, raises labor's marginal productivity, increases the labor hired, enlarges the surplus, and so on, through the cycle until all surplus labor is absorbed into the industrial sector. Beyond this point Q_{L3}, the labor supply curve (S_{Lk}) is upward sloping and additional laborers can be attracted only with a higher wage. As productivity increases beyond MRP_{L3} to MRP_{L4}, the MRP_L (or demand for labor) curve intersects the labor supply curve at a wage w_T and at a quantity of labor Q_{L4} in excess of surplus rural labor.[21]

In the Lewis model, capital is created by using surplus labor (with little social cost). Capital goods are created without giving up the production of consumer goods. However, to finance surplus labor, additional credit may sometimes be needed.

The significance of Lewis's model is that growth takes place as a result of structural change. An economy consisting primarily of a subsistence agricultural sector (which does not save) is transformed into one predominantly in the modern capitalist sector (which does save). As the relative size of the capitalist sector grows, the ratio of profits and other surplus to national income grows.

CRITIQUE

Critics question the theoretical underpinning of the Lewis model, the assumption of an unlimited labor supply. They believe the capitalist wage rate may rise before all surplus rural labor is absorbed. As workers with zero marginal productivity migrate from the subsistence agricultural sector, those workers remaining in this sector will then divide *constant* output among *fewer persons* resulting in a *higher wage*. Industrial wages, then, must increase to motivate rural workers to migrate. Or Lewis's critics argue that the larger industrial labor force contributes to greater food demand, but the capacity to produce food is unchanged. Thus food prices rise. Accordingly the industrial sector must increase wages to pay for the increased price of food. Lewis overestimates the extent that the availability of cheap rural migrant labor can stimulate industrial growth.

THE FEI-RANIS MODIFICATION

How can LDCs maintain subsistence output per farm worker in the midst of population expansion? John Fei and Gustav Ranis, in their modification of the Lewis model, contend that the agricultural sector must grow, through technological progress, for output to grow as fast as population; technical change increases output per hectare to compensate for the increase in labor per land, which is a fixed resource. Fei and Ranis label w_k from 0 to Q_{L3} an **institutional wage** supported by nonmarket factors such as the government minimum wage or labor union pressure. This institutional wage can remain infinitely elastic even when the marginal revenue productivity of labor is greater than zero; this wage remains at the same level as long as marginal productivity is less than the wage. However, the threshold for both agricultural and industrial sectors occurs when the marginal revenue

---

[21]W. Arthur Lewis, "Economic Development with Unlimited Supplies of Labor," *Manchester School* 22 (May 1954): 139–91.

productivity in agriculture equals the wage. At this point, the **turning point** or **commercialization point**, industry abandons the institutional wage, and together with agriculture, must pay the market rate. Similar to the Lewis model, the advent of fully commercialized agriculture and industry ends industrial growth (or what Fei-Ranis label the takeoff into self-sustained growth).[22]

One problem is to avoid increasing the average product of labor in agriculture and the industrial institutional wage that would halt industrial expansion. Fei and Ranis solve this with a sleight of hand; the LDC maintains a constant institutional wage until Q_{L3} but at the expense of realism: each migrating farm worker takes his or her own subsistence bundle to the industrial sector.

How do Fei and Ranis prevent rises in food prices (and the agricultural terms of trade) from increasing the industrial wage? Fei-Ranis propose a balanced growth between agriculture and industry. However, agricultural growth increases farm income, undermining the restraints on the institutional wage.

APPLICATION OF THE LEWIS-FEI-RANIS MODEL TO JAPAN

Fei and Ranis believe their model applies to Japan from 1888 to 1930. Indeed, unlike Lewis's assumption, the marginal productivity of labor in Japanese agriculture during this period was always positive. And Japan's industry paid a low premium for labor after 1873, when land reform displaced a large number of landless workers, who could no longer lease land. Since much of industry's wage laborers—women, second and third sons with no inheritance rights, or off-farm, part-time workers—merely supplemented household income, employers paid them less than subsistence wages.

However, subsistence levels rose over time during the late nineteenth and early twentieth centuries as the minimum maintenance expected by society increased with growth. The relatively stable agricultural (and thus industrial) real wages can be attributed partly to technical progress and increased productivity in agriculture (and cheap food from colonies Taiwan and Korea after 1911), which enabled the industrial sector to buy food without declining terms of trade. These low real industrial wages increased industrial profits, business savings, and labor-intensive manufactured export competitiveness, consistent with the Lewis-Fei-Ranis model. Indeed the large wage differential between France and Italy on the one hand and Japan on the other was a major contributor to Japan's comparative advantage in textiles, a labor-intensive commodity.

In Japan, over a normal range, where product and labor demand increased gradually, **labor supply elasticities** (percentage change in quantity supplied/percentage change in wage) were high (though not infinite, with a perfectly horizontal supply, as in Lewis-Fei-Ranis), benefiting from vast reserves in the agricultural and informal industrial sectors. But the 1915–19 increase in demand for Japanese industrial products and labor resulting from World War I was too substantial to be satisfied by labor from the elastic portion of the supply curve. Wage equilibrium could only be attained at the inelastic portion of the labor supply curve, thus increasing industrial wages and subsequently, through greater food demand by new workers, increasing agricultural product (especially rice), and labor prices. In the 1920s and early 1930s, industrial wages—rigid in the downward direction because

[22]Gustav Ranis and John C.H. Fei, "A Theory of Economic Development," *American Economic Review* 51 (September 1961): 533–65; and John C. H. Fei and Gustav Ranis, *Development of the Labor Surplus Economy* (Homewood, Ill.: Irwin, 1964).

of emerging unions—remained high, while agricultural (and informal industrial sector) wages declined from their war peak. Nevertheless, during the 1920s and early 1930s, Japan's rapid increase in labor productivity relative to labor remuneration increased its export competitiveness, especially in textiles. Following the war and recovery years from 1935 to 1955, the labor surplus ended and industrial sector supply turned inelastic permanently, as innovation-led demand for industrial products and labor increased rapidly, while labor supply growth from agriculture and population growth was drying up.[23]

In Japan, unlike Lewis-Fei-Ranis, the capitalist wage rate was raised during World War I before all surplus rural labor was absorbed. As workers with low (not zero, as in Lewis's model) marginal productivity migrated from the subsistence agricultural sector, that sector then divided its growing output among fewer persons, resulting in a gradually increasing wage. Industrial wages then had to increase to motivate rural workers to migrate. The larger industrial labor force contributed to a growing food demand that rose more rapidly than the capacity to produce food, resulting in food price increases. Accordingly, the industrial sector had to raise wages to pay for the increased price of food. In the Japanese case, the Fei-Ranis model overestimated the time that cheap labor could stimulate industrial growth.

Indeed empirical studies by neoclassical critics show that: (1) both farm and industrial wages fluctuate in response to changes in supply and demand, and (2) the supply curve is upward sloping, showing a positive relationship between the wage and quantity of labor. The supply curve is not infinitely elastic, as for portions of the supply curves in Figure 5–1, but inelastic, meaning that the percentage change in quantity is less than the percentage change in wage.[24] Evidence by these critics suggest that the period of unlimited supply of labor is more restricted than either Lewis or Fei-Ranis indicate.

Baran's Neo-Marxist Thesis

Africa, Asia, and Latin America were not of major interest to Marx. He regarded production in these regions as feudal and backward compared to the more progressive modes of capitalism. Thus he saw the introduction of European capitalism in these regions as beneficial. But in the twentieth century, Marxian analysis came to encompass an international class struggle, including the conflict between rich and poor countries. Vladimir Ilich Lenin, who not only furnished intellectual and organizational leadership for the revolutionary takeover of power by the

---

[23]E. Wayne Nafziger, *Learning from the Japanese: Japan's Pre-War Development and the Third World* (Armonk, N.Y.: M.E. Sharpe, 1995), pp. 103–05; Miyohei Shinohara, *Structural Changes in Japan's Economic Development* (Tokyo: Kinokuniya, 1970); E. Patricia Tsurumi, *Factory Girls: Women in the Thread Mills of Meiji Japan* (Princeton, N.J.: Princeton University Press, 1990); Yujiro Hayami, *A Century of Agricultural Growth in Japan: Its Relevance to Asian Development* (Tokyo: University of Tokyo Press, 1975); Ryoshin Minami, *The Turning Point in Economic Development: Japan's Experience* (Tokyo: Kinokuniya, 1973); Kazushi Ohkawa and Henry Rosovsky, *Japanese Economic Growth: Trend Acceleration in the Twentieth Century* (Stanford: Stanford University Press, 1973); and Miyohei Shinohara, *Growth and Cycles in the Japanese Economy* (Tokyo: Kinokuniya, 1962).

[24]Bent Hansen, "Marginal Productivity Wage Theory and Subsistence Theory in Egyptian Agriculture," *Journal of Development Studies* 2 (July 1966): 367–407; Bent Hansen, "Employment and Wages in Rural Egypt," *American Economic Review* 59 (June 1969): 298–313; and Alan Richards, "The Egyptian Farm Labor Market Revisited," *Journal of Development Economics* 43 (April 1993): 239–61.

Communist party in Russia in October 1917 but was also chairman of the party from then until his death in 1924, provided much of this new Marxian revision. He argued that it was essential to recognize the difference between the monopoly capitalism of his period and the competitive capitalism of Marx's day. According to Lenin, a logical outgrowth of the monopoly stage of industrial and financial capitalism is the imperialist domination of poor countries by rich countries.

THESIS

The late U.S. Marxist, Paul A. Baran, incorporated Lenin's concepts of imperialism and international class conflict into his theory of economic growth and stagnation. For Baran capitalist revolution, homegrown variety, in LDCs was unlikely because of Western economic and political domination, especially in the colonial period. Capitalism arose not through the growth of small competitive firms at home, but through the transfer from abroad of advanced monopolistic business. Baran felt that as capitalism took hold, the bourgeoisie (business and middle classes) in LDCs, lacking the strength to spearhead thorough institutional change for major capital accumulation, would have to seek allies among other classes.

Thus in certain instances, the bourgeoisie would ally itself with the more moderate leaders of the workers and peasants to form a progressive coalition with a New Deal orientation (such as the Congress party governments under Prime Minister Jawaharlal Nehru, 1947–64, in India). At the outset, such a popular movement would be essentially democratic, antifeudal, and anti-imperialist and in support of domestic capitalism. However, the indigenous capitalist middle classes would ultimately be either unwilling or unable to provide the leadership for a sustained economic development that would also greatly reduce poverty and liberate the masses. In time the bourgeoisie, frightened by the threat of labor radicalism and populist upheaval and the possible expropriation of their property, would be forced into an alliance with the landed interests and the foreign bourgeoisie in their midst, whose governments could provide economic and military assistance to stave off impending disaster.

The differences within this counterrevolutionary coalition would not interfere with the overriding common interest in preventing socialism. Even so the coalition would be unable to raise the rate of capital accumulation significantly. A progressive income tax system to eliminate nonessential consumption; channeling savings from the landed aristocracy into productive investment; and undertaking substantial public investment in sectors where private capital does not venture, where monopolistic controls block expansion, or where infrastructure is required would be beyond the coalition's ability or desire. Thus this conservative alliance thrusts the popular forces even further along the road of radicalism and revolt, leading to further polarization. Finally Baran theorizes that the only way out of the impasse may be worker and peasant revolution, expropriating land and capital, and establishing a new regime based on the "ethos of collective effort," and "the creed of the predominance of the interests of society over the interests of a selected few."[25]

---

[25]Paul A. Baran, *The Political Economy of Growth* (New York: Monthly Review Press, 1957). His views are more succinctly presented in "On the Political Economy of Backwardness," *Manchester School* 20 (January 1952): 66–84, reprinted in A. N. Agarwala and S. P. Singh, *The Economics of Underdevelopment* (London: Oxford University Press, 1958), pp. 75–92.

CRITIQUE

Although Baran's approach explains the difficulties that some reformed capitalist LDCs face in spurring economic development, the theory fails to examine a number of economic and political conflicts of interest. Although there are certainly many local agents, managers, merchants, industrialists, bureaucrats, and politicians who benefit considerably from foreign-controlled capital and technology, there are also some local capitalists whose interests compete with foreign business. These capitalists and their allies frequently lead movements for independence. (For example, the Ivory Coast cocoa farmers who opposed the formation of French cocoa plantations were major supporters of the nationalist Democratic party in the 1950s.) After independence these nationalist elements may become even stronger as colonial economic ties are gradually weakened. Economic policy under a coalition of domestic capitalists, politicians, and bureaucrats may erode the power of foreign capital. The allies and competitors of foreign business people are often locked in economic and political conflict.

Baran also ignores the probability that power is more frequently transferred from one elite to another when revolution occurs, rather than from the advantaged classes to the politically dispossessed masses: Very few of the Soviet and Chinese revolutionary leaders were workers or poor peasants.

For Baran the society closest to "a new social ethos [that] will become the spirit and guide of a new age"[26] is the Soviet Union after 1917. He argues that despite the political violence used by Stalin in the 1930s, and the loss of several million lives during this period, the collectivization of agriculture in the Soviet Union was the only possible approach to economic growth, given an irrational and illiterate peasantry. However, he ignores the substantial growth in both agriculture and industry from 1921 to 1928 under the Soviet New Economic Policy of market socialism. This policy consisted of widespread reliance on market prices, limited private ownership (especially in agriculture), and state ownership of most of the largest industrial enterprises. After Stalin began collectivization, agricultural production declined, the peasant's standard of living dropped significantly, and even the savings agriculture contributed to the industrial sector probably did not increase. There were widespread violence, famine, forced labor, and purges during collectivization. Although the performance of Soviet agriculture since then has improved, the relatively slow growth in agricultural productivity has frustrated Soviet leadership in its attempt to increase average consumption levels to those expected in a high-income economy.

Baran does not ask whether a more gradual, less-centralized approach to agricultural production would have resulted in more rapid development. But perhaps such a question cannot be resolved. Some historians argue that raising living levels, increasing life expectancy, and improving literacy during economic growth have inevitable human costs. The economic transition may be marked by squalor, poverty, unhealthy environment, high infant mortality rate, and a high premature death rate among the working poor, as occurred during Europe's Industrial Revolution, or by the disruption, famine, and death among peasants in the Soviet Union in the 1930s. But in any case, the human costs cannot be avoided.

Several Marxian economists have argued that the Russian Revolution of 1917 did not erase divergent class interests. One French economist argues that the

---

[26]Paul A. Baran, "On the Political Economy of Backwardness," *Manchester School* 20 (January 1952): 84.

Soviet Union abandoned the socialist road, creating a new ruling class—made up of the Communist party, the *Praesidium*, and the bureaucracy—whose economic interests are antagonistic to those of Soviet workers.[27]

Dependency Theory

Celso Furtado, a Brazilian economist for the U.N. Economic Commission for Latin America, was an early contributor to the Spanish and Portuguese literature in **dependency theory** in the 1950s and 1960s. According to him, since the eighteenth century, global changes in demand resulted in a new international division of labor in which the peripheral countries of Asia, Africa, and Latin America specialized in primary products in an enclave controlled by foreigners while importing consumer goods that were the fruits of technical progress in the central countries of the West. The increased productivity and new consumption patterns in peripheral countries benefited a small ruling class and its allies (less than a tenth of the population), who cooperated with the DCs to achieve modernization (economic development among a modernizing minority). The result is "peripheral capitalism, a capitalism unable to generate innovations and dependent for transformation upon decisions from the outside."[28]

A major dependency theorist, Andre Gunder Frank, is a U.S. expatriate recently affiliated with England's University of East Anglia. Frank, writing in the mid-1960s, criticized the view of many development scholars that contemporary underdeveloped countries resemble the earlier stages of now-developed countries. Many of these scholars viewed modernization in LDCs as simply the adoption of economic and political systems developed in Western Europe and North America.

For Frank the presently developed countries were never *under*developed, though they may have been *un*developed. His basic thesis is that underdevelopment does *not* mean traditional (that is, nonmodern) economic, political, and social institutions but LDC subjection to the colonial rule and imperial domination of foreign powers. In essence Frank sees underdevelopment as the effect of the penetration of modern capitalism into the archaic economic structures of the third world.[29] He sees the deindustrialization of India under British colonialism, the disruption of African society by the slave trade and subsequent colonialism, and

---

[27]Charles Bettelheim, *Class Struggles in the USSR*, I (New York: Monthly Review Press, 1978).

[28]Celso Furtado, *Economic Development of Latin America: A Survey from Colonial Times to the Cuban Revolution* (Cambridge: Cambridge University Press, 1970), and *The Economic Growth of Brazil: A Survey from Colonial to Modern Times*, trans. by Ricardo W. de Aguiar and Eric Charles Drysdale (Berkeley and Los Angeles: University of California Press, 1968). The quote is from a short synopsis in Celso Furtado, "The Concept of External Dependence in the Study of Underdevelopment," in Charles K. Wilber, ed., *The Political Economy of Development and Underdevelopment* (New York: Random House, 1973), pp. 118–23.

[29]Excellent anthropological support for dependency analysis is provided by Edwin N. Wilmsen, *Land Filled with Flies: A Political Economy of the Kalahari* (Chicago: University of Chicago Press, 1989). The author, who worked in Botswana's Kalahari for more than fifteen years, criticizes ethnologists for analyzing the San-speaking peoples (or Bushmen) on the rural fringe of southern African economies without considering their historical context and contemporary condition. In previous millennia, the San were enmeshed in the pastoralist economies of the region through production and kinship networks. The poverty, remoteness, and foraging of the San are not unchanging attributes bequeathed by ancient ancestors, Wilmsen contends, but results of subjugation under capitalist penetration and state expansion during the past four to five centuries.

the total destruction of Incan and Aztec civilizations by the Spanish conquistadors as examples of the creation of underdevelopment.[30]

More plainly stated, the economic development of the rich countries contributes to the underdevelopment of the poor. Development in an LDC is not self-generating nor autonomous but ancillary. The LDCs are economic satellites of the highly developed regions of Northern America and Western Europe in the international capitalist system. The Afro-Asian and Latin American countries least integrated into this system tend to be the most highly developed. For Frank, Japanese economic development after the 1860s is the classic case illustrating his theory. Japan's industrial growth remains unmatched: Japan, unlike most of the rest of Asia, was never a capitalist satellite.

Brazil best illustrates the connection between the satellite relationship and underdevelopment. Since the nineteenth century, the growth of major cities, São Paulo and Rio de Janeiro, has been satellite development—largely dependent on outside capitalist powers, especially Britain and the United States. As a result, regions in interior Brazil have become satellites of these two cities and through them, of these Western capitalist countries.

Frank suggests that satellite countries experience their *greatest* economic development when they are *least* dependent on the world capitalist system. Thus Argentina, Brazil, Mexico, and Chile grew most rapidly during World War I, the Great Depression, and World War II, when trade and financial ties with major capitalist countries were weakest. Significantly the most underdeveloped regions today are those that have had the closest ties to Western capitalism in the past. They were the greatest exporters of primary products to, and the biggest sources of capital for, developed countries and were abandoned by them when for one reason or another business fell off. Frank points to India's Bengal; the one-time sugar-exporting West Indies and Northeastern Brazil; the defunct mining districts of Minas Gerais in Brazil, highland Peru, and Bolivia; and the former silver regions of Mexico as examples. He contends that even the *latifundium*, the large plantation or hacienda that has contributed so much to underdevelopment in Latin America, originated as a commercial, capitalist enterprise, not a feudal institution, which contradicts the generally held thesis that a region is underdeveloped because it is isolated and precapitalist.

It is an error, Frank feels, to argue that the development of the underdeveloped countries will be stimulated by indiscriminately transferring capital, institutions, and values from developed countries. He suggests that, in fact, the following economic activities have contributed to underdevelopment, not development:

1. Replacing indigenous enterprises with technologically more advanced, global, subsidiary companies.
2. Forming an unskilled labor force to work in factories and mines and on plantations.
3. Recruiting highly educated youths for junior posts in the colonial administrative service.
4. Workers migrating from villages to foreign-dominated urban complexes.
5. Opening the economy to trade with, and investment from, developed countries.

---

[30]Andre Gunder Frank, *Latin America: Underdevelopment or Revolution?* (New York: Monthly Review Press, 1969), a collection of essays, most of which were first published in the mid-1960s.

According to Frank, a third-world country can develop only by withdrawing from the world capitalist system. Perforce such a withdrawal means a large reduction in trade, aid, investment, and technology from the developed capitalist countries.

CRITIQUE

Many economic historians would agree with Frank that colonies paid dearly for economic dependency under foreign rule. They grant that development was not self-directed. Production was directed toward external rather than domestic needs, economic policies inhibited local industrial activity and led to uneven ethnic and regional economic progress; an elite oriented to foreign interests arose. However these costs were offset, at least in part, by the development of schools, roads, railroads, and administrative service under the colonial powers.

Moreover it is unfair to compare the experience of these countries under colonialism to what might have happened without foreign domination. The internal economic and political weaknesses of Afro-Asian and Latin American countries during the last part of the nineteenth and early part of the twentieth centuries probably made it inevitable that most of them would be economically dependent on some foreign power. The acute underdevelopment of Afghanistan, Thailand, and Ethiopia, which were not colonized, though they were influenced by the West, suggests that colonialism by itself may not have had so negative an impact as Frank indicates. Furthermore cutting economic ties with developed capitalist countries, as Frank recommends, is more likely to inhibit than expedite LDC development. To be sure, the People's Republic of China (through 1976) and the Soviet Union (since the 1930s) were not much hurt by a policy of economic self-sufficiency because they had large resource bases. However Frank's recommendation is often costly for small countries. Ghana's President Kwame Nkrumah lost a 1957 wager to President Felix Houphouet-Bogney of the neighboring Ivory Coast, similar in resource endowment to Ghana, that history would judge Ghana, which cut economic ties with capitalist countries, more successful economically than the Ivory Coast, dependent on the French for the majority of industrial investment (through the early 1970s) and for international trade. The Ivory Coast outperformed Ghana in annual growth: from 1950 to 1960, 1.5 percent to −0.3 percent; from 1960 to 1970, 4.2 percent to −0.3 percent; and from 1970 to 1980, 1.4 percent to −3.2 percent.[31] Moreover Cuba also stagnated during a period of drastically reduced economic ties to foreign capital. On the other hand, Taiwan and South Korea both experienced rapid real growth and decreased income inequality during the 1960s and 1970s while highly dependent on trade, assistance, and investment from the United States and other capitalist countries.[32]

Some changes to cut dependence have not had the anticipated effect. Dependence has taken new forms in the last quarter of the twentieth century. Beginning in the mid 1970s, Nigeria took several steps that, on the face of it, should have re-

---

[31]E. Wayne Nafziger, *Inequality in Africa: Political Elites, Proletariat, Peasants, and the Poor* (Cambridge: Cambridge University Press, 1988), pp. 54, 72–74.

[32]Bill Warren, a Marxist economist, argues that the LDC state can control foreign multinational corporations, using contact with advanced capitalist economies to strengthen the development of an indigenous capitalist class that can play a leading role in industrialization. *Imperialism: Pioneer of Capitalism* (London: Verso, 1980).

duced its dependence on the West. The Lagos government cut substantially the share of its trade with the colonial power, Britain. Lagos acquired majority equity holdings in local petroleum extracting, refining, and distribution and promulgated an indigenization decree shifting the majority of ownership in manufacturing from foreign to indigenous hands. But these measures did not greatly reduce dependence on the West. Nigeria's trade was still virtually all with capitalist DCs (with the United States replacing Britain as the chief trading partner). In contrast to more diversified exports in the 1960s, petroleum comprised more than 80 percent of export value for the 1970s. Moreover only 15 to 20 percent of the petroleum industry's total expenditure on goods and services was spent on locally produced items, which do not include most basic requirements, such as drilling rigs, platforms, heavy structures, underwater engineering systems, and other advanced technologies. Further multinational corporate (MNC) ownership was replaced by MNC–state joint enterprises, which enriched private middlemen and women and enlarged the patronage base for state officials but did little to develop Nigerian administrative and technological skills for subsequent industrialization. Kenya, Tanzania, Zaïre, Malawi, and Bangladesh made even less progress than Nigeria in using indigenization requirements to reduce external dependence.[33]

There are, however, several instances where countries might have developed more rapidly with less dependence on foreign economic initiative. Pakistan, Bangladesh, Honduras, Guatemala, Zaïre, and the Philippines were probably hurt by excessive economic dependence on the United States and other Western countries. But the solution to these problems is not withdrawal from the world capitalist system but rather, a more selective policy in dealings with capitalist countries. Trade, economic aid, capital movements, and technological borrowing from developed countries should be such that investment is directed into priority industries. Discouraging foreign monopoly power, encouraging domestic enterprise, preventing heavy debt burdens, avoiding substantial technological dependence on outsiders, and protecting infant domestic industries should all be part of this selective policy. (Chapters 16–18 discuss further foreign trade and investment strategies.)

What characteristics of dependent economies are not found in independent ones? Frank defines dependence in a circular manner. The LDCs are underdeveloped because they are dependent. But the features Frank concentrates on in defining dependence are those characteristic of underdevelopment. Thus the theory does not offer an independent and verifiable explanation of the processes causing underdevelopment.

Are there degrees of economic dependence? Dependency theory fails to distinguish between regional powers in the third world, such as Brazil and OPEC countries, Venezuela, Libya, Saudi Arabia, and Nigeria, and more dependent countries, such as Senegal, Niger, Uganda, Nepal, and Lesotho.

Finally, most developed countries are also dependent on foreign economic ties. In fact Canada and Belgium may be more dependent on foreign investment than India or Pakistan, but Frank does not consider them dependent countries. Rather than divide the world into dependent and independent countries, it seems more sensible to think in terms of a continuum of dependence from the weakest LDC to the most powerful capitalist country.

---

[33]E. Wayne Nafziger, *Inequality in Africa: Political Elites, Proletariat, Peasants, and the Poor* (Cambridge: Cambridge University Press, 1988), 53–54.

The Neoclassical Counterrevolution

In the 1980s, the governments of economic conservatives, American President Ronald Reagan, British Prime Minister Margaret Thatcher, Canadian Prime Minister Brian Mulroney, German Chancellor Helmut Kohl, and a series of Japanese Liberal Democratic Party prime ministers coincided with a **neoclassical counterrevolution** in economic policy and analysis. "Liberal" here, and among Europeans, refers to **economic liberalism** (the ideology of Adam Smith, Milton Friedman, and Ludwig von Hayek), which stresses freedom from the state's economic restraint (see Chapter 3's discussion of factors influencing capitalism), and not left-of-center politics and economics, as used in North America. (Another usage refers to the "liberal" arts and sciences worthy of a free person.) The governments of the United States, Canada, Western Europe, Japan, Australia, and New Zealand, the high-income members of the **Organization for Economic Cooperation and Development (OECD)**, largely supportive of the market, privatization, supply-side economics, and other neoclassical positions, were influential as majority holders in two international financial institutions created at Bretton Woods, New Hampshire in July 1944 as part of a new post-World War II international economic order, the **World Bank** and **International Monetary Fund (IMF)**. The World Bank (or International Bank for Reconstruction and Development) initially envisioned as a source for loans to areas devastated during World War II, is now the major source of development loans to LDCs. The IMF, an agency charged with promoting exchange stability to provide short-term credit for international balance of payments deficits, is a lender of last resort, where borrowers agree to adopt acceptable adjustment policies. Neoclassicists dominated policy positions in the World Bank and IMF, and even had substantial influence in the United Nations Development Program (UNDP) and the regional development banks (especially African, Asian, and Middle Eastern), although failing to penetrate the United Nations Conference on Trade and Development (UNCTAD) and International Labor Organization (ILO), which like the 1960s and 1970s, are still dominated by third-world ideologies demanding a more just world economic order.

The neoclassicists contend that slow or negative growth results from poor resource allocation from nonmarket prices and excessive LDC state intervention. They argue that promoting competitive free markets, privatizing public enterprises, supporting exports and free international trade, liberalizing trade and exchange rates, allowing exchange rates to attain a market-clearing rate, removing barriers to foreign investment, rewarding domestic savings, reducing government spending and monetary expansion, and removing regulations and price distortions in financial, resource, and commodity markets will spur increased efficiency and economic growth. The World Bank and International Monetary Fund point to South Korea, Taiwan, Singapore, Hong Kong, Malaysia, Thailand, and Indonesia as examples of the free market approach, although we have seen in Chapter 3 that governments have played major roles in their economic development.

Neoclassicism's policies are reflected in the **Washington consensus**, a term coined by Washington's Institute of International Economics' economist John Williamson. This consensus includes the World Bank, the IMF, and the United States government, based in Washington, D.C.,[34] and other major Bank-IMF share-

[34]John Williamson, "Democracy and the 'Washington Consensus'," *World Development* (August 1993): 1329–36; and John Williamson, ed., *The Political Economy of Policy Reform* (Washington, D.C.: Institute for International Economics, 1994), pp. 26–28.

holders, the high-income OECD governments, although perhaps not the OECD bureaucracy itself in Paris, France.

Following are the components of the neoclassical Washington consensus:

1. *Price decontrol.* Neoclassicists favor immediate lifting of controls on commodity, factor, and currency prices.
2. *Fiscal discipline.* Budget deficits of governments or central banks should be small enough to be financed without using inflationary financing.
3. *Public expenditure priorities.* LDCs should reduce government spending, and redirect expenditures from politically sensitive areas like administration, defense, indiscriminate subsidies, and "white elephants" to infrastructure, primary health, and education.
4. *Tax reform.* This includes broadening of the tax base, improved tax administration, sharpening of tax incentives, reduced marginal tax rates, diminished tax evasion and loopholes, and taxing interest on assets held abroad.
5. *Financial liberalization.* The immediate objectives are to abolish preferential interest rates for privileged borrowers and charge nominal interest rates in excess of inflation rates, while the ultimate objective is market-determined interest rates to improve capital's allocative efficiency.
6. *Exchange rates.* Countries need a unified, competitive rate to spur a rapid expansion in exports.
7. *Trade liberalization.* LDCs should replace quantitative restrictions with tariffs, and progressively reduce tariffs until they achieve a uniform low tariff rate (about 10 to 20 percent).
8. *Domestic savings.* Fiscal discipline, cutbacks in government spending, tax reform, and financial liberalization divert resources from the state to highly-productive private sectors, where savings rates are higher. The neoclassical growth model, discussed below, emphasizes the importance of savings and capital formation for rapid economic development.
9. *Foreign direct investment.* Neoclassicists favor abolishing barriers to the entry of foreign firms; additionally, foreign firms should compete with domestic firms on equal terms.
10. *Privatization.* State enterprises should be privatized.
11. *Deregulation.* Governments should abolish regulations that impede new-firm entry and restrict competition unless safety or environmental protection justifies regulations.
12. *Property rights.* The legal system should provide secure property rights without excessive costs to all land, capital, and buildings.[35]

Williamson, prodded by both economists from Washington and LDCs, indicates that "Washington consensus" is a misnomer, and that these policies more accurately reflect a "universal convergence" of DC and LDC (especially Latin American) capitals,[36] albeit with support from the three major Washington institutions. Indeed, there is widespread (although not universal) consensus among economists

[35]John Williamson, "Democracy and the 'Washington Consensus'," *World Development* (August 1993): 1329–36.

[36]John Williamson, "Democracy and the 'Washington Consensus'," *World Development* (August 1993): 1329.

favoring more reliance on market prices to improve the efficiency of resource allocation, monetary and fiscal discipline, improved tax administration, trade and exchange liberalization, and secure and exclusive user or property rights. While few economists argue with the need for selective deregulation, opponents of neoclassicals feel they fail to realize the extent to which externalities, public goods, and income distribution limit the scope of deregulation. Additionally, while many of these opponents support liberalization of entry and improved competition policy for activities previously restricted to the public sector, they oppose the neoclassical emphasis on rampant privatization.

Critics see other problems with the neoclassicals. Cutbacks in government spending may depress the economy, and usually requires that spending on education, nutrition, and social services be reduced. The neoclassicals' concern with decontrol and deregulation may turn a blind eye toward preventing industrial concentration. Even where privatization is desirable, government may want to proceed slowly to avoid a highly concentrated business elite being created from newly privatized firms falling into a few hands, as was true in Nigeria and many other African countries during the 1970s. The emphasis on openness to foreign investment and abolition of lending to preferred domestic borrowers may increase monopolistic power within the economy and restrict opportunities for domestic capitalists and entrepreneurs to learn from experience. Paul Mosley, Jane Harrigan, and John Toye argue that, given LDC labor and resource immobility, immediate liberalization of external trade and supply-side stimulation in "one glorious burst" result in rising unemployment, inflation, and capital flight, and the undermining of efforts to bring the international balance of payments into adjustment.[37] While few would dispute the advantages of a *single* country striving for competitive exchange rates to expand exports, a given LDC may face an export trap, in which its export growth faces competition from other LDCs under pressure to expand exports. Furthermore, critics charge that the neoclassical model for liberalization and adjustment hurts disadvantaged portions of the population without providing safety nets for the poor.

Neoclassicals generally favor comprehensive change to liberalization, an immediate "big bang" or "shock therapy" (see Chapter 20) rather than a gradual adjustment in price decontrol, market creation, reduction in government spending, monetary restriction, deregulation, legal changes, and privatization. Historical experience in the nineteenth-century and twentieth-century West and Japan indicate that economic liberalization requires changes in economic institutions, which can only occur step by step. As economic historian Douglass C. North argued in his Nobel lecture:

> Neoclassical theory is simply an inappropriate tool to analyze and prescribe policies that will induce development. It is concerned with the operation of markets, not with how markets develop. How can one prescribe policies when one doesn't understand how economies develop?[38]

Much more needs to be said about neoclassical position, the leading approach in economics departments in the United States, Canada, and the United

---

[37]Paul Mosley, Jane Harrigan, and John Toye, *Aid and Power: The World Bank and Policy-based Lending*, vol. 1 (London: Routledge, 1991), pp. 110–16.

[38]Douglass C. North, "Economic Performance Through Time," *American Economic Review* 84 (June 1994): 359–68, with quotation on p. 359.

Kingdom, and among the world's major lending institutions, and an important influence among economists in most of the rest of the world. But the subject is too large to be covered in a single chapter. Chapters 6 and 7 examine income distribution policies, Chapters 8–12 factor market policies, Chapter 13 environmental policies, Chapter 14 domestic savings policies, Chapter 15 monetary and fiscal policies, Chapter 16–18 international trade and exchange-rate liberalization, Chapter 19 government planning, and Chapter 20 policies toward financial stabilization, external adjustment, and privatization. The neoclassical agenda is at the center of these controversies about prices, markets, ownership, and financial policies. These controversies will help you arrive at a clearer position concerning neoclassical economics.

The Neoclassical Growth Theory

MIT economist Robert Solow won a Nobel prize for his formulation of the **neoclassical theory of growth**, which stressed the importance of savings and capital formation for economic development, and for empirical measures of sources of growth. Unlike the Harrod-Domar model of growth, discussed in this chapter's appendix, which focused on capital formation, Solow allowed changes in wage and interest rates, substitutions of labor and capital for each other, variable factor proportions, and flexible factor prices. He showed that growth need not be unstable, since as the labor force outgrew capital, wages would fall relative to the interest rate, or if capital outgrew labor, wages would rise. Factor price changes and factor substitution mitigated the departure from the razor's edge of the Harrod-Domar growth path.

Since aggregate growth refers to increases in total production, we can visualize growth factors if we examine the factors contributing to production. We do this in a **production function** stating the relationship between capacity output and the volume of various inputs.

Solow used the following Cobb–Douglas production function, written in the 1920s by mathematician Charles Cobb and economist Paul Douglas (later U.S. Senator from Illinois), to distinguish between the sources of growth—labor quantity and quality, capital, and technology. The equation is

$$Y = TK^{\alpha}L^{\beta} \qquad (5\text{--}1)$$

where Y is output or income, T the level of technology, K capital, and L labor. T is neutral in that it raises output from a given combination of capital and labor without affecting their relative marginal products. The parameter and exponent α is $(\Delta Y/Y)/(\Delta K/K)$, the elasticity (responsiveness) of output with respect to capital (holding labor constant). (The symbol Δ means increment in, so that, for example, $\Delta Y/Y$ is the rate of growth of output and $\Delta K/K$ the rate of growth of capital.) The parameter β is $(\Delta Y/Y)/(\Delta L/L)$, the elasticity of output with respect to labor (holding capital constant).[39] If we assume $\alpha + \beta = 1$, which represents constant returns to scale (that is, a 1 percent increase in both capital and labor increases output by 1 percent, no matter what present output is), and perfect competition, so that production factors are paid

[39]Charles Cobb and Paul Douglas, "A Theory of Production," *American Economic Review* (supplement) 18, no. 1 (March 1928): 139–65; and A.P. Thirlwall, *Growth and Development with Special Reference to Developing Countries* (New York: Wiley, 1977), pp. 52–54.

their marginal products, then α also equals capital's share and β labor's share of total income. (Constant returns to scale, where output and *all* factors of production vary by the same proportion, still entail diminishing returns, where *increments* in output fall with each successive change in *one* variable factor.) The Cobb-Douglas production function allows capital and labor to grow at different rates.[40]

The neoclassical model predicts that incomes per capita between rich and poor countries will converge. But empirical economists cannot find values for parameters and variables (such as α, β, and capital formation rates) that are consistent with neoclassical Equation 5–1 and Chapter 3's evidence of lack of convergence (See Box 5–1).

BOX 5-1

We can illustrate the neoclassical bias toward convergence if we compare the United States and the Philippines in 1992. The United States has 110 times the Philippines' net national product (*Y*), 3.67 times the Philippines' labor force (*L*), and, according to neoclassical assumptions, the same level of technology (*T*). A growth rate by the United States at the same rate as the Philippines' requires either capital formation rates or β values that are not plausible.

A benchmark for β is 0.6, so that α is 0.4. Plugging these values and *Y* and *L* into Equation 5–1 requires that *K* (capital stock) in the United States be 18,050 times that of the Philippines for the U.S. to attain the same growth rate as that of the Philippines. But assume, as the neoclassicals do, that the capital requirement per unit of output is fixed, so that the ratio of capital to income is the same as the ratio of savings or investment to additional income (savings and investment rates are the same, given the neoclassical assumption of a **closed economy**, one with no foreign trade or investment); then the U.S. capital stock is only 92 times that of the Philippines'. For the Philippines' savings rate to be its 1992 rate (18 percent) and for *K* in the U.S. to be 18,050 times that of the Philippines, the neoclassical model requires the United States to save 2,943 percent, a preposterous figure, instead of its 1992 figure, 15 percent.

What are α and β if the United States' net national product is 110 times that of the Philippines, the U.S. labor force is 3.67 times that of the Philippines, and U.S. capital stock 92 times that of the Philippines?[41] The answer is α = 1.05 and β = –0.05. But a negative β is absurd, meaning that labor's share and marginal product are both negative.

---

[40]Robert Solow, "A Contribution to the Theory of Economic Growth," *Quarterly Journal of Economics* (February 1956): 65–94; Robert Solow, *Growth Theory: An Exposition* (New York: Oxford University Press, 1970); Charles P. Kindleberger and Bruce Herrick, *Economic Development* (New York: McGraw-Hill, 1977), p. 81; and Hollis Chenery, Sherman Robinson, and Moshe Syrquin, *Industrialization and Growth: A Comparative Study* (New York: Oxford University Press, 1986), p. 17.

[41]Relative labor, capital, and NNP are from World Bank, *World Development Report, 1994* (New York: Oxford University Press, 1994).

Can we modify neoclassical assumptions to arrive at plausible numbers that are consistent with no convergence? Gregory Mankiw, David Romer, and David Weil argue that while the direction of the variables, the growths in capital and labor, is correct, the magnitudes of these growths on income growth are excessive. These three economists propose an augmented Solow neoclassical model, which includes human capital as an additional explanatory variable to physical capital and labor.[42]

Human capital, as well as physical capital, can yield a stream of income over time. Nobel laureate Theodore W. Schultz argues that a society can invest in its citizens through expenditures on education, training, research, and health that enhance their productive capacity.[43] While there are diminishing returns to physical capital by itself, there are constant returns to all (human and physical) capital.[44]

Given the fact that such a large percentage of capital stock is human capital, Mankiw et al. expected that adding a human capital variable, the fraction of the working age population that attends secondary school, would improve the explanation of the model. Mankiw et al.'s augmented model substantially reduces labor's share of income from about 0.60 to 0.33. They modify Equation 5–1 to

$$Y = TK^{1/3}L^{1/3}H^{1/3} \qquad\qquad (5\text{--}2)$$

where H is human capital. H's positive correlation with savings rates and population growth substantially alters the results. Adding human capital, which explains 80 percent of the variation between rich and poor countries, does indeed give plausible values for the neoclassical growth model.[45] Mankiw et al.'s model means that, with similar technologies and rates of capital and labor growths, income growth should converge, but much more slowly than Solow's model (Equation 5–1).

CRITIQUE

But while Mankiw et al. salvaged the neoclassical growth model, it still has several weaknesses, including the assumptions that markets are perfectly competitive (essential for computing the marginal products that are components of α, β, and the human capital exponent), that technological change is exogenous (explained outside the model), and that the level of technology is the same throughout the world. Indeed, neoclassical technical progress takes place completely independent of decisions by people, firms, and governments.

The New (Endogenous) Growth Theory

The University of Chicago's Robert Lucas finds that international wage differences and migration are difficult to reconcile with neoclassical theory. If the same technology were available globally, skilled people embodying human capital would *not*

[42]N. Gregory Mankiw, David Romer, and David N. Weil, "A Contribution to the Empirics of Economic Growth," *Quarterly Journal of Economics* 107 (May 1992): 407–37.

[43]Theodore W. Schultz, *Transforming Traditional Agriculture* (New Haven, Conn.: Yale University Press, 1964).

[44]Robert E. Lucas, Jr., "On the Mechanics of Economic Development," *Journal of Monetary Economics* 22 (July 1988): 3–42.

[45]N. Gregory Mankiw, David Romer, and David N. Weil, "A Contribution to the Empirics of Economic Growth," *Quarterly Journal of Economics* 107 (May 1992): 407–37.

move from LDCs, where human capital is scarce, to DCs, where human capital is abundant, as these people do now. Nor would a given worker be able to earn a higher wage after moving from the Philippines to the United States.[46] Moreover, Harvard's Robert Barro and Xavier Sala-i-Martin observe that diminishing returns to capital in the neoclassical model should mean substantial international capital movements from DCs, with high capital-labor ratios, to LDCs, with low capital-labor ratios. These capital movements should enhance the convergence found in Solow's model, in contrast to the lack of convergence found in the real world.[47] Additionally, most LDCs attract no net capital inflows, and many LDCs even experience domestic capital flight. New growth theorists think their model is closer to the realities of international flows of people and capital than the neoclassical model.

Paul Romer, a University of California-Berkeley economist, believes that if technology is **endogenous**, explained within the model, economists can elucidate growth where the neoclassical model fails. When the level of technology is allowed to vary, you can explain more of growth, as DCs have higher level than LDCs. Variable technology means that the speed of convergence between DCs and LDCs is determined primarily by the rate of diffusion of knowledge.[48] For **new growth theorists** like Romer, **innovation** or technical change, the embodiment in production of some new idea or invention that enhances capital and labor productivity, is the engine of growth.

Neoclassical theorists assume that technological discoveries are global public goods, so that all people can use new technology at the same time. Indeed, it is technologically possible (but not historically accurate) for every person and firm to use the internal-combustion engine, the transistor, the microcomputer, and other innovations. For new growth economists, however, technological discovery results from an LDC's government policies (the neoclassical growth theorists have no role for the state) and industrial research.

Neoclassical economists assume that the innovator receives no monopoly profits from their discoveries. However, because individuals and firms control information flows, petition for patents to restrict use by rivals, and charge prices for others to use the technology, new growth economists assume a temporary monopoly associated with innovation (see Chapter 12's discussion of the Schumpeterian entrepreneur). Note the concentration of high-technology industries in particular locations such as the Silicon Valley, in Santa Clara County, Western California, between Palo Alto and San Jose, and Route 128, which runs around Greater Boston. Private and government support for technological concentration and control breaks down the assumption of perfect competition, as well as the ability to compute factor shares.

Neoclassical economists emphasize capital formation. New growth economists, on the other hand, stress external economies to capital accumulation that

---

[46]Robert E. Lucas, Jr., "On the Mechanics of Economic Development," *Journal of Monetary Economics* 22 (July 1988): 3–42; and Paul M. Romer, "The Origins of Endogenous Growth," *Journal of Economic Perspectives* 8 (Winter 1994): 11.

[47]Robert J. Barro and Xavier Sala-i-Martin, "Convergence," *Journal of Political Economy* 100 (April 1992): 223–51. Robert J. Barro, N. Gregory Mankiw, and Xavier Sala-i-Martin, "Capital Mobility in Neoclassical Models of Growth," *American Economic Review* 85 (March 1995): 103–15, who examine samples of U.S. states and OECD countries (but not DCs and LDCs together), find that, in neoclassical models, the quantitative effect of including capital mobility in explaining convergence is small.

[48]Paul M. Romer, "The Origins of Endogenous Growth," *Journal of Economic Perspectives* 8 (Winter 1994): 8–9; Paul M. Romer, "Increasing Returns and Long-Run Growth," *Journal of Political Economy* 94 (October 1986) 1002–37; and Paul M. Romer, "Endogenous Technological Change," *Journal of Political Economy* 98 (1990): S71-S102.

can permanently keep the marginal product of physical or human capital above the interest rate, and prevent diminishing returns from generating stagnation.[49]

CRITIQUE

The endogenous growth model, like Mankiw et al.'s neoclassical model enhanced by human capital, generates plausible numbers and is consistent with persistent differences in income per capita between nations (that is, no or little convergence between nations). Indeed both models are consistent with a large number of observations concerning aggregate output and capital. Howard Pack, however, considers endogenous growth theory as only a rich expansion of neoclassical growth theory rather than a powerful organizing framework about actual growth. Also, as Solow argues, the knife-edge character of the model means that any disequilibrium can cause the model to break down.[50] Moreover, technology is growth in output unexplained by the increase in measured factors of production. Could we explain technical advance by increased investment in resources, such as research and development (R&D)? Surely purposive, profit-seeking investment in knowledge is a key to explaining technological progress.[51] Others suggest international trade, government macroeconomic policies, learning by doing, or other variables discussed in future chapters. Furthermore, the endogenous growth theory, similar to the neoclassical growth theory, fails to discuss how changes in incentives or institutions affect the variables of the model and the rate of economic growth.

Solow contends that "the 'production' of new technology may not be a simple matter of inputs and outputs." Indeed, R&D is an inadequate measure of resources devoted to increasing productivity. A producer's investment in research and development may contribute to growth that is disseminated to other producers. In many instances, however, as in microcomputers, economies may require substantial time before production reorganization contributes to increased productivity. Moreover, some investment in R&D may net no growth at all. Furthermore, some LDCs may be able to increase capital and labor productivity by using existing technologies without any new investment in R&D. For Solow, the lack of correspondence between investment in technology and economic growth means that much of R&D is, as neoclassicists contend, exogenous to the economy.[52] Neither the new growth theorists' measures of R&D nor the neoclassicals' measures of human capital explain much of the extraordinary growth of Asian NICs—South Korea, Taiwan, and Singapore—during the last quarter of the twentieth century.[53] Econometric models have not yet been able to break down technological innovations and economic growth into measured inputs, and it is doubtful that they will.

[49]Paul M. Romer, "The Origins of Endogenous Growth," *Journal of Economic Perspectives* 8 (Winter 1994): 3–22; and Gene M. Grossman and Elhanan Helpman, "Endogenous Innovation in the Theory of Growth," *Journal of Economic Perspectives* 8 (Winter 1994): 23–44.

[50]Howard Pack, "Endogenous Growth Theory: Intellectual Appeal and Empirical Shortcomings," *Journal of Economic Perspectives* 8 (Winter 1994): 55–56; and Robert M. Solow, "Perspectives on Growth Theory," *Journal of Economic Perspectives* 8 (Winter 1994): 50–51.

[51]Howard Pack, "Endogenous Growth Theory: Intellectual Appeal and Empirical Shortcomings," *Journal of Economic Perspectives* 8 (Winter 1994): 55–72; and Gene M. Grossman and Elhanan Helpman, "Endogenous Innovation in the Theory of Growth," *Journal of Economic Perspectives* 8 (Winter 1994): 24.

[52]Robert M. Solow, "Perspectives on Growth Theory," *Journal of Economic Perspectives* 8 (Winter 1994): 45–54, with quotation on p. 52.

[53]Howard Pack, "Endogenous Growth Theory: Intellectual Appeal and Empirical Shortcomings," *Journal of Economic Perspectives* 8 (Winter 1994): 60–63.

Summary

1. English classical economist David Ricardo feared eventual stagnation from slow capital accumulation, and diminishing returns from population growth on fixed natural resources. However, he failed to see the possibility of sustained, rapid, economic growth because his theory understated scientific discoveries and technological progress.

2. Marx saw history dialectically—as progressing from feudalism to capitalism to socialism on the basis of class conflict. The oppressed classes overthrow the classes controlling the prevailing means of production. Nevertheless, the socialist revolution did not take place in the most advanced capitalist countries, nor did workers overthrow capitalism when they became a majority of the labor force, as Marx expected.

3. Rostow's economic model has five stages; its central historical stage is the take-off, a decisive period of increased investment, rapid growth in leading sectors, and institutional change during which the major blocks to steady growth are finally overcome. Rostow's theory has several weaknesses: insufficient empirical evidence concerning conditions needed for takeoff; imprecise definitions; no theoretical ground for a society's movement from one stage to another; and the mistaken assumption that economic development in LDCs will parallel the early stages of DC development.

4. The vicious circle theory contends that a country is poor because its income is too low to encourage potential investors and generate adequate saving. However, high income inequality, funds spent on prestige projects and the military, and numerous products requiring few economies of scale suggest that the savings potential of LDCs is much greater than this theory envisions.

5. Balanced growth advocates argue that a big push is needed to begin economic development because of indivisibilities in demand and infrastructure. Critics indicate that most LDCs do not have the resources essential for launching such a big push.

6. Hirschman supports a deliberate unbalancing of the economy to facilitate economic decision making and investment. However, he fails to stress the importance of agricultural investment.

7. For Lewis, economic growth takes place as a result of growth in the size of the industrial sector, which saves, relative to the subsistence agricultural sector, which saves nothing. In the Lewis model, an unlimited supply of surplus farm labor migrates to urban areas for wages in excess of rural, subsistence wages. This supply of cheap labor to the industrial sector is the basis for profits, and capital accumulation. However, critics question Lewis's premise of zero marginal productivity of labor and believe that the capitalist wage rate will rise before all surplus rural labor is absorbed.

8. Fei and Ranis, too, believe that the capitalist wage will increase before surplus labor is absorbed, unless agriculture and industry can achieve balanced growth. However, contrary to the Lewis-Fei-Ranis model, Japan raised its capitalist wage rate before all surplus rural labor was absorbed.

9. For Baran, the coalition of the bourgeoisie and landed classes, helped by foreign capitalist governments, is incapable of undertaking the capital formation and political reform required for rapid economic growth and alleviation of mass poverty. Although Baran's vision of a ruling progressive coalition is intriguing,

he underestimates the conflicts of interest and class antagonism that are likely to occur under its rule.

10. Furtado's dependency theory contends that increased productivity and new consumption patterns resulting from capitalism in the peripheral countries of Asia, Africa, and Latin America benefit a small ruling class and its allies.

11. Frank's dependency approach maintains that countries become underdeveloped through integration into, not isolation from, the international capitalist system. However, despite some evidence supporting Frank, he does not adequately demonstrate that withdrawing from the capitalist system results in faster economic development.

12. The neoclassical counterrevolution to Marxian and dependency theory emphasized reliance on the market, private initiative, and deregulation in LDCs. Neoclassical growth theory emphasizes the importance of increased saving for economic growth. The Washington institutions of the World Bank, International Monetary Fund, and the United States government have applied neoclassical analysis in their policy-based lending to LDCs.

13. The new endogenous growth theory arose from concerns that neoclassical economics neglected the explanations of technological change and accepted an unrealistic assumption of perfect competition. The new growth theory, however, does no better than an enhanced neoclassical model in measuring the sources of economic growth.

Terms to Review

- theory
- classical theory
- invisible hand
- law of diminishing returns
- laissez-faire
- iron law of wages
- surplus
- historical materialism
- reserve army of the unemployed
- preconditions stage
- takeoff
- vicious circle
- virtuous circle
- demonstration effect
- balanced growth
- unbalanced growth
- price elasticity of demand
- big push thesis
- indivisibilities
- external economies
- infrastructure
- backward linkages
- forward linkages
- institutional wage
- commercialization (turning) point
- labor supply elasticities
- dependency theory
- neoclassicism
- neoclassical counterrevolution
- economic liberalism
- Organization for Economic and Cooperation and Development (OECD)
- World Bank
- International Monetary Fund (IMF)
- Washington consensus
- neoclassical theory of growth
- production function
- closed economy
- human capital
- endogenous
- new growth theory
- innovation
- Harrod-Domar growth model
- ICOR (incremental capital output ratio)
- accelerator theory of investment

Questions to Discuss

1. Is Ricardian classical economic theory applicable to LDCs?

2. How valid is the assumption that the development of LDCs will parallel the earlier stages of today's DCs?

3. Choose one developed country (or one LDC that Rostow says has already experienced takeoff). How well does Rostow's stage theory explain that country's economic growth?

4. Which historical theory—Marx's or Rostow's—is more useful in explaining Western economic development? Contemporary LDC development?

5. Are some of today's LDCs closer to Marx's feudal stage than his capitalist stage? What might a Marxist recommend for a LDC in the feudal stage? Would a Leninist or Baranist prescription for a feudal LDC be any different from Marx's?

6. How might Marxian economic analysis (like Mao's or Bettelheim's) threaten political elites in socialist countries?

7. How valid is Baran's theory in explaining contemporary underdevelopment in Asia, Africa, and Latin America? Are revolution and a Soviet-type government essential for removing this underdevelopment?

8. How valid is Baran's theory in explaining the weaknesses of New-Deal-type regimes in LDCs?

9. How does Andre Gunder Frank differ from Karl Marx in judging Western capitalism's influence in Asia, Africa, and Latin America?

10. For which country has dependence on Western capitalist economies been most costly? For which country has dependence on Western capitalist economies been most beneficial? On the basis of arguments about these two countries, how persuasive is Frank's dependency theory?

11. What are some potential LDC vicious circles? How plausible are these as barriers to development?

12. How are wages determined in the subsistence and capitalist sectors in the Lewis model?

13. What is Lewis's explanation for the expansion of the industrial capitalist sector? Why do critics think that the Lewis model overstates rural-urban migration and industrial expansion?

14. How well does the Lewis-Fei-Ranis model explain Japan's economic growth in the early part of the twentieth century?

15. How important are supply and demand indivisibilities in influencing LDC investment strategies?

16. What is the neoclassical theory of economic development? theory of economic growth? What are the policy implications of the neoclassical theory of development and growth? How effective have neoclassical policy prescriptions been for stimulating economic growth in developing countries?

17. What were the weaknesses of the neoclassical theory of growth and development that gave rise to the new endogenous growth theory? How does the new growth theory address the neoclassical weaknesses? What are the strengths and weaknesses of new growth theory?

18. Choose a country or world region. Which economic development theory best explains development in that country or region?

Guide to Readings

Higgins (note 18) has a detailed discussion and evaluation of the models of classical economists, Marx, Rostow, and balanced and unbalanced growth theorists. Irma Adelman's book devoted to *Theories of Economic Growth and Development* (Stanford: Stanford University Press, 1961) analyzes the classical and Marxian models, as well as several other major theories. Enke (note 4) has a concise outline and critique of the classical approach.

Rostow's stage theory was criticized by economists and historians at the 1963 International Economic Association meetings in Konstanz, West Germany. The papers have been compiled in a book edited by Rostow (note 11).

Nurkse's book (note 14) presents his views of the vicious circle and balanced growth theories. Nurkse's summary article, Rosenstein–Rodan's article on indivisibilities (note 15), Fleming's criticism of balanced growth (note 18), Myint's article (note 13), Rostow's presentation of his stage theory in condensed form, Lewis's article (note 21), and Baran's article on economic backwardness are included in Agarwala and Singh (note 25).

The major statements of the dependency theory are three sources by Furtado (note 28), Frank (note 30), and Andre Gunder Frank, *Capitalism and Underdevelopment in Latin America: Historical Studies of Chile and Brazil* (New York: Monthly Review Press, 1969). A useful critique and bibliography of dependence theory are in Sanjaya Lall, "Is 'Dependence' a Useful Concept in Analyzing Underdevelopment," *World Development* 3 (November–December 1975): 799–810.

James Weaver and Kenneth Jameson discuss competing approaches for explaining economic development, including orthodox and Marxist theories, in *Economic Development: Competing Paradigms* (Washington, D.C.: University Press of America, 1981).

Lewis (note 21) and two sources from Ranis and Fei (note 22) present the Lewis-Fei-Ranis model.

On neoclassical growth theory, see two references from Solow (note 40) and Mankiw et al. (note 41). Lucas and Romer (note 46) discuss new growth theory. For a highly accessible discussion and bibliography of both neoclassical and new growth theory, see articles by Paul M. Romer, Gene M. Grossman and Elhanan Helpman, Robert M. Solow, and Howard Pack in the *Journal of Economic Perspectives*, 8 (Winter 1994) (see notes 49 and 50). On convergence see Romer (note 49) and Robert J. Barro and Xavier Sala-i-Martin, "Convergence," *Journal of Political Economy* 100 (April 1992): 223–51.

Mohsin S. Khan, Peter J. Montiel, and Nadeem U. Haque present IMF-World Bank macroeconomic models in "Adjustment with Growth: Relating the Analytical Approaches of the IMF and the World Bank," *Journal of Development Economics* 32 (January 1990): 155–79. For various macroeconomic adjustment models, including those for Iran, Venezuela, Singapore, and South Korea, see Mohsin S. Khan, Peter J. Montiel, and Nadeem U. Haque, eds.,

Macroeconomic Models for Adjustment in Developing Countries (Washington, D.C.: International Monetary Fund, 1991).

John Weeks, "Fallacies of Competition: Myths and Maladjustment in the 'Third World'," an Inaugural Lecture delivered on October 13, 1993, School of Oriental and African Studies, University of London, England, criticizes neoclassical development economics and the Washington consensus.

Some may prefer to include Joseph A. Schumpeter's theory of growth and business cycles (Chapter 12) with the theories of this chapter.

David Lim, *Explaining Economic Growth: A New Analytical Framework* (Cheltenham, U.K.: Edward Elgar, 1996) finds that the newly industrializing countries of East Asia have more distorted prices than the slower–growing countries of Asia, a challenge to the Washington consensus.

The Harrod-Domar Model

Capital formation and the **ICOR, the incremental capital output ratio,** the inverse of the ratio of increase in output to investment are fundamental variables in the **Harrod-Domar growth model**. If Y is income, K capital stock, and I investment, then the *ICOR* is $(\Delta K / \Delta Y)$, the increment in capital divided by the increment in income, the same as $(I/\Delta Y)$, since $\Delta K \equiv I$ by definition.

Evsey D. Domar emphasizes that present investment, while contributing to aggregate demand today, also provides new productive capacity. If this capacity is not adequately used, it discourages future investment, thus increasing surplus capital and depressing the economy. But if investment increases at the correct rate, aggregate demand will be sufficient to use fully the newly added capacity. Domar indicates the rate at which investment would have to grow for this process to take place. Investment must grow at a constant percentage rate

$$\frac{\Delta I}{I} = \left(\frac{1}{ICOR} \right)(\alpha) \tag{5–3}$$

since α, the marginal propensity to save, the ratio of the increment in savings to the increment in income, and the ICOR are both constant.

Roy F. Harrod is also concerned with keeping total spending and productive capacity in balance, but he focuses on the growth path of income, unlike Domar's concentration on the growth rate of investment. In the Harrod model, the equilibrium (or warranted) growth rate keeps planned savings equal to planned investment, that is,

$$sY_t = ICOR\left(Y_t - Y_{t-1}\right) \tag{5–4}$$

$$\frac{\left(Y_t - Y_{t-1}\right)}{Y} = \frac{s}{ICOR} \tag{5–5}$$

where s is (S_t/Y_t), the average propensity to save.

Harrod goes beyond Domar's explanation of what investment must be for sustainable growth to include a theory of what determines investment. He calls his notion the **accelerator theory of investment;** that is, investment today (I_t) is partly dependent on income today minus that of yesterday ($Y_t - Y_{t-1}$), reflected in the *ICOR* relationship.

Harrod also discusses what happens if the actual growth rate does not equal the warranted rate, that is, planned savings does not equal planned investment. He concludes that the warranted growth path is like a razor's edge, since a departure of the actual growth rate [$(Y_t - Y_{t-1})/Y_t$] from the warranted path causes a further departure in the same direction, throwing the economy into a period of either explosive growth (producing inflation) or stagnation.

The model's instability follows from some peculiar assumptions about producer behavior. If producers guessed correctly yesterday about demand and their supply just equaled market demand, they will plan today to increase their output by the *same percentage* as they increased it yesterday. If they produced too much, they will reduce yesterday's growth rate of output and again produce too much today because demand will fall below expectations. If they produced too little yesterday, so there was excess demand, today's output growth will increase over yesterday's and there will again be excess demand. One possibility Harrod considers is that the warranted growth path may not be attainable because of limitations in the growth of capacity, that is, his "natural" growth rate.

There are several problems with the Harrod–Domar model. The first is Harrod's assumption about producer behavior, including the premise that producers do not modify behavior as they learn how the economy previously responded to divergences between warranted and actual growths. Harrod's behavioral assumptions may be even less relevant where the state has a major role in planning output expansion. The second problem is that Harrod's accelerator has no lag, implying that capital goods are produced simultaneously with the increased output requiring this production. A third problem, which is also characteristic of the Domar model, is the assumption of fixed capital-labor proportions, which omits the possibility of adjusting capital-labor ratios to avoid surplus capital, and output ceilings that might cause the warranted rate to be the actual rate. Models that allow for substitution between factors—such as the neoclassical growth model and others using a Cobb–Douglas approach—overcome this last problem of the Harrod–Domar model.[54]

---

[54]Roy F. Harrod, "An Essay in Dynamic Theory," *Economic Journal* 49 (March 1939): 14–33; Evsey D. Domar, "The Problem of Capital Accumulation," *American Economic Review* 37 (March 1947): 34–55; Gardner Ackley, *Macroeconomic Theory* (New York: Macmillan, 1961), pp. 513–26; and Edward Shapiro, *Macroeconomic Analysis* (New York: Harcourt, Brace, Jovanovich, 1978), 402–13. I am grateful for the help of Edgar S. Bagley.

PART II: POVERTY ALLEVIATION AND INCOME DISTRIBUTION

CHAPTER 6

Poverty, Malnutrition, and Income Inequality

Scope of the Chapter

The World Bank's *World Development Report* states that against the background of substantial LDC growth in the past two decades,

> it is all the more staggering—and all the more shameful—that more than one billion people in the developing world are living in poverty. . . . Progress in raising average incomes, however welcome, must not distract attention from this massive and continuing burden of poverty. . . . In the countries that have participated in [recent] overall economic progress [such as Indonesia and China], poverty has declined and the incomes even of those remaining in poverty have increased. . . . But in many countries economic performance was weaker, and the number in poverty fell more slowly. Where rapid population growth was an important factor, as in much of Sub-Saharan Africa, consumption per head stagnated and the number in poverty rose.[1]

Economic growth is the most important factor contributing to poverty reduction. Nevertheless, LDCs cannot solve poverty without attention to income and property distribution, for poverty rose in a number of countries in the 1970s, 1980s, and 1990s even when growth targets were met or surpassed. As indicated in Chapter 2, GNP growth can be a misleading indicator of development, since GNP is heavily weighted by the income shares of the rich. Gary S. Fields finds it regrettable that standard studies of country development provide great detail about macroeconomic conditions and the balance of payments without providing "information on who has benefitted how much from economic growth and . . . who has been hurt how much by economic decline."[2]

---

[1] World Bank, *World Development Report, 1990* (New York: Oxford University Press, 1990), p. 1.
[2] Gary S. Fields, "Poverty and Income Distribution: Data for Measuring Poverty and Inequality Changes in the Developing Countries," *Journal of Development Economics* 44 (June 1994): 87.

Estimates of income distribution in most developing countries are, at best, approximations of the underlying distribution we wish to measure. Despite efforts since the early 1970s to investigate income inequality, these data are even weaker than national income statistics. The International Labor Organization suggests that using many of these data to make policy is like trying to run through the forest in the dark without a flashlight.[3] Many of the official figures of government and international agencies on income distribution are not reliable or compatible over time or space.[4] Frequently the sample procedure for looking at inequalities is not adequate. Also income is not only understated for subsistence farmers (see Chapter 2) but also for the rich, who often understate income for tax purposes.

Moreover, scholars often do not indicate how income and the units sharing it are defined. Also, the factual basis of the estimates is sometimes unclear. Some figures appear to be produced on a very slender basis, but are frequently cited, gaining credence with each subsequent citation. A case in point is World Bank economist Montek S. Ahluwalia (1974), whose source for Sierra Leone cites the *Freetown Daily Mail*, which drew its information from the advance report of a 1966–68 household survey of the urban Western province, not representative of a primarily rural country. Additionally, the report measured only money income. Furthermore, it is not possible to compute Ahluwalia's figures from the original data.[5]

Economists need minimal standards for data admissibility. Fields indicates the following: (1) the data base must be an actual household survey or census, (2) the data must be national in coverage, and (3) to compare across time, surveys, measures, and the income concept and recipient unit must be constant. For time-series consumption or income, household data and poverty lines need to be adjusted for inflation, frequently with high inflation rates. While economists would prefer surveys to collect information on noncash income such as food and other goods produced at home, we may sometimes have no choice but to accept household surveys that ask for cash income.[6]

Nevertheless, a few careful studies can help us answer some questions about differences in poverty and income inequality and suggest policies to reduce them. Indeed, regions such as sub-Saharan Africa, which lack measures of incidence, intensity, and intrapoor income distribution, are also likely to have weak or nonexistent antipoverty policies.[7] We begin by discussing the concept and amount of absolute poverty in the world. We go on to consider the concepts and extent of income inequality and to look at differences in poverty and inequality among the following: (1) by country; (2) countries in early and late stages of economic development; (3) low-, middle-, and high-income countries; (4) DCs and LDCs; (5) by

---

[3]International Labor Organization, Jobs and Skills Program for Africa, *First Things First: Meeting the Basic Needs of the People of Nigeria* (Addis Ababa, 1981), p. 29.

[4]Terence Moll, "Mickey Mouse Numbers and Inequality Research in Developing Countries," *Journal of Development Studies* 28 (July 1992): 689–704; and Jacques Lecaillon, Felix Paukert, Christian Morrisson, and Dimitri Germidis, *Income Distribution and Economic Development: An Analytical Survey* (Geneva: International Labor Office, 1984).

[5]Douglas Rimmer, *The Economies of West Africa* (London: Weidenfeld and Nicolson, 1984), p. 43.; and Montek S. Ahluwalia, "Income Inequality: Some Dimensions of the Problems," in Hollis Chenery, Montek S. Ahluwalia, C.L.G. Bell, John H. Duloy, and Richard Jolly, eds., *Redistribution with Growth* (London: Oxford University Press, 1974), p. x.

[6]Gary S. Fields, "Poverty and Income Distribution: Data for Measuring Poverty and Inequality Changes in the Developing Countries," *Journal of Development Economics* 44 (June 1994): 89–90, 97.

[7]Michael Lipton and Jacques van der Gaag, eds., *Including the Poor—Proceedings of a Symposium Organized by the World Bank and the International Food Policy Research Institute* (Washington, D.C.: World Bank, 1993), p. 3.

world region; (6) between slow- and fast-growing countries; and (7) by gender. We analyze accompaniments of absolute poverty, identify subgroups within a country's population that are most hurt by poverty, and present several case studies of policies developing countries have used to influence poverty and income distribution. Finally, we suggest policies for reducing poverty and improving income distribution and discuss the relationship between inequality and political instability.

Global Absolute Poverty

Absolute poverty, a different concept from income inequality, is below the income that secures the bare essentials of food, clothing, and shelter. Other essentials may be added, as in the standard for Indonesia, Bangladesh, Nepal, Kenya, Tanzania, and Morocco (the Afro-Equa-Bengal) discussed below. Thus, determining this level is a matter of judgment, so that it is difficult to make comparisons between countries. Moreover, what is considered poverty varies according to the living standards of the time and region. World Bank economists Martin Ravallion, Gaurav Datt, and Dominique van de Walle show that national poverty lines increase with mean consumption, although poverty lines are below the mean in all cases. Accordingly, many Americans classified as poor by their government are materially better off than many Americans of the 1950s or Africans today who are not considered poor.

Recognizing that the perception of poverty has evolved historically and varies tremendously across cultures, Ravallion, Datt, and van de Walle set an **extreme poverty line** and a **poverty line**. The lower line, the extreme poverty line, recognized as the absolute minimum by international standards, is based on a standard set in India, the country with the most extensive literature on the subject, and close to the poverty line of perhaps the poorest country, Somalia. The definition used by the Bank is based on previous work by its economists Montek S. Ahluwalia, Nicholas G. Carter, and Hollis B. Chenery. These economists, who assume a population with a "normal" distribution by age and gender, define the extreme poverty line as the income needed to attain basic nutritional needs, that is, a daily supply of 2,250 calories per person, a figure of 275 purchasing-power adjusted dollars or I\$275 per capita in 1985.[8] The 2,250 calories would be met by the following diet: 5 grams of leafy vegetables, 110 grams of other vegetables (potatoes, root vegetables, gourds, and so on), 90 grams of milk, 35 grams of oil, 35 grams of sugar, 10 grams of flesh foods (fish and meats), 45 grams of pulses (peas or other legumes), and 395 grams of cereals (rice, corn, millet, or wheat). To illustrate, the 395 grams of cereals might consist of about 2 cups of hot prepared rice, equivalent in weight to 54 percent of the total diet.[9]

---

[8]Partha Dasgupta, *An Inquiry into Well-Being and Destitution* (Oxford: Clarendon Press, 1993), p. 404, indicates that undernourishment studies for LDCs focus on calorie deficiency, since "diets are such that protein requirements could be expected to be met if calorie needs were met." He also discusses tropical calorie requirements for maintenance, for physical activities, and for heavy manual work for a male subsistence farmer (pp. 422–23).

[9]The figure for flesh foods is an average for a population that includes high Hindu castes who do not eat meat for religious reasons. For these castes, pulses combined with additional cereals make up the amino acids provided by meat. R. Rajalakshmi, *Preschool Child Malnutrition* (Baroda, India: University of Baroda Press, 1975), pp. 106–9, refers to a usual adult Indian diet. I am grateful for the help of nutritionist Meredith Smith in preparing this material.

For constructing a least-cost diet, see Patrick J. Gormely, "Are High-Protein Foods Economically Efficient?" *Food Policy* 3 (November 1978): 280–88.

Data on income distribution for 1985 indicate that 33 percent of the Indian population was below the extreme poverty line (or potentially undernourished).

The World Bank's upper poverty line, the Afro-Equa-Bengal poverty line, below which persons are designated as poor, was 370 purchasing-power adjusted dollars or I\$370 per capita in 1985. This poverty line provides for consumption in excess of the bare physical minimum, but varies from country to country, reflecting the cost of participating in the everyday life of society. The Afro-Equa line is more subjective, including indoor plumbing and potable water as a "necessity" in some countries but not in others. At the upper poverty line, 55 percent of the 1985 Indian population was below the poverty line.

Given information on income distribution, poverty is determined by finding the percentage of the population with an income of less than I\$370, and extreme poverty (at the India-based standard) by finding the share of the population with an income of less than I\$275. The assumption is that two persons with the same purchasing-power adjusted income (not including nonincome factors, such as access to public services) living in different countries will have the same measured poverty. Thirty-one percent, or 1.073 billion people in the developing world, and 22 percent of the total world population, were poor in 1985; 31 percent, or 1.116 billion people in LDCs, and 22 percent of the world, were poor in 1990; 30 percent, or 1.438 billion people in developing countries, and 25 percent of the world, were poor in 1996; and 24 percent, or 1.210 billion people in LDCs, or 20 percent of the world's population, were projected to be poor in 2000. In 1985, 18 percent, or 633 million people in developing countries, and 13 percent of the world, were in extreme poverty. These measures of poverty leave out many persons who are deprived *relative* to others around them. Indeed Ravallion, Datt, and van de Walle contend that, given the Afro-Equa I\$370 poverty standard, poverty in DCs is negligible.[10] Figure 6–1 shows the case where the left tail of the DC (right) curve exceeds the poverty line (P), which corresponds to 30 percent of the population in the LDC (left) curve.

---

[10]Martin Ravallion, Gaurav Datt, and Dominique van de Walle, "Quantifying Absolute Poverty in the Developing World," *Review of Income and Wealth* 37 (December 1991): 345–61; World Bank, *World Development Report, 1990* (New York: Oxford University Press, 1990), pp. 26–29, 139; and World Bank, *World Development Report, 1992* (New York: Oxford University Press, 1992), p. 30; and Montek S. Ahluwalia, Nicholas G. Carter, and Hollis B. Chenery, "Growth and Poverty in Developing Countries," *Journal of Development Economics* 6 (September 1979): 299–341.

There are several problems with defining a poverty line in terms of income needed to ensure a given supply of calories: (1) There is a substantial variation in the age and gender composition from one population to another; (2) caloric intakes at a given level of expenditure vary considerably; (3) specifying a single caloric norm is questionable; (4) variations in caloric requirements for the same individual occur; and (5) other nutrients, such as protein, vitamins, and minerals, are not considered. Nevertheless Nevin S. Scrimshaw and Lance Taylor in "Food," *Scientific American* 243 (September 1980): 81 indicate that as income rises, the consumption of other nutrients rises along with caloric consumption.

The adequacy of calories and other nutrients also depends on non-nutritional factors as well, including potable water, immunization, general medical care, sanitation, and personal hygiene. Partha Dasgupta, *An Inquiry into Well-Being and Destitution* (Oxford: Clarendon Press, 1993), p. 405.

For criticisms of the World Bank approach and a proposal for an improved method of measuring poverty, see V. V. Bhanoji Rao, "Measurement of Deprivation and Poverty Based on the Proportion Spent on Food: an Explanatory Exercise," *World Development* 9 (April 1981): 337–53. See also Harold Alderman, "New Research on Poverty and Malnutrition: What Are the Implications for Policy?" in Michael Lipton and Jacques van der Gaag, eds., *Including the Poor—Proceedings of a Symposium Organized by the World Bank and the International Food Policy Research Institute* (Washington, D.C.: World Bank, 1993), pp. 115–131.

FIGURE 6-1   Income Distribution in Rich and Poor Countries

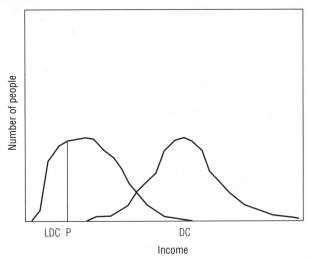

Concepts and Measures of Poverty: Amartya Sen's Approach

Harvard University economist-philosopher Amartya K. Sen contends that traditional welfare economics, which stresses the revealed preferences or desire-based
utilities of individuals in their acts of choice, lacks enough information about people's preferences to assess the social good. Accordingly, as an alternative, Sen's
welfare theory relies not on individuals' attainments (for example, of basic needs)
but individuals' capabilities, an approach he believes can draw on a richer information base. For Sen, living consists of a vector of interrelated functionings (beings and doings), such as being adequately nourished, avoiding premature mortality, appearing in public without shame, being happy, and being free. Yet Sen
does not assign particular weights to these functionings, as well-being is a "broad
and partly opaque concept," which is intrinsically ambiguous.

Sen focuses on a small number of basic functionings central to well-being: to
be adequately fed and sheltered and in good health. GNP per capita, which measures **capabilities**, does not correlate closely with these functionings, which indicate attainments, Sen contends. One example is life expectancy, a proxy for health,
which, at 75 years, is almost as high for Costa Rica as for the U.S. (76 years), which
has an income per head 12 times as high. Moreover, men in the Harlem district of
New York City, despite the capability sets and choices available to the U.S. society,
have less chance of living to 40 years than men in Bangladesh. This is not because
Harlem has a lower GNP per capita than Bangladesh, Sen explains, but because of
the high urban crime rate, inadequacy of medical attention, racism, and other factors that reduce Harlem's basic attainments.[11] Although people in Harlem have a

---

[11]According to the United States Justice Department's Bureau of Justice Statistics, in the U.S., African-
American men aged 12 to 24 years were victims of homicide at a rate of 114.9 per 100,000 in 1992, compared to 11.7 per 100,000 for white men of the same age, and 8.5 per 100,000 for the general U.S. population. "Blacks at Higher Risk of Murder, Report Says," *Kansas City Star* (December 9, 1994), p. A4.

Bruce P. Corrie discusses "The Human Development Index for the Black Child in the United
States," an HDI for each of the fifty states based on poverty rates, low birthweight, incarceration rates,
and unemployment rates for African-Americans, in *Challenge* (January-February 1994): 53–55.

greater command of resources than those in Bangladesh, the costs of social functionings, which include avoiding public shame and participating in the life of the community, are higher for Harlem residents (as well as U.S. residents generally, Sen argues) than for Bangladeshis.[12]

For Sen, poverty is not low well-being but the inability to pursue well-being because of the lack of economic means. This lack may not always result from a deficiency of capabilities. An extreme example will illustrate this even more clearly than that of the Harlem case. If Mr. Richman has a high income, but squanders it so that he lives miserably, it would be odd to call him "poor." Here poverty is the failure of basic capabilities to reach minimally acceptable levels.[13]

Sen argues against relying only on poverty percentage or **head-count approach** (H) to measure poverty and deprivation, the approach of World Bank economists, Montek S. Ahluwalia, Nicholas G. Carter, and Hollis B. Chenery.[14] As D.L. Blackwood and R.G. Lynch assert in their criticism of Ahluwalia et al.: "Poverty does not end abruptly once an additional dollar of income raises a family's (or individual's) income beyond a discretely defined poverty line. It is more accurate to conceive of poverty as a continuous function of varying gradation."[15] In addition to (H), Sen contends, we need an **income-gap approach** (I), which measures the additional income needed to bring the poor up to the level of the poverty line. This gap can be expressed in per capita terms, that is, as the average shortfall of income from the poverty line. Having measures of H, as well as I, should reduce the strong temptation government faces to concentrate on the *richest* among the poorest, thus merely minimizing the percentage of the population in poverty (minimizing H) rather than minimizing the average deprivation of the poor (I). For Sen, adding an empirical measure, I, should improve policy effectiveness.

Table 6–1 from the World Bank (1990), which by then had become convinced of the validity of Sen's critique of Bank-type analyses of poverty, illustrates both the headcount and income-gap concepts. While 30 percent of sub-Saharan Africa's population was extremely poor (using the India-based lower poverty line), a transfer of 4 percent of GNP by the sub-Sahara would bring the income of every extremely poor person exactly up to the lower poverty line.

Ravallion, Datt, and van de Walle show that the LDCs' 1-percent extreme poverty (Indian-standard) gap (Table 6–1) could be reduced by a 1-percent transfer from LDC consumption *or* a one-half of one-percent transfer from world consumption. This assumes perfect nondistortionary targeting to the extreme poor. Alas, we do not have the perfect information essential to identify and target the poor. Yet we not only have information on which countries have extreme poverty, but even more detailed information on the regions, classes, and communities of

[12]Robert Sugden, "Welfare, Resources, and Capabilities: A Review of *Inequality Reexamined* by Amartya Sen," *Journal of Economic Literature* 31 (December 1993): 1947–62; C. McCord and H.P. Freeman, "Excess Mortality in Harlem," *New England Journal of Medicine* 322 (18 January 1990); and Amartya Sen, *Inequality Reexamined* (Cambridge, Mass.: Harvard University Press, 1992). Sen's 1992 book is the capstone of years of work, including *On Economic Inequality* (Oxford: Clarendon Press, 1973): *Poverty and Famines: An Essay on Entitlement and Deprivation* (Oxford: Clarendon Press, 1981); *On Ethics and Economics* (Oxford: Blackwell, 1987).

[13]Amartya Sen, *Inequality Reexamined* (Cambridge, Mass.: Harvard University Press, 1992), pp. 102–16.

[14]Montek S. Ahluwalia, Nicholas G. Carter, and Hollis B. Chenery, "Growth and Poverty in Developing Countries," *Journal of Development Economics* 6 (September 1979): 299–341.

[15]D.L. Blackwood and R.G. Lynch, "The Measurement of Inequality and Poverty: A Policy Maker's Guide to the Literature," *World Development* 22 (April 1994): 569.

TABLE 6–1 How Much Poverty Is There in the Developing Countries? The Situation in 1985

Region	Lower Poverty Line (India Standard) Extremely Poor			Upper Poverty Line (Afro-Equa-Bengal Standard) Poor (Including Extremely Poor)			Social Indicators		
	Number (millions)	Head Count Index (percent)	Poverty Gap	Number (millions)	Head-Count Index (percent)	Poverty Gap	Under 5 Mortality (per thousand)	Life Expectancy (yrs)	Net Primary Enrollment Rate (percent)
Sub-Saharan Africa	120	30	4	184	48	11	196	50	56
East Asia	120	9	0.4	182	13	1	96	67	96
China	80	8	1	136	13	2	58	69	93
South and Southeast Asia	300	29	3	532	49	10	172	56	74
India	250	33	4	404	53	12	199	57	81
Eastern Europe	3	4	0.2	5	7	0.4	23	71	90
Middle East and North Africa	40	21	1	60	31	2	148	61	75
Latin America	50	12	1	110	19	1	75	66	92
All developing countries	633	18	1	1,073	31	3	121	62	83

Note: the poverty line in 1985 is I$275 per capita a year (or 275 purchasing-power adjusted dollars) for the extremely poor and I$370 per capita a year for the poor.

The headcount index is defined as the percentage of the population below the poverty line.

The poverty gap is defined as the aggregate income shortfall of the poor as a percentage of aggregate consumption. Under 5–year mortality rates are for 1980–85, except for China and South Asia, where the period is 1975–80.

Source: World Bank, *World Development Report, 1990* (New York: Oxford University Press, 1990), p. 29, with adjustments for population estimates and subsequent revisions in the number and headcount index of the poor.

the extreme poor. However, as the next section indicates, gains from transfers or distribution-neutral growth could be wiped out by the steady increase in global income inequality.[16]

A third empirical measure Sen recommends is the distribution of income among the poor, as measured by the Gini coefficient (G). Combining G, H, and I, which together represent the Sen measure for assessing the seriousness of absolute poverty, satisfies Sen's three axioms for a poverty index: (1) the focus axiom, which stipulates that the measure depend only on the incomes of the poor, (2) the monotonicity axiom, which requires that the poverty index increase when the incomes of the poor decrease, and (3) the weak transfer axiom, which requires that the poverty measure be sensitive to changes in the income distribution of the poor (so that a transfer of income from a lower-income poor household to a higher-income household increases the index).

---

[16]Martin Ravallion, Gaurav Datt, and Dominique van de Walle, "Quantifying Absolute Poverty in the Developing World," *Review of Income and Wealth* 37 (December 1991): 345–61.

The Lorenz Curve and Gini Index (G): Measures of the Distribution of Income

This discussion, however, is not limited to the income distribution of the poor but focuses on the Gini as a tool for measuring the overall income concentration among both nonpoor and poor.

Indices of income distribution measure relative poverty rather than absolute poverty. Income inequalities are often shown on a **Lorenz curve** (see Figure 6–2). If income distribution were perfectly equal, it would be represented by the 45° line (a). If one person, represented at the extreme right, received all the income, the Lorenz curve would follow half the perimeter of the box, the x-axis, and the right line parallel to the y-axis (e). In practice Lorenz curves are located between the 45° line and the line of complete inequality. Table 6–2, columns 2 and 3, shows the personal income distribution of two countries. Next to sparsely-populated Botswana,

FIGURE 6–2   Lorenz Curves for Bangladesh, Brazil, and the World

The Lorenz curve indicates a higher income inequality for the world than for Brazil, the country (with data) that has the world's highest personal income inequality. Curve *b* shows the income inequality for Bangladesh, the country with the world's lowest personal income inequality.

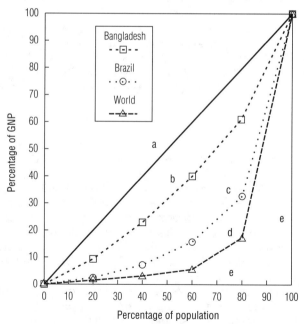

Sources: World Bank, *World Development Report, 1993* (New York: Oxford University Press, 1993), pp. 296–97; and United Nations Development Program, *Human Development Report, 1992* (New York: Oxford University Press, 1992), p. 36.

TABLE 6-2 Personal Income Distribution for Bangladesh, Brazil, and the World

(1) Population Quintile	(2) Bangladesh (1988–89) (percent)	(3) Brazil (1991) (percent)	(4) World (1989) (percent)
1	9.5	2.1	1.4
2	13.4	4.9	1.8
3	17.0	8.9	2.3
4	21.6	16.8	11.8
5	38.5	67.3	62.7
Total	100.0	100.0	100.0
Gini coefficient	0.26	0.57	0.87

Sources: World Bank, *World Development Report, 1993* (New York: Oxford University Press, 1993), pp. 296–97; and United Nations Development Program, *Human Development Report, 1992* (New York: Oxford University Press, 1990), p. 36.

with 1.5 million people, Brazil is the country with data that has the world's highest personal income inequality. (South Africa, which may be as high, lacks personal income distribution data; however, the richest 5 percent of the population, mostly white, owns 88 percent of all assets.)[17] Bangladesh is the country with the lowest inequality.

Income concentration for some DCs, such as Japan, may be as low or even lower than that for Bangladesh; however, most DC measures of income inequality, which are for households rather than persons, are not comparable to measures available for the majority of LDCs. Economists would prefer surveys of larger units, the household, to that of the individual, so that low-earning members of high-earning families are not classified as poor. Data on household income allow researchers to express poverty on a per-capita basis, at least if information is available for researchers to adjust income for household size. Still one problem of household income data is the risk that researchers will ignore inequality *within* households.[18]

Table 6–2's data are arranged in ascending order from population quintile 1 (the 20 percent or one-fifth with the lowest income) to quintile 5 (the 20 percent with the highest income). These data are plotted on curves *b* and *c* in Figure 6–2.

At present most measures of income distribution are for countries, or regions within a country, but there is a growing perception of the global economy as an international system. LDC populations who demand a new international economic order assume that the welfare of a jute farm laborer in Bangladesh, a foundry worker in Brazil, a textile manufacturer in Kenya, and a cabinet minister in India are linked to decisions made by bankers, industrialists, and economic policymakers in the United States, Western Europe, and Japan. Developing countries compare their living standards to those of developed nations. Accordingly there is some validity to the concept of a world distribution of income.

Income inequality for the world exceeds that for any single country. The top 20 percent of the world's income-earning households receive 63 percent of the

[17]United Nations Development Program, *Human Development Report, 1993* (New York: Oxford University Press, 1993), p. 27.

[18]Gary S. Fields, "Poverty and Income Distribution: Data for Measuring Poverty and Inequality Changes in the Developing Countries," *Journal of Development Economics* 44 (June 1994): 89.

global income, and the bottom 40 percent receive only 3 percent. In Brazil, the top 20 percent of the households receive 67 percent of the income, and the bottom 40 percent, 7 percent. Brazil's curve c is to the left of the world's curve d in Figure 6–2.

When x and y are Lorenz curve coordinates (based on cumulative values, not the incremental values listed in Table 6–2), and Δx and Δy are corresponding increments passing through these coordinates, then the **Gini index of inequality**

$$G = \frac{2}{10,000} \sum (x - y) \Delta x \qquad (6\text{–}1)$$

Summations are taken as many times as there are Δx increments between the limits.[19] The Gini index is the area between curve a and the Lorenz curve as a proportion of the entire area below curve a. It ranges from a value of zero, representing equality, to 1, representing maximum inequality. The 1989 Gini for the world, 0.87, which increased from 0.69 in 1960 to 0.71 in 1970 to 0.79 in 1980, exceeds that for Brazil, 0.57. The global income distribution is more unequal than that within any single country, as cross-national disparities in GNP per capita are added to those of internal inequalities.[20]

Global Growth, Transfers, and Income Inequality

We discussed above the transfers essential to eliminate extreme poverty. With regard to applying growth to wipe out poverty, Ravallion, Datt, and van de Walle estimate that a 1-percent LDC per capita consumption growth, with income inequality unchanging, would reduce the poverty percentage, H, by 2 percent yearly. But the world Gini concentration is high and has been increasing steadily since 1960; the ratio of the share of the world's richest fifth to that of the world's poorest fifth almost doubled in the three decades before 1989 (Table 6–3 and Figure 6–3). And income concentration is expected to continue to increase through the last years of the twentieth century. Indeed Ravallion et al. estimate that the elasticity of the poverty gap with regard to the Gini index

$$\left(\text{Eq. } 6\text{–}1 \right) \qquad \frac{\dfrac{\left(H_2 - H_1 \right)}{\text{average } H}}{\dfrac{\left(G_2 - G_1 \right)}{\text{average } G}}$$

[19]Richard L. Merritt and Stein Rokkan, *Comparing Nations: The Use of Quantitative Data in Cross-National Research* (New Haven: Yale University Press, 1966), p. 364.

[20]Indeed between-country inequalities were by far the most significant component of world income inequalities (79 percent in 1965 and 86 percent in 1992). Within-country inequalities comprised 21 percent of global inequalities in 1965 and 14 percent in 1992. Roberto Patricio Korzeniewicz and Timothy P. Moran, "A Disaggregation of the World Distribution of Income into Between- and Within-Country Components, 1965–1992," Paper presented to the International Studies Association, Chicago, February 24–26, 1995.

For the method of calculating a global income distribution with national distributions given, see ibid.; Margaret E. Grosh and E. Wayne Nafziger, "The Computation of World Income Distribution," *Economic Development and Cultural Change* 34 (January 1986): 347–59; and Henri Theil, "World Income Inequality and Its Components," *Economic Letters* 2 (1979): 99–102.

TABLE 6-3	Global Income Disparity, 1960–89 Percentage of global income			
	World's Poorest 20%'s Share (%)	World's Richest 20%'s Share (%)	Richest to Poorest Ratio	Gini Coefficient
1960	2.3	70.2	30 to 1	0.69
1970	2.3	73.9	32 to 1	0.71
1980	1.7	76.3	45 to 1	0.79
1989	1.4	82.7	59 to 1	0.87

Source: United Nations Development Program, *Human Development Report, 1992* (New York: Oxford University Press, 1992), p. 36.

8.4 (where *1* is the earlier time period and *2* is the later time period), is so high that the effect of a growth of 16 percent in mean consumption, 1985–2000, on poverty would be offset by a 4.3 percent increase in the Gini index.[21]

FIGURE 6-3 Global Economic Disparities
Distribution of economic activity, 1989—percentage of world total (Quintiles of population ranked by income)

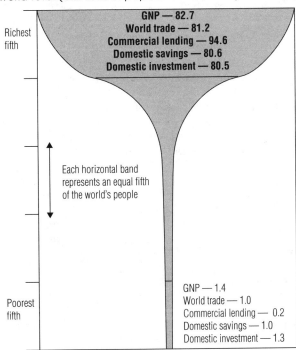

Source: United Nations Development Program, *Human Development Report, 1992* (New York: Oxford University Press, 1992), p. 35.

[21]Martin Ravallion, Gaurav Datt, and Dominique van de Walle, "Quantifying Absolute Poverty in the Developing World," *Review of Income and Wealth* 37 (December 1991): 345–61.

Early and Late Stages of Development

Nobel economist Simon Kuznets hypothesized that during industrialization, inequality follows an inverted U-shaped curve, first increasing and then decreasing with economic growth. Initially, growth results in lower income shares for the poor and higher income shares for the rich.[22] Irma Adelman's and Cynthia Taft Morris's explanation for the **Kuznets curve** presupposes that LDCs are characterized by a dual economy (Chapter 4) in which the modern sector's income and productivity are significantly higher than the traditional sector's. They indicate that when economic growth and migration from the traditional to the modern sector begin in a subsistence agrarian economy (production mostly for the use of the cultivator and his family) through the expansion of a narrow modern sector (primarily manufacturing, mining, and processing), income inequality typically increases. Income inequalities have especially worsened where foreign exploitation of natural resources triggered growth. Data indicate that the income shares of the poorest 60 percent and middle 20 percent decline significantly in such a context while the share of the top 5 percent increases strikingly—particularly in low-income countries with a sharply dualistic economy dominated by traditional or foreign elites.[23]

Once countries move beyond this early stage, further development generates no particular increase nor decrease in shares for the top 5 percent. At the very highest income level of a developing country, broad-based social and economic advances usually operate to its relative disadvantage, at least if the government *enlarges* its role in the economic sphere. However, according to Adelman and Morris, the share of the top 5 percent increases if more natural resources become available for exploitation.

Middle-income groups are the primary beneficiaries of economic development beyond the early, dualistic stage. The first more widely based social and economic advances typically favor the middle sector.

As indicated earlier, the relative position of the poorest 60 percent typically worsens when growth begins. The modern sector competes with the traditional sector for markets and resources, and the result is a decline in the income *shares* of the poor. Such a decline occurred when peasants became landless workers during the European land consolidation of the sixteenth through the nineteenth centuries and when high-yielding varieties of grains were first used on commercial farms in India and Pakistan. Even when economic growth becomes more broadly based, the poorest segments of the population increase their income shares only when the government expands its role, widening opportunities for education and training for lower-income groups.[24]

Do country data over time provide evidence that inequality follows an inverted U-shaped curve as economic development takes place? Time–series data

---

[22]This proposition was first advanced by Simon Kuznets, "Economic Growth and Income Inequality," *American Economic Review* 45 (March 1955): 1–28.

[23]Irma Adelman and Cynthia Taft Morris, *Economic Growth and Social Equity in Developing Countries* (Stanford: Stanford University Press, 1973), contend that income, not just income shares, falls in early stages of growth, but their evidence does not support this.

[24]Irma Adelman and Cynthia Taft Morris, *Economic Growth and Social Equity in Developing Countries* (Stanford: Stanford University Press, 1973), pp. 178–83; and Irma Adelman and Cynthia Taft Morris, "Growth and Impoverishment in the Middle of the Nineteenth Century," *World Development* 6 (March 1978): 245–73.

for individual countries are scarce and unreliable, and many LDCs have not yet arrived at a late enough stage of development to test the declining portion of the upside-down U curve. However, the time–series data available suggest the plausibility of the inverted U-shaped curve for DCs. Income concentration in Britain, Germany, Belgium, the Netherlands, and Denmark increased from preindustrialization to early industrialization and decreased from early to late industrialization. Indeed, in late nineteenth century Europe, inequality was very high and was highest in Britain, where the top 10 percent received 50 percent of the income and the bottom 20 percent 4 percent. This distribution is close to that of Brazil and Panama today, where the top 10 percent receive 40 to 50 percent and the bottom 20 percent 2 percent. Second, the most reliable data for today's LDCs suggest that since 1970, inequality rose in low-income and lower-middle-income Bangladesh, the Philippines, Colombia, and Thailand and fell in middle-income Taiwan, supporting the inverted U, but declined in low-income and lower-middle-income Pakistan, Costa Rica, and Peru and increased in middle-income Argentina, Brazil, and Mexico, exceptions to the inverted U.[25] Thus, while the historical growth of early industrializing Europe followed an inverted U, the evidence for today's LDCs is too mixed and inconclusive to confirm the Kuznets curve.

Low-, Middle-, and High-Income Countries

INCOME INEQUALITY IN LOW-, MIDDLE-, AND HIGH-INCOME COUNTRIES

Evidence for the Kuznets curve is stronger when we classify a group of countries *in a given time period* by per capita income levels. The relationship between inequality (as measured by the Gini index) and gross domestic product per capita is an inverted U skewed to the right (Figure 6–4). Figure 6–4, based on World Bank estimates of income distribution in 54 countries during the 1980s and early 1990s, exemplifies the upside-down U relationship. Ahluwalia ranks income inequality as high if the income share of the poorest 40 percent is less than 12 percent of GNP; moderate if it is between 12 and 17 percent; and low if 17 percent and above.[26] Table 6–4, which includes the same 54 countries, indicates 27 percent of low-income countries, 30 percent of middle-income countries, and 0 percent of high-income

---

[25]Jeffrey G. Williamson, *Inequality, Poverty, and History: The Kuznets Memorial Lectures of the Economic Growth Center, Yale University* (Oxford: Basil Blackwell, 1991), pp. 10–13; World Bank, *World Development Report, 1993* (New York: Oxford University Press, 1993), pp. 296–97; R.M. Sundrum, *Income Distribution in Less Developed Countries* (London: Routledge, 1992), pp. 117–21; Simon Kuznets, "Quantitative Aspects of the Economic Growth of Nations: VIII, Distribution of Income by Size," *Economic Development and Cultural Change* 11, no. 2, part 2 (January 1963): 58–67; Jacques Lecaillon, Felix Paukert, Christian Morrisson, and Dimitri Germidis, *Income Distribution and Economic Development: An Analytical Survey* (Geneva: International Labor Office, 1984), pp. 42–43; Cynthia Taft Morris and Irma Adelman, *Comparative Patterns of Economic Development, 1850–1914* (Baltimore: Johns Hopkins University Press, 1988); and Gary S. Fields, *Poverty, Inequality, and Development* (Cambridge: Cambridge University Press, 1980), pp. 78–98.

[26]Montek S. Ahluwalia, Nicholas G. Carter, and Hollis B. Chenery, "Growth and Poverty in Developing Countries," *Journal of Development Economics* 6 (September 1979): 299–341; and Montek S. Ahluwalia, "Income Inequality," in Hollis Chenery, Montek S. Ahluwalia, C. L. G. Bell, John H. Duloy, and Richard Jolly, eds., *Redistribution with Growth* (London: Oxford University Press, 1974), pp. 1–22.

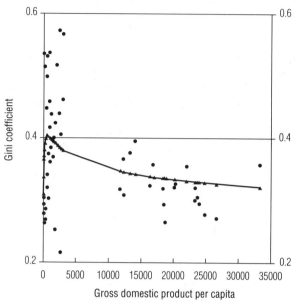

FIGURE 6–4   Income Inequality and per Capita Income
As per capita income increases, income inequality (the
Gini index) first increases and then decreases. The trend
line for the predicted Gini is an inverted U skewed to
the right.

GNP per capita is for 1991, and Gini coefficient for latest
available data, 1981–1991, for personal distribution of GNP.
Gini = 0.6089 – 17.0296 (1/GNP per capita) –0.0278 ln(GNP per capita)
      (0.0941)   (8.997)   (0.0107)
with the coefficients for (1/GNP per capita) and ln (GNP per capita)
significant at the 1 percent level.
Source: World Bank, *World Development Report, 1993*
(New York: Oxford University Press, 1993), pp. 238–39, 296–97.

countries have high income inequality. On the other hand, 71 percent of low-income countries, 20 percent of middle-income countries, and 70 percent of high-income countries have low inequality. Accordingly income inequality increases as we move from low- to middle-income countries and declines from middle- to high-income countries, confirming the inverted U. The cross-sectional and DC time-series data but *not* the LDC time-series data support the hypothesis that inequality follows an inverted U-shaped curve as per capita income increases.

The variance around the estimated curve is greater from low to middle levels of development. Indeed, if we exclude Latin America, the proportion of middle-income countries with high inequality falls from 20 percent to 10 percent, a figure less than that for low-income countries' high concentration, now 21 percent (Table 6–4). Could the inverted U at a given time be a historical artifact, reflecting the fact that Latin America countries, who comprise a majority of middle-income

TABLE 6-4 Differences in Income Inequality between High-, Middle-, and Low-Income Countries

High Inequality—Share of Lowest 40 Percent Less Than 12 Percent				Moderate Inequality—Share of Lowest 40 Percent Between 12 Percent and 17 Percent				Low Inequality— Share Of Lowest 40 Percent, 17 Percent and Above			
Country	Lowest 40%	Middle 40%	Top 20%	Country	Lowest 40%	Middle 40%	Top 20%	Country	Lowest 40%	Middle 40%	Top 20%

Developing countries (personal income or expenditure distribution shares):
Low-income countries (less than U.S. $650):

Country	Lowest 40%	Middle 40%	Top 20%	Country	Lowest 40%	Middle 40%	Top 20%	Country	Lowest 40%	Middle 40%	Top 20%
Tanzania (1991)	8.1	29.1	62.8	Sri Lanka (1985–86)	13.3	30.6	56.1	Ethiopia (1981–82)	21.3	37.5	41.2
Kenya[a] (1981–83)	9.1	30.0	60.9					Uganda (1989–90)	20.6	37.5	41.9
Honduras (1989)	8.7	27.8	63.5					Nepal (1984–85)	22.0	38.5	39.5
Lesotho (1986–87)	11.0	27.6	61.4					Bangladesh (1988–89)	22.9	38.6	38.5
								Rwanda (1983–85)	22.8	38.3	38.9
								India (1989–90)	21.3	37.5	41.2
								China (1990)	17.4	40.8	41.8
								Ghana (1989–90)	18.3	37.6	44.1
								Pakistan (1991)	21.3	39.1	39.6
								Indonesia (1990)	20.8	37.0	42.2

Middle-income countries (U.S. $650-U.S. $8,000):

Country	Lowest 40%	Middle 40%	Top 20%	Country	Lowest 40%	Middle 40%	Top 20%	Country	Lowest 40%	Middle 40%	Top 20%
Guatemala (1989)	7.9	29.1	63.0	Philippines (1988)	16.6	35.6	47.8	Ivory Coast (1988)	19.2	38.6	42.2
Panama (1989)	8.3	31.9	59.8	Dominican Republic (1989)	12.1	32.2	55.7	Morocco (1990–91)	17.1	36.7	46.2
Chile (1989)	10.5	26.5	63.0	Peru (1985–86)	14.1	34.7	51.2	Poland (1989)	23.0	40.9	36.1
Botswana (1985–85)	6.0	27.6	66.4	Colombia (1988)	12.7	34.3	53.0	Hungary (1989)	25.7	40.0	34.3
Brazil (1989)	7.0	25.7	67.3	Jamaica (199)	15.9	35.8	48.3				
Mexico (1984)	11.9	32.2	55.9	Tunisia (1990)	16.3	37.4	46.3				
				Thailand (1988)	15.5	33.8	50.7				
				Costa Rica (1989)	13.1	36.2	50.7				
				Malaysia (1989)	12.9	33.4	53.7				
				Venezuela (1989)	14.3	36.3	49.4				
				Yugoslavia (1989)	16.0	39.9	44.1				

TABLE 6-4   Continued

Country	High Inequality—Share of Lowest 40 Percent Less Than 12 Percent			Country	Moderate Inequality—Share of Lowest 40 Percent Between 12 Percent and 17 Percent			Country	Low Inequality— Share Of Lowest 40 Percent, 17 Percent and Above		
	Lowest 40%	Middle 40%	Top 20%		Lowest 40%	Middle 40%	Top 20%		Lowest 40%	Middle 40%	Top 20%

Developed countries (household income distribution shares):
High-income countries (more than U.S. $8,000)

Country				Country	Lowest 40%	Middle 40%	Top 20%	Country	Lowest 40%	Middle 40%	Top 20%
				New Zealand (1981–82)	15.9	39.4	44.7	Israel (1979)	18.1	42.3	39.6
				Hong Kong (1980)	16.2	36.8	47.0	Spain (1980–81)	19.4	40.5	40.1
				Singapore (1982–83)	15.0	36.0	49.0	United Kingdom (1979)	17.3	43.2	39.5
				Australia (1985)	15.5	42.3	42.2	Italy (1986)	18.8	40.2	41.0
				United States (1985)	15.7	42.4	41.9	Netherlands (1983)	20.1	41.6	38.3
				Switzerland (1982)	16.9	38.5	44.6	Belgium (1978–79)	21.6	42.4	36.0
								France (1979)	18.4	40.7	40.9
								Canada (1987)	17.5	42.3	40.2
								Germany (Federal Republic) (1984)	19.5	41.9	38.6
								Denmark (1981)	17.4	44.0	38.6
								Finland (1981)	19.4	43.9	37.7
								Norway (1979)	19.0	44.2	36.8
								Sweden (1981)	21.2	41.9	36.9
								Japan (1979)	21.9	40.6	37.5

[a]Based on household income distribution shares.

Source: World Bank, *World Development Report, 1993* (New York: Oxford University Press, 1993), pp. 238–39, 296–97.

countries, tend to have high income concentration?[27] Economic historian Jeffrey G. Williamson argues that cross-sectional data are not likely to show that inequality rises systematically; correlations between income inequality and early modern

---

[27]Harry T. Oshima, "The Impact of Technological Transformation on Historical Trends in Income Distribution of Asia and the West," *Developing Economies* 23 (September 1994): 237–55, shows a Kuznets curve for Asia with similar pattern to, but below, that of the West. Oshima also argues that electronic technologies of automation, computers, and robots, by making middle managers, wholesalers, intermediaries, supervisors, clerks, secretaries, typists, and some manual workers redundant while improving the problem-solving capacity of workers on the factory floor, increased inequality in the United States, adding an upward tail to the inverted U. However, Japan's Ginis have not increased, perhaps reflecting substantially different employment and retraining policies by firms.

economic growth "are bound to be poor since history has given less developed countries very different starting points."[28] Indeed, there is much more variation in relative inequality *within* country income groups than *between* them. (We discuss factors other than income below.) Income level is an imprecise predictor of a country's income inequality.[29]

INCOME INEQUALITY IN DEVELOPED AND DEVELOPING COUNTRIES

The overwhelming majority of developed (high-income) countries have low income inequality (and none have high income inequality), while only about two-fifths of the developing countries have low inequality (and one-fourth to one-third high inequality). The income shares of the poor are higher and their variance lower in DCs than in LDCs. While Table 6–4's conclusion that the poorest 40 percent in high-income countries receive 18 percent compared to 18 percent for low-income countries is not distorted, the indication that poor in middle-income countries receive 13 percent overstates their equality. First, in LDCs personal and household income concentrations are approximately the same, whereas in DCs concentrations for persons is less than for households, since household size increases rapidly from lower- to upper-income classes. Suppose that DCs, whose income distribution is ranked by households, would have followed the approach of the LDCs in having their income distribution data ranked by persons. Then DC distribution data would have been even more egalitarian vis-à-vis LDC data than what appears in Figure 6–4 and Table 6–4. Second, in DCs, inequalities measured over a lifetime are markedly lower than those measured over a year, while in LDCs inequalities do not vary with the period chosen. Third, LDC life expectancies are highly correlated with average incomes, frequently contributing to interethnic, metropolitan-rural, and skilled-unskilled working life disparities of 10 to 15 years; in DCs these disparities are usually not so great. (In the United States, where these disparities are greater than for DCs generally, a 76.5-year life expectancy for white Americans compares to an African-American life expectancy of 70.8 years.) Fourth, progressive income taxes (with higher tax *rates* for higher incomes) and social welfare programs make income more equal in developed countries than Table 6–4 indicates. Fifth, however LDC (especially in a low-income country) urban-rural income discrepancies are overstated, since rural in-kind incomes are undervalued and rural living costs are usually 10 to 20 percent lower than urban costs. Sixth, retained corporate profits, which accrue disproportionately to upper-income classes, and are a significant fraction of GNP in DCs and many middle-income countries but usually omitted in income distribution estimates, contribute to overstating equality in high-income countries. Thus overall the first four distortions are probably balanced by the fifth and sixth distortions, so that the comparison in Table 6–4 of DCs' and low-income countries' income distributions is unchanged. However, middle-income countries are affected so little by distortions 5 and 6 that these are outweighed by the first four distortions, which increase the disparity in income concentrations between DCs and

[28]Jeffrey G. Williamson, *Inequality, Poverty, and History: The Kuznets Memorial Lectures of the Economic Growth Center, Yale University* (Oxford: Basil Blackwell, 1991), p. 8.

[29]Gary S. Fields, *Poverty, Inequality, and Development* (Cambridge: Cambridge University Press, 1980), p. 67.

middle-income countries in Table 6–4.[30] These distortions make the inverted U even more pronounced than data suggest.

Absolute Poverty in Developing Countries

Information on relative income inequality in developing countries does not indicate much about the extent of absolute poverty. Current interest in income distribution reflects a concern that nutrition, shelter, health, education, sanitation, and so forth, meet certain minimum standards.

Previously in this chapter, we defined the concept of an international poverty line based on the income (I\$370 per capita in 1985) to provide consumption for essentials in excess of a bare physical minimum. According to this standard, 30 percent of the developing world (Latin America, Africa, non-Japanese Asia, and parts of Eastern Europe) was poor in 1996 (see Table 6–5).

TABLE 6-5   Population below the Poverty Line in Developing Countries, 1996

	GNP per Capita, 1992 (U.S. dollars)	Population 1996 (millions)	Percentage of Population in Poverty[a]	Number of People in Poverty (millions)
South and Southeast Asia				
(all countries)	310	1757	41	716
Afghanistan	..	19	53	10
Bangladesh	180	122	78	95
India	310	955	40	382
Indonesia	670	197	25	49
Malaysia	2790	20	16	3
Myanmar (Burma)	..	46	35	16
Nepal	170	22	60	13
Pakistan	420	134	28	38
Philippines	770	70	54	38
Sri Lanka	540	19	40	8
Thailand	1840	60	30	18
Vietnam	..	77	54	42
East Asia				
(excluding Japan)	780	1447	8	117
China	470	1221	9	110
South Korea	6790	46	5	2
Sub-Saharan Africa				
(all countries)	530	601	49	292
Botswana	2790	2	46	1
Burundi	210	6	84	5
Cameroon	820	14	37	5
Chad	220	6	54	3
Ethiopia (including Eritrea)	110	62	60	40

---

[30]Jacques Lecaillon, Felix Paukert, Christian Morrisson, and Dimitri Germidis, *Income Distribution and Economic Development: An Analytical Survey* (Geneva: International Labor Office, 1984), pp. 34–52; Simon Kuznets, "Demographic Aspects of the Size Distribution of Income: An Exploratory Essay," *Economic Development and Cultural Change* 25 (October 1976): 1–44; United Nations Development Program, *Human Development Report, 1993* (New York: Oxford University Press, 1993), pp. 18, 26; United Nations Development Program, *Human Development Report, 1994* (New York: Oxford University Press, 1994), p. 98, the last two sources of which give figures on black-white disparities in the United States. In 1992, GDP per capita, in purchasing-power adjusted dollars, was \$22,000 for whites and \$17,100 for blacks, while infant mortality rates for whites was 8 per 1000 and for blacks 19.

TABLE 6-5   Continued

	GNP per Capita, 1992 (U.S. dollars)	Population 1996 (millions)	Percentage of Population in Poverty[a]	Number of People in Poverty (millions)
Ghana	450	18	42	8
Kenya	310	31	52	16
Lesotho	590	2	55	1
Madagascar	230	15	43	6
Malawi	210	11	82	9
Mali	310	10	54	5
Mozambique	60	17	59	10
Nigeria	320	104	40	42
Rwanda	250	8	85	7
Somalia	. .	10	60	6
Sudan	. .	30	84	25
Tanzania	110	30	58	17
Zaïre	. .	45	70	32
Zambia	. .	9	64	6
West Asia and North Africa (all countries)	1950	394	32	124
Algeria	1840	30	23	7
Egypt	640	62	23	14
Jordan	1120	4	16	1
Morocco	1030	30	37	11
Tunisia	1720	9	17	2
Latin America (all countries)	2690	487	36	183
Argentina	6050	35	16	6
Bolivia	680	9	60	5
Brazil	2770	159	47	74
Chile	2730	14	10	1
Colombia	1330	37	42	16
Costa Rica	1960	4	28	1
Dominican Republic	1050	8	55	4
Ecuador	1070	11	56	6
El Salvador	1170	6	52	3
Guatemala	980	11	70	8
Haiti	. .	7	72	5
Honduras	580	6	37	2
Mexico	3470	96	30	29
Nicaragua	340	4	20	1
Panama	2420	3	44	1
Paraguay	1380	5	36	2
Peru	950	24	32	8
Uruguay	3340	3	13	0.4
Venezuela	2910	22	31	7
Eastern Europe (excluding LDCs part of the former Soviet Union)[b]	. .	101	6	6
All developing countries (excluding the former Soviet Union)	1040	4787	30	1438

[a]Poverty percentages based on 1992. These were applied to the 1996 population figures in column 2 to calculate the 1996 poverty estimates in column 4.

[b]Data are lacking for the former Soviet Union.

Sources: All country poverty data are from United Nations Development Program, *Human Development Report, 1994* (New York: Oxford University Press, 1994), pp. 73, 134–35, 174–75; world regional data from World Bank, *World Development Report, 1992: Development and the Environment* (New York: Oxford University Press, 1992), p. 30; World Bank, *World Development Report, 1990* (New York: Oxford University Press, 1990), pp. 19, 139; and population data from Population Reference Bureau, *1993 World Population Data Sheet* (Washington, D.C.: Population Reference Bureau, 1993). World regional data sometimes had to be adjusted to be consistent with the aggregation of country data.

Michael P. Todaro, *Economic Development* (New York: Longman, 1994), p. 147, combines creditable but disparate sources on poverty rates, such as Eliana Cardoso and Ann Helwege, "Below the Line: Poverty in Latin America," *World Development* 20 (January 1992): 19–37, and World Bank, *World Development Report, 1990* (New York: Oxford University Press, 1990), pp. 19, 139, into one table, implying a parallel that is lacking.

If we can identify countries with large numbers of poor and the poverty groups within countries—our goal in the next several sections—we can more readily ascertain the types of policies and the population groups to target to reduce international poverty. Most of the poor are from countries with low levels of per capita income. Only a relative few are from nations with a highly unequal income distribution. In Table 6–5, India, China, and Bangladesh, all with low income inequality, comprise 41 percent of the poor (and 48 percent of the LDC population). Indeed India and Bangladesh, with 22 percent of the population, account for 33 percent of the poor. However, absolute poverty is present even in upper-middle income countries. High income inequality may make poverty an equally serious problem for a country with several times the per capita income of another. If China's data are accurate, 9 to 10 percent of the peoples of both China and Chile are considered poor, notwithstanding a GNP per head in Chile that is seven times China's. Highly-populated India and Nigeria, together with Colombia, have poverty rates of about 40–42 percent, although Colombia's 1992 GNP per head, $1,290, is four times that of either India or Nigeria. Moreover, though Mexico and Pakistan both have about one-third of their population poor, Mexico's income per capita is 2.5 times that of Pakistan's (Table 6–5).

Regions of the World

Table 6–6 indicates LDC numbers of poor and poverty rates and their changes from 1985 to projections for 2000. Poverty rates, which probably did not fall during the slow or negative growth of the 1980s, fell during the early 1990s, and are expected to fall in the late 1990s. South and Southeast Asia had the highest poverty rate in 1985, 52 percent compared to sub-Saharan Africa's 48 percent, while in 1990, South and Southeast Asia's rate was 49 percent compared to the sub-Sahara's 49 percent. There was a substantial margin of error, as South and Southeast Asia's 1985 poverty rate was in the range 51–53 percent, and sub-Saharan Africa's 1985 range was 20–77 percent (both with a 95-percent confidence level). Development economists generally believe that the most serious LDC poverty problems are in sub-Saharan Africa and South Asia.

West Asia and North Africa's (the Middle East's) poverty rate was third highest, 31 percent, in 1985 (with 13–51 percent range at the 95-percent level), and Latin America's rate fourth highest, 28 percent in 1985 (with 23–38 percent range). The two regions switched rankings in the 1990s, with Latin America the third highest in 1990, with 34 percent, compared to the Middle East's 33 percent; Latin America's poverty rate increased relative to the Middle East's in the 1990s. The lowest poverty rate among LDCs was Eastern Europe with 7 percent (with 8–11 percent range) in 1985 and 1990, and the second lowest rate was East Asia, with China comprising a majority of the population, 13 percent (with no range) in 1985 and 11 percent in 1990.[31] Chapter 7 indicates that China's reversal of urban bias may have reduced the urban-rural gap and thus overall income inequality from 1979, the beginning of agricultural reform, to 1985. While economists disagree on what happened to inequality, none doubt that China's rapid economic growth decreased poverty.

---

[31]Martin Ravallion, Gaurav Datt, and Dominique van de Walle, "Quantifying Absolute Poverty in the Developing World," *Review of Income and Wealth* 37 (December 1991): 354–55.

TABLE 6-6 Poverty in the Developing World, 1985-2000								
	Percentage of Population Below the Poverty Line				*Number of Poor (millions)*			
Region	*1985*	*1990*	*1996*	*2000*	*1985*	*1990*	*1996*	*2000*
All developing countries	31	31	30	24	1,073	1,166	1,438	1,210
South and Southeast Asia	52	49	41	37	532	562	716	511
East Asia	13	11	8	4	182	169	117	73
Sub-Saharan Africa	48	48	49	50	184	216	292	304
Middle East and North Africa	31	33	32	31	60	73	124	137
Latin America	28	34	38	36	110	141	183	181
Eastern Europe[a]	7	7	6	6	5	5	6	4
World	22	22	25	20	1,073	1,166	1,438	1,210

The poverty line, I$370 annual income per capita in 1985 purchasing power dollars, is based on estimates of Afro-Equa-Bengal poverty lines. In 1990 prices, the poverty line would be approximately I$420 annual income per capita.

[a]Does not include the former U.S.S.R.

Sources: United Nations Development Program, *Human Development Report, 1994* (New York: Oxford University Press, 1994), pp. 73, 134–35, 174–75; United Nations Development Program, *Human Development Report, 1992* (New York: Oxford University Press, 1992), p. 30. Estimates for 1996 are the author's, based on data from the same sources. The upward revisions of poverty rates for Latin America for the 1980s and early 1990s in the *Human Development Report, 1994* necessitated adjusting World Bank estimates for Latin America, LDCs, and the world for 1985.

Negative growth contributed to increases in poverty rates in sub-Saharan Africa, Latin America, and the Middle East from 1985 to the 1990s. Growth in Asia (especially China and other parts of East Asia) contributed to falling poverty rates there.

Slow and Fast Growers

As already indicated, countries at earlier and lower levels of development are more likely to experience increases in income inequality. However, higher rates of economic growth, which are only weakly correlated with GNP per capita, are not associated with either greater equality or inequality. Both fast growers, such as Malaysia, Chile, and Botswana, and slow growers, such as Brazil, Tanzania, Kenya, Honduras, Guatemala, Dominican Republic, and Panama have high income inequalities. And slow-growing Ethiopia, Uganda, Ghana, the Ivory Coast, Poland, and Hungary and fast-growing China, Taiwan, India, Pakistan, Indonesia, and Israel have low income inequalities.

To be sure, Alberto Alesina and Dani Rodrik find that income inequality is negatively correlated with subsequent economic growth among DCs. But when less reliable data from LDCs are included, the coefficient is no longer statistically significant at the 5 percent level. Moreover, the lack of significance holds true for both democracies and nondemocracies.[32]

Women, Inequality, and Male Dominance

Development economics assumes that government policies should be directed to resource allocation among households or families. Partha Dasgupta, however, stresses the allocation of food, education, health care, and work between men and women, young and old, boys and girls, and lower- and higher-birth-order children. Most data are biased, Dasgupta contends, because they fail to show this major source of interpersonal inequality. In many parts of the world, income inequality would be 30 to 40 percent higher if intrahousehold distribution were included. Gender ideologies commonly support the notion that men have the right to personal spending money (sometimes even when overall income is inadequate), while women's income is for collective purposes. According to Dasgupta, the higher infant mortality and other age-specific death rates for females relative to males in India, China, and the Middle East indicate a substantial antifemale bias in nutrition and health care. Indeed M.R. Rosenzweig and T.P. Schultz argue that the lower rates of returns to female relative to male labor explains the low survival rates among girls.[33]

In most precolonial Afro-Asian societies, patriarchal authority severely limited the power of women, who were protected if they were deferential to the patriarchs. Yet some societies gave women clearly defined economic roles, allowing wealth accumulation and limited economic authority.

Most Afro-Asian women lost their limited power under colonialism. Men received land titles, extension assistance, technical training, and education. When men left farms to seek employment, as in South Africa, women remained burdened with responsibility for the family's food. A few women, especially West African market traders, became wealthy, but the majority worked long hours to survive. In the 1930s through 1950s, colonial authorities colluded with patriarchal indigenous leaders to increase control over women. In some instances, where they had an independent economic base, women used traditional female organizations and methods, not confrontation to male authority, to oppose both European and local authorities. Women played a prominent role in many of the early nationalist struggles, especially when colonialists threatened their economic interests.

After independence low female literacy (two-thirds that for men, now three-fourth of men's in LDCs), limited economic opportunity, and domestic burdens relegated women to the lowest economic rungs, even in countries claiming to be socialist, such as Ethiopia, which allocated land to male family heads during land

---

[32]Alberto Alesina and Dani Rodrik, "Distributive Politics and Economic Growth," *Quarterly Journal of Economics* 109 (May 1994): 465–90.

[33]Partha Dasgupta, *An Inquiry into Well-Being and Destitution* (Oxford: Clarendon Press, 1993), p. 17, 311; Amartya Sen, *Inequality Reexamined* (Cambridge, Mass.: Harvard University Press, 1992), pp. 122–25; M.R. Rosenzweig and T.P. Schultz, "Market Opportunities, Genetic Endowments and the Intra family Allocation of Resources: Child Survival in Rural India," *American Economic Review* 72 (September 1982): 803–15; and Daisy Dwyer and Judith Bruce, eds., *A Home Divided: Women and Income in the Third World* (Stanford, Calif.: Stanford University Press, 1988), pp. 1–11.

reform in the 1970s. Government agricultural policy favored male heads of households and development plans often ignored women. Moreover, male migration to urban areas or to neighboring countries (as in Yemen, the Sudan, and Botswana) place women at a further disadvantage. Nevertheless economic or political crises sometimes benefit women, as men seek new alliances between sexes in rebuilding weak economies and polities.

The International Labor Organization estimates that women comprised 513 million, or 34 percent (roughly an unchanging proportion during the late twentieth century) of the LDC labor force of 1,510 million and 766 million, or 36 percent, of the global labor force of 2,129 million in 1990. Females receive an average income half that of males in LDCs (three-fourths in Latin America), partly from **crowding,** the tendency to discriminate against women (and minorities) in well-paying jobs, forcing them to increase the supply of labor for menial or low-paying jobs. Though women are frequently the backbone of the rural economy, in a modernizing economy, they enjoy few advantages. While men seek wage employment in cities, women play the dominant role in small-scale farming, often on smaller plots and with lower returns than male-headed households. Women's workloads are heavy as a result of childbearing (five children in the average rural LDC family), carrying water (two hours spent daily by many African women), collecting wood, increased weeding from new crop varieties, and other farm tasks due to growing rural population pressures. Additionally, when technological innovations increase the productivity of cash crops, men frequently divert hectarage from women's food crops. Moreover, women as a rule receive lower returns to training and education (university rates of return are negative for Kenyan women) because of discrimination, withdrawal from the labor force, and having to live in the same place as their husbands. Furthermore, in Accra, Ghana female workers shoulder most of the responsibility for cooking, cleaning, laundry, and other housework, while two-thirds of the male workers do not do any housework,[34] a pattern similar to that in many other cultures.

One striking demographic feature of the contemporary world that reflects the unequal treatment of women is the enormous geographic variation in the ratio of females to males. Medical evidence indicates that, given similar care, women have lower death rates than men. Thus in North America and Europe, although men outnumber women at birth, women have lower mortality rates, outnumbering men by 105 to 100.

---

[34]Jane L. Parpart, "Women and the State in Africa," in Donald Rothchild and Naomi Chazan, eds., *The Precarious Balance* (Boulder, Colo.: Westview, 1986), pp. 278–92; United Nations, Department of International Economic and Social Affairs, *World Survey on the Role of Women in Development* (New York, 1986), pp. 12, 70; Jacques Lecaillon, Felix Paukert, Christian Morrisson, and Dimitri Germidis, *Income Distribution and Economic Development: An Analytical Survey* (Geneva: International Labor Office, 1984), pp. 80–81; David E. Bloom and Adi Brender, "Labor and the Emerging World Economy," *Population Bulletin* 48 (October 1993): 8–9; William J. House and Tony Killick, "Social Justice and Development Policy in Kenya's Rural Economy," in Dharam Ghai and Samir Radwan, eds., *Agrarian Policies and Rural Poverty in Africa* (Geneva: International Labor Office, 1983), pp. 31–69; Arne Bigsten, *Education and Income Determination in Kenya* (Aldershot, England: Gower, 1984), pp. 134–47; Eugenia Date-Bah, "Sex Inequality in an African Urban Labour Market: The Case of Accra-Tema," Geneva, International Labor Organization, World Employment Program 2–21/Working Paper 122, pp. 59–65; E. Wayne Nafziger, *Inequality in Africa: Political Elites, Proletariat, Peasants, and the Poor* (Cambridge: Cambridge University Press, 1988), pp. 45–46, 124–26; Idriss Jazairy, Mohiuddin Alamgir, and Theresa Panuccio, *The State of World Rural Poverty: An Inquiry into its Causes and Consequences*, Published for the International Fund for Agricultural Development (New York: New York University Press, 1992), pp. 78–84; and Katherine Terrell, "Female-Male Earnings Differentials and Occupational Structure," *International Labor Review* 131(4–5) (1992): 387–404.

In many LDCs, however, the ratio of females to males is lower: 1.02 in sub-Saharan Africa, 0.98 in North Africa, 0.94 in China, Bangladesh, and the Middle East, 0.91 in Pakistan, and 0.93 in India, but 1.04 in Kerala state, known for its progressive policies toward females (Chapter 2). Amartya Sen uses sub-Saharan Africa as a benchmark to estimate "missing" women in female-deficit LDCs. He estimates 44 million missing females in China and 37 million in India.

The missing women reflect these cultures' antifemale biases. In China, where the state irregularly enforces a "one couple, one child" policy, expectant couples may use sonograms to identify the gender of the fetus, sometimes aborting female children. Also a small fraction of Indian and Chinese couples practice female infanticide. Additionally, Amartya Sen found that in Bombay, India, women had to be more seriously ill than men to be taken to a hospital. India, China, and some other LDCs with low female to male ratios have a bias in nutrition and health care that favors males. Discrimination against women in schools, jobs, and other economic opportunities lies behind the bias against the care of females within the family.[35]

The findings about intra-family distribution suggest the error of merely directing resources to the household as a unit or to the nominal household head. Policymakers interested in inequality cannot stand clear of the issue of internal distribution within a household but may need to examine policies to see whether they discriminate against women or children.[36]

Accompaniments of Absolute Poverty

The 1.4 billion people living in absolute poverty suffer the following deprivations:

1. Three- to four-fifths of their income is spent on food; the diet is monotonous, limited to cereals, yams, or cassavas, a few vegetables, and in some regions, a little fish or meat.

2. About 60 percent are undernourished and hundreds of millions are severely malnourished. Energy and motivation are reduced; performance in school and at work is undermined; resistance to illness is low; and the physical and mental development of children is often impaired.

3. One of every 10 children born die within the first year; another dies before the age of 5; and only five reach the age of 45.

4. Beginning in 1975, the World Health Organization and UNICEF expanded immunization against the major diseases of the developing world. Immunization rates increased rapidly, and deaths from these diseases fell substantially in LDCs from the 1980s to the 1990s. Still fewer than 50 percent of the children in absolute poverty are vaccinated against measles, diphtheria, and whooping cough, which have been virtually eliminated in rich countries. These diseases are still frequently fatal in developing countries. A case of measles is 35 times more likely to kill a child in a low-income country than in the United States.

5. Two-thirds of the poor lack access to clean and plentiful water and even a larger proportion lack an adequate system for disposing of their feces. Lack of sanita-

---

[35]Amartya Sen, "The Economics of Life and Death," *Scientific American* 268 (May 1993): 40–47.

[36]Daisy Dwyer and Judith Bruce, eds., *A Home Divided: Women and Income in the Third World* (Stanford, Calif.: Stanford University Press, 1988), p. 3.

tion, a problem of virtually all the poor, contributes to 900 million diarrheal diseases yearly. These diseases cause the death of 3 million children annually, most preventable with adequate sanitation and clean water.

6. Average life expectancy is about 45 years, compared to 77 years in developed countries.

7. Only about one-third to two-fifths of the adults are literate.

8. Only about four of every 10 children complete more than 4 years of primary school.

9. The poor are more likely to be concentrated in environmentally marginal and vulnerable areas, face higher rates of unemployment and underemployment, and have higher fertility rates than those who are not poor.[37]

Indeed, you should remember that as we analyze the problems of LDCs in subsequent chapters, the problems of the LDCs' poor are even more severe than those of LDCs generally.

Identifying Poverty Groups

1. Almost two-fifths of the world's absolute poor live in South Asia, mainly in India and Bangladesh. One-fifth live in sub-Saharan Africa, with Nigeria and Ethiopia with the largest number of poor. The remainder (each region with roughly one-tenth) are divided among Latin America (Brazil and Mexico the major contributors), Southeast Asia (with the Philippines and Indonesia the largest numbers), the Middle East, and East Asia (primarily China). By the year 2000, one-third of the world's poor is projected to live in the sub-Sahara, which will be the world region with the largest number of poor.

2. Some minority groups are overrepresented among the poor; these include the Indians in Latin America and the outcastes in India.

3. Four-fifths of the poor live in rural areas, most of the rest in urban slums—but almost all in crowded conditions. The rural poor are the landless workers, sharecroppers, tenants, and small land owners. The urban poor include the unemployed, irregularly employed, menial workers, some small shopkeepers, artisans, and traders.

4. Compared to the lowest income classes in DCs, a much smaller percentage of the poor in the LDCs are wage laborers, or unemployed and searching for work (see below, on policies). Most of the poor work long hours as farmers, vendors, artisans, or hired workers. A few self-employed may own a small piece of land, some animals, or some tools, but many of the poor own no land and have virtually no assets.

---

[37]World Bank, *World Development Report, 1993* (New York: Oxford University Press, 1993); World Bank, *World Development Report, 1992* (New York: Oxford University Press, 1992), p. 5; World Bank, *World Development Report, 1990* (New York: Oxford University Press, 1990); World Bank, *World Development Report, 1980* (New York: Oxford University Press, 1980), p. 33; United Nations Development Program, *Human Development Report, 1993* (New York: Oxford University Press, 1993); United Nations Children Fund (UNICEF), *The State of the World's Children, 1994* (Oxford: Oxford University Press, 1994); and Robert S. McNamara, presidential address to the World Bank, Washington, D.C., September 30, 1980, pp. 2–21.

United Nations Children Fund (UNICEF), *The State of the World's Children, 1995* (Oxford: Oxford University Press, 1995), pp. 24–27, indicates the progress in reducing diarrhea through oral rehydration therapy and lessons for the mothers of infants.

5. Most of the poor are illiterate: They have not completed more than a year or two of school. As a result, their knowledge and understanding of the world are severely circumscribed.

6. Women are poorer than men, especially in one-quarter of the world's households where women alone head households. The female labor force is small, employed in the lowest paid jobs, and characterized by a far greater unemployment rate than the male labor force. In households with an adult male, females are often given more menial work and males are favored in the distribution of food and other consumer goods (see Chapter 7).

7. Forty percent of the poor are children under 10, living mainly in large families. For example, in Pakistan, the poorest 10 percent of households averaged 7.7 members, of whom 3.6 were children under 10. The corresponding national averages were 6.1 and 2.2.

8. Even when living with an extended family, the elderly are poorer than other groups.

9. Many of the poor are beyond the gaze of the casual visitor to a village—away from roads, away from markets, or living on the outskirts of the village.[38] Indeed Alan G. Hill contends that the wretched Sahel Africans presented dramatically on Western television screens represented the normal misery for poor populations in remote rural areas, discovered only when "the destitute collect on roadsides, in refugee camps or on the outskirts of towns and cities."[39]

Case Studies of Countries

INDONESIA AND NIGERIA

The contrast between the success of two populous oil-exporting countries, Indonesia and Nigeria, in changing poverty rates, is instructive. The differences are a result of dissimilar economic growth and income distribution records ensuing largely from disparate polices. From 1973 to 1992, Indonesia's yearly growth was 5.7 percent while Nigeria's was 1.4 percent. Personal income concentration in Indonesia fell from a Gini of 0.46 in 1971 to 0.41 in 1976 to 0.30 in 1990. While Nigeria lacks income distribution data, information on the ratio of Nigerian industrial to agricultural labor productivity indicate an increase from 2.5:1 in 1966 to 2.7:1 in

---

[38]The rural poor often live in remote regions afar from services and thus lack sufficient weight to influence political decisions. Idriss Jazairy, Mohiuddin Alamgir, and Theresa Panuccio, *The State of World Rural Poverty: An Inquiry into its Causes and Consequences*, Published for the International Fund for Agricultural Development (New York: New York University Press, 1992), p. 29.

[39]World Bank, *World Development Report, 1990* (New York: Oxford University Press, 1990); United Nations Development Program, *Human Development Report, 1993* (New York: Oxford University Press, 1993); World Bank, *World Development, 1980* (New York: Oxford University Press, 1980), pp. 33–35; Irene Tinker, Michèle Bo Bramsen, and Myra Buvini´c, *Women and World Development* (New York: Praeger, 1976); Alan G. Hill, *Demographic Responses to Food Shortages in the Sahel*, ESD 801/13 (Rome: Food and Agriculture Organization, 1978), p. 1; Peter Hendry, "Food and Population: Beyond Five Billion," *Population Bulletin* 43 (April 1988): 8; and Per Pinstrup-Anderson, *World Food Trends and Future Food Security*, Food Policy Report (Washington, D.C.: International Food Policy Research Institute, 1994), p. 1.

1970 to 7.2:1 in 1975, after a fourfold increase in petroleum prices during four months in 1972–73; the ratio probably fell again in the 1980s.[40]

Before 1973, both countries had more than 40 percent of GNP originating in agriculture. Both countries experienced an oil boom during 1973–75 and 1979–81. While Indonesia's agricultural output increased 3.7 percent yearly from 1973 to 1983, output in Nigeria declined 1.9 percent and agricultural exports, 7.9 percent yearly over the same period. From 1983 to 1992, Indonesia's agricultural output rose 2.8 percent and farm exports 6.2 percent annually; Nigeria's agricultural production grew 4.1 percent and farm exports fell 2.9 percent annually over the same period. Furthermore, agricultural imports as a share of total imports rose from 3 percent in the late 1960s to 17 percent in the 1980s and the 1990s in Nigeria, while in Indonesia the share increased only from 1 percent to 4 to 5 percent over the same period.

Several differences in agricultural pricing and investment explain Indonesia's more favorable agricultural development. The real value of the Nigerian naira appreciated substantially in the early 1970s and early 1980s, depreciating relative to the dollar only under pressure in 1986, while Indonesia's rupiah's real value increased more slowly, and depreciated vis-à-vis the dollar starting from 1978 to 1983. Additionally, Indonesia invested a substantial amount of government funds in agriculture, including a General Rural Credit Program which loaned to rural people at commercial rates, while less than 10 percent of the Nigerian plan's capital expenditures were in agriculture. The attempt by Nigeria, beginning in the mid 1980s, to increase incentives and investment in agriculture had little initial impact.[41] The country will require sustained policy changes to reverse the effects of years of neglect.

Indonesia reduced it poverty incidence from 59 percent in 1975 to 25 percent in 1996, while Nigeria's incidence rose from 35 percent in 1975 to 40 percent in 1996. A major contributor to reduced rural poverty in Indonesia was the dramatic increase in rice yields. For example, in Balearjo, East Java, from 1953 to 1985, rice yields increased from 2 to 6 tons of paddy per hectare for the wet season crops, while the daily wage rose from 2 to 4 kilograms of rice. On the other hand, despite the oil boom, Nigeria's nutritional levels barely increased from the mid 1960s to the late 1970s, with the poorest 30 to 40 percent of rural households and many in the new urban slums being seriously undernourished and impoverished. Average calorie intake in Nigeria, especially in the otherwise more prosperous south where diets relied heavily on roots and tubers, did not improve between 1952 and 1985. Indeed average consumption levels in 1985 were lower than in the 1950s.[42]

In 1986–90, the **terms of trade** (price index of exports divided by the price index of imports) of Nigeria, with petroleum comprising more than 90 percent of its exports, fell to one-third to one-sixth the 1981 oil-driven peak, spurring a 4-year

[40]Shail Jain, *Size Distribution of Income: A Compilation of Data* (Washington, D.C.: World Bank, 1975), p. 55; World Bank, *World Development Report, 1982* (New York: Oxford University Press, 1982), p. 158; World Bank, *World Development Report, 1993* (New York: Oxford University Press, 1993), p. 296; Victor P. Diejomaoh and E.C. Anusionwu, "Education and Income Distribution in Nigeria," in Henry Bienen and Victor P. Diejomaoh, eds., *The Political Economy of Income Distribution in Nigeria* (New York: Holmes and Meier, 1981), pp. 373–420.

[41]World Bank, *World Development Report, 1986* (New York: Oxford University Press, 1986), p. 72; and E. Wayne Nafziger, *The Debt Crisis in Africa* (Baltimore: Johns Hopkins University Press, 1993), pp. 52–53.

[42]World Bank, *World Development Report, 1994* (New York: Oxford University Press, 1994), p. 42.

slump comparable to the West's Great Depression of the 1930s. The more diversified Indonesian economy, with some 35 to 55 of exports manufactures or non–oil primary products, continued to grow throughout the late 1980s and early 1990s, gradually reducing poverty rates.[43] While many of Nigeria's insecure military or civilian political elites (turning over frequently from coups), civil servants, and intermediaries for foreign capital had to rely on the state's economic levers to build patronage networks to survive,[44] Indonesia enjoyed greater political continuity and policy predictability, and less political intervention in economic policy decisions,[45] from the 1960s through the 1990s.

MALAYSIA, PAKISTAN, AND BRAZIL

Table 6–5 shows the comparison in the income distributions of Pakistan, Malaysia, and Brazil. Pakistan, with low inequality, reduced its incidence of poverty from 54 percent in 1962 to 28 percent in 1996. Malaysia, with moderate inequality, decreased its poverty rate from 37 percent in 1973 to 16 percent in 1996, while the same rate in Brazil, with high inequality, only fell from 50 percent in 1960 to 47 percent in 1996.

Economists break down reductions in poverty rates into the part attributable to growth and the part attributable to changes in income inequality. From 1960 to 1980, before its negative growth of the 1980s, annual growth in Brazil was 5.1 percent compared to Malaysia's 4.3 percent. Brazil's poverty rate during the same period fell from 50 percent to 21 percent. However, if Brazil's inequality had fallen as in Malaysia, Brazilian poverty would have fallen by 43 percentage points rather than by 29. Thus, both the pattern and rate of growth are important determinants of changes in poverty rates.[46]

We can illustrate how growth patterns affect poverty rates by a stylized graph comparing income distribution relative to the poverty line in Pakistan and Brazil. Figure 6–5 shows the **cumulative distribution function**, that is, the percentage of persons who receive no more than a particular income, expressed as a

---

[43]Montek S. Ahluwalia, Nicholas G. Carter, and Hollis B. Chenery, "Growth and Poverty in Developing Countries," *Journal of Development Economics* 6 (September 1979): 312–13; World Bank, *World Development Report, 1990* (New York: Oxford University Press, 1990), pp. 40–43; International Labour Office, Jobs and Skills Program for Africa, First Things First: Meeting the Basic Needs of the People of Nigeria (Addis Ababa, 1981); Peter Matlon, "The Structure of Production and Rural Incomes in Northern Nigeria," in Henry Bienen and Victor P. Diejomaoh, eds., *The Political Economy of Income Distribution in Nigeria* (New York: Holmes and Meier, 1981), pp. 323–72; E. Wayne Nafziger, *Inequality in Africa: Political Elites, Proletariat, Peasants and the Poor* (Cambridge: Cambridge University Press, 1988), pp. 10, 26, 34, 123–24; E. Wayne Nafziger, *The Debt Crisis in Africa* (Baltimore: Johns Hopkins University Press, 1993), pp. 27–28, 67–69; E. Wayne Nafziger, "The Economy," in Helen Chapin Metz, ed., *Nigeria: A Country Study* (Washington, D.C.: Library of Congress, 1991), pp. 155–202, 331–35; World Bank, *Trends in Developing Countries, 1993* (Washington, D.C., 1993), pp. 237–38, 369–70; and Table 7–4.

[44]The Pius Okigbo panel that probed the Central Bank of Nigeria reported that $12.4 billion of oil revenues had disappeared beyond budgetary oversight, 1988 to mid 1994. "Nigeria's Missing Billions," *Economist* (22 October 1994): 50. Previous panels investigating corruption have also found billions missing.

See also Peter M. Lewis, "Economic Statism, Private Capital, and the Dilemmas of Accumulation in Nigeria," *World Development* 22 (March 1994): 437–45; and Sayre P. Schatz, "Pirate Capitalism and the Inert Economy of Nigeria," *Journal of Modern African Studies* 22 (March 1984): 45–57.

[45]Howard Pack, "Productivity or Politics: The Determinants of the Indonesian Tariff Structure," *Journal of Development Economics* 44 (August 1994): 441–51.

[46]World Bank, *World Development Report, 1982* (New York: Oxford University Press, 1982), p. 110; and World Bank, *World Development Report, 1990* (New York: Oxford University Press, 1990), pp. 47–48.

FIGURE 6-5   Different Initial Conditions: The Impact
on Poverty Reduction

Heavy concentration of poor
just below poverty line

The Pakistani case

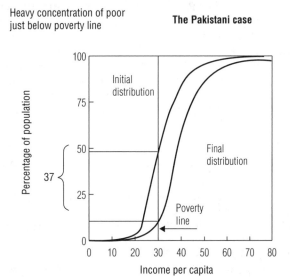

Lower concentration of poor
just below poverty line

The Brazilian case

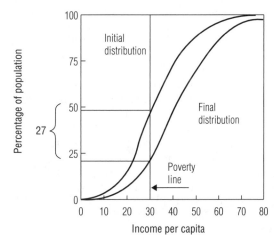

Source: World Bank, *World Development Report, 1990*
(New York: Oxford University Press, 1990), p. 47–48.

function of that income. For example, when the poverty line is set at 30, the curve
on the left in each figure shows that 50 percent of the population is poor. A 50 percent increase in income will shift the distribution function to the right. The reduction in the poverty rate is 37 percentage points in the upper graph (the Pakistani
case) but only 27 percentage points in the lower graph (the Brazilian case).

The difference in outcome arises from differences in the slope of the distribution function at the poverty line. If the slope is very steep, implying less inequality

in the region of the poverty line, as in the upper graph showing Pakistan, a large number of people is concentrated just below the line, and the poverty rate falls substantially. If the slope is less steep, implying greater inequality around the poverty line, as in the lower graph showing Brazil, few people are located immediately below the poverty line. In this case the same increase in income moves only a few of the poor above the line, and the reduction in the poverty rate will be much smaller.

For example, starting from the distributions available in the early 1990s, a 10 percent increase in the incomes of the poor in Pakistan would reduce the poverty rate by about 7 percentage points. Where the distribution is more unequal, as in Brazil, the corresponding figure would be only 3 percentage points.[47]

SRI LANKA

From independence in 1948 to 1977, Sri Lanka, which spent about half of its recurrent governmental expenditures for food subsidy, health, and educational programs, made much progress in meeting its population's basic needs. In the late 1960s and early to middle 1970s, about 20 percent of these expenditures (10 percent of GNP) was for food subsidies, including a free ration of 0.5–1.0 kilograms of rice per week for each person (the remainder sold at a subsidized price). Unlike its large, diverse neighbor, India, Sri Lanka's food programs effectively fed the poor and those in rural areas. The direct ration provided about 20 percent of the calories and 15 percent of the incomes of the poorest 20 percent of the population. In contrast to programs that redistribute cash or assets, there were fewer political obstacles to food redistribution.

One percent of Sri Lanka's population, compared to 25 percent in Bangladesh, subsisted on less than 1,700 calories per day in 1970. The food subsidy program reduced mortality and malnutrition greatly. The mortality rate was much lower in Sri Lanka than in Bangladesh, although when cuts in the ration and subsidy were made during periods of high food prices in Sri Lanka, mortality rates increased significantly.[48]

Yet Sri Lanka's basic needs policies were achieved at the expense of resources needed for employment and investment. High enrollment rates and weak curricula contributed to a secondary-school-graduate unemployment rate of over 25 percent and to an overall unemployment rate of 20 percent in 1977. Additionally low food prices hurt agricultural growth, and high business taxes and pervasive government controls discouraged investment. After 1977, governments cut food subsidies and other social spending as part of a strategy for improving farm incentives and attracting foreign investment. Additionally, Sri Lanka's social programs were also hurt by severe ethnic conflict.

INDIA

In India, the constitution of 1949 and 5-year plans (beginning in 1951) stressed removing injustices, abolishing poverty, and improving income distribution. Begin-

---

[47]The explanation for Figure 6.5 is from World Bank, *World Development Report, 1990* (New York: Oxford University Press, 1990), p. 47, except I have labelled the upper graph the Pakistani case and the lower graph the Brazilian case.

[48]Paul Iseman, "Basic Needs: The Case of Sri Lanka," *World Development* 8 (March 1980): 237–58; and World Bank, *World Development Report, 1980* (New York: Oxford University Press, 1980), p. 62.

ning in the 1950s, numerous programs were undertaken to achieve these goals, including land reform, village cooperatives, community development, credit and services for the rural poor, educational and food subsidies, minimum wages, rural employment programs, and direct provision for upgrading health, sanitation, nutrition, drinking water, housing, education, transport, communication, and electricity for the poor. As Inderjit Singh states

> Those who benefited from . . . antipoverty programs were usually those who had the grassroots power. Deciding who was "poor" and therefore eligible for aid depended on the administrators of these programs, generally the rural elite. So, rather than being a neutral agent for the distribution of gains, government became a trough where different social groups fed in relation to their economic power. Many antipoverty programs in India—such as the Drought Areas Program, the Rural Works Program, and special credit programs—delivered the greater share of their benefits to the richer, not the poorer, segments of society.[49]

But overall progress was limited: Income shares for the poor dropped from the 1950s through the late 1970s, while according to government studies, no appreciable dent was made on absolute poverty.

In India's democracy, the poor pressured political leaders to adopt programs aimed at improving the lot of weaker sections of the population. However, the landed and business classes dominated the government service and legislatures, and it was not in their interest to administer effectively programs that helped the underprivileged at their expense. Thus by 1970, only 0.3 percent of the total land cultivated had been distributed under land legislation. Furthermore, laws were frequently enacted with loopholes and exemptions that allowed land transfers to relatives, keeping land concentrated in the hands of a few families. Also large moneylenders, farmers, and traders controlled village cooperatives and used most of the social services and capital provided by community development programs.[50]

The fastest poverty reduction probably occurred after liberalization reforms spurred growth, beginning first in the mid-1980s with limited delicensing and price decontrol, but culminating in the New Industrial Policy in 1991, assumed in response to International Monetary Fund and World Bank pressure for India to reduce its chronic deficit on international balance on goods, services, and income (or exports minus imports of goods and services). As of 1994, however, there were no official studies available to verify economists' intuition that faster post-reform growth had reduced poverty.

---

[49]Inderjit Singh, The Great Ascent: The Rural Poor in South Asia (Baltimore: Johns Hopkins University Press, 1990), p. xviii.

[50]Pranab K. Barhan, "India," in Hollis Chenery, Montek S. Ahluwalia, C. L. G. Bell, John H. Duloy, and Richard Jolly, eds., *Redistribution with Growth* (London: Oxford University Press, 1974), pp. 255–62; and David Morawetz, *Twenty-five Years of Economic Development, 1950 to 1975* (Baltimore: Johns Hopkins Press, 1977), pp. 39–41. For studies indicating a decline in the income and asset shares of the poor, see India, Ministry of Agriculture and Irrigation, *Report of the National Commission on Agriculture, 1976* (New Delhi, 1976); and R. P. Pathak, K. R. Ganapathy, and Y. U. K. Sarma, "Shifts in Patterns of Asset-Holdings of Rural Households, 1961–62 to 1971–72," *Economic and Political Weekly* 12 (March 19, 1977): 507–17.

Policies to Reduce Poverty and Income Inequality

As we discussed in an earlier section, the inverted U-shaped curve descriptive of income inequality rises in early stages of development and drops later on. Moreover income inequality worsens as income increases from low to middle levels and then improves as income advances from middle to high levels.

This pattern, however, may be a consequence of deliberate economic policies. Greater inequality is probably a result of past policies that incorrectly assumed benefits would eventually trickle down to the poor. Furthermore many LDCs emphasized the growth of the urban-oriented, highly technological, highly mechanized production of Western-style consumer goods. They neglected production patterns based on indigenous tastes, processes, and factor endowments. This section outlines some policies that may succeed in reducing poverty and income inequality.

Socialist economists argue that high income inequality is inevitable in a capitalist society, with its gulf between incomes from capital, land, and entrepreneurship, on the one hand, and wage earners, on the other. However, empirical evidence indicates that *evolutionary* policy changes in a mixed or capitalist LDC, such as Taiwan, South Korea, and early post-World War II Japan, can reduce poverty and income inequality substantially.[51]

As might be expected, the initial distribution of assets and income is crucial in determining income inequality. People who already own property, hold an influential position, and have a good education are in the best position to profit as growth proceeds. Thus a society with high income inequality is likely to remain unequal or become more so, whereas one with small disparities may be able to avoid large increases in inequality. It simply may not be possible to grow first and redistribute later, because early social and economic position may have already fixed the distribution pattern. To reduce poverty and income inequality, a society may need to enact land reform (discussed in Chapter 11), mass education, and other such programs straightaway rather than waiting until after growth is well under way.[52]

Capital and Credit.   In LDCs generally, the poor live primarily from their labor and the rich on returns from property ownership. Not only do the poor have little capital, their poverty also limits their ability to respond to good investment opportunities, such as new seed varieties, fertilizer, tools, or their children's education.

Government efforts to supplant traditional moneylenders in providing credit for the poor have had only limited success. Even public agencies require collateral. People with few assets can rarely meet such a standard. Furthermore, the substantial staff time needed to process and supervise loans and perhaps

---

[51]Montek S. Ahluwalia, Nicholas G. Carter, and Hollis B. Chenery, "Growth and Poverty in Developing Countries," *Journal of Development Economics* 6 (September 1979), 299–341; Irma Adelman and Sherman Robinson, *Income Distribution Policy in Developing Countries: A Case Study of Korea* (Stanford: Stanford University Press, 1978); and Charles R. Frank, Jr., and Richard C. Webb, eds., *Income Distribution and Growth in the Less-Developed Countries* (Washington, D.C.: Brookings Institution, 1977).

[52]David Morawetz, *Twenty-five Years of Economic Development, 1950 to 1975* (Baltimore: Johns Hopkins University Press, 1977), p. 41; E. Wayne Nafziger, "Class, Caste, and Community of South Indian Industrialists: An Examination of the Horatio Alger Model," *Journal of Development Studies* 11 (January 1975): 131–48; and Alberto Alesina and Dani Rodrik, "Distributive Politics and Economic Growth," *Quarterly Journal of Economics* 109 (May 1994): 465–90.

arrange technical assistance, as well as the higher risk of bad debts, make it difficult for these credit programs to be self-supporting. Moreover, the limited amount of subsidized credit has frequently not wound up in the hands of the poor, but of more influential groups.

Some credit programs (the MicroFund in Manila, Philippines and the Association for Development of Microenterprise or ADEMI in Santo Domingo, Dominican Republic, both established in 1989) provide training and technical aid for the urban poor, especially women, in **microenterprises** (very small firms). Indonesia's Badan Kredit Kecamatan (BKK), founded in 1982, provides individuals (primarily low-income women) tiny initial loans (a $5 limit) quickly on the basis of character references from local officials without collateral. The BKK is profitable but still reaches the poor, as the smallness of the loan and strictness of the terms cull out the nonpoor. In the early 1980s, the Small-Scale Enterprise Credit Program in Calcutta raised the average income of new borrowers 82 percent within 2 years, while the Kupedes program for Indonesian microenterprises, established in 1988, increased average borrower incomes from $74 to $183 after 3 years. These four lending institutions were supported with limited subsidies to help cover their initial administrative costs but not otherwise to subsidize interest rates.

Group lending is one way to avoid subsidies in providing credit for the poor. Under such schemes, similar to the Grameen Bank of Bangladesh established in 1988, peer borrowing groups of five or so people with joint liability approve loans to other members as a substitute for the bank's screening process. The group members discuss all loan requests, scrutinize the investment plan and creditworthiness of the borrower, and save an established percentage of the loan, which remains on deposit during the borrowing. Failure to repay by any member jeopardizes the group's access to future credit. The Grameen Bank received limited subsidies from international lenders, used to start up the group and offer interest rates several points below the market. As of 1991, Grameen had more than 1,000 branch offices, served more than one million clients (more than 90 percent of whom were women), and had a repayment rate of 92 percent.[53]

The poor can increase investment through risk pooling. In addition to spreading risk throughout the extended family, people spread risk by (usually informal) reciprocal relationships within **patron-client** (superior-subordinate) **systems** and lineage and village communities.[54]

Public investment in roads, schools, electricity, potable water, irrigation projects, and other infrastructure, if made in underprivileged areas, can provide direct benefits for the poor, increase their productivity, or provide jobs for them.[55]

Education and Training.   As Chapter 5 contended, investment in education, training, and other forms of human capital yields a stream of income over time. Universal, free, primary education is a major way of redistributing human capital

[53]World Bank, *World Development Report, 1990* (New York: Oxford University Press, 1990), pp. 66–69; Maria Otero and Elisabeth Rhyne, *The New World of Microenterprise Finance: Building Healthy Financial Institutions for the Poor* (West Hartford, Conn.: Kumarian Press, 1994); Idriss Jazairy, Mohiuddin Alamgir, and Theresa Panuccio, *The State of World Rural Poverty: An Inquiry into its Causes and Consequences*, Published for the International Fund for Agricultural Development (New York: New York University Press, 1992), p. 206; and Katherine Lammers, "Microenterprise Development," M.A. report, Kansas State University, 1994, pp. 24–28.

[54]Partha Dasgupta, *An Inquiry into Well-Being and Destitution* (Oxford: Clarendon Press, 1993), pp. 204–38.

[55]World Bank, *World Development Report, 1980* (New York: Oxford University Press, 1980), pp. 41–42.

to the relative benefit of the poor. High primary enrollment rates are associated with relatively high income shares for the bottom 40 percent of the population (see Chapter 10).[56]

In parts of low-income West Africa, the government not only subsidizes the universities but also provides free tuition and living allowances for the students, whose parents usually have incomes that are higher than the national average and rarely originate from the low-income peasant agricultural sector. Student living allowances comprise nearly half the funds that West African governments spend on higher education. Sub-Saharan Africa spends 22 percent of its public educational budget on higher education although only 2 percent of those aged 18 to 23 attend school at that level. Moreover, during the economic recession and fiscal constraints of the 1980s and early 1990s, Ghana, Tanzania, and Mali, as well as countries suffering from war such as Ethiopia, Mozambique, Somalia, and Liberia, reduced primary enrollment rates. Moreover, the Brazilian government spends 23 percent of its public education budget on higher education but only 9 percent on secondary education. In addition, the top one-fifth income earners in Chile, Uruguay, Costa Rica, and the Dominican Republic receive more than one-half of the subsidies for higher education, while the poorest quintile receives less than one-tenth. Furthermore, many resource-poor low-income countries have sacrificed quality of education at the primary level, often lacking instructional competence, basic mathematics, science, and language textbooks, and other teaching materials.[57]

Employment Programs.   Unemployment in LDCs is a major concern. It leads to economic inefficiency and political discontent as well as having obvious implications for income distribution. Open unemployment, in which a person without a job actively seeks employment, is largely an urban phenomenon in LDCs. The unemployed are mainly in their teens and early twenties and usually primary or secondary school graduates. It is rare for unemployed youth to seek an urban job without family support.

Some policies to reduce unemployment include faster industrial expansion, public employment schemes, more labor-intensive production in manufacturing, a reduction in factor price distortion, greater economic development and social services in rural areas, a more relevant educational system, greater consistency between educational policy and economic planning, and more reliance on the market in setting wage rates (see Chapter 10). Public works programs for expanding employment can provide a safety net for the poor and help LDCs respond to recessions and macroeconomic shocks.[58]

Health and Nutrition.   LDCs increase efficiency and equity by shifting funds from advanced curative medicine in urban hospitals to basic health services such as preventive care, simple health information, an improved health environment, and nontraditional or middle-level health practitioners in numerous rural clinics. The demand by the poor for medical care is highly price elastic so that when fees

---

[56]Montek S. Ahluwalia, "Income Inequality," in Hollis Chenery, Montek S. Ahluwalia, C. L. G. Bell, John H. Duloy, and Richard Jolly, eds., *Redistribution with Growth* (London: Oxford University Press, 1974), p. 17; and George Psacharopoulos and Maureen Woodhall, *Education for Development: An Analysis of Investment Choice* (New York: Oxford University Press, 1985), pp. 258–64.

[57]World Bank, *World Development Report, 1990* (New York: Oxford University Press, 1990), p. 79.

[58]World Bank, *World Development Report, 1990* (New York: Oxford University Press, 1990), p. 118.

are more than nominal, the poor will be the first to drop out. Charging higher fees to the rich for hospital care, however, can generate substantial revenue.[59] Sickness and insufficient food limit the employment opportunities and earning power of the poor. Food subsidies or free rations increase the income of the poor, lead to better health and nutrition, permit people to work more days in a year, and enhance their effectiveness at work. However, because of the expense of food programs, they are not likely to be continued unless food production per capita is maintained or raised. Poverty is a terribly circular affliction.

Population Programs.   Chapter 8 maintains that the living levels of the poor are improved by smaller family size, since each adult has fewer dependents.

Research and Technology.   The benefits of research and new technology in reducing poverty are most apparent in agriculture. The introduction of high-yielding varieties of wheat and rice—the **Green Revolution**—has expanded food supplies and reduced food prices for the poor, and increased wage rates and, in some instances, small farmer incomes. But much more research is needed to improve the productivity of food crops on which many low-income farmers depend and to increase jobs and cheap consumer goods output in industry.

Migration.   As development proceeds, more jobs are created in the industrial, urban sector, so people move to the cities. Despite some problems, the living standards of migrants employed in the cities, though low, tend to be above those of the rural poor. Generally city workers send money home, so that farmland has to support fewer people, both of which benefit the rural poor. Yet policies of urban bias, discussed in the next chapter, spur more migration than what is socially desirable.

Taxes.   Chapter 15 discusses tax schemes, such as the progressive income tax, to reduce income inequality.

Transfers and Subsidies.   In developed countries, antipoverty programs include income transfers to the old, the very young, the ill, the handicapped, the unemployed, and those whose earning power is below a living wage. But except for some middle-income countries, such as Brazil and Turkey, most developing countries cannot support such programs. For example, in Bangladesh, where more than three-fourths of the population is poor and undernourished (see Table 6–5), welfare payments to bring the population above the poverty line would undermine work incentives and be prohibitively expensive.

An alternative approach is subsidizing or rationing cheap foodstuffs. Subsidizing foods that higher income groups do not eat benefits the poor. For example, sorghum, introduced into ration shops in Bangladesh in 1978, was bought by nearly 70 percent of low-income households but by only 2 percent of high-income households.[60]

Emphasis on Target Group.   Another strategy for improving the lot of the poor is to target certain programs for the poorest groups. India has an affirmative action program favoring the placement of outcastes and other economically "backward castes

[59]World Bank, *World Development Report, 1990* (New York: Oxford University Press, 1990), pp. 86–87.
[60]World Bank, *World Development Report, 1980* (New York: Oxford University Press, 1980), pp. 42–45, 51, 62.

and tribes" when openings in educational institutions and government positions occur. A number of countries, including India, use industrial incentives and subsidies to help economically backward regions and train business people from underprivileged groups. Some countries have tried to improve female literacy and educational rates. Others have stressed health and nutritional programs for expectant and nursing mothers and children. Improvements in pensions, provident funds, and social security benefit the elderly (although in Brazil politically-unassailable social security has become a fiscal nightmare, excluding most of the poor, who, however, provide a large share of the financing).[61] Upgrading housing in urban areas can increase real income among the poor. Finally, some LDCs, in a reversal of the policies of the 1950s and 1960s, have stressed development in the rural areas where most poor live.

The success of public intervention to target groups depends on political support. From 1948 to 1977, Sri Lanka spent about 10 percent of its GNP on food subsidies, including a free ration of 0.5–1.0 kilograms (1.1–2.2 pounds) of rice weekly for each person, with the remainder sold at a subsidized price. But in the late 1970s, to reduce the adverse effect of low food prices on agricultural growth, the Junius Jayewardene government replaced this universal food subsidy with a less costly targeted food stamp program, that gradually eroded in value with inflation over time. The middle class, which no longer gained from the more cost-effective program, withdrew its crucial political support. Similarly, a food subsidy directed to the poor in Colombia was so tightly targeted that it lacked an effective political constituency, and was abolished at a change of government.[62] In the 1980s and 1990s, Indians have increasingly opposed the job and university-entrance reservation of 22.5 to 52 percent (the amount varying by state), and many employers have instituted hiring policies to circumvent the job reservation.

Michael Lipton and Jacques van der Gaag, consultants for the World Bank, explain that

> Targeting is not simply a Scrooge-like way to limit the fiscal cost of reducing poverty. It can also prevent undue dependency among the poor and wrong incentives. Conversely, incentives can be used to improve targeting. Where the rich avoid the use of public health clinics because of crowding or low-quality care, these clinics can be used as distribution centers for, say, food stamps. This kind of self-targeting has proved effective in Jamaica. [Ehtisham] Ahmad warns of the risk, however, that such a scheme, although it may avoid leakage to the rich, may exclude or deter many of the poor.[63]

---

[61]Michael Lipton and Jacques van der Gaag, eds., *Including the Poor—Proceedings of a Symposium Organized by the World Bank and the International Food Policy Research Institute* (Washington, D.C.: World Bank, 1993), p. 31.

[62]World Bank, *World Development Report, 1990* (New York: Oxford University Press, 1990), pp. 91–92.

Undoubtedly, the disruption of production and deterioration of well-being from Sri Lanka's ethnic conflict and civil war have been major contributors to a substantial increase in malnutrition in the 1980s and 1990.

[63]Michael Lipton and Jacques van der Gaag, eds., *Including the Poor—Proceedings of a Symposium Organized by the World Bank and the International Food Policy Research Institute* (Washington, D.C.: World Bank, 1993), p. 9, citing work in their edited volume by Timothy Besley and Ravi Kanbur, "The Principles of Targeting," pp. 67–90, and Ehtisham Ahmad, " Protecting the Vulnerable: Social Security and Public Policy," pp. 359–77.

Another problem is assessing and verifying low incomes, difficult enough in DCs with their literate populations accustomed to filling in tax forms. As an example, Timothy Besley and Ravi Kanbur point to "a coupon program that distributed food every two weeks through government-run supermarkets [using] income to determine who could participate in Recife, Brazil. The program revealed several problems. . . It is difficult to target income if income reporting is arbitrary. . . A coupon program requires extensive bookkeeping and administrative cost." Building on this experience, the Brazilian government modified the program successfully, reaching very low-income neighborhoods without coupons. Any leakage to the nonpoor was less expensive than administering the cumbersome coupon program.[64]

Judy L. Baker and Margaret Grosh found that in Latin America, geographic targeting (especially when the size of unit used in making decisions was small) was as effective as means tests in insuring that benefits go to the poorest 40 percent of the population. Due to its simplicity and cost-effectiveness, geographic targeting may be a legitimate alternative to self-targeting.[65]

Workfare. Self-targeting involves designing schemes based on self-regulation that only the poor will pass. One program that provides food security while relying on self-selection by the poor is food or other income in exchange for work. A work requirement, combined with low wages, guarantees that only the poor will apply for jobs where they cannot otherwise be identified, thus allowing a greater coverage of the poor with a given budget. However, when India's statutory minimum wage doubled in 1988, Maharashtra state's Employment Guarantee Scheme doubled the wage rate for food-for-work recipients but because this wage did not effectively ration jobs to the most needy, scheme administrators used informal rationing.[66] Kirit Parikh and T.N. Srinivasan's simulation showed that a well-designed, well-executed, and well-targeted works program improves the welfare of the rural poor and increased economic growth, even if the resources are raised through additional taxation. Even if the works program means other investment foregone, the sacrifice in growth is modest and the effect on the welfare of the poor is positive.[67] In some Indian villages, employment guaranteed workfare served to stabilize income, reducing the "hungry season." A study of a food-for-work program in Bangladesh found that the foregone earnings of participants in the program were one-third of their earnings.[68]

Integrated War on Poverty. A study by Irma Adelman and Sherman Robinson indicates that, taken singly, most of these policies cannot end rising income

---

[64]Timothy Besley and Ravi Kanbur, "The Principles of Targeting," in Michael Lipton and Jacques van der Gaag, eds., *Including the Poor—Proceedings of a Symposium Organized by the World Bank and the International Food Policy Research Institute* (Washington, D.C.: World Bank, 1993), p. 71.

[65]Judy L. Baker and Margaret E. Grosh, "Poverty Reduction through Geographic Targeting: How Well Does it Work?" *World Development* 22 (July 1994): 983–95; and Margaret E. Grosh, *Administering Targeted Social Programs in Latin America: From Platitudes to Practice* (Washington, D.C.: World Bank, 1994).

[66]Michael Lipton and Jacques van der Gaag, *Including the Poor: Proceedings of a Symposium Organized by the World Bank and the International Food Policy Research Institute* (Washington, D.C.: World Bank, 1993), pp. 34–35; and Timothy Besley and Ravi Kanbur, "The Principles of Targeting," in ibid., pp. 78–79.

[67]Kirit Parikh and T.N. Srinivasan, "Poverty Alleviation Policies in India," in Michael Lipton and Jacques van der Gaag, *Including the Poor: Proceedings of a Symposium Organized by the World Bank and the International Food Policy Research Institute* (Washington, D.C.: World Bank, 1993), pp. 403–06. See also Amartya Sen, "The Economics of Life and Death," *Scientific American* 268 (May 1993): 40–47.

[68]World Bank, *World Development Report, 1990* (New York: Oxford University Press, 1990), pp. 96–100.

inequality occurring with development. Only a total mobilization of government policies toward programs to help the poor directly—a war on poverty—succeeds in reducing income inequality and increasing absolute incomes. And successful countries, such as Taiwan, South Korea, Israel, and Singapore, all redistributed before growth. For Adelman and Robinson, the redistributed asset changes with the level of economic development. At first when the economy is primarily agricultural, land is redistributed. With further development, the primary asset is physical capital. At a later stage, the redistribution of human capital through education and training for the poor is emphasized.[69]

Adjustment Programs.   Chapters 17, 18, and 20 discussed how the IMF and World Bank compel LDC experiencing a chronic external deficit and debt problem to undertake economic reform, structural adjustment, and macroeconomic stabilization policies. The evidence suggests that adjustment programs are initially likely to reduce real wages and worsen the condition of the poor. To be sure, the World Bank **Social Dimensions of Adjustment Projects (SDA)** attempts to find policy instruments to achieve economic development and poverty reduction, with emphasis on short-term compensation where adjustment programs have immediate costs for identifiable groups. However, LDC planners find it politically difficult to compensate the poor for the impact of adjustment programs. To illustrate, in Ghana, the **Program of Action to Mitigate the Social Costs of Adjustment (PAMSCAD),** beginning in 1988, provided limited funds for public works, food-for-work projects, and retrenched public-sector workers but little for projects to offset declining health care and potable water, malnourishment among women and children, and adjustment costs by the poorest classes. For the redistributive effect of Ghana's adjustment programs struck at powerful vested interests, who fought back to regain their ascendancy at the expense of the poor. The IMF and World Bank were aware of the internal politics of adjustment that resulted in privileged interest groups but not the poor being effective in receiving compensation for adjustment.[70] In the future, these international agencies must insist that LDC adjustment programs also include provisions for compensating the poor.

---

[69]Irma Adelman and Sherman Robinson, *Income Distribution Policy in Developing Countries: A Case Study of Korea* (Stanford: Stanford University Press, 1978).

[70]James P. Grant, *The State of the World's Children, 1989* (New York: Oxford University Press, 1989), pp. 18–20; Paul Streeten, "A Survey of the Issues and Options," in Simon Commander, ed., *Structural Adjustment and Agriculture: Theory and Practice in Africa and Latin America* (London: Overseas Development Institute, 1989), pp. 16–17; World Bank, *Adjustment Lending: An Evaluation of Ten Years of Experience* (Washington, D.C., 1988), pp. 29–49; Trevor W. Parfitt, "Lies, Damned Lies and Statistics: The World Bank/ECA Structural Adjustment Controversy," *Review of African Political Economy,* no. 47 (Spring 1990), p. 13; Joan M. Nelson, "The Politics of Pro-poor Adjustment," in Joan M. Nelson and contributors, *Fragile Coalitions: The Politics of Economic Adjustment* (New Brunswick, N.J.: Transaction Books, 1989), pp. 102; Food and Agriculture Organization of the United Nations, *The State of Food and Agriculture, 1990* (Rome, 1991), p. 114; J.L.S. Abbey, "Ghana's Experience with Structural Adjustment: Some Lessons," in James Pickett and Hans Singer, eds., *Towards Economic Recovery in Sub-Saharan Africa: Essays in Honor of Robert Gardiner* (London: Routledge, 1990), p. 39; Tsatsu Tskikata, "Ghana," in Adebayo Adedeji, Sadig Rasheed, and Melody Morrison, eds., *Human Dimensions of Africa's Persistent Economic Crisis* (London: Hans Zell, 1990), p. 161; and E. Wayne Nafziger, *The Debt Crisis in Africa* (Baltimore: Johns Hopkins University Press, 1993), pp. 174–75.

Income Equality Versus Growth

Some development economists maintain that inequality, by spurring high investment rates, benefits the poor, since accumulation raises productivity and average material welfare. Gustav F. Papanek, an advisor to Pakistan during the late 1950s and early 1960s, asserted a conflict "between the aims of growth and equality" such that "great inequality of incomes is conducive to increased savings."[71] Mahbub ul Haq, an eloquent World Bank spokeperson for meeting LDC basic needs in the 1970s and 1990s, contended while Pakistani planner in the 1960s: "The underdeveloped countries must consciously accept a philosophy of growth and shelve for the distant future all ideas of equitable distribution and welfare state. It should be recognized that these are luxuries which only developed countries can afford." His conclusion was "additional output should be distributed in favor of the saving sectors." His was "basically a philosophy of growth as opposed to a philosophy of distribution [and] is indispensable in a period of 'take-off'."[72] In the 1980s, as Pakistani planner, he stated views similar to those he held in the 1960s.

University of California, Los Angeles, economist Deepak Lal concluded from comparative studies "that growth does 'trickle down,' whilst growth collapses lead to increasing poverty." Additionally, "direct transfers and social expenditures to alleviate poverty were found not to have made any appreciable dent on poverty." Indeed expanding entitlements have "the effect of 'killing the goose that laid the golden egg'." A part of his finding is the "Director's law" stating "that most politics (except for the Platonic variety) leads to income transfers from the poor and the rich to the middle class." For Lal, "it is not surprising that a common finding of many empirical studies of poverty redressed in countries with the most widespread welfare systems is that these programs far from relieving absolute poverty have tended to institutionalize it."[73] Lal's conclusions about growth trickling down to the poor and the inefficacy of welfare programs contradict studies by the World Bank and International Labor Office.[74]

Adelman and Morris oppose a strategy of waiting for later stages of development to emphasize income distribution.[75] And Cambridge economist Joan Robinson argues that even if you assume that inequality spurs capital accumulation and growth, it may not be prudent for the LDC poor to favor inequality, thus

---

[71]Gustav F. Papanek, *Pakistan's Development: Social Goals and Private Incentives* (Cambridge, Mass.: Harvard University Press, 1967).

[72]Mahbub ul Haq, *The Strategy of Economic Planning: A Case Study of Pakistan* (Karachi, Pakistan: Oxford University Press, 1966).

[73]Deepak Lal, "The Political Economy of Poverty, Equity, and Growth in 21 Developing Countries: A Summary of Findings," Paper presented to an American Economic Association panel on "Economics of Growth and Stagnation," Washington, D.C., December 29, 1990.

[74]Hollis Chenery, Montek S. Ahluwalia, C. L. G. Bell, John H. Duloy, and Richard Jolly, eds., *Redistribution with Growth* (London: Oxford University Press, 1974); Montek S. Ahluwalia, Nicholas G. Carter, and Hollis B. Chenery, "Growth and Poverty in Developing Countries," *Journal of Development Economics* 6 (September 1979): 299–341; World Bank, *World Development Report, 1980* (New York: Oxford University Press, 1980); World Bank, *World Development Report, 1990* (New York: Oxford University Press, 1990); Michael Lipton and Jacques van der Gaag, eds., *Including the Poor—Proceedings of a Symposium Organized by the World Bank and the International Food Policy Research Institute* (Washington, D.C.: World Bank, 1993); and Jacques Lecaillon, Felix Paukert, Christian Morrisson, and Dimitri Germidis, *Income Distribution and Economic Development: An Analytical Survey* (Geneva: International Labor Office, 1984).

[75]Irma Adelman and Cynthia Taft Morris, *Economic Growth and Social Equity in Developing Countries* (Stanford: Stanford University Press, 1973).

risking their children's health and nutrition to bequeath a fortune to their grandchildren. Promoting saving through inequality is more costly than other alternatives such as government policies to promote both equality and capital formation.[76]

Torsten Persson and Guido Tabellini argue that inequality is harmful for growth, since in a society with substantial distributional conflict, political leaders are compelled to produce economic policies that tax investment and growth promotion to redistribute income.[77] In sub-Saharan Africa, in the 1970s through the early 1980s, shrinking economic pie slices and growing distributional conflict added pressures to national leaders, whose response was usually not only antiegalitarian but also antigrowth, hurting small farmers' incentives, taking peasant savings for government industry, building government enterprises beyond management capacity, using these inefficient firms to give benefits to clients, and allocating educational funds to maintain the standing of their children and block the upward mobility of the children of workers and farmers. Regime survival in a politically fragile system required marshalling elite support at the expense of economic growth. Spurring peasant production through market prices and exchange rates interfered with national leaders' ability to build political support, especially in cities.[78] Yet the link between stagnation and inequality in Africa may be exceptional. Still we cannot be certain that there is generally a tradeoff between growth and equality. Data are not of sufficient quality to enable us to generalize about the relationship between growth and equality in LDCs.

Generally accelerating economic growth through stable macroeconomic policies is perhaps the most satisfactory *political* approach to reducing poverty and dampening distributional conflict. A number of upper-middle-income countries, such as South Korea, Taiwan, Malaysia, and Thailand, have decreased poverty a great deal through rapid economic growth; and historically workers gain more from a larger GNP pie than from a larger share of a pie that remains the same size. When the income pie is not enlarged, any gains the underprivileged classes make are at the expense of the more privileged classes: Such a redistribution from the higher to lower income classes is difficult to achieve politically. However, when the GNP pie grows, the piece of pie can be larger for both privileged and underprivileged groups. Chapters 8 to 20 focus on ways of accelerating growth. As the next section indicates, the questions of poverty, inequality, and government policy are intertwined with those of political order.

Inequality and Political Instability

Only rarely has peasant discontent led to revolutionary insurrection. China's civil war (1927–49) is a modern example. Yet given the substantial income inequalities within many developing states, the noteworthy point may not be the few economically deprived that rebel against political authority, but the vast majority who do not. Karl Marx expected that as workers united and became more powerful and comprised a majority of the population, they would revolt and appropriate capital

---

[76]Joan Robinson, *An Essay on Marxian Economics* (London: Macmillan, 1949).

[77]Torsten Persson and Guido Tabellini, "Is Inequality Harmful for Growth," *American Economic Review* 84 (June 1994): 600–21.

[78]E. Wayne Nafziger, *Inequality in Africa: Political Elites, Proletariat, Peasants and the Poor* (Cambridge: Cambridge University Press, 1988).

and land. Yet wage earners did not revolt when they were in a majority in the West, and there is no indication that this will occur among workers in the developing world. The state has the military and police power to neutralize or suppress rebellion. Furthermore, the economically disadvantaged are rarely united, since their interests vary; and in any event, the political elite can usually reward potentially restive groups who cooperate with it and thus remains in control. The poor remain unorganized; the state remains intact.

Despite the popularly *perceived* economic discrepancy between what ought to be and what is, a tension termed **relative deprivation,** actual political violence rarely occurs. The likelihood of powerfully felt relative deprivation, common experiences and beliefs that sanction violence, the ideological support of other groups, protection from retribution, and cues for violence all determine whether or not the deprived will rebel.[79] Furthermore, the political leadership does not simply rule by force and fraud but represents the interests and purposes of important and influential groups in society. Usually the power elite sees to it that the ideological positions of the media, schools, and religious communities do not contradict its interest. Prevailing political and religious ideologies legitimate inequalities associated with class, occupation, and caste.

Despite all of these tendencies to maintain political stability, representatives of the developing world increasingly stress the inequalities, injustices, and tensions of the *global* economy and polity when explaining poverty and underdevelopment in their own countries. Their views of income distribution and class antagonisms go beyond differences within countries to include greater discrepancies between countries. Rich countries are seen as controlling the international economy, and most of the U.S. and Canadian readers of this book are viewed as members of an international upper class and beneficiaries of an unjust international order.

Thus people who perceive a highly interrelated global system dominated by rich countries are not surprised when political enmities and disorder in Latin America, Africa, and the Middle East threaten the material comforts and political tranquility of middle-class affluent people in DCs. This perception is a far cry from that of most Westerners, for whom riots, terrorism, holding hostages, and armed attacks directed against rich countries are often capricious, arbitrary, and inexplicable. Herman E. Daly argues that the wide gap in economic well-being between the rich and poor, the increasing material aspirations of poor countries, and the rich's tenacious defense of their living standards are a threat to all of our human activities, a threat to "spaceship earth" itself (see Chapter 13).[80]

Summary

1. The current definition of the international extreme poverty line is the income needed for a daily supply of 2,250 calories per person in India. Based on this figure, in 1985 about 0.6 billion of the 3.5 billion population in LDCs were poor.

2. People in absolute poverty are undernourished and have low resistance to disease. A high infant mortality rate, a life expectancy of about 40 years, and illiteracy characterize this group.

---

[79]Ted Robert Gurr, *Why Men Rebel* (Princeton: Princeton University Press, 1970).

[80]Herman E. Daly, *Steady-state Economics: The Economics of Biophysical Equilibrium and Moral Growth* (San Francisco: W. H. Freeman, 1977).

3. The current definition of the international poverty line provides for consumption in excess of the bare physical minimum, but varies from country to country, reflecting the cost of participating in the everyday life of society. This poverty line includes indoor plumbing and potable water as a "necessity" in some countries. If you use this less standardized definition of poverty, 1.1 billion people in LDCs were poor in 1985.

4. Amartya Sen's concept of poverty focuses on capabilities rather than attainments, meaning that a high-income person who squanders his resources so that he lives miserably would not be considered poor.

5. Sen argues that policy makers need the following measures of poverty: headcount or poverty percentage, income-gap or the additional income needed to bring the poor up to the level of the poverty line, and Gini coefficient or concentration of income among the poor.

6. Only 1.4 percent of the real income in the world goes to the poorest 20 percent of the world's population, while the richest 20 percent receives 82.7 percent of it. Income inequality worldwide exceeds that for any single country.

7. Early economic development in LDCs often results in increasing poverty for the lowest income groups. Inequality follows an inverted U-shaped pattern, first increasing and then decreasing with growth in per capita income.

8. Although middle-income countries tend to have higher income inequality than low-income countries, inequality increases in low-income states with economic development.

9. Developed countries have lower income inequality than developing countries.

10. Although absolute poverty is present in upper-middle-income countries with high inequalities, such as Mexico and Brazil, most absolute poverty is in India, Bangladesh, Pakistan, and parts of sub-Saharan Africa, which have low per capita income.

11. The rate of economic growth is not associated with the degree of income inequality.

12. Minority groups, rural residents, women, children, the elderly, and the illiterate are highly represented among the world's poor.

13. Women comprise 34 percent of the LDC labor force and receive an average income half that of men, partly because of discrimination.

14. Taiwan's and South Korea's stress on land reform, education, and labor-intensive manufacturing, and Indonesia's emphasis on rural development have succeeded in increasing the income shares of the poorest segments of their populations. On the other hand, many of India's programs to aid the poor were circumvented by administrators, landlords, and business people whose economic interests were threatened by such efforts.

15. Policies used to reduce poverty and income inequality include credit for the poor, universal primary education, employment programs, rural development schemes, progressive income taxes, food subsidies, health programs, family planning, food research, inducements to migration, income transfers, affirmative action programs, targeting programs for the poorest groups, and workfare schemes for which only the poor will qualify. However an integrated war on poverty requiring a total mobilization of government policies toward programs to help the poor is probably necessary if poverty and inequality are to be substantially reduced.

16. Designing "safety nets" for the poor is an essential component to facilitate widespread support for economic adjustment and stabilization programs.
17. Economists disagree on whether there is a tradeoff or interlink between equality and growth. Most economists agree, however, that accelerating economic growth through stable macroeconomic policies is the most satisfactory political approach to reducing poverty and reducing distributional conflict.
18. Despite the vast poverty and inequality in LDCs, the economically disadvantaged rarely rebel against the state.

Terms to Review

- absolute poverty
- poverty line
- extreme poverty line
- Kuznets curve
- Sen's concept of capabilities
- headcount approach
- income-gap approach
- Lorenz curve
- Gini index of inequality
- elasticity of the poverty gap with regard to the Gini index
- cumulative distribution function

- international balance on goods and services
- microenterprises
- group lending
- Green Revolution
- terms of trade
- crowding
- Social Dimensions of Adjustment Projects (SDA)
- Program of Action to Mitigate the Social Costs of Adjustment (PAMSCAD)
- relative deprivation

Questions to Discuss

1. What is an international poverty line? What are some of its advantages and disadvantages?
2. Why do World Bank economists use two separate poverty lines? Indicate the major differences between the two poverty lines.
3. What is meant by absolute poverty? What are some characteristics of absolute poverty?
4. Assess the reliability and validity of LDC statistics on poverty and income inequality.
5. Is poverty synonymous with low well-being?
6. Indicate the advantages of using the headcount approach, income-gap approach, *and* Gini coefficient to depict poverty as opposed to using only the headcount approach.
7. Design a program for gathering information on poverty and income distribution for low-income countries (or a particular low-income country), indicate data and measures you would stress, and explain how this information can be used to influence government policy.
8. Evaluate the relative success of developed and developing countries, low- or middle-income countries, countries in early or late stages of development,

countries from differing regions of the world, and countries in transition compared to Afro-Asian-Latin American countries in reducing poverty and income inequality in recent decades.

9. How do Irma Adelman and Cynthia Taft Morris show how economic growth in a dual economy explains the Kuznets curve?

10. Does the rising segment of the inverted U-shaped curve imply that the poor suffer from economic growth?

11. Why are cross-national income distribution data for different per capita income levels *at a given time* inadequate for generalizing about income distribution changes with economic development over time?

12. Which policies do you think are most effective in reducing poverty and income inequality in developing countries?

13. Discuss why LDC women have higher poverty rates than men. What LDC policies would reduce female poverty rates?

14. Is there a tradeoff between LDC policies seeking to reduce income inequality and those trying to stimulate growth? Does the tradeoff vary between different LDCs?

15. What conditions do you think are necessary for economic inequalities to contribute to political upheaval?

Guide to Readings

Data on LDC poverty and income distribution are included in Ravallion, Datt, and van de Walle (note 10); the appendix to the World Bank's annual *World Development Report*; the United Nations Development Program's annual *Human Development Report*; an edited volume by Lipton and van der Gaag (note 7); Eliana Cardoso and Ann Helwege, "Below the Line: Poverty in Latin America," *World Development* 20 (January 1992): 19–37; Lecaillon, Paukert, Morrisson, and Germidis (note 4); Ahluwalia, Carter, and Chenery (note 14); and Chenery et al. (note 5).

N. Kakwanit, "Measuring Poverty: Definitions and Significance Tests with Application to Côte d'Ivoire," in Michael Lipton and Jacques van der Gaag, eds., *Including the Poor—Proceedings of a Symposium Organized by the World Bank and the International Food Policy Research Institute* (Washington, D.C.: World Bank, 1993), pp. 43–66; and Blackwood and Lynch (note 15) have an excellent assessment of mathematical measures of poverty and income inequality. For critiques of the literature, see Moll (note 4), Lecaillon et al. (note 4), Lipton and van der Gaag (note 7); and Alderman (note 10).

Sen (five works cited in notes 12 and 35) is the foremost analyst of concepts and measures of poverty and welfare; his contribution is evaluated by Sugden (note 12). Dasgupta (note 8) reconciles the theoretical considerations of welfare economics and political philosophy with the empirical evidence concerning poverty and deprivation. T.N. Srinivasan, "Destitution: a Discourse," *Journal of Economic Literature* 32 (December 1994): 1842–55, has an insightful review of Dasgupta's work. Fields (note 2) has an excellent survey of the literature.

Kuznets (note 22) first hypothesized that over time, inequality within a country follows an inverted U-shaped curve. Williamson (note 25), Adelman and Morris (two citations in note 24), and Sundrum (note 25) use historical data to examine Kuznets' hypothesis.

The *World Development Report, 1990* focuses on a discussion of LDC poverty, including policies to reduce poverty. Major studies of policies for improving income distribution include Chenery et al. (note 5), Adelman and Robinson, Frank and Webb (note 51), and Margaret E. Grosh, "Five Criteria for Choosing among Poverty Programs," World Bank Policy Research Department Working Paper 1201, October 1993. Graham Pyatt and Erik Thorbecke discuss planning to reduce poverty in *Planning Techniques for a Better Future* (Geneva: International Labor Office, 1976). See Paul Clements for "A Poverty-Oriented Cost-Benefit Approach to the Analysis of Development Projects," *World Development* 23 (April 1995): 577–92.

R. M. Sundrum, *Growth and Income Distribution in India* (Newbury Park, Calif.: Sage, 1987), analyzes poverty and income distribution in India. Nafziger (note 34) focuses on explanations for income inequality in sub-Saharan Africa.

UNICEF's annual *The State of the World's Children* (note 37) indicates accompaniments of absolute poverty, especially among the third world's children. Dasgupta (note 8), Dwyer and Bruce (note 36), Tinker, Bramsen, and Buvinić (note 39), and Parpart (note 34) examine gender income differentials in developing countries.

On the effect of LDC structural adjustment and reform on poverty, see Lipton and van der Gaag (note 66), the Food and Agriculture Organization of the United Nations, Nafziger, Nelson, Commander, and Adedeji, Rasheed, and Morrison (note 70), and various World Bank publications. For more on the role of microenterprises in economic development, see Otero and Rhyne, World Bank (note 53), and Carl Liedholm and Donald Mead (cited in Chapter 12).

Dominique van de Walle and Kimberly Nead, eds., *Public Spending and the Poor: Theory and Evidence* (Baltimore: Johns Hopkins University Press, 1995), ask whether public spending in LDCs helps redistribute income to the poor, and whether targeting specific poverty groups can improve the impact of spending on the poor. Some economists recommend self-targeting schemes, such as public employment programs; however, Martin Ravallion and Gaurav Datt show that these work schemes reduce poverty less than universal cash handouts. Giovanni Andrea Cornia and Frances Stewart make a plea for measuring the errors of excluding the poor and not just the leakage of benefits to the nonpoor.

CHAPTER 7

Rural Poverty and Agricultural Transformation

In LDCs, 3.1 billion (63 percent of 4.9 billion) people and 1.15 billion (80 percent) poor people live in rural areas. And in most developing countries, the agricultural population is growing, pressing on a limited arable land base.

But the rural poor become urban poor as they migrate to densely populated cities in their search for employment. The urban population as a percentage of the LDC population grew from 27 percent in 1975 to 35 percent in 1992, and is projected to increase to 40 percent in 2000 and 47 percent in 2010 (Chapter 9). Without comprehensive rural development, the International Fund for Agricultural Development estimates that the number of rural poor could grow to 1.31 billion of 3.24 billion rural people in 2000.[1]

Clearly, any approach to reduce poverty and accelerate economic growth should focus on rural development. But another major focus needs to be income distribution, increasing the productivity and income of the rural poor. For this to occur, the LDC rural poor need increased access to productive resources, land and capital, and technology. This chapter concentrates on both increased rural relative to urban income and reduced intrarural inequalities as components of a strategy to reduce rural poverty.

Scope of the Chapter

This chapter examines rural poverty and indicates policies to ameliorate it. Our approach is tenfold:

1. We look at the nature of poverty in rural areas in LDCs (though the information available is limited).
2. We identify major rural groups comprising the poor.

---

[1] Idriss Jazairy, Mohiuddin Alamgir, and Theresa Panuccio, *The State of World Rural Poverty: An Inquiry into its Causes and Consequences*, Published for the International Fund for Agricultural Development (New York: New York University Press, 1992), p. 1.

170

3. We discuss the differences between rural and agricultural development.

4. We show that present-day, rural-urban differences in LDCs are greater than in the West in the nineteenth century.

5. We compare agricultural productivity in DCs and LDCs and in China and India.

6. We examine the transition from subsistence to specialized farming to clarify what farming is like in LDCs.

7. We compare the growth of food production per capita in LDCs and DCs.

8. We examine the determinants of the growth in food demand.

9. We discuss factors contributing to low income in rural areas.

10. Finally and perhaps most importantly, we examine policies that might increase income and reduce poverty in rural areas.

Major Rural Groups in Poverty

The widespread assumption among development economists in the 1960s and 1970s that agrarian societies are characterized by roughly uniform poverty is a myth.[2] Rural society is highly differentiated, comprising a complex structure of rich landowners, peasants, sharecroppers, tenants, and laborers, in addition to artisans, traders, and plantation workers. In most LDCs, it is the small landholders (with less than 3 hectares or 7 acres), the near-landless, the landless, and the agricultural laborers who comprise the poor. According to the International Fund for Agricultural Development (IFAD), 52 percent of the LDC rural poor consist of smallholder farmer households (many of whom are in marginal areas where rainfall is inadequate, soils are fragile and vulnerable to erosion, and desertification is a serious risk), 24 percent of landless households, 7 percent of indigenous ethnic tribals, 6 percent of nomadic pastoralists, 4 percent of small and artisanal fishers, and 6 percent of internally displaced refugees. Sub-Saharan Africa has a disproportional share of smallholder poor and Latin America of landless poor. Households headed by women, a category which overlaps with the other IFAD categories, comprise 12 percent of the rural poor and are often counted among the poorest of the poor.[3] As pointed out in Chapter 6, women have fewer opportunities for schooling, lack physical mobility, and often work more than 14 hours a day with household chores, growing food crops, and working in the labor force at low wages.[4]

No Asian, African, and Latin American country with a majority of the labor force in agriculture had more than three hectares of cropland per agricultural workers in 1990 save two (Afghanistan and Botswana). This is a far cry from the

---

[2]See Henry J. Bruton, *Principles of Development Economics* (Englewood Cliffs, N.J.: Prentice Hall, 1965), p. 100.

[3]Polygyny, the taking of several wives, persists in many parts of sub-Saharan Africa. In Africa's "polygyny belt," which stretches from Senegal in the west to Tanzania in the east, a substantial fraction of married women are in polygynous unions. In African societies where women do not own land, men control access to land; wives, in effect, pay their husband a share of farm output in exchange for cultivation rights. According to Hanan G. Jacoby, "The Economics of Polygyny in Sub-Saharan Africa: Female Productivity and the Demand for Wives in Côte d'Ivoire," *Journal of Political Economy* 105 (October 1995): 938–971, in the Ivory Coast, the demand for wives increases with a man's wealth and the availability to him of farms on which the labor of wives can be productive.

[4]Idriss Jazairy, Mohiuddin Alamgir, and Theresa Panuccio, *The State of World Rural Poverty: An Inquiry into its Causes and Consequences,* Published for the International Fund for Agricultural Development (New York: New York University Press, 1992), pp. xviii–xix, 406–07.

40 hectares per agricultural worker in the United States in 1910, the time productivity reached a level where the number of farm workers began to fall.[5] Unsurprisingly, almost 40 percent of the LDC rural population is in poverty.

Yet because rural income fluctuates with the season, annual weather variations, and the illness or death of major breadwinners, the static picture of poverty portrayed by data at a given time is deceptive. In central India, 88 percent of the agricultural households were poor at least 1 year between 1975 and 1983, 44 percent for 6 or more years, and 19 percent poor every year, although the average poverty rate was 50 percent. Thus transient poverty is substantial, and a substantial share of the population moves out of poverty (25 percent in the central Indian study) or from nonpoor to poor (16 percent in central India) in any given year.[6] Yet central India's poverty fluctuated around a trend of declining rural poverty, resulting from agricultural growth and falling rural inequality.[7]

Rural and Agricultural Development

Rural development is not the same as agricultural development. The agrarian community requires a full range of services such as schools, shops, banks, machinery dealers, and so on. Often rural areas use surplus agricultural labor, either seasonally or full-time, in industry. Thus in Maoist China from 1958 to 1976, rural development was based on the people's commune, which provided economies of scale for social services and mobilized underemployed labor for manufacturing, constructing machine tools, building roads and dams, and digging irrigation chemicals. Since the rural reform in 1979, China's rural population has depended even more heavily on nonfarm incomes. In India, off-farm employment comprised almost 50 percent of small farmers' income and more than 50 percent of their labor. In LDCs generally, many farmers are employed part-time, and other family members full-time, in off-farm enterprises. Thomas P. Tomich, Peter Kilby, and Bruce F. Johnston indicate that farm income comprises only 57 percent of rural household income in African and Asian LDCs, with the ratio of farm income to nonfarm income to urban transfers 4:2:1.[8] Finally some farmers actually live in urban areas. Thus rural development includes more than agricultural income growth.

Rural-Urban Income Differentials
in Nineteenth-Century Europe and Present-Day LDCS

Contemporary rural-urban differentials in LDCs are much greater than they were in Europe in the nineteenth century. Output per person outside agriculture, as a multiple of the figure in agriculture, is eight in Africa and four in Asia and Latin

[5]Thomas P. Tomich, Peter Kilby, and Bruce F. Johnston, *Transforming Agrarian Economies: Opportunities Seized, Opportunities Missed* (Ithaca, N.Y.: Cornell University Press, 1995).

[6]World Bank, *World Development Report, 1990* (New York: Oxford University Press, 1990), pp. 34–36.

[7]Inderjit Singh, *The Great Ascent: The Rural Poor in South Asia* (Baltimore: Johns Hopkins University Press, 1990), pp. 26–35.

[8]Inderjit Singh, *The Great Ascent: The Rural Poor in South Asia* (Baltimore: Johns Hopkins University Press, 1990), p. 91; and Thomas P. Tomich, Peter Kilby, and Bruce F. Johnston, *Transforming Agrarian Economies: Opportunities Seized, Opportunities Missed* (Ithaca, N.Y.: Cornell University Press, 1995).

America. It was two in Europe in the nineteenth century.[9] However, discrepancies between urban and rural areas in income per person are not so high as nonagricultural-agricultural differences indicate because (1) urban agriculturalists have a lower average income than others in urban areas; (2) rural nonagriculturalists have a higher average income than others in rural areas; and (3) rural worker participation rates (which include proportionally more women and children) are high.

Agricultural Productivity in DCs and LDCs

How does agricultural productivity differ between LDCs and DCs? Agricultural output per worker in developing countries is one–thirtieth of that in developed countries and one-seventy-eighth of that in North America (the United States and Canada) (Table 7–1). Obviously world agriculture is highly diverse. On the one hand is the highly efficient agriculture of the affluent countries where high levels of capital accumulation, technical knowledge, and worker productivity permit a small farm population to feed entire nations. In contrast is the low-productive

TABLE 7-1 Agricultural Output per Agricultural Worker—World and Regions, 1964-66 to 1991-93 (1979-81 world = 100)

Region	Agricultural Output per Agricultural Worker						
	1964–66	*1969–71*	*1974–76*	*1979–81*	*1984–86*	*1989–91*	*1991–93*
Developed and transitional economies	341	456	564	696	881	1072	1140
Developed countries	568	756	965	1277	1590	1920	2075
North America	2152	2678	3041	3521	4200	4997	5486
Western Europe	325	437	550	717	919	1121	1583
Oceania Developed	3009	3483	3563	3764	4322	4700	5078
Japan and Asia Developed	107	146	190	261	348	424	448
Other	218	210	292	460	394	442	403
Transitional Economies	177	239	289	321	420	513	507
Eastern Europe	191	230	308	392	498	563	529
Former Soviet Union	193	279	319	327	435	552	573
Developing Countries	45	48	51	55	61	67	70
Africa	53	56	56	53	54	59	59
Latin America	202	221	243	278	290	328	335
Asia Developing	35	38	40	44	51	57	60
Oceania Developing	76	81	85	95	102	106	106
World	82	90	95	100	107	113	114

Note: The values of the world and regional aggregates of agricultural production are computed by using international commodity prices, which assigns a single "price" to each commodity. The values obtained are expressed in international dollars (as explained in Chapter 2) at the 1979–81 average prices.

Source: L. Naiken, "Agricultural Output per Agricultural Worker," Rome: Food and Agriculture Organization of the United Nations, July 1994. I am grateful to L. Naiken for compiling this table for this book.

[9]Michael Lipton, *Why Poor People Stay Poor: A Study of Urban Bias in World Development* (London: Maurice Temple Smith, 1977), pp. 435–37.

agriculture in most Asian and African countries that barely sustains the population, including a minority off the farm, at a subsistence level. The major factors raising LDC agricultural labor productivity are (1) new biological-chemical-mechanical inputs in production, (2) new technical and organizational knowledge from greater specialization, and (3) expanded markets for agricultural output.[10]

Small-Scale LDC Agriculture

The evolution of agricultural production commonly occurs in three stages: (1) **peasant farming,** where the major concern is survival; (2) **mixed farming;** and (3) **commercial farming.**[11] If you have seen only the highly specialized, mechanized farms of the United States and Canada, it may be hard for you to visualize the subsistence agriculture that is the livelihood of most farmers in LDCs (and was for most farmers in North America in the late eighteenth and early nineteenth centuries). On the traditional peasant farm, output and consumption are almost identical, and the staple crop (usually wheat, barley, sorghum, rice, or corn) is the chief source of food. Land and labor are the key production factors, and capital is small. Labor, however, is underutilized except for peak seasons, such as planting and harvest. Cultivators—small owners, tenants, or sharecroppers—farm only as much land as their families can work without hired labor.

For many this way of life is changing. An increasing number of peasants, pressured by a growing rural population per cultivated hectare, attracted by productivity gains from new capital and technology, and stirred by mass communications to higher consumer expectations, are producing crops for the market. Yet change does not take place so rapidly as the Western observer expects. Peasant resistance to change, which appears irrational to the Westerner, may in fact be prudent. The prime objective of the peasant is not to maximize income but his or her family's chance of survival.

Attempts to improve the situation of subsistence farmers by an indiscriminate introduction of cash crops often result in a greater risk to the survival of the peasant's family without any major increase in its average consumption. In parts of South Asia and Latin America, peasants who grow cash crops earn so little that at least three-quarters of their income is spent on food. In fact commercial farming is often a more precarious operation than subsistence farming: Prices fluctuate, necessary materials are scarce, and the weather remains unpredictable. Extension agents who introduce new varieties, cultivation, or management practices for trials on peasant farms should generally experiment with only a small part of a farmer's land, so that the innovations are not unduly risky and so the farmer can compare the results with traditional practices.[12]

For many mixed farming rather than highly specialized commercial farming is the first step away from subsistence agriculture. Production branches off into other enterprises besides the staple crop, such as fruits, vegetables, and animal husbandry. This change begins with improved productivity through technological advances,

[10]Thomas P. Tomich, Peter Kilby, and Bruce F. Johnston, *Transforming Agrarian Economies: Opportunities Seized, Opportunities Missed* (Ithaca, N.Y.: Cornell University Press, 1995).

[11]This discussion draws on Raanan Weitz, *From Peasant to Farmer: A Revolutionary Strategy for Development* (New York: Columbia University Press, 1971), pp. 6–28.

[12]Inderjit Singh, *The Great Ascent: The Rural Poor in South Asia* (Baltimore: Johns Hopkins University Press, 1990), p. 109.

capital formation, or using resources underemployed in subsistence farming, and it varies depending on the particular conditions of the farm. For example, if the staple crop is grown only part of the year, new crops may be introduced in the slack season to use idle land and family labor, or more crops may be grown as a result of mixed cropping, irrigation, or using new seed varieties. Reducing labor requirements in the peak seasons by introducing simple labor-saving techniques can lead to new enterprises, such as cattle or poultry farming. Improved seeds, fertilizer, and irrigation may yield more food and free some land for cash crops. Thus the farmer will have a marketable surplus for cash income. By spreading the work load more evenly throughout the year, diversified farming uses more of the available labor. Mixed farming can also provide more security to the operator. If one crop is destroyed by pests, disease, or natural calamity or sells at a low price, others may do better.

The specialized farm, the most advanced agricultural phase in a market economy, usually emphasizes cultivating one crop. Such a farm is capital intensive, uses advanced technology, and takes advantage of economies of scale and expanding national and international markets. The farmer no longer grows crops for the family but for the market.

Concentrating on one major crop appears quite risky. It seems to return the farm to the unbalanced work schedule and dependence on a single crop of the subsistence phase. However, the specialized farm uses labor-saving devices that decrease the work load at peak periods, so that the slack season can be used for other activities, such as plowing, fertilizing, maintaining equipment, and catching up with the latest literature. Furthermore, some of the risks of one-crop farming can be overcome by insurance policies, pesticides, market research, and irrigation. Also, the income from specialized farming is so much higher than from other forms of farm production that it outweighs occasional losses from bad weather or price fluctuations.

Even when agricultural output per person grows, the transition from peasant to specialized farmer usually increases the number of landless laborers. Indeed, the change of many farm cultivators to hired workers during growing commercialization may be partly responsible for the increased rural poverty noted in South and Southeast Asia in the 1960s and 1970s, and reduced nutrition for workers in newly-established plantations in Sri Lanka and Zimbabwe. And often women lose with commercialization, even when they were important decision makers before the change.[13] Thomas P. Tomich, Peter Kilby, and Bruce F. Johnston, however, argue that commercialization has only a small positive effect on calorie intake but does not worsen LDC household welfare.[14]

Growth of Average Food Production in DCs and LDCs

Both agricultural and food outputs per worker in LDCs are fractions of the same measures in DCs. How does the *growth* of food production per capita in LDCs compare to that in DCs? Figure 7–1 indicates that food output per person in developing

[13]Hans P. Binswanger and Joachim von Braun, "Technological Change and Commercialization in Agriculture: Impact on the Poor," in Michael Lipton and Jacques van der Gaag, *Including the Poor: Proceedings of a Symposium Organized by the World Bank and the International Food Policy Research Institute* (Washington, D.C.: World Bank, 1993), pp. 171–80.

[14]Thomas P. Tomich, Peter Kilby, and Bruce F. Johnston, *Transforming Agrarian Economies: Opportunities Seized, Opportunities Missed* (Ithaca, N.Y.: Cornell University Press, 1995).

FIGURE 7-1   Growth in Food Production per Capita, 1960-91 (1960 = 100)
Per capita food production grew by 9 percent in developed countries from 1962 to 1989, and by 14 percent in developing countries during the same period (22 percent in Latin America; 41 percent in East Asia,
excluding Japan and China; 11 percent in South and Southeast Asia; and -20 percent in sub-Saharan
Africa, the only world region where calorie intake, even if equally distributed, is below minimal nutritional
standards). Although the graph shows year-to-year fluctuations, the figure for per capita food output for
a given year *t* is an average of the figures for year *t* – 2 through *t* + 2.

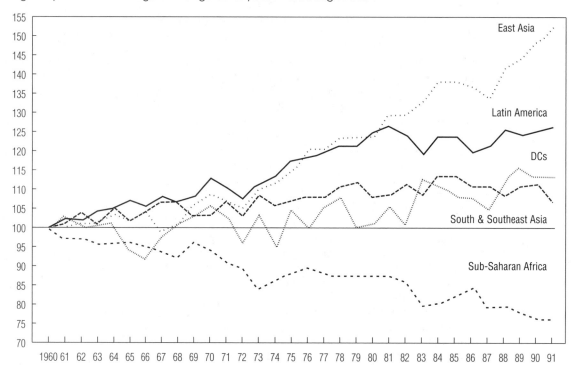

Sources: U.S. Department of Agriculture, International Economic Division, *World Indices of Agricultural and Food
Production, 1950–85* (Washington, D.C., 1986); U.S. Department of Agriculture, Economic Research Service,
World Indices of Agricultural and Food Production, 1976–85 (Washington, D.C., 1986); U.S. Department of Agri-
culture, Economic Research Service, *World Indices of Agricultural and Food Production, 1977–86* (Washington,
D.C., 1988); and Food and Agriculture Organization of the U.N. (FAO), *The State of Food and Agriculture, 1993*
(Rome, 1993), pp. 206–09.

countries grew at an annual rate of 0.5 percent from 1962 to 1989, and in developed
countries, at a rate of 0.3 percent per year. (Of course since the vagaries of weather
make farm production volatile, alarmists can always distort figures to show reduction in per capita grain production by beginning with a bumper crop, as in 1970 to
1971 in India, and ending with a poor harvest, as in 1972 to 1973 or 1979 to 1980. To
avoid distortions due to weather fluctuations, I use a 5-year moving average in
which food output in the year 1989, for instance, is computed as an average of the
outputs of 1987 through 1991.)

    Food output per capita increased from 1962 to 1989, in all LDC regions ex-
cept sub-Saharan Africa, where it declined 0.8 percent annually. Africa's daily

calorie consumption per capita, 2,116 (compared to 2,115 in the early 1960s and 2,197 in the mid 1970s), was 92 percent of the requirement by the Food and Agriculture Organization (FAO) of the United Nations, 1988–90; calorie consumption in all other LDC regions exceeded FAO requirements. Only South Africa, Congo, the Ivory Coast, Benin, Mauritania, Mali, and Guinea had a daily consumption that was not less than the minimum required;[15] Ethiopia's was only 71 percent of the minimum, Mozambique 77 percent, Angola and Rwanda 80 percent, Somalia 81 percent, and Sudan 83 percent.[16]

The International Fund for Agricultural Development has developed the **food security index (FSI)**, which combines food production and consumption variables to measure national, composite food security. The FSI "combines measures of calorie availability (in relation to requirement), the growth of per capita daily energy supply, food production, food staples self-sufficiency, and variability of food production and consumption." Countries which have high food production potential or import capacity and which experience a low variability of production and consumption would have a high value of FSI.[17]

Africa's FSI is low (and falling since the 1960s) not only because of large food deficits but also because of domestic output and foreign-exchange reserve fluctuations, as well as foreign food-aid reductions. Cereal consumption per capita has had a high coefficient of variation since 1965. In 1989, Economic Commission for Africa Executive Secretary Adebayo Adedeji spoke of "the humiliation it has brought to Africa in having to go round with the begging bowl for food aid."[18] Relief agencies indicates 20 million deaths from severe malnutrition in 1991 in six African countries where food trade was disrupted by domestic political conflict—Ethiopia, Liberia, Sudan, Somalia, Angola, and Mozambique. The 5 million or so refugees annually fleeing civil wars, natural disasters, and political repression (including before 1990, South Africa's destabilization) added to Africa's food shortages.[19]

Illustrative of the enormity of the sub-Sahara's difference from other LDCs is that while the sub-Sahara and India both produced 50 million tons of foodgrains in 1960, in 1988 India produced 150 million tons (after the Green Revolution and other farm technological improvements) and sub-Saharan Africa (with faster population growth) was still stuck at little more than 50 million tons. India's yield per hectare increased by 2.4 percent yearly, while the sub-Sahara's grew at a negligible annual

---

[15]United Nations Development Program, *Human Development Report, 1994* (New York: Oxford University Press, 1994), pp. 118–20, 132–33, 207–08; and Economic Commission for Africa, *ECA and Africa's Development, 1983–2008: A Preliminary Perspective Study* (Addis Ababa, 1983), p. 9.

[16]United Nations Development Program, *Human Development Report, 1994* (New York: Oxford University Press, 1994), p. 27.

[17]Idriss Jazairy, Mohiuddin Alamgir, and Theresa Panuccio, *The State of World Rural Poverty: An Inquiry into its Causes and Consequences*, Published for the International Fund for Agricultural Development (New York: New York University Press, 1992), pp. 27, 398–99, 464–65.

[18]Colin Kirkpatrick and Dimitris Diakosavvas, "Food Insecurity and Foreign-Exchange Constraints in Sub-Saharan Africa," *Journal of Modern African Studies* 23 (June 1985): 326–42; and Adebayo Adedeji, *Towards a Dynamic African Economy: Selected Speeches and Lectures, 1975–1986* (London: Frank Cass, 1989), p. 2.

[19]Patricia Daley, "The Politics of the Refugee Crisis in Tanzania," in Horace Campbell and Howard Stein, eds., *Tanzania and the IMF: The Dynamics of Liberalization* (Boulder, Colo.: Westview, 1992), p 115; and Thomas Goliber, "Africa's Expanding Population: Old Problems, New Policies," *Population Bulletin* 44 (November 1989): 10–11.

rate of 0.1 percent. Thus, the sub-Sahara, which was a parity with India in 1960, produced only about one-third of Indian output in 1988.[20] According to Table 7–1, the average North American agricultural worker produces 93 times as much farm output as the average African.

Africa's deteriorating food position began before the droughts in the Sahel, the Sudan, and Ethiopia in 1968 to 1974 and in 1984 to 1985. While the roots of Africa's food crisis can be traced back to colonialism, the continuing crisis is due to African governments' neglect of agriculture. Colonial policy contributed to today's agricultural underdevelopment. (1) Africans were systematically excluded from participating in colonial development schemes and producing export crops and improved cattle. British agricultural policy in Eastern Africa benefitted European settlers and ignored and discriminated against African farmers; in Kenya, this meant prohibiting Africans from growing coffee until 1933. (2) Colonial governments compelled farmers to grow selected crops and work to maintain roads. (3) Colonialism often changed traditional land tenure systems from communal or clan to individual control. This created greater inequalities from new classes of affluent farmers and ranchers, and less secure tenants, sharecroppers, and landless workers. (4) Colonialists failed to train African agricultural scientists and managers. (5) Research and development concentrated on export crops, plantations, and land settlement schemes, neglecting food production and small farmers and herders. (6) Europeans reaped most of the gains from colonial land grants and export surpluses from agriculture.[21] As indicated later in this chapter, the contemporary neglect of Africa's agriculture results partly from the political advantage to state leaders to intervene in the market to improve prices and incomes that urban classes receive relative to farmers.

Agricultural economists, who agree on the rising global trend in foodgrain output per person from the early 1950s through the 1980s, noticed a fall in average grain production during the late 1980s and early 1990s. The debate between Malthusians, such as Lester R. Brown, and their critics, such as Tim Dyson, is whether this adverse agricultural trend will deepen in the late 1990s and early twenty-first century, leading to massive famines.[22] The controversy, discussed in connection with Figure 8–8, examines the sustainability of the contemporary global agricultural system, including regional trends, population growth, environmental and resource limitations, and agricultural technological gains.[23]

World food production, which grew between the 1950s and the early 1990s, is expected to continue growing in the late 1990s and the first decade of the twenty-first century in both LDCs and DCs. Meanwhile food demand per capita will continue to rise, though not so rapidly as increases in GNP.

---

[20]Hans Singer, "The Role of Food Aid," in James Pickett and Hans Singer, eds., *Towards Economic Recovery in Sub-Saharan Africa: Essays in Honor of Robert Gardiner* (London: Routledge, 1990), pp. 178–81.

[21]Carl K. Eicher and Doyle C. Baker, *Research on Agricultural Development in sub-Saharan Africa: A Critical Survey,* East Lansing: Michigan State University International Development Paper no. 1, 1982, pp. 20–23; and Dharam Ghai and Samir Radwan, eds., *Agrarian Policies and Rural Poverty in Africa* (Geneva: International Labor Office, 1983), pp. 16–21.

[22]Lester R. Brown, "Grain Harvest Plummets," in Lester R. Brown, Hal Kane, and David Malin Roodman, eds., *Vital Signs, 1994: The Trends that are Shaping Our Future*, Worldwatch (New York: Norton, 1994), pp. 26–27; and Tim Dyson, "Population Growth and Food Production: Recent Global and Regional Trends," *Population and Development Review* 20 (June 1994): 397–411.

[23]Pierre Crosson, "Demand and Supply: Trends in Global Agriculture," *Food Policy* 19 (April 1994): 105–19.

The growth in food demand or

$$\dot{D} = \dot{P} + \alpha \dot{E} \qquad (11-1)$$

where $\dot{P}$ is population growth, α the income elasticity of demand for food (change in the quantity of food demanded per capita/quantity of food demanded per capita)/(change in per capita income/per capita income) and $\dot{E}$ per capita income growth, all expressed in yearly figures. In empirical studies, estimates for α vary widely (from 4 percent to 85 percent), depending on location, type of survey, and income levels. Table 7–2 indicates the range of elasticities in LDCs for selected commodities. For International Food Policy Research Institute economist Harold Alderman, α averages 0.48 for LDC average incomes.[24] If the annual figures are 2 percent for population growth, 2.08 percent for income per capita growth, and 0.48 for α, than food demand growth is 2 percent + 1 percent or 3 percent yearly.

TABLE 7–2	Income Elasticities in Developing Countries for Selected Commodities[a]
Item	*Income elasticity*
Wheat	0.04–0.98
Rice	0.01–0.30
Beef	0.75–1.85
Poultry	0.40–2.20
Pork	0.50–0.97
Milk	1.50–2.50
Eggs	0.80–1.20
Fish	0.61–1.50
Shrimp	1.25
Fruit	1.22–2.50
Sugar	1.50–2.00
Vegetables	0.10–0.92
Vegetable oils	0.50–1.81
Beverages	0.74
Cocoa	0.75
Manufactures	0.74–3.38

[a]The percentage increase in quantity demanded as a result of a 1 percent increase in income. The estimates are based on studies of developing countries. The range of estimates reflects differences in per capital income levels among countries.

Source: World Bank, *Global Economic Prospects and the Developing Countries, 1994* (Washington, D.C., 1994), p. 39.

---

[24]Harold Alderman, "New Research on Poverty and Malnutrition: What Are the Implications for Policy?" in Michael Lipton and Jacques van der Gaag, *Including the Poor: Proceedings of a Symposium Organized by the World Bank and the International Food Policy Research Institute* (Washington, D.C.: World Bank, 1993), pp. 118–19.

The LDC **food deficit** is expected to be 4.5 percent of food consumption in LDCs by 2000. East, Southeast, and South Asia show a surplus, and Latin America's relative deficit is smaller in 2000 than in 1980. Yet the LDCs' *absolute* deficit, especially in sub-Saharan Africa and the Middle East, increased from 1980 to 2000 (Table 7–3). The major developing countries with food deficits in the 1990s and first decade of the twenty-first century are indicated in Chapter 8, which examines the population-food balance in more detail. Food importers, such as Britain, Germany, and Japan, generate enough industrial surplus to maintain a high level of nutrition.

An American Association for the Advancement of Science symposium argues that annual food production is enough to feed everyone on earth adequately if distribution were more equal. However while *intra*regional distribution would be adequate for Asia and Latin America, sub-Saharan Africa's caloric intake, if equally distributed, would still be below minimal nutritional standards.[25] Chapter 8's discussion of the food-population balance and the following section on Sino-

TABLE 7–3   Food Consumption and Food Deficits in Developing Countries, 1980 and 2000 (million metric tons and percentages)

	1980			2000[a]		
Region	*Food Consumption (m.m.t.)*	*Food Deficit (Food Consumption Minus Production) (m.m.t.)*	*Food Deficit/ Food Consumption (percent)*	*Food Consumption (m.m.t.)*	*Food Deficit (Food Consumption Minus Production) (m.m.t.)*	*Food Deficit/ Food Consumption (percent)*
East and Southeast Asia	110.8	0.6	0	180	(31)	(7.2)
China	313.9	15.0	4.8	494	(7)	(1.4)
South Asia	188.0	3.3	1.8	310	(13)	(10.0)
Middle East	86.9	18.9	21.7	183	64	35.0
Sub-Saharan Africa	78.3	5.9	6.8	160	47	29.4
Latin America	115.9	8.2	7.1	214	9	4.2
Total	893.8	51.9	5.7	1541	69	4.5

[a]Consumption projections assume a trend based on 1966–80 average annual growth rate of real GNP per capita.

Note: ( ) indicates surplus.

Source: Leonardo A. Paulino, *Food in the Third World: Past Trends and Projections to 2000*, Research Report 52, International Food Policy Research Institute, Washington, D.C., June 1986.

---

[25]Philip H. Abelson, ed., *Food: Politics, Economics, Nutrition, and Research* (Washington, D.C.: American Association for the Advancement of Science, 1975); and U.S. Department of Agriculture, Economics, Statistics, and Cooperative Service, International Economic Division, *Food Problems and Prospects in sub-Saharan Africa: The Decade of the 1980's* (Washington, D.C.: U.S. Agency for International Development, 1980).

Indian comparisons suggest that local food shortages are due not so much to inadequate world production as to deficiencies in food distribution. Although worldwide food output per capita should grow in the 1990s and the first decade of the 2000s, inequality in food distribution means that some people in LDCs will be undernourished.

Still the projections in Table 7–3, while consistent with the bleakness of other food data, especially on Africa, should not obscure the fact that the crises in urban food supply, overall food production, and external imbalances are somewhat distinct. With rapid urbanization and changes in urban diets and the importation of much of urban food supply, we can expect food imports to rise from 1980 to 2010, regardless of food output trends. African farmers are largely self-sufficient in basic calories; price changes have little impact on the output of subsistence crops, since most production is for self-consumption. Export crops drive cash income and capacity to import. The fact that grain imports are 25 to 30 percent of grain consumed in Africa does not mean that imported cereals sustained one-quarter of the population. Rising cereal imports, helped by falling food import prices, meant increased cereals consumed in urban areas (rice and wheat), and a shift in Madagascar, Southern Nigeria, Ghana, and Uganda from coarse grains (sorghum and millet), roots, and tubers.[26]

Fish Catches

Foodgrain output figures omit fish, an important source of high-quality protein throughout the world and one-fourth of the animal protein in the developing world. LDCs ate 56 million tons of fish in 1990, the majority of the world's catch of 97 million tons, which was a fivefold increase over 40 years but a 3-percent decline from 1989, the peak harvest (as of 1994). World fish tonnage compared to 143 tons of red meat, 34 million tons of fowl, 35 tons of hen eggs, and 539 tons of milk in 1990. Since 85 percent of the fish is harvested without practicing husbandry, fish, if available, has cost advantages over other kinds of food. China's fish catches, which grew rapidly in the 1980s, were 12.1 million tons compared to 10.4 million tons in the former Soviet Union, 10.3 million tons in Japan, 6.9 tons in Peru, 5.9 tons in the United States, and 5.2 million tons in Chile in 1990. In comparison, the whole of Africa produced only 4.3 million tons in 1990, with the leading catches Morocco, with 0.6 million tons; Ghana 0.4 million tons, and Nigeria 0.3 tons. During the 1980s, coastal states, which extended national management of fish resources within their zones, gained large benefits in the redistribution of the seas' wealth at the expense of Eastern Europe, former Soviet republics, and other countries with limited open access to the seas.[27] Overall this limit of fish catches results from an overuse of a common property resource, the earth's bodies of water, discussed in Chapter 13.

---

[26]Vali Jamal, "Getting the Crisis Right: Missing Perspectives on Africa," *International Labor Review* 127, no. 6 (1988): pp. 657–70.

[27]Food and Agriculture Organization of the U.N. (FAO), *The State of Food and Agriculture, 1992* (Rome, 1992), pp. 16–39, 127–64; Anne E. Platt, "Fish Catch Stable," in Lester R. Brown, Hal Kane, and David Malin Roodman, eds., *Vital Signs, 1994: The Trends That Are Shaping Our Future*, Worldwatch Institute (New York: Norton, 1994), pp. 32–33; and "World Fishing Flounders," *Economist* (June 23, 1984): pp. 70–71.

Food in India and China

During the Chinese Cultural Revolution from 1966 to 1976, some Western economists accepted the official claim that the country had no malnutrition. French economist Al Imfeld maintained that "in contrast to India, China has eliminated hunger."[28] The best evidence indicates that food production per capita in China fell more than 12 percent between the 1930s and the late 1970s. Although growth in food production per capita of the world's most populated country, China from 1952 to 1984, was slightly faster than that of the second most populated country, neighboring India, breaking down the analysis into the pre-1977 to 1979 period, when China had primarily cooperative and collective farming, and the period after the 1979 agricultural reforms, is more revealing. India's annual growth in food output per person, from 1954 to 1977, was 0.4 percent compared to China's 0.3 percent.[29] (The 5-year moving average avoids much influence from the abnormal growth just following China's post-1949 war rehabilitation and India's recovery from disruption due to the 1947 Indian-Pakistani partition or following China's reforms and India's post-1978 liberalization.)

Yet because China's food grain output per person in the early 1950s was roughly 25 to 30 percent higher than India's, China's average *level* of food output per person remained higher than India's through the 1980s. Furthermore, since income inequalities are less in China than India, the percentage of the population that is malnourished is lower than in India. Nevertheless, China's Communist Party Central Committee admitted that in 1977, about one hundred million people, or more than one-tenth of China's population, did not have enough to eat,[30] thus contradicting Imfeld's contention.

Stanford economist John G. Gurley argues that "the Chinese have what is in effect an insurance policy against pestilence, famine, and other disasters."[31] But though China normally has had a lower malnutrition rate and distributes food more equally than does India, China was more subject to famine than is India.

Amartya K. Sen emphasizes that having enough to eat does not depend on merely egalitarian income distribution or low poverty rates but on society's system of entitlement. **Entitlement** refers to the set of alternative commodity bundles that a person can command in a society using the totality of rights and opportunities that he or she possesses. An entitlement helps people acquire capabilities (like being well nourished). In a market economy, the entitlement limit is based on ownership of factors of production and exchange possibilities (through trade or a shift in production possibilities). For most people, entitlement depends on the ability to find a job, the wage rate, and the prices of commodities bought. In a welfare or socialist economy, entitlement also depends on what families can obtain from the state through the established system of command. A hungry, destitute person will be *entitled* to some-

---

[28]Al Imfeld, *China as a Model of Development,* trans. Matthew J. O'Connell (New York: Orbis, 1976), p. 157.

[29]E. Wayne Nafziger, "India versus China: Economic Development Performance," *Dalhousie Review* 65 (Fall 1985): 366–92, with updated information from U.S. Department of Agriculture, International Economic Division, *World Indices of Agricultural and Food Production, 1950–85* (Washington, D.C., 1986); and U.S. Department of Agriculture, Economic Research Service, *World Indices of Agricultural and Food Production, 1977–86* (Washington, D.C., 1988).

[30]Christopher Howe, *China's Economy: A Basic Guide* (New York: Basic Books, 1978), pp. xxiii, 180–84; Dwight H. Perkins, *China's Agricultural Development: 1368–1968* (Chicago: Aldine, 1969); Nick Eberstadt, "Has China Failed?" *New York Review of Books,* 26 (April 5, 1979): 33–46; and A. Doak Barnett, *China's Economy in Global Perspective* (Washington, D.C.: Brookings Institute, 1981), p. 305.

[31]John G. Gurley, *China's Economy and the Maoist Strategy* (New York: Monthly Review Press, 1976), p. 134. The book is based on essays written during the Cultural Revolution.

thing to eat, not by society's low Gini concentration and a high food output per capita, but by a relief system offering free food. Thus in 1974, thousands of people died in Bangladesh despite its low inequality, because floods reduced rural employment along with output, and inflation cut rural laborers' purchasing power.

Sen argues that food is "purchased" with political pressure as well as income. Accordingly one-third of the Indian population goes to bed hungry every night and leads a life ravaged by regular deprivation. India's social system takes nonacute endemic hunger in stride; there are no headlines nor riots. But while India's politicians do not provide entitlements for chronic or endemic malnutrition, they do so for potential severe famine through food imports, redistribution, and relief. In Maoist China, the situation was almost the opposite. Its political commitment ensured lower regular malnutrition through more equal access to means of livelihood and state-provided entitlement to basic needs of food, clothing, and shelter. In a normal year, China's poor were much better fed than India's. Yet if there were a political and economic crisis that confused the regime so that it pursued disastrous policies with confident dogmatism, then it could not be forced to change its policies by crusading newspapers or effective political opposition pressure, as in India.

Famines result from a failure of the entitlement system. Sen, using Beijing University figures, calculates an extra mortality of 14–16 million people from famine in China from 1959 to 1961 (see Fig. 7–2), greater in absolute or relative terms than the 3 million extra mortality in India's largest twentieth-century famine, the Great Bengal Famine of 1943. So although China was more successful than India before 1977 to 1979 in eliminating regular malnutrition, China has had more famines than India.[32]

FIGURE 7–2 **Grain Production Per Person, China and India, 1950–94**

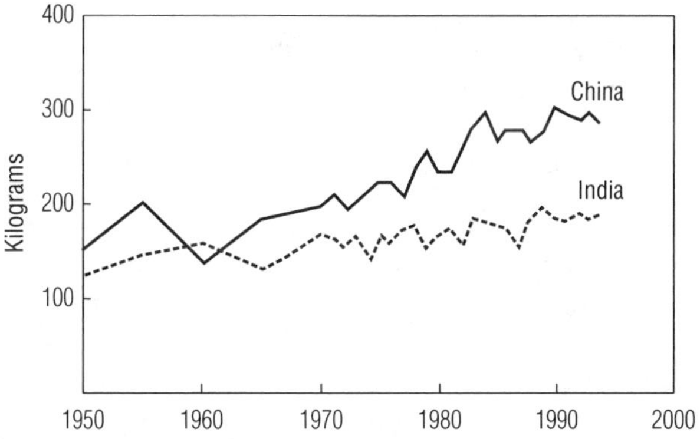

Source: Lester R. Brown, *Who Will Feed China? Wake-up Call for a Small Planet,* Published for Worldwatch (New York: Norton, 1995), p. 29. Reprinted by permission.

[32]Amartya K. Sen, "Development: Which Way Now?" *Economic Journal* 93 (December 1983): 757–60; and Amartya K. Sen, *On Economic Inequality* (Oxford: Clarendon Press, 1983). For further discussion of Sen's entitlement theory of famine, see Peter Bowbrick, "The Causes of Famine: A Refutation of Professor Sen's Theory," *Food Policy* 11 (May 1986), 105–24; Amartya K. Sen, "The Causes of Famine: A Reply," *Food Policy* 11 (May 1986), 125–32; Peter Bowbrick, "Rejoinder: An Untenable Hypothesis on the Causes of Famine," *Food Policy* 12 (February 1987), 5–9; Amartya K. Sen, "Reply: Famine and Mr. Bowbrick," *Food Policy* 12 (February 1987), 10–14; Stephen Devereux, "Entitlements, Availability, and Famine: A Revisionist View of Wollo, 1972–74," *Food Policy* 13 (August 1988), 270–82; and Erhun Kula, "The Inadequacy of The Entitlement Approach to Explain and Remedy Famines," *Journal of Development Studies* 25 (October 1988), 112–16.

China's per capita food production dropped sharply during the 1959 to 1961 famine (1960's figure was 25 percent below 1952's), resulting in widespread malnutrition. The cause of this decline was not only bad weather, floods, and drought, but also poor quality work during the emphasis on collective labor-intensive projects during the Great Leap Forward (GLF) from 1958 to 1960. Reservoir construction work destroyed soil, rivers, and existing irrigation systems. Reservoir and water conservation work raised underground water levels, led to alkalized, salinized, and water-logged soil, halted stream and river flows, left irrigation channels unfinished, and failed to provide for drainage. Moreover, GLF water projects removed land from cultivation. Yet the GLF political pressure for agricultural success made local officials unwilling to report food shortages.[33]

In reforms beginning in 1979 (see Chapter 20), China decontrolled farm prices for farm commodities, encouraged direct sale by peasants to the market, and instituted a household responsibility system, which allowed farmers more freedom to choose both farm and nonfarm activities. From 1977 to 1984, even India's 3.0–percent annual growth in food output per capita under a modest post-1978 liberalization was outstripped by China's 4.6-percent growth, which was not so rapid as gains in oilseed, livestock, and cotton output. Indeed China reversed its pre-1979 dependence on imported grains, exporting corn, other coarse grains, and soybeans. These remarkable gains were achieved with few increased farm inputs (see Chapter 20).[34] Even after 1984, longer-term leasing contracts, subleasing of land by peasants, free-market pricing for most farm products, and greater nonfarm options for the rural population was accompanied by rapid although decelerated growth in foodgrain output per person. China's price decontrol of food inputs and outputs, while only partial, reinforces the World Bank's emphasis in the Berg report (discussed later in the chapter) of "getting prices right."

Rural Poverty by Regions of the World

If we use the upper poverty line discussed in Chapter 6, rural poverty as a percentage of the population of Latin America, Africa, and Asia (excluding Japan) was 37 percent in 1996 (Table 7–4), compared to 18 percent for urban poverty. The highest rural poverty rate, 66 percent, was in sub-Saharan Africa, the region with the greatest rural-urban discrepancy in poverty rates. Latin America, also with a substantial discrepancy, had a rural poverty rate of 59 percent, South and Southeast Asia 44 percent, the Middle East 34 percent, and East Asia 11 percent.

[33]Jan S. Prybyla, *The Political Economy of Communist China* (Scranton, Pa.: International Textbook, 1970), pp. 264–69; A. Doak Barnett, *China's Economy in Global Perspective* (Washington, D.C.: Brookings Institute, 1981), pp. 271, 302; and Nicholas R. Lardy, *Agriculture in China's Modern Economic Development* (Cambridge: Cambridge University Press, 1983), pp. 152–53.
[34]World Bank, *World Development Report, 1986* (New York: Oxford University Press, 1986), pp. 104–6. Chinese-Indian comparisons come from E. Wayne Nafziger, "India versus China," *Dalhousie Review* 65: 366–92, with later data from U.S. Department of Agriculture, *World Indices of Agricultural and Food Production, 1950–85* (Washington, D.C., 1986); and U.S. Department of Agriculture, *World Indices of Agricultural and Food Production, 1977–86* (Washington, D.C., 1988).

TABLE 7-4 Population below the Poverty Line in Rural Areas in Developing Countries, 1996

	Rural Population 1996 (millions)	*Percentage of Rural Population in Poverty*	*Number of Rural People in Poverty (millions)*
South and Southeast Asia (all countries)	1291	44	574
Afghanistan	15	60	9
Bangladesh	100	86	86
India	707	41	290
Indonesia	138	27	37
Laos	3.7	83	3.1
Malaysia	11	22	2
Myanmar (Burma)	34	33	11
Nepal	19	61	12
Pakistan	90	29	26
Philippines	39	64	25
Sri Lanka	15	46	7
Thailand	46	34	16
Vietnam	62	60	37
East Asia (excluding Japan)	998	11	107
China	879	12	102
North Korea	9	21	2
South Korea	12	4	0.5
Sub-Saharan Africa (all countries)	415	66	272
Angola	8	65	5
Benin	3.3	65	2.2
Botswana	1.5	53	0.8
Burkina Faso	9	90	8
Burundi	6	86	5
Cameroon	8	40	3
Central African Republic	1.7	90	1.6
Chad	4.0	56	2.2
Congo	1.5	79	1.2
Ethiopia (including Eritrea)	54	63	34
Ghana	12	54	6
Guinea	5	70	3
Kenya	23	55	13
Lesotho	1.6	56	0.9
Madagascar	11	50	6
Malawi	10	90	9
Mali	7	60	4
Mauritania	1.2	86	1.0
Mozambique	12	65	8
Niger	8	34	3
Nigeria	66	51	33
Rwanda	8	91	7
Senegal	5	70	4
Sierra Leone	3.4	66	2.2
Somalia	7	71	5
Sudan	23	85	20

TABLE 7-4 Continued

	Rural Population 1996 (millions)	Percentage of Rural Population in Poverty	Number of Rural People in Poverty (millions)
Tanzania	23	60	14
Togo	3.2	30	1.0
Uganda	17	80	14
Zaïre	32	90	27
Zambia	5	80	4
Zimbabwe	8	59	5
West Asia and North Africa (all countries)	244	34	83
Algeria	14	24	3
Egypt	35	53	18
Iran	29	30	9
Iraq	6	31	2
Jordan	1.2	15	0.2
Lebanon	0.5	23	0.1
Morocco	16	45	7
Syria	7	54	4
Tunisia	3.9	14	0.5
Turkey	23	14	3
Yemen	9	30	3
Latin America (all countries)	190	59	112
Argentina	5	21	1.0
Brazil	37	73	27
Bolivia	4.3	86	3.7
Chile	2.1	25	0.5
Colombia	11	45	5
Costa Rica	2.1	36	0.8
Cuba	2.8	33	0.9
Dominican Republic	3.0	70	2.1
Ecuador	5	47	2
El Salvador	3.3	74	2.4
Guatemala	7	73	5
Haiti	4.9	80	3.9
Honduras	3.3	56	1.9
Jamaica	1.2	78	0.9
Mexico	25	51	13
Nicaragua	1.6	19	0.3
Panama	2.3	70	1.6
Paraguay	2.6	52	1.3
Peru	7	52	4
Uruguay	0.3	29	0.1
Venezuela	1.8	61	1.2
All developing countries (excluding Eastern Europe and the former Soviet Union)	3138	37	1148

Source: United Nations Development Program, *Human Development Report, 1994* (New York: Oxford University Press, 1994), pp. 134–35, 148–49.

Factors Contributing to Low Income and Poverty in Rural Areas

Average income in rural areas is substantially less than in urban areas in LDCs. Rural inequality is greater than urban inequality in Latin America but less in the rest of the developing world.[35] Not surprisingly in LDCs as a whole, there are higher poverty rates in rural areas than in cities. This section discusses why this is so.

LACK OF RESOURCES AND TECHNOLOGY

Agricultural income and productivity in LDCs are low because of minimal capital per worker and inadequate technology. Small farm *owners* receive limited credit and tenants, sharecroppers, and landless laborers receive almost none. There is little research and development to improve technology appropriate for small farmers, partly because they lack effective demand and political power.

CONCENTRATION OF CAPITAL, LAND, AND TECHNOLOGY

Agricultural technology and capital are concentrated among large farmers. The development of commercial agriculture, as in the case of the high-yielding seed varieties of the Green Revolution (discussed in Chapter 8), compelled some cultivators to work for a wage, and made many other farmers even more marginal than they had been. Many of the poor are smallholder farmers, including a substantial share of women, who work long hours and are already deeply involved in agricultural production, but lack the productive resources (fertilizer, better seeds, equipment, tools, land, and skills) and new technology to escape from their poverty trap. Although still less than urban inequality, rural income inequality has increased since 1970.[36]

Incomes of farm households are highly correlated with the amount of nonfarm income (urban wages, remittances, and so forth), especially Kenya and Nigeria. Indeed, household nonfarm income is the key to determining farm productivity and household incomes in Kenya. Farm families receiving urban wages bought land, hired farm labor, financed innovations, purchased farm inputs, and increased farm income. Most farm families without a regularly employed person earn no more than enough to satisfy the necessities of life. A study of northern Nigerian villages found that off-farm income accounts for nearly 40 percent of the total income of the top quintile (fifth), but only 22 to 27 percent of income of the four bottom quintiles, while a western central Nigerian survey indicated rural family income and capital per hectare correlated significantly with the percentage of income from nonfarm sources.[37] Indeed, studies in Nigeria, South Korea, Taiwan, Thailand, and Sierra Leone indicate that because of rural nonfarm

---

[35]Shail Jain, *Size Distribution of Income: A Compilation of Data* (Washington, D.C.: World Bank, 1975).

[36]Ibid.; International Labor Office, *Profiles of Rural Poverty* (Geneva, 1979); and Idriss Jazairy, Mohiuddin Alamgir, and Theresa Panuccio, *The State of World Rural Poverty: An Inquiry into its Causes and Consequences*, Published for the International Fund for Agricultural Development (New York: New York University Press, 1992), pp. xix–xx, 105–06.

[37]E. Wayne Nafziger, *Inequality in Africa: Political Elites, Proletariat, Peasants, and the Poor* (Cambridge: Cambridge University Press, 1988), p. 85; Paul Collier and Deepak Lal, *Labour and Poverty in Kenya, 1900–1980* (Oxford: Clarendon Press, 1986), pp. 249–50; and Peter Matlon, "The Structure of Production and Rural Incomes in Northern Nigeria," in Henry Bienen and V. P. Diejomaoh, *The Political Economy of Income Distribution in Nigeria* (New York: Holmes & Meier, 1981), pp. 323–72.

income, income inequality is not as high as inequality in landholdings would suggest.[38]

Landholdings are severely concentrated in many LDCs (see Chapter 6). This is especially true in Latin America, where the average farm size is over 80 hectares or 200 acres (20 times larger than in Afro-Asia) (Table 7–5), and size dispersion is substantial (Gini coefficient = 0.84, if you include the holding of landless as zero).[39] In Brazil a small fraction of landholders (16 percent) commands 87 percent of agricultural land. Land inequality is greater than data indicate because many small holders sharecrop or lease their holdings, and many rural have no land at all.[40] Since the colonial period more than 100 years ago, most of Latin America has been characterized by **latifundios,** large land-grant estates owned by the few, and **minifundios,** small poor holdings that rarely provide adequate employment for a family (see Table 7–6). To obtain a subsistence income, holders of *minifundios* generally work as seasonal labor on the *latifundios.* And of course, these large estates, characterized by extensive cultivation, high capital intensity, and much unused land, have a higher output per agricultural worker.

In the last few decades, the many *latifundios* have increased their capitalization and levels of technology. Moreover, in some Latin American countries, a well-capitalized medium-scale sector has emerged. Yet despite these changes and a smattering of land redistribution, Latin America still has a high degree of land concentration.[41]

LOW EDUCATIONAL AND SKILL LEVELS

Average incomes in urban areas are higher than in rural areas, where skill levels and demands are lower. Years of schooling, a major indicator of skill and productivity (see Chapter 10), are fewer in rural than in urban areas. For example, in India the city-born child has twice the chance of receiving a primary or secondary education as the one born in a rural community and eight times the chance of receiving a university education. More and better quality schools are available to city children than to rural children. In addition much rural schooling is irrelevant to its community's economic needs. Some economists even question how much rural areas benefit from a child's education, since the most able and educated young people usually emigrate to the cities.[42]

RURAL-URBAN MIGRATION

Attracted by the prospect of better-paying jobs in urban areas, rural emigrants tend to have education, skill, and income that are higher than average in the rural areas. Poorer villagers are often at a disadvantage in migrating: (1) They simply

---

[38]Thomas P. Tomich, Peter Kilby, and Bruce F. Johnston, *Transforming Agrarian Economies: Opportunities Seized, Opportunities Missed* (Ithaca, N.Y.: Cornell University Press, 1995).

[39]Lyn Squire, *Employment Policy in Developing Countries: A Survey of Issues and Evidence* (New York: Oxford University Press, 1981), p. 156; and Robert Repetto, "Population, Resources, Environment: An Uncertain Future," *Population Bulletin* 42 (July 1987): 14.

[40]Robert Repetto, "Population, Resources, Environment: An Uncertain Future," *Population Bulletin* 42 (July 1987): 13–14.

[41]Idriss Jazairy, Mohiuddin Alamgir, and Theresa Panuccio, *The State of World Rural Poverty: An Inquiry into its Causes and Consequences,* Published for the International Fund for Agricultural Development (New York: New York University Press, 1992), pp. 109–13.

[42]Michael Lipton, *Why Poor People Stay Poor: A Study of Urban Bias in World Development* (London: Maurice Temple Smith, 1977), pp. 259–60; 446.

TABLE 7–5   Distribution of Agricultural Landholding by Percentile Groups of Households

Country	Year	Lowest (First) Quintile (twenty percent)	Second Quintile	Third Quintile	Fourth Quintile	Fifth Quintile	Gini Co-efficient
		Distribution of Landholding by Percentile					
		Groups of Households					
Bangladesh	1983–1984	2.3	5.4	12.5	23.6	56.2	0.50
Bolivia	1978	5.8	5.8	5.8	9.3	73.3	0.55
Botswana	1971	6.9	6.9	6.9	13.4	65.9	0.50
Brazil	1980	0.3	1.0	3.1	7.2	88.4	0.75
Cameroon	1984	3.6	9.3	15.0	21.6	50.5	0.42
Chile	1987	2.8	2.8	2.8	15.5	76.1	0.64
Colombia	1983–1984	0.4	1.3	3.8	12.6	81.9	0.70
Costa Rica	1984	0.8	0.8	7.1	12.1	79.2	0.67
Dominican Republic	1981	1.2	3.4	3.4	3.4	88.6	0.70
Ecuador	1987	1.0	1.6	4.2	9.6	83.6	0.69
Egypt, Arab Republic	1984	11.2	11.2	11.2	11.2	55.2	0.35
El Salvador	1985	5.1	5.1	5.1	10.6	74.1	0.57
Ethiopia	1984	7.7	15.1	18.3	23.9	35.0	0.25
Ghana	1984	7.8	7.8	7.8	18.6	58.0	0.44
Guatemala	1979	0.8	1.6	3.3	4.2	90.1	0.72
Haiti	1971	0.8	0.8	0.9	30.0	67.5	0.65
Honduras	1980–1981	2.9	2.9	3.8	11.4	79.0	0.64
India	1976–1977	4.1	4.1	6.3	20.3	65.2	0.55
Indonesia	1983	3.0	6.2	11.3	24.0	55.5	0.49
Iraq	1982	2.4	16.1	18.1	18.1	45.3	0.35
Ivory Coast	1988	5.9	9.5	17.6	23.6	43.4	0.36
Jordan	1983	1.3	4.4	9.0	20.0	65.3	0.57
Korea, Republic of	1980	5.7	12.7	16.0	25.0	40.6	0.33
Malawi	1980–1981	5.2	11.1	15.5	24.0	44.2	0.36
Malaysia	1976	3.1	6.1	11.9	16.8	62.1	0.51
Mexico	1970	5.1	5.1	5.1	8.0	76.7	0.58
Morocco	1981–1982	6.8	6.8	6.8	21.6	58.0	0.47
Myanmar (Burma)	1989–1990	4.7	7.4	12.3	24.2	51.4	0.44
Nepal	1982	2.6	2.6	7.7	19.8	67.3	0.59
Niger	1980	5.9	11.7	18.6	28.9	34.9	0.30
Nigeria	1973–1974	1.6	6.8	24.2	32.4	35.0	0.37
Pakistan	1980	2.8	7.2	11.5	19.3	59.2	0.50
Panama	1981	0.1	0.4	2.2	9.3	88.0	0.74
Peru	1984[a]	3.3	3.3	3.3	17.1	73.0	0.61
Philippines	1981	3.2	8.1	11.6	20.4	56.7	0.48
Sri Lanka	1982	2.8	2.8	8.7	18.3	67.4	0.58
Syrian, Arab Republic	1979	1.9	3.9	7.2	18.6	68.4	0.59
Thailand	1978	4.0	8.3	16.3	24.2	47.2	0.41
Tunisia	1980	3.0	3.0	9.4	16.2	68.4	0.58
Turkey	1980	2.1	6.1	11.4	21.3	59.1	0.52
Uganda	1984[b]	4.5	4.5	4.5	12.0	74.5	0.59
Zambia	1981	18.0	18.0	18.0	18.0	28.0	0.08

[a]Private holdings.

[b]Based on four regions only (Busoga, Kigezi, Masaka, and Teso).

Source: Idriss Jazairy, Mohiuddin Alamgir, and Theresa Panuccio, *The State of World Rural Poverty: an Inquiry into its Causes and Consequences*, Published for the International Fund for Agricultural Development (New York: New York University Press, 1992), pp. 416–17.

TABLE 7-6 *Minifundios*, Medium-sized Farms, and *Latifundios* in the Agrarian Structure of Selected Latin American Countries, 1966

	Minifundios[a]		Medium-sized and Family farms[b]		Latifundios[c]	
	Percent of Farms	Percent of Occupied Land	Percent of Farms	Percent of Occupied Land	Percent of Farms	Percent of Occupied Land
Argentina	43.2	3.4	56.8	59.7	0.8	36.9
Brazil	22.5	0.5	72.8	40.0	4.7	59.5
Colombia	64.0	4.9	34.7	45.6	1.3	49.5
Chile	36.9	0.2	56.2	18.5	6.9	81.3
Ecuador	89.9	16.6	9.7	38.3	0.4	45.1
Guatemala	88.4	14.3	11.5	44.9	0.1	40.8
Peru	88.0	7.4	10.9	10.2	1.1	82.4

[a]Employ less than two people.

[b]Family farms employ two to four people and medium-sized farms four to twelve workers.

[c]Employ more than twelve people.

Source: Celso Furtado, *Economic Development in Latin America* (New York: Cambridge University Press, 1970), pp. 54–55.

cannot afford to migrate—acquiring job information, emigrating, and searching for work are expensive propositions, especially if they are financed at the high interest rates charged by the village moneylender. And of course emigrés must subsist as they wait for their first paychecks. (2) Their families find it more difficult to release them from work. (3) They are not so well educated as most other villagers. Many urban employers use education to screen job applicants, even for unskilled work (see Chapter 10). Even when the poorer villagers surmount these obstacles and move to the city, they frequently do not stay. Poverty forces them back to the village. The jobless, ill, pregnant, and elderly eventually return to relatives in the rural areas, eroding average incomes already reduced by the large economic burden from high rural birth rates.[43]

POLICIES OF URBAN BIAS

British economist Michael Lipton argues that the most significant class conflicts and income discrepancies are not between labor and capital, as Karl Marx contended, but between rural and urban classes. Despite development plans that proclaim agriculture as the highest priority sector, and political rhetoric that stresses the needs of the poor rural masses, government allocates most of its resources to cities, a policy of **urban bias.** Planners and politicians in LDCs are more likely to respond to the concerns of the more powerful, organized, and articulate urban dwellers. Thus farmland is diverted from growing millet and beans for hungry villagers to produce meat and milk for urban middle and upper classes or to grow cocoa, coffee, tea, sugar, cotton, and jute for export. Scarce capital is spent on high-

---

[43]Ibid., pp. 66, 147–49, 231–35.

ways and steel mills instead of on water pumps, tube wells, and other equipment essential for growing food. High-cost administrative and management talent is used to design office buildings and sports stadiums rather than village wells and agricultural extension services.

Urban bias may take these forms:

1. Policies that raise industrial prices relative to the prices of farm goods. Government may set price ceilings on food and guarantee minimum prices for industrial goods. High taxes and low prices force agriculture to transfer income and capital to industry and social infrastructure. The most frequently cited model for such policies is the Soviet Union of the 1930s, which used low prices, sales taxes, and government monopsony purchases to divert the surplus from agriculture into heavy-industry output and investment growth unmatched by any Western country. But in the 1970s direct and indirect taxation of agriculture as a percentage of agricultural value added exceeded 40 percent in Ghana, with 62 percent; the Ivory Coast, with 51 percent, Egypt, with 49 percent, Pakistan, with 48 percent; Sri Lanka, with 44 percent; and Thailand, with 43 percent.[44]

2. Concentration of investment in industry. Although over half of the LDC population is in agriculture, only about 20 percent of investment is in agriculture.

3. Tax incentives and subsidies to pioneering firms in industry, but not in agriculture.

4. Setting below-market prices for foreign currency, which reduces domestic currency receipts from agricultural exports. This policy lowers the price of capital goods and other foreign inputs, which benefits large industrial establishments with privileged access to import licenses. In Pakistan such a foreign exchange policy coupled with industrial price guarantees resulted in the transfer of about 70 percent of agricultural savings and over 24 percent of its gross product to the nonagricultural sector in 1964 and 1965.

5. Tariff and quota protection for industry, contributing to higher fertilizer, seed, equipment, materials, and consumer prices for farmers.

6. Spending more for education, training, housing, plumbing, nutrition, medical care, and transport in urban areas than in rural areas (see Chapter 9).[45] Thus life expectancy, an indicator of the quality of the health care system, varies widely among regions. Buenos Aires had a 1985 life expectancy of 75 years; the rest of Argentina, 69; the poor rural areas, 63; and Argentina as a whole, 70. Algiers's life expectancy is 68; the rest of Algeria, 61; the poor rural areas, 58; and Algeria generally, 61.

SEASONAL POVERTY AND HUNGER

Ironically *moderate* undernourishment is higher in rural than urban areas, since it is more likely to result from inadequate income than food shortages. However, Food and Agriculture Organization (FAO) studies of several LDCs indicate that,

[44]World Bank, *World Development Report, 1990* (New York: Oxford University Press, 1990), pp. 58–59; and Michael Lipton, *Why Poor People Stay Poor: A Study of Urban Bias in World Development* (London: Maurice Temple Smith, 1977).

[45]World Bank, *World Development Report, 1990* (New York: Oxford University Press, 1990), pp. 58–59; and Keith Griffin and Azizur Rahman Khan, eds., *Growth and Inequality in Pakistan* (London: Macmillan, 1972).

because of greater access to subsistence food production, the percentage of the population suffering *severe* malnourishment in rural areas is lower than in urban areas.[46]

Yet there is substantial hunger in rural areas. A "hungry season" before the beginning of a new harvest is widespread in many LDCs, especially in West Africa. Poor rural households are caught in a poverty trap in which selling labor and obtaining credit at high interest rates to ensure survival through the hungry season results in less income and high interest payments in future years. The poverty trap is circular. Initially farmers sacrifice self-sufficiency to produce cash crops. Accordingly they no longer grow early maturing crops that would fill the hunger gap between harvests. Poor farm families are also more vulnerable than previously as a result of individualized consumption replacing community or clan sharing. Furthermore, poor farm families cannot afford to purchase food just before harvests, when cash resources are lowest and prices are highest. At this juncture, many poor farmers neglect their own farms and sell their labor to richer farmers. They accept a lower income from their own farm to guarantee short-term survival. Reduced calorie and protein consumption during a period of more work leads to weight loss and greater chances of contracting diseases. The situation may become worse each year.[47]

Policies to Increase Rural Income and Reduce Poverty

This section focuses on increasing average rural incomes and reducing the percentage of the rural population in poverty by improving income distribution.

AGRARIAN REFORM AND LAND REDISTRIBUTION

In most developing countries, arable land per person of the agricultural population declined between 1965 and 1995. Many LDCs have exhausted their land frontier; in other countries, the cost of new land development was too high to be economically viable.[48]

Moreover, in many LDCs, landholdings are severely concentrated: A small fraction of landholders own the bulk of the land. However most holdings are less than 2 hectares apiece. The U.N. Food and Agricultural Organization (FAO) indicates that in Latin America, the region with highest concentration, 1.3 percent of the landowners hold 71.6 percent of the land under cultivation. In Bangladesh, India, Indonesia, South Korea, Nepal, Sri Lanka, Yemen, and many other Asian countries, as well as Kenya, marginal farmers, those with less than one hectare of

---

[46]Food and Agriculture Organization of the United Nations, *The Fourth FAO World Food Survey* (Rome, 1977), pp. 29–46.

[47]Derek Byerlee, Carl Eicher, and David Norman, "Farm Systems in Developing Countries" (unpublished manuscript, 1982); and Mark Newman, Ismael Ouedraogo, and David Norman, "Farm-level Studies in the Semiarid Tropics of West Africa," Proceedings of the Workshop on Socioeconomic Constraints to Development of Semiarid Tropical Agriculture, International Crop Research Institute for Semiarid Tropics (ICRISAT), Hyderabad, India, February 19–23, 1979, pp. 241–63.

[48]Idriss Jazairy, Mohiuddin Alamgir, and Theresa Panuccio, *The State of World Rural Poverty: An Inquiry into its Causes and Consequences*, Published for the International Fund for Agricultural Development (New York: New York University Press, 1992), pp. 105–06.

operational landholdings, hold more than half of the land but substantially less than half of *cultivated* land.[49]

Furthermore, many developing countries have failed to define property rights to agricultural land, a failure that adversely affects land use and improvement. As Theodore Panayotou contends:

> Property rights are a precondition for efficient use, trade, investment, conservation, and management of resources [such as land]. No one would economize on, pay for, invest in, or conserve a resource without an assurance that he has secure and exclusive rights over it, that he can recover his costs through use, lease, or sale, and that such rights will be enforced.[50]

Sub-Saharan Africa suffers more than Asia and Latin America from insecure and uncertain land rights. Sara Berry observes that:

> In Africa, unfortunately, many insecurities now exist presently around the land because the land laws passed by many governments are ambivalent, confusing, inconsistent, inapplicable or badly applied. As a result access to, and control of land takes place . . . within a framework of conflicting legal and political principles and practices.[51]

The rural poor can increase their income if they are provided access to productive resources, the most important of which is land. According to the International Fund for Agricultural Development, the rural poor can improve their access to land "through land redistribution (from larger holdings above a certain size), adjudication of traditional land systems (basically privatization of land previously held under customary tenure), settlement schemes (setting up poor families on newly developed and/or government-owned land and allocating land to them for cultivation and/or grazing), and . . . establishment of individual usufruct [use] rights or community rights."[52] These measures can reduce income inequality.

Yet poverty stems not only from unequal land distribution but also from low farmer productivity. Frequently the land tenure system provides the cultivator little incentive for innovation, long-term investment, harder work, increased fertilization, and improved seeds. And in many instances, landowners raise rents and crop shares when production goes up. The cultivator gains little from higher production.

Giving the poor more land has been tried in a number of countries, with mixed results. Land reform has frequently failed because of the political opposition

---

[49]Idriss Jazairy, Mohiuddin Alamgir, and Theresa Panuccio, *The State of World Rural Poverty: An Inquiry into its Causes and Consequences*, Published for the International Fund for Agricultural Development (New York: New York University Press, 1992), pp. 107, 110.

[50]Theodore Panayotou, *Green Markets: The Economics of Sustainable Development* (San Franciso: Institute for Contemporary Studies, 1993), p. 35.

[51]Sara Berry, "The Food Crisis and Agrarian Change in Africa: A Review Essay," *African Studies Review* 27 (August 1984): 92.

[52]Idriss Jazairy, Mohiuddin Alamgir, and Theresa Panuccio, *The State of World Rural Poverty: An Inquiry into its Causes and Consequences*, Published for the International Fund for Agricultural Development (New York: New York University Press, 1992), p. 106.

of landlords (as in India), the transfer of holdings to relatives, or because the new landowners do not have access to credit, water, fertilizer, extension assistance, and other services. However, in the early 1950s in Japan, Taiwan, and South Korea, where land redistribution was coupled with credit and extension services for small farmers, incomes rose substantially.

By the 1960s, economists believed that redistributing land to small farmers led to lower crop yields. However, subsequent research indicates that land redistribution to the poor *usually* increases LDC agricultural output, at least after a period of adjustment, for two reasons: (1) a small farmer who receives security of ownership is more likely to undertake improvements; and (2) small farms often use more labor per hectare—labor that otherwise might not have been used. When small-sized farms have lower productivity per hectare, it is more often because farmers are illiterate and thus tend to adopt technological innovations more slowly or because they have virtually no access to credit. Furthermore, land fragmentation eventually inhibits productivity.

From 1954 to 1974, Kenya replaced the colonial land tenure system with a new system in which Africans acquired land from Europeans in the central and western highlands. The government assisted Africanization, purchasing land from the former owners and redistributing land to smallholders under the "one million acre settlement program." Thousands of hectares were transferred to Africans through land settlement schemes, large-scale individual purchases, land buying companies, and cooperatives. The landless were not the main beneficiaries. Indeed, many tenants, squatters, and other landless peasants were evicted with land privatization. For the political leadership redistributed most of the land to itself, allies, and clients, many of whom had no experience in farming. The Kenyan case illustrates how politics can limit the success of programs that ostensibly redistribute land to the cultivator.

Alternatives to distributing individual land parcels center on creating cooperatives or revising land tenure or rental rules. But these methods are limited. Quite often cooperatives are dominated by moneylenders and landed interests, or they have management and incentive problems.

Changing rental systems is difficult. Many LDC tenants farm the landowner's land under a **sharecropping** system. Sharecropping may include tenure arrangements where the landlord provides the land, some equipment, and a proportion of seed and fertilizer in exchange for a proportion of the final crop. However, in West Bengal, India, the most common sharecropping arrangement has been one where the landlord only leased land to the sharecropper, lived away from the village, and returned to the village periodically to collect the share of the crop, often payable in kind.[53] Revised land tenure rules that give the tenant farmer greater security, and thus more incentive to invest, are hard to enforce. Numerous landless workers may be willing to replace existing tenants and forego the revised rules, and landlords may try to make up for lost rent in other tenant transactions. They may raise interest on money lent to tenants or lower wages. Or as Inderjit Singh notes in India: "In areas where redistribution is most desirable there is little land available to distribute." Despite the difficulties, land and tenure reforms can still be used to reduce poverty in many

---

[53]Atul Kohli, *The State and Poverty in India: The Politics of Reform* (Cambridge: Cambridge University Press, 1987), p. 133.

LDCs,[54] especially where increased capital per farmer and improved technology enable the cultivator to gain without the landowner losing.

CAPITAL

Agriculturalists have often assumed that the success of mechanization in raising production in the United States and Canada can be duplicated in LDCs. However, as Chapter 9 contends, technology developed for DCs frequently is not suitable for LDCs, where labor tends to be low cost and capital is expensive. In these countries, planning has to be such that production increases from new machinery justify its high cost.

Here are a few sensible policy guidelines. When farms are small, improve farm implements rather than use tractors and combines. If costly machinery is used, it should be rented to all farmers to spread the cost over enough units to be economical. New machinery is more likely to pay for itself if it is used during planting and harvesting to reduce labor shortages rather than during slack farm seasons, when labor is at a surplus. Moreover, machinery prices should probably not be subsidized. Eastern Nigerian farm settlement schemes in the 1960s, for instance, used tractors and earthmovers when they were subsidized, but returned to labor-intensive means of clearing and cultivation when machinery was priced more realistically.[55]

Poor farmers typically have less access to public capital than affluent farmers. As indicated in Chapter 5, direct social investment (roads, schools, and so on) in poor rural areas will increase income and jobs.

CREDIT

The major source of credit for many small farmers is the village moneylender-large landlord, who may charge interest rates of 5 to 10 percent per month. Still, some small farmers prefer this credit to bank or government credit, since repayment schedules are more flexible. Frequently moneylender and debtor are bound by a semipermanent patron-client relationship, in which the creditor provides virtually unconditional access to money in emergencies and for marriage celebrations for daughters in the family. (Remember the discussion of Balayya in Chapter 1.)

Commercial farmers cannot make a profit if they pay usurious interest rates. Yet these farmers have a unique need for credit that may require a separate loan agency. Expenses for the time between sowing and harvest frequently have to be

---

[54]World Bank, *World Development Report, 1980* (New York: Oxford University Press, 1980), p. 41; Montek S. Ahluwalia, "Income Inequality," in Hollis Chenery, Montek S. Ahluwalia, C. L. G. Bell, John H. Duloy, and Richard Jolly, eds., *Redistribution with Growth* (London: Oxford University Press, 1974), p. 24; R. Albert Berry and William R. Cline, *Agrarian Structure and Productivity in Developing Countries*, a study prepared for ILO (Baltimore: Johns Hopkins University Press, 1979); Idriss Jazairy, Mohiuddin Alamgir, and Theresa Panuccio, *The State of World Rural Poverty: An Inquiry into its Causes and Consequences*, Published for the International Fund for Agricultural Development (New York: New York University Press, 1992), p. 112; E. Wayne Nafziger, *Inequality in Africa: Political Elites, Proletariat, Peasants, and the Poor* (Cambridge: Cambridge University Press, 1988), pp. 47, 170; Clarence Zuvekas, Jr., *Economic Development: An Introduction* (New York: St. Martin's, 1979), p. 220; and Inderjit Singh, *The Great Ascent: The Rural Poor in South Asia* (Baltimore: Johns Hopkins University Press, 1990), p. 1.

[55]Uma Lele, *The Design of Rural Development: Lessons from Africa* (Baltimore: Johns Hopkins University Press, 1975), p. 35; and Clarence Zuvekas, Jr., *Economic Development: An Introduction* (New York: St. Martin's, 1979), p. 217.

financed, and since small farmers have little fixed capital, they must offer their land as collateral. Yet government loans boards rarely accept such collateral, since it is difficult politically to foreclose land if the farmer fails to repay. Farming is also subject to risks, such as weather, that cannot be controlled.

Government-administered credit may be necessary to pay for technological innovation, such as high-yielding varieties of grain, as well as the extension help, storage facilities, irrigation, and fertilizer required to take advantage of a new technique. Despite great need, government-administered credit programs are rarely self-supporting and have a limited success.[56] Still there are a few exceptions, successful group lending schemes which lend to small farms and enterprises, such as the Grameen Bank of Bangladesh (see Chapter 6).

RESEARCH AND TECHNOLOGY

The section in Chapter 8 on the food-population balance will emphasize the importance of research and technology, especially as generated by an international network of agricultural research centers, in improving agricultural technology. Here we want to stress that the technology used should depend on available resources. For example, Japan, with a ratio of farm workers per cultivated hectare almost 50 times as high as that of United States, has emphasized biological and chemical technology (such as new seeds and fertilizer) rather than mechanical technology. For the majority of LDCs with high worker-land ratios, the Japanese approach is more sensible than that of the United States.[57]

The introduction of new technology in rural areas is often quite risky. Understandably farmers are reluctant to accept change unless their risks are adequately covered. From long experience, peasants have reason to be skeptical of the findings of experimental research farms. In a number of instances in LDCs, peasant income has fallen, sometimes threatening household survival, when innovation occurred. Too often the new methods were not adapted to local farming conditions: They were inadequately tested in a different soil, climate, and environment and had adverse side effects that destroyed any benefit they may have had. When family survival is at stake, it is more important to avoid any probability of crop failure than to maximize long-run output.

Clearly introducing new technology requires active initial monitoring, so that probable social and economic effects are foreseen: While on-farm tests are required, small farmers are free to experiment with only a fraction of their landholdings, using the remainder to produce food by the old techniques in case the experiment should fail.

Perhaps China best illustrates the importance of adequate agricultural research policies. From the 1950s through the late 1980s, China had a very slow growth in food output per person. During that period, Chinese agricultural institutes were isolated from international institutes and did little basic agricultural research. During the height of the Cultural Revolution from 1966 to 1970, some leading agricultural scientists were sent to rural areas to learn from the peasants and workers. At about the same time, the matriculation of agricultural students was disrupted because the educational system was shut down. Deng Xiaoping, China's

[56]Guy Hunter, ed., *Agricultural Development and the Rural Poor: Declaration of Policy and Guidelines for Action* (London: Overseas Development Institute, 1978), p. 83.

[57]Yujiro Hayami and Vernon W. Ruttan, *Agricultural Development: An International Perspective* (Baltimore: Johns Hopkins University Press, 1971), pp. 111–28.

foremost political leader during the late 1970s, 1980s, and early 1990s, argued that lagging research and low-quality education, especially in agriculture, constitute the "greatest crisis" in contemporary China.[58] China's dilemma underscores the importance of fundamental agricultural research, either undertaken in local research institutes or borrowed and adapted from abroad.

Chapter 8 also takes up these issues. It too stresses the importance of technology that matches resources and social conditions. Farmers need to be more directly involved in selecting research topics. Also the LDC agricultural institutes must develop and adapt technology suitable for small farmers and laborers and disseminate this technical information.[59] Additionally, institutes need to stress research on foods, such as cassava and millets, that loom large in poor people's budgets.[60]

EXTENSION SERVICES

Extension personnel must take the results of agricultural research to the farmers. The agent's role is crucial and varied. Agents must contact and speak with farmers; pass on simple technical information; be able to demonstrate it personally; identify difficulties; know sources of technical advice and training; identify farmers who are good credit risks; arrange for fertilizer, seeds, and other inputs from government depots; and clearly report farm problems and characteristics to researchers and planners.

Unfortunately agricultural extension programs in LDCs are not very successful. Extension agents are often few and far between, ill paid, ill trained, and ill equipped to provide technical help. In many instances, they are beholden to the large, influential farmers and neglect the small farmers, who have far less education and political power. They especially neglect women, even though women manage a sizable proportion of farm activities, particularly food crops, in traditional agriculture.

Extension services based on the U.S. model are not effective. Edward B. Rice has found that in Latin America and other LDCs, the independent extension service based on the U.S. model introduces few innovations and contributes little to rapid growth. He suggests that extension personnel might be more effective if integrated with development organizations, such as loan banks, irrigation authorities, seed and fertilizer distribution centers, agrarian reform agencies, or cooperative organizations.[61]

ACCESS TO WATER AND OTHER INPUTS

Irrigation increases agricultural productivity. It enlarges the land area under cultivation, permits the growth of several crops per year, and regulates the flow of water. Water may be essential with fertilization and improved seed use, and

---

[58]Christopher Howe, *China's Economy: A Basic Guide*, (New York: Basic Books, 1978), pp. 26–27, 81.

[59]Guy Hunter, ed., *Agricultural Development and the Rural Poor: Declaration of Policy and Guidelines for Action* (London: Overseas Development Institute, 1978), pp. 78–82; and World Bank, *World Development Report, 1990* (New York: Oxford University Press, 1990), p. 69.

[60]Timothy Besley and Ravi Kanbur, "The Principles of Targeting," in Michael Lipton and Jacques van der Gaag, *Including the Poor: Proceedings of a Symposium Organized by the World Bank and the International Food Policy Research Institute* (Washington, D.C.: World Bank, 1993), p. 81.

[61]Ibid., p. 55; Edward B. Rice, *Extension in the Andes: An Evaluation of Official U.S. Assistance to Agricultural Extension Services in Central and South America* (Cambridge, Mass.: MIT Press, 1974); World Bank, *World Development Report, 1978* (New York: Oxford University Press, 1978), p. 43; and Uma Lele, *Design of Rural Development: Lessons from Africa* (Baltimore: Johns Hopkins University Press, 1979) pp. 62–63.

water-right reform are often necessary for land reform to be successful. But investment in irrigation and focus on water distribution vary substantially between the two continents with a predominantly agricultural population: 35 percent of cropland in Asia is irrigated, but only 5 percent in sub-Saharan Africa.[62] But even in Asia, water access and availability can often be problematic for small farmers. For example, in Pakistan's century-old irrigation system in the Indus River basin, large, influential farmers get first chance at available water, wasting it, since cost is unrelated to used amount. Even if water access were not a problem, the small farmer seldom has the savings, credit, or incentive to invest in wells and other water projects. When government funds are inadequate, water courses deteriorate. Obviously water rights management and user fees must be planned to avoid inequity and inefficiency. Competent technical management must foresee salinity or sedimentation problems. But even when these matters are competently handled, irrigation is not a panacea for LDC agriculture. Many irrigation systems in LDCs have failed to increase agricultural output to pay for their high construction and operating costs. These enduring monuments to failure underline the need for detailed preinvestment feasibility studies of irrigation projects, including careful estimates of capital, personnel, inputs, and maintenance costs over time and how to increase output (see Chapters 11 and 19).

Aside from water access, farmers require other inputs such as seeds and fertilizer. These are generally supplied through government ministries or agencies. In this case, government must guarantee input quality, accessibility, and quantity.[63] The Nigerian bureaucracy failed to plan for its Operation Feed the Nation in 1979: One-half million tons of imported fertilizer were delivered 2 months too late for the planting season.

TRANSPORT

The LDC crops, otherwise competitive with those in other countries, often cannot enter world markets because of high transport costs. Investment in roads, railroads, port dredging, canals, and other transport can lower the cost of producing farm goods and delivering them to markets. The U.S. Midwest became a center of specialized production of corn, wheat, beef, and pork in the mid–nineteenth century only after several decades of road, railroad, steamboat, and canal expansion. Bolivia illustrates the transport problem for LDCs. Agricultural commodities in Bolivia's lush subtropical and tropical eastern lowlands are at a competitive disadvantage because of high transport costs: Crops must get over the Andes mountains to the west or travel the great distance to the eastern coasts of Brazil and Argentina. Farmers near La Paz pay about twice, and those in remote rural areas of Bolivia several times, the price of fertilizer paid in the United States or Mexico. Thus agricultural export potential in Bolivia is severely limited.[64]

[62]Thomas P. Tomich, Peter Kilby, and Bruce F. Johnston, *Transforming Agrarian Economies: Opportunities Seized, Opportunities Missed* (Ithaca, N.Y.: Cornell University Press, 1995).

[63]World Bank, *World Development Report, 1978* (New York: Oxford University Press, 1978, pp. 40–42; Clarence Zuvekas, Jr., *Economic Development: An Introduction* (New York: St. Martin's, 1979), p. 216; and Douglas Ensminger and Paul Bomani, *Conquest of World Hunger and Poverty* (Ames: Iowa State University Press, 1980), p. 63.

[64]Clarence Zuvekas, Jr., *Economic Development: An Introduction* (New York: St. Martin's, 1979), p. 135, 230.

MARKETING AND STORAGE

Poor marketing channels and insufficient storage facilities often hamper grain sales outside the region of production and limit production gains from the improved seeds of the Green Revolution.[65] For example, the lack of storage and drying facilities in the Philippines in the 1960s prevented many farmers from growing two rice crops a year. And in northern India, the increase in wheat production in 1968 required that the crop be stored in schools or in the open air. As much as one-third of this crop was destroyed by rats and rain.

Government must plan for the impact of new seeds and improved agricultural techniques on marketing and storage. Government can provide the infrastructure, such as roads and grain bins; set uniform grades and standards that sharpen the incentive to improve product quality; supply national price information; and help farmers decide which crops to plant, when to sell, and what storage facilities to build.

Many LDCs have established official marketing boards to buy crops from farmers to sell on the world market. However, these boards have a tendency to demand a monopsony position to ensure financial success and frequently accumulate funds to transfer from agriculture to industry. Nevertheless, the boards can stabilize crop prices and provide production and market research, promotion, extension assistance, and other services.

Many government marketing institutions in LDCs have been established to replace open markets considered inefficient, antisocial, and subject to exploitation by middlemen and women. However, a government should examine whether its use of scarce capital and skilled personnel to establish such an enterprise to replace the private intermediary is socially beneficial. Ironically such marketing institutions are more likely to eliminate the small, competitive grain trader than the agent or distributor for the large, influential agribusiness. Furthermore, the private middleman or woman operating in a competitive market is likely to have a smaller markup than the state enterprise, which frequently has a monopoly. Moreover, empirical evidence indicates that the farm market is relatively efficient in transmitting price information, providing incentives, allocating production among commodities, and rationing goods among consumers.

PRICE AND EXCHANGE RATE POLICIES

Irma Adelman's and Sherman Robinson's simulations of the effect of government policy interventions warn against confining rural development projects to those that only increase agricultural productivity—making more machinery and credit available; improving irrigation, fertilizer, and seeds; adding new technology; enhancing extension services; and so on. Increased agricultural production and an inelastic demand (see Figure 7–3) are likely to reduce the agricultural terms of trade as well as rural real income and to increase urban-rural inequalities in the short run.[66] Thus to reduce rural poverty, production-oriented programs must be

---

[65]This section draws from Yujiro Hayami and Vernon W. Ruttan, *Agricultural Development*, pp. 216, 267; Guy Hunter, ed., *Agricultural Development and The Rural Poor: Declaration of Policy and Guidelines for Action* (London: Overseas Development Institute, 1978), pp. 89–91; and Uma Lele, *The Design of Rural Development: Lessons from Africa* (Baltimore: Johns Hopkins University Press, 1975), pp. 100–101.

[66]Irma Adelman and Sherman Robinson, *Income Distribution Policy in Developing Countries: A Case Study of Korea* (Stanford: Stanford University Press, 1978), pp. 128–46.

FIGURE 7-3   Increased Agricultural Supply When Demand is Inelastic

When the relevant range of a demand curve (*D*) is inelastic (that is, when the percentage change in price exceeds the percentage change in quantity demanded), an increase in agricultural supply will reduce agricultural income or total revenue. Note that the area of the total revenue (price times quantity) rectangles decreases in size as supply increases from S_1 to S_2.

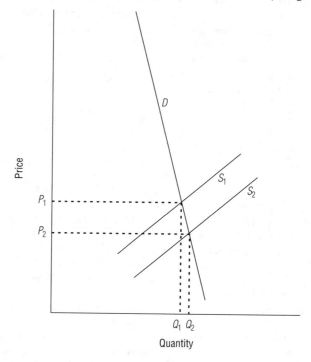

combined with price and exchange rate policies, improved rural services, land reform, farmer cooperation, and more rural industry.

Empirical studies indicate a high *long-run* **elasticity of supply** (that is, a high percentage change in quantity supplied in response to a 1-percentage change in price) in LDC agriculture. Long-run means the farmer can vary the hectares devoted to a given crop.

In response to consumer pressure, LDC governments frequently establish maximum producer, wholesale, or retail prices for food. But the long-run effects of such policies, given high supply elasticity, may raise prices by discouraging domestic production and increasing reliance on imports. This effect occurred in Argentina in the late 1940s. Subsequent government measures to increase relative farm prices in the early 1950s did not stimulate output as expected because farmers felt the more favorable prices would not be permanent. Subsidizing food is the only way of reducing consumer food prices without harming production incentives (even in socialist countries).

The benefits of research, technology, extension and credit programs, and so on can be lost with ill-conceived pricing policies. Technological development is more efficient when farm input and output prices are competitive. Researchers and extension agents are more likely to innovate when farm prices clear the market than when they are controlled. Lastly farmers tend to press research institutions for technological innovations with a high payoff—for example, those that save resources with an inelastic supply.[67]

The World Bank's Berg report criticizes African states for keeping farm prices far below market prices, dampening farm producer incentives, using marketing boards to transfer peasant savings to large industry, and setting exchange rates that discourage exports and encourage **import substitutes** (domestic production replacing imports). World Bank economist Kevin M. Cleaver shows that the **real exchange-rate change** (domestic inflation divided by foreign inflation times the percentage change in the foreign exchange price of domestic currency), from 1970 to 1981, is negatively related to agricultural (and overall) growth rates. Kenya and Lesotho, whose farm exports remained competitive as the real value of their domestic currency depreciated, grew faster than Ghana and Tanzania, whose real domestic currency value appreciated (increased).[68] These state interventions into the price system hurt farmers, increasing industry and agricultural income differentials.[69]

Agricultural resource allocation is highly affected by the foreign exchange rate. As discussed in Chapters 9 and 18, a domestic price for foreign currency lower than equilibrium price reduces farm export receipts and wastes capital goods imports by those people acquiring foreign currency.

IMPROVING RURAL SERVICES

Urban areas have far more schools, medical services, piped water, and so on, than rural areas. If rural, middle, and lower classes opposed the urban bias of the national political leadership, they might be able to increase their share of social investment. It is especially important to narrow the educational gap existing between the rural and urban child. As argued in Chapter 10, increasing the share of public educational expenditures in rural areas redistributes income to the poor. And if rural schools begin to place a greater emphasis on curricula that prepare children for rural employment, the rural areas will retain *and* attract more skilled people.

---

[67]Yujiro Hayami and Vernon W. Ruttan, *Agricultural Development: An International Perspective* (Baltimore: Johns Hopkins University Press, 1971), pp. 56–59; and Clarence Zuvekas, Jr., *Economic Development: An Introduction* (New York: St. Martin's, 1979), pp. 233–34.

[68]World Bank, *Accelerated Development in sub-Saharan Africa: An Agenda for Action* (Washington, D.C., 1981); and Kevin M. Cleaver, "The Impact of Price of Exchange Rate Policies on Agriculture in sub-Saharan Africa," World Bank Staff Working Paper no. 728, Washington, D.C., 1985.

[69]Mahmood H. Khan and Mohsin S. Khan, "Agricultural Growth in Sub-Saharan African Countries and China," International Monetary Paper on Policy Analysis and Assessment, Washington, D.C., April 1995, argue that African states will need to cease intervening into farm prices, while substantially investing in infrastructure and water, changing property rights, and applying new technologies widely.

COOPERATIVE AND COLLECTIVE FARMS

Many LDCs have favored large farms, believing they can take advantage of internal economies of scale. However, Nancy L. Johnson and Vernon W. Ruttan show, on the basis of case studies of large farms in capitalist and socialist economies, that except for very specific circumstances, economies of scale in large-scale farming do not exist. Because labor and machines are both mobile in agriculture, the monitoring costs for supervising hired labor is expensive, contributing to scale diseconomies absent in mass manufacturing. Moreover, farm hands must work independently, anticipating problems and reacting to different situations as they arise, a skill more difficult to teach than factory labor. Furthermore, the annual cycle of preparing the seedbed, planting, and harvest requires that farm tasks be done sequentially, limiting specialization gains.[70]

Agricultural policymakers in Tanzania, Ethiopia, Mozambique, Ghana, Nigeria, and other African countries, many of whom misunderstood these economies of farm size, have emphasized large capital-intensive estates, which have contributed to the decline in African agricultural output per capita.[71] As an example, from 1967 to 1976, Tanzania launched **ujamaa** (literally "familyhood") socialism, which emphasized land nationalization and communal village production units. *Ujamaa* failed, as its egalitarian goals collided with the actions of the state bureaucracy, whose mushrooming racketeering, embezzlement, and accumulation took place at the same time that both peasant prices and the transfer of resources from agriculture to the state fell.[72]

Farmers can sometimes reduce diseconomies of scale through machinery. Thus, in Brazil, mechanized plows allowed those farming hard *cerrado* soils to plow in advance of the rains and reduce runoff, and in North America, grain dryers lengthen harvest. More generally, there are economies in the use of lumpy inputs such as machinery or management; in access to inputs, credit, services, storage facilities, marketing, or distribution; and where processing or marketing economies are transmitted backwards to the farm. Still, Johnson and Ruttan believe that optimal-sized farms are generally owner-operators, who can achieve economies of scale in purchasing and marketing cooperatives.[73]

Cooperatives.   The **cooperative**, involving the least radical break from the individual or family farm, may include the common use of facilities, pooling land, the combined purchase of inputs, or the shared marketing of crops. The cooperative

---

[70]Nancy L. Johnson and Vernon W. Ruttan, "Why are Farms so Small?" *World Development* 22 (May 1994): 691–706.

[71]Thomas P. Tomich, Peter Kilby, and Bruce F. Johnston, *Transforming Agrarian Economies: Opportunities Seized, Opportunities Missed* (Ithaca, N.Y.: Cornell University Press, 1995).

James Kaising Kung, "Egalitarianism, Subsistence Provision, and Work Incentives in China's Agricultural Collectives," *World Development* 22 (February 1994): 175–87, however, shows that collective agriculture in China failed, not because of the difficulties of monitoring work effort in a team, but because of the way the state impoverished the peasantry through a policy of extracting agricultural produce and a flawed remuneration system that rewarded work by piece rate rather than by time worked.

[72]E. Wayne Nafziger, *The Debt Crisis in Africa* (Baltimore: Johns Hopkins University Press, 1993), pp. 117–19.

[73]Nancy L. Johnson and Vernon W. Ruttan, "Why are Farms so Small?" *World Development* 22 (May 1994): 691–706.

ownership or hire of a tractor, irrigation channel, peanut sheller, or grain harvester divides high overhead costs.[74] Many countries in the transition from socialism have existing cooperatives, which can be converted to voluntary, member-owned and controlled organizations that small farmers in a market economy to benefit from large-scale internal and external economies.

Collective Farms or Communes.   Here the state or community owns the land and capital. Pre-1985 Soviet Union and Maoist China are the chief exemplars of collectivism. Soviet leader Joseph Stalin introduced the **collective farm** (*kolkhoz*) in 1929. Between 1921 and 1928, a new class of *kulaks* (prosperous small landholders) and private traders whom the party could not control had arisen. Collectivization was Stalin's way of regaining control. The Chinese stressed the slogan, "Learn from the Soviet Union," but their people's commune (or collective farm) was shaped over several years (1949–59). The Chinese commune, with an average of 15,000 members, consisted of several production brigades divided into decentralized production teams of 100 to 400 people, the basic unit of production and distribution.
   Why did the Stalinist Soviet Union and Maoist China collectivize their farms?

1. To use official price policies to increase saving. (However, the net result of these policies was income transfer from rural to urban areas. Recall that the Soviet Union used low prices to squeeze agriculture for the benefit of heavy industry.)
2. To exploit internal economies of scale in production and social services. The Soviet *kolkhoz,* usually more than 400 hectares, used tractors, combines, an accountant, an engineer, and sometimes an agronomist. The Chinese commune was large enough for a tractor station, high school, hospital, credit cooperative, radio station, reservoir, dam, hydroelectric power station, processing plant, sawmill, and a variety of rural industries. But the economies of farm production failed to materialize.
3. To employ underutilized farm workers in rural industry during the off-season (as on the Chinese communes). The rural underemployed stayed home, reducing the blight, population density, and pressure on food prices in urban areas that result when they migrate.
4. To enable the state to control the grain market. This control was especially important in the Soviet Union, where the Communist leadership *believed* (perhaps erroneously) that peasant marketing declined during the steep drop in farm prices relative to industrial prices from 1922 to 1924.

Most economists doubt that the benefits of collective agriculture surpassed the costs. During the Soviet collectivization of 1929 to 1933, the forcible collection

---

[74]Clarence Zuvekas, Jr., *Economic Development: An Introduction* (New York: St. Martin's, 1979), p. 34; and Guy Hunter, ed., *Agricultural Development and the Rural Poor: Declaration of Policy and Guidelines for Action* (London: Overseas Development Institute, 1978), p. 60. The remainder of this section uses Jan S. Prybyla, *The Chinese Economy: Problems and Policies* (Columbia: University of South Carolina Press, 1978), pp. 43–46, 60–64; Paul R. Gregory and Robert C. Stuart, *Soviet and Post-Soviet Economic Structure and Performance* (New York: HarperCollins, 1994); E. L. Wheelwright and Bruce McFarland, *The Chinese Road to Socialism: Economics of the Cultural Revolution* (New York: Monthly Review Press, 1970), pp. 43–65; Alec Nove, *An Economic History of the U.S.S.R.* (Middlesex, U.K.: Penguin, 1972); Christopher Howe, *China's Economy, a Basic Guide* (New York: Basic Books, 1978) pp. xxiii–xxv; and Carmelo Mesa-Lago, *Cuba in the 1970s: Pragmatism and Institutionalization* (Albuquerque: University of New Mexico Press, 1978), pp. 97–101.

of grain, the confiscation of farm property, the arrest and deportation of real and alleged kulaks, the destruction of tools and livestock, the class warfare between peasants and kulaks, the administrative disorder, the disruption of sowing and harvest, and the accompanying famine led to the deaths of about 5 million people. Gross agricultural output per person declined from 1928 to 1937. Although Soviet agricultural performance improved from 1937 to 1991, the average level of food productivity per hectare was still below Western countries such as Italy. In the early 1990s, the Russian leadership was divided on agricultural policy, especially in light of peasant aversion to the risks of reform. In China, although industrial output per capita grew by 8.3 percent per year between 1952 and 1975, food output per person increased only 0.2 percent per year. Moreover, small private plots in the Soviet Union and Maoist China produced a disproportionate share of vegetables, livestock, and peasant's money income, albeit with more labor per hectare than on the collective. Furthermore, in both socialist Poland and Yugoslavia, farmers resisted collectivization. In these countries, the private sector accounted for more than four-fifths of the agricultural area and output. To be sure, the Soviet people were adequately nourished, and Maoist China met the nutritional needs of its poorest 40 percent better than most other low-income countries. Nevertheless, the low productivity of pre-1989 Eastern European and Soviet agriculture compared to capitalist North America and Western Europe (Table 7–1), together with the slow pre-1979 growth in Chinese food output per person, suggests the failure of collective agriculture as a model for developing countries.

Collectivism's advantages proved to be much less than their proponents claimed. Low farm prices and the transfer of agricultural savings to industry hampers agricultural growth. The few economies of large-scale production can be achieved instead through cooperatives, renting machinery, and technical and managerial assistance provided by extension agents. Local or provincial government or private enterprise can provide many of the social services mentioned. Even in a mixed or capitalist economy, off-farm employment opportunities can be made available to farmers during the slack season. Although the state leadership may wish to control the grain market for political reasons, there is no evidence that this increases agricultural efficiency and growth.

There are other problems with the collective farms. The link between individual initiative and effort on the one hand, and income on the other, is not so powerful as on the individually or family-owned farm. Also the collectivist system for paying labor is complicated, time consuming, and cumbersome: The output of the production unit is usually distributed by work points based on the type of task and work performance. Disputes concerning its accuracy and equity are common. Additionally there are marked differences in average income between collective farms. Effort and efficiency cannot usually overcome poor location and soil. Moreover, collective farm investment tends to be made for political reasons rather than prospective rates of return. Furthermore, collective farms are rewarded on the basis of output rather than efficiency (which considers cost) and demand for what is produced.

In China, from 1979 to 1983, production teams (usually the size of a village) distributed the land they had farmed collectively for more than two decades under contract for long-term use rights to individual households, the **household responsibility system**. The local authorities allocated land to households on the basis of equal division by population (adjusted by age and gender), equal division by labor force participation, or some combination of the two methods. Martin

Gaynor and Louis Putterman show that these methods of equal distribution of land correspond to optimal incentives for increasing the productivity of land.[75]

Moreover, ironically despite Deng Xiaoping's repudiation of Mao's slogans of egalitarianism and increasing moral (not material) incentives, Martin King Whyte thinks Deng's decollectivization and price decontrol probably reduced China's income inequality. While Mao attacked privilege among encrusted bureaucrats and intellectuals, his opposition to financial incentives reduced income, especially among peasants. Mao's urban bias policies widened the urban-rural gap from the mid-1950s to the mid-1970s. While post-1979 agricultural reforms encouraged enterprising peasants "to get rich" and widen intrarural income differentials, the rapid growth of agricultural income vis-à-vis industrial income reduced the difference between town and countryside, perhaps even reducing overall income inequality. Additionally relaxing restrictions on urban emigration permitted rural families from depressed areas to reduce populations and benefit from nonfarm remittances.[76] As implied before, market-oriented reforms may cut inequalities fostered by the state's town-biased allocation system.

State Farms. Partly because of the cumbersome way of paying wages on the collective farm, the Soviet Union gradually increased the percentage of land in **state farms** from the early 1950s to the late-1980s. By the late 1970s, over one-half of the country's total cultivated land was used for state farms. Their workers, as well as an increasing number of collective farm workers, were being paid a fixed wage, which protected peasant income against the effects of weather fluctuations and soil deficiencies, and increased peasant resistance to the uncertainties of market reform.

RURAL INDUSTRY

As discussed in Chapter 9, demand for agricultural labor grows slowly (and in later stages may even decrease). Technical advances and capital accumulation displace some farm labor. The LDC demand for food grows slowly, since its income elasticity (percentage change in per capita food purchases relative to percentage change in per capita income) is only about one-half. On the other hand, population growth in rural areas is usually more rapid than in LDCs as a whole, so the labor supply usually grows rapidly. Off-farm employment must expand to take care of these extra workers. In the 1970s and 1980s, nonfarm activities comprised 79 percent of rural employment in Latin America, 34 percent in Asia, and 19 percent in Africa.[77]

Public works projects and small- and medium-scale manufacturing, agribusiness, and processing increase relative incomes and reduce unemployment

---

[75]Martin Gaynor and Louis Putterman, "Productivity Consequences of Alternative Land Division Methods in China's Decollectivization," *Journal of Development Economics* 42 (December 1993): 357–86.

[76]Martin King Whyte, "Social Trends in China: The Triumph of Inequality?" in A. Doak Barnett and Ralph N. Clough, eds., *Modernizing China: Post-Mao Reform and Development* (Boulder, Colo.: Westview, 1986), pp. 103–23.

[77]Peter Hazell and Steven Haggblade, "Farm-Nonfarm Growth Linkages and the Welfare of the Poor," in Michael Lipton and Jacques van der Gaag, *Including the Poor: Proceedings of a Symposium Organized by the World Bank and the International Food Policy Research Institute* (Washington, D.C.: World Bank, 1993), pp. 190–92; and World Bank, *World Development Report, 1990* (New York: Oxford University Press, 1990), pp. 60–61.

and underemployment in rural areas. Since 1958, China has had a policy of "walking on two legs," with large urban manufacturing augmented by a "second leg," small- and medium-sized industry on the rural communes. India has limited industrial expansion and new enterprises in metropolitan areas, while firms locating in industrially "backward" nonmetropolitan areas are given favored access to materials and facilities.

Industries and retail enterprises complementary to agriculture—firms producing and selling basic consumer items, blacksmithing, repair, and maintenance shops—are certainly worth developing. However, many industrial operations cannot be competitive without the materials, power, markets, financial institutions, communication network, and skilled labor usually concentrated in major urban centers. For example, except in a few metropolitan areas in Nigeria, the electricity supply is too unreliable for many enterprises, including those using plastic injector molding machines, iron-smelting furnaces, or refrigerators. In the 1980s, Deng Xiaoping admitted that the emphasis by rural communes during the Chinese Cultural Revolution on making their own lathes and tractors was very uneconomical, even given the high transport and distribution costs.

POLITICAL CONSTRAINTS

Improved rural social services, greater price incentives, effective farm cooperatives, and public spending on research, credit, rural industry, extension services, irrigation, and transport are frequently not technical, but political, problems. The political survival of state leaders in fragile LDCs requires marshaling the support of urban elites (civil servants, private and state corporate employees, business people, professionals, and skilled workers) through economic policies that sacrifice income distribution and agricultural growth. Moreover, LDCs may lack the political and administrative capability, especially in rural areas, to undertake programs to reduce poverty. Established interests—large farmers, moneylenders, and the urban classes—may oppose the policy changes and spending essential to improving the economic welfare of the small farmer, tenant, and landless workers.

Additionally, state intervention in the market is an instrument of political control and assistance. Government, quasi-government corporations, and private business pressure political elites for inexpensive food policies to keep down wages, and governments sometimes use troops to quell food-related riots (as in Brazil, Egypt, and Tunisia in the mid-1980s). Unrest by urban workers over erosion of their purchasing power has threatened numerous LDC governments. Real wage declines under Nigeria's Abubakar Tafewa Balewa government in 1964 and the Yakubu Gowon government in 1974 to 1975, as well as Ghana's Kofi Busia government in 1971, contributed to political unrest and violence that precipitated military coups. Politicians may also help emerging industry reduce raw material or processing costs. Market intervention provides political control for elites to use in retaining power, building support, and implementing policies.

In 1954 in Ghana, Kwame Nkrumah's Convention People's Party (CPP) passed a bill freezing cocoa producer prices for 4 years, anticipating use of the increased revenues for industry. But the CPP government undercut the newly formed opposition party in the cocoa-growing regions by selectively providing subsidized inputs—loans, seeds, fertilizer, and implements—for prospective dissidents. Additionally, state farm programs in each constituency in the 1960s made available public resources to organize support for the Nkrumah government.

Market-clearing farm prices and exchange rates, whose benefits are distributed indiscriminately, erode urban political support and secure little support from the countryside. In comparison, project-based policies allow benefits to be selectively apportioned for maximum political advantage. Government makes it in the interest of numerous individuals to cooperate with programs that harm the interest of producers as a whole.[78]

Rural dwellers, who are often politically weak and fear government reprisals, rarely organize to oppose antirural policies. While poor farmers have little tactical power, rich ones have too much to lose from protest. Moreover, they have less costly options—selling in black markets, shifting resources to other commodities, or migrating to urban areas. Yet eventually rural classes harmed by state market intervention may have to mobilize to oppose the urban and large-farm bias of many contemporary LDC political leaders.

Summary

1. Rural inequality is probably less than urban inequality in LDCs as a whole. Nevertheless rural populations have a higher percentage in poverty than urban populations, because of much lower average incomes in rural areas. Most rural poverty is concentrated among agricultural laborers, the landless, and the near landless.

2. Output per person outside agriculture as a multiple of that in agriculture, which is eight in Africa and four in Asia and Latin America, was only about two in Europe in the nineteenth century.

3. Because of high levels of capital accumulation, technical knowledge, and worker productivity, agricultural output per worker in developed countries is about thirty times as high as in developing countries.

4. Subsistence farming dominated LDC agriculture in the past. The major goal of the peasant farmer has not been to maximize income, but the family's probability of survival. Nevertheless, many peasants, attracted by the potential for improving productivity and living standards, have begun to produce more crops for the market.

5. Food production per capita in the developed countries grew at a rate of 9 percent from 1962 to 1989, compared to 14 percent in developing countries during the same period. Growth rates for both India and China are positive, though generally slower than for LDCs before the late 1970s, and more rapid than other LDCs after liberalization in the late 1970s. Agricultural economists noticed a fall in global average foodgrain production during the late 1980s and early 1990s, but they do not know if foodgrain output per person will grow or decline in the late 1990s and early twenty-first century.

6. Colonial and postcolonial policies biased against agriculture helped contribute to sub-Saharan Africa's decline in food output per capita from the early 1950s to

[78]Robert H. Bates, *Markets and States in Tropical Africa: The Political Basis of Agricultural Policies* (Berkeley and Los Angeles: University of California Press, 1981); Douglas Rimmer, *The Economies of West Africa* (London: Weidenfeld and Nicolson, 1984); E. Wayne Nafziger, *Inequality in Africa: Political Elites, Proletariat, Peasants, and the Poor* (Cambridge: Cambridge University Press, 1988), pp. 140–56, 173–75; and Peter Hendry, "Food and Population: Beyond Five Billion," *Population Bulletin* 43 (April 1988): 11.

the early 1990s. Africa's food security is low because of substantial fluctuations in domestic production and foreign-exchange reserves and reductions in food aid.

7. Two-thirds of sub-Saharan Africa's rural population and more than one-half of Latin America's rural population live in poverty. East Asia has the lowest rural poverty rate among LDC regions.

8. Inadequate capital (including that for health and social services), lack of technology, low educational and skill levels, the brain drain to urban areas, food price policies, below-market foreign exchange rates, and governmental urban bias contribute to low incomes in rural areas. Land concentration, the bias of technology toward large farmers, and large seasonal variations in income also affect rural poverty rates.

9. Policies that would increase rural income and reduce rural poverty are manifold. Land reform and redistribution, developing labor-intensive capital equipment, establishing rural credit agencies, agricultural research centers that conduct on-farm tests, institutes to develop and adapt technology for small farmers, an extension service integrated with development agencies, an irrigation authority that conducts careful feasibility studies of proposed projects, and government ministries that provide suitable and timely inputs to farmers are estimable goals. So, too, farm commodity and foreign exchange prices close to market-clearing rates; greater expenditure on social and educational services in rural areas; redistributing land to the rural poor; establishing agro industries, basic consumer goods industries, and other small industries in rural areas; and investment in marketing, transport, and storage facilities for agricultural commodities would improve the lot of the rural poor.

10. Well-planned, cooperative ventures can help small farmers improve productivity by allowing them to take advantage of economies of large-scale production. Collective farms have the same advantage and also use farm workers in rural industry during the slack season. However, collectivism has not generally increased productivity because of some inherent disincentives.

11. Production-oriented rural development projects such as small-farmer credit, agricultural innovations and new technology, and improved extension services are likely to reduce agricultural terms of trade and thus reduce rural incomes in the short run. To increase incomes of the rural poor, production-oriented programs need to be combined with policies to improve relative agricultural prices and rural income distribution.

The following subjects related to food and agriculture are covered in subsequent chapters: the food-population balance (Chapter 8); disguised unemployment in agriculture and rural-urban migration (Chapter 9); natural resources and the environment (Chapter 13); and the substantial dependence of many low-income countries on primary product exports (Chapter 18).

Terms to Review

- peasant farming
- mixed farming
- commercial farming
- food security index (FSI)
- food deficit
- import substitutes
- real exchange-rate change
- entitlement

- *latifundios*
- *minifundios*
- urban bias
- sharecropping
- elasticity of supply
- *ujamaa*

- cooperative
- *kolkhoz*
- collective farm
- kulak
- household responsibility system
- state farm

Questions to Discuss

1. Give arguments in favor of LDCs concentrating their antipoverty programs in rural areas.
2. Why is agricultural productivity in DCs so much higher than in LDCs?
3. How would the theory of a peasant economy differ from that of a commercial farm economy?
4. What do you expect the trend in food output per capita and food consumption per capita to be in LDCs in the next decade? What LDC regions are most vulnerable in the next decade? What LDC regions are most invulnerable in the next decade?
5. Explain and compare India's progress since the early 1950s in increasing average food output and reducing hunger to China's progress.
6. Explain sub-Saharan Africa's negative growth in food output per person between the early 1950s and the early 1980s.
7. What factors contribute to the high incidence of rural poverty in LDCs?
8. Indicate the forms of urban bias in LDCs. Give examples of policies of urban bias (or rural bias) in your own country or another one you know well. Has such a policy bias hampered development?
9. What policies are most effective in increasing rural income and reducing rural poverty? What strategies are needed to prevent rural development policies from increasing rural poverty through reduced agricultural terms of trade?
10. Is Soviet and Chinese collectivism (similar to that before 1975) practicable in LDCs? Compare and explain China's agricultural progress in the Maoist period (1949–76) to that of the period after the 1979 agricultural reforms.

Guide to Readings

Data on food output and imports in DCs and LDCs are in publications by the U.S. Department of Agriculture (similar to those cited in the note to Figure 7–1), the International Food Policy Research Institute (see note to Table 7–3), and the Food and Agriculture Organization of the United Nations. For a discussion of measuring food production, consumption, and demand in LDCs, see Robert E. Evenson and Carl E. Pray, "Food Production and Consumption: Measuring Food Production (with Reference to South Asia)," *Journal of Development Economics* 44 (June 1994): 173–97; and Howarth E. Bouis, "The Effect of Income on Demand for Food in Poor Countries: Are Our Food Consumption

Databases Giving us Reliable Estimates?" *Journal of Development Economics* 44 (June 1994): 199–226.

On Africa's food problem, see Ghai and Radwan, Eicher and Baker (note 21), Lele (note 55), and World Bank, *Adjustment in Africa: Reforms, Results, and the Road Ahead* (Oxford: Oxford University Press, 1994). Material on food and agriculture in China is contained in Howe; Eberstadt (note 30); Lardy (note 33); Sylvan Wittwer, Yu Youtai, Sun Han, and Wang Lianzheng, *Feeding a Billion: Frontiers of Chinese Agriculture* (East Lansing: Michigan State University Press, 1987); and Carl Riskin, *China's Political Economy: The Quest for Development since 1949* (Oxford: Oxford University Press, 1987). Gregory and Stuart (note 74) discuss food and agriculture in Russia.

Lipton's thesis on urban bias (note 44) is assessed in a special issue of the *Journal of Development Studies* 29 (July 1993).

Some of the major works on rural poverty in LDCs are Jazairy, Alamgir, and Panuccio (note 1), Lipton (note 44), and the World Bank's annual *World Development Report.* Weitz (note 11) has a thorough treatment of the evolution from peasant to specialized farmers. Excellent discussions of agricultural policies are in Lele (note 55); Hunter (note 56); Hayami and Ruttan (note 57); Lipton (note 44); Tomich, Kilby, and Johnston (note 5); John H. Sanders, Sunder Ramaswamy, and Barry I. Shapiro, *The Economics of Agricultural Technology in Semi-Arid Sub-Saharan Africa* (Baltimore: Johns Hopkins University Press, 1996); and Inderjit Singh, *The Great Ascent: the Rural Poor in South Asia* (Baltimore: Johns Hopkins University Press, 1990).

Ajit Kuman Ghose, ed., *Agrarian Reform in Contemporary Developing Countries,* prepared for the ILO (London: Croom Helm, 1983), pp. 3–28; M. R. El Ghonemy, K. H. Parsons, R. P. Sinha, N. Uphoff, and P. Wignaraja, *Studies on Agrarian Reform and Rural Poverty* (Rome: Food and Agriculture Organization of the United Nations, 1984), pp. 19–57; and Berry and Cline (note 54) discuss agrarian reform.

PART III: FACTORS OF GROWTH

CHAPTER 8 Population and Development

Chapters 8 to 13 analyze factors that influence economic growth. The next three chapters examine the role of the human population in economic growth. This chapter examines how population growth affects economic development and how fertility affects labor force participation and development. Chapter 9 looks at how population growth affects labor force growth and unemployment, and Chapter 10 at what factors affect labor skills—a major component of population quality.

Between 1980 and 1996, the world's population grew at 1.7 percent per year, from 4.4 billion to 5.8 billion. During the same period, LDC population grew at 2.3 percent per year, from 3.2 billion to 4.6 billion. This chapter explains this phenomenal growth rate and looks at its implications.

Scope of the Chapter

After a brief historical sketch, we consider population growth in DCs and LDCs and by world regions. Next we explain the rapid growth in LDCs by looking at trends in death and birth rates during a period of demographic (population) transition. With this background, we assess the effect of population growth on economic development and review the work of classical economist Thomas Robert Malthus, who argues that population growth outstrips economic growth. In this connection, we discuss the present and future balance between food and population. Population growth also affects urbanization, labor force growth, and the number of dependents workers must support; we look at all of these elements, too. In the last section, we consider the relative merits of birth control programs and socioeconomic development in reducing population growth.

World Population Throughout History

Throughout most of our existence, population grew at a rate of only 0.002 percent (or 20 per million people) per year. This growth was subject to substantial fluctuations from wars, plagues, famines, and natural catastrophes. However, since about 8000 B.C.E., population growth rates have accelerated. Worldwide population reached one billion in the early nineteenth century, millions of years after our appearance on earth. The second billion was added about a century later, in 1930. The third billion came along in only 30 years, in 1960; the fourth took only 15 years, in 1975; the fifth, 11 years, in 1986; and the sixth billion 12 years, in 1998 (see Figure 8–1). Eighty percent of the world's population lives in LDCs.

Population Growth in Developed and Developing Countries

Figure 8–2 indicates the great variation in birth rates, death rates, and population growth among nations. Countries can be roughly divided into three groups: (1) the DCs and transitional economies, consisting of countries in Europe, North

FIGURE 8–1   World Population Growth through History
The graph shows how explosive population growth has been in the last 200 years. World population grew at an annual rate of about 0.002 percent between the appearance of humankind and 8000 B.C.E., 0.05 percent between 8000 B.C.E. and 1650, 0.43 percent between 1650 and 1900, 0.91 percent between 1900 and 1950, 1.93 percent between 1950 and 1980, and is growing 1.62 percent per year between 1980 and 2000.

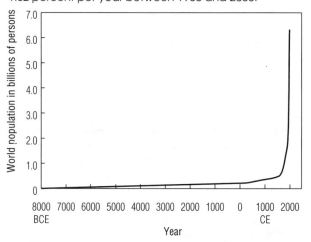

Sources: Based on Paul R. Ehrlich, Anne H. Ehrlich, and John P. Holdren, *Ecoscience: Population, Resources, Environment* (San Francisco: W. H. Freeman, 1977), p. 183; Warren S. Thompson and David T. Lewis, *Population Problems* (New York: McGraw-Hill, 1965), p. 384; Alexander Morris Carr-Saunders, *World Population: Past Growth and Present Trends* (Oxford: Clarendon Press, 1936), pp. 15–45; U.S. Bureau of the Census, *World Population: 1977—Recent Demographic Estimates for the Countries and Regions of the World* (Washington, D.C., 1978), p. 15; U.S. Bureau of the Census, *Illustrative Projections of World Populations in the Twenty-first Century* (Washington, D.C., 1979), p. 17; World Bank, *World Development Report, 1987* (New York: Oxford University Press, 1987), pp. 254–55; and World Bank, *World Development Report, 1994* (New York: Oxford University Press, 1994), pp. 210–11.

FIGURE 8-2 Population Growth in Developed and Developing Countries
A population growth rate of 0.8–1.8 percent per year divides the DCs from the LDCs.

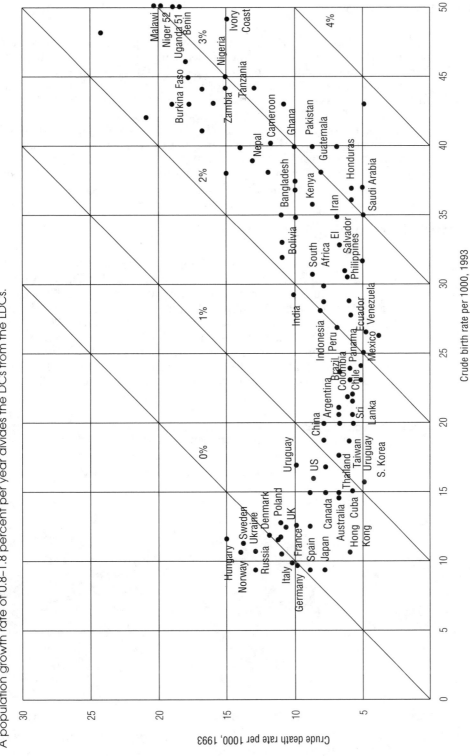

Source: World Bank. *World Development Report, 1995* (New York: Oxford University Press, 1995), pp. 212–13, and author's estimates for Cuba and Taiwan.

213

America, Australia, New Zealand, and Japan, with population growth rates below 0.8 percent per year; (2) Argentina, Chile, Uruguay, Cuba, China, Taiwan, South Korea, Thailand, Indonesia, and Sri Lanka, with annual rates between 0.8 and 1.8 percent, whose demographic behavior is closer to DCs than to LDCs; and (3) the bulk of the LDCs—most of Africa, Asia, and Latin America, with population growth rates of at least 1.9 percent per year.

A major distinction between the three groups is the birth rate. (Following the conventional use, **crude birth and death rates** denote a number per 1,000, *not* percent.) the DCs' and transitional countries' crude birth rate are no more than 16 per thousand. Most developing countries have birth rates of at least 25 per 1,000. Countries in category 2 generally fall between these two figures.

World Population by Region

The world's population is unevenly distributed geographically. Figure 8–3 shows regional distribution in 1950 and 1994, and projected distribution in 2025. The most rapidly growing regions are in the developing world: Asia, Africa, and Latin America. Their share of the global population increased from 70.0 percent in 1950 to 80.1 percent in 1994, and is expected to reach 85.2 percent in 2025. Since 1950, Asia, Africa, and Latin America grew at a rate of 2.2 percent per year, a rate that doubles population in 33 years. Such growth is unprecedented in world history.

Africa is expected to have the most rapid growth, 1994 to 2025, 2.6 percent annually. Its present rate, 2.9 percent yearly, is the result of a traditionally high

FIGURE 8–3   World Population by Region: 1950, 1994, and 2025 (projected)
Asia's, Africa's, and Latin America's share of the world population is increasing over time.

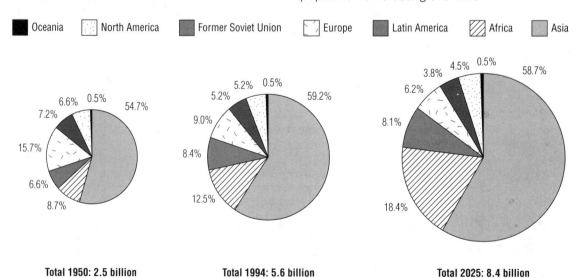

Sources: United Nations, Department of Economic and Social Affairs, *Demographic Yearbook, 1976* (New York, 1977), p. 115; Paul R. Ehrlich, Anne H. Ehrlich, and John P. Holdren, *Ecoscience: Population, Resources, Environment* (San Francisco: W. H. Freeman, 1977), pp. 200–201; and Population Reference Bureau, *World Population Data Sheet, 1994* (Washington, D.C., 1994).

crude birth rate, 42 per 1,000 (with only 21 percent of married women using contraceptives), and a crude death rate, 13 per thousand. The death rate plummeted in the last four decades because of improvements in health, nutrition, medicine, and sanitation. While growth in Latin America until 2025 is projected at 1.2 percent annually, its present yearly rate, 2.0 percent per year, is based on 27 births and 7 deaths per 1,000. Although Asia's annual growth, 1.7 percent (birth rate of 25 and death rate of 8), will decline to 1.3 percent in the 31 years, 1994 to 2025, it is by far the most heavily populated region, with almost 60 percent of the world's people.[1]

Population size is a factor in shifting political and military power from the North Atlantic to Asia and the Pacific. The percentage of people living in North America and Europe (excluding the former Soviet Union) declined from 23.0 percent in 1900 to 14.2 percent in 1994, and is expected to decrease to 10.6 percent in 2025. Six Asian countries plus the Russian Federation (partly in Asia) are on the list of the ten largest countries in the world. China and India constitute 37.5 percent of the world's population (Table 8–1).

Most of the large increases in population between 1994 and 2025 are expected in the developing world. India's addition to population during this period should exceed U.S. total population in 2025. China, Nigeria, Pakistan, Bangladesh,

TABLE 8–1 Population of the Twenty-three Largest Countries in the World: 1996 and 2025 (projected)

	Total Population, 1996 (millions) (world ranking in parentheses)	Projected Population, 2025 (millions) (world ranking in parentheses)
China	1218 (1)	1504 (1)
India	956 (2)	1376 (2)
U.S.	264 (3)	338 (3)
Indonesia	206 (4)	288 (4)
Brazil	161 (5)	200 (8)
Russian Federation	147 (6)	142 (10)
Pakistan	134 (7)	276 (5)
Japan	126 (8)	126 (13)
Bangladesh	122 (9)	211 (7)
Nigeria	104 (10)	246 (6)
Mexico	96 (11)	138 (11)
Germany	81 (12)	73 (21/22)
Vietnam	77 (13)	107 (14)
Philippines	72 (14)	105 (15)
Iran, Islamic Rep.	66 (15)	152 (9)
Turkey	64 (16)	98 (17)
Egypt	62 (17)	98 (18)
Thailand	61 (18)	74 (19)
Ethiopia	59 (19)	133 (12)
U.K.	59 (20)	62 (25)
France	58 (21)	59 (27)
Italy	57 (22)	56 (28)
Ukraine	51 (23)	48 (33)

Source: Population Reference Bureau, *1994 World Population Data Sheet* (Washington, D.C., 1994)

---

[1]Population Reference Bureau, *1994 World Population Data Sheet* (Washington, D.C., 1994).

Iran, and Indonesia will each grow more from 1994 to 2025 than the United States, the world's third largest country. Africa will grow the fastest of any region, with Nigeria, Ethiopia, Zaïre (rising to sixteenth with 105 million), Egypt, Tanzania (rising to twentieth with 74 million), and South Africa (rising to twenty-first/twenty-second with 73 million). Also Myanmar (Burma) will rank twenty-third (with 72 million).

The Demographic Transition

In the ancient and medieval periods, famine, disease, and war were potent checks to population growth throughout the world. During the Black Death (1348–50), for example, Europe lost one-fourth to one-third of its population.

After 1650, the population of Western countries increased more rapidly and steadily. The rate increased first in England (especially from 1760 to about 1840), then in other parts of Western Europe, and later in several areas Europeans had settled—the United States, Canada, Australia, and New Zealand. However, between 1930 and the present, population growth rates declined in these Western countries in about the same order in which they had increased.[2] On the other hand, except for China and Japan, non-Western countries did not experience initial rapid population growth until after 1930.

The **demographic transition** is a period of rapid population growth between a preindustrial, stable population characterized by high birth and death rates and a later, modern, stable population marked by low fertility and mortality. The rapid natural increase takes place in the early transitional stage when fertility is high and mortality is declining. Figure 8–4 illustrates the four-stage demographic transition theory.

STAGE 1: HIGH FERTILITY AND MORTALITY

We were in this stage throughout most of our history. Although annual population growth was only 5 per 10,000 between 1 C.E. and 1650 C.E., growth in eighteenth- and nineteenth-century Western Europe was about 5 per 1,000, and birth and death rates were high and fairly similar. High mortality in North America is not so historically remote, as the following quote illustrates:

> Abraham Lincoln's mother died when she was thirty-five and he was nine. Prior to her death she had three children: Abraham's brother died in infancy and his sister died in her early twenties. Abraham's first love, Anne Rutledge, died at age nineteen. Of the four sons born to Abraham and Mary Todd Lincoln, only one survived to maturity. Clearly, a life with so many bereavements was very different from most of our lives today.[3]

High mortality rates were inevitable in the absence of modern sanitation, medicine, industry, agriculture, trade, transportation, and communication. Premodern socioeconomic groups, such as village communities, tribes, lineages, and

[2]Warren S. Thompson and David T. Lewis, *Population Problems* (New York: McGraw-Hill, 1965), pp. 396–418.
[3]David M. Heer, *Society and Population* (Englewood Cliffs, N.J.: Prentice Hall, 1975), p. 56.

FIGURE 8-4 The Demographic Transition in Representative Developed and Developing Countries

The following shows the transition from a preindustrial, stable population (stage 1) to a late expanding population (stage 3) for both developed (Sweden) and developing (Mexico) countries, and to a later, modern stable population for the DC.

Stage 1—early stable (Sweden before 1810, Mexico before 1920). Birth and death rates are high. Death rates vary widely due to famines, epidemics, and disease. The average life expectancy is 30–35 years.

Stage 2—early expanding (Sweden, c. 1810–65; Mexico, 1920–70). Birth rates remain high. Death rates fall rapidly as a result of advances in health, medicine, nutrition, sanitation, transportation, communication, commerce, and production. Since techniques that reduce deaths can be dispersed more quickly to recently modernizing countries, the decline in the death rate is steeper in developing countries than in developed countries. Stage 2 is the period of most rapid population explosion. Stage 2 may take 50–100 years in the developed country and 15–50 years in the developing country.

Stage 3—late expanding (Sweden, c. 1865–1980; Mexico, 1970–?). Death rates continue to decline. By the end of the period, average life expectancy is at least 70 years. Birth rates fall rapidly, reflecting not only more effective contraceptives and more vigorous family planning programs, but also the increased cost of children, enhanced mobility, higher aspirations, and changing values and social structure associated with urbanization, education, and economic development. Population growth is positive but decelerating. Except for such countries as China, Taiwan, South Korea, Thailand, Indonesia, Sri Lanka, Cuba, Uruguay, Chile, and Argentina, which have birth rates of 25 per 1,000 population or less, most developing countries (including Mexico) are at the beginning of stage 3. Developed countries are further along in stage 3, but only a few (noted below) have finished stage 3. Developed countries that have completed this stage have taken at least 50 years to do so.

Stage 4—late stable (Sweden, c.1980–, Mexico?) Both death and birth rates are low and nearly equal. Birth rates, however, may fluctuate. Eventually the population is stationary. Only a few countries in Europe (Germany, Austria, Sweden, Denmark, Belgium, Britain, Greece, Italy, Spain, Russia, Ukraine, and Bulgaria) are close to equality in birth and death rates.

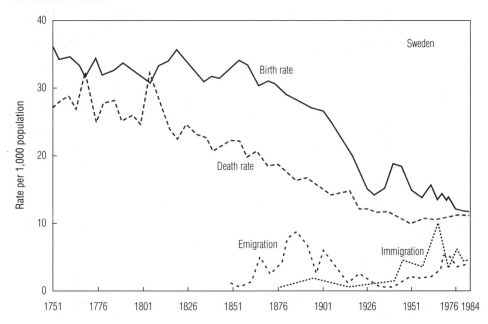

FIGURE 8–4 Continued

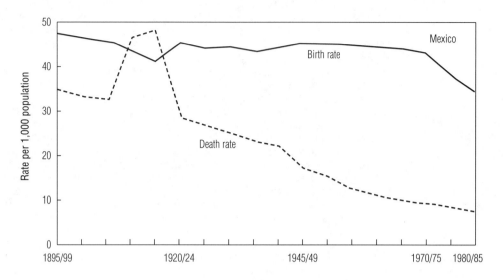

principalities, were small and largely self-sufficient. Even so, food shortages brought on by floods, droughts, insect plagues, and warfare, although confined to a small locality, were very serious. Roads and vehicles for transporting surplus food from other areas were rarely adequate to the need during these times.

For such populations to survive, fertility must at least match mortality. Thus it is not surprising that prevailing ideology, values, religion, and social structure in the ancient, medieval, and early modern world supported high birth rates. Large families were considered a blessing from God. A woman gained acceptance in her husband's family, as well as her community, by bearing children. However, values and institutions supporting high fertility changed slowly as mortality rates declined. We bear the burden of these outmoded views today, long after they have lost their original function.

Preindustrial Western continental Europe had lower birth and death rates than have twentieth-century developing countries in a comparable stage of development (shown in Figure 8–4). Early and near-universal marriage are practiced in these developing countries in contrast to the nineteenth-century European pattern of late marriage or sometimes no marriage at all.[4] This difference accounts, in part, for the LDCs' higher birth rates.

STAGE 2: DECLINING MORTALITY

This stage began in nineteenth-century Europe as modernization gradually reduced mortality rates. Food production increased as agricultural techniques improved. The introductions of corn and the potato, either of which could sustain a large family on a small plot of land, were especially important at this time. Improvements in trade, transportation, and communication meant people were less

---

[4]Michael S. Teitelbaum, "Relevance of Demographic Transition Theory for Developing Countries," *Science* 188 (May 2, 1975): 420–25.

vulnerable to food shortages. Death from infectious diseases, such as tuberculosis and smallpox, declined as nutrition and medical science improved, and after the introduction and adoption of soap, cheap kitchen utensils, and cotton clothing led to better personal hygiene. Drainage and land reclamation reduced the incidence of malaria and respiratory diseases.[5]

Mortality rates decreased about a century earlier in developed countries than developing countries. However, today's LDCs have lowered their mortality rates much more rapidly once they began. Figure 8–5 indicates a gradual, long-term reduction in Western death rates, with Denmark's declining from 27 to 11 and France's from 26 to 12, over a period of 130 years (1830–1960). Sri Lanka's and India's mortality rates, however, decreased sharply from 1915 to 1995—Sri Lanka's from 30 to 6, and India's from 47 to 9 (infants 500 to 74), per 1,000 population. These rapid declines are based on techniques that the developed countries acquired over decades—improved agriculture, transport, commerce, medicine, sanitation, and so forth.

**FIGURE 8–5   Changes in Death Rates (selected
countries)**

Mortality rates declined in LDCs faster than in DCs.

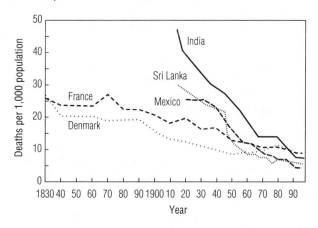

Sources: Warren S. Thompson and David T. Lewis, *Population Problems* (New York: McGraw-Hill, 1965); United Nations, *Demographic Yearbook, 1976* (New York, 1976); World Bank, *World Development Report, 1979* (Washington, D.C., 1979); World Bank, *World Development Report, 1982* (New York: Oxford University Press, 1982); World Bank, *World Development Report, 1988* (New York: Oxford University Press, 1988); World Bank, *World Development Report, 1992* (New York: Oxford University Press, 1992); World Bank, *World Development Report, 1994* (New York: Oxford University Press, 1994); and World Bank, *World Development Report, 1995* (New York: Oxford University Press, 1995).

---

[5]Paul R. Ehrlich, Anne H. Ehrlich, and John P. Holdren, *Ecoscience: Population, Resources, Environment* (San Francisco: W. H. Freeman, 1977), pp. 186–92.

Why have some LDC death rates dropped to 5–9 per 1,000, below those of many industrialized countries? With a stable population, these mortality rates would be consistent with a life expectancy of more than 100 years! These low death rates are possible because birth rates higher than replacement levels create an age structure more youthful than exists in a stable population (one only replacing itself). (Figure 8–9 shows that DCs, with a more stable population, have an older population than the LDCs.) If the death rates for specific age groups were applied to a stable population, death rates in LDCs would be, in fact, in excess of 10 per 1,000.

In the late 1930s, average life expectancy in developing countries was 32 years compared to 56 in developed countries. Life expectancy in LDCs increased to 63 in 1994, compared to 76 in the developed countries (Table 8–2). Since World War II, mortality rates have dropped sharply in developing countries because of declines in infant mortality and better medical treatment for major infectious diseases—malaria, cholera, yellow fever, typhoid fever, smallpox, tuberculosis and other respiratory ailments. Despite such improvements, Figure 8–6 shows that people still live longer in rich countries. The positive relationship between life expectancy and income per capita persists until income reaches a certain level, perhaps corresponding to some critical level of health practice and economic productivity. Beyond this level, there appears to be little, if any, positive relationship between average income and life expectancy. Accordingly, although developed, and a few developing, countries have a life expectancy figure of over 70 years, the only countries with a life expectancy between 35 and 70 years are developing countries.

It may be several decades before lowered mortality rates are matched by a decline in fertility rates. One element in this decades-long process—values and institutions supporting high fertility rates—are quite resistant to change. It is much easier in the contemporary world to lower a mortality rate than to change a value system that promotes fertility. The technology needed to increase life expectancy is widely available to all developing countries. They have access to the accumu-

TABLE 8-2   Life Expectancy at Birth, by Region, 1935–39, 1950–55, 1965–70, 1975–80, 1985–90, and 1994

Region	*Years*					
	1935–39	*1950–55*	*1965–70*	*1975–80*	*1985–90*	*1994*
South Asia	30	41	46	49	56	60
East Asia	30	45	55	61	71	71
Africa	30	36	43	47	54	55
Latin America	40	52	60	64	68	68
China	n.a.[a]	48	60	64	70	70
Developing countries	32	42	49	54	61	63
Developed countries	56	65	70	73	76	76

[a]Not available.

Sources: David Morawetz, *Twenty-Five Years of Economic Development* (Baltimore: Johns Hopkins University Press, 1977), p. 48; World Bank, *World Tables, 1980* (Baltimore: Johns Hopkins University Press, 1980), pp. 442–47; John W. Sewell, Stuart K. Tucker, and contributors for the Overseas Development Council, *Growth, Exports, and Jobs in a Changing Economy: Agenda, 1988* (New Brunswick, N.J.: Transaction Books, 1988), pp. 246; and Population Reference Bureau, *1994 World Population Data* (Washington, D.C., 1994).

FIGURE 8-6 Life Expectancy in Developed and Developing Countries

Among LDCs life expectancy increases with average income. Beyond a certain income level, there is little relationship between average income and life expectancy.

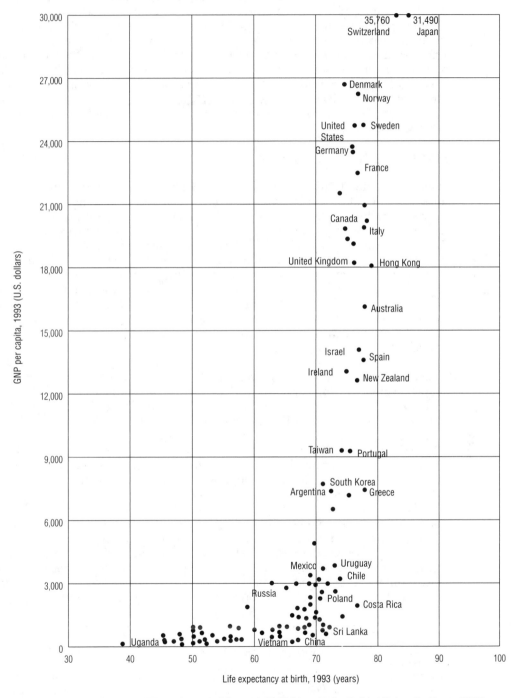

Source: World Bank, *World Development Report, 1995* (New York: Oxford University Press, 1995), pp. 162–63.

lated improvements in health, medicine, agriculture, and industry of the nineteenth century and the much more radical innovations of this century—immunization, pesticides, high-yielding grain varieties, and so on. To illustrate our thesis, the Allied powers (in the 1940s) and the World Health Organization (in the 1950s) sprayed a new insecticide, DDT, over large areas of Sri Lanka to destroy malaria-carrying mosquitos. The cost was less than two dollars per head. Malaria was largely eradicated, contributing in part to a steep decline in Sri Lanka's death rate from 21.7 per 1,000 in 1945, to 14.6 in 1948, to 9.1 in 1959 (see Figure 8–5). Since most people desire health and long life, new life extension methods are easily and quickly adopted.[6]

STAGE 3: DECLINING FERTILITY

Stage 3, declining fertility, of the demographic transition did not begin in Europe for several decades, and in some instances, a century, after the beginning of declining mortality in stage 2. However, in developing countries, stage 3 has followed much more rapidly stage 2. Nevertheless, stage 2 was more explosive, since the initial birth rate was higher and the drop in death rate steeper.

What are the most important determinants of fertility decline? There are two competing answers. Organized **family-planning programs,** which provide propaganda and contraceptives to reduce the number of births, is one answer. The other is motivating birth control through the more complicated processes of education, urbanization, modernization, and economic development. This view is expressed in the slogan of the 1974 World Population Conference held in Bucharest, "Development is the best contraceptive."

Those who support family planning programs point to the substantial decline in the world's **total fertility rate (TFR)**—the number of children born to the average woman during her reproductive years—from the 1960s to the 1990s, even in the poorest developing countries. To the surprise of many demographers, the TFR of most of 113 developing countries, and all thirty five developed countries, decreased, so that the world's TFR dropped from 4.6 births per woman in 1968, to 4.1 in 1975, to 3.6 in 1987, to 3.1 in 1995. In the early 1960s, a number of developing countries began major family planning programs. At least one study suggests that declines in crude birth rates in developing countries were strongly associated with substantial, organized, family planning efforts.[7]

However, other evidence indicates that fertility also decreases with economic development, modernization, urbanization, and industrialization. For example, Figure 8–7 indicates that among developing countries (those with a 1992 GNP per capita of less than $9,000), average income and fertility are negatively related; that is, low income is associated with high fertility rates. The relative importance of family planning programs versus economic development for population control is discussed in a later section on strategies for reducing fertility.

[6]Michael S. Teitelbaum, "Relevance of Demographic Transition Theory for Developing Countries," *Science* 188 (May 2, 1975): 420–25.

[7]Amy Ong Tsui and Donald J. Bogue, "Declining World Fertility: Trends, Causes and Implications," *Population Bulletin* 33, no. 4 (October 1978): 1–55; World Bank, *World Development Report, 1988* (New York: Oxford University Press, 1988), pp. 276–77; Peter Hendry, "Food and Population: Beyond Five Billion," *Population Bulletin* 43 (April 1988): 14; and Population Reference Bureau, *1995 World Population Data Sheet* (Washington, D.C., 1995).

FIGURE 8-7   Fertility Rates in Developed and Developing Countries

Fertility rates decline as average income rises.

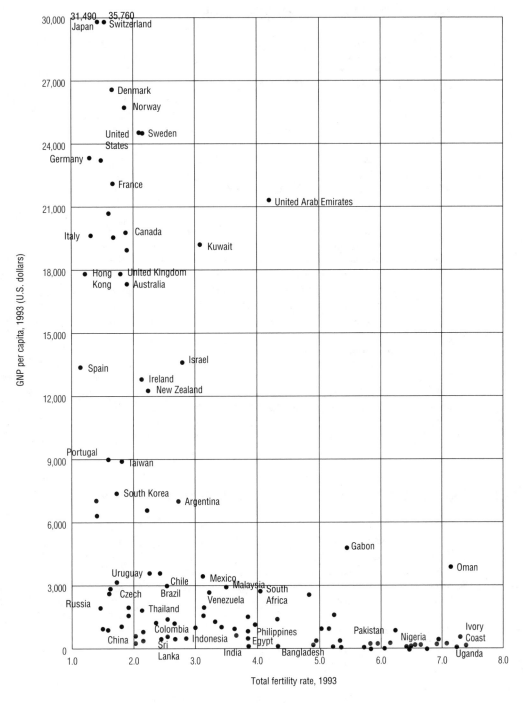

Source: World Bank, *World Development Report, 1995* (New York: Oxford University Press, 1995), pp. 162–63, 212–13.

THE DEMOGRAPHIC TRANSITION IN THE 1990S

In the early 1990s, most countries were still in stage 3 of the demographic transition. Virtually all countries had experienced some decline in mortality. The highest death rates in the world, primarily in sub-Saharan Africa, were in the lower 20s, substantially below mortality in stage 1. We cannot always identify precisely what stage a country is in. However, even the most demographically backward countries were in the latter part of stage 2, if not in the earlier part of stage 3, by the 1990s. On the other hand, only Germany, Austria, Sweden, Denmark, Belgium, Britain, Greece, Italy, Spain, Russia, Ukraine, and Bulgaria were in stage 4—low, stable population growth—with virtually equal fertility and mortality rates.

BEYOND STAGE 4: A STATIONARY POPULATION

World Bank projections indicate that most developing countries will not reach an exact replacement rate before 2020 to 2040. At this rate, the average woman of child-bearing age bears only one daughter—her replacement in the population. However **population momentum** or growth continues after **replacement-level fertility** has been reached because previous fertility rates have produced an age structure with a relatively high percentage of women in or below reproductive age. Thus most developing countries will not have a **stationary population** (where growth is zero) until 2075 to 2175, about 5 to 14 decades after attaining exact replacement level.

Let us examine this process more fully. Take as an example China, a country with a population of 1,117 million and a total fertility rate of 5–6 in the early 1970s that fell precipitously to 2.0 in 1994–95. If it retained replacement-level fertility in 2000, its population would then be 1,279 million. Even if it maintains this fertility level, population will grow to 1,508 million by 2050, and 1,570 million by 2105, the year a stationary population level is reached. The LDCs can expect substantial future population growth even if measures are undertaken immediately to reduce fertility rates.[8]

Is Population Growth an Obstacle to Economic Development?

Does population growth hamper economic development as classical economist Thomas Robert Malthus contends, or does population spur innovation and development as Julian L. Simon argues? This section examines some possible costs of high fertility rates and rapid population growth, including (1) diminishing returns to natural resources, with an adverse impact on average food consumption; (2) increased urbanization and congestion; (3) a higher labor force growth rate and higher unemployment; and (4) a working population that must support a larger number of dependents.

---

[8]Thomas W. Merrick, "World Population in Transition," *Population Bulletin* 41 (April 1986): 6; World Bank, *World Development Report, 1980* (New York: Oxford University Press, 1980), pp. 142–43, 162–63; World Bank, *World Development Report, 1988* (New York: Oxford University Press, 1988), pp. 274–75; and Thomas Frejka, "The Prospects for a Stationary Population," *Scientific American* 228, no. 3 (March 1973): 15–23.

POPULATION AND FOOD

The Malthusian View.   The best-known work on the food and population balance is Malthus's *Essay on the Principle of Population* (1798, 1803). The essay, written in reaction to the utopian views of his father's friends, was one reason economics came to be referred to as the dismal science. Malthus's theory was that population, which increased geometrically—1, 2, 4, 8, 16, 32, and so on—outstripped food supply, which grew arithmetically: 1, 2, 3, 4, 5, 6. For Malthus, a clergyman as well as an economist, the only check to population growth would be wars, epidemics, infanticide, abortion, and sexual perversion, unless people practiced moral restraint, that is, later marriages and abstention. Even then he believed living standards would remain at a subsistence level in the long run.[9]

However, Malthus failed to envision the capital accumulation and technical progress that would overcome diminishing returns on land. Rough estimates are that between 1650 and 1996, the world's food production multiplied 13 to 15 times, while population increased only eight times. The world's cultivated land probably doubled or tripled during this period, largely from increases in cultivation in the United States, Canada, Australia, and New Zealand. Output per hectare probably increased at least fourfold during these 336 years through irrigation, multiple cropping, improved seeds, increased use of commercial fertilizer, better farm implements, and other agricultural innovations. Malthus also underestimated the extent to which education, economic modernization, industrialization, urbanization, and improved contraception would reduce fertility rates.

Present and Future Population-Food Balance.   Some scientists believe the Malthusian population and food relationship is applicable to the contemporary world. For them the rapid population growth of LDCs since World War II confirms Malthus's thesis. Few economists saw statistical evidence of a return of the Malthusian specter before the 1990s, but then many economists were startled by trend lines which suggested that the long-term increase in foodgrain (rice, wheat, and coarse grains) output per person, especially prominent since World War II, was beginning to fall in the mid-1980s. Tim Dyson, using a 5-year moving average (where the figure for a given year *t* is an average of the figures for year *t*-2 through *t*+2 except for years at the extremities), shows this fall in Figure 8–8. Optimist Dyson and pessimist Lester R. Brown agree on the outline of the trend line, but disagree on how to interpret it. Brown notes the reduced effective demand for food in developing areas such as Africa and Latin America, which faced falling average incomes in the 1980s, as well as the earth's rapid population growth, increasing average costs from and diminishing returns to growing biochemical energy and fertilizer use, less sustainable farming practices, and limits in expanded agricultural hectarage reaching the limits of its carrying capacity. Dyson notes a decline in average grain production from peak production to 1990, even when calculated using 5-year moving averages, in all regions except Asia. However, for Dyson, low world grain prices, and reduced grain price supports, the withdrawal of cultivated land, and the cessation of subsidized overseas sales by the largest grain producer, the United States, were responsible for the lion's share of the declining trend since the 1980s. Still, the declining trend line in sub-Saharan Africa, Latin America, and North America since the 1980s, suggest reason for concern.

---

[9]Thomas Robert Malthus, *Essay on the Principle of Population* (Homewood, Ill.: Irwin, 1963).

FIGURE 8-8   World Per Capita Cereal Production: Annual Estimates and 5-year Averages, 1951–92

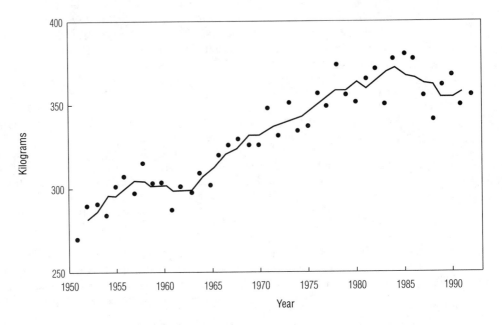

Note: Averages for 1952 and 1991 are calculated from data for 1951–53 and 1990–92, respectively.
Source: Tim Dyson, "Population Growth and Food Production: Recent Global and Regional Trends," *Population and Development Review* 20 (June 1994): 398.

Moreover, the decline in fish catches per capita since 1990 (Chapter 7), and the leveling off in soybeans and meat production since the late 1980s also reinforce the pessimistic scenario based on grain output data.[10]

Thus, we need to ask whether average food production will rise or fall through the 1990s and the first decade of the twenty-first century when world population growth is expected to increase 1.4 percent per year?[11] Major studies of world food supply disagree about whether, with present trends in resource availability and environmental limitation, together with expected technological improvements, food increases should stay ahead of population growth in the first quarter of the twenty-first century.

---

[10]Lester R. Brown, "Facing Food Insecurity," in Lester R. Brown et al., *State of the World, 1994*, Worldwatch Institute (New York: Norton, 1994), pp. 177–97, 248–51; Tim Dyson, "Population Growth and Food Production: Recent Global and Regional Trends, *Population and Development Review* 20 (June 1994): 397–411; and Lester R. Brown, Anne E. Platt, Hal Kane, and Sandra Postel, "Food and Agricultural Resource Trends," in Lester R. Brown, Hal Kane, and David Malin Roodman, eds., *Vital Signs, 1994*, Worldwatch Institute (New York: Norton, 1994), pp. 26–41, especially Lester R. Brown, "Grain Harvest Plummets," pp. 26–27. Dennis T. Avery, "Don't Worry, Eat and Be Happy," *Wall Street Journal* (December 11, 1995), p. A12, thinks that the fall in foodgrain output per capita in the early 1990s merely reflects a shift from the consumption of grains to that of "luxury" food like meat, milk, and eggs, but he provides no evidence for this view.

[11]World Bank, *World Development Report, 1994* (New York: Oxford University Press, 1994), pp. 230–31.

Simon's View.   Some economists' optimism about technological change makes them not only believe that output will continue to grow more rapidly than population but also that population growth stimulates per capita output growth. Simon argues that the level of technology is enhanced by population. More people increase the stock of knowledge through additional learning gains compounded by the quickening effect of greater competition and total demand spurring "necessity as the mother for invention." Division of labor and economies of large-scale production increase as markets expand. In short as population size rises, both the supply of, and demand for, inventions increase thereby increasing productivity and economic growth. Because population growth spurs economic growth, Simon's model requires no government interference and is consistent with a **laissez-faire** population policy.

While Simon criticizes the Club of Rome's *Limits to Growth* (Chapter 13) for underestimating technical change, he goes to the other extreme by assuming that population growth causes technological progress. Indeed, Simon's assumption that technological progress arises without cost contradicts the second law of thermodynamics, which states that the world is a closed system with ever-increasing entropy or unavailable energy (see Chapter 13). Moreover, Simon's model, like that of the Club of Rome, yields the intended results because they are built into the assumptions. Simon's premise is that "the level of technology that is combined with labour and capital in the production function must be influenced by population directly or indirectly."[12]

Food Research and Technology.   There are reasons to be concerned about the Malthusian balance in LDCs. About 80 percent of the world's expenditures on agricultural research, technology, and capital are made in developed countries. Vernon Ruttan's study indicates that these expenditures bear directly on the greater agricultural labor productivity in DCs. This greater productivity has little to do with superior resource endowment.[13] To be sure, some agricultural innovations used in DCs can be adapted to LDCs. However, these innovations must be adapted carefully in the developing countries. Usually LDCs need their own agricultural research, since many of their ecological zones are quite different from those of North America and Europe. The discovery of improved seed varieties and the improvement of agricultural methods in third-world countries are mainly the work of an **international network of agricultural research centers.** The principal food commodities and climate zones of the developing world have been brought into this network. Such donors as the World Bank, the U.N. Development Program, the Ford Foundation, the Rockefeller Foundation, the U.S. Agency for International Development, and agencies of other governments have financed the network. Its goals are to continue and extend the work generally known as the **Green Revolution—** the development of high-yielding varieties of wheat and rice. Prototypes of these

---

[12]Julian L. Simon, *Theory of Population and Economic Growth* (Oxford: Basil Blackwell, 1986) (quote on p. 3); Julian L. Simon, "The Case for More People," *American Demographics* 1 (November/December 1979): 26–30; H. W. Arndt, Review of Simon's *Theory of Population and Economic Growth, Population and Development Review* 13 (March 1987): 156–58; and John Ermisch, Review of Simon's *Theory of Population and Economic Growth, Population Studies* 41 (March 1987): 175–77.

[13]Vernon Ruttan, "Induced Technical and Institutional Change and the Future of Agriculture," in the Fifteenth International Conference of Agricultural Economists, *Papers and Reports* (Sao Paulo, Brazil, 1972).

centers are International Center for the Improvement of Maize and Wheat (CIM-MYT), the Mexican institute, founded in 1943, where a team led by Nobel Peace Prize winner Norman Borlaug developed dwarf wheats; and International Rice Research Institute (IRRI) in the Philippines, founded in 1960, which stresses research on rice and the use of multiple cropping systems. Economists in India, Pakistan, the Philippines, and Mexico argue that foodgrain growth would not have kept up with population growth in the 1960s, 1970s, and 1980s without the improved packages of high-yielding seed varieties, fertilizers, pesticides, irrigation, improved transport, and extension.

The network, however, has had difficulties in helping national research centers adapt its research to local conditions and encourage its adoption by farmers. Furthermore many crop scientists in developing countries leave local research centers because of low salaries, politics on the job, government roadblocks to research, small budgets, and other grievances.[14]

Network critics charge that research projects emphasize high-yielding grain varieties that benefit the large commercial farmers. To elaborate, scientists tended to develop these varieties as part of a package, which included capital inputs, such as irrigation, fertilizers, tractors, mechanical pumps, threshers, reapers, combines, pesticides, and so on. For example, in India and Pakistan, new wheat varieties were adapted to cropland under controlled irrigation—land owned primarily by relatively affluent Punjabi farmers. Some of the negative effects of the package were increased land concentration, displacement of farm labor, and rising rural unemployment and emigration.

Moreover Cornell University scientists David Pimentel and Marcia Pimentel contend that the adverse environmental side effects of pesticides, a foundation of the Green Revolution, call into question its long-run sustainability and continuing yield growth. A part of the strategy of the Green Revolution is large monocultures and year-round plantings of a single crop, which increase pest outbreaks and exacerbate the pressure for pesticides. Many LDCs, like DCs before them, have subsidized the use of pesticides, which disproportionately benefit wealthy farmers and large companies. In addition, those pests that survive have a genetic makeup allowing them to detoxify the poison and dominate in succeeding generations, shielding them from pesticides. Furthermore pesticides upset nature's method of control by wiping out pest predators and swelling other populations that were initially small to pest status. For example, in northeastern Mexico, cotton production required increased insecticide applications but increased the outbreak of tobacco budworms, a secondary pest, which replaced the eradicated boll weevil. In Egypt, DDT use to control the bollworm spurred the white fly to explode into a major pest.

Much of the substantial percentage of pesticides that do not reach their host become environmental contaminants. Pesticides not only damage their targets but have a toxic effect on wildlife, plants, groundwater, and soil and water organisms. Pesticides can interfere with the endocrine and immune systems of animals, while atrazine at low levels harm whole ecosystems, inhibiting algae and plankton growth and the reproduction of fish and other organisms. The alternative to pesticide application, integrated pest management, using crop rotation, multiculture

---

[14]Nicholas Wade, "International Agricultural Research," in Philip H. Abelson, ed., *Food: Politics, Economics, Nutrition, and Research* (Washington, D.C.: American Association for the Advancement of Science, 1975), pp. 91–95; and World Bank, *World Development Report, 1982* (New York: Oxford University Press, 1982), pp. 57–77.

planting, field sanitation, and biological control through natural predators, requires substantial investment in research and technology.[15]

The net impact of new high-yielding grain varieties may still be positive. They did mitigate food shortages in South Asia during the 1970s and 1980s. But LDCs need to closely scrutinize the health and environmental impact of the Green Revolution's package of seeds, fertilizers, pesticides, water use, and infrastructure costs.

Food Distribution.   There is more than enough food produced each year to feed everyone on earth adequately, yet millions are hungry. Food distribution is the difficulty. The Japanese, who are well nourished, consume about the same amount of calories and protein per person as the world average. James D. Gavan and John A. Dixon estimate that calorie and protein availability in India would have exceeded minimal requirements if distribution had not been so unequal.[16] Furthermore although Brazil, a country with high income inequalities, has almost six times the GNP per capita of China, it has a large amount of malnutrition; and China, with lower income inequalities, has little. In general malnutrition is strongly correlated with poverty, which in turn is correlated with inequality in income distribution. Except for sub-Saharan Africa, food shortages are not due to inadequate production but to deficiencies in food distribution.

Unequal food distribution means that some countries and localities are likely to face food deficits. Despite increased agricultural productivity in developing countries, their absolute food deficits are expected to increase, especially in Bangladesh, Nigeria, and most other sub-Saharan African countries. Domestic food deficits by themselves need not mean undernourishment if a country can afford to import food. However, with higher prices for farm inputs and increased capital goods imports for industrialization, many developing countries may not have the foreign currency to import enough food to relieve the deficit.

Energy Limitations.   Higher energy prices could seriously weaken our assumptions about the global food balance. The substantial gains made in food productivity in the four decades after World War II were partly dependent on cheap, abundant energy supplies. World average food output may be ceasing to grow as energy and other resource limitations become more binding. Obviously the energy-intensive U.S. food system cannot be exported intact to developing countries. Two scientists estimate that to feed the entire world with a food system like that of the United States would require 80 percent of today's entire world energy expenditures.[17]

---

[15]"Food and Agriculture," in World Resources Institute, United Nations Environment Program, and the United Nations Development Program (Allen L. Hammond, ed.), *World Resources, 1994–95* (New York: Oxford University Press, 1994), pp. 111–18; and David Pimentel and Marcia Pimentel, "Adverse Environmental Consequences of the Green Revolution," in Robert Dorfman and Nancy S. Dorfman, eds., *Economics of the Environment: Selected Readings* (New York: Norton, 1993), pp. 497–500.

[16]James D. Gavan and John A. Dixon, "India: A Perspective on the Food Situation," in Philip H. Abelson, ed., *Food: Politics, Economics, Nutrition, and Research* (Washington, D. C., American Association for the Advancement of Science, 1975), pp. 49–57.

[17]John S. Steinhart and Carol E. Steinhart, "Energy Use in the U.S. Food System," in Philip H. Abelson, ed., *Food: Politics, Economics, Nutrition, and Research* (Washington, D. C., American Association for the Advancement of Science, 1975), pp. 33–42.

Lower tillage agriculture in the United States in the 1980s and 1990s might reduce this figure a few percentage points.

A Recapitulation.   In the four decades after World War II, the world avoided the Malthusian specter but did not show evidence to support Simon's view that population growth spurred output growth. Indeed there is reason to be wary about the population-food balance for future years in LDCs. The uncertainty concerning future growth in agricultural productivity, especially in sub-Saharan Africa, probably means that we should continue our efforts at population control.

URBANIZATION AND CONGESTION

LDCs are congested and overpopulated in certain areas and especially so in major cities. Although 31 percent of the population of Africa is urban, it remains the least urbanized of the six continents. Yet some scholars argue that urban growth in Africa hampers economic development, employment growth, and the alleviation of poverty. In the early 1980s, highways to the central business district in Lagos, Nigeria, were so choked with traffic that it took 4 to 5 hours for a taxi to drive 24 kilometers (15 miles) from the international airport in rush-hour traffic. Although the premium on space in the inner city made it almost impossible for the working poor to afford housing there, the cost of transport made it difficult to live even on the outskirts of Lagos. Ironically the demand for transport (and congestion) in Lagos fell in the 1980s as a result of an economic depression triggered by reduced real oil export prices!

  Urban areas in LDCs are not only experiencing a rapid natural increase in population but are also serving as a magnet for underemployed and poorly paid workers from the rural areas. Combatting increased congestion may actually increase gross product; usually the costs of congestion are *not* subtracted from national income. A World Bank study estimates that urban populations in LDCs will triple between 1975 and 2000 (see Chapter 9.)[18] Overurbanization means it is necessary to limit population growth not just in cities but in an entire nation.

RAPID LABOR FORCE GROWTH AND INCREASING UNEMPLOYMENT

The LDC labor force growth rate is 1.9 percent per year, more than the rate of population growth, 1.6 percent yearly.[19] The vast pool cannot be readily absorbed by industry, resulting in increased unemployment and underemployment. Chapter 9 indicates some of the political and social problems, as well as economic waste, ensuing from such underemployment. These problems underscore the urgent need to reduce population growth.

THE DEPENDENCY BURDEN

Although the LDC labor force is growing rapidly, the number of children dependent on each worker is high. High fertility rates create this dependency burden. The **dependency burden** is an index of this load. It is the proportion of the total population aged 0 to 14 years, and 65 years and older, which are considered nonworking years. Figure 8–9 compares the dependency ratio in developing and de-

---

[18]Michael A. Cohen, "Cities in Developing Countries: 1975–2000," *Finance and Development* 13 (March 1976): 13.

[19]World Bank, *World Development Report, 1994* (New York: Oxford University Press, 1994), pp. 210–11.

FIGURE 8-9   Dependency Loads
Dependency loads are higher for LDCs than DCs.

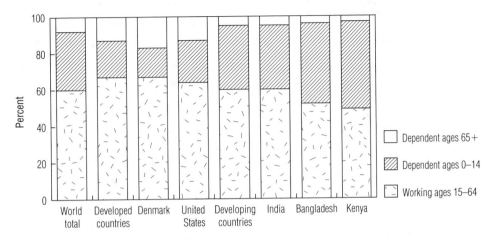

Source: Based on Population Reference Bureau, *World Population Data Sheet, 1994* (Washington, D.C., 1994).

veloped countries. For example, 65 percent of the population in the United States is in the working ages, 15 to 64 years old, compared to 49 percent in Kenya. Despite the higher elderly percentage in the United States, dependency in Kenya is more burdensome, since 49 percent of its population is aged 0 to 14 compared to only 22 percent in the United States. Kenya, with a high birth rate (44 per 1,000 in 1994), has more people in the dependent ages than in the working ages. The United States, with a lower birth rate (16 per 1,000), has only about half as many persons in the dependent ages as in the working ages. Another way of viewing age structure is a **population age pyramid** showing the percentage distribution of a population by age and sex (Figure 8–10).

Some LDCs narrowed the base of the pyramid in the 1970s, 1980s, and 1990s. For example, in 1960, when the birth rate in Costa Rica was 47 per 1,000, it had a population structure with a wider base and a narrower peak than Kenya's pyramid in the left of Figure 8–10. However, after the country launched a vigorous family-planning program in 1968, the birth rate dropped to 29 per 1,000 from 1978 to 1987 (26 per 1,000 in 1994) so that the two bottom bars, corresponding to ages 0 to 9, narrowed substantially.

Of course the ratio of the labor force to population is not only a function of dependency ratios. Because of cross-national differences in the participation of women, old people, youths, and children in the labor force, countries with similar dependency ratios may have different ratios of labor force to population.

Dependency loads vary within developing countries according to income. The living standards of the poor are hurt by high fertility and large families. Each adult's earnings support more dependents than is the case in richer families. Thus, in peninsular Malaysia in 1980, 71 percent of the richest 10 percent (by household) were 15 to 64 years old compared to only 45 percent for the poorest 10 percent.[20]

---

[20]World Bank, *World Development Report, 1980* (New York: Oxford University Press, 1980), pp. 42–43.

FIGURE 8-10 Population Distribution by Age and Sex, 1990

DCs, like Denmark and the United States, with low birth rates, have older populations than the LDCs, like Kenya,, with high birth rates. Denmark, with a near **stationary population** or near zero growth, has roughly equal numbers of people in all age ranges, tapering off gradually at the older ages. The United States, with a **constrictive population** and slow growth, has small numbers of people in the younger ages. Kenya, with an **expansive population** or rapid growth, has large numbers of people in the younger ages.

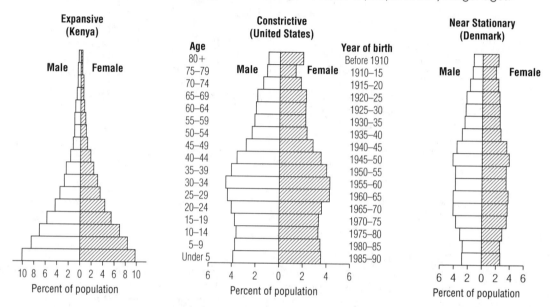

Source: Arthur Haupt and Thomas T. Kane, *Population Handbook: International Edition* (Washington, D.C.: Population Reference Bureau, 1991), p. 10.

Figure 8–11, which plots the relationships between age and service require-ments, shows the higher educational and health costs of caring for those 15 years or under. Thus the high dependency ratio in Bangladesh means that a substantial proportion of its resources must be diverted to provide schools, food, health care, and social services for the young. Households in Bangladesh have a large number of consumers per earning member, which means a high ratio of consumption to income. Very little income is left over for savings or capital formation.[21]

Oxford economist Robert Cassen argues that

[South] Korea provides a contrasting example. If Korea had maintained its 1960 fertility level until 1980, the number of primary school children would have been one-third larger, and expenditure on primary education (at the same cost per pupil) would have been higher by 1 percent of GDP. In fact, however, Korea ef-fectively promoted fertility decline through publicly funded family planning programs at the same time that socioeconomic change made smaller families at-

---

[21]In 1996, 215 million (5 percent) of the LDCs' population was aged 65 years and over, compared to 162 million (13 percent) of the DCs' population. In 2025, demographers expect those 65 years and over in LDCs to be 534 million (or 8 percent), and those in DCs to be 275 million (or 20 percent). Computed from World Bank, *World Population Projections: Estimates and Projections with Related Demographic Statis-tics, 1994–95* (Baltimore: Johns Hopkins University Press, 1994), pp. 62–65.

FIGURE 8-11   Population Age Profile and Service Requirements: Bangladesh, 1975

Bangladesh's high birth rate necessitates high spending levels on food, health care, and education for children. (Total population, 74 million)

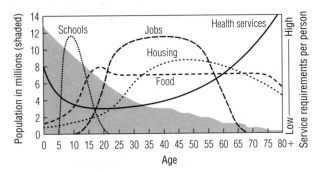

Source: Madgda McHale and John McHale, "World of Children," *Population Bulletin* 33, no. 6 (January 1979): 14.

tractive. It was thus able to improve both the extent and the quality of education, helping to lay the foundations for its manufacturing success.[22]

Overall neither Malthusian pessimism or Simon's optimism is warranted. Simon's model fails to consider how population growth increases the costs of agricultural resources, congestion, environmental degradation, labor force underemployment, and the burden of dependency. On the other hand, the two centuries since Malthus wrote have demonstrated that technological innovation, capital accumulation, and birth control more than compensate for diminishing returns to fixed land.[23] Whether this trend will continue through the beginning of the twenty-first century depends on economic, population, and environmental policies.[24]

---

[22]Robert Cassen, "Population and Development: Old Debates, New Conclusions," in Robert Cassen and contributors, *Population and Development: Old Debates, New Conclusions*, Overseas Development Council U.S.-Third World Policy Perspectives (New Brunswick, N.J.: Transaction, 1994), p. 12.

[23]However, in the relatively unsettled areas of Asiatic Russia, inland Brazil, Australia, and Canada, population growth may be subject, other things being equal, to increasing returns and growing per capita income, resulting from increased division of labor.

[24]Regressions of the effect of population growth on the growth of GNP per capita, from 1965 to 1987, in Assaf Razin and Efraim Sadka, *Population Economics* (Cambridge, Mass.: MIT Press, 1995), p. 8, provide support for the pessimists' points of view. However, regressions of the effect of population growth on economic growth, 1965 to 1984, in David E. Bloom and Richard B. Freeman, "The Effects of Rapid Population Growth on Labor Supply and Employment in Developing Countries," *Population and Development Review* 12 (September 1986): 403–5, provide no support for either the optimists' or pessimists' points of view. The findings of Robin Barlow, "Population Growth and Economic Growth: Some More Correlations," *Population and Development Review* 20 (March 1994): 153–65, are more mixed, indicating that while past fertility rates are positively related to economic growth, present population growth is negatively related to economic growth. Marvin Goodfriend and John McDermott, "Early Development," *American Economic Review* 85 (March 1995): 116–33, find that population growth may increase or decrease GNP per capita, depending on the relative size of the preindustrial and market sectors. Income per capita is an average of output from a diminishing-return preindustrial technology and an increasing-returns market technology. On the other hand, the enhanced neoclassical growth model of N. Gregory Mankiw, David Romer, and David N. Weil, "A Contribution to the Empirics of Economic Growth," *Quarterly Journal of Economics* 112 (May 1992): 407–37, shows that higher population growth lowers income per capita because the available capital must be spread more thinly over the population of workers.

Strategies for Reducing Fertility

Increasing urban congestion, rapid labor force growth, a high dependency burden, and uncertainty about food output growth indicate the importance of limiting population growth in LDCs. The only possible approach here is a reduction in fertility. Let us examine two strategies: (1) birth control programs and (2) socioeconomic development.

BIRTH CONTROL PROGRAMS

From time immemorial, societies have had available a number of contraceptive methods. Intercourse without penetration and coitus interruptus have been known and practiced in one form or another in nearly all societies. Abortion; high celibacy rates; no marriage at all; late marriage; sanctions against the remarriage of widows; and taboos against coitus outside marriage, while nursing an infant, or on certain religious holidays have all been used to reduce fertility. Ireland, with land and food shortages throughout much of the eighteenth, nineteenth, and early twentieth centuries, had less and later marriage than other parts of Europe. In the early twentieth century, the average Irish bridegroom was over 30. Marriage had to be postponed until the son could obtain land and independence from his father.

Moreover, a large number of premodern cultures have practiced infanticide (a control on family size, though not births). In some preindustrial cultures a newborn child is not considered a member of society, so that destruction of the child is viewed psychologically in much the same light as we view abortion.

Furthermore, chemical and mechanical contraceptives were known and applied in many primitive and peasant societies. Women in nineteenth-century Martinique and Guiana used rather effectively a douche containing lemon juice mixed with a decoction of the husks of the mahogany nut. However, some of these contraceptives—the vaginal insertion of an okralike seed pod, rags of finely chopped grass, or dung—were clumsy, sexually unsatisfactory, or unhealthy. By and large, the technology of preindustrial societies was not equal to providing a chemical or mechanical contraceptive that was cheap, satisfactory, effective, and readily available.[25]

But since most of these societies had high mortality rates, population growth rates were low anyway. However, maintaining a stable population today requires lowered fertility rates and more adequate contraceptives. Because of the cost of modern contraceptives and their social benefits, many LDC governments subsidize birth control devices, so that users receive them free or for a nominal cost.

Modern Contraceptives.   In the 1990s, the abortion-inducing drug (available in a few countries), the injectable drug, the oral contraceptive (the Pill), the intrauterine device (IUD), abortion, and sterilization were all used as methods of birth control. Condoms, diaphragms, spermicides, coitus interruptus, and the rhythm method are cheap but less effective than the first grouping.

Male sterilization via vasectomy, which involves a 10-minute outpatient operation with local anesthesia, is relatively inexpensive. It is usually irreversible, safe, and has no effect on subsequent sexual performance. Vasectomies have been

---

[25]Kingsley Davis and Judith Blake, "Social Structure and Fertility: An Analytical Framework," *Economic Development and Cultural Change* 4 (April 1956): 211–35.

widely used in India. Female sterilization, a more expensive and more serious operation, is rarely performed in LDCs (although post-1980 India is an exception).

The IUD is an effective contraceptive and except for male sterilization, the cheapest (though it has to be inserted by medical personnel). However, because of high rates of expulsion or removal, use of the IUD requires follow-up. A study in the early 1970s in Lucknow, India, indicates that less than one-half of the women using IUDs retained them for as long as a year and only about one-fourth for as long as two years.[26]

The oral contraceptive, nearly 100 percent effective if taken on schedule, is more expensive than the IUD. The Pill must be taken daily except for an interval of several days per month, a difficult system for people in both DCs and LDCs.

Abortion is expensive and where illegal, performed under conditions hazardous to the woman's life and health. However, it is a widely used method of birth control, as indicated by estimates of four abortions for every 10 live births in the world in 1971.[27] In 1988, in Hungary, a nominally Roman Catholic country, there were seven abortions for every 10 live births.[28] In the 1990s, more than two-thirds of the world's population live in countries where abortions are legal.

Family-Planning Programs. Cassen estimates that 100 million or 15 percent of the world's couples, in which women are of reproductive age, wish to limit their fertility and need to be provided improved access to contraceptives.[29] By the 1990s, developing countries comprising 95 percent of their population had embarked on official family-planning programs to reduce population growth. India established a program in 1951, Pakistan in 1960, South Korea in 1961, China and North Vietnam in 1962, and a wave of others occurred thereafter.[30] In 1979, there may have been as many as 40 million new users of birth control devices and methods provided by family-planning programs worldwide, including sterilizations, IUDs, the Pill, abortion, condoms, or others.

The six Asian countries—China, Taiwan, South Korea, Thailand, Indonesia, and Sri Lanka—whose total fertility rates (2–3) are almost as low as those in developed countries (see Figure 8–7), all launched family-planning programs in the 1960s that substantially reduced fertility rates during the subsequent decade. In

---

[26]Joginder S. Uppal, *Economic Development in South Asia* (New York: St. Martin's, 1977), p. 48.

[27]Timothy King, coordinator, *Population Policies and Economic Development* (Baltimore: Johns Hopkins University Press, 1974).

[28]Arthur Haupt and Thomas T, Kane, *Population Handbook: International Edition* (Washington, D.C.: Population Reference Bureau, 1991), p. 22.

[29]Robert Cassen, "Population and Development: Old Debates, New Conclusions," in Robert Cassen and contributors, *Population and Development: Old Debates, New Conclusions*, Overseas Development Council U.S.-Third World Policy Perspectives (New Brunswick, N.J.: Transaction, 1994), p. 6.

[30]World Bank, *World Development Report, 1984* (New York: Oxford University Press, 1984), p. 127.

In Pakistan, women have not accepted family planning, even in the 1990s, as customs that restrict female education and labor force participation encourage high fertility as the surest route to economic security. Deborah Maine, Lynn Freedman, Farida Shaheed, and Schuyler Frautschi, "Risk, Reproduction, and Rights: The Uses of Reproductive Health Data," in Robert Cassen and contributors, *Population and Development: Old Debates, New Conclusions*, Overseas Development Council U.S.-Third World Policy Perspectives (New Brunswick, N.J.: Transaction, 1994), p. 217. The 1988–93 percentage of married women of childbearing age using contraception in Pakistan, however, was only 14 percent, compared to 43 percent in India, 83 percent in China, and 77 percent in South Korea. World Bank, *World Development Report, 1994* (New York: Oxford University Press, 1994), pp. 212–13.

1962, China advocated "birth planning" to protect the health of mothers and children. During the Cultural Revolution from 1966 to 1976, many neighborhood groups collectively set targets for births and awarded the privilege of having babies to "deserving couples." Even in rural areas, where contraceptives dispensed by health care centers included "paper pills," sheets of water-soluble paper impregnated with oral contraceptives, over one-half of the couples practiced contraception. The "one couple, one child" policy, adopted in 1979, includes an array of rewards and sanctions, from community pressure and intimidation (sometimes from designated grandmotherly figures) to deprivation of educational benefits and job opportunities. The policy has been enforced more or less in urban areas, but rarely in rural areas. China's birth control programs reduced the crude birth rate from 36 per 1,000 in 1960 to 19 in 1986 (a greater success than India's). In 1973, contraceptive users as a percentage of women of reproductive age exceeded 50 percent in Taiwan and reached 30 percent in South Korea. This progress in family planning contributed to a decrease in crude birth rate from the lower 40s to the teens per 1,000 in both countries between 1960 and 1988. Sri Lanka's relatively strong family-planning program resulted in a decline in the birth rate from 36 to 24 per 1,000 between 1960 and 1988, while Indonesia's program was instrumental in a reduction from 47 to 28 and Thailand's in a fall from 46 to 29 during the same period.[31]

Some of the momentum in support of LDC family planning was lost in the 1990s. United Nations Secretary-General Boutros Boutros-Ghali, under pressure from LDCs' increasing ambivalence about family planning, issued a draft *Agenda for Development* in 1994 that indicated that population growth was a potential problem but remained silent on population policies.[32] The direction that LDC population programs will go in the future is not certain.

Negative Externalities in Childbearing.   Chapter 5 mentioned external economies or externalities, cost advantages that an individual or firm conveys to other units within the economy. **Negative externalities** or external diseconomies are costs that an actor (for example, a couple) imposes on the rest of society. By having more children, a couple may increase its voice in local decisions, its claim to village common resources, and its economic security (especially during old age). At the same time, for society, more children diverts spending on physical and human capital, increases environmental degradation, and reduces wages (by increasing labor relative to other resources).[33]

Negative externalities associated with childbearing mean that for a couple, the cost of preventing an extra (marginal) birth exceeds the benefit, while for society the benefit of preventing a marginal birth exceeds the cost. In this situation, so-

---

[31]Paul R. Ehrlich, Anne H. Ehrlich, and John P. Holdren, *Ecoscience: Population, Resources, Environment* (San Francisco: W. H. Freeman, 1977); World Bank, *World Development Report, 1979* (Washington, D.C., 1979), pp. 56–58; Population Reference Bureau, *1988 World Population Data Sheet* (Washington, D.C., 1988); and Kaval Gulhati and Lisa M. Bates, "Developing Countries and the International Population Debate: Politics and Pragmatism," in Robert Cassen and contributors, *Population and Development: Old Debates, New Conclusions*, Overseas Development Council U.S.-Third World Policy Perspectives (New Brunswick, N.J.: Transaction, 1994), pp. 71–72.

[32]"Population in the UN's 'Agenda for Development'," *Population and Development Review* 20 (September 1994): 683–86.

[33]Nancy Birdsall, "Government, Population, and Poverty: A Win-Win Tale," in Robert Cassen and contributors, *Population and Development: Old Debates, New Conclusions*, Overseas Development Council U.S.-Third World Policy Perspectives (New Brunswick, N.J.: Transaction, 1994), pp. 256–61.

ciety would gain by the state subsidizing contraceptives for family planning programs so that the relationship between marginal cost and marginal benefit for a couple corresponds to the marginal cost-benefit relationship for society.

Cost-Effectiveness of Family-Planning Programs.   How cost-effective are family-planning programs? Does the social marginal benefit of a program exceed its social marginal cost? Suppose the present value of benefits from preventing a birth is $100, a figure equal to the saved hospital, medical, food, educational, and other costs minus the expected earnings of the person whose birth was prevented.[34] Assume the cost of providing contraceptives to prevent one birth amounts to $50. If a subsidy of $40 induces a family not to have another child, program costs would still be only $90 per prevented birth, $10 less than the $100 the birth would cost a society.

Simulation models developed by Stephen Enke indicate high returns to investment in birth control programs.[35] As a result of slowed population growth, labor force growth also slows—decreasing the ratio of labor to capital and natural resources and increasing labor's marginal productivity. In addition, slowing population growth reduces the ratio of nonworking dependents to the economically productive population (a ratio discussed earlier in this chapter). Nevertheless, Enke's models overstate the returns to family-planning programs. Frequently they attribute to these programs prevented births that would not have occurred anyway because traditional methods of birth control would have succeeded. The models also understate the increased cost per user as the programs reach out to families resistant to birth control and overstate the net benefits of a prevented birth to society. Underestimating overhead costs in the population centers and understating the present value of future earnings are also problems.[36]

Motivation to Limit Family Size.   A successful family-planning program requires more than making a supply of contraceptives available; it also requires a demand for birth control. A number of programs in developing countries, especially in highly populated South Asia, have had only a limited impact on reducing fertility, partly because of a lack of motivation to limit family size. India's program encountered active resistance during the early 1960s. Opposition, which led occasionally to riots, had numerous causes. The programs were directed by Western instead of local medical services. Frequently religious and ethnic minorities viewed the program as discriminatory, and peasants believed that it was contrary to their economic interests. However, India's program was reorganized in 1965 with strong governmental support. Incentive payments were increased. For example, transistor radios were given to the users as well as persons who "motivated" the use of the birth control devices. A "cafeteria" approach to contraceptive methods

[34]To obtain present value, evaluate the present worth of each part of the stream of future receipts and expenditures. Thus if the interest rate is 15 percent, the present value of earnings of $5,000 18 years into the future is, $5,000/(1 + .15)^{18}$, or $404.03. The present value of $1,000 spent on food, housing, health care, schooling, and other items 8 years into the future is $1,000/(1 + .15)^8$, or $326.90. Once the present worth of future receipts and expenditures for every year is known, simply add together all these separate, discounted values. See Chapter 11.

[35]Stephen Enke, "The Economics of Government Payments to Limit Population," *Economic Development and Cultural Change,* 8 no. 4 (July 1960): 239–48; and Stephen Enke, "The Economic Aspects of Slowing Population Growth," *Economic Journal* 76 (March 1966): 44–56.

[36]Clarence Zuvekas, Jr., *Economic Development: An Introduction* (New York: St. Martin's, 1979), pp. 92–93.

and devices was used. Funding increased, so that by 1975 there were 50,000 family-planning centers and subcenters throughout the country. Nevertheless, despite the effort, the birth rate fell from 44 to only 33 per 1,000 between 1960 and 1988, a drop not much in excess of countries investing little in family-planning programs. Furthermore, the public outcry following a sterilization campaign in 1976 and 1977 set back the entire family-planning program by more than a decade.

The varying success of organized family-planning efforts in developing countries indicates that making contraceptives available is not enough to reduce fertility rates. Couples will not use contraceptives unless they are motivated to limit births. The next section discusses ways in which socioeconomic change affects birth control decisions.

SOCIOECONOMIC DEVELOPMENT

Children in a Peasant Society. In most low-income countries, especially in South and Southeast Asia, farming is predominantly peasant agriculture. Peasants cultivate bits of land they usually do not own. Agricultural methods are traditional, technology stagnant, and little capital is available. Compared to their counterparts in urban society, children in a peasant society are more likely to be perceived as an economic asset. Boys as young as 8 to 10 years tend or herd animals, weed, pick, and sell produce. Girls fetch water, prepare meals, tend to younger children, and sometimes farm. Children place fewer economic demands on a peasant family. Food is raised domestically; housing is constructed by the family from local materials; and the cost of education, entertainment, and travel is negligible. Although the family may receive a dowry when a daughter marries out of the village, major financial security is usually provided by sons, who add to the family's farm output or earn money from trade or another occupation. Having a larger family permits more income and asset transfer to balance temporary deficits or surpluses. When social insurance is inadequate, the larger the family, the smaller the risk of a poverty-ridden old age.

The literate, urban white-collar worker in South and Southeast Asia is more likely to limit family size than is an illiterate peasant in the same region. Consider, for example, the family in a two-room apartment in Delhi, India, with husband and wife employed and their children expected to get an education. The cost of children is more for this family than for one in a less densely populated village in rural southeastern India. Childrearing, particularly when children are too young to attend school, interferes with work for women outside the home. In addition, children are more likely to interfere with the urban worker's aspirations for a better job or geographic mobility.

Indian village values support high fertility. In much of rural India, the status of the new bride in her husband's village is tied to having children, especially sons. A son not only provides added security for old age, but also performs essential religious rites on the death of a parent.

As child mortality rates fall, fewer births are needed to achieve any given desired family size. Parents may need only two to three children to be virtually certain of a surviving son, in contrast to the six to eight essential when death rates are high.

In general modernization affects the birth rate. For example, as Table 8–3 indicates, fertility in India declines with increased income, education, urban living, and improved occupational status. This argument supports Nobel laureate

TABLE 8-3 Average Number of Children Born per Couple, by Selected Characteristics, in India, 1961–65 (by income, education, residence, and occupation)

Characteristics	Average Number of Children
Household income and expenditure (1960–61)	
Up to Rs 10 per month	3.40
Rs 11–20 per month	3.02
Rs 21–30 per month	2.95
Rs 30 and over per month	2.70
Educational level attained by women (1961)	
Illiterate	3.5
Primary school	3.4
Secondary school	3.1
College	3.0
Postgraduate	2.5
Residence (1963–64)	
Urban	3.19
Rural	3.76
Occupation of head of household	
Agriculture	4.4
Industry	4.2
Professional—law, medicine, teaching	3.7
Average for all occupations	4.3

Source: Joginder S. Uppal, *Economic Development in South Asia* (New York: St. Martin's, 1977), p. 41.

Gary S. Becker's view that the change in the demand for children rather than the supply of contraceptives is the primary cause of the change in fertility.[37]

Income Distribution.   A number of studies indicate that fertility is lower when income distribution is more even. Income redistribution to lower classes increases the percentage of the population above the poverty level. Increased economic security and higher income for the poor mean having children is not the only way of securing one's old age. Higher absolute incomes and redistribution policies (discussed in Chapters 6 and 7) increase lower-class literacy, mobility, and urbanization, factors reducing birth rates. Thus in Taiwan, high enrollment rates in schools,which reduce child labor, are associated with lowered fertility.[38] Furthermore, with allowances for time lags, low birth rates increase income equality by decreasing unemployment and increasing per capita expenditure on training and education.

Taiwan and the Philippines illustrate this relationship between income distribution and fertility. In the early 1970s, per capita income in Taiwan was approximately the same as in the Philippines. However, there was a considerable discrepancy between the income distribution in the two countries. The top 10 percent

---

[37]Gary S. Becker, *A Treatise on the Family*, enlarged edition (Cambridge, Mass.: Harvard University Press, 1991), p. 141.

[38]Julian L. Simon, "Income, Wealth, and Their Distribution as Policy Tools in Fertility Control," in Ronald G. Ridker, ed., *Population and Development: The Search for Selective Interventions* (Baltimore: Johns Hopkins University Press, 1976), pp. 36–76.

of the population in the Philippines was significantly richer than the same group in Taiwan, but the bottom 20 percent was more than twice as well-off in Taiwan. Moreover, in comparison to the Philippines, which had a high farm tenancy rate, in Taiwan, as a result of land reform in the 1950s, nearly all farmers owned their land. These facts explain why Taiwan's fertility rate is lower than the Philippines'.[39] More people had reached a socioeconomic level in Taiwan that promoted birth control. And income inequality is lower in low-fertility South Korea (which also had a low farm tenancy rate), Taiwan, China, Thailand, Indonesia, Sri Lanka, Argentina, Chile, Uruguay, and Cuba than in high-fertility Venezuela, Mexico, Brazil, Colombia, Panama, Peru, Ecuador, El Salvador, and Honduras (Figure 8–2).

Religion.   When factors measuring modernization are held constant, religion explains few cross-national fertility differences. Thus fertility rates in predominantly Roman Catholic Latin America, France, Portugal, and Poland, given their level of development, are about what demographers would expect. And Catholic Spain and Italy had the lowest total fertility rates in the world, 1.2, in 1995. Yet religious (prolife) politics (along with a belief that population was neutral in development) influenced the U.S. government, previously the major donor to LDC population programs, to refuse to finance family planning programs in LDCs from 1984 to 1992. Washington feared that aid to these programs might promote or condone abortion or coercive population control. This withdrawal of U.S. aid reduced funding for the United Nations Population Fund and other family planning programs in LDCs. In 1993, President William J. Clinton rescinded this policy. The following year the United States Agency for International Development (USAID) identified "stabilizing world population growth and protecting human health" as one of the five areas that were keys to sustainable development.[40] The policy of the United States government toward LDC family planning is likely to be in flux during the late 1990s.

A Summary of Variables.   Interestingly enough, a study by Anne D. Williams indicates income is not important in reducing a fertility rates when other factors are held constant.[41] How then do we explain the negative relationship between per capita income and fertility in Figure 8–7? Variables *positively* associated with income, such as education and literacy, occupational status, women in the labor force, urbanization, and income equality, are all *negatively* correlated with fertility. On the other hand, child mortality rates and children in the labor force—*negatively* related to income—are *positively* associated with the birth rate.

The Role of Women.   A major theme of the International Conference on Population and Development, held in Cairo, Egypt in 1994, was that countries wishing to reduce birth rates should empower women socially and economically. Female

[39]William Rich, "Smaller Families through Jobs and Justice," *International Development Review,* 14, no. 4 (1972/73): 10–15; and D. Gale Johnson, "Effects of Institutions and Policies on Rural Population Growth with Application to China," *Population and Development Review* 20 (September 1994): 503–31.

[40]Peter Hendry, "Food and Population: Beyond Five Billion," *Population Bulletin* 43 (April 1988): 32; Population Reference Bureau, *1995 World Population Data Sheet* (Washington, D.C., 1995); "Rescission of the US 'Mexico City Policy'," *Population and Development Review* 19 (March 1993): 215–16; and "USAID's Strategy for Stabilizing World Population Growth and Protecting Human Health," *Population and Development Review* 20 (June 1994): 483–87.

[41]Anne D. Williams, "Determinants of Fertility in Developing Countries," in M. C. Keeley, ed., *Population, Public Policy, and Economic Development* (New York: Praeger, 1976), pp. 117–57.

equality is associated with high levels of female education and labor-force participation, both variables related to low fertility.

DEVELOPMENT OR FAMILY PLANNING?

What policies then can a developing country pursue to lower fertility rates? Programs promoting social and economic development by improving health, nutrition, education, female rights, and urban development will lower fertility rates. In addition, improving income distribution—including more educational and job opportunities for women, the underprivileged classes, and lower-income groups—will also contribute to a reduced birth rate. In a sense, lower fertility is a by-product of strategies widely considered socially desirable in themselves.

Which is more important in contributing to reduced fertility, family planning or socioeconomic development? We cannot choose one as more important, since birth reduction depends on both. Birth control devices offered by family-planning agencies will not be accepted if the social and economic circumstances of the population are such that reduced fertility does not seem an advantage. On the other hand, people wanting smaller families must have access to birth control devices and information. Developing countries serious about reducing fertility need both family-planning programs and policies promoting socioeconomic development and increased income equality.

The reader should keep in mind that development and population are interacting variables. Each affects the other.

Summary

1. Population growth in the second half of the twentieth century, especially among LDCs, is unprecedented in human experience. The developing world has a current population growth rate in excess of 2 percent per year. More than one-half of the world's population lives in Asia.

2. The demographic transition is a period of rapid population growth occurring between a preindustrial, stable population characterized by high fertility and mortality rates and nearly equal birth and death rates in a late modern period. The fast growth takes place in the early transitional stage, when fertility rates remain high but mortality rates decline.

3. Contemporary LDC population growth has been more explosive than that of the DCs during their early transitional period because of a sharper drop in mortality rates in LDCs. Today's developing countries were able to take advantage of advances in food production, new pesticides, improvements in transport and communication, improved nutrition, better personal hygiene, medical innovations, and immunization in a short time—many of which were not available to DCs during their early demographic transition.

4. Fertility decreases with economic development, urbanization, industrialization, mobility, literacy, female labor force participation, reduced income inequality, and greater family-planning efforts. However these efforts are not likely to be successful unless socioeconomic development and improved income distribution make birth control seem advantageous. Development and family-planning programs have both contributed to the decrease in LDC fertility rates since the 1960s.

5. The young age structure in LDCs means that their populations will continue to grow even after the average woman of childbearing age bears only enough daughters to replace herself.

6. Malthus's predictions that population would outgrow food supply were wrong in the past because he did not foresee that technological change, capital accumulation, and voluntary birth control would maintain a safe food and population balance. Present agricultural production is sufficient to feed everyone on earth adequately. However, deficiencies in food distribution between and within nations, inadequate agricultural research, and limited energy make future food availability in LDCs rather uncertain, especially in sub-Saharan Africa.

7. Simon, who contends that population growth stimulates technology, division of labor, and economic growth, argues against a LDC government population policy. However, Simon's assumptions contradict the second law of thermodynamics, which states that the world is a closed system with ever-increasing entropy.

8. Increased urbanization and congestion, rapid labor force growth, growing unemployment, and high dependency burdens are some major costs of high fertility rates and rapid population growth. That 35 to 40 percent of LDC population is 0–14 years old compared to only 20 to 25 percent in the DCs means that resources have to be diverted from capital formation to take care of the young in the LDCs.

Terms to Review

- crude birth rate
- crude death rate
- family-planning programs
- total fertility rate
- demographic transition
- replacement-level fertility
- population momentum

- stationary population
- international network of agricultural research centers
- Green Revolution
- dependency ratio
- population age pyramid
- laissez-faire

Questions to Discuss

1. What factors have contributed to a rising LDC population growth rate since 1950? Why has the LDC population growth rate not slowed down much in recent years?

2. Explain the demographic transition theory. At what stages in the theory are LDCs? Why are they in different stages?

3. Compare and contrast the historical population growth patterns of DCs and today's LDCs. Why are the patterns different?

4. What, if any, is the statistical relationship between birth rate and GNP per capita? Between birth rate and income distribution? What are the reasons for these relationships?

5. Why would population continue to grow for several decades after it reaches a replacement-level fertility?

6. What are some of the costs of a high fertility rate and rapid population growth?

7. How well does Malthusian population theory explain Western population growth? Contemporary LDC population growth?

8. What do you expect to happen to food production per capita (especially in LDCs) in the late twentieth century?

9. Discuss and evaluate views of economic optimists like Simon who argue that LDC governments do not need a policy to limit population growth.

10. Which policies are more important for reducing fertility: family-planning programs or socioeconomic development?

Guide to Readings

Robert Cassen and contributors, *Population and Development: Old Debates, New Conclusions*, Overseas Development Council U.S.-Third World Policy Perspectives (New Brunswick, N.J.: Transaction, 1994), provide a survey of the research on the relationship between population and development. Thomas W. Merrick, "Population Dynamics in Developing Countries," in ibid., pp. 80–86, discusses the demographic transition. Teitelbaum (note 4) expounds and criticizes the theory of demographic transition. Allen C. Kelley, "Economic Consequences of Population Change in the Third World," *Journal of Economic Literature* 36 (September 1988): 1685–1728, summarizes the literature on the economic effects of population growth.

The annual *World Population Data Sheet* from the Population Reference Source (note to Figure 8–2) is a handy, up-to-date source of basic LDC demographic statistics. Other sources are World Bank, *World Population Projections: Estimates and Projections with Related Demographic Statistics, 1994–95* (Baltimore: Johns Hopkins University Press, 1994), and subsequent volumes; the United Nations, *Demographic Yearbook* (note to Figure 8–3); United States Bureau of the Census, *World Population* (note to Figure 8–1); and World Bank, *World Development Report* publish current world population statistics periodically. The World Bank discusses *Averting the Old Age Crisis: Policies to Protect the Old and Promote Growth* (New York: Oxford University Press, 1994).

Joseph Chamie, "Demography: Population Databases in Development Analysis," *Journal of Development Economics* 44 (June 1994): 131–46, points out that users of existing population databases often undertake faulty analyses because of the weakness of database sources. Chamie also discusses other aspects of the strengths and weaknesses of these databases.

Wolfgang Lutz provides a basic analysis of "The Future of World Population," in *Population Bulletin* 49 (June 1994): 1–47.

Lant H. Pritchett, "Desired Fertility and the Impact of Population Policies," *Population and Development Review* 20 (March 1994): 1–55, presents evidence that actual fertility in LDCs closely coincides with desired fertility. John Bongaarts, "The Supply-Demand Framework for the Determinants of Fertility: An Alternative Implementation," *Population Studies* 47 (November 1993):

437–56, provides an excellent introduction to the supply and demand approach to fertility, including an analysis of Richard Easterlin's model.

Bloom and Freeman (note 24) summarize the effect of rapid population growth on LDC labor force growth.

The *Population Bulletin* frequently provides timely surveys of the LDC population and labor force. The *Population and Development Review* is probably the best journal to browse for the latest analyses of the relationships between population and economic development.

D. Gale Johnson, "Effects of Institutions and Policies on Rural Population Growth with Application to China," *Population and Development Review* 20 (September 1994): 503–31, is an excellent demographic study of China's population.

Partha Dasgupta surveys "The Population Problem: Theory and Evidence," in *Journal of Economic Literature* 33 (December 1995): 1879-1902.

9

Employment, Migration and Urbanization

Questions concerning population and the labor force are intertwined. The dependency burden of the working population depends on fertility rates, and labor force growth is a function of natural population increase and migration. Labor skills are a major component of population quality. This chapter examines employment, unemployment, underemployment, and labor migration, while the next chapter considers the quality of labor resources.

Before the main body of the chapter, however, we want to introduce Chapters 9–13. For now the discussion shifts from poverty alleviation, income distribution, and the population problem (Chapters 6–8), to the factors that contribute to economic growth (Chapters 9–13).

The Production Function

As Chapter 5 indicated, we can visualize growth factors in a **production function** stating the relationship between capacity output and the volume of various inputs.

$$Y = F\left(L,\ K,\ N,\ E,\ T\right) \qquad (9\text{--}1)$$

means that output (or national product) (Y) during a given time period depends on the input flows of labor (L), capital (K), natural resources (N), and entrepreneurship (E); and prevailing technology (T).

The formula implies that each input, such as labor (L), is homogeneous. We could assume that L represents a number of labor units in which a skilled person is more than one unit. More realistically, though, L stands for a list of skills, together with the number of individuals possessing each skill, available during the unit of time.

Capital goods—plant, equipment, machinery, buildings, and inventories—are produced goods used as inputs in further production. To avoid circularity, where the value of capital is determined by its output potential, the *stock* of capital

245

consists of a heterogeneous complex of specific capital goods. Variable K, however, refers to the *flow* of capital services available for production during the period.

Analogous to the other inputs in our equation, N is a heterogeneous complex of natural resources. Although the **stock** of natural resources, at least nonrenewable resources, may be gradually depleting, only the **flow** per unit of time is relevant for the production function.

If technology is fixed, the flow of natural resources places an absolute limitation on physical production in such industries as steel and aluminum. New discoveries or techniques may allow increased exploitation of natural resources, so that the flow of N increases per time period; on the other hand, advances in technology, such as transistors and silicon chips, may reduce the natural resources required per unit of output.

Entrepreneurship is the production resource coordinating labor, capital, natural resources, and technology. Variable E lends itself even less to quantification than the other production factors.

Technology (T), or technical knowledge, connotes the practical arts, ranging from hunting, fishing, and agriculture through manufacturing, communication, and medicine. T can be a direct production input, as in Equation 9–1, or a variable affecting the relationship between inputs L, K, N, and E and output Y. From the latter perspective, technologies are skills, knowledge, procedures, and activities for transforming inputs into outputs, and an increased T reduces inputs per output.[1]

The scale of production is a variable that might have been included in Equation 9–1. With a given technology, increasing the inputs—labor, capital, natural resources, and entrepreneurship—by some multiple may not result in the same multiplication in output because of economies or diseconomies of scale.

Since our focus is on income or production per worker (or per person), we could restate Equation 9–1 with the independent variable Y/L or Y/P (with P, population). In this case, the production function would become more complex.

The next two chapters concentrate on the role of the labor force in economic development. Chapter 11 discusses capital and technology, Chapter 12 entrepreneurship, and Chapter 13 natural resources, land, and the environment in economic growth.

Employment Problems in LDCS

You cannot understand LDC unemployment unless you realize how it is different from that in the West. The openly unemployed in LDCs are usually 15 to 24 years old, educated, and residents of urban areas. The unemployed in LDCs, usually supported by an extended family in a job search, are less likely to be from the poorest one-fifth of the population than in DCs.

Still, the employment problem is of major concern to developing countries. Obviously providing adequately paid, productive jobs for the very poor is a major way of reducing poverty and inequality in LDCs. High unemployment rates represent a vast underutilization of human resources; the unemployed, who are most often young, urban, educated males, are a potential source of social unrest and political discontent.[2]

---

[1] Martin Fransman, *Technology and Economic Development* (Boulder, Colo.: Westview, 1986), p. 23.

[2] E. Wayne Nafziger, *The Economics of Political Instability: The Nigerian-Biafran War* (Boulder, Colo.: Westview, 1983).

In the West, economic development was accompanied by a large internal and international migration from rural areas, where technical progress freed labor, to urban areas, where rapid, industrial expansion increased labor demand. Many economists expected that rapid industrialization would resolve the employment problem in LDCs. Unfortunately for reasons to be discussed below, this strategy of rapid industrial growth did not have the same results in LDCs as in the West.

Scope of the Chapter

The next two sections of this chapter discuss the types of underutilized labor and the extent of LDC unemployment and underemployment. The subsequent section examines whether LDC industrial expansion can absorb labor force growth. Following that, we look at disguised unemployment in agriculture. We review the Lewis model and examine the Harris–Todaro model of rural-urban migration and consider why Western explanations for unemployment may not apply to LDCs. After that, we explain LDC unemployment by looking at LDC technology, factor-price distortions, and educated labor markets. The final section considers policies to reduce unemployment.

Dimensions of Unemployment and Underemployment

The openly **unemployed** are those without work (not even one hour in paid employment, self-employment, or unpaid apprenticeship) who are actively seeking and currently available for work among a specified age range (usually covering those age groups corresponding to substantial participation in economic activity) during a specified reference period (either one day or one week). LDC unemployment, according to estimates from International Labor Organization data, rose from 36 million in 1960 to 66 million in 1980 to 91 million in 1992–93, an increase of 153 percent, while unemployment as a percentage of the labor force increased from 7.4 percent in 1970 to 7.8 percent in 1980 to 8.2 percent in 1992–93. The Economic Commission for Africa estimates 1975 unemployment rates of 10.8 percent in Africa, 6.9 percent in Asia, and 6.5 percent in Latin America, while 1992/93 unemployment rates from International Labor Organization statistics were 12.2 percent in Africa, 7.0 percent in Asia, and 8.1 percent in Latin America.[3] Yet unemployment rates moved cyclically, peaking during periods of recession and adjustment to chronic balance-of-payments deficits.[4]

These unemployment rates have substantial margins of error. Statistics from the usual sources, household surveys, while generally more reliable than data from unemployment registries or insurance systems, may be deficient because of inadequate infrastructure, errors in the sampling method, and the inexperience and lack of training of interviewers and supervisors.[5]

---

[3]Yves Sablo, "Employment and Unemployment, 1960–90," *International Labor Review* 112 (December 1975): 408–17; Economic Commission for Africa, *ECA and Africa's Development, 1983–2000: A Preliminary Perspective Study* (Addis Ababa, 1983), pp. 7–59; and International Labor Office, *World Labor Report, 1995* (Geneva, 1995).

[4]Susan Horton, Ravi Kanbur, and Dipak Mazumdar, "Labor Markets in an Era of Adjustment," *International Labor Review* 130(5–6) (1991): 531–58.

[5]International Labor Office, *World Labor Report, 1995* (Geneva, 1995), pp. 15–21.

Who are the unemployed in LDCs? Mainly city residents—unemployment in urban areas is twice that of rural areas. Most unemployed are first-time entrants to the labor force: The unemployment rate for youths, 15 to 24, is twice that of people over 24. The unemployed are often women—although there are fewer unemployed females than males, the rate for women is higher. Finally the unemployed are fairly well educated. Unemployment correlates with education until after secondary levels, when it begins to fall.[6] These patterns are explained later in the chapter.

Most countries distinguish people who work short hours from those who work full time. Students, retired people, and houseworkers who work a few hours usually do not identify themselves with their employment status. Part-time workers are people who voluntarily work short hours.

To the unemployed, we must add the **underemployed,** those who work less than they would like to work. The **visibly underemployed** are workers who are compelled to work short hours as an alternative to being out of a job. **Invisible underemployment** results from an inadequate use of workers' capacities.

Readers should be skeptical of journalists' reports of combined unemployment and underemployment rates in excess of 50 percent in a depressed country. One reason to be skeptical is that there are no operational guidelines for measuring underemployment, so that most such rates are meaningless.[7]

Underutilized Labor

Besides the openly unemployed, Edgar O. Edwards identifies three forms of labor underutilization or underemployment: the visibly active but underutilized—those who are "marking time," including,

1. Disguised unemployment. Many people seem occupied on farms or employed in government on a full-time basis even though the services they render may actually require much less than full time. Social pressures on private industry also may result in disguised unemployment. The concept is discussed in more detail below.
2. Hidden unemployment. Those who are engaged in nonemployment activities, especially education and household chores, as a "second choice," primarily because job opportunities are not (a) available at the levels of education already attained; or (b) open to women, due to discrimination. Thus educational institutions and households become "employers of last resort." Moreover, many students may be among the less able. They cannot compete successfully for jobs, so they go to school.
3. The prematurely retired. This phenomenon is especially apparent in the civil service. In many LDCs, retirement age is falling as longevity increases, primarily as a means of creating job opportunities for younger workers.[8]

The remainder of the chapter focuses on the openly unemployed, the underemployed, and the disguised unemployed.

---

[6]Lyn Squire, *Employment Policy in Developing Countries: A Survey of Issues and Evidence* (New York: Oxford University Press, 1981), pp. 66–69.

[7]International Labor Office, *World Labor Report, 1995* (Geneva, 1995), pp. 12–21.

[8]Edgar O. Edwards, ed., *Employment in Developing Nations* (New York: Columbia University Press, 1974), pp. 10–11.

Labor Force Growth, Urbanization, and Industrial Expansion

Growing LDC unemployment is caused by the labor force growing faster than job opportunities. By 2000 the LDC labor force will have increased more than 2.5 times—from 500 million in 1950 to 1,325 million (Figure 9–1). Today's developing countries must contend with a much more rapid labor force growth than the industrialized countries had at a similar stage in their growth. The labor force in Western Europe, North America, and Japan grew at 0.8 percent a year in the nineteenth century compared to 1.9 percent per year in the developing countries in 1992–96. (Labor force growth lags behind population growth. China's 1980 to 1985 labor force growth of 2.5 percent yearly was a reflection of population growth in the early to mid-1960s, while the 1985 to 2000 annual labor force growth of 1.4 percent is linked to the declining 1970 to 1985 population growth that accompanied an expedited family-planning program. The echo of East Asia's reduced labor force growth at the turn of the twenty-first century is the falling 1.4-percent yearly population growth that occurred from 1980 to 1985.) It took almost 90 years for the labor force to double in industrialized countries; it now takes about 38 years in the developing countries.[9]

In the United States, the labor force participation for females over age 15 surged from 34 percent in 1950 to 57 percent in 1991. The story, however, is quite

FIGURE 9–1   Labor Force Estimates and Projections, 1950–2000

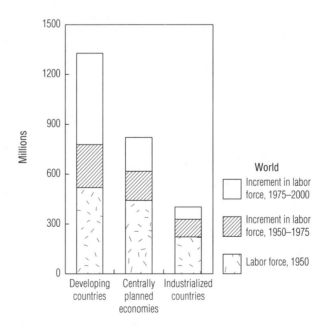

Source: World Bank, *World Development Report, 1979* (Washington, D.C., 1979) p. 48.

---

[9]World Bank, *World Development Report, 1994* (New York: Oxford University Press, 1994), pp. 210–11.

different in developing countries, where 80 percent of the world's women live. There is substantial variation in LDC female participation rates and some of these data are unreliable. Still, population economists think that female participation rates in Asia (except China) and Africa fell from 1950 to 1990. In sub-Saharan Africa, where women comprised 42 percent of the agricultural labor force but only 27 percent of the nonagricultural labor force (in 1985), the growth of industrial and services shares in the labor force has diminished female labor force participation. In the Middle East, where traditional culture discourages or prohibits women from leaving the safety and sanctity of their homes to work for others, economic growth may even reduce female labor force participation.

According to the International Labor Office and Population Reference Bureau, the female share of the world's labor force (*not* the same as the uncertain global female labor participation rate) stayed roughly constant during the last half of the twentieth century, increasing from 35 percent in 1950 to 36 percent in 1990 (and projected to be 35 percent in 2025). In LDCs, the female share of the labor force increased from 33 percent in 1950 to 34 percent in 1990 (and was projected to 34 percent in 2025).[10]

Economic growth is usually accompanied by a decline in the proportion of labor force in agriculture and an increase in the share of labor in the more productive industrial and services sector. Yet in 1990–92, 66 percent of the labor force in low-income countries was in agriculture and only 10 percent in industry, while in middle-income countries, 46 percent was in agriculture and 25 percent in industry (see Table 4–1).

Annual industrial employment expanded at 0.5 percent of the total labor force in developing countries in 1987–92—higher than the 0.3 percent figure for industrialized Europe at the turn of the twentieth century.[11]

Because of fast labor force growth, industry in today's developing countries absorbs only 20 to 35 percent of the increased labor force, compared to about 50 percent in Europe in 1900. Let us illustrate. Assume the labor force is growing at 2.7 percent per year, the rate for sub-Saharan Africa from 1992 to 2000 (see Table 9–1). Assume agricultural employment remains constant, so that growth is in industry and services. The nonagricultural sector in sub-Saharan Africa in the 1990s employs 33 1/3 percent of the labor force. This sector would have to increase its total employment 8.1 percent per year to absorb a labor force growth of 2.7 percent (that is 0.33 1/3 × 0.081 = 0.027). Table 9–2 indicates that although two sub-Saharan countries increased manufacturing output by 11 percent or more per year, this growth substantially exceeds manufacturing employment growth in all sub-Saharan countries. Indeed only two LDCs, South Korea and Taiwan, increased manufacturing employment by more than 8 percent. Both countries have had a rapid rate of industrial growth and an emphasis on labor-intensive manufactures, especially in exports. Since *nonagricultural* employment rarely grows faster than *manufacturing* employment, achieving the needed employment growth in most LDCs is difficult.[12]

[10]David E. Bloom and Adi Brender, "Labor and the Emerging World Economy," *Population Bulletin* 48 (October 1993): 8–9.

[11]United Nations Development Program, *Human Development Report, 1990* (New York: Oxford University Press, 1990), pp. 157, 167; and United Nations Development Program, *Human Development Report, 1994* (New York: Oxford University Press, 1994), pp. 163, 174. [0.54]

[12]Peter Gregory, "An Assessment of Changes in Employment Conditions in Less-Developed Countries," *Economic Development and Cultural Change* 28 (July 1980): 673–700; World Bank, *World Development Report, 1979* (Washington, D.C.: 1979), p. 46; and United Nations Development Program, *Human Development Report, 1994* (New York: Oxford University Press, 1994), pp. 162–63.

TABLE 9-1 Growth of the Labor Force, 1950–2000

	Average Annual Percentage Growth Rate				
	1950–60	*1960–70*	*1970–80*	*1980–92*	*1992–2000*
East Asia and Pacific[a]	2.1	2.4	2.4	2.1	1.8
South and Southeast Asia	1.4	1.7	1.8	2.1	1.9
Latin America and Caribbean	2.2	2.4	3.1	2.5	2.3
Middle East and North Africa	1.6	1.9	3.0	3.2	3.2
Sub-Saharan Africa	1.7	2.2	2.4	2.5	2.7
Developing Europe	1.1	0.8	1.4	1.1	0.2
Developing countries	1.6	1.8	2.3	2.2	1.9
Developed countries	n.a.[b]	1.2	1.3	0.6	0.4

[a]Excludes Japan.

[b]Not available.

Sources: World Bank, *World Development Report, 1979* (Washington, D.C., 1979), p. 47; Lyn Squire, *Employment Policy in Developing Countries: A Survey of Issues and Evidence* (New York: Oxford University Press, 1981), pp. 44–45; World Bank, *World Development Report, 1988* (New York: Oxford University Press, 1988), pp. 282–83; and World Bank, *World Development Report, 1994* (New York: Oxford University Press, 1994), pp. 210–11.

TABLE 9-2 Industrialization and Employment Growth in Developing Countries

Region/Countries	*Annual Manufacturing Output Growth[a] (in percentage) 1963–69*	*Annual Manufacturing Employment Growth (in percentage) 1963–69*
Africa		
Algeria	−0.5	−27.0
Egypt	11.2	0.7
Ethiopia	12.8	6.4
Ghana	10.6	6.3
Kenya	6.4	4.3
Nigeria	14.1	5.7
Uganda	6.6	4.8
Asia		
Korea, Rep. of	18.4	13.0
India	5.9	3.3
Israel	12.1	3.0
Pakistan	12.3	2.6
Philippines	6.1	4.8
Taiwan	16.8	13.3
Thailand	10.7	−12.0
Latin America		
Brazil	6.5	1.1
Chile	4.8	4.2
Colombia	5.9	2.8
Costa Rica	8.9	2.8
Dominican Rep.	1.7	−3.3
Ecuador	11.4	6.0
Panama	12.9	7.4

[a]More precisely annual growth rate in the contribution of manufacturing to GNP.

Source: David Morawetz, "Employment Implications of Industrialization in Developing Countries," *Economic Journal* 84 (September 1974): 492–95.

Sluggish employment growth in the industrial and services sectors has contributed to high rates of urban unemployment, underemployment, and low rural productivity. The rest of this chapter explores the relationship between rural development and productivity, and labor migration from rural to urban areas and the consequent rising urban unemployment.

Disguised Unemployment

Many economists believe **disguised unemployment,** that is, **zero marginal revenue productivity of labor,** is endemic among LDC agricultural labor: Withdrawing a labor unit from agriculture does not decrease output. *Disguised unemployment* was a term first used during the Great Depression to describe workers in DCs who took inferior jobs as a result of being laid off. Between the 1930s and early 1950s, LDCs had little visible industrial unemployment, so economists surmised that the LDC counterpart of mass unemployment in the West was disguised unemployment: People continued to work on the farm despite depressed conditions. At that time, foreign experts viewed LDC agricultural production as inefficient. Compared to workers in advanced economies, agricultural workers in LDCs seemed to be producing little and appeared to be idle much of the time. Some agricultural economists assumed that peasant agriculture could be organized to employ all farm workers 10 hours a day, 6 days a week, all year long. But disguised unemployment had many mistaken premises. Many observers misunderstood the seasonality of LDC agricultural work and the difference in economic behavior between subsistence and commercial farmers (Chapter 7).[13]

The theoretical basis for zero marginal productivity of labor was the concept of **limited technical substitutability of factors.** Economic theory frequently assumes that you can produce a good with an infinite number of combinations of capital and labor, adjusting continuously by substituting a little more of one factor for a little less of another. However, in practice, there may be only a few productive processes available to an LDC, these being perhaps highly mechanized processes developed in the capital-abundant West. The extreme case is where production requires an unalterable ratio of capital to labor, so that the capital available to the economy cannot fully employ those in the labor force.[14] In peasant agriculture, labor less than fully employed is supposedly reflected in disguised unemployment.

However, the assumption of rigid factor proportions in LDC agriculture is not correct. Jacob Viner notes,

> I find it impossible to conceive of a farm of any kind on which, other factors of production being held constant . . . it would not be possible, by known methods, to obtain some addition to the crop by using additional labor in more careful selection and planting of the seed, more intensive weeding, cultivating, thinning, and mulching, more painstaking harvesting, gleaning and cleaning of the crop.[15]

[13]Charles H. C. Kao, Kurt A. Anschel, and Carl K. Eicher, "Disguised Unemployment in Agriculture: A Survey," in Carl K. Eicher and Lawrence Witt, eds., *Agriculture in Economic Development* (New York: McGraw-Hill, 1964), pp. 129–44.

[14]R.S. Eckhaus, "The Factor-Proportions Problem in Underdeveloped Areas," *American Economic Review* 45 (September 1955): 539–65.

[15]Jacob Viner, "Some Reflections on the Concept of Disguised Unemployment," *Indian Journal of Economics* 38 (July 1957): 19.

Whether or not disguised unemployment exists depends on how an economist defines the term *marginal unit.* Zero marginal productivity in agriculture is much less plausible if it refers to a *marginal hour of work* rather than a *marginal worker.* It is not difficult to imagine a village or clan applying simple and unchanging techniques and capital equipment to a plot of land whose size has remained the same for years. Since financial incentives do not work and frequent negotiations would be costly, tasks are assigned by custom. People of the same age and sex work about the same amount of time and get the same wage. Everyone is fed to a subsistence level as long as enough food is available. If population and the labor force increase, for example, by one-fifth, each worker's hours decrease by one-fifth. Output does not change. However, even if an extra worker's output is zero, an extra hour's output may be considerable. Where hours worked is the relevant measure, labor has a positive marginal productivity.

Even though capital-labor ratios are alterable in agriculture, they might not be so in industry, especially in such sectors as steel or chemicals. The last resort for labor not employed in profit-maximizing industry is with the clan, or extended family, in agriculture. Agriculture's absorption of this labor means marginal productivity and wage that will be lower than in industry. Yet the possibilities of substantial labor-intensive agricultural jobs, as Viner indicates, means that the marginal product of agricultural labor would be positive.

Do field investigations support this supposition? Several studies between 1930 and the early 1950s purported to show that LDC output in agriculture remained constant or increased with reduced labor. But these studies lacked evidence that capital formation and the level of technology remained constant.[16] Obviously labor's marginal productivity can be positive—even if output expands with less labor—if capital and technology increase.

Rural-Urban Migration

While overall the LDC labor force grows at an annual rate of 1.9 percent, the urban labor force and population are growing annually by 3.4 percent! The urban share of total LDC population has grown from 27 percent in 1975 and 35 percent in 1992 to 40 percent in 2000 (77 percent in Latin America, 37 percent in Asia, and 38 percent in Africa, compared to 76 percent in DCs and 48 percent for the world total), and is projected to increase to 47 percent in 2010 and 57 percent in 2025.[17] From 1975 to 2000, the number of cities in LDCs with populations over 1 million has been increasing from 90 to 300. Table 9–3 indicates that 27 LDC urban agglomerations will have populations of at least 10 million and three agglomerations (Bombay, India; Shanghai, China; and Mexico City) at least 15 million by 2000.

Low returns to agriculture and the prospect of higher wages in industry spur migration from rural to urban areas. A substantial proportion of the growth in the

---

[16]Charles H. C. Kao, Kurt A. Anschel, and Carl K. Eicher, "Disguised Unemployment in Agriculture: A Survey," in Carl K. Eicher and Lawrence Witt, eds., *Agriculture in Economic Development* (New York: McGraw-Hill, 1964), pp.129–44.

[17]World Bank, *World Development Report, 1994* (New York: Oxford University Press, 1994), pp. 210–11, 222–23; United Nations Development Program, *Human Development Report, 1994* (New York: Oxford University Press, 1994), pp. 148–49; United Nations, Department of Economic and Social Information and Policy Analysis, *World Urbanization Prospects: The 1992 Revision—Estimates and Projections of Urban and Rural Populations and of Urban Agglomerations* (New York: United Nations, 1993), pp. 74–75, 106–07; and Michael A. Cohen, "Cities in Developing Countries: 1975–2000," *Finance and Development* 13 (March 1976): 12–15.

TABLE 9-3   Populations of Urban Agglomerations, 1950, 1970, 1990, 2000, and 2010 (in millions)—ranked by 1990 population

Urban Agglomeration	1950	1970	1990	2000	2010
Tokyo, Japan	6.9	16.5	25.0	28.0	28.9
São Paulo, Brazil	2.4	8.1	18.1	22.6	25.0
New York, U.S.	12.3	16.2	16.1	16.6	17.2
Mexico City, Mexico	3.1	9.1	15.1	16.2	18.0
Shanghai, China	5.3	11.2	13.4	17.4	21.7
Bombay, India	2.9	5.8	12.2	18.1	24.4
Los Angeles, U.S.	4.0	8.4	11.5	13.2	13.9
Buenos Aires, Argentina	5.0	8.4	11.4	12.8	13.7
Seoul, Rep. of Korea	1.0	5.3	11.0	12.9	13.8
Rio de Janeiro, Brazil	2.9	7.0	10.9	12.2	13.3
Beijing, China	3.9	8.1	10.9	14.4	18.0
Calcutta, India	4.4	6.9	10.7	12.7	15.7
Osaka, Japan	4.1	9.4	10.5	10.6	10.6
Paris, France	5.4	8.5	9.3	9.5	9.6
Tianjin, China	2.4	5.2	9.2	12.5	15.7
Jakarta, Indonesia	1.6	3.9	9.2	13.4	17.2
Moscow, Russian Federation	5.4	7.1	9.0	9.8	10.4
Metro Manila, Philippines	1.5	3.5	8.9	12.6	16.1
Cairo, Egypt	2.4	5.3	8.6	12.6	16.1
Delhi, India	1.4	3.5	8.2	11.7	15.6
Karachi, Pakistan	1.3	3.9	7.9	11.9	17.0
Lagos, Nigeria	0.6	2.1	7.7	13.5	21.1
London, U.K.	8.7	8.6	7.3	7.3	7.3
Bangkok, Thailand	1.4	3.2	7.1	9.9	12.7
Chicago, U.S.	4.9	6.7	6.8	7.0	11.0
Teheran, Iran, Islamic Rep.	1.1	3.4	6.7	8.7	11.9
Dakha, Bangladesh	0.5	1.6	6.6	11.5	17.6
Istanbul, Turkey	1.1	2.8	6.5	9.3	11.8
Lima, Peru	1.0	3.0	6.5	8.4	10.1
Essen, Germany	5.3	6.6	6.4	6.6	6.7

The 30 largest urban agglomerations also include (in millions): Milan, Italy 3.6, Berlin, Germany 3.3, Philadelphia, U.S. 2.9, Detroit, U.S. 2.8, Naples, Italy 2.8, Manchester, U.K. 2.5, Birmingham, U.K. 2.3, Boston, U.S. 2.2, and Hamburg, Germany, 2.2 in 1950; Milan, Italy 5.5, Philadelphia, U.S. 4.0, Saint Petersburg, Russian Federation 4.0, Detroit, U.S. 4.0, Naples, Italy 3.6, Shengyang, China 3.5, and Hong Kong 3.5 in 1970; Hyderabad, India 6.7 in 2000; and Hyderabad, India 9.4, Lahore, Pakistan, and Madras, India 8.4 in 2010.

Source: United Nations, Department of Economic and Social Information and Policy Analysis, *World Urbanization Prospects: The 1992 Revision—Estimates and Projections of Urban and Rural Populations and of Urban Agglomerations* (New York: United Nations, 1993), pp. 126–27, 139–43.

urban labor force is because of such migration, especially in predominantly agricultural countries that are newly industrializing. Thus migration to the cities is a larger contributor than natural population growth to urban labor growth in sub-Saharan Africa, the least industrialized LDC region, than it is in more industrialized Latin America, where natural increase is the major source of urban growth.[18]

[18]The merging or expansion of villages can create a statistical illusion of townward migration. For example, two villages of 2,000 each can, through natural increase, expand their built-up areas until they meet to form a single village of 5,000, the usual threshold for reclassification as an urban area. Bombay and Delhi, India, and Kuala Lampur, Malaysia, contain villagelike enclaves. Michael Lipton, *Why Poor People Stay Poor: A Study of Urban Bias in World Development* (London: Temple Smith, 1977), pp. 225–26.

THE LEWIS MODEL

Remember the Lewis model in Chapter 5 that explained how LDC economic growth originated from the increase in the size of the industrial sector relative to the subsistence agricultural sector. The Lewis model also explains migration from rural to urban areas in developing countries. The simplest explanation for rural-urban migration is that people migrate to urban areas when wages there exceed rural wages. Arthur Lewis elaborates on this theory in his explanation of labor transfer from agriculture to industry in a newly industrializing country. In contrast to those economists writing since the early 1970s, who have been concerned about overurbanization, Lewis, writing in 1954, is concerned about possible labor shortages in the expanding industrial sector.

THE HARRIS–TODARO MODEL

The Lewis model does not consider why rural migration continues despite high urban unemployment. John R. Harris and Michael P. Todaro, whose model views a worker's decision to migrate on the basis of wages *and* probability of unemployment, try to close this gap in the Lewis model. They assume that migrants respond to urban-rural differences in expected rather than actual earnings. Suppose the average unskilled rural worker has a choice between being a farm laborer (or working his or her own land) for an annual income of Rs. 3,000 or migrating to the city where he or she can receive an annual wage of Rs. 6,000. Most economists, who assume full employment, would deduce that the worker would seek the higher paying urban job. However, in developing countries with high unemployment rates, this supposition might be unrealistic. Assume that the probability of the worker getting the urban job during a 1-year period is 20 percent. The worker would not migrate, since the **expected income** is Rs. 6,000 × .20, or Rs. 1,200, much less than Rs. 3,000 (3,000 × a probability of 1) on the farm. But if the probability of success is 60 percent, expected urban earnings would be Rs. 6,000 × .60, or Rs. 3600. In this case, it would be rational for the farm worker to seek the urban job. And since most migrants are young (under 25), it would be more realistic to assume an even longer time span in the decision to migrate. The migrant may consider lifetime earnings. Thus if the present value of expected lifetime earnings in the urban job is greater than on the farm, it would be rational to migrate.

According to Harris and Todaro, creating urban jobs by expanding industrial output is insufficient for solving the urban unemployment problem. Instead they recommend that government reduce urban wages, eliminate other factor price distortions, promote rural employment, and generate labor-intensive technologies, policies discussed below.[19]

CRITICISMS OF THE HARRIS–TODARO MODEL

Even without amenities, an ILO study indicates that the ratio of average urban to rural income is more than 2 in Asia and Latin America and 4–5 in Africa (after adjustments for living costs). Assuming a ratio of 2, urban unemployment must be

---

[19]John R. Harris and Michael P. Todaro, "Migration, Unemployment, and Development: A Two-sector Analysis," *American Economic Review* 60, no. 1 (March 1970): 126–42; and Michael P. Todaro, "Income Expectations, Rural-Urban Migration and Employment in Africa," *International Labor Review* 104 (November 1971): 387–413.

50 percent to equate urban and rural expected income. But LDC urban unemployment rarely exceeds 10 to 20 percent, indicating migration does not close the urban and rural expected wage gap. We can explain the gap by adding to the Harris–Todaro urban **formal** and rural sectors the urban **informal sector,** where petty traders, tea shop proprietors, hawkers, street venders, artisans, shoe shiners, street entertainers, garbage collectors, repair persons, cottage industrialists, and other self-employed generate employment and income for themselves in activities with little capital, skill, and entry barriers. These small enterprisers have low start-up costs and profit margins, negotiate agreements outside the formal legal system, and hire workers at less than the legal minimum wage. A substantial share of the LDC urban labor force is relegated to the informal sector: 34 percent of Mexico City's; 45 percent of Bogota, Colombia's; 43 percent of Calcutta, India's; and 50 percent of Lagos, Nigeria's.

The informal-sector's labor supply is affected primarily by wages and population growth in the rural sector. The substantial absorption of rural emigrants in the informal sector explains why migration stops long before rural expected incomes attain urban formal sector ones. Many migrants are neither unemployed nor receiving the prevailing formal sector wage but are working in informal jobs, which facilitate their entry into the urban economy.[20]

THE EFFECT OF OTHER AMENITIES

The decision to migrate is not based merely on differences in earnings. Workers considering migration will look at many other factors; they will compare housing, shops, transport, schools, hospitals, and other amenities in the two places. This decision encompasses much more than the difficulty of keeping youths on the farm once they have seen the bright lights of Paris, Lagos, New Delhi, or São Paulo. In fact it is rare in developing countries for a rural youth to seek a city job without family support. Typically job applicants are sent to the city by their families to diversify family income. While in the city, they may stay with relatives during the job search. The Western stereotype of young urban immigrants as rebels against the family is not common in developing countries, where young people rarely have cars or money essential for independence and they depend heavily on the family for employment, a good marriage, and economic security.

The concentration of social services in LDC urban areas has led to over-urbanization, especially in Africa. A visitor who ventures beyond an African capital city is likely to be shocked by the economic and social disparity existing between the city and the hinterlands. For example, in 1968, the eight-story, 500-bed Centre Hospitalier Universitaire, one of the largest and most modern hospitals in Africa, was built in the affluent section of Abidjan. But the project's funds, given by the French government, were originally intended for 12 regional hospitals in the Ivory Coast. Housing, transport, sewerage, fuel, and staple foods are often

---

[20]Jacques Lecaillon, Felix Paukert, Christian Morrisson, and Dimitri Germidis, *Income Distribution and Economic Development: An Analytical Survey* (Geneva: International Labor Office, 1984), pp. 54–57; N. Vijay Jagannathan, *Informal Markets in Developing Countries* (New York: Oxford University Press, 1987), pp. 57–58; S. V. Sethuraman, *The Urban Informal Sector in Developing Countries* (Geneva: International Labor Office, 1981), p. 17; William E. Cole and Richard D. Sanders, "Internal Migration and Urban Employment in the Third World," *American Economic Review* 75 (June 1985): 481–94; and Malcolm Gillis, Dwight H. Perkins, Michael Roemer, and Donald R. Snodgrass, *Economics of Development* (New York: Norton, 1987), pp. 190–91.

government subsidized in urban areas, where their cost is far more than in rural areas.[21]

Western Approaches to Unemployment

The classical view of employment, prevalent in the West for about 100 years before the Great Depression, was that in the long run, an economy would be in equilibrium at full employment. Flexible wage rates responding to demand and supply ensured that anyone who wanted to work would be employed at the equilibrium wage rate. In the idealized world of classical economics, there would never be involuntary unemployment!

John Maynard Keynes's general theory of income and employment was a response to failure of the classical model in the West in the 1930s. In the Keynesian model, a country's employment increases with GNP. Unemployment occurs because aggregate (total) demand by consumers, businesses, and government for goods and services is not enough for GNP to reach full employment. The Keynesian prescription for unemployment is to increase aggregate demand through more private consumption and investment (by reduced tax rates or lower interest rates) or through more government spending. As long as there is unemployment and unutilized capital capacity in the economy, GNP will respond automatically to increased demand through higher employment.[22]

However, Keynesian theory has little applicability in the LDCs. First, businesses in LDCs cannot respond quickly to increased demand for output. The major limitations to output and employment expansion are usually on the supply side, in the form of shortages of entrepreneurs, managers, administrators, technicians, capital, foreign exchange, raw materials, transportation, communication, and smoothly functioning product and capital markets. In fact, where there are severe limitations in supply response (where output or supply is price inelastic), increased spending may merely result in higher inflation rates.

Second, open unemployment may not be reduced even if spending increases labor demand. As indicated previously, open unemployment occurs primarily in urban areas. However, labor *supply* in urban areas responds rapidly to new employment opportunities. The creation of additional urban jobs through expanded demand means even more entrants into the urban labor force, mainly as migrants from rural areas.

Third, LDCs cannot rely so much as DCs do on changes in fiscal policy (direct taxes and government spending) to affect aggregate demand and employment. Direct taxes (personal income, corporate income, and property taxes) and government expenditures make up a much smaller proportion of GNP in LDCs than in DCs (see Chapter 15).

Fourth, as the discussion concerning Table 9–2 suggested, employment growth is likely to be slower than output growth. In fact in some instances, increasing employment may decrease output. In the 1950s, when Prime Minister Jawaharlal Nehru asked economists on the Indian Planning Commission to expand employment, they asked him how much GNP he was willing to give up. The

---

[21]Josef Gugler and William G. Flanagan, *Urbanization and Social Change in West Africa* (London: Cambridge University Press, 1978).

[22]Michael P. Todaro, *Economic Development in the Third World* (London: Longman, 1977). pp. 174–79, has a thorough discussion of the classical and Keynesian theories of employment.

idea of a tradeoff between output and employment, which astounded the Indian prime minister, is consistent with a planning strategy in which capital and high-level technology are substituted for labor in the modern sector. For example, milling rice by a sheller machine rather than pounding by hand increases output at the expense of employment. However, this tradeoff between employment and output may not be inevitable, as we indicate in the discussion of employment policies.

Causes of Unemployment in Developing Countries

This section focuses on the reasons for urban unemployment in LDCs. As indicated earlier, the LDC urban labor force is growing at about 4 percent per year due to population increases and rural-urban migration. The first two parts of this section indicate why this labor supply cannot be absorbed. Then we look at supply and demand factors that contribute to high unemployment rates among the educated in LDCs.

THE UNSUITABILITY OF TECHNOLOGY

As indicated in Chapter 4, most LDCs are dual economies having a modern manufacturing, mining, agricultural, transportation, and communication sector. But organizational methods and ideas, management systems, machines, processes, and so on, are imported from the DCs to run this modern sector. This technology was designed primarily for the DCs, which have high wages and relatively abundant capital. But as we have pointed out before, technology developed for DCs may not be suitable for LDCs, where wages are low and capital is scarce. On the basis of capital resources available, Frances Stewart estimates that the appropriate capital stock per person in the United States might be eight times that of Brazil, 20 times that of Sri Lanka, and over 45 times that of Nigeria and India.[23]

Often LDCs do not adopt more appropriate technology because of the rigid factor requirements of the production processes in many industries. There simply may be no substitute for producing a good with a modern, highly capital-intensive technique. China learned this the hard way during its Great Leap Forward in 1958 to 1960, which actually resulted in a great leap backward in industrial output. At that time, China emphasized labor-intensive projects that included digging canals, repairing dams, leveling mountains, and building backyard furnaces. Take the case of iron and steel. In 1958, iron and steel utensils and fixtures were taken from Chinese households for use in hundreds of thousands of backyard, steel-and iron-smelting blast furnaces. To one observer, these furnaces shone like innumerable glowworms in the night. However, by 1959, China's backyard furnaces were producing only one-fourth of the planned annual output of 20 million tons of pig iron. Some of this metal was too brittle even to use for simple farm tools. By 1960, the backyard furnaces were abandoned in order to concentrate on large, conventional smelting, blast, and open-hearth furnaces.[24]

---

[23]Frances Stewart, "Technology and Employment in LDCs," in Edgar O. Edwards, ed., *Employment in Developing Nations* (New York: Columbia University Press, 1974), pp. 86–88.

[24]Jan S. Prybyla, *The Political Economy of Communist China* (Scranton, Pa.: International Textbook, 1970), pp. 256, 276–77, 299.

When capital-labor ratios in industry are inflexible, the small amount of capital available in LDCs may not make it possible to employ all the labor force.

FACTOR PRICE DISTORTIONS

However, even when there is a wide choice of various capital-labor combinations, LDCs may not choose labor-intensive methods because of **factor price distortions** that make wages higher and interest rates and foreign exchange costs lower than market-clearing rates.

High Wages in the Modern Sector.   Marx's collaborator, Friedrich Engels, who wrote in the late nineteenth century, referred to Britain's regularly employed industrial proletariat, with its wages and privileges in excess of other European workers, as a **labor aristocracy.** Today some scholars apply Engels's concept to LDCs, pointing out that urban workers tend to be economically far better off than the rural population.

It is true that the prevailing wage for unskilled labor in the modern sector in LDCs is frequently in excess of a market-determined wage because of minimum wage legislation, labor union pressure, and the wage policies of foreign corporations operating in these countries. Often trade unions try to influence wages in the modern sector through political lobbying rather than collective bargaining. Frequently unions became political during a colonial period, when the struggle for employment, higher wages, and improved benefits was tied to a nationalist movement. After independence was gained, the political power of the unions often led to the widespread establishment of official wage tribunals, which frequently base a minimum living wage on the standards of more industrialized countries rather than on market forces in their own country. When foreign firms pay higher wages than domestic firms, the motive may be to gain political favor, avoid political attack, and prevent labor strife, as well as to ensure getting workers of high quality.

In many LDCs, the income of workers paid the legal minimum wage is several times the country's per capita GNP. Even when we adjust for the average number of dependents supported by these workers, the per capita incomes of their households are still usually in excess of the average for the country as a whole. This disparity exists because the minimum wage (when enforced) usually applies to only a small fraction of the labor force, workers in government and in firms with, say, 15 to 20 or more employees. The wage structure for these workers in the **formal sector** is usually higher than those with comparable jobs in the **informal sector.** Wage-employment studies indicate that wages higher than equilibrium reduce employment in the formal sector.

Stabilization and wage-price decontrol during the 1980s and early 1990s, usually under International Monetary Fund and World Bank auspices, contributed to reductions in aggregate demand, real wages, and inflation rates. Food prices increased and real wages fell as Africa decontrolled agricultural and industrial prices during the 1980s. Compared to 1980, real nonagricultural wages dropped considerably during adjustment programs—in Tanzania by 40 percent to 1983; in Zambia, 33 percent to 1984; in Malawi, 24 percent by 1984; in Kenya, 22 percent by 1985; in Zimbabwe, 11 percent by 1984; in Mauritius, 10 percent by 1985; and in Swaziland, 5 percent by 1983.[25] Also compared to 1980, Latin America

---

[25]E. Wayne Nafziger, *The Debt Crisis in Africa* (Baltimore: Johns Hopkins University Press, 1993), pp. 156–58.

underwent substantial real-wage reductions—in Bolivia by 50 percent to 1986, and in Chile by 27 percent to 1986.[26] Unfortunately, adjustment programs that contributed to these real-wage losses were accompanied by reduced government social spending that removed social safety nets, such as food subsidies, health expenditures, and free primary education. Thus, any country reducing wage distortions needs programs to protect the basic needs of urban wage earners during the transition and help them retrain for jobs in expanding sectors. For example, while the adjustments of the 1980s in Africa and Latin America reduced the incomes of wage earners in domestic-oriented industries, public sector employees, and informal-sector workers, these same adjustments increased the incomes of commercial farmers, their wage labor, export-oriented industries, and traders benefiting from exchange-rate and price changes.[27]

Low Capital Costs.   Capital costs in LDCs may be artificially low. Programs encouraging investment, such as subsidized interest rates, liberal depreciation allowances, and tax rebates are common. But at least as important are policies that keep the **price of foreign exchange,** that is, the price of foreign currency in terms of domestic currency, lower than equilibrium.

The LDC central bank restrictions on imports and currency conversion, although ostensibly made to conserve foreign exchange, may actually create foreign currency shortages by keeping the foreign exchange price too low. For example, such restrictions may allow Nigeria to keep the foreign exchange rate at ₦25 = $1 rather than a market-clearing rate of ₦50 = $1. This low price of foreign currency means that an imported machine tagged at $1,000 costs ₦25,000, instead of ₦50,000 (at equilibrium exchange rates). The low foreign exchange price gives importers of capital goods (as well as other goods) an artificial inducement to buy. However, since most countries assign a high priority to importing capital goods, these importers have a better chance of acquiring licenses for foreign exchange from the central bank than do other importers (see Chapter 18).

The low foreign exchange price and the official preference for imported capital goods combine to make the actual price of capital cheaper than its equilibrium price. And when this occurs with wages higher than market rates, LDCs end up using more capital-intensive techniques and employing fewer people than would happen at equilibrium factor prices. Distortions in these prices and fairly inflexible factor requirements for some production processes result in higher unemployment. The end effect is increased income inequalities between property owners and workers and between highly paid workers and the unemployed.

Removing Capital Cost Distortions in India.   In 1991–95, as part of liberalization, the World Bank and IMF required India to reduce distortions of capital, foreign exchange, and other financial markets. For India, this meant raising the real rate of interest to a competitive level, substantial devaluation of the rupee, and reduced protection.

Several entrepreneurs unable to expand because of a lack of credit during non-price rationing of bank loans have been able, since 1991, to acquire capital for

[26]Susan Horton, Ravi Kanbur, and Dipak Mazumdar, "Labor Markets in an Era of Adjustment," *International Labor Review* 130(5–6) (1991): 549.

[27]Simon Commander, "Prices, Markets, and Rigidities: African Agriculture, 1980–88," in Simon Commander, ed., *Structural Adjustment and Agriculture: Theory and Practice in Africa and Latin America* (London: Overseas Development Institute, 1989), p. 239.

innovation and expansion. Others, including managers of large private capital-intensive steel enterprises, have complained about how higher rates of interest have choked off planned expansion. Overall the higher interest rates have rationalized bank lending. However, several small- and medium-sized entrepreneurs have complained about the continuing subsidies for competitors in the public sector (for example, steel), where lower decontrolled prices after 1991 has meant many units in this sector continue to expand despite generating surplus less than a competitive rate of interest.

The liberalized foreign-exchange regime (higher rupee price of the dollar and delicensing of many foreign purchases) is a welcome change for a South Indian marble products producer, who has reduced his time for clearing imported machines through Indian customs from an average of one month before 1991 to two days since 1993. Several other entrepreneurs have found that foreign-currency decontrol has created easier access to imports to improve plant and machinery (albeit at higher rupee prices) and spurred them to seek markets overseas.[28]

In India, state-owned enterprises have opposed financial liberalization, fearing a substantial decline in output with a withdrawal of favorable access to bank credit. Labor unions are disproportionately represented by workers in state-owned enterprises and in government, who generally enjoy relatively high wages and secure jobs. Unions are important political agents, providing financial and electoral support for political parties, such as the Congress Party. The fact that public firms and large private firms with longstanding access to input licenses are supported by politically powerful unions threatens bank, interest-rate, and foreign-exchange deregulation in India.

UNEMPLOYMENT AMONG THE EDUCATED

The overall secondary school enrollment rate in LDCs is about 45 percent. Regrettably, scattered studies suggest that LDCs, especially those with secondary enrollment rates over 40 percent (Korea and Taiwan are exceptions), have unemployment rates of well over 10 percent among persons with some secondary schooling. Sri Lanka (where the overwhelming majority of youths receive some secondary education), India, and Malaysia have unemployment rates in this educational group in excess of 20 percent. The unemployment rate for people with some primary education may be close to 10 percent; for those with some postprimary education even lower; and those with no schooling lower yet.[29] Even so, there is no evidence of a rising unemployment trend among the educated in LDCs, although there is an indication of higher unemployment in particular countries that have instituted universal primary education or rapidly expanded secondary enrollment during the past decade.

Unemployment among the educated appears to be associated with how the labor market adjusts to an influx of school graduates (and dropouts). While political pressures force many LDC public education systems to expand, there are rarely enough jobs for these people once they graduate. Job aspirations among the educated simply cannot be met. During the initial years of educational expansion and replacement of foreigners by locals just after independence from colonial rule,

---

[28]E. Wayne Nafziger and R. Sudarsana Rao, "Indian Entrepreneurship and Innovation under Licensing and Liberalization in India," *Indian Economic Journal* 44 (October-December 1996).

[29]Lyn Squire, *Employment Policy in Developing Countries: A Survey of Issues and Evidence* (New York: Oxford University Press, 1981), p. 70.

graduates were readily absorbed in high-level positions in the civil services, armed forces, government corporations, schools, and private business. However, in subsequent years, there have been far fewer vacancies at these levels.

High unemployment among the educated is in part due to the fact that the wage structure may adjust slowly, especially if the public sector is the major employer of educated workers. Frequently in government service, wages are based on the cost of acquiring the training essential to meet the legal requirements for the job rather than on labor supply and productivity. The signals from this perverse wage-setting mechanism do not provide consistency between educational output and employment opportunities. Furthermore, graduates may be encouraged to wait for well-paid jobs rather than immediately accept a job that pays much less. If the wage difference is high enough and the probability of obtaining a higher paid job is sufficiently large, a period of job seeking will yield a higher expected, lifetime income.

These explanations are consistent with the unemployment patterns indicated earlier. Illiterate people cannot wait for a better paid job. They remain on the farm or take the first job offer. At the other extreme, highly trained people are scarce enough in most LDCs that university graduates get well-paid jobs immediately. But those in between, primary and secondary school graduates (or dropouts), are neither assured of high-paying jobs nor completely out of the running for them. Thus there may be a substantial payoff in a full-time search for a job. The educated unemployed tend to be young, with few dependents, and supported by their families. Most eventually find work, usually within 2 years, although some have to lower their job expectations. Mark Blaug, P. R. G. Layard, and Maureen Woodhall found that while 65 percent of secondary school graduates in India were unemployed in the first year after completing their education, only 36 percent were in the second year, 20 percent in the third, 11 percent in the fourth, 6 percent in the fifth, and 2 percent in the sixth. Except for possible political discontent, the costs associated with this unemployment are not so serious as they might appear.[30]

Policies for Reducing Unemployment

POPULATION POLICIES

As we have already said, rising LDC unemployment is caused by slowly growing job opportunities and a rapidly growing labor force. Family planning programs and programs to improve health, nutrition, education, urban development, income distribution, and opportunities for women can reduce fertility and population growth, thus decreasing labor force size 15 to 20 years hence (Chapter 8). Such fertility reduction should be pursued.

POLICIES TO DISCOURAGE RURAL-URBAN MIGRATION

Unemployment can be reduced by decreasing rural-urban migration. The key to such a decrease is greater rural economic development. As indicated in Chapter 7, this development can be facilitated by eliminating the urban bias in development

---

[30]World Bank, *World Development Report, 1980* (New York: Oxford University Press, 1980), p. 51; and Mark Blaug, P. R. G. Layard, and Maureen Woodhall, *The Causes of Graduate Unemployment in India* (London: Allen Lane, Penguin Books, 1969), p. 90.

projects; removing price ceilings on food and other agricultural goods; setting the foreign exchange price close to a market-clearing rate; increasing capital-saving, technological change in agriculture; locating new industries in rural areas; and providing more schools, housing, food, sewerage, hospitals, health services, roads, entertainment, and other amenities.

However, such expenditures to reduce urban migration may reach diminishing returns quickly. Unemployment among even a fraction of urban migrants may be preferable to widespread low worker productivity in rural areas. In some instances, the problem of urban migration may be a political not an economic one.

APPROPRIATE TECHNOLOGY

In general **appropriate technologies** in LDCs use more unskilled labor than in DCs. The use of more appropriate technology can be stimulated by (1) intraindustry substitution, (2) interproduct substitution, (3) greater income equality, (4) providing fewer refined products and services, (5) government purchase of labor-intensive goods, (6) making sounder choices among existing technologies, (7) factor substitution in peripheral or ancillary activities, (8) using less-modern equipment, (9) the local generation of technologies and, (10) the local adaptation of technologies. In addition policies reducing factor price distortion, as discussed in a subsequent section, encourage the use of more appropriate technology. Let us examine the items in this list more carefully.

1. Encouraging the production of more labor-intensive goods within each industry is possible (for example, manufacturing cotton shirts rather than nylon and sandals instead of fancy leather shoes).

2. A single need may be fulfilled by several goods whose production varies in labor intensity. Housing needs may be more or less fulfilled by the sidewalks of Calcutta, caves, mud huts, multistory apartments, single-family houses, or palaces. In Calcutta bamboo-reinforced mud huts with tin roofs are more labor-intensive (and affordable) than Western-style, single-family dwellings.

3. Macroeconomic studies indicate that goods consumed by the poor are somewhat more labor-intensive than those consumed by the rich. Government policies, including progressive taxes, the subsidized distribution of public goods and essential commodities, and high tariffs or excise taxes on luxury items, may improve income equality. Such policies are likely to increase the demand for labor-intensive goods, such as cotton shirts, sandals, mud huts, and ungraded rice, and reduce the demand for more capital-intensive, luxury goods, particularly imports.[31]

4. One can remove luxury components from existing goods and services. Poor-quality soap produced with labor-intensive techniques can perhaps substitute for Western detergents. Traditional medicine as practiced by barefoot doctors in China may be used instead of the high-income medicine from the West.

5. Government can influence employment by directing official purchases toward labor-intensive goods.

6. Planners or entrepreneurs may choose a more labor-intensive existing technology. However, David Morawetz's survey concludes that the substitution of labor

---

[31]David Morawetz, "Employment Implications of Industrialization in Developing Countries," *Economic Journal* 84, (September 1974): 505–6, 512–14; and Edgar O. Edwards, *Employment in Developing Nations* (New York: Columbia University Press, 1974), p. 29.

for capital is drastically limited depending on the good specified for production. Labor-intensive methods in textiles, brick making, road building, and iron and steel output may be greatly limited if high-quality products are to be produced.[32]

7. Peripheral and ancillary activities, such as materials receiving, handling, packaging, and storage probably offer more factor substitution than materials processing. It is usually possible to use people instead of fork lifts and conveyer belts.

8. Using less modern equipment from DCs (for example, animal-drawn hay rakes or precomputer office equipment) offers some possibilities for more labor-intensive approaches. However, older equipment in good condition is usually not readily available from the industrialized countries.

9. The LDCs can generate technology locally. During the Cultural Revolution from 1966 to 1976, Chinese managers, engineers, and workers were compelled to be inventive, since they were cut off from the outside world. Although Chinese factory workers learned to make their own tools and machines, it was later admitted that this approach was more costly than using available technology.

    The LDCs open to outside techniques can generate some technology through industry research or research organizations designed specifically to producing technology appropriate to their needs and resources. However, many government institutes have failed in developing appropriate technology. Industrial research is usually best done in the context of the producing unit by entrepreneurs, managers, engineers, technicians, and marketing specialists familiar with the industry and the work force. But even this work on labor-intensive technology will not be carried out if factor and product prices are distorted (see below).

    Perhaps the most successful example of generating appropriate technology is the high-yielding wheat varieties used in the Green Revolution in Mexico, India, and Pakistan. Appropriate technology institutes have also been effective in developing natural resources and infrastructure where there is little incentive for private research.

10. Foreign technology may be scaled down to fit LDC skills and resources. Such adaptations in South and Southeast Asia include a 5-horsepower tiller, a low-lift water pump, a McCormick-style thresher, and a jeep-type vehicle.[33]

Sometimes adaptation may, however, require costly use of scarce engineers, managers, and other skilled persons. It may be cheaper to transfer the technology outright rather than to spend the resources to modify it.

Nor may appropriate technologies always save capital, since it is not the only scarce factor in LDCs. Skilled entrepreneurs, managers, government administrators, and labor may be scarce as well. Thus capital-intensive, machine-paced, or process-oriented operations, which save on scarce management, may be appropriate in some cases. For example, modern factory methods for making shoes and wooden furniture use more capital per worker than cottage methods but save on skilled labor, since each operative needs a narrower range of skills than the shoemaker or carpenter who makes the whole product. Thus if skilled labor is a limitation, using the more modern, capital-intensive methods may be suitable.[34]

[32]David Morawetz, "Employment Implications of Industrialization in Developing Countries," *Economic Journal* 84 (September 1974), 515–23.

[33]Amir U. Khan, "Appropriate Technologies: Do We Transfer, Adapt, or Develop?" in Edgar O. Edwards, ed., *Employment in Developing Nations* (New York: Columbia University Press, 1974), pp. 223–33.

[34]David Morawetz, "Employment Implications of Industrialization in Developing Countries," *Economic Journal* 84 (September 1974), 517.

To conclude this section, there is some scope for more appropriate technology to increase the use of labor. Nevertheless, cheaper alternative technologies to those used in DCs are not as widely available as many economists have thought.

POLICIES TO REDUCE FACTOR PRICE DISTORTION

The LDCs can increase employment by decreasing distortions in the prices of labor and capital. These distortions can be reduced through the following policies: (1) curtailing wages in the organized sector, (2) encouraging small-scale industry, (3) decreasing subsidies to capital investors, (4) revising worker legislation—reviewing termination practices and severance payment requirements, (5) reducing social security programs and payroll taxation, (6) increasing capital utilization and, (7) setting market-clearing exchange rates.

1. Reducing wages increases employment opportunities when the price elasticity of labor demand (minus the percentage change in the quantity of labor demanded divided by the percentage change in the wage for a unit of labor) is greater than one (or elastic). However, wage cuts are not effective when labor demand is inelastic. Labor demand is more inelastic (1) when product demand is inelastic, (2) the smaller the fraction labor is of total cost, (3) the less other factors can be substituted for labor, (4) when factor supplies other than labor are inelastic, and (5) the more inflexible the product's administered price.[35] Moreover, although there may be some labor aristocrats around, they do not comprise the bulk of LDC wage earners. Furthermore, care should be taken not to weaken the ability of trade unions to protect worker rights and income shares against powerful employers.

2. Encouraging the informal sector, especially small-scale industry, usually reduces unit wage costs and has a favorable employment effect. Firms with less than 50 workers employ over half the industrial labor force in LDCs, including 71 percent in Colombia, 70 percent in Nigeria, and 40 percent in Malaysia (43 percent in Japan and 34 percent in Switzerland!).

   Small firms have a more favorable employment effect than large firms, because they require less capital and more labor per unit of output and because their factor prices are much closer to market prices. Wage legislation often does not apply to, or is not enforced in, small firms; their wages are lower than in large ones. Additionally, the small firm's less-subsidized capital costs are close to market rates.

   Government can encourage small-scale industry through such policies as industrial extension service, technical help, and preferred, official buying. However, subsidized credit and imports for small firms merely encourage the use of more capital-intensive techniques.[36]

3. As just implied, a country can decrease capital-intensive techniques and unemployment by not subsidizing capital and credit.

4. A number of economists contend that worker legislation in many LDCs holds back industrial employment growth as much as high wages. Such legislation makes it difficult to fire an employee and requires large severance pay when termination occurs. These economists reason that employers may not hire extra workers when they see opportunities for sales expansion if they know that they

---

[35]Paul A. Samuelson, *Economics* (New York: McGraw-Hill, 1980), p. 525.
[36]David Morawetz, "Employment Implications of Industrialization in Developing Countries," *Economic Journal* 84 (September 1974), 524–26.

will not be able to release them if the expansion is only temporary. So far evidence fails to demonstrate that the effect of these worker policies is positive.

5. A reduction in social security payments and payroll taxes will increase the demand for, and supply of, labor at a given wage and thus increase employment. However, the cost of these policies would be a reduction in overall savings and an increase in poverty among the aged, physically impaired, and in families losing a bread winner.

6. The LDCs can reduce foreign trade and currency restrictions to raise the price of foreign exchange to a market-clearing rate. This rate discourages using foreign-made capital goods by raising their domestic currency price. This increase in the price of capital will stimulate the greater use of labor-intensive techniques. Furthermore, a foreign exchange rate close to equilibrium is probably a more effective policy for promoting exports and import replacements than subsidies, tariffs, quotas, and licenses, all of which distort the efficient allocation of resources.

Additionally, a simple way of increasing employment is to utilize capital stock more intensively by working two or three shifts rather than one. Since LDCs appear to have low capital utilization rates compared to DCs, employment could be substantially increased if there were enough skilled managers and foremen for extra shifts.

EDUCATIONAL POLICY

The challenge here is to reform the educational system to achieve a balance between LDC educational output and labor needs. Several strategies are suggested.

1. Where politically feasible, educational budgets in many LDCs should grow more slowly and be more oriented toward primary education and scientific and technical learning. The problem of unemployed secondary school graduates and dropouts is usually greatest where secondary education has expanded rapidly in recent years. In addition many secondary school graduates are trained in the humanities and social sciences but lack the scientific, technical, and vocational skills for work in a modern economy. Even though rapidly expanding primary education may increase unemployment, such a negative effect is somewhat offset by the higher literacy rate achieved and increased income equality. (See also Chapter 10, which indicates that the rate of return to primary education in LDCs is generally higher than to secondary education.)

2. Subsidies for secondary and higher education should be reduced, since they encourage a surplus of educated people, some of whom become unemployed. In addition as indicated in Chapter 10, they redistribute income to the rich. However, in order to improve income distribution, subsidies might be made for scholarships for the poor.

3. Increase the flexibility of pay scales. Occupational choice should change with shifts in supply and demand. When there is a surplus of engineers or lawyers (as in India in the early 1970s), salaries should fall, so that both graduates and prospective students will shift to another field.

4. Inequalities and discrimination in both education and employment should be minimized. To reduce the burden on the educational system and improve its performance, LDCs should pursue policies that encourage greater reliance on job-related learning experiences for advancement; they should use successful work experience as a criterion for educational advancement and reduce discrimination in hiring and promotion. In some instances where the highly educated are se-

verely underutilized, it is because ethnic, regional, and sex discrimination keeps the most qualified workers from finding appropriate jobs.

5. Job rationing by educational certification must be modified. Frequently overstated job specifications make overeducation necessary for employment. Requiring a secondary education to sweep the factory floor or a university degree to manage a livestock ranch is counterproductive. Employers should be encouraged to set realistic job qualifications, even though the task of job rationing may be made somewhat more difficult.[37]

The policies on migration, education, technology, and factor price distortions discussed in the last four sections may not always be politically feasible. Governments sometimes lose the political support they need to function when they revise labor codes, curtail wages, eliminate capital subsidies, adjust foreign exchange rates, reduce secondary and higher education subsidies, or make government pay scales more flexible.

GROWTH-ORIENTED POLICIES

Clearly South Korea and Taiwan achieved rapid employment growth partly through policies like those we have discussed and partly through rapid economic growth. Other things being equal, faster rates of growth in production contribute to faster employment growth. But other things are not always equal, as suggested by our discussion on rural-urban migration, appropriate technology, factor prices, and the educated labor market.

Summary

1. Production depends on the flow of natural resources, capital, labor, entrepreneurship, and technology per unit of time.

2. The openly unemployed, those without a job who are actively looking for one, are usually urban, 15–24 years old, and among the well educated.

3. The underemployed, the visibly active but underutilized, the impaired, and the unproductive are all underutilized in LDC labor forces.

4. The labor force grows faster than job opportunities, so unemployment grows. About one-third percent of the labor force in low-income countries (excluding China and India) is employed outside agriculture. The labor force in these countries is growing at about 2.5 percent per year. If employment in agriculture remains constant, the industrial sector must increase employment by about 7.5 percent per year to absorb this extra labor. Industrial employment rarely grows this fast in these countries.

5. Although many economists believe that there is widespread disguised unemployment, or zero marginal productivity, in LDC agriculture, the available evidence does not support the contention.

6. Rural-urban migration contributes almost as much to the rapid growth of the urban labor force in LDCs as population growth. Lewis argues that an unlimited

[37]Edgar O. Edwards and Michael P. Todaro, "Education, Society, and Development: Some Main Themes and Suggested Strategies for International Assistance," *World Development* 2 (January 1974): 29–30; and Lyn Squire, *Employment Policy in Developing Countries: A Survey of Issues and Evidence* (New York: Oxford University Press, 1981), pp. 194–205.

supply of underutilized farm labor migrates to urban areas for wages only slightly in excess of rural wages. Harris and Todaro indicate, however, that farm workers considering a move to an urban area consider urban-rural differences in unemployment as well as wages.

7. Keynesian unemployment from deficient aggregate demand is not important in LDCs because of the slow response in output to demand increases, ineffective fiscal policy, rural-urban migrants in the labor market, and possible tradeoffs between employment and output from inappropriate technology.

8. Technology designed for the industrialized countries, which have a relative abundance of capital and scarcity of labor, is often not suitable for LDCs, with their abundant labor and scarce capital. This inappropriate technology increases unemployment. However, in some instances, such as in the iron and steel industries, the capital-labor ratios may be invariable. The LDCs must use the same technology as DCs in such a case.

9. Capital may be priced higher and labor priced lower than equilibrium prices in LDCs because of government wage and social legislation, trade union pressures, and a low price for foreign exchange.

10. The LDC unemployment is higher among the educated than the uneducated because the educated may have unrealistic earnings expectations or job preferences and because wages paid to educated workers are often inflexible.

11. Policies to reduce unemployment include programs to reduce fertility; encourage rural development and amenities; substitute labor-intensive production techniques for capital-intensive approaches; substitute products that use labor more intensively; redistribute income to the poor; increase official purchases from small-scale, labor-intensive firms; generate new technology locally; adapt existing technology; curtail wages in the organized sector; decrease subsidies to capital; increase capital utilization; set equilibrium foreign exchange rates; resist pressures for a too rapid expansion of upper-level education and refuse to subsidize this level of education; increase the share of spending for primary schooling; stress scientific and technical education; improve wage flexibility at the higher levels; and reduce job rationing by educational certification.

Terms to Review

- unemployment
- underemployment
- disguised unemployment
- zero marginal productivity of labor
- limited technical substitutability of factors
- expected income

- Keynesian theory of income and employment
- factor price distortions
- labor aristocracy
- formal sector
- informal sector
- price of foreign exchange
- appropriate technology

Questions to Discuss

1. What inputs determine the level of national product in a given year? Are these inputs stocks or flows?

2. What supply and demand factors for industrial labor explain rising LDC unemployment rates?

3. How widespread is disguised unemployment in LDCs?

4. Explain urban-rural migration in LDCs.

5. What factors contribute to high urban unemployment in LDCs? Why are macroeconomic theories based on Western experience inadequate in explaining this high unemployment?

6. What policies can LDC governments undertake to reduce the unemployment rate?

7. Explain why rural-urban migration persists in light of substantial urban unemployment (for example, 15 percent or more). How would the Harris–Todaro model explain this situation? Evaluate the Harris–Todaro model.

8. What is the urban informal sector? How does the informal sector labor market affect (or how is it affected by) labor markets in the urban formal and rural sectors?

9. What causes unemployment among the educated in LDCs? What educational policies will reduce this unemployment?

10. What is Lewis's explanation for rural-urban migration? Why do critics think that the Lewis model overstates rural-urban migration?

Guide to Readings

World Development Report, 1979, pp. 46–58, and Morawetz (note 34) analyze the inability of modern industry to provide adequate employment opportunities for the rapidly growing LDC labor force. Policies to reduce unemployment are discussed in these two sources in addition to Squire (note 6) and the edited volume by Edwards (note 8), especially Stewart (note 23). Unemployment among the educated is treated by Edwards and Todaro (note 37) and the *World Development Report, 1980*, pp. 46–51.

Kao, Anschel, and Eicher (note 13) have a comprehensive review of the theoretical and empirical literature on disguised unemployment in agriculture. Lewis (chapter 5, note 21), and Harris and Todaro (note 19) discuss the determinants of migration from rural and urban areas. See also Oded Stark, "Rural-to-Urban Migration in LDCs: A Relative Deprivation Approach," *Economic Development and Cultural Change* 32 (January 1984): 475–86; and Oded Stark and David Levhari, "On Migration and Risk in LDCs," *Economic Development and Cultural Change* 31 (October 1982): 191–96.

Lisa Peattie, "An Idea in Good Currency and How It Grew: The Informal Sector," *World Development* 15 (July 1987): 851–60, discusses different concepts of the informal sector and why they are so fuzzy. For a critique, see Nasreen Khundker, "The Fuzziness of the Informal Sector: Can We Afford to Throw Out the Baby with the Bath Water? (A Comment)," *World Development* 16 (October 1988): 1263–65.

10

C H A P T E R

Education, Training, and Human Capital

Scope of the Chapter

Nobel laureate Simon S. Kuznets argues that the major stock of an economically advanced country is not its physical capital but "the body of knowledge amassed from tested findings and discoveries of empirical science, and the capacity and training of its population to use this knowledge effectively.[1] The contrast in economic growth between Japan and Germany, on the one hand, and third-world countries, on the other after World War II illustrates the importance of labor quality. Although much of the physical capital in Germany and Japan was in ruins or depleted, their economies grew rapidly after the war, since the skill, experience, education, training, health, discipline, and motivation of the existing labor force remained intact.

Why is labor productivity higher in DCs such as Japan and Germany than in LDCs? In this chapter, we are not interested in productivity differences attributed to capital and land. Rather we focus on the effect of variables, such as (1) formal education and training; (2) socialization, childrearing, motivation, and attitudes; and (3) the health and physical condition of the labor force, including a section on HIV infection and the AIDS epidemic.

Education and Training

INVESTMENT IN HUMAN CAPITAL

Remember the discussion of human capital in Chapter 5. Theodore W. Schultz argues that

> Capital goods are always treated as produced means of production. But in general the concept of capital goods is restricted to material factors, thus excluding

---

[1]Simon S. Kuznets, "Toward a Theory of Economic Growth," in Robert Lekachman, ed., *National Policy for Economic Welfare at Home and Abroad* (Garden City, N.Y.: Doubleday, 1955), p. 39.

the skills and other capabilities of man that are augmented by investment in human capital. The acquired abilities of a people that are useful in their economic endeavor are obviously produced means of production and in this respect forms of capital, the supply of which can be augmented.[2]

ECONOMIC RETURNS TO EDUCATION

Education helps individuals fulfill and apply their abilities and talents. It increases productivity, improves health and nutrition, and reduces family size. Schooling presents specific knowledge, develops general reasoning skills, causes values to change, increases receptivity to new ideas, and changes attitudes toward work and society. But our major interest is its effect in reducing poverty and increasing income.

World Bank economists George Psacharopoulos and Maureen Woodhall indicate that the average return to education (and human capital) is higher than that to physical capital in LDCs but lower in DCs. Among human investments, they argue that primary education is the most effective for overcoming absolute poverty and reducing income inequality. This is especially true in Bangladesh and sub-Saharan Africa, where less than three-fourths of the children of primary school age are enrolled in school.

Yet in the 1960s, planners in developing countries favored secondary and higher education that met the high-level labor requirements of the modern sector rather than establishing literacy and general education as goals for the labor force as a whole. Psacharopoulos, in a study in 1994 on the social rates of return to educational investment, indicates the highest average returns are from primary education. He shows that returns to primary education were 18 percent per year, secondary education 13 percent, and higher education 11 percent (Table 10–1). The higher rates of returns to primary education are consistent with diminishing returns to increased dollars per pupil. Public expenditure per student is more for higher and secondary education than for primary education. Sub-Saharan Africa

TABLE 10-1   Average Social Returns to Education

Region	Primary Education	Secondary Education	Higher Education
Sub-Saharan Africa	24	18	11
Asia	20	13	12
Latin America and the Caribbean	18	13	12
Organization for Economic Cooperation and Development	14	10	9
World	18	13	11

Note: In all cases, the figures are "social" rates of return: The costs include foregone earnings (what the students could have earned had they not been in school) as well as both public and private outlays; the benefits are measured by income before tax. (The "private" returns to individuals exclude public costs and taxes, and are usually larger.)

Source: George Psacharopoulos, "Returns to Investment in Education: A Global Update," *World Development* 22 (September 1994): 1328.

---

[2]Theodore W. Schultz, *Transforming Traditional Agriculture* (New Haven: Yale University Press, 1964).

spends 100 times as much per pupil for higher education as for primary education! (See Table 10–2.) Africa's higher education costs result partly from an inability to achieve economies of scale. Thus in the 1970s, in Ghana educating 20,000 students cost $3,500 per student, while in India, 2,700,000 (with a network of local affiliated colleges to major universities in each state) cost only $250 per student.[3] On the other hand, returns to primary education reach a point of diminishing returns, declining as literacy rates increase (Table 10–1).

John B. Knight, Richard H. Sabot, and D.C. Hovey argue that studies by Psacharopoulos and Woodhall are based on methodologically flawed estimates. While average rates of return on primary education were higher than that to secondary education, the marginal rates of returns to the cohort entering into the labor market were lower for primary education than for secondary education. In the 1960s and 1970s, primary graduates were in scarce supply; a primary-school certificate was a passport to a white-collar job. In the 1990s, however, after decades of rapid educational expansion and the displacement of primary graduates by secondary graduates, primary completers are fortunate to get even the most menial blue-collar wage job. As education expands and as secondary completers displace primary completers in many occupations, successive cohorts of workers with primary-school certificates "filter down" into lesser jobs and lower rates of return. However, secondary graduates, who have acquired more occupation-specific human capital, resist the reduction of scarcity rents and the compression of the occupational wage structure with educational expansion. Thus

TABLE 10–2   Public Expenditures on Elementary and Higher Education per Student, 1976

Region	Higher (Postsecondary) Education	Elementary Education	Ratio of Higher to Elementary Education
Sub-Saharan Africa	3819	38	100.5
South Asia	117	13	9.0
East Asia	471	54	8.7
Middle East and North Africa	3106	181	17.2
Latin America and Caribbean	733	91	8.1
Industrialized countries	2278	1157	2.0
U.S.S.R. and Eastern Europe	957	539	1.8

Note: Figures shown are averages (weighted by enrollment) of costs (in 1976 dollars) in the countries in each region for which data were available.

Source: World Bank, *World Development Report, 1980* (New York: Oxford University Press, 1980), p. 46.

---

[3]George Psacharopoulos and Maureen Woodhall, *Education for Development: An Analysis of Investment Choices* (New York: Oxford University Press, 1985), pp. 21–22, 196–97; George Psacharopoulos, "Returns to Education: A Further International Update and Implications," *Journal of Human Resources* 20 (Fall 1985): 583–604; and George Psacharopoulos, "Returns to Investment in Education: A Global Update," *World Development* 22 (September 1994): 1325–43.

The returns to investment in primary education are especially high in countries such as Bangladesh, "where mass illiteracy prevails." United Nations Economic and Social Commission for Asia and the Pacific, *Human Resources Development: Intersectoral Coordination and Other Issues* (New York, 1992), p. 38.

Knight, Sabot, and Hovey question whether LDCs should place a priority on investment in primary education.[4]

How do educational differentials in lifetime earnings vary internationally (assuming a 10-percent annual interest rate on future earnings)? In the late 1960s, the ratio of higher educational to primary education earnings in Africa (8–10) was much higher than Latin American (4–5), Asian (3–6), and North American (3) ratios. Indeed in Africa, where university and even secondary graduates have been scarce, the premium to graduates of both levels of education (highly subsidized) is high, while the premium is low for both levels in North America.[5]

NONECONOMIC BENEFITS OF EDUCATION

As we have hinted at earlier, schooling is far more than the acquisition of skills for the production of goods and services. Education has both consumer-good and investment-good components. The ability to appreciate literature or to understand the place of one's society in the world and in history—although they may not help a worker produce steel or grow millet more effectively—are skills that enrich life, and they are important for their own sakes. People may be willing to pay for schooling of this kind even when its economic rate of return is zero or negative.

Some returns to education cannot be captured by increased individual earnings. Literacy and primary education benefit society as a whole. In this situation where the social returns to education exceed private returns, there is a strong argument for a public subsidy.

EDUCATION AS SCREENING

It may be inadequate to measure social rates of return to education through the wage, which does not reflect added productivity in imperfectly competitive labor markets. In LDCs access to high-paying jobs is often limited through educational qualifications. Education may certify an individual's productive qualities to an employer without enhancing them. In some developing countries, especially in the public sector, the salaries of university and secondary graduates may be artificially inflated and bear little relation to relative productivity. Educational requirements serve primarily to ration access to these inflated salaries. Earnings differences associated with different educational levels would thus overstate the effect of education on productivity.

On the other hand, using educational qualifications to screen job applicants is not entirely wasteful and certainly preferable to other methods of selection, such as class, caste, or family connections. Moreover, the wages of skilled labor relative to unskilled labor have steadily declined as the supply of educated labor has grown. Even the public sector is sensitive to supply changes: Relative salaries of teachers and civil servants are not so high in Asia, where educated workers are more abundant, as in Africa, where they are more scarce.

---

[4]John B. Knight, Richard H. Sabot, and D.C. Hovey, "Is the Rate of Return on Primary Schooling Really 26 Per Cent?" *Journal of African Economies* 1 (August 1992): 192–205; and John B. Knight and Richard H. Sabot, *Education, Productivity, and Inequality: The East African Natural Experiment* (Oxford: Oxford University Press, 1990), pp. 170–71.

[5]Keith Hinchliffe, "Education, Individual Earnings, and Earnings Distribution," *Journal of Development Studies* 11 (January 1975): 152–56.

The World Bank, which surveys seventeen studies in LDCs that measure increases in annual output based on 4 years of primary education versus no primary education, tries to eliminate the screening effect by measuring productivity directly rather than wages.[6] All these studies were done in small-scale agriculture where educational credentials are of little importance. The studies found that, other things being equal, the returns to investment in primary education were as high as those to investment in machines, equipment, and buildings. These studies conjectured that primary education helps people to work for long-term goals, to keep records, to estimate the returns of past activities and the risks of future ones, and to obtain and evaluate information about changing technology. All in all, these studies of farmer productivity demonstrate that investment in education pays off in some sectors even where educational qualifications are not used as screening devices.

M. Boissière's, J. B. Knight's, and R. H. Sabot's study in Kenya and Tanzania, which separates skills learned in school from its screening effect, shows that earning ability increases substantially with greater literacy and numeracy (as measured by tests given by researchers), both in manual and nonmanual jobs. These skills enable mechanics, machinists, and forklift drivers, as well as accountants, clerks, and secretaries, to do a better job. But cognitive skills, especially literacy and numeracy, are not certified by schooling but discovered on the job by the employer, who is willing to pay for them by giving a wage premium over time. Earnings do not, however, increase much with increased reasoning ability (measured by Raven's Progressive Matrices' pictorial pattern matching, for which literacy and numeracy provide no advantage) or increased years of school.

In both countries, learning school lessons, not just attending school and receiving certification, substantially affects performance and earnings in work. However, earning differences between primary and secondary graduates could reflect screening or alternatively unmeasured noncognitive skills acquired in secondary education.[7] Research in countries at other levels of economic development is essential before we can generalize about the effects of screening and cognitive achievement.

EDUCATION AND EQUALITY

The student who attends school receives high rates of return to what his or her family spends. Yet poor families who might be willing to borrow for more education usually cannot. A simple alternative is for government to reduce the direct costs of education by making public schooling, especially basic primary education, available and free. Expanding primary education reduces income inequality and favorably affects equality of opportunity. As primary schooling expands, children in rural areas, the poorest urban children, and girls will all have more chance of going to school. In general, public expenditures on primary education redistribute income toward the poor, who have larger families and almost no access to pri-

---

[6]The next three sections rely on World Bank, *World Development Report, 1980* (New York: Oxford University Press, 1980), pp. 46–53; Henry J. Bruton, *Principles of Development Economics* (Englewood Cliffs, N.J.: Prentice-Hall, 1965), pp. 205–21; M. Boissière, J. B. Knight, and R. H. Sabot, "Earnings, Schooling, Ability, and Cognitive Skills," *American Economic Review* 75 (December 1985): 1016–30; and E. Wayne Nafziger, *Inequality in Africa: Political Elites, Proletariat, Peasants, and the Poor* (Cambridge: Cambridge University Press, 1988), pp. 133–35.

[7]M. Boissière, J. B. Knight, and R. H. Sabot, "Earnings, Schooling, Ability, and Cognitive Skills," *American Economic Review* 75 (December 1985): 1016–30.

vate schooling.[8] Public spending on secondary and higher education, on the other hand, redistributes income to the rich, since poor children have little opportunity to benefit from it (Table 10–3).

The links between parental education, income, and ability to provide education of quality mean educational inequalities are likely to be transmitted from one generation to another. Public primary school, while disproportionately subsidizing the poor, still costs the poor to attend. Moreover, access to secondary and higher education is highly correlated with parental income and education. In Kenya and Tanzania, those from a high socioeconomic background are more likely to attend high-cost primary schools, with more public subsidy; better teachers, equipment, and laboratories; and higher school–leaving examination scores; which admit them to the best secondary schools and the university. The national secondary schools, which receive more government aid and thus charge lower fees, take only 5 percent of primary school graduates. Additionally, the explicit private cost for secondary school graduates to attend the university (highly subsidized) is low, and the private benefit is high. Yet this cost (much opportunity cost) of secondary and higher education is still often a barrier to the poor. Moreover, those with affluent and educated parents cannot only finance education more easily, but are more likely to have the personal qualities, good connections, and better knowledge of opportunities to receive higher salaries and nonmanual jobs. Climbing the educational ladder in Kenya, Tanzania, and many other LDCs depends on income as well as achievement.

Even if girls never enter the labor force, educating them may be one of the best investments a country can make in future economic welfare. Studies indicate clearly that educating girls substantially improves household nutrition and reduces fertility and child mortality.[9] Yet in most parts of the developing world, especially South Asia, the Middle East, and Africa, the educational bias in favor of male enrollment is pronounced (Figure 10–1). Parents view education for their daughters as less useful than for their sons. Frequently they fear that education

TABLE 10–3   Public Education Spending per Household (in dollars)

Income Group[a]	Malaysia, 1974[b]		Colombia, 1974[c]	
	Primary	*Presecondary*	*Primary*	*University*
Poorest 20 percent	135	4	48	1
Richest 20 percent	45	53	9	46

[a]Households ranked by income per person.

[b]Federal costs per household.

[c]Subsidies per household.

Source: World Bank, *World Development Report, 1980* (New York: Oxford University Press, 1980), p. 50.

---

[8]George Clarke, "More Evidence on Income Distribution and Growth." Policy Research Working Paper 1064, World Bank, Policy Research Department, Washington, D.C., 1992; World Bank, *World Development Report, 1980* (New York: Oxford University Press, 1980), pp. 46–53; and World Bank, *The East Asian Miracle: A World Bank Policy Research Report* (New York: Oxford University Press, 1993), p. 197.

[9]United Nations Economic and Social Commission for Asia and the Pacific, *Socio-Cultural Impact of Human Resources Development* (New York, 1992), pp. 16–19.

FIGURE 10-1   Enrollment Ratios by Region, 1960–91
Enrollment ratios are generally higher in East Asia and lower in sub-Saharan Africa than other LDC regions. These ratios are higher among males than females, especially in South Asia, the Middle East, and Africa.

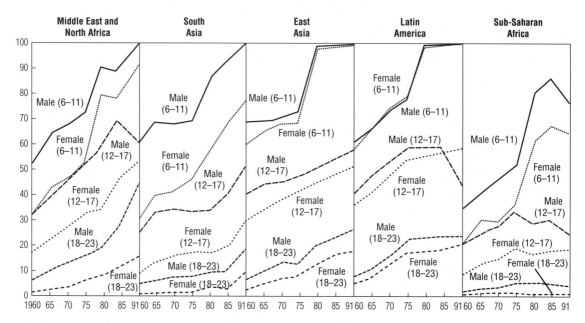

Sources: World Bank, *World Development Report, 1980* (New York: Oxford University Press, 1980), p. 47; World Bank, *World Development Report, 1983* (New York: Oxford University Press, 1983), pp. 266–67; World Bank, *World Development Report, 1988* (New York: Oxford University Press, 1988), pp. 280–81; and World Bank, *World Development Report, 1994* (New York: Oxford University Press, 1994), pp. 216–17.

will harm a daughter's marriage prospects or domestic life. A girl's education may result in fewer economic benefits, especially if she faces job discrimination, marries early and stops working, or moves to her husband's village. However, educating her does increase the opportunity for paid employment, and families waste no time in educating their daughters when cultural change reduces the bias against woman in the labor market.

SECONDARY AND HIGHER EDUCATION

While primary education in LDCs is important, secondary and higher education should not be abandoned. Despite the high numbers of educated unemployed in some developing countries, especially among humanities and social sciences (but not economics!) graduates,[10] there are some severe shortages of skilled peo-

---

[10]George Psacharopoulos, "Returns to Education: A Further International Update and Implications," *Journal of Human Resources* 20 (Fall 1985): 590–91, 603–4, indicates that the average returns to human capital investment for fourteen DCs and LDCs are higher for economics than six other fields, which suggests that unemployment rates for economic graduates are also low.

ple. Although these shortages vary from country to country, quite often the shortages are in vocational, technical, and scientific areas.[11]

One possible approach to reduce the unit cost of training skilled people is to use more career in-service or on-the-job training. The following discussion suggests other ways.

In most countries, government subsidizes students beyond the primary level. Yet the families of these students are generally much better off than the national average (Table 10–3). For example, in Tunisia, the proportion of children from higher income groups is nine times larger in universities than in primary schools. These students should probably be charged tuition and other fees to cover the costs of their higher education, since its individual rewards are large. Charging these richer students allows government to spend more on poorer children, who can be granted scholarships. These policies may be difficult to implement. Parents of postprimary children are usually politically influential and will probably resist paying greater educational costs.

Correspondence courses can dramatically reduce the cost of some postprimary schooling, including teacher training. Such courses may not be feasible for lab subjects and the like; however where they are possible, they can usually be provided at a fraction of the cost of traditional schools and allow would-be students to earn income while continuing their education. Studies indicate that Brazil, Kenya, and the Dominican Republic have all conducted correspondence courses that have effectively taught people in remote areas.

In many instances, LDCs can reduce the number of university specializations, relying instead on foreign universities for specialized training in fields where few students and expensive equipment lead to excessive costs per person. However, care must be taken to prevent either a substantial brain drain from LDCs to DCs (more on this later) or a concentration of foreign-educated children among the rich and influential.

Educational options will widen as LDCs increase their investment in telecommunications. The electronic and video media offer extensive future opportunities for enhanced schooling, learning, and continuing education.

PLANNING FOR SPECIALIZED EDUCATION AND TRAINING

The following three skill categories require little or no specific training. The people having these skills move readily from one type of occupation to another.

1. The most obvious category comprises skills simple enough to be learned by short observation of someone performing the task. Swinging an ax, pulling weeds by hand, or carrying messages are such easily acquired skills that educational planners can ignore them.
2. Some skills require rather limited training (perhaps a year or less) that can best be provided on the job. These include learning to operate simple machines, drive trucks, and perform some construction jobs.

---

[11]United Nations Economic and Social Commission for Asia and the Pacific, *Human Resources Development: Intersectoral Coordination and Other Issues* (New York, 1992), pp. 38–51, notes substantial shortages of people with scientific and technological education in China and South Asia. Farmers and informal-sector entrepreneurs and workers in rural areas especially benefit from simple technical training.

3. Another skill category requires little or no specialized training but considerable general training—at least secondary and possible university education. Many administrative and organizational jobs, especially in the civil service, require a good general educational background, as well as sound judgment and initiative. Developing these skills means more formal academic training than is required in the two previous categories.

We have already discussed how public expenditures are best allocated between primary, secondary, and postsecondary education to ensure these skill levels, but we add that *highly* specialized training and education are usually not essential in these skill categories.

It is very important how a LDC develops the more specialized skills it will need in its labor force. There is a wide range of skills especially relevant to LDCs that require specific training and among which there is very little substitution. Most professionals—medical doctors, engineers, accountants, teachers, lawyers, social workers, and geologists—are included in this category. Generally a person with these skills has gone through 12 to 20 years of training, several of which have involved specialized training. The skill has been created at great cost, and the worker's productivity depends very much on the general pattern of the country's economic development.

Educational and personnel planning are most pressing where little substitution among skills is possible. For example, if a country has large oil deposits and its educational system produces only lawyers, sociologists, and poets but no geologists and petroleum engineers, establishing an oil industry will be difficult unless the country can import the needed technicians.

The fixed input-output planning method uses past information to derive a relationship between specialized human inputs and outputs. This approach first estimates the future level and composition of output. The assumed input-output relationship then enables the planner to estimate the demand for persons to fill the expected jobs. Given the length of training required for highly skilled jobs, the production of highly trained persons to fill them is nearly fixed in the short run. However, plans might be made for, say, 5 years, 10 years, and 20 years hence, with educational programs to meet the needs of specialized personnel. These programs would include training teachers by the time needed.

Yet the fixed input-output approach does not recognize some possibilities for substitution. First, if the supply of teachers is inadequate or too costly, planners might hire foreign teachers or send students abroad. Second, one category of high-level skills may substitute for another—nurses or paramedics for a medical doctor, technicians for an engineer, and elementary teachers trained in postprimary teachers' colleges for university graduates in education. Third, it is not necessarily true that the array of skills produced should adapt to the desired output composition. Perhaps the relationship can be reversed, especially in an economy open to international trade and specialization. For example, if a country has an abundance of potters and brass workers and a scarcity of chemical engineers, it may be less costly, especially in the short run, to export pottery and brass goods and import chemicals. Other alternatives would be to hire foreign chemical engineers or provide economic incentives to encourage foreign enterprises to produce chemicals domestically.[12]

---

[12]This and the next two sections rely heavily on Henry J. Bruton, *Principles of Development Economics* (Englewood Cliffs, N. J.: Prentice Hall, 1965), pp. 205–21.

ACHIEVING CONSISTENCY IN PLANNING FOR EDUCATED PERSONNEL

What can be done to reduce the shortages and surpluses of particular types of high-level personnel in LDCs? Various government departments (or ministries) must coordinate their activities.[13] For example, the Department of Education's planning may conflict with that of the Department of Economic Planning. Educational policy may be to turn out historians, psychologists, and artists, while the development plan calls for engineers, accountants, and agronomists.

Chapter 9 mentioned some of the distortions that occur in the market for educated labor. The educated may have unrealistic earning expectations and job preferences, and wage rates may adjust slowly to changes in the supply and demand for skills. Chapter 9 suggested certain policies to handle this market distortion. These included slower growth in educational budgets, orientation toward scientific and technical learning, a reduction in subsidies for secondary and higher education to high- and middle-income students, a modification of job rationing by educational certification, and more flexible wages.

In most LDCs, the supply and demand for high-level personnel could be equalized if wages were adjusted to productivity. For example, in Kenya a primary school teacher is paid one-third as much as a secondary school teacher, and in Cyprus, the primary teacher earns 48 percent of a clerical officer's salary, while one in New Zealand makes 414 percent.[14] Another example is that existing wages in LDC agriculture departments frequently encourage the rare extension worker skilled in analyzing plant or animal diseases or in designing farm machinery to seek an urban desk job. A shift in wage structure will not only spur job shifts among the presently employed, but will also encourage changes in spending for education and training. But even if wages are more closely related to productivity, the long gestation period required for the production of some skills may cause difficulty. Yet the market might still work effectively if government keeps people informed about future trends in the supply and demand for skilled labor.

VOCATIONAL AND TECHNICAL SKILLS

It is often inefficient to rely heavily on schools to develop vocational skills. Technical skills change rapidly, and vocational and technical schools often find it difficult to keep up. Frequently these institutions should simply provide generalized training as a basis for subsequent on-the-job training or short courses. On-the-job training balances supply and demand. Firms train people for only those slots already in existence or virtually certain to come into existence. Training processes operating independently of specific job demands are less effective, and the instructors in such situations may have no idea of the needs of the firms where students will ultimately be placed.

Where on-the-job training is not possible, short-term training institutions for people already at work are often superior to vocational or technical schools. A firm's production may be substantially disrupted if an entrepreneur in a small firm or a key management person in a large firm leaves for long-term training.

---

[13]United Nations Economic and Social Commission for Asia and the Pacific, *Human Resources Development: Intersectoral Coordination and Other Issues* (New York, 1992).

[14]Peter Heller and Alan Tait, "Government Employment and Pay: Some International Comparisons," *Finance and Development* 20 (September 1983): 44–47.

Thus it is best perhaps to offer a short course oriented toward those skills that are lacking. The key person's productivity will improve, and production will not be appreciably impaired.

Another approach may be to use extension agents to teach specific knowledge and skills to an owner, manager, or technician in a firm or farm. The extension agent can visit the enterprise, provide one-on-one instruction at the extension center, or have the client consult with a technical or management expert. I have observed leatherworking, woodworking, and shoemaking experts in Nigeria's industrial extension centers helping small-scale entrepreneurs, who had capital and management experience, master the mechanical skills and establish the production line essential for their firms to expand.

Should vocational training or extension programs be subsidized? We know that even in the case of small farmers or industrialists, the recipient of such assistance is usually economically better off than average. Subsidies are questionable. However, there may be some economic rationale for subsidies to programs that provide direct entrepreneurial and technical assistance to small productive units. Thus a small firm may not be able to pay a highly specialized person; however if this person's scarce managerial and technical skills are used in 30 or 40 firms a year, the economic cost per firm is likely to be low. Furthermore, given the external economies and the difficulty of billing each firm for the service, there may be merit in not charging for it at all.

REDUCING THE BRAIN DRAIN

The market for persons with scientific, professional, and technical training is an international one. In 1962, U.S. immigration laws were liberalized to admit persons having certain skills. The result is that almost half a million individuals with professional, scientific, and engineering training migrated to the United States between 1962 and 1980. Altogether other Western countries may have attracted just as many skilled immigrants. The overwhelming majority of these people came from LDCs, especially Asian countries, such as South Korea, India, the Philippines, and Taiwan. George J. Borjas indicates that United States immigrants, who have usually been educated abroad, do not receive their marginal products as wages, thus importing "free" human capital into the U.S.[15]

According to Herbert B. Grubel and Anthony B. Scott's marginal product approach, the developing country does not lose from the emigration of high-level personnel, or **brain drain.** In a competitive economy, a worker earns an income equivalent to his or her marginal product. Since the emigrant removes both contribution to national product and the income that gives a claim to this share, the income of those remaining behind is not reduced. In fact the welfare of the people born in the country increases, since the emigrant increases his or her income.[16]

Another approach is that emigration is an "overflow" of high-level persons who would otherwise be underutilized and discontented in their home countries.[17] For example, it is argued that someone like European-based Pakistani Nobel physicist Abdus Salam would not have had at home the research and li-

[15]George J. Borjas, "The Economics of Immigration," *Journal of Economic Literature* 32 (December 1994): 1667–1717.

[16]Herbert B. Grubel and Anthony D. Scott, "The International Flow of Human Capital." *American Economic Review* 56 (May 1966): 268–74.

[17]George B. Baldwin, "Brain Drain or Overflow," *Foreign Affairs* 48 (January 1970): 358–72.

brary facilities and intellectual stimulation from colleagues needed for his special-ized work in chromodynamics (see Box 10.1).

However there are several reasons to question these two analyses. Criticisms 1–3, following, are of the marginal product model, and 4 deals with the overflow approach.

1. The marginal product model assumes that individuals pay the full cost of their education. Yet in most LDCs the government subsidizes schooling. When edu-cated persons emigrate, the country loses human capital, a cost borne by its tax-payers in the past.

2. Many LDC labor markets are not competitive but nearly **monopsonistic** (one buyer), with only one major employer, the government. In this situation, mar-ginal product is in excess of the wage. Accordingly, the country loses more out-put than income from emigration.

3. High-level technical, professional, and managerial skills increase the productiv-ity of other production factors, such as capital and unskilled labor. Thus emigra-tion of high-level personnel reduces the productivity of other factors.

4. The overflow theory probably applies to only a fraction of the skilled people who emigrate. Furthermore, government could reduce overflow by encouraging students and trainees to take programs relevant to the home country, and DCs might provide refresher conferences, seminars, workshops, and training to the LDCs' highly-skilled personnel to reduce their emigration to DCs (see Box 10.1).

All in all, there is reason for LDC concern about the brain drain. They might undertake several policies.

1. Scholarships and training grants can be awarded only within the country, except where needed programs are not available. Students studying abroad should re-ceive scholarships funds only for programs of study relevant to the home country.

2. Many students sent abroad could go to another LDC offering the needed spe-cialization.

BOX 10-1

Abdus Salam, who became famous among particle physicists in 1950, returned to Pakistan soon thereafter but was isolated, doing little more rewarding than manage the college soccer team. In 1954, he reluc-tantly returned to Britain. In the early 1960s, after his pathbreaking the-ories won him the Nobel, he persuaded the International Atomic En-ergy Agency to establish the International Center for Theoretical Physics (ICTP) in Trieste, Italy, where LDC physicists, rejuvenated by month-long conferences featuring lectures, workshops, and seminars by the world's leading physicists, are provided alternatives to emigra-tion. "Physics for the Poor," *Economist* (November 18, 1989): 99–100; and Author's visit to ICTP, July 31-August 4, 1995.

Few other beneficiaries of the brain drain have been able to make the contribution Dr. Salam did to his home country and other LDCs.

3. Even when the student is sent to a developed country for graduate study, joint degree programs between universities in DCs and LDCs, in which research is done locally under the supervision of a scholar living in the LDC, would improve the chance of that student's remaining at home.

4. The government can provide temporary salaries to its foreign-educated graduates in their job searches, guarantee employment in the home country, or financially assist recruiters seeking nationals abroad.

5. Eliminating discriminatory policies and barriers to free inquiry might encourage highly educated nationals abroad to return.

Some policies to reduce the brain drain may have negative effects. For example, the insights and creativity garnered from overseas study and travel may have to be sacrificed.

Socialization and Motivation

Socialization is the process whereby personality, attitudes, motivation, and behavior are acquired through child rearing and social interaction. In this process, the group imparts its expectations to the individual concerning food habits, religion, sexual attitudes, world view, and work attitudes. Do cross-national differences in labor productivity and work commitment result from different socialization processes?

COMMITMENT TO WORK

During the colonial period, many Western government officials, managers, and economists argued that Afro-Asians were not motivated by economic incentives and lacked a commitment to work. Many of these Westerners opposed raising native wages on the grounds that the labor supply curve was backward bending at an early stage. The prevailing view was that Afro-Asians would work less if wages were increased because they had few wants and valued their leisure. If there were some validity to the **backward-bending labor supply curve** during the early part of this century, it was because of Western colonial policy. Traditionally many peasants sold no agricultural products; instead they farmed for consumption by the family, clan, or village. However, when the colonial government required money taxes, the peasant had either to produce what the European traders would buy or work at least part-time for the colonial government or a foreign firm. Not surprisingly many worked for money only long enough to pay the enforced tax. Accordingly, if wages per hour were raised, they worked fewer hours and disappeared to their villages sooner.

The supply curve for labor for most individuals, whether in LDCs or DCs, is backward bending at some point. Most people take part of their higher income in leisure. However, despite the backward bending *individual* curve, the *aggregate* supply curve of labor is upward sloping (that is, more hours of work are forthcoming at higher wages).[18]

---

[18]J.H. Boeke, *Economics and Economic Policy of Dual Societies* (New York: Harper Row, 1953), presents a theory of sociocultural dualism, which features a clash between indigenous social systems in the East and imported Western social systems. He argues that Indonesia and other Eastern societies have limited wants, contributing to a backward-sloping labor supply curve. Evidence from Benjamin Higgins, *Economic Development: Problems, Principles, and Policies* (New York: Norton, 1968), pp. 227–41, undermines Boeke's theory of Eastern "limited wants."

ATTITUDES TOWARD MANUAL WORK

Gunnar Myrdal, the Swedish economist who won the Nobel prize partly for his detailed inquiry into Asian poverty, argues that a major barrier to high labor productivity is a class system in which the elite are contemptuous of manual work.[19] The implication is that upper- and middle-class Westerners, who are more likely to carry their own briefcases, mow their lawns, and repair their automobiles, have different attitudes.

Yet affluent Europeans and North Americans may do more manual work than affluent Asians simply because cheap labor is not readily available to them. In general, unskilled labor is more abundant in LDCs than in DCs. However, Northern Europeans have hired Turkish, Croatian, and Italian "guest workers" to do menial jobs; farmers in the southwestern United States Hispanics to do "stoop" work; and American parents foreign nannies for child care. Furthermore, as the minimum wage for cooks, nannies, gardeners, and other servants increases in LDCs, as in Nigeria during the oil boom of the 1970s, elites in LDCs increasingly resort to manual work themselves. Thus attitudes toward manual work may differ between DCs and LDCs, but these appear to be primarily related to the supply of cheap labor.

CREATIVITY AND SELF-RELIANCE

Psychologists argue that differences in skills and motivations are created by the child's environment. Cultures vary widely in approaches to child rearing and training. We cannot reject out of hand the possibility that cross–national differences in labor productivity may be affected by attitudes and capabilities derived from different socialization processes.

Some childhood development scholars suggest that the environment in traditional societies, such as exist in most LDCs, produces an authoritarian personality. Children brought up in these societies view the world as consisting of arbitrary forces rather than one that can be rationally manipulated. They are less likely to be independent, self-reliant, creative, imaginative, and reliable than children from societies that encourage reasoning and initiative. These theories are discussed in more detail when we look at entrepreneurship and innovation (see Chapter 12).

Health and Physical Condition

Life expectancy is probably the best single indicator of national health levels. As indicated in Chapter 8, life expectancy in LDCs increased steadily between the 1930s and 1990s. These increases were more the result of general improvements in living conditions than in medical care. Nevertheless, medical progress has been considerable, especially in controlling communicable diseases. By 1975, plague and smallpox were virtually eliminated, and malaria and cholera kill fewer people today than they did in 1950.

Poor nutrition and bad health contribute not only to physical suffering and mental anguish, but also to low labor productivity. A mother malnourished during pregnancy, and inadequate food during infancy and early childhood may lead to disease as well as deficiencies in a child's physical and mental development.

---

[19]Gunnar Myrdal, *Asian Drama: An Inquiry into the Poverty of Nations*, vol. 2 (Middlesex, Eng.: Penguin Book, 1968), pp. 1020–1285.

Future productivity is thereby impaired. Furthermore, malnutrition and disease among adults saps their energy, initiative, creativity, and learning ability and reduces their work capacity.

Malnourishment is mostly a problem among the poor. Millions of people in LDCs suffer from malnutrition, not because they do not know what to eat or because the right kind of food is not available, but because they cannot afford it. Some one billion of the world's people are trapped in a vicious circle of poverty, malnutrition, and low productivity.

Nutrition economists think that the *proportion* of people in LDCs suffering from malnutrition has fallen since 1960, although Africa and Latin America experienced setbacks in the 1980s (Chapter 7). It is clear that with improved transport and communication and greater awareness of the need for emergency food aid, fewer people starve to death as a result of severe food crises and famines today than in 1960. Yet countries with any lengthy disruption in planting, harvesting, and food distribution—as often happens with internal political conflict, such as in Sudan, Somalia, Angola, Rwanda, and Bosnia in the early 1990s—remain vulnerable to starvation.

Obviously good health and nutrition are intertwined with a country's economic and social development. Although people are healthier and nutrition has probably not declined in LDCs since the 1960s, progress has been slow—with the result that labor productivity has grown slowly. And overall the physical and mental well-being among the poorest segments of LDC population has improved but modestly. In Abidjan, Ivory Coast, the probability of dying between 1–4 years of age is fifteen times greater in slum areas than in affluent areas where housing and health standards are comparable to DCs.[20]

AIDS

According to the World Health Organization (WHO), 66 percent of the world's 8.8 million people infected with HIV (human immunodeficiency virus) in 1990 lived in sub-Saharan Africa and an additional 18 percent lived in other LDCs. WHO projects that in 2000 HIV prevalence will be 26 million, with 12 million from the sub-Sahara. In the third world, AIDS is primarily a disease of heterosexual adults, with substantial infection of young children at the time of their birth. An HIV-infected adult develops AIDS (acquired immunodeficiency syndrome) on average in 6 to 10 years. In 1990, about 75 percent of the world's 0.4 million AIDS-related deaths were in sub-Saharan Africa. In 2000, WHO projects that half of the 1.8 AIDS-related deaths will be from sub-Saharan Africa.[21]

---

[20]David Morawetz, *Twenty-five Years of Economic Development, 1950 to 1975* (Baltimore: Johns Hopkins University Press, 1977), pp. 44–50; Shlomo Reutlinger, "Malnutrition: A Poverty or a Food Problem," *World Development* 5 (1977): 715–24; Shlomo Reutlinger and Marcelo Selowsky, *Malnutrition and Poverty: Magnitude and Policy Options* (Baltimore: Johns Hopkins University Press, 1976), pp. 8–9; Johanna T. Dwyer and Jean Mayer, "Beyond Economics and Nutrition: The Complex Basis of Food Policy," in Philip H. Abelson, ed., *Food: Politics, Economics, Nutrition, and Research* (Washington, D.C.: American Association for the Advancement of Science, 1975), pp. 74–78; Halfdan Mahler, "People," *Scientific American* 243 (September 1980) 66–77; and Peter Hendry, "Food and Population: Beyond Five Billion," *Population Bulletin* 43 (April 1988): 8.

[21]World Bank, *World Development Report, 1993* (New York: Oxford University Press, 1993), pp. 33–34.

HIV infection rates are increasing rapidly in South and Southeast Asia. In Thailand, one adult in 50 is infected with HIV. UNICEF, *The State of the World's Children, 1995* (Oxford: Oxford University Press, 1995), p. 22.

World Bank researchers Martha Ainsworth and Mead Over analyze the effect of AIDS on sub-Saharan Africa. AIDS infection rates in Africa is highest among urban high-income, skilled men and their partners. Projections of infection rates for the late 1990s or first decade of the twenty-first century are difficult because of uncertainties about HIV infection rates among different socioeconomic groups, fertility rates of HIV-infected women, and the incubation period before AIDS-related deaths. Yet while some subnational areas where infection rates are extremely high may experience negative population growth, no African country is likely to experience zero or negative population growth from AIDS deaths. Still, Ainsworth and Over forecast a steep rise in mortality rates among economically active adults and young children in Africa.[22] Moreover, the World Bank's *World Development Report* contends that the AIDS epidemic, through its effect on savings and productivity, poses a threat to the economic growth of many countries already under economic distress. World Bank simulations indicate a slowing of growth of income per capita by an average 0.6 percentage point yearly in the 10 worst-affected countries in sub-Saharan Africa during the early 1990s. Tanzania, whose income per capita fell 0.2 percent a year from AIDS in the early 1990s, is projected to suffer a growth slowdown of 0.1 to 0.8 percentage points annually in the late 1990s. The slowdown from AIDS results from the health care costs, the loss of skilled adults in their prime working years, the withdrawal of children from school to help at home, the cost of caring for orphans, and other costs. Additionally, in Tanzania, despite the fact that the government pays a large share of health costs, the death from AIDS of an adult affects the next generation, as children withdraw from school to help at home. Prevention measures, such as education on safer sex, promotion of condom use, prevention and treatment of sexually transmitted diseases, and reduction of blood-borne transmission, are cost-effective, especially if targeted at people at particularly high risk of acquiring and transmitting HIV infection, such as sex workers, migrants, the military, truck drivers, and drug users who share needles.[23]

Summary

1. Despite destruction of physical capital during World War II, the economies of Germany and Japan grew rapidly in the postwar period because their labor forces—with high degrees of skill, experience, education, health, and discipline—remained intact.

2. Investment in human capital includes expenditures on education, training, research, and health, enhancing a people's future productivity.

3. Economists who analyze the relative rates of returns to investment to primary education and secondary education in LDCs disagree on whether LDCs should put greater priority on primary education. Psacharopoulos and Woodhall, who find that the higher average returns are from primary education, argue for more emphasis on primary education. Knight, Sabot, and Hovey, however, question this emphasis in a study that shows that the marginal rates of returns to the cohort entering into the labor market were lower for primary education.

[22]Martha Ainsworth and Mead Over, "AIDS and African Development," *World Bank Research Observer* 9 (July 1994): 203–40.

[23]World Bank, *World Development Report, 1993* (New York: Oxford University Press, 1993), pp. 20, 100–05.

4. While employers sometimes use secondary and university education as a screening device, they discover and pay wage premiums for literacy and numeracy, even in manual work.

5. Public expenditure per student for higher education in LDCs is about ten times as high as for primary education.

6. In LDCs the expansion of primary education redistributes benefits from the rich to the poor, while the growth of secondary and higher education redistributes income from the poor to the rich. In light of this pattern, LDCs may want to charge their richer citizens for the full cost of secondary and higher education.

7. In most LDCs, boys are sent to school far more often than girls. Yet a number of studies indicate that educating girls has a high payoff in improving nutrition, reducing fertility and child mortality, and increasing labor force productivity.

8. One planning method for producing specialized skills is to use input-output relationships to determine future demand for various types of high-level personnel. However, assuming a fixed input-output relationship does not recognize the possibility of substituting one skill for another or adapting output to skills array.

9. If wages are adjusted more closely to productivity, LDC educational planning is easier.

10. On-the-job training tends to balance demand for, and supply of, training. In addition extension agents and training at short-term vocational or technical institutions can help people improve their skills without appreciably disrupting production.

11. Some economists argue that LDCs do not lose from the brain drain, since the worker earns an income equal to his or her marginal product. However, we can question this analysis, since marginal product may exceed the wage, high-level skills increase the productivity of other production factors, and government highly subsidizes education in developing countries.

12. There is no evidence of a backward bending supply curve for labor unique to LDCs. Furthermore, the aggregate supply curve of labor in LDCs is clearly upward sloping.

13. Although affluent Asians may be more likely to consider manual work degrading than affluent Westerners, these attitudes appear to be primarily related to the more abundant supply of cheap labor in Asia.

14. Poor nutrition and health reduce labor productivity. However, health has improved, and nutrition has probably not deteriorated in LDCs since the 1960s.

15. HIV infection and AIDS-related deaths have had a substantial adverse impact on economic growth in some developing countries, especially in Africa.

Terms to Review

- education as screening
- brain drain
- monopsonistic
- socialization
- backward-bending labor supply curve

Questions to Discuss

1. Would you expect the returns to a dollar of investment in education to vary from those in industrial plant, machinery, and equipment? Would noneco-

nomic educational benefits affect the decision under perfect competition to equalize the expected marginal rate of return per dollar in each investment?

2. Does empirical evidence on the rates of return to education show that LDCs should put a priority on primary education relative to secondary and university education? Would you expect the relative returns to primary education, on the one hand, and secondary and post-secondary education, on the other hand, to change as economic development takes place?

3. To what extent is education a screening device for jobs rather than a way of increasing productivity in LDCs? How might the importance of screening and enhancing productivity vary by educational and skill level, sector, or world region in the developing world?

4. How does LDC government investment in educational expansion affect income distribution?

5. What are some of the ways that an LDC can increase its rate of returns to investment in secondary and higher education?

6. What advice would you give to the top official in the Department of Education in a LDC who is designing a long-run program of education, training, and extension in his country? (You may either focus on LDCs in general, a particular LDC world region, or a particular LDC.)

7. How might government wage policies contribute to unemployment and underutilization of labor among the educated?

8. How can LDCs reduce the brain drain?

9. How do you explain cross-national differences in labor productivity?

10. What investments can an LDC government make to increase the health and reduce the incidence of disease in the LDC? Examine these investments in the light of the opportunity cost for other investments, including those in social capital.

Guide to Readings

Theodore W. Schultz, *The Economic Value of Education* (New York: Columbia University Press, 1963); Schultz, "Investment in Human Capital," *American Economic Review* 51 (March 1961): 1–17; and Gary S. Becker, *Human Capital* (New York: Columbia University Press, 1975), are some of the major works on investment in human capital. Jere R. Behrman and Mark R. Rosenzweig, "Labor Force: Caveat Emptor: Cross-Country Data and Education and the Labor Force," *Journal of Development Economics* 44 (June 1994): 147–71, assess LDC data on education and the labor force. Boissière, Knight, and Sabot (note 7); Knight and Sabot (note 4); Knight, Sabot, and Hovey (note 4); Psacharopoulos and Woodhall (note 3); Psacharopoulos (note 3); and the *World Development Report, 1980* (note 6) analyze returns to education. *World Development Report, 1980,* pp. 32–64, has an excellent discussion of current issues in human resource development, especially in education, training, health, and nutrition. This report, United Nations Economic and Social Commission for Asia and the Pacific (note 3), Bruton (note 6), and works by Edwards, and Edwards and Todaro cited in the readings for Chapter 9 consider the question of educational planning.

Partha Dasgupta, *An Inquiry into Well-being and Destitution* (Oxford: Clarendon Press, 1993) focuses on the relationship between nutrition, energy requirements, and worker productivity, with the implications of malnutrition for incentives, institutional reform, and income redistribution. He uses the findings of nutitionists on the link between food needs and work capacity to reconstruct modern resource allocation theory. See also United Nations Economic and Social Commission for Asia and the Pacific (note 9) for a discussion of nutrition.

Morawetz, Reutlinger, Mahler, and Reutlinger and Selowsky (note 20), Alan Berg, *Malnutrition: What Can Be Done? Lessons from World Bank Experience* (Baltimore: Johns Hopkins University Press, 1987), and Nevin S. Scrimshaw and Lance Taylor, "Food," *Scientific American* 243 (September 1980): 78–88, analyze nutrition, health, and economic development. Burton A. Weisbrod and Thomas W. Helminiak, "Parasitic Diseases and Agricultural Labor Productivity," *Economic Development and Cultural Change* 25 (April 1977): 505–22, measure the impact of parasitic diseases on labor productivity. The effect of tropical climate on human efficiency is examined in Chapter 13. The *World Development Report, 1993* (note 21) and Ainsworth and Over (note 22) analyze the effect of AIDS on developing countries.

World Development 3 (October 1975) and the *Journal of Development Economics* 2 (September 1975) are entirely devoted to a discussion of the brain drain. *IDS Bulletin* 20 (January 1989) focuses on adjusting LDC education to the economic crisis.

Kusum Nair, "Asian Drama—A Critique," *Economic Development and Cultural Change* 17 (July 1969): 453–56, presents a skillful argument against Myrdal's discussion (note 19) of Asian attitudes toward manual work.

The effect of childhood environment on the creativity and self-reliance of the labor force is discussed by David C. McClelland, *The Achieving Society* (Princeton: D. Van Nostrand, 1961), and Everett E. Hagen, *On the Theory of Social Change: How Economic Growth Begins* (Homewood, Ill.: Dorsey Press, 1962). See also Chapter 12.

11

Capital Formation, Investment Choice, and Technical Progress

The rapid economic growth of Japan and a few Western countries since the mid–nineteenth century has not been equaled by other countries. Since then the United States, Canada, Japan, and most Western European countries experienced real growth rates in gross national product per capita in excess of 1 percent per year, a rate that means a rise to more than four times initial value by 2000 (Chapter 3). The most important sources of this growth were capital formation and increased knowledge and technology. But now such continuous rapid growth may be more difficult. Given limited mineral resources, improved technology, and increased capital accumulation will be essential for expanding (and perhaps just maintaining) real planetary product per capita in the future. Technical advances, such as better mining techniques (especially for using ocean resources), may mitigate our limited mineral supplies; and microminiaturization with integrated circuits (for substantial reductions in materials required), and the development of renewable power sources based on the sun, either directly through solar cells, or indirectly through water power, wind power, and photosynthesis, will help us use our resources more wisely.

Scope of the Chapter

This chapter analyzes the relationships between capital, technology, and economic development. The first section summarizes studies that review how capital formation and technical progress contribute to economic growth and indicates why the contribution of the two differs in DCs and LDCs. The second part tries to identify the composition of the **growth in total factor productivity**, usually labeled **technical progress**—the residual factor in growth, the increased worker productivity arising from factors other than increases in capital per worker-hour. Third, we consider technical change as a prolonged process of learning by doing. The fourth section asks whether growth can be attributed only to increases in measured inputs. Fifth, we define research, development, and invention, and their relationship to technical change.

The sixth section looks at the investment criterion, maximum labor absorption, and some of its inadequacies. Next we discuss social benefit-cost analysis, the planner's most comprehensive gauge for investment choice. We raise questions about the appropriate discount rate and how to treat risk and uncertainty. Subsequently, we indicate how private profitability must be adjusted for externalities, income distribution, indivisibilities, monopoly, savings effects, and factor price distortions to obtain social profitability. Our final section analyzes and assesses shadow prices, a way of adjusting prices more closely to social costs and benefits.

Capital Formation and Technical Progress As Sources of Growth

In the 1950s, U.N. economists considered capital shortage the major limitation to LDC economic growth. By capital they meant tools, machinery, plant, equipment, inventory stocks, and so on, but not human capital.

On the basis of nineteenth- and twentieth-century Western growth, however, British economic historian Sir Alex Cairncross, writing in 1955, questioned whether capital's role was central to economic growth. To be sure, he agreed with U.N. economists that capital and income grow at about the same rate. But he felt that capital increases do not explain economic growth, that, in fact, the reverse was true: The amount of capital responds to increases in its demand, which depends on economic growth.[1]

Since 1955, econometricians have tried to resolve this controversy with studies measuring how factor growth affects output growth. The studies' primary concern has been to determine the relative importance of the two major sources of economic growth—capital formation and technical progress.

Initial attempts at statistical measurement in the West and Japan in the late 1950s and 1960s indicated that capital per worker-hour explained 5 to 33 percent of growth in output per worker-hour. Scholars usually attributed the residual, 67 to 95 percent, to technical progress.[2] A development economist used this evidence to argue that capital formation has been stressed too much and technical progress too little.[3]

Studies of non-Western economies published after 1960 contradict findings based on Western data. These studies indicate that the contribution of capital per

[1]Alex Cairncross, "The Place of Capital in Economic Progress," in Leon H. Dupriez, ed., *Economic Progress: Papers and Proceedings of a Round Table Held by the International Economic Association* (Louvain, France: Institut de Recherches Economiques et Sociales, 1955), pp. 235–48.

[2]Moses Abramovitz, "Resources and Output Trends in the United States since 1870," *American Economic Review* 44 (May 1956): 5–23; Robert Solow, "Technical Change and the Aggregate Production Function," *Review of Economics and Statistics* 39 (August 1957): 312–20; and Henry J. Bruton, "Productivity Growth in Latin America," *American Economic Review* 57 (December 1967): 1099–1116.

[3]Everett E. Hagen, *The Economics of Development* (Homewood, Ill.: Irwin, 1980), pp. 201–3.

worker to growth, even among fast-growing East Asian NICs, is 50 to 90 percent, while that of the residual is only 10 to 50 percent.[4]

For command economies Russia/the Soviet Union, pre-1989 Eastern Europe, and pre-1976 China, the residual is even smaller than for the third-world countries of Asia, Africa, and Latin America. Virtually all growth in these economies can be attributed to increases in capital and other inputs, and only a tiny fraction to technical innovation.

The aggregate models used in studies of the sources of economic growth in developed and developing countries are rough tools. Yet these studies point in the same general direction. First the major source of growth per worker in developing countries is capital per worker; increased productivity of each unit of capital per worker is of less significance. Second the major source of growth per worker in developed countries is increased productivity, with increases in capital per worker being relatively unimportant. Accordingly capital accumulation appears to be more important and technical progress less important as a source of growth in developing countries than in developed countries.

In 1965, Nobel prize winner John R. Hicks argued that econometric studies of growth sources in Western countries understate capital formation's contribution to growth. Since many significant advances in knowledge are embodied in new capital, its separation from technical progress may lead to underestimating its contribution. Furthermore, accumulation of new capital is frequently offset by a decrease in value in old capital, partly from obsolescence. Thus, Hicks contended, it is very wrong to give the impression to an LDC, having relatively small amounts of old capital, that capital accumulation is a matter of minor importance.[5] Econometric studies of LDCs done since 1965 seem to confirm Hicks's point. The rates of capital growth in developing countries (as well as Israel, which received substantial inflows of funds in the 1950s) were rapid enough to offset some of the understatement of capital in the production function. Developing countries concerned about rapid economic growth ignore capital accumulation at their peril. Chapters 14 and 15 concentrate on policies to increase capital formation in LDCs.

Components of the Residual

Studies of Western growth find that the residual is a major contributor to economic growth. However, to label this residual technical knowledge without explaining it is to neglect a major cause of economic growth. Critics in the early 1960s objected to elevating a statistical residual to the engine of growth, thus converting ignorance

---

[4]Angus Maddison, *Economic Progress and Policy in Developing Countries* (London: Allen and Unwin, 1970); Sherman Robinson, "Sources of Growth in Less Developed Countries: A Cross Section Study," *Quarterly Journal of Economics* 85 (August 1971): 391–408; Alwyn Young, "The Tyranny of Numbers: Confronting the Statistical Realities of the East Asian Growth Experience," *Quarterly Journal of Economics* 110 (August 1995): 641–80. See also Dale W. Jorgenson, *Productivity*, vol. 2, *International Comparisons of Economic Growth* (Cambridge, Mass.: MIT Press, 1995); and Hollis Chenery, Sherman Robinson, and Moises Syrquin, *Industrialization and Growth* (New York: Oxford University Press, 1986).

[5]John R. Hicks, *Capital and Growth* (New York: Oxford University Press, 1965).

In contrast, Edward F. Denison, *Estimates of Productivity Change by Industry: An Estimate and an Alternative* (Washington, D.C.: Brookings, 1988), p. 39, would remove all contributions of advances in knowledge from capital accumulation and attribute these improvements to technical progress.

into knowledge.[6] Accordingly, in recent years some economists have labeled this residual total factor productivity rather than technical progress.

What does this residual include? Edward F. Denison has studied the contribution that 23 separate sources made to growth rates in nine Western countries for the period from 1950 to 1962.[7] His estimates, particularly of labor quality, are based on reasonable and clearly stated judgments rather than on econometric exercises. Thus he *assumes* that three-fifths of the earnings differentials between workers of the same age, geographical area, and family economic background are the result of education. Moreover, individuals in the labor force having the same years of school and hours in school per year obtained at the same age are considered to have an equivalent education, no matter when or where they received their education. Furthermore, 70 percent of the decrease in average hours worked is assumed to be offset by productivity increases. The reader aware of Denison's assumptions and approximations can benefit from his work; he is careful in handling empirical data, stating assumptions, and in investigating how results may be sensitive to variations in assumptions.

In all DCs, growth in national income per worker is attributed more to increases in output per unit of input (the residual factor) than to increases in inputs, labor, capital, and land. Denison indicates that sources for increased output per worker for the United States or Northwestern Europe include advances in knowledge, economies of scale, improved allocation of resources, reduction in the age of capital, and decreases in the time lag in applying knowledge. Other empirical studies have included organizational improvements, increased education and training, and learning by experience.

Western and Japanese total factor productivity growth slowed down after 1973. Martin Neil Baily and Robert J. Gordon show that 10 percent of the slowdown in annual productivity growth in the United States from 1948–73 to 1973–87 results from the understatement in productivity gains in the manufacture of computer power. However, the understatement of productivity improvement in the use of computers in nonmanufacturing sectors is virtually nil.[8]

Learning by Doing

Technical change can be viewed as a prolonged learning process based on experience and problem solving. Each successive piece of capital equipment is more productive, since learning advances are embodied in new machines. Learning not only takes place in research, educational, and training institutions, but also through using new capital goods. Japan, which copied Western techniques for producing toys, cameras, and electronics after World War II, has become a leader in these industries through this kind of hands-on learning.

A **learning curve** measures how much labor productivity (or output per labor input) increases with cumulative experience. Thus a Swedish ironworks increased its output per worker-hour 2 percent per year despite no new investment

---

[6]Thomas Balogh and Paul P. Streeten, "The Coefficient of Ignorance," *Bulletin of the Oxford Institute of Statistics* 25 (May 1963): 99–107.

[7]Edward F. Denison, *Why Growth Rates Differ: Postwar Experience in Nine Western Countries* (Washington, D.C.: Brookings Institution, 1967).

[8]Martin Neil Baily and Robert J. Gordon, "The Productivity Slowdown, Measurement Issues, and the Explosion of Computer Power," *Brookings Papers on Economic Activity* 2 (1986): 347–420.

and no new production methods for 15 years. Likewise U.S. Air Force engineers assume a constant relative decline in labor required for an airplane body as the number of airframes previously produced increases. A constant relative decline in labor requirements as output expands means labor costs approach zero as cumulative production tends to infinity—a nonsensical idea if output runs were long, but since in practice they tend to be less than 20 years, economists can safely use this form of the learning curve. Furthermore, British scholars of technical progress, Charles Kennedy and A. P. Thirlwall, argue that, even where learning by doing from a good ends, where product types are constantly changing, we can assume there is no aggregate limit to the learning process.[9]

Because of external economies, that is, cost reductions spilling over to other goods and producers (Chapter 5), firms whose workers learn by using capital equipment cannot hold on to some of the benefits of this learning. The **social profitability** (profits adjusted for divergences between social and private benefits and costs) of investment exceeds profitability to the firm. Thus investment rate under competitive conditions may be lower than the one optimal for society or the one prevailing with central planning. A capitalist government may wish to subsidize investment to the point that its commercial profitability equals its social profitability.

Growth As a Process of Increase in Inputs

Some economists contend that virtually all economic growth can be explained by increases in inputs. In Chapters 5 and 10, we discussed the importance of the human capital input in increasing labor quality and economic growth. Theodore W. Schultz, in his presidential address to the American Economic Association in 1961, suggests that most of the residual can be attributed to investment in this input rather than to technical progress. He argues that

> Studies of economic growth based on increases in man-hours worked and on increases in capital restricted to structures, equipment, and inventories, presumably with quality held constant, do not take account of the important changes that occur over time in the quality of labor and of material capital goods. The advance in knowledge and useful new factors based on such knowledge are all too frequently put aside as if they were not produced means of production but instead simply happened to occur over time. This view is as a rule implicit in the notion of technological change.[10]

Economists contending that output is explained by increases in input attribute the growth in total factor productivity to research, education, and other forms of human capital. Indeed Mankiw, Romer, and Weil's empirical evidence (see Chapter 5) indicates that the overwhelming share of economic growth is

---

[9]Kenneth Arrow, "The Economic Implications of Learning by Doing," *Review of Economic Studies* 29 (June 1962): 154–94; and Charles Kennedy and A. P. Thirlwall, "Technical Progress: A Survey," *Economic Journal* 82 (March 1972): 38–39.

[10]Theodore W. Schultz, "Investment in Human Capital," *American Economic Review* 51 (March 1961): 1–17; and Theodore W. Schultz, *Transforming Traditional Agriculture* (New Haven: Yale University Press, 1964).

explained by increases in inputs, human capital, physical capital, and labor. Dale W. Jorgenson and Zvi Griliches show that if quantities of output and input are measured accurately, the observed growth in total factor productivity in the United States is negligible, accounting for only 3.3 percent of economic growth. However, in reply to Denison's careful analysis, Jorgenson and Griliches admit they erred in adjusting for changes in utilization of capital and land. Still adjusting for the error leaves substantial scope for the importance of the growth of factor inputs.[11] Moreover, for developing countries, a much larger growth share is explained by increased inputs.

From one perspective, capital includes anything that yields a stream of income over time. Investment is net addition to material, human, and intellectual capital. Improvements in people's health, discipline, skill, and education; transfers of labor to more productive activities; and the discovery and application of knowledge constitute human and intellectual capital. Economic development, then, may be viewed as a generalized process of capital accumulation.[12] This approach is valuable, since it emphasizes the relative return from alternative resource investments.

Zvi Griliches, in his 1994 presidential address to the American Economic Association, lamented that measuring growth is difficult and data are scanty. Nevertheless, he noted that, thanks to some pioneering studies, economists know much more about the sources of input growth than they did in the 1960s.[13]

The Cost of Technical Knowledge

Countries at different levels of technical learning use the same technology at widely varying levels of efficiency. The same steel mill costs three times as much to erect in Nigeria as in South Korea, and once it operates, is only half as productive.[14]

Choices among technologies, which continually change, are poorly defined. Technical knowledge, which is unevenly distributed internationally and *intra*nationally, is acquired only at a cost and is almost always incomplete, so that any person's knowledge is smaller than the total in existence. Less-developed areas can almost never acquire technical knowledge in its entirety, since blueprints, instructions, and technical assistance fail to include technology's implicit steps. Learning and acquiring technology does not result automatically from buying, producing, selling, and using but requires an active search to evaluate current routines for possible changes. Search involves people gathering intelligence by purchasing licenses, doing joint research, experimenting with different processes and

[11]Dale W. Jorgenson and Zvi Griliches, "The Explanation of Productivity Change," *Review of Economic Studies* 34 (July 1967): 249–83; Edward F. Denison, "Some Major Issues in Productivity Analysis: An Examination of Estimates by Jorgenson and Griliches," *Survey of Current Business* 52 (May 1972): 37–64; and Dale W. Jorgenson and Zvi Griliches, "Issues in Growth Accounting: A Reply to Edward F. Denison," *Survey of Current Business* 52 (May 1972): 65–94.

[12]Harry G. Johnson, "Development as a Generalized Process of Capital Accumulation," in Gerald M. Meier, *Leading Issues in Economic Development* (New York: Oxford University Press, 1976), pp. 542–47.

[13]Zvi Griliches, "Productivity, R&D, and the Data Constraint," *American Economic Review* 84 (March 1994): 1–23.

[14]Sanjaya Lall, "Promoting Technology Development: The Role of Technology Transfer and Indigenous Effort," *Third World Quarterly* 14(1) (1993): 95–108.

designs, improving engineering, and so forth. The LDC firms and governments obtain technical knowledge through transfer from abroad as well as internal innovation, adaptation, and modification. Paradoxically LDCs can only buy information from abroad before its value is completely assessed, since this implies possessing the information.

The **price of knowledge,** determined in the wide range between the cost to the seller (often a monopolist) of producing knowledge and the cost to the buyer of doing without, depends on the respective resources, knowledge, alternatives, and bargaining strengths of both parties. Selling knowledge, like other public goods, does not reduce its availability to the seller but does decrease the seller's monopoly rents.[15]

Research, Invention, Development, and Innovation

Technical progress results from a combination of research, invention, development, and innovation. **Basic research** consists of systematic investigation aimed at fuller knowledge of the subject studied. **Applied research** is concerned with the potential applications of scientific knowledge, frequently to commercial products or processes. **Development** refers to technical activities that apply research or scientific knowledge to products or processes.[16] Some research and development results in **invention,** devising new methods or products. At times invention may require development. The commercial application of invention is innovation, discussed in Chapter 12.

According to one study, investment in agricultural research in the United States from 1940 to 1950 yielded a return of at least 35 percent per year, while that in hybrid corn research from 1910 to 1955 yielded at least 700 percent yearly.[17] In his 1968 presidential address to the American Economic Association, Kenneth E. Boulding speculated that the rate of return on the small investment in economic research was several hundred percent per year over the period from 1945 to 1965.[18]

Despite these spectacular results, *organized* research and development (abbreviated as R and D) as a whole has had only a modest impact on the rate of economic growth, since much of it generates no new knowledge. Denison estimates that only 7.5 percent of U.S. per capita growth from 1929 to 1957 can be attributed to organized R and D.[19] Today over half of these expenses are for defense and

---

[15]R. R. Nelson, "Innovation and Economic Development: Theoretical Retrospect and Prospect," IDB/CEPAL Studies on Technology and Development in Latin America, Buenos Aires, 1978, p. 18; and Martin Fransman, *Technology and Economic Development* (Boulder, Colo.: Westview, 1986).

[16]Charles Kennedy and A. P. Thirlwall, "Technical Progress: A Survey," *Economic Journal* 82 (March 1972): 11–72.

[17]Zvi Griliches, "Research Costs and Social Returns: Hybrid Corn and Related Innovations," *Journal of Political Economy* 66 (October 1958): 419–31.

[18]Kenneth E. Boulding, *Economics as a Science* (New York: McGraw-Hill, 1970), p. 151, emphasizes the great depressions prevented by economic research. The rate of return on economic research has probably decreased, however, since Boulding wrote. In the late 1970s, an economic adviser to the Carter administration, Alfred Kahn, admitted that economists do not know how to reduce inflation substantially without increasing unemployment. A number of difficult economic problems exist in developing countries. However, in contrast to U.S. economic issues, few of these problems have been researched, suggesting that returns to economic research in the third world would be high.

[19]Edward F. Denison, *The Sources of Economic Growth in the United States and the Alternatives before Us* (New York: Committee for Economic Development, 1962).

space programs, which have had only incidental benefits to civilian production. Furthermore, many economists are skeptical that creativity flourishes in the institutionalized R and D setting. Much technical progress results from on-the-job problem solving and performance improvement rather than from work done in R and D departments. Moreover, a very large portion of privately financed R and D is irrelevant to measured growth. And in developing countries, where R and D is usually a smaller percentage of GNP, its contribution to growth is likely to be less. However, these countries may be able to purchase or borrow technology from abroad (as discussed in Chapter 16).

Yet studies like Denison's assume R and D spending is a flow cost used to produce output in a given year rather than an asset that accumulates through time. Thus these studies, which assume current spending alone measures innovation, leave out accumulated knowledge.[20]

A firm's size, monopoly power, and product diversification will determine how much R and D it does. If it is large, monopolistic, and diverse, the enterprise is more likely to capture the benefits from R and D.[21]

However, in competitive product markets like grain, the individual producer can appropriate only a small fraction of the benefits accruing from research. For example, Griliches indicates that consumers received almost all of the social returns of government-sponsored research on hybrid seed corn in the United States.[22] Corn farmers, or even the hybrid seed corn industry, would probably not have undertaken the research, since private rates of return were far below social rates. When such a divergence in these rates exists, the case for government investment in research is strong.

In the 1950s and 1960s, U.S. and British technological leaders, with the highest ratio of R and D spending to GNP, had some of the lowest rates of productivity growth. There are potential advantages for countries that are **technology followers,** like early post–World War II Japan, and South Korea and Taiwan, in the last quarter of the twentieth century. While followership requires an early emergence of indigenous technological capacity, it may not require deep levels of knowledge.

Since World War II, rapidly growing Japan and Germany have been large net importers of technology, while slow-growing Britain and the United States are not, suggesting that part of the latters' industrial problems is too little awareness of others' inventions and development.[23]

However, the catch-up process is self-limiting because as a follower catches up, the possibility of making large leaps by acquiring best-practice technology becomes smaller and smaller. The potential for rapid growth by a follower, such as Japan, weakens as its technological level converges toward that of the leader, the United States.[24] As Japan has shifted to leadership in numerous industrial sectors, it has had to orient its technological policies and educational system toward original research at the technical frontier, which is more expensive than followership.

---

[20]M. I. Kamien and N. L. Schwartz, *Market Structure and Innovation* (Cambridge: Cambridge University Press, 1982), p. 51.

[21]Charles Kennedy and A. P. Thirlwall, "Technical Progress: A Survey," *Economic Journal* 82 (March 1972): 61–62.

[22]Zvi Griliches, "Research Costs and Social Returns: Hybrid Corn and Related Innovations," *Journal of Political Economy* 66 (October 1958): 419–37.

[23]Lawrence G. Franko, *The Threat of Japanese Multinationals—How the West Can Respond* (Chichester, U.K.: Wiley, 1983), p. 24.

[24]Moses Abramovitz, "Catching Up, Forging Ahead, and Falling Behind," *Journal of Economic History* 46 (June 1986): 387–89.

Investment Criteria

Investable resources can be used in a number of ways: to build steel mills or fertilizer plants, to construct schools, to expand applied research, to train agricultural extension agents, and so on. And since there are not enough resources to go around, we must choose among investments. The rest of this chapter indicates how we can make these choices in an economically rational way.

MAXIMUM LABOR ABSORPTION

In LDCs labor—often underemployed and having low alternative costs—is usually considered the abundant factor, and capital, the scarce factor. Thus we might expect LDCs to specialize in labor-intensive goods (that is, those with high labor-capital ratios). Specifically this means that LDCs should replace the capital-intensive industrial techniques common in DCs with more labor-intensive approaches.

As discussed in Chapter 10, appropriate technology for LDCs should fit their factor proportions. According to E. F. Schumacher, the advocate of small is beautiful (Chapter 2), an **intermediate technology** is needed—techniques somewhere between Western capital-intensive processes and the LDCs' traditional instruments.[25] In practice however, many LDCs use capital-intensive methods. Sometimes entrepreneurs, bound in inertia, may not question existing capital-intensive designs. But these techniques have other attractions in LDCs as well.

1. Business people often want to use the most advanced design without knowing that it may not be the most profitable. James Pickett, D. J. C. Forsyth, and N. S. McBain, on the basis of field research in Africa, attribute this attitude to an **engineering mentality.**

    Engineers . . . are professionally driven by . . . "the half-artistic joy in technically perfecting the productive apparatus." . . . The engineer's interest is in technical efficiency—in extracting the maximum amount of sucrose from a given input of sugar cane; and from this standpoint machines are often more reliable than men. . . . A decision is taken, for example, to establish a plant of some given productive capacity in a developing country. Engineers trained according to developed country curricula are asked to design the plant. They produce blueprints for a limited number of alternatives, each of which is a variant on current "best-practice" technique. The alternatives are submitted to economic . . . scrutiny, the most attractive chosen, and another capital-intensive, technologically inappropriate plant is established.[26]

2. For many commodities, there may be no substitute for a highly capital-intensive production process, as the ratio of capital to labor is unalterable (Chapter 10). With fixed factor proportions, a given amount of capital may not fully employ

---

[25]E. F. Schumacher, "Industrialization through 'Intermediate Technology,' " in Ronald Robinson, ed., *Industrialization in Developing Countries,* Cambridge University Overseas Studies Committee Conference on Role of Industrialization in Development, Cambridge, U.K., 1965, pp. 91–96.

[26]James Pickett, D. J. C. Forsyth, and N. S. McBain, "The Choice of Technology," *World Development* 2 (March 1974): 47–54.

The economist rejects the technically most efficient process where less costly inputs or improved revenue prospects increase social profitability. Economic efficiency implies that the use of a resource should be expanded when the extra social revenue associated with it exceeds the extra social cost, and contracted when the reverse occurs, even if this implies substituting crude labor-intensive machines for the "best-practice" sucrose-extracting machines.

the labor force. Yet there may be no other technologies available using higher ratios of labor to capital to produce the specified commodities.

3. Capital-intensive methods embodying technical advances may be cheaper per output unit than either traditional labor-intensive approaches or newly designed intermediate technologies. Business people may find that modifying existing technologies is more expensive than using them without alteration. For as Chapter 12 indicates, adapting existing Western technology to LDC conditions often requires substantial (and sometimes costly) creativity.

4. Automatic machinery may reduce the need for skilled workers, managers, or administrators, all of whom are scarce in developing countries. Conserving on expensive personnel may be as important as conserving capital in LDCs (see Chapter 10).

5. Although LDC labor is abundant and its wage is lower than in DCs, it is not necessarily cheaper to hire because its productivity may be lower. The **efficiency wage** (the wage rate divided by the productivity of labor) and wage costs per unit of output may differ little between LDCs and DCs.[27]

6. Factor-price distortions may make capital, especially from abroad, cheaper than its equilibrium price. The reasons for these distortions, as indicated in Chapter 9, include minimum wage legislation, pressure from organized labor, subsidies to capital, and artificially low foreign exchange prices.

Thus maximizing a project's labor intensity is not a sound investment criterion. Nevertheless, LDC planners need to examine carefully technologies in which labor can be substituted for capital.

Yet most of the global stock of new technology is capital intensive. Buddhadeb Ghosh and Chiranjib Neogi recommend that a country acquire new technology even if capital intensive, but modify through local R and D until it discovers the appropriate technology.[28]

SOCIAL BENEFIT-COST ANALYSIS

Suppose society has a given amount of resources to invest to raise output. The objective is to allocate these limited resources to achieve the largest possible increase in the economy's capacity to produce goods and services. A standard approach, **social benefit-cost analysis,** more comprehensive than the just-discussed labor absorption criterion, states that you maximize the net social income (social benefits minus social costs) associated with a dollar of investment.

The **net present value** (V) of the stream of benefits and costs is calculated as

$$V = B_0 - C_0 + \frac{B_1 - C_1}{(1+r)} + \frac{B_2 - C_2}{(1+r)^2} + \ldots \frac{B_T - C_T}{(1+r)^T} = \sum_{t=0}^{T} \frac{B_t - C_t}{(1+r)^t} \qquad (11\text{--}1)$$

where B is social benefits, C is social costs, r is the social discount rate (the interest rate set by planners), t is time, and T is the life of the investment project.

[27]A.P. Thirlwall, *Growth and Development with Special Reference to Developing Economies* (Boulder, Co.: Lynne Rienner, 1995), pp. 233–34.

[28]Buddhadeb Ghosh and Chiranjib Neogi, "Productivity, Efficiency, and New Technology: The Case of Indian Manufacturing Industries," *Developing Economies* 31 (September 1993): 308–25.

Interest on capital reflects a discount of future income relative to present income, because more capital invested now means society produces a higher income in the future. Thus even where there is no risk or inflation, a dollar's worth of future income is never worth so much as today's dollar. Future values are always discounted, and the more distant the payoff, the greater the discount.

Suppose an irrigation project results in a net stream of $200 per year for 20 years, but nothing thereafter. The total net income stream is $200 \times 20 = \$4,000$ over the investment life. Assume, however, that the discount rate is 15 percent. This discounts the $200 annual net return to $173.91 in the first year, $99.43 in the fifth year, $49.44 in the tenth year, $24.58 in the fifteenth year, and $12.22 in the twentieth year. The discounted value of the total income stream over the 20-year period is not $4,000, but only $1,251.87.

Now to return to decisions about investment, you should rank investment projects by their V (Table 11-1 shows how to rank two hypothetical investment

TABLE 11-1 **Present Value of Hypothetical 20-Year Net Income Streams from Two Alternative $1 Million Investment Projects in Year 0 Discounted at 15 Percent per Year**

| | Textile Factory ($1 million initial K) | | | Sugar Refinery ($1 million initial K) | |
Year	Net Income $(B_t - C_t)$	Net Income (discounted to year 0)	Year	Net Income $(B_t - C_t)$	Net Income (discounted to year 0)
1	125,000	108,696	1	175,000	152,174
2	125,000	94,518	2	175,000	132,325
3	125,000	82,190	3	175,000	115,065
4	125,000	71,469	4	175,000	100,057
5	125,000	62,147	5	175,000	87,006
6	125,000	54,041	6	175,000	75,657
7	200,000	75,187	7	175,000	65,789
8	200,000	65,380	8	175,000	57,208
9	200,000	56,852	9	175,000	49,746
10	200,000	49,437	10	175,000	43,257
11	200,000	42,989	11	175,000	37,615
12	200,000	37,381	12	175,000	32,709
13	200,000	32,506	13	175,000	28,442
14	200,000	28,266	14	175,000	24,733
15	200,000	24,579	15	175,000	21,506
16	200,000	21,373	16	175,000	18,701
17	200,000	18,585	17	175,000	16,262
18	200,000	16,161	18	175,000	14,141
19	200,000	14,053	19	175,000	12,296
20	200,000	12,220	20	175,000	10,693
	3,550,000	$V = 968,030$		3,500,000	$V = 1,095,382$

$$\frac{V}{K} = \frac{968,030}{1,000,000} = 0.97 \qquad\qquad \frac{V}{K} = \frac{1,095,382}{1,000,000} = 1.10$$

Even though the summation of *undiscounted* net incomes is higher for the textile factory than the sugar refinery, planners should invest in the refinery, since its present value is higher. The example illustrates the importance of higher net incomes in the first few years before the discount factor is very high.

projects by V). Choose projects with the highest ratio of V to K (the amount of capital to be allocated), then the next highest V/K, and so on, until the funds to be invested are exhausted.[29] Thus a government agency choosing among investment projects, say, high-yielding varieties of seeds, oil wells, textile factories, sugar refineries, flour mills, primary education, and training industrial managers, should be guided by the following rule: *Maximize the contribution to national product arising from a given amount of investment.*

What Discount Rate to Use?   The present value of the net income stream is critically dependent on the **discount** (or interest) **rate** used. To illustrate, the present value of an investment of $1,000, with a net income stream of $130 per year over the next 20 years, can change from more than $1,000 to less than $1,000, if the discount rate is raised from 10 percent to 15 percent.

   The influential manual written by Oxford professors Ian M. D. Little and James Mirrlees for the OECD (an organization of developed capitalist countries) indicates that the discount rate should be set high enough to equate new capital formation (investment) with the supply of domestic savings and capital imports available (say K_1 in Figure 11–1). At a given discount rate (r), V/K diminishes (the

FIGURE 11-1   *V/K*, Discount Rates, and Capital Projects
Planners should choose a discount rate (for example, *r* = 0.125 above) so that the marginal project included has a V/K = 1 *and* just uses up the total investment funds available.

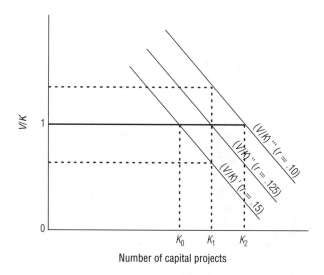

---

[29]After the projects are ranked, you may be able to increase the present value of all projects by shifting resources from projects with low V/K to those with high V/K. Assume project A has a V/K of 1.8 and project B of 1.0. Switching a marginal dollar from project B to project A means that V/K for that dollar investment is increased from 1.0 to 1.8. Switches can continue until V/K is maximized; V/K is equalized for the last dollar invested in each project. However, in practice, where the project size is lumpy or discontinuous, as in the case of a dam or steel mill, these switches may not be possible.

V/K curve is downward sloping) as capital projects increase. The *V/K* schedule rises (shifts to the right) as discount rates decrease and falls (shifts to the left) as discount rates increase.

Given the supply of savings and capital imports, planners should choose a discount rate so that the number of investment projects is consistent with a *V/K* equal to one; that is, present value of the net income stream is equal to the value of the capital invested (Equation 11–1). A too-low discount rate ($r = 10$ percent in Figure 11–1) results in excessive demand for investment, K_1K_2 and often a large international balance of payments deficit. For *V/K* to equal 1 (in Figure 11–1) at the point corresponding to the number of capital projects available, K_1, the discount rate must be 12.5 percent. A too-high discount rate ($r = 15$ percent) results in too little investment, K_0, so that the discount rate must be lowered to 12.5 percent to spur decisionmakers to use the savings and capital imports available.

Little and Mirrlees think most LDCs should use a real, or inflation-adjusted, interest rate of 10 percent. To illustrate, suppose $100 today and $200 next year are equivalent in buying power. A real interest rate of 10 percent would require a nominal interest rate of 120 percent per year so that $220 would be repaid next year for a loan of $100 today.

In practice they suggest the trial use of three rates—high, medium, and low—to sort out projects that are obviously good and obviously bad. The marginal ones can be put off until the planners see how large the investment program will be and whether any better projects come along to displace the marginal ones.[30]

Risk and Uncertainty.   It is difficult to rank investment projects whose net income streams are risky or uncertain. **Risk** is a situation where the probabilities of future net returns occurring are known. To calculate *V* (Equation 11–1), decisionmakers can specify the whole set of alternative net income streams, computing the expected present value of the alternative outcomes, each weighted by its probability. This approach is especially appropriate for risk-indifferent government planners who have numerous projects, a long time in which to work, and considerable borrowing capacity in the event of unexpected shortfalls, especially since governments (or even giant corporations) can pool risk. Indeed the larger the population, the lower the projects' risk per individual citizen. To be sure, private individuals bear some risks, for example, students enrolled in courses in mechanics, farmers using high-yielding varieties of rice, and slum dwellers resettled in public housing. Moreover, individual risks from public investments vary depending on the distribution of income, preferences, and tax rates.[31] Decision makers can, however, adjust expected present value for risk-taking or aversion. For example, the risk averter can place less value on probability distributions with a wide dispersion around the mean.

Many LDC investment choices are characterized by **uncertainty,** where the probabilities of net returns occurring are unknown. Yet this does not mean that planners must forgo project appraisal. While the outcome of a particular investment

[30]Ian M. D. Little and James A. Mirrlees, *Social Cost Benefit Analysis,* vol. 2 of *Manual of Industrial Project Analysis in Developing Countries* (Paris: Organization for Economic Cooperation and Development, 1968); George B. Baldwin, "A Layman's Guide to Little/Mirrlees," *Finance and Development* 9 (March 1972): 20; and Armen A. Alchian and William R. Allen, *University Economics: Elements of Inquiry* (Belmont, Calif.: Wadsworth, 1972), pp. 467–68.

[31]Kenneth J. Arrow and Robert C. Lind, "Uncertainty and the Evaluation of Public Investment Decisions," *American Economic Review* 60 (June 1970): 364–78.

may be uncertain, the risk of the entire investment program is negligible. Although the characteristics of success are uncertain, the ingredients for outright failure (political unacceptability, management incompetence, and so on) may not be. Meticulous feasibility studies of the project will help planners evaluate their abilities to respond to difficulties (often unforeseen). Although planners may not be able to rank some projects by V/K, they may still be able to make careful nonquantitative comparisons between projects.[32]

Differences Between Social and Private Benefit-Cost Calculations

Under restrictive assumptions, the invisible hand of the market, dependent on thousands of individual decisions, will guide producers toward maximum social welfare. In an economy that consists of perfectly competitive firms that: (1) produce only final goods, (2) render no external costs or benefits to other production units, (3) produce under conditions of constant (marginal opportunity) costs, and (4) pay market-clearing prices for production factors, a private firm that maximizes its rate of return will also maximize the increase in national product.

However, the social and private profitability of any investment are frequently different. When Equation 11–1 is used for the private firm rather than national-planning authorities, B becomes benefits and C costs incurred by the firm from the project, and r becomes the prevailing rate of interest that the firm pays on the capital market. Private investors want to maximize the commercial profitability of the investment. On the other hand, the national planner is likely to consider not only the internal rate of return to a given investment project, but also its effect on the profitability of other production units and on consumers. The following discussion examines the divergence between private and social marginal productivity.

EXTERNAL ECONOMIES

As indicated in Chapter 5, external economies are cost advantages rendered free by one firm to another producer or a consumer. So though the irrigation authority may not recover its investment in dams, reservoirs, canals, pumps, and tubewells directly, increased farm yields because of improved water supplies may make the social profitability of their investment quite high. Likewise revenues generated by vaccinating people for measles, rubella, polio, and cholera may not cover costs but may substantially increase net social benefits by improving the health and productivity of the population. On the other hand, the costs of external diseconomies, such as environmental pollution arising from iron smelting, chemical, and fertilizer plants, must be added to direct costs to arrive at any investment's net social impact.

The Dakha, Bangladesh, municipal authorities should consider externalities when they decide whether to build an underground railway of a given design. Officials can estimate the initial capital outlays spread over 8 years (compounding to

---

[32]Pan A. Yotopoulos and Jeffrey B. Nugent, *Economics of Development: Empirical Investigations* (New York: Harper & Row, 1976), pp. 376–77; and Frank Knight, *Risk, Uncertainty, and Profit* (Boston: Houghton Mifflin, 1921).

get the value of K in year 0) and against which must be set the stream of future net social benefits (gross benefits less operating costs) spread over 40 years but discounted to year 0.

Net social benefits will exceed net financial benefits if only because a lower fare would produce greater social benefits while reducing net receipts. The largest net benefit occurs when the fare is equal to the marginal operating cost, which varies throughout the day. But it is less cumbersome to hold the fare constant at average operating cost (or above average at peak hours, with a concessionary rate for other times).

Part of the annual gross benefit of the railway is the total receipts expected in each of the 40 years (say, 50 cents per ride times the number of riders). External benefits include the difference between 50 cents and the most people are prepared to pay for alternative road transport (auto, taxi, bus, bicycle, and rickshaw—a human-powered carriage) and the time, comfort, and safety benefits to riders (or to road users from less congestion).

If the capitalized value were $200 million in year 0 and the discount rate is correct, Dakha should build the underground if the sum of discounted future net benefits exceeds $200 million.

How do we calculate benefit cost if the railway adds equipment and other capital costs during the life of the underground? E. J. Mishan favors putting capital costs and operating costs together and entering all payments and external diseconomies as costs and all gross receipts and external economies as benefits. Thus we invest if net benefits $(B - C)$, which replace V in Equation 11–1, are at least zero.[33]

Planners be forewarned. Politicians have discovered the concept of *external economies*, using vague references to them to support inviable steel plants, dams, or port projects in their local districts. But even though planning agencies are generally responsible to the political leadership, careful feasibility studies, including evidence of the existence and the extent of externalities, can make a planning agency's recommendations difficult to override.

DISTRIBUTIONAL WEIGHTS

The social value of an investment may depend on who receives its benefits and bears its costs. In Equation 11–1 consumer goods produced for the rich count as much as for the poor. A government may express its goals of improving income distribution by weighing an investment's net benefits to the poor more heavily than to the rich.[34]

INDIVISIBILITIES

The returns to many indivisible investment projects, such as bridges, dams, rail lines, and electrical plants, depend on economies of scale in the use of technology, capital, or labor (see Chapter 5). Electricity can be generated, for example, in small-scale coal or oil-based steam plants or in large-scale hydroelectric or nuclear power plants.

---

[33]E. J. Mishan, *Cost-Benefit Analysis: An Informal Introduction* (London: Allen and Unwin, 1982); Edward M. Gramlich, *A Guide to Benefit-Cost Analysis* (Englewood Cliffs, N.J.: Prentice Hall, 1990).

[34]United Nations, Industrial Development Organization, *Guidelines for Project Evaluation* (New York, 1972), pp. 75–80, 135–48.

The benefit-cost calculation still applies in the presence of indivisibilities. However, they make the role of engineers and others who formulate the project more important. Thus, before evaluating a project on the basis of a given technology and scale, the project evaluator should be certain to ask engineers and others if all feasible technologies and scales have been considered.[35]

MONOPOLY

A **monopoly** is a single seller of a product without close substitutes; an **oligopoly** has few sellers, with interdependent pricing decisions among the larger firms in the industry. Unlike pure competition, where the individual firm faces a horizontal (perfectly elastic) demand curve, the pure monopolist faces a downward-sloping demand curve. Prices are higher and outputs lower in monopolistic resource and product markets than they are under pure competition.

Monopolistic restraints are frequent in LDCs, especially in the early stages of manufacturing. In many instances, industrial concentration is a by-product of official government policy, especially of fiscal incentives and controls. Also large firms know how to deal with the bureaucracy. Rare is the LDC government with the political ability and willpower to pursue antimonopoly policies. But if such a course *is* followed, trusts can be broken up; subsidies or preferential licensing of monopolistic pioneer companies eliminated; foreign ownership shares reduced; foreign companies made to divest themselves of ancillary production or marketing channels; or nationalization of monopolies undertaken.

However, nationalized enterprises may still behave as a private monopolist in pricing and output policies. In other instances, a monopoly may be natural, as when internal economies of scale bring about a continuously falling average cost curve that makes having more than one firm in an industry inefficient. Examples of these **natural public monopolies** may be telephone, electricity, water, or postal service. In these cases, fixed production and distribution costs are so large that large-scale operations are necessary for low unit costs and prices. Where competition is inappropriate, LDC governments can place monopolies under public ownership or regulation, so that consumers benefit from scale economies. Government can further reduce resource misallocation from public monopolies if they are required to use competitive pricing policies—where marginal cost is equal to price.

Planners must realize that monopolistic behavior at a later stage in the production process can affect benefits at an earlier stage. Suppose an irrigation project leads to growing more sugar beets, so more sugar is refined. If the sugar refiner has a monopoly, the sugar beet farmers' demand for irrigation water will not be a sufficient indication of such a project's merits. If refiners were producing sugar competitively, they would use more beets, in turn increasing the demand for water. Obviously the more monopolistic an industry, the more scope there will be for improving allocation through antimonopoly policies and marginal cost pricing. Even though economists can recommend such improvements, their only recourse in calculating benefit cost is to accept present and future prices and correct them for measurable externalities.[36]

---

[35]Pan A. Yotopoulos and Jeffrey B. Nugent, *Economics of Development: Empirical Investigations* (New York: Harper & Row, 1976), p. 374.

[36]A. R. Prest and R. Turvey, "Cost-Benefit Analysis: A Survey," *Economic Journal* 75 (December 1965): 683–735; E. J. Mishan, *Cost-Benefit Analysis: An Informal Introduction* (London: Allen & Unwin, 1982), pp. 111–53, and Karl E. Case and Ray C. Fair, *Principles of Economics* (Englewood Cliffs, N.J.: Prentice Hall, 1996), pp. 322–46.

SAVING AND REINVESTMENT

The usual benefit-cost analysis does not consider the effect of an investment's income streams on subsequent saving and output. Let us compare the irrigation project discussed above to a rural luxury housing project. Assume both projects have the same annual net income streams over a 20-year investment life. Let us focus only on the $200 annual net return ($99.43 discounted to the present) in the fifth year. Suppose that the commercial farmers whose incomes increased by $200 from the irrigation project invest $100 in farm machinery and buildings, which in turn increases net farm earnings for the next 20 years. Assume though that all of the income from the luxury housing project is spent on consumer goods. Should the additional income (discounted back to the present) attributed to the commercial farmers' investment not also be included in the net income streams of the initial irrigation project? On the other hand, that none of the net earnings from luxury housing is reinvested would make that project less desirable.

Though it is not usually done, benefit-cost analysis can consider the effect of a project's net returns on subsequent saving and output.[37] In some instances, the savings effect will conflict with the distributional effect, since higher income recipients usually save and reinvest more. Furthermore, since the income streams are even further in the future, their discounted value may be small, especially with high interest rates. Although accurate prediction is not possible, we can consider how much people are likely to save from income resulting from a particular investment project.

FACTOR PRICE DISTORTIONS

Chapter 9 indicated that wages in LDCs are frequently higher, and interest rates and foreign exchange costs lower, than market-clearing rates. Because of these distortions, the private investor may use more capital goods and foreign inputs and less labor than is socially profitable.

Shadow Prices

Prices do not measure social benefits and costs of an investment project if external economies and diseconomies, indivisibilities, monopolies, and price distortions are present. Prices observed in the market adjusted to take account of these differences between social cost-benefit and private cost-benefit calculations are **shadow prices.**

Planners use shadow (or accounting) prices to rectify distortions in the price of labor, capital, and foreign exchange. The following examples illustrate how this adjustment is usually made. The shadow wage for unskilled industrial labor, based on its alternative price in agriculture, may be only Rs. 0.50 per hour when the prevailing wage is Rs. 1.00 per hour. Even though business people borrow money at subsidized rates from government loan boards at only a 12-percent interest rate, the shadow interest rate, based on the cost of capital on the world market, may be 18 percent. The shadow (equilibrium) foreign exchange rate may be Rs. 26 = $1, while the actual rate, repressed by import and exchange restrictions,

---

[37]Walter Galenson and Harvey Leibenstein, "Investment Criteria, Productivity, and Economic Development," *Quarterly Journal of Economics* 69 (August 1955): 343–70; and Otto Eckstein, "Investment Criteria for Economic Development and the Theory of Intertemporal Welfare Economics," *Quarterly Journal of Economics* 71 (February 1957): 56–85.

may be Rs. 13 = $1. Thus the foreign-made computer purchased by a domestic firm for only Rs. 26,000 ($2,000) has a shadow price of Rs. 52,000. Correspondingly the accounting price of raw jute exported for $1,000 a ton is Rs. 26,000 compared to the Rs. 13,000 received by the seller at the official exchange rate.

Little and Mirrlees determine the shadow prices of both inputs and outputs by their world prices, since these "represent the actual terms on which the country can trade." However, they argue that, since traded goods are valued in world prices, nontraded goods must be similarly valued, in order to "ensure that we are valuing everything in terms of a common yardstick."[38]

Very few economists favoring the use of shadow prices question Little's and Mirrlees's valuations of goods that are or could be traded. But to value nontraded items in world prices involves a lot of trouble for doubtful advantage. Usually input-output data and purchasing power equivalents do not exist, so we cannot accurately value local goods in terms of world prices. In most countries, it is probably simpler and sufficiently accurate to (1) use world prices for inputs and outputs that are traded; (2) convert these values into domestic currency at an exchange rate (using a market rate if the official rate is badly out of line); and (3) value at domestic factor costs (shadow or market prices as appropriate) for nontraded inputs. In most investment projects, any distortions in the values of nontraded inputs are not likely to be important.[39]

Shadow pricing can open up Pandora's box. To illustrate, the shadow price of capital may depend on a distorted wage whose shadow rate requires calculation, and so on for other factors. Scarce planning personnel may have more important tasks than computing shadow prices from a complex system of interindustry equations, especially when data are lacking and shadow rates continually change. In addition a government that, say, hires labor on the basis of a shadow wage lower than the wage paid increases its payroll costs and budget deficit.[40]

Many developed capitalist countries have prices near enough to equilibrium that shadow prices are not needed for government planning. It would seem much easier for LDC governments to change foreign exchange rates, interest rates, wages, and other prices to equilibrium prices, which would make planning less cumbersome and time consuming and improve the efficiency of resource allocation.

Chapter 9 discussed how to decrease factor price distortions by (1) cutting wages and fringe benefits, (2) reducing interest rate subsidies, and (3) increasing the price of foreign exchange to an equilibrium rate. Yet price distortions are difficult to remove. Low elasticities of demand for urban labor may limit how much wage reductions expand employment (see Chapter 9). Increased foreign exchange prices (say, from Rs. 13 = $1 to Rs. 26 = $1) will not improve the balance of trade (exports minus imports of goods) if sums of the export and import demand elasticities are too low. An inelastic demand for an LDC's exports results in only a modest increase in rupee export receipts, which may not compensate for the in-

[38]Ian M. D. Little and James A. Mirrlees, *Social Cost Benefit Analysis,* vol. 2 of *Manual of Industrial Project Analysis in Developing Countries* (Paris: Organization for Economic Cooperation and Development, 1968), p. 92.

[39]George B. Baldwin, "A Layman's Guide to Little/Mirrlees," *Finance and Development* 9 (March 1972): 16–21.

[40]Wolfgang F. Stolper, *Planning without Facts: Lessons in Resource Allocation from Nigeria's Development* (Cambridge, Mass.: Harvard University Press, 1966), pp. 82–90.

crease in rupee import payments from inelastic import demand (that is, a relatively small quantity decline in response to the relatively large rupee price increase from the increased foreign exchange price). In LDCs import demand elasticity is often low as a result of high tariffs, extensive quantitative and other trade restrictions, and exchange controls.

Moreover, equilibrium prices may conflict with other policy goals. The LDC governments may not want to weaken labor unions' ability to protect the rights and shares of workers against powerful employers. Subsidized capital may be part of a government plan to promote local enterprise. Young, growing debtor nations borrowing capital to increase future productivity (for example, the United States and Canada in the late nineteenth century) may not be able to attain a foreign exchange rate that eliminates an overall balance of payments deficit.

Furthermore, existing distortions may be supported by economic interests too powerful for government to overcome. These interests may include organized labor, local enterprises receiving subsidies, industries competing with imports, firms favored with licensed foreign inputs, industrial and import licensing agencies, and central banks.

The LDC governments may be faced with a choice between the Scylla of cumbersome shadow price calculations and the Charybdis of factor price modification. Although the case for adjusting LDC prices nearer to their equilibrium rate is strong, the technical and political obstacles to doing so are often formidable.

Summary

1. The growth in total factor productivity is the increased worker productivity arising from factors other than increases in capital per worker.
2. Capital formation and technical progress are major factors responsible for the rapid economic growth of the West and Japan in the last 125–150 years.
3. Economic growth cannot be explained merely by increases in inputs.
4. Econometric studies of *developed* countries indicate that the increase in the productivity of each worker per unit of capital is a more important source of growth than the addition in capital per worker. Major explanations for this increase in productivity are advances in knowledge, greater education and training, learning by experience, organizational improvement, economies of scale, and resource shifts.
5. However, research on the sources of growth in *developing* countries provides evidence that the contribution of capital per worker is more important to economic growth than that of worker productivity per unit of capital. Reasons for the greater contribution of capital to growth in LDCs are higher marginal productivity of capital and higher growth rates of capital.
6. Technical progress results from a combination of research, development, invention, and innovation.
7. Technical knowledge acquired from abroad is costly and usually incomplete.
8. LDC planners must examine existing technologies for possible substitution of labor for capital. Nevertheless, the maximization of labor absorption is inadequate as an investment criterion. Labor-intensive techniques may sometimes not be used because of fixed capital-labor ratios in the industry, the high cost of adapting and modifying existing technologies, scarce administrative and

managerial resources needed to implement labor-intensive techniques, and distortions that increase the price of labor relative to that of capital.

9. Social benefit-cost analysis chooses investment projects that maximize the discounted net social benefits per unit of capital invested.

10. The discount rate should be set high enough to equate investment with savings and capital imports.

11. The investment planner who wants to avert risk can place less value on probability distributions with a wide relative dispersion around the average.

12. Market prices must be adjusted for externalities, distribution, indivisibilities, monopolies, and factor price distortions to obtain shadow prices. These prices aid the planner in adjusting returns away from commercial profitability to social profitability.

13. Computing shadow prices is usually a cumbersome and time-consuming task. Setting factor and foreign exchange prices closer to equilibrium rates may be more effective in improving resource allocation.

Terms to Review

- production function
- capital goods
- stocks
- flows
- entrepreneurship
- technology
- total factor productivity growth
- technical progress
- learning curve
- social profitability
- price of knowledge
- basic research
- applied research
- development
- invention

- technological followership
- maximum labor absorption
- intermediate technology
- engineering mentality
- efficiency wage
- social benefit-cost analysis
- present value (*V*) of the net income stream
- discount rate
- risk
- uncertainty
- monopoly
- oligopoly
- natural public monopolies
- shadow prices

Questions to Discuss

1. What factors explain the rapid long-term growth in gross national product per capita of the West and Japan?

2. What is the relative importance of capital formation and technical progress as sources of economic growth? in the West? in LDCs?

3. Why is capital accumulation more important as a source of growth in LDCs than in DCs? Why is technical progress less important?

4. What contributes to growth in output per worker-hour besides increases in capital per worker-hour?

5. How do economists conceptualize technical knowledge? What effect does cost have in technology search?

6. What implications does learning by doing have for LDC domestic and international technological policies?

7. Can growth be conceptualized as a process of increase in inputs?

8. How is the price of knowledge determined?

9. What are some of the advantages and disadvantages of technology followership?

10. What criterion would you recommend that a planner use in allocating investable resources among different projects and sectors in a less developed economy?

11. What is the maximum labor absorption investment criterion? What are its flaws?

12. What are the attractions of capital-intensive techniques in capital scarce LDCs?

13. What is social benefit-cost analysis? Explain how it is used to rank alternative investment projects.

14. How would Sichuan (China) provincial authorities decide whether to build a bridge across the Yangtze River in a major city, Chongqing?

15. What are the differences between social and private benefit-cost calculations?

16. How do planners choose what discount rate to apply to investment projects?

17. What are shadow prices? Give some examples. What is a planning alternative to the use of shadow prices? Evaluate this alternative.

Guide to Readings

A.P. Thirlwall, *Growth and Development with Special Reference to Developing Countries* (New York: Wiley, 1977), pp. 48–80; and Henry J. Bruton, *Principles of Development Economics* (Englewood Cliffs, N.J.: Prentice-Hall, 1965), pp. 11–21, provide a more detailed analysis of the aggregate production function.

Michael Kremer uses the space shuttle *Challenger* as a metaphor for production in "The O-Ring Theory of Economic Development," *Quarterly Journal of Economics* 108 (August 1993): 551–75. The *Challenger* has thousands of components, but exploded because the temperature at which it was launched was so low that one component, the O-rings, malfunctioned. In a similar fashion, Kremer proposes a production function where "production consists of many tasks, [either simultaneous or sequential], all of which must be successfully completed for the product to have full value" (p. 551). To illustrate, a violinist who plays off key or misses the beat can ruin a whole symphony orchestra. This production function does not allow the substitution of quantity (two mediocre violinists, copyeditors, chefs, or goalkeepers) for quality (one good one). Kremer thinks the O-ring theory can explain why rich countries specialize in more complicated products, have larger firms, and have astonishingly higher worker productivity than poor countries.

Griliches (note 13) examines research and development, technical progress, and growth in productivity. Martin Fransman, *Technology and Economic*

Development (Boulder, Colo.: Westview, 1986); and Giovanni Dosi, Christopher Freeman, Richard Nelson, Gerald Silverberg, and Luc Soete, eds., *Technical Change and Economic Theory* (London: Pinter, 1988), are important analyses of technical progress, while Kennedy's and Thirlwall's survey (note 9) of technological change is excellent though dated. Arrow (note 9) is the classic article on learning by doing. A. P. Thirlwall, *Growth and Development with Special Reference to Developing Countries* (New York: Wiley, 1977), pp. 48–80, has an excellent survey of the literature on sources of growth in developing countries.

Richard Layard and Stephen Glaister, eds., *Cost-Benefit Analysis* (Cambridge: Cambridge University Press, 1994), have an up-to-date benefit–cost textbook. Other manuals providing guidelines for investment choice and benefit-cost analysis are Gramlich (note 33), Mishan (note 33), Little and Mirrlees (note 30), and UN, *Guidelines* (note 34). Baldwin's essay (note 30) provides a brief, simple explanation of benefit-cost analysis, while Morawetz (see note, Chapter 9), includes employment considerations in his analysis. Arrow and Lind (note 31) analyze the effect of uncertainty on public investments. Chapter 14 indicates some serious limitations in using the incremental capital-output ratio (ICOR) as an investment criterion. Henry J. Bruton, *Principles of Development Economics* (Englewood Cliffs, N.J.: Prentice-Hall, 1965), pp. 281–316; Yotopoulos and Nugent, pp. 369–92 (note 32); and A.P. Thirlwall, *Growth and Development with Special Reference to Developing Countries* (New York: Wiley, 1977), pp. 169–211, in ascending level of difficulty, provide surveys of technological choice, investment criterion, and resource allocation. On capital accumulation and economic development, see Shanti S. Tangri and H. Peter Gray, eds., *Capital Accumulation and Economic Development* (Boston: Heath, 1967).

E. F. Schumacher, "Industrialization through 'Intermediate Technology'" (note 25), *Small Is Beautiful—Economics as If People Mattered* (New York: Harper & Row, 1973), and *Good Work* (New York: Harper & Row, 1979), make a strong case for using intermediate technology, especially in LDCs.

CHAPTER 12
Entrepreneurship, Organization, and Innovation

Perhaps one day a saga may be written about the modern captain of industry. Perhaps, in the civilization which succeeds our own, a legend of the entrepreneur will be thumbed by antiquarians, and told as a winter tale by the firelight, as today our sages assemble fragments of priestly mythologies from the Nile, and as we tell to children of Jason's noble quest of the Golden Fleece. But what form such a legend may take it is not at all easy to foresee. Whether the businessman be the Jason or the Aetes in the story depends on other secrets which those unloved sisters keep hid where they store their scissors and their thread. We have, indeed, the crude unwrought materials for such a legend to hand in plenty, but they are suitable, strange to say, for legends of two sharply different kinds. The Golden Fleece is there, right enough, as the background of the story. But the captain of industry may be cast in either of two roles: as the noble, daring, high-souled adventurer, sailing in the teeth of storm and danger to wrest from barbarism a prize to enrich his countrymen; or else as a barbarous tyrant, guarding his treasure with cunning and laying snares to entrap Jason, who comes with the breath of a new civilization to challenge his power and possession.[1]

The entrepreneur, with a dream and will to found a private kingdom, to conquer adversity, to achieve success for its own sake, and to experience the joy of creation, is a heroic figure in economic development, according to Joseph A. Schumpeter—sometime finance minister in an Austrian Socialist government and professor of economics in Bonn, Tokyo, and at Harvard.[2] In a similar vein, Harvard psychologist David C. McClelland perceives the efforts of the entrepreneur, in controlling production in both capitalist and socialist economies, as largely responsible for rapid economic growth. For McClelland, the entrepreneur, driven by an inner

[1]Maurice Dobb, *Capitalist Enterprise and Social Progress* (London: George Routledge and Sons, 1926), p. 3.

[2]Joseph A. Schumpeter, *The Theory of Economic Development* (Cambridge, Mass.: Harvard University Press, 1961). (First German ed., 1911.)

urge to improve, is motivated by profits as a measure of achievement rather than as a source of enrichment.[3]

Economic historians emphasize that such Schumpeterian captains of industry as John D. Rockefeller (oil), Andrew Carnegie (steel), Cornelius Vanderbilt (railroads), James B. Duke (tobacco and power), and Jay Gould and J. P. Morgan (finance) led the 50-year economic expansion before World War I that made the United States the world's leading industrial nation. Rockefeller combined managerial genius, capacity for detail, decisiveness, frugality, and foresight with a ruthless suppression of competition, the use of espionage and violence to gain competitive advantages, and a general neglect of the public interest to become the symbol of the virtues and vices of these "robber barons."[4]

But surely an economy does not require Rockefellers, Vanderbilts, and Goulds for rapid development. The functions of entrepreneurship, organization, and innovation are not limited to the large private sector but can be exercised by the Argentine flour miller, the Malaysian cobbler, or the Chinese government planner and factory manager. Except in an anarchist utopia, the need for entrepreneurship is free of ideology.

Despite exceptions, such as Jamshedjee Tata, responsible for India's first steel mill in 1911, the political, cultural, and technological milieu was not right for vigorous, industrial, entrepreneurial activity in present LDCs, especially prior to 1950.

Scope of the Chapter

The **entrepreneur** can be viewed in at least four ways: (1) as the coordinator of other production resources—land, labor, and capital; (2) as the decision maker under uncertainty; (3) as the innovator; and (4) as the gap filler and input completer. The last two concepts, which are the most relevant for economic development, are discussed in the first two sections of this chapter.

We next look at entrepreneurial functions in LDCs. After this we consider the family as an entrepreneurial unit. The multiple entrepreneurial function is then discussed. The next two sections examine McClelland's and Hagen's analyses of the effect of social and psychological factors on entrepreneurship. Subsequent sections consider the entrepreneur's socioeconomic profile—occupational background, religious and ethnic origin, social origin and mobility, education, and sex. The last section discusses technological mobilization and innovation in socialist and transitional economies.

Entrepreneur As Innovator

The rapid economic growth of the Western world during the past century is largely a story of how novel and improved ways of satisfying wants were discovered and adopted. But this story is not just one of inventions or devising new methods or products. History is replete with inventions that were not needed or that, more frequently, failed to obtain a sponsor or market. For example, the Stanley Steamer, invented early in the twentieth century, probably failed not because it was inferior

---

[3]David C. McClelland, *The Achieving Society* (Princeton, N.J.: D. Van Nostrand, 1961).

[4]Gerald D. Nash, ed., *Issues in American Economic History: Selected Readings* (Boston: Heath, 1964), pp. 347–48.

to the automobile with the internal combustion engine but because the inventors, the Stanley brothers, did not try to mass produce it. No, to explain economic growth, we must emphasize innovation rather than invention. Economists have paid little systematic attention to the process of **innovation**—the embodiment in commercial practice of some new idea or invention—and to the innovator.

SCHUMPETER'S THEORY

Schumpeter is the exceptional economist who links innovation to the entrepreneur, maintaining that the source of private profits is successful innovation and that innovation brings about economic growth.[5] He feels that the entrepreneur carries out new economic combinations by: (1) introducing new products, (2) introducing new production functions that decrease inputs needed to produce a given output, (3) opening new markets, (4) exploiting new sources of materials, and (5) reorganizing an industry.

The Schumpeterian model begins with a **stationary state,** an unchanging economic process that merely reproduces itself at constant rates without innovators or entrepreneurs. This model assumes perfect competition, full employment, and no savings nor technical change; and it clarifies the tremendous impact of entrepreneurs on the economic process. In the stationary state, no entrepreneurial function is required, since the ordinary, routine work, the repetition of orders and operations, can be done by workers themselves. However, into this stationary process, a profit-motivated entrepreneur begins to innovate, say, by introducing a new production function that raises the marginal productivity of various production resources. Eventually such innovation means the construction of new plants and the creation of new firms, which imply new leadership.

The stationary economy may have high earnings for management, monopoly gains, windfalls, or speculative gains, but has no entrepreneurial profits. Profits are the premium for innovation, and they arise from no other source. Innovation, however, sets up only a temporary monopoly gain, which is soon wiped out by imitation. For profits to continue, it is necessary to keep a step ahead of one's rivals—the innovations must continue. Profits result from the activity of the entrepreneur, even though he or she may not always receive them.

New bank credit finances the innovation, which, once successfully set up, is more easily imitated by competitors. Innovations are not isolated events evenly distributed in time, place, and sector; they arise in clusters, as a result of lowered risk. Eventually the waves of entrepreneurial activity not only force out old firms but exhaust the limited possibilities of gain from the innovation. As borrowing diminishes and loans are repaid, the entrepreneurial activity slackens and finally ceases. Innovation, saving, credit creation, and imitation explain economic growth, while their ebb and flow determine the business cycle.

THE SCHUMPETERIAN ENTREPRENEUR
IN DEVELOPING COUNTRIES

According to Schumpeter, his theory is valid only in capitalist economies prior to the rise of giant corporations. Thus it may be even less appropriate for mixed and capitalist LDCs, since many industries in these countries, especially in

---

[5]Joseph A. Schumpeter, *The Theory of Economic Development* (Cambridge, Mass.: Harvard University Press, 1961); and Joseph A. Schumpeter, *Business Cycles,* 2 vols. (New York: McGraw-Hill, 1939).

manufacturing, are dominated by a few large firms. It seems unrealistic to preclude the possibility that innovation may mean expansion of already-existing firms. In fact, in the real world, characterized by imperfect competition, an established organization would frequently have an advantage in developing new techniques, markets, products, and organizations.

Furthermore, Schumpeter's concept of the entrepreneur is somewhat limited in developing countries. The majority of LDC Schumpeterian entrepreneurs are traders whose innovations are opening new markets. In light of technical transfers from advanced economies, the development of entirely new combinations should not unduly limit what is and is not considered entrepreneurial activity.

People with technical, executive, and organizational skills may be too scarce in less-developed countries to use in developing new combinations in the Schumpeterian sense. And in any case, fewer high-level people are needed to adapt combinations from economically advanced countries.

STAGES IN INNOVATION

Technical advance involves (1) the development of pure science, (2) invention, (3) innovation, (4) financing the innovation, and (5) the innovation's acceptance. Science and technical innovation interact; basic scientific advances not only create opportunities for innovation, but economic incentives and technical progress can affect the agenda for, and identify the payoffs from, scientific research. Links from production to technology and science are often absent in LDCs. Yet low-income countries can frequently skip stages 1 and 2 and sometimes even stage 3, so that scarce, high-level personnel can be devoted to adapting those discoveries already made.[6]

Entrepreneur As Gap-Filler

The innovator differs from the manager of a firm, who runs the business along established lines. Entrepreneurs are the engineers of change, not its products. They are difficult to identify in practice, since no one acts exclusively as an entrepreneur. Though they frequently will be found among heads or founders of firms, or among the major owners or stockholders, they need not necessarily hold executive office in the firm, furnish capital, or bear risks.

Entrepreneurship indicates activities essential to creating or carrying on an enterprise where not all markets are well established or clearly defined, or where the production function is not fully specified nor completely known. Nobel economist Ronald H. Coase identifies two major coordinating instruments within the economy: the entrepreneur, who organizes within the firm through command and hierarchy, and the price mechanism, which coordinates decisions between firms. The choice between organization within the firm or by the market (that is, the "make or buy" decision) is not given or determined by technology but mainly reflects the transactions costs of using the price system, including the cost of discovering what prices are.[7]

---

[6]W. Robert Maclaurin, "The Sequence from Invention to Innovation and Its Relation to Economic Growth," *Quarterly Journal of Economics* 67 (February 1953): 97–111; and Martin Fransman, *Technology and Economic Development* (Boulder, Colo.: Westview, 1986), pp. 47–48.

[7]Ronald H. Coase, "The Nature of the Firm," *Economica N.S.* 4 (1937): 386–405. He argues that "a firm . . . consists of the system of relationships which comes into existence when the direction of resources is dependent on an entrepreneur. . . . As a firm gets larger, there may be decreasing returns to the entrepreneur function, that is, the costs of organizing additional transactions within the firm may rise" (pp. 388–89).

An entrepreneur (an individual or groups of individuals) has the rare capability of making up for market deficiencies or filling gaps. There is no one-to-one correspondence between sets of inputs and outputs. Many firms operate with a considerable degree of slack.[8] Thus the entrepreneur, especially in LDCs, may need to seek and evaluate economic opportunities; marshall financial resources; manage the firm; and acquire new economic information and translate it into new markets, techniques, and products, since it may not be possible to hire someone to do these tasks. To illustrate, if an upper skiving machine is essential for making men's fine leather shoes; if no one in the country produces this machine; and if imports are barred, then only entrepreneurs who know how to construct the machine can enter the fine leather footwear industry.

The entrepreneur must also be an "input completer." For any given economic activity, a minimum quantity of inputs must be marshaled. If less than the minimum is available, the entrepreneur steps in to make up for the lack of marketable inputs by developing more productive techniques; accumulating new knowledge; creating or adopting new goods, new markets, new materials, and new organizational forms; and creating new skills—all important elements in economic growth. As indicated in Chapter 11, growth cannot be explained merely by increases in standard inputs, such as labor and capital. Entrepreneurial gap filling and input completing help explain why labor and capital do not account for all outputs. No fixed relationship between inputs and outputs exists, partly because entrepreneurial contributions cannot be readily quantified, predicted, planned for, or controlled.

Functions of the Entrepreneur

As we hinted earlier, we feel Schumpeter's concept of the entrepreneur should be broadened to include those who adapt and modify already existing innovations.[9] Most business activity in a nonstationary state requires some innovation. Each firm is uniquely located and organized, and its economic setting changes over time. Absolute imitation is therefore impossible, and techniques developed outside the firm must be adapted to its circumstances. This necessity is especially apparent when a LDC firm borrows technology from an advanced economy with different, relative factor prices—for example, a higher labor price relative to capital. These adaptations require, if you will, innovation if defined in a less restrictive sense than Schumpeter used it.

In a changing economy, it is difficult to distinguish between the adaptations of day-to-day management and the entrepreneur's creative decisions. Thus the following list of thirteen entrepreneurial roles includes some management functions.

Exchange relationships

1. Seeing market opportunities (novel or imitative)
2. Gaining command over resources

---

[8]Harvey Leibenstein, "Allocative Efficiency versus 'X-Efficiency'," *American Economic Review* 56 (June 1966): 392–415; and Harvey Leibenstein, "Entrepreneurship and Development," *American Economic Review* 58 (May 1968): 72–83.

[9]Although Schumpeter did not consider the imitator to be an entrepreneur, he did contrast the imitating entrepreneur with the innovating entrepreneur. Entrepreneurs who adapt innovations already in existence could be said to be involved in both imitation and innovation.

3. Marketing the product and responding to competition
4. Purchasing inputs

Political administration
5. Dealing with the public bureaucracy (concessions, licenses, taxes, and so forth)
6. Managing human relations in the firm
7. Managing customer and supplier relations

Management control
8. Managing finances
9. Managing production (control by written records, supervision, coordinating input flows with customer orders, maintaining equipment)

Technological
10. Acquiring and overseeing plant assembly
11. Minimizing inputs with a given production process—industrial engineering
12. Upgrading processes and product quality
13. Introducing new production techniques and products

The economist who analyzes Western economies frequently limits the entrepreneurial function to activities 1 and 2: It is assumed that the remaining skills can be purchased in the marketplace. But the extent to which the entrepreneur can delegate these activities to competent subordinates depends on many variables: the scale of production; how well developed the market is for such highly skilled labor; the social factors governing how responsible hired personnel will be; and the entrepreneur's efficiency in using high-level managerial employees. Since many of the markets for skilled people in developing countries are not well developed, entrepreneurs frequently have to perform these tasks themselves. Studies of entrepreneurs in LDCs indicate that production, financial, and technological management are least satisfactory.[10]

Family As Entrepreneur

The family enterprise, which is widespread in less-industrialized countries, is usually small and managed primarily by the father or eldest son. As the dominant form of economic organization in nineteenth-century France, the family firm was conceived of as a fief to maintain and enhance the position of the family, and not as a mechanism for wealth and power.[11] However, some of the leading industrial conglomerates in developing countries are family owned. For example, India's largest private manufacturers are usually members of old trading families, who control several companies. Frequently family members specialize their roles according to industry, location, or management function.

Family entrepreneurship can mobilize large amounts of resources, make quick, unified decisions, put trustworthy people into management positions, and

---

[10]Peter Kilby, ed., *Entrepreneurship and Economic Development* (New York: Free Press, 1971), pp. 1–40.
[11]David S. Landes, "French Entrepreneurship and Industrial Growth in the Nineteenth Century," *Journal of Economic History* 9 (May 1949): 45–61.

constrain irresponsibility. Thus among the Ibo people in Nigeria, families guarantee that debts are paid, and their solidarity provides strong sanctions against default, since individual failure reflects on family reputation. The extended family frequently funds apprentice training and initial capitalization, although it may hinder the firm's expansion by diverting resources to current consumption.[12]

In India, the extended family involved in business activity is usually methodical in choosing its investments in the human capital of its children. The family may use its income and enterprises to provide the training, education, travel, and business experience of its children, and to purchase plant and equipment that is most appropriate for the young business person's entrepreneurial development. As youngsters, the children in business families are exposed to a business milieu and learn about the family enterprises. Where the family has sufficient income, it enrolls the children in excellent schools, frequently encouraging its offspring to study law, economics, engineering, or business administration at the university, and sometimes even providing foreign travel and training. A family with several children may diversify their educations among subjects relevant for business. During school vacations and after graduation, each son, and increasingly in the last two decades each daughter, is moved from job to job within the family's production units, gradually increasing the child's responsibility. Moreover, families sometimes arranges marriages to further alliances with other prosperous business families.[13]

Family entrepreneurship, however, may be conservative about taking risks, innovating, and delegating authority. Paternalistic attitudes in employer-employee relationships prevail, and family-owned firms are often reluctant to hire professional managers. This reluctance, however, may reflect the critical shortage of professionals and managers in LDCs—especially those who can occupy positions of authority without ownership—rather than the idiosyncrasies of the family. In addition, most family firms are too small to afford outside managers. And we must add that paternalism and authoritarianism are feudal legacies characteristic of many enterprises in developing countries, and not unique to family businesses.

Multiple Entrepreneurial Function

Frequently today with the increased complexity of business firms, the entrepreneurial function may be divided among a business hierarchy. Such a hierarchical functioning might be more appropriately labeled **organization** rather than entrepreneurship. Organization connotes not only the constellation of functions, persons, and abilities used to manage the enterprise, but also how these elements are integrated into a common undertaking.[14] Organization may be either profit or social service oriented, giving the concept applicability to both private and public sectors.

---

[12]E. Wayne Nafziger, "The Effect of the Nigerian Extended Family on Entrepreneurial Activity," *Economic Development and Cultural Change* 18 (October 1969): 25–33.

[13]E. Wayne Nafziger, "Class, Caste, and Community of South Indian Industrialists: An Examination of the Horatio Alger Model," *Journal of Development Studies* 11 (January 1975): 131–48.

[14]Frederick Harbison, "Entrepreneurial Organization as a Factor in Economic Development," *Quarterly Journal of Economics* 64 (August 1956): 364–79.

Achievement Motivation, Self-Assessment, and Entrepreneurship

Psychological evidence indicates that in early childhood, a person unconsciously learns behavior that is safest and most rewarding and that such learning substantially influences adult behavior. For example, the individual who is encouraged to be curious, creative, and independent as a child is more likely to engage in innovative and entrepreneurial activity as an adult. Although a society may consciously attempt to nurture imagination, self-reliance, and achievement orientation in child rearing and schooling, scholars used to consider this process slow and uncertain at best and requiring at least a generation before it would affect entrepreneurship and economic growth.

McClelland contends that a society with a generally high **need for achievement** or urge to improve produces more energetic entrepreneurs, who, in turn, bring about more rapid economic development. He argues that entrepreneurs can be trained to succeed. Scholars are quite skeptical of the validity of McClelland's findings. Nevertheless, achievement motivation training (along with practical training in management, marketing, and finance and assistance in project conception and planning) is more and more a part of programs at entrepreneurship development centers.[15]

Boyan Jovanovic finds that differences in entrepreneurial ability, learned over time, determine a person's entry of exit into business. From business experience, people acquire more precise estimates of their ability, expanding output as they revise their ability estimates upward, and contracting with downward revisions of ability.[16]

Theory of Technological Creativity

HAGEN'S THEORY

On the Theory of Social Change (1962), by economist Everett E. Hagen, uses psychology, sociology, and anthropology to explain how a traditional agricultural society (with a hierarchical and authoritarian social structure where status is inherited) becomes one where continuing technical progress occurs. Since the industrial and cultural complex of low-income societies is unique, they cannot merely imitate Western techniques. Thus economic growth requires widespread adaptation, creativity, and problem solving, in addition to positive attitudes toward manual labor.

Hagen suggests that childhood environment and training in traditional societies produce an authoritarian personality with a low need for achievement, a high need for dependence and submission, and a fatalistic view of the world. If parents perceive children as fragile organisms without the capacity for understanding or managing the world, the offspring are treated oversolicitously and prevented from taking the initiative. The child, repressing anger, avoids anxiety by obeying the commands of powerful people.

---

[15]David C. McClelland, *The Achieving Society* (Princeton, N.J.: D. Van Nostrand, 1961); and David C. McClelland and David G. Winter, *Motivating Economic Achievement* (New York: Free Press, 1971). See E. Wayne Nafziger, *Entrepreneurship, Equity, and Economic Development* (Greenwich, Conn.: JAI Press, 1986), pp. 61–70, for an elaboration of criticisms of the McClelland approach.

[16]Boyan Jovanovic, "Selection and Evolution of Industry," *Econometrica* 50 (May 1982): 649–670.

Events that cause peasants, workers, and lower elites to feel they are no longer respected and valued may catalyze economic development. For Hagen this process occurs over many generations. Increasingly adults become angry and anxious; and sons retreat and reject their parents' unsatisfying values. After several generations, women, reacting to their husbands' ineffectiveness, respond with delight to their sons' achievements. Such maternal attitudes combined with paternal weakness provide an almost ideal environment for the formation of an anxious, driving type of creativity. If sons are blocked from other careers, they will become entrepreneurs and spearhead the drive for economic growth.[17]

A CRITIQUE

One problem with Hagen's theory is that loss of status respect is an event so broadly defined that it may occur once or twice a decade in most societies. Nor does the theory explain groups, such as seventeenth-century English Catholics, who lost status but did not become entrepreneurs. Furthermore, the interval between status loss and the emergence of creativity varies from 30 to 700 years, so that Hagen's hypothesis fits almost any case.

Although Hagen charges economists with ethnocentrism, he applies a Western-based personality theory to vastly different societies and historical periods. In addition his case studies provide no evidence of changes in parent-child relationships and child-training methods during the early historical periods of status loss. Moreover, one economic historian convincingly argues that the position, training, and discipline of the child in modern Germany, Austria, and Sweden resemble those described in Hagen's traditional society.[18] Finally, Hagen slights the effect on entrepreneurial activity of changes in economic opportunities, such as improved transport, wider-reaching markets, the availability of foreign capital and technology, and social structure. But despite its inadequacies, Hagen's work has made economists more aware of the importance of noneconomic variables in economic growth.

Occupational Background

Many studies of industrial entrepreneurs in developing countries indicate trade was their former occupation.[19] A trading background gives the entrepreneur a familiarity with the market, some general management and commercial experience,

---

[17]Everett E. Hagen, *On the Theory of Social Change: How Economic Growth Begins* (Homewood, Ill.: Dorsey Press, 1962).

[18]Alexander Gerschenkron, Review of Hagen, *On the Theory of Social Change, Economica* 32 (February 1965): 90–94.

[19]The following studies were consulted: Yusif A. Sayigh, *Entrepreneurs of Lebanon: The Role of the Business Leader in a Developing Economy* (Cambridge, Mass.: Harvard University Press, 1962); Alec P. Alexander, "Industrial Entrepreneurship in Turkey: Origins and Growth," *Economic Development and Cultural Change* 8 (July 1960): 349–65; Alec P. Alexander, *Greek Industrialists: An Economic and Social Analysis* (Athens: Center of Planning and Economic Research, 1964); Peter Kilby, *African Enterprise: The Nigerian Bread Industry* (Stanford: Hoover Institution, 1965); John R. Harris, "Industrial Entrepreneurship in Nigeria" (Ph.D. diss., Northwestern University, 1967); James J. Berna, *Industrial Entrepreneurship in Madras State* (New York: Asia Publishing House, 1960); E. Wayne Nafziger, *Class, Caste, and Entrepreneurship: A Study of Indian Industrialists* (Honolulu: University Press of Hawaii, 1978); Gustav F. Papanek, "The Development of Entrepreneurship," *American Economic Review* 52 (May 1962): 46–58; and John J. Carroll, *The Filipino Manufacturing Entrepreneur, Agent and Product of Change* (Ithaca: Cornell University Press, 1965).

sales outlets and contacts, and some capital. A number of traders entered manufacturing to ensure regular supplies or because they can increase profits. Frequently a major catalyst for this shift was government policy following independence from colonial control. At that time, governments often encouraged import substitution in manufacturing through higher tariffs, tighter import quotas, and an industrial policy that encourages the use of domestic inputs. Even with government encouragement, traders going into manufacturing often have had trouble setting up a production line and coordinating a large labor force.

Writers on entrepreneurship occasionally mention a "trader mentality" that leads to an irrational preference for the quick turnover rather than the long-run returns that manufacturing offers. Frequently, however, the trader may lack industrial management and technical skills. In addition the business milieu, social overhead services, and government policies may not encourage industry. It is not irrational for entrepreneurs to prefer trade to manufacturing if they believe incomes are higher in trade. For some traders, an industrial venture may await government programs in technical and management training, industrial extension, and financial assistance.

In most developing countries, numerous young people are apprenticed to learn such skills as baking, shoemaking, tinsmithing, blacksmithing, tanning, and dressmaking from a parent, relative, or other artisan. Even though some have argued that artisans trained in this way have less drive and vision and direct relatively small firms, some of them have, nonetheless, become major manufacturers. This transformation is especially pronounced in early phases of industrialization, such as in England's Industrial Revolution and today's less-developed countries. The scale of the enterprise may gradually expand over several years or even generations. Even so, relatively few artisans can make the leap from the small firm owner to manufacturer. However, artisans and their students benefit from industrial innovation as well as from training and extension programs. Apprentice systems inevitably improve with the introduction of new techniques. Economists should not overlook these artisans, since they contribute to industrial growth.

In general, most successful industrial entrepreneurs have borne or shared chief responsibility for the management of at least one enterprise prior to their present activity, whether this work was in another manufacturing unit or in handicrafts, trade, transport, or contracting. Few industrialists, however, were once farmers. Except for landowners, very few farmers have had the funds to invest in industry. And even landlords are poorly represented. They tend to place a high value on consumption and real estate expenditure and lack experience in managing and coordinating a production process with specialized work tasks and machinery and in overseeing secondary labor relations.

Few people in developing countries move from government employment to entrepreneurship. In studies in Lebanon, Turkey, Greece, Pakistan, and India, less than 10 percent of the entrepreneurs were once in the civil service. Frequently, potentially capable entrepreneurs in government service have relatively high salaries, good working conditions, attractive fringe benefits, and tenure. Leaving such a job to enter entrepreneurial activity involves substantial risk.

Empirical studies indicate that an even smaller fraction of industrial entrepreneurs were previously blue-collar workers. Blue-collar workers are most likely to become entrepreneurs because of "push" factors, such as the lack of attractive job options or the threat of persistent unemployment, rather than "pull" factors, such as the prospect of rapidly expanding markets.

Religious and Ethnic Origin

WEBER'S THESIS: THE PROTESTANT ETHIC

Capitalism is an economic system where private owners of capital and their agents, making decisions based on private profit, hire legally free, but capital–less, workers. Max Weber's *The Protestant Ethic and the Spirit of Capitalism* (1904–05) tried to explain why the continuous and rational development of the capitalist system originated in Western Europe in about the sixteenth century.[20] Weber noted that European businessmen and skilled laborers were overwhelmingly Protestant and that capitalism was most advanced in Protestant countries, such as England and Holland. He held to the view, discussed in Chapter 3, that Protestant asceticism was expressed in a secular vocation. Although Puritans (or ascetic Protestants) opposed materialism as much as the Roman Catholic Church, they did not disapprove of accumulating wealth. They did however restrict extravagance and conspicuous consumption and frowned on laziness. These attitudes resulted in a high savings rate and continued hard work—both factors favorable to economic progress.

Calvinists (Reformed churches and Presbyterians), Pietists, Methodists, Baptists, Quakers, and Mennonites made up the major ascetic Protestant denominations. Sixteenth-century French reformer John Calvin taught that those elected by God were to be diligent, thrifty, honest, and prudent, virtues coinciding with the spirit essential for capitalist development.

CRITIQUE OF WEBER

The Protestant Reformation and the rise of capitalism, though correlated, need not indicate causation. A third factor—the disruption of the Catholic social system and loss of civil power—may have been partly responsible for both. Alternatively, the Protestant ethic may have changed to accommodate the needs of the rising capitalist class. Another explanation is that the secularization, ethical relativism, and social realism of Protestantism may have been as important as its "this-worldly" asceticism in explaining its contribution to economic development.

MARGINAL INDIVIDUALS AS ENTREPRENEURS

Despite criticisms Weber's work has stimulated scholars to ask important questions about how entrepreneurial activity is affected by religious, ethnic, and linguistic communities. One question concerns marginal ethnic and social groups, that is, those whose values differ greatly from the majority of the population. To what extent do **marginal individuals,** because of their ambiguous position, tend to be innovative?

In a confirmation of Weber's study, Hagen finds that Nonconformists (Quakers, Methodists, Congregationalists, Baptists, Anabaptists, and Unitarians), with only 7 percent of the population, contributed 41 percent of the leading entrepreneurs during the English Industrial Revolution (1760–1830). Other marginal communities disproportionally represented in entrepreneurial activity include Jews in

---

[20]Max Weber, *The Protestant Ethic and the Spirit of Capitalism,* translated by Talcott Parsons in 1930 (New York: Charles Scribner's Sons, 1958).

medieval Europe, Huguenots in seventeenth- and eighteenth-century France, Old Believers in nineteenth-century Russia, Indians in East Africa before the 1970s, Chinese in Southeast Asia, Lebanese in West Africa, Marwaris in Calcutta, and Gujaratis in Bombay. Refugees from the 1947 partition between India and Pakistan, and the exchange of minorities between Turkey and Greece in the 1920s, were overrepresented among industrialists in these four countries. Displaced Armenians, Jews, Europeans, Palestinians, and Arab expatriates, escaping persecution, political hostility, and economic depression, were responsible for the rise in entrepreneurial activity in the Middle East between 1930 and 1955. For migrants the challenge of a new environment may have a beneficial educational and psychological effect, and the geographical dispersion of friends and relatives may allow the rejection of local values, obligations, and sanctions that impede rational business practice.

In the contemporary world, most dominant communities value economic achievement. Thus leading business communities include the Protestants of Northern and Western European origin living in the United States, and Hindu high castes in India. In Lebanon in 1959, the politically dominant Maronites and other Christians comprised 80 percent of the innovative entrepreneurs, although only 50 percent of the population. The Yorubas and Ibos, the largest ethnic communities in the more industrialized region of southern Nigeria, are the leading entrepreneurs.

Unlike the preceding groups, aliens have usually not been innovative in industry requiring large fixed investment, which can easily be confiscated. Furthermore, the technical change they introduce is usually not imitated by other groups. The English Nonconformists, Huguenots, Old Believers, Marwaris, Gujaratis, and the south Asian and Mediterranean refugees mentioned previously are not considered alien groups, since their roots have been in their country's culture. Even though there are instances where aliens have made important contributions to technical change, there is no evidence they are generally more innovative than natives.

Are marginal individuals especially innovative? Since no one has conducted a systematic worldwide test, we simply cannot say.

Social Origins and Mobility

THE UNITED STATES

The dominant American folk hero has been the person who goes from rags to riches through business operations. One of the most celebrated was the steel magnate Andrew Carnegie (1835–1919), an uneducated immigrant, the son of a workingman, forced to seek employment at a young age. Through cleverness and hard work, he rose from bobbin boy to messenger to assistant railroad superintendent to industrial leader. For him, "The millionaires who are in active control started as poor boys and were trained in the sternest but most efficient of all schools— poverty."[21] Even so, his story is atypical. The Horatio Alger stories of the nineteenth century are largely legend. The typical successful industrial leader in the late nineteenth and early twentieth centuries was usually American by birth, Eng-

---

[21]Andrew Carnegie, *The Empire of Business* (New York: Doubleday, Page, and Co., 1902), p. 109.

lish in national origin, urban in early environment, educated through high school, and born and bred in an atmosphere in which business and a relatively high social status were intimately associated with his family life.[22]

OTHER CAPITALIST AND MIXED ECONOMIES

It should not be surprising that industrialists outside the United States have a similar sociological profile. Innovators during the English Industrial Revolution were primarily sons of men in comfortable circumstances.[23] Industrial entrepreneurs from Greece, Nigeria, Pakistan, India, and the Philippines had an occupational and family status substantially higher than the population as a whole. Industrial corporate managers, mostly from families having the funds to pay for a university education, generally have an even higher socioeconomic status than entrepreneurs.

SOCIALIST COUNTRIES

In the Soviet Union in 1936, one of the few studies with reliable information on parental occupational origins, sons of white-collar employees, professionals, or businessowners had six times the representation in industrial, executive positions that the sons of manual workers and farmers had. This situation existed despite the 1917 revolution, which had ostensibly overturned the existing class structure.[24] Even in China, capitalists, supporting the 1949 revolution who had not been allied to foreign interests, continued (except for the Cultural Revolution, 1966–76) to receive interest on their investments and to be paid fairly high salaries for managing joint public-private enterprises. Members and children of the prerevolutionary Chinese bourgeoisie still hold a large number of positions in industry, administration, and education, despite attacks on their privileges from 1966 through 1976.[25]

ADVANTAGES OF PRIVILEGED BACKGROUNDS

The entrepreneur or manager frequently profits from having some **monopoly advantage.** This advantage (except for inherited talent) is usually the result of greater opportunities, such as (1) access to more economic information than competitors, (2) superior access to training and education, (3) a lower discount of future earnings, (4) larger firm size, and (5) lucrative agreements to restrict entry or output. All five are facilitated by wealth or position.[26]

Accordingly in India, high castes, upper classes, and large business families use such monopoly advantages to become industrial entrepreneurs in disproportionate numbers. In one Indian city, 52 percent of these entrepreneurs (in contrast

[22]William Miller, ed., *Men in Business: Essays on the Historical Role of the Entrepreneur* (New York: Harper & Row, 1962).

[23]Everett E. Hagen, *On the Theory of Social Change: How Economic Growth Begins* (Homewood, Ill.: Dorsey Press, 1962).

[24]David Granick, *The Red Executive: A Study of the Organization Man in Russian Industry* (New York: Anchor Books, 1961).

[25]Jan Deleyne, *The Chinese Economy* (New York: Harper & Row, 1971); and Thomas P. Lyons, *Economic Integration and Planning in Maoist China* (New York: Columbia University Press, 1987).

[26]Maurice Dobb, *Capitalist Enterprise and Social Progress* (London: George Routledge and Sons, 1926).

to only 11 percent of blue-collar workers) were from high Hindu castes, which comprise only 26 percent of the total population. None of the entrepreneurs, but a disproportionate share of blue-collar workers, was from low-caste backgrounds (that is, Harijans and Protestant or Roman Catholic Christians). This lopsided distribution of business activity—shown in Table 12–1, which reflects differences in economic opportunities between the privileged and less-privileged portions of the population—is typical of many other countries as well.

Entrepreneurial activity is frequently a means of moving one or two notches up the economic ladder. Research indicates that the socioeconomic status of entrepreneurs is higher than their parents' status, which is substantially higher than that of the general population.

Education

Most studies indicate a higher level of education among entrepreneurs than for the population as a whole, and a direct relationship between education and the entrepreneur's success. People with more education probably make sounder business decisions; in addition their verbal skills are better and make acquiring new ideas and methods, corresponding and conversing in business relationships, and understanding instruction manuals and other routine, written information easier. Finally, the educated entrepreneur probably has a sound mathematical background, facilitating computation and recordkeeping.

However, the education of the entrepreneur may be negatively related to success in crafts requiring a lengthy apprenticeship such as weaving, blacksmithing, goldsmithing, shoemaking, and leathermaking. Time and money spent

TABLE 12–1　Caste and Religious Community of Entrepreneurs and Workers in an Indian City

Caste/Religion	Percentage of Entrepreneurs	Percentage of Blue-Collar Workers	Percentage of Total Population
High Hindu			
Brahmin (priest)	20.4	2.2	21.4
Kshatriya (ruler, warrior)	9.3	8.9	2.3
Vaishya (trader)	22.2	0.0	2.2
Middle Hindu			
Sudra (artisan, peasant)	27.8	57.8	56.9
Low Hindu			
Harijan (outcaste)	0.0	15.5	11.2
Non-Hindu			
Muslim	13.0	6.7	1.3
Christian (high caste)	1.8	0.0	0.1
Christian (low caste)	0.0	8.9	4.5
Sikh, Parsi, other	5.5	0.0	0.1
Total	100.0	100.0	100.0

Source: E. Wayne Nafziger, *Class, Caste, and Entrepreneurship: A Study of Indian Industrialists* (Honolulu: University Press of Hawaii, 1978), p. 65.

on formal education may represent relinquished opportunities in training more closely related to entrepreneurial activities.[27]

Education may limit entrepreneurship by giving people other occupational choices. Thus in the early 1960s, when Nigerians were replacing the remaining Britons in the civil service, Nigeria's few university graduates turned to these jobs with their high salary, security, prestige, and other perquisites rather than to entrepreneurial activity with its relatively low earnings and high risk. On the other hand, in areas where university graduates are in excess supply, such as south India, some choose entrepreneurship to avoid unemployment or blue-collar jobs.

Gender

In the United States, there are relatively few women in business—not merely because of sex discrimination (though that plays a part) but because of the whole female socialization pattern in America. Some feminists charge that girls are brought up to aspire to be secretaries, nurses, dancers, and kindergarten teachers rather than to start a business.

In many developing countries, the percentage of female businesspersons is lower than in the United States. Despite certain exceptions, such as the concentrations of female traders in some large open-air market places in West Africa, only a small proportion of large-scale entrepreneurs in LDCs are women.

Most LDCs have cultural norms dictating how males and females should behave at work. Frequently a woman's physical mobility and social contact are restricted in LDCs. The anthropologist Johanna Lessinger states that in India women are not allowed to deal directly with strange men, since it is assumed that all unmonitored contact between unrelated men and women must be sexual.[28] Furthermore, according to Lessinger, Indian women are viewed as naturally weaker, more emotional, less socially adept, less rational, and inferior to men. These views have been used not only to limit competition between women and men in business, but also, in some instances, to justify a woman's restriction to the household.

Moreover the culture may view the characteristics of the successful entrepreneur—shrewdness, quick judgment, gregariousness, and force of personality—as inconsistent with those of a good and proper woman. Even where a woman is determined to be an entrepreneur, she is daily reminded that she is going against the norm: Sexual harassment is likely if she steps beyond the bounds of accepted behavior. Although a woman can get around these restrictions by surrounding herself with relatives, neighbors, and other women who can vouch for her good behavior, this strategy is cumbersome for the entrepreneur, who must be mobile. In addition to these social restrictions, the LDC businesswoman may be refused credit by bankers and suppliers. In general, despite some slight variations, these

---

[27]E. Wayne Nafziger, *African Capitalism: A Case Study in Nigerian Entrepreneurship* (Stanford: Hoover Institution, 1977).

    E. Wayne Nafziger and Dek Terrell, "Entrepreneurial Human Capital and the Long-Run Survival of Firms in India," *World Development* 24 (April 1996), argue that, in India, firms founded by better educated (usually better connected) entrepreneurs are *less* likely to survive. The explanations are not only the greater opportunities by entrepreneurs in other pursuits but also to the reduction of returns from government connections and other forms of rent seeking during India's economic liberalization.

[28]Johanna Lessinger, "Women Traders in Madras City," unpublished paper, Barnard College, 1980.

attitudes toward female entrepreneurial activity are prevalent in developing countries.

Technological Mobilization in Socialist Economies

Chapter 20 will indicate how difficult it was to motivate innovative activity in centrally planned economies such as the Soviet Union. Soviet managers resisted innovation, since resources diverted to technological change usually threatened the rewards for plan fulfillment.

From 1966 to 1970, the early years of the Cultural Revolution, China's leaders took control of industrial innovation and management from the professional managerial elite. Management changed from one person to a "three-in-one" revolutionary committee, consisting of government officials, technicians, and workers. Campaigns urged workers to invent or improve machines, tools, and processes—a policy that began after Soviet technicians took their blueprints and withdrew from unfinished factories in 1960.

According to the Chinese press in the late 1960s, numerous technical activists among the workers, previously unrecognized, introduced new techniques, persevered when criticized by bureaucrats and peers, and received support from the Communist party. Through its help, they acquired more sophisticated technical advice and frequently received further training and education leading to promotion.[29] Since the 1978 industrial reforms, professional managers and technicians reasserted their authority and quelled the innovation of technical activists.

As Chapter 20 will indicate, China's **individual economy** has grown rapidly as the number of privately self-employed in cities and towns increased about fiftyfold from 1978 to 1988. While privately owned and operated proprietorships could employ only five outside the family, vertically or horizontally integrated cooperatives and corporations had higher employment limits that varied by locality. In 1984, Wan Runnan persuaded six Academy of Sciences engineering colleagues to join him in borrowing $5,400 and renting a small office to found the Beijing Stone Group Company, which grossed $85.5 million sales in electronic equipment, earned $6.7 million after taxes, employed 800, and had 15 subsidiaries (including Japan and Hong Kong) by 1987. The Stone Group controlled ownership and provided technical knowledge for joint ventures with Japan's Mitsui in producing an English–Chinese electronic typewriter, word processors, and printers suitable for China, and software. Chinese law and social sanctions limit annual after-tax income of company President Wan to $8,500, yet as an entrepreneur, he had independence, prestige, and an income 25 times his academy salary.[30] However, Wan, who allied with dissident Chinese students and intellectuals, went into exile in June 1989 as a leader of the Chinese Democratic Front opposing the Chinese government, and the government suppressing private enterprise.[31]

---

[29]Richard P. Suttmeir, *Research and Revolution: Science Policy and Societal Change in China* (Lexington, Mass.: Heath, 1974).

[30]Harry Harding, *China's Second Revolution: Reform after Mao* (Washington, D.C.: Brookings Institution, 1987), pp. 124–28; Thomas B. Gould, "China's Private Entrepreneurs," *China Business Review* (November-December 1985): 46–50; Shi Zulin, "Individual Economy in China," paper presented to the U.S. People to People Economics Delegation, Beijing, May 14, 1987; and Adi Ignatius, "Fast-growing Chinese Electronics Firm Emulates IBM," *Wall Street Journal* (June 3, 1988): 10.

[31]Merle Goldman, "Vengeance in China," *New York Review of Books* 36 (November 9, 1989): 5–9; and Adi Ignatius, "Computer Whiz Leads China's Opposition," *Wall Street Journal* (August 22, 1989): p. A1.

Summary

1. The political and cultural milieu in LDCs was generally not conducive to large-scale industrial entrepreneurship before 1950 or so. Although LDC governments should encourage their entrepreneurs, it is not essential that they be captains of industry as glorified by Schumpeter.

2. To Schumpeter the entrepreneur is an innovator, one who carries out new combinations. These innovations are the source of private profit and economic growth. However, LDCs need not unduly emphasize developing new combinations, since some technology can be borrowed or adapted from abroad.

3. Coase identifies the entrepreneur, who organizes within the firm, and the price mechanism as the two major coordinating instruments within the economy. The choice between organization within the firm or by the market reflects the transactions costs of using the price system.

4. The entrepreneur differs from the manager of a firm, who runs the business on established lines. The entrepreneur can fill gaps, complete inputs, and make up for market deficiencies.

5. Since they assume that most skills needed for an enterprise can be purchased in the market, Western economists frequently limit the entrepreneurial function to perceiving market opportunities and gaining command over resources. However, LDC entrepreneurs may have to provide some basic skills themselves, such as marketing, purchasing, dealing with government, human relations, supplier relations, customer relations, financial management, production management, and technological management, which are all skills in short supply in the market.

6. Although the family enterprise has the advantage of quick, unified decision making, its disadvantages include a conservative approach to taking risks, reluctance to hire professional managers, and paternalism in labor relationships.

7. McClelland contends that a society with a generally high need for achievement produces energetic entrepreneurs who bring about rapid economic growth. Some training institutions have used achievement motivation training as a part of programs at centers to develop entrepreneurship.

8. Hagen argues that societies where children are raised democratically, so that they are encouraged to take initiative and be self-reliant, are more likely to produce entrepreneurs. However, critics are skeptical about Hagen's claim that this creativity is linked to a prior period of lost status.

9. Industrial entrepreneurs in LDCs come from a wide variety of occupational backgrounds, including trade, sales, and crafts. Few manufacturing entrepreneurs, however, come from farming, government employment, or factory work.

10. According to Weber, the spirit of the modern capitalist entrepreneur in Western Europe in the sixteenth century was found disproportionally among Puritans, whose religious asceticism manifested itself in worldly activity. Despite criticism of Weber's thesis, his work has stimulated scholars to ask questions about how differences between religious and ethnic groups affect entrepreneurial activity. One such question, concerning the representation of marginal ethnic and social groups in entrepreneurial activity, has not been satisfactorily answered.

11. Generally entrepreneurs come from a much higher socioeconomic background than the general population. In addition they tend to be upwardly mobile.

12. Although education can increase the entrepreneurial supply by making available skills needed for business, it can decrease this supply by increasing a person's job options.

13. Cultural norms in LDCs defining how women should behave at work limit female entrepreneurial activity. (Such problems occur in developed countries as well.)

14. Organization and innovation are important for growth in socialist as well as capitalist economies. It had been difficult for socialist countries, particularly the Soviet Union, to motivate managers and technicians to innovate.

15. Under China's post-1978 industrial reform, self-employed individuals can innovate, start a new enterprise, combine capital and personnel, and eventually, albeit with certain limits, expand the firm. The last part of the twentieth century and the first part of the twenty-first century will indicate whether individual entrepreneurial activity will expand or whether the Communist party, state, and bureaucracy will resist this capitalist encroachment.

Terms to Review

- entrepreneur
- innovation
- stationary state
- multiple entrepreneurial function
- organization

- need for achievement
- marginal individuals
- monopoly advantage
- China's individual economy

Questions to Discuss

1. What is Schumpeter's theory of economic development? What is the role of the entrepreneur in this theory? How applicable is Schumpeter's concept of the entrepreneur to developing countries?

2. Which steps in the process of developing technical advances are essential for LDCs? Which steps in the process can they skip in full or in part?

3. What is meant by the entrepreneur as gap-filler? Why is this entrepreneurial concept more relevant to LDCs than DCs?

4. What are the functions of the entrepreneur in LDCs? How might these functions differ from those of the entrepreneur in DCs?

5. What are the advantages and disadvantages of family enterprises in LDCs?

6. What are some of the noneconomic factors affecting entrepreneurship in LDCs?

7. What are the socioeconomic factors that affect the supply of industrial entrepreneurs in mixed and capitalist LDCs?

8. Are marginal individuals more innovative than nonmarginal individuals as entrepreneurs?

9. Is the concept of entrepreneurship applicable to socialist economies?

Guide to Readings

The United Nation's *Journal of Development Planning* no. 18 (1988), edited by Harvey Leibenstein and Dennis Ray, devotes a whole issue to entrepreneurship and economic development, including Dennis Ray's "The Role of Entrepreneurship in Economic Development," pp. 3–18; William J. Baumol, "Is Entrepreneurship Always Productive?" pp. 85–94; Lois Stevenson, "Women and Economic Development: A Focus on Entrepreneurship," pp. 113–26; E. Wayne Nafziger, "Society and the Entrepreneur," pp. 127–52; Linsu Kim, "Entrepreneurship and Innovation in a Rapidly Developing Country," pp. 183–94; Peter Kilby, "Breaking the Entrepreneurial Bottleneck in Late-Developing Countries: Is There a Useful Role for Government?" pp. 221–50; and several other articles. Harris's survey of empirical studies of entrepreneurship (note 19), primarily in LDCs, is the most comprehensive available. Kilby's discussion of various perspectives on entrepreneurship (note 10) is not so exhaustive as the Harris survey but emphasizes the correlation of the theoretical literature from a large number of disciplines with existing empirical literature. In addition Schumpeter, McClelland, and Hagen summarize their views on entrepreneurship in short articles in the Kilby volume. Nafziger (note 19) sketches the concept of the entrepreneur in the history of economic theory and in contemporary economic analysis. Carl Liedholm and Donald Mead have a survey, *Small Scale Industries in Developing Countries: Empirical Evidence and Policy Implications*, prepared for the U.S. Agency for International Development (East Lansing, Mich.: Michigan State University, 1987).

Gene M. Grossman and Elhanan Helpman, *Innovation and Growth in the Global Economy* (Cambridge, Mass.: MIT Press, 1991), analyze the contribution of innovation to economic growth.

CHAPTER

13

Natural Resources and the Environment: Toward Sustainable Development

This chapter analyzes land, natural resources, and the environment as economic resources in LDCs, and whether development is sustainable, given natural resource depletion and environmental damage.

1. We look at differences between land, natural resources, and capital.
2. We assess the effect of changing real oil prices on consumption in the 1970s, 1980s, and 1990s.
3. We analyze the adverse impact that Dutch disease in a booming export sector can have on other sectors of the economy.
4. We define sustainable development and examine the impact of poverty on the environment.
5. We identify market imperfections that contribute to environmental degradation.
6. We examine the change in pollution with economic growth, and specify a decision-making rule for abating pollution.
7. We discuss how to place a monetary value on pollution discharges.
8. We discuss the growth of arid and semiarid lands.
9. We examine economic development in tropical climates.
10. We analyze policy toward environmental resources, such as biodiversity and climate, that are global public goods.
11. We consider the extent to which growth is limited by a scarcity of natural resources.
12. We look at measures of economic welfare that consider resource depletion and environmental damage.

330

13. We examine the ethical dilemmas of rich nations in a world of limited resources and income inequalities.

Importance of Natural Resources

Simon Kuznets writes that economic growth "is unlikely to be inhibited by an absolute lack of natural resources,"[1] as Japan, Switzerland, Singapore, and Israel have grown rapidly despite a paucity of natural resources. Yet Kuwait and the United Arab Emirates have some of the world's highest per capita incomes, while those in Saudi Arabia and Libya are higher than most other LDCs'. Still incomes and revenues in these oil exporting states varied widely from 1970 to 1996, following boom and bust cycles similar to those in Texas, Louisiana, Oklahoma, and Alberta.

Land, Natural Resources, and Environmental Resources

Land and **natural resources** are considered nonproducible, since unlike capital, they cannot be replenished through production. In practice, however, the line between these resources and capital is blurred. Thus we say land is nonproducible, but in some major port cities, such as Singapore, Bombay, and Boston, where land was scarce, landfills extended overall area. Although only about 11 percent of the earth's land area is cultivated, new arable land is continually created through drainage, irrigation, and the use of fertilizer, new seeds, and new machinery. New techniques and cheap transport have made economical the exploitation of resources that were previously unused.

Land and natural resources, although often lumped together, have highly distinguishable properties. Land is immobile and potentially renewable. Natural resources, on the other hand, are mobile, but most are nonrenewable—they cannot be replenished at a rate fast enough to be meaningful in terms of the human life span. Nonrenewable energy sources include petroleum, coal, lignite, peat, natural gas liquids, terrestrial heat flows, oil shale, tar sands, uranium, and thorium.

Resource flows, or renewable energy sources, consist of photochemical energy stored in plants and animals (for example, food, wood, animal excrement, and vegetable fuel), and sun, water (including tidal energy), wind, and animal power.[2] Some economists do not like calling them renewable resources, preferring the term resource flows, for even if they cannot be exhausted, they lack regenerative capacity (i.e, humans cannot regenerate these flows). Solar energy may be stored by trees, fossil fuels, or algae, and may be artificially stored by batteries or hot water tanks, but the stock of solar energy is the sun itself; our consumption of solar energy has no effect on the stock or our future consumption.

Environmental resources are resources provided by nature that are indivisible. An ecosystem, an ozone layer, or the lower atmosphere cannot be allocated unit by unit (as you would allocate oil or copper) or consumed directly, but people consume the services these resources provide. We can view some resources in

---

[1]Simon S. Kuznets, "Toward a Theory of Economic Growth," in Robert Lekachman, ed., *National Policy for Economic Welfare at Home and Abroad* (Garden City, N.Y.: Doubleday, 1955), p. 36.
[2]Earl Cook, *Man, Energy, Society* (San Francisco: W. H. Freeman, 1976), pp. 17, 51.

more than one category, as trees may be renewable resources yet the forest ecosystem an indivisible environmental resources.[3]

Petroleum

The fourfold price increase in crude petroleum over four months in 1973 and 1974 sent many LDC economies reeling. The LDC imports of fuels and lubricants (largely petroleum) as a percentage of total merchandise imports more than doubled from 8.0 percent in 1970 to 17.5 percent in 1977. The **balance of trade** (merchandise exports minus merchandise imports) for oil-importing LDCs dropped from −$18.0 billion in 1973 to −$42.2 billion in 1974 to −72.1 billion in 1980, while it rose in oil-exporting countries from $18.9 billion in 1973 to $87.1 billion in 1974 to $170.8 billion in 1980. For India oil import payments as a percentage of export receipts more than doubled from 18.6 percent in 1973 to 38.4 percent in 1974. Yet oil-importing LDCs recovered some from the 1973 to 1974 shock, growing as fast as oil-exporting LDCs from 1973 to 1980. Non-oil LDCs' balance of trade recovered during the collapse in oil prices in the 1980s, falling to −$35.7 billion in 1983 and −$9.2 billion in 1986, before turning positive in 1987 to 1988 (and 1990), while oil-exporting countries' positive trade balance dropped throughout the 1980s and early 1990s, turning negative in 1994 and 1995 (Table 13–1). While oil-importing LDCs maintained their growth from the 1970s to 1980s, oil-exporting countries' growth, the major determinant of which is the oil export price (Fig. 13–1), declined to a negative rate.[4]

The Organization of Petroleum Exporting Countries (OPEC) is a **cartel** whose members agree to limit output and fix prices. Though founded in 1960, OPEC achieved its major success through concerted action to increase oil prices in 1973 and 1974. During the 1970s, OPEC countries took over ownership of the oil concessions within their territories, and international oil companies became a combination of contractor and sales agent for these countries.

However, during the 1980s and early 1990s, conservation, the development of alternative energy sources, and a recession among much of the **high-income Organization of Economic Cooperation and Development (OECD)**—the United States, Canada, Western Europe, Japan, Australia, and New Zealand—dampened the growth of oil demand.[5] At the same time, the income and commodity terms of trade of oil-exporting LDCs fell, increasing the external debt they owed DCs, their banks, the International Monetary Fund, and the World Bank and the policy leverage of these institutions, contributing to pressures for OPEC liberalizing and providing improved terms for foreign oil producers. Meanwhile OPEC was finding it more difficult to enforce prices and quotas, since members, such as Iran and

---

[3]James R. Kahn, *The Economic Approach to Environmental and Natural Resources* (Fort Worth, Tex.: Dryden Press, 1995), p. 5.

[4]Alireza Rahimibrougerdi, "An Empirical Investigation of the Effects of Major Exogenous Shocks on the Growth of Non-Oil- and Oil-Exporting Developing Countries from 1965 to 1985" (Ph.D. diss., Kansas State University, 1988), pp. 147–68.

[5]In the late 1970s and 1980s, the Environmental Defense Fund, arguing that promoting conservation was cheaper than building new power stations, prodded California's regulators to link Pacific Gas and Electric Company (PG&E)'s profits to its energy efficiency. PG&E's conservation promotion became a model for electrical utilities and their regulators all over the world. "Low-hanging Fruit," *Economist* (August 31, 1991): S13-S19.

TABLE 13-1   Balance of Trade by Country Group, 1970–95 (billions of U.S. dollars)[a]

Country Group	1970	1971	1972	1973	1974	1975	1976	1977	1978	1979	1980	1981	1982
Developed countries	−6.7	−5.7	−7.4	−13.5	−54.7	−19.4	−45.5	−51.2	−29.2	−85.2	−67.0	−19.7	−14.9
Oil-exporting developing countries	7.7	10.8	11.1	18.9	87.1	58.5	70.5	62.1	106.5	170.0	170.8	124.9	64.4
Oil-importing developing countries	−14.2	−19.5	−16.4	−18.0	−42.2	−55.6	−41.5	−42.0	−61.5	−91.6	−72.1	−77.0	−57.0

Country Group	1983	1984	1985	1986	1987	1988	1989	1990	1991	1992	1993	1994	1995
Developed countries	−16.6	−43.9	−38.3	−10.8	−30.6	−12.3	−40.9	−40.0	5.9	43.4	95.4	104.4	102.6
Oil-exporting developing countries	44.2	54.7	55.7	15.0	37.2	21.3	43.4	73.4	37.5	24.6	31.5	−53.5	−56.4
Oil-importing developing countries	−35.7	−17.2	−20.5	−9.2	2.0	2.5	−5.3	22.4	−28.9	−43.7	−71.3	−67.5	−67.7

[a]Socialist countries and transitional countries of Eastern Europe and the former Soviet Union are not included.

Sources: International Monetary Fund, *International Financial Statistics Yearbook, 1981* (Washington, D.C., 1981), pp. 67–73; International Monetary Fund, *World Economic Outlook* (Washington, D.C., October 1988), pp. 93, 106; and International Monetary Fund, *World Economic Outlook* (Washington, D.C., October 1994), pp. 153, 158.

Nigeria, that faced mounting debt, political, or military problems, exceeded their quotas or offered discounts below posted prices, and major nonmember producers, such as China, the United Kingdom, Mexico, and Norway, increased their production shares.

FIGURE 13-1   Real Petroleum Prices, 1971–2004 (projected) (1971=100)

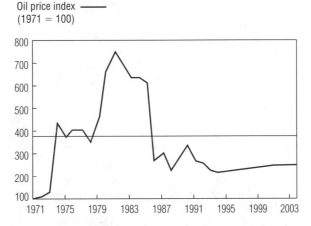

Oil price index ——
(1971 = 100)

Source: World Bank, *Global Economic Prospects and the Developing Countries* (Washington, D.C., 1995), p. 73.

Saudi Arabia (population 19 million), with 35 percent of the world's estimated reserves (Table 13–2) and the lowest cost production, has a dominant role in
OPEC pricing. When members violate OPEC agreements, the Saudis can increase
production and lower prices, as from 1986 to 1988, threatening to drive high-cost
producers out of the market. Still, even the Saudis were hurt by increased government spending and substantial royal perquisites amid negative growth during the
1980s and early 1990s, facing major debt problems after the Persian Gulf War of
1991. Trying to predict the responses of the Saudis and OPEC's weaker members
indicates the difficulty of predicting how successful price collusion and future
price trends will be.

Energy use depends on both income and price effects (with conservation
measures being part of the price impact). The price elasticity of demand for energy
increases with response time. Thus in the first several months of the abrupt 1973 to
1974 oil price increase, the elasticity of demand for energy was close to zero

TABLE 13–2   The World's Twenty-Six Leading Crude Oil Countries (by 1994 production and 1995 estimated proven crude oil reserves, millions of barrels)

Country	1994 Production	1995 Reserves
Saudi Arabia[a]	2.97	259
U.S.	2.42	23
Russia	2.12	41
Iran[a]	1.31	89
China	1.07	24
Mexico	.99	51
Norway	.92	7
Venezuela[a]	.92	64
United Kingdom	.87	5
United Arab Emirates[a]	.82	98
Kuwait[a]	.74	94
Nigeria[a]	.73	16
Canada	.63	7
Indonesia[a]	.55	6
Libya[a]	.50	21
Algeria[a]	.43	8
Egypt	.32	3
Oman	.29	3
Brazil	.25	1
Argentina	.24	1
Malaysia	.23	1
India	.22	4
Syria	.21	1
Australia	.21	1
Iraq[a]	.20	100
Other	1.76	45
Total world	21.92	973

[a]OPEC members (also includes Gabon).

The second leading producer, the United States, is a net oil importer, and the majority of both Russian and Chinese
productions is consumed domestically.

Sources: United States Department of Energy/Energy Information Administration, *International Petroleum Statistics
Report* (March 1995); American Petroleum Institute, *Basic Petroleum Data Book*, VIII, *Petroleum Industry Statistics*
(Washington, D.C., 1995), section IV; and *Economist* (August 1, 1992): 89.

(*growth* in amount demanded decreased little). Over the next 7-year period, price elasticities were about 0.4 percent in DCs and 0.3 percent in LDCs (*growth* in quantity demanded dropped substantially). The full effect of changing energy prices takes place 15 to 25 years later, when demand elasticities (in response to 1973–74 prices) may well be twice as high as for the 7-year period.[6]

Dutch Disease

Michael Roemer analyzes **Dutch disease,** named when the booming North Seas' gas export revenues in the 1970s appreciated the guilder, making Dutch industrial exports more costly in foreign currencies and increasing foreign competition and unemployment. Analogously, the United States suffered from a similar disease from 1980 to 1984, experiencing a farm export crisis and deindustrialization from the decline of traditional U.S. export industries (automobiles, capital goods, high technology, railroad and farm equipment, paint, leather products, cotton fabrics, carpeting, electrical equipment and parts, and basic chemicals) during substantial capital inflows strengthening the dollar.[7] Yet LDCs are less likely to catch Dutch disease from capital inflows than from a major world price increase, a cost-reducing technological change, or a major discovery of a primary resource. The pathology might better be called the Indonesian, Nigerian, Mexican, Venezuelan (from petroleum), Thai (rice, rubber, tin), Malaysian (rubber, tin), Brazilian (coffee, sugar), Colombian (coffee), Ivory Coast (coffee, cocoa, wood), Bangladesh (foreign aid inflows), Egyptian (tourism, remittances, foreign aid inflows), Jordanian (remittances), Zambian, Zaïrian (copper), Ghanaian (cocoa), or Kenyan (tourism, coffee) disease, an economic distortion resulting from dependence on one to three booming exports.

Roemer's three-sector model shows that growth in the booming export sector reduces the price of foreign exchange, retarding other sectors' growth by reducing incentives to export other commodities and replace domestic goods for imports and raising factor and input prices for nonbooming sectors. Moreover, labor moves from the lagging export and import substitution sectors to the booming and nontradable sectors. Other ill effects of the export boom may be relaxed fiscal discipline, increased capital-intensive projects, and wage dualism. Government can minimize the negative effects of Dutch disease by investing in the lagging traded goods sector before the natural resource is exhausted, so that the rest of the economy can capture the potential benefits of the export boom.[8]

---

[6]Robert Stobaugh, "After the Peak: The Threat of Imported Oil," in *Energy Future: Report of the Energy Project at the Harvard Business School*, ed. Robert Stobaugh and Daniel Yergin (New York: Random House, 1979), pp. 31–33; and World Bank, *World Development Report, 1981* (New York: Oxford University Press, 1981), pp. 36–37.

[7]Chapter 18's discussion of infant entrepreneurship indicates that Mexico and Argentina suffered from a similar disease, a foreign-investment blitz, in the early 1990s. Chile, however, limited the impact of this illness through stringent controls on capital inflows.

[8]Michael Roemer, "Dutch Disease in Developing Countries: Swallowing Bitter Medicine," in Mats Lundahl, *The Primary Sector in Economic Development* (New York: St. Martin's, 1985), pp. 234–52. See also Ronald Findlay, "Primary Exports, Manufacturing, and Development," in Mats Lundahl, *The Primary Sector in Economic Development* (New York: St. Martin's, 1985), pp. 218–33; and W. Max Corden and J. Peter Neary, "Booming Sector and Deindustrialisation in a Small Open Economy," *Economic Journal* 92 (December 1982): 825–48.

Oil booms have proven a blessing for many oil-exporting countries but a curse for others. In 1976, Nigeria's head of state, General Olusegun Obasanjo, responding to political unrest and an overheated economy, pointed out that petroleum revenue was not a cure-all. "Though this country has great potential she is not yet a rich nation.... Our resources from oil are not enough to satisfy the yearnings, aspirations and genuine needs of our people, development and social services."[9]

Oil revenues increased average material welfare, widened employment opportunities, and increased policy options. But they also altered incentives, raised expectations, and distorted and destabilized non-oil output, frequently in agriculture. Chapter 6 indicated exchange-rate, pricing, investment, and incentive policies that Indonesia undertook, but that Nigeria failed to take, to counter successfully the adverse effects of Dutch disease.

The Dutch disease from the oil boom in the 1970s may seem a mild case of influenza for Nigeria, Mexico, and Venezuela compared to **reverse Dutch disease** from the oil bust of the 1980s. For a top Nigerian economic official, striking it rich on oil in the 1970s was "like a man who wins a lottery and builds a castle. He can't maintain it, and then has to borrow to move out."[10] Dependence on one or two exports makes these countries especially vulnerable to external price shocks.

Poverty and Environmental Stress

The 1987 United Nations Commission on Environment and Development, chaired by Norwegian Prime Minister Gro Harlem Brundtland, coined the term **sustainable development**, referring not only to the survival of the human species, but also maintaining the productivity of natural, produced, and human assets from generation to generation. But grinding poverty and impatience spur people to strive for immediate gain, forgetting long-term social sustainability. In order to survive, impoverished people degrade and destroy their immediate environment, cutting down forests for fuelwood and export earnings, overusing marginal agricultural land, migrating to shrinking areas of vacant land, and destroying habitat for biological species essential for pharmeceuticals and seed varieties.[11] Additionally, they forego maintenance of vegetation, forests, and the biosphere. At subsistence levels of living, when people's survival is at stake, hand-to-mouth economics prevail in which the future is infinitely discounted; people overexploit natural resources and underinvest in conservation and regeneration, leading to resource depletion and species loss. In this economic climate, people make irreversible decisions, foreclosing options by logging and mining of rainforests and other economic options that reduce species.[12] More than 100 million people in LDCs experi-

[9]Alan Rake, "And Now the Struggle for Real Development," *African Development* 10 (December 1976): 1263; and E. Wayne Nafziger, *The Economics of Political Instability* (Boulder, Colo.: Westview, 1983), p. 187.

[10]Flora Lewis, "Oil Crisis of '73 Wreaking Economic Havoc," *Kansas City Times* (November 22, 1988), p. 7. See David Evans, "Reverse Dutch Disease and Mineral-Exporting Developing Economies," *IDS Bulletin* 17 (October 1986): 10–13, on reverse Dutch diseases from depressed primary product prices.

[11]Richard B. Norgaard, *Sustainability and the Economics of Assuring Assets for Future Generations*, World Bank Policy Research Working Paper 832, Washington, D.C., 1992, pp. 38–40; and World Commission on Environment and Development, *Our Common Future* (New York: Oxford University Press, 1987), p. 28.

[12]Theodore Panayotou, *Green Markets: The Economics of Sustainable Development* (San Francisco: Institute for Contemporary Studies, 1993), pp. 46–54; and Christopher Flavin, *Slowing Global Warming: A Worldwide Strategy* (Washington, D. C.: Worldwatch Institute, 1989).

ence acute firewood shortages. In the late 1980s, a study of Nepalese hill villages with severe deforestation indicated one-quarter of the household labor normally devoted to agriculture was diverted to fuelwood collection.[13]

The World Bank lists the following adverse effect of environmental degradation on health and productivity: (1) water pollution contributes to more than 2 million deaths and billions of illnesses a year; water scarcity to poor household hygiene, added health risks, and limits on economic activity; and water pollution and scarcity to declining fisheries, municipal and rural household costs of providing safe water, and aquifer depletion leading to irreversible compaction; (2) excessive urban particulate matter is responsible for 300 to 700 thousand premature deaths annually and for half of childhood chronic coughing; smoky indoor air affects 400 to 700 million people, mainly women and children in poor rural areas; and air pollution has many acute and chronic health impacts, restricts vehicle and industrial activity during critical episodes, and affects forests and water bodies through acid rain; (3) solid and hazardous wastes acutely increase health risks locally, such as diseases spread by rotting garbage and blocked drains; and pollute groundwater resources; (4) soil degradation reduces nutrition for poor farmers on depleted soils and increases susceptibility to drought, while decreasing field productivity in tropical soils, contributing to offsite siltation of reservoirs, river-transport channels, and other hydrological investments; (5) deforestation leading to localized flooding, contributing to death and disease; and losing sustainable logging potential, erosion prevention, watershed stability, and carbon sequestration provided by forests; (6) reduced biodiversity, contributing to loss of new drugs and genetic resources, and reduced ecosystem adaptability; and (7) atmospheric changes, shifting vector-borne diseases, increasing risks from climatic natural diseases, and increasing diseases from ozone depletion (estimated to contribute to as much as 300 thousand additional cases of skin cancer and 1.7 million cases of cataracts a year worldwide).[14]

Poverty and insecurity contribute to lack of capital and labor to conserve the environment. Poor, landless people are forced to cultivate marginal lands, lacking other alternatives. Low-income countries will pay little, if any, to avoid climatic and biological resources degradation.

Grassroots Environmental Action

The transition to sustainable development generally requires local participation in managing resources. United Nations Research Institute for Social Development (UNRISD) researchers Dharam Ghai and Jessica M. Vivian contend that low-income local people operating small-scale schemes based on longstanding knowledge of the soil and terrain usually resist large-scale commercialization (dams, irrigation projects, fishing trawlers, timber) by government or firms that fail to consult local people or bear the costs of degradation. Grassroots action in defense of the environment, especially in democracies such as India, can have a significant impact, even in the face of opposition of entrenched interest groups whose profits lie in overexploiting resources. Local people who are not just

---

[13]Stephen Mink, "Poverty and the Environment," *Finance and Development* 30 (December 1993): 8–9.
[14]World Bank, *World Development Report, 1992* (New York: Oxford University Press, 1992), p. 4.

defending the "environment" in the abstract but their livelihood and their way of life are difficult for ruling elites to quell.[15]

How do we reconcile UNRISD findings with those of the Brundtland Commission? Robin Broad, who conducted field work in rural communities across the Philippines argues that the poor who live in a stable ecosystem, with secure long-term user rights (see below) will behave responsibly toward the environment. However, when events and institutions transform poor people "into marginal people living in vulnerable and fragile ecosystems," they will destroy and degrade their environment.[16]

Market Imperfections and Policy Failures as Determinants of Environmental Degradation

Resource and environmental economist Theodore Panayotou argues that environmental degradation originates from market distortions, defective economic policies, and inadequate property rights definitions—that is, that environmental problems are, at heart, economic problems. Market and policy failures mean a disassociation of scarcity and prices, benefits and costs, rights and responsibilities, and actions and consequences. People maximize profits by shifting costs onto others; and appropriate common and public property resources without compensation. Market failures are institutional failures partly attributable to the nature of certain resources and partly to the failure of the government to establish fundamental conditions for efficient markets and use instruments (taxes, regulations, public investment, and macroeconomic policies) to bring costs and benefits that institutions fail to internalize into the domain of the market. Policy failures are cases of misguided government intervention in fairly well-functioning markets or unsuccessful attempts to mitigate market failure which results in worse outcomes. However, society's goals cannot be eliminating environmental deterioration altogether but rather accounting for all costs from diminished quantity and quality and lost diversity of natural resources, considering the productivity and sustainability of alternative resource uses, and insisting that environmental costs are borne by those who generate them. Growth must be derived from increased efficiency and innovation rather than by shifting environmental costs onto others.[17]

Following are six market imperfections that contribute to environmental degradation.

(1) Externalities. Externalities refer to economic activities conveying direct and unintended costs and benefits to other individuals and firms. Chapters 5 and 11's concept of external economies also includes negative externalities or **external diseconomies**. These diseconomies include air pollution (from steel plants and automobile exhausts), water pollution, and depletion of fisheries by overfishing.

You can trace almost all resource problems to discrepancies between the private and social valuation of resources. In general, overexploitation, inefficient use,

---

[15]Dharam Ghai and Jessica M. Vivian, eds., *Grassroots Environmental Action: People's Participation in Sustainable Development* (London: Routledge, 1992).

[16]Robin Broad, "The Poor and the Environment: Friends or Foes?" *World Development* 22 (June 1994): 811–22.

[17]Theodore Panayotou, *Green Markets: The Economics of Sustainable Development* (San Francisco: Institute for Contemporary Studies, 1993).

inadequate conservation, and the lack of investment in the regeneration of natural resources arise from the failure of either the market or government to price resources according to social scarcity.

Government should identify spillovers (externalities) ignored in calculating private benefit-cost or user costs over time (where current resource use affects the future resource available), and internalize these costs or charge them to the current consumers and producers through taxation or modifying prices (rather than future generations or innocent bystanders from the present generation). Examples include the state levying taxes on polluters or charging a surcharge for pesticide use.[18] Government here has a more active role than when operating under Coase's theorem (Box 13-1).

(2) Common Property Resources. Biologist Garrett Hardin's **"tragedy of the commons"** implies that just as the herders' cattle eventually overgraze a pasture open to all, so do businesses and individuals overpollute atmosphere and overuse biosphere free for all to use.[19] Individuals exploit an unpaid or open access

---

BOX 13-1

Coase's Theorem

Coase's theorem asserts that if society defines property rights clearly, then markets will produce efficient outcomes such that people will pay for negative externalities they impose on others. Efficient outcomes include considering transaction costs discussed under (6) of market imperfections. Ronald H. Coase, "The Problem of Social Cost," in Robert Dorfman and Nancy S. Dorfman, eds., *Economics of the Environment: Selected Readings* (New York: Norton, 1993), pp. 109–38 (first published in the *Journal of Law and Economics*, 1960). Panayotou and Dorfman agree with the rule that people should pay for costs they shift to others, but unlike Coase, see an essential role for the state in allaying market failure. Theodore Panayotou, *Green Markets: The Economics of Sustainable Development* (San Francisco: Institute for Contemporary Studies, 1993); and Robert Dorfman, "Some Concepts from Welfare Economics," in Robert Dorfman and Nancy S. Dorfman, eds., *Economics of the Environment: Selected Readings* (New York: Norton, 1993), pp. 79–96.

---

[18]Theodore Panayotou, *Green Markets: The Economics of Sustainable Development* (San Francisco: Institute for Contemporary Studies, 1993), pp. 39–45; and Robert Dorfman, "Some Concepts from Welfare Economics," in Robert Dorfman and Nancy S. Dorfman, eds., *Economics of the Environment: Selected Readings* (New York: Norton, 1993), pp. 79–96.

[19]Garrett Hardin, "The Tragedy of the Commons," *Science* 162 (December 13, 1968): 1244–45.

John Peirson, "Development and the Environment," in A.P. Thirlwall, *Growth and Development with Special Reference to Developing Economies* (Boulder, Colo.: Lynne Rienner, 1994), p. 218, points out that free open access to grazing land need not necessarily destroy the usefulness of land. Overgrazing depends on the private costs of raising cattle, their market value, and the ability of the land to support large numbers of cattle.

resource as if they were facing an infinite discount rate. Indeed, having large families, while harmful to society, is optimal for a couple exploiting the commons. Families, factories, fishers, and herders, which generate environmental costs, should bear the costs they convey to others through the degradation of air, water, and pastures.

During the last quarter of the twentieth century, West Africa, facing foreign exchange shortages, has exported substantial amounts of timber. Additionally, tens of thousands of West Africans cut down timber to mitigate acute firewood shortages. West Africa's rate of tropical deforestation during the 1980s was 0.8 percent yearly; by 1997, few of these forests remained.[20]

From time immemorial, cultures have discovered the dangers of common-property tenure and have developed property rights, sometimes group tenure or coordination of hunting and gathering, to protect their resources. In the evolution of humankind, only those cultures survived which developed institutions to limit common-property resource use.[21]

(3) Public Goods.   Many environmental resources are public goods, which are characterized by nonrivalry and nonexclusion in consumption. Nonrivalry means that one individual's consumption of the good (lighthouses, biodiversity of species, oceans) does not diminish the amount of good available for others to consume. Nonexclusion means that if one person is able to consume the good (the atmosphere, flood protection, national defense, and police fire protection), then others cannot be excluded from consuming it.[22]

(4) Irreversibility.   Many environmental and natural resource goods cannot be reproduced in the future if we fail to preserve them now. The market makes inadequate provision for the future of a rare phenomena of nature (the Grand Canyon), a threatened specie (the elephant), or an ecosystem (the tropical rainforest) essential for the survival of a specie. We should place a high value on retaining options to use goods or services that would be difficult or impossible to replace and for which there are no close substitutes.[23] Logging or mining of the tropical rainforest, the habitat for about half of the world's biological species, destroys the species which are essential for the pharmeceuticals and seed varieties that humankind needs in the future.

(5) Undefined User Rights.   People will not pay for or conserve a resource without the assurance of secure and exclusive rights over it. The overuse of common property resources ensues from legally unclear ownership and user rights to

[20]Theodore Panayotou, "The Population, Environment, and Development Nexus," in Robert Cassen and contributors, *Population and Development: Old Debates, New Conclusions*, Overseas Development Council U.S.-Third World Policy Perspectives (New Brunswick, NJ: Transaction, 1994), pp. 151–52; Carl Tham, "Poverty, Environment, and Development," in Uner Kirdar, ed., *Change: Threat or Opportunity for Human Progress* (New York: United Nations, 1992), pp. 25–37; and World Bank, *World Development Report, 1992* (New York: Oxford University Press, 1992), p. 6.

[21]H. Scott Gordon, "The Economic Theory of a Common-Property Resource: The Fishery," in Robert Dorfman and Nancy S. Dorfman, eds., *Economics of the Environment: Selected Readings* (New York: Norton, 1993), pp. 97–108.

[22]James R. Kahn, *The Economic Approach to Environmental and Natural Resources* (Fort Worth, Tex.: Dryden, 1995), p. 18.

[23]John V. Krutilla, "Conservation Reconsidered," in Robert Dorfman and Nancy S. Dorfman, eds., *Economics of the Environment: Selected Readings* (New York: Norton, 1993), pp. 188–98.

an asset. In Thailand, subsistence farmers, without long-term tenure rights, "mined" the soil because they lacked incentives for more sustainable practices. In Pakistan's Indus River basin (Chapter 7) and California's valleys, the delivery of water from large public irrigation projects to farmers at low, subsidized costs results in its wasteful use. Pakistan's large, influential farmers get access to water at the expense of the rights of small farmers because user (or ownership) rights to water are not explicitly defined in terms of prices, quantities to be used, and rights of upstream and downstream users. The use of water at one point along an irrigation channel affects its uses at other points, that is, one use has an opportunity cost in terms of other uses given up.[24] The similar underpricing of rights to discharge pollutants into the atmosphere, rights that can be efficiently allocated through transferable emissions permits, is discussed below.

(6) High Transactions Costs. Transactions costs are the costs of information, coordination, bargaining, monitoring, and enforcement of contracts. If set-up costs are high, markets based on voluntary agreement and exchange fail to emerge. The costs of parceling out the sea to individual fishers and enforcing property rights over a mobile resource, such as water, may be prohibitively high. Moreover, when millions of people burn carbon-based fuels whose pollution, which migrates across borders, affect millions of victims, the costs of negotiations between the many parties involved are going to be significant.[25]

Panayotou lists the following economic manifestations of environmental degradation and the corresponding solutions to the environmental problems:

Economic manifestations of environmental degradation	*Solutions to environmental problems*
(1) overuse, waste, and inefficiency coexisting with growing resource scarcity and shortages, as in Thailand, Indonesia, Philippines, India, and Pakistan	eliminate market distortions that spur overuse of common property resources
(2) an increasingly scarce resource put to inferior, low-return, and unsustainable uses, when superior, high-return, and sustainable uses exist (for example, Brazil's conversion of valuable forests in the Amazon to ranches, reducing soil fertility)	eliminate perverse fiscal incentives offered by the Brazilian government

[24]J.H. Dales, "Land, Water, and Ownership," in Robert Dorfman and Nancy S. Dorfman, eds., *Economics of the Environment: Selected Readings* (New York: Norton, 1993), pp. 225–40; Theodore Panayotou, *Green Markets: The Economics of Sustainable Development* (San Francisco: Institute for Contemporary Studies, 1993), pp. 35–38, 67–70; and Lester R. Brown, Christopher Flavin, and Sandra Postel, *Saving the Planet: How to Shape an Environmentally Sustainable Global Economy*, Worldwatch Institute (New York: Norton, 1991), p. 87.

[25]Theodore Panayotou, *Green Markets: The Economics of Sustainable Development* (San Francisco: Institute for Contemporary Studies, 1993), pp. 34, 43–44; and James R. Kahn, *The Economic Approach to Environmental and Natural Resources* (Fort Worth, Tex.: Dryden, 1995), p. 46.

Economic manifestations of environmental degradation	*Solutions to environmental problems*
(3) exploitation of a renewable resource capable of sustainable management as an extractive resource (such as tropical forests mined without concern for regeneration and future harvests)	cease underpricing or oversubsidizing the resource (such as water and ranch land)
(4) a resource put to single use when multiple uses would generate a larger net benefit (as illustrated by a tropical forest that could be used for fruits, latex, water and soil conservation, and biological diversity rather than just timber)	eliminate price distortions through subsidies or underpricing
(5) investments in the protection and enhancement of the resource base (through reducing erosion and improving irrigation) are not undertaken even though they would generate a positive net present value by increasing productivity and enhancing sustainability	government taxes and subsidizes to make internal and social profitability coincide
(6) a larger amount of effort and cost is incurred when a smaller amount of effort and cost would have generated a higher level of output and profit and less damage to the resource (fisheries and common pastures)	government fees to reduce common-property and open-access resources, which lead to overuse
(7) local communities, tribal and indigenous groups, and women are displaced and deprived of customary rights of access to resources, forests although because of their specialized knowledge and self-interest, they are most cost-effective managers of the resource	prevent central government from assuming ownership and management of tropical and other common-property resources
(8) public projects are undertaken that do not generate benefits to compensate all affected (including the environment) sufficiently to make them decidedly better off with that project than without it (for example, future generations are not fully compensated)	government needs to (a) create green markets to make people bear the costs they transmit to others and to encompass the needs of the future, and (b) prevent state ownership from contributing to the "tragedy of the commons"

Economic manifestations of environmental degradation	Solutions to environmental problems
(9) resources and byproducts are not recycled, even when recycling would generate both economic and environmental benefits	government should embody the disposal price in the price the consumer pays, and should charge for unrecycled waste
(10) unique sites and habitats are lost and animal and plant species go extinct without compelling economic reasons	provide market signals so that species of such value that their irreversible loss cannot be justified would be properly evaluated[26]

Pollution

As argued above, pollution problems result from divergences between social and commercial costs, divergences arising under both capitalism and socialism. In the mid-1980s more than half the rivers of socialist Poland were too polluted even for industrial use. Stalinism and subsequent state management in the Soviet Union meant cheaply priced resources and ruthless treatment of land, air, and water. Indeed, the former Soviet Union best illustrates the "tragedy of the commons," in which everybody's property is nobody's property. Worldwatch researchers Lester R. Brown, Christopher Flavin, and Sandra Postel contend that the world's worst water quality is in the former Soviet Union's Aral Sea basin. The accumulation of agricultural pesticides in local water supplies has caused birth defects, miscarriages, kidney damage, and cancer. According to Murray Feshbach and Alfred Friendly, Jr., *Ecocide in the USSR: Health and Nature Under Siege*, these pesticides and defoliants have so contaminated the rivers feeding the Aral Sea that mothers in the region who breast-feed their babies run the risk of poisoning them. Furthermore, three-quarters of the former Soviet Union's surface water was unfit to drink and one-third of the underground water sources were contaminated. Nuclear accidents at Chernobyl and Kyshtym spread radioactive fallout over large hectares of agricultural land and killed thousands of people (see Chapter 20 on the former Soviet Union's reduced life expectancy). Feshbach and Friendly argue that air, land, and water were systematically poisoned, which also meant a substantial loss of diverse species, another legacy the former Soviet Union still lives with.[27]

Hardin's tragedy takes something—trees, grass, or fish—out of the commons. The reverse of the tragedy of the commons is pollution, which puts chemical, radioactive, or heat wastes or sewage into the water, and noxious and dangerous fumes into the air. For the firm, the cost of discharging wastes is much less

---

[26]Theodore Panayotou, *Green Markets: The Economics of Sustainable Development* (San Francisco: Institute for Contemporary Studies, 1993), pp. 8–23.

[27]Lester R. Brown, Christopher Flavin, and Sandra Postel, *Saving the Planet: How to Shape an Environmentally Sustainable Global Economy*, Worldwatch Institute (New York: Norton, 1991), pp. 26–27; and Murray Feshbach and Alfred Friendly, Jr. (with Lester Brown), *Ecocide in the USSR: Health and Nature Under Siege* (New York: Basic Books, 1991), pp. xi-25.

than purifying wastes before releasing it. Without a clear definition of ownership and user rights and responsibilities, an economy "fouls its own nest."[28]

Production and consumption create leftovers or residuals that are emitted into the air or water or disposed of on land. Pollution of air and water is excessive not in an absolute sense but relative to the capacity of them to assimilate emissions and to the objectives of society. Thus, under frontier conditions, with little population density, pollution may not be a problem. As population density becomes more salient, a country can charge a high enough price for use of a resource to limit effluents to a level that can be assimilated without damage to capacity.[29]

Urban air pollution is a major form of environmental degradation. The megacities of the world, urban areas with more than 10 million people, lie under clouds of industrial and vehicular pollution, generated primarily by fossil fuels. This pollution in densely populated areas is often visible, obviously human made, and poses immediate health risks to people living in the vicinity. The amount of this air pollution depends on pollution reduction efforts, choice of fuels, available technologies, topography, weather, and climate. The most serious health problems result from exposure to suspended particulate matter (SPM), consisting of small, separate particles from sooty smoke or gaseous pollutants. Health consequences include a high incidence of respiratory diseases such as coughs, asthma, bronchitis, and emphysema, and increased death rates among children, elderly, and the weak. Particulates, especially the finer ones, can carry heavy metals, many of which are poisonous or carcinogenic, into the deeper, more sensitive parts of the lungs. Sooty smoke from incomplete fuel combustion and vehicle exhausts such as diesel engines, are anthroprogenic sources of SPM. Liquid SPM contributes to the damage of buildings, habitat, and fish, as well as humans. Enterprises and vehicle owners can reduce particulate emissions by installing control equipment, such as dust removal equipment in coal-fired utilities, or by switching to fuels other than coal.[30]

The finer, more hazardous SPM and (probably) airborne lead increase with GDP per capita until you get to the levels of middle-income countries, and decrease beyond these levels. Sulphur dioxide (SO_2) has a similar relationship to country income, except it begins to decline with lower-middle income countries. Sulphur dioxide is emitted with the burning of fossil fields from automobile exhausts, nonferrous ore smelting, and petroleum refining. More than 600 million people, including those in major cities such as Beijing, Mexico City, and Seoul, live in urban areas where SO_2 levels exceed World Health Organization guidelines. The downturn in SPM, airborne lead, and SO_2 levels is not due to changes in output composition but to tighter government restrictions such as the installation of control equipment, the switching to fuels other than coal, and limits on lead additives to gasoline.[31]

[28]Garrett Hardin, "The Tragedy of the Commons," *Science* 162 (December 13, 1968): 1244–45.

[29]Barry C. Field, *Environmental Economics: An Introduction* (New York: McGraw-Hill, 1994), p. 24; and Theodore Panayotou, *Green Markets: The Economics of Sustainable Development* (San Francisco: Institute for Contemporary Studies, 1993), p. 7.

[30]Gene M. Grossman, "Pollution and Growth: What Do We Know?" in Ian Goldin and L. Alan Winters, eds., *The Economics of Sustainable Development*, published for the OECD (Cambridge: Cambridge University Press, 1995), pp. 19–50; and World Resources Institute, United Nations Environment Program, and the United Nations Development Program, *World Resources, 1994–95*, edited by Allen L. Hammond (New York: Oxford University Press, 1994), p. 197.

[31]Gene M. Grossman, "Pollution and Growth: What Do We Know?" in Ian Goldin and L. Alan Winters, eds., *The Economics of Sustainable Development* (Cambridge: Cambridge University Press, 1995), pp. 27–35; and World Resources Institute, United Nations Environment Program, and the United Nations Development Program, *World Resources, 1994–95*, edited by Allen L. Hammond (New York: Oxford University Press, 1994), p. 198.

The major forms of freshwater pollution are pathogens (disease agents, usually micro-organisms) in raw sewage, industrial and agricultural contaminants from heavy metals and synthetic organic compounds in drinking water and aquatic organisms, and excessive nutrients in sewage, agricultural runoff, and industrial discharge. In India, 114 towns dump their human waste and untreated sewage directly into the Ganges, so that this holy river is among the most polluted in the world. Almost two billion people in developing countries drink contaminated water, the primary cause of the death of children. LDCs discharge more than 90 percent of their urban sewage without adequate treatment. Waterborne pathogens from human and animal feces can cause gastroenteritis, typhoid, dysentery, cholera, hepatitis, amoebic dysentery, schistosomiasis, and giardiasis, which are responsible for a substantial fraction of LDC deaths each year. Fecal contaminants rise with GDP per capita (and industrialization and urbanization) until a country reaches upper-middle or high income status, after which these contaminants drop sharply, largely as a result of investments in water and sewage treatment. The relationship between heavy metals, toxic chemicals, and excess nutrients in rivers and income is mixed, although lead, cadmium, and nickel concentrations generally fall with income.[32]

Policy makers need to consider alternative costs of using scarce resources and costs of the damage to the productivity of resource as waste disposal increases beyond a certain threshold. Moreover, prevention is often more cost-effective than rehabilitation, and some environmental costs are irreversible.[33]

Consider a resource flow, based on periodic rain and snow, year after year, the basis for a river, which flows down from the mountains, through farms, to a city. State authorities do not face a problem of resource allocation, as long as the river flow exceeds withdrawals of water for use, and the water is not contaminated. However, once water is scarce and users face excess demand, the water authority needs to charge a price and define user rights to the water. Take Figure 13–2, which shows a demand curve for a fixed supply of water (L_0) available at zero cost. Here the price where the quantity demanded is equal to the fixed quantity supplied is P_0. However, if government only charges a price P_1, then the quantity demanded is L_1, and the water shortage is L_0L_1.[34] This is a frequent problem, as illustrated by irrigation water in Pakistan and southern California, where farmers waste water sold to them at a subsidized price.

No policy maker wants to pay the staggering costs often essential to restore waste sites to pristine conditions. Instead policy makers try to attain an optimal environmental quality, which considers the tradeoff between the damage that people suffer from pollution and the cost of reducing emission in terms of the resources that could have been used in other ways.

Figure 13–3 shows a **marginal damage (MD) function**, upward sloping to the right, which indicates the change in dollar (or other domestic currency) cost resulting from a unit change in pollution emissions, measured here in tons per year (but sometimes measured as ambient concentration, such as parts per million). Air

[32]Gene M. Grossman, "Pollution and Growth: What Do We Know?" in Ian Goldin and L. Alan Winters, eds., *The Economics of Sustainable Development*, published for the OECD (Cambridge: Cambridge University Press, 1995), pp. 35–45; and Al Gore, *Earth in the Balance: Ecology and the Human Spirit* (New York: Plume, 1993), p. 110.

[33]Theodore Panayotou, *Green Markets: The Economics of Sustainable Development* (San Francisco: Institute for Contemporary Studies, 1993), p. 7.

[34]James R. Kahn, *The Economic Approach to Environmental and Natural Resources* (Fort Worth, Tex.: Dryden Press, 1995), pp. 375–78.

FIGURE 13-2   A Water Shortage Caused by a Low Price

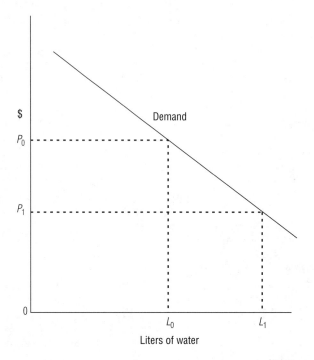

FIGURE 13-3   The Efficient Level of Pollution Emissions

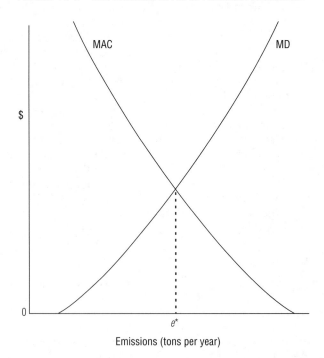

pollution damages human health, degrades materials and buildings, worsens the visual environment, and disrupts or destroys nonhuman ecosystems, including crops, animals, insects, and genetic stock.

How do we measure dollar cost? Let's look only at the damage to people's health. The most obvious cost is excess illness or death from diseases such as lung cancer, chronic bronchitis, emphysema, and asthma from elevated levels of pollutants, such as sulfur dioxide, asbestos fibers, and radon emissions.[35] We can calculate the (discounted) cost of extra days lost from deaths and illnesses (person-days of work lost times the daily output foregone, usually estimated by the daily wage), medical expense, and nonpecuniary costs, such as pain and suffering.

Figure 13–3 also shows abatement costs, the costs of reducing pollution emissions into the environment. The **marginal abatement cost (MAC) function**, upward sloping to the left, indicates the change in dollar cost to change pollution emissions by one unit (for example, one ton per year). Abatement is defined widely to include all ways of reduction emission including changing production technology, switching inputs, recycling residuals, treating wastes, abandoning a site, and so forth. Where the MAC curve intersects the horizontal axis is the uncontrolled pollution emission level, where nothing is abated. As the curve slopes upward to the left from zero MAC, the marginal (or extra) cost of the first units of emission reduction is relatively low. Think of a steel plant. The firm might attain the first small reduction in pollution by putting a screen or filter on the smokestack. But as pollution levels fall further the marginal cost of achieving additional reductions increases. For example, a 30 to 40 percent reduction in emissions might require investment in new technology to reduce effluents. Reducing emissions 60 to 70 percent might require new treatment technology in addition to all previous steps taken. A 90 percent reduction might require costly equipment for recycling virtually all pollution emitted in the plant. The extreme option for a single plant is to cease operations, thereby achieving zero emissions. Thus the larger the reduction in emissions, the greater the marginal cost of producing further reductions.[36]

The efficient level of pollution emission or minimal social cost is where marginal damages are equal to marginal abatement costs (that is, where emissions are e^*). Why? Emissions higher than e^* expose society to additional damages whose costs are in excess of abatement costs reduce (MD>MAC). Emissions lower than e^* mean that society incurs extra abatement costs in excess of foregone damage (MAC>MD).

Government needs to enforce and administer emission regulations, and firms need to keep records of abatement costs and emission reductions. To analyze minimal costs from society's viewpoint, you should include transactions costs, such as enforcement and administrative costs, in the marginal abatement cost function; the result is that the efficient level of emissions increases (or moves to the right).[37]

To achieve minimal social cost (MAC = MD), the government's pollution control board might charge individuals (such as automobile consumers) or firms a price that approximates the marginal social cost or damage of pollution. Once prices are set for sources and amounts of pollution, the polluter can adjust in any way it pleases, either by finding the cheapest means of reducing or eliminating

[35]Barry C. Field, *Environmental Economics: An Introduction* (New York: McGraw-Hill, 1994), pp. 86–88.

[36]Barry C. Field, *Environmental Economics: An Introduction* (New York: McGraw-Hill, 1994), pp. 90–93.

[37]Barry C. Field, *Environmental Economics: An Introduction* (New York: McGraw-Hill, 1994), pp. 93–100.

pollutions, or paying fines. Using a market system to charge for pollution spurs private firms to make socially efficient decisions.[38]

Contingent Valuation

The ability to place a monetary value on pollution discharges or other forms of ecological degradation is a cornerstone of the economic approach to the environment.[39] But a damage function relating the cost to the amount of, say, pollution emissions, while conceptually straightforward, is often difficult to measure.

Contingent valuation uses questionnaires from sample surveys to elicit the willingness of respondents to pay for a hypothetical program, such as a public good (for example, the environment). Economists can use interviews to simulate a market to determine how much people would pay for additional quantities of a public good. Values revealed by survey respondents may allow economists to draw a market demand schedule.[40]

But it would not work to approach people at a mall in São Paulo, Brazil, ask them to drop their shopping bags, and inquire about how much they are willing to pay to preserve the tropical rainforest in the Amazon River basin or a penguin in the Antarctica. W. Michael Hanemann argues that people are more willing to tell you whether they would pay some particular amount in increased taxes than to specify the maximum amount they or society generally should pay for the program. A self-contained referendum is preferable. The enumerator should ask the Brazilian voter a concrete question such as: "If it costs you $10 taxes annually for the next twenty years for a program that will preserve 50 million hectares (124 million acres) of the Amazon River basin rainforest, would you vote for it?" The survey should use different dollar amounts for different respondents so as to trace a demand schedule that indicates willingness to pay at various prices.[41]

Economists have some objections to the contingent valuation method. Answering survey questions requires effort, so that some people become impatient, uninterested, or tired. Different people perceive the same questions differently, and the choice of words is so important in conveying meaning. People may respond by making up answers rather than evincing true economic preferences, whatever these may be.

How important is scope? Do people respond the same when you ask about preserving one rainforest or two rainforests, or one rainforest, then another rainforest? Peter A. Diamond and Jerry A. Hausman argue that contingent valuation surveys do not measure the preferences they attempt to measure. For example, the sequence in which a question is asked helps determine the answer: people asked a first question to pay to preserve the visibility at the Grand Canyon were willing to pay more than those asked the third question about the Canyon. How much people were willing to pay to save the seal depended on the sequence of questions

---

[38]Larry E. Ruff, "The Economic Common Sense of Pollution," in Robert Dorfman and Nancy S. Dorfman, eds., *Economics of the Environment: Selected Readings* (New York: Norton, 1993), pp. 20–36.

[39]W. Michael Hanemann, "Valuing the Environment through Contingent Valuation," *Journal of Economic Perspectives* 8 (Fall 1994): 19–43.

[40]Paul R. Portney, "The Contingent Valuation Debate: Why Economists Should Care," *Journal of Economic Perspectives* 8 (Fall 1994): 3–17.

[41]W. Michael Hanemann, "Valuing the Environment through Contingent Valuation," *Journal of Economic Perspectives* 8 (Fall 1994): 22–24.

about seal and whale preservation. People's stated willingness to pay does gregate. Thus people are willing to pay more to preserve three wildernesses separately than the three together. Diamond and Hausman conclude that contingent valuation is deeply flawed. At a minimum, contingent valuation surveys need to be pretested so that the questions are as precise as possible. Even with careful preparation, the contingent valuation method can only find an approximate value for what is invariably difficult to measure precisely. The more you rely on measurable costs (for example, medical costs plus wages foregone for a certain number of person-years lost from air pollution), the more confidence you will have in your valuation.[42]

Arid and Semiarid Lands

A desert is a region supporting little vegetation because of insufficient rainfall (less than 25 centimeters or 10 inches of rain annually) and dry soil. About 23 percent of the earth's land area is desert, or **arid land,** and an additional 20 percent is semiarid. In 1996, about 14 percent of the world population (810 million people) lived in arid or semiarid lands. According to U.N. estimates, about 100 million people live on almost useless lands—lands damaged by erosion, dune formation, vegetational change, and salt encrustation. Perhaps 60 million of these 100 million people, because of their dependence on agriculture, face the gradual loss of their livelihoods as fields and pastures turn into wastelands.

LDCs risk large amounts of nondesert land being turned into desert. When you disturb imperiled ecological systems with increased human activity, you can disrupt infiltration of rainwater, increase surface runoff, lower groundwater levels, dry up surface water, and lose topsoil and soil nutrients, perhaps contributing to hunger and even famine.[43]

In the last half-century, particularly since the late 1960s, the Sahara Desert has expanded southward into the areas of the African Sahel (parts of Mauritania, Senegal, Mali, Burkina Faso, Niger, and Chad). Such encroachment in Africa, as well as in the Middle East, Australia, and the Americas, results more from irresponsible land use patterns—deforestation, overgrazing, overcultivating, and shortsighted farming practices—than from climatic fluctuations.[44]

Tropical Climates

Geographically the **tropics** lie in a band 2,500 kilometers (4,000 miles) wide on each side of the equator, but climatically they are wider. There are three types of tropical climates, all hot but widely varied in rainfall. The wet equatorial climate, a band 1,100 kilometers (1,800 miles) wide centered on the equator, is characterized by

[42]Peter A. Diamond and Jerry A. Hausman, "Contingent Valuation: Is Some Number Better than No Number?" *Journal of Economic Perspectives* 8 (Fall 1994): 45–64; and W. Michael Hanemann, "Valuing the Environment through Contingent Valuation," *Journal of Economic Perspectives* 8 (Fall 1994): 27–28, 34–36.

[43]United Nations, *Global Outlook, 2000: An Economic, Social, and Environmental Perspectives* (New York, 1990), pp. 87–88.

[44]Erik Eckholm and Lester R. Brown, *Spreading Deserts—The Hand of Man* (Washington, D.C.: Worldwatch Institute, 1977). I have updated these estimates to 1996.

constant rainfall (190 to 300 centimeters, or 75 to 120 inches, a year) and humidity. A monsoon strip, alternately wet and dry, lies 1,100 kilometers on either side of the wet equatorial tropics. Still farther north and south are the arid tropics, about 1,600 kilometers (2,500 miles) wide, where rain-fed agriculture is practically impossible.

In 1945, the geographer Ellsworth Huntington contended that different climates, through their direct effects on human energies and achievement, determined different levels of civilization. He argued that the highest level of achievement is affected by the degree to which the weather is moderate and variable.[45] Following strong reaction against his theories, few recent scholars have tried to explain or even declare a relationship between climate and human achievement. At present they do not know if hot tropical weather has a direct adverse impact on our work efficiency, creativity, and initiative.

However, Andrew W. Kamarck enumerates other less questionable notions about why economic underdevelopment occurs in the tropics.[46] There is no winter in the tropics. Weeds, insect pests, and parasitic diseases that are enemies to crops, animals, and people are not exterminated. This disadvantage outweighs any benefit that might accrue from luxuriant plant growth. Intestinal parasites occur in nearly all domestic animals in the tropics. They retard the development of young animals, reduce yields of milk and meat, impair the working capacity of draft animals, and kill many infected animals. For example, trypanosomiasis, a disease carried by the tsetse fly, inhibits farm and transport development because it attacks cattle and transport animals in much of tropical Africa. Gigantic swarms of locusts can fly over 1,900 kilometers (1,200 miles) nonstop and attack crops anywhere from West Africa to India.

In the tropics, soil is damaged by the sun, which can burn away organic matter and kill microorganisms, and by torrential rains, which can crush soil structure and leach out minerals. And when the lush tropical vegetation is removed, soil deteriorates unless recent alluvial or volcanic overflow replenishes it. Thus reddish and yellowish brown laterite soils predominate in large parts of the humid tropics.

Disease is also a factor in economic underdevelopment in the tropics. This region offers far more hospitable conditions for human disease than the temperate zones. The incidence of parasitic infections in temperate zones is much lower than in the tropics, since winter kills most parasites. At least three-fourths of the adult population of the tropics is infected with some form of parasite. In fact infectious, parasitic, and respiratory diseases account for about 44 percent of the deaths in LDCs but only 11 percent in DCs. For example, about 200 million people suffer from bilharzia, a disease carried by a parasitic worm, that may produce severe, irreversible liver damage, an enlarged spleen, and a bloated abdomen, while the rest of the body becomes emaciated. River blindness, a fly-borne infection, affects approximately 20 million people, mostly in large river valleys in tropical Africa, and causes partial or total blindness. Because constant warm temperature plays a part in this parasite's life cycle, the fly cannot successfully carry this infection into temperate areas. Amoebic and bacillary dysentery spread more rapidly in tropical areas than in temperate zones. The idea that only visitors "not used to the water" suffer from dysentery is fiction.[47] Overall these parasitic dis-

---

[45]Ellsworth Huntington, *Mainsprings of Civilization* (New York: Wiley, 1945).

[46]Most of this section relies on Andrew M. Kamarck, *The Tropics and Economic Development: A Provocative Inquiry into the Poverty of Nations* (Baltimore: Johns Hopkins University Press, 1976), and its updating.

[47]Everett E. Hagen, *Economics of Development* (Homewood, Ill.: Irwin, 1975), p. 191.

eases substantially impair the health, well-being, and productivity of people living in the tropics.

Poor soil and plant, animal, and human diseases endemic in the tropics explain some of their underdevelopment. An exception is the industrialized highlands of southern Brazil. Although they are located in the tropics, their altitudes foster a cool climate similar to the eastern Appalachians in the United States.

No doubt problems of plague (like desert locusts, which spread from Ethiopia-Sudan in 1985 through much of the Sahara, Northern Africa, and Saudi Arabia by 1988), disease, and soil can be ameliorated by international cooperative research and centralized services in tropical agriculture and medicine. Clearly capital transfer or adaptation of existing research and technology from developed temperate countries is limited as a spur to tropical economic growth until these other problems are dealt with.

Global Public Goods: Climate and Biodiversity

Many environmental resources are **public goods**, which are characterized by nonrivalry and nonexclusion in consumption. Nonrivalry means that one individual's consumption of the good does not diminish the amount of good available for others to consume. Nonexclusion means that if one person is able to consume the good, then others cannot be excluded from consuming it.[48]

While carbon emissions and rainforest and specie destruction are internal public bads within an individual tropical country, these forms of environmental degradation also have adverse impact on climate change and biological diversity for other countries, both within the region and throughout the globe. The atmosphere and biosphere are **global public goods** since nations cannot exclude other nations from the benefits of their conservation or from the costs of their degradation.

We cannot expect interregional or global public goods to be provided in sufficient quantity by an individual tropical country in the free market, since many benefits spill over to other countries. In tropical regions such as West Africa, the ecology of the desert and the tropical rainforest are interconnected. Climatologists Yongkang Xue and Jagadish Shukla indicate that afforestation in southern Nigeria and southern Cameroon's tropical rainforest reduce the drought of the sub-Saharan border or Sahel, including northern Nigeria, northern Cameroon, Niger, and Chad. In addition, afforestation in this rainforest also affects global climate and stock of species.[49]

BIOLOGICAL DIVERSITY

The earth's four biological systems—forests, grasslands, fisheries, and croplands— supply all of our food and much of the raw materials for industry (with the notable exceptions of fossil fuels and minerals). Each of these systems is fueled

---

[48]James R. Kahn, *The Economic Approach to Environmental and Natural Resources* (Fort Worth, Tex.: Dryden Press, 1995), p. 18.

[49]Yongkang Xue and Jagadish Shukla, "The Influence of Land Surface Properties on Sahel Climate. Part 1: Desertification," *Journal of Climate* 6 (December 1993): 2232–45; and Yongkang Xue and Jagadish Shukla, "The Influence of Land Surface Properties on Sahel Climate. Part 2: Afforestation," Center for Ocean-Land-Atmosphere Studies, Calverton, Md., 1993.

by photosynthesis, where plants use solar energy to combine water and carbon dioxide to form carbohydrates, a process which supports all life on earth. Lester R. Brown, Christopher Flavin, and Sandra Postel argue that unless we manage the basic biological system of converting solar energy into biochemical energy more intelligently, the earth will never meet the basic needs of 5.8 billion people.[50]

Sustainability requires a multitude of species and genetic stock with which to experiment. **Biodiversity** includes genetic diversity, the variation between individuals and populations within a species (for example, the thousands of traditional rice varieties in India); species diversity, differing types of plants, animals, and other life forms within a region; ecosystem diversity, a variety of habitats within a grassland, marsh, woodland, or other area; and functional diversity, the varying roles of organisms within an ecosystem.[51]

Diversity is important for two reasons. First, the diversity of species bestows stability in ecosystems. Species are entwined like a woven fabric; they cannot be seen in isolation from their ecosystem. Examples of this interdependence are the food chain, plant dependence on birds and insects for pollination, the habitat dependency of animals and insects, and the protection of species from natural enemies. Greater genetic diversity means a species is more likely to survive threats such as droughts and floods. Species diversity, the world's available gene pool, is one of the planet's irreplaceable resources.

According to biologist David Hartnett, the connections between species are intricate and far-reaching. Hunters who almost annihilated the sea otter in the United States' Pacific Coast in the early twentieth century affected the rest of the ecosystem adversely. Sea otters fed on sea urchins, which fed on kelp and sea grass. As the sea otter became virtually extinct, the sea urchin population exploded, decimating the population of sea grass and kelp that were critical habitat for coastal fish that bald eagles and harbor seals ate. Thus, the virtual extinction of the sea otter, through a complex chain, endangered the bald eagle.[52]

Second, as genetic and species diversity in plants and animals is reduced, potential advances in medicine, agriculture, and biotechnology are also reduced. Genetic diversity provides the farm economy with options other than heavy pesticide use or substantial crop loss in the face of infestation. Species diversity provides humankind with more choices for medicines, cosmetics, industrial products, fuel, building materials, food, and other products, and more protection against plant enemies. More than half of the world's species are in the 6 percent of the earth's land surface in tropical forests, primarily in Colombia, Brazil, Madagascar, the Himalayas, the Philippines, Malaysia, Borneo, and Australia. Scientists have found as many ant species from a single leguminous tree in Peru as ant diversity in all of the British isles. In a one-hectare (2.5 acre) plot in Kalimantan, Indonesia, another scientist found 700 tree species, about equal to the number native to all of North America. Forty percent of the species in tropical rainforests disappeared from 1985 to 2000, mostly from burning and clearing. Thus, tropical defor-

---

[50]Lester R. Brown, Christopher Flavin, and Sandra Postel, *Saving the Planet: How to Shape an Environmentally Sustainable Global Economy*, Worldwatch Environmental Alert Series (New York: Norton, 1991), pp. 73–74.

[51]World Resources Institute, United Nations Environment Program, and the United Nations Development Program (Allen L. Hammond, ed.), *World Resources, 1994–95* (New York: Oxford University Press, 1994), pp. 147–48.

[52]I am grateful to David Hartnett for this material.

estation (through population growth, fuelwood consumption, and slash-and-burn agriculture) is a major force behind the biological crisis.[53]

Geneticist Edward O. Wilson estimates that deforestation in the late twentieth century has reduced species 10,000 times faster than the natural extinction rate that existed before humans appeared; the diversity of species destroyed by human activity in the last 10,000 years will take 100 million years to recover.[54] World Resources Institute researchers Kenton R. Miller, Walter V. Reid, and Charles V. Barber argue that rapid deforestation and specie loss mean we are "eating our seed corn, squandering in a heedless evolutionary moment the forest's genetic capital, evolved over billions of years."[55] The U.S. Department of Agriculture estimates that 96 percent of the commercial vegetable varieties it listed in 1903 are now extinct; the Green Revolution in Mexico and South Asia, which promoted a limited number of high-yielding varieties of grain, dropped thousands of traditional crop varieties. Crop breeders need a diversity of crop varieties to breed new varieties that resist evolving pests and diseases. Nearly all the coffee trees in South America are descended from a single tree in an Amsterdam botanical garden 200 years ago, a potentially serious problem when a new disease begins attacking coffee trees.[56]

Developing countries have focused on the critical role of biological resources in economic development. These countries' governments have questioned DC multinational corporations' policies of obtaining diverse agricultural genetic material free of charge from a gene-rich third world country, and then selling the patented seed varieties from the material back to the country of origin at substantial prices. While most of the cost of conserving biodiversity would fall to LDCs, since these biological resources are largely within their borders, LDCs want DCs to pay much more of the price of conserving these resources, since, LDCs argue, DCs receive the lion's share of the benefits from these resources. DC corporations often take indigenous knowledge about products of nature, alter these products in a laboratory, and patent the altered product, LDC leaders charge. Initially, the United States did not sign the Convention on Biological Diversity at the 1992 U.N. Conference on Environment and Development because of concerns about intellectual property rights for those developing and patenting new drugs, funding for conservation of biological resources under control of DCs, control of national governments over access to genetic resources, and the obligation of all parties to provide access to and transfer biotechnology.[57] In 1993, however, President Bill Clinton

---

[53]World Resources Institute, United Nations Environment Program, and the United Nations Development Program (Allen L. Hammond, ed.), *World Resources, 1994–95* (New York: Oxford University Press, 1994), pp. 147–48; Edward O. Wilson, "Threats to Biodiversity," *Scientific American* (September 1989): 108–110; and United Nations, *Global Outlook 2000: An Economic, Social, and Environmental Perspective* (New York, 1990), p. 95.

[54]Edward O. Wilson, "Threats to Biodiversity," *Scientific American* (September 1989): 108–115.

[55]Kenton R. Miller, Walter V. Reid, and Charles V. Barber, "Deforestation and Species Loss," in Robert Dorfman and Nancy S. Dorfman, eds., *Economics of the Environment: Selected Readings* (New York: Norton, 1993), pp. 501–17, with quotation on p. 502.

[56]World Resources Institute, United Nations Environment Program, and the United Nations Development Program (Allen L. Hammond, ed.), *World Resources, 1994–95* (New York: Oxford University Press, 1994), pp. 147–64; and United Nations, *Global Outlook, 2000: An Economic, Social, and Environmental Perspective* (New York: United Nations Publications, 1990), pp. 94–95.

[57]World Resources Institute, United Nations Environment Program, and the United Nations Development Program (Allen L. Hammond, ed.), *World Resources, 1994–95* (New York: Oxford University Press, 1994), pp. 154–60.

signed the convention, while including a memorandum of understanding concerning protection of MNC intellectual property.

Overall the best strategy is to buy "insurance policies" by reducing loss of species and protecting habitats from undue conversion, fragmentation, and degradation. Over time, the preservation of biological diversity provides the genetic, biological, and ecosystem stocks for solutions to all sorts of future human problems.[58]

"GLOBAL WARMING" (GLOBAL CLIMATE CHANGE)[59]

Human activities affect the earth's climate. While most environmental risks are local or regional, some risks, such as the costs from greenhouse gases, are global in scope. Indeed William D. Nordhaus contends that humankind, through injecting greenhouse gases into the atmosphere, is playing dice with the universe.[60] Air pollutants and volcanic eruptions that originate from human activity change the temperature and climate, which spur shifts in ocean circulation, which feeds back to affect climate variables.[61]

If humankind continues its present rates of carbon emissions, the likelihood of serious harms to human welfare through global warming from the buildup of greenhouse gases and the costs of postponing measures to limit the buildup of these gases is high. The United Nations wants nations to adopt immediate measures to limit the growth of these gases.[62]

The Greenhouse Effect.   The earth reflects some sunlight and absorbs other. Where absorption is not matched by radiation back into space, the earth gets warmer until the radiation matches the absorbed incoming sunlight. Some atmospheric gases transparent to sunlight absorb radiation in the infrared spectrum, blocking outward radiation and warming the atmosphere. The greenhouse effect is the phenomenon by which the earth's atmosphere traps infrared radiation or heat. As a metaphor, the smudgepot effect is preferable to the greenhouse, according to Thomas C. Schelling. On a clear day in January in Orange County, California, the earth, and the adjacent atmosphere warm nicely, but warmth radiates rapidly away during the clear nights and frost may threaten the orange trees. Smudgepots, burning cheap oil on windless nights, produce carbon dioxide and other substances, that absorb the radiation and protect the trees with a blanket of warm air. Greenhouses trap the air warmed by the earth's surface and keep it from rising to be replaced by cooler air.[63]

Greenhouse gases include carbon dioxide (CO_2), methane, nitrous oxide, and water vapor, that keep the earth habitable, and chlorofluorocarbons (CFCs);

---

[58]Richard B. Norgaard, *Sustainability and the Economics of Assuring Assets for Future Generations*, World Bank Policy Research Working Paper 832, Washington, D.C., 1992, p. 51; and David Hartnett.

[59]My thanks to chemist Ken Klabunde for comments on this section.

[60]William D. Nordhaus, "Reflections on the Economics of Climate Change," *Journal of Economic Perspectives* 7 (Fall 1993): 11–25.

[61]World Resources Institute, United Nations Environment Program, and the United Nations Development Program, *World Resources, 1994–95*, edited by Allen L. Hammond (New York: Oxford University Press, 1994), p. 197.

[62]United Nations, *Global Outlook 2000: An Economic, Social, and Environmental Perspective* (New York, 1990), pp. 77–78.

[63]Thomas C. Schelling, "The Economics of Global Warming," in Robert Dorfman and Nancy S. Dorfman, eds., *Economics of the Environment: Selected Readings* (New York: Norton, 1993), p. 465.

the problem is the excessive concentration of these gases. In 1990, carbon dioxide (from coal, oil, natural gas, and deforestation) added 57 percent of the "greenhouse effect." CFCs, from foams, aerosols, refrigerants, and solvents, which progressively deplete the stratospheric ozone layer, contributed 25 percent. Methane, from wetlands, rice, fossil fuels, livestock, and landfills, added 12 percent, and nitrous oxide, from fossil fuels, fertilizers, and deforestation, 6 percent.

CO_2 absorbs infrared or heat radiations, so that increasing concentrations of CO_2 change the temperature of the earth's surface, reducing temperature differentials between the equator and the poles and decreasing atmospheric cycling, providing the potential for dramatic climatic and ecological effects. The facts of the greenhouse effect, temperature changes, and that human activity is a major contributor are not in dispute, but the magnitude of climate change on the natural environment and human welfare is in dispute.[64]

Major Contributors to Greenhouse Gases.   Developed and transitional countries, with one-fifth of the world's population, consume more than four-fifths of the world's natural resources. The demand for goods by these countries is responsible for much of the destruction of tropical rainforests for energy, minerals, logs, plantation agriculture, and fast-food hamburgers from cattle-ranching. The loss of tropical rainforests not only reduces species and genetic materials and sometimes threaten the livelihood of indigenous peoples, but also diminishes carbon absorption, that is, the ability of the earth to remove excess CO_2.[65]

---

[64]Christopher Flavin, *Slowing Global Warming: A Worldwide Strategy* (Washington, D. C.: Worldwatch Institute, 1989; World Resources Institute, United Nations Environment Program, and the United Nations Development Program, *World Resources, 1994–95*, edited by Allen L. Hammond (New York: Oxford University Press, 1994), pp. 199–205; Allen V. Kneese, "Analysis of Environmental Pollution," in Robert Dorfman and Nancy S. Dorfman, eds., *Economics of the Environment: Selected Readings* (New York: Norton, 1993), pp. 37–56; Thomas C. Schelling, "The Economics of Global Warming," in Robert Dorfman and Nancy S. Dorfman, eds., *Economics of the Environment: Selected Readings* (New York: Norton, 1993), pp. 464–83; and Yoshiki Ogawa, "Economic Activity and the Greenhouse Effect," in Robert Dorfman and Nancy S. Dorfman, eds., *Economics of the Environment: Selected Readings* (New York: Norton, 1993), pp. 484–96.

Another greenhouse gas, ozone, is found in the troposphere, the lower part of the atmosphere up to 15 kilometers above the ground. But the ozone problem is even more confusing than the problem of carbon emission, since high ozone levels in the troposphere are bad, but high concentrations in the stratosphere, 15–50 kilometers above ground, are good. Ozone is a naturally occurring gas, and in the stratosphere is concentrated into the ozone layer, which is like a thick belt around the earth. This ozone protects the earth from ultraviolet radiation from the sun, but in the lower atmosphere ozone concentrations are harmful to health and vegetation (increasing skin cancers), and contribute to the formation of "acid rain." Increased ultraviolet (UV) radiation also has a potentially disturbing effect on ecosystems. UV radiation damages DNA, growth, and reproduction, and interferes with the single-celled algae's (phytoplankton's) process of photosynthesis, thus reducing the fish stock which feed on the algae. Ultraviolet radiation also contributes to lower photosynthetic activity and reduced vegetation growth in land-based ecosystems. R. Kerry Turner, David Pearce, and Ian Bateman, *Environmental Economics: An Elementary Introduction* (Baltimore: Johns Hopkins University Press, 1993), pp. 281, 285–86.

[65]Russell Train, "Preserving Biological Diversity in the Developing World," in Peter H. Raven, Linda R. Berg, and George B. Johnson, *Environment* (Fort Worth: Harcourt Brace Jovanovich, 1993), p. 262.

The metaphor of Al Gore, *Earth in the Balance: Ecology and the Human Spirit* (New York: Plume, 1993), p. 95, is that between the human lung, which inhales oxygen and exhales carbon dioxide, and that of the engines of civilization, which have automated breathing. The wood, coal, oil, natural gas, and gasoline that fuel our civilization convert oxygen into CO_2. Trees and other plants pull CO_2 out of the atmosphere and replace it with oxygen, transforming the carbon into wood. But as we destroy forests, we are damaging the earth's ability to remove excess CO_2. In a sense, earth has two lungs, the forests and ocean, that are being seriously injured, impairing the earth's ability to "breathe."

DCs, with 49 percent, and the transitional countries of Eastern Europe and the former Soviet Union, with 25 percent, produce the lion's share of the globe's carbon dioxide (CO_2) emissions, whose major sources are fossil fuels. The United States (with 5 trillion metric tons emitted in 1991), the former Soviet Union, China, Japan, Germany, India, the United Kingdom, Iraq, Canada, and Italy are the largest emitters of CO_2; but on a per–capita basis the United Arab Emirates, Iraq, the U.S., and Canada are the leading four emitters[66] (see Figure 13–4). In general, carbon dioxide emissions per capita increase with income per capita; the increase is steep after a GNP per capita of $10,000 in 1992.[67]

CO_2 emissions depend on fuel mix (natural gas emits less carbon than oil, which emits less than coal), energy intensity, afforestation, economic growth, and population growth. After the high energy prices of the 1970s, Japan (and, to a lesser extent, the United States) reduced carbon emissions (and energy imports)

FIGURE 13–4   Seventeen Countries with the Highest Per Capita Industrial Emissions of Carbon Dioxide (CO_2) (1991)

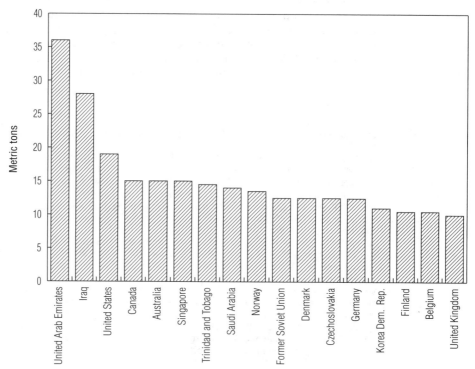

Source: World Resources Institute, United Nations Environment Program, and the United Nations Development Program, *World Resources, 1994-95,* edited by Allen L. Hammond (New York: Oxford University Press, 1994), pp. 362–63.

---

[66]World Resources Institute, United Nations Environment Program, and the United Nations Development Program, *World Resources, 1994–95,* edited by Allen L. Hammond (New York: Oxford University Press, 1994), pp. 202–04, 362–63.

[67]John Peirson, "Development and the Environment," in A.P. Thirlwall, *Growth and Development with Special Reference to Developing Economies* (Boulder, Colo.: Lynne Rienner, 1994), p. 212.

through technological change oriented toward reduced energy intensity. On the other hand, population growth was important in increasing emissions in many developing countries, such as India. In the early 1990s, greenhouse gas emissions fell in Eastern Europe and the former Soviet Union as a result of the near collapse of their economies; since emissions will grow again as economic growth resumes, these transitional economies need other solutions.[68]

Costs of Global Climate Change from Increased Carbon Emissions. Estimating the cost of reducing global carbon emissions is difficult. Models that estimate these costs include assumptions about how variables such as population and energy demand changes, and how the world will evolve over a long period with and without a control program. In this discussion, we can barely provide a sense for how these variables and climate interact.

Globally averaged surface temperatures increased 0.6 degrees Celsius during the twentieth century, but most of these changes were in the last quarter of the century. The speed by which climate system has changed over the last generation is as substantial as climate changes that occur naturally over a period of 1,000 years.

Yet economic change is less dependent on changes in average temperature than on variables that accompany or result from these changes, such as precipitation, water levels, the amplitude of weather volatility, and extremes of droughts or freezes. Scientists focus on average temperature change, which is a useful index of climate change that is highly correlated with or causally related to more important variables.[69]

How much will global temperatures change during the twenty-first century? While forecasts vary, the scientific consensus is that, in the absence of drastic cuts in the annual global emissions of greenhouse gases, *some* global warming will occur in the twenty-first century. Given that atmospheric carbon dioxide has a long half-life, even reductions in emissions still increase the accumulation of greenhouse gases.[70] The consensus forecast among scientists is that, even with modest control measures, temperatures will rise 2.5–5.5 degrees Celsius (4.5–9.9 degrees Fahrenheit) from the late twentieth century to the late twenty-first century.

Scientists expect that if 1990s' annual CO_2 emission rates continue, then CO_2 in the atmosphere will double from the 1990s to sometime in the twenty-first century. Most of the scientists' global climate models ask: What effect will this doubling have on temperature and other variables? The most widely accepted change

---

[68]Yoshiki Ogawa, "Economic Activity and the Greenhouse Effect," in Robert Dorfman and Nancy S. Dorfman, eds., *Economics of the Environment: Selected Readings* (New York: Norton, 1993), pp. 484–96; and World Resources Institute, United Nations Environment Program, and the United Nations Development Program (Allen L. Hammond, ed.), *World Resources, 1994–95* (New York: Oxford University Press, 1994), p. 200.

[69]Christopher Flavin, *Slowing Global Warming: A Worldwide Strategy* (Washington, D. C.: Worldwatch Institute, 1989; Thomas C. Schelling, "The Economics of Global Warming," in Robert Dorfman and Nancy S. Dorfman, eds., *Economics of the Environment: Selected Readings* (New York: Norton, 1993), pp. 464–71; and William D. Nordhaus, "Reflections on the Economics of Climate Change," *Journal of Economic Perspective* 7 (Fall 1993): 11–25.

[70]James M. Poterba, "Global Warming Policy: A Public Finance Perspective," *Journal of Economic Perspectives* 7 (Fall 1993): 47–63; John P. Weyant, "Costs of Reducing Global Carbon Emissions," *Journal of Economic Perspectives* 7 (Fall 1993): 27–46; and World Resources Institute, United Nations Environment Program, and the United Nations Development Program, *World Resources, 1994–95*, edited by Allen L. Hammond (New York: Oxford University Press, 1994), p. 200.

is a temperature increase of 3-degrees Celsius, with a range of 1.5 degrees either side. This 3-degree Celsius change is much more than the variation (no more than 1 degree) in any century in the last 10,000 years. While most North Americans are used to substantial temperature shifts from winter to summer, they may not realize how substantial a 3 degrees Celsius average change is. What is now New York City was covered by one kilometer of ice during an ice age, although global temperatures were only 6 degrees Celsius colder than today.[71]

In 1985, a Villach, Austria, conference of scientists foresaw the following effect of global warming in the twenty-first century:

> Many important economic and social decisions are being made today on long-term projects—major water resource management activities such as irrigation and hydro-power, drought relief, agricultural land use, structural designs and coastal engineering projects, and energy planning—based on the assumption that past climatic data, without modification, are a reliable guide to the future. This is no longer a good assumption.[72]

Economist Schelling argues, however, that the vulnerability to climate change in the twenty-first century will be less than if this same change had occurred in the twentieth century, when global shares of gross product and the labor force in agriculture were higher. He estimates that the effect of global warming on health and nutrition in the United States and other DCs in the mid–twenty-first century would be negligible. Indeed, for Schelling, carbon dioxide enrichment, by enhancing photosynthesis, will increase agricultural yields for many cultivated plants in the Northern hemisphere, the location of most DCs. He assumes that if climatic changes are continuous over a century, then Kansas's climate may become like Oklahoma's, Nebraska's like Kansas's, and South Dakota's like Nebraska's, but Oklahoma, Kansas, Nebraska, and South Dakota will not become like Oregon, Louisiana, or Massachusetts; climate change, thus, will be gradual rather than abrupt. Some economists contend that northern nations, such as Canada and Russia, will benefit from the increased warmer-season crops and correspondingly greater agricultural yields from global warming. Schelling even concludes that DCs have no self-interest in expensively slowing CO_2 emission rates.[73]

---

[71]Thomas C. Schelling, "The Economics of Global Warming," in Robert Dorfman and Nancy S. Dorfman, eds., *Economics of the Environment: Selected Readings* (New York: Norton, 1993), pp. 465–69; Al Gore, *Earth in the Balance: Ecology and the Human Spirit* (New York: Plume, 1993), p. 91; Christopher Flavin, *Slowing Global Warming: A Worldwide Strategy* (Washington, D. C.: Worldwatch Institute, 1989); and Richard Schmalensee, "Symposium on Global Climate Change," *Journal of Economic Perspectives* 7 (Fall 1993): 3–10.

[72]"The Villach Conference," *Search* 17 (1985): 183–84, in G.I. Pearman, ed., *Greenhouse: Planning for Climate Change* (East Melbourne, Australia: CISRO Publications, 1988), p. 162.

[73]Thomas C. Schelling, "The Economics of Global Warming," in Robert Dorfman and Nancy S. Dorfman, eds., *Economics of the Environment: Selected Readings* (New York: Norton, 1993), pp. 466–73; James M. Poterba, "Global Warming Policy: A Public Finance Perspective," *Journal of Economic Perspectives* 7 (Fall 1993): 47–63; and William D. Nordhaus, "Economic Approaches to Greenhouse Warming," in Rudiger Dornbusch and James M. Poterba, eds., *Global Warming: Economic Policy Responses* (Cambridge, Mass.: MIT Press, 1991), pp. 33–67.

Robert Mendelsohn, William D. Nordhaus, and Daigee Shaw, "The Impact of Global Warming on Agriculture: a Ricardian Analysis," *American Economic Review* 84 (September 1994): 753–71, provide evidence that global warming may have economic benefits for U.S. agriculture, even without CO_2 fertilization.

The London *Economist* and *Wall Street Journal*[74] agree with Schelling, although uncertainties associated with disruptions of ecosystems in both DCs and LDCs, mentioned below, raise questions about Schelling's sanguineness.

What about the LDCs of the south? Lester Brown and his colleagues argue from trends in the late 1980s and early 1990s that the earth's rapid population growth, increasing average costs from and diminishing returns to growing biochemical energy and fertilizer use, less sustainable farming practices, and limits in expanded agricultural hectarage mean that the earth is reaching the limits of its carrying capacity. These changes, exacerbated by adverse climatic changes, indicates concern about average food levels in LDCs, especially in sub-Saharan Africa and Latin America.[75] Moreover, parasitic and other vector-borne diseases, including possibly malarial mosquitos, are sensitive to climatic changes. Those damaged the most by global climate changes are human settlements most vulnerable to energy reductions and most exposed to natural hazards, such as coastal or river flooding (Bangladesh, China, Egypt, and island nations), severe drought, landslides, severe wind storms (China), and (Bangladesh) tropical cyclones, whose frequency is likely to increase 50 percent from the present to the mid-twenty-first century from a doubling in human-generated carbon dioxide emissions. If we add to all this the melting of polar ice caps, the effects of flooding on Bangladesh and other LDCs are even more substantial.[76] Brown and his colleagues argue that the LDCs of the south are the major nations suffering from global warming, even though they produce only a small fraction of the world's annual carbon emissions. Why should global warming flood the homelands of Bangladeshis who have never used electricity, they ask.[77]

But global climate change will increase drought, heat waves, and tropical storms, raise sea level, and shift vegetation zones so as to disrupt grain and other crop production.[78] Consider the rise in sea level.

Titus et al. assert that

> A rise in sea level would inundate wetlands and lowlands, accelerate coastal erosion, exacerbate coastal flooding, threaten coastal structures, raise water tables, and increase the salinity of rivers, bays, and aquifers. [A] rise in sea level would enable saltwater to penetrate further inland and upstream in rivers,

---

[74]"Stuck in the Greenhouse," *Economist* (August 31, 1991): 28–30; Thomas Kamm, "Rio Eco-Fest: Some Big Problems Await World Leaders at the Earth Summit," *Wall Street Journal* (May 29, 1992): A1; Patricia Adams, "Rio Agenda: Soak the West's Taxpayers," *Wall Street Journal* (June 3, 1992): A14; David Stipp and Frank Edward Allen, "Forecast for Rio: Scientific Cloudiness," *Wall Street Journal* (June 3, 1992): B1; Alan Murray, "The Outlook: An Alternative Agenda for the Rio Summit," *Wall Street Journal* (June 8, 1992): A1; and George Melloan, "How about Some Concern over Ecojournalism?" *Wall Street Journal* (June 22, 1992): A13.

[75]Lester R. Brown, "Facing Food Insecurity," in Lester R. Brown et al., *State of the World, 1994*, Worldwatch Institute (New York: Norton, 1994), pp. 177–97, 248–51; and Lester R. Brown, Anne E. Platt, Hal Kane, and Sandra Postel, "Food and Agricultural Resource Trends," in Lester R. Brown, Hal Kane, and David Malin Roodman, eds., *Vital Signs, 1994*, Worldwatch Institute (New York: Norton, 1994), pp. 26–41, especially Lester R. Brown, "Grain Harvest Plummets," pp. 26–27.

[76]John Topping, "Likely Impact of Global Warming on Developing Countries," in Uner Kirdar, ed., *Change: Threat or Opportunity for Human Progress* (New York: United Nations, 1992), pp. 129–44.

[77]Lester R. Brown, Christopher Flavin, and Sandra Postel, *Saving the Planet: How to Shape an Environmentally Sustainable Global Economy* (New York: Norton, 1991).

[78]Christopher Flavin, *Slowing Global Warming: A Worldwide Strategy* (Washington, D.C.: Worldwide Institute, 1989).

bays, wetlands, and aquifers, which would be harmful to some aquatic plants and animals, and would threaten human uses of water.[79]

Part of this is the fact that overflowing oceans will increase the salt water content of previously freshwater inland rivers, deltas, and of aquifers. The effect of climate changes on these water systems are unpredictable.

Still several economic models have estimated that doubling CO_2 would reduce GNP in the United States by 1.0–1.3 percent in the last decade of the twenty-first century. Yet these studies may underestimate the impact of specialization and international trade in reducing losses. Studies of the effect of global climate change on developing countries are more fragmentary. Probably, however, LDCs, with a larger share of GNP in agriculture and other sectors exposed to climate change than in the United States, are more vulnerable.[80]

Predictions about when doubling CO_2 will occur vary from model to model. Indeed, generally the authors of these models would be the first to admit that their estimates are fraught with a large margin of error. Models cannot predict changes in prices, an important determinant of welfare. Ultimately population increase, the relationship between population and food productivity, changes in energy demand, and other premises about how events will unfold are as important as carbon abatement cost functions in determining GNP. Scientists do not even agree on the carbon emissions attributable to various sources. Nor do scientists know the extent to which greenhouse gases adversely affect human productivity and welfare. Furthermore, many costs, such as sea-level rise, electricity operational cost, capital cost, and costs of preserving coastal wetlands, old growth forests, and biological diversity, are difficult to quantify.[81]

Uncertainties abound. Except for some opportunistic weeds, plants may not migrate as fast as climate.[82] Animals may not be able to adapt to changing plant systems. Humans may not easily adapt to changes in plants, animals, and entire ecosystems, and some countries may ban migration from nations adversely affected.

Will change be as continuous as the climate models suppose? If substantial changes are exacerbated by positive feedbacks, the models might explode. Indeed, Yale economist William D. Nordhaus worries about the reliability of climate models, "because climate appears to be heading out of the historical range of temperatures witnessed during the span of human civilizations."[83]

---

[79]James G. Titus et al. "Greenhouse Effect and Sea Level Rise: Potential Loss of Land and the Cost of Holding Back the Sea," *Coastal Management* 3(1) (1992): 8–11.

[80]William D. Nordhaus, "Reflections on the Economics of Climate Change," *Journal of Economic Perspective* 7 (Fall 1993): 14–18.

[81]Richard D. Morgenstern, "Towards a Comprehensive Approach to Global Climate Change Mitigation," *American Economic Review* 81 (May 1991): 140–45; William D. Nordhaus, "Reflections on the Economics of Climate Change," *Journal of Economic Perspectives* 7 (Fall 1993): 11–25; and Thomas C. Schelling, "The Economics of Global Warming," in Robert Dorfman and Nancy S. Dorfman, eds., *Economics of the Environment: Selected Readings* (New York: Norton, 1993), p. 473.

[82]Edward O. Wilson contends that global warming will displace four North American trees—yellow birch, sugar maple, beech, and hemlock, which will fail to migrate rapidly enough. "Threats to Biodiversity," *Scientific American* (September 1989): 112–24.

[83]William D. Nordhaus, "Reflections on the Economics of Climate Change," *Journal of Economic Perspective* 7 (Fall 1993): 14.

See also S. Schneider, "The Future of Climate: Potential for Interaction and Surprises," *Global Environmental Change* 4(1) (1994), who argues that history is replete with unforseen ecological changes.

Policy Approaches.   The consensus of the scientific community is that green-house gases are harmful, even though the exact magnitude of the harm is uncertain. Again, the best strategy is to reduce greenhouse gas emissions by buying "insurance policies" against the worst possible damage. Additionally, scientists need to continue research so as to estimate optimal greenhouse-gas abatement more precisely.

The Rio de Janeiro, Brazil, Earth Summit of 1992 allocated annual carbon emission targets on the basis of 1990 levels, rewarding the high polluters; however, future emissions are to be based on 1990 population, so as not to reward population growth. Nordhaus, however, shows that other approaches, such as carbon taxes or international markets for tradeable emission permits discussed below, are cheaper than the Rio method, which is less expensive than stabilizing climate so that the change in global average temperature is limited to 1.5 degrees Celsius in the twenty-first century.[84]

Green Taxes.   This proposal, a tax on fossil fuel proportional to the carbon emitted when the fuel is burned, relies on market-based incentives that spur people to reduce emissions at least cost rather than on direct regulations, such as the Rio approach, that engender inefficiencies. Government decision-makers, adjusting for market imperfections, should try to tax or fine emitters so they bear the costs they transmit to others. What rule should government adopt? Remember the rule for minimal social cost discussed previously: the efficient level of emission is where marginal abatement cost equals marginal damage. These marginal values are, however, even more difficult to estimate for greenhouse-gas emitters than for other polluters. Polluters can adjust any way they please, through amelioration (including migration and shifting land use and industry patterns), abatement (such as reflecting more incoming sunlight back into space), prevention (investing in emission control), or paying the carbon tax.[85]

As Figure 13–5 shows, the carbon tax shifts the supply curve to the left from S_1 to S_2, increasing the price from P_1 to P_2, and reducing consumption from Q_1 to Q_2 in the short run. In the long run, as firms leave the coal and other fossil fuel industries, supply shifts further to the left, to S_3, and the price increases even further, to P_3.[86]

The taxes would increase the prices of virtually all goods and services, but would substitute for other taxes. The total tax burden would be the same, but shift the burden away from income toward environmentally damaging activities, reducing environmental degradation. However, since the carbon tax is regressive, so

---

[84]Alan S. Manne and Richard G. Richels, "International Trade in Carbon Emission Rights: A Decomposition Procedure," *American Economic Review* 81 (May 1993): 135–39; and William D. Nordhaus, "Reflections on the Economics of Climate Change," *Journal of Economic Perspective* 7 (Fall 1993): 20–24.

[85]Thomas C. Schelling, "The Economics of Global Warming," in Robert Dorfman and Nancy S. Dorfman, eds., *Economics of the Environment: Selected Readings* (New York: Norton, 1993), p. 478; and James M. Poterba, "Global Warming Policy: A Public Finance Perspective," *Journal of Economic Perspectives* 7 (Fall 1993): 47–63.

Another emphasis is insurance, which compensates those adversely affected by flooding or other climate changes. Graciela Chichilnisky and Geoffrey Heal, "Global Environment Risks," *Journal of Economic Perspectives* 7 (Fall 1993): 65–86.

[86]Dale W. Jorgenson, Daniel T. Slesnick, and Peter J. Wilcoxen, "Carbon Taxes and Economic Welfare," in Martin Neil Baily and Clifford Winston, eds., *Brookings Papers on Economic Activity: Microeconomics 1992* (Washington, D.C.: Brookings Institution, 1992), pp. 393–431, 451–54; and "Economists Propose Taxes to Avert Global Warming," *The Margin* (Spring 1993): 32–33.

FIGURE 13-5   Levying a Carbon Tax on Petroleum

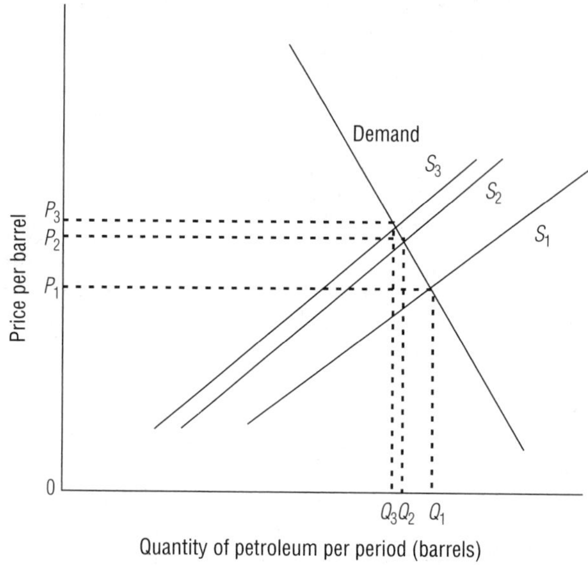

Quantity of petroleum per period (barrels)

that the poor pay a higher percentage of their income in taxes than the rich, government might allocate some revenues from the taxes to compensate the poor.

Lester R. Brown, Christopher Flavin, and Sandra Postel contend that

> Environmental taxes are appealing because they can help meet many goals efficiently. Each individual producer or consumer decides how to adjust to the higher costs. A tax on [carbon] emissions, for instance, would lead some factories to add controls, others to change their production processes, and still others to redesign products so as to generate less [carbon]. In contrast to regulations, environmental taxes preserve the strengths of the market. Indeed, they are what economists call corrective taxes: they actually improve the functioning of the market by adjusting prices to better reflect an activity's true cost.[87]

The government can reduce the substantial GNP cost of a carbon tax increased gradually to allow time to institute new technologies when capital equipment is normally replaced. Phasing in the carbon taxes over, say, 5 to 10 years would ease the economic impact and allow for gradual adjustment.[88]

International Tradeable Emission Permits.   Harvard's Martin Feldstein opposes the 1992 Rio treaty because it sets physical targets rather than using marginal or "least cost" principles of abatement. The principle of least-cost reduction

[87]Lester R. Brown, Christopher Flavin, and Sandra Postel, *Saving the Planet: How to Shape an Environmentally Sustainable Global Economy*, Worldwatch Institute (New York: Norton, 1991), p. 142.

[88]John P. Weyant, "Costs of Reducing Global Carbon Emissions," *Journal of Economic Perspectives* 7 (Fall 1993): 27–46; "Greenery and Poverty," *Economist* (September 18, 1993): 80; and Lester R. Brown, Christopher Flavin, and Sandra Postel, *Saving the Planet: How to Shape an Environmentally Sustainable Global Economy*, Worldwatch Institute (New York: Norton, 1991), pp. 141–49, with quotation on pp. 142–43.

rests on the scientific fact that a ton of carbon emitted anywhere on the globe contributes equally to global greenhouse gases. Once countries negotiate emission rights, Feldstein favors international tradeable emission permits to achieve the least marginal cost per unit of abatement. A change from a regulatory system to transferable discharge permits should provide incentives for emitters to adopt new control techniques to reduce emissions at lower cost, since they can sell excess permits. Emitters facing steep control costs will purchase permits from emitters having less costly options, thereby subsidizing the more efficient control of emissions by low-cost emitters.[89]

Stanford's John P. Weyant examined the implications of the Energy Modeling Forum 12, a composite of fourteen major models of global climate change, for the cost of global carbon emissions control. He found that the Rio approach of stabilizing emissions at 1990 levels in each country cost 2.5 percent of world GDP by the year 2043. However, the economic optimal approach, which uses tradeable emission permits, allowing an equalization of the marginal cost of control across all nations, achieves the same target levels at two thirds the costs, or a loss of only 1.7 percent of world GDP.[90]

Multilateral Aid and Agreements in Funding Global Common Property Resources in Tropical Countries. DCs and transitional countries are the major carbon emitters. D.S. Mahathir Mohamed, Malaysian prime minister in 1992, contended that if humankind is to clean up the global environment, "those most responsible for polluting [the environment] must bear the burden proportionately. Eighty percent of Earth's pollution is due to the industrial activities of the North."[91] The World Bank concurs, arguing that the North should bear the burden of finding and implementing solutions to global warming, ozone depletion, and other environmental problems.[92]

To be sure, the share of LDC emissions will increase in the late part of the twentieth century and early decades of the twenty-first century. However, low-income countries, primarily located in the tropics, will pay little to avoid long-term environmental degradation. Tropical countries are not just poor, but their environmental problems, such as rainforest and specie destruction, are not just public bads internal to the country, but also global public bads. Tropical countries receive only a portion of the gain from maintaining tropical rainforests or reforestation to limit greenhouse gases, adverse climate change, and the loss of biological resources. Since tropical rainforests are global public goods, affecting global climate and genetic stock, we cannot expect individual tropical countries to provide forests in sufficient quantities, since much of the gains spill over to other countries.

If DCs want to protect themselves against the risk of explosive harm and care about LDC economic and environmental vulnerability, they will want to contribute resources to invest in reducing environmental degradation. Indeed, DC contributions to technological transfer, such as switching LDCs from high-carbon

---

[89]Martin Feldstein, "The Case for a World Carbon Tax," *Wall Street Journal* (June 4, 1992): A10; and Thomas H. Tietenberg, "Transferable Discharge Permits and the Control of Stationary Source Air Pollution," in Robert Dorfman and Nancy S. Dorfman, eds., *Economics of the Environment: Selected Readings* (New York: Norton, 1993), pp. 241–70.

[90]John P. Weyant, "Costs of Reducing Global Carbon Emissions," *Journal of Economic Perspectives* 7 (Fall 1993): 34–36.

[91]D.S. Mahathir Mohamed, "Ending Eco-Imperialism at Rio," *Kansas City Star* (June 3, 1992): C-5.

[92]World Bank, *World Development Report, 1992* (New York: Oxford University Press, 1992), p. 3.

to low-carbon fuels, could add to DC national income. Additionally, DC aid might include concessional aid to tropical LDCs to help avoid global damage from tropical deforestation and species loss, while partially compensating tropical countries for forgoing private gain. This compensation can reduce the tropics' sacrifice of immediate basic needs. As discussed in Chapter 17, some DC governments and nongovernmental organizations have undertaken debt-for-nature swaps in Africa and Latin America. In the 1990s, DCs purchased portions of the debts of tropical countries in exchange for their preservation of tropical rainforest and its biodiversity.

Humankind generally has an interest in providing funds to preserve these tropical global common-property resources. DCs need to focus on agreements to reduce global public bads associated with deforestation and specie destruction in tropical regions. These countries might regard their spending as investment in ecosystems that influence the productivity of the common resources of humanity. Such agreements would benefit the world as a whole, but would particularly benefit tropical countries in reducing their environmental degradation and adverse climate change.

Still international environmental agreements to fund and regulate global public goods have had a mixed record. The **Montreal Protocol**, signed in 1987 and strengthened in 1990, to reduce ozone depletion through the cutting of chlorofluorocarbon (CFC) production, enjoyed widespread compliance among the predominant CFC producers, the DCs, which had already developed cost-effective substitutes. However, the **International Convention on Climate Change (ICCC)**, signed in 1994, which required national inventories on greenhouse gas emissions, has not been so successful, partly because of the ICCC's substantial costs and complexity, and opposition, especially in the United States, to taxes on carbon emissions. The institutions for implementation, enforcement, and financing the ICCC are thus far poorly developed.[93] In addition, the Global Environment Facility established in 1991, under which funding for global public goods might take place, has had only limited success, partly because of the lack of funding and difficulties in agreeing how to divide the funding.

No single nation acting alone can stabilize greenhouse gas emissions. Additionally, unilateral national policies do not achieve the least-cost method of reducing emissions. Moreover, international competition to attract industry through less stringent emissions standards may undermine environmental policy-making. Thus, a supranational approach is essential. However, coordinated international action is difficult to achieve.[94]

Harold Demsetz thinks it is unlikely that users of a global common property resource (such as air and water) would agree to manage the resource even though it is in the interest of all to cooperate in reducing use of the resource. While all users benefit, each user will earn even higher returns by **free riding** on the virtuous behavior of the remaining cooperators. Global optimality requires global cooperation, yet the incentives facing individual countries work in the opposite direction. As with the international nuclear nonproliferation treaty or ICCC, we might expect the united action by users to be unstable. Demsetz argues that the only way out of the common property dilemma is intervention by the state. How-

[93]World Resources Institute, United Nations Environment Program, and the United Nations Development Program (Allen L. Hammond, ed.), *World Resources, 1994–95* (New York: Oxford University Press, 1994), pp. 202–03.

[94]James M. Poterba, "Global Warming Policy: A Public Finance Perspective," *Journal of Economic Perspectives* 7 (Fall 1993): 48–49.

ever, the world lacks an international government which can dictate the environmental policies of individual states.[95]

Still a number of countries may collude to sign an international environmental agreement even where a number of countries do not cooperate. Countries may agree to pursue the global optimality strategy if all other countries in previous periods abide by this strategy. Also countries can punish those that refuse to abide by whaling conventions, nonproliferation treaties, or other environmental agreements by import embargos or other sanctions. Concerns about fairness can reduce the free-rider problem. Furthermore, a non-cooperator may find it advantageous to join the agreement if strengthening it increases others' abatement levels in excess of the abatement costs the country incurs. Or pulling out of a treaty may result in less abatement by other countries, so that the cost of pulling out exceeds the benefits.[96] If major nations fail to make commitments to a global environmental accord and choose to free ride on the actions of other nations, the prospects for the success of environmental agreements are limited.[97]

Limits to Growth

The nineteenth-century English, classical economists feared eventual economic stagnation or decline from diminishing returns to natural resources. The concept of diminishing returns was the foundation for Malthus's *Essay on the Principles of Population* (1798, 1803) which argued that population growth tended to outstrip increases in food supply. Economists have long disputed whether diminishing returns and Malthusian population dynamics place limits on economic growth.

THE CLUB OF ROME STUDY

In the early 1970s, the influential Club of Rome, a private international association organized by Italian industrialist Aurelio Peccei, commissioned a team of scholars at MIT to examine the implication of growth trends for our survival. The study, *The Limits to Growth*, based on computer simulations, uses growth trends from 1900 to 1970 as a base for projecting the effects of industrial expansion and population growth on environmental pollution and the consumption of food and nonrenewable resources. The study and its sequel in 1992 suggest that as natural resources diminish, costs rise, leaving less capital for future investment. Eventually new capital formation falls below depreciation, so that the industrial base, as well as the agricultural and services economies, collapse. Shortly after population drops precipitously because of food and resource shortages. *Limits* concludes that if present growth continues, the planetary limits to growth will be reached sometime in the twenty-first century, at which time the global economic system will break down.

---

[95]Harold Demsetz, "Toward a Theory of Property Rights," *American Economic Review* 57 (May 1967): 347–59; and Scott Barrett, "International Cooperation for Environmental Protection," in Robert Dorfman and Nancy S. Dorfman, eds., *Economics of the Environment: Selected Readings* (New York: Norton, 1993), pp. 445–63.

[96]Scott Barrett, "International Cooperation for Environmental Protection," in Robert Dorfman and Nancy S. Dorfman, eds., *Economics of the Environment: Selected Readings* (New York: Norton, 1993), pp. 454–63.

[97]James M. Poterba, "Global Warming Policy: A Public Finance Perspective," *Journal of Economic Perspectives* 7 (Fall 1993): 48–49.

The message of *Limits* is that since the earth is finite, any indefinite economic expansion must eventually reach its limits. Exponential growth can be illustrated by the following. Take a sheet of paper and continue to fold it in half 40 times. Most of you will give up long before the fortieth time, at which time the paper's thickness, initially one millimeter, will stretch to the moon! In a similar vein, we can appreciate *Limits'* contention that without environmental controls, economic growth and the attendant exponential increase in carbon dioxide emissions from burning fossil fuel, thermal pollution, radioactive nuclear wastes, and soluble industrial, agricultural, and municipal wastes severely threatens our limited air and water resources.

The previous pages have explored some of the limits associated with the overuse of common-property resources, the "tragedy of the commons." No one can ignore the warnings to humankind to pay attention to these limits.

Yet many of the assumptions the MIT scholars make are seriously flawed. For example, their estimates indicate that they apparently believe that *proven* petroleum reserves represent *all* the petroleum reserves of the world. However, **proven reserves** are not satisfactory for making long-term projections, since they are only the known reserves that can be recovered profitably at prevailing cost and price levels. Proven reserves are no more than an assessment of the working inventory of minerals that industry is confident is available. Profit-motivated, commercial exploration tries to find only sufficient new reserves to meet the industry's requirements over its forward planning period (typically 8 to 12 years), plus any new reserves that promise to be more profitable than previous discoveries.

Thus it is not surprising that proven reserves are rather meager in comparison to the reserves that can ultimately be recovered. Thus we have the spectacle in 1864 of W. Stanley Jevons, one of the great economists of the nineteenth century, predicting that England's industry would soon grind to a halt with the exhaustion of England's coal. A modern example of this disparity between proven and ultimately recoverable reserves is that in 1970, the proven reserves of lead, zinc, and copper were much larger than those in 1949, even though the amount of these metals mined between 1949 and 1970 was greater than proven reserves in 1949.

A further criticism of the MIT team is that their model analyzes the world's population, capital stock, natural resources, technology, and output without discussing differences by world region. It also treats food output as a single entity, ignoring differences between cereals, fruits, vegetables, and animal products.

Another flaw in the MIT study is the assumption of exponential growth in industrial and agricultural needs, but the arbitrary placement of nonexponential limits on the technical progress that might accommodate these needs. As Robert Cassen contends, "Only where specific binding constraints cannot be compensated for by human ingenuity do economies encounter effective limits to growth."[98]

A complex computer model only aids understanding if its assumptions are valid. Critics argue that *Limits* is not a "rediscovery of the laws of nature," as the

---

[98]Robert Cassen, "Population and Development: Old Debates, New Conclusions," in Robert Cassen and contributors, *Population and Development: Old Debates, New Conclusions*, Overseas Development Council U.S.-Third World Policy Perspectives (New Brunswick, N.J.: Transaction, 1994), p. 7.

authors' press agents claim, but a "rediscovery of the oldest maxim of computer science: Garbage In, Garbage Out."[99]

DALY'S IMPOSSIBILITY THEOREM

Herman E. Daly more clearly indicates the assumptions, calculations, and causal relationships behind limits to economic growth and unlike *Limits,* goes on to calculate their effect on increased international conflict.[100] According to him, a U.S.-style, high mass consumption, growth-oriented economy is impossible for a world of 5.8 billion people. The stock of mineral deposits in the earth's crust and the ecosystem's capacity to absorb enormous or exotic waste materials and heat drastically limit the number of person-years that can be lived at U.S. consumption levels. Daly believes that how we apportion these person-years of mass consumption among nations, social classes, and generations will be the dominant political and economic issue of the future. The struggle for these limited high-consumption units will shape the nature of political conflict, both within and between nation-states.

Daly's argument that the entire world's population cannot enjoy U.S. consumption levels—the **impossibility theorem**—can be illustrated in the following way. Today it requires about one-third of the world's flow of nonrenewable resources and 26 percent of **gross planetary product** (the gross production value of the world's goods and services) to support the 5 percent of the world's population living in the United States. On the other hand, the 80 percent of the world's population living in LDCs use only about one-seventh of the nonrenewable resources and produce only 17 percent of the gross planetary product.[101] Present resource flows would allow the extension of the U.S. living standard to a maximum of 15 percent of the world's population with nothing left over for the other 85 percent.

Daly argues that natural capital is the limiting factor in economic evolution. Thus, we need to concentrate on increasing output per natural capital, since we cannot substitute physical capital or labor for natural capital. Daly illustrates the impossibility of continuing growth in the use of natural capital by pointing out that humans directly use or destroy about 25 percent of the earth's **net primary productivity (NPP)**, the total amount of solar energy converted into biochemical energy through the photosynthesis of plants minus the energy these plants use for

---

[99]Donella H. Meadows, Dennis L. Meadows, Jørgen Randers, and William W. Behrens, III, *The Limits to Growth* (New York: Universe Books, 1972); Donella H. Meadows, Dennis L. Meadows, and Jørgen Randers, *Beyond the Limits: Confronting Global Collapse, Envisioning a Sustainable Future* (Post Mills, Vt.: Chelsea Green Publishing, 1992); Colin Robinson, "The Depletion of Energy Resources," in *The Economics of Natural Resource Depletion,* ed. D. W. Pearce (New York: Wiley, 1975), pp. 28–31; A. J. Surrey and William Page, "Some Issues in the Current Debate about Energy and Natural Resources," in *The Economics of Natural Resource Depletion,* ed. D. W. Pearce (New York: Wiley, 1975), pp. 56–64; Julian L. Simon, *The Ultimate Resource* (Princeton: Princeton University Press, 1981); Colin Clark, *Population and Depopulation,* The 11th Monash Economics Lecture, Monash University, Clayton, Victoria, Australia, October 3, 1977; and the last quote is from Peter Passell, Marc Roberts, and Leonard Ross, Review of *Limits to Growth, New York Times Book Review* (April 2, 1972).

[100]Herman E. Daly, *Steady-State Economics: The Economics of Biophysical Equilibrium and Moral Growth* (San Francisco: W. H. Freeman, 1977).

[101]Chapter 2 indicates that cross-cultural comparisons of income understate the gross national product per capita of the poor countries. Even when figures are adjusted for these distortions, the share of the poorest countries increases only from 17 percent to 20 percent.

their own life.[102] Other land-based plants and animals are left with the remainder, a shrinking share. At a 1.6-percent yearly population growth, population and humankind's proportion of NPP doubles in 43 years; another doubling means humanity's share of NPP is 100 percent, which is not possible. Indeed, Daly thinks humankind's share of net productivity is already unsustainable.[103]

For some the solution to this dilemma is to increase world resource flows sixfold, the amount needed to raise world resource use per capita to that in the United States. However, to increase resource flows this much, the rest of the world would have to attain the capitalization and technical extracting and processing capacity of the United States. Such an increase in capital would require a tremendous increase in resource flows during the accumulation period. Harrison Brown estimates that it would take more than 60 years of production at 1970 rates to supply the rest of the world with the average industrial metals per capita embodied in the artifacts of the ten richest countries. Furthermore, due to the law of diminishing returns, a sixfold increase in net, usable resources, energy, and materials implies a much greater than sixfold increase in gross resources and environmental impact. Enormous increases in energy and capital devoted to mining, refining, transportation, and pollution control are essential for mining poorer grade and less-accessible minerals and disposing safely of large quantities of wastes.[104]

Brown's estimates are based on rough input-output relationships with no allowance for new discoveries and technological improvements. Nevertheless, the required increases in resource flows suggest the difficulty, if not impossibility, of the world attaining a U.S.-style consumption level by the early- to mid-twenty-first century.

ENTROPY AND THE ECONOMIC PROCESS

The application of the physical law of **entropy** to production shows, from a scientific perspective, the finite limits of the earth's resources. What goes into the economic process represents valuable natural resources; what is thrown out is generally waste. That is, matter-energy enters the economic process in a state of low entropy and comes out in a state of high entropy. To explain, entropy is a measure of the *unavailable* energy in a thermodynamic system. Energy can be free energy, over which we have almost complete command, or bound energy, which we cannot possibly use. The chemical energy in a piece of coal is free energy because we can transform it into heat or mechanical work. But when the coal's initial free energy is dissipated in the form of heat, smoke, and ashes that we cannot use, it has been degraded into bound energy—energy dissipated in disorder, or a state of high entropy. The second law of thermodynamics states that the entropy of a closed system continuously increases, or that the order of such a system steadily

---

[102]This definition is from Sandra Postel, "Carrying Capacity: Earth's Bottom Line," *Challenge* (March-April 1994), pp. 4–12.

[103]Herman E. Daly, "From Empty-World Economics to Full-World Economics: Recognizing an Historical Turning Point in Economic Development," in Robert Goodland, Herman Daly, Salah El Serafy, and Bernd von Droste, *Environmental Sustainable Economic Development: Building on Brundtland* (Paris: UNESCO, 1993), pp. 29–38.

[104]Harrison Brown, "Human Materials Production as a Process in the Biosphere," *Scientific American* 223, no. 3 (September 1970): 195–208.

turns into disorder. The entropy cost of any biological or economic enterprise is always greater than the product. Every object of economic value—a fruit picked from a tree or a piece of clothing—has a low entropy. Our continuous tapping of natural resources increases entropy. Pollution and waste indicate the entropic nature of the economic process. Even recycling requires an additional amount of low entropy in excess of the renewed resource's entropy.[105]

We have access to two sources of free energy, the stock of mineral deposits and the flow of solar radiation intercepted by the earth. However, we have little control over this flow. The higher the level of economic development, the greater the depletion of mineral deposits and hence the shorter the expected life of the human species. For theorist Nicholas Georgescu–Roegen, every time we produce a Cadillac, we destroy low entropy that could otherwise be used for producing a plow or a spade. Thus we produce Cadillacs at the expense of future human life. Economic abundance, a blessing now, is against the interest of the human species as a whole. We become dependent on, and addicted to, industrial luxuries, so that, according to Georgescu–Roegen, the human species will have a short but exciting life.

Georgescu–Roegen's perspective is one not of decades but of millennia, since his preoccupation is with our survival as a species. But even if we have little concern beyond the lifetime of our great-grandchildren, we ignore pessimists such as Daly and Georgescu-Roegen at our peril.

Natural Asset Deterioration and the Measurement of National Income

The most widely used measure of economic progress, gross product, has major failings as a measure of economic welfare. Chapter 2 indicates that GNP or GDP is overstated since a number of items included in their national incomes are intermediate goods, reflecting the costs of producing or guarding income. Gross product assigns a positive value to any economic activity, whether it is productive, unproductive, or destructive.

Former World Bank President Barber B. Conable contends that

Unfortunately, [gross product figures] are generally used without the caveat that they represent an income that cannot be sustained. Current calculations ignore the degradation of the natural resource base and view the sales of nonrenewable resources entirely as income. A better way must be found to measure the prosperity and progress of mankind.[106]

The expenditures on smog eradication, water purification, health costs from air pollution, and the reduction of traffic congestion that add to national income are really costs of economic growth. The 1989 Alaskan oil spill actually increased GNP, since much of the $2.2 billion spent on labor and equipment for the cleanup added to income. Shifting from the automobile to the bicycle and light rail transport

---
[105]Nicholas Georgescu-Roegen, *The Entropy Law and the Economic Process* (Cambridge, Mass.: Harvard University Press, 1971).
[106]"A Call for New Measures of Progress," San Francisco: Redefining Progress, 1995.

would probably enhance urban life but reduce GNP. The quality of services and sustainability of consumer services are more important indicators of progress.[107]

Economists subtract depreciation when factories, buildings, and other capital equipment depreciate (age and fall into disrepair), but make no similar subtraction for the deterioration of forests, soil, air quality, and other natural resources, the loss of biology diversity, and other environmental degradation. When people cut trees and sell timber, the proceeds count as income but there is no subtraction from GNP to get NNP. Natural wealth is whittled away with no debit for the loss of species and the deterioration of the forest, depletion of soil nutrients, and depreciation of economic assets that could provide revenue long into the future if managed well. We need a measure of regeneration of atmosphere and other natural assets. World Resources Institute economist Ronald Repetto points out the failure to distinguish between natural asset destruction and income generation makes GNP "a false beacon, and can draw those who steer by it onto the rocks." Indonesia, Nigeria, Kenya, Bolivia, Colombia, Ethiopia, Ghana, and other countries dependent on primary products—fuels, timber, minerals, and agricultural crops—for 75 percent or more of exports are most in danger of running aground. Nigeria overcut its forests so that timber, a major export of the 1960s and early 1970s, virtually disappeared from export accounts in the 1980s and 1990s. A country can still register GNP growth while heading toward ecological bankruptcy.[108]

THE INDEX OF SUSTAINABLE ECONOMIC WELFARE (ISEW)

Conable and other critics argue that we need better ways to measure the progress of humanity than GNP. The United Nations is working for a method to incorporate resource depletion and environmental degradation into gross product statistics by the turn of the twenty-first century. In the meantime we must rely on pioneering studies of a few countries.

Ronald Repetto and his colleagues examined the implications for Indonesia of a more accurate measure of income and wealth. Repetto et al. found that when you considered the depletion of only three natural resources—forests, soils, and petroleum—the average annual growth of Indonesia's GNP per capita from 1971 to 1984 fell from 4.8 percent to 1.7 percent. If coal, mineral ores, and other nonrenewable-resource exploitation and fisheries deterioration had been included, average GNP would have fallen even more.[109]

---

[107]Lester R. Brown, Christopher Flavin, and Sandra Postel, *Saving the Planet: How to Shape an Environmentally Sustainable Global Economy* (New York: Norton, 1991), p. 124; and Frank Bracho, "Towards More Effective Development Indicators," in The Caracas Report on Alternative Development Indicators, *Redefining Wealth and Progress: New Ways to Measure Economic, Social and Environmental Change* (New York: The Bootstrap Press, 1989).

[108]Lester R. Brown, Christopher Flavin, and Sandra Postel, *Saving the Planet: How to Shape an Environmentally Sustainable Global Economy* (New York: Norton, 1991), pp. 121–24; Robert Repetto et al., *Wasting Assets: Natural Resources in the National Income Accounts* (Washington, D.C.: World Resources Institute, 1989); and Partha Dasgupta, "Optimal Development and the Idea of Net National Product," in Ian Goldin and L. Alan Winters, eds., *The Economics of Sustainable Development* (Cambridge: Cambridge University Press, 1995), pp. 111–46.

[109]Ronald Repetto et al., *Wasting Assets: Natural Resources in the National Income Accounts* (Washington, D.C.: World Resources Institute, 1989). Repetto et al. find that Indonesia's annual GNP growth fell from 7.1 percent to 4 percent. I have adjusted these figures for population growth to get the per capita figures.

Daly and John Cobb developed the **Index of Sustainable Economic Welfare** or **ISEW** per capita, a more comprehensive indicator of well-being that takes into account average consumption, the flow of consumer services, income distribution, sustainable investment, housework and nonmarket transactions, changes in leisure time, the cost of unemployment and underemployment, the lifespan of consumer durables and infrastructure, defensive (commuting, automobile accident) costs, air and water pollution, resource depletion, and long-term environmental damage, including greenhouse-gas emission and ozone depletion. Daly, John Cobb, Clifford Cobb, and Ted Halstead think ISEW per capita in the United States rose continuously for almost two centuries, although, lacking a long-term series, their measure only shows the steady 31-percent increase for the three decades from 1950 to 1969 (Figure 13–6). ISEW per capita peaked during the decade 1966 to 1976, with more than $7,000, while GDP per capita was $11,000 to $13,000. However, from 1976 to 1992, while GDP per capita rose to more than $16,000, ISEW per capita fell 40 percent to just in excess of $4,000, increasing the gap between the two measures

FIGURE 13–6   Gross Domestic Product Per Capita vs. Index of Sustainable Economic Welfare Per Capita in the United States, 1950–1992 (in 1982 U.S. dollars)

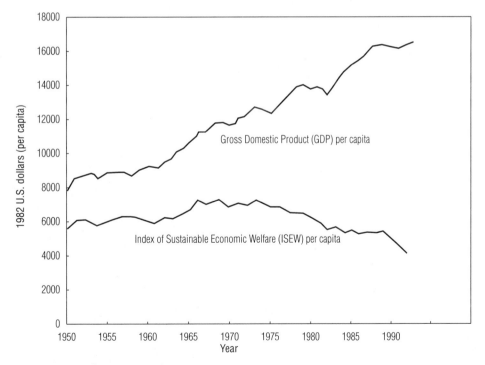

Sources: The Genuine Progress Indicator: Summary of Data and Methodology (San Francisco: Redefining Progress, 1995); and Herman E. Daly and John B. Cobb, Jr., *For the Common Good: Redirecting the Economy Toward Community, the Environment, and a Sustainable Future* (Boston: Beacon Press, 1989), pp. 418–20.

substantially.[110] The major growths of the subtractions from GDP include depletion of nonrenewable resources, long-term environmental economic damage, ozone depletion, loss of wetlands, and loss of farmland (Table 13–3).

ISEW or an alternative measure to adjust gross product for resource depletion and environmental damage require much more research, conceptualization, and measurement. Many of the estimates used for ISEW components have large margins of error. The measures of damage of water quality, for example, are crude. Some ISEW variables are not complete. Thus the measure of environmental damage does not include estimates of depletion of genetic diversity, or urban and farmland runoff. There are conceptual problems in estimating the value of nonrenewable resources, the prices of these resources, and the number of years to exhaust resources. Moreover, many assumptions are conjectures that play a substantial role in the final numbers. Nevertheless, once national-income statisticians include environmental and resource variables in their measures of economic welfare, we can expect continuing improvements in their concepts and methods.

TABLE 13–3 **Components of the Index of Sustainable Economic Welfare Per Capita (in 1982 Dollars) in the United States, 1950, 1969, 1992**

	1950	*1969*	*1992*
Weighted Personal Consumption (+)	4333.7	8049.7	9368.7
Personal Consumption	(4814.7)	(7188.4)	(10642.8)
Income Distribution Index	(111.1)	(89.3)	(113.6)
Value of Housework (+)	4611.5	4419.3	4708.4
Services of Household Capital (+)	356.6	693.2	1579.0
Services of Government Capital (+)	90.0	155.9	158.5
Loss of Leisure Time (-)	47.3	0.0	554.0
Cost of Underemployment (-)	64.4	165.8	534.0
Cost of Consumer Durables (-)	530.0	827.9	1733.3
Cost of Commuting (-)	256.1	306.4	453.4
Cost of Personal Pollution Control (-)	0.0	7.9	43.1
Cost of Automobile Accidents (-)	135.3	201.3	274.1
Cost of Water Pollution (-)	142.5	159.9	138.2
Cost of Air Pollution (-)	327.7	333.5	164.4
Cost of Noise Pollution (-)	34.2	45.4	44.2
Loss of Wetlands (-)	151.7	301.4	557.5
Loss of Farmland (-)	94.6	200.8	302.2
Depletion of Nonrenewable Resources (-)	708.6	1646.9	2975.5
Long-term Environmental Damage (-)	1105.3	1570.0	2411.8
Cost of Ozone Depletion (-)	15.1	214.6	815.5
Loss of Forests (-)	203.6	169.7	225.5
Net Capital Investment (+)	87.3	283.7	94.7
Net Foreign Lending (+) or Borrowing (-)	+0.7	–8.4	–455.7
ISEW per capita	5663.4	7441.7	4226.5

Source: Clifford Cobb and Ted Halstead, *The Genuine Progress Indicator: Summary of Data and Methodology* (San Francisco: Redefining Progress, 1994), pp. 38–39.

---

[110]Herman E. Daly and John B. Cobb, Jr., *For the Common Good: Redirecting the Economy toward Community, the Environment, and a Sustainable Future* (Boston: Beacon Press, 1994), with updating of the figures by Clifford Cobb and Ted Halstead, and renaming of ISEW per capita the Genuine Progress Indicator (GPI) in *The Genuine Progress Indicator: Summary of Data and Methodology* (San Francisco: Redefining Progress, 1994).

Adjusting Investment Criteria for Future Generations

Nobel economist Jan Tinbergen states that "two things are unlimited: the number of generations we should feel responsible for and our inventiveness."[111] The long run in economic analysis tends to be as little as 10 to 25 years, but for the biologist and geologist at least many generations. Critics argue that using the economist's time preference will only hasten the conversion of natural environments into low-yield capital investments. The economist's investment choice, based on maximizing present value, assumes that current generations hold all rights to assets and should efficiently exploit them. But markets do not necessarily provide for equity between generations. Most depleted mineral and biological wealth, especially biodiversity, is all but impossible to recapture after it is destroyed, thus reducing natural assets in the future. Using conventional investment criteria, in which benefits and costs are discounted at a substantial positive rate of interest, automatically closes off the future. If discounted at 15 percent annually, the present value of a dollar five years from now is $0.50, 16 years from now $0.11, and 33 years from now only $0.01.

Economists such as California Berkley's Richard B. Norgaard contend that conventional investment criteria, based on meeting this generation's preference for consumption over time, is *not* justifiable when the future's needs are at stake. We need to distinguish between investment for this generation's time preference and investment to transfer resources and species to future generations. A possible rule of the thumb that considers the preferences of future generations would be one where assets—natural, produced, and human capital—in each time period or generation must be at least as productive as that in the preceding period of generation. Each generation would be obligated to pass on to the next generation a mix of assets which provides the potential for equal or greater flows of income. For Norgaard, this means legislation to protect individual species, set aside land for parks and reserves, and establish social conservation agencies to institutionalize protection of the rights of future generations.[112] Humankind, once meeting the constraint of sustainability, should then select investment projects with the highest social rates of return based on more conventional economic criteria.

John V. Krutilla thinks that today's investment behavior will be motivated by the desire to leave an estate to descendants that will yield collective consumption goods of appreciating future values.[113] Nobel economist Robert Solow argues that we need not leave the world as we found it in detail nor should each generation leave undiminished the natural resources and plant and animal species existing on earth, as humans can substitute one input for another in production.[114] In fact, Harvard's Larry Summers believes that you can use conventional investment criteria if you compute environmental spillovers (external costs and benefits)

[111]Jan Tinbergen, "Foreword," in Donella Meadows, Dennis L. Meadows, and Jorgen Randers, *Beyond the Limits: Confronting Global Collapse, Envisioning a Sustainable Future* (Post Mills, Vt.: Chelsea Green, 1992), p. x.

[112]Richard B. Norgaard, *Sustainability and the Economics of Assuring Assets for Future Generations*, World Bank Working Paper 832, January 1992, pp. 27, 37–38, 48.

[113]John V. Krutilla, "Conservation Reconsidered," in Robert Dorfman and Nancy S. Dorfman, eds., *Economics of the Environment: Selected Readings* (New York: Norton, 1993), pp. 188–98.

[114]Robert M. Solow, "Sustainability: An Economist's Perspective," in Robert Dorfman and Nancy S. Dorfman, eds., *Economics of the Environment: Selected Readings* (New York: Norton, 1993), pp. 179–87.

accurately.[115] If people feel the market does not value the rainforest in the Amazon River basin highly enough, the Brazilian government can set land or user prices, purchase the land for a reserve, tax nearby factories' pollutants, or request aid from a global environment facility to prevent irreversible damage to the forest's biodiversity and carbon sequestration.

While the costs of preserving endangered species and curbing carbon emissions are incurred in the immediate future, major benefits do not occur until well into the twenty-first century, so that benefit-cost ratios are highly dependent on the interest (or discount) rate. Cambridge economist Partha Dasgupta indicates that for the discount rate to be valid, people need to know something concrete about feasible development paths and about productivity of capital. In practice, these paths are so uncertain and so prone to irreversible damage that the present generation should stress preserving the future generations' options.[116] Growth must come from increased efficiency and innovation rather than by shifting costs of environmental degradation to innocent bystanders or future generations.

Living on a Lifeboat

What impact do limited resources have on the ethics of whether or not rich countries should aid poor countries? Hardin, who uses the metaphor of living on a lifeboat, argues that food, technical, financial, and other assistance should be *denied* to desperately poor countries as a way of ensuring the survival of the rest of the human species. Hardin sees the developed nations as a lifeboat with a load of rich people. In comparison,

> The poor of the world are in other, much more crowded lifeboats. Continuously . . . the poor fall out of their lifeboats and swim for a while in the water outside, hoping to be admitted to a rich lifeboat, or in some other way to benefit from the "goodies" on board.[117]

Hardin sees only three options for the passengers on the rich lifeboat, filled to perhaps 80 percent of its capacity:

1. Take all the needy aboard so that the boat is swamped and everyone drowns—complete justice, complete catastrophe.
2. Take on enough people to fill the remaining carrying capacity. However, this option sacrifices the safety factor represented by the extra capacity. Furthermore, how do we choose whom to save and whom to exclude?
3. Admit no more to the boat, preserve the small safety factor, and assure the survival of the passengers. This action may be unjust, but those who feel guilty are free to change places with those in the water. Those people willing to climb aboard would have no such qualms, so the lifeboat would purge itself of guilt as the conscience-stricken surrender their places.

---

[115]Larry Summers, "Summers on Sustainable Growth," *Economist* (May 30, 1992): 65

[116]Partha Dasgupta, "Optimal Development and the Idea of Net National Product," in Ian Goldin and L. Alan Winters, eds., *The Economics of Sustainable Development* (Cambridge: Cambridge University Press, 1995), pp. 111–43.

[117]Garrett Hardin, "Living on a Lifeboat," *Bio Science* 24 (October 1974): 561–68.

This ethical analysis aside, Hardin supports the **lifeboat ethic** of the rich on practical grounds: The poor (that is, the LDCs) are doubling in numbers every 36 years, the rich (DCs), every 254 years. During the next 36 years, the 3.8 to 1 ratio of those outside to those inside the rich lifeboat will increase to 6.8 to 1.[118]

Hardin's premises about population growth are faulty. He expresses concern that some of the "goodies" transferred from the rich lifeboat to the poor boats may merely "convert extra food into extra babies."[119] To be sure, agriculturalists express concern that the continuing increased food output per capita since World War II may be ceasing during the 1990s. Moreover, LDC population growth after World War II was caused by falling mortality rates, not greater fertility (which instead has been dropping). Furthermore, evidence indicates that economic assistance to LDCs generally facilitates development, thus reducing the fertility rate rather than increasing it (see Chapters 7 and 8).

In addition, Hardin's lifeboat metaphor is flawed. In contrast to Hardin's lifeboats that barely interact, nations in the real world interact enormously through trade, investment, military and political power, and so on. His metaphor is not realistic enough to be satisfactory. Hardin must admit that the rich lifeboats are dependent on the poor lifeboats for many of the materials and products of their affluence. Furthermore, the rich lifeboats command a disproportional share of the world's resources. Indeed one seat on the lifeboat (that is, access to a given amount of nonrenewable resources) can support ten times the population from an LDC as from the DC. Daly and Georgescu–Roegen would argue that it is North Americans, not Africans and South Asians, who most endanger the stability of the lifeboat. The average person in the United States or Canada, for instance, consumes about 130 times as much energy per capita as the average citizen of Bangladesh (see the last column, Table 2–1). Also Hardin fails to acknowledge that the carrying capacity of the planet, unlike that of the lifeboat, is not fixed but can increase with technical change. Indeed, technical assistance can enhance output in the poor countries without hurting the rich countries. Finally Hardin's rich lifeboat can raise the ladder and sail away. In the real world, we may not be able to abandon the poor. Rich countries can provide economic aid, including assistance for education, public administration, family planning, and environmental resources, particularly global public goods (see earlier this chapter and Chapter 16).

Summary

1. Land and natural resources are distinguishable. Land is immobile and potentially renewable. Natural resources are mobile, but most are nonrenewable.

2. Environmental resources are resources provided by nature that are indivisible.

3. Oil crises in the 1970s worsened the balance of trade deficit, debt burden, and inflation rate and slowed the growth rate of oil-importing LDCs, but the oil glut in the 1980s and early 1990s reduced these problems for some oil importers.

4. Dutch disease is the adverse competitive effect that local currency appreciation due to a booming export sector has on other exports and import substitutes.

---

[118]The doubling time and ratios are based on 1994 population growth figures in Population Reference Bureau, *1994 World Population Data Sheet* (Washington, D.C., 1994).

[119]Garrett Hardin, "Living on a Lifeboat," *Bio Science* 24 (October 1974): 564.

5. Sustainable development refers to maintaining the productivity of natural, produced, and human assets from generation to generation. Norgaard argues that conventional investment criteria are not adequate for considering the consumption needs of future generations.

6. Panayotou contends that environmental degradation originates from market distortions, defective economic policies, and inadequate property rights definitions, meaning that environmental problems are basically economic problems.

7. External diseconomies, overuse of an open access resource, underproduction of public goods, the irreversibility of rare phenomena of nature, murky owner and user rights to an asset, and high transactions costs are market imperfections that contribute to environmental degradation. Pollution problems result from divergences between social and commercial costs. These divergences even occur under socialism; indeed the Soviet Union's ruthless treatment of land, air, and water illustrate how everybody's property may become nobody's property.

8. The efficient level of pollution emission is where marginal damages are equal to marginal abatement costs.

9. Many economists object to contingent valuation, the use of questionnaires from sample surveys to elicit the willingness of respondents to pay for an environmental good, as deeply flawed.

10. About 14 percent of the world population lives on arid or semiarid land. Increases in arid lands in the last several decades are traceable to overcultivation, deforestation, and so forth.

11. Economic underdevelopment in the tropics is partly a matter of geography. There is no winter to exterminate weeds and insect pests. Parasitic diseases are endemic and weaken the health and productivity of people. The heat and torrential rains damage the soils, removing needed organic matter, microorganisms, and minerals.

12. Tropical countries generally will not provide global public goods, such as the atmosphere or biosphere, in sufficient quantity, since many benefits spill over to other countries. Rich countries have an interest in providing funds to preserve tropical global common-property resources. However, because they may earn higher returns from free riding, users of global common property resources rarely agree to commit resources to manage global resources in the interest of all.

13. Developed and transitional countries produce a disproportional share of the world's carbon dioxide emissions that contribute to global warming. In the absence of drastic cuts in the annual global emissions of carbon dioxide, scientists expect increases in globally averaged surface temperatures in the twenty-first century that are several times these increases in previous centuries. The developing countries of the south are expected to be the major nations suffering from global warming, even though they produce only a small fraction of the globe's carbon emissions.

14. Market-based "green taxes" are more efficient than physical targets in reducing carbon emissions. Many economists think that international tradeable emission permits are the economically optimal approach to levying "green taxes" on carbon emitters.

15. The Club of Rome's study, *The Limits to Growth*, concluded that the global economic system will collapse during the twenty-first century. However, a major shortcoming of the study is the assumption of exponential growth in industrial

and agricultural needs and the arbitrary placement of nonexponential limits on the technical progress that might accommodate these needs.

16. Daly's impossibility theorem argues that there are not enough resources in the world to support the whole world at U.S.-style consumption levels.

17. Our continuous use of natural resources increases entropy, a measure of the unavailable energy in a thermodynamic system. Georgescu–Roegen argues that luxury production decreases the expected life span of the human species.

18. The Index of Sustainable Economic Welfare (ISEW) per capita is a comprehensive indicator of well-being that subtracts depletion of nonrenewable resources, long-term environmental economic damage, ozone depletion, loss of wetlands, and loss of farmlands from GNP. Economists estimate that ISEW per capita has fallen in the United States since 1976.

19. Lifeboat ethics, used as an argument for denying economic assistance to LDCs, is based on a number of flawed premises. Rich nations command a disproportional share of the world's resources, depend economically on poor nations, and have access to technical knowledge that can increase LDC productivity without decreasing their own.

Terms to Review

- land
- natural resources
- resource flows
- environmental resources
- balance of trade
- cartel
- Organization of Economic Cooperation and Development (OECD)
- Dutch disease
- reverse Dutch disease
- sustainable development
- externalities
- external diseconomies
- common property resources
- tragedy of the commons
- public goods
- user rights
- transactions costs
- Coase's theorem
- marginal damage (MD)
- marginal abatement cost (MAC)
- contingent valuation

- arid land
- tropics
- global public goods
- biodiversity
- global warming
- greenhouse effect
- greenhouse gases
- green taxes
- international tradeable emission permits
- Montreal Protocol
- International Convention on Climate Change (ICCC)
- free riding
- proven reserves
- Daly's impossibility theorem
- gross planetary product
- net primary productivity (NPP)
- entropy
- Index of Sustainable Economic Welfare (ISEW)
- lifeboat ethic

Questions to Discuss

1. Indicate in broad outline the movements of *real* world crude petroleum prices in the last quarter of a century. What impact have these prices had on oil-importing LDCs?

2. Assume you are asked as an economic practitioner to analyze a patient with Dutch disease. Analyze the causes of the disease, describe the patient's symptoms, and prescribe an antidote to improve the patient's health. Also do the same for reverse Dutch disease.

3. What is meant by "sustainable development?" What implications should sustainable development have for investment criteria?

4. What are the market imperfections that contribute to environmental degradation?

5. What is meant by Hardin's "tragedy of the commons"? Identify environmental problems associated with this tragedy.

6. Theodore Panayotou contends that "Ultimately, excessive environmental damage can be traced to 'bad' economics stemming from misguided government policies and distorted markets." Discuss what Panayotou means by this statement, how accurate his view is, and what the policy implications of this view is. Give examples of misguided government policies and distorted markets, and the reasons for these policies and markets.

7. How do pollution levels vary with economic growth?

8. What decision-making rule minimizes social cost where pollution is involved? Assess the position that optimal level of pollution emission is zero.

9. Discuss and assess the methods for estimating the monetary values of pollution discharge and ecological degradation.

10. How does geography affect economic development in the tropics? What measures are needed to overcome these adverse effects?

11. Discuss the concept of global public goods, give examples of those that have environmental implications, and indicate the implications of global public goods for international funding programs. In your analysis, focus especially on global public goods in tropical countries.

12. What program would you design for global optimal greenhouse-gas abatement?

13. Assess the arguments for and against the use of international tradeable emission permits in abating global greenhouse gases.

14. Discuss the role of green markets, green taxes, and green aid in reducing market imperfections concerning the environment and resource use. Discuss the possibility of using green markets, green taxes, and green aid in multilateral agreements.

15. How severely will a shortage of natural resources limit economic growth in the next half-century, especially in LDCs?

16. Indicate the adjustments that Daly and Cobb make to compute the Index of Sustainable Economic Welfare (ISEW). How do these adjustments affect measures of net economic welfare? Evaluate ISEW per capita as a measure of economic welfare that is an alternative to gross product per capita.

Guide to Readings

The *International Petroleum Statistics Report* (note to Table 13–2) and the periodical *Petroleum Economist* provide data and analysis of the petroleum industry.

Roemer, Findlay, and Corden and Neary (note 8) examine Dutch disease in LDCs. The *IDS Bulletin* 17 (October 1986) has three articles dealing with

Dutch disease: Evans (note 10); Ahmad Jazayeri, "Prices and Output in Two Oil-Based Economies: The Dutch Disease in Iran and Nigeria," pp. 14–21; and Alan Gelb, "From Boom to Bust—Oil Exporting Countries over the Cycle, 1970–84," pp. 22–29.

The annual *Vital Signs* and *State of the World* by Lester R. Brown and associates at the Worldwatch Institute, (New York: Norton); Brown, Flavin, and Postel (note 27); and World Resources Institute, U.N. Environmental Program, and the U.N. Development Program (note 51) provide information on the relationship between the world's resources, environment, and population, and assess the sustainability of the planet. All sources, especially the last, discuss the global public goods of climate and biodiversity. Wilson (note 54) is a definitive source on biodiversity. Schelling (note 63), Ogawa (note 64), Poterba (note 70), Weyant (note 70), Nordhaus (note 60), Flavin (note 64), Morgenstern (note 81), Demsetz (note 95), Mendelsohn, Nordhaus, and Shaw (note 73), and Turner, Pearce, and Bateman (note 64) have economic analysis and policy recommendations concerning the problem of global climate change. Gore (note 65) has analyses, tables, and figures on global warming of interest to lay readers. Barrett (note 95) discusses the pitfalls associated with international environmental agreements.

The World Bank (note 14) analyzes the effect of environmental degradation on health and productivity in LDCs.

On the concept of sustainable development, see Herman E. Daly, "Ecological Economics and Sustainable Development," in C. Rossi and E. Tiezzi, eds., *Ecological Physical Chemistry, Proceedings of an International Workshop, 8–12 November 1990, Siena, Italy* (Amsterdam: Elsevier Science Publishers, 1991), pp. 182–89; the World Commission on Environment and Development (note 11); and Robert M. Solow, "Sustainability: An Economist's Perspective," in Robert Dorfman and Nancy S. Dorfman, eds., *Economics of the Environment: Selected Readings* (New York: Norton, 1993), pp. 179–87. The edited book by Goldin and Winters (note 31) applies rigorous economic analysis to the question of sustainable development.

Dorfman and Dorfman's edited readings on the environment are excellent in discussing economic principles, policies, benefit-cost analysis and measurement, and a global analysis related to the environment. Other excellent survey sources on environmental economics include Kahn (note 3), Field (note 35), and Turner, Pearce, and Bateman (note 64). Field, pp. 84–105, analyzes the marginal conditions for optimal pollution abatement.

Panayotou (note 12) has a clear and concise explanation of market distortions and policy failures that are the root causes of severe environmental degradation. Ghai and Vivian (note 15) examine the management of environmental resources on the local level in LDCs.

Hardin has written the classic essay (note 19) on the "tragedy of the commons." Alan Randall, "The Problem of Market Failure," in Dorfman and Dorfman, pp. 144–61, has a comprehensive analysis of market imperfections that contribute to environmental degradation. Dales (note 24) discusses the role of ownership and user rights in reducing environmental damage.

The *Journal of Economic Perspectives* (Fall 1994) has a concise summary of the literature on contingent valuation (see notes 39–42).

Feshbach and Friendly (note 27) have an exhaustive survey of environmental degradation in the former Soviet Union.

Kamarck (note 46) has written the definitive study on economic development in the tropics.

Norgaard (note 11) discusses the effect of environmental public goods and bads on investment criteria.

Does scarcity of natural resources place substantial limitations on future economic growth? Although the best-known analyses of the yes answer to this question are studies by Meadows et al. (note 99), the arguments by Daly (note 100) and Georgescu–Roegen (note 105) are more compelling. On the negative side of this question is Simon (note 99). Short articles by growth optimist J. E. Stiglitz and pessimist Daly, plus a critique by Georgescu–Roegen, are in V. Kerry Smith, *Scarcity and Growth Reconsidered* (Baltimore: Johns Hopkins University Press, 1979), pp. 36–105. Clear expositions for the two sides, written for the lay reader, are Georgescu–Roegen, "The Entropy Law and the Economic Process," in H. E. Daly, ed., *Essays toward a Steady-State Economy* (Cuernavaca, Mexico: Centro Intercultural de Documentacion, 1971); and Simon, "The Scarcity of Raw Materials," *Atlantic Monthly* (June 1981): 33–41.

On ways to measure economic welfare that include environmental degradation and resource depletion, see Repetto et al. (note 109), Daly and Cobb (note 110), and Cobb and Halstead (note to Table 13–3).

CHAPTER 14

Sources of Capital Formation

In this chapter we discuss the requirements and sources of capital formation. We will use national-income equations to show the relationship between saving, investment, and the international balance on goods, services, and income (that is, exports minus imports of goods and services).

The following equation shows income (Y) equal to expenditures (or aggregate supply equal to aggregate demand). National income, when calculated on the expenditure side, is

$$Y = C + I + \left(X - M\right) \tag{14-1}$$

where C = consumption, I = domestic capital formation (or investment), X = exports of goods and services, and M = imports of goods and services.

Savings (S) is that part of national income that is not spent for consumption, viz.

$$S = Y - C \tag{14-2}$$

Hence

$$Y = C + S \tag{14-3}$$

Thus national income is equal to

$$C + I + \left(X - M\right) = C + S \tag{14-4}$$

If we subtract C from both sides of the equation,

$$I + \left(X - M\right) = S \tag{14-5}$$

Subtracting X from and adding M to both sides results in

$$I = S + \left(M - X\right) \tag{14-6}$$

If M exceeds X, the country has a deficit in its balance on goods, services, and income. It may finance the deficit by borrowing, attracting investment, or receiving grants from abroad (surplus items). Essentially

$$M - X = F \tag{14-7}$$

where F is a **capital import,** or inflow of capital from abroad. Substituting this variable in Equation 14–6 gives us

$$I = S + F \tag{14–8}$$

Equation 14–8 states that a country can increase its new capital formation (or **investment**) through its own domestic savings and by inflows of capital from abroad. (When a politically or economically unstable LDC exports capital through capital flight, there is an outflow of domestic savings; a net outflow means F is negative in Equation 14–8.)

Scope of the Chapter

A major goal of this chapter is to compare output devoted to consumer goods versus capital goods (those that increase the system's capacity). Both kinds of items are urgently needed in LDCs. Increased consumption is important because large parts of the population live close to subsistence. Greater capital formation raises the productivity of consumer goods output in the future. The heart of the issue is the conflict between resources for present consumption and future consumption (present saving).

The first section of this chapter examines a widely used method for calculating capital requirements, the *ICOR* approach. The remainder of the chapter discusses how an economy can increase its rate of capital formation.

Capital Requirements

W. Arthur Lewis's model (see Chapter 5) focuses on increasing capital formation as a percentage of national income. He contends that

> The central problem in the theory of economic development is to understand the process by which a community which was previously saving and investing 4 or 5 percent of its national income or less, converts itself into an economy where voluntary saving is running at about 12 to 15 percent of national income or more. This is the central problem because the central fact of economic development is rapid capital accumulation (including knowledge and skills with capital).[1]

We can illustrate the need for raising the investment rate if we examine Roy Harrod's equation:[2]

$$G = \frac{i}{ICOR} \tag{14–9}$$

where G is the rate of economic growth, i investment as a percentage of income, and **ICOR, the incremental capital output ratio,** the inverse of the ratio of increase in output to investment (see the discussion of the Harrod-Domar model in the Appendix to Chapter 5). If Y is income, K capital stock, and I investment, then

---

[1]W. Arthur Lewis, "Economic Development with Unlimited Supplies of Labor," *Manchester School* 22 (May 1954): 139–91.

[2]Roy F. Harrod, "An Essay in Dynamic Theory," *Economic Journal* 49 (March 1939): 14–33

$G = (\Delta Y/Y)$, $i = (I/Y)$, and the *ICOR* is $(\Delta K/\Delta Y)$, the increment in capital divided by the increment in income, the same as $(I/\Delta Y)$, since $\Delta K \equiv I$ by definition.[3] Thus Equation 14–9 is an identity

$$\frac{\Delta Y}{Y} \equiv \frac{\dfrac{I}{Y}}{\dfrac{I}{\Delta Y}} \qquad (14\text{–}10)$$

Assume that the *desired rate of growth in GNP per capita* is 4 percent per year. As a rough approximation, we can add this desired figure to *population growth per year* (say, 2 percent) to get *G*, the *targeted rate of growth in total income per year* (6 percent).

The *ICOR*, used to calculate the investment rate required to achieve the economic growth target, is a simple and crude empirical ratio between added capital stock and the resulting increase in output per year. For reasons indicated below, *ICOR*s range widely, from about 2 to 7. At best a 2-percentage-point increase in investment rate in a year may increase growth by 1-percentage point. Here an *i* (**investment rate**) of 12 percent, divided by *ICOR* 2 results in the targeted growth rate of 6 percent (Equation 14–9). At worst it may require a 7-percentage point increase in investment rate to increase growth by 1 percentage *point*. However, a growth target of 6 percent with an *ICOR* of 7 requires an investment rate of 42 percent—rarely, if ever, attained. (See Table 14–1 for investment rates by country groups, and Figure 14–1, which shows a drop in saving and investment in the early 1980s, during global depressed demand and a rising LDC debt overhang.)

TABLE 14-1 Saving and Investment Rates by Country Group, 1960 and 1992[a]

	Gross Domestic Saving/ Gross Domestic Product, 1960	Gross Domestic Investment/ Gross Domestic Product, 1960	Gross Domestic Saving/ Gross Domestic Product, 1992	Gross Domestic Investment/ Gross Domestic Product, 1992
Low-income countries	0.17	0.19	0.27	0.27
China and India[b]	0.19	0.21	0.32	0.30
Other low-income	0.09	0.11	0.18	0.22
Middle-income countries[c]	0.19	0.20	0.24	0.23
High-income countries	0.22	0.21	0.22	0.21

[a]Figures are weighted averages for the country groups.

[b]Figures for 1960 and 1991 for China.

[c]Figures for 1960 and 1990.

Sources: World Bank, *World Development Report, 1994* (New York: Oxford University Press, 1994), pp. 178–79; World Bank, *World Development Report, 1993* (New York: Oxford University Press, 1993), pp. 254–55; World Bank, *World Development Report, 1992* (New York: Oxford University Press, 1992), pp. 234–35; and World Bank, *World Development Report, 1982* (New York: Oxford University Press, 1982), pp. 118–19.

---

[3]Since *actual* savings (income not spent for consumption) equals *actual* investment (output not used for consumption), you can substitute *s*, savings as a percentage of income, for *i*. This adjustment gives you the fundamental Harrod equation, discussed in the appendix to Chapter 5.

FIGURE 14-1   Domestic Saving and Investment in
Developing Countries[a]

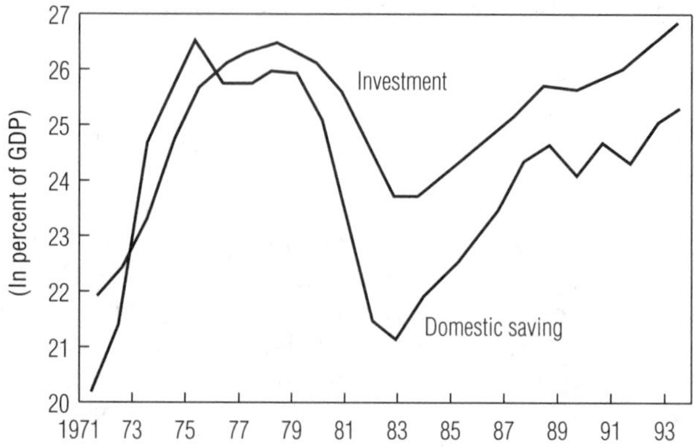

[a]Three-year centered moving average.
Source: International Monetary Fund, *World Economic Outlook, October 1993* (Washington, D.C., 1993), p. 73.

A major condition for the takeoff in Walter W. Rostow's theory of economic growth is a sharp increase in investment as a percentage of national income, say, from 5 percent or less to over 10 percent (see Chapter 5). Both Lewis and Rostow emphasize that abrupt increases in growth rates during the West's industrial revolution (late eighteenth through late nineteenth centuries) resulted from increased investment rates. But there is little historical evidence of an abrupt increment in either growth rate or investment rate (as we indicated in our discussion of Rostow's theory in Chapter 5).

Nevertheless, we can see the importance of investment rates of over 10 percent if we look at it from the following perspective, similar to Rostow's. Assume that the *ICOR* for an economy in its early stages of economic development is 3.5. If population grows by 2 percent per year, it is essential for overall economic growth to be 2 percent annually for income per capita to remain constant. Thus, to sustain income per capita, a country must invest 7 percent of national income, since according to Equation 14–9, $(i/ICOR) = (7 \text{ percent}/3.5) = 2$ percent. Attaining a mere 1-percent growth rate in income per capita (or a 3-percent overall growth rate) requires investing 10.5 percent of national income. Thus under plausible assumptions concerning *ICORs* and population growth, investment as a proportion of national income should exceed 10 percent to achieve even a 1-percent per capita growth.

The weighted average of the domestic savings rate in low-income countries (other than China and India) is 18 percent. When you add the rate of foreign capital inflow to income, 4 percent (see Equation 14–8), you get an investment rate of 22 percent (Table 14–1). Of the 88 LDCs for which there are data in the *World Development Report, 1994*, only 3 had investment rates of less than 10 percent. In 1960, the year that Rostow first published the *Stages,* only 10 of 85 countries had investment rates of less than 10 percent.

However, Rostow assumed that *net* investment rates of over 10 percent, *not gross* investment rates, were relevant in determining growth rates. **Depreciation** (or capital consumption) must be subtracted from **gross investment** to give **net investment**. Data on depreciation, and thus net investment, are poor.

If you put aside an outlier country, the Congo, the net investment rate for LDCs is 60 percent of gross investment rate (see Table 14–2), which suggests that a gross investment rate of about 16 percent roughly corresponds to a net investment rate of 10 percent. Most LDCs have attained this result—64 percent (25 out of 39) of the low-income countries in *World Development Report, 1994* have a gross investment rate of at least 16 percent, and 87 percent (46 out of 53) of the middle-income countries. Yet in 1960, only half of the LDCs had a gross investment rate of 16 percent or above. Fourteen percent (4 out of 27) of today's low-income countries had an investment rate of at least 16 percent in 1960, while 68 percent (36 out of 53) of today's middle-income countries attained this rate. Thus rough calculations suggest that several low-income countries have net investment rates below Rostow's

TABLE 14–2   Rates and Sources of Capital Formation, ca. 1990

	(1) Gross Investment as a Perentage of Gross Domestic Product	Percentage of Capital Formation Financed by			Percentage Components of Domestic Net Saving		
		(2) Foreign Saving	(3) Depreci- ation	(4) Domestic Net Saving (5+6+7)	(5) Cor- porate Saving	(6) Gov- ernment Saving	(7) House hold Saving
Developed countries							
Australia	0.21	0.19	0.71	0.10	−0.07	0.01	0.16
Belgium	0.20	−0.08	0.48	0.60	0.29	−0.23	0.54
Canada	0.21	0.17	0.55	0.28	0.06	−0.11	0.33
Finland	0.27	0.18	0.55	0.27	0.13	0.13	0.01
France	0.20	0.01	0.63	0.36	0.18	−0.02	0.20
Germany FR	0.22	−0.14	0.56	0.58	0.14	0.04	0.40
Japan	0.33	−0.04	0.44	0.60	0.06	0.25	0.29
Netherlands	0.21	−0.18	0.50	0.68	0.26	−0.10	0.52
Norway	0.20	−0.17	0.73	0.44	0.21	0.22	0.01
Sweden	0.21	0.16	0.55	0.29	0.07	0.24	−0.02
Switzerland	0.29	−0.13	0.36	0.77	0.20	0.12	0.45
United Kingdom	0.19	0.19	0.58	0.23	−0.02	0.10	0.15
United States	0.17	0.11	0.71	0.18	0.06	−0.16	0.28
Developing countries							
Congo	0.19	0.94	1.21	−1.15	−0.45	−0.60	−0.10
Costa Rica	0.28	0.34	0.09	0.57	0.04	−0.01	0.54
India	0.24	0.10	0.43	0.47	0.06	−0.17	0.58
Malta	0.33	0.12	0.14	0.74	0.24	0.20	0.30
Paraguay	0.07	−0.60	0.92	0.68	0.21	0.15	0.32
Philippines	0.22	0.22	0.34	0.44	0.10	0.10	0.24
South Africa	0.20	−0.11	0.85	0.26	0.23	0.02	0.01
Thailand	0.37	0.19	0.21	0.60	0.16	0.25	0.19
Vanuatu	0.44	0.15	0.22	0.63	0.28	0.16	0.19

Source: United Nations, *National Accounts Statistics: Main Aggregates and Detailed Tables, 1992* (New York, 1992), Parts I and II.

threshold of 10 percent, although there are not nearly so many of them in the early 1990s as there were in the 1950s and early 1960s.[4]

The *ICOR*, used to express simple relationships in Equation 14–9, varies with economic development and falls with the expansion (rises with the contraction) of the business cycle. A.P. Thirwall questions whether we can treat the *ICOR* as an independent variable to be used as a parameter in investment planning. Is not the *ICOR* a dependent variable determined by the rates of investment and economic growth?[5]

The *ICOR* has other limitations. A low *ICOR* (that is, little investment per unit of increased output) may not necessarily indicate highly productive capital. First, the *ICOR* excludes the costs of inputs other than capital. An *ICOR* may be low because complementary factors—entrepreneurship, management, labor, and technical knowledge—are high per unit of capital, not because the capital projects chosen have high yields. Second, as with the private benefit-cost analysis discussed in Chapter 11, *ICOR* ignores externalities and interdependencies among different projects. Third, *ICORs* may be misleading because of variations in capital utilization. Thus two otherwise similar manufacturing plants may have different *ICORs* because of differences in the number of shifts worked per day, the utilization of capacity in a given shift, and so forth. Fourth, the *ICOR* neglects the timing of costs and benefits and ignores those beyond the period measured (usually only 1 year).

Consider the firm in Table 14–3 choosing between investing $10,000 in a pickup truck or 10 bullocks and wagons. For an enterprise, the *Y* in the *ICOR's* denominator is *not* net output but its **value added** (output minus purchases from other enterprises). The conventional *ICOR*, computed for 1 year, is ($I/\Delta Y$), or (10,000/4,000) = 2.50 for the truck, and (10,000/3,000) = 3.33 for the bullocks with wagons. However, because of frequent monsoons, rough roads, and the high cost of spare parts, the truck's investment life is only 5 years and the bullocks' and wagons', 15 years. The longer life of the bullock project makes the discounted value of its value added greater, $17,542.11, compared to $13,408.64 for the truck.

The *ICORs* can be computed for longer than 1 year but are still misleading because timing of inputs and outputs is ignored. Let us assume the investment life of the pickup truck is 10 years instead of 5 years, so that its net value added is $40,000. If computed over a 15-year period, the *ICOR* for the bullock project is lower, 10,000/45,000 (or 0.22), compared to 10,000/40,000 (or 0.25) for the truck. Yet because its returns are earlier, the truck's present value added (discounted at a rate of 15 percent per year), $20,075.08, is greater than the bullocks' and wagons' $17,542.11.

The *ICOR* for a particular type of industrial project, or even at an aggregate level, is often unstable, varying with changes in capacity utilization over the period of the business cycle. The *ICOR* may also be subject to long-run change: some economists argue that the *ICOR* would fall with economic development due to economies of scale, external economies, and improvements in labor skills. Other economists, however, contend that the *ICOR* would rise from diminishing returns as capital-labor ratios grow with economic growth. The little evidence

---

[4]World Bank, *World Development Report, 1979* (Washington, D.C.: International Bank for Reconstruction and Development, 1979), pp. 134–35; and World Bank, *World Development Report, 1994* (New York: Oxford University Press, 1994), pp. 178–79.

[5]A.P. Thirlwall, *Growth and Development with Special Reference to Developing Economies* (Boulder, Colo.: Lynne Rienner, 1995), p. 114.

TABLE 14-3   Comparison of the ICORs and the Present Discounted Values
of Two Projects

	One Pickup Truck	Ten Bullocks and Ten Wagons
Initial investment	$10,000	$10,000
Annual value added	$ 4,000	$ 3,000
Investment life	5 years	15 years
Total value added over one investment life	$4,000 × 5 = $20,000	$3,000 × 15 = $45,000
Net value added discounted to the present (15 percent discount rate)	$13,408.64	$17,542.11

available suggests that long-run changes in the *ICOR* are small, with factors contributing to a rise and a fall in the ratio tending to offset each other. If the ratio stays fairly constant over long period, say 10 to 15 years, you can use the *ICOR* in an equation, such as 14–9, to estimate capital requirements.[6] Still, the *ICOR* is a rough tool rather than a precise instrument for investment planning. The *ICOR* approach is simple, but economists must use it with care, if they are to clarify relationships in the development process.

Of course costs and benefits could be discounted to the present so that the *ICOR* were the reciprocal of the private marginal product criterion. Further we could adjust for externalities so that an *ICOR* investment criterion became the reciprocal of the social benefit-cost criterion (see Chapter 11), so that the rankings of investment projects by the two criteria would be similar.

How does a country determine its desired investment rate? For some countries, the investment rate goal is set a bit higher than a past rate or close to the rate attained by another country in a comparable situation. One resolution of the issue is to devote as many resources as possible to capacity-increasing projects, while also trying to increase the utilization of existing capital and improving the methods applied to old capital.[7]

How to Increase the Rate of Capital Formation

How can a LDC government increase net capital formation as a percentage of national income? This section discusses several ways of achieving this goal. Although the first measure assumes no government role in capital formation decisions, remaining measures do involve some government action.

---

[6]A.P. Thirlwall, *Growth and Development with Special Reference to Developing Economies* (Boulder, Colo.: Lynne Rienner, 1995), p. 116.

T.N. Srinivasan, "Data Base for Development Analysis: An Overview," *Journal of Development Economics* 44 (June 1994): 10–13, points out that World Bank and International Monetary Fund data indicate an increased savings and investment in LDCs from the 15 years before 1973 to the period after 1973, accompanied by a reduction in growth rates. Do these trends suggest an increasingly inefficient use of capital (increased *ICOR*)? Not necessarily. Srinivasan suggests that the unreliability of data on savings, investment, and growth, especially in light of substantial black-market transactions in many LDCs, preclude any firm inference about trends.

[7]W.B. Reddaway, *The Development of the Indian Economy* (London: Allen & Unwin, 1962).

FREE MARKET INDUCEMENT: THE CLASSICAL MECHANISM

The nineteenth-century English classical economists assumed a purely competitive economy. They believed that government interference in privately made saving and investment decisions would hurt economic efficiency and that indeed the capital formation rate corresponding to these decisions meant full employment and optimal economic growth. Classical premises concerning savings and investment have made a comeback among contemporary economists, so that many of them favor minimal intervention in the capital market.

Household Saving.   Classical economists analyzed saving by households, a major source of net capital formation then and now (see Table 14–2). They argued that the interest rate equalizes household saving supply and business investment demand. A higher interest rate rewards thrift, resulting in an upward, supply-of-savings curve. A lower interest rate decreases the cost of business borrowing, so that investment demand is downward sloping. The intersection of demand and supply determines the interest rate and the amount of saving households make available to businesses.

Retained Earnings.   Classical economists also recognized a business's retained earnings as a major source of capital formation. Business saving, which consists of corporate saving as well as saving from unincorporated business (a small fraction of household saving), is the leading source of net capital formation (see Table 14–2).

Remember Lewis's model in which labor migrates when urban wages exceed rural wages (Chapter 5). He assumes that the capitalist saves all surplus (profits, interest, and rent), and the worker saves nothing. The model is based on the classical tradition, positing no technical change, a prevailing wage at subsistence, zero saving by wage earners, and economic development based on increasing capital per worker (Chapter 5). But the problem with Lewis's model is that wages are likely to increase well before surplus agricultural labor is hired by the capitalist sector. When wages rise, there is a profit squeeze, and saving and growth in the capitalist sector are reduced.

Contemporary Attitudes toward the Classical Approach.   A number of contemporary economists criticize the classical approach, especially its view of the determination of capital formation rates. For Keynesian and new Keynesian economists, the interest rate is determined by the demand for, and supply of, money. They reject the classical view that the interest rate equates the saving plans of households and the investment plans of businesses. Keynesians believe these plans are largely unrelated to the interest rate. They point out that saving plans usually do not coincide with investment plans, since savers and investors are different groups motivated by different considerations. Saving depends on income; investment is a function of its expected rate of return. Keynesian economists do not expect a market economy's actual saving to equal the amount needed for society's desired economic growth.

Although classical economists advocated investments in infrastructure, such as roads and canals, they generally emphasized a free market with minimal government intervention—a view having little appeal to leaders and economists in developing countries. The LDCs are even less inclined than DCs to accept the saving decisions of households and businesses based on the market. Perhaps they are reluctant to do so because they think that governments taking an active role in increasing capital formation rates generate high saving rates. In any event, the rest of our discussion of ways of increasing capital formation stresses government-initiated measures.

CAPITAL IMPORTS

The LDCs may prefer to increase capital formation without the pain of reducing current consumption, that is, with capital inflows from abroad or by exploiting idle resources. The success of importing capital, discussed in Chapter 16, depends on how much capacity increases in the future, so that a country can raise domestic saving to export capital.

EXPLOITING IDLE RESOURCES

Redundant Labor. According to Ragnar Nurkse, a government should use labor with low or zero marginal productivity in agriculture to work on capital projects, such as roads, railways, houses, and factories. Workers on these projects continue to depend on their relatives on the farm for food. It is as if workers in capital goods production carry their own subsistence bundles with them. In essence new capital formation, or saving, is created at virtually no cost.[8]

The problem with Nurkse's theory is that we can expect those remaining on the farm *and* those beginning work on capital projects to increase consumption. To persuade idled agricultural laborers to work harder off the farm probably requires money wages. In fact just as in the Lewis model, these laborers will leave the farm only if they receive a wage exceeding the subsistence that all members of the rural community receive (see Chapter 9). Those remaining on the farm will inevitably increase their consumption as existing output (barely reduced by the withdrawal of labor) is spread over fewer people. Thus financial and social costs of the capital projects are actually greater, and the potential for saving less, than Nurkse anticipates.

Although in theory government could use taxes or low agricultural procurement prices to prevent those staying on the farms from consuming more, in practice government cannot capture the saving potential from unutilized labor except in economies like the Soviet Union. Even there, from 1929 to 1933, immediate gains from forced agricultural saving were more than offset when peasants disrupted production; they ate a major form of agricultural capital stock—animal herds. Chapter 7 discussed other disruptions to Soviet farm output.

Another problem with Nurkse's approach is that employing previously unutilized farm labor activates resources with high alternative costs. The workers on the capital project will need some capital (such as crude tools) to build the roads, railways, houses, and factories. In addition, entrepreneurs, supervisors, and planners will be needed to initiate, plan, and administer the project. Furthermore, if workers move to the city, its housing, transport, schools, hospitals, and other services will have to be expanded.

Unused Capital Capacity. Visitors to many capital poor LDCs are shocked by the evidence of widespread capital underutilization: earthmovers rusting away for lack of servicing or spare parts; empty housing projects; abandoned irrigation

---

[8]Ragnar Nurkse, *Problems of Capital Formation in Underdeveloped Countries* (New York: Oxford University Press, 1967), first published 1953.

ditches; and factories producing at a fraction of capacity because of mechanical breakdowns, materials shortages, or insufficient markets. Surely, they ask, cannot output be increased through wiser capital utilization?

Yet existing capacity is not fully utilized for many reasons. LDCs use more capital than is socially most profitable because technology transferred from DCs is not suited to their needs and because of factor price distortions and low foreign exchange prices (see Chapters 9 and 11). Furthermore, many developing countries can profitably absorb only so much additional capital. The small size of the construction industry, poor transport and communication facilities, irregular power, slow and undependable deliveries, unsatisfactory servicing of equipment, and inadequate housing for foreign personnel constitute major technical limitations to more effective use of existing and potential capital. LDCs also lack skilled people; competent civil servants, innovative entrepreneurs, experienced managers and technicians, and educated workers. However, in the long run, expanding educational and training facilities, transportation and communication, and other infrastructure should increase **absorptive capacity.**

Factories producing textiles, shoes, motor vehicles, beer, soft drinks, paper products, and so on, could reach full capacity by running 24 hours a day, running three shifts instead of one. Even so, more managers, supervisors, technicians, and other skilled persons in short supply in most LDCs would be needed.

In the short run, some of these skilled people can be hired from abroad. Still it is difficult and expensive to find foreigners who will work and respond well in the local culture and economy. Furthermore using foreign specialists may prevent local workers from getting experience, learning, and control of domestic production—a long-run benefit that would increase the future ability of the country to use capital effectively.

Labor with low marginal productivity in agriculture cannot be easily utilized cheaply; increasing capital utilization is difficult, and the success of capital imports depends on increasing future capacity. Thus increasing saving usually requires diverting resources from consumption, discussed in the remainder of this chapter.

MORAL SUASION

Many poor countries have a substantial but unexploited capacity to save. Societies spending resources for guns, tanks, cathedrals, or palaces surely could divert funds into productive investment (Chapter 5). Moreover, households in low-income countries accumulate assets of one kind or another that represent saving—for a rainy day, marriage festivities, religious observances, and other purposes. Many a poor rural Indian woman wears a lifetime of savings in the form of a gold necklace.

Political leaders have often stirred up the populace to sacrifice for a war effort. Could not some of this enthusiasm support the program for economic development? The government could convince people that development is taking place, that saving is bearing fruit. Sound national economic management, coupled with a social security system, might make people less insecure about economic emergencies, so that they might invest more in productive activity.[9]

---

[9]Some of the material from this and subsequent sections is from Henry J. Bruton, *Principles of Development Economics* (Englewood Cliffs, N.J.: Prentice Hall, 1965), pp. 154–58.

Persuasion is more likely to be effective, especially among lower- and middle-income groups, if real personal income is increasing. It is easier to convince people to save when income is going up than when it is constant, since saving would then mean a decrease in consumption.[10]

IMPROVEMENT IN THE TAX SYSTEM

Saving is unconsumed current production. Taxation is one form of saving (a part of S in the national accounts Equation 14–4). Improving the tax system increases saving.

An Emphasis on Direct Taxes.   In the West, a major source of government revenue is direct taxes—those levied on property, wealth, inheritance, and personal and corporate income. Many LDCs lack the administrative or political capacity to raise large amounts of revenue in this way. Nonetheless, direct taxes, especially on affluent individuals and enterprises, increase government revenue substantially. Chapter 15 discusses some of the problems involved in collecting taxes.

Taxes on Luxuries.   Through luxury taxes, government can reduce the resources that would have been used for air conditioners, automobiles, and the like. An excise tax, levied on the production or sale of the individual luxury commodity, is the most common luxury tax. A luxury tax levied only on imports should probably be avoided, since it would stimulate domestic investment in luxury goods.

A word of caution is necessary. Excessively widespread and steep taxes on nonessential goods may either encourage evasion and smuggling or adversely affect incentives—most people will not work harder if they cannot spend the extra income earned.

Sales (or Turnover) Taxes.   From the six decades after the early 1930s, the Soviet Union used high sales taxes on, and government monopoly purchases of, farm goods to capture agricultural saving. Some LDC governments use agricultural marketing boards with monopsony buying power to set low purchase prices for farm goods in order to sell them later on the world market for a substantial profit. However, such action may hamper the growth of agricultural output. Furthermore, the substantial price spread gives rise to smuggling. As an example, in 1975, Ethiopia was the largest exporter of sesame seeds in the world, though it produced little of this crop domestically. Two-thirds of the sesame seeds were smuggled from the Sudan, where the Sudan Oil Seed marketing board paid prices significantly below world prices.[11]

The value-added tax, discussed in Chapter 15, is more uniform and distorts resource allocation less than the sales tax but has the same advantage of potentially capturing saving for government. However, the value-added tax is even more difficult to administer in LDCs than the sales tax.

---

[10]Economists, especially from DCs, should be careful about prescribing expenditure reductions for marriage feasts, religious observances, cathedrals, mosques, and so on, in order to increase productive investment for material goods.

[11]Based on Food and Agriculture Organization of the United Nations, *Trade Yearbook*, Rome, 1952–1980, and calculated by Abdalla Sidahmed, who brought this example to my attention.

A well-designed tax program can help government acquire resources for capital formation, and eliminate obstacles to private saving. However, such improvements in tax machinery are a long, slow process.

DEVELOPING FINANCIAL INTERMEDIARIES

Many people hold physical assets or money as a precaution against a rainy day. Traditionally many LDC savers hold assets in gold, jewels, or foreign bank accounts. These holdings will probably be shifted to stocks, bonds, or short-term saving deposits once people are convinced that a piece of paper represents a legitimate claim to an asset, which can be relatively liquid.

People are more likely to save if financial instruments and institutions exist. **Financial intermediaries** are institutions that serve as middlemen between savers and investors; examples are commercial banks, savings banks, community savings societies, development banks, stock and bond markets, mutual funds, social security, pension and provident funds, insurance funds, and government debt instruments.

These financial intermediaries need not merely be "demand-following"—responding merely to investor and saver demand—but may be "supply-leading," facilitating entrepreneurship and capital formation that would otherwise not occur.[12] As an example, in the last decades of the nineteenth century in Russia, the czar's minister of finance created state banks that actively sought to lend to local and foreign entrepreneurs in heavy industry. And development banks in LDCs, such as the Industrial Credit and Investment Corporation of India established in 1954, have financed both local and foreign private ventures, although these have usually been limited to large-scale enterprises.

INCREASING INVESTMENT OPPORTUNITIES

In many instances, an investment opportunity will generate saving that otherwise would not be made. Government subsidies, tariffs, loans, training facilities, technical and managerial help, and construction of infrastructure may increase saving because prospective entrepreneurs perceive higher investment returns. As an example, a small-town shoemaker whose capital consists of a hammer, pliers, knife, rasp, bench, and other simple tools may begin to save to buy skiving, sewing, tacking, lasting, and pulling-over machines once the government has provided electricity in the area or has set up an industrial extension center to help the shoemaker order machines, design production lines, repair and maintain machines, and manage a labor force.

REDISTRIBUTING INCOME

The government can encourage particular sectors and economic groups by its tax, subsidy, and industrial policies. It can redistribute income to people with a high propensity to save or stimulate output in sectors with the most growth potential and in which saving and taxation are high.

---

[12]Hugh T. Patrick, "Financial Development and Economic Growth in Underdeveloped Countries," *Economic Development and Cultural Change* 14 (January 1966): 174–77.

LOCAL FINANCING OF SOCIAL INVESTMENT

Political integration and national loyalty are often weak in many young LDC nations. In such cases, government frequently lacks the political will and administrative ability essential for expanding tax revenue (see Chapter 15). However, local government can levy taxes that the central government cannot *if* the funds are used to finance schools, roads, or other social overhead projects that clearly benefit local residents. In fact, some new urban services, such as roads, sewers, aqueducts, street lighting, and parks, can be financed by special assessments on those businesses, property owners, and individuals that benefit most from construction.[13]

INFLATIONARY FINANCING

The banking system can provide credit and the treasury can print money to lend to those with high rates of saving and productive investment. Creating new money, although inflationary, increases the proportion of resources available to high savers, so that real capital formation rises. However, this approach is not sustainable, and it is fraught with perils, as Chapter 15 indicates.

CONFISCATION, FOREIGN EXCHANGE CONVERSION RESTRICTIONS, AND INDIGENIZATION DECREES

Expropriating private capital can increase capital formation if foreign companies have repatriated a large proportion of earnings abroad or if domestic investors have dissipated much of their income in luxury consumption or investment in luxury housing or foreign assets. Martin Bronfenbrenner argues that confiscating capital did not kill the "goose that laid the golden egg" in the Soviet Union and China.[14] In fact expropriation seems to have permitted these countries to industrialize faster than most other non-Western economies.

Bronfenbrenner uses an arithmetic model of confiscation. He assumes a plausible quantitative relationship between national income, income shares, and saving in LDCs. He shows that productive investment rates can be significantly increased in societies whose income distributions include high property income (profits, rents, and interest), only a small proportion of which are plowed back into economic development. The model assumes that saving originates only in this sector, which makes up 15 percent of national income. One-third of this property share (or 5 percent of national income) comprises net saving. Of this 5 percent, 2 percent is invested productively. After government confiscates all capital goods without compensation, all property income can be invested. Even if the share of property income declines by one-third, to 10 percent of national income, as a result of less efficient management by government, this 10 percent can be productively invested. Thus the previous rate of productive investment (2 percent) is multiplied by a factor of five.

---

[13]William G. Rhoads and Richard M. Bird, "Financing Urbanization by Benefit Taxation," in Richard M. Bird and Oliver Oldman, eds., *Readings on Taxation in Developing Countries* (Baltimore: Johns Hopkins University Press, 1975), pp 453–63.

[14]Martin Bronfenbrenner, "The Appeal of Confiscation in Economic Development," *Economic Development and Cultural Change* 3 (April 1955): 201–18.

Confiscation runs counter to Western moral premises and economic interest. Yet the temptation to confiscate may be great, especially when the value of existing private assets relative to potential, future private investment is high. However, LDCs are less likely to benefit from the confiscation of foreign capital when (1) its returns are high enough to satisfy both foreign investors and domestic political leaders; (2) the country is highly dependent on future funds and personnel from abroad; (3) when foreign companies provide knowledge and technology not otherwise available; or (4) the country is vulnerable to military, political, or economic retaliation by the foreign power losing from expropriation.

This list suggests that in practice the net benefits from confiscation are often negligible or even negative, especially for small countries. The loss of foreign trade, aid, and investment resulting from international economic sanctions is difficult to replace. And countries such as Cuba, which confiscated foreign enterprise after the 1959 revolution, no longer can benefit from close economic ties with the Soviet Union and other socialist countries. Indeed, even during the period of Soviet patronage, despite some gains, the overall, economic growth of postrevolutionary Cuba was slow, partly because Cuba no longer exported sugar to the United States and other Western countries. Furthermore, once expropriation has occurred, domestic economic mismanagement may ruin whatever benefits may have accrued. Wasteful government spending and public enterprise losses from inefficiency and corruption may severely limit the state's productive investment.

The LDC governments can be selective in confiscation policies. They can exempt companies from countries that, it is expected, may one day provide significant aid and investment or exempt all foreign companies. Moreover capital outflows from foreign companies can be reduced, short of confiscation, by restricting the conversion of profits, dividends, royalties, management fees, and other earnings into foreign currency but at the cost of discouraging foreign investment and reducing allocative efficiency, which dampens exports and import substitutes (see Chapter 16).

Another LDC strategy, short of confiscation, is an **indigenization** decree requiring majority local ownership in certain sectors and reserving other sectors entirely for local enterprises. The primary objectives of indigenization are greater self-reliance and self-sustaining growth.

But even many LDC nationals believe indigenization's prospects are poor, since if complete, it means doing without international aid, capital, imported technology, and imported consumer goods. Zaïre nationalized its largest copper-producing firm, a Belgian concern, GECAMINES (Général de Carriers et des Mines du Zaïre), in 1967. While its dominant position and privileged access to inputs made it financially profitable, the firm used more foreign exchange than it generated, was highly capital intensive, had large excess capacity, and was not well integrated with other Zaïrian sectors.

Zaïre's 1973 nationalization of palm oil changed it from a leading export to a net import by 1977. Government-appointed Zaïrian plantation managers, most of whom lacked interest and competence, systematically depleted the plantations' working capital to rescue their own financial position, hedging against future loss of power.[15]

---

[15]Claude Ake, "The Political Context of Indigenization," in Adebayo Adedeji, ed., *Indigenization of African Economies* (London: Hutchinson University Library for Africa, 1981), pp. 32–41; and Guy Gran, ed., *Zaïre: The Political Economy of Underdevelopment* (New York: Praeger, 1979).

The Nigerian Enterprises Promotion Decrees of 1972, 1977, and 1981 shifted the manufacturing sector from foreign majority ownership in the 1960s to indigenous majority ownership in the mid- and late 1970s, even though some foreigners naturalized, converted equity into debt holdings, or used other loopholes to continue ownership or control. Chibuzo S. A. Ogbuagu argues that indigenization became an instrument for a few civil servants, military rulers, business people, and professionals to amass considerable wealth by manipulating state power. Several top politicians and military officers benefiting from fraud resigned to join business or were forced from government because of conflicts of interest. Ironically an indigenization policy designed partly to reduce foreign concentration created Nigerian monopolies and oligopolies, especially among those with the wealth and influence to obtain capital and government loans to purchase foreign shares.

Additionally Nigerian entrepreneurs still lacked the capital and management and technical skills to replace foreigners effectively in most industries reserved for them by law. As a result, some industries covered under previous indigenization acts were reclassified under the 1981 law to permit more foreign participation. Many Nigerians acquiring shares in indigenized companies were content with dividends paid to them by foreign managers. So most Nigerians increased shares of foreign firms without the enterprising zeal and managerial or technical know-how to take on the higher responsibility of running the economy.[16]

Given the insistence of DC governments and businesses, commercial banks, the World Bank, and other multilateral lending agencies on an IMF "seal of approval" of LDC policies before investing and making loans and grants, the cost of confiscation, foreign exchange restrictions, and indigenization decrees is greater in the 1990s than it was in the 1970s and early 1980s.

Summary

1. A country can increase its new capital formation through domestic saving or by inflows of capital from abroad.

2. The *ICOR* (incremental capital-output ratio) is the ratio of investment to increments in national income. If an economy's *ICOR* is 3.5, a targeted rate of overall growth of 3 percent (2 percent for population growth and 1 percent for growth in output per capita) requires 10.5 percent of national income to be invested. Crude estimates indicate that two-thirds of present LDCs have net investment rates of at least 10 percent, compared to about one-half of LDCs in 1960.

3. The *ICOR* has limitations as a guide for figuring capital requirements because it (1) excludes the cost of inputs other than capital, (2) ignores externalities, (3) does not consider variations in capital utilization, and (4) neglects the timing of costs and benefits.

4. In both DCs and LDCs, the major source of domestic net saving is household saving, with corporate saving second, and government saving third.

5. The English classical economists believed that government interference in capital formation decisions made by private individuals in the market would hurt efficiency and growth.

---

[16]Chibuzo S.A. Ogbuagu, "The Nigerian Indigenization Policy: Nationalism or Pragmatism?" *African Affairs* 82 (April 1983): 241–66; and E. Wayne Nafziger, *Inequality in Africa: Political Elites, Proletariat, Peasants, and the Poor* (Cambridge: Cambridge University Press, 1988), pp. 88–90.

6. Some contemporary leaders and economists in LDCs do not accept the saving decisions of households and businesses arising from the market. The following are some of the measures LDC governments can take to increase saving rates: (1) exploitation of unused capital capacity, (2) moral suasion, (3) increased collection of personal income, corporation, and property taxes, (4) taxes on luxuries, (5) sales taxes, (6) development of financial intermediaries, (7) increased investment opportunities, (8) redistribution of income to people or sectors with high saving or tax rates, (9) increased local financing of social investment, (10) inflationary financing for high savers, (11) restrictions on converting profits, dividends, royalties, management fees, and other earnings into foreign currency, (12) indigenizing local ownership, and (13) confiscation of private capital. Needless to say, governments must consider the costs associated with any one of these measures.

Terms to Review

- capital import
- investment
- investment rate
- gross investment
- net investment
- depreciation

- incremental capital-output ratio (ICOR)
- value added
- absorptive capacity
- financial intermediaries
- indigenization

Questions to Discuss

1. Using national income equations, show two ways of explaining capital inflow from abroad.
2. Use the equation stating economic growth equals investment rate divided by the incremental capital-output ratio to explain why Walter Rostow's theory of economic growth emphasizes a sharp increase in investment rate from 5 percent to over 10 percent of national income. What are some criticisms of Rostow's emphasis on this increased investment rate?
3. What is the incremental capital-output ratio (*ICOR*)? What problems occur when using *ICORs* to estimate capital requirements?
4. What measures can LDC governments take to increase net capital formation as a percentage of national income?
5. How useful is the Lewis model in explaining early growth in capital formation in developing countries?
6. How adequate is the market for making saving decisions in LDCs?
7. Is there much potential for using previously idle resources to increase LDC capital formation rates?
8. How can LDCs improve the tax system to increase saving?
9. Evaluate foreign exchange conversion restrictions, indigenization decrees, and confiscation of foreign-owned private capital as measures for increasing productive capital formation.

Guide to Readings

The annual *World Development Report* of the World Bank has information on LDC saving and investment rates. Yotopoulos and Nugent, pp. 393–95 (note 32, Chapter 11), and V. R. Panchamukhi, *Capital Formation and Output in the Third World* (New Delhi, Radiant, 1986), critically review *ICORs* and growth.

Adelman and Enke (guide to Chapter 5) discuss the classical approach to saving decisions. The Lewis-Fei-Ranis model (Chapter 5) analyzes the increase in saving in a dual economy. Bruton, pp. 121–73 (note 9) is a good source for ideas on how to raise rates of capital formation in LDCs.

Monetary, Fiscal, and Incomes Policy, and Inflation

Monetary policy affects the supply of money (basically currency plus commercial bank demand deposits) and the rate of interest. **Fiscal policy** includes the rate of taxation and level of government spending. **Incomes policy** consist of anti-inflation measures that depend on income and price limitations, such as moderated wage increases.

The DC governments use monetary and fiscal policies to achieve goals for output and employment growth and price stability. Thus during a recession, with slow or negative growth, high unemployment, and surplus capital capacity, these governments reduce interest rates, expand bank credit, decrease tax rates, and increase government spending to expand aggregate spending and accelerate growth. On the other hand, DC governments are likely to respond to a high rate of inflation (general price increase) with increased interest rates, a contraction of bank credit, higher tax rates, decreased government expenditures, and perhaps even wage-price controls in order to reduce total spending.

The DCs do not often attain their macroeconomic goals because of ineffective monetary and fiscal tools, political pressures, or contradictory goals. Thus we have the quandary during **stagflation** or inflationary recession (a frequent economic malady in the West during the 1970s and 1980s) of whether to increase aggregate spending to eliminate the recession or decrease spending to reduce inflation.

Countries may use incomes policy—wage and price guidelines, controls, or indexation, and exchange-rate fixing in the short run and stabilization in the medium-run—with moderate inflation (positive inflation, say, no more than 100 percent annually) and high inflation (for example, more than 5.9 percent monthly or 100-percent yearly price increase), as in Nicaragua, Peru, and Bolivia (1980–92), Argentina (1980–91), Brazil (1980–93), Poland (1982, 1990), Mexico (1983, 1986), Russia (1992–94), Ukraine, Kazakhstan, Romania, and Bulgaria (the early 1990s). According to Rudiger Dornbusch, **hyperinflation,** which occurred in postwar Germany, Austria, Hungary, Russia, and Poland in the early 1920s; postwar China, Greece, and Hungary in the mid- to late 1940s; and Yugoslavia (the late 1980s and early 1990s), Russia (1992–93), and Brazil (1992–93), corresponds roughly to an inflation of 20 percent monthly or 792 percent annually.[1]

Scope of the Chapter

The LDCs encounter even greater limitations than DCs in using monetary and fiscal policies to achieve macroeconomic goals. The first section of this chapter discusses some of the limitations of monetary policy in LDCs. Second we look at the low tax rates in LDCs. The third section examines tax policy goals, including limitations LDCs face in using various taxes. Political constraints on implementing tax policies are mentioned in the fourth section. A fifth part on government expenditures indicates the limits of using spending policies to stabilize income and prices. The sixth section, on the problem of inflation, analyzes accelerated worldwide inflation since 1970; the demand-pull, cost-push, ratchet, structural, expectational, political, and monetary explanations for inflation; the benefits and costs of inflation; and the relationship between inflation and growth.

Limitations of Monetary Policy

In DCs central banks (like the Bank of England or the U.S. Federal Reserve) can increase the supply of money by buying government bonds, lowering the interest rate charged commercial banks, and reducing these banks' required ratio of reserves to demand deposits. The increased money supply and decreased interest rate should increase investment spending and raise output and employment during recession. And a decreased money supply should curtail investment, so that inflation is reduced.

The banking system, often limited in its ability to regulate the money supply to influence output and prices in DCs, is even more ineffective in LDCs. Usually the money market in developing countries is externally dependent, poorly organized, fragmented, and cartelized (more on this last point when we discuss financial repression later in the chapter).

1. Many of the major commercial banks in LDCs are branches of large private banks in DCs, such as Citicorp or Barclay's Bank. Their orientation is external: They are concerned with profits in dollars, pound sterling, or other convertible currency, not rupees, nairas, pesos, and other currencies that cannot be exchanged on the world market.
2. Many LDCs are so dependent on international transactions that they must limit the banking system's local expansion of the money supply to some multiple of foreign currency held by the central bank. Thus the government cannot always control the money supply because of the variability of foreign exchange assets.
3. The LDC central banks do not have much influence on the amount of bank deposits. They generally make few loans to commercial banks. Furthermore, since securities markets are usually not well developed in LDCs, the central bank usually buys and sells few bonds on the open market.

---

[1]Rudiger Dornbusch, *Stabilization, Debt, and Reform: Policy Analysis for Developing Countries* (Englewood Cliffs, N.J.: Prentice Hall, 1993), pp. 1, 13–29; and Jeffrey D. Sachs and Felipe Larrain B., *Macroeconomics in the Global Economy* (Englewood Cliffs, NJ: Prentice Hall, 1993), pp. 729–39.

4. Commercial banks generally restrict their loans to large and medium enterprises in modern manufacturing, mining, power, transport, construction, and plantation agriculture. Small traders, artisans, and farmers obtain most of their funds from close relatives or borrow at exorbitant interest rates from local money lenders and landlords. Thus LDC banking systems have less influence than DCs on the interest rate, level of investment, and aggregate output.

5. Demand deposits (checking accounts) as a percentage of the total money supply are generally lower in LDCs than DCs. In the United States, they make up three-fourths of the total money supply, but in most developing countries, the figure is less than half. Checks are not widely accepted for payment in LDCs. Generally commercial banks in LDCs control a smaller share of the money supply than in DCs.[2]

6. The links between interest rate, investment, and output assumed in DCs are questionable in LDCs. Investment is not very sensitive to the interest rate charged by commercial banks, partly because a lot of money is lent by money-lenders, landlords, relatives, and others outside the banks. Furthermore, because of supply limitations, increases in investment demand may result in inflation rather than expanded real output. The LDCs often face these limitations at far less than full employment because of poor management, monopolistic restraints, bureaucratic delay, and the lack of essential inputs (resulting from licensing restrictions on foreign exchange or domestic materials).

Tax Ratios and GNP Per Capita

We have seen the monetary policy limitations in LDCs. Fiscal policy—taxation and government spending—comprises another tool for controlling income, employment, and prices. Tax policy also has other purposes—raising funds for public spending being the most obvious one. The next four sections examine changes in tax revenues as an economy develops, factors to be considered in formulating tax policy, political obstacles to tax collections, and patterns of government spending in DCs and LDCs.

The concept of systematic state intervention to stimulate economic development has been a major part of the ideology of many developing countries. Yet perhaps surprisingly, taxes as a percentage of GNP in LDCs are generally less than in DCs. According to Table 15–1, tax revenue as a percentage of GNP is 17.9 percent for developing countries and 27.5 percent for developed countries.[3]

Among the sample of LDCs, the tax ratio is 16.3 percent for low-income countries and 21.5 percent for middle-income countries. If we exclude Eastern Europe, percentages range from a high of 59.4 percent for Botswana, with substantial diamond and gold revenues in a sparsely populated country (Portugal with 37.9 percent and Israel, technically a high-income country 37.7 percent are next) to a

---

[2]U Tun Wai, "Interest Rates in the Organized Money Markets of Underdeveloped Countries," *International Monetary Fund Staff Papers* 5 (August 1956): 249–78, and U Tun Wai, "Interest Rates Outside the Organized Money Markets of Underdeveloped Countries," *International Monetary Fund Staff Papers* 6 (November 1957): 80–125; excerpts of which are reprinted in Gerald M. Meier, *Leading Issues in Economic Development* (New York: Oxford University Press, 1976), pp. 299–305.

[3]Tax revenues include contributions. The tax ratios in the study, which adjusts "off-budget" items to improve the ratios' comparability, are at least rough indicators of the true rankings.

TABLE 15-1   Central Government Current Revenue by Revenue Source and Current Revenue as Percentage of GNP, 1992 (Classified by Country Income Categories)

	Source of Revenue (by Percentage)						
	Income, Profit, Capital Gains	*Social Security*	*Goods and Services*	*International Trade and Transactions*	*Other[b]*	*Nontax Revenue[7]*	*Revenue as Percentage of GNP*
Low-income countries	26.9	0.2	32.4	20.7	1.1	18.7	16.3
Middle-income countries	26.9	13.3	32.0	8.3	1.0	18.5	21.5
High-income countries	41.1	32.6	14.1	1.2	2.5	8.5	27.5

Note: Percentages are based on countries with information. Forty percent had data among low-income countries, 48 percent among middle-income countries, and 95 percent among high-income countries. Countries in each country income category are weighted by population.

[a]*Other taxes* include employers' payroll or labor taxes, taxes on property, and taxes not allocated to other categories.

[b]Nontax revenue comprise receipts that are not a compulsory nonrepayable for public purposes, such as fines, administrative fees, or entrepreneurial income from government ownership of property. Proceeds of grants and borrowing, funds arising from the repayment of previous lending by governments, incurrence of liabilities, and proceeds from the sale of capital assets are not included. Ibid., pp. 236–37.

Source: World Bank, *World Development Report, 1994* (New York: Oxford University Press, 1994), pp. 162–63, 182–83.

low of 9.7 percent for El Salvador and Myanmar (Burma), 9.6 percent for Nepal, and 9.1 percent for each Madagascar and Chad, and perhaps even lower for countries such as Uganda (where government ceased to operate in many areas during a civil war in the early 1980s) and Ghana, without reliable statistics. Data also indicate that the tax ratio for a given country increases with economic growth.[4]

The increase in tax ratio with GNP per capita is a reflection of both demand and supply factors—demand for **social goods** (collective goods like education, highways, sewerage, flood control, and national defense) and the capacity to levy and pay taxes.

Wagner's law, named for the nineteenth century German economist Adolph Wagner, states that as real GNP per capita rises, people demand relatively more social goods and relatively fewer private goods. A poor country spends a high percentage of its income on food, clothing, shelter, and other essential consumer goods. After these needs have been largely fulfilled, an increased proportion of additional spending is for social goods.[5]

---

[4]Vito Tanzi, "Quantitative Characteristics of the Tax Systems of Developing Countries," in David Newbery and Nicholas Stern, eds., *The Theory of Taxation for Developing Countries* (New York: Oxford University Press, 1987), pp. 205–41; David B. Perry, "International Tax Comparisons," *Canadian Tax Journal* 28 (January-February 1980): 89–93; Alan A. Tait, Wilfred L. M. Gratz, and Barry J. Eichengreen, "International Comparisons of Taxation for Selected Developing Countries, 1972–76," *International Monetary Fund Staff Papers* 26 (March 1979): 123–56; and Raja J. Chelliah, Hessel J. Baas, and Margaret R. Kelly, "Tax Ratios and Tax Effort in Developing Countries, 1969–71," *International Monetary Fund Staff Papers* 22 (March 1975): 187–205. See Table 15–1.

[5]Adolph Wagner, "Three Extracts on Public Finance," in Richard A. Musgrave and Alan Peacock, eds., *Classics in the Theory of Public Finance* (New York: Macmillan, 1958), pp. 1–16. Wagner wrote in the 1880s.

Goals of Tax Policy

The most important taxation goal in LDCs is to mobilize resources for public expenditure. According to the IMF, the amount of these resources is determined by GNP per capita, the share of the mining sector in GNP, the share of exports in GNP, and tax policy. Part of this section looks at how tax policies affect public spending. In addition we consider the impact of taxes on stability of income and prices. However, achieving these crucial taxation goals must be viewed in light of other goals, such as improved income distribution, efficient resource allocation, increased capital and enterprise, and administrative feasibility. The LDC governments must consider all of these goals when designing tax schemes to achieve rapid economic growth, to improve the lot of the poor, and to stabilize prices.

MOBILIZING RESOURCES
FOR PUBLIC EXPENDITURE

A major reason that tax ratios increase with GNP per capita is that richer countries rely more heavily on taxes with greater elasticity (that is, percentage change in taxation/percentage change in GNP). An **elastic tax,** whose coefficient exceeds one, rises more rapidly than GNP. **Direct taxes**—primarily property, wealth, inheritance, and income taxes (such as personal and corporate taxes)—are generally more elastic than **indirect taxes** such as import, export, turnover, sales, value-added, and excise taxes (except for sales or excise taxes on goods purchased mostly by high-income groups).

Direct taxes account for 29.2 percent of the revenue sources in LDCs and 47.9 percent in DCs (where revenue means central government current revenue, a concept that understates these and subsequent figures when compared to *all* revenue from *all* levels of government). The leading direct taxes, the corporate income and personal taxes and capital gains taxes, comprise 26.9 percent of total LDC revenue sources compared to 41.1 percent of DC sources. Accordingly the average ratio of direct taxes to GNP is 4.8 percent in low-income countries, 6.3 percent in middle-income countries, and 10.4 percent in high-income countries. While data are lacking, a major problem of economies in transition to a market economy, such as Russia and China, is to devise a tax system that will yield the revenue that was raised previously from the turnover tax (Chapter 14) and surpluses from government enterprises that set monopoly prices.

The major source of tax for LDCs is international trade, an indirect tax comprising 16.9 percent of the total—with import duties about 80–85 percent of trade taxes and the remainder export duties. Other important indirect taxes—excise, sales, value-added, and other taxes on production and internal transactions—account for 32.4 percent of the total (see Table 15–1).

In recent decades, a number of LDCs have introduced the **value-added tax**, a tax on the difference between the sales of a firm and its purchases from other firms. The appeals of the value-added tax are: simplicity, uniformity, the generation of buoyant revenues, and the enabling of a gradual lowering of other tax rates throughout the system (for example, the lowering or elimination of the distortions of a **cascade tax**). One example of a cascade is the simplest sales tax that takes a straightforward percentage of all business turnover, so that tax on tax occurs as a taxed product passes from manufacturer to wholesaler to retailer.[6]

Although personal income taxes rarely comprise more than 7 percent of GNP in LDCs, they often account for 7 to 10 percent of GNP in the DCs. In most DCs, the income tax structure is **progressive,** which means that people with higher incomes pay a higher percentage of income in taxes. For example, in 1988, a married couple with two children in the United States earning $12,500 would pay no tax; one earning $25,000 would pay $1,826 (7.3 percent); one earning $50,000, $8,553 (17.1 percent); one earning $100,000, $19,280 (19.9 percent); and one earning $200,000, $54,314 (27.2 percent). Many people feel the progressive tax is just—that those with higher incomes should bear a larger tax burden, since they have a much greater ability to pay. Moreover, a progressive income tax has an elasticity greater than one, so that a rising GNP pushes taxpayers into higher tax brackets. Let us examine the personal income tax and others in light of overall tax policy goals before discussing some of the administrative and political reasons why LDCs rely so little on the individual income tax.

STABILITY OF INCOME AND PRICES

As we said earlier, developed countries use fiscal and monetary policies to achieve macroeconomic goals of economic growth, employment, and price changes. When there is high unemployment, the government can increase spending and decrease taxes to increase aggregate demand and employment. In times of inflation, government can reduce spending and increase taxes to decrease aggregate demand and diminish price rises.

At times fiscal policy has a limited effect in stabilizing employment and prices in DCs, and not surprisingly, it is even less effective in LDCs. There are several reasons for this ineffectiveness.

First, as indicated above, tax receipts as a share of GNP in LDCs are typically smaller than in DCs.

Second, LDCs, relying more on indirect taxes (leaving aside for now the value-added tax), have less control than DCs over the amount of taxes they can raise. Personal and corporate income taxes can generally not be used to stabilize aggregate spending, since they comprise only 5.1 percent of GNP in LDCs. Furthermore LDC indirect taxes are subject to wide variation—especially taxes on international trade, which are frequently affected by sharp fluctuations in volume and price (see Chapter 4). In the 1970s, Zaïre raised about four-fifths of its revenue from export taxes. However, when the price of its leading export, copper, fell by 40 percent from 1974 to 1975, export receipts dropped 40 percent, too, resulting in a 36-percent decline in export tax revenue and a 19-percent decline in total government revenue.[7]

Third, prices and unemployment are not so sensitive to fiscal policy in LDCs as in DCs. Chapter 9 details (and we reiterate here) why expansionary fiscal policies (increased government spending and decreased tax rates) may have only a

---

[6]Alan A. Tait, *Value Added Tax: International Practice and Problems* (Washington, D.C.: International Monetary Fund, 1988), pp. 4–15, 194–97; and Murray L. Weidenbaum and Ernest S. Christian, Jr., "Shifting to Consumption as a Federal Tax Base: An Overview," in Murray L. Weidenbaum, David G. Raboy, and Ernest S. Christian, Jr., *The Value-Added Tax: Orthodoxy and New Thinking* (Boston: Kluwer Academic Publishers, 1989), pp. 1–16.

[7]World Bank, *World Tables, 1980* (Baltimore: Johns Hopkins University Press, 1980).

limited effect in reducing unemployment in LDCs: (1) There are major supply limitations, such as shortages of skills, infrastructure, and efficient markets; (2) creating urban jobs through expanded demand may result in more people leaving rural areas; (3) employment may not rise with output because of factor price distortions or unsuitable technology; and (4) government may set unrealistically high wages for educated workers. On the other side of the coin, although contractionary fiscal policies may reduce Keynesian demand-pull inflation, they are not likely to reduce cost-push, ratchet, and structural inflation (discussed below).

Generally tax policy, as monetary policy, is a very limited tool for achieving income and price stability.

IMPROVING INCOME DISTRIBUTION

The progressive personal income tax takes a larger proportion of income from people in upper-income brackets and a smaller proportion from people in lower-income brackets. Thus income distribution after taxes is supposed to be less unequal than before taxes.

Excise taxes or high import tariffs on luxury items redistribute income from higher-income to lower-income groups. These taxes are especially attractive when the income would otherwise be spent on lavish living and luxury imports.

The broad-based **sales tax** is usually levied as a fixed percentage of the price of retail sales. The sales tax, used widely by state and local governments in the United States, and the value-added tax, a major tax source of the European Union, is usually **regressive,** in that people with lower incomes pay a larger percentage of income in taxes. Since the poor save a smaller proportion of income than the rich, a LDC government wanting to use the tax system to reduce income inequality should not rely much on a value-added or general sales tax. However, the regressive feature of the tax can be modified by exempting basic consumer goods, such as food and medicine. But this modification is often opposed by treasury officials because it reduces revenues substantially and is costlier to administer.

EFFICIENCY OF RESOURCE ALLOCATION

One goal of a tax system is to encourage efficient use of resources or at least to minimize inefficiencies. Export taxes reduce the output of goods whose prices are determined on world markets. Such taxes shift resources from export to domestic production with a consequent loss of efficiency and foreign exchange earnings.[8]

Import duties raise the price of inputs and capital goods needed for agricultural and industrial exports and domestic goods. The price of locally produced goods requiring imported inputs increases, altering consumer choice.

An economy maximizes output and optimizes resource efficiency when price equals marginal cost. If government raises revenue from indirect taxes, price cannot equal marginal cost in all industries. However, indirect taxes can be levied at uniform rates on all final goods and exemptions and differential rates applied only to improve income distribution or encourage rapidly growing sectors. In this way, price will be proportional to marginal costs in all industries, and a minimum distortion of consumer choice will occur. Essentially a sales tax distorts efficiency least if it is broad based; that is, if it applies to the final sale of producer goods as

---

[8]John F. Due and Ann F. Friedlaender, *Government Finance: Economics of the Public Sector* (Homewood, Ill.: Irwin, 1981), p. 548.

well as to consumer goods and services. A uniform tax rate based on value added has a similar effect to the sales tax on resource allocation and tax incidence, but it is usually more difficult for LDC governments to administer.[9]

INCREASING CAPITAL AND ENTERPRISE

The LDC governments can mobilize saving through direct taxes (on personal income, corporate profits, and property), taxes on luxury items, and sales and value-added taxes. These taxes result in a higher rate of capital formation if government has a higher investment rate than the people taxed. Moreover the state can use taxes and subsidies to redistribute output to sectors with high growth potential and to individuals with a high propensity to save (see Chapter 14).

The government can use tax policy to encourage domestic and foreign entrepreneurship. Tax revenues can be used for transport, power, and technical training to create external economies for private investment. Government development banks, development corporations, and loans boards can lend capital to private entrepreneurs. **Fiscal incentives** to attract business, especially from abroad, include tax holidays (for the first few years of operation), income averaging (where losses in one year can be offset against profits in another), accelerated depreciation, import duty relief, lower tax rates for reinvested business profits, and preferred purchases through government departments. The LDC governments may limit these incentives to enterprises and sectors that are of high priority in their development plan.

Surveys suggest that fiscal incentives have, at best, only a slight effect on the amount of investment. Moreover subsidized investment may crowd out existing firms or firms that might have been willing to invest without subsidy. Using tax incentives successfully requires careful economic planning, skillfully structuring taxes, competent tax administration, quick decisions on applications, and no political favoritism.[10]

Is there a conflict between the redistributive effect of the progressive income tax and increased capital accumulation? As we indicated in Chapter 14, profits are a major source of new capital formation. Since for the successful business person, expansion takes precedence over the desire for higher consumption, taxes on profits affect consumption far more than saving. Nicholas Kaldor even argues that progressive taxation, by curbing luxury spending that distorts the investment pattern, may even stimulate capital accumulation. Before progressive taxation, too much capital is invested in industries catering to the rich. After taxation some investment shifts from luxury production to necessities.[11] Thus while there are conflicts between income redistribution and capital accumulation, they are probably less than is commonly believed in LDCs.

---

[9]Charles E. McLure, Jr., "The Proper Use of Indirect Taxation," in Richard M. Bird and Oliver Oldman, eds., *Readings on Taxation in Developing Countries* (Baltimore: Johns Hopkins University Press, 1975), pp. 339–49. See also John F. Due, "Value-Added Taxation in Developing Economies," in N. T. Wang, ed., *Taxation and Development* (New York: Praeger, 1976), pp. 164–86.

[10]S. M. S. Shah and J. F. J. Toye, "Fiscal Incentives for Firms in Some Developing Countries: Survey and Critique," in J. F. J. Toye, ed., *Taxation and Economic Development* (London: Frank Cass, 1978), pp. 269–96; and Walter W. Heller, "Fiscal Policies for Underdeveloped Countries," in Richard M. Bird and Oliver Oldman, eds., *Readings on Taxation in Developing Countries* (Baltimore: Johns Hopkins University Press, 1975), pp. 5–28.

[11]Nicholas Kaldor, "Will Underdeveloped Countries Learn to Tax?" in Richard M. Bird and Oliver Oldman, eds., *Readings on Taxation in Developing Countries* (Baltimore: Johns Hopkins University Press, 1975), p. 33.

According to Alberto Alesina and Dani Rodrik, the conflict does not occur because lower disposable (after-tax) income inequality causes lower savings, but because of pressures for redistribution by the majority of the population when incomes and wealth are highly unequal. Alesina and Rodik contend that any conflict results from the fact that a greater inequality of wealth and income contributes to increased political pressures for redistribution and higher rates of taxation on holders of capital and land, and the ensuing lower rates of growth.[12]

ADMINISTRATIVE FEASIBILITY

Some developed countries use income taxes (especially the progressive personal tax) to mobilize large amounts of resources for public expenditures, improve income distribution, stabilize income and prices, and prevent inefficient allocation that comes from a heavy reliance on indirect taxes. However, few LDCs rely much on income taxes, because they have trouble administering them.[13]

The following conditions must be met if income tax is to become a major revenue source for a country: (1) existence of a predominantly money economy, (2) a high standard of literacy among taxpayers, (3) widespread use of accounting records honestly and reliably maintained, (4) a large degree of voluntary taxpayer compliance, and (5) honest and efficient administration. Even DCs, to say nothing of LDCs, have trouble fulfilling these conditions.[14] Tanzania under President Julius K. Nyerere from 1974 to 1985, was probably the only African country that used its tax system to redistribute income to low-income classes.

Several LDCs have used value-added taxes (VAT) to raise a substantial fraction of revenues. Chile and South Korea both began using the value-added tax in the 1970s; Chile raises almost 40 percent and South Korea about 25 percent of their tax revenues from the VAT. Colombia, Argentina, Uruguay, Mexico, Peru, Haiti, Honduras, Turkey, and Indonesia mobilize one-sixth to one-fourth of their tax moneys from VAT. Stanford University's Ronald McKinnon recommends that former socialist countries such as Russia, that have relied heavily on enterprise taxes, adopt the VAT. The value-added tax, which is less difficult to administer, permits the central government to tax all forms of enterprise income uniformly.[15]

The most frequently used approach for levying the VAT is the subtractive-indirect (the invoice and credit) method. Under this approach, the firm issues invoices for all taxable transactions, using these invoices to compute the tax on total sales. But the firm is given credit for the VAT paid by its suppliers. To a substantial

---

[12]Alberto Alesina and Dani Rodrik, "Distributive Politics and Economic Growth," *Quarterly Journal of Economics* 109 (May 1994): 465–90.

[13]Given our consciousness concerning how much the U.S. Internal Revenue Service and the Canadian personal income tax service emphasize tax enforcement and penalties, many students from the U.S. and Canada are surprised to learn that the two countries have some of the highest rates of personal income tax compliance in the world.

[14]Richard Goode, "Personal Income Tax in Latin America," in Joint Tax Program, Organization of American States/Inter-American Development Bank/Economic Commission for Latin America, *Fiscal Policy for Economic Growth in Latin America* (Baltimore: Johns Hopkins University Press, 1962), pp. 157–71; and Vito Tanzi, "Personal Income Taxation in Latin America: Obstacles and Possibilities," *National Tax Journal* 19 (June 1966): 156–62.

[15]Ronald I. McKinnon, *The Order of Economic Liberalization: Financial Control in the Transition to a Market Economy* (Baltimore: Johns Hopkins University Press, 1993), pp. 134–35, who, however, recognizes that Russian socialist enterprises have not established the accounting conventions for making distinctions between profits, interest, rents, wages, and salaries.

degree, the VAT is self-enforcing, as the firm has an incentive to present invoices to subtract the VAT on purchases from the VAT on sales; these invoices provide a check on VAT payments at earlier stages. In Turkey, an additional cross-match is by consumers, who with receipts for purchases, can offset a proportion of the VAT paid on their retail purchases against their income-tax liability.[16]

Taxes on international trade are the major source of tax revenue in LDCs, especially for low-income countries with poor administrative capacity. Import duties can restrict luxury goods consumption, which reduces saving and drains foreign exchange.[17] However, government can exempt the import of capital goods and other inputs needed for the development process. Export taxes, on the other hand, can substitute for income taxes on (commercial) farmers, as, for example, in Ghana.

Exports and imports usually pass through a limited number of ports and border crossings. A relatively small administrative staff can measure volume and value and collect revenue. To be sure, traders may underinvoice goods or seek favors or concessions from customs officials. However, these problems are not so great as those encountered with an income, sales, or value-added tax.

The LDCs may be able to administer excise taxes if the number of producers is small. Rates are usually specific rather than percentage of value to simplify collection. The principal excises in LDCs, just as in DCs, are motor fuel (often for road finance), cigarettes, beer, and liquor. However, as the economy develops, introducing more excise taxes complicates administration and discriminates against consumers of taxed items.

The inadequacies of segmented excise taxes have led a number of developing countries to introduce sales taxes. In the poorest countries, using a retail tax is impossible. Enumerating, let alone collecting from, the numerous, very small, uneducated peddlers, traders, and shopkeepers is the major difficulty. Thus a number of African countries have levied a sales tax on manufacturers, where numbers are fewer and control is easier. But this tax discriminates between products, favors imports, and interferes with the allocation of functions by production stage. Other countries restrict the sales tax to large retail firms, which also introduces distortions and inequities.[18]

The value-added tax faces similar administrative problems, especially among the numerous retailers in low-income countries. The cost of compelling compliance among these retailers, who may pay for their purchases out of the till and keep no records of cash transactions, are substantial relative to the tax collected. LDCs also face pressures for multiple rates (lower rates on essential goods like food, higher rates on luxury goods, differential geographical rates) and exemptions (for small traders, and for activities in the public interest such as postal services, hospitals, medical and dental care, schools, cultural activities, and noncommercial radio and television). Foreign trade adds a further complication. Many LDCs fully rebate VAT paid in the exporter's domestic market where the

---

[16]Alan A. Tait, *Value Added Tax: International Practice and Problems* (Washington, D.C.: International Monetary Fund, 1988); and Murray L. Weidenbaum and Ernest S. Christian, Jr., "Shifting to Consumption as a Federal Tax Base: An Overview," in Murray L. Weidenbaum, David G. Raboy, and Ernest S. Christian, Jr., *The Value-Added Tax: Orthodoxy and New Thinking* (Boston: Kluwer Academic Publishers, 1989), pp. 1–16.

[17]Note, however, some of the unintended side effects of a tax on luxury items (Chapter 18).

[18]John F. Due and Ann F. Friedlaender, *Government Finance: Economics of the Public Sector* (Homewood, Ill.: Irwin, 1981), pp. 539–48.

importing country also levies VAT rates. Finally, few poor countries have the capability to administer, collect, audit, monitor, and hear appeals from value-added taxpayers and evaders.[19]

Political Constraints to Tax Policy

Politics may be as obstructive as administration in using direct taxes in LDCs. Property owners and the upper classes often successfully oppose a progressive income tax or sizable property tax, introduce tax loopholes beneficial to them, or evade tax payments without penalty.

The United States has a reputation for less legal tax avoidance and illegal evasion than most of the third world. However, a Brookings Institution study indicates that even in the United States taxes as a percentage of income remain nearly constant for virtually all income levels because of tax loopholes and the effect of indirect taxes. Furthermore, the U.S. Internal Revenue Service assumes that the average U.S. citizen is rather resistant to taxation. Tax evasion is low because of the high probability and serious consequences of being caught.[20]

Tax collection in an LDC depends not only on the appropriate tax legislation, but also, more importantly, on administrative capability and political will. A noted tax authority wrote that

> In many underdeveloped countries the low revenue yield of taxation can only be attributed to the fact that the tax provisions are not properly enforced, either on account of the inability of the administration to cope with them, or on account of straightforward corruption. No system of tax laws, however carefully conceived, is proof against collusion between the tax administrators and the taxpayers; an efficient administration consisting of persons of high integrity is usually the most important requirement for obtaining maximum revenue, and exploiting fully the taxation potential of a country.[21]

Expenditure Policy

Many Afro-Asian leaders after independence were convinced that colonialism meant slow economic growth, largely as the result of laissez-faire capitalism (implying a minimum of government interference into the economy). These leaders focused populist and anti-imperialist sentiments in these countries into an ideol-

---

[19]VAT also has an immediate inflationary effect on the economy. Alan A. Tait, *Value Added Tax: International Practice and Problems* (Washington, D.C.: International Monetary Fund, 1988); and Murray L. Weidenbaum and Ernest S. Christian, Jr., "Shifting to Consumption as a Federal Tax Base: An Overview," in Murray L. Weidenbaum, David G. Raboy, and Ernest S. Christian, Jr., *The Value-Added Tax: Orthodoxy and New Thinking* (Boston: Kluwer Academic Publishers, 1989), pp. 1–16.

[20]Joseph A. Pechman and Benjamin A. Okner, *Who Bears the Tax Burden?* (Washington, D.C.: Brookings Institution, 1974); and Vito Tanzi, "Personal Income Taxation in Latin America," in Richard M. Bird and Oliver Oldman, eds., *Readings On Taxation in Developing Countries: Obstacles and Possibilities* (Baltimore: Johns Hopkins University Press, 1975), pp. 234–36.

[21]Nicholas Kaldor, "Taxation for Economic Development," *Journal of Modern African Studies* 1 (May 1963): 23.

ogy of African or Asian socialism. This socialism, frequently misunderstood by outsiders, usually did not imply that government was to own a majority of land and capital. Nor did it mean that tax revenue was a large proportion of GNP. As we indicated earlier, Wagner's law of demand and administrative limits on tax collections restricted the social goods sector in most of these economies.

What socialism in the third world often meant was systematic planning (see Chapter 19) by the state to assure a minimum economic welfare for all its citizens. Yet World Bank statistics indicate that LDC governments spend a relatively small percentage of GNP on health, welfare, social security, and housing (in low-income countries, the 1992 expenditures on these categories were 1.2 percent of GNP and 6.7 percent of the central government budget; in middle-income countries, 5.8 percent of GNP and 24.5 percent of the budget; and in high-income countries, 15.6 percent of GNP and 49.6 percent of the budget), and a relatively large share on education, electricity, gas, water, transport, communication, and training programs (see Table 15–2). Doubtless in countries where a large part of the population is poor, welfare and social security payments to bring everyone above the poverty line would not only undermine work incentives but would also be prohibitively expensive (see Chapter 6). Moreover as we have said before, infrastructure and education are important investments creating external economies in early stages of development.[22]

TABLE 15–2 Central Government Current Expenditure by Expenditure Categories and Current Expenditure as Percentage of GNP, 1992 (Classified by Country Income Categories)

	Percentage of Expenditure						
	Defense	*Education*	*Health*	*Housing, Amenities, Social Security, and Welfare*	*Economic Services[b]*	*Other[a]*	*Total Expenditure as Percentage of GNP[c]*
Low-income countries	13.8	4.8	2.1	4.6	21.2	53.5	18.5
Middle-income countries	9.5	13.2	5.1	19.4	16.0	36.8	23.8
High-income countries	14.9	5.0	14.2	35.4	6.8	23.7	31.6

Note: Percentages are based on countries with information. Forty percent had data among low-income countries, 48 percent among middle-income countries, and 95 percent among high-income countries. Countries in each country income category are weighted by population.

[a]*Other* covers general public services, interest payments, and items not included elsewhere; for some economies *other* also includes amounts that could not be allocated to other components, or adjustments from accrual to cash accounts. World Bank, *World Development Report, 1994* (New York: Oxford University Press, 1994), p. 236.

[b]*Economic services* comprise expenditure associated with the regulation, support, and more efficient operation of business, economic development, redress of regional imbalances, and creation of employment opportunities. Activities include research, trade promotion, geological surveys, and inspection and regulation of particular industry groups. Ibid., p. 236.

[c]Excludes consumption expenditure by state and local governments. Central government expenditure includes government's gross domestic investment and transfer payments. Ibid., p. 236.

Source: World Bank, *World Development Report, 1994* (New York: Oxford University Press, 1994), pp. 162–63, 180–81.

---

[22]Richard A. Musgrave and Peggy B. Musgrave, *Public Finance in Theory and Practice* (New York: McGraw-Hill, 1980), p. 813.

Military expenditures have a high foregone cost in resources for social programs in LDCs. In 1990–92, low-income countries spent 2.4 percent of GNP on defense (Ethiopia 12.4 percent and Mozambique, then fighting rebels supported by white-ruled South African-supported rebels, 11.9 percent[23]), an amount in excess of spending for health, education, housing, welfare, amenities, and social security. Low-income countries spent 10.4 percent of import expenditures on armaments, and have 40 percent more armed forces (generally with above-average education) than teachers.[24]

Can government vary spending to regulate income, employment, and prices? Sound investment projects in education, power, transport, and communication are difficult to prepare and require a long lead time. Furthermore as indicated, macroeconomic variables are not so sensitive to demand management in LDCs as in DCs. Spending policy, just as monetary and tax policies, is a limited instrument for influencing economic growth and price stability.

Inflation

ACCELERATED LDC INFLATION SINCE 1970

Inflation is the rate of increase in the general level of prices, measured by the **consumer price index (CPI)**, the average price of a basket of goods and services consumed by a representative household, or by the **GDP deflator**, which compares the average price of the GDP basket today and in a base period. During the 1950s and the 1960s, economists considered inflation as a phenomenon affecting individual countries in isolation. To be sure, inflation in Latin America was 22 percent per year from 1960 to 1970. But if we exclude the 41 percent annual inflation rate of the contiguous region of Brazil-Uruguay-Argentina-Chile, Latin America's annual rate for the decade was only 5 percent, comparable to that of Afro-Asia, that is, 6 percent (see Table 15–3). However, LDC annual inflation has accelerated, increasing from 9 percent in the 1960s to 26 percent in the 1970s to 76 percent, 1980 to 1992. Most of this increase came from rapid inflation in Latin America, 47 percent annually in the 1970s and 230 percent, 1980 to 1992! The DC inflation rates, while increasing from 4 percent in the 1960s to 9 percent in the 1970s, fell to 4 percent, 1980 to 1992.

Instability in the international economy during most of the 1970s exacerbated inflation. In 1971, the post-1945 Bretton Woods system of fixed exchange rates broke down. It was replaced by a floating exchange rate system, under which DCs experienced large swings in exchange rates. H. Johannes Witteveen, while president of the International Monetary Fund in 1975, argued that exchange fluctuations in an imperfectly competitive world exacerbated inflation by increasing prices in countries with a depreciating currency, but not decreasing prices in countries with an appreciating currency. Poor world harvests in 1972 to

---

[23]Economic Commission for Africa, *South African Destabilization: The Economic Cost of Frontline Resistance to Apartheid*, Addis Ababa, 1989, estimates that the nine Southern African Development Coordination Conference (SADCC) states—Angola, Botswana, Lesotho, Malawi, Mozambique, Tanzania, Swaziland, Zambia, and Zimbabwe—lost $60 billion (or one-fourth) their gross domestic product from South Africa's destabilization.

[24]United Nations Development Program, *Human Development Report, 1994* (New York: Oxford University Press, 1994), pp. 47–60, 170–71.

1973 increased food prices, wage rates, and cost-push inflation substantially in 1972 to 1974. Higher oil prices also pushed up costs and prices, especially in industry and power, in 1973 to 1975. Worldwide inflation remained high between 1975 and 1978, a period when, according to a Brookings Institution study, the effect of oil prices was not important. Inflation in the DCs radiated out to the LDCs through trade links.[25] Yet from 1978 through the end of the 1980s (as in the 1960s), inflation rates varied too widely among LDCs (note the differences between Latin America and Afro-Asia in Table 15–3) to attribute to a common cause. We cannot blame Paraguay's rapid inflation in the early 1950s; Brazil's, Uruguay's, Chile's, and Bolivia's in the decade before 1974; or Brazil's, Argentina's, Peru's, Bolivia's, and Israel's inflations in the 1980s and early 1990s at more than 100 percent yearly, on international instability. Let us examine several causes in the following sections.

TABLE 15-3   Inflation Rates in Developed and Developing Countries, 1960-92

	Average Annual Rate of Inflation[a] (percent)					
	1960–70		*1970–80*		*1980–92*	
Country groups						
Developed countries	4.3		9.1		4.3	
Developing countries	8.9		26.2		75.7	
Latin America		22.5		46.7		229.5
Afro-Asia		6.1		13.9		8.9
Developing countries by region						
Latin America	22.5		46.7		229.5	
Brazil		46.1		38.6		370.2
Excluding Brazil		9.3		50.9		157.2
Africa	5.3		14.2		14.7	
Asia	6.4		13.9		7.6	
India		7.1		8.4		8.5
Excluding India		5.3		16.2		7.2
Middle East	2.5		17.0		10.1	

Note: China is not included in 1960–70 for developing countries, Afro-Asia, and Asia. In 1960–92, developing countries include developing Europe. Central Asia from the former Soviet Union is included among developing countries but not Afro-Asia in 1980–92. The Middle East is included in the Afro-Asian total.

[a]GNP deflator.

Sources: World Bank, *World Development Report, 1981* (New York: Oxford University Press, 1981), pp. 134–35, 181; World Bank, *World Development Report, 1988* (New York: Oxford University Press, 1988), pp. 222–23; and World Bank, *World Development Report, 1994* (New York: Oxford University Press, 1994), pp. 162–63.

---

[25]United Nations, Department of International Economic and Social Affairs, *World Economic Survey, 1980–1981* (New York, 1981), pp. 37–39; H. Johannes Witteveen, "Inflation and the International Monetary System," *American Economic Review* 65 (May 1975): 108–14; and William R. Cline and Associates, *World Inflation and the Developing Countries* (Washington, D.C.: Brookings Institution, 1981).

DEMAND-PULL INFLATION

The next seven sections consider the (1) demand-pull, (2) cost-push, (3) ratchet, (4) structural, (5) expectational, (6) political, and (7) monetary explanations for inflation, and what government can do to reduce each.

Demand-pull inflation results from consumer, business, and government demand for goods and services in excess of an economy's capacity to produce. The International Monetary Fund, when financing the international payments deficit for a rapidly inflating LDC, requires contractionary monetary and fiscal policies—reduced government spending, increased taxes, a decreased money supply, and a higher interest rate—to curb demand. Sometimes these demand restrictions do not moderate inflation. The LDC government may have to decrease substantially the employment rate and real growth to reduce the inflation rate. As a result, many LDC economists question the importance of demand-pull inflation and look for other causes of inflation.

COST-PUSH INFLATION

The presence of cost-push and structural (supply-side) inflationary pressures may explain why a contraction in demand may cause unemployment and recession rather than reduce inflation. **Cost-push inflation** means prices increase even when demand drops or remains constant, because of higher costs in imperfectly competitive markets.

Labor unions may force up wages although there is excess labor supply—particularly by applying political pressure on government, the major employer and wage-setter in the modern sector. Higher food prices may also come into play, as during the poor worldwide harvests in 1972 to 1973. If food costs more, workers may press for higher wages.

Similarly, large businesses may increase prices in response to increased wage and other costs, even though demand for their products does not increase. Because of labor's and business's market power, economists sometimes label cost-push inflation "administered price" or "seller's" inflation.

Economists may blame rising costs from demand pull on cost push. Increased aggregate demand for finished goods and services expands business's derived demand for raw materials and labor. When their short-run supply is inelastic, costs go up before finished-good prices rise. Despite appearances, here excess demand, not cost, is inflation's cause.[26]

RATCHET INFLATION

A ratchet wrench only goes forward, not backward. Analogously prices may rise, but not go down. Assume aggregate demand remains constant but demand increases in the first sector and decreases in the second. With **ratchet inflation,** prices rise in the first sector, remain the same in the second, and increase overall.

The LDC governments could use antimonopoly measures and wage and price controls to moderate cost-push and ratchet inflationary pressures. Yet they may lack the political and administrative strength to attack monopolies and restrain wages. Several LDCs have instituted price controls but usually with mixed

---

[26]Maxwell J. Fry, *Money, Interest, and Banking in Economic Development* (Baltimore: Johns Hopkins University Press, 1988), pp. 330–31.

results. Price controls should be limited to highly imperfect markets, rather than competitive markets, where these controls cause shortages, long lines, and black markets. In addition some business firms circumvent price controls by reducing quality, service, or in some instances, quantity (for example, the number of nuts in a candy bar). Most LDC governments lack the administrative machinery and research capability to obtain the essential data, undertake the appropriate analysis, change price ceilings in response to movements in supply and demand in thousands of markets, and enforce controls.

STRUCTURAL INFLATION: THE CASE OF LATIN AMERICA

Some Latin American economists, especially from the United Nations Economic Commission for Latin America (ECLA), criticize the orthodox prescriptions of the International Monetary Fund for attaining macroeconomic and external equilibrium (Chapters 17, 18, and 20). These economists also argue that structural rigidities, not demand-pull, cost-push, or ratchet inflation, cause rapid inflation in Latin America. Structural factors include the slow and unstable growth of foreign currency earnings (from exports) and the inelastic supply of agricultural goods. A price rise from these factors is termed **structural inflation.**

Sluggish growth in foreign exchange earnings relative to import demand occurs because a disproportional share of exports in Latin America are primary products (food, raw materials, minerals, and organic oils and fats) other than fuels (see Chapter 4). The slow growth in demand for these primary exports decreases the country's terms of trade, that is, the ratio of its export prices to its import prices. Government restricts imports to adjust to foreign exchange shortages. Import demand, which grows with national income, exceeds import supply, and inflation sets in. Even expanding the supply of **import substitutes** (domestic production replacing imports) increases prices and input costs above import prices. The slow growth of export income necessitates frequent exchange-rate devaluation, which increases import prices.[27] In addition export sluggishness keeps export tax revenues down, reducing government saving and further increasing inflation.

Food output is especially unresponsive to price rises—a second structural rigidity in LDC economies. This supply inelasticity is largely due to defective land tenure patterns, such as concentrated land ownership, poor production incentives, and insecure tenancy.

All of these factors—deterioration in terms of trade, cost of import substitution, devaluation, and rise in agricultural prices—initiate cost-push inflation. Structuralists, many of whom support financially repressive policies discussed below, contend that contractionary monetary and fiscal policies, such as those advised by the International Monetary Fund, depress the economy and exacerbate political discontent without going to the heart of the problem, the need for fundamental structural change—land reform, expanding the industrial sector, antimonopoly measures, and improved income distribution.[28]

---

[27]Economists from the United States, which has a low propensity to import from increased GNP, often fail to comprehend the cost-push inflationary impact of the devaluation (and the increased domestic currency cost of foreign inputs) on a country which has a high ratio of imports to GNP.

[28]Much of the analysis of structural inflation in this section borrows from Roberto de Oliveira Campos, "Economic Development and Inflation with Special Reference to Latin America," in Organization for Economic Cooperation and Development, *Development Plans and Programmes* (Paris: OECD Development Center, 1964), pp. 129–37, reprinted in Gerald M. Meier, *Leading Issues in Economic Development* (New York: Oxford University Press, 1984), pp. 268–73.

Critics of the structuralists argue that the pressure on food supplies is not pe-culiar to Latin America. In fact the United Nations and the U.S. Department of Agriculture indicate both total and per capita food production grew about as rapidly in Latin America in the 1970s and 1980s as in any other region of the de-veloping world.[29]

In addition, Latin American export growth has not been sluggish. From 1970 to 1993, the real value of exports from Latin America grew 3.6 percent annually, its terms of trade increased slightly (0.21 percent annually), and the real purchasing power of export earnings increased 3.8 percent yearly.[30]

Moreover, when export growth is sluggish, the cause is not structural but an overvalued domestic currency relative to foreign exchange. Assume the market-clearing exchange rate is 50 pesos per dollar and the actual exchange rate 25 pesos per dollar. The farmer selling $1,000 worth of sugar cane on the world market re-ceives only 25,000 pesos at the existing exchange rate rather than 50,000 pesos at an equilibrium rate. Devaluing the domestic currency to reflect the market ex-change rate would spur farmers and other producers to export.

All in all, cost-push inflation generated by import substitution, decline in the terms of trade, and inelastic agricultural supplies are of limited use in explaining the chronic high rates of inflation found in many Latin American countries.

EXPECTATIONAL INFLATION

Inflation gains momentum once workers, consumers, and business people expect it to continue. **Inflationary expectations** encourage workers to demand higher wage increases. Business managers expecting continued inflation grant workers' demands, pass cost increases on to consumers, buy materials and equipment now rather than later, and pay higher interest rates because they expect to raise their prices. Lenders demand higher interest rates because they expect their money to be worth less when the loan is repaid, after prices have risen. Consumers purchase durable goods in anticipation of higher future prices. Thus once started, expecta-tions can engender an inertia that makes it difficult to stop an inflationary spiral.[31]

A major justification for wage-price controls is to break the vicious circle of inflationary expectations among workers, consumers, and business people. But as noted earlier, few LDC wage-price controls are effective, and people may view any success controls have as an aberration rather than as a basis for changing long-run expectations.

---

[29]Figure 7–1, and United Nations, Department of International Economic and Social Affairs, *World Eco-nomic Survey, 1980–1981* (New York, 1981), p. 28.

[30]Computed from International Monetary Fund, *World Economic Outlook* (Washington, D.C.: October 1988), pp. 59–137; and International Monetary Fund, *World Economic Outlook* (Washington, D.C.: Octo-ber 1994), pp. 119–186. See also William R. Cline and Associates, *World Inflation and the Developing Countries* (Washington, D.C.: Brookings Institution, 1981). See also the discussion of the long-run terms of trade in Chapter 8.

[31]Karl E. Case and Ray C. Fair, *Principles of Economics*, 2nd ed. (Englewood Cliffs, N.J.: Prentice Hall, 1996), pp. 761–62; Daniel R. Fusfeld, *Economics* (Lexington, Mass.: Heath, 1976), p. 332; and Robert L. Heilbroner and James K. Galbraith, *The Economic Problem* (Englewood Cliffs, N.J.: Prentice Hall, 1990), pp. 398–99.

See, however, Ana Dolores Novaes, "Revisiting the Inertial Inflation Hypothesis for Brazil," *Jour-nal of Development Economics* 42 (October 1993): 89–110, who argues that inertia explains only a small portion of continuing inflation.

POLITICAL INFLATION

In the 1950s, 1960s, and early 1970s, some Chileans explained their chronic hyper-inflation as "a 'struggle' or even 'civil war' between the country's major economic interest groups." Albert O. Hirschman contends that in Latin America, inflation, as civil war, can be caused by "a group which wrongly believes that it can get away with 'grabbing' a larger share of the national product than it has so far received." When communication between economic groups is poor, one or more classes may overestimate its strength and make excessive money demands that can be worked out only through inflation. Such a process may reduce tension that may otherwise result in revolution or war. Many LDC ministers of labor have averted a political strike by granting inflationary wage increases.[32]

Social tensions and class antagonisms causing this **political inflation** are too deep seated to be cleared up by short-run government policies. In fact the political threat of the conflict may be so great that the government may have little choice but to tolerate persistent inflation.

MONETARY INFLATION

According to Dornbusch

> Milton Friedman argues that inflation is always and everywhere a monetary phenomenon. That is barely true in some cases and very true in others. The art is to know which is which. In the United States monetarism comes out of the corner after inflation has happened, because then a monetary expansion can clearly be documented and held responsible. There is always some lag in the link between inflation and money that will oblige. But when there is no inflation even though money has grown rapidly, monetarists stay in hiding. In the United States experience, monetarism does not do a lot for us, no more at least than the prediction that it is colder in winter than in summer.[33]

Similarly in LDCs, monetarism has little explanatory value except during high inflation, as during the late 1980s or early 1990s in Latin America, the former Soviet Union, and parts of Eastern Europe and Africa. According to Robert Mc-Nown and Myles S. Wallace, monetary growth outweighs real shocks in explaining price increases during high inflation, as occurred in Brazil, Chile, Argentina, and Israel in the 1970s and 1980s.[34] High inflation not only occurs during civil war, revolution, deep social unrest, and weak government, but also with external shocks (such as the German reparation payments in the 1920s, the oil price hikes of 1973–75 and 1979–80, and the debt crisis and high real interest rates of the 1980s). Monetary expansion contributes to inflation, while rapid inflation wipes out the real value of tax revenues, increasing budget deficits and accelerating

---

[32]Albert O. Hirschman, *Journeys toward Progress: Studies of Economic Policy-Making in Latin America* (New York: Twentieth Century Fund, 1963), pp. 192–223.

[33]Rudiger Dornbusch, *Stabilization, Debt, and Reform: Policy Analysis for Developing Countries* (Englewood Cliffs, N.J.: Prentice Hall, 1993), p. 1.

[34]Robert McNown and Myles S. Wallace, "National Price Levels, Purchasing Power Parity, and Cointegration: A Test of Four High Inflation Economies," *Journal of International Money and Finance* 8 (1989): 533–45.

money growth, thus strengthening the link between financing the budget and the growth of money.[35]

INCOMES POLICIES AND EXTERNAL STABILIZATION

The price of foreign exchange plays an important role in spurring on inflation. In many instances, hyperinflation is triggered by a balance-of-payments crisis and the resulting currency collapse. The increased price of foreign inputs to domestic production provides a stimulus to cost-push inflationary pressures.

Stabilizing high inflation requires budgetary and monetary control, increasing tax yields, external support (to reduce supply-side limitations), structural (supply-side, many middle- to long-run) reforms (Chapter 20), and incomes policies to reduce inflationary inertia. Providing external loans so the country has ample reserves for imports is one way to provide assurance for the foreign-exchange and capital markets, and increase the likelihood the reserves do not have to be used. Incomes policies, such as freezing exchange rates, wages, and prices for a few months can effectively supplement domestic budget cuts. Relying on demand management (contractionary monetary and fiscal policies) alone without incomes policies will create an extraordinary depression. Dornbusch suggests fixing the price of foreign exchange without overvaluation for two to three months rate (to reduce inflation inertia), then eventually using a **crawling peg**, which depreciates home currency continuously so the exchange rate facilitates external competitiveness.[36] Mexico used a crawling peg in 1993–94 but in the face of rising U.S. interest rates in 1994, the band within which the peso price of the dollar could "crawl" (read increase) to maintain balance-of-payments equilibrium was too narrow, thus triggering a foreign-exchange crisis in late 1994 and early 1995.[37] In 1991, Argentina pegged the peso to the dollar and established a currency board to limit domestic currency issue to 100 percent of foreign currency and reserve assets, policies that generated an "inflation miracle"—slashing inflation from 3,080 percent annually in 1989 and 2,315 percent in 1990 to 172 percent in 1991, 25 percent in 1992, 11 percent in 1993, and 4 percent in 1994! However, critics contend that after peso stabilization, Argentina suffered from a loss of competitiveness from a peso overvalued relative to dollar, as suggested by a shift from a trade surplus of $8.6 billion in 1990 to a trade deficit of $3.7 billion in 1993.[38] Here

---

[35]Ibid., pp. 1–2; and Jeffrey D. Sachs and Felipe Larrain B., *Macroeconomics in the Global Economy* (Englewood Cliffs, N.J.: Prentice Hall, 1993), pp. 732–27.

[36]Rudiger Dornbusch, *Stabilization, Debt, and Reform: Policy Analysis for Developing Countries* (Englewood Cliffs, N.J.: Prentice Hall, 1993), pp. 1–3, 13–29.

Ronald I. McKinnon, *The Order of Economic Liberalization: Financial Control in the Transition to a Market Economy* (Baltimore: Johns Hopkins University Press, 1993), pp. 106–07, recommends indexing the peg to the change in the domestic general price index relative to the change in the foreign general price index.

An International Monetary Fund panel analyzing the use of exchange rates to stabilize prices in high-inflation economy was skeptical about fixing the price of foreign exchange for any length of time. In some instances, the IMF panel granted, a country could successfully use the exchange rate as an anchor when this policy was accompanied by a credible program of fiscal restraint. "Using Exchange Rate Anchors in Adjustment Programs: When and How?" *IMF Survey* (November 20, 1995), pp. 361–63.

[37]Nora Lustig (Brookings Institution economist), "The Decision to Devalue the Mexican Peso Was a Necessary Attempt to Avert Fiscal Crisis," *Kansas City Star* (January 6, 1995): p. C-5.

[38]"Creating Credibility," *Economist* (20 July 1994): 76; International Monetary Fund, *World Economic Outlook, May 1992* (Washington, D.C., 1992); p. 19; and International Monetary Fund, *World Economic Outlook, October 1994* (Washington, D.C., 1994); p. 25.

using a crawling peg for the peso after a short initial period of a fixed peg might have prevented a deterioration in the trade balance.

BENEFITS OF INFLATION

Inflation need not be all bad. In fact would we not welcome inflation if it contributed to economic growth and higher material well-being? As a matter of fact, Robert A. Mundell's monetarist model indicates that rapid inflation may add 1 percentage point to annual, real economic growth by spurring extra capital formation.[39]

Some economists argue that inflation can promote economic development in the following ways.

1. The treasury prints money or the banking system expands credit so that a modernizing government can raise funds in excess of tax revenues. Even if real resources remain constant, inflationary financing allows government to control a larger resource share by bidding resources away from low-priority uses.

2. Government can use inflationary credit to redistribute income from wage earners who save little to capitalists with high rates of productive capital formation. Business people usually benefit from inflation, since product prices tend to rise faster than resource prices. For example, wages may not keep up with inflation, especially in its early stages when price increases are greater than anticipated. Furthermore, inflation reduces the real interest rate and real debt burden for expanding business.

3. Inflationary pressure pushes an economy toward full employment and more fully utilizes labor and other resources. Rising wages and prices reallocate resources from traditional sectors to rapidly growing sectors.

COSTS OF INFLATION

Yet inflation can be highly problematical.

1. Government redistribution from high consumers to high savers through inflationary financing may work during only the early inflationary stages. When people expect continued inflation, they find ways of protecting themselves against it. Wage demands, automatic cost-of-living adjustments, for example, reflect inflationary expectations. Retirees and pensioners pressure government to increase benefits to keep up with inflation. Government may respond to other political interests to control increases in the prices of food, rents, urban transport, and so forth. Official price ceilings inevitably distort resource allocation, frequently resulting in shortages, black markets, and corruption.

2. Inflation imposes a tax on the holders of money. Government or business people benefiting from inflationary financing collect the real resources from the **inflation tax.** People attempt to evade the tax by holding onto goods rather than money. Yet to restore the real value of their money, people would have to accumulate additional balances at a rate equal to inflation.

---

[39]Robert A. Mundell, "Growth, Stability, and Inflationary Finance," *Journal of Political Economy* 73 (April 1965): 97–109.

3. Inflation distorts business behavior, especially investment behavior, since any rational calculation of profits is undermined. Entrepreneurs do not risk investing in basic industries with a long payoff period but rather in capital gains assets (for example, luxury housing) as a protection against inflation. Business people waste much effort forecasting and speculating on the inflation rate, or in hedging against the uncertainties involved.[40]

4. Inflation, especially if it is discontinuous and uneven, weakens the creation of credit and capital markets. Uncertainties about future price increases may damage the development of savings banks, community savings societies, bond markets, social security, pension funds, insurance funds, and government debt instruments. For example, Brazil's annual growth rate in GNP per capita declined from 11 percent in 1968 to 1973 to 5 percent in 1973 to 1979, partly from the adverse impact of inflation on savings. Nominal interest rates remained almost constant while annual inflation accelerated from 13 percent in 1973 to 44 percent in 1977. Because of the resulting negative *real* interest rates, savings were reduced and diverted from productive investment.[41]

5. Monetary and fiscal instruments in LDCs are usually too weak to slow inflation without sacrificing real income, employment, and social welfare programs.

6. Income distribution is usually less uniform during inflationary times. Inflation redistributes income, at least in the early stages, from low-income workers and those on fixed income to high-income classes. This redistribution may not increase saving, since the rich may buy luxury items with their increased incomes. A study of seven LDCs (including Brazil, Uruguay, Argentina, and Chile) by the Organization for Economic Cooperation and Development concluded that "there is no evidence anywhere of inflation having increased the flow of saving."[42]

7. Inflation increases the prices of domestic goods relative to foreign goods—decreasing the competitiveness of domestic goods internationally and usually reducing the **international balance of merchandise trade** (exports minus imports of goods). Inflation also discourages the inflow of foreign capital, since the real value of investment and of future repatriated earnings erodes. The large international deficits that often come with rapid inflation can increase debt burdens and limit essential imports.

With inflation in excess of 30 percent a year in the mid-to-late 1970s, Brazil depreciated the cruzeiro relative to the U.S. dollar at a steady, predictable rate to keep domestic prices competitive. However, devaluation stimulated inflation through the increased demand for Brazilian goods and cost-push pressures from higher import prices. Furthermore Brazilian inflation was too erratic for steady exchange-rate changes to prevent fluctuations in real export and import prices. Yet

---

[40]Harry G. Johnson, "Is Inflation the Inevitable Price of Rapid Development or a Retarding Factor in Economic Growth?" *Malayan Economic Review* 11 (April 1965): 22–28, reprinted in Gerald M. Meier, *Leading Issues in Economic Development* (New York: Oxford University Press, 1976), pp. 311–15.

[41]World Bank, *World Development Report, 1981* (New York: Oxford University Press, 1981); and William R. Cline, "Brazil's Aggressive Response to External Shocks," in William R. Cline and Associates, *World Inflation and the Developing Countries* (Washington, D.C.: Brookings Institution, 1981), pp. 102–05.

[42]Ian Little, Tibor Scitovsky, and Maurice Scott, *Industry and Trade in Some Developing Countries: A Comparative Study* (London: Oxford University Press, 1970), p. 77.

most LDCs are not even so capable as Brazil in managing monetary, fiscal, and exchange-rate policies to limit the evils of inflation.

THE DYNAMICS OF INFLATION

Once high inflation occurs, the disintegration of financial institutions (such as bond markets, lending agencies in domestic currency, savings banks, and holding money as a store of value) exacerbates inflation further. If there is any delay between the accrual and payments of taxes, their real value erodes disastrously (1996 taxes paid in 1997 wreaks havoc with the real value of tax collection). As inflation accelerates, contracts or indexation lags shorten (to avoid real wages declining as inflation erodes the purchasing power of the constant nominal payments), which causes inflation to accelerate. Under extreme inflation, governments may abandon domestic currency for U.S. dollars or another foreign currency, which means the government must continue to increase inflation to get any seigniorage. As economic institutions collapse and wage contracts and financial asset maturities shrink, hyperinflation becomes inevitable. The erosion of the real value of taxation, the shortening of contracts, and financial adaptation to inflation all react perversely to widen the deficit and accelerate the inflation rate explosively.[43]

INFLATION AND GROWTH: EMPIRICAL EVIDENCE

As indicated above, Mundell's monetarist model suggests that inflation can increase real economic growth. However, the empirical evidence is mixed, depending on the time period, country group, and range of inflation examined. Opposing Mundell's work, Henry C. Wallich's study of 43 countries from 1956 to 1965, finds a negative relationship between inflation and real economic growth. A. P. Thirlwall's and C. A. Barton's review of 51 countries from 1958 to 1965 finds no significant correlation between inflation and growth. But U Tun Wai's study of 31 LDCs from 1946 to 1954, and Graeme S. Dorrance's research on 49 DCs and LDCs from 1953 to 1961, indicate a positive relationship between the two variables.[44]

However, Thirlwall, Barton, Tun Wai, and Dorrance find that among LDCs, growth declines when annual inflation exceeds 10 percent. Figure 15–1, which is consistent with this, shows that inflation rates are negatively related to real growth rates in high-inflation Latin America. While Afro-Asia's inflation is also negatively related to growth (Figure 15–2), the x coefficient is not significant at the 5 percent level; indeed the negative relationship is a result of countries whose inflation rate exceeds 10 percent annually. The evidence suggests that inflation in

---

[43]Rudiger Dornbusch, *Stabilization, Debt, and Reform: Policy Analysis for Developing Countries* (Englewood Cliffs, N.J.: Prentice Hall, 1993), pp. 18–24.

[44]Henry C. Wallich, ""Money and Growth: A Country Cross-Section Analysis,"*Journal of Money, Credit, and Banking* 1 (May 1969): 281–302; A.P. Thirlwall and C. A. Barton, ""Inflation and Growth: The International Evidence," *Banca Nazionale del Lavoro Quarterly Review* no. 99 (September 1971): 263–75; U Tun Wai, ""The Relation between Inflation and Economic Development: A Statistical Inductive Study," *International Monetary Fund Staff Papers* 7 (October 1959): 302–17; and Graeme S. Dorrance, ""Inflation and Growth: The Statistical Evidence," *International Monetary Fund Staff Papers* 13 (March 1966): 82–102.

FIGURE 15-1   Growth and Inflation in Latin America
Growth rates are negatively related to inflation rates in
Latin America.

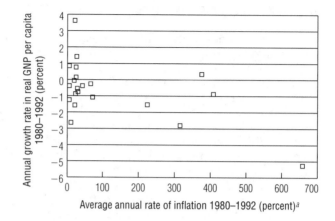

^aMeasured by the implicit GDP price deflator.
Inflation rate = 0.0541 – 0.0057 Real growth rate
              (1.4848) (0.0019)
Source: World Bank, *World Development Report, 1994*
(New York: Oxford University Press, 1994), pp. 162–63.

FIGURE 15-2   Growth and Inflation in Afro-Asia
Growth rates are not related to inflation rates in
Afro-Asia.

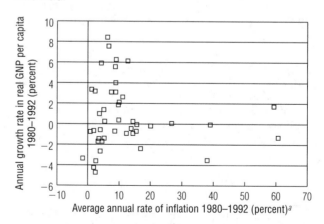

^aMeasured by the implicit GDP price deflator.
Inflation rate = 11.6358—0.3073 Real growth rate
              (13.8115) (0.6564)
Source: World Bank, *World Development Report, 1994*
(New York: Oxford University Press, 1994), pp. 162–63.

LDCs has *not* contributed to economic growth but may inhibit growth, especially at annual percentage rates in the double digits.[45]

Financial Repression and Liberalization

The LDC money markets tend to be highly oligopolistic even when dominated by domestic banks and lenders. Government **financial repression**—distortions of the interest rates, foreign exchange rates (Chapter 18), and other financial prices—reduce the relative size of the financial system and the real rate of growth.

Frequently the motive for LDC financial restriction is to encourage financial institutions and instruments from which the government can expropriate **seigniorage** (or extract resources from the financial system in return for controlling currency issue and credit expansion). Under inflationary conditions, the state uses reserve requirements and obligatory holdings of government bonds to tap savings at low or negative *real* interest rates. Authorities suppress private bond and equity markets through transactions taxes, special taxes on income from capital, and inconducive laws to claim seigniorage from private holders assets. The state imposes interest rate ceilings to stifle private sector competition in fund raising. Imposing these ceilings, foreign exchange controls, high reserve requirements, and restrictions on private capital markets increases the flow of domestic resources to the public sector without higher taxes or interest rates, or the flight of capital overseas (see Chapter 17).

Under financial repression, banks engage in nonprice rationing of loans, facing pressure for loans to those with political connections but otherwise allocate credit according to transaction costs, all of which leave no opportunity for charging a premium for risky (and sometimes innovative) projects. Overall these policies also encourage capital-intensive projects (Chapter 9) and discourage capital investment. The LDC financially repressive regimes, uncompetitive markets, and banking bureaucracies not disciplined by market and profit tests may encourage adopting inefficient lending criteria. The high arrears, delinquency, and default of many LDC (especially official) banks and development lending institutions result from (1) failure to tie lending to productive investment, (2) neglect of marketing, (3) delayed loan disbursement and unrealistic repayment schedules, (4) misapplication of loans, (5) ineffective supervision, (6) apathy of bank management in recovering loans, and (7) irresponsible and undisciplined borrowers, including many who (for cultural reasons or misunderstanding government's role) fail to distinguish loans from grants. Additionally Argentina's, Brazil's, Chile's, Uruguay's, Mexico's, Turkey's, Thailand's, and pre–World War II Japan's bank-lending policies have suffered from collusion between major corporations and banks.

---

[45]Jeffrey R. Nugent and Constantine Glezakos, "Phillips Curves in Developing Countries," *Economic Development and Cultural Change* 30 (January 1982): 321–34.

Could the causal relationship lead from growth to inflation rather than the other way around? Thirlwall and Barton argue that "if growth is a supply phenomenon, higher growth should lower inflation not exacerbate it. Real growth by itself cannot be the cause of inflation unless it sets in motion forces which themselves generate rising prices and persist"—such as shortages in the produce and factor markets. Attempts to expand demand in excess of the growth rate of productive potential can cause inflation, but it is a non sequitur to argue from this that real growth causes inflation. A. P. Thirlwall and C. A. Barton, "Inflation and Growth: the International Evidence," *Banca Nazionale del Lavoro Quarterly Review* no. 99 (September 1971): 269–70.

Combating financial repression, which is as much political as it is economic, can reduce inflation. Financial liberalization necessitates abolishing ceilings on interest rates (or at least raising them to competitive levels), introducing market incentives for bank managers, encouraging private stock and bond markets, and lowering reserve requirements. At higher (market-clearing) interest rates, banks make more credit available to productive enterprises, increasing the economy's capacity and relieving inflationary pressures. Trade liberalization, which threatens (often) politically influential import-competing industrialists, increases product competition and reduces import prices (see Chapter 20), reducing input prices and cost-push inflation[46] (Box 15–1 gives examples of how liberalization in India affects individual firms.)

But liberalization also requires greater restrictions by the monetary and fiscal authorities. The central bank and finance ministry must regulate the growth of banks and other enterprises that grant credit, create checkable deposits, and provide cash on demand. An independent board should replace government industrial departments in managing foreign exchange, in order to restrict the excessive bidding for foreign currency by enterprises desperate to find a nondepreciating liquid financial asset to hold during high inflation. The central government must limit spending, maintaining a balanced budget, especially in the transition to a liberal market economy. As the private sector increases in size relative to the state sector, the fiscal authorities need to maintain their collection of turnover and excess profits taxes on state enterprises until the transition to a new tax system that raises revenue from both private and government firms. In the early 1990s, Russia's failure to restrict the creation of "wildcat" banks and unregulated quasi-bank intermediaries, to restrain the holding of foreign-exchange liquid assets, to collect revenues, and to limit state spending contributed to inflation rates in excess of 700 percent annually from early 1992 to late 1993.[47] (See Chapter 20 for more discussion of optimal sequences in the transition from state socialism to a market economy.)

Still, mild financial repression—specifically repression of interest rates and contest-based credit allocation—contributed to rapid growth in Japan (both before and after World War II), South Korea, and Taiwan. But each of these economies had competent and politically-insulated bankers and government loan bureaucrats to select and monitor projects, and apply export performance as a major

---

[46]Ronald I. McKinnon, *The Order of Economic Liberalization: Financial Control in the Transition to a Market Economy* (Baltimore: Johns Hopkins University Press, 1993), pp. 43–83; Maxwell J. Fry, *Money, Interest, and Banking in Economic Development* (Baltimore: Johns Hopkins University Press, 1988), pp. 7–18, 261–335; Ronald I. McKinnon, *Money and Capital in Economic Development* (Washington, D.C.: Brookings Institution, 1973); Edward S. Shaw, *Financial Deepening in Economic Development* (New York: Oxford University Press, 1973); Mario I. Blejer, "Liberalization and Stabilization Policies in the Southern-Cone Countries: An Introduction," *Journal of Interamerican Studies and World Affairs* 25 (November 1983): 441; Felipe Morris, "India's Financial System: An Overview of Its Principal Structural Features," Washington, World Bank Staff Working Paper no. 739, 1985, p. 21; David Gill, "Securities Market Structural Issues and Challenges," paper prepared for the annual meeting of the International Federation of Stock Exchanges, Toronto, September 12–14, 1983: and Yoon Je Cho, "The Effect of Financial Liberalization on the Efficiency of Credit Allocation: Some Evidence from Korea," *Journal of Development Economics* 29 (July 1988): 101–10.

[47]Ronald I. McKinnon, *The Order of Economic Liberalization: Financial Control in the Transition to a Market Economy* (Baltimore: Johns Hopkins University Press, 1993), pp. 1–10, 120–61, 213; International Monetary Fund, *World Economic Outlook, October 1993* (Washington, D.C., 1993), pp. 86–90; and International Monetary Fund, *World Economic Outlook, May 1995* (Washington, D.C., 1995), pp. 52–58.

BOX 15-1

Examples of the Effect of Liberalization in India on Individual Firms

Because of longstanding restrictions, Indian companies have not participated in the borderless Asian-Pacific economy (discussed in Chapter 3), and have been at a major disadvantage in winning contracts overseas. In 1990, one year before India's liberalization program, TRP Software, Limited, a Calcutta data systems and software company, undertook a detailed study to bid to design information management services for the municipal government of a major Australian city. Foreign-exchange restrictions prevented TRP's director, J.T. Banerjee, from taking more than one trip to the city to do the planning. Nevertheless, TRP took advantage of India's low-salaried professional designers, software engineers, and systems analysts to put together a highly competitive package for the Australian city. Other firms from countries without foreign-exchange restrictions sent executive officers to Australia with the design and bid. Because of the prohibitive amount of time necessary to receive Reserve Bank of India foreign-exchange permission for the trip, TRP had to rely on an express package service, which delivered the firm's bid 10 minutes late, thus losing the opportunity to win the contract.

In 1991, in response to an international balance of payments crisis, India undertook liberalization. TRP no longer faced limitations in competing overseas. A number of other firms found that foreign-currency decontrol had facilitated acquiring imports to improve plant and machinery (albeit at higher rupee prices) and spurred them to try markets overseas. The liberalized foreign-exchange regime was a welcome change for a southern marble products entrepreneur, who reduced his time for clearing imported machines through Indian customs from one month before 1991 to two days since 1993.

In the 1960s and 1970s, the Indian government tried to influence industrial output by physical controls operated partially through a licensing system. The purposes of these controls were to guide and regulate production according to targets of the Five Year plans, and to promote balanced economic development between the different regions of the country. Jagdish Bhagwati explains that the 1991 economic reform was not a return to laissez-faire policies, but an effort to prevent the government from counter-productive intervention.[48]

India's licensing policy enticed entrepreneurs to focus on making profits from long-term government-granted **monopoly rents,** such as those from influence and connections to acquire licenses rather than from innovation, which provides only a temporary monopoly gain.

---

[48]Jagdish Bhagwati, *India in Transition: Freeing the Economy* (Oxford: Clarendon Press, 1993), p. 98.

Most firms that failed to acquire licenses or quotas were unable to survive. On the other hand, several manufacturing firms with input licenses continued to operate, although variable cost exceeded revenue in manufacturing. They could still make a profit by acquiring inputs on the controlled market and selling them on the free market for higher prices. A number of firms were producing enough to give the appearance of being genuine manufacturing firms, while making their profits on buying and selling controlled inputs.[49]

A manager of one of the largest industrial conglomerates complained about a major plank of India's financial liberalization, the increase in interest rates charged by banks, which had been previously state-owned. This industrial aggregate, which had adapted to the sluggishness of license-protected monopoly production, would no longer be profitable at these higher interest rates.

For entrepreneurs in India, liberalization measures have been a two-edged sword, resulting in the entry or expansion of firms previously blocked, and eliminating many inefficient firms formerly protected through monopoly rents from a licensing regime. Some entrepreneurs have gained and some have lost from liberalization. The major advantage of liberalization, however, is to reduce the number of entrepreneurs who survive from monopoly rents and to increase the number of entrepreneurs who survive as a result of innovation, efficiency, and production managerial ability.

yardstick for allocating credit.[50] Few other LDCs have the institutional competence to ration credit based on performance; usually the public accuses financial officers who allocate funds at below-market rates of nepotism, communalism, and other forms of favoritism.

Moreover, reducing financial and price repression can, in the short run, spur inflation. Financial liberalization, through abolishing ceilings on interest rates, encouraging private stock and bond markets, creating other new financial intermediaries, lowering reserve requirements, and decontrolling exchange rates, means government loses part of its captive inflation tax base.[51]

---

[49]E. Wayne Nafziger, *Class, Caste, and Entrepreneurship: A Study of Indian Industrialists* (Honolulu: University Press of Hawaii, 1978), pp. 108–19; and E. Wayne Nafziger and R. Sudarsana Rao, "Industrial Entrepreneurship and Innovation under Licensing and Liberalization in India," *Indian Economic Journal* 44 (October-December 1996). My colleagues and I conducted interviews of Indian entrepreneurs and managers in 1971 and 1993. J.T. Banerjee is a pseudonym I use for an entrepreneur I interviewed; likewise, TRP Software is not the real name of Mr. Banerjee's firm.

[50]World Bank, *The East Asian Miracle: Economic Growth and Public Policy* (New York: Oxford University Press, 1993), pp. 237 -41, 356–58; Toru Yanagihara, "Anything New in the *Miracle* Report: Yes and No," *World Development* 22 (April 1994): 665–66; and Jene Kwon, "The East Asia Challenge to Neoclassical Orthodoxy," *World Development* 22 (April 1994): 641.

[51]Rudiger Dornbusch, *Stabilization, Debt, and Reform: Policy Analysis for Developing Countries* (Englewood Cliffs, N.J.: Prentice Hall, 1993), pp. 21–22.

Islamic Banking

While Islam, like early medieval Christianity, interprets its scriptures to ban interest, it encourages profit as a return to entrepreneurship together with financial capital. Moreover, like Western banks, Islamic banks are financial intermediaries between savers and investors and administer the economy's payment system. Bank depositors are treated as if they were shareholders of the bank. Islamic banks receive returns through markup pricing (for example, buying a house, then reselling it at a higher price to the borrower and requiring the borrower to repay over 25 years) or profit-sharing, interest-free deposits (mutual-fund-type packages for sale to investor-depositors). These banks operate alongside traditional banks in more than 50 countries (including Malaysia), but in Ayatollah Ruhollah Khomeini's Iran (1979–89) and Mohammad Zia ul-Haq's Pakistan (1985–88), the government eliminated interest-based transactions from the banking system. Interest-free banking can improve efficiency, since profit shares are free from interest rate controls. Indeed World Bank and International Monetary Fund economist Mohsin S. Khan argues that Islamic banking, with its equity participation, is more stable than Western banking, since shocks are absorbed by changes in the values of deposits held by the public.[52]

However, Timur Kuran, Faisal Professor of Economics and Islamic Thought at the University of Southern California, questions whether the Muslim scripture, the Qur'an, bans interest and earning money without assuming risk. According to Kuran, Islamic banks pay profit shares to account holders from income received mostly from bonds and other interest-bearing assets. Moreover, in countries, such as Turkey, "where Islamic banks compete with conventional banks, the ostensibly interest-free returns of [Islamic banks] essentially match the explicitly interest-based returns of [conventional banks]."[53]

Profit sharing is problematic where businesses use double bookkeeping for tax evasion, making their profits difficult for banks to determine.[54] Because many borrowers hide information about their actual profits, many Islamic banks shun profit and loss sharing even in the presence of huge tax incentives. Indeed Kuran finds that Islamic banks and enterprises do business much like their secular counterparts. Kuran asks why economic Islamization has generated so much excitement and participation without bringing about major substantive changes? The

---

[52]Maxwell J. Fry, *Money, Interest, and Banking in Economic Development* (Baltimore: Johns Hopkins University Press, 1988), p. 266; Zubair Iqbal and Abbas Mirakhor, "Islamic Banking," Washington, D.C., International Monetary Fund Occasional Paper 49, March 1987; and Mohsin S. Khan, "Islamic Interest-Free Banking," *International Monetary Fund Staff Papers* 33 (March 1986): 1–27.

Geoffrey A. Jehle, "*Zakāt* and Inequality: Some Evidence from Pakistan," *Review of Income and Wealth*, Series 40 (2) (June 1994): 205–15, finds that *zakāt*, one of the five Muslim pillars of the faith that mandates that believers give alms to the poor, reduces income inequality in Pakistan, both within and between provinces. However, the great bulk of giving and receiving is done by the poor and near-poor among themselves. Timur Kuran, "Islamic Economics and the Islamic Subeconomy," *Journal of Economic Perspectives* 9 (Fall 1995): 163–64, finds that the equalizing effect of *zakāt* has been disappointing, because of low rates, vast loopholes, widespread evasion, the high costs of administering a system which loses substantial sums to official corruption, and the diversion of revenue to finance causes other than poverty reduction, including religious education and pilgrimages to Mecca.

[53]Timur Kuran, "Islamic Economics and the Islamic Subeconomy," *Journal of Economic Perspectives* 9 (Fall 1995): 155–73, with quotation on p. 161.

[54]Mohsin S. Khan, "Islamic Interest-Free Banking," *International Monetary Fund Staff Papers* 33 (March 1986): 1–27.

main reasons, he contends, are the desire of politicians to demonstrate a commitment to Islamic ideals, the efforts of Muslim business people who feel they behave in un-Islamic ways to assuage their guilt, and the attempts to foster networks of interpersonal trust among those with a shared commitment to Islam.[55]

Summary

1. Central banks in LDCs generally have less effect on expenditure and output than in DCs because of an externally dependent banking system, a poorly developed securities market, the limited scope of bank loans, the low percentage of demand deposits divided by the total money supply, and the relative insensitivity of investment and employment to monetary policies.

2. Tax revenue as a percentage of GNP in LDCs is about 18 percent compared to 28 percent in DCs.

3. The increase in tax ratios with GNP per capita reflects both the growth in the demand for public services and the capacity to levy and pay taxes.

4. Direct taxes (such as taxes on property, wealth, inheritance, and income) account for about one-third of revenue sources in LDCs and about two-thirds in DCs. Major indirect taxes in most LDCs are those on international trade, production, and internal transactions, which, however, distort resource allocation. Direct taxes generally have a higher elasticity (that is, percentage change in taxation/percentage change in GNP) than indirect taxes.

5. Some DCs use the progressive income tax to mobilize large amounts of public resources, improve income distribution, stabilize income and prices, and prevent inefficient use of resources, often arising from a heavy reliance on indirect taxes. However, import, export, and excise taxes are the major sources of tax revenue in LDCs. Most LDCs lack the administrative capacity to emphasize an income tax.

6. A number of LDCs have introduced the value-added tax, a tax on the difference between the sales of a firm and its purchases from other firms. The appeals of the value-added tax are simplicity, uniformity, and the generation of substantial revenues.

7. Developing countries cannot use fiscal policy to stabilize income and prices so effectively as developed countries can. The LDC governments have less control over the amount of taxes raised and less scope for speeding up or delaying expenditures.

8. A relatively small percentage of government spending in LDCs is on health, social security, and welfare, and a relatively high percentage on infrastructure.

9. The annual inflation rate in LDCs increased from less than 10 percent in the 1960s to over 20 percent in the 1970s and over 70 percent in the 1980s and early 1980s, with the highest inflation rates in Latin America.

10. Demand-pull is not an adequate explanation for inflation in LDCs. Inflation may be cost push (from the market power of businesses and unions), ratchet (from rigid prices downward), or structural (slow export growth and inelastic food supply), with added momentum, once started, from inflationary expectations. Policies to moderate inflation include market-clearing exchange rates, wage-

---

[55]Timur Kuran, "Islamic Economics and the Islamic Subeconomy," *Journal of Economic Perspectives* 9 (Fall 1995): 155–73.

price controls, antimonopoly measures, land reform, structural change from agriculture to industry, and improved income distribution. With the possible exception of exchange-rate policy, most LDCs lack the administrative and political strength to undertake these policies, especially in the immediate future.

11. Countries with high rates of inflation may use incomes policy—wage and price guidelines or controls, and exchange-rate fixing—together with monetary and fiscal stabilization to reduce increases in the price index.

12. Some economists argue that inflation can promote economic growth by redistributing income from low savers to high savers. However, inflation distorts resource allocation, weakens capital markets, imposes a tax on money holders, undermines rational business behavior, increases income inequality, hurts the balance of trade and, beyond the early stages of inflation, probably does not redistribute income to high savers.

13. There is not enough evidence to support the hypothesis that inflation contributes to economic growth.

14. The LDC money markets are often highly oligopolistic and financially repressive, distorting interest rates, foreign exchange rates, and other financial prices. Government protects oligopolistic banks to be able to tap savings at low interest rates. If political elites have the will to undertake financial liberalization, they can reduce inflation and spur growth.

Terms to Review

- monetary policy
- fiscal policy
- incomes policy
- hyperinflation
- stagflation
- Wagner's law
- social goods
- elastic tax
- direct taxes
- indirect taxes
- value-added tax (VAT)
- cascade tax
- progressive tax
- regressive tax
- sales tax
- fiscal incentives
- inflation

- consumer price index (CPI)
- GDP deflator
- demand-pull inflation
- cost-push inflation
- ratchet inflation
- structural inflation
- inflationary expectations
- political inflation
- inflation tax
- crawling peg
- import substitutes
- international balance of merchandise trade
- monopoly rents
- financial repression
- seigniorage
- social goods

Questions to Discuss

1. What prevents LDC use of monetary, fiscal, and incomes policies from attaining goals of output and employment growth, and price stability?

2. Why are taxes as a percentage of GNP generally lower for LDCs than for DCs?

3. What are the goals of LDC tax policy? What obstacles do LDCs encounter in reaching their tax policy goals?

4. Why are direct taxes as a percentage of GNP generally lower, and indirect taxes as a percentage of GNP, generally higher, for LDCs than DCs? Why is heavy reliance on indirect taxes as sources of revenue often disadvantageous to LDCs?

5. Indicate the benefits and difficulties associated with using value-added taxes in developing countries.

6. What tax measures can LDCs take to reduce income inequality? To increase capital and enterprise?

7. What, if any, is the tradeoff between tax policies that reduce income and wealth concentration and those that increase capital formation?

8. Why is health, social security, and welfare spending as a percentage of GNP less in LDCs than DCs? Why is health, social security, and welfare spending as a percentage of total government spending less in LDCs than DCs?

9. Why are military expenditures as a percentage of GNP high in low-income countries?

10. Why did the LDC inflation rate increase from the 1960s to the 1980s?

11. How do you expect inflation in the 1990s to compare to that of the 1980s?

12. What causes LDC inflation? Which causes are most important? How might LDCs reduce inflation?

13. Why was inflation so rapid in Latin America in the 1960s, 1970s, and 1980s?

14. In what way might inflation avert civil war or political violence?

15. How important are monetary factors in contributing to LDC inflation?

16. What are the costs and benefits of inflation? Which are greater for LDCs, costs or benefits?

17. What is the role of the foreign-exchange rate in stabilizing inflation?

18. What is the empirical relationship between inflation and growth?

19. Compare the monetary, fiscal, and incomes policies to use in high inflation countries to policies to use in countries with low inflation.

20. Explain the political and economic reasons for frequent LDC government financial repression and the effects it has on economic development. Indicate policies for LDC financial liberalization and ways in which they could affect inflation and real growth.

21. What effect might financial liberalization have on individual firms in LDCs?

Guide to Readings

Tun Wai (note 44) discusses the limitations of monetary policy in LDCs. Vito Tanzi, *Fiscal Policy in Open Developing Economies* (Washington, D.C.: International Monetary Fund, 1990), discusses fiscal policy in LDCs. Fry (note 46); Newbery and Stern (note 4); Stephen R. Lewis, Jr., *Taxation for Development: Principles and Applications* (New York: Oxford University Press, 1984); and Eprime Eshag, *Fiscal and Monetary Policies and Problems in Developing Countries* (Cambridge: Cambridge University Press, 1983), are excellent general works on LDC monetary and fiscal policies. Tanzi; Perry; Tait, Gratz, and Eichengreen; Chelliah, Baas, and Kelly (note 4); and the World Bank (note to Table 15–1) discuss tax rate figures in DCs and LDCs. Tait (note 6) examines international practices and problems associated with the value-added tax. Shah and Toye (note 10) analyze fiscal incentives to increase capital and enterprise in developing countries. World Bank, *World Development Report, 1989,* discusses LDC financial systems. Alesina and Rodrik (note 12) have an excellent article on tax policy, income distribution, and capital formation.

Recent information on inflation is available from the International Monetary Fund's annual *World Economic Outlook* (note 30) and the United Nation's annual *World Economic Survey* (note 29); and on inflation, revenues, and expenditures the World Bank's annual *World Development Report* (note to Table 15–1).

De Oliveira Campos (note 28) analyzes the controversy between monetarists and structuralists concerning Latin American inflation. *World Development* 15 (August 1987) devotes a special issue to inflation in Latin America. Eliana A. Cardoso analyzes "Hyperinflation in Latin America," in *Challenge* 32 (January/February 1989): 11–19. McNown and Wallace (note 33) use cointegration to examine price levels and purchasing power parity in high inflation economies. See Jeffrey D. Sachs and Felipe Larrain B., *Macroeconomics in the Global Economy* (Englewood Cliffs, N.J.: Prentice Hall, 1993), on definitions of inflation and stopping high inflation. Dornbusch (note 1) analyzes how to stabilize an LDC experiencing high inflation. Novaes (note 31) examines the role of inertia in inflation.

Johnson (note 40) has a systematic discussion of arguments for and against inflation. A. P. Thirlwall, *Growth and Development with Special Reference to Developing Countries* (New York: Wiley, 1977), pp. 283–87, summarizes evidence on the relationship between inflation and economic growth.

McKinnon (1993) (note 46) analyzes optimal strategies for financial liberalization in LDCs and transitional economies. Fry, McKinnon (1973), Shaw, and Blejer (note 46) also examine financial repression and liberalization and their impacts on development.

Kuran (note 53) has an excellent review article and bibliography on Islamic banking and economics.

The United Nations Development Program, pp. 47–60, 170–71 (note 24), discusses military spending and the peace dividend with the end of the Cold War.

Pierre-Richard Agénor and Peter J. Montiel, *Development Macroeconomics* (Princeton, N.J.: Princeton University Press, 1996), discuss market structure, behavioral functions, exchange–rate management, stabilization, structural reforms, and economic growth in an open–economy developing country.

PART V: THE INTERNATIONAL ECONOMIES OF DEVELOPMENT

CHAPTER

16

Balance of Payments, Aid, and Foreign Investment

Scope of the Chapter

This chapter discusses international aid and investment. We look first at DC–LDC economic interdependence. The second section discusses capital inflows, and the third, their roles in reducing savings and foreign exchange gaps. The fourth section reviews the balance of payments. Finally the last section analyzes how to finance the deficit.

North–South Interdependence

The countries of the North (DCs) and the South (third world) are economically interdependent. Even the United States, which, together with Japan, has the lowest *ratio of international trade to GNP* among DCs, depended more on the third world in the early 1990s than in the early 1970s. The U.S. merchandise imports as a percentage of GNP, which increased from 6 percent in 1970 to 12 percent in 1980, fell to 9 percent in 1987 before rising again to 10 percent in 1994. However, U.S. exports to third-world countries (excluding Eastern Europe and the former Soviet Union) as a percentage of the total increased from 31 percent in 1970 to 38 percent in 1975 to 41 percent in 1981 before dropping to 34 percent in 1986 and 34 percent in 1990, but rising to 40 percent in 1994. The U.S. imports from the third world increased from 25 percent in 1970 to 42 percent in 1975 (soon after the 1973–74 great oil price hike) to 46 percent in 1981 before declining to 34 percent in 1986, as oil prices fell and the United States became more competitive with dollar depreciation, but increasing to 39 percent in 1990 and 42 percent in 1993. Although the

431

share of U.S. *trade with the third world* was slightly less than Japan's 55 percent, it was more than the European Union, Canada, Australia, or New Zealand.[1]

In 1993, 54 percent of U.S. petroleum consumption was imported, of which 80 percent was from the third world. In about the same year, imports from the third world as a percentage of total consumption were high for a number of vital minerals—100 percent for strontium, 83 percent of columbium, 88 percent for natural graphite, 86 percent for bauxite and alumina, 80 percent for manganese ore, 74 percent for tin, 62 percent for flourspar, 58 percent for barite, 57 percent for diamonds, and 51 percent for cobalt.[2]

In 1980, an independent commission, consisting of twenty diplomats from five continents chaired by former West German Chancellor Willy Brandt, stressed that interdependence created a mutual interest by both North and South in reforming the world economic order. However in the 1980s LDC governments remained dissatisfied with the lack of progress made by North–South conferences in reshaping old international economic institutions (or setting up new ones) to implement the Brandt Commission recommendations or the U.N. General Assembly's call for a new international economic order in the mid–1970s (see Chapter 18). Among northern governments, the United States, still the world's major trader, banker, investor, and aid-giver, despite a relative decline in international economic power from the late 1940s to the 1990s, was the most vocal in arguing that major changes in international economic institutions were not in the U.S. interest and perhaps of limited benefit even to LDCs. Keep this background in mind as we discuss external financing and technology in LDCs.

Capital Inflows

The LDCs obtain a capital inflow from abroad when institutions and individuals in other countries give grants or make loans or (equity) investments to pay for a balance on goods and services deficit (or import surplus). Thus in 1991, Ghana received grants and transfers of $451 million and a net inflow of capital of $367 million to pay for a merchandise deficit of $365 million, a service deficit of $363 million, and a reduction in official liabilities by $90 million. [See Table 16–1 for the **international balance of payments statement,** an annual summary of a country's international economic and financial transactions. A double-entry bookkeeping system ensures that current (income) and capital accounts equal zero.]

This inflow of foreign funds enables a country to spend more than it produces, import more than it exports, and invest more than it saves (Equations 14–1–14–8), and thus fills the gaps that limit development. A study by three MIT economists in-

---

[1]United States President, *Economic Report of the President, 1995* (Washington, D.C.: GPO, 1995), pp. 274–397; and World Bank, *Global Economic Prospects and the Developing Countries, 1995* (Washington, D.C., 1995), 78–91.

[2]Sources for this section are the U.S. Council for Economic Advisers, *The Economic Report of the President, 1982* (Washington, D.C.; U.S. Government Printing Office, 1982), p. 233; U.S. Council for Economic Advisers, *The Economic Report of the President, 1994* (Washington, D.C.; U.S. Government Printing Office, 1994), p. 205; U.S. Department of State, "Trade Patterns of the West, 1977," Special Report no. 48 (Washington, D.C.: Bureau of Public Affairs, 1978); John W. Sewell, Stuart K. Tucker, and contributors, *Growth, Exports, and Jobs in a Changing World Economy* (New Brunswick, N.J.: Transaction Books, 1988), pp. 216–19; U.S. Department of Commerce, *U.S. Foreign Trade Highlights, 1993* (Washington, D.C.: GPO, 1994); and Independent Commission on International Development Issues (Brandt report), *North–South: A Program for Survival* (Cambridge, Mass.: MIT Press, 1980).

TABLE 16-1   Ghana's International Balance of Payments, 1991 ($ million)

	Goods and Services Account	Current Account	Capital Account (+ increases in foreign liabilities)
	(− Debits or Payments)		
Merchandise exports	+948		
Merchandise imports	−1313		
Service exports minus service imports (net travel, transport, investment income, and other services)	−363		
Balance on goods, services, and income		−728	
Net grants, remittances, and unilateral transfers		+451	
Balance on current account		−277	
Net capital inflows			+367
Net official reserve asset change			−90
		−277	+277

Source: Africa Research Bulletin (Economic Series) (13 September 1991): 10501.

dicates that without **capital goods imports** (electrical, mechanical, and transport equipment, machinery, and instruments, not the same as capital imports in Equations 14–7 and 14–8), LDCs run an export surplus. The World Bank estimates that foreign capital as a share of LDC total capital formation was 10 to 20 percent in the 1960s and 1970s, although this share declined to 8 to 12 percent in the 1980s and the 1990s.[3]

But when a country imports capital, domestic saving declines. Two economists who have noticed this relationship argue that using foreign capital makes a country less thrifty. They suggest that foreign capital distorts the composition of capital, frustrates indigenous entrepreneurship, and inhibits institutional reform.[4]

Their explanation is wrong. A careful look shows that an increase in capital inflow associated with a decrease in domestic saving occurs because of the way economists define these aggregates. From Equation 14–8,

$$S = I - F \qquad (16-1)$$

where S is saving, I is investment, and F is capital imports. Investment does not rise because the increase in capital formation from the capital inflow is counter-

---

[3]F. Desmond McCarthy, Lance Taylor, and Cyrus Talati, "Trade Patterns in Developing Countries, 1964–82," *Journal of Development Economics* 27 (October 1987): 5–39; World Bank, *World Development Report, 1988* (New York: Oxford University Press, 1988), pp. 230–31; World Bank, *World Development Report, 1984* (New York: Oxford University Press, 1984), pp. 226–27; and World Bank, *World Development Report, 1994* (New York: Oxford University Press, 1994), pp. 178–79.

[4]K. B. Griffin and J. L. Enos, "Foreign Assistance: Objectives and Consequences," *Economic Development and Cultural Change* 18 (April 1970): 313–27.

balanced by the negative foreign investment, or an increase in foreign claims on the country.

Two Gaps

Hollis B. Chenery and Alan M. Strout, in a model based on empirical evidence from 50 LDCs from 1957 to 1962, identify three development stages in which growth proceeds at the highest rate permitted by the most limiting factors. These factors are (1) the skill limit (see Chapter 14 on inability to absorb additional capital), (2) the savings gap (investment minus savings), and (3) the foreign exchange gap (imports minus exports).

In stage 1, foreign skills and technology reduce the skill limit. The authors, however, focus on stage 2, **investment-limited growth,** and stage 3, **trade-limited growth**—both stages where foreign aid and capital can reduce the gap that limits accelerated growth.

But why differentiate between the two gaps, since Equations 14–7 and 14–8 imply that the *actual* savings gap is always equal to the *actual* foreign exchange gap? The answer is that gap analysis does not focus on *actual* shortages but rather on discrepancies in plans between savers and investors, and exporters and importers. Planned saving depends on income and income distribution, but planned investment is determined by the expected rates of return to capital. Export plans depend on international prices and foreign incomes, but import plans are determined by international prices, domestic income, and income distribution. Given the independence of decisions, it is not surprising that the excess of planned investment over saving might differ from the amount that planned imports exceed exports.

Chenery's and Strout's evidence indicates that at early development stages, growth is likely to be investment limited. If planned investment minus planned saving is greater than planned imports minus planned exports at a given GNP, then all the investment will not be realized. Actual investment equals actual saving plus foreign borrowing at a lower level of GNP than would have been realized if there had been a small savings gap. The required foreign assistance equals the larger of the two gaps, the savings gap. This import of capital will remove the limitation that investment places on growth.

If on the other hand the foreign exchange gap is larger than the savings gap, imports will fall, reducing the foreign capital and inputs available for the development effort. In this case, growth is trade limited. Capital imports equal to the foreign exchange gap will remove the limitation that trade places on growth.

In reality foreign borrowing reduces both the savings and foreign exchange gaps by equal amounts. A machine acquired by international transfer represents both an import for which no foreign exchange needs to be expended and an investment good that does not have to be offset by domestic saving.

The Chenery–Strout, three-stage approach only approximates reality in the many LDCs, where the three limitations often coexist or interact with one another. In fact limits may vary from one sector to another. One sector may be limited by a savings gap, another by a foreign exchange gap, and a third by a skill constraint.

Furthermore the **two-gap analysis,** which focuses on an aggregate approach, does not look at specific needs that foreign funds can meet. Moreover, the emphasis on external development limitations diverts attention from internal economic factors that are often important constraints on growth. Nevertheless, the Chenery–Strout three-stage and two-gap approaches, even though stereotypical, can be useful tools in analyzing foreign capital requirements in a number of different LDCs.[5]

Stages in the Balance of Payments

As we have said, foreign loans enable a country to spend more than it produces, invest more than it saves, and import more than it exports. But eventually the borrowing country must service the foreign debt. Debt service refers to the interest plus repayment of principal due in a given year. Sometimes a country can arrange debt relief, convert debt into equity, or postpone payment by rescheduling the debt or borrowing in excess of the debt due for the year (see Chapter 17). In rare instances, a country may repudiate its debts despite potential economic sanctions and credit restraints (see Chapter 14), or more frequently simply default as sub-Saharan Africa did on more than half its scheduled debt in 1990![6]

Paying back the loan requires a country to produce more than it spends, save more than it invests, and export more than it imports. Doing this need not be onerous, however. In fact it is typical for a newly industrializing country to encounter a growing debt. The United States, from the Revolutionary War until after the Civil War, was a **young and growing debtor nation,** borrowing from England and France to finance an import surplus for domestic investments, such as railroads and canals. However, the United States proceeded to a subsequent stage, **mature debtor nation,** 1874 to 1914, when the economy's increased capacity facilitated the export surplus to service the foreign debt. Similarly, contemporary industrializing countries effectively using capital inflows from abroad should usually be able to pay back loans with increased output and productivity.[7]

Sources of Financing the Deficit

Exports minus imports of goods and services equal the **international balance on goods, services, and income.** Aid, remittances, loans, and investment from abroad finance a LDC's balance on goods and services deficit.

Both oil-importing developed and developing countries had a deficit in 1974, mainly as a result of the quadrupling of oil prices over 4 months in 1973

---

[5]Hollis B. Chenery and Alan M. Strout, "Foreign Assistance and Economic Development," *American Economic Review* 56 (September 1966): 679–733; Charles P. Kindleberger and Bruce Herrick, *Economic Development* (New York: McGraw-Hill, 1977), pp. 296–98; Gerald M. Meier, *International Economics: The Theory of Policy* (New York: Oxford University Press, 1980), pp. 331–34; and Gerald M. Meier, *Leading Issues in Economic Development* (New York: Oxford University Press, 1976), pp. 333–44.

[6]E. Wayne Nafziger, *The Debt Crisis in Africa* (Baltimore: Johns Hopkins University Press, 1993), p. 17.

[7]Since the last quarter of 1985, the United States has been the world's largest net debtor. Robert L. Heilbroner and James K. Galbraith, *The Economic Problem* (Englewood Cliffs, N.J.: Prentice Hall, 1990), pp. 112–13. By the end of 1994, the U.S. net debt was $681 billion. Economists do not know how to fit this U.S. debt period into a balance of payments stage theory. Because of the widespread use of the dollar for international payments and reserves, global companies and central banks sometimes have accumulated dollar assets even when the United States has a persistent deficit in its balance on goods and services. Foreigners may eventually discontinue providing credit to the United States, which would have to reduce consumption to increase savings and reduce its foreign debt.

and 1974. However from 1975 through 1980, while the DCs had surpluses, the oil-importing LDCs had deficits. These deficits continually increased over this period (except for 1976 and 1977), and middle-income LDCs had higher deficits, partly because oil comprised a larger proportion of their total imports than was the case in low-income countries. Middle-income countries' larger deficit was financed disproportionately by commercial loans, with low-income countries receiving primarily aid.[8]

In the 1980s and 1990s, LDCs had a deficit every year except 1980. The deficit increased during the U. S. and other DCs' recession, 1981–82, but fell from 1983 to 1990; in the 1990s the deficit increased again. Oil-exporting countries had surpluses, 1980 to 1986, but these balances shifted to deficits from 1987 to 1995 (except 1990), as real oil prices virtually collapsed (Figure 13–1). The major sources of financing, loans at bankers' standards, declined during most of the 1980s (see Table 16–2), as commercial banks became more cautious with loan write-offs, write-downs, and asset sales by several highly indebted LDCs. Low-income countries received fewer foreign capital resources, as their primary source, aid, as a percentage of GNP declined in the major donor group, the Organization for Economic Cooperation and Development (OECD). However, loans at bankers' standards, primarily to East Asia, Southeast Asia, Latin America, the Middle East, and Eastern Europe, increased during the early 1990s. (Keep in mind that Table 16–2 is in current-price U.S. dollars, which inflated at 80 percent, or 4 percent annually, from 1980 through 1994.)

CONCESSIONAL AID

Aid, or **official development assistance (ODA),** includes development grants or loans made at concessional financial terms by official agencies. Military assistance is not considered part of official aid, but technical cooperation is.

The Grant Element of Aid.   Economists distinguish **concessional loans**, which have at least a 25-percent **grant element**, from loans at bankers' standards. In 1992, the average grant component of the **bilateral aid** (given directly by one country to another) member countries of the OECD gave to developing countries was 93.7 percent. Of the $41.2 billion the OECD contributed, $32.9 billion were outright grants. In addition loans totaling $8.3 billion had a grant component of 69 percent, or $5.7 billion. (The grant element of the loan depends on how much the interest rate is below commercial rates, the length of the grace period in which interest charges or repayments of principal is not required, how long the repayment period is, and the extent to which repayment is in local, inconvertible currency.)

Calculating the grant component of OECD aid or ODA to developing countries in 1992 is fairly simple. Adding the product of $32.9 billion multiplied by 1.00 (the grant component of gifts) to the product of $8.3 billion multiplied by 0.69 (the grant component of loans) equals $38.6 billion, the total grant element of aid

---

[8]World Bank, *World Development Report, 1981* (New York: Oxford University Press, 1981), pp. 49–63.

TABLE 16-2 Developing Countries' Balance on Goods and Services Deficit and Finance Sources, 1980–96 ($ billions)

Item	Year																
	1980	1981	1982	1983	1984	1985	1986	1987	1988	1989	1990	1991	1992	1993	1994	1995	1996
Balance on goods, services, and income deficit	(12.9)[a]	66.5	103.0	83.1	56.0	49.2	70.9	32.9	52.9	64.0	29.3	86.7	109.3	128.9	123.4	117.2	123.4
Financed by																	
Private transfers	12.3	11.7	8.3	10.2	11.9	11.1	15.2	17.6	18.1	19.7	16.0	-0.1	-0.7	6.8	2.7	4.5	4.7
Official development assistance	5.4	7.0	8.3	9.8	10.8	13.9	15.0	15.6	17.2	18.2	26.1	3.1	35.7	31.2	32.8	34.4	35.5
Private direct investment	4.3	18.1	20.3	13.1	14.0	11.2	9.9	13.0	16.6	15.9	19.4	29.0	37.4	52.3	56.2	47.2	43.9
Loans (commercial and official) at bankers' standards	99.2	113.3	80.3	52.7	47.6	51.2	38.8	47.7	22.7	45.6	56.1	90.9	108.3	135.5	76.5	57.7	81.2
Short-term borrowing	-89.0	-104.0	-75.8	-21.7	-19.3	-16.6	-14.9	-5.4	-6.2	-5.9	-35.0	39.8	-17.0	-32.3	6.4	0.4	-4.6
Changes in reserves[b]	-45.1	20.4	61.6	19.0	-9.0	-21.6	6.9	-55.6	-15.5	-29.5	-53.3	-76.0	-54.4	-64.6	-51.2	-34.8	-37.3

[a]() refers to balance on goods, services, and income surplus.

[b]Minus sign (−) indicates an increase in reserves.

Source: International Monetary Fund, *World Economic Outlook, 1988* (Washington, D.C., 1988), pp. 97, 108; and International Monetary Fund, *World Economic Outlook, May 1995* (Washington, D.C., 1995), pp. 161–67.

(grants plus loans). Divide $38.6 billion by $41.2 billion (total aid) to equal 0.937, the grant component of aid to developing countries.[9]

OECD Aid.   During the 1980s, OECD countries contributed four-fifths of the world's bilateral (and almost three-fifths of all) official development assistance to LDCs. However, in the early 1990s, after the collapse of centralized socialism and a decade or so of falling surpluses in the Organization of Petroleum Exporting Countries, the OECD contributed 98 percent of all aid (with OPEC providing 2 percent).[10] The OECD aid increased from $6.9 billion in 1970 to $8.9 billion in 1973 to $13.6 billion in 1975 to $26.8 billion in 1980, but declined to $25.9 billion in 1981 and to $21.8 billion in 1985, before increasing to $47.1 billion in 1988 and $60.8 billion in 1992, but declined to $56.0 billion in 1993. As a percentage of GNP, it dropped from 0.34 percent of GNP in 1970 to a post-1960s low of 0.30 percent of GNP in 1973. In 1975, this figure increased to 0.33 percent and in 1980 to 0.37 percent before declining to 0.35 percent in 1985, but rebounding to 0.39 percent in 1986, but fell to 0.34 percent in 1988 and 0.33 percent during all 3 years, 1990–92, before declining to 0.30 percent in 1993. The most recent figures cited are less than half of the 0.70 percent target the OECD accepted in the 1970s and continually reconfirmed in the 1980s and early 1990s.[11] In 1993, only Denmark, Norway, Sweden, and the Netherlands exceeded this target. Canada, with $2.3 billion, ranked seventh among OECD nations in ODA as a percentage of GNP, with 0.45 percent (see Table 16–3).

Although annual U.S. foreign aid (ODA) in the 1960s, 1970s, and 1980s was larger than that of any other country, in the early 1990s, Japan gave more foreign aid than any other country. In 1993, Japan's foreign aid was $11.3 billion, compared to the second-ranking U.S.'s $9.7 billion. As a percentage of GNP (0.15 per-

---

[9]Sources for the section on concessional aid are Organization for Economic Cooperation and Development, *Efforts and Policies of the Members of the Development Assistance Committee: Development Cooperation: 1994 Report*, Report by James H. Michel, Chair of the Development Assistance Committee (Paris: Organization for Economic Cooperation and Development, 1995); Organization for Economic Cooperation and Development (report by John P. Lewis), *Development Cooperation: Efforts and Policies of the Members of the Development Assistance Committee* (Paris, November 1981); OECD (report by Rutherford M. Poats), *Development Cooperation: Efforts and Policies of the Members of the Development Assistance Committee* (Paris, November 1982); OECD, *Resources for Developing Countries, 1980, and Recent Trends* (Paris, June 1981); Overseas Development Council (Roger D. Hansen and Contributors), *U.S. Foreign Policy and the Third World: Agenda, 1982* (New York: Praeger, 1982), pp. 225–46; Overseas Development Council (John W. Sewell and the Staff), *The United States and World Development: Agenda, 1980* (New York: Praeger, 1980), pp. 215–37; Organization for Economic Cooperation and Development, *Financing and External Debt of Developing Countries: 1987 Survey* (Paris, 1988); Organization for Economic Cooperation and Development, *Financing and External Debt of Developing Countries: 1986 Survey* (Paris, 1987); and Society for International Development, *Survey of International Development* 15 (January/February 1978).

[10]During peak years in the 1970s and early 1980s, OPEC countries contributed one-fourth and the socialist countries of the Soviet Union and Eastern Europe one-seventh of world ODA. In 1993, China, South Korea, Taiwan, Turkey, Egypt, India, Israel, and a growing number of other countries provided ODA. However, countries outside OPEC and the high-income OECD provided only a small fraction of one percent of global ODA in 1993. Organization for Economic Cooperation and Development, *Efforts and Policies of the Members of the Development Assistance Committee: Development Cooperation: 1994 Report*, Report by James H. Michel, Chair of the Development Assistance Committee (Paris: Organization for Economic Cooperation and Development, 1995), p. 107; and E. Wayne Nafziger, *The Economics of Developing Countries* (Englewood Cliffs, N.J.: Prentice Hall, 1990), pp. 357–58.

[11]In 1961, U.S. President John F. Kennedy proposed that the 1960s be the First Decade of Development. Although he pledged that the United States would devote 1 percent of its GNP to the effort, the U.S. share has never exceeded half that share. Gerald Piel, "Worldwide Development or Population Explosion: Our Choice," *Challenge* 38 (July/August 1995): 13–22.

TABLE 16-3 Official Development Assistance (ODA) from OECD DAC (Development Assistance Committee) Countries (1993)

	ODA ($ million)	ODA as Percent of GNP
Japan	11,259	0.26
U.S.	9,721	0.15
France	7,915	0.63
Germany	6,954	0.37
Italy	3,043	0.31
United Kingdom	2,908	0.31
Netherlands	2,525	0.82
Canada	2,373	0.45
Sweden	1,769	0.98
Denmark	1,340	1.03
Spain	1,213	0.25
Norway	1,014	1.01
Australia	953	0.35
Belgium	808	0.39
Switzerland	793	0.33
Austria	544	0.30
Finland	355	0.45
Portugal	246	0.29
New Zealand	98	0.25
Ireland	81	0.20
Luxembourg	50	0.35
DAC countries	55,963	0.30

Note: Figures include forgiveness of non-ODA official debt, which comprises about 3 percent of ODA. Chapter 17 discusses debt forgiveness.

Source: Organization for Economic Cooperation and Development, *Efforts and Policies of the Members of the Development Assistance Committee: Development Cooperation: 1994 Report*, Report by James H. Michel, Chair of the Development Assistance Committee (Paris: Organization for Economic Cooperation and Development, 1995), pp. A9–A10, B2.

cent), foreign aid in the United States ranks last among OECD members. The U.S. citizens spend more on participant sporting activities and supplies in a year than their government spends annually on foreign aid. Furthermore, aid as a percentage of GNP in the United States has generally declined steadily with 0.50 percent in 1965, 0.32 percent in 1970, 0.26 percent in 1975, 0.27 percent in 1980, 0.24 percent in 1985, 0.21 percent in 1988, 0.20 percent in 1991, and 0.15 percent in 1993. During the same period, other OECD countries maintained a aid to GNP percentage in excess of 0.40 percent before falling to 0.39 percent in 1992 and 0.38 percent in 1993. The real value of U.S. aid dropped from the 1960s to the 1970s, then leveled out in the 1980s, but fell again in the 1990s. In the rest of the OECD countries, real aid increased continually from the 1960s, before falling slightly in the 1990s.[12]

---

[12]Organization for Economic Cooperation and Development, *Efforts and Policies of the Members of the Development Assistance Committee: Development Cooperation: 1994 Report*, Report by James H. Michel, Chair of the Development Assistance Committee (Paris: Organization for Economic Cooperation and Development, 1995); and Overseas Development Council, *U.S. Foreign Policy and the Third World: Agenda, 1982* (New York: Praeger, 1982).

Why Give Aid?   Development assistance is under renewed attack. Traditional critics view it as too softhearted to be hardheaded. Some leftists see aid as imperialist support for repressive LDC regimes, rather than as a way of spurring economic development for the masses. Critics of all persuasions charge that aid is ineffective: It does not do what it sets out to do.

Let us examine this issue more carefully. Foreign aid is usually in the national self-interest. Economic aid, like military assistance, can be used for strategic purposes—to strengthen LDC allies, to shore up the donor's defense installations, to improve donor access to strategic materials, and to keep LDC allies from changing sides in the international political struggle. Assistance can be motivated by political or ideological concerns—to influence behavior in international forums; to strengthen cultural ties; or to propagate democracy, capitalism, socialism, or Islam. (A political and strategic motivation—to promote democracy and private enterprise and minimize Soviet influence in the third world—was important in congressional approval of President Harry Truman's call in 1949 for U.S. "Point Four" economic assistance to LDCs.) Furthermore aid supports economic interests by facilitating private investment abroad, improving access to vital materials, expanding demand for domestic industry, and subsidizing or tying exports. (Tied aid, since it prevents the recipient country from using funds outside the donor country, is worth less than its face value. In some instances, aid may be tied to importing capital-intensive equipment, which may reduce employment in the recipient country. In 1992, as a share of total bilateral aid, tied aid comprised 31.5 percent of OECD aid and 50.1 percent of U.S. aid.[13])

Some aid—emergency relief, food aid, assistance for refugees, and grants to least-developed countries—is given for humanitarian reasons. Most OECD countries have a small constituency of interest groups, legislators, and bureaucrats pressing for aid for reasons of social justice. For example, some of the support for Point Four and subsequent aid came from humanitarian groups in the United States.

It is difficult to separate humanitarian motives from the self-interested pursuit of maintaining a stable, global political system. Rich countries have an interest in pursuing a world order that avoids war (especially a nuclear holocaust), acute world population pressures, widespread hunger, resource depletion, environmental degradation, and financial collapse. Economic aid is one aspect of this drama.

Many of the major aid recipients of the United States represent countries that the United States consider important strategic interests (see Box 16–1). In 1994, the U.S. Agency for International Development tried to identify strategic, humanitarian, and economic interests in United States aid. Long-term objectives of aid included encouraging broad-based economic growth, promoting peace, building democracy, promoting U.S. prosperity through trade, protecting the environment, providing humanitarian assistance, aiding post-crisis transition in the former socialist countries, stabilizing world population growth, and protecting human health.[14] AIDs and other epidemic diseases, and drugs, such as cocaine, marijuana, and heroin, reflect threats to the quality of life in DCs, as well as LDCs.

---

[13]Organization for Economic Cooperation and Development, *Efforts and Policies of the Members of the Development Assistance Committee: Development Cooperation: 1994 Report*, Report by James H. Michel, Chair of the Development Assistance Committee (Paris: Organization for Economic Cooperation and Development, 1995), p. 29.

[14]The document, "Strategies for Sustainable Development," is summarized in "USAID's Strategy for Stabilizing World Population Growth and Protecting Human Health," *Population and Development Review* 20 (June 1994): 483–87.

BOX 16–1

The 1992–93 Rank Ordering of the Aid Recipients of the United States, Japan, and the OECD

United States	Japan	OECD
Israel	Indonesia	Egypt
Egypt	China	Indonesia
El Salvador	Philippines	China
Somalia	Egypt	Israel
Philippines	Thailand	Philippines
Colombia	India	India
India	Pakistan	Former Yugoslavia
Jamaica	Bangladesh	Mozambique
Pakistan	South Korea	Tanzania
Panama	Malaysia	Bangladesh
Zambia	Vietnam	Thailand
Ethiopia	Sri Lanka	Pakistan
Bolivia	Kenya	Zambia
Bangladesh	Peru	Morocco
Turkey	Nepal	Ivory Coast

Source: Organization for Economic Cooperation and Development, *Efforts and Policies of the Members of the Development Assistance Committee: Development Cooperation: 1994 Report*, Report by James H. Michel, Chair of the Development Assistance Committee (Paris: Organization for Economic Cooperation and Development, 1995), pp. H16–H31.

Major motives for Japanese aid are international responsibility as a major world economic power, export promotion, resource acquisition, overall economic security, bilateral influence, and recipient political stability. As listed below, Japan's aid programs are biased toward Asia. A low proportion of Japan's aid goes to least developed countries, which are primarily in Africa. Japan's aid also focuses on loans, so that the grant element of aid is low.

Despite Japan's leadership in aid expenditures, aid programs in Japan are understaffed, politically muddled, and administratively complex. The programs are fragmented into competing ministries that are excessively centralized, yet no ministry has total oversight of the program.

Japan's historical memory of rapid economic growth through using strong internal leadership and control to learn and adapt from the West has shaped Japan's foreign aid programs. A strong emphasis by Japan, which attributes its economic success to self direction, is to promote self-reliance among its aid recipients. The Keidanren, Japan's Federation of Economic Organizations, the main business grouping in Japan and a major contributor to Japan's aid philosophy, argues that Japan's aid "is based on the belief that the developing countries themselves should play the leading role in their economic development and that Japan's [overseas development assistance] is designed to complement their self-help efforts to end poverty."[15] Still, we cannot take the Keidanren's and aid officials' stress on recipient self-reliance totally at face value, as some of Japan's foreign economic policies in Asia foster dependence, as Chapter 18's discussion on the Asian borderless economy indicates.

Aid to Enhance Global Public Goods.   Global public goods provide an especially strong argument for foreign aid. **Public goods** are characterized by nonrivalry and nonexclusion in consumption. Nonrivalry means that one individual's consumption of the good does not diminish the amount of good available for others to consume. Nonexclusion means that if one person is able to consume the good, then others cannot be excluded from consuming it.[16] As pointed out in Chapter 13, the atmosphere and biosphere are **global public goods**, since nations cannot exclude other nations from the benefits of their conservation or from the costs of their degradation. In addition, family planning programs (Chapter 8) and programs that further global peace and security also have global public goods components.

The Effectiveness of Aid.   How effective has aid been? In some instances, aid has exceeded an LDC's capacity to absorb it. Moreover, aid can delay self-reliance, postpone essential internal reform, or support internal interests opposed to income distribution. Specifically, food aid can undercut prices for local food producers.

Elliott R. Morss argues that the effectiveness of aid to sub-Saharan Africa declined after 1970, as aid programs placed more burden on scarce local management skills and put less emphasis on recipients' learning by doing. After 1970, donors switched from program support (for example, to infrastructure or agriculture) to project assistance, which entailed more specific statements of objectives and means of attaining them, more precise monitoring and evaluation, more foreign control over funds, and more local personnel and resources committed to projects. Furthermore each of the major bilateral, multilateral, and nongovernmental organizations has competing requirements.

When donors underwrite most of the development budget, they insist on continual, extensive project supervision and review, so that recipient government agencies are more answerable to them than to their own senior policy officials. Donors frequently recommend and supervise poorly conceived projects. But even when well conceived, LDC officials fail to learn how to do something until they have the power to make their own decisions. Morss argues that the proliferation of donors and requirements has resulted in weakened institutions and reduced management capacity. For example, in 1981, Malawi, lacking the indigenous capacity to manage 188 projects from 50 different donors, hired donor country personnel (sometimes with donor salary supplements) to take government line positions to manage projects. However, Malawi has not been able to increase its capacity to run its own affairs and establish its own policies.[17]

---

[15]Alan Rix, *Japan's Foreign Aid Challenge: Policy Reform and Aid Leadership* (London: Routledge, 1993), with quotations on pp. 38–39; and Organization for Economic Cooperation and Development, *Efforts and Policies of the Members of the Development Assistance Committee: Development Cooperation: 1994 Report*, Report by James H. Michel, Chair of the Development Assistance Committee (Paris: Organization for Economic Cooperation and Development, 1995).

[16]James R. Kahn, *The Economic Approach to Environmental and Natural Resources* (Fort Worth, Tex.: Dryden Press, 1995), p. 18.

[17]Elliot R. Morss, "Institutional Destruction Resulting from Donor and Project Proliferation in sub-Saharan African Countries," *World Development* 12 (April 1984): 465–70.

Nevertheless, evidence suggests that aid has been essential to many low-income countries in reducing savings and foreign exchange gaps. Furthermore low-income recipient countries continue to press for more aid from rich countries.

Reasons for the Decline in Aid. In 1995 the OECD chided the United States for setting a poor example by cutting its aid budget and warned that the move might have contributed to other OECD countries following suit. In blunt language, the OECD indicated that the United States' "seeming withdrawal from traditional leadership is so grave that it poses a risk of undermining political support for development cooperation" by other donor countries.[18]

How do we explain what James H. Michel, Chair of the OECD's Development Assistance Committee called the "sharp decline in spending by the industrialized democracies for official development assistance."[19] We can only speculate about the reasons. For the United States, political influence has declined dramatically since 1946, when Europe and Japan were war devastated and few LDCs were independent, so U.S. economic aid has come to have less influence too. In any event, the post-1970 U.S. Congress, and at times the president, were increasingly skeptical about aid's value in strengthening allies, influencing international behavior, improving U.S. access to markets and raw materials, promoting capitalism, maintaining global stability, and building a world order consistent with U.S. preferences. Indeed Michel suggests that Americans and other DCs lack "a firm conviction . . . that increasing the security of the people who inhabit the developing world is a major and concrete part of meeting . . . threats" to the North's quality of life. In the United States, even some liberals, churches, and humanitarian organizations traditionally in favor of economic aid stopped supporting it in the 1980s and 1990s because they increasingly perceived it as benefiting large U.S. corporations and conservative countries suppressing human rights.

Moreover, aid levels have fallen with the end of the Cold War and the competition for influence between the West and Russia. Russia has substantially reduced its aid to LDCs, with the collapse of socialism and subsequent negative growth in the 1990s. On the other hand, military security is less important as a motivator for aid from the U.S. and its allies. Additionally, DCs have allocated aid to Eastern Europe and the former Soviet Union in their transition to market economies at the expense of the developing countries of Africa, Asia, and Latin America. Germany has shifted its emphasis to reintegrating its eastern states within the federation, and the European Union is focusing more on economic opportunities within Eastern Europe.

Furthermore, the United States and other OECD countries have achieved many of their goals through means other than aid—specifically through their dominant shares in two major international financial institutions, the International Monetary Fund and World Bank. The conditions set by these lending institutions have ensured that LDCs and Eastern Europe undertake many of the market

[18]Organization for Economic Cooperation and Development, *Efforts and Policies of the Members of the Development Assistance Committee: Development Cooperation: 1994 Report*, Report by James H. Michel, Chair of the Development Assistance Committee (Paris: Organization for Economic Cooperation and Development, 1995); and Steven Greenhouse, "Rich Nations Criticize U.S. On Foreign Aid," *New York Times* (April 8, 1995): p. 4.

[19]Organization for Economic Cooperation and Development, *Efforts and Policies of the Members of the Development Assistance Committee: Development Cooperation: 1994 Report*, Report by James H. Michel, Chair of the Development Assistance Committee (Paris: Organization for Economic Cooperation and Development, 1995), p. 1.

reforms, stabilization, privatization, and external adjustment that high-income OECD countries want.

Aid to Low- and Middle-Income Countries.   Real concessional aid to LDCs rose from $31.3 billion in fiscal year 1972–73 to $48.2 billion in 1982–83 to $59.1 billion in 1992–93 (in 1992 prices). The share of low-income countries in total aid increased from about half in 1972–73 and 1982–83 to 72.9 percent in 1992–93, an indication of substantial reallocation away from relatively prosperous LDCs in the last decade or two.

In 1992–93, 36.6 percent of the aid went to sub-Saharan Africa, the region with the largest number of least-developed countries; 27.1 percent to Asia; 13.4 percent to Latin America, with only one least-developed country; and 23.0 percent to the Middle East, with no least-developed countries. The listing in Box 16–1 indicates that while only four of the top 13 recipients of aid (with at least $1 billion received) in 1992–93—Mozambique, Tanzania, Bangladesh, and Zambia—were least developed countries, nine of the 13 (including the least developed) were low-income countries.

Low-income countries received $10.42 official development assistance per capita in 1992–93, and middle-income countries $7.76. Donors, however, gave only $2.31 aid per capita to populous China and India, whose populations comprise almost two-thirds of low–income countries. (Donors defend this small figure on the grounds that these two countries could not be given as much as other low–income countries without destroying the effectiveness of the flows to other recipients.) If India and China are excluded from low-income countries, per capita assistance to low-income countries is $24.75.

Aid to low-income countries (including least developed but not India and China) was 33.2 percent of their gross investment and 7.3 percent of GNP in 1992–93. This percentage of GNP is 13 times as high as India and China and 22 times as high as that for middle-income countries. For Mozambique, a country of 17 million, aid was 112 percent of GNP! For Zambia, a country of 10 million, aid was 25 percent of GNP; for Honduras, a country of 6 million, aid was 9 percent of GNP.[20]

Multilateral Aid.   In 1992, $17.5 billion, some 32.2 percent of OECD development assistance (and 0.11 percent of GNP) went to **multilateral agencies**, those involving several donor countries. For the United States, 32.9 percent of ODA (and 0.07 percent of GNP) went to these agencies. In 1992, the rank order of concessional aid by major multilateral agencies was the **International Development Association (IDA**, the World Bank's concessional window, primarily for low-income countries, which has usually extended credit for 50 years, with a 10-year grace period, no interest charge, and a nominal service charge) $4.8 billion; the **Commission of the European Communities (CEC**, for aid primarily to the European Community's former colonies in Africa, the Caribbean, and the Pacific), $4.2 billion; the World Food Program; the United Nations Development Program; the United Nations High Commission for Refugees; the Asian Development Fund;

[20]Organization for Economic Cooperation and Development, *Efforts and Policies of the Members of the Development Assistance Committee: Development Cooperation: 1994 Report*, Report by James H. Michel, Chair of the Development Assistance Committee (Paris: Organization for Economic Cooperation and Development, 1995); World Bank, *World Bank Atlas, 1995* (Washington, D.C., 1994); World Bank, *World Development Report, 1994* (New York: Oxford University Press, 1994).

UNICEF (the United Nations Children's Fund); the International Monetary Fund (IMF) soft-loan window; the African Development Fund; and the United Nations Relief and Works Agency.

The overwhelming share of IMF resources is for loans at bankers' standards. However, IMF concessional funds include member contributions (but rarely the United States) for structural adjustment facilities, discussed in Chapter 17, and a trust fund from the sale of IMF gold. Donor countries and agencies often form a funding consortia, frequently under World Bank auspices; a fractional share for concessional aid can soften the overall payment terms of the financial package. Multilateral agencies and consortia generally coordinate technical and financial contributions of individual donor countries with one another and with the recipient's economic program. Aid administered in this way reduces the amount of bidding donor countries make for favors from recipient countries and softens adverse political reactions if a particular project fails.

Congress members sometimes object to U.S. loss of donor control over aid channeled through multilateral agencies and consortia. Other OECD members, however, perceive the United States as dominant in shaping the Washington consensus (Chapter 5) that establishes policies for multilateral agencies and consortia. The United States, as the largest shareholder, can veto loan or concessional funds from the IMF or World Bank. And, as Chapter 17 indicates, some LDCs think the United States and other DCs use external resources to set conditions for LDC domestic economic policies by requiring an IMF "seal of approval" before OECD countries, their commercial banks, or multilateral agencies will loan, aid, or arrange debt rescheduling and writeoffs.

Food Aid. The economist stressing basic-needs attainment is quite interested in food as foreign aid. As indicated in Chapter 7, there is more than enough food produced each year to feed adequately everyone on earth. However, food is so unevenly distributed that malnutrition and hunger exist in the same country or region where food is abundant.

During the 1960s, the United States sold a sizable fraction of its agricultural exports under a concessionary Public Law 480, where LDC recipients could pay for the exports in inconvertible currency over a long period. The U.S. real food aid, as well as food reserves measured in days of world consumption, dropped from the 1960s to the 1970s, 1980s, and early 1990s, partly because U.S. farm interests wanted to reduce surplus grain stocks.

Although annual food aid in the later 1970s, 1980s, and early 1990s was below that of the 1960s, food and agricultural aid (including that from the United States) increased in real terms from the 1960s to the late 1970s and 1980s. In the late 1970s, 1980s, and the early 1990s, food and agricultural aid was one-fourth of worldwide economic aid. Although most of this was to increase LDC food and agricultural production, such aid cannot meet the most urgent short-term needs. Direct food aid is essential for meeting these needs.

In the 1980s and early 1990s, about three-quarters of the food aid went to low-income countries; it amounted to about one-third of their cereal imports. Projections in Chapters 7 and 8 indicate that food deficits are likely to increase in the 1990s. Yet in the 1980s and early 1990s, the United States, which provides the bulk of total food aid, reduced its food assistance.

Critics of food aid argue that it increases dependence, promotes waste, does not reach the most needy, and dampens local food production. Nevertheless food aid has frequently been highly effective. It plays a vital role in saving human lives during famine or crisis and if distributed selectively, reduces malnutrition. Unfortunately poor transport, storage, administrative services, distribution networks, and overall economic infrastructure hinder the success of food aid programs, but the concept itself is not at fault. Furthermore, dependence on emergency food aid is less than that from continuing commercially imported food.

Yet food aid programs need improvement. A World Bank study contends that transitory food insecurity is linked to fluctuations in domestic harvests, world prices, and foreign exchange earnings. The study recommends that international donors emphasize supporting recipient programs safeguarding food security (especially for highly vulnerable people such as lactating women and children under 5 years), investing in projects that promote growth and directly benefit the poorest people, improving the international trade environment (including food price stabilization), and integrating food aid with other aid programs and national institutions and plans, while domestic governments should stress the redistribution of income to relieve afflicted people. The World Bank would not make food self-sufficiency a priority for the recipient LDC but emphasizes preventing substantial food price increases through imports if cheaper.

Moreover, local recipients should receive food they like. The Bank suggests that recipient governments exchange donated food for cash and buy local foods, thus reducing transport costs and waste.[21]

WORKERS' REMITTANCES

Remittances from nationals working abroad help finance an LDC's balance on goods and services deficit. These remittances, primarily from migrants to Europe and the oil-affluent Persian Gulf, from Latin American migrants to oil-exporting Venezuela, from Central American migrants to the United States, and from neighboring countries' migrants to South Africa, Nigeria, Gabon, and the Ivory Coast, amounted to $29 billion to oil-importing LDCs in 1992. In 1992, remittances as a percentage of merchandise exports were 187 percent in Ethiopia, 178 percent in Egypt, 86 percent in Jordan, 45 percent in Bangladesh, 30 percent in Sudan, 20 percent in Pakistan, 11 percent in India, 25 percent in Portugal, 24 percent in Greece, 89 percent in Benin, 161 percent in El Salvador, 8 percent in Mexico, 20 percent in Turkey, and 54 percent in Morocco. For most of the first seven countries listed, this percentage fell during the oil price slump of the 1980s and early 1990s. The last three countries are vulnerable to European and North American backlash to guest workers. The average propensity to save (saving/income) among Turkish and Pakistani emigrants was several times that of their domestic counterparts. The **average propensity to remit** (remittances/emigrant income) was still 11 percent for Turkish workers and 50 percent for Pakistanis, and enabled the living standards and investment rates of the emigrants' families to increase substantially.[22]

---

[21]World Bank, *Poverty and Hunger: Issues and Options for Food Security in Developing Countries* (Washington. D.C., 1986); John W. Sewell, Stuart K. Tucker, and contributors, *Growth, Exports, and Jobs in a Changing World Economy* (New Brunswick, N.J.: Transaction Books, 1988), pp. 235–40; and Organization for Economic Cooperation and Development, *Financing and External Debt: 1987 Survey* (Paris, 1988), pp. 7–40.

[22]World Bank, *World Development Report, 1981* (New York: Oxford University Press, 1981), p. 51; and World Bank, *World Development Report, 1994* (New York: Oxford University Press, 1994), pp. 186–95.

PRIVATE INVESTMENT AND MULTINATIONAL CORPORATIONS

Private foreign investment, a source for financing the balance on goods and services deficit, consists of **portfolio investment,** in which the investor has no control over operations, and **direct investment,** which entails managing the operations. In the nineteenth century, Western European investment in the young growing debtor nations, the United States and Canada, was primarily portfolio investment, such as securities. Today DC investment in LDCs is virtually all private direct investment. **Multinational corporations** (MNCs), business firms with a parent company in one country and subsidiary operations in other countries, are responsible for this direct investment.

The United States accounted for 52 percent of the world's stock of foreign direct investment (FDI) capital in 1971, 40 percent in 1983, and only 25 percent in 1993. DCs comprised 97 percent of world FDI capital stock in 1983 and 93 percent in 1993. After the U.S., the rank order of 1993 FDI capital stock was Japan, the United Kingdom, Germany, and France. The 7 percent of FDI stock held by LDCs included South Africa, India, South Korea, Hong Kong, Singapore, Brazil, Argentina, Colombia, Peru, the Philippines, Taiwan, the OPEC countries, and others.[23]

The United States had both the largest inward and outward flows of foreign direct investment in 1993. China ranked second in 1992 inward flows (or first in 1992 flows to LDCs), $11 billion, 22 percent of total FDI flows to developing countries in 1992. Other leading LDC hosts to inward flows were Singapore $5.6 billion, Mexico $5.4 billion, Malaysia $4.5 billion, Argentina $4.2 billion, Thailand $2.1 billion, Hong Kong $1.9 billion, Indonesia $1.8 billion, Brazil $1.5 billion, and Nigeria $0.9 billion. Seventy-six percent of 1992 FDI inward flows to developing countries (excluding Eastern Europe and the former Soviet Union) were concentrated in these 10 LDCs. By region, 57 percent of the FDI flows of $25 billion to developing countries in 1992 was to the fastest growing host, Asia (excluding the Middle East), 34 percent was to Latin America, and only 6 percent in Africa,[24] where the risk premium is high. Overall, LDCs were hosts for 32 percent of 1993 inflows of foreign direct investment.

In 1993, China was the second largest exporter among LDCs; the export share of foreign affiliates in total national exports increased from 13 percent in 1990 to 28 percent or $25.2 billion in 1993. The future rate of FDI growth in China will depend largely on its political stability, the consistency of its economic policies, its macroeconomic management, and its integration into the world economy.[25]

---

[23]C. Fred Bergsten, Thomas Horst, and Theodore H. Moran, "Home-Country Policy toward Multinationals," in Robert E. Baldwin and J. David Richardson, eds., *International Trade and Finance: Readings* (Boston: Little, Brown, 1981), pp. 267–95; Paul Streeten, "Multinationals Revisited," in Robert E. Baldwin and J. David Richardson, eds., *International Trade and Finance: Readings* (Boston: Little, Brown, 1981), pp. 308–15; and United Nations Conference on Trade and Development (UNCTAD), *World Investment Report, 1994: Transnational Corporations, Employment and the Workplace* (New York: United Nations, 1994); and John H. Dunning, "Transnational Corporations in a Changing World Environment: Are New Theoretical Explanations Required?" in Teng Weizao and N.T. Wang, eds., *Transnational Corporations and China's Open-Door Policy* (Lexington, Mass.: Lexington, 1988), pp. 28–29.

[24]Only 0.6 percent of the FDI flows to developing countries were to least developed countries.

[25]United Nations Conference on Trade and Development (UNCTAD), *World Investment Report, 1994: Transnational Corporations, Employment and the Workplace* (New York: United Nations, 1994), pp. 14–68.

Some economists question whether FDI sources can sustain the flows to LDCs (especially to China) of the late 1980s and early 1990s for any period thereafter. Many MNCs were attracted by large and growing markets and low-cost labor-intensive production in China and other East and Southeast Asian countries. However, the advantages of market growth and cheap labor may decline in the future.

Most of the world's business community believed that no one could afford to ignore the enormous investment opportunities in China. For many an MNC, investment in China represented an effort to get its "foot in the door" to insure the potential to expand in what could be one of the largest markets in the early twenty-first century. If MNCs, after having obtained a minimal presence in China, reduce investment flows substantially, China could experience a shock to its balance-of-payments, export growth, and growth in GNP. Moreover, China's overdependence on foreign capital and technology might reduce domestic savings and innovation.

Some LDC governments are ambivalent, or even hostile, toward MNCs. To be sure, these corporations bring in capital, new technology, management skills, new products, and increased efficiency and income; however MNCs usually seek to maximize the profits of the parent company, rather than the subsidiaries'. It may be in the interest of the parent company to limit the transfer of technology and industrial secrets to local personnel of the subsidiary, to restrict its exports, to force it to purchase intermediate parts and capital goods from the parent, and to set intrafirm (but international) transfer prices to shift taxes from the host country. Still, during the last decade or so, some MNCs have concentrated increasing research and development in affiliates, even in LDCs. For example, in the late 1980s and early 1990s, many MNCs in Japan, where a strong yen made exports less competitive, strengthened their research and development capabilities in affiliates and allied enterprises in Asian developing countries (see Chapter 18 on the Asian borderless economy.)

Most foreign investment is from large corporations. The largest MNCs, with hundreds of branches and affiliates throughout the world, have an output comparable to the LDC with which they bargain. Exxon, Shell, Mobil, British Petroleum, General Motors, Ford, Toyota, General Electric, Matsushita, Hitachi, IBM, Itochu, Marubeni, Mitsui, and Nissho Iwai,[26] each have an annual output exceeding that of most third-world countries (Table 16–4). Thus for instance, Ford would not negotiate investment in Thailand as an inferior party but as roughly an equal in economic power and size.[27] Furthermore, MNCs are increasingly footloose, shifting investments from one country to another as tax rates, wages, and other costs change.[28]

MNCs are important actors on the international scene. The UNCTAD estimates that in 1992, MNC foreign production accounted for 21 percent of world output and that MNC intrafirm trade was one-third of international trade. Four-

---

[26]The last four are among the 15 or so Japanese trading companies that specialize in foreign trade and are responsible for more than half of Japan's foreign trade.

[27]Strictly speaking one must subtract purchases of inputs from other firms from Ford's production to get its value added, so that the figure is comparable to Thailand's GNP, which does not double count the production of inputs supplied by one firm to another.

[28]Richard J. Barnet and John Cavanagh, *Global Dreams: Imperial Corporations and the New World Order* (New York: Touchstone, 1994).

TABLE 16–4 Ranking of Developing Countries and Multinational Corporations according to Production in 1992[a] ($ billions)

1. China	546.1	30. *Mobil*	64.1
2. Brazil	426.3	31. *Daimler-Benz[b]*	63.1
3. Russian Federation	374.0	32. *Matsushita Electric[b]*	60.8
4. Mexico	295.0	33. *Phillip Morris*	59.1
5. South Korea	293.8	34. Venezuela	58.8
6. India	273.9	35. *British Petroleum[b]*	58.6
7. Argentina	200.3	36. *Hitachi[b]*	58.4
8. *Itochu Corporation[b]*	165.8	37. *General Electric*	57.1
9. Taiwan	165.4	38. *Volkswagen[b]*	54.7
10. *Marubeni[b]*	149.4	39. *Siemens[b]*	50.3
11. *Mitsui[b]*	147.8	40. Malaysia	50.2
12. *General Motors*	132.4	41. *Nissan Motor[b]*	50.2
13. Iran	131.1	42. Philippines	49.5
14. Saudi Arabia	126.2	43. Algeria	48.4
15. Indonesia	123.5	44. Colombia	44.4
16. Turkey	115.8	45. *RTZ[b]*	44.0
17. *Exxon*	115.7	46. *Unilever[b]*	43.7
18. Thailand	106.7	47. *Chevron*	41.4
19. South Africa	106.3	48. *Fiat[b]*	40.1
20. *Ford*	100.1	49. *Veba[b]*	39.4
21. *Royal Dutch Shell[b]*	96.6	50. *Solvay[b]*	39.0
22. Ukraine	94.8	51. *Nestle[b]*	38.4
23. *Nissho Iwai[b]*	91.6	52. *Du Pont*	37.8
24. *Toyota Motor Co.[b]*	81.3	53. Chile	37.1
25. *Grand Metropolitan[b]*	79.8	54. *Toshiba[b]*	37.0
26. Greece	75.1	55. *Chrysler*	36.9
27. Poland	73.3	56. *Texaco*	36.8
28. Portugal	73.0	57. Egypt	35.0
29. *IBM*	64.5	58. All other LDCs less than	35.0

[a]GNP for countries and gross sales for corporations, not strictly comparable. As indicated in note 26, one must subtract purchases of inputs from other firms from a multinational corporation's production to get its value added, so that the figure is comparable to a developing country's GNP.

[b]Corporations based outside the United States—Itochu, Marubeni, Mitsui, Nissho Iwai, Toyota, Matsushita, Hitachi, Nissan, Toshiba (Japan), Shell, Unilever (Netherlands/U.K.), Grand Metropolitan, RTZ (U.K.), Daimler-Benz, Siemens, Veba (Germany), Fiat (Italy), Solvay (Belgium), and Nestle (Switzerland).

Source: World Bank, *World Development Report, 1994* (New York: Oxford University Press, 1994), pp. 162–63; and United Nations Conference on Trade and Development (UNCTAD), *World Investment Report, 1994: Transnational Corporations, Employment and the Workplace* (New York: United Nations, 1994), pp. 6–7. Author's estimate for Taiwan.

fifths of Africa's 1983 commodity trade was handled by MNCs. Thirty-eight percent of total U.S. imports in 1977 consisted of intrafirm transactions by MNCs based in the United States. Over one-third of these transactions were from LDCs. Moreover, MNCs play an important role in LDC manufacturing exports, responsible for 20 percent of Latin America's manufactured exports. Indeed U.S. affiliates alone accounted for 7.2 percent of 1977 LDC manufacturing exports, 35.7 percent of Mexico's, and 15.2 percent in Brazil, but only 1.5 percent in South Korea.[29]

The markets MNCs operate in are *often* international **oligopolies** with competition among few sellers whose pricing decisions are interdependent. International economists contend that large corporations invest overseas because of international imperfections in the market for goods, resources, or technology. The MNCs benefit from monopoly advantages, such as patents, technical knowledge, superior managerial and marketing skills, better access to capital markets, economies of large-scale production, and economies of **vertical integration** (that is, cost savings from decision coordination at various production stages). An example of vertical integration is from crude petroleum marketing backward to its drilling and forward to consumer markets for its refined products. UNCTAD argues, however, that in the 1990s, with substantial improvements in communication and information technologies, MNCs have moved to even more complex integration, coordinating "a growing number of activities in a wider array of locations." Multinationals are increasingly establishing stand-alone affiliates, linked by ownership to the parent but otherwise operating largely as independent concerns within the host economy. These affiliates arrange their own subcontractors, suppliers, and marketing, with some even located in third countries.[30]

From 1988 to 1992, LDCs, under pressure by creditors to privatize public enterprises, sold 17 percent of their medium-sized and large state-owned enterprises to foreign direct investors. In Eastern Europe and the former Soviet Union, 1988 to 1992, FDI from privatizing state-owned enterprises comprised 67 percent of total FDI inflows to that region.[31]

Additionally in some industries, control over global marketing and financing still gives MNCs much power in determining the supply and price of LDC primary exports. For example, three conglomerates account for 70–75 percent of the global banana market; six corporations, 70 percent of cocoa trade; and six MNCs, 85–90 percent of leaf tobacco trade.[32]

Yet ironically in some instances, MNCs may increase competition because their intrafirm transactions break down barriers to free trade and factor movement between countries. On the other hand, once MNCs are established in an economy, they may exploit their monopolistic advantages and enhance concentration. Thus MNCs, which accounted for 62 percent of manufacturing's capital stock

[29]United Nations Conference on Trade and Development (UNCTAD), *World Investment Report, 1994: Transnational Corporations, Employment and the Workplace* (New York: United Nations, 1994); United Nations Conference on Trade and Development Seminar Program, *Intra-firm Transactions and Their Impact on Trade and Development*, May 1978, Report Series no. 2, UNCTAD/OSG/74; Paul Streeten, "Multinationals Revisited," in Robert E. Baldwin and J. David Richardson, eds., *International Trade and Finance: Readings* (Boston: Little, Brown, 1981), pp. 308–15; Economic Commission for Africa (ECA), *Commodity Market Structures, Pricing Policies, and Their Impact on African Trade*, E/ECA/TRADE/3 (Addis Ababa, 1983); Magnus Blomstrom, Irving Kraus, and Robert Lipsey, "Multinational Firms and Manufactured Exports from Developing Countries," National Bureau of Economic Research Working Paper no. 2493, Cambridge, Mass. 1988; and United Nations Center on Transnational Corporations, *Transnational Corporations and International Trade: Selected Issues* (New York, 1985), pp. 3–8.

[30]United Nations Conference on Trade and Development (UNCTAD), *World Investment Report, 1993: Transnational Corporations and Integrated International Production* (New York: United Nations, 1993), pp. 5, 118–21, with quotation from p. 5.

[31]United Nations Conference on Trade and Development (UNCTAD), *World Investment Report, 1994: Transnational Corporations, Employment and the Workplace* (New York: United Nations, 1994), p. 26.

[32]Economic Commission for Africa, *Commodity Market Structures, Pricing, Policies and Their Impact on African Trade*, E/ECA/TRADE/3 (Addis Ababa, 1983).

in Nigeria in 1965, contributed to high rates of industrial concentration. Yet a subsidiary's production that dominates a LDC industry may be only a fraction of the parent company's output and peripheral to the MNC's decision-making process.[33]

You may have already sensed that leaders in LDCs do not agree on whether MNCs are beneficial or not. Some emphasize that MNCs provide scarce capital and advanced technology essential for rapid growth. Others believe such dependence for capital and technology hampers development. In the next two sections, we summarize the benefits and costs of MNCs in less-developed countries.[34]

The Benefits of MNCs.   MNCs can help the developing country to

1. Finance a savings gap or balance of payments deficit.
2. Acquire a specialized good or service essential for domestic production (for example, an underwater engineering system for offshore oil drilling or computer capability for analyzing the strength and weight of a dam's components).
3. Obtain foreign technology and innovative methods of increasing productivity.
4. Generate appropriate technology by adapting existing processes or by means of a new invention.
5. Fill part of the shortage in management and entrepreneurship.
6. Complement local entrepreneurship by subcontracting to ancillary industries, component makers, or repair shops; or by creating forward and backward linkages.
7. Provide contacts with overseas banks, markets, and supply sources that would otherwise remain unknown.
8. Train domestic managers and technicians.
9. Employ domestic labor, especially in skilled jobs.
10. Generate tax revenue from income and corporate profits taxes.
11. Enhance efficiency by removing impediments to free trade and factor movement.
12. Increase national income through increased specialization and economies of scale.

The Costs of MNCs.   Some economists and third-world policy makers have questioned whether MNC benefits exceed costs. These critics charge that MNCs have a negative effect on the developing country because they

1. Increase the LDC's technological dependence on foreign sources, resulting in less technological innovation by local workers.

---

[33]Charles P. Kindleberger, "The Theory of Direct Investment," in Robert E. Baldwin and J. David Richardson, eds., *International Trade and Finance: Readings* (Boston: Little, Brown, 1974), pp. 267–85; and E. Wayne Nafziger, *African Capitalism: A Case Study in Nigerian Entrepreneurship* (Stanford: Hoover Institution, 1977), pp. 55–60.

[34]Sources for these two sections are Ronald Müller, "The Multinational Corporation and the Underdevelopment of the Third World," in Charles K. Wilber, ed., *The Political Economy of Development and Underdevelopment* (New York: Random House, 1979), pp. 151–78; Paul Streeten, "The Multinational Enterprise and the Theory of Development Policy," *World Development* 1 (October 1973): 1–14; Sanjaya Lall, "Less-Developed Countries and Private Foreign Direct Investment: A Review Article," *World Development* 2 (April-May 1974): 41–48; and Edward F. Buffie, "Direct Foreign Investment, Crowding Out, and Underemployment in the Dualistic Economy," *Oxford Economic Papers* 45 (October 1993): 639–67.

2. Limit the transfer of patents, industrial secrets, and other technical knowledge to the subsidiary, which may be viewed as a potential rival.[35] For example, Coca-Cola left India in 1977 rather than share its secret formula with local interests (although in 1988–89 it reentered India, but without sharing its formula, to forestall dominance by Pepsi Cola's minority-owned joint venture).

3. Enhance industrial and technological concentration.

4. Hamper local entrepreneurship and investment in infant industries.

5. Introduce inappropriate products, technology, and consumption patterns (see Box 16–2).

6. Increase unemployment rates from unsuitable technology (see Chapter 9).

7. Exacerbate income inequalities by generating jobs and patronage and producing goods that primarily benefit the richest 20 percent of the population.

8. Restrict subsidiary exports when they undercut the market of the parent company.

9. Understate tax liabilities by overstating investment costs, overpricing inputs transferred from another subsidiary, and underpricing outputs sold within the MNC to another country.

10. Distort intrafirm transfer prices to transfer funds extralegally or to circumvent foreign exchange controls.

11. Require the subsidiary to purchase inputs from the parent company rather than from domestic firms.

12. Repatriate large amounts of funds—profits, royalties, and managerial and service fees—that contribute to balance of payments deficits in the years after the initial capital inflow.

13. Influence government policy in an unfavorable direction (for example, excessive protection, tax concessions, subsidies, infrastructure, and provision of factory sites).

14. Increase foreign intervention in the domestic political process.

15. Divert local, skilled personnel from domestic entrepreneurship or government service.

16. Raise a large percentage of their capital from local funds having a high opportunity cost.

On the last point, Ronald Müller's evidence from Latin America indicates that MNCs contribute only 17 percent, and local sources 83 percent, of the financial capital. However Müller includes as local capital the subsidiary's reinvested earnings and depreciation allowances. If this source is excluded, local financing accounts for 59 percent of total capital. Still if the figure is representative of developing countries as a whole, MNCs contribute less than generally believed. Moreover even if local individuals and financial institutions contribute only 20 to 30 percent, this amount represents substantial funds that invested elsewhere might better meet the country's social priorities.

Southern Africa illustrates MNC cost. Between 1960 and 1985, almost half the Western MNC investment in Africa was in the Republic of South Africa, supporting not only apartheid there but also harming the neighboring countries'

---

[35]Owen T. Adikibi, "The Multinational Corporation and Monopoly of Patents in Nigeria," *World Development* 16 (April 1988): 511–26.

| | |

BOX 16-2

Infant Feeding and the Multinationals

Critics charge that multinational corporations introduce inappropriate consumption patterns in LDCs and point to the infant formula industry as a major example.

According to the U.N. Food and Agriculture Organization (FAO),

> Breast milk is a commodity of very high nutritious value and low production cost which is almost perfectly equitably distributed among the needy—something that . . . cannot be said about supplies of other types of food. . . . In India, a low-paid working woman would have to use her total income in order to purchase formula milk in sufficient quantities.

The World Health Organization contended that major MNCs have used unfair marketing gimmicks to persuade women to buy infant formula for bottle feeding. Labels display bouncing, blue-eyed, white babies, suggesting to poor third-world mothers that their own children can attain robust good health if fed the formula. Some companies have offered scholarships and travel allowances to have rural health officials promote the formulas. Companies often give a new mother free formula as she leaves the hospital. Such a mother may start off her baby on the formula only to discover that when the samples run out, she cannot revert to breast feeding because her milk dries up in about a week if suckling is discontinued.

However, to use infant formula effectively, a mother must read the directions on a can, mix the powder with the right amount of purified water, refrigerate the fluid, and feed it to her baby in a sterilized bottle, nearly an impossibility for most poor women in LDCs.

Breast-fed infants are rarely malnourished except when the mother is severely underfed. And bottle feeding infants under such unsanitary circumstances as exist in many LDCs means the infant is subject to diarrhea and gastrointestinal tract infection, which lead to an increased incidence of protein energy malnutrition.

According to FAO, the drastic decline in breast feeding in many urban areas has dramatically increased infant malnutrition in low-income groups. In 1975, in a West African city hospital, 90 percent of the infants below the age of 6 months with diarrhea and dehydration were bottle fed, even though more than three-fourths of urban infants that age were breast fed. In the baby's second year, corresponding to the weaning age, severe cases of malnutrition occur with the highest frequency.

In May 1981, the assembly of the World Health Organization voted over U.S. objection for a voluntary commercial code to ban advertising and restrict marketing practices in the infant formula industry. Some code supporters estimate that implementing it could save the lives of as many as one million infants a year. And while infant formula MNCs, under pressure from consumer groups and other critics, agreed in the early to mid-1980s to restrict LDC marketing practices, in the late 1980s and early 1990s, several consumer lobbyists charged the MNCs with reneging. In response to another incident, a U.S. MNC paid the Indian government $470 million for a toxic chemical gas leak at a Bhopal pesticide plant that killed 2,500 people on December 3, 1984. Although responsibility of the infant feeding and pesticide MNCs may be overstated and not representative of the impact of MNCs in other industries, these cases illustrate why many LDCs want to restrict the flow of foreign investment.

Sources: Food and Agriculture Organization of the United Nations, *The Fourth FAO World Food Survey,* FAO Food and Nutrition Series No. 10 (Rome, 1977), pp. 43–45; *Dollars and Sense* (May–June 1981), pp. 12–14; Ward Morehouse and M. Arun Subramaniam, *The Bhopal Tragedy* (New York: Council on International and Public Affairs, 1986); "How Union Carbide Fleshed Out its Theory of Sabotage at Bhopal," *Wall Street Journal* (July 7, 1988), p. 1; Amrita Basu, "Bhopal Revisited: The View from Below," *Bulletin of Concerned Asian Scholars* 26 (January-June 1994): 3–13.

development. The MNCs and the Pretoria government viewed South Africa as the core for their expanding activities throughout other parts of southern Africa, which provided labor, a market, and raw materials. The MNCs with subsidiaries also in South Africa's neighboring countries dominated their banking systems, invested much of these countries' financial capital in South Africa, shipped raw materials for processing from them to South Africa, and neglected their manufacturing and (sometimes) mining industries. These neighbors bought capital goods, some consumer goods, and even foodstuffs from South African MNCs. Until the 1980s, the international copper companies in Zambia, Zaïre, Botswana, and Namibia built most fabricating factories in South Africa or the West.[36]

The MNCs and LDC Economic Interests.   The MNC benefits and costs vary among classes and interest groups within a LDC population. Sometimes political elites welcome a MNC because it benefits them through rake-offs on its contract, sales of inputs and services, jobs for clients, and positions on the boards of directors (even though the firm harms the interests of most of the population). However, as political power is dispersed, elites may have to represent a more general public interest.

Since the early 1970s, there has been a shift in bargaining power away from the MNCs to third-world governments, which have increased their technical and economic expertise and added alternative sources of capital and technology. An increasing share of MNC investment is in joint ventures with LDC government or business. And LDCs have appropriated more of the monopoly rents from public

---

[36]Ann Seidman and Neva Seidman Makgetla, *Outposts of Monopoly Capitalism: Southern Africa in the Changing Global Economy* (Westport, Conn.: Lawrence Hill, 1980).

utilities and mineral production. In the 1970s, the most visible change was the shift in the ownership of OPEC oil concessions from the international oil companies to OPEC member governments (see Chapter 13). Moreover, as a result of increasing LDC restrictions, some of the MNC role has shifted from equity investment, capital ownership, and managerial control of overseas facilities to the sale of technology, management services, and marketing. As LDCs become more selective in admitting MNCs, and more effective at bargaining, they increase the benefits and reduce the costs of MNCs.[37]

Some economists, however, would argue that, since the mid-1980s, the bargaining power has shifted back somewhat to MNCs. Under IMF stabilization loans and IMF-World Bank adjustment loans, LDCs have faced pressures to privatize and open their economies to foreign capital investment, policies which provide more opportunities for DC-based multinational companies.

Alternatives to MNC Technology Transfer. The LDCs can receive technology from MNCs without their sole ownership. Joint MNC-local country ventures can help LDCs learn by doing. Yet frequent contractual limits on transferring patents, industrial secrets, and other technical knowledge to the subsidiary, which may be viewed as a potential rival, may hamper learning benefits. **Turnkey projects**, where foreigners for a price provide inputs and technology, build plant and equipment, and assemble the production line so that locals can initiate production at the "turn of a key," are usually more expensive and rarely profitable in LDCs (which usually lack an adequate industrial infrastructure). Other arrangements include management contracts, buying or licensing technology, or (more cheaply) buying machinery in which knowledge is embodied. The late nineteenth-century Japanese government, which received no foreign aid, introduced innovations by buying foreign technology or hiring foreign experts directly. More recently in the 1980s, the Chinese government-owned Jialing Machinery Factory in Chongqing improved the engineering of its motorcycles substantially by buying technical advice, machines, parts, and licensing technology from Japan's Honda Motor Company. Additionally nonmarket sources of foreign knowledge include imitation, trade journals, and technical and scientific exchange, as well as feedback from foreign buyers or users of exports—all virtually costless.[38]

Sanjaya Lall's conclusion is sensible

> The correct strategy then must be a judicious and careful blend of permitting TNC [MNC] entry, licensing and stimulation of local technological effort. The stress must always be—as it was in Japan—to keep up with the best practice technology and to achieving production efficiency which enables local producers

[37]Paul Streeten, "Multinationals Revisited," in Robert E. Baldwin and J. David Richardson, eds., *International Trade and Finance: Readings* (Boston: Little, Brown, 1981), pp. 308–15.

[38]Gerald L. Nordquist, "Visit to Jialing Machinery Factory, May 24, 1987," in Louis de Alessi, delegation leader, Report of the May 13–30, 1987 American People to People Economics Delegation to the People's Republic of China, Spokane, Wash., Citizen Ambassador Program, 1987, pp. 66–71; E. Wayne Nafziger, "The Japanese Development Model: Its Implications for Developing Countries," *Bulletin of the Graduate School of International Relations, International University of Japan,* no. 5 (July 1986): 1–26; and Martin Fransman, *Technology and Economic Development* (Boulder, Colo.: Westview, 1986), pp. 11–14, who indicates major modes of transferring knowledge through the market.

(regardless of their origin) to compete in world markets. This objective will necessitate TNC presence in some cases, but not in others.[39]

Loans at Bankers' Standards.   Nonconcessional loans from abroad finance a deficit in the balance on goods and services account. For LDCs the ratio of official aid to commercial loans declined for a decade and a half after 1970: from 1.40 in 1970 to 0.66 in 1973 to 0.55 in 1975 to 0.36 in 1978 to 0.23 in 1984. Subsequently the ratio of official aid to commercial loans rose from 0.23 in 1984 to 0.33 in 1987 to 0.47 in 1990, before falling to 0.43 in 1994. The increasing trend after the mid-1980s mostly reflected the fall in private lending discussed below rather than substantial growth in concessional assistance. By the late 1980s and early 1990s, low-income countries, with more than twice the population of middle-income countries, received twice the official assistance that middle-income countries did, in contrast to the 1970s, when aid was evenly divided among the country categories. However, all but a small fraction of commercial loans (that is, loans at bankers' standards) were to middle-income countries having high credit ratings.[40]

Two sources of lending fell in the late 1980s: (1) private lending as commercial bankers became unwilling to finance in the face of debt rescheduling and default (Chapter 17), recent nonperforming loans, and the change from syndicated to more selective lending by individual banks, and (2) official (or officially supported) export credit finance (a part of short-term borrowing in Table 16–2) as the creditworthiness of oil exporters declined with oil-price reductions, LDC imports decreased (with slower growth and rising debt), and interest rates for bank finance fell.[41] In the 1990s, in response to debt rescheduling and write-downs (discussed in Chapter 17), loans at bankers' standards to LDCs rose modestly.

Bilateral Flows.   OECD official development assistance is only a part of the total net flow of resources to LDCs. As indicated earlier, 0.30 percent of the 1993 GNP of OECD countries was foreign aid. However, additional net flows included private capital—0.33 percent of GNP, nonconcessional official flows—0.04 percent of GNP, and private voluntary agencies—0.03 percent of GNP. Thus the total net flow was 0.70 percent of GNP.[42]

---

[39]Sanjaya Lall, *Multinationals, Technology and Exports: Selected Papers* (New York: St. Martin's Press, 1985), p. 76.

[40]Sources for the section on loans are Organization for Economic Cooperation and Development, *Development Cooperation: Efforts and Policies of the Members of the Development Assistance Committee* (Paris, November 1982); Organization for Economic Cooperation and Development, *Resources for Developing Countries, 1980 and Recent Trends* (Paris, June 1981); Overseas Development Council, *U.S. Foreign Policy and the Third World: Agenda, 1982* (New York: Praeger, 1982), pp. 225–46; Overseas Development Council, *The United States and World Development; Agenda, 1982* (New York: Praeger, 1982), pp. 215–37; World Bank, *World Development Report, 1981* (New York: Oxford University Press, 1981), pp. 49–63; World Bank, *Annual Report, 1980* (Washington, D.C.: 1980); International Monetary Fund, *World Economic Outlook* (Washington, D.C., 1988), pp. 96–109; and International Monetary Fund, *World Economic Outlook, May 1995* (Washington, D.C., 1995), pp. 161–67.

[41]Organization for Economic Cooperation and Development, *Financing and External Debt of Developing Countries: 1985 Survey* (Paris, 1986), pp. 23–24.

[42]Organization for Economic Cooperation and Development, *Efforts and Policies of the Members of the Development Assistance Committee: Development Cooperation: 1994 Report*, Report by James H. Michel, Chair of the Development Assistance Committee (Paris: Organization for Economic Cooperation and Development, 1995), pp. C3-C4.

The Eurocurrency Market. **Eurodollars** are dollars deposited in banks outside the United States. More generally **Eurocurrency** deposits are in currencies other than that of the country where the bank (called a Eurobank) is located. The Eurobank system began in the early 1950s when the Soviet Union, using the U.S. dollar for international trade and fearing the U.S. government might block its deposits in U.S. banks, transferred its dollars to English banks. These (and subsequently other European) banks could lend these dollars to MNCs, banks, governments, and other borrowers. Banks increased their profits by avoiding national exchange controls, reserve requirements, and bank interest ceilings, and depositors were attracted by receiving higher interest rates. In the early 1990s, dollars comprised two-thirds of the more than $6 trillion deposits in this unregulated financial market, which is located in Europe (London, Zurich, Paris, Amsterdam, and Luxembourg), Hong Kong, Singapore, Tokyo, Kuwait, Nassau, Panama, Grand Cayman, Bahrain, and (in 1981 after U.S. banks could accept Eurodeposits) New York City. Eurobanks have played a role in lending to LDCs, including recycling petrodollars to oil-importing LDCs in the mid-1970s. While the absence of reserve requirements provides substantial potential for the multiple expansion of bank deposits (and world inflation), in practice most loan funds are deposited outside Eurobanks, thus leaking out of the system.[43]

Funds from Multilateral Agencies. In 1944, 44 nations established the **World Bank**, envisioned primarily as a source for loans for post-World War II reconstruction; and the **IMF**, an agency charged with providing short-term credit for international balance of payments deficits (see Chapter 5). Neither institution was set up to solve the financial problems of developing countries; nevertheless, today virtually all financial disbursements from the World Bank are to LDCs, and the IMF is the lender of last resort for LDCs with international payments crises.

The World Bank is a well-established borrower in international capital markets, issuing bonds denominated in U.S. dollars, but guaranteeing a minimal Swiss franc value when the dollar depreciates. In the early 1990s, the Bank, which is the largest source of long-term developmental finance for LDCs, provided about 40 percent of the total net resources to LDCs. It lent more than $30 billion to LDC governments annually, including funds for social investments, such as irrigation and flood control in Indonesia, a hydroelectric plant in Colombia, a mass transit rail system in Brazil, port facilities in Slovenia, a water supply system in Thailand, and a college of fisheries in the Philippines. Furthermore, the World Bank has used its technical and planning expertise to upgrade projects to meet banking standards. A World Bank affiliate, the International Finance Corporation, has invested $2–3 billion annually in agencies to stimulate private enterprise, such as the Industrial Credit and Investment Corporation of India, mentioned in Chapter 14. These amounts do not include soft loans (or concessional aid) of more than $5 billion annually made by another World Bank affiliate, the **International Development Association.**

The IMF provides ready credit to a LDC with balance of payments problems equal to the **reserve tranche**—the country's original contribution of gold—or

---

[43]Paul R. Krugman and Maurice Obstfeld, *International Economics: Theory and Policy* (New York: HarperCollins, 1994), pp. 642–51; Peter B. Kenen, *The International Economy* (Englewood Cliffs, Prentice-Hall, 1989), pp. 453–54, 468–70; Wilfred J. Ethier, *Modern International Economics* (New York: London, 1988), pp. 498–509; and Daniel R. Fusfeld, *Economics: Principles of Political Economy* (Glenview, Ill.: Scott, Foresman, and Co., 1988), pp. 799–801.

25 percent of its initial contribution or quota. Beyond that other credit lines include the first credit tranche, with 25 percent of the quota, granted on adoption of a program to overcome international payments difficulties; an **extended facility,** with 150 percent of the quota, based on a detailed medium-term program; a **supplementary financing facility subsidy account,** 140 percent of quota (financed by repayments from trust fund loans and voluntary contributions) to support standby arrangements for eligible low-income LDCs under previous programs; a **compensatory and contingency financing facility (CFF),** 75 percent of quota, to finance a temporary shortfall in export earnings or excess costs of cereal imports beyond the country's control; **buffer stock financing,** 50 percent of the quota, to stabilize export earnings; an **oil facility,** funds borrowed from oil-exporting countries to lend at competitive interest rates to LDCs with balance of payments deficits; and a **subsidy account,** contributed by 25 DCs and capital surplus oil exporters that makes available interest subsidies to low-income countries.[44] To illustrate, the financial intermediation of the IMF enabled India to borrow $2.85 billion from Saudi Arabia in 1981 at an interest rate of 11 percent, compared to 18 percent in the commercial markets.

Yet between 1983 and 1985, most special funding beyond direct IMF credits dried up, with net lending to LDCs falling from $11.4 billion to $0.2 billion, reducing IMF leverage to persuade LDCs to undertake austerity in the face of internal political opposition. However, from 1986 to 1988, the IMF added a **structural adjustment facility (SAF)** which provides concessional assistance as a portion of a package of medium-term macroeconomic and adjustment programs to low-income countries facing chronic balance of payments problems; an **enhanced structural adjustment facility** for the poorest IMF members making adjustments; and restored the CFF with an average grant element of 20 percent. The first two facilities were financed by recycling the IMF Trust Fund (from the sale of IMF gold) and by Japan and European countries with external surpluses, but not the United States, which had an international deficit and was opposed to IMF long-term concessional aid. As an example of how this aid works, in 1988, the IMF approved $85 million ($35 million as SAF and $18 million as supplementary funding) for Togo, whose export earnings from cocoa, coffee, palm products, and peanuts had declined from 1985 to 1987.[45]

While the third world's (LDCs and high-income oil-exporters) collective vote in the IMF, based on member quotas, is 40 percent, LDCs often support DCs in laying down conditions for borrowing members in order not to jeopardize the IMF's financial base. In 1988, in exchange for IMF lending, Togo agreed to reduce its fiscal deficit, restrain current expenditures, select investment projects more rigorously, privatize some public enterprises, and liberalize trade. The LDC critics, supported by the Brandt Commission, charge that the IMF presumes that international payments problems can be solved only by reducing social programs, cutting subsidies, depreciating currency, and restructuring similar to Togo's 1988 program. According to the Brandt report, the Fund's insistence on drastic measures in short time periods imposes unnecessary burdens on low-income countries that

---

[44]Herbert G. Grubel, *International Economics* (Homewood, Ill.: Irwin, 1981), pp. 531–33.

[45]Richard E. Feinberg, "An Open Letter to the World Bank's New President," in Richard E. Feinberg and contributors, *Between Two Worlds: The World Bank's Next Decade* (New Brunswick, N.J.: Transaction Books, 1986), pp. 14–18; World Bank, *World Development Report, 1988* (New York: Oxford University Press, 1988), p. 141; and *IMF Survey* (February 8, 1988), p. 33, (April 4, 1988), p. 110, (August 19, 1988), p. 273, and (September 26, 1988), p. 302.

not only reduce basic-needs attainment, but also occasionally lead to "IMF riots" and even the downfall of governments.[46] Surely the IMF must be satisfied that a borrower can repay a loan. And there may be few alternatives to monetary and fiscal restrictions or exchange-rate devaluation for eliminating a chronic balance of payments deficit. Furthermore, as Chapters 17 and 20 indicates, the IMF's structural adjustment lending puts more emphasis on growth and efficiency and less on reducing domestic demand and attaining external balance.

Other major multilateral sources of nonconcessional lending in 1993 were the Inter-American Development Bank, the Asian Development Bank, and the European Union.

Private Loans.   In the 1960s, the LDC balance on goods and services deficit was financed primarily by flows from official or semiofficial sources in the form of grants, concessional loans, and market loans. In contrast, primarily private loans financed deficits in the late 1970s and the early 1980s, but there is no pattern since then. The ratio of private flows to official flows from OECD countries increased from 0.64 in 1964 to 1966 to 0.87 in 1970 to 1.35 in 1975 to 1.95 in 1979, before falling to 1.78 in 1983 and 0.59 in 1987, rising to 2.50 in 1991, but falling to 1.02 in 1993.

In the 1960s, private finance consisted mainly of suppliers' credits and direct foreign investment. Commercial bank lending increased after 1967 but rose even more dramatically in 1973 to 1975. However, the share of commercial bank lending and other private flows declined during the 1980s, because of DC bankers' concerns about the creditworthiness of heavily indebted countries and the LDCs' reluctance to increase their debt burden to private lenders.

Summary

1. An independent commission chaired by Willy Brandt contends that the reform of the world economic order is in the mutual interest of both DCs and LDCs. In the 1980s, some DC governments, especially the United States, did not agree that major reform was in their interest.

2. A capital inflow enables a country to invest more than it saves and import more than it exports.

3. A newly industrializing country that effectively uses an inflow of foreign funds should usually be able to pay back its debt from increased output and productivity.

4. Exports minus imports of goods and services equal the international balance on goods and services. Aid, remittances, loans, and investment from abroad finance a balance on goods and services deficit.

5. Countries give concessional aid to LDCs for reasons of national economic and political interest, humanitarianism, and global political maintenance.

6. In 1986, the grant component of concessional aid to LDCs by high-income Organization for Economic Cooperation and Development (OECD) countries (the West and Japan) was 94 percent.

---

[46]International Development *Report* (Brandt report), *North-South: A Program for Survival* (Cambridge, Mass.: MIT Press, 1980), pp. 215–16.

7. The OECD official aid remained between 0.30 percent and 0.39 percent of GNP from 1970 to 1993. For the United States, this percentage decreased from 0.32 percent in 1970 to 0.24 percent in 1985 to 0.15 percent in 1993, the lowest percentage among high-income OECD countries. These aid proportions are far below the 0.70 percent aid target.

8. The major multilateral agencies providing concessional aid to LDCs were the International Development Association (a World Bank affiliate), the Commission of the European Communities, and the United Nations.

9. Although the United States still accounts for the largest share of the world's foreign, private investment, its share declined between 1971 and 1993.

10. The largest multinational corporations have an economic strength comparable to that of the LDCs with which they bargain. The foreign production of MNCs accounts for about 21 percent of world output and intrafirm trade for about 33 percent of international manufacturing trade.

11. Although MNCs in developing countries provide scarce capital and advanced technology for growth, doing so may increase LDC dependence on foreign capital and technology. The LDCs need a judicious combination of MNCs, joint MNC–local ventures, licensing, and other technological borrowing and adaptation.

12. Developing countries increased their reliance on commercial loans from the early 1970s to the mid-1980s, but reduced their reliance on these loans thereafter.

Terms to Review

- capital import
- investment
- General Agreements on Tariffs and Trade
- capital goods imports
- international balance of payments statement
- two-gap analysis
- investment-limited growth
- trade-limited growth
- young debtor nation
- mature debtor nation
- international balance on goods, services, and income
- aid (official development assistance)
- grant element of aid
- concessional loans
- Organization for Economic Cooperation and Development (OECD)
- Council for Mutual Economic Assistance (CEMA)
- bilateral aid
- public goods
- global public goods
- multilateral agencies
- average propensity to remit
- portfolio investment
- direct investment
- multinational corporations
- oligopoly
- vertical integration
- turnkey projects
- Eurodollars
- Eurocurrency
- World Bank
- International Development Association (IDA)
- Commission of the European Communities (CEC)
- International Monetary Fund (IMF)
- reserve tranche
- IMF extended facility
- IMF supplementary financing facility subsidy account
- IMF compensatory and contingency financing facility (CFF)
- IMF buffer stock financing
- IMF oil facility

- IMF subsidy account
- IMF structural adjustment facility (SAF)

- IMF enhanced structural adjustment facility

Questions to Discuss

1. Using national income equations, explain an inflow of capital from abroad in terms of expenditures-income, investment-saving, and import-export relationships. Indicate the relationships between expenditures and income, investment and saving, and imports and exports for a country paying back a foreign loan. Does repaying the loan have to be burdensome?

2. To what extent does the Brandt Commission's view of DC and LDC interdependence conflict with Frank's view of LDC dependence?

3. How can foreign aid, capital, and technology stimulate economic growth? How could the roles of foreign aid, capital, and technology vary at different stages of development?

4. What are Chenery's and Strout's two gaps? How do foreign aid and capital reduce these two gaps? What are the strengths and weaknesses of the two-gap analysis?

5. What are sources for financing an international balance on goods and services deficit? Which was the most important source for LDCs in the 1990s?

6. How effective has DC aid been in promoting LDC development? How effective has food aid been?

7. What are the costs and benefits for donor countries giving aid to LDCs? Do the costs outweigh the benefits? Choose one donor country. What are the costs and benefits for this country giving aid? Do the costs outweigh the benefits?

8. What is the trend for OECD aid as a percentage of GNP since 1970?

9. Compare economic aid to low- and middle-income countries in the early 1990s. How do you explain the difference?

10. How important was multilateral aid as a percentage of total economic aid during the 1990s?

11. What are the costs and benefits to LDCs of MNC investment? How has the balance between costs and benefits changed in the last decade or so?

12. What was the trend in the ratio of official aid relative to commercial loans to LDCs in the 1970s, 1980s, and 1990s? How important is multilateral lending as a source of nonconcessional loans?

13. How important has the World Bank been as a source of funds for LDCs? How important has the International Monetary Fund (IMF) been as a source of funds for LDCs? Do you think there should be any changes in World Bank and IMF roles in LDC development?

Guide to Readings

The UNCTAD annual report (note to Table 16–4); Sanjaya Lall, "Promoting Technology Development: the Role of Technology Transfer and Indigenous

Effort," *Third World Quarterly* 14(1) (1993): 95–108; Lall (note 39); John H. Dunning, *International Production and the Multinational Enterprise* (London: Allen and Unwin, 1981); Baldwin and Richardson (note 33); and Michael E. Porter, *The Comparative Advantage of Nations* (London: Macmillan, 1990), have useful background on the multinational corporation.

Chenery and Strout (note 5) analyze the savings and foreign exchange gaps.

Data on aid and loans to LDCs and their balance of payments are in periodic volumes from the IMF (note to Table 16–2), OECD (note to Table 16–3), Overseas Development Council (note 9), and World Bank, *World Development Report* (note 20). Rix (note 15) has an excellent analysis of Japan's foreign aid. Weizao and Wang (note 23) discuss MNCs in China. Robert Cassen and associates, *Does Aid Work?* (Oxford: Clarendon Press, 1994), examine the effectiveness of aid.

17 The External Debt Crisis

Scope of the Chapter

Chapter 16 mentioned that the LDCs' persistent deficit on the balance on goods, services, and income, together with a decline in loans at bankers' standards after 1983, exacerbated the LDC debt crisis. This chapter discusses the definition of external debt, the origins of the debt crisis, how capital flight exacerbates the debt problem, the U.S. bankers' and LDC governments' perspective on the crisis, indicators of debt, net transfers, the major LDC debtors, the roles of World Bank and IMF lending and policies, proposals to resolve the debt crisis, and the distributional effects of the debt crisis and relief measures.

Definitions of External Debt and Debt Service

A country's **total external debt (EDT)** includes the stock of debt owed to nonresident governments, businesses, and institutions and repayable in foreign currency, goods, or services. EDT includes both short-term debt, with a maturity of one year or less; long-term debt, with a maturity of more than one year; and the use of IMF credit, which denotes repurchase obligations to the IMF. External debt includes public and publicly guaranteed debt, as well as private debt.[1]

Debt service is the interest and principal payments due in a given year on long-term debt.

---

[1]World Bank, *World Debt Tables: External Finance for Developing Countries, 1993–94*, vol. 1, *Analysis and Summary Tables* (Washington, D.C., 1993), pp. ix, 158–59.

Origins of the Debt Crisis

The LDC external debt increased from $49 billion in 1970 to $157 billion in 1976 to $816 billion in 1982 to $908 billion in 1984 to $1,216 billion in 1986[2] for several reasons.

1. External debt accumulates with international balance on goods, services, and income deficits. LDC international deficits increased from a series of global shocks, including the 1973 to 1974 and 1979 to 1980 oil price rises (which reduced non-oil-producing LDCs' terms of trade) and the recession of the industrialized countries, 1980–83, and continuing slow growth during the remainder of the 1980s (with sharply falling commodity prices, slowed export expansion, and increased OECD protectionism).

2. As indicated in Chapter 16, DCs relied more on private bank and other commercial loans, increasing their ratio to official aid from 1970 to the mid-1980s. Official development assistance (ODA) declined sharply in 1982–83 during the DCs' recession, when LDC external debt grew at a faster rate.[3]

3. Like Iowa farmers and Pennsylvania small business people, LDCs reacted to the input price hikes of 1973 to 1975 by increasing their borrowing. The quadrupling of world oil prices in 1973 to 1974 poured tens of billions of petrodollars into the global banking system, which were "recycled" as loans to LDCs and U.S. farmers and business people at low rates of interest. They were lured by **negative world real interest rates,** the nominal rates of interest minus the inflation rate, −7 percent in 1973, −16 percent in 1974, and −5 percent in 1975. Many of these debts came due in the early 1980s when high nominal rates of interest, together with low inflation rates, resulted in high real interest rates (9–12 percent in 1982 to 1985).[4]

The average interest rate for fixed-interest loans (generally subsidized or long term) rose from 4 percent (1970) to 6 percent (1981) to 7 percent (1986). From 1971 to 1981, interest rates on floating-interest loans (primarily from commercial sources) increased from 8 percent to 18 percent. The decrease in the average loan maturity from 20 years in 1970 to 16 years in 1986, as well as a reduction in the average grace period over the same period from 6 years to 5 years, also aggravated the problem of debt service.[5]

---

[2]LDC debt continued to increase (in nominal terms) to $1,411 billion in 1989 to $1,662 billion in 1992.

Organization for Economic Cooperation and Development, *Financing and External Debt of Developing Countries: 1987 Survey* (Paris, 1988), p. 218; World Bank, *World Development Report, 1978* (New York: Oxford University Press, 1978), pp. 96–97; World Bank, *World Development Report, 1988* (New York: Oxford University Press, 1988), pp. 258–59; and World Bank, *World Debt Tables: External Finance for Developing Countries, 1993–94*, vol. 1, *Analysis and Summary Tables* (Washington, D.C., 1993), pp. 170–71.

[3]Overseas Development Council (ODC), *U.S. Foreign Policy and the Third World: Agenda, 1982* (New York: Praeger, 1982), 225–468; and International Monetary Fund, *World Economic Outlook, October 1988* (Washington, D.C., 1988), pp. 96–109.

[4]Ann O. Krueger, "Origins of the Developing Countries' Debt Crisis," *Journal of Development Economics* 27 (October 1987): 169; Alireza Rahimibrougerdi, "An Empirical Investigation of the Effects of Major Exogenous Shocks on the Growth of Nonoil- and Oil-Exporting Developing Countries from 1965 to 1985" (Ph.D. diss., Kansas State University, 1988), pp. 6, 83; John Cavanagh, Fantu Cheru, Carole Collins, Cameron Duncan, and Dominic Ntube, *From Debt to Development: Alternatives to the International Debt Crisis* (Washington, D.C.: Institute for Policy Studies, 1985), p. 25.

[5]World Bank, *World Development Report, 1988* (New York: Oxford University Press, 1988), pp. 260–61.

4. The inefficiency and poor national economic management indicated before in Nigeria, Zaïre, and Ghana, as well as in Latin American military governments, in the 1970s, meant no increased capacity to facilitate the export surplus to service the foreign debt. Argentina's substantial increase in public spending in the 1970s, financed by borrowing from abroad, increased external debt and reduced export capacity.

Chapter 20 indicates that the efficiency of public enterprise is potentially comparable to that of private enterprise, given a certain size firm, but that public firms are more likely to choose an excessive scale of operations, have easier access to state financing to mute bankruptcy, and more pressure to provide jobs and contracts to clients and relatives than private enterprises. Few LDCs achieve the high quality of economic management by the civil service and economic policy making insulated from political pressures achieved by Taiwan and South Korea (see Chapter 3). In the early 1980s, before World Bank- and IMF-imposed reforms, government employment as a percentage of total nonagricultural employment was 54 percent in Africa, 36 percent in Asia, and 27 percent in Latin America, compared to 24 percent in the OECD.[6]

To illustrate, in Nigeria, government expenditures as a percentage of GDP rose from 9 percent in 1962 to 44 percent in 1979 but fell to 17 percent from World Bank structural adjustment programs, such as the one in effect from 1986 to 1990, which emphasized privatization, market prices, and reduced government expenditures. Nigeria had centralized power during its 1967–70 civil war with the breakup of regions, and in the 1970s, as the oil boom enhanced the center's fiscal strength. Expansion of the government's share of the economy did little to increase political and administrative capacity, but it did increase incomes and jobs that political elites could distribute to their clients.[7]

5. The adjustment essential to export more than was imported and produce more than was spent required translating government spending cuts into foreign exchange earnings and competitive gains, usually necessitating reduced demand and wages, real currency depreciation, and increased unemployment. But when many other LDCs go through the same adjustment process, the benefit to any given LDC was less. In 1985, for example, the pressure on debtor countries to increase export revenues contributed to a glut in primary products and a collapse of their prices.

Mexico reduced real wages 40 percent, increased the unemployment rate, and depreciated the peso from 1980 to 1987 to increase its external competitiveness by 40 percent. Currency depreciation also raised the nominal interest rate essential to spur Mexicans to hold pesos rather than U.S. dollars. Few countries were willing to contract domestic employment and real wages to return the balance on goods and services account to equilibrium.[8]

---

[6]Peter Heller and Alan Tait, "Government Employment and Pay: Some International Comparisons," *Finance and Development* 28 (September 1983): 44–47.

[7]Central Bank of Nigeria, *Annual Reports and Statements of Accounts* (Lagos, 1960–80) (annual); Nigeria, Office of Statistics, *Digest of Statistics* (Lagos, 1960–80) (quarterly); Chibuzo S.A. Ogbuagu, "The Nigerian Indigenization Policy: Nationalism or Pragmatism?" *African Affairs* 82 (April 1983), pp. 241–66; and E. Wayne Nafziger, *The Debt Crisis in Africa* (Baltimore: Johns Hopkins University Press, 1993), p. 50.

[8]World Bank, *World Development Report, 1985* (New York: Oxford University Press, 1985), pp. 62–63; Rudiger Dornbusch, "International Debt and Economic Instability," Proceedings of a Federal Reserve Bank of Kansas City symposium, Jackson Hole, Wyoming, August 27–29, 1986, pp. 71–75; and Jeffrey D. Sachs, "The Debt Crisis at a Turning Point," *Challenge* 31 (May/June 1988), 20.

6. When debts are denominated in U.S. dollars, their **appreciation** (increased value relative to other major currencies) from 1980 to 1984 increased the local and non-dollar currency cost of servicing such debts. Or as in 1985 to 1988, nondollar debts increased when measured in dollars that **depreciate** (reduce their value relative to other major currencies). For example, the dollar value of Indonesia's 1985 debt to the Japanese, ¥1,250 billion) increased from $5 billion to $10 billion in 1988, as the dollar depreciated from ¥250 = $1 to ¥125 = $1.

7. International lenders required LDC governments to guarantee private debt. When private borrowers defaulted, the state's external debt service increased.

8. Overvalued domestic currencies and restrictions on international trade and payments dampened exports, induced imports, and encouraged capital flight from LDCs, exacerbating the current account deficit and external debt problems. One indicator of overvaluation, the black market exchange rate vis-à-vis the official nominal exchange rate, appreciated in Sub-Saharan Africa from 1.36 in 1971 to 1.53 in 1980 to 2.10 in 1983, before falling (often at World Bank/International Monetary Fund insistence) to 1.38 in 1985. These exchange-rate distortions reduced export competitiveness while spurring applications for artificially cheap foreign capital and inputs.[9]

9. The lack of coordination by leading DCs in exchange-rate and financial policies under the world's post-1973 **managed floating exchange-rate system** (an international currency system where central banks intervene in the market to influence the price of foreign exchange) resulted in gyrating exchange rates and interest rates. Efforts to set **target zones** within which key DC exchange rates will float have only increased destabilizing capital movements and unstable exchange-rate changes when inevitably rates approach zone boundaries. This global instability increased external shocks and undermined long-run LDC planning.[10]

10. Substantial capital flight from foreign aid, loans, and investment (discussed below).

Capital Flight

Some bankers and economists feel it is futile to lend more funds to LDCs if a large portion flows back through capital flight. John T. Cuddington estimates that Mexico's **propensity to flee** attributable to additional external borrowing, 1974 to 1984, was 0.31, meaning that 31 cents from a dollar lent by foreign creditors left the country through capital flight![11] The Organization for Economic Cooperation and Development suggests that the $70 billion capital flight from Latin America, 1982, was double the interest portion of the Latin debt-service payments for that year. Capital flight intensifies foreign exchange shortages and damages the collective interest of the wealthy classes that buy foreign assets. Reversing capital flight will

---

[9]World Bank and U.N. Development Program, *Africa's Adjustment and Growth in the 1980s* (Washington, D.C., 1989), pp. 12–17.

[10]Deena Khatkhate, "International Monetary System—Which Way?" *World Development* 15 (December 1987): vii–xvi.

[11]John T. Cuddington, *Capital Flight: Estimates, Issues, and Explanations,* Princeton Studies in International Finance no. 58, Princeton University, 1986.

not eliminate the debt crisis but can reduce debt burdens and commercial bankers' justification for resisting increased exposure to debtor countries.[12]

DEFINITIONS

The many methods of exporting capital illegally include taking currency overseas, sometimes in a suitcase, directly investing black-market money, and false invoicing in trade documents. Which of the domestic holdings of foreign assets (property, equity investment, bonds, deposits, and money) should be classified as domestic capital flight rather than normal capital outflows? Defining **capital flight** as resident capital outflow makes it easier to conceptualize and measure than alternative definitions that characterize it as illegal, abnormal, or undesirable to government or due to overinvoicing imports or underinvoicing exports. Using the World Bank's estimates of capital flight as equal to current account balance, net foreign direct investment, and changes in reserves and debt, the largest capital flights, 1976 to 1984, were from Argentina, Venezuela, Mexico, Indonesia, Syria, Egypt, and Nigeria, while net flights from Brazil (whose real devaluation in 1980 was substantial), South Korea (whose exchange rate remained close to a market-clearing rate), Colombia, and the Philippines were negative.[13]

Whenever international capital markets are highly integrated and transaction costs are low, private individuals will have strong incentives to circumvent what appears to be arbitrary barriers to capital movements, as even the United States found in the 1960s when interest equalization taxes and foreign credit restraint programs resulted in Eurocurrency and Eurobond market expansion to satisfy the offshore demand for funds.[14]

CAUSES

Resident capital outflows result from differences in perceived risk-adjusted returns in source and haven countries. We can attribute these differences to slow growth, overvalued domestic currencies, high inflation rates, confiscatory taxation, discriminatory interest ceilings or taxes on residents, financial repression, default on government obligations, expected currency depreciation, limitations on convertibility, poor investment climate, or political instability in source countries, all exacerbated by the United States' abandoning income taxation on nonresident bank-deposit interest and much other investment income and (in the early 1980s) paying high interest rates. In 1982, Mexico's devaluation and inflation "almost totally wiped out the value of obligations denominated in Mexican pesos." The domestic entrepreneurial energies lost from these policies were substantial.[15]

---

[12]Donald R. Lessard and John Williamson, eds., *Capital Flight and Third-World Debt* (Washington, D.C.: Institute for International Economics, 1987); John Williamson and Donald R. Lessard, *Capital Flight: The Problem and Policy Responses* (Washington, D.C.: Institute for International Economics, 1987); Bank of International Settlements, *Annual Report, 1988* (Geneva, June 1989), pp. 135–36; and R.T. Naylor, *Hot Money and the Politics of Debt* (London: McClelland & Stewart, 1989), pp. 330–31.

[13]Robert Cumby and Richard Levich, "On the Definition and Magnitude of Recent Capital Flight," in Donald R. Lessard and John Williamson, eds., *Capital Flight and Third-World Debt* (Washington, D.C.: Institute for International Economics, 1987), pp. 27–67.

[14]Donald R. Lessard and John Williamson, eds., *Capital Flight and Third-World Debt* (Washington, D.C.: Institute for International Economics, 1987).

[15]John Williamson and Donald R. Lessard, *Capital Flight: The Problem and Policy Responses* (Washington, D.C., Institute for International Economics, 1987), with quotation from p. 21.

ZAÏRIAN PATHOLOGY

Zaïre, whose capital flight cannot be tracked statistically, is a blatant example of flight from LDCs desperately needing foreign exchange to resolve debt problems. Thus foreign exchange from smuggling Zaïrian goods, such as diamonds, abroad is so widespread that a neighbor, Congo, became a diamond exporter of some importance in the 1970s and early 1980s without having any diamond deposits! For two decades the country stumbled from one debt crisis to another, lacking the capacity to pay debt service, which was $375-$625 million annually in the 1980s.[16]

For Pierre Dikoba, Zaïrian President Mobutu Sese Seko's "loot[ing] the country" explained the torn tin roof, malarial mosquitoes, and the lack of furniture, books, and pictures in Kinshasa primary school where he taught in 1991. In 1988, U.S. House Foreign Affairs Chair Howard Wolpe asserted: "Literally hundreds and hundreds of millions of dollars have vanished into the hands or bank accounts of the president and his collaborators." Peter Körner and colleagues estimated Mobutu's 1984 overseas wealth at four to six billion dollars, invested in Swiss bank accounts and Western real estates, enough to solve Zaïre's debt crisis. Indeed, if Mobutu and his allies had not taken out of the country a large proportion of funds the Zaïrian government borrowed abroad, Zaïre might not have had a debt crisis. In 1977, President Mobutu denounced the Zaïrian disease, stating that "everything is for sale, everything is bought in our country. And in this traffic, holding any slice of public power constitutes a veritable exchange instrument, convertible into illicit acquisition of other goods."[17]

HOW TO REDUCE FLIGHT

Source countries need robust growth, market-clearing exchange rates and other prices, an outward trade orientation, dependable positive real interest rates, fiscal reform (including lower taxes on capital gains), taxes on foreign assets as high as domestic assets, more efficient state enterprises, other market liberalization, supply-oriented adjustment measures, a resolution of the debt problem, and incorruptible government officials.[18] Haven countries can lower interest rates and cease tax discrimination favoring nonresident investment income, while their banks can refuse to accept funds from major LDC debtor countries.

Just listing policies for source and haven countries suggests the difficulty of the problem. For Rimmer de Vries, capital flight is the caboose, not the locomotive, meaning that capital flight is symptomatic of the financial repression and economic underdevelopment at the root of the debt crisis, not the cause of it.[19] We

[16]E. Wayne Nafziger, *The Debt Crisis in Africa* (Baltimore: Johns Hopkins University Press, 1993), pp. 92–93; and World Bank, *World Debt Tables: External Finance for Developing Countries, 1993–94*, vol. 2, *Country Tables* (Washington, D.C., 1993), p. 500.

[17]Edward T. Pound, "Zaïre's Mobutu Mounts All-Out PR Campaign to Keep His U.S. Aid," *Wall Street Journal* (March 7, 1990): p. A–4; Joe Davidson, "In Zaïre, Corrupt and Autocratic Rule, Backed by U.S., Has Led Straight to Ruin," *Wall Street Journal* (December 17, 1991): p. A–11; Susanne Erbe, "The Flight of Capital from Developing Countries," *Intereconomics* 20 (November/December 1985), 268–75; and Peter Körner et al., *The IMF and the Debt Crisis: A Guide to the Third World's Dilemma*, trans. Paul Knight (Atlantic Highlands, NJ: Zed Books, 1986), p. 137.

[18]John Williamson and Donald R. Lessard, *Capital Flight: The Problem and Policy Responses* (Washington, D.C.: Institute for International Economics, 1987), pp. 28–58.

[19]Rimmer de Vries, as part of a panel on policy issues in Donald R. Lessard and John Williamson, eds., *Capital Flight and Third-World Debt* (Washington, D.C., Institute for International Economics, 1987), p. 188.

have another vicious circle—low growth, capital flight, and foreign exchange restrictions that hamper growth. Ironically John Williamson and Donald R. Lessard, despite recommendation of financial and exchange-rate liberalization, indicate that sometimes LDCs may have to use **exchange controls,** which limit domestic residents' purchase of foreign currency, to limit the exodus of new savings.[20] The Africa Research Bulletin urges the United States to remove tax policies favoring nonresident bank deposits and Switzerland to lift secrecy protection for bank deposits (dubbed Africa's second AIDS epidemic, "acquired Investments Deposited in Switzerland") of African politicians and economic malfeasors facing judicial due process for criminal activity."[21]

The Crisis from the U.S. Banking Perspective

U.S. regulations restricting interstate commercial bank activity and the rates that banks could pay for deposits enhanced incentives for American and European banks in the 1960s and 1970s to expand into the market for dollar deposits (or Eurodollars, as discussed in Chapter 16) located in cities of Europe, East Asia, the Middle East, Nassau, Panama, Bahrain (and later New York City) that comprise a regulatory no-man's-land. The successive waves of new U.S., European, and Japanese banks entering the Eurocurrency market, with no reserve requirements, fueled credit expansion, especially in the 1970s. European, Japanese, and American regional banks challenging leading American bank domination sought new markets in the 1970s. After 1974, as capital-surplus oil-exporting countries recycled petrodollars to expand credit supply while Western demand for credit contracted, bankers viewed LDCs as a new frontier for lending. LDC borrowers were attractive, as they paid a premium over DC borrowers and were thought to pose little risk since borrower or guarantor governments, deemed incapable of bankruptcy, would service their debt. Ruling elites in Latin America and sub-Saharan Africa were lured by the use of easy bank credit to enhance coalition building while postponing large debt servicing for (perhaps) a future regime.[22]

During the 1980s, the inability of the LDCs to pay debt was a major international economic concern of American journalists and scholars. A complete writeoff of Third World debts in the early 1980s would have wiped out many major U.S. commercial banks, which had more exposure to LDC debt than banks in any other country. Yet in the early 1990s, Harvard economist Benjamin J. Cohen asked: Whatever happened to the Third World debt crisis?[23] A partial answer is that, for LDCs, little has changed. In Africa and a few countries in Latin America, the debt overhang still keeps standards of living down and limits the investment needed to end stagnation. Meanwhile, however, LDC debt repudiation no longer threatens money-center banks of New York City, such as Citicorp, Manufacturers Hanover, and Chase Manhattan. These banks have reduced their exposure to Third World borrowers, so their defaults endanger neither bank credit ratings and stock prices

---

[20]John Williamson and Donald R. Lessard, *Capital Flight: The Problem and Policy Responses* (Washington, D.C., Institute for International Economics, 1987), p. 57.

[21]*Africa Research Bulletin (Economic Series)* 28 (October 15, 1991): 10550.

[22]E. Wayne Nafziger, *The Debt Crisis in Africa* (Baltimore: Johns Hopkins University Press, 1993), p. 75.

[23]Benjamin J. Cohen, "What Ever Happened to the LDC Debt Crisis?" *Challenge* 34 (May-June 1991): 47–51.

nor the stability of the U.S. banking system. The policy of the United States in the 1980s focused on saving its banks and averting a debtors' cartel. By 1987 the major creditor banks no longer had to continue lending to LDCs or participate in debt rescheduling to forestall their own collapse. Thus, while the U.S. government and commercial banks have abandoned their preoccupation with the debt crisis, debt continues to increase in the Third World generally, while the crisis has improved only a little in Africa and parts of Latin America.

During the 1980s, when commercial banks held 72 percent of Latin American debt, U.S. banks (holding 36 percent) and British banks, but few continental European banks, were vulnerable to Latin default. LDC debts to U.S. banks as a percentage of their capital grew from 110 percent in 1978 to 154 percent in 1982, before falling to 114 percent in 1986 to 63 percent in 1988. For the nine major U.S. banks, this percentage was even higher: 163 percent in 1978, 227 percent in 1982, 154 percent in 1986, and 198 percent in 1988.

Assume a bank's LDC debt-capital ratio is 100 percent, and the bank writes off 60 percent of LDC debt but none of the other debts. If the loan-capital ratio is 1,200 percent (this ratio typically varies between 1,000 and 1,700 percent for U.S. banks), then bad loans as a percentage of capital are at the precarious level of 5 (60/1,200) percent.

In response to nonperforming LDC loans and petrodollar shrinkage from low world oil prices, U.S. banks reduced their loans to oil-importing LDCs from $121 billion in 1982 to $118 billion in 1984 to $100 billion in 1986. Indeed, the United States, which ranked first in the world in commercial bank lending to LDCs from 1970 to 1983, fell to second place from 1984 to 1989, with only about half the loans to that of Japan. However, during the remainder of the 1980s, LDC loans ceased to fall with major loan restructuring. Also U.S. bank exposure to LDC foreign debt declined in the mid-1980s from loan writeoffs, writedowns, and asset sales.[24]

In 1988, Latin American, Philippine, and Polish loans held by U.S. banks sold at a 40 to 70 percent discount on the second hand market, indicating market expectation of partial default. Secondary market prices of bank debts of severely indebted countries (based on present value of debt service/annual GNP in excess of 80 percent *or* present value of debt service/annual export ratio more than 200 percent)[25] ranged from 4 percent for Peru and 6 percent for the Ivory Coast to 24 percent for Nigeria to 64 percent for Chile. Steadily increasing discounts for LDC bank debt, the reduction of commercial lending to LDCs, and the increasing interest and principal arrears throughout the late 1980s indicate how much debtor countries' creditworthiness had deteriorated. Banks charged a rising risk premium for LDC borrowers, including interest rates 1 to 2 percentage points in excess of the **London Interbank Offered Rate (LIBOR)**, a virtually riskless interest

[24]Rudiger Dornbusch, "International Debt and Economic Instability," in *Debt, Financial Stability, and Public Policy*, proceedings of a Federal Reserve Bank of Kansas City symposium, Jackson Hole, Wyoming, August 27–29, 1986, pp. 63–86; "Debt Breakthrough," *Wall Street Journal* (December 30, 1987): pp. 1, 4; John W. Sewell, Stuart K. Tucker, and contributors, *Growth, Exports, and Jobs in a Changing World Economy: Agenda, 1988* (New Brunswick, N.J.: Transaction Books, 1988), p. 231; Willem H. Buiter and T. N. Srinivasan, "Rewarding the Profligate and Punishing the Prudent and Poor: Some Recent Proposals for Debt Relief," *World Development* 15 (March 1987): 412; and *IMF Survey* (January 25, 1988), p. 17, and (December 12, 1988), p. 385.

[25]World Bank, *World Debt Tables: External Finance for Developing Countries, 1993–94*, vol. 1, *Analysis and Summary Tables* (Washington, D.C., 1993), p. 165.

rate used as a standard for comparing other interest rates, for Brazil, Argentina, and Mexico, and as much as 9 percentage points for other LDCs.[26]

The Crisis from the LDC Perspective

But while DC banks improved their financial position in the late 1980s, external LDC debt increased to more than $1 trillion in the late 1980s. GNP per capita declined in Latin America and Africa during the 1980s, designated a "lost development decade." While severely indebted countries (SICs) of the 1980s grew faster than DCs, 1965–80, SICs declined sharply during the early 1980s, stagnated during the late 1980s, and declined 1988–93, while DCs grew. Living standards fell especially in sub-Saharan Africa (largely corresponding to the low-income severely indebted countries in Table 17–1), where the debt overhang contributed to the fall in health spending, child nutrition, and infant survival among the poor in the early 1980s, and the decline in real wages, employment rate, and health and educational expenditure shares in the late 1980s. In 1989, the Economic Commission for Africa's Executive Secretary Adebayo Adedeji observed that Africa would not recover without lifting the "unbearable albatross" of debilitating debt burdens, low export prices, and net capital outflow (including capital transfer to the West by the wealthy and politically influential).[27] About the same time, several African countries imposed debt service ceilings or debt moratoria, or simply defaulted on debt.

TABLE 17–1   Average Annual Growth of Severely Indebted Countries in Real GNP per Capita by Income Category (percent per year)

	1965–80	*1980–85*	*1985–88*	*1988–93*
Severely indebted countries				
Low-income	2.5	−4.6	−1.6	−0.5
Middle-income	3.8	−2.2	0.9	−0.4
Total	3.5	−2.8	0.2	−0.4
High-income countries	2.7	1.7	2.7	2.3

Sources: United States President, Council of Economic Advisors, *Economic Report of the President, 1990* (Washington, D.C.: U.S. Government Printing Office, 1990), p. 236; World Bank, *World Debt Tables: External Finance for Developing Countries, 1993–94*, vol. 1, *Analysis and Summary Tables* (Washington, D.C., 1993), pp. 170–233; and World Bank, *World Development Report, 1994* (New York: Oxford University Press, 1994), pp. 162–213.

---

[26]Dharam Ghai, ed., *The IMF and the South: The Social Impact of Crisis and Adjustment* (London: Zed Books, 1991), p. 2.

However, as Ash Demirgüc-Kunt and Enrica Detragiache, "Interest Rates, Official Lending, and the Debt Crisis: A Reassessment," *Journal of Development Economics* 44 (August 1994): 261–85 point out, commercial lenders charged South Korea, Indonesia, and Turkey lower interest rates than the market rate. Indeed, during the 1980s, these countries sometimes even paid interest rates below LIBOR. The three countries benefited from considerable official borrowing, with substantial concessional components, from DC donors.

[27]United Nations Children's Fund (UNICEF), *The State of the World's Children, 1989* (New Delhi, India, 1989); and Ernest Harsch, "After Adjustment," *Africa Report* 34 (May/June 1989): 47.

Additionally, some Latin America countries (dominant among severely in-debted middle-income countries in Table 17–1) experienced a deterioration in so-cial indicators during the 1980s. In mid-1985, Peru's President Alan Garcia limited debt payment to 10 percent of exports. Brazil's President Sarney put a moratorium on interest payments for 12 months in February 1987, explaining his country's im-patience by indicating that "a debt paid with poverty is an account paid with democracy."[28] Creditors cut Brazil's short-term credits, although the U.S. Federal Reserve and Treasury arranged a short-term debt settlement a year later (1988). At a meeting of leaders of debtor nations in late 1987, Argentine President Raul Al-fonsin indicated that the West must recognize how "current economic conditions impede our development and condemn us to backwardness. We cannot accept that the south pay for the disequilibrium of the north."

Debt Indicators

The **debt-service ratio** is the interest and principal payments due in a given year on long-term debt divided by that year's exports of goods and services. This ratio for LDCs increased from 9 percent in 1970 to 13 percent in 1979 to 18 percent in 1983 to 20 percent in 1986 and to 23 percent in 1988, before falling to 21 percent in 1989 and 19 percent for each of the years, 1990 to 1993. In 1992, the actual debt-service ratios were 30 percent in Latin America, 25 percent in the Middle East, 21 percent in South and Southeast Asia, 17 percent in Sub-Saharan Africa, 16 percent in Eastern Europe and the former Soviet Union, 13 percent in East Asia, 32 percent in severely indebted middle-income countries, and 19 percent in severely in-debted low-income countries. (Countries are classified as severely, moderately, or slightly indebted countries on the basis of ratios of the present value of external debt to GNP and the present value of external debt to exports.)

Sometimes, as in sub-Saharan Africa, lower debt-service ratios reflect sub-stantial default or debt rescheduling. For example, in 1990, while Latin America's *actual* debt-service ratio, 27 percent, exceeded the sub-Sahara's 24 percent, the sub-Sahara's *scheduled* debt payments percentage, 66 percent, was more than twice Latin America's 30 percent.[29]

Another measure of the burden of debt is debt service as a percentage of GNP—5 percent in Latin America, the Middle East, and both severely *and* moder-ately indebted low-income countries; 4 percent in sub-Saharan Africa and East Asia; and 3 percent in South and Southeast Asia. Four to five percent represents a substantial burden, especially for countries whose exports and national products are growing slowly. (See below for a discussion of South Korea, Malaysia, and African countries).

Another indicator of debt burden, debt as a percentage of LDC GNP, in-creased from 12 percent in 1970 to 24 percent in 1980 to 33 percent in 1984 to 37 percent in 1986 and 1989, before leveling off to 37–38 percent for each of the years, 1990 to 1992, and increasing to 40 percent in 1993. Debt was more than five times

---

[28]Gustav Ranis, "Latin American Debt and Adjustment," *Journal of Development Economics* 27 (October 1987): 189–99; and Guillermo O'Donnell, "Brazil's Failure: What Future for Debtors' Cartels?" *Third-World Quarterly* 9 (October 1987): 1157–66.

[29]World Bank, *World Debt Tables: External Finance for Developing Countries, 1993–94*, vol. 1, *Analysis and Summary Tables* (Washington, D.C., 1993), pp. 164–209; and E. Wayne Nafziger, *The Debt Crisis in Africa* (Baltimore: Johns Hopkins University Press, 1993), pp. 16–17.

GNP in Nicaragua and Mozambique, more than twice GNP in Zambia, Tanzania, Ivory Coast, Mauritania, and Sierra Leone, and just in excess of GNP in Congo, Laos, Jordan, Madagascar, Egypt, Honduras, Panama, Nigeria, Bulgaria, and Ecuador, in 1992.[30]

Net Transfers

Net transfers are net international resource flows (investment, loans, and grants) minus net international interest payments and profit remittances. As a result of substantial debt servicing, net transfers were negative from Latin America from 1986 to 1990 and from developing countries generally from 1986 to 1988.

Since the lion's share of the poorest LDCs has been in sub-Saharan Africa, the majority of its net resources flows have been concessional since 1984. This concessional aid contributed to positive net transfers in the sub-Sahara every year from 1980 to 1993.

Still, the International Monetary Fund received net transfers from sub-Saharan Africa, 1983 to 1993, as repayment obligations exceeded new loans, even though the Fund introduced concessional adjustment facilities in the late 1980s. During the same period, however, net transfers from the World Bank (including the International Development Association concessional window) to the sub-Sahara was large and positive every year, thus partially offsetting the Fund's net transfer *from* the sub-Sahara. The World Bank's aversion to negative net transfers to the most debt-distressed world region may be deliberate, even though the Bank refuses to confirm the policy, perhaps for fear of establishing a precedent.[31]

Major LDC Debtors

Who have been the major LDC debtors? In 1992, the rank order was Brazil ($121 billion), Mexico ($113 billion); Indonesia, India, China, Argentina, Turkey, Poland, and South Korea (each with over $40 billion of debt). The 33 countries indicated in Table 17–2 accounted for 72 percent of the total LDC debt. Yet none of these countries is least developed. Indeed middle-income countries accounted for 70 percent of the $1.7 trillion outstanding debt of LDCs in 1992. Low-income countries listed in Table 17–2 include five severely indebted countries Egypt, Nigeria, Sudan, Zaïre, and Nicaragua, and moderately indebted (but populous) Indonesia, Bangladesh, India, and Pakistan, and China.[32]

---

[30]International Monetary Fund, *World Economic Outlook* (Washington, D.C., 1988), pp. 122–32; Jeffrey D. Sachs, "The Debt Crisis at a Turning Point," *Challenge* 31 (May/June 1988): 17–26; World Bank, *World Development Report, 1988* (New York: Oxford University Press, 1988), pp. 258–59; and World Bank, *World Debt Tables: External Finance for Developing Countries, 1993–94*, vol. 1, *Analysis and Summary Tables* (Washington, D.C., 1993), pp. 33, 79–81, 170.

[31]World Bank, *World Debt Tables: External Finance for Developing Countries, 1993–94*, vol. 1, *Analysis and Summary Tables* (Washington, D.C., 1993), pp. 171–232; and E. Wayne Nafziger, *The Debt Crisis in Africa* (Baltimore: Johns Hopkins University Press, 1993), pp. 34, 211.

[32]World Bank, *World Debt Tables: External Finance for Developing Countries, 1993–94*, vol. 1, *Analysis and Summary Tables* (Washington, D.C., 1993), pp. 170, 222; and vol. 2, *Country Tables* (Washington, D.C., 1993), pp. xxii–xxiv.

**TABLE 17-2   Total External Public Debt (EDT) by Country—Less-Developed Countries, 1980–1992
($ billions) ($10 billion or more in 1992, ranked by 1992 debt)**

Country	1980	1982	1985	1987	1989	1990	1991	1992
Brazil	71	93	106	124	111	116	117	121
Mexico	57	86	97	109	94	106	115	113
Indonesia	21	26	34	50	53	67	76	84
India	21	27	41	56	64	69	72	77
China	5	8	17	35	45	53	61	69
Argentina	27	44	51	58	65	62	65	68
Turkey	19	20	26	41	41	49	50	55
Poland	n.a.	n.a.	33	43	43	49	53	49
South Korea	29	37	47	40	33	35	40	43
Egypt	21	29	42	52	52	40	41	40
Thailand	8	12	18	20	23	28	36	39
Venezuela	29	32	35	35	32	33	34	37
Philippines	17	25	27	30	29	30	32	33
Portugal	10	14	17	18	20	24	29	32
Nigeria	9	13	20	31	32	35	34	31
Algeria	19	18	18	24	27	28	28	26
Pakistan	10	12	13	17	18	21	23	24
Hungary	10	10	14	20	20	21	23	22
Morocco	10	12	17	21	22	23	21	21
Peru	9	12	13	17	19	20	21	20
Malaysia	7	13	20	23	16	16	18	20
Chile	12	17	20	21	18	19	18	19
Ivory Coast	7	8	10	13	14	17	18	18
Colombia	7	10	14	17	17	17	17	17
Syria	4	3	11	16	17	17	17	17
Former Yugoslavia	18	20	22	22	19	18	16	16
Sudan	5	7	9	12	14	15	16	16
Iran	5	5	6	6	7	9	11	14
Bangladesh	4	5	7	10	11	12	13	13
Ecuador	6	8	9	10	11	12	12	12
Bulgaria	n.a.	n.a.	4	8	10	11	12	12
Nicaragua	2	3	6	8	10	11	11	11
Zaïre	5	5	6	9	9	10	11	11

Former Soviet Union not included.

n.a. = data not available.

Sources: World Bank, *World Debt Tables: External Finance for Developing Countries, 1993–94*, vol. 1, *Analysis and Summary Tables* (Washington, D.C., 1993), pp. 76–78, and vol. 2, *Country Tables* (Washington, D.C., 1993); and World Bank, *World Debt Tables, 1990–91: External Debt of Developing Countries*, vol. 2, *Country Tables* (Washington, D.C., 1990).

Between January 1980 and September 1993, 64 LDCs (including transitional economies) renegotiated their foreign debts through multilateral agreements with official creditor groups (the **Paris Club)** or with commercial banks (under **London Club** auspices), lengthening or modifying repayment terms. These countries included most sub-Saharan countries, and the countries listed in Table 17–2, except for South Korea, China, India, Indonesia, Malaysia, Thailand, Iran, Syria, Portugal, and Hungary.[33]

---

[33]World Bank, *World Debt Tables: External Finance for Developing Countries, 1993–94*, vol. I, *Analysis and Summary Tables* (Washington, D.C.: 1993), pp. 94–111.

Yet ironically for some countries, a high rank among LDC debtors indicated a high credit rating among commercial banks. South Korea, which borrowed at sub-market interest rates and received substantial overseas development assistance,[34] has shown that heavy borrowing can be serviced as long as exports and GNP grow rapidly. Although South Korea's debt rose from $1.8 billion in 1970 to $15 billion in 1979 to $40 billion in 1982 to $47 billion in 1986 (before falling to $33 billion in 1989 and rising to $43 billion), its exports grew so rapidly that its debt-servicing capacity improved considerably. Indeed, in 1992, Korea and fast-growing Malaysia's debt-service ratios were each only 7 percent, compared to the following high debt-service ratios for slow growers: Bolivia 39 percent, Honduras 35 percent, the Philippines 28 percent, and from Africa, Uganda 41 percent, the Ivory Coast and Tanzania 32 percent, Nigeria 31 percent, Zambia 29 percent, Ghana 27 percent, Kenya 25 percent, and Malawi 24 percent.[35] A large debt need not be a problem so long as foreign creditors believe an economy can roll over the debt or borrow enough to cover debt service and imports.

While only four major debtors were from sub-Saharan Africa, its external debt ($194 billion, about one and one-half times Brazil's 1992 figure) was probably as burdensome as any other world region. By the end of 1986, two-thirds of the 45 countries under the IMF African Department had credit outstanding averaging 134 percent of their quotas[36] (compared to only 25 percent unconditional borrowing rights, the reserve tranche). In the 1970s and early to mid-1980s, rulers of Nigeria ($25 billion debt in 1986), Zaïre ($7 billion 1986 debt, most principal and interest from 1971–74 borrowing), and Ghana ($3 billion debt) squandered their loan funds, sometimes expanding patronage for intermediaries and contractors so rapidly that they lost track of millions of dollars borrowed from abroad. During Nigeria's second republic (civilian government), 1979 to 1983, the ports sometimes lacked the capacity for imports like cement going to government agencies controlled by politicians distributing benefits to clients. The countries had to reschedule their debts—Ghana in 1974, after an abrupt decline in the prices of cocoa exports; Zaïre, in 1980 to 1987, after several years of depressed copper export prices; and Nigeria, in 1983 and 1986, after a prolonged oil price slump. Compared to Asian-Latin debtors, the three African countries have poorer credit ratings among commercial banks because of poor national economic management, as reflected in previous balance of payments crises, and a slow growth in output and exports.

World Bank and IMF Lending and Adjustment Programs

Throughout most of the post–World War II period, the World Bank emphasized development lending to LDCs, while the International Monetary Fund (IMF) lent resources to help DCs and LDCs cope with balance of payments crises. In the late

---

[34]Ash Demirgüç-Kunt and Enrica Detragiache, "Interest Rates, Official Lending, and the Debt Crisis: A Reassessment," *Journal of Development Economics* 44 (August 1994): 261–85.

[35]Organization for Economic Cooperation and Development, *Financing and External Debt of Developing Countries: 1987 Survey* (Paris, 1988); World Bank, *World Development Report, 1981* (New York: Oxford University Press, 1981), p. 60; World Bank, *World Debt Tables: External Finance for Developing Countries, 1993–94*, vol. 1, *Analysis and Summary Tables* (Washington, D.C., 1993), pp. 234–37, and vol. 2, *Country Tables*.

[36]Organization for Economic Cooperation and Development, *Financing and External Debt of Developing Countries: 1987 Survey* (Paris, 1988), p. 72; and Karamo N. M. Sonko, *Debt, Development and Equity in Africa* (Lanham, Md.: University Press of America, 1994).

1970s, 1980s, and 1990s, LDCs with chronic external deficits and debt overhang whose creditors failed to reschedule debt required economic adjustment (structural or sectoral adjustment, macroeconomic stabilization, or economic reform), imposed domestically or (usually) by the World Bank or International Monetary Fund. In 1979, World Bank introduced **structural adjustment loans (SALs)** and soon thereafter **sectoral adjustment loans (SECALs).** SECALs emphasized reforms in trade, agriculture, industry, public enterprise, finance, energy, education, or other sectors. SALs were no longer tied to specific projects, but to support the balance of payments through 15–20 year loans, with 3–5 years' grace, and interest rates only 0.5 percent above the Bank's borrowing costs except for a front-end fee on new commitments. Structural adjustment policies emphasized growth and improved allocative efficiency as well as controlling domestic demand and improving the current account.[37]

In the 1980s and 1990s, the Bank led donor coordination, increasing the power of external leverage. Although IMF direct credits to LDCs fell in the mid-1980s, the IMF retained substantial influence because of IMF–World Bank cooperation and a required IMF "seal of approval" for virtually all commercial bank, bilateral, and multilateral aid and loans. In 1986–87, the IMF used trust funds and funds from surplus DC countries for SALs to LDCs (especially in Africa) experiencing unanticipated external shocks.[38]

Chapter 20 analyzes World Bank and IMF adjustment policies further.

Resolving the Debt Crisis

Although in the 1970s and early 1980s, creditors took a case-by-case approach to the debt crisis, beginning in the mid-1980s, several policymakers had advocated debt relief plans. We focus here on several proposals, beginning with two plans named for American treasury secretaries, the Baker Plan (1985), which emphasized expanded lending for LDC debtors, and the Brady Plan (1989), stressing debt write-offs and write-downs, together with cancellation, rescheduling, and exchanges of debt as enablers.

BAKER PLAN

In the early 1980s, the U.S. government had no strategy besides declaring that debtors should pay the full interest due to American banks. However by 1985, Washington had realized the limitations that the debt crisis placed on Latin American growth and on demand for U.S. exports. Peru's President Garcia's 1985 U.N. speech posing the problem as "democracy or honoring debt" forced U.S. political leaders to focus on tradeoffs. Some U.S. bankers and Treasury officials feared a debtors' cartel. In response, at the October 1985 IMF–World Bank meeting, Secretary of the Treasury James A. Baker, III, unveiled a U.S. proposal, which called for Inter-American Development Bank, IMF credits and new surveillance (the inspi-

---

[37]Mohsin S. Khan, "Macroeconomic Adjustment in Developing Countries: A Policy Perspective," *The World Bank Research Observer* 2 (January 1987): 26–27; and E. Wayne Nafziger, *The Debt Crisis in Africa* (Baltimore: Johns Hopkins University Press, 1993), pp. xxi–xxii.

[38]Richard E. Feinberg, "An Open Letter to the World Bank's New President,"in Richard E. Feinberg and contributors, *Between Two Worlds: The World Bank's Next Decade* (New Brunswick, N.J.: Transaction Books, 1986), pp. 14–18.

ration for IMF structural adjustment lending beginning in 1986), World Bank structural adjustment loans, contributions from trade surplus countries like Japan, and additional commercial bank lending, to help the highly indebted middle-income countries. Baker provided for the IMF to continue to coordinate new bank lending, but with some centralization, so as to avoid the free-rider problem, in which individual banks could benefit by new loans from other banks. Countries receiving funds were not to sacrifice growth, as the package of budget restraint, tax reform, liberalized trade and foreign investment, the privatization of some state-owned enterprises, and setting public-sector prices closer to the market would promote efficiency without making contractionary financial policy necessary. The IMF, though under pressure from the U.S. Federal Reserve Board and Treasury and a Mexican threat of debt repudiation, contributed $1.7 billion to a $12 billion "growth-oriented" package of adjustment and structural reform, which included $6 billion from commercial banks. But the Baker initiative did not address how to go from the initial lending package to subsequent inducements for voluntary capital flows. Also, the approach did not help the poorest countries (who reduced borrowing because of low creditworthiness), and its terms did not take into account past management performance. Moreover, Latin American debtors considered the new resources inadequate and asked for a lower interest rate spread over the Eurodollar London rate (or LIBOR) and a ceiling on debt service payments.[39]

Brazil's moratorium on debt payments in early 1987 drove secondary market prices for debt down and restrained new-money packages. In response, in 1987, Secretary Baker called for a "menu approach," including bonds for new money and debt-equity conversion, in which bank participation was tailored to individual bank interests. A limited amount of structural reform (reduced tariffs, privatization) took place, especially in Latin America. In Latin America, those countries with larger foreign resource transfers had faster growth in the late 1980s.

The Baker Plan, which stressed saving U.S. banks at the expense of the IMF, the World Bank, multilateral banks, and Japanese creditors, was vastly underfunded. Yet the plan did, however, forestall a major write-off of Third World debts that threatened the nine major U.S. banks in the early 1980s. Latin American debtors ceased threatening to form a cartel. This lessened the concerns of top creditor banks about LDC default and gave them time to reduce gradually their exposure to LDC borrowers. Baker also reduced the vulnerability of money-center banks by enlisting the IMF, World Bank, and DC lenders in an effort to reduce bad debts. Indeed, in the next few years these multilateral agencies and lenders strengthened their sanctions against unilateral LDC default. The insistence of the World Bank, bilateral lenders, banks, and export credit agencies on IMF approval of macroeconomic stabilization (usually involving credit and budgetary restraints) left LDC borrowers few other funding sources. Furthermore, the Baker initiative made time available for the U.S. Federal Reserve and bank regulators to

---

[39]Jeffrey D. Sachs, "The Debt Crisis at a Turning Point," *Challenge* 31 (May/June 1988): 17–26; Willem H. Buiter and T. N. Srinivasan, "Rewarding the Profligate and Punishing the Prudent and Poor: Some Recent Proposals for Debt Relief," *World Development* 15 (March 1987), 411–17; Gustav Ranis, "Latin American Debt and Adjustment," *Journal of Development Economics* 27 (October 1987): 189–99; Gerald K. Helleiner, "Summary of the U.N. Secretary-General's Advisory Group Report on Financial Flows for Africa," in North-South Institute, *Structural Adjustment in Africa: External Financing for Development*, Ottawa, Canada, February 25–26, 1988, p. 30; and William R. Cline, "The Baker Plan and Brady Reformulation: An Evaluation," in Ishrat Husain and Ishac Diwan, eds., *Dealing with the Debt Crisis* (Washington, D.C.: World Bank, 1989), pp. 176–86.

support U.S. money-center banks through measures such as increased reserve requirements.[40]

Thus, by 1987, Harry Huizanga could say that "bank stock prices to a large extent already reflect the low quality of developing-country loans. Thus no major U.S. bank goes under if it gets a return on its developing-country debt that is consistent with developing-country prices observed in the secondary market."[41] More importantly, the Baker Plan's averting a possible debtors' cartel and widespread unilateral LDC default enabled the top creditor banks to reduce their LDC-debt exposure, so they could boycott reschedulings and new-money packages and insist on LDC full servicing while no longer fearing their own collapse. Ironically, the major money-center banks' new-found immunity from LDC defaults contributed to the death of Baker's efforts to spur increased bank lending to LDCs.

BRADY PLAN

By the 1980s, commercial banks no longer deemed most balance-of-payments financing compatible with their fiduciary obligations, so net commercial credit to LDCs continually fell, becoming negative between 1983 and 1989. In March 1989, U.S. Treasury Secretary Brady presented a plan for debt, debt-service reduction, and new-money packages on a voluntary and case-by-case basis, relying on World Bank, IMF, and other official support. The Brady Plan asked commercial banks to reduce their LDC exposure through voluntary debt reduction or writeoffs whereby banks exchanged LDC debt for cash or newly created bonds partly backed by the IMF or the World Bank, or debtor countries converted or bought back debt on the secondary market.[42] While the IMF and World Bank were to set guidelines on debt exchanges, negotiations of transactions were to be in the marketplace, according to Brady.[43]

Debtor countries preferred debt reduction to new money, which enlarged debt and constrained growth. Debt overhang acted as a tax on investment and income increases. In the early 1980s, when financial flows dried up, many debtors needed trade surpluses to service debt.

The World Bank and IMF set aside $12 billion (one-fourth of policy-based lending) for discounted debt buybacks, with $12 billion matching funds from the Bank and $4.5 billion from the Japanese government; thus total Brady Plan government or multilateral resources were $28 billion, 1990 to 1992. In 1989, Mexico was the first country to benefit from the plan, receiving $3 billion from the World Bank and Inter-American Development Bank and $2 billion from the Japanese to

---

[40]John F. Weeks, "Losers Pay Reparations, or How the Third World Lost the Lending War," in John F. Weeks, ed., *Debt Disaster? Banks, Governments, and Multilaterals Confront the Crisis* (New York: New York University Press, 1989), pp. 41–63; Karin Lissakers, "Background to the Debt Crisis: Structural Adjustment in the Financial Markets," in ibid., pp. 67–73; and Paul M. Sacks and Chris Canavan, "Safe Passage through Dire Straits: Managing an Orderly Exit from the Debt Crisis," in ibid., pp. 176–86.

[41]Harry Huizinga, "The Commercial Bank Claims on Developing Countries: How Have Banks Been Affected?" in Ishrat Husain and Ishac Diwan, eds., *Dealing with the Debt Crisis* (Washington, D.C.: World Bank, 1989), p. 129.

[42]Harry Huizinga, "The Commercial Bank Claims on Developing Countries: How Have Banks Been Affected?" in Ishrat Husain and Ishac Diwan, eds., *Dealing with the Debt Crisis* (Washington, D.C.: World Bank, 1989), pp. 129–32.

[43]World Bank, *World Debt Tables, 1989–90: External Debt of Developing Countries*, vol. 1, *Analysis and Summary Tables* (Washington, D.C., 1989), 24.

issue conversion bonds, which could purchase debt with a $10 billion face value for a secondary market price of $5 billion (that is, 50 percent of face value).[44]

However, replacing commercial bank debt with World Bank/IMF funds reduces flexibility for recipients, as debt to the Bank and Fund, which require first claim on debt servicing, cannot be rescheduled. Still, the increase of IMF quotas by 50 percent in 1990 made more short-term funds available for debt reduction.[45]

DC commercial banks have faced increasing constraints on lending in the early 1990s, with slower DC growth, a perception of low creditworthiness of debtor countries, difficulties of implementing reform programs, increased regulatory and competitive pressure of banks, the effect of depressed secondary market prices of LDC loans on bank share prices, the reluctance of U.S. and Japanese banks to increase exposure to highly indebted LDCs, the riskiness of new-money approaches, and the free-rider problems of banks collecting full interest due without contributing to fresh-money loans (see below). Furthermore, commercial banks concentrated loan arrangements on Brazil and Mexico rather than smaller Latin American or Sub-Saharan debtors. Indeed, the financing gap in sub-Saharan Africa widened through 1990, and in Latin America through at least 1993.[46]

Debt-reduction measures include the exchange of foreign debts against domestic assets (debt-equity conversions), which can contribute to accelerating inflation and higher interest rates if assets acquired by the creditor are private but guaranteed by government. The exchange of discounted foreign debt for another foreign asset requires that the new asset be more secure and that its probability of servicing be larger than that of the old debt.

Buying back a debt at a discount with foreign exchange is not feasible for most LDC debtors, who have little foreign exchange available. Few creditors have been willing to reduce interest rates on existing debt instruments. Attracting reflows of flight capital may require higher risk premiums and high real interest rates. Moreover, reflows may be put in highly liquid form rather than in investments in expanding productive capacity.[47]

CANCELING DEBT

According to Harvard University's Jeffrey D. Sachs, advisor to Latin American and Eastern European economies, LDCs facing a substantial debt overhang might be better off defaulting on a portion of the debt than undertaking austere domestic adjustment or timely debt servicing. About 20 countries undertook such unilateral action in the 1980s. Many LDC leaders felt there was no IMF adjustment program for full debt servicing that makes the country better off than forgoing the program by partially suspending debt payments. Any IMF program may be too tight relative to other options for the debtor government.

---

[44]William R. Cline, "The Baker Plan and Brady Reformulation: An Evaluation," in Ishrat Husain and Ishac Diwan, eds., *Dealing with the Debt Crisis* (Washington, D.C.: World Bank, 1989), pp. 187–91; and World Bank, *World Debt Tables, 1989–90: External Debt of Developing Countries*, vol. 1, *Analysis and Summary Tables* (Washington, D.C., 1989), 21.

[45]Food and Agriculture Organization of the U.N. (FAO), *The State of Food and Agriculture, 1990* (Rome, 1991), p. 6.

[46]World Bank, *World Debt Tables, 1989–90: External Debt of Developing Countries*, vol. 1, *Analysis and Summary Tables* (Washington, D.C., 1989), 12; and World Bank, *World Debt Tables: External Finance for Developing Countries, 1993–94*, vol. 1, *Analysis and Summary Tables* (Washington, D.C., 1993), 170–89.

[47]Ishrat Husain and Saumya Mitra, "Future Financing Needs of the Highly Indebted Countries," in Ishrat Husain and Ishac Diwan, eds., *Dealing with the Debt Crisis* (Washington, D.C., 1989), pp. 199–209.

The precedent for defaulting on debt is the 1930s. Countries that stopped paying their debt service recovered from the Great Depression more quickly than countries that resisted default and had virtually identical access to post-World War II capital markets.

However, country default in the 1990s is more costly than it was in the 1930s, when debt was held among scattered bondholders ranging from retired individuals to large corporations, so that creditor collusion was virtually impossible. Currently debt is, in contrast, largely held by an oligopoly of international commercial banks, which hold the lion's share of LDC international reserves, dispense LDC credit, maintain close communication with each other, and coordinate action with the IMF and DC central banks. Moreover, contemporary LDCs face a relatively prosperous, not a depressed and divided, North. Furthermore, today's bank cartel insists on a case-by-case approach, thus increasing their bargaining power vis-á-vis debtors.

Yet the debtor may be able to avoid sanctions when the lender agrees to debt reduction or cancellation or the conversion of loans to grants. Sachs maintains that the best strategy for the IMF (or other international agencies) would be a program based on partial and explicit debt relief, which can serve as a carrot for political turnaround. William R. Cline doubts, however, that these agencies can use debt relief as a "policy bribe" in exchange for economic reform. Indeed, creditor sanctions on debtor behavior are very ineffective. The IMF's Joshua Greene admitted that assessing African debt for rescheduling is so hopeless that it would be simpler to forgive the entire debt.[48]

Should DCs or multilateral agencies use concessional aid for debt relief or cancellation? Most large debtors are middle-income countries, and *not* among the poorest states. Thus UNCTAD emphasized widespread debt renegotiation to cancel or reschedule debts of least-developed (largely overlapping with IDA-eligible) countries.[49]

From 1978 through 1990, 14 Organization for Economic Cooperation and Development (OECD) countries canceled more than $2 billion of concessional debt (mostly under Paris Club auspices), about one-fifth of concessional loans to IDA-eligible countries in sub-Saharan Africa. Sweden, Canada, the Netherlands, Belgium, the United Kingdom, Germany, Denmark, Norway, and Finland were major contributors to debt forgiveness to the sub-Sahara. OECD nations also gave recipients concessional aid to buy commercial bank debt instruments at heavily discounted prices.[50]

---

[48]Jeffrey D. Sachs, "Conditionality, Debt Relief, and the Developing Country Debt Crisis," in Jeffrey D. Sachs, *Developing Country Debt and the World Economy* (Chicago: University of Chicago Press, 1989), p. 279; Robert Devlin, *Debt and Crisis in Latin America: The Supply Side of the Story* (Princeton, NJ: Princeton University Press 1989), p. 233; Robert Devlin, "Economic Restructuring in Latin America in the Face of the Foreign Debt and the External Transfer Problem," *CEPAL Review*, no. 32 (August 1987): pp. 91–93; Carlos F. Diaz-Alejandro, "Latin American Debt: I Don't Think We Are in Kansas Anymore," *Brookings Papers*, no. 2 (1984): p. 382; William R. Cline, "Latin American Debt: Progress, Prospects, and Policy," in Sebastian Edwards and Felipe Larrain, eds., *Debt, Adjustment and Recovery: Latin America's Prospects for Growth and Development* (Oxford: Basil Blackwell, 1989), p. 45; and Joshua Greene, "The African Debt Problem: What Are the Issues and Strategies for Resolution?" Paper presented to the African Studies Association meeting, St. Louis, November 23–26, 1991.

[49]United Nations Conference on Trade and Development (UNCTAD), *Trade and Development Report, 1978* (New York, 1978).

[50]Charles Humphreys and John Underwood, "The External Debt Difficulties of Low-Income Africa," in Ishrat Husain and Ishac Diwan, eds., *Dealing with the Debt Crisis* (Washington, D.C.: World Bank, 1989, p. 45; and World Bank, *World Debt Tables, 1989–90: External Debt of Developing Countries*, vol. 1, *Analysis and Summary Tables* (Washington, D.C., 1989), pp. 24, 44.

RESCHEDULING DEBT

Between 1986 and 1992, LDCs rescheduled $493 billion external debt stock, with Latin America the largest beneficiary with $315 billion rescheduled and Europe and Central Asia (that is, Eastern Europe and the former Soviet Union) the second largest with $71 billion (but the largest in 1992 and some years beyond). Seventeen percent of this represented debt reduction, both official and commercial.[51]

In 1988 in Toronto, Canada, the **G7** (**Group of Seven** major industrialized countries—the United States, Canada, Japan, the United Kingdom, Germany, France, and Italy) agreed to reschedule concessional debt, canceling it at least in part, with the balance to be repaid with a 25-year maturity including 14 grace years. The **Toronto terms** included a "menu" of the following three supposedly equivalent rescheduling options for low-income debt-distressed countries (primarily in Africa) with an acceptable ongoing World Bank/IMF adjustment program: (1) partial writedowns (forgiveness of one-third the eligible debt service plus rescheduling the remainder at market interest rates, with a 14-year maturity with 8 years' grace, and market interest rates), (2) longer terms (rescheduling eligible debt service at market interest rates, but with a 25-year maturity), and (3) rescheduling of debt at lower interest rates (3.5 percentage points below or one-half market rates, whichever provides the smaller reduction), with repayment maturity of 14 years and 8 years' grace. At Toronto, the United States agreed for the first time to allow other creditors to apply concessional interest rates for reschedulings, but the U.S. chose option (2), inferior to the other options. Since Toronto terms applied only to debt maturing within 18 months of the consolidation period, the reduction in actual debt service was only about $100 million annually in 1989–90.[52]

TRINIDAD TERMS

In 1990, British Chancellor John Major proposed the following **Trinidad terms** for low-income debt-distressed countries: (1) rescheduling of the entire stock of debt in one stroke instead of renegotiating maturities only as they fall due at 15-to-18-month intervals, (2) increasing the debt cancellation from one-third to two-thirds of outstanding debt stock, (3) capitalizing all interest payments at market rates on the remaining one-third debt stock for 5 years and requiring phased repayment with steadily increasing principal and interest payments tied to debtor-country export and output growth, and (4) stretching repayments of the remaining one-third debt stock to 25 years with a flexible repayment schedule. The present value of the eligible (poorest) sub-Saharan African countries would be reduced by $18 billion

[51]World Bank, *World Debt Tables: External Finance for Developing Countries, 1993–94*, vol. 1, *Analysis and Summary Tables* (Washington, D.C., 1993), 173, 185, 189.

[52]Carol Lancaster, *African Economic Reform: The External Dimension* (Washington, D.C.: Institute for International Economics, 1991), pp. 43–44; United Nations, *Financing Africa's Recovery: Report and Recommendations of the Advisory Group on Financial Flows for Africa* (New York, 1988), pp. 45–47; Gerald K. Helleiner, "Summary of the U.N. Secretary-General's Advisory Group Report on Financial Flows for Africa," in North-South Institute, *Structural Adjustment in Africa: External Financing for Development*, Ottawa, Canada, February 25–26, 1988, p. 31; Percy S. Mistry, "African Debt Revisited: Procrastination or Progress?" Paper prepared for the North-South Roundtable on African Debt Relief, Recovery, and Democracy, Abidjan, Ivory Coast, July 8–9, 1991, pp. 16–18; World Bank, *World Debt Tables, 1989–90: External Debt of Developing Countries* (Washington, D.C., 1990), 93–94; and Stephen Haggard and Robert Kaufman, "The Politics and Stabilization and Structural Adjustment," in Jeffrey D. Sachs, *Developing Country Debt and the World Economy* (Chicago: University of Chicago Press, 1989), pp. 264–66.

(rather than $2 billion under Toronto terms). Percy S. Mistry, a former World Bank official, indicates that the Trinidad terms "represent a significant departure from business-as-usual by a weighty creditor country."[53]

After the United States and Japan objected to the G7 nations adopting Trinidad terms, Prime Minister Major announced in late 1991 that Britain would unilaterally implement these terms to $18 billion bilateral debt of poor African countries. In late 1994, the G7 and Paris Club adopted Trinidad terms.

EGYPT-POLAND TERMS

In 1990, during the Persian Gulf War, the U.S. government extended generous terms to two middle-income countries, canceling $6.7 billion in military debt owed by Egypt (a "debt for war" swap) and 70 percent of the $3.8 billion U.S. government debt of Poland (favored because of the large Polish-American communities in Chicago and other politically crucial northern states), thus allowing both to evade IMF prescriptions. Mistry sees no economic explanation for bilateral creditors' "desultory foot-dragging over the debt crises of Africa and Latin America," whose countries are subject to an IMF and World Bank short leash, while finding more than $13 billion for Egypt and Poland at terms more generous than Toronto terms. For Mistry, this piecemeal approach involved an "embarrassing ad hoc improvisation when G–7 decides to favor debtor countries for some expedient political reasons (e.g., Poland and Egypt) and, by the same token, to punish others using the Damoclean sword of debt as a tool for foreign policy leverage)." These selective initiatives set no precedents for poorer countries in Africa and Latin America but instead, according to Mistry, impart chaos to international debt management.[54]

COMMERCIAL BANK LENDING

As indicated, net commercial credit to LDCs continually fell in the 1980s and early 1990s. In the late 1980s, commercial banks reduced balance-of-payments financing, instead offering financial instruments more tailored to the banks' regulatory, accounting, and tax situation. Yet the debt from an earlier period was still substantial, so that nominal debt stock was not falling. Moreover, 49 percent of 1993 LDC (60 percent of Latin American and 26 percent of sub-Saharan) debt outstanding was to private creditors.[55]

One approach, the market-based "menu" approach—buybacks, debt-equity swaps, debt exchanges, and exit bonds discussed below—allows commercial banks and debtor countries to fine-tune instruments case-by-case. However, buybacks and debt-equity swaps actually increase banks' short-term financing re-

---

[53]Percy S. Mistry, "African Debt Revisited: Procrastination or Progress?" Paper prepared for the North-South Roundtable on African Debt Relief, Recovery, and Democracy, Abidjan, Ivory Coast, July 8–9, 1991, p. 18.

[54]Percy S. Mistry, "African Debt Revisited: Procrastination or Progress?" Paper prepared for the North-South Roundtable on African Debt Relief, Recovery, and Democracy, Abidjan, Ivory Coast, July 8–9, 1991, quoted from pp. 3, 6, and 37; Food and Agriculture Organization of the U.N. (FAO), *The State of Food and Agriculture, 1990* (Rome, 1991), p. 7; and Carol Lancaster, *African Economic Reform: The External Dimension* (Washington, D.C.: Institute for International Economics, 1991), pp. 52–54.

[55]World Bank, *World Debt Tables: External Finance for Developing Countries, 1993–94*, vol. 1, *Analysis and Summary Tables* (Washington, D.C., 1993), 171, 175, 187.

quirements. Moreover, creditors have used the menu mainly for major Latin American debtors, with little application to Africa.[56]

DEBT EXCHANGES

Debt-Equity Swaps.   Debt-equity swaps involve an investor exchanging at the debtor country's central bank the country's debt purchased at discount in the secondary market for local currency, to be used in equity investment.[57] From 1982 to the early 1990s, the active market for the swapping or selling of commercial bank claims on LDCs grew rapidly. Usually, with a swap, a DC commercial bank (Citicorp led here) sells an outstanding loan made to a debtor-country government agency to a multinational corporation, which presents the loan paper to the debtor's central bank, which redeems all or most of the loan's face value in *domestic currency* at the market exchange rate. The investor, by acquiring equity in an LDC firm, substitutes a repayment stream depending on profitability for a fixed external obligation. Yet many bankers doubt that a country that lacks foreign exchange for debt service would make exchange available for repatriating corporate income.[58] MIT's Rudiger Dornbusch even argues that the U.S. government has been "obscene in advocating debt-equity swaps and in insisting that they be part of the debt strategy." According to him, the U.S. Treasury has made these swaps a dogma, and the IMF and World Bank, against their staffs' advice, have simply caved in.[59]

Debt Buybacks.   In late 1989 the World Bank created a **Debt Reduction Facility (DRF)** for **IDA-eligible countries**, countries poor enough to be eligible for International Development Association concessional lending. The DRF provides grants to eligible countries (21 sub-Saharan African countries, a few Latin countries, and Bangladesh) of as much as $10 million to buy back commercial debt instruments. Since much of the debt of these countries has been discounted by 80 to 90 percent, a small amount of cash has substantial impact in reducing debt stocks and service. The debt facility is open to countries with a World Bank or IMF adjustment program and (in the Bank's judgment) a credible debt-management program.

Here are a few examples. Niger bought back its commercial bank debt of $108 million at 18 cents per dollar with $10 million DRF and $9.5 million from France and Switzerland in early 1991. Uganda completed a buyback of $153 million in debt obligation, 89 percent of its outstanding commercial bank debt, at 12 cents on the dollar with DRF, European Union, German, Dutch, and Swiss funds in early 1993. Bolivia eliminated most of its commercial bank debt by retiring $170 million at 16 cents per dollar with DRF, U.S. Agency for International Development, Swedish, Swiss, and Dutch funds in mid-1993. Yet creditors and donors

---

[56]Ishrat Husain and John Underwood, "The Problem of Sub-Saharan Africa's Debt—and the Solutions," unpublished paper, Washington, D.C., World Bank, 1992, p. 29; and Michel H. Bouchet and Jonathan Hay, "The Rise of the Market-Based 'Menu' Approach and Its Limitations," in Ishrat Husain and Ishac Diwan, eds., *Dealing with the Debt Crisis* (Washington, D.C.: World Bank, 1989), pp. 146–51.

[57]Stijn Claessens and Ishac Diwan, "Market-Based Debt Reduction," in Ishrat Husain and Ishac Diwan, eds., *Dealing with the Debt Crisis* (Washington, D.C.: World Bank, 1989), p. 271.

[58]World Bank, *World Debt Tables, 1989–90: External Debt of Developing Countries*, vol. 1, *Analysis and Summary Tables* (Washington, D.C., 1989), p. 18; and *IMF Survey* (July 11, 1988), p. 226.

[59]Rudiger Dornbusch, "Discussion," in John Williamson, ed., *Latin American Adjustment: How Much Has Happened?* (Washington, D.C.: Institute for International Economics, 1990), p. 324.

were reluctant to use the resources of the facility to avoid setting precedents for large debtors, such as Brazil, Mexico, Argentina, and middle-income countries where exposure is larger.[60]

Who benefits from a self-financed debt buyback? Paul R. Krugman and Maurice Obstfeld argue that creditors gain and a heavily indebted country loses from buying back part of its own debt on the secondary market. The debtor loses even if a donor provides aid (if that aid has an opportunity cost within the debtor country) to a debtor country to buy back part of its debt. The case of Bolivia in 1988 shows how a buyback plan meant to help a debtor can degenerate into a large giveaway to creditors. In 1988 Bolivia received $34 million from donors to buy back a portion of its commercial debt. Before the buyback was planned, the market valued Bolivia's foreign debt of $757 million at 7 cents on the dollar or $53 million. After the buyback, the remaining debt sold for 12 cents on the dollar, a value on the market of $43.4 million. Bolivia's benefit from the $34 million gift was the reduction in its total expected debt payments from $53 million to $43.4 million, equal to $9.6 million. Creditors received the lion's share of the gain, $24.4 million, that is, the $34 million bought back minus the $9.6 million reduction in expected debt payments.[61]

Debt-for-Nature Swaps.   While DCs contribute disproportionately to carbon dioxide, methane, and nitrous oxide emissions that exacerbate global warming (Chapter 13), LDC emissions are also a problem. LDC leaders argue that DC interest in resolving the debt problem and the environmental crisis provides an opportunity to connect the two issues. Developing countries might repay debt in local currency, with half the proceeds made available to an international environmental fund that spends to protect the local environment and the remaining local-currency payments made available for population or development projects. David Bigman suggests that G7 and other industrial countries use a tax on fossil fuels to finance the environmental fund and an environmental protection corps of young DC volunteers serving for one year.[62]

Inevitably, growth in low-income countries will increase environmental pressures. The prevailing environmental problems are desertification (from irregular rainfall and overuse), deforestation (reduced forest and woodland cover, deteriorating soil protection, and fuelwood shortages), contamination and loss of groundwater, and urban and water pollution (especially from inadequate sewerage treatment and industrial discharges).[63]

---

[60]United Nations, *Financing Africa's Recovery: Report and Recommendations of the Advisory Group on Financial Flows for Africa* (New York, 1988), pp. 45–47; World Bank and United Nations Development Program, *Africa's Adjustment and Growth in the 1980s* (Washington, D.C., 1989), pp. 14–16; Charles Humphreys and John Underwood, "The External Debt Difficulties of Low-Income Africa," in Ishrat Husain and Ishac Diwan, eds., *Dealing with the Debt Crisis* (Washington, D.C., 1989), pp. 45, 52–53, 57; World Bank, *World Debt Tables, 1989–90: External Debt of Developing Countries*, vol. 1, *Analysis and Summary Tables* (Washington, D.C., 1989), pp. 31, 41–49; World Bank, *World Debt Tables: External Finance for Developing Countries, 1993–94*, vol. 1, *Analysis and Summary Tables* (Washington, D.C., 1993), pp. 38–39; and E. Wayne Nafziger, *The Debt Crisis in Africa* (Baltimore: Johns Hopkins University Press, 1993), pp. 97–98.

[61]Paul R. Krugman and Maurice Obstfeld, *International Economics: Theory and Practice*, 3rd ed. (New York: HarperCollins, 1994), pp. 703–04.

[62]David Bigman, "A Plan to End LDC Debt and Save the Environment Too," *Challenge* 33 (July/August 1990): 33–37.

[63]African Development Bank and Economic Commission for Africa (ECA), *Economic Report on Africa, 1988*, Abidjan and Addis Ababa, March 1988, pp. 29–98.

Environmental stress increases with population growth. Reducing government expenditures to cope with the debt crisis also reduces resources, especially imports, available for accelerating economic growth, cutting environmental degradation, or slowing population growth. From 1987 to 1993, nongovernmental international environmental organizations and DC governments raised $128 million at an initial cost of $47 million (an average discount of 62 percent) to purchase debt instruments in 31 LDCs, mostly in Latin America. For example, in 1992, an environmental organization bought $2.2 million of Brazil's commercial debt (at a 66 percent discount) to establish the Grande Sertão Verde National Park in northern Brazil.[64]

Debt-for-Development Swaps.   Here an international agency buys LDC debt in the secondary market at substantial discount, exchanging the debt at a prearranged discount with the debtor country, which issues a bond or other financial instruments. In the early 1990s, UNICEF purchased debt to finance child development programs in Bolivia, Jamaica, Madagascar, the Philippines, and Sudan, such as health, sanitation, and primary education. Harvard University bought $5 million of Ecuadorian debt for $775,000, a discount of 84 percent, to finance for ten years traveling expenses and stipends for 20 Ecuadorian students at Harvard and 50 Harvard students and faculty to perform research in Ecuador.[65]

Other Debt Exchanges.   Other types of conversions include debt-debt conversions, in which foreign currency debt is exchanged for obligations in domestic currency, informal debt conversions by private companies and citizens, and exit bonds for creditor banks wishing to avoid future concerted lending. A debtor country can offer to settle arrears with individual banks by trading debts for long-term bonds, with a long grace period and an amortization period of 25 to 35 years.

An exit bond is a buyback financed by future cash flows. Debtor countries invite banks to bid to exchange their loans for bonds with a future stream of interest payments on a reduced principal (say) fully secured by U.S. Treasury securities. The African Development Bank initiated this type of securitization in Africa.[66]

CONCERTED ACTION

Debt reduction is the restructuring of debt to reduce expected present discounted value of the debtor's contractual obligations. The general commercial debt reduction (encompassing other than the largest debtors) envisioned under the Brady Plan failed because of the lack of multilateral coordination. Bilateral arrangements are subject to free-rider problems, where nonparticipating banks benefit from

[64]World Bank, *World Debt Tables: External Finance for Developing Countries, 1993–94*, vol. 1, *Analysis and Summary Tables* (Washington, D.C., 1993), p. 115.
[65]World Bank, *World Debt Tables: External Finance for Developing Countries, 1993–94*, vol. 1, *Analysis and Summary Tables* (Washington, D.C., 1993), pp. 114–17.
[66]World Bank, *World Debt Tables, 1989–90: External Debt of Developing Countries*, vol. 1, *Analysis and Summary Tables* (Washington, D.C., 1989), p. 18; World Bank, *World Debt Tables, 1991–92: External Debt of Developing Countries*, vol. 1, *Analysis and Summary Tables* (Washington, D.C., 1991), p. 126; and Stijn Claessens and Ishac Diwan, "Market-Based Debt Reduction," in Ishrat Husain and Ishac Diwan, eds., *Dealing with the Debt Crisis* (Washington, D.C.: World Bank 1989), p. 271.

increased creditworthiness and value of debt holdings. Banks are willing to reduce LDC debt, but only if their competitors do likewise.[67]

The solution lies in concerted debt reduction, where all banks owed a debt participate jointly on a prorated basis. For debt relief, just as in U.S. bankruptcy, settlements (under Chapter 11 of the Bankruptcy Reform Act of 1978), concerted efforts are more effective than individual deals by creditors with debtors, and rebuilding of debtor productive capacity more effective than legalistic solutions.[68]

Debt reduction can improve creditor welfare, as a large debt overhang can worsen debtor economic performance, and diminish the creditor's expected returns. Just as in bankruptcy, decentralized market processes rarely result in efficient debt reduction, since each individual creditor is motivated to press for full payment on its claims, even if collective creditor interests are served by reducing the debt burden. The bankruptcy settlement cuts through the problem of inherent collective inaction and enforces a concerted settlement on creditors. Bankruptcy proceedings (under U.S. law) force individual creditors to give up some legal claims, reducing the contractual obligations of debtors, and thus preserving debtor capacity to function effectively and thereby service as much of the debt as possible. The debt overhang prevents countries from returning to the loan market; the most effective way to revive lending is to reduce the debtor's debt-servicing burden. We should apply the lesson of bankruptcy to sovereign debt overhang, even though debtor LDCs face a liquidity rather than a solvency problem. A major objective in debt reorganization is to reverse investment and productivity declines resulting from poor creditworthiness. Debt reduction may be the only feasible alternative, as banks, lacking incentives, are becoming increasingly resistant to new-money packages, and debtors lack incentives to undertake tough reforms designed to increase debt-servicing payments abroad. DCs can best support moderate political leaders by reducing debt so that debtor countries have an incentive to undergo reform and offer long-term benefits to their publics.

Before 1989, major creditors undertook insufficient joint action to attain success in debt reduction. From 1989 to 1993, to avoid damaging precedents for other LDC debtors, creditors generally worked out debt-reduction packages with selected large debtors, such as Mexico, Brazil, Venezuela, and Nigeria.

The inherent barrier to voluntary schemes with small debtors is that the nonparticipating creditor who holds on to its original claims (which will rise in value) will be better off than those participating in collective debt reduction. *Creditor participants pay the cost of debt reduction, while all creditors share the benefits.*

As of 1994, the World Bank and IMF have made only limited progress in coordinating concerted debt reduction for smaller debtors. A wider Debt Reduction Consortium (DRC) could amalgamate consultative groups (CG) chaired by the World Bank, the Paris Club, London Club, and roundtables chaired by the United Nations Development Program. Debt relief needs to shift its focus from the Paris Club to another organization, such as the CG, where debtor countries have a better opportunity to present their case and creditors a wider perspective on the debt question. An additional problem in organizing debt relief is that DC governments and commercial banks no longer have the urgency to address the LDC debt crisis, since it no longer endangers the DC banking system. Moreover, global concerted

---

[67]Jeffrey D. Sachs, "Making the Brady Plan Work," *Foreign Affairs* 69 (Summer 1989), pp. 87–104.

[68]Jeffrey D. Sachs, "Efficient Debt Reduction," in Ishrat Husain and Ishac Diwan, eds., *Dealing with the Debt Crisis* (Washington, D.C.: World Bank, 1989), p. 239–40; and Sidney Dell, *International Development Policies: Perspectives for Industrial Countries* (Durham, N.C.: Duke University Press, 1991), p. 139.

efforts proposed in the 1930s and 1990s—a special international lending facility, injections of new funds, debt buybacks, and conversions of existing assets into new assets with different contingencies—have had limited success because of disagreements about who should fund and control the administration.[69]

THE ENTERPRISE FOR THE AMERICAS INITIATIVE

In June 1990, U.S. President George Bush announced the **Enterprise for the Americas Initiative (EAI)**, which included reducing part of the $12 billion official debt owed the United States by Latin American countries undergoing World Bank/ IMF reforms. To be eligible for debt relief, the Latin American country needed to: (1) receive IMF approval for a standby agreement, extended arrangement, or structural adjustment facility, (2) obtain World Bank approval for a structural or sectoral adjustment program, and (3) agree to a satisfactory financing program for debt service reduction with its commercial bank lender.

Under the EAI, the country exchanges United States Agency for International Development or other U.S. official concessional debt for new and restructured debt with a reduced face value. The United States, which determines the discount or amount forgiven case by case, charges a concessional interest rate on the new debt, which cannot be further restructured. The country must pay the principal on the new debt in U.S. dollars. However, as in the case of Bolivia, Chile, and Jamaica in the early 1990s, a country with an Environmental Framework Agreement with the U.S. government can pay interest in local currency, depositing the funds to finance debt-for-nature projects. From 1991 through 1993, the United States wrote down 54 percent of the $1.6 billion official debt of Chile, Bolivia, Jamaica, Colombia, El Salvador, Uruguay, and Argentina.[70]

THE POLICY CARTEL

Mosley, Harrigan, and Toye refer to the International Monetary Fund and World Bank as a "managed duopoly of policy advice." Before arranging LDC debt write-offs and write-downs, the World Bank, DC governments, or commercial banks require the IMF's "seal of approval" in the form of a stabilization program. This requirement creates a monopoly position leaving debtors little room to maneuver. Latin American and African debtors would benefit from the strengthening of independent financial power within the world economy. Yet the Bretton Woods institutions, the World Bank and IMF, as charged by their DC and LDC shareholders, do not use their resources to write down or cancel debts. Both institutions must be satisfied that a borrower can repay a loan. There may be few alternatives to financial restrictions, devaluation, price liberalization, and deregulation for eliminating a chronic debt crisis.

---

[69]Carol Lancaster, *African Economic Reform: The External Dimension* (Washington, D.C.: Institute for International Economics, 1991), pp. 55–56; Percy S. Mistry, "African Debt Revisited: Procrastination or Progress?" Paper prepared for the North-South Roundtable on African Debt Relief, Recovery, and Democracy, Abidjan, Ivory Coast, July 8–9, 1991, p. 15; Barry Eichengreen and Richard Portes, "Dealing with Debt: The 1930s and the 1980s," in Ishrat Husain and Ishac Diwan, eds., *Dealing with the Debt Crisis* (Washington, D.C.: World Bank, 1989), pp. 69–86; and E. Wayne Nafziger, *The Debt Crisis in Africa* (Baltimore: Johns Hopkins University Press, 1993), pp. 20–21, 193–95.

[70]World Bank, *World Debt Tables: External Finance for Developing Countries, 1993–94*, vol. 1, *Analysis and Summary Tables* (Washington, D.C., 1983), 35–36, 115.

This section does not exhaust the policy approaches for resolving the debt crisis. The reader should consult Chapters 16, 18, and 20 for factors influencing LDC external adjustment, with emphasis on sections that discuss direct foreign investment, concessional aid, DCs' reduced trade barriers against LDCs, and LDC trade and exchange-rate policies to avoid biases against exports.

Distributional Effects

The U.N. Conference on Trade and Development has proposed widespread debt renegotiation to cancel or reschedule debts, especially of the least-developed countries. Since the late 1970s, the Paris Club, comprising of ad hoc meetings of representatives of creditor countries, has increased arrangements to reschedule or consolidate official debts. Sweden, Canada, and the Netherlands have even canceled the debts of some of the poorest countries as a form of development assistance.

Yet these measures affected only a small fraction of total LDC debt, since private creditors hold the majority of the debt. But Jeffrey D. Sachs is critical of such measures as the Baker plan, which saves banks at the expense of the IMF, the World Bank, and Japanese creditors. Moreover, both Baker and Brady proposals emphasize middle-income countries in financial trouble rather than poor countries or more prudent South Korea. Additionally, many LDCs adversely affected by external shock or growth deceleration, including Bangladesh, and most of low-income sub-Saharan Africa, borrowed less by choice than necessity (low credit-worthiness).[71]

Why should DCs or multilateral agencies use concessional aid for debt relief or cancellation? Most of the large debtors are *not* among the poorest countries but are instead middle income. Many countries with debt crises have not managed their economies very well.

Latin America's and sub-Saharan Africa's debt crises have forced many countries to curtail poverty programs, even though few of these programs have been funded by foreign borrowing. In 1985, Tanzanian President Julius K. Nyerere asked, "Must we starve our children to pay our debt?" The UNICEF found that child malnutrition increased and primary school enrollment rates declined in the 1980s in many least-developed countries as external debt constraints cut spending on services most needed by the poor.[72]

In 1989, in response to increased poverty in adjusting countries, IMF Managing Director Michel Camdessus asserted:

> The first [conviction] is that adjustment does not have to lower basic human standards. . . . My second conviction is that the more adjustment efforts give proper weight to social realities—especially the implications for the poorest—the

[71]Jeffrey D. Sachs, "The Debt Crisis," *Challenge* 31 (May/June 1988), 19; and Willem H. Buiter and T. N. Srinivasan, "Rewarding the Profligate," *World Development* 15 (March 1987), 414.

[72]Manuel Pastor, Jr., "The Effects of IMF Programs in the Third World: Debate and Evidence from Latin America," *World Development* 15 (February 1987): 249–62; E. Wayne Nafziger, *Inequality in Africa: Political Elites, Proletariat, Peasants, and the Poor* (Cambridge: Cambridge University Press, 1988), pp. 61–63; UNICEF, *The State of the World's Children, 1989* (New Delhi: 1989); and Jeffrey Sachs and Andrew Berg, "The Debt Crisis: Structural Explanations of Country Performance," *Journal of Development Economics* 29 (November 1988): 217–306; and Marcelo Selowsky, "Comment on The Debt Crisis: Structural Explanations of Country Performance," *Journal of Development Economics* 29 (November 1988): 307–09.

more successful they are likely to be. . . . People know something about how to ensure that the very poor are spared by the adjustment effort. In financial terms, it might not cost very much. Why? Because if you look at the share of the poorest groups in the distribution of these [adjusting] countries income, it is a trifling amount. . . . Unfortunately it is generally "everyone else," and not the poverty groups, that is represented in government.[73]

Mosley, Harrigan, and Toye observe that statements such as this by Camdessus "almost certainly exaggerate the extent to which the Fund at the operational level has moved or will move away from this traditional brief," that is the required internal changes for restoration of a sustainable macroeconomic recovery.[74] Indeed the IMF (and World Bank) stress income distribution and basic needs in their publications but have few systematic studies of the effects of adjustment on poverty and income inequality and few programs to ensure that adjusting countries protect the income and social services of the poor. Bank and Fund adjustment programs may need to support income transfers for the poor, as most LDCs (except for some upper-middle countries such as Brazil and Turkey) lack the resources to support income transfers for the poor. For example, in the poorest African countries, where the majority of the population lives close to subsistence, welfare payments to bring the population above the poverty line would undermine work incentives and be prohibitively expensive. The World Bank's Social Dimensions of Adjustment Projects (SDA), discussed in Chapter 6, if enacted more widely in the future, is a step toward compensating the poor for losses from adjustment programs.

Summary

1. Some of the causes of the debt crisis have been global shocks and instability in the 1970s and 1980s, a decline in the ratio of official aid to commercial loans, increased real interest rates from the 1970s to the 1980s, inefficiency, poor economic management, overvalued domestic currencies, and capital flight.

2. Lending to LDCs (especially Latin American) may be undermined by capital flight because perceived risk-adjusted returns are higher in haven countries than in LDCs. Equilibrium exchange rates, fiscal reform, increased efficiency of state enterprises, and nondiscriminatory haven country policies can help reduce flight, but ironically exchange controls may also be necessary sometimes.

3. LDCs, especially Latin American, had an increase in their real external debt in the 1970s and 1980s. The LDC debt service ratio more than doubled between 1970 to 1986. The exposure of several major U.S. commercial banks to losses from LDC loan write-offs or write-downs has been substantial.

4. The ratio of debt service to GNP is not always a good indicator of the debt burden. Many large LDC debtors borrowed heavily because of their excellent international credit ratings.

---

[73]Quoted in James P. Grant, *The State of the World's Children, 1989* (New York: Oxford University Press, 1989), pp. 18–20.

[74]Paul Mosley, Jane Harrigan, and John Toye, *Aid and Power: The World Bank and Policy-based Lending*, vol. 1 (London: Routledge, 1991), 54.

5. Middle-income countries account for 70 percent of the total outstanding debt of all LDCs. Yet the debt burden for low-income countries, such as the majority of sub-Saharan African countries, which have poor credit ratings, may be as heavy as for middle-income countries.

6. In the 1980s and early 1990s, at least 64 LDCs renegotiated their foreign debts through multilateral agreements with official creditor groups.

7. In the late 1970s through the 1990s, developing countries with chronic external deficits required economic adjustment, imposed domestically or by the World Bank or International Monetary Fund. In 1979, the World Bank began structural adjustment loans and soon thereafter sectoral adjustment loans. IMF loans of last resort were conditioned on an LDC implementing an acceptable macroeconomic stabilization programs. Additionally, in 1986–87, the IMF initiated structural adjustment loans for LDCs experiencing unanticipated external shocks.

8. Finance officials in DCs instituted several plans for resolving the debt crisis. The Baker plan (1985) emphasized new loans from multilateral agencies and surplus countries, while the Brady plan (1989) stressed debt reduction or write-downs. One strategy for debt write-offs was debt equity swaps, which involved selling an outstanding loan to a private company, which acquired equity interest in a LDC firm.

9. Debt write-downs require multilateral coordination among creditors to avoid the free-rider problem in which nonparticipating creditors benefit from the increased value of debt holdings.

10. Mosley, Harrigan, and Toye refer to the IMF and World Bank as a "managed duopoly of policy advice." Before the World Bank, DC governments, or commercial banks arrange LDC debt write-downs, they require that the IMF approve the LDC's stabilization program.

Terms to Review

- total external debt (EDT)
- debt service
- London Interbank Offered Rate (LIBOR)
- debt-service ratio
- net transfers
- Paris Club
- London Club
- negative world real interest rates
- currency appreciation
- currency depreciation
- managed floating exchange-rate system
- target zones
- capital flight
- propensity to flee
- exchange controls

- structural adjustment loans (SALs)
- sectoral adjustment loans (SECALs)
- Baker plan
- Brady plan
- Group of Seven (G7)
- Toronto terms
- Trinidad terms
- Egypt-Poland terms
- debt exchanges
- debt-equity swaps
- debt buybacks
- debt-for-nature swaps
- debt-for-development swaps
- Debt Reduction Facility
- IDA-eligible countries
- Enterprise for the Americas Initiative (EAI)

Questions to Discuss

1. Discuss the nature and origins of the LDCs' external debt problem. What impact has the debt crisis had on LDC development? On DCs?
2. Define the major debt indicators. How useful is each of these indicators as a measure of the debt burden?
3. Who are the major LDC debtors? Explain the reasons for the discrepancies between the leading LDC debtors and LDCs with the greatest debt burdens.
4. What is capital flight? What relevance does it have for the debt problem? What can source and haven countries do to reduce capital flight?
5. What plan should the international community adopt to resolve the debt crisis? In your answer, consider the Baker and Brady Plans, debt cancellation and rescheduling, and debt exchanges, as well as the roles of the World Bank, International Monetary Fund, and DCs in the effort at resolution.
6. What impact has incurring major external debt by LDCs had on income distribution? What impact have attempts to reduce the debt crisis had on income distribution?

Guide to Readings

The OECD (note 35), World Bank (note 1), IMF (note 3), *IMF Survey*, UNICEF (note 27), UNCTAD (note 49), and FAO (note 45) are major periodic statistical sources on the LDC external debt crisis. You can find useful analyses of the debt problem in Cohen (note 23), Dornbusch, Buiter and Srinivasan (note 24), Ranis (note 28), Ghai (note 26), Helleiner (note 52), Sachs (note 52), Nafziger (note 16), Krueger (note 4), Pastor (note 72), Weeks (note 40), Williamson (note 59), Husain and Diwan (note 41), Krugman and Obstfeld (note 61), Mosley, Harrigan, and Toye (note 74), Giovanni Andrea Cornia, Richard Jolly, and Frances Stewart, eds., *Adjustment with a Human Face: Protecting the Vulnerable and Promoting Growth*, 2 vols (Oxford: Clarendon Press, 1987); Simon Commander, ed., *Structural Adjustment and Agriculture: Theory and Practice in Africa and Latin America* (London: Overseas Development Institute, 1989); Horace Campbell and Howard Stein, eds., *Tanzania and the IMF: The Dynamics of Liberalization* (Boulder, Colo.: Westview, 1992); and John Loxley, "The IMF and World Bank Conditionality and sub-Saharan Africa," in Peter Lawrence, ed., *World Recession and the Food Crisis in Africa* (London: James Currey, 1986), pp. 96–103.

The Institute of International Economics in Washington, D.C., provides many useful monographs on debt problems, including Lessard and Williamson, and Williamson and Lessard (note 12) and William R. Cline, *Mobilizing Bank Lending to Debtor Countries* (Washington, D.C.: Institute for International Economics, 1987). The *International Monetary Fund Staff Papers,* a quarterly journal, frequently has articles discussing LDC debt.

International Trade

Scope of the Chapter

This chapter discusses arguments for and against tariff protection, the shift in LDCs' terms of trade, import substitution and export expansion in industry, DC import policies, expansion of primary export earnings, trade in services, protection of intellectual property rights, foreign exchange-rate policies, LDC regional integration, the Asian and North American borderless economies, protection of infant entrepreneurship, and the new international economic order.

Arguments for and against Tariffs

ARGUMENT FOR FREE TRADE: COMPARATIVE ADVANTAGE

International economists still accept the doctrine of **comparative advantage** formulated by Adam Smith and David Ricardo, English classical economists of the late eighteenth and early nineteenth centuries.

Assume a world of two countries (for example, a LDC like Pakistan and a DC like Japan) and two commodities (for example, textiles and steel). Other classical assumptions include

1. Given productive resources (land, labor, and capital) that can be combined in only the same fixed proportion in both countries.
2. Full employment of productive resources.
3. Given technical knowledge.
4. Given tastes.
5. Pure competition (so the firm is a pricetaker).
6. No movement of labor and capital between countries but free movement of these resources within a country.
7. Export value equal to import value for each country.
8. No transportation costs.

The theory states that world (that is, two-country) welfare is greatest when each country *exports products whose comparative costs are lower at home than abroad* and *imports goods whose **comparative costs** are lower abroad than at home.*

International trade and specialization are determined by *comparative costs,* not *absolute costs.* Absolute cost comparisons require some standard unit, such as a common currency (for example, textiles $5 a meter in Pakistan and $10 in Japan). But you cannot compare absolute costs without an exchange rate (such as a Pakistani rupee price of the Japanese yen).

Assume that before international trade, the price of textiles is Rs. 50 per yard in Pakistan and ¥300 in Japan, and the price of steel per ton is Rs. 200 and ¥400 (shown in Table 18–1).

We cannot conclude that both textiles and steel are cheaper in Pakistan simply because it takes fewer rupees than yen to buy them. The two currencies are different units of measuring price, and there is no established relationship between them. If Japan issued a new currency, converting old yen into new ones at a ratio of 100:1, both products would then sell for fewer yen than rupees, even though the real situation had not changed.

It is easy to compare relative prices, however. The ratio of the price of steel to that of textiles is 4:3 in Japan and 4:1 in Pakistan. Hence the relative price of steel is lower in Japan than in Pakistan, and the relative price of textiles is lower in Pakistan than in Japan. Thus Pakistan has a comparative cost advantage in textiles and Japan a comparative cost advantage in steel.

To demonstrate that the LDC (Pakistan) gains when exporting textiles in exchange for Japanese steel, we must use an exchange rate (for example, rupee price of the yen) to convert comparative prices into absolute price differences. Pakistanis will demand Japanese steel if they can buy yen for *less than* half a rupee per 1 yen. Why? Because steel is *absolutely* cheaper in Japan than in Pakistan. If, for example, people purchase 1 yen for one-fourth of a rupee, Japanese steel sells for Rs. 100 (¥400)—cheaper than the Pakistani steel price or Rs. 200. On the other hand, the Japanese will buy Pakistani textiles if they can sell 1 yen for *more than* one-sixth of a rupee. At an exchange rate of 1 yen per one-fourth of a rupee for example, the Japanese can buy Pakistani textiles for ¥200 (Rs. 50)—cheaper than the Japanese price of ¥300.

International trade takes place at any exchange rate between half a rupee per 1 yen (the maximum rupee price per yen to induce Pakistanis to trade) and one-sixth of a rupee per 1 yen (the minimum rupee price per yen to induce the Japanese to trade). Within this range, the *absolute* price of steel is lower in Japan than in Pakistan, and the *absolute* price of textiles is lower in Pakistan than in Japan, so both countries gain from trade.

This exchange-rate range is not arbitrary. If it is *more than* half a rupee per 1 yen, there is no trade, since Pakistan does not demand any Japanese goods. If it is *less than* one-sixth of a rupee per yen, there is no trade, since Japan demands no Pakistani goods.

TABLE 18–1   Comparative Costs of Textiles and Steel in Pakistan and Japan

	Pakistan	*Japan*
Textiles (price per meter)	Rs. 50	¥300
Steel (price per ton)	Rs. 200	¥400

Given our assumption, if relative prices are the same in the two countries before trade, there will be no trade. If, for example, the relative prices of steel and textiles are Rs. 200 and Rs. 50 in Pakistan, and ¥1,200 and ¥300 in Japan, there is no exchange rate at which both countries demand a good from the other.

Pakistan gains (or at least does *not* lose) by specializing in and exporting textiles, in which it has a comparative cost advantage, and by importing steel, in which it has a comparative cost disadvantage. Pakistan obtains steel more cheaply by using its productive resources to produce textiles, and trading them at a mutually advantageous rate for steel, rather than by producing steel at home.

Although the theory can be made more realistic by including several countries, several commodities, imperfect competition, variable factor proportions, increasing costs, transport costs, and so on, these changed assumptions complicate the exposition but do *not* invalidate the principle of free trade according to a country's comparative advantage. For example, the **factor proportions theory** or **Heckscher–Ohlin theorem,** introduced by two Swedish economists, shows that a nation gains from trade by exporting the commodity whose production requires the intensive use of the country's relatively abundant (and cheap) factor of production and importing the good whose production requires the intensive use of the relatively scarce factor. International trade is based on differences in factor endowment, such as Pakistani labor abundance and Japanese capital abundance. Pakistan has a comparative advantage in labor-intensive goods (textiles) and Japan a comparative advantage in capital-intensive goods (steel), meaning textile opportunity costs (measured by steel output forgone per textile unit produced) are greater in Japan than in Pakistan.[1]

Does foreign investment in LDCs follow comparative advantage? Japanese economist Kiyoshi Kojima argues that whereas U. S. MNCs invest abroad because of monopoly advantages from patents, technology, management, and marketing (see Chapter 16), Japanese MNCs invest in LDCs to take advantage of their comparative advantage in natural resources or in labor-intensive commodities, a pattern that promotes trade and specialization.[2]

Comparative advantage may be based on a **technological advantage** (as in Japan, the United States, and Germany), perhaps a Schumpeterian innovation like a new product or production process that gives the country a temporary monopoly in the world market until other countries are able to imitate. The **product cycle model** indicates that while a product requires highly skilled labor in the beginning, later as markets grow and techniques become common knowledge, a good becomes standardized, so that less-sophisticated countries can mass produce the item with less skilled labor. Advanced economies have a comparative advantage in nonstandardized goods, while LDCs have a comparative advantage in stan-

---

[1] Eli F. Heckscher, "The Effect of Foreign Trade on the Distribution of Income," in H. S. Ellis and L. M. Metzler, *Readings in the Theory of International Trade* (Homewood, Ill.: Irwin, 1950), pp. 272–300 (original article published in 1919); and Bertil Ohlin, *Interregional and International Trade* (Cambridge: Harvard University Press, 1933). For an elaboration of the theory of comparative advantage, the Heckscher-Ohlin thesis, and the Leontief paradox contradicting that thesis, see Peter B. Kenen, *The International Economy,* 3rd ed. (Cambridge: Cambridge University Press, 1994), pp. 19–85.

For a discussion of the effect of trade on wages in DCs and LDCs, see Gary Burtless, "International Trade and the Rise in Earnings Inequality," *Journal of Economic Literature* 33 (June 1995): 800–16; and Adrian Wood, *North-South Trade, Employment, and Inequality: Changing Fortunes in a Skill-Driven World* (New York: Oxford University Press, 1994).

[2] Kiyoshi Kojima, *Japanese Direct Foreign Investment: A Model of Multinational Business Operations* (Tokyo: Charles E. Tuttle, 1978), pp. 134–51.

dardized goods.[3] Product cycle is illustrated by specialization in cotton textiles shifting from England (the mid-eighteenth to mid-nineteenth centuries) to Japan (the late-nineteenth to early-twentieth centuries) to South Korea, Taiwan, China, Hong Kong, and Singapore (beginning in the 1960s) subsequently joined by Thailand (in the 1980s). Automobiles shifted from the United States (through the late 1960s) to Japan (the mid-1970s through the late 1980s), with the next shift uncertain—a shift among DCs with a global seamless network producing a world car, or to developing countries such as South Korea. Foreign investment and technological transfer by U.S. automobile companies in Japan (for example, General Motors with Isuzu and Ford with Mazda) and Japanese companies in South Korea (Mitsubishi with Hyundai) have helped shift comparative advantage. Indeed Japanese economist Miyohei Shinohara speaks of a **boomerang effect,** imports in reverse or intensification of competition in third markets arising from Japanese enterprise expansion in, and technology exports to, other Asian countries.[4] But Japanese economist Shojiro Tokunaga and his collaborators regard this competitive intensification from third markets as part of a Japanese-led specialized international division of knowledge that enables Japanese companies to maintain competition in the face of yen appreciation (see below).

California-Berkeley economist Paul Romer argues that the theory of comparative advantage, by focusing only on existing goods, understates the advantages of free trade and the costs of trade restrictions. Trade barriers thwart the potential introduction of new goods and productive activities from abroad. Given imperfect competition and barriers to entry, fixed costs restrict the otherwise almost limitless number of goods that innovative entrepreneurs can introduce. If tariffs, quantitative restrictions, and administrative barriers prevent a new good from ever appearing, the harm includes the entire consumer and producer surplus, not just the static loss from forgone specialization in goods enjoying a comparative advantage.[5]

Contemporary theory implies that (1) less-developed countries gain from free international trade and (2) lose by tariffs (import taxes), subsidies, quotas, administrative controls, and other forms of protection. But theory holds that free trade has benefits other than more efficient resource allocation. It leads to greater productivity because it disperses new ideas. It introduces new goods and productive activities, widens markets, improves division of labor, permits more specialized machinery, overcomes technical indivisibilities, utilizes surplus productive capacity, and stimulates greater managerial effort because of foreign, competitive pressures.[6]

ARGUMENTS FOR TARIFFS

Despite their apparent advantage, few LDCs pursue free trade policies. This section evaluates some major arguments for tariffs. Because of a basic symmetry in argument, subsequent arguments for tariffs except the revenue argument also

---

[3]Raymond Vernon, "International Investment and International Trade in the Product Cycle," *Quarterly Journal of Economics* 2 (May 1966): 190–207.

[4]Miyohei Shinohara, *Industrial Growth, Trade, and Dynamic Patterns in the Japanese Economy* (Tokyo: University of Tokyo Press, 1982), pp. 32–33, 72–75, 127–28.

[5]Paul Romer, "New Goods, Old Theory, and the Welfare Costs of Trade Restrictions," *Journal of Development Economics* 43 (February 1994): 5–38.

[6]Hla Myint, "The 'Classical Theory' of International Trade and the Underdeveloped Countries," *Economic Journal* 68 (June 1958): 317–37; and Harvey Leibenstein, "Allocative Efficiency vs. 'X-Efficiency'," *American Economic Review* 56 (June 1966): 392–415, discussed in Chapter 13.

constitute cases for protective devices such as subsidies (including supporting industrial policy by the state).

The most frequent rationale for tariffs is to protect infant industries. Alexander Hamilton, the first U.S. secretary of the treasury, criticized Adam Smith's doctrine of **laissez-faire** (governmental noninterference) and free trade. Hamilton supported a tariff, passed in 1789, partly designed to protect manufacturing in his young country from foreign competition. **Infant industry arguments** include (1) increasing returns to scale, (2) external economies, and (3) technological borrowing.

Increasing Returns to Scale. A new firm in a new industry has many disadvantages: It must train specialized management and labor, learn new techniques, create or enter markets, and cope with the diseconomies of small-scale production. Tariff protection gives a new firm time to expand output to the point of lowest long-run average cost.

An argument against this notion is illustrated by a world of two countries, each of which initially produces a different good with decreasing costs at the lowest long-run average cost. Assume that later both countries levy tariffs to start an infant industry in the good produced by the other country, so that the market is divided and both countries produce both goods well below lowest average cost output. In this case, the world loses specialization gains and economies of scale. The world would be better off if each country specialized in one decreasing-cost product, exchanging it for the decreasing-cost product of the other country.

But some may ask if infant industry protection would not be warranted for the firm in a newly industrializing country competing with firms in well-established industrial countries. In this instance, however, tariff protection, by distributing income from consumers to producers, amounts to a subsidy to cover the firm's early losses. Why should society subsidize the firm in its early years? If the enterprise is profitable over the long run, losses in the early years can be counted as part of the entrepreneur's capital costs. If the enterprise is not profitable in the long run, however, would not resources be better used for some other investment?

Yet government might still want to protect infant industry. First, government support may cover part of the entrepreneur's risk when average expected returns are positive but vary widely. Second, the state may support local technological learning and knowledge-creating capabilities. Third, government planners may better forecast the future success of the industry than private entrepreneurs but protect or subsidize private investment to avoid direct operation of the industry themselves. Fourth, protecting the new industry may create external economies, or promote technological borrowing, both discussed below.

External Economies. These are production benefits that do not accrue to the private entrepreneur. One example is technological learning, measured by a learning curve that shows how much unit costs fall with the increased labor productivity from cumulative experience. This curve, which is downward sloping over time, is a source of dynamic increasing returns. Related to these, external economies also include the training of skilled labor, and lower input costs to other industries, all of which cannot be appropriated by the investor but may be socially profitable even if a commercial loss occurs. Government can make a rational case for protecting or subsidizing such investment. The argument can, however, easily be abused by political leaders who discover immeasurable externalities for pet projects.

Technological Borrowing. Classical economists assumed a given technology open to all countries. In reality much of the world's rapidly improving technology is concentrated in a few countries.

Much international specialization is based on differences in technology rather than resource endowment. Assume both Italy and Indonesia can produce corn, but only Italy has the technical capacity to manufacture transistor radios. Thus Italy trades radios, in which it has a comparative advantage, for Indonesia's corn. Yet Indonesia has the necessary labor and materials, so that if Italy's technology could be acquired, Indonesia's comparative advantage would shift to radios. If Indonesia levies a tariff on transistor radios, Italian companies may transfer capital and technology to produce radios behind Indonesia's tariff wall. Once Indonesia acquires this technology, its average costs will be lower than those in Italy.

Critics raise one question: If Indonesia is open to foreign investment and if foreign technology gives Indonesia a comparative advantage, why is a tariff necessary to induce the foreign entrepreneur to produce radios there? Should not the foreign radio manufacturer see the opportunity and bring capital and technology to Indonesia?

Tariffs (subsidies, exchange controls, and quantitative restrictions) may shelter inefficient technological transfers from abroad. In India, in the 1960s, protection conferred such monopoly power on automobile manufacturers Hindustan Motors and Premier Automobiles (in a joint venture with Fiat and later Nissan) that they subtracted value from raw materials and purchased inputs. The automobile industry had an **effective rate of protection** (that is, protection as a percentage of valued added by production factors at a processing stage) of 2,612 percent;[7] indeed the foreign-exchange cost of the inputs used in producing a domestic automobile was higher than the foreign-exchange cost of buying an automobile directly from abroad! India acquired few technical learning gains from protection, which instead supported technological sloth. Moreover, India's high rates of protection reduced the rupee price of the dollar below the equilibrium price, thus shortchanging (or discriminating against) exporters who exchanged their dollars for rupees. Below we discuss protection of infant entrepreneurship as an alternative to protecting infant industry.

Politically it is difficult to end tariff protection for infant industries. When governments feel compelled to protect infant industry, they could instead provide subsidies which are politically easier to remove rather than tariffs.

Intraindustry Trade. Ironically, about one-fourth of international trade consists of **intraindustry trade**, exchanges by two countries (primarily DCs) within the same industry (or standard industrial classification). Examples include the automobile (Germany exports Mercedes-Benz to the United States, which exports Fords to Germany), office machinery, and running-shoe industries. Intraindustry trade plays a particularly large role in trade in manufactured and high-technology goods among DCs. The markets for these goods are **monopolistically competitive**, an industry structure characterized by a large number of firms, no barriers to entry, and **product differentiation**, where corporations proliferate models, styles, brand names, and other positive distinguishing traits, such as image, service, and unique taste or components, sometimes enhancing different identities through

---

[7]Jagdish N. Bhagwati and Padma Desai, *India: Planning for Industrialization—Industrialization and Trade Policies since 1951* (London: Oxford University Press, 1970), pp. 335–67.

advertising. Product differentiation assures each firm a monopoly in its particular product within an industry and is thus somewhat insulated from competition. Each firm takes the prices charged by its rivals as given, ignoring the effect of its own price on its competitors' prices. Monopolistic competition assumes that although each firm faces competition from other producers, it behaves as if it were a monopolist. Thus, Mexico, in which General Motors, Ford, Chrysler, Toyota, Nissan, and Volkswagen offer substantially different yet competing automobiles, is characterized by monopolistic competition.

Intraindustry trade among DCs, which is a major source of gains from trade, arise (1) when countries are at similar stages of economic development, usually similar in their relative factor supplies (abundant human capital and sparse unskilled labor), so that there is little interindustry trade, and (2) when gains from economies of large-scale production and product choice are substantial.[8]

What are the implications of intraindustry trade for developing countries? Perhaps only a few newly industrialized countries (NICs), such as South Korea, Taiwan, and Singapore, have attained the human capital abundance, technological sophistication, and level of demand that would allow them to gain from specialized intraindustry trade in differentiated products. But once you have reached the DC "big leagues," where the technological frontier changes incessantly, you probably gain more by the bracing challenge of rivals than by building a wall of protection around you. William Lewis's study of global manufacturing competitiveness concluded: "Global competition breeds high productivity; protection breeds stagnation."[9]

Changes in Factor Endowment. A government might levy a tariff so that entrepreneurs modify their output mix to match a shifting comparative advantage due perhaps to a change in resource proportions. Thus as its frontier pushed westward and capital expanded, the United States changed from a country rich in natural resources, exporting a wide variety of metals and minerals, to a capital-rich country. Analogously the rapid accumulation of capital and technology may alter comparative advantage from labor-intensive to capital- and technology-intensive goods. Thus in the 1950s and 1960s, Japan's Ministry of International Trade and Industry (MITI) tried to establish capital- and technology-intensive industries, which appeared not to be to Japan's static comparative advantage but offered more long-run growth because of rapid technical change, rapid labor productivity growth, and a high **income elasticity of demand** (percentage change in quantity demanded/percentage change in income). South Korea followed a similar strategy in the 1960s, 1970s, and 1980s, but established performance standards for each industry protected (Chapter 3).

We must ask why private entrepreneurs would not perceive the changing comparative advantage and plan accordingly. Even in Japan, while MITI facilitated the output of memory chips for semiconductors, it did not encourage electronics production and tried to consolidate Japan's automobile production into a few giant corporations, attempting to prevent Soichiro Honda from producing cars! Indeed while MITI was accommodating and supportive, private entrepre-

---

[8]Karl E. Case and Ray C. Fair, *Principles of Economics* (Englewood Cliffs, N.J.: Prentice Hall, 1996), pp. 350–76; Robert L. Heilbroner and James K. Galbraith, *The Economic Problem*, 9th ed. (Englewood Cliffs, N.J.: Prentice Hall, 1990), pp. 575–76; and Paul R. Krugman and Maurice Obstfeld, *International Economics: Theory and Policy*, 3rd ed. (New York: HarperCollins, 1994), pp. 119–33.

[9]William Lewis, "The Secret to Competitiveness," *Wall Street Journal* (October 22, 1993): p. A14.

neurs invested and coordinated the essential resources.[10] Government protection (or subsidy) is appropriate only if government foresees these changes better than private entrepreneurs.

Revenue Sources.   As indicated in Chapter 15, tariffs are often a major source of revenue, especially in young nations with limited ability to raise direct taxes. In fact, U.S. tariffs in 1789, despite Hamilton's intentions, did more to raise revenue than protect domestic industry.

Even for a government unconcerned about the losses a tariff imposes on other people, tariffs have limits. At the extreme, a prohibitive tariff brings no revenue. And a tariff that maximizes revenue in the short run will probably not do so in the long run. In the short run, before domestic production has moved into import-competing industries, demand is often inelastic (that is, the absolute value of the percentage change in quantity is less than the absolute value of the percentage change in price). However once productive resources adjust, demand elasticities increase; and a greater relative quantity decrease—in response to the increased price from the tariff—occurs. Thus a government setting a maximum revenue tariff must take account of the long-run movement of production resources.[11]

Improved Employment and the Balance of Payments.   A rise in tariff rates diverts demand from imports to domestic goods, so that the balance on goods and services (exports minus imports), aggregate demand, and employment increase.[12] The economic injury to other countries, however, may provoke retaliation. Furthermore the effects of import restrictions and increased prices spread throughout the economy, so that domestic- and export-oriented production and employment decline. In fact, Lawrence B. Krause's study of the U.S. economy indicates that jobs lost by export contraction exceed jobs created by import replacement.[13] It is probably more effective to use policies discussed in Chapter 9, and when possible, financial policies (Chapter 15) for employment and home currency devaluation to improve employment and the balance of payments.[14]

Reduced Internal Instability.   The sheer economic cost of periodic fluctuations in employment or prices from unstable international suppliers or customers may justify tariffs to reduce dependence on foreign trade. According to the World Bank, commodities accounting for one-third of LDC nonfuel primary exports fluctuated in price by over 10 percent from one year to the next, 1955 to 1976. By encouraging import substitution, tariff protection can reorient the economy toward more stable domestic production. Losses in allocative efficiency might be outweighed by the greater efficiency implicit in more rational cost calculations and

---

[10]Charles L. Schultze, "Industrial Policy: A Dissent," *Brookings Review* 2 (Fall 1983): 3–12.

[11]Arguments 1–3 and 5–6 are from John Black, "Arguments for Tariffs," *Economic Journal* 69 (June 1959): 191–208; and Charles P. Kindleberger, *International Economics* (Irwin: Homewood, Ill., 1963), pp. 124–34.

[12]When demand is elastic, the percentage decline in the quantity imported exceeds the percentage increase in price from the tariff, so that import value, price multiplied by quantity, falls. When demand is inelastic, import payments increase, but by less than the government's gain in tariff revenue.

[13]John Black, "Arguments for Tariffs," *Economic Journal* 69 (June 1959): 199–200; and Lawrence B. Krause, *Brookings Papers on Economic Activity* (Washington, D.C.: Brookings Institution, 1971), pp. 421–25.

[14]Jagdish Bhagwati, "Free Trade: Old and New Challenges," *Economic Journal* 104 (March 1994): 231–46, argues that the case for protection is valid only when the distortion is foreign, not domestic, for surely the country has some policy discretion in changing domestic distortion.

investment decisions. Yet such a policy may be costly. Tariffs on goods with inelastic demand, such as necessities, increase import payments.

Policymakers should compare the costs of alternative ways of stabilizing the internal economy, such as holding reserves. A LDC with adequate foreign exchange reserves can maintain its purchasing power during times of low demand for its exports. Moreover a country can use reserves from import commodities to offset the destabilizing effects of sudden shortages on domestic prices and incomes.[15]

National Defense.   A developing country may want to avoid dependence on foreign sources for essential materials or products that could be cut off in times of war or other conflict. A tariff in such a case is only worthwhile if building capacity to produce these goods takes time. Otherwise the LDC should use cheaper foreign supplies while they are available.

Policymakers will want to examine alternatives to a national defense tariff, such as stockpiling strategic goods or developing facilities to produce import substitutes without using them until the need arises.

In a period of rapid technical change in military and strategic goods, a government must ask whether it is worth increasing costs through tariffs to avoid hypothetical future dangers. Would it not be better to divert these resources to investment, research, and technical education to increase the economy's overall strength and adaptability?

Extracting Foreign Monopoly or Duopoly Profit.   An LDC facing a foreign monopoly supplier of a good may levy a tariff to transfer some of the monopoly profit to revenue for the LDC. While world welfare falls, the home country levying the tariff increases its welfare at the expense of the foreign producer.

Assume an LDC firm is competing against a foreign firm: (1) in a duopoly, that is, where there are two firms in an industry, (2) where price and output decisions are interdependent, and (3) where both are characterized by internal economies of scale, that is, a falling average-cost curve. A tariff can increase exports for the protected firm in any foreign market in which the firm operates. However, if the foreign country retaliates with a tariff, the two firms are likely to maintain previous market shares, with a greatly reduced volume of trade.[16]

Antidumping.   **Dumping** is selling a product cheaper abroad than at home. Why should a country object to it? If a foreign country is supplying cheap imports favorable to consumers, should not such action be considered as a reduction in foreign comparative costs? Yes and no. If the foreign supplier is dumping as a temporary stage in a price war to drive home producers out of business and establish a monopoly, a country may be justified in levying a tariff.[17]

---

[15]World Bank, *World Development Report, 1978* (New York: Oxford University Press, 1978), pp. 19–20; and John Black, "Arguments for Tariffs," *Economic Journal* 69 (June 1959): 206–8.

[16]Dennis R. Appleyard and Alfred J. Field, Jr., *International Economics* (Homewood, Ill.: Irwin, 1992), pp. 162–69; James A. Brandner and Barbara J. Spencer, "Tariffs and the Extraction of Foreign Monopoly Rents under Potential Entry," *Canadian Journal of Economics* 3 (August 1981): 371–89; and Paul R. Krugman, "Import Protection as Export Promotion: International Competition in the Presence of Oligopoly and Economies of Scale" in Henryk Kierzkowski, ed., *Monopolistic Competition in International Trade* (Oxford: Oxford University Press, 1984), pp. 180–93.

[17]John Black, "Arguments for Tariffs," *Economic Journal* 69 (June 1959): 201–4.

Reduced Luxury Consumption.   Government may wish to levy a tariff to curtail the consumption of luxury goods. As indicated in Chapter 15, however, an excise tax is probably preferable to a tariff on luxuries, which would have the unintended effect of stimulating domestic luxury goods production.

CONCLUSION

From our arguments, it should now be clear that tariff protection need not necessarily be attributed to analytical error or the power of vested interests, but may be based on some genuine exceptions to the case for free trade. Yet many of the most frequent arguments for tariffs, such as protecting infant industry, are more limited than many LDC policymakers suppose. In fact a critical analysis of the arguments for tariffs provides additional support for liberal trade policies.

The Application of Arguments for and against Free Trade to Developed Countries

Because of the lack of validity of infant-industry and revenue arguments, the case for free trade is even more powerful for DCs than for LDCs. What about arguments, used by opponents to trade expansion in the United States, for protection against goods embodying cheap labor or using polluting processes that American law prohibits?

Surely law, culture, and relative resource prices and proportions are at the heart of differences that contribute to comparative advantage and disadvantage. To be sure, under restrictive assumptions, free trade lowers the wage of the scarce factor, which in DCs is labor.[18] However, free trade increases national income. A rich country can use taxes and subsidies, unemployment compensation, and training programs to see that neither dislocated workers nor the rest of the population loses from external competition.[19]

No international trading rules prohibit the U.S. Congress from passing laws to protect the environment. However, these rules on the environment "are designed to prevent environmental measures from becoming a new handmaiden of protection."[20] To improve global standards, environmentalists need to support a global environmental organization.[21]

---

[18]Wolfgang Stolper and Paul Samuelson, "Protection and Real Wages," *Review of Economic Studies* 9 (1941): 58–73.

[19]For a symposium on DC income inequality and trade, see Richard B. Freeman, "Are Your Wages Set in Beijing?" *Journal of Economic Perspectives* 9 (Summer 1995): 15–32; J. David Richardson, "Income Inequality and Trade: How to Think, What to Conclude," *Journal of Economic Perspectives* 9 (Summer 1995): 33–55; and Adrian Wood, "How Trade Hurt Unskilled Workers," *Journal of Economic Perspectives* 9 (Summer 1995): 57–80.

[20]Gary Clyde Hufbauer and Jeffrey J. Schott, *NAFTA: An Assessment*, rev. ed. (Washington, D.C.: Institute for International Economics, 1993), p. 94.

[21]Daniel C. Esty, "The Case for a Global Environmental Organization,"in Peter B. Kenen, ed., *Managing the World Economy: Fifty Years After Bretton Woods* (Washington, D.C.: Institute for International Economics, 1994), pp. 287–309.

Shifts in the Terms of Trade

One sign of the peripheralness of many LDCs is their international trade vulnerability, which is exacerbated by a high export primary commodity concentration ratio (the three leading primary products as a percentage of total merchandise exports, as discussed in Chapter 4). The high commodity concentration of LDCs is associated with volatile export prices and earnings. Developing countries are vulnerable to relative international price instability not only because of their dependence on volatile primary product exports but also because exports are highly concentrated in a few commodities and directed to a few countries. The resulting wide swings in export prices have had a disastrous effect on government budgets and external balances.

A measure of relative export prices, the **commodity terms of trade,** equals the price index of exports divided by the price index of imports. If export prices increase 10 percent and import prices 21 percent, the commodity terms of trade drop 9 percent, that is, $1.10/1.21 = 0.91$.

Soon after World War II, Raul Prebisch, then Director General of the Economic Commission for Latin America, and Hans Singer, with the U.N. Department of Economic and Social Affairs, argued that the commodity terms of trade of countries (mainly LDCs) producing primary goods (food, raw materials, minerals, and organic oils and fats) decline in the long run. The trend, taken from a League of Nations statistical series, is inferred from the inverse of the rising terms of trade, 1876–1880 to 1938, of Britain, a manufactures exporter and primary product importer.

The **Prebisch–Singer thesis** states that the terms of trade deteriorated historically because of differences in the growth of demand for, and the market structure in, primary and manufacturing production. **Engel's law** indicates that as income increases, the proportion of income spent on manufactured goods rises and the proportion spent on primary products falls. If resources do not shift from primary to manufacturing output, there will be an excess supply of, and declining relative price in, primary products and an excess demand for, and increasing relative price in, manufactured goods. Moreover, the predominantly non-oil primary products that LDCs export and the manufactured products exports by DCs and a few newly industrializing countries are not priced the same way. Although global marketing for most primary products is oligopolistic, the LDC farmer is a price taker, with no influence on market price; however widespread commodity productivity gains can result in lower prices. On the other hand, most industrial production and marketing are relatively monopolistic, with productivity gains leading to higher prices.[22]

Is the Prebisch–Singer thesis adequate? Can we arrive at a historical law based on Britain's relatively declining primary product prices for a seven-decade period? If we exclude the depressed prices of the 1930s, the price fall from the 1870s is not really so great. Furthermore, the increase in the British commodity terms of trade shown by the League of Nations data may be partly an artifact of the inadequate measure. The data do not adequately account for qualitative improvements

---

[22]United Nations, Department of Economic Affairs, *Relative Prices of Exports and Imports of Underdeveloped Countries* (New York, 1949); Raul Prebisch, "The Economic Development of Latin America and Its Principal Problems," *Economic Bulletin for Latin America* 7, no. 1 (February 1962):1–22 (first published in 1950); and Hans W. Singer, "The Distribution of Gains between Investing and Borrowing Countries," *American Economic Review* 40, no. 2 (May 1950): 473–85. Ragnar Nurkse's *Patterns of Trade and Development* (New York: Oxford University Press, 1961), contributed to these ideas.

taking place predominantly in manufactured goods. Although there was little difference between a bushel of grain in 1880 and 1938, new and improved manufactured goods were developed during the period. Additionally, international shipping costs fell with the opening of the Suez and Panama canals and the development of refrigeration and steamships. Since international transport rates enter only import prices (measured with the cost of insurance and freight, c.i.f.), but not exports, falling rates would reduce import prices more than export prices. The two factors result in an upward bias in the British terms of trade. Yet John Spraos's careful statistical study for the United Nations shows that, when we adjust for the problems mentioned, the League of Nations data would still indicate a deterioration of primary producers' terms of trade, although by a smaller magnitude than Prebisch and Singer thought. Figure 18–1 shows a declining trend for the price of *non-oil* commodities relative to exports of manufactures since 1948.

However Spraos's figures for Britain's relative primary prices rose between 1939 and 1973, just after the League's figures. Thus Spraos concludes that while Prebisch and Singer got the direction of changes in the terms of trade from 1876–1880 to 1938 right, if we extend the data to 1973, the falling commodity terms of trade for primary products are open to doubt.[23] Pier Giorgio Ardeni and Brian Wright, though, using a statistical approach that does not assume stationarity of

FIGURE 18–1 **Non-oil Commodity Prices Relative to Unit Value of Manufactures Exports, 1948–1992**[a]

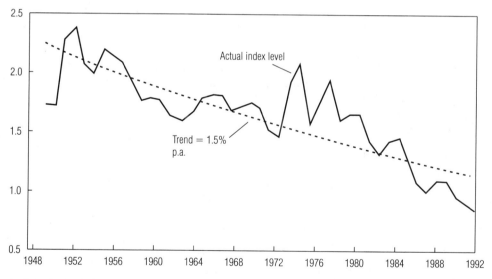

[a]Index of thirty-three non-oil commodity prices deflated by the unit value of manufactures index. 1987 = 1.0
Source: World Bank, *Global Economic Prospects and the Developing Countries, 1993* (Washington, D.C., 1993), p. 58.

---

[23]W. Arthur Lewis, "World Production, Prices and Trade, 1870–1960," *Manchester School* 20 (May 1952): 105–38; Pan A. Yotopoulos and Jeffrey B. Nugent, *Economics of Development—Empirical Investigations* (New York: Harper & Row, 1976), pp. 342–45; and John Spraos, *Inequalising Trade? A Study of Traditional North/South Specialisation in the Context of Terms of Trade Concepts* (Oxford: Clarendon Press, 1983).

the underlying data, reinforce both the validity of the Prebisch-Singer finding through 1938 and for data extended through 1988.[24]

Are other more complex measures more useful than the commodity terms of trade? As illustrated above, if export prices increase 10 percent and import prices 21 percent for a decade, the commodity terms of trade, 1.10/1.21, drop to 0.91. However, if the *quantity* of exports expands by 10 percent for the decade, the **income terms of trade** (the value index of exports divided by the price index of imports) are $(1.10 \times 1.10)/1.21 = 1.00$. This figure means the country has the same export purchasing power as it did a decade ago. Although oil-importing, middle-income countries had a decline in commodity terms of trade, from 1970 to 1980, a rapid expansion in export volume enabled them to increase **export purchasing power.**[25] Income terms of trade are also an appropriate measure when the country's export commodities have a large share of the world market (Brazil's coffee and Saudi Arabia's oil), so that export prices depend on export quantum.

The country might be interested in whether it increases the quantity of imports available per factors employed in export production. Assume that output per combined factor inputs increases by 10 percent over the decade. The commodity terms of trade, 0.91, multiplied by 1.10 yields 1.00, the **single factoral terms of trade.** This figure implies that the output of a given amount of the country's productive resources can purchase as many imports as it did a decade ago.

Thus a country's commodity terms of trade may decline at the same time that export purchasing power and single factoral terms of trade increase.

Although the degree of monopoly may differ between DCs and LDCs, the argument for deteriorating terms of trade depends on the change in, *not* the extent of, monopoly power in primary and secondary production. There is no evidence that industrial monopoly power increases more rapidly than agricultural monopoly power.

The view that LDCs export primary products whose terms of trade are declining and DCs export manufacturers with increasing terms of trade is oversimplified in many ways.

Charles Kindleberger's evidence does not support deteriorating long-run terms of trade for *primary product exporters.* He does, however, find that the LDCs are especially vulnerable to declining terms of trade because they cannot easily shift resources to accord with shifting patterns of comparative advantage.[26] Primary-product export concentration, the dependence of LDC primary exports on foreign multinational corporations for processing, marketing, and financing, and limitations on the expansion of processing indicate the LDCs' inability to shift resources with changing demand and technologies.

Although a larger proportion of exports from developing countries are primary products than from DCs, LDCs still account for less than one-half of the world's primary products (see Chapter 4).

Table 18–2 indicates that major exporters of one primary good, crude petroleum, made extraordinary improvements in their terms of trade in the 1970s. In fact a country's international trade position in oil overwhelmed other factors in determining its direction in the commodity terms of trade. The 1979 terms of trade of petroleum exporters were three to four times 1970 levels and those of petro-

[24]Pier Giorgio Ardeni and Brian Wright, "The Prebisch-Singer Hypothesis: A Reappraisal Independent of Stationarity Hypothesis," *Economic Journal* 102 (July 1992): 803–12.

[25]World Bank, *World Development Report, 1981* (New York: Oxford University Press, 1981), p. 21.

[26]Charles P. Kindleberger, *The Terms of Trade: A European Case Study* (New York: Wiley, 1956).

TABLE 18-2   Terms of Trade,^a 1979, 1989, 1994 (1970 = 100)

	1979	*1989*	*1994*
Developing countries^b	150	123	117
Africa	126	99	84
Asia	98	90	92
Latin America	140	113	100
Middle East	305	233	179
Oil-importing developing countries	94	82	81
Oil-exporting developing countries	357	256	216
Developed countries	93	100	123

^aCommodity terms of trade. A value in excess of 100 in 1979 and an increasing value from 1979 to 1989 or from 1989 to 1994 indicate increases in the terms of trade, while a value below 100 in 1979 and a declining value from 1979 to 1989 or from 1989 to 1994 indicate decreases.

^bExcludes China 1970–79 but includes China 1979–94.

Source: Calculated from International Monetary Fund, *World Economic Outlook, October 1988* (Washington, D.C., 1988), pp. 133, 140; and International Monetary Fund, *World Economic Outlook, October 1994* (Washington, D.C., 1994), pp. 145–48.

leum-importing countries decreased over the same period (although slightly less than those of DCs). However, the terms of trade for both oil-exporting and oil-importing developing countries fell in the 1980s and early 1990s, while the terms of trade for DCs rose during the same periods.

A single country, such as nineteenth-century Japan, exporting agricultural and light manufacturing goods, would often be a price taker with substantial scope in expanding export receipts alongside a long-run elastic supply curve. Could not a single primary-producing country today assume that it can expand export volume without adversely affecting price? The World Bank admonishes third-world governments to "get prices right," allowing prices to reach a market-clearing rate, rejecting past policies of setting minimum prices for industrial goods, fixing price ceilings on food, and setting low prices for foreign currency, which discourage primary product exports. However, today this single-country analysis suffers from a fallacy of composition: What is true of the individual case is not necessarily true of all cases combined. Thus, while policies promoting domestic-currency prices favorable to primary-product exporters might help a given country (whose global market share is probably too small to affect world price adversely), the adoption of these policies by numerous poor countries under pressure to improve external balances results in a market glut from increased export volume, which reduces total export receipts when the price elasticity of demand (the absolute value of the percentage change in quantity demanded divided by the percentage change in price) is less than one (inelastic). Inelastic demand can be illustrated by the doubling of cocoa exports (in tons), thereby reducing their prices per ton 75 percent so that total export receipts fall by 50 percent.

Import Substitution and Export Expansion in Industry

Given the slow growth of exports, many LDC governments try to industrialize and improve their international balance of payments by import substitution (replacing imports by domestic industry) and export expansion.

The simplest base for early industrial expansion is producing consumer goods for a market previously created by imports. It becomes more difficult, however, to undertake successive import substitution, which usually involves intermediate and capital goods that require more capital-intensive investments with larger import contents.

Import substitution can be justified on many grounds—increasing returns to scale, external economies, technological borrowing, internal stability, and other tariff arguments already presented—but is subject to the same rejoinders. Studies indicate that most LDCs have carried import substitution to the point where gains to local industrialists are less than losses to consumers, merchants, inputs buyers, and taxpayers. Indeed India, which emphasized import substitution, generated self-reliant but socially wasteful technology that would have been written off in a more competitive environment.[27]

A study by the National Bureau of Economic Research (NBER) of fifteen LDCs indicates that export promotion is generally more effective than highly protected import substitution in expanding output and employment. NBER empirical data confirm the Heckscher-Ohlin theorem, in which LDCs in early stages of growth are most likely to have a comparative advantage in exporting labor-intensive goods and importing capital- or skilled-labor-intensive commodities. A strategy that substitutes domestic output for imports, then, emphasizes the production of goods more likely to use considerably more capital per unit of labor. Export promotion includes the following advantages: (1) international competition, which encourages quality control, new products and techniques, and good management, (2) cost economies from increased market size, (3) information provided by DC users can improve export technology and product quality, (4) cost to society is more visible than protection, and (5) efficient firms are not limited by domestic demand growth. Export promotion relies on pricing incentives, such as market exchange rates, export subsidies, and concessional credit, which provide a uniform bias among export activities.[28]

As an example, during most of the 1980s, Mexico provided incentives for import substitutes and implicitly discouraged export development. South Korea on the other hand provided virtually no incentives for import substitution while heavily encouraging export activity through capital subsidies, depreciation allowances, and import duty exemptions. From 1980 to 1992, Mexico's real annual growth rates were 1.6 percent in industry and -0.2 percent overall, compared with Korea's 11.6 and 8.5 percents—spurred by scale economies, international competition, price flexibility, and no agricultural and foreign exchange shortages associated with export promotion.[29] Deepak Lal's and Sarath Rajapatirana's later study comparing the four export-promoting NICs (Taiwan, South Korea, Hong Kong, and Singapore) to moderately import-substituting Southern-Cone countries (Argentina, Chile, and Uruguay) and Sri Lanka reinforce the NBER findings for the 1970s and 1980s, when the NICs not only grew more

[27]Sanjaya Lall, *Multinationals, Technology, and Exports* (New York: St. Martin's Press, 1985), p. 18.

[28]Martin Fransman, *Technology and Economic Development* (Boulder, Colo.: Westview, 1986), pp. 75–93.

[29]Anne O. Krueger, Hal B. Lary, Terry Monson, and Narongchai Akrasanee, eds., *Trade and Employment in Developing Countries,* vol. I, *Individual Studies* (Chicago: University of Chicago Press, 1981); Anne O. Krueger, *Foreign Trade Regimes and Economic Development: Liberalization Attempts and Consequences* (Cambridge: Ballinger, 1978); and World Bank, *World Development Report, 1994* (New York: Oxford University Press, 1994), pp. 162–65.

rapidly but also recovered more quickly from the shocks of oil price rises and world recession.[30]

Still the transition from import replacements to export expansion (and free trade) is difficult. It takes time to expand capacity, reallocate resources, acquire physical inputs, develop skills, upgrade procedures, and learn by doing before new competitive export industries based on comparative advantage can emerge. We can expect export expansion to be slow, since most potential exporters have to produce for a domestic market first.[31]

Inward-looking policies have been costly to LDCs, increasing their dependence on just a few exports and on the protection and monopoly power of foreign capital. Moreover, protection reduces the domestic-currency price (peso or shilling) of foreign exchange, thus discouraging exporters. Import restrictions increase local demand for import-competing sectors' production and use of domestic resources, increasing the price of domestic inputs and foreign-exchange (dollar) price of domestic currency, thus reducing exports. Indeed, the World Bank's Dean DeRosa argues that this fall in exports matches the protection-induced fall in imports in the sub-Sahara. In the 1980s, the mean tariff, customs surcharge, surtax, stamp tax, other fiscal charges, and tax on foreign-exchange transactions in sub-Saharan countries were 33 percent of value. Since nontariff barriers (quantitative restrictions, foreign-exchange restrictions, minimum price systems, and state trading monopolies) affect 81 percent of tariff line items, the total protective and exchange-rate distortions caused by the sub-Sahara's import barriers were substantial. DeRosa estimates that sub-Saharan Africa loses 15–32 percent of its potential export revenue because of import protection.[32] Emphases on export expansion activities have the following advantages: (1) competitive pressures tend to improve quality and reduce costs, (2) information provided by DC users can improve export technology and product quality, (3) cost economies develop from increased market size, and (4) increased imports of productive inputs result from the greater availability of foreign-exchange earnings.[33]

Yet DeRosa and other Bank/Fund liberalizers fail to realize that Africa's emphasis on import substitution instead of export expansion is a result of an export trap: declining export purchasing power is due to rapid LDC primary-product export growth and a DC tariff structure biased against LDC expansion in primary-product processing and light manufactures. For African industrial export expansion to be successful, DCs must reduce protectionist policies. If DCs had dropped manufacturing tariffs on Africa in 1989 by 5 percentage points, an IMF simulation model estimates the following effects:[34]

---

[30]Deepak Lal and Sarath Rajapatirana, "Foreign Trade Regimes and Economic Growth in Developing Countries," *World Bank Research Observer* 2 (July 1987): 189–217. Peter C. Y. Chow's econometric study demonstrates that export growth promotes both industrial and overall economic growth in the NICs. "Causality between Export Growth and Industrial Development: Empirical Evidence from the NICs," *Journal of Development Economics* 26 (June 1987): 155–63.

[31]Heinz Gert Preusse, "The Indirect Approach to Trade Liberalization: Dynamic Consideration on Liberalization-cum-Stabilization Policies in Latin America," *World Development* 16 (August 1988): 883–97; and Staffan B. Linder, *An Essay on Trade and Transformation* (New York: Wiley, 1961).

[32]Dean DeRosa, "Protection in Sub-Saharan Africa Hinders Exports," *Finance and Development* 28 (September 1991): 42–45.

[33]Martin Fransman, *Technology and Economic Development* (Boulder, Colo.: Westview, 1986), pp. 75–93.

[34]International Monetary Fund, *World Economic Outlook, October 1990* (Washington, D.C., 1990), pp. 74–75.

	1990	*1991*	*Average 1992–95*
current account balance/export	+1.0%	+0.8%	0%
debt/export	-9.2%	-11.3%	-9.5%
debt service/export	-1.5%	-1.7%	-1.4%
real GNP	+1.2%	+1.6%	+1.6%
export volume	+2.6%	+3.4%	+3.3%
import volume	+3.0%	+4.1%	+4.5%

In the late nineteenth century, Japan faced Western tariffs at least as high as contemporary DC tariffs levied against LDC exports. However, late nineteenth-century protection in the West did not discriminate so systematically against the early stages of processing primary products, such as textiles, as contemporary DC protection does.

Most LDC policymakers perceive the International Monetary Fund and World Bank strategies as focusing on a narrow range of agricultural and light industrial exports. Countries adopting Bank/Fund structural adjustment, including agricultural export expansion through currency devaluation and price decontrol, face severe competition from other LDCs whose adjustment programs required similar policies.[35] Although expanding primary-product and light-manufacturing exports and achieving market-clearing exchange rates were strategies successful in Japan, 1868–1912, which had little competition from other LDCs, today's low-income countries face export expansion limitations from numerous LDC competitors producing commodities in markets with low income and price elasticities.

The LDC manufactured exports grew more rapidly than primary products from 1970 to 1992. Most developing countries with rapid industrial growth emphasized the expansion of manufactured exports. This expansion, however, was concentrated in relatively few LDCs, primarily middle-income countries. Manufactured exports were 49 percent of total merchandise exports in middle-income countries compared to 39 percent for low-income countries other than China and India (see Table 18–3).

Manufactured export volume increased annually by 1.9 percent from 1970 to 1980, and 3.9 percent from 1980 to 1992, in the low-income countries other than China and India, and by 4.0 percent and 3.7 percent, respectively, in the middle-income countries. In the 1960s, the most successful LDC expansion was in labor-intensive manufactured exports, such as textiles, clothing, footwear, and simple consumer goods; in the 1970s and 1980s, these exports were joined by machinery, transport equipment, and paper manufacturers. Expansion of this kind often means the comparative advantage shifts from the innovating country to a LDC after the technology is disseminated internationally. We must attribute much of this export expansion to multinational corporations—sometimes operating in joint ventures with LDCs but most certainly selling technology, subcontracting, making components, breaking down production processes, and providing multinational marketing. These exports tend to be concentrated in a relatively few markets in the West and Japan.

---

[35]Cadman Atta Mills, "Structural Adjustment in Sub-Saharan Africa," Economic Development Institute Policy Seminar Report No. 18, Washington, D.C., World Bank, 1989; World Bank, *Accelerated Development in Sub-Saharan Africa: An Agenda for Action* (Washington, D.C., 1981); and World Bank, *World Development Report, 1991* (New York: Oxford University Press, 1991).

TABLE 18-3 Structure of Merchandise Exports, 1992 (by country group)

	Percentage Share of Merchandise Exports				
Country Group	Fuels, Minerals, and Metals	Other Primary Commodities	Textiles and Clothing	Machinery and Transport Equipment	Other Manufactures
Low-income countries (other than China and India)	40	21	21	2	16
China and India	10	15	29	13	33
Middle-income countries	32	19	10	18	21
High-income countries	7	11	5	43	34

Source: World Bank, *World Development Report, 1994* (New York: Oxford University Press, 1994), pp. 190–91.

In 1992 Taiwan, South Korea, Hong Kong, and Singapore, comprising less than 2 percent of LDC population, accounted for 35 percent of LDC clothing and textile exports and 50 percent of total LDC manufactured export. If we add the exports of China, Spain, Malaysia, Indonesia, Brazil, and Thailand, the figure for total LDC manufactured exports reaches 93 percent.

Because of their large populations, China's and India's manufactured output and manufactured exports per capita are below average for LDCs. On the other hand, two other LDCs not on the list of leading manufactures exporters, Mexico and Argentina, oriented primarily toward domestic markets, are relatively advanced industrially.[36]

DC Import Policies

The **General Agreements on Tariffs and Trade (GATT)/World Trade Organization (WTO) system** administers rules of conduct in international trade. GATT, founded in 1947, is to continue in the transition together with WTO, established in 1995, until WTO becomes all-encompassing.

GATT/WTO applies only to economies where market prices are the rule, thus denying membership to countries where the state is the predominant international trader. The United States led the effort resulting in the denial of charter (1995) membership in the WTO to China, which despite its post-1979 economic reforms, still had extensive price distortion and widespread state control of production.

Under GATT/WTO, LDCs have called for DCs to remove or reduce trade barriers against third-world exports, especially manufactured and processed goods. The World Bank estimates the cost of DC protection against LDCs ranges from 2.5 percent to 9 percent of their GNP.[37]

---

[36]World Bank, *World Development Report, 1988* (New York: Oxford University Press, 1988), pp. 236–37, 244–45; and World Bank, *World Development Report, 1994* (New York: Oxford University Press, 1994), pp. 162–63, 186–87, 190–91.

[37]World Bank, *World Development Report, 1988* (New York: Oxford University Press, 1988), p. 16.

For LDCs, industrial comparative advantage may lie in the processing of natural-resource-based goods. For example, Pakistan might export textiles and yarn, Zambia might export refined copper, and Tanzania might export coffee essences or extracts. The Tokyo Round tariff cuts negotiated under GATT in 1974 to 1979 reduced DC tariffs to an average of 5–6 percent of value. Yet the low rate is misleading. First, tariff rates were much higher on labor-intensive goods in which LDCs are more likely to have a comparative advantage. Second the effective rate of protection, a measure of protection at each processing stage, is usually higher than the nominal rate for manufactured and processed goods, since DC tariff rates rise as imports change from crude raw materials to semimanufactures to finished goods.[38] Tokyo Round effective protection on LDC commodities according to processing state was 3 percent on stage 1 (the raw material, for example, raw cotton), 23 percent on stage 2 (low-level processing, as of cotton yarn), 20 percent on stage 3 (high-level processing, as of cotton fabrics), and 15 percent on stage 4 (the finished product, for example, clothing). DC effective rates of protection, which are highest at low levels of processing where poor countries concentrate their industrial activities, have encouraged importing raw materials at the expense of processing, especially at lower levels. Fifty-four percent of DC imports from LDCs are at stage 1, 29 percent at stage 2, 9 percent at stage 3, and 8 percent at stage 4. Zambia, which had the largest nonagricultural share (84 percent) of 1992 GDP in the low-income sub-Sahara and a high elasticity of employment growth with respect to nonagricultural output growth, expanded from consumer goods to intermediate and capital goods. But high effective protection rates on processing have diverted Zambia's industrial growth from exports to import substitution. Indeed, until the late 1980s, MNCs with subsidiaries in Zambia, Zaïre, Botswana, and Namibia built most of the fabricating and processing plants in South Africa and in the West. High protection rates on processing have also diverted India, Pakistan, Sri Lanka, and Indonesia, each of which has a nonagricultural sector with a share in 1992 GDP of at least 68 percent, from exports to import substitution. GATT's **Uruguay Round** negotiations, 1986–94, which reduced overall DC tariffs to 4 percent, resulted in modest liberalization in the trade of industrial goods; yet high effective rates of tariffs may frequently still remain at stages 2 and 3, and nontariff barriers may continue.[39]

Suppose an industrialized country has no tariff on raw cotton imports but a 5-percent tariff on cotton yarn imports. Assume raw cotton sells for $600 per ton and cotton yarn for $700 a ton, with $100 value added by the cotton yarn industry. The 5-percent nominal cotton yarn tariff (or $35), although only a small fraction of total sales value, is a 35-percent effective tariff rate on the $100 value added. It allows the domestic, DC, cotton yarn producer to be much less efficient than the foreign producer and still retain the home market. World Bank data in-

---

[38]See Bela Balassa, *The Structure of Protection in Developing Countries* (Baltimore: Johns Hopkins University Press, 1971); Ian Little, Tibor Scitovsky, and Maurice Scott, *Industry and Trade in Some Developing Countries* (London: Oxford University Press, 1970); and Sebastian Edwards, "Openness, Trade Liberalization, and Growth in Developing Countries," *Journal of Economic Literature* 31 (September 1993): 1362–63, for examples that show that the degree of protection granted to manufacturing value added was significantly higher than suggested by data on nominal import tariffs.

[39]World Bank, *World Development Report, 1994* (New York: Oxford University Press, 1994), p. 166; and United Nations Conference on Trade and Development, *Trade and Development Report, 1994* (New York, 1994), p. X.

dicate that although the effective protection rate of post–Tokyo Round tariffs was 2 percent for raw materials, it was 15–20 percent for processed and manufactured products.[40]

Other disturbing developments have been the new trade restrictions—the **Multifiber Arrangement (MFA),** "voluntary" export restraints, trigger price arrangements, antidumping duties, industrial subsidies, and other **nontariff barriers (NTBs)**—introduced in the 1970s, 1980s, and 1990s. In 1987, DC use of NTBs affected about 25 percent of nonfuel imports from LDCs compared to 21 percent of those from other DCs. Indeed, in the late 1980s, 80 percent of the exports of Bangladesh, one of the poorest countries in the world, were subject to DC nontariff barriers. The MFA, established in 1974 and made increasingly restrictive in 1978, 1982, and 1986, allowed bilateral agreements (often arising from economic pressures brought to bear by rich countries) and unilateral ceilings on any product category to limit "disruptive" textile and clothing imports;[41] under Uruguay Round agreements, MFA is to be phased out by 2005. In 1989, the Super 301 provision of the U.S. Omnibus Trade and Competitiveness Act, which directed the President to identify unfair traders, threatened trade sanctions against Brazil for import licensing and India for foreign investment and insurance company restrictions; for Columbia University economist Jagdish Bhagwati, the U.S. threat represented "aggressive unilateralism."[42] **Trigger price mechanisms,** such as the one the United States uses to prevent "unfair" price competition from steel imports, require foreign importers to pay antidumping duties on prices determined to be below domestic production cost. Subsidies, used widely by Norway, Belgium, France, and the United Kingdom, have the same protective effect as tariffs.

Since the early 1970s, the DCs have adopted a **generalized system of tariff preferences (GSP)**, by which tariffs on selected imports from LDCs are lower than those offered to other countries. The GSP of the European Community (EC), which agreed in 1975 to accept certain products from 51 African, Caribbean, and Pacific countries without tariffs, covered 22 percent of the total value of merchandise imports from LDCs; the GSP of the United States was 12 percent (low-income countries, GSP accounted for only 0.5 percent of these imports in 1985); and that of all OECD countries was 7 percent from LDCs, in 1985.[43] The U.S. graduated the four Asian tigers (Taiwan, South Korea, Hong Kong, and Singapore) from GSP in 1989, and let GSP expire in 1993.[44] In the mid-1990s, the European Union (formerly the EC) redirected its GSP from the Asian industrializing countries to the poorest

---

[40]World Bank, *World Development Report, 1987* (New York: Oxford University Press, 1987), p. 136; Gerald M. Meier, *International Economics—The Theory of Policy* (New York: Oxford University Press, 1980), pp. 118–19; and World Bank, *World Development Report, 1981* (New York: Oxford University Press, 1981), pp. 22–34.

[41]*IMF Survey* (December 12, 1988), pp. 386–89; Tim Carrington, "Developed Nations Want Poor Countries to Succeed on Trade, But Not Too Much," *Wall Street Journal* (September 20, 1993): p. A-10; and World Bank, *World Development Report, 1987* (New York: Oxford University Press, 1987), pp. 136–37.

[42]Jagdish Bhagwati, "The Fraudulent Case against Japan," *Wall Street Journal* (January 6, 1992): p. A–14.

[43]World Bank, *World Development Report, 1986* (New York: Oxford University Press, 1986), pp. 142–42; World Bank, *World Development Report, 1981* (New York: Oxford University Press, 1981), pp. 28–30; and Jan S. Hogendorn, *Economic Development* (New York: Harper & Row, 1987), p. 405.

[44]During the period when Taiwan, South Korea, and Hong Kong were eligible for the GSP, they received 44 percent of its total benefit. Idriss Jazairy, Mohiuddin Alamgir, and Theresa Panuccio, *The State of World Rural Poverty: An Inquiry into its Causes and Consequences*, Published for the International Fund for Agricultural Development (New York: New York University Press, 1992), p. 11.

developing countries.[45] Thus far GSP benefits have been modest, but expanding the scheme could accelerate LDC industrial export growth, even as Uruguay Round trade barrier restrictions make GSP less valuable. Despite the apparent economic value to LDCs of the Tokyo and Uruguay Rounds' tariff reduction and GSP gains, LDCs were hurt by renewed DC protectionist policies, especially during the 1980 to 1982 and 1991 to 1993 global recessions. The increased tariffs and other trade restrictions DCs used to divert demand to domestic production especially hurt LDC primary and light manufacturing export expansion.

Expanding Primary Export Earnings

The Organization of Petroleum Exporting Countries (OPEC) was fairly successful in the 1970s in maintaining prices and limiting output (Chapter 13). Here we do not concentrate on oil but on other primary products, the major focus of those economists concerned about LDC export expansion.

STAPLE THEORY OF GROWTH

The export of staples, such as primary or primary-product-intensive commodities, is sometimes a major engine of growth. The **staple theory of growth** was first used to explain the association between expanding primary production (wheat) and economic growth in late nineteenth-century Canada.[46] Other examples of staple exports stimulating growth include English textiles (the late eighteenth century); U.S. cotton (the early nineteenth century) and grain (after the Civil War); Colombian coffee (the last half of the nineteenth century); Danish dairy products (the last half of the nineteenth century); Malaysian rubber and Ghanaian cocoa (first half of the twentieth century); and Korean, Taiwanese, and Hong Kong textiles (after 1960). The recent examples of Bangladesh jute, Sri Lankan tea, Zambian copper, and Cuban sugar, however, suggest that staple export expansion does not necessarily trigger rapid economic growth.

Integrated Program for Commodities

Exporters of primary products other than minerals and petroleum frequently face *short-run* demand and supply inelasticities and thus greater price (Chapter 4) and income (price multiplied by quantity) fluctuations than manufactures exporters. In 1976, in the face of OPEC success, low foreign aid, and the perception that commodity markets were biased against LDCs, the United Nations Conference on Trade and Development (UNCTAD) proposed an **integrated program for commodities**—consisting of output restrictions or export quotas, international buffer stocks, a common fund, and compensatory financing—to stabilize and increase

---

[45]Organization for Economic Cooperation and Development, *Efforts and Policies of the Members of the Development Assistance Committee: Development Cooperation: 1994 Report*, Report by James H. Michel, Chair of the Development Assistance Committee (Paris: Organization for Economic Cooperation and Development, 1995), p. 44.

[46]Harold Innis, *Problems of Staple Production in Canada* (Toronto: Ryerson Press, 1933); and Melville H. Watkins, "A Staple Theory of Economic Growth," *Canadian Journal of Economics and Political Science* 29 (May 1963):141–58.

primary commodity prices and earnings. Emphasis was on 10 **core commodities**—cocoa, coffee, tea, sugar, cotton, jute sisal, rubber, copper, and tin—chosen on the basis of wide price fluctuations, large shares in LDC primary exports, or high export concentration in LDCs.

Primary-product commodity prices are more volatile than prices of manufactures (Figure 18–2). The 1970s was particularly turbulent for commodity prices, with two oil shocks and severe macroeconomic disturbances. Since the mid-1980s, however, commodity price variability has been closer to average levels during the post-World-War-II period while still above the levels from the late 1940s through 1970.[47]

Cartels.   The Organization of Petroleum Exporting Countries (OPEC) is a **cartel** whose members have agreed to limit output and fix prices. During most of the 1980s and 1990s, OPEC was not effective as a cartel.

The number of primary commodities for which collusion would be effective or feasible is small. The prime candidates for a successful price-raising cartel appear to be the tropical beverages, coffee, cocoa, and tea, if action were taken to avoid substitution among them. Even though there are competitive threats from coffee grain mixtures and cocoa substitutes, these three beverages have long-run import demand inelasticities. When demand is inelastic, supply reductions increase the price and total revenues. The long gestation between new planting and production contributes to high prices spurring increased investment and subsequent oversupply followed by prolonged periods of low prices.[48] Past efforts suggest that the major difficulty for a beverage cartel controlling supply would be disagreements between traditional and new producers about market shares. Evidence from one study indicates that the major beneficiaries of such a cartel would be middle-income countries.

FIGURE 18–2   Instability Index for Manufactures and Primary-Product Commodities

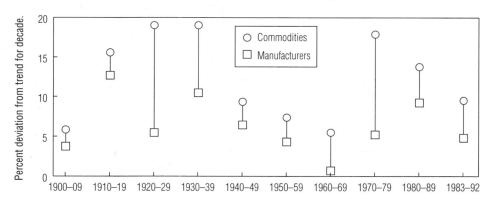

Source: World Bank, *Global Economic Prospects and the Developing Countries, 1994* (Washington, D.C., 1994), p. 52.

---

[47]World Bank, *Global Economic Prospects and the Developing Countries, 1994* (Washington, D.C., 1994), pp.52–53.
[48]World Bank, *Global Economic Prospects and the Developing Countries, 1994* (Washington, D.C., 1994), p. 52.

Danish economist Karsten Laursen argues that sugar, rubber, fiber, and metal cartels are not likely to increase prices because the *long-run* demand elasticity for the *imports* of these goods is high, since potential substitutes are many.[49]

Buffer Stocks. Some international agreements among commodity producer governments provide for funds and storage facilities to operate a **buffer stock** to stabilize prices. The buffer stock management buys and accumulates goods when prices are low and sells when prices are high to maintain prices within a certain range.

A 1975 U.N. General Assembly resolution asks for buffer stocks to secure more "stable, remunerative, and equitable" prices for LDC exports.[50] There are however several major problems with such a program.

First, because of overoptimism or pressure from producer interests, buffer stock management often sets prices above long-run equilibrium, and stocks overaccumulate.

Second, the costs of storage, interest, and (for some commodities) spoilage are high. Laursen estimates that the annual costs for buffer stocks for the 10 core commodities, $900 million, would exceed the gains to producers ($250 million) and consumers ($75 million) by more than $500 million.

Third, the objective of commodity stabilization is not clear. Stability may refer to international commodity prices, producers' money income or real income, export earnings, or export purchasing power. Stabilizing one of these variables may sometimes mean destabilizing another. For example, price stability destabilizes earnings if demand is price elastic.

Fourth, by reducing risk, price stability may intensify competition and increase investment, decreasing the long-run equilibrium price. On the other hand, price stability, especially in jute, sisal, cotton, and rubber, may prevent consumers from seeking synthetic substitutes.[51]

Common Fund. The integrating factor in the commodity program is the common fund used to finance international buffer stock agreements. According to UNCTAD, buffer stocks would be cheaper if financed by a common fund than if financed individually, because the fund could (1) take advantage of different phasing of financial flows between stock accounts, (2) obtain better borrowing terms than individual buffer stocks, (3) support new international commodity agreements, and (4) facilitate lending from one commodity agency to another.

Yet the economies attributed to common financing compared to individual financing are relatively small. And the capital requirements for the 10 core commodities, based on Laursen's estimate, are tens of billions of dollars, far in excess of available resources. Furthermore, most of the fund's resources might be used by a small number of commodities that loom large in international commodity trade

---

[49]Karsten Laursen, "The Integrated Program for Commodities," *World Development* 8 (April 1978): 423–35.

[50]"The United Nations Seventh Special Session: A Hopeful Step Forward in the Process of Laying the Foundation for an Alternative World Economic Order," *Survey of International Development* 12 (September–October 1975): 1–4.

[51]Karsten Laursen, "The Integrated Program for Commodities," *World Development* 8 (April 1978): 423–35; World Bank, *World Development Report, 1978* (New York: Oxford University Press, 1978), p. 19; and Gerald Meier, *International Economics—The Theory of Policy* (New York: Oxford University Press, 1980), p. 312.

at the expense of the others. The little funding available in the late 1980s was used for only two commodities, cocoa and rubber.

Compensatory Financing.   Chapter 16 mentioned the IMF's compensatory and contingency financing facility, used to finance a temporary shortfall in domestic food supplies (to purchase cereal imports) or in export earnings beyond a country's control, or to bolster IMF-supported adjustment programs. From 1976 to 1986, LDCs borrowed $12 billion from the facility, one-third of total IMF credit. The borrowing limit may be only a drop in the bucket, however, for countries like copper-exporting Zambia that are so vulnerable to a single commodity's sharply fluctuating price.

Another scheme to stabilize export earnings is the European Union's **Stabex,** covering 48 primary products from 66 African, Caribbean, and Pacific countries, all former colonies of European Union members. To qualify for support, a commodity must have accounted for at least 6.5 percent of a country's total exports in the preceding year, or 2.0 percent for least developed, landlocked, or island countries. Stabex transfers to the 35 least-developed countries are in the form of grants and to the other countries, interest-free loans to be repaid over 7 years with 2 years' grace.[52]

Nevertheless, except for compensatory and contingency financing, use of these measures were limited, and had little effect in improving primary commodity stability or remuneration.

AGRICULTURAL PROTECTION

Just as in the industrial sector, DC protectionism is a major barrier to LDC export expansion in the primary-product sector. Perhaps the most important step countries could take would be to eliminate trade barriers against primary products. Robert McNamara, in his 1976 presidential address to the World Bank's board of governors, estimated that LDC gains from completely free access of their agricultural products to DC markets would be more than $15 billion in 1985.

However, while tariffs, quotas, and administrative barriers constitute the main barrier to LDC industrial exports, subsidies are the major impediment to LDC exports in agriculture. In 1990, the net producer subsidy equivalents for the United States were 44 percent in wheat, 49 percent in rice, and 62 percent in milk; for the European Union, 46 percent for wheat, 60 percent in rice, and 69 percent in milk; and for Japan, 99 percent for wheat, 87 percent for rice, and 85 percent for milk. But the Uruguay Round of GATT trade negotiations made only meager progress in liberalizing agricultural trade. Brazil, for example, objects to its competitive losses from subsidies of soybeans, poultry, and oilseeds by the United States and other DCs. Still, under the Uruguay Round, DCs will reduce the volume of subsidized exports by 21 percent from 1994 to 2000.

But we should not only focus on DC protection against agriculture. A simulation by World Bank economists indicates that LDCs, whose trade barriers are biased against other LDCs' agricultural goods, would realize even much larger

---

[52]Karsten Laursen, "The Integrated Program for Commodities," *World Development* 8 (April 1978): 423–35; World Bank, *World Development Report, 1980,* (New York: Oxford University Press, 1980), p. 20; World Bank, *World Development Report, 1986* (New York: Oxford University Press, 1986), pp. 139–42; and World Bank, *Global Economic Prospects and the Developing Countries, 1994* (Washington, D.C., 1994), pp. 58–59, 67.

efficiency gains by free agricultural trade within the developing world than by free farm trade between DCs and LDCs.[53]

Services and Intellectual Property Rights

During the last quarter of the twentieth century, the United States has had a persistent comparative advantage and surplus in the trade of services and as the world's leader in patents, trademarks, and copyrights, forms of **intellectual property rights**, has been vulnerable to losses of economic returns from unprotected rights and piracy. As a result, during GATT's Uruguay Round, the U.S. took leadership in efforts to liberalize trade among services and to establish international rules to enforce protection of intellectual property rights enforcement worldwide. Trade in services amounts to 20 percent ($1 trillion of $5 trillion of 1993 total world trade),[54] but GATT made little progress before the Uruguay Round in opening markets to management consulting, legal, accounting, engineering, advertising, insurance, financial, transport, trade, and tourism services, and software. LDCs opposed liberalizing services not only because of the opposition of strong vested interests but because of the fear of losses from technological learning gains. Yet joint ventures and consultants' contracts with foreigners could provide an impetus for development of these LDC services.

The Uruguay Round provides 10 to 20 years of protection of patents, trademarks, copyrights, biotechnological products, and other innovative products. The agreement guarantees creators of intellectual products and creative works a limited exclusive economic right. These provisions will increase LDC costs of: royalty payments to foreigners, payments for products manufactured under license or imported, and enforcement and administrative costs. Arun Ghosh, an Indian economist, complains that while Americans are urged to substitute generic for brandname drugs, third-world countries will need to increase their payments for product patents for life-saving drugs. LDCs may, however, gain from DCs' greater incentives to invest in LDCs and license patented inventions to their entrepreneurs. Yet many economists think DCs will transfer less technology to LDCs after the Uruguay Round agreement than before.[55]

Foreign Exchange Rates

International trade requires one national currency to be exchanged for another. An Indian firm, for example, uses local currency, rupees, to buy the dollars needed to purchase a computer from a U.S. company.

---

[53]Robert S. McNamara, address to the Board of Governors (Washington, D.C.: World Bank, October 1976); United Nations Conference on Trade and Development (UNCTAD), *Trade and Development Report, 1991* (New York, 1991), p. 152; John H. Jackson, "Managing the Trading System: The World Trade Organization and the Post-Uruguay Round GATT Agenda," in Peter B. Kenen, ed., *Managing the World Economy: Fifty Years After Bretton Woods* (Washington, D.C.: Institute for International Economics, 1994), pp. 131–51; and World Bank, *World Development Report, 1976* (New York: Oxford University Press, 1976), pp. 122–32, 144.

[54]"A Disquieting New Agenda for Trade," *Economist* (July 16, 1994): 63–64.

[55]United Nations Conference on Trade and Development, *Trade and Development Report, 1994* (New York, 1994), p. 154; Martin Rosenberg, "In Trade Debate, Expect Fireworks," *Kansas City Star* (November 13, 1994): pp. A–1, A–6; Arun Ghosh, "What Is Sauce for the Goose Is Not Sauce for the Gander," *Economic and Political Weekly* (Bombay) 28 (August 21, 1993): 1696–97; and "The Uruguay Round's Key Results," *Wall Street Journal* (December 15, 1993): p. A–6.

PRESENT EXCHANGE-RATE SYSTEM

The rules for today's international monetary system tolerate several ways of determining the exchange rate. The world's present managed floating exchange-rate system (mentioned in Chapter 17) is a hybrid of six exchange-rate regimes: (1) the single floats of major international currencies, the U.S. dollar, Canadian dollar, British pound, and Japanese yen; (2) the joint float (with a 15-percent spread) of the European Monetary System (German, French, Danish, Italian, Irish, and Benelux currencies) against the U.S. dollar; (3) the independent (for example Australia, the Philippines, Bolivia, Nigeria, Zaïre, and South Africa) or managed float (for example, Pakistan, India, Indonesia, China, Egypt, Mexico, Argentina, and South Korea) of minor currencies; (4) the frequent adjustment (usually depreciation) of currencies according to an indicator (for example, Brazil, Chile, and Colombia); (5) pegging currencies to a major currency, especially to a dominant trading partner (38 are pegged to the U.S. dollar, 14 to the French franc, and five to other currencies); and (6) pegging currencies to a **basket** (composite) **of currencies,** most notably **special drawing rights (SDRs),** bookkeeping entries in the accounts of member countries of the IMF used as an internationalized currency by central banks for official transactions (with the IMF and other central banks).[56]

DOMESTIC CURRENCY OVERVALUATION

The domestic currency (Nigerian naira) price of foreign (U.S. dollar) currency, for example, ₦50 = \$1, is the **price of foreign exchange.** In a free market, this exchange rate is determined by the intersection of D_1, the demand for foreign currency (depending on the demand for foreign goods, services, and capital); and S_1, the supply of foreign currency (depending on foreign demand for domestic goods, services, and capital). (See Figure 18–3.)

Nigeria's increased demand for U.S. computers or insurance, *or* a reduced U.S. demand for Nigerian oil or cocoa, increases the foreign exchange rate, for example, from ₦50 = \$1 to ₦51 = \$1.

A country's central bank may keep down the price of foreign exchange by using **exchange controls** to limit its citizens' purchase of foreign currency for foreign equipment, materials, consumer goods, and travel. Assume that the market-clearing price of foreign exchange (with no exchange controls) is ₦50 = \$1, determined by D_1 and S_1. To avert a balance of payments crisis and domestic currency devaluation, however, a country may repress demand to D_2 through exchange controls and trade restrictions, so that the actual price of foreign exchange is ₦25 = \$1, at the intersection of D_2 and S_1.

Overvaluing the domestic currency relative to foreign currency, however, may discourage import substitution and exports. At the rate of ₦25 = \$1, the exporter selling cocoa for \$10 a kilogram earns only ₦250, rather than ₦500 at the market exchange rate. Additionally the domestic steel firm imports a computer whose world price is \$5,000 at only ₦125,000 rather than ₦250,000.

---

[56]International Monetary Fund, *International Financial Statistics* 41 (October 1988): 22; and Lloyd B. Thomas, Jr., *Money, Banking, and Economic Activity* (Englewood Cliffs, N.J.: Prentice Hall, 1986), pp. 554–63.

Developing countries, supported by France, have been on the losing side of some bitter disputes at the IMF about allocating new SDRs for LDC aid.

**FIGURE 18-3   Determining the Price of Foreign
Exchange under the Market and
Exchange Controls**

If allowed to float freely, the exchange rate will be
₦50 = $1, at the intersection of D_1 and S_1. Controls on
currency transactions by domestic citizens can repress
demand to D_2, which intersects S_1 at a price of foreign
exchange ₦25 = $1. This rate, however, is likely to dis-
courage exports and encourage attempts to obtain
import licenses.

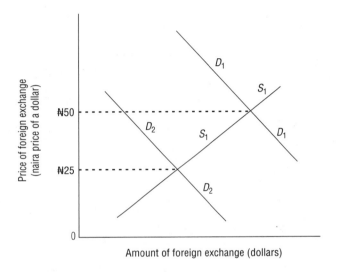

Amount of foreign exchange (dollars)

AVOIDING BIAS AGAINST EXPORTS

Most LDCs' prices of foreign exchange are lower than market rates (for example,
₦25 = $1 is lower than ₦50 = $1), meaning they are biased against exports. These
submarket exchange rates mean that the price ratio of nontraded to traded goods
increases, so that imports and competitors to exports are cheaper in domestic currency. Some notable exceptions to low exchange rates argue in favor of adjusting
exchange rates so they do not discriminate against exports. The yen in rapidly
growing, early modern (Meiji) Japan (1868–1912) chronically depreciated vis-à-
vis the U.S. dollar, which meant that the real exchange rate (see below) remained
virtually unchanged. Fortuitously for Japan, during most of this period, the yen's
standard was silver, which declined relative to gold. Moreover Japan's modest
trade restrictions (which reduced the demand for dollars and by themselves
overvalued the yen) were offset by export promotion schemes (which increased
the demand for yen). Doubtlessly, these foreign exchange policies help explain
why Japan's annual real average growth rates in exports during the Meiji period
were at least twice those of either the United States or Britain. Additionally studies on effective rates of protection and effective subsidies indicate that South

Korea, virtually the most rapidly growing LDC after World War II, discriminated *in favor* of exports.[57]

DOMESTIC CURRENCY DEVALUATION

The country with an overvalued currency could impose compensating duties and surcharges on imported inputs and capital instead of relying on exchange controls, licenses, or quotas that implicitly subsidize the successful applicant. But these duties and surcharges, tax incentives, subsidies, loans, and technical assistance may stimulate import replacements and exports less than an overvalued domestic currency inhibits these activities. Devaluing the domestic currency to its equilibrium rate in order to ration imports through the market, encourage import substitution, and promote exports may be preferable to inducements under an overvalued currency regime. Additionally, domestic currency depreciation would increase labor-intensive production and employment (Chapter 9), improve investment choice (Chapter 11), and reduce structural inflation but probably reduce real wages (Chapter 15).

THE REAL EXCHANGE RATE

We cannot calculate LDC currency depreciation or appreciation vis-à-vis the dollar over time by looking at changes in the nominal exchange rates. To illustrate, in 1968 (the base year), ₦1 = $1.40, while the consumer price indices in both the United States and Nigeria were 100. By 1979, ₦1 = $1.78 (a 27 percent increase for the naira compared to 1968), while the U.S. consumer price index was 208.5 and Nigeria's was 498.0. The **real exchange rate** (the nominal exchange rate adjusted for relative inflation rates at home and abroad), calculated as

> dollar price of naira in base year X percentage change in dollar price of naira from base year to terminal year X (Nigerian consumer price index/U.S. consumer price index)

was ₦1 = $1.40 in 1968, and ₦1 = $4.25 (1.40 × 1.27 × 2.39) in 1979, which was an increase of 3.04, meaning the value of the naira vis-à-vis the dollar more than tripled over the 11-year period. With further **real appreciation,** as Nigerian non-oil exports became less competitive and imports more competitive, Nigeria depreciated the naira in 1986 under World Bank adjustment to bring it closer to the 1969 real exchange rate. However, with rapid inflation in the late 1980s and early 1990s, the Abuja government stubbornly resisted the more rapid naira devaluation necessary to maintain a stable real exchange rate.

---

[57]E. Wayne Nafziger, *Learning from the Japanese: Japan's Prewar Development and the Third World* (Armonk, NY: M.E. Sharpe, 1995), pp. 129–52; E. Wayne Nafziger, "The Japanese Development Model: Its Implications for Developing Countries," *Bulletin of the Graduate School of International Relations, I.U.J.* no. 5 (July 1986): 1–26; Martin Fransman, *Technology and Economic Development* (Boulder, Colo.: Westview 1986), pp. 76–85; Larry E. Westphal and K. S. Kim, "Industrial Policy and Development in Korea," Washington, World Bank Staff Working Paper no. 263, 1977; and Chong Hyun Nam, "Trade and Industrial Policies and the Structure of Protection in Korea," in W. Hong and C. B. Krause, *Trade and Growth of the Advanced Developing Countries in the Pacific Basin: Papers and Proceedings of the Eleventh Pacific Trade and Development Conference* (Seoul: Korea Development Institute, 1981), pp. 46–73.

DUAL EXCHANGE RATES

Currency depreciation can have short-run costs, especially in an economy that adjusts slowly. Inflation and shortages may appear before consumers switch to replacements for foreign food and other consumer goods, before export and import substitution industries expand capacity to take advantage of more favorable prices, and before buyers of imported inputs and capital goods can shift to domestic suppliers. These transitional problems have led some economists to suggest a **dual exchange rate,** with the first a near market rate, used to reduce controls, spur exports and import substitutes, and increase efficiency; and the second, perhaps the old rate overvaluing domestic currency, set to dampen short-run inflationary pressures from price inelastic foreign goods like food, industrial inputs, and capital goods (or their domestic substitutes shifting to exports) or to maintain foreign exchange commitments for foreign corporations repatriating interest and dividends.[58] In 1983, in response to an overvalued cedi, Ghana instituted a dual exchange rate (with a surcharge on nonessential imports and a bonus to exporters), while also increasing farm producer prices, removing price distortions on oil and other goods, and reducing deficit financing. By 1984, inflation fell and growth accelerated. Despite protest from labor unions about its effect on the cost of goods previously consumed, Ghana widened the distance between the two exchange rates in 1985 and 1986. These measures improved the balance on goods and services in 1986.[59] However, dual rates maintain some price distortions, postpone resource adjustments, and spur people to acquire foreign currency cheaply in one market and sell it expensively in the other.

EXCHANGE-RATE ADJUSTMENT AND OTHER PRICES

Let the student be warned: Market-clearing exchange rates may not provide enough signals for improving the efficiency of resources use if domestic prices of goods and services, wages, interest rates, and other prices are not flexible.[60] The **theory of the second best** states that if economic policy cannot satisfy all the conditions necessary for maximizing welfare, then satisfying one or several conditions may not increase welfare (that is, may not lead to a second-best position). This theory indicates that liberalizing one price (for example, the exchange rate) while other prices are still repressed may be worse than having all prices distorted.

The Impossible Trinity: Exchange-Rate Stability, Free Capital Movement, and Monetary Autonomy

Since 1979, the European Monetary System (EMS) has aimed to maintain stable exchange rates, free capital mobility, and national control over monetary policy among members, labeled an **impossible trinity** by OECD economist Helmut

[58]Nicholas Kaldor, "An Exchange-Rate Policy for India," *Economic and Political Weekly* (Bombay) 19 (July 14, 1984): 1093–95.

[59]E. Wayne Nafziger, *Inequality in Africa: Political Elites, Proletariat, Peasants, and the Poor* (Cambridge: Cambridge University Press, 1988), pp. 153–54.

[60]T. N. Srinivasan, "Economic Liberalization in China and India: Issues and an Analytical Framework," *Journal of Comparative Economics* 11 (September 1987), 427–43.

Reisen.[61] On the average of once per year, however, weak-currency countries could no longer maintain the tight coordination of their currencies with the German mark, contributing to a crisis in the foreign-exchange or capital markets. The French or Italian treasury, then, has confronted the prospect of capital controls, increased interest rates in the face of high unemployment, or devaluing the currency or widening currency spreads (as in mid-1993, when European finance ministers pretended that the increase from 2.5 percent to 15 percent in the range allowed around parity did not mean abandoning a fixed exchange-rate system).

During the 1980s and early 1990s, countries such as Taiwan and Singapore, however, demonstrated their ability to maintain exchange-rate stability against the dollar or a basket of currencies.[62] Most other LDCs are too vulnerable to external price and demand shocks to maintain stability of their currencies vis-a-vis major DC currencies.[63] However, the other extreme, relinquishing control over financial policies, is just as bad. The francophone West African countries in the CFA (*communaute financiere africaine*) franc zone paid a heavy price in growth forgone by maintaining their currencies fixed at CFAF50 equal to one French franc from 1948 to 1994. During much of this period, the CFA countries lacked the autonomy to use monetary, fiscal, and exchange-rate policies to stimulate demand. By the mid-1980s, the United Nations contended that "after several years of unsuccessful adjustment, it became increasingly apparent that the center-piece of the franc zone—the fixed exchange rate against the French franc—was seriously impeding the adjustment effort." Since the mid-1980s, the CFA countries experienced real currency appreciation vis-à-vis DCs and neighboring countries and falling terms of trade, contributing to chronic current-account deficits.[64] From 1960 to 1994, distorted exchange-rate prices contributed to the negative or negligent economic growth of Chad, Niger, Benin, Burkina Faso, Central African Republic, Mauritania, Ivory Coast, and Senegal.

REGIONAL INTEGRATION IN THE SOUTH

Some LDC economists stress that the fact that in 1992 only 24 percent (or $183 billion) of LDC total exports went to other LDCs (and only 31 percent, or $125 billion, in 1984) indicates the substantial output gain potential from greater *intra*-LDC trade (and factor movements).[65] Many LDC leaders, frustrated by DC protectionism, poor terms of trade, a lack of internal economies of scale, and the slow growth of industrial specialization and exports, have advocated **economic integration,** a grouping of nations that reduces or abolishes barriers to trade and

---

[61]Helmut Reisen, "Southeast Asia and the 'Impossible Trinity,'" *International Economic Insights* 4 (May/June 1993): 21–23. His view is supported by Bryon Higgins, "Was the ERM Crisis Inevitable?" *Federal Reserve Bank of Kansas City Economic Review* (Fourth Quarter 1993): pp. 27–40.

[62]Helmut Reisen, "Southeast Asia and the 'Impossible Trinity,'" *International Economic Insights* 4 (May/June 1993):21–23.

[63]In 1995, the International Monetary Fund, drawing lessons from the global effects of Mexico's financial crisis, indicated that LDCs should consider placing temporary controls on foreign capital flows to avoid disruptions from capital flight. David Wessel, "IMF Urges Developing Nations to Study Controls on Inflows of Foreign Capital," *Wall Street Journal* (August 22, 1995), pp.. A2, A4.

[64]United Nations, *World Economic and Social Survey, 1994: Current Trends and Policies in the World Economy* (New York, 1994), pp. 47–50.

[65]World Bank, *World Development Report, 1986* (New York: Oxford University Press, 1986), pp. 196–97, 202–03; World Bank, *World Development Report, 1994* (New York: Oxford University Press, 1994), pp. 186–87; and World Bank, *Global Economic Prospects and the Developing Countries, 1994* (Washington, D.C., 1994), p. 80.

resource movements only among member countries. Integration ranges along a continuum from its loosest form, a preferential trade arrangement, to a free trade area, a customs union, a common market, an economic union, and to the most advanced integration, a complete economic and monetary union.

A **preferential trade arrangement,** illustrated by the Preferential Trade Area for Eastern and Southern African States (PTA), launched in 1984, provides lower tariff and other trade barriers among member countries than between members and nonmembers. A **free trade area**, such as the North American Free Trade Agreement (NAFTA) signed in 1993 between the United States, Mexico, and Canada, removes trade barriers among members, but each country retains its own barriers against nonmembers. Other examples are the Latin American Free Trade Association (LAFTA—Mexico and most of South America, founded in 1960), which stagnated for years and was dissolved in 1980; the Economic Union of Caribbean Countries (CARIFTA), established as a free trade area in 1968 but converted into a common market in 1973 before eventually disintegrating; and the Southern African Development Community (SADC), established in 1992. A **customs union,** exemplified by the European Community (EC), 1957 to 1970, and the Southern African Customs Union (SACU), goes beyond the free trade area to retain common trade barriers against the rest of the world. A **common market** moves a step beyond a customs union by allowing free labor and capital movement among member states. Examples include not only the EC since 1970, but also the Central American Common Market (CACM), established in 1960 but paralyzed because of hostilities between some members; the East African Community (EAC), established in 1967 but experiencing tensions until its disintegration in 1977; and the Economic Community of West African States (ECOWAS), created in 1975, whose internal opposition has delayed strides toward trade liberalization and free factor movement. An **economic union**, not yet achieved by the European Union or EU despite its name, goes further by unifying members' monetary and fiscal policies. The success of the United States, whose 1789 constitution made 13 states a **complete economic and monetary union,** and that of the EU have partly served as a spur to increased economic integration by LDCs.[66]

There have been attempts by groups of LDC nations to further regional economic cooperation, including the following cases short of economic integration. The Association of South East Asian Nations (ASEAN), formed in 1967, which includes Indonesia, Malaysia, the Philippines, Singapore, Thailand, and seven other member states, has a **complementation agreement,** largely unimplemented, under which the organization allocates and shares the costs of starting large-scale infant industries.[67] The Lagos Plan of Action, begun by the Organization of African Unity heads of governments in 1980, aims to speed up regional economic integration and cooperation as necessary instruments for collective self-reliance.

Few LDC attempts at economic integration have succeeded, mainly because less advanced nations are discontented that the most advanced members of the union receive (or are thought to receive) the lion's share of the benefits. In the EAC, the overwhelming amount of new industrial investment went to the relatively de-

---

[66]Dominick Salvatore, *International Economics* (Englewood Cliffs, N.J.: Prentice Hall, 1995), pp. 299–328; and S. K. B. Asante, *The Political Economy of Regionalism in Africa: A Decade of the Economic Community of West African States (ECOWAS)* (New York: Praeger, 1986), pp. 24–28.

[67]Malcolm Gillis, Dwight H. Perkins, Michael Roemer, and Donald R. Snodgrass, *Economics of Development* (New York: Norton, 1987), pp. 471–72.

Vietnam joined ASEAN in 1995. ASEAN's goal is a free-trade association by 2000.

veloped center, Nairobi, and other cities in Kenya. Working out agreements to compensate members with the smallest shares of gains, or to assign some industries to each member country, is difficult. Moreover the market size of many unions, such as the EAC, CACM, and CARIFTA, is too small to attract industries that require substantial internal economies of scale. A related dilemma is an externally oriented transport system that lacks adequate intraregional transportation facilities.[68] Furthermore, although theory indicates the union gains most from specialization reallocation from less efficient producers exiting the industry and shifting their resources to activities with a greater comparative advantage, most LDCs perceive this "creative destruction" as harmful. Thus while regional integration in the South can reduce dependence on DCs, expand industry, increase efficiency and competition, and improve bargaining power, LDCs are unlikely to use this form of South–South integration for major gains in the last decade of the twentieth century.

We turn now to a consideration of LDCs involved in efforts at regional economic integration with DCs. We include, however, LDC free trade areas in the Western hemisphere, because of our later concern with the possibility of economic integration within the Americas.

NAFTA provides for free trade of goods and most services, although a fraction will only be phased in over 5 to 15 years. Additionally, NAFTA agrees to free capital movement (although not in oil, dominated by the state-owned *Petroleos Mexicanos* or Pemex until 2003), but not free labor migration. The Mercado Comun del Sur (Mercosur) agreement, signed in 1991 by Brazil, Uruguay, Argentina, and Paraguay, provides for progressive tariff reduction (with a number of exceptions) and free movement of people. The Andean Group, founded in 1969 and reinvigorated in 1990, includes Bolivia, Colombia, Ecuador, and Venezuela (Peru withdrew in 1992), which achieved regional free trade in 1992. The Central American Common Market (CACM), revived in the late 1980s, consists of El Salvador, Costa Rica, Guatemala, Honduras, Nicaragua, and (in a limited way) Panama. CACM has agreed to gradually reduce intra-CACM tariffs and restrictions to the free movement of labor. In 1989, Trinidad and Tobago, Barbados, Jamaica, Bahamas, Guyana, and six small Caribbean countries created the Caribbean Community (Caricom). Caricom has integrated its currencies, pegging them to the U.S. dollar. Moreover, despite delayed implementation, Caricom has reduced intra-community tariffs and moved toward a common tariff schedule on nonmembers. Furthermore, a number of Western Hemisphere countries have made agreements across regional groups, and Chile has bilateral agreements with Argentina, Mexico, Venezuela, and Colombia to liberalize trade and promote investment.[69]

The **Lomé Convention,** the arrangement of the EU with 66 of its African, Caribbean, and Pacific (ACP) former colonies (omitting several rich or populous Asian members of the British Commonwealth), grants preferences to the EU market for manufactured and primary goods, and special arrangements, such as rights to sell quotas of sugar at a fixed price usually above the world price.[70] In the late 1990s, Poland, Hungary, the Czech Republic, and possibly Slovakia may join the EU, benefiting from the consumer demand from an affluent population of

[68]Mordechai E. Kreinin, *International Economics: A Policy Approach* (San Diego: Harcourt Brace Jovanovich, 1987), pp. 394–96.

[69]Gary Clyde Hufbauer and Jeffrey J. Schott, *Western Hemisphere Economic Integration* (Washington, D.C.: Institute for International Economics, 1994); and Gary Clyde Hufbauer and Jeffrey J. Schott, *NAFTA: An Assessment*, rev. ed. (Washington, D.C.: Institute for International Economics, 1993).

[70]World Bank, *World Development Report, 1986,* (New York: Oxford University Press, 1986), pp. 140–44.

350–400 million and from free movement across borders. Other aspirants are Bulgaria, Romania, Estonia, Latvia, Lithuania, and the Mediterranean islands Malta and Cyprus.

In principle, GATT opposes preferential trade pacts raising barriers to the trade of third countries. What are the implications of the Lomé Convention (and other free trade arrangements) for nonmember countries? The convention may reduce world (and probably LDC) total welfare by **trade diversion** from a ACP beneficiary country displacing imports from a lowest cost third country.[71] NAFTA diverts some U.S. sourcing from lower-cost Korea, Taiwan, and Asian and Caribbean countries to Mexico. However Lomé, NAFTA, and LDC regional economic groups are also responsible for some **trade creation,** in which a beneficiary country's firms displace inefficient domestic producers in a member country.

Regional free trade is usually superior to bilateralism but generally inferior to worldwide free trade in global efficiency in the allocation of resources.[72] In 1994, the United States agreed to proceed toward free trade with both Western Hemisphere and Asia-Pacific Economic Cooperation (APEC) nations in the early decades of the twenty-first century. Institute for International Economics economists Gary Clyde Hufbauer and Jeffrey J. Schott examine the sequence from existing free trade arrangements to a Western Hemisphere Free Trade Area (WHFTA) or APEC free trade area. The question is: Should the U.S. proceed with bilateral negotiations or conduct enlargement talks through NAFTA? Hufbauer and Schott oppose the United States, the dominant country in WHFTA and APEC, negotiating the expansion of NAFTA country by country. These bilateral negotiations would divide WHFTA-APEC countries, and would spawn disparate rules that would create enormous confusion in the global trading system. Not the least of this confusion would be the movement of capital and labor back and forth as NAFTA (or its successor) and other regional groups continually change the composition of their membership.[73] While it will only gradually become apparent what enlargements are politically feasible, the United States (and LDCs generally) will benefit from the goal of maximizing the global trading community.

We can use some of the same concepts in regional integration to analyze **special** duty free **economic zones (SEZs)** in Puerto Rico, India, Taiwan, the Philippines, the Dominican Republic, Mexico, Panama, Brazil, and (since 1979) coastal cities of China.[74] Indeed although China's SEZs stimulate technological learning and increase domestic incomes from foreign trade and investment, they suffer some backwash effects from outflows of labor, capital, and skills from the rest of China that remind economists of the costs of dualism discussed in Chapter 4.

---

[71]Gerhard Pohl and Piritta Sorsa, "Is European Integration Bad News for Developing Countries?" *World Bank Research Observer* 9 (January 1994): 147–55; and A.J. Hughes Hallett, "The Impact of EC-92 on Trade in Developing Countries," *World Bank Research Observer* 9 (January 1994): 121–46.

[72]Economists are not certain how much sub-Saharan Africa, at the periphery of the world economy, will benefit from increased worldwide free trade under GATT/WTO. The sub-Sahara may lose from the increased prices of staples imported from DCs, and may gain little from export expansion because of low income and price elasticities of demand for primary products. United Nations, *World Economic and Social Survey, 1994: Current Trends and Policies in the World Economy* (New York, 1994), p. 85. The probability of trade diversion would be exacerbated if Africa is left out of a Western Hemisphere-Asian free trade area. All this strengthens the case for concessional aid and debt relief for least-developed countries, primarily from the sub-Sahara.

[73]Gary Clyde Hufbauer and Jeffrey J. Schott, *Western Hemisphere Economic Integration* (Washington, D.C.: Institute for International Economics, 1994), pp. 176–83.

[74]Y. C. Jao and C. K. Leung, eds., *China's Special Economic Zones: Policies, Problems, and Prospects* (Hong Kong: Oxford University Press, 1986).

The Asian and North American Borderless Economies

In Chapter 16 we discussed the role of multinational corporations in an integrated global economy. While Africa and South Asia have received only minimal benefits from this integration, a number of Asian economies are integrated into MNC production shifts in the product cycle. Since the devaluation of the U.S. dollar relative to the yen beginning in late 1985, Japanese companies have tried to retain their international price competitiveness in manufacturing products by organizing a borderless Asian economy. This borderless system encompasses a new international division of knowledge and function that selects the more sophisticated activities, including R&D-intensive and technology-intensive industries for the newly industrializing countries (NICs), South Korea, Taiwan, Hong Kong, and Singapore, while assigning the less sophisticated, labor-intensive, low value-added production and assembly, which use more standardized and obsolescent technologies, to China and the ASEAN four, Indonesia, Malaysia, the Philippines, and Thailand.

According to Japanese official definitions used in the early 1990s, Japanese foreign direct investment does not necessarily depend on majority ownership, but can involve only 10 percent ownership if the Japanese corporation either has at least one part-time director, furnishes the technology, provides financial assistance, executes an exclusive agency agreement, or purchases products, raw materials, or parts from the production facility abroad. Moreover, the Japanese company does not even need any equity holding to be involved in foreign direct investment if the firm provides loans exceeding one year to a firm abroad whose management is influenced by the Japanese corporation through long-term contract.[75]

Sony, an example of this global seamless network, has factories for audio, television, and video products and parts in Taiwan, Korea, Thailand, Malaysia, and Singapore, the major distribution warehouse in Singapore, and linkage of these units on-line with Japanese, U.S., European, and Southeast Asian companies as well as important cooperating firms.[76] In a similar fashion, a Pontiac Le Mans bought in the United States embodies routine labor and assembly operations in South Korea, advanced components (engines, transaxles, and electronics) from Japan, styling and design engineering from Germany, small components from Taiwan, Singapore, and Japan, advertising and marketing services from Britain, and data processing from Ireland and Barbados.[77]

Despite the advantages to the ASEAN four, the borderless economy contributes to a widening gap between modern branches of industry, such as electronics, and traditional branches within the country. To be sure, ASEAN labor

---

[75]Tokunaga Shojiro, "Japan's FDI-Promoting Systems and Intra-Asia Networks: New Investment and Trade Systems Created by the Borderless Economy," in Tokunaga Shojiro, ed., *Japan's Foreign Investment and Asian Economic Interdependence* (Tokyo: University of Tokyo Press, 1992), pp. 5–48; and Steven Schlossstein, *Asia's New Little Dragons: The Dynamic Emergence of Indonesia, Thailand, and Malaysia* (Chicago: Contemporary Books, 1991), pp. 32, 152. Schlossstein uses the metaphor of a flying geese formation of the East and Southeast Asian economies, with Japan at the lead, the NICs toward the front, and the ASEAN four close behind.

[76]Tokunaga Shojiro, "Japan's FDI-Promoting Systems and Intra-Asia Networks: New Investment and Trade Systems Created by the Borderless Economy," in Tokunaga Shojiro, ed., *Japan's Foreign Investment and Asian Economic Interdependence* (Tokyo: University of Tokyo Press, 1992), pp. 37–38.

[77]Robert B. Reich, *The Work of Nations: Preparing Ourselves for 21st-Century Capitalism* (New York: Alfred A. Knopf, 1991), p. 113.

learns how to produce inputs and parts to precise specifications for Japanese high-tech industry. However, the ASEAN four have left technical details to their foreign business partners, so that these countries lack the ability to adapt and innovate, which is concentrated in Japan and the NICs.

Another factor limiting ASEAN's gains from the borderless system is the fact that Japanese (and other DC) MNCs raise the lion's share of their funds from the local capital market. The most successful of the South and Southeast Asian countries are Thailand and Malaysia. Both countries have attracted high-technology industries such as computers, electronics, and semiconductors as a part of the Japanese-directed borderless economy. Indeed in 1993, Malaysia was third to the United States and Japan in producing semiconductors (primarily for Japanese companies, such as Hitachi, Toshiba, and NEC) and the world's leading exporter of computer chips. But both Thailand and Malaysia pay relatively little attention to bottom-up development of indigenous manufacturing techniques. The development of indigenous technological capability requires, similar to Meiji Japan, a conscious and aggressive strategy of technical innovation.[78]

Malaysia and Thailand's positions in an international division of labor (as a part of Japan's borderless economy since the mid-1980s) seem to be based, as in late-nineteenth-century Japan, on near-market exchange-rates that expedite labor-intensive exports. Malaysia and Thailand have enjoyed limited prosperity while, however, sacrificing their economic autonomy to less-sophisticated, labor intensive, low value-added production in a Japanese-organized division of knowledge. However, Takeshi Aoki and Tessa Morris-Suzuki, contributors to Shojiro Tokunaga (ed.), *Japan's Foreign Investment and Asian Economic Interdependence*, contend that the short-run prosperity from integration within the Japanese-led trading system came at the expense of the technological learning and skill acquisition essential for rapid growth in the late 1990s and early twenty-first century. Aoki mentions the inadequate spending on R&D, the lack of indigenous mastery of industrial technology, the few Malay entrepreneurs, the sparse linkages within the industrial economy, and the substantial shortage of skilled workers, technicians, and engineers as major obstacles to Malaysia's future growth. For Morris-Suzuki, some major barriers to Thailand's prospective development are the concentration of technological transfer within multinational enterprises rather than local firms, the lack of innovation and adaptation by indigenous personnel, the falling R&D capability, the poor communications facilities, and the low secondary-school enrollment rates. Indeed, Malaysia and Thailand have emphasized peripheral intermediation in technologically complex industrial production rather than indigenous innovation and technology generation in less complex industry that provides more scope for gains from learn-

---

[78]Tessa Morris-Suzuki, "Japanese Technology and the New International Division of Knowledge in Asia," in Tokunaga Shojiro, ed., *Japan's Foreign Investment and Asian Economic Interdependence* (Tokyo: University of Tokyo Press, 1992), pp. 145–48; Steven Schlossstein, *Asia's New Little Dragons: The Dynamic Emergence of Indonesia, Thailand, and Malaysia* (Chicago: Contemporary Books, 1991), p. 232; Tokunaga Shojiro, "Japan's FDI-Promoting Systems and Intra-Asia Networks: New Investment and Trade Systems Created by the Borderless Economy," in Tokunaga Shojiro, ed., *Japan's Foreign Investment and Asian Economic Interdependence* (Tokyo: University of Tokyo Press, 1992), pp. 158–63; Aoki Takeshi, "Japanese FDI and the Forming of Networks in the Asia-Pacific Region: Experience in Malaysia and Its Implications," in Tokunaga Shojiro, ed., *Japan's Foreign Investment and Asian Economic Interdependence* (Tokyo: University of Tokyo Press, 1992), p. 97; and World Bank, *The East Asian Miracle: Economic Growth and Public Policy* (New York: Oxford University Press, 1993), pp. 238–39.

ing.[79] Ironically, for Malaysia and Thailand to follow the early Japanese model means less dependence on technology, capital, and imports from Japanese multinational corporations.

Promotion and Protection of Infant Entrepreneurship

The dynamic gains from learning management and technology by doing, for countries such as Malaysia, Thailand, India, and Latin American countries are likely to be substantial, although they may be difficult to measure. Much of this dynamic learning can come from being open to international trade.

Importing from technologically advanced economies improves an LDC's industrial efficiency. Moreover, LDC engineers and technicians may import a foreign machine, tear it apart, learn how it was put together, and modify it to fit local circumstances. The product-cycle model, discussed above, suggests that technological borrowing can proceed from imported product to a copy, usually inferior in quality, to slow improvement, with finer grades and specialties, which come with experience, improved endowment of human and physical capital, and a shift in comparative advantage. Examples of LDCs following this sequence include Japan in the 1880s and 1890s and the early decades of the twentieth century, and the Asian tigers after 1970.

The country responds to the exacting demand of foreign consumers, as Japan's textile industry did in the 1920s and 1930s, reorienting itself from silk to cotton and rayon goods demanded by American women. Or third-world labor learns to produce inputs and parts to precise specifications. In the late nineteenth-century, the Japanese improved their technology by working with Western firms.[80] Later, in the 1980s and 1990s, as mentioned before, ASEAN labor learned to meet the specifications of advanced Japanese industry.

One alternative to protecting infant industry from foreign competition through tariffs is protecting **infant entrepreneurship** through restrictions on foreign investment. To be sure, limiting foreign capital by requiring majority local ownership in certain sectors, reserving other sectors entirely for local enterprise, and limiting repatriation of the profits of foreign capital and the earnings of foreign personnel (see Chapter 14) may discourage overseas investment and enterprise.

Still, as the *Wall Street Journal* indicated in mid-1994, "the foreign-investment blitz has been a mixed blessing for Mexico and Argentina, which have seen their currencies appreciate greatly against the dollar. The overvalued currencies make exports from Mexico and Argentina more expensive and imports cheaper." As a

---

[79]Tessa Morris-Suzuki, "Japanese Technology and the New International Division of Knowledge in Asia," in Tokunaga Shojiro, ed., *Japan's Foreign Investment and Asian Economic Interdependence* (Tokyo: University of Tokyo Press, 1992), pp. 135–52;and Aoki Takeshi, "Japanese FDI and the Forming of Networks in the Asia-Pacific Region: Experience in Malaysia and Its Implications," in Tokunaga Shojiro, ed., *Japan's Foreign Investment and Asian Economic Interdependence* (Tokyo: University of Tokyo Press, 1992), pp. 73–110.

[80]E. Wayne Nafziger, *Learning from the Japanese: Japan's Pre-War Development and the Third World* (Armonk, N.Y.: M.E. Sharpe, 1995), pp. 38–39, 43, 47, 137; William W. Lockwood, *The Economic Development of Japan: Growth and Structural Change, 1868–1938* (Princeton, N.J.: Princeton University Press, 1954), pp. 331–32; and "Of Strategies, Subsidies and Spillovers," *Economist* (March 18, 1995): p. 78.

result, both countries ran huge deficits in their international goods, services, and income accounts in the early 1990s.[81]

In contrast to Mexico and Argentina, Chile favored local entrepreneurs and capitalists without drastic restrictions on foreign capital. While economic liberalization in Chile in the early 1990s surpassed that of virtually all other Latin American countries, Chile had the most stringent controls among Latin countries on incoming capital, protecting local enterprise without distorting the foreign-exchange rate substantially. In 1994, the Chilean government required foreign companies (or Chilean companies with foreign collaborators) to offer a minimum issue of $25 million on the Chilean stock exchange and have approval from two foreign credit-rating agencies. Additionally, the foreign company had to pay a hefty capital-gains tax and wait 1 year to repatriate their funds abroad. Foreign investment was $21 billion in Mexico, $15 billion in Brazil, $11 billion in Argentina, and $4 billion in Venezuela, while only $1 billion in Chile in 1993. At the same time, however, Chilean entrepreneurs and savers responded with high levels of domestic capital formation and new ventures, and moderated the boom-and-bust and balance-of-payment cycles associated with foreign investment in the 1980s. In late 1994, UNCTAD was still not clear how much LDC protection of domestic entrepreneurship and regulation of trade-related foreign investment were allowed under GATT's Uruguay Round.[82]

Black Markets and Illegal Transactions

Black markets for foreign exchange form in response to restrictions on trade (tariffs, quotas, and administrative controls) and controls on currency transactions (as in Figure 18–3). In mid-1983, the premium for the black market relative to the official market for foreign exchange was 310 percent in Nigeria (that is, the black-market rate, ₦2.95 = $1 was 410 percent of the official rate, ₦0.72 = $1), 72 percent in Ecuador, 27 percent in Pakistan, 26 percent in Mexico, 6 percent in Morocco, and 3 percent in Malaysia. The imposition of exchange and trade restrictions creates incentives to overinvoice imported goods (depositing excess foreign-currency proceeds in foreign bank accounts) and smuggle. Illegal trade creates a demand for illegal currency, which stimulates its supply, leading to the establishment of a black market if the central bank is unable or unwilling to meet all the demand at the official price of foreign exchange. The major sources for the supply of illegal foreign currency comprise export smuggling, underinvoicing exports, overinvoicing imports, exchanges by foreign tourists or diversion of remittances through unofficial channels, and diversion by government officials in exchange for bribes or favors. Black markets for foreign exchange have several adverse effects on government authorities: the cost of enforcement, the loss of tariffs revenue, the encouragement of government corruption and rent-seeking, and the loss of income to government on foreign currency transactions. Liberalizing the official market for foreign exchange, an action which usually depreciates the domestic currency, will usually reduce the black-market premium for foreign exchange.[83]

[81]Matt Moffett, "Chile Stays Wary of Foreign Investment," *Wall Street Journal* (June 9, 1994), p. A10.

[82]Ibid.; and United Nations Conference on Trade and Development, *Trade and Development Report, 1994* (New York, 1994), p. 136.

[83]Pierre Agenor, *Parallel Currency Markets in Developing Countries: Theory, Evidence, and Policy Implications* (Princeton, N.J.: Princeton University International Finance Section, 1992), pp. 5–25.

In Colombia, however, the black market has consistently paid a premium for the domestic currency, the peso.

While estimates are imprecise, illegal and black-market transactions are important components of international trade. The Overseas Development Council (ODC) estimates 1990 illegal narcotics (coca, cocaine, marijuana, and heroin) exports as 186 percent of legal export earnings in Colombia, 184 percent in Bolivia, 136 percent in Jamaica, 121 percent in Mexico, 90 percent in Peru, and 39 percent in Pakistan. The opium and heroin export percentage in the Golden Triangle (Burma, Thailand, and Laos) and illegal export percentages in some other LDCs are also substantial.[84] For many LDCs, official measures of balance-of-payments components must be suspect.

A New International Economic Order:
The U.N. General Assembly Versus the New Liberalism

Since the rise of national states during the early modern period, world leaders have tried to change the world economic order. Nations formed alliances and fought global wars in part to influence this order. In 1944, U.S. Secretary of the Treasury Harry White, British Chancellor of the Exchequer John Maynard Keynes, and other allied finance ministers met at Bretton Woods, New Hampshire to sketch a framework for the international economy after World War II, all but ignoring the newly independent and other emerging nations of the third world that would become of importance in subsequent decades.

Since the 1970s, there have been at least two major visions of the new international economic order (NIEO): that of the **Group of 127 (G127)** less-developed countries of Africa, Asia, and Latin America that are members of the U.N. Conference on Trade and Development and the liberal approach of the Group of Seven (G7) (and allies in Europe, Australia, and New Zealand). Our sketch of these two images of the world economic order will also include a definition of what this order encompasses.

THE U.N. CONCEPT

An early demand by developing countries for a new international economic order was in response to dissatisfaction with their record during the United Nations' first development decade, from 1960 to 1970, when these countries and international agencies emphasized internal economic policies. Their call for a new order intensified in the mid-1970s, when their modest gains from previous years were threatened by worldwide inflation, a fourfold increase in oil prices in 1973 to 1974, and the subsequent deterioration in LDC foreign exchange and debt position. Leaders of developing countries increasingly attributed LDC underdevelopment to a weak position in the international economic system.

The U.N. General Assembly's sixth and seventh special sessions (1974–75) adopted a declaration on principles and programs for a change in the international economic order. The international economic order comprises all economic relations and institutions linking people from different nations, including the World Bank and the U.N. Development Program that lend capital to LDCs; the International Monetary Fund (IMF), which provides credit to ease short-term international payments imbalances; the General Agreements on Tariffs and Trade

---

[84]Overseas Development Council, *U.S. Foreign Policy and Developing Countries: Discourse and Data 1991* (Washington, D.C., 1991), p. 30; and *Economist* (October 8, 1988), p. 22.

(GATT), which administers international-trade rules; bilateral and multilateral trade, aid, banking services, currency rates, capital movements, and technological transfers; multilateral aid consortiums; and international commodity stabilization agreements. Third-world countries wanted more policy influence in international institutions, more control over international economic relations, and a restructured world order that emphasized their needs.

One of the LDCs' aims has been to be less dependent on rich countries. The U.N. declaration proclaims that every state has permanent sovereignty over its natural resources and economic activities. Furthermore, each state is entitled to control its natural resources and their exploitation, "including the right to nationalization or transfer of ownership to its nationals." Although OPEC achieved full local ownership and a price-setting producer cartel that raised prices and revenues substantially in the mid to late 1970s, the cartel's effectiveness broke down due to several members' lack of discipline in the 1980s and 1990s (violating the agreement, ignoring quotas, and undercutting prices) and the expansion of non-OPEC oil exploration and energy substitutes. No other raw material producers' group has been able to achieve even the temporary success that OPEC did in controlling its resources and setting prices.

In 1974, when the U.N. General Assembly declared principles for the new order, it also adopted a plan of action. Clearly for many DCs the U.N. ratification implied only vague intentions, not the plan's implementation, which required discussions and painstaking negotiations in a number of international forums. But progress on specific measures during the 1970s, 1980s, and 1990s has been limited due to LDC division, substantial DC opposition, and the weakness of the U.N. General Assembly. The U.N. recommendations and assessment of the progress in meeting them can be divided into the following five categories: (1) transfer of real resources, (2) science and technology, (3) industrialization, (4) food and agriculture, and (5) international trade.[85]

DEVELOPMENT AID AND LDC INFLUENCE

The U.N. resolution contains many proposals for increasing the flow of development assistance from developed to developing countries. On the first proposal, for a greater volume and predictability of financial aid, DCs contributed 0.30 percent of GNP in 1993 compared to the 0.70-percent U.N. target.[86] Contrary to the demand, donors did not increase aid much to least-developed countries, and major creditor countries have devised only limited ways of mitigating LDC debt burdens. International organizations, such as the World Bank Group and the U.N. Development Program, did enhance the real value of assistance, as the resolution called for.

The share of SDRs as international reserves increased more slowly than the NIEO resolution envisioned. However, when the IMF demonetized gold in the

[85]Jan Tinbergen, coordinator, *Reshaping the International Order: A Report to the Club of Rome* (New York: E. P. Dutton, 1976); "Principles for a 'New International Economic Order' Adopted by Sixth Special Session of the United Nations General Assembly," *Survey of International Development* 11 (May-June 1974): 1–4; and "The United Nations Seventh Special Session: A Hopeful Step Forward in the Process of Laying the Foundation for an Alternative World Economic Order," *Survey of International Development* 12 (September-October 1975): 1–4, summarize these recommendations.

[86]Organization for Economic Cooperation and Development, *Efforts and Policies of the Members of the Development Assistance Committee: Development Cooperation*, Report by James H. Michel, Chair of the Development Assistance Committee (Paris: Organization for Economic Cooperation and Development, 1995), pp. A9–A10.

late 1970s, a portion of the proceeds from its gold sales was used to aid LDCs. In a small way, as the U.N. plan of action asks, international institutions have begun to reflect the greater political, economic, and population weight of Asia, Latin America, and Africa. The IMF, known as the "rich man's club," allotted directorships to Saudi Arabia, China, and the LDCs generally.

From 1974 to 1994, bilateral aid increased slowly, and aid given to multilateral agencies declined if measured in real terms or as a percentage of the donors' GNP. In addition aid volume remained unpredictable. Moreover, creditors rescheduled or canceled only a little of the LDC debt.

SCIENCE AND TECHNOLOGY

While LDC governments have improved their ability to negotiate contracts favorable to transferring science and technology, this transfer has not, as the United Nations requested, increased dramatically. Scientific and technological applications, concentrated largely in the DCs, are bases for their high productivity and the profitability of their large businesses. Contrary to the NIEO statement, DC businesses resist sharing their techniques or devoting their efforts to solving LDC scientific and technological problems when they do not have economic control. Nor have DCs adopted an international code of conduct for transferring technology nor put many resources into strengthening LDC scientific and technological infrastructure, as the U.N. resolved.

FOREIGN INVESTMENT

The DCs have resisted redeploying most industries that survive only by tariffs and subsidies to LDCs, and where redeployment has been undertaken by MNCs, it has tended to be concentrated in a limited number of countries—most often South Korea, Taiwan, Singapore, Brazil, and Mexico. As LDCs increase their expertise in the economic ministries, many have devised and enforced industrial policies to limit MNCs to participation in investment projects consistent with the laws, regulations, and development programs of the developing countries. However, the GATT's Uruguay Round agreement in 1994 may reduce scope for LDC industrial policy, especially requirements that goods produced domestically embody a certain percentage of local content and that the imports of foreign firms be limited to the amount of foreign exchange generated through exports.[87]

FOOD AND AGRICULTURAL AID

Total food and agricultural aid to LDCs did not increase between 1974 and 1994, as the NIEO resolution asked, while direct food aid dropped. The DCs did not adopt trade policies more conducive to LDC expansion of export earnings.

INTERNATIONAL TRADE

A limited number of LDCs have been successful in export promotion, stressed by the United Nations. While LDCs made few gains in increasing primary product export price stability, it is doubtful that this NIEO goal should be a LDC priority.

---

[87]"Trade Agreement Mandates Broad Changes," *IMF Survey* (January 10, 1994): p. 3.

Finally, LDCs made only modest gains in their goal of improving export income stability.

THE LIBERAL CONCEPT

Industrialized countries, led by the United States, opposed much of the NIEO agenda, such as strengthening multilateral commodity stabilization and income enhancement and supranational codes of conduct as threatening DC prices and incomes and the interests of DC-based firms. Additionally, the bargaining power of LDCs, weak even in 1974, eroded with their increased debt and credit costs in the 1980s. These events coincided with the dominance of **liberalism**, a child of late eighteenth- and nineteenth-century classical economic liberalism, as expounded by Adam Smith and David Ricardo (Chapter 5), with their emphases on a free-market economy, government noninterference in prices, and the private ownership of land and capital. These emphases, beginning about 1980, were not just an extension of the domestic economics of U.S. President Ronald Reagan and British Prime Minister Margaret Thatcher to Western-dominated multilateral aid and lending programs by the International Monetary Fund and World Bank, but also an LDC response to the failure of price controls, government licenses and regulation, and massive subsidies to public enterprises. The fall of centralized state socialism in communist Eastern Europe in the late 1980s and the former Soviet Union in the early 1990s reinforced the liberal view DCs held regarding necessary changes in the world economic order. In Chapter 20, we will discuss further the policy implications of liberalism.

Summary

1. The LDCs generally gain from a free trade policy wherein they produce goods in which they have a comparative advantage. Factor endowment and technology help determine a country's comparative advantage.

2. Exceptions to the free trade argument include increasing returns to scale, external economies, potential technological borrowing, changes in factor endowment, a revenue tariff, increased employment, improved balanced of trade, greater domestic stability, national defense, antidumping, and reduced luxury consumption. Yet most of these tariff arguments are weaker than many LDC economic policymakers think.

3. In the more than 100 years since the last quarter of the nineteenth century, the commodity terms of trade (price index of exports/price index of imports) of primary product exporters have probably fallen.

4. Export promotion is generally more effective than import substitution in expanding output and employment.

5. Rapid growth in LDC manufactured exports in the last few decades was primarily concentrated in middle-income countries, such as Taiwan, South Korea, Hong Kong, Singapore, Spain, Brazil, Thailand, Indonesia, and Malaysia.

6. Although the generalized system of tariff preferences and the 1970s' Tokyo Round negotiations reduced DC tariffs on selected LDC imports, these gains may have been outweighed by losses from protectionist policies set up during the 1980s. Additionally, DCs increased nontariff trade barriers against LDC imports, especially labor-intensive goods, in the late 1970s, 1980s, and 1990s.

7. For DCs with no tariff on LDC primary products but a substantial tariff on manufacturing and processing that uses primary goods as inputs, the nominal rate of protection is less than the effective rate of protection.

8. Expanding primary exports stimulated rapid economic growth in a number of Western countries in the nineteenth century, but this approach has had a more limited impact on growth in today's LDCs.

9. Although the IMF's and European Union's compensatory financing schemes have helped stabilize LDC export earnings, a common fund has not been established, and buffer stock agreements have been of limited value.

10. Agricultural subsidies in the United States, European Union, and Japan are major barriers against LDC farm exports.

11. The LDCs with a foreign exchange price below the market-clearing price can improve import rationing, encourage import substitution, and promote exports by depreciating their currencies. Yet the gains may be limited if domestic prices are still repressed.

12. Regional economic integration among LDCs or of LDCs with DCs have the potential for limited gains in LDC economic growth. However, regional free trade, while superior to bilateral trade agreements, is inferior to worldwide free trade in global efficiency.

13. Developing countries gain from integration within the Asian and North American borderless economies. However, members of these economies need to ensure that they do not sacrifice their economic autonomy and gains from learning to integration as a peripheral economy within a Japanese- or U.S.-organized borderless economy.

Terms to Review

- tariffs
- comparative advantage
- comparative costs
- factor proportions theory
- Heckscher–Ohlin theorem
- technological advantage
- product cycle theory
- boomerang effect
- income elasticity of demand
- laissez-faire
- infant industry arguments
- effective rate of protection
- commodity terms of trade
- Prebisch–Singer thesis
- Engel's law
- income terms of trade
- export purchasing power
- single factoral terms of trade
- dumping

- General Agreements on Tariffs and Trade/World Trade Organization system
- nontariff barriers (NTBs)
- Multifiber Arrangement (MFA)
- trigger price mechanism
- generalized system of tariff preferences (GSP)
- staple theory of growth
- integrated program for commodities
- core commodities
- cartel
- buffer stocks
- Stabex
- intellectual property rights
- basket of currencies
- special drawing rights (SDRs)
- price of foreign exchange (exchange rate)
- exchange controls

- real exchange rate
- real appreciation
- dual exchange rate
- theory of the second best
- multiple exchange rate
- impossible trinity
- economic integration
- preferential trade arrangements
- free trade area
- customs union
- common market
- economic union
- complete economic and monetary union
- complementation agreement
- trade diversion
- trade creation
- Lomé Convention
- special economic zones (SEZs)
- Asian borderless economy
- infant entrepreneurship
- Group of 127
- new international economic order
- liberalism

Questions to Discuss

1. What are the major arguments for and against tariffs in LDCs? in DCs?
2. Present the four arguments for tariffs you consider strongest and then indicate their weaknesses.
3. Discuss the adequacy of using a model with three factors—land, labor, and capital—in determining comparative advantage. How would we extend the Heckscher–Ohlin model to explain LDC comparative advantage more realistically?
4. Discuss whether a capital poor LDC would better import capital-intensive goods from abroad, attract capital from abroad, subsidize and spur production shifting comparative advantage to these goods, or use liberalized policies for capital and other factor markets.
5. Do LDCs face historically deteriorating terms of trade?
6. Which is more effective in expanding LDC output and employment: export expansion or import substitution? What policies avoid biases against exports?
7. Name and then characterize those LDCs that were most successful in expanding exports in the last quarter of the twentieth century.
8. Why is the nominal rate of tariff protection a poor gauge of the effective rate of protection for processed and manufactured goods?
9. Why are nominal exchange-rate changes inadequate when calculating currency depreciation or appreciation? Indicate how to calculate the real exchange rate.
10. What DC changes in tariff policies would aid LDC development?
11. How much progress has the GATT/WTO system made in facilitating the trade expansion of LDCs since 1960? What changes would you recommend to the GATT/WTO system to expand LDC trade further?
12. Why has the integrated program for commodities not been more successful in expanding LDC primary product export earnings?
13. Indicate the nature of the present international exchange-rate system and how it affects LDCs.
14. Under what circumstances might a LDC gain from depreciating its currency? What are some of the advantages of depreciation?

15. Discuss the advantages and disadvantages of dual (or other multiple) exchange rates.

16. Why may efforts to achieve a market-clearing exchange rate not improve economic efficiency and growth in a domestic economy that is otherwise not liberalized?

17. Discuss why LDCs have made so few gains in their attempts at regional economic integration.

18. Can an LDC attain all three of the following goals: stable exchange rates, free capital mobility, and national control over monetary policy? If not, which goals should have the highest priorities and what should be the tradeoffs between the various goals?

19. Should GATT encourage the expansion of regional integration among LDCs? If not, what alternatives would you recommend?

20. What policies might an LDC undertake to reduce the premium for the black market for foreign exchange?

21. What changes do LDCs want in the international economic order? What progress has been made in implementing these demands? Are any of the demands inconsistent? Are any contrary to LDC interests?

22. Discuss the relative merits of the positions of liberals and the U.N. General Assembly concerning changes in the international economic order.

23. Indicate the advantages and disadvantages of LDCs becoming members of the Asian or Western Hemisphere borderless economy.

Guide to Readings

Sebastian Edwards, "Openness, Trade Liberalization, and Growth in Developing Countries," *Journal of Economic Literature* 31 (September 1993): 1358–1393, has an excellent survey of the literature.

Paul R. Krugman and Maurice Obstfeld, *International Economics: Theory and Policy*, 3rd ed. (New York: HarperCollins, 1994), pp. 11–86, clearly explain the theory of comparative advantage. Ravi Batra, "The Fallacy of Free Trade," *Review of International Economics* 1(1) (1992): 19–31, argues against free trade for the United States. Black (note 13), Bhagwati (note 14), and Paul Krugman, "Does the New Trade Theory Require a New Trade Policy," *World Economy* 15 (July 1992): 423–41, evaluate arguments for tariffs. Romer (note 5) discusses the welfare costs of trade restrictions.

Peter B. Kenen, ed., *Managing the World Economy: Fifty Years After Bretton Woods* (Washington, D.C.: Institute for International Economics, 1994), has a number of useful articles about international trade policy including articles by Esty on a global environmental organization (note 21), by Jackson on GATT/WTO after the Uruguay Round (note 53), and Barry Eichengreen and Peter B. Kenen, "Managing the World Economy under the Bretton Woods System: An Overview," pp. 3–57.

Agenor (note 83) examines the black market for foreign exchange in LDCs. Other studies of this black market include J.B. Macedo, "Exchange Rate Behavior with Currency Inconvertibility," *Journal of International Economics* 12 (February 1982); P. Montiel, Pierre Agenor, and Nadeem Ul Haque, *Informal Financial Markets in Developing Countries: A Macroeconomic Analysis* (Oxford: Blackwell, 1993); and Mark Pitt, "Smuggling and the Black Market for Foreign Exchange," *Journal of International Economics* 16 (1984): 243–57.

Yotopoulos and Nugent (note 23), Spraos (note 23), and Giorgio Ardeni and Wright (note 24) have good discussions of the concepts and controversies concerning terms of trade and the Prebisch-Singer thesis.

Krueger et al., *Trade and Employment* (note 29), and Lal and Rajapatirana (note 30) have useful analyses of the effect of alternative international trade strategies on output and employment. DeRosa (note 32) and the IMF (note 34) estimate potential LDC export revenue losses from DC protectionism.

Nafziger, 1995 (note 57), examines how developing Japan used international trade and exchange-rate policies to attain rapid economic growth. Tokunaga Shojiro and his collaborators (note 75) discuss the role of Asian LDCs in the Japanese-led Asian borderless economy. World Bank, *The East Asian Miracle: Economic Growth and Public Policy* (note 78) indicate the international economic policies the Asian tigers, Malaysia, and Thailand used in their rapid growth during the last four decades of the twentieth century. See the series of articles assessing *The East Asian Miracle* in *World Development*, April 1994.

The IMF's *World Economic Outlook, International Financial Statistics,* and *IMF Survey,* the World Bank's annual *World Development Report (WDR)* and *Global Economic Prospects and the Developing Countries,* UNCTAD's annual *Trade and Development Report,* the annual U.N. *World Economic Survey,* and the Bank's and Fund's quarterly *Finance and Development,* have recent information on international trade data and policies. The 1994 U.N. World Economic Survey summarizes the Uruguay Round negotiation on pp. 79–88. The Organization for Economic Cooperation and Development, *The New World Trading System: Readings* (Paris, OECD, 1994), discusses changes in the WTO/GATT trading system.

Tinbergen; the *Survey of International Development,* May-June 1974; and *Survey of International Development,* September-October 1975) (note 85) indicate the major components of the U.N. General Assembly's demand for a new international economic order. For an overview of primary commodity problems, see Alfred Maizels, "Commodities in Crisis: An Overview of the Main Issues," *World Development* 15 (May 1987): 537–50. Laursen (note 49) discusses and evaluates the components of UNCTAD's integrated program for commodities. On international commodity agreements, buffer stocks, production and export controls, GSP, the Lomé Convention, the IMF's compensatory financing facility, and Stabex, consult the 1986 *World Devlopment Report,* pp. 133–44 (note 52). On the last two topics, see Adrian P. Hewitt, "Stabex and Commodity Export Compensation Schemes: Prospects for Globalization," *World Development* 15 (May 1987): 617–32.

Reisen (note 61) explains the difficulty of LDCs' maintaining stable exchange rates, free capital mobility, and national control over monetary policy.

Hufbauer and Schott (1994) (note 69) and Hufbauer and Schott (1993) (note 69) have a thorough analyses of the impact of NAFTA on member countries and the costs and benefits of following various sequences toward Western hemisphere economic integration. Hughes Hallett (note 71) and Pohl and Sorsa (note 71) examine what effect the European Union has on trade diversion and creation in LDCs.

George J. Borjas and Valerie A. Ramey, "Foreign Competition, Market Power, and Wage Inequality," *Quarterly Journal of Economics* 110 (November 1995): 1075-1110, show that foreign competition in highly concentrated industries was an important factor contributing to the increase in the returns to skills and increases in wage inequality in the United States.

Jeffrey A. Miron and Jeffrey Zwiebel, "The Economic Case Against Drug Prohibition," *Journal of Economic Perspectives* 9 (Fall 1995): 175-92, argue that a free market for currently illegal drugs would reduce violence and property crimes. The prohibition of drugs increases their cartelization, thus increasing the marginal benefit and diminishing the marginal cost of violence.

Paul A. David, "Clio and the Economics of QWERTY," *American Economic Review* 75 (May 1995): 332-37, indicates that comparative advantage is path dependent, in which historically remote events influence subsequent patterns of specialization. An early Milwaukee printer, Christopher Latham Sholes, designed the typewriter's topmost row of letters to spell QWERTYUIOP to reduce jamming from rapid typing in the dominant right hand and to provide salespersons easy access to the typewriter's brand name in one row. The market position of QWERTY, which established it over other keyboards, has provided continuing advantage so that even today QWERTY dominates computer keyboard layouts. David contends there are many other instances where sequences of choices made close to the beginning of the process determined the path of subsequent location and technological change. See also Paul Krugman, *Peddling Prosperity: Economic Sense and Nonsense in the Age of Diminished Expectations* (New York: W.W. Norton, 1994), pp. 221-44.

CHAPTER 19

Planning and the Market

Most people want to control and plan their economic future. The complexity of contemporary technology and the long time between project conception and completion require planning, either by private firms or government.[1]

Development planning is the government's use of coordinated policies to achieve national economic objectives, such as reduced poverty or accelerated economic growth. A plan encompasses programs discussed previously—antipoverty programs, family planning, agricultural research and extension, employment policies, education, local technology, savings, investment project analysis, monetary and fiscal policies, entrepreneurial development programs, and international trade and capital flows. Planning involves surveying the existing economic situation, setting economic goals, devising economic policies and public expenditures consistent with these goals, developing the administrative capability to implement policies, and (where still feasible) adjusting approaches and programs in response to ongoing evaluation.

Planning takes place in socialist but also in capitalist and mixed, private–public LDCs. Capitalist countries plan in order to correct for externalities, redistribute income, produce public goods (for example, education, police, and fire protection), provide infrastructure and research for directly productive sectors, encourage investment, supply a legal and social framework for markets, maintain competition, compensate for market failure, and stabilize employment and prices.

Usually the country's head of government (prime minister or president) assigns the plan to a planning office that includes politicians, civil servants, economists, mathematicians, statisticians, accountants, engineers, scientists, educators, social scientists, and lawyers, as well as specialists in various industries, technologies, agriculture, international trade, and ethnology.

In the 1950s, economists stressed an expert planning agency independent of political and bureaucratic pressures. After many a sophisticated plan lay on the shelf unused, the emphasis shifted to a planning commission directly responsible to politicians and integrated with government departments of industry, finance, commerce, petroleum, agriculture, health, education, and social welfare, as well as with regional and local government departments and planners.

---

[1]John Kenneth Galbraith, *The New Industrial State* (Boston: Houghton Mifflin, 1967).

Economists are ambivalent about integrating the central bank into the government's monetary and fiscal planning. On the one hand, most economists favor the integration of monetary policy with the government administration's fiscal policies. Still since many economists fear that political and administrative leaders will not be vigilant in fighting inflation, these economists recommend that the central bank operate independently of the head of state and government departments.

Takatoshi Ito contends that under presidential administration (similar to that of the United States), the incumbent party manipulates financial policy in its effort to be reelected, while a parliamentary state (such as that in Japan or India) does not manipulate policies in anticipation of approaching elections, but instead waits to call general elections until times of autonomous economic expansion. Thus, parliamentary governments manipulate the timing of elections, while presidential governments manipulate the timing of economic policies.[2]

Do financial policies in democratic states differ from those under authoritarian regimes? Political scientists find no difference between the macroeconomic policies of established democratic and authoritarian governments, but countries undergoing transitions to democracy pursued more expansionary monetary and fiscal policies than before and after the transition and compared to established regimes.[3]

State Planning As Ideology for New States

Economic planning in LDCs was limited prior to their independence (often gained during the 1950s and 1960s). The British and French used development plans (worked out by territorial governments with help from London and Paris) as a basis for colonial aid after World War II. But the plans, prepared by administrators with little or no planning background, were usually just lists of investment projects. And no attempt was made to integrate the various economic sectors. However, they did have the virtue of being carried out, in contrast to many postindependence plans.

Many intellectuals, nationalist leaders, and politicians believed that laissez-faire capitalism rigidly adhered to during the colonial period was responsible for slow LDC economic growth. So once independence was granted, nationalists and anticolonialists pushed for systematic state economic planning to remove these deep-seated, capitalistic obstacles. Such sentiments were expressed in a statist (usually called socialist) ideology that stressed government's role in assuring minimum economic welfare for all citizens.

Many third-world leaders, even from mixed economies, such as Nigeria, Kenya, India, and Sri Lanka, agreed with Kwame Nkrumah (Ghana's president, 1957–66) who wrote that "the vicious circle of poverty, which keeps us in our rut of impoverishment, can only be broken by a massively planned industrial undertaking." He was skeptical of the market mechanism's effectiveness, argued for the

---

[2]Takatoshi Ito, *The Japanese Economy* (Cambridge, Mass.: MIT Press, 1992), pp. 89–95.

[3]Richard Sandbrook, *The Politics of Africa's Economic Stagnation* (Cambridge: Cambridge University Press, 1985); Larry Diamond, Juan J. Linz, and Seymour Martin Lipset, eds., *Democracy in Developing Countries*, 2 vols. (Boulder, Colo.: Lynne Rienner, 1988); and Stephan Haggard and Robert R. Kaufman, "Economic Adjustment in New Democracies," in Joan M. Nelson and contributors, *Fragile Coalitions: The Politics of Economic Adjustment* (New Brunswick, N.J.: Transaction Books, 1989), pp. 57–77.

"uncounted advantages of planning," and contended that government interference in the economic growth of developing countries is "universally accepted." Vigorous state planning would remove the distorting effects of colonialism and free an LDC from dependence on primary exports.[4]

And since in many LDCs, the business class was weak at independence, the argument for a major state role in spearheading economic development was strengthened. Yet decisions concerning government size were usually based less on economic reasoning than on ruling elites' interests. Most third-world elites were politicians, professional administrators, and bureaucrats and wanted to protect their interests from business people. Elites perceived anarchy in the market, which reinforced by their lack of control, produced a statist ideology.

Afro-Asian Socialism

African and Asian socialism did not coincide with the Western socialist concept of the ownership of most capital and land by the state (see Chapter 2). Instead the Afro-Asian variety usually included the following: a high-level of state ownership of the **commanding heights** (major sectors of heavy industry, metallurgy, military industries, mining, fuel, transport, banking, and foreign trade), a penchant for public control of resource allocation in key sectors, a deemphasis on foreign trade and investment, a priority on inward-looking production, and a rapid indigenization of high-level jobs.[5]

Dirigiste Debate

From after World War II to the early 1980s, many development economists favored a major role for the LDC state in promoting macroeconomic stability, national planning, and a sizable public sector. In the early 1980s, a series of World Bank and IMF reports emphasized reversing the LDC government sector's overextension.[6] Indeed, World Bank and IMF conditions for balance of payments lending to LDCs sometimes required privatization of LDC state-owned enterprises, a part of policy reforms that stressed state enterprise reform and competition policies in both private and public sectors.[7]

The emphasis on privatization, discussed in Chapter 20, began with the 1981 to 1986 World Bank presidency of former New York bank president A. W. Clausen and continued under former U.S. Congress person Barber B. Conable (1986–91), former New York bank president Lewis T. Preston (1991–95); and former New York investment banker James D. Wolfensohn (1995–). The emphasis was not just an application of President Reagan's and Prime Minister Thatcher's economic views to U.S., British, and Western-dominated multilateral aid and lending programs, but

---

[4]Kwame Nkrumah, *Neo-Colonialism: The Last Stages of Imperialism* (London: Nelson, 1965).

[5]Shankar N. Acharya, "Perspectives and Problems of Development in sub-Saharan Africa," *World Development* 9 (February 1981): 117–18.

[6]An early report signaling the Bank's emphasis on the private sector was the World Bank, *Accelerated Development in sub-Saharan Africa: An Agenda for Action* (Washington, D.C., 1981).

[7]Paul Mosley, "Privatisation, Policy-based Lending, and World Bank Behaviour," in Paul Cook and Colin Kirkpatrick, eds., *Privatisation in Less-Developed Countries* (Sussex, U.K.: Wheatsheaf, 1988), pp. 125–26.

also an LDC response to the failure of public enterprise to match expectations. Frequently LDC governments provided massive subsidies to public enterprises that had been expected to produce an investible surplus.

University of London and University of California—Los Angeles economist Deepak Lal criticizes development economists' *dirigiste* dogma: a view that standard economic theory does not apply to LDCs, the price mechanism has to be supplanted by direct government controls, and resource allocation is of minor importance in designing public policies. Lal contends that the demise of development economics would be conducive to LDC economics and economies.[8]

Critics charge that Lal does not define development economists to include all authors applying economics to LDCs but only those authors with whom he disagrees. Moreover, Lal's description of their views is a caricature: Dudley Seers, an example of Lal's *dirigistes*, rejects a *rigid adherence* to standard economic theory (see Chapter 1), favors income transfers rather than price controls to redistribute income, and criticizes detailed physical planning. Nor is Lal correct in attributing Taiwan's and South Korea's success to little governmental direction, nor the World Bank in linking rapid growth in Malawi in the 1970s to low interference in prices. Taiwan and Korea both promulgated land reform in the late 1940s and early 1950s; provided subsidies for farm products and their inputs beginning in the 1960s; and actively used government incentives, controls, and protection to promote industries for export expansion since World War II. Critics of the World Bank argue that Malawi's agricultural policy in the 1970s had sizable price distortions and the transferring resources from peasant agriculture to commercial agriculture and industry overstated the growth accompanying falling peasant agricultural productivity and declining average real incomes for the population as a whole. The discussion in this chapter reflects a growing consensus among development economists on planning, the market, and the public sector somewhere between the views of Lal and his straw men and women, the *dirigistes*.[9]

Scope of the Chapter

We look first at state planning as an ideology for nations that have gained independence since World War II. The second section examines Soviet planning and the third Indian planning and their implications for LDCs. The fourth part outlines promarket and proplanning arguments. Fifth, we look at the need for indicative planning in most nonsocialist LDCs. Sections 6–8 analyze planning goals and instruments, plan duration, and the limitations of planning models. In section 9,

---

[8]Deepak Lal, *The Poverty of "Development Economics"* (London: Institute of Economic Affairs, 1983).

[9]Frances Stewart, "The Fragile Foundations of the Neoclassical Approach to Development," *Journal of Development Studies* 21 (January 1985): 282–92; Clive Hamilton, "Class, State, and Industrialisation in South Korea," *IDS Bulletin* 15 (April 1984): 38–43; Martin Fransman, "Explaining the Success of the Asian NICs: Incentives and Technology," *IDS Bulletin* 15 (April 1984): pp. 50–56; Mick Moore, "Agriculture in Taiwan and South Korea: The Minimalist State," *IDS Bulletin* 15 (April 1984): 57–64; Robert Wade, "Dirigisme Taiwan-style," *IDS Bulletin* 15 (April 1984): 65–70; World Bank, *World Development Report, 1983* (New York: Oxford University Press, 1983), pp. 60–63; Jonathan Kydd and Robert Christiansen, "Structural Change in Malawi since Independence: Consequences of a Development Strategy based on Large-Scale Agriculture," *World Development* 10 (May 1982): 355–74; and Jonathan Kydd, "Malawi in the 1970s: Development Policies and Economic Change," paper presented to a Conference on Malawi: An Alternative Pattern of Development, Edinburgh University, Centre of African Studies, May 24–25, 1984.

we examine LDC economic data, emphasizing development of an input-output table. The last two sections deal with public policies toward the private sector and public expenditures.

Soviet Planning

Until the late 1980s, many LDCs turned to the Soviet Union for lessons in state planning. From 1928 through Mikhail Gorbachev's economic restructuring (perestroika) during the late 1980s, the Soviet **controlling plan** authorized what each key sector enterprise produced and how much it invested. Yet even Soviet planning, probably more comprehensive than any other country ever attained, was not so totally planned and rigidly controlled as you might think. Soviet planning began modestly. During the 1918 to 1921 civil war, enterprises ignored planning directives. Not until 1925 to 1926 did Gosplan, the State Planning Committee of the USSR, which consults with ministries, republics, and enterprises, have the personnel and authority to plan detailed input-output relationships.

In the centrally planned key sectors (heavy industry, much of light industry, and a small part of agriculture) in the quarter century after World War II, there was much local, extraplan discretion—government simply could not control all operations details. For example, bad weather or shortages sometimes prevented delivery of essential materials so that enterprise managers adjusted by hoarding, bartering, and other informal arrangements. In the late 1980s, over half of Soviet GNP remained out of the purview of planners and under the control of local officials, enterprises, and even private markets. These activities, however, generally depended on state policies for financial controls, purchasing, pricing, wage schedules, labor mobility, education and training, turnover taxes, foreign trade, and so forth.[10]

Leon Trotsky recognized the difficulties of comprehensive Soviet centralized planning early in its history. Trotsky, Communist party leader exiled by Joseph Stalin, criticized Soviet bureaucratic and centralized economic management:

> If there existed the universal mind that projected itself into the scientific fancy of Laplace; a mind that would register simultaneously all the processes of nature and of society, that could measure the dynamics of their motion, that could forecast the results of their interreactions, such a mind, of course, could *a priori* draw up a faultless and exhaustive economic plan, beginning with the number of hectares of wheat and down to the last button for a vest. In truth, the bureaucracy often conceives that just such a mind is at its disposal; that is why it so easily frees itself from the control of the market and of Soviet democracy. . . . The innumerable living participants of the economy, state as well as private, collective as well as individual, must give notice of their needs and of their relative strength not only through the statistical determination of plan commissions but by direct pressure of supply and demand. The plan is checked, and, to a considerable measure, realized through the market. . . . Economic accounting is unthinkable without market relations.[11]

---

[10]Paul R. Gregory and Robert C. Stuart, *Soviet and Post-Soviet Economic Structure and Performance* (New York: HarperCollins, 1994).

[11]Leon Trotsky, *The Soviet Economy in Danger* (New York: Pioneer Publishers, 1931), pp. 29–30, 33.

While Soviet leader Gorbachev (1985–91) believed that economic restructuring was essential in reversing slow U.S.S.R. growth after 1970, he decentralized without providing the enterprise freedom and market incentives that were essential.

Indian Planning

In 1950, India was the first major mixed LDC to have its own planning commission. Decades before he took office, Jawaharlal Nehru, prime minister after India's independence in 1947, had been attracted by English democratic socialism as well as Soviet industrial planning. India's economic policies for its first 5-year plans (and several interim plans) through 1978 suffered from the paradox of inadequate attention to programs in the public sector and too much control over the private sector. Thus we had Indian planners frequently choosing public sector investments on the basis of rough, sketchy, and incomplete reports, with little or no benefit–cost calculations for alternative project locations. And the government, having selected the project, often failed to do the necessary detailed technical preparation and work scheduling related to the project. The bureaucracy was slow and rigid, stifling quick and imaginative action by public sector managers. (Even public firms had to apply for materials and capital import licenses a year or so in advance.) Poorly stated criteria for awarding input licenses and production quotas led to charges of bribery, influence peddling, and ethnic or political prejudice. Key public sector products were often priced lower than scarcity prices, increasing waste and reducing savings. Furthermore, political involvement in public enterprises meant unskilled labor overstaffed many projects.

Jagdish N. Bhagwati and Padma Desai's study shows that such planning problems led to profit rates for public enterprises that were lower than for indigenous, private operations even when adjusted for commercial and social profit discrepancies. This inefficiency explains why the Indian public sector, despite its domination of large industry, made no net contribution to the country's 1990 total capital formation; indeed Table 14–2 suggests that dissavings from public sector losses, which the government budget covered, reduced capital formation!

Indian planners on the other hand tried to influence private investment and production through licensing and other controls. These controls were intended to regulate production according to plan targets, encourage small industry, prevent concentrated ownership, and achieve balanced regional economic development.

The Indian government's award of materials and input quotas at below-market prices (before the 1991 reform) hampered private industrial efficiency.

1. It subsidized some firms and forced others to buy inputs on the black market or do without.
2. Favoring existing firms discouraged new-firm entry. And inefficient manufacturers sold controlled inputs on the free market for sizable profit.
3. Business people were unproductive, since they were dealing with government agencies and buying and selling controlled materials.
4. Capital was often underutilized, since government encouraged building excess capacity by awarding more materials to firms with greater plant capacity.
5. Entrepreneurs inflated materials requests, expecting allotments to be reduced by a specific percentage.

6. Business people used or sold all materials within the fiscal year to avoid quota cuts the following years.

7. A shortage of controlled inputs could halt production, since the application process took several months.

8. Large companies, which were better organized and informed than small enterprises, took advantage of economies of scale in dealing with the public bureaucracy.

9. Entrepreneurial planning was difficult because of quota delay and uncertainty.[12]

India's planners distrusted the market in resource allocation, especially when scarcities were acute. Central planners, however, lack the information essential that more decentralized decision makers have. Once the licensing system was created, politicians, bureaucrats, and sheltered businesses and their workers used centralized planning logic to define their own interest and to oppose reform, and Indian economists also rationalized the system. India's concern about avoiding monopolistic concentration contributed to the detailed physical planning that meant the virtual elimination of contested markets by foreign and other domestic competitors.[13]

India has increasingly realized the inadequacies of the bureaucracy in controlling private output and prices, and the costs of licensing and quota policies. In the 1980s, the Indian government slowly increased efficiency and savings through improved public sector plans and relaxed production and materials licensing, import restrictions, and other controls on private business, improving consumption and savings. Yet these policies increased economic growth only slightly. Growth rates appeared to accelerate more rapidly after 1991, when India's stabilization and policy reforms included rupee devaluation and increasing convertibility, import barrier reductions, the privatization of numerous state enterprises, the deregulation of industry, decreased restrictions on foreign investment, the liberalization of capital markets, and cutbacks in income and wealth taxes.

The Market Versus Detailed Centralized Planning

While the Soviet experience indicates how much of an economy remains beyond the control of central planners, the Indian experience suggests the costs of intervention in mixed economies. The inability to work out in-depth programs in the public sector, and excessive private-sector regulation, are endemic in many other mixed economies, including Nigeria and Pakistan.

The plan and the market are separate ways of coordinating transactions. Using the market adds certain costs: discovering relevant prices and negotiating and concluding separate contracts for each exchange transaction. To reduce risks and other costs, managers (together with suppliers and workers) sign long-term contracts rather than making agreements for each separate transaction. Planning and organizing eliminate certain costs of the market system but also increase large-scale diseconomies—diminishing returns to management. A balance between

---

[12]Jagdish N. Bhagwati and Padma Desai, *India: Planning for Industrialization—Industrialization and Trade Policies since 1951* (London: Oxford University Press, 1970); and E. Wayne Nafziger, *Class, Caste, and Entrepreneurship: A Study of Indian Industrialists* (Honolulu: University Press of Hawaii, 1978), pp. 114–19.

[13]Jagdish Bhagwati, *India in Transition: Freeing the Economy* (Oxford: Clarendon Press, 1993), pp. 53–54.

using the market and a planning organization is reached when "the costs of organizing an extra transaction . . . become equal to the costs of carrying out the same transaction by means of an exchange in the open market."[14] In this section, we focus on the free market as an alternative to state planning.

PROMARKET ARGUMENTS

The market efficiently allocates scarce resources among alternative ends. First, consumers receive goods for which they are willing to pay. Second, firms produce commodities to maximize profits. If the resulting income distribution is acceptable, consumption and production are socially efficient. Third, production resources hire out to maximize income. Fourth, the market determines available labor and capital. Fifth, the market distributes income among production resources and thus among individuals.

The market provides incentives for economic growth. Consumers try to increase income to acquire more goods. Investors and innovators profit from the market. People invest in human capital and firms in material capital, since such capital earns an income.

The market stimulates growth and efficiency automatically, without a large administration on centralized decision making. Thus, it conserves on skilled personnel, a scarce resource in LDCs. The market needs little policing other than a legal system enforcing contracts. When government abandons the market and starts allocating scarce goods and concessions (for example, foreign currency, licenses, and materials), corruption, favoritism, bribery, and black markets are more likely to thrive.

Ronald Coase, economist from the University of Chicago, argues that planning agencies and firms reach rapidly diminishing returns to management under centralized planning. Coase's position is:

> Firms exist because some transactions internal to firms are less costly than similar transactions carried out in markets. The limits of the firm depend on cost comparisons at these margins. . . . "Central planning" within firms is disciplined by competition among them, so long as resources are free to move to their highest valued uses.[15]

But under Soviet-type economy-wide central planning, most resources lack this freedom. Moreover, Oliver Williamson argues that the number of prices essential to decentralize a complex organization increases multiplicatively with size. The major cost explosion is that of monitoring labor and managers. When state so-

---

[14]R. H. Coase, "The Nature of the Firm," *Economica N.S.* 4 (1937): 386–405, reprinted in George J. Stigler and Kenneth E. Boulding, eds., *Readings in Price Theory* (Chicago: Irwin, 1952), pp. 331–51 (quote on p. 341); and Oliver E. Williamson, "The Modern Corporation: Origins, Evolution, Attributes," *Journal of Economic Literature* 21 (December 1981): 1537–68.

[15]Sherwin Rosen, "Transactions Costs and Internal Labor Markets," in Oliver E. Williamson and Sidney G. Winter, eds., *The Nature of the Firm: Origins, Evolution, and Development* (New York: Oxford University Press, 1991), p. 76, in a book devoted to Ronald H. Coase, "The Nature of the Firm," *Economica N.S.* 4 (1937): 386–405.

cialism suppresses the market, the cost of monitoring people explodes, as reward and penalty systems no longer result in self-enforcing contracts.[16]

PROPLANNING ARGUMENTS

Market decisions do not produce the best results when the market fails, as with environmental degradation, measles vaccinations, and labor training. Social profitability exceeds private profitability when external economies (for example, vaccinations and the training of labor) are rendered free by one firm to a consumer or another producer. External diseconomies (pollution, let us say) mean private profitability exceeds social profitability (see Chapters 5, 11, and 13). National planners can choose investment projects for social profitability rather than for their internal market rates of return.

Social and private profitability also diverge in a market economy when there are monopolistic restraints and other market failures. A monopolist produces less and charges higher prices than does a competitive firm. National planners reduce a project's monopoly profits but increase net social benefits by expanding output and lowering prices to the competitive equilibrium. Industry and enterprise managers in a planned economy will however restrict output volume if they are rewarded on the basis of profits.[17]

Additionally, government needs to produce the public or collective goods, schools, defense, sewage disposal, and police and fire protection that the market fails to produce (see Chapter 20).

Moreover, the free market may not produce so high a savings rate as is socially desirable. A government generating surplus from its own production, setting low procurement prices for state trading monopsonies, and levying turnover taxes can usually save in excess of households and firms. Centrally planned economies have had higher rates of saving than market economies.

Furthermore, relying on the market assumes that people are well informed and want to maximize gains. Should not centralized planning replace the market in LDCs where this assumption is false? The answer is not clearcut. If prospective private entrepreneurs lack information and motivation, the planner's role may be enlarged. On the other hand, the planning agency can ease its task by disseminating information to make the market work more effectively. Although the peasant preoccupied with family survival may not be an income maximizer (Chapter 7), empirical studies demonstrate that the LDC industrialist, trader, and commercial farmer respond to income and price incentives, suggesting that the market works well.

---

[16]Oliver E. Williamson, "Hierarchical Control and Optimum Firm Size," *Journal of Political Economy* 75 (April 1967): 123–39; and discussion of Williamson's views by Sherwin Rosen, "Transactions Costs and Internal Labor Markets," in Oliver E. Williamson and Sidney G. Winter, eds., *The Nature of the Firm: Origins, Evolution, and Development* (New York: Oxford University Press, 1991), p. 82. See also H.B. Malmgren, "Information, Expectations and the Theory of the Firm," *Quarterly Journal of Economics* 76 (August 1961): 399–421.

[17]Harry G. Johnson, *Money, Trade, and Economic Growth* (London: George Allen & Unwin, 1962), pp. 152–63; Oskar Lange and Fred M. Taylor, *On the Economic Theory of Socialism*, Benjamin E. Lippincott, ed. (New York: McGraw-Hill, 1965); and Abram Bergson, "Market Socialism Revisited," *Journal of Political Economy* 75, no. 5 (October 1967): 657–65.

MARKET SOCIALISM

The income distribution the market produces—partly dependent on the skills and property of the privileged and wealthy (Chapter 11)—may not be just or socially desirable. Yet the greater income inequality of capitalist economies may result less from the market than from unequal holdings of land and capital. Polish economist Oskar Lange's model of decentralized **market socialism** combined the advantages of market allocation with more uniform income distribution by dividing the returns from social ownership of nonhuman, productive resources among the whole population. Lange's approach assumed that individuals allocated their limited income among consumer goods and services and provided labor services just as in capitalist economies. Socialist enterprises produced where product price equaled marginal cost (the competitive profit maximization rule), while combining factor inputs to minimize the average cost of production. Industrial authorities chose the rate of expansion or contraction of the industry as a whole. Central planners used trial and error to set prices at equilibrium (where shortages and surpluses disappeared), adjusted prices for externalities through taxes and subsidies, and allocated returns from property owned collectively by society.

Critics argued that pricing consistent with maximum profits would encourage monopolistic behavior by enterprise and industry managers in concentrated industries; planning decisions would not be compatible with political freedom; and central planners would have the impossible task of setting millions of prices for individual products and subproducts.[18] But decentralized enterprises could set prices rather than central planners, who need only intervene to prevent monopoly pricing. One example close to Lange's model, the Soviet New Economic Policy, 1921 to 1927, which enabled the economy to recover rapidly from the chaos and disruption of revolution and civil war, was later replaced because the Communist party bureaucracy lacked control over the economy.

WORKER-MANAGED SOCIALISM: THE FORMER YUGOSLAVIA

Economists in the former Yugoslavia, the nearest contemporary approximation of Lange's model, argued that socialist planning must be managed by workers to be democratic and must use the market for resource allocation to be efficient. The Yugoslav experience with worker-managed socialism is instructive, despite the breakup of the country in the 1990s from ethnic conflict.

From 1948 to 1951, each firm elected a workers' council, which hired a professional manager to carry out the council's decision. Workers shared in income from the enterprise, after subtracting material and other costs, based on a democratically agreed-on income distribution determined by the intensity and quality of people's labor. Individuals sought employment anywhere, and firms were free to hire a particular person. Generally the labor-managed firm maximized net income per member.[19]

---

[18]Oskar Lange and Fred M. Taylor, *On the Economic Theory of Socialism,* Benjamin E. Lippincott, ed. (New York: McGraw-Hill., 1965); and Paul R. Gregory and Robert C. Stuart, *Soviet Economic Structure and Performance* (New York: Harper & Row, 1974), pp. 311–19.

[19]Branko Hôrvat, Mihailo Markovic, and Rudi Supek, *Self-Governing Socialism,* 2 vols. (White Plains, N.Y.: International Arts and Sciences Press, 1975); especially Branko Hôrvat, "An Institutional Model of a Self-Managed Socialist Economy," pp. 307–27, and Jaroslav Vanek, "Identifying the Participatory Economy," pp. 135–40, in Branko Hôrvat, Mihailo Markovic, and Rudi Supek, *Sociology and Politics; Economics,* vol. 2 (White Plains, N.Y.: International Arts and Sciences Press, 1975).

From 1959, a decade after worker management began, until 1979, Yugoslavia's real GNP grew 6 percent annually, and the labor force was transformed from primarily peasant agriculture into modern sector employment. During the 1980s, however, real GNP per capita declined, the unemployment rate averaged 10 to 15 percent, strikes were widespread, annual inflation averaged more than 35 percent, and total external debt was the tenth largest in the world ($21 billion in 1988). Workers' councils were limited by state regulations (including prices) and by political intervention of the League of Communists of Yugoslavia (LCY). Moreover, Yugoslavia's 1976 reform established the basic organizations of associated labor (BOs), a separate autonomous planning unit for each department in the firm. The BOs, in addition to workers' council, trade union, business managers, their administrative and technical staff, the LCY, and the local community, complicated enterprise decision making, introducing multiple checks and balances, so that the firm's hierarchy was ill defined. The need for consensus among so many units gave many people (for example, discontented, even striking work units, such as janitors or carpenters) the capacity to impede and few people the power to implement policies. When coalitions broke down, the state (federation, province, or local community) or LCY bureaucracy could dissolve disruptive workers' councils, recall business managers, or withhold infrastructure or funds.

Other weaknesses of the Yugoslav self-managed socialism were the lack of participation of rank-and-file employees in important policymaking, the dependence of pay on factors outside BO control (for example, closing down production because suppliers failed to deliver an essential input), the unconcern for long-run performance (considerable turnover of workers, who lack ownership shares in the firm), neglect of externalities, widely varying income among workers doing the same job in different firms, lack of a labor market, the state's soft budget constraint (an absence of financial penalties for enterprise failure), restricted entry of new firms to increase competition, collusion between vertically and horizontally linked firms, investment choice based on negotiations not benefit-cost analysis, overborrowing (resulting from no interest charge), disincentives to expand employment, too little investment from current surplus, and too many incentives for highly capital-intensive production (from pressures to distribute higher incomes per member).[20]

CONCLUSION

Despite Yugoslavia's experience during the 1980s, market socialism's appeal is enhanced by China's post-1978 market-oriented reforms (Chapters 7 and 20), especially in agriculture. Market socialism may appeal to LDCs that oppose private ownership but lack the administrative service and planning capability to run a centralized socialist economy. Still, since "socialism with Chinese characteristics" is evolving in an ad hoc manner, we cannot be certain how long LDCs will have a prominent market socialist model.

---

[20]Martin Schrenk, "The Self-Managed Firm in Yugoslavia," in Gene Tidrick and Chen Jiyuan, eds., *China's Industrial Reform* (New York: Oxford University Press, 1987), pp. 339–69; Alec Nove, *The Economics of Feasible Socialism* (London: Allen and Unwin, 1983), pp. 133–41, and Rammath Narayanswamy, "Yugoslavia: Self-Management or Mismanagement?" *Economic and Political Weekly* 23 (October 1, 1988), 2052–54.

Indicative Plans

The weaknesses of Soviet planning discussed before may have been minor compared to those of LDC planning agencies in the 1970s and 1980s that insisted that partial planning give way to comprehensive planning. For in economies with a large private sector, government planning can only be partial. Chapter 3 pointed out the difficulty of applying Fel'dman's Soviet planning model to mixed LDCs where planning did not represent a binding commitment by a public department to spend funds. Few third-world planning commissions have had the skills and authority needed for Soviet-type planning.

Most mixed or capitalist developing countries are limited to an **indicative plan,** which indicates expectations, aspirations, and intentions, but falls short on authorization. Indicative planning may include economic forecasts, helping private decision makers, policies favorable to the private sector, ways of raising money and recruiting personnel, and a list of proposed public expenditures—usually not authorized by the plan, but by the annual budget.

Planning Goals and Instruments

Planning sets economic goals. Since government hires the planners, political leaders set the goals, which may or may not reflect the people's priorities. Possible planning goals include rapid economic growth, reduced poverty and income inequality, high basic-needs attainment, greater educational attainment, greater employment, price stability, lower international economic dependence, greater regional balance, and adequate environmental quality. Some of the goals, such as reduced poverty and inequality and high basic-needs attainment are complementary rather than independent. Yet where there are conflicts between goals, political leaders must decide what relative weight to give to each goal. In this case, about all planning professionals can do is interpret economic data to identify goals (for example, the need to reduce a region's rural poverty, cope with a balance of payments crisis, or slow down inflation), clearly state them, and formulate the costs of one goal in terms of another.

Planners face such questions as follow: How much real growth should be sacrificed to reduce the rate of inflation by 1 percentage point? How much would increased capital formation lessen low-income consumption? How much GNP would have to be given up to achieve an acceptable level of independence from world markets? How much output should be sacrificed to attain a desired level of environmental quality?

Planners often express goals as **target variables**—for example, annual GNP growth of 6 percent; output growth of manufacturing, 8 percent and of agriculture, 5 percent; poverty reduced by 1 percentage point of the population; and a balance of payments deficit not in excess of $200 million. Goals are achieved through **instrument variables,** such as monetary, fiscal, exchange rate, tariff, tax, subsidy, extension, technology, business incentive, foreign investment, foreign aid, social welfare, transfer, wage, labor training, health, education, economic survey, price control, quota, and capital-rationing policies.[21]

---

[21]Hollis B. Chenery, "Development Policies and Programs," *Economic Bulletin for Latin America* 3, no. 1 (March 1958): 55–60.

The Duration of Plans

The availability of instrument variables depends on the length of time in which the goals are to be achieved. To slow down labor force growth takes 15 to 20 years, to build a dam a decade, but to increase free rice allotments per capita may take only a few weeks.

Short-term plans focus on improving economic conditions in the immediate future (the next calendar or budget year); **medium-term plans,** on the more distant future (say, a 5-year plan); and **long-term** (or perspective) **plans,** on the very distant future (15, 20, or more years).

Long-term goals must serve as a background for medium- and short-term plans. Medium-term plans, which often coincide with government office terms, are such that investment returns begin to occur after the first year or so of the plan. These plans can be more precise than long-term plans.

A medium-term plan can be a **rolling plan,** revised at the end of each year. As a planning commission finishes the first year of the plan, it adds estimates, targets, and projects for another year to the last year. Thus planners would revise the 5-year plan for 1997 to 2001 at the end of 1997, issuing a new plan for 1998 to 2002. In effect a plan is renewed at the end of each year, but the number of years remains the same as the plan rolls forward in time.

However, a rolling plan involves more than a mechanical extension of an existing plan. It requires rethinking and revising the whole plan each year to set targets for an additional year. Built into the rolling plan are a regular review and revision procedure (in effect needed for all plans, whatever their range). Yet rolling plans have sometimes proved too difficult for most LDCs to manage. A simpler way of bringing a medium-term plan up to date is by implementing part of it through the short-term plan.

Short-term (usually annual) plans carry out government policy in connection with a detailed budget. The size and composition of an annual plan are determined primarily by finances, plan expertise, and the progress made in feasibility studies and projects started in previous periods.[22]

Planning Models and Their Limitations

Planners need a bird's eye view of macroeconomic relationships before determining programs, expenditures, and policies, and a simple aggregate model can provide this overall perspective. Most macroeconomic models for the United States are complicated, sometimes consisting of hundreds of variables and equations. But most LDCs cannot afford such complexity. And even if skills, funds, and data were available, the planners' policy control in mixed and capitalist LDCs is too limited for a comprehensive aggregate model to have much practical value.

Nobel laureate W. Arthur Lewis criticizes planning agencies in data-poor, mixed LDCs that hire economists to formulate a complex macroeconomic model. He believes the time spent is not worth the effort. He ironically notes that

---

[22]Jan Tinbergen, *Development Planning,* trans. by N. D. Smith (London: World University Library, 1967), pp. 36–38; and Albert Waterston, *Development Planning: Lessons of Experience* (Baltimore: Johns Hopkins University Press, 1969), pp. 120–33.

The principal danger of a macroeconomic exercise lies in its propensity to dazzle. The more figures there are in a Plan, produced by an army of professionals who have labored mightily to make them consistent, the more persuasive the Plan becomes. Attention shifts from policy to arithmetic. Consistency can be mistaken for truth. Revision is resisted. Yet the Plan is not necessarily right merely because its figures are mutually consistent. . . . Once the point is grasped that mathematical exercises do not of themselves produce truth, a Plan with figures is no more dangerous than a Plan without figures.[23]

Many planners still think that planning primarily involves agreeing on macroeconomic targets for investment and output. Lewis notes that when Nigeria's First National Development Plan, 1962 to 1968, was published,

Argument broke out as to whether the planners had "chosen" the right rate of growth whether they had used the right capital-output ratios, and whether they had determined correctly the amount of capital which private entrepreneurs would be required to invest. All such discussion misconceives what the government can actually do.[24]

For Nigeria, characterized in the 1960s by its Economic Planning Unit head as "planning without facts," Lewis maintains that you can make nearly as good a development plan without national income projections, capital-output ratios, and other such econometric manipulations as with them.[25]

Generally macroeconomic planning models used in LDCs with large private sectors have been ineffective. Actual policies and economic growth in such countries have little relationship to the plan's instrument and target variables. Much of LDC economic growth since the early 1960s has gone in directions unforeseen by the plan or if included in the plan, would have occurred even in the plan's absence![26]

Thus mixed LDC planners should generally not be judged by how well they have reached their target growth rates. The U.N. Center for Development Planning, Projections, and Policies observed that Nigeria's real growth in gross domestic product from 1970 to 1974 was 12.3 percent per year compared to an annual target of only 6.2.[27]

But this rapid growth had little to do with plan investments. The Nigerian government spent only 63 percent of planned public capital. Planners did not clearly identify feasible industrial projects nor give details of supporting government policies. And poor coordination and personnel shortages resulted in inadequate preparatory work by accountants, economists, engineers, managers, and planners. In reality most Nigerian growth could be explained by factors largely

[23]W. Arthur Lewis, *Development Planning: The Essentials of Economic Policy* (London: Allen and Unwin, 1966), pp. 16–17.

[24]W. Arthur Lewis, *Reflections on Nigeria's Economic Growth* (Paris: Development Center of the Organization for Economic Cooperation and Development, 1967), p. 35.

[25]Ibid., 35–36; and Wolfgang F. Stolper, *Planning without Facts: Lessons in Resource Allocation from Nigeria's Development* (Cambridge, Mass.: Harvard University Press, 1966).

[26]Clarence Zuvekas, Jr., *Economic Development: An Introduction* (New York: St. Martin's, 1979), p. 191.

[27]Center for Development Planning, Projections, and Policies, "Implementation of Development Plans: The Experience of Developing Countries in the First Half of the 1970s," *Journal of Development Planning* no. 12 (1977): 1–69.

outside the planners' purview—the unexpectedly rapid oil growth and sharply increasing oil prices.

Nonetheless, macroeconomic models may be useful in forecasting and projections, enabling decision makers to see the economy from a national perspective. And if a forecast is based on consultation with the economic ministries and private firms, as in early post-World War II Japan, it may give investors greater confidence in the economy's forward movement. But although planning models have some value, Lewis contends that the most important parts of the plan are the documents showing how to improve data collection, raise revenue, recruit personnel, and select and implement projects—topics discussed below.

Three professionals play an especially important role in planning: (1) the person with treasury experience, used to dealing with government departments and planning public expenditures; (2) the practical economist familiar with the unique problems that emerge in LDCs to help formulate public policies; and (3) the econometrician to construct **input-output tables** to clarify intersectoral economic relations.[28]

Economic Data

Economic data in many LDCs are of little value. Since some facts needed for decision making may be unavailable, planners may have to improvise.

As pointed out in Chapter 2, small errors in GNP may have a major impact on economic growth.

Planning in a country with poor economic data should concentrate on organizing an effective census bureau and department of statistics, hiring practical field investigators and data analysts, and taking periodic economic surveys. Sound development planning requires information on national income, population, investment, saving, consumption, government expenditure, taxes, exports, imports, balance of payments, and performance of major industries and sectors, as well as their interrelationships.[29]

THE INPUT-OUTPUT TABLE

The most useful technique for describing these interrelationships is the input-output table, illustrated with interindustry transactions in Papua New Guinea (see Table 19–1). When divided horizontally, the table shows how the output of each industry is distributed among other industries and sectors of the economy. At the same time, when divided vertically, it shows the inputs to each industry from other industries and sectors.

Table 19–1 is more simplified than usually used in planning, but it is realistic in other respects. It consolidates an original 46 productive sectors into 11. An input-output table used for planning typically includes from 40 to 200 sectors, depending on how much aggregation (or consolidation) is desired.

[28]W. Arthur Lewis, *Development Planning: The Essentials of Economic Policy* (London: Allen and Unwin, 1966), pp. 16–17.

[29]Graham Eele, "The Organization and Management of Statistical Services in Africa: Why Do They Fail?" *World Development* 17 (March 1989): 431–38, opposes government departments distinguishing between data collection and policy analysis.

TABLE 19–1 Input-Output Table, Papua New Guinea ($ million; purchasers' values)

Outputs / Inputs	1 Ag	2 Ffm	3 Mfg.	4 Bc	5 Tc	6 Cm	7 Eh	8 Gs	9 Os	10 Be	11 Nmp	Net Current Exp.[a]	Pers. Cons.	Public	Private[b]	Exports	Total Output
			Purchases by Intermediate Users											Gross Domestic Capital (Final Demand Purchases)			
Sales of intermediate inputs by processing sectors																	
1 Agriculture	1.89		7.86				0.51	0.35		0.13			17.56		6.20	80.21	114.71
2 Fishing, forestry, mining	0.04		10.53	0.05			0.06	0.04					3.46		0.10	209.80	224.08
3 Manufacturing	9.05	1.66	17.01	40.51	12.21	2.65	2.43	7.04	1.61	2.61			76.52	1.10	2.60	46.78	223.78
4 Building construction	0.48	0.56	0.36	0.61	0.22	0.66	1.15	15.19	1.05	0.08				61.10	57.27		138.73
5 Transport, communication	3.91	0.83	6.32	3.47	3.51	1.51	4.80	14.54	0.21	11.80			16.94	0.40	0.30	13.17	81.71
6 Commerce	6.43	3.00	25.52	7.43	4.11	0.70	0.40	0.24	0.33	1.60			23.99	1.30	8.55	5.41	89.01
7 Education, health		0.10							0.06			60.40	4.70			0.10	65.36
8 Govt. services, N.E.I.	0.77	0.34	0.22	0.95	0.41	1.59	0.01	0.17	5.51	0.35		106.55		11.60		0.36	128.83
9 Other services			0.03		0.15	8.31	0.19	0.71		9.33		7.60	20.71			7.81	54.84
10 Business expenses	1.45	4.08	6.86	7.25	2.80	13.94	0.52	1.92	4.48							3.87	47.17
11 Nonmarket production													219.00	35.70	4.40		259.10
Payments for Primary Inputs																	
Wages & salaries																	
Indigenes	18.31	8.65	14.54	12.57	9.87	8.19	18.43	23.58	13.05								127.19
Nonindigenes	3.34	9.90	20.66	14.78	15.82	11.69	26.34	46.19	11.11								159.83
Operating surplus[c]	58.03	122.12	44.47	7.76	7.56	31.39	1.84	0.31	12.57		259.10						545.15
Depreciation	2.91	32.52	8.97	5.54	9.89	4.74	0.08	0.25	2.76								67.66
Net indirect tax	0.55	7.22	19.79	1.85	1.46	1.19	0.06	0.04	0.49	1.02			13.16	0.20	3.48	2.34	52.85
Imports, c.i.f.	7.55	33.10	40.64	35.96	13.70	2.45	8.54	18.26	1.61	20.25			96.43	24.60	60.02	9.51	372.62
Sales by final buyers															-0.42	0.42	
Total input	114.71	224.08	223.78	138.73	81.71	89.01	65.36	128.83	54.84	47.17	259.10	174.55	492.47	136.00	142.50	379.78	2,572.62

[a]Net current expenditures of public authorities, missions, and financial enterprises.

[b]Including additions to stocks.

[c]Including indigenous nonmarket income.

Source: M. L. Parker, "An Interindustry Approach to Planning in Papua New Guinea," *Economic Record* 50 (September 1974): 369.

Even most sectors from a 200-row, 200-column table require aggregation from several industries. Furthermore, sector worksheets may vary widely in detail and quality. The sectoral relationships of inputs to output for a data-poor economy's first table may be based not only on published sources, government department documents, and interviews and surveys, but also on estimates from similar economies or even educated guesses.

Frequently disaggregation, that is, having a detailed breakdown of industries and sectors, may be an advantage. If the table is used to forecast, a detailed classification by industry would reveal bottlenecks that might occur during output expansion.[30] Thus the disaggregated input-output table would show how much the electronics and wire industries must be expanded beyond existing capacities for telecommunications to grow.

The upper left-hand quadrant of Table 19–1 records interindustry transactions—the delivery of output from all sectors (industries) to all other sectors of the economy for production use. In this quadrant, sectoral outputs become inputs in other sectors.

The columns show the structure of inputs for a given sector. Thus the agricultural sector uses $0.04 million of inputs from the fishing, forestry, and mining sector, $9.05 million from the manufacturing sector, $0.48 million from building and construction, $3.91 million from transport and communication, $6.43 million from commerce, $0.77 million from governmental services, and $1.45 million from business expenses. In addition various agricultural units use $1.89 million inputs from other parts of agriculture.

The rows on the other hand show the output distribution of the same sectors. The first row of Table 19–1 shows the output of agriculture to be used in the same sector ($1.89 million), in manufacturing ($7.86 million), in education and health ($0.51 million), in government services ($0.35 million), and business expenses ($0.13 million).

To read the table, remember the following simple rules:

1. To find the amount of purchases from one sector by another, locate the *purchasing industry* at the top of the table, then read *down the column* until you come to the *processing industry*. (For example, the education and health sector purchases $4.80 million of inputs from transport and communication.)

2. To find the amount of sales from one sector to another, locate the *selling industry* along the left side of the table, then read *across the row* until you come to the *buying industry*. (Thus the building construction industry sells $0.36 million of output to the manufacturing industry.)

While the upper-left quadrant records the sale of intermediate inputs from one sector to another, the major part of the lower-left quadrant gives the payment, by sectors, to foreigners for imports and to production factors for wages, salaries, profits, interest, and rent. In the farthest column right, total factor payments (such

---

[30]The treatment here borrows from William H. Miernyk, *The Elements of Input-Output Analysis* (New York: Random House, 1965), pp. 8–57; A. P. Thirlwall, *Growth and Development with Special Reference to Developing Economics* (New York: Wiley, 1977), pp. 219–34; Zoltan Kenessey, *The Process of Economic Planning* (New York: Columbia University Press, 1978), pp. 278–90; W. Duane Evans and Marvin Hoffenberg, "The Interindustry Relations Study for 1947," *Review of Economics and Statistics* 34 (May 1952), pp. 97–142; M. Jarvin Emerson and F. Charles Lamphear, *Urban and Regional Economics: Structure and Change* (Boston: Allyn and Bacon, 1975), pp. 11–24; and Wassily Leontief, *Input-Output Economics* (New York: Oxford University Press, 1966).

as $127.19 million wages and salaries to indigenes) and depreciation all involve payments by intermediate industries. Total imports ($372.62 million) and net indirect taxes ($52.85 million) in the last column, however, include direct payments by final demand (consumption, investment, and export) purchases, as well as intermediate purchases.

Intermediate inputs from the upper left plus primary inputs from the lower left equal total inputs, for example, $114.71 million for agriculture. This figure equals agriculture's total output, $114.71 million, the sum of intermediate inputs and final demand, which consists of consumption, capital formation, exports, and net current expenditure of public authorities, missions, and financial enterprises. Total input equals total output for all intermediate input sectors.

You would not expect the total of any of the individual rows of the primary inputs to equal the total of any of the final demand columns. But the individual differences must cancel out for the entire economy. As is true of any single processing sector, *total* outlays must equal *total* outputs for the economy as a whole.

The total output in the input-output table for Papua New Guinea, $2,752.62 million, is far in excess of GNP for the same year, $952.68 million, calculated on the income side as factor payments (wages and salaries, and operating surplus), depreciation, and net indirect taxes, or on the expenditures side as final demand purchases minus imports. Every effort is made to eliminate double counting in computing the components of GNP. But since the input-output table measures all *transactions* between sectors of the economy, the value of goods and services produced in a given year is counted more than once. Since some goods will enter into more than one transaction, their value must be counted each time a different transaction takes place. What we have is an accumulation of value added at each stage of the production process until the good is acquired through final demand.

THE INPUT-OUTPUT TABLE'S USES

Analysis based on the input-output table has a number of uses in planning. Data needed to construct the table provide sectoral information that may become invaluable in other aspects of planning. But even more important, if the plan sets a certain level of final demand and indicates which sectors are to produce it, then the detailed interrelationships and deliveries can be well approximated by tracking through the table the direct and indirect purchases needed. Doing this allows the planner to explore the implications of alternative development strategies. Input-output analysis provides a set of consistent projections for an economy. It broadly indicates the economic structure that might emerge given a particular development strategy. Input-output analysis shows the sectoral changes that must occur in the growth process in a way no aggregate macroeconomic model can do.

Assume that planners in Papua New Guinea wish to double building and construction from $138.73 million to $277.46 million. This expansion requires additional fishing, forestry, and mining production of $0.05 million, manufacturing output of $40.51 million, building and construction of $0.61 million, $27.35 million in wages and salaries, and $35.96 million of foreign exchange for imports (to name just a few of the added inputs column 4, Table 19–1, indicates are needed). However, when the manufacturing sector sells more of its output to the building and construction industry, manufacturing industry's demand for the products of agriculture, fishing, forestry, mining, and so on, will likewise increase—the amount of the increase depending on the technical coefficient that relates the amount from an intermediate sector needed for every unit of manufacturing output. (This calculation can be made from information in column 3, Table 19–1.) These effects will spread throughout the processing sector.

Tracing the effects of increased demand throughout the input-output model can provide planners with other valuable estimates. It can help them calculate the effects of intermediate sector expansion on changes in import requirements, balance of payments, employment, investment demand, and national income that go beyond the immediate, direct impact. Rather than using the laborious step-by-step approach, planners can use high-speed electronic calculating equipment to compute a matrix showing the total requirements, direct and indirect, per dollar of demand.

THE INPUT-OUTPUT TABLE'S VALIDITY

There are several assumptions underlying input-output analysis that raise questions about its validity. First, the technical coefficients are fixed, which means no substitution between inputs occurs (such as capital for labor, or building and construction for manufacturing inputs). Furthermore, input functions are linear, so that output increases by the same multiple as inputs. Production is subject to constant returns to scale. Moreover, the marginal input coefficient is equal to the average, implying no internal economies or diseconomies of scale. Second, there are no externalities, so that the total effect of carrying out several activities is the sum of the separate effects. Third, there are no joint products. Each good is produced by only one industry, and each industry produces only one commodity. Fourth, there is no technical change, which rules out the possibility of, say, new, improved agricultural methods reducing the industrial and commercial inputs required per output unit.

Even though we may question the validity of these assumptions, the errors may not be substantial, especially in a period of 5 years or less. For example, there may not be much substitutability between inputs in the short run while relative factor prices and the level of technology are relatively constant. If input coefficients can be derived at regular and frequent intervals, some of these problems can be overcome.

THE TIME LAPSE IN ESTIMATES

The United States failed to incorporate results of its 1991 input-output survey into the national accounts until 1996. For DCs that revise input-output tables annually, the timeliness of the United States would receive a low grade. For many LDCs, not only are the input-output tables out of date but also baseline expenditure surveys in both urban and rural areas, industrial structure, transport, construction, and small-scale industry. Some LDCs have estimates that are 15 to 20 years old, while others still rely on the original benchmark estimates of the 1960s or early 1970s.[31] One of an LDC's highest priorities should be to establish a census and statistics department to gather periodic economic data.

---

[31]Alan Heston, "National Accounts: A Brief Review of Some Problems in Using National Accounts Data in Level of Output Comparisons and Growth Studies," *Journal of Development Economics* 44 (June 1994): 44–45.

Public Policies Toward the Private Sector

In most LDCs, even many claiming to be socialist, the private sector, comprised, at least, of most of agriculture, is larger than the public sector. Planners may set targets for production, employment, investment, exports, and imports for the private sector but usually have no binding policies to affect the target. Beyond forecasting, the usefulness of target figures for the private sector depends on the reliability of data, the persuasiveness of the planning process, and policy control over the private sector.

Private sector planning means government trying to get people to do what they would otherwise not do—invest more in equipment or improve their job skills, change jobs, switch from one crop to another, adopt new technologies, and so on.

Some policies for the private sector might include the following:

1. Investigating development potential through scientific and market research, and natural resources surveys;
2. Providing adequate infrastructure (water, power, transport, and communication) for public and private agencies;
3. Providing the necessary skills through general education and specialized training;
4. Improving the legal framework related to land tenure, corporations, commercial transactions, and other economic activities;
5. Creating markets, including commodity markets, security exchanges, banks, credit facilities, and insurance companies;
6. Seeking out and assisting entrepreneurs;
7. Promoting better resource utilization through inducements and controls;
8. Promoting private and public saving;
9. Reducing monopolies and oligopolies.[32]

Public Expenditures

Planners should ask each government department to submit proposals for expenditures during the plan period. Departments should estimate potential financial (and social) costs and benefits. Each government agency or enterprise should conduct feasibility studies of prospective investment projects in the same detail as would private business. Additionally, government must estimate the effect of new capital programs on future, recurrent expenditures. Chapter 20 examines issues associated with public enterprises.

Since the total cost of the various departmental proposals will probably exceed available funds, planners must set priorities. An individual project should be evaluated in relation to other projects, and not in isolation. Wolfgang F. Stolper, University of Michigan professor serving as Nigeria's chief planner in the 1960s, stresses that planning decisions are "more-or-less," not "either-or." Planners should "rarely condemn a project outright but [should] mainly question its size and timing," and make it depend on other decisions simultaneously taken.[33]

---

[32]W. Arthur Lewis, *Development Planning: The Essentials of Economic Policy* (London: Allen and Unwin, 1966), pp. 13–24.

[33]Wolfgang F. Stolper, "Problems of Development Planning," in Gerald M. Meier, *Leading Issues in Economic Development* (New York: Oxford University Press, 1976), p. 822.

An LDC needs government executives, administrators, and technicians experienced in conceiving projects, starting them, keeping them on schedule, amending them, and evaluating them. Without competent government administration, there is no basis for development planning.

Summary

1. Development planning is the government's coordinated policies to achieve national economic goals, such as rapid economic growth. Planning involves surveying the economy, setting goals, devising economic policies, and public spending. It also means implementing and evaluating planning policies.

2. For planning to work, the planning commission must be responsible to political leaders and integrated with government departments and economics ministries.

3. Planners must usually tell political leaders what the tradeoffs are among multiple economic goals.

4. A state planning ideology arose in LDCs as a reaction to nationalist perceptions of slow economic growth under colonial capitalism.

5. Lal argues that development economics is dominated by *dirigiste,* those in favor of government intervention into LDC prices. Critics of Lal respond that while development economists often reject a rigid adherence to Western economic theory, they usually reject price controls, although they put more emphasis on planning than Lal does.

6. Planning in many mixed LDCs has failed because detailed programs for the public sector have not been worked out, and excessive controls are used in the private sector.

7. Even Soviet "controlling" planning, which took years to develop, was still subject to decentralized management discretion, even before the Gorbachev era.

8. The plan and market are separate ways of coordinating transactions. Although the market allocates scarce resources efficiently among alternative means, it may not work so well as planning in considering externalities, correcting for market failure, mobilizing saving, and adjusting for monopolies. Thus planning eliminates certain costs of the market but also increases large-scale diseconomies through diminishing returns to management.

9. The choice for developing countries is usually not between the plan or the market, but between various combinations of the two.

10. Worker-managed socialism helped contribute to Yugoslavia's rapid economic growth from 1959 to 1979, but 1976 reforms, increasing checks and balances and bureaucraticizing enterprise decision making, hampered policy implementation and increased worker dissatisfaction.

11. Most LDCs have too few resources, skills, and data to benefit from complex macroeconomic planning models. Yet a simple aggregate model may be useful as a first step in drawing up policies and projects.

12. An input-output table is useful for assessing the effects of different development strategies on exports, imports, the balance of payments, employment, national income, and sectoral investment demand and output.

13. Most LDCs with a large private sector are limited to an indicative plan that states expectations, aspirations, and intentions but authorizes little public spending.

14. In most mixed and capitalist LDCs, documents showing how to improve data collection, raise revenue, recruit personnel, and select and implement projects are more important for successful planning than planning models.

Terms to Review

- development planning
- commanding heights
- *dirigiste*
- controlling plan
- market socialism
- worker-managed socialism
- indicative plan
- target variables

- instrument variables
- short-term plans
- medium-term plans
- long-term plans
- rolling plans
- input-output table
- intermediate inputs

Questions to Discuss

1. Why did many political leaders of states gaining independence after World War II emphasize state planning?
2. Why might a capitalist LDC want to plan?
3. What is the *dirigiste* debate? Indicate Lal's characterization of the *dirigistes* and the response of Lal's critics.
4. Why have so few LDCs been successful at detailed centralized planning?
5. What problems have mixed economies had in using Soviet-type planning?
6. What problems occur when using widespread controls to influence private investment and production in a mixed or capitalist economy?
7. What are the advantages and disadvantages of the market as an alternative to state planning? What economic systems could combine some of the advantages of both planning and the market? How effective are these systems?
8. Indicate the strengths and weaknesses of market socialism and worker-managed socialism in LDCs. How might an LDC avoid Yugoslavia's economic problems of the 1980s?
9. What are the roles of political leaders and planning professionals in formulating an economic plan?
10. What instruments do planners use to achieve goals?
11. Illustrate how the instrument variables used depend on the plan's duration.
12. Why is the use of complex macroeconomic planning models in LDCs limited?
13. What are the most important parts of the plan in a mixed or capitalist LDC?
14. What is an input-output table? Of what value is input-output analysis to a planner? What are some of the weaknesses of the input-output table as a planning tool?
15. What policies can planners undertake to encourage the expansion of private sector production?
16. What advice would you give to the person in charge of development planning in an LDC with a large private sector?

Guide to Readings

Lewis (note 23) has useful suggestions for planning in a mixed and capitalist LDC.

Miernyk offers an elementary explanation of input-output analysis (note 30), and Thirwall and Kenessey provide concise applications to LDC planning (note 30). Heston (note 31) critiques input-output data and national accounts in LDCs.

R. M. Sundrum, *Growth and Income Distribution in India: Policy and Performance since Independence* (Newbury Park, Calif.: Sage Publications, 1987), looks at India's growth and planning; Janos Kornai focuses on Hungary's socialist market economy in "The Dual Dependence of the State-Owned Firm in Hungary," in Tidrick and Jiyuan, eds. (note 20); Schrenk (note 20) examines the former Yugoslavia's worker-managed socialism; and Paul R. Gregory and Robert C. Stuart, *Soviet and Post-Soviet Economic Structure and Performance* (New York: HarperCollins, 1994), analyze Soviet economic planning. Lange and Taylor (note 18), Hôrvat, Vanek (note 19), and Nove (note 20) discuss market socialism. The *Journal of Development Studies* 24 (July 1988), devotes a special issue to "Markets within Planning: Socialist Economic Management in the Third World." E. V. K. FitzGerald, M. Wuyts (eds.), Charles Bettelheim, Gary Littlejohn, Max Spoor, David Kaimowitz, Maureen Mackintosh, Gordon White, and Nelson P. Moyo include analyses of China, Vietnam, Nicaragua, Mozambique, Zimbabwe, and more general market socialist models.

Stewart (note 9) responds to Lal's critique of *dirigisme* (note 8). The contributors to Peter J. Boettke, ed., present their views of *The Collapse of Development Planning* (New York: New York University Press, 1994).

Coase, Williamson (two sources), and Williamson and Winter (notes 14, 15, and 16), though focusing on the firm, have implications for the relative costs of monitoring and other transactions under the plan and the market.

C H A P T E R **20**

Stabilization, Adjustment, Reform, and Privatization

Chapter 17 mentioned problems of economic **adjustment**, including structural or sectoral adjustment, macroeconomic stabilization, and economic liberalization and reform. Adjustment often requires developing and transitional countries to borrow from and meet conditions set by the World Bank and International Monetary Fund as a last resort. Chapter 5 examined the policies that form the Washington consensus of the World Bank, IMF, and United States government.

In this chapter, we discuss adjustment and stabilization programs of third-world countries of Asia, Africa, and Latin America, with particular emphasis on World Bank and IMF adjustment programs. After that, we analyze public enterprises, looking at public enterprises and the role of public goods, the importance of government sector, the concept of the state-owned enterprises, the size of the state-owned sector, arguments for public enterprise, the performance of private and public enterprises, the determinants of public enterprise performance, privatization, some pitfalls of privatization, and public enterprises and multinational corporations. The third portion of the chapter examines adjustment, stabilization, and liberalization in the economies of transition, especially Russia, China, and Poland. A final section looks at lessons third-world countries can learn from the Russian, Polish, and Chinese transitions to the market.

The World Bank

In 1975, the World Bank established an interest subsidy account (a "third window") for discount loans for poorest countries facing oil price increases.[1] In 1979 to 1983, structural adjustment loans accounted for only 9 percent of Bank lending and had little impact on the most highly indebted countries. Although the Bank set up a Special Program of Assistance (SPA) in 1983 to ease the debt crisis, by the late 1980s critics, including some U.S. economists and members of Congress,

---

[1]Jonathan E. Sanford, "Feasibility of a World Bank Interest Subsidy Account to Supplement the Existing IDA Program," *World Development* (July 1988): 787–96.

voiced dissatisfaction with the Bank's minimal financial contribution to debt relief arrangements. The leadership of the Bank, while pointing out that 45 percent of its loans were to heavily indebted countries, argued, however, that the Bank's primary role was development lending to poor countries, not financial guarantees for commercial bank loans to middle-income countries.[2]

After 1987, the World Bank group (including its soft-loan window, the International Development Association or IDA), the IMF (Structural Adjustment Facility), and bilateral donors concentrated the SPA on low-income debt-distressed Sub-Saharan Africa. The SPA increased confinancing of adjustment with other donors, and provided greater debt relief, including cancellation of debt from aid and concessional rescheduling for commercial debt from creditor governments. Also, as discussed in Chapter 17, in 1989 the Bank created a Debt Reduction Facility for the poorest debt-distressed countries.

International Monetary Fund

A **balance of payments equilibrium** refers to an international balance on the goods and services balance over the business cycle, with no undue inflation, unemployment, tariffs, and exchange controls. Countries with chronic balance of payments deficits eventually need to borrow abroad, often from the IMF as the lender of last resort. In practice a member borrowing from the IMF, in excess of the reserve tranche, agrees to certain performance criteria, with emphasis on a long-run international balance and price stability. IMF standby arrangements assure members of the ability to borrow foreign exchange during a specified period up to a specified amount if they abide by the arrangement's terms. IMF **conditionality,** a quid pro quo for borrowing, includes the borrower's adopting adjustment policies to attain a viable payments situation—a necessity for preserving the revolving nature of IMF resources. These policies may require that the government reduce budget deficits through increasing tax revenues and cutting back social spending, limiting credit creation, achieving market-clearing prices, liberalizing trade, devaluing currency, eliminating price controls, or restraining public-sector employment and wage rates. The Fund monitors domestic credit, the exchange rate, debt targets, and other policy instruments closely for effectiveness. Even though the quantitative significance of IMF loans for LDC external deficits has been small, the seal of approval of the IMF is required before the World Bank, regional development banks, bilateral and multilateral lenders, and commercial banks provide funds.

Policies generally shift internal relative prices from nontradable to tradable goods, promoting exports and "efficient" import substitution. While policies generally move purchasing power from urban to rural areas, consumers to investors, and labor to capital, subgroups within these categories may be affected very differently; moreover, government functionaries who oversee and administer programs still possess discretion in distributing rewards and sanctions. Conditions attached to IMF credits sometimes provoke member discontent, as in Nigeria's antistructural adjustment "riots" in mid-1989.

The DCs' collective vote, based on members quotas, is 60 percent. And LDCs often support DCs in laying down conditions for borrowers so as not to jeopardize

---

[2]"World Bank gives Debtors Condition for More Lending," *Wall Street Journal* (July 1, 1988): p. 19; and Walter S. Mossberg, "World Bank's Conable Runs into Criticism on Poor Nations' Debt," *Wall Street Journal* (June 21, 1988), pp. 1, 24.

the IMF's financial base. Still, many African and Latin American borrowers say that IMF conditionality is excessively intrusive. Thus, for example, in 1988, in exchange for IMF lending to finance a shortfall in export earnings from cocoa, coffee, palm products, and peanuts, Togo relinquished much policy discretion, agreeing to reduce its fiscal deficit, to restrain current expenditures, to select investment projects rigorously, to privatize sundry public enterprises, and to liberalize trade. Yet the IMF must be satisfied that a borrower can repay a loan. Lacking adjustment by surplus nations, there may be few alternatives to monetary and fiscal restrictions or domestic-currency devaluation for eliminating a chronic balance-of-payments deficit.[3]

Critics from LDCs, supported by the Brandt Commission (see Chapter 16), charged that the IMF presumes that international payments problems can be solved only by reducing social programs, cutting subsidies, depreciating currency, and restructuring similar to Togo's 1988 program. According to the Brandt report, the IMF's insistence on drastic measures in short time periods imposes unnecessary burdens on low-income countries that not only reduce basic-needs attainment but occasionally lead to "IMF riots" and the downfall of governments. These critics prefer that the IMF concentrate on results rather than means.[4]

Despite a decline in funds from the 1970s to the 1980s, the IMF maintained or even increased its leverage for enforcing conditions on borrowers in the 1980s. For during the 1980s and early 1990s, World Bank loans consolidated conditions set by the IMF. The IMF became gatekeeper and watchdog for the international financial system, as IMF standby approval served as a necessary condition for loans or aid by others.[5] Moreover, the World Bank led donor coordination between DCs and the Bank and Fund, increasing their external leverage. Many low-income recipients, especially from Africa, lacked personnel, abdicating responsibility for coordinating external aid, and increasing the influence of the Bank, IMF, and other donors.

Internal and External Balance

A country needs to adjust whenever it fails to attain balance of payments and domestic macroeconomic equilibria, that is equilibra referring to both external and internal balances. Following is a simplified explanation of how to attain both external and internal balance.

---

[3]E. Wayne Nafziger, *The Debt Crisis in Africa* (Baltimore: Johns Hopkins University Press, 1993), pp. 101–02.

[4]Independent Commission on International Development Issues (Brandt Report), *North-South: A Program for Survival* (Cambridge, Mass.: MIT Press, 1980), pp. 215–16; and Cadman Atta Mills, "Structural Adjustment in Sub-Saharan Africa," Economic Development Institute Policy Seminar Report No. 18, Washington, D.C.: World Bank, 1989, p. 10.

[5]John Loxley, "The IMF and World Bank Conditionality and Sub-Saharan Africa," in Peter Lawrence, ed., *World Recession and the Food Crisis in Africa* (London: James Currey, 1986), pp. 96–103; Economic Commission for Africa, *Survey of Economic and Social Conditions in Africa, 1983–1984*, E/ECA/CM.11/16, Addis Ababa, April 1985; and John F. Weeks, "Losers Pay Reparations, or How the Third World Lost the Lending War," in John F. Weeks, ed., *Debt Disaster? Banks, Government, and Multilaterals Confront the Crisis* (New York: New York University Press, 1989), p. 57.

An example of skillfully playing the World Bank against the IMF for public relations gains involved President Ibrahim Babangida, who from 1985 to 1986 conducted a year-long dialogue with the Nigerian public, resulting in a rejection of IMF terms for borrowing. The Babangida military government secured standby approval from the IMF but rejected its conditions, while agreeing to impose similar terms "on its own" approved by the Bank. In October 1986, the Bank, with Western commercial and central support, delivered $1,020 million in quickly disbursed loans and $4,280 million in 3-year project loans. E. Wayne Nafziger, *The Debt Crisis in Africa* (Baltimore: Johns Hopkins University Press, 1993), p. 130.

Remember national-income equation 14–5

$$S = I + \left(X - M\right) \tag{20-1}$$

where S = Savings, I = domestic investment, X = exports of goods and services, and M = imports of goods and services.

If we subtract I from both sides of the equation,

$$S - I = X - M \tag{20-2}$$

or savings minus investment equals the international balance on goods and services.

Internal balance refers to full employment (and price stability); **external balance** refers to exports equal to imports. Figure 20–1, a simple model of Keynesian macroeconomic income determination, shows the relationships between income and expenditures and internal and external balances. Figure 20–1's upward-sloping line shows net domestic savings, Savings (S) minus Investment (I). The downward-sloping line shows net exports, Exports (X) minus Imports (M). (Savings and imports depend on income; investment is dependent on the interest rate and the expected rate of return; and exports are dependent on foreign income.) The intersection of $S - I$ with $X - M$ indicates net savings and net exports on the vertical axis, and on the horizontal axis, an equilibrium income (Y_E) short of the full-employment level of income (Y_F).

A simple algebraic manipulation changes our equation to the macroeconomic equilibrium where

$$S + M\left(\text{leakages}\right) = I + X\left(\text{injections}\right), \tag{20-3}$$

aggregate demand equals aggregate supply, or expenditures equal income.

Countries facing a persistent external deficit can (1) borrow overseas without changing economic policies (feasible if the deficit is temporary), (2) increase

FIGURE 20-1   Internal and External Balances

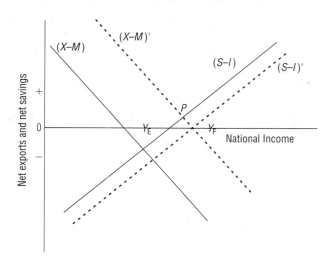

trade restrictions and exchange controls, which reduce efficiency and may violate international rules but may be tolerated in LDCs, or (3) undertake contractionary monetary and fiscal policies or **expenditure-reducing policies** [a shift of the $(S - I)$ curve upward and to the left], which sacrifice internal goals of employment and growth for external balance. Remedy (3), which critics call "leeching" after the nineteenth-century medical practice of using bloodsuckers to extract "unhealthy blood" from the sick, works with sufficient regularity to be considered the creditor community's least-risk choice. An economy, if depressed sufficiently, will at some point reduce its balance-of-payments deficit. And indeed, World Bank evidence for thirty countries, 1980–85, indicates that LDCs undergoing adjustment gave up domestic employment and spending objectives to cut their payments deficits.[6] If the deficit is chronic, additional borrowing without policy change only postpones the need to adjust. When the World Bank or IMF requires improved external balance, in the short run (2 years or so), the agency may condition its loan on (4) **expenditure switching**, that is, switching spending from foreign to domestic sources, through devaluing local currencies. For long-term adjustment, the Bank or Fund prescribes supply-side adjustments through infrastructure, market development, institutional changes, price (including interest rate) reforms, reduced trade and payments controls, and technology inducement to improve efficiency and capacity to facilitate growth with external balance, but these changes take too much time for short-run adjustment.

Consider the intersection of $(X - M)$ and $(S - I)$ in Figure 20–1, corresponding to an external deficit with unemployment. To attain both external or internal balances, the country combines expenditure-switching (depreciating domestic currency) and expenditure-increasing (expansionary monetary and fiscal) policies.

Depreciating the currency—for example, increasing the shilling's (domestic currency) price of the dollar from Sh15 = \$1 to Sh20 = \$1—results in the country's export prices falling in dollars. If the sums of the price elasticities of demand for exports plus imports are at least roughly equal to one, the country's goods and services balance will improve. Thus net exports $(X - M)$ increase (say) to $(X - M)'$, an international surplus. At the same time the net exports and net savings schedules intersect at a point further to the right (P), corresponding to higher income and employment, but still at less than full employment.

Increasing demand through reduced interest rates or a rising government budget deficit (higher government spending or lower tax rates), an expenditure-increasing policy, lowers net savings $(S - I)$ to $(S - I)'$. The new net savings and net exports schedules intersect at a full employment level of income, Y_F, with a zero balance of goods and services balance, attaining both internal and external balances.

Critique of the World Bank and IMF Adjustment Programs

Many LDC critics feel the IMF focuses only on demand while ignoring productive capacity and long-term structural change. These critics argue that the preceding model of two balances shows the cost of using austerity programs—contractionary

---

[6]John F. Weeks, "Losers Pay Reparations, or How the Third World Lost the Lending War," in John F. Weeks, ed., *Debt Disaster? Banks, Governments, and Multilaterals Confront the Crisis* (New York: New York University Press, 1989), p. 61; and World Bank, *Adjustment Lending Policies for Sustainable Growth* (Washington, D.C., 1988), pp. 1–3.

monetary and fiscal policies—prescribed by the IMF. Additionally these governments object to the Fund's market ideology and neglect of external determinants of stagnation and instability. Moreover, IMF austerity curtails programs to reduce poverty and stimulate long-run development. Yet while the IMF has perceived its role as providing international monetary stability and liquidity, not development, the concessional component of its structural adjustment loans, which began in 1986, emphasized development more. However, in their Declaration of Uruguay, October 27–29, 1988, the seven largest Latin American countries contended that "the conditionality of adjustment programs, sector lending, and restructuring agreements often entails measures that are inadequate and contradictory, making the economic policies more difficult in an extremely harsh economic climate."[7]

Beginning in the 1950s, **structural economists** from the United Nations Economic Commission for Latin America (ECLA) criticized IMF orthodox premises that external disequilibrium was short-term, generated by excess demand, requiring primarily contractionary monetary and fiscal policies and currency devaluation. ECLA economists emphasized the necessity for long-run institutional and structural economic change—accelerating the growth of export earnings, improving the external terms of trade, increasing the supply elasticity of food output through land reform, reducing income inequality, and expanding the industrial sector and antimonopoly measures before shorter-run financial and exchange-rate policies would be effective.

The new structuralist critique of the 1980s and 1990s also stresses the long-run transformation of the economy. Critics viewed the Latin American payments crisis as resulting from a long-term structural crisis in export supply and wanted IMF programs to stress these long-run changes and avoid austerity programs.[8] (See also the prescription by Latin American structural economists for structural inflation, discussed in Chapter 15.)

To avoid heavy social costs, the United Nations Children's Fund (UNICEF) urges **adjustment with a human face**, including IMF and World Bank adjustment programs emphasizing the restoration of LDC growth while protecting the most vulnerable groups, as well as growth-oriented adjustment, such as expansionist monetary and fiscal policies and World Bank/IMF loans sufficient to avoid a depressed economy. According to UNICEF, the empowerment and participation of vulnerable groups—the landless, the urban poor, and women—are essential to improve policies and protect these groups and children, especially the undernourished.[9]

---

[7]*IMF Survey* (November 14, 1988), p. 354.

[8]Mary Sutton, "Structuralism: The Latin American Record and the New Critique," in Tony Killick, ed., *The Quest for Economic Stabilisation* (London: Overseas Development Institute, 1984), pp. 16–67; Jennifer Sharpley, "Kenya, 1975–81," in Tony Killick, Graham Bird, Jennifer Sharpley, and Mary Sutton, *The IMF and Stabilisation: Developing Country Experiences* (London: Overseas Development Institute, 1984), pp. 164–216; and Roberto de Oliveira Campos, "Economic Development and Inflation with Special Reference to Latin America," in Organization for Economic Cooperation and Development, *Development Plans and Programs* (Paris: OECD Development Center, 1964), pp. 129–37, reprinted in Gerald M. Meier, *Leading Issues in Economic Development* (New York: Oxford University Press, 1984), pp. 268–73.

[9]Giovanni Andrea Cornia, Richard Jolly, and Frances Stewart, "An Overview of the Alternative Approach," in Giovanni Andrea Cornia, Richard Jolly, and Frances Stewart, eds., *Adjustment with a Human Face: Protecting the Vulnerable and Promoting Growth*, vol. 1 (Oxford: Clarendon Press, 1987), pp. 131–46; Frances Stewart, "Alternative Macro Policies, Meso Policies, and Vulnerable Groups," in Cornia, Jolly, and Stewart, eds., ibid., pp. 147–64; and Frances Stewart, "Are Adjustment Policies in Africa Consistent with Long-run Development Needs?" Paper presented to the American Economic Association, Washington, D.C., December 30, 1990.

In its criticisms of World Bank and IMF adjustment programs, the United Nations Economic Commission for Africa (ECA) offered an African Alternative Framework to Structural Adjustment Programs for Socio-Economic Recovery and Transformation (AAF-SAP), in 1989. Like the structuralists, ECA rejected the orthodox prescription for Africa's poorly structured economies. Like UNICEF, ECA complained that

> the major transitional adverse social consequences of structural adjustment programs are: declining per capita income and real wages, rising unemployment and underemployment; deterioration in the level of social services as a result of cuts on social public expenditures; falling educational and training standards; rising malnutrition and health problems; and rising poverty levels and income inequalities. . . . Many African governments have had to effect substantial cuts in their public social expenditures such as education, health and other social services in order to release resources for debt service and reduce their budget deficits. From the point of view of long-term development, the reduction in public expenditures on education . . . necessitated by stabilization and structural investment programs, has meant a reversal of the process, initiated in the early 1960s, of heavy investment in human resources development. . . . Today, per capita expenditure on education in Africa is not only the lowest in the world but is also declining. . . . All indications are to the effect that structural adjustment programs are not achieving their objectives.[10]

Indeed, ECA Executive Secretary Adebayo Adedeji argued that structural adjustment "has produced little enduring poverty alleviation and certain [of its] policies have worked against the poor."[11]

The ECA objected to the World Bank's and IMF's adjustment programs emphasizing deregulating prices, devaluing domestic currency, liberalizing trade and payments, promoting domestic savings, restricting money supply, reducing government spending, and privatizing production. These programs, ECA argued, fail in economies like those of Africa with a fragile and rigid production structure not responsive to market forces.

The ECA called for a holistic alternative to failed Bank and IMF structural adjustment programs, with an emphasis on increased growth and long-run capacity to adjust. Yet the ECA's list of policy instruments, while ambitious, was short on specifics. But the ECA emphasized adjustment programs as primarily the responsibility of Africans, who may set up programs in partnership with outside agencies, rather than having these agencies do the formulating, designing, implementing, and monitoring.[12]

---

[10]Economic Commission for Africa, *African Alternative Framework to Structural Adjustment Programs for Socio-Economic Recovery and Transformation (AAF-SAP)*, E/ECA/CM.15/6/Rev. 3, Addis Ababa, April 10, 1989, p. 24.

[11]Adebayo Adedeji, *Towards a Dynamic African Economy: Selected Speeches and Lectures, 1975–1986* (London: Frank Cass, 1989), pp. 21–25.

[12]Economic Commission for Africa, *African Alternative Framework to Structural Adjustment Programs for Socio-Economic Recovery and Transformation (AAF-SAP)*, E/ECA/CM.15/6/Rev. 3, Addis Ababa, April 10, 1989, pp. i–iii, 26–46, and 49–53.

Empirical Evidence

IMF and World Bank adjustment programs seek to restore viability to the balance of payments and maintain it in an environment of price stability and sustainable rates of growth. How successful have these programs been?

John Loxley found little evidence that IMF programs restored growth and external balance or spurred bank credit inflows in the 1970s, as only five of 23 sub-Saharan African countries reached growth targets; 13 of 18, inflation targets; and 11 out of 28 trade targets. For Thorvaldur Gylfason, the economic performance of 32 LDCs signing IMF standby agreements, 1977–79, was not significantly better than 10 other LDCs.[13]

Robin A. King and Michael D. Robinson used the World Bank's *World Debt Tables* (1984) to compare LDCs rescheduling and not rescheduling debt, 1976–81. They found that reschedulers attained desired outcomes of slower import and debt-service growths but had undesirable slower export (with a 3-year lag) and GNP growths, as well as reduced foreign-exchange inflows due to increased risk.[14]

Adjustment programs resulting in switching expenditures from foreign to domestic sources (usually through devaluation) are supposed to improve the external balance while increasing growth. A World Bank study of 54 LDCs receiving adjustment lending during 1980–87 indicated that more than half of the recipients improved their current account; however, their average growth was slower than before despite being significantly higher in the short run (though no more sustained) than non-recipients'. Also recipients' export growth and import decline were faster than others', although some recipients' import reduction resulted from lack of foreign exchange. Moreover, while recipients' social indicators were generally higher than others', recipients' calorie intake stagnated or declined during the 1980s, a trend worse than other LDCs experienced.[15]

The World Bank also measured the net change in performance of countries receiving adjustment loans (ALs) in the 3 years before to the 3 years after receiving ALs and compared this change to countries not receiving these loans. Among low-income countries generally, current-account balances and debt-service ratios improved faster, growth was slower, and inflation faster among recipients than the comparison groups. Middle-income countries receiving ALs, however, had faster growth (though faster inflation) than the comparators. For both low-income and middle-income countries, the burden of adjustment fell heavily on investment.

IMF studies suggest that demand-restraining monetary and fiscal policies reduce growth until the long lags associated with exchange-rate, interest-rate, resource-allocation (such as increasing agricultural producer prices), and other market reforms stimulate growth. The 1987 real exchange rate of countries undergoing Bank adjustments depreciated on average by about 40 percent from their

[13]John Loxley, "The IMF and World Bank Conditionality and sub-Saharan Africa," in Peter Lawrence, ed., *World Recession and the Food Crisis in Africa* (London: James Currey, 1986), pp. 96–103; and Thorvaldur Gylfason, *Credit Policy and Economic Activity in Developing Countries with IMF Stabilization Programs,* Princeton Studies in International Finance No. 60, Princeton, N.J.: Princeton University, 1987.

[14]Robin A. King and Michael D. Robinson, "Assessing Structural Adjustment Programs: A Summary of Country Experience," in John F. Weeks, ed., *Debt Disaster? Banks, Governments, and Multilaterals Confront the Crisis* (New York: New York University Press, 1989), pp. 110–15.

[15]World Bank, *Adjustment Lending: An Evaluation of Ten Years of Experience* (Washington, D.C., 1988), pp. 2–4.

1965–81 levels. Changes in exchange rates and interest rates improved resource allocation and restructured the economy toward exportables and import substitutes, stimulating investment and growth.[16]

Simon Commander's study finds commercial (especially export and import-replacement) farmers, their wage labor, and traders benefiting from exchange-rate and other adjustments. Public-sector employees, domestic-goods producers, and informal-sector workers tend to be hurt by adjustment.[17]

United Nations Conference on Trade and Development (UNCTAD) maintained that the economic performance of the 12 least-developed countries with consecutive structural adjustment programs throughout the 1980s did not differ significantly from least-developed countries as a whole. Further, Riccardo Faini, Jaime de Melo, Abdelhak Senhadji, and Julie Stanton's study of 93 LDCs undertaking adjustment before 1986, controlling for initial conditions and external factors, found no evidence of a statistically better (or worse) performance for World Bank/IMF loan recipient countries.[18]

UNICEF contends that

> the common aim of these [World Bank/IMF economic adjustment] measures is to improve the balance of payments, repay debts and reduce inflation. Important national objectives—such as expanding and protecting employment, ensuring a minimum income for households and providing basic public services—have become secondary. Ironically, the result has often been an aggravation of the economic crisis and a parallel human crisis as unemployment rises, incomes of the most vulnerable groups fall, import-dependent industries cut production, public services are curtailed, and public discontent and political instability grow.[19]

Another UNICEF study shows that from 1980 to 1985, during a period of negative growth resulting from external debt limiting social spending, child welfare deteriorated in most of sub-Saharan Africa; that is, rates of infant mortality, child death, child malnutrition, primary school dropout, illiteracy, and nonimmunization all increased. The fall in birth weight occurring throughout the sub-Sahara also indicated declining welfare. Moreover, an ECA paper indicates that killer diseases like yaws and yellow fever, virtually eliminated by the end of the 1950s, reemerged in the 1980s.[20]

---

[16]Ibid., pp. 18–36.

[17]Simon Commander, "Prices, Market and Rigidities: African Agriculture, 1979–88," in Simon Commander, ed., *Structural Adjustment and Agriculture: Theory and Practice in Africa and Latin America* (London: Overseas Development Institute, 1989), p. 239.

[18]United Nations Conference on Trade and Development, *Trade and Development Report*, 1991 (New York, 1991), p. 8; and Riccardo Faini, Jaime de Melo, Abdelhak Senhadji, and Julie Stanton, *World Development* (August 1991): 957–67.

[19]UNICEF, *The State of the World's Children* (New Delhi, 1989), p. 21.

[20]Giovanni Andrea Cornia, "Economic Decline and Human Welfare in the First Half of the 1980s," in Giovanni Andrea Cornia, Richard Jolly, and Frances Stewart, eds., *Adjustment with a Human Face: Protecting the Vulnerable and Promoting Growth*, vol. 1 (Oxford: Clarendon Press, 1987), 11–47; and Reginald Herbold Green, "The Human Dimension as the Test of and a Means of Achieving Africa's Economic Recovery and Development: Reweaving the Social Fabric, Restoring the Broken Pot," in Adebayo Adedeji, Sadig Rasheed, and Melody Morrison, eds., *The Human Dimensions of Africa's Persistent Economic Crisis* (London: Hans Zell Publishers, 1990), p. 3.

Frances Stewart uses World Bank data to ask whether Bank/IMF policies restore external equilibrium and internal balance as well as long-term development. She finds no difference in the fall in GNP per capita, 1980–87, between sub-Saharan countries undergoing strong Bank/Fund adjustment programs and those with weak programs. Additionally, during the period, real domestic investment and export earnings fell, the fiscal deficit remained large, debt continued to accumulate, and the current account did not improve, despite falling imports, in sub-Saharan countries undertaking adjustment. When Stewart deplores that "after undergoing tough programmes, many countries found themselves with reduced real income, increased poverty, deteriorating social conditions, reduced growth potential and often with no significant improvements in their external accounts," she was describing the situation in Nigeria (before the 1989–91 oil price recovery), Zambia, and Tanzania in the 1980s. She concludes that, irrespective of the cause, Bank/Fund policies did not meet their short-run objectives and were undermining growth potential, 1980–87.[21]

Paul Mosley, Jane Harrigan, and John Toye and Food and Agriculture Organization of the U.N. (FAO) criticized methods for evaluating World Bank/IMF adjustment programs. Comparing performance before and after adjustment, though useful and informative, has a strong static bias, FAO pointed out. The questions to ask are: How would the economy have performed without the policy reforms? How does this performance compare with the actual performance? Moreover, comparing adjusting to nonadjusting countries ignores the conditions when adjustment policies were initially implemented, the different economic and political characteristics of the countries and the different policies.[22]

Mosley, Harrigan, and Toye reject comparing LDC World Bank recipients with LDC nonrecipients; the results will be misleading because recipients are not representative of LDCs generally. For example, perhaps only the most desperate countries apply for Bank adjustment loans (ALs), or the Bank may eliminate from consideration economies that are too weak to undergo programs. For this reason, Mosley et al.'s comparisons were based on selecting recipient countries with similar characteristics to 1980–86 recipients. To illustrate, the Ivory Coast was paired with Cameroon, Kenya with Tanzania, Pakistan with Egypt, and Thailand with Malaysia. Another problem, the linkage of Bank ALs to other finance programs, such as the IMF stabilization agreement, was disentangled by regression analysis, which holds other influences constant.

Although both adjustment loan recipient and control groups grew more slowly in the early 1980s than in the late 1970s, the AL group had a significantly worse growth experience than the control group. Among the AL-assisted countries in which compliance with policy conditionality was high, growth was even more unfavorable compared to the relevant control group. While the standard deviations were large, the AL countries had a greater fall in investment rates (from cutting the government development budget, from the multiplier effect in lowering aggregate domestic demand, and from the lesser constraints on spending on consumer import goods compared to project aid), but a more substantial improvement in current-account balance, a lesser decline in real export growth, and

[21]Frances Stewart, "Are Adjustment Policies in Africa Consistent with Long-run Development Needs?" Paper presented to the American Economic Association, Washington, D.C., December 30, 1990.

[22]Food and Agriculture Organization of the U.N. (FAO), *The State of Food and Agriculture, 1990* (Rome, 1991), p. 115.

greater reduction in real import growth than non-AL countries (with all differences here and subsequently significant at the 5 percent level).[23]

Mosley, Harrigan, and Toye's regression-based results, which examine growth in all adjustment-loan countries, in sub-Saharan African countries, and in middle-income countries (with time lags varying from zero to 2 years) as a function of financial flows, compliance with Bank conditionality, and extraneous variables (weather and terms of trade), are consistent with their paired comparisons. Bank financial flows are negatively correlated but compliance with Bank conditions positively correlated with growth, so overall Bank program effects are nil (or perhaps negative, since the negative money effect is immediate, while the positive compliance effect, from price-based and other reforms, is lagged at least a year and uncertain to materialize). The authors explain the surprising negative effects of money flows by showing that they reduce pressures for policy reform and appreciate the real dollar price of domestic currency (as in "Dutch disease," discussed in Chapter 13). The same study found that Bank financial flows have a strong negative effect and compliance with Bank reform a strong positive impact on export growth in the immediate period, but the relationships are reversed for a longer period (1 or 2 years); the net effect of Bank programs on export growth is negative in the same and next years but positive 2 years hence. IMF standby credit, while positively related to middle-income countries' growth, is negatively correlated with sub-Saharan growth. Both weather and terms of trade improvement have a positive effect on growth.[24]

FAO, which examines the critical period after 1981–83, divided LDCs into healthy adjusters, who reduced internal and external deficits without jeopardizing growth, so savings and export earnings rose; unhealthy adjusters, who decreased the external deficit by restricting imports and investment, thus threatening the long-term capacity to expand; and deteriorators, whose internal and external deficits increased. Deteriorators appreciated their currencies in real terms, unhealthy adjusters' currencies did not change, and healthy ones depreciated currencies, resulting in the most success in improving their trade balances. Income distribution shifts following devaluation (for example, from urban to rural residents) sometimes contributed to a recession, at least in the short run.

While savings rates declined from the 1970s to the 1980s, they recovered substantially after 1981–83 in the healthy adjusters, while falling uninterruptedly among unhealthy adjusters and deteriorators. LDC import and investment rates declined during the depression of 1981–83, afterward recovering unevenly and contributing to growth in the healthily adjusting Latin American countries but not recovering in any major African country grouping.[25]

The assessment of World Bank/IMF adjustment programs is mixed, with Bank studies indicating their effectiveness but several independent empirical studies failing to show the success of these programs. These studies, taken as a whole, show that the record of growth, external balance, and social indicators of countries with strong Bank/IMF adjustment programs was no better than those with weak or no adjustment programs. Moreover, Bank/Fund programs reduce investment and social spending. Yet, the World Bank and IMF could argue that

[23]Paul Mosley, Jane Harrigan, and John Toye, *Aid and Power: The World Bank and Policy-based Lending*, vol. 1 (London: Routledge, 1991), 181–207.

[24]Ibid., pp. 208–32.

[25]Food and Agriculture Organization of the U.N., *The State of Food and Agriculture, 1990* (Rome, 1991), pp. 115–49.

these countries would have done worse with programs organized by national planners. Turning this statement on its head, many LDC leaders see no evidence that national planners do any worse than the Bank and Fund, but at least national adjustment plans provide indigenous people with experience and learning benefits. In the 1990s, the Bank and Fund have put more emphasis on increasing recipient capability to plan adjustment programs. Future research needs to assess this new emphasis by the World Bank and IMF.

The Sequence of Trade, Exchange Rate, and Capital Market Reform

Although price controls, exchange-rate misalignments, and government budget deficits contributed to the debt crisis, the immediate freeing of markets and contraction of spending may not resolve the disequilibrium. Many adjusting countries feel that the World Bank and IMF focus only on demand reduction. After 1981, the IMF emphasized shock treatment for demand restraint in low-income Africa, rarely providing financing for external adjustments, and cut programs from 3 years to 1 year. One year is not enough for adjustment. Demand restrictions, inflation deceleration, and currency depreciation do not switch expenditures to exports and import substitutes or expand primary production quickly enough to have the desired effect on prices and trade balance. Studies indicate that, even in DCs (for example, the United States, 1985–1988), the current-account improvement from devaluation usually takes about 2 to 5 years, usually beginning with a worsening trade balance in the first year. The time for adjustment is due to the lags between changes in relative international prices (from exchange-rate changes) and responses in quantities traded. Lags involve time for recognition, decision (assessing the change), delivery, replacement (waiting to use up inventories), and production.[26]

Trade liberalization in the midst of stabilization, even if politically possible, may perpetuate a government budget crisis. As Mosley, Harrigan, and Toye argue, given resource immobility, early liberalization of international trade and supply-side stimulation in "one glorious burst" result in rising unemployment, inflation, and capital flight and the subsequent undermining of adjustment programs. This trade-reform failure is consistent with the theory of the second best. An application of this theory suggests that trade liberalization while other prices are still controlled may be worse than having all prices distorted (see Chapter 18).

Mosley, Harrigan, and Toye and FAO suggest the following trade, exchange, and capital market liberalization sequence: (1) liberalizing imports of critical capital and other inputs, (2) devaluing domestic currency to a competitive level, while simultaneously restraining monetary and fiscal expansion to curb inflation and convert a nominal devaluation to a real devaluation,[27] (3) promoting exports through liberalizing commodity markets, subsidies, and other schemes, (4) allocating foreign exchange for maintaining and repairing infrastructure for production

[26]Herbert G. Grubel, *International Economics* (Homewood, Ill.: Irwin, 1981), pp. 349–88.

[27]Ronald I. McKinnon, *The Order of Economic Liberalization: Financial Control in the Transition to a Market Economy* (Baltimore: Johns Hopkins University Press, 1993), p. 5, emphasizes the importance of strict budget balance rather than moderate deficit financing. Tighter fiscal discipline is essential, he argues, to improve the expectations of the government's potential creditors, either foreign or domestic.

increases, (5) removing controls on internal interest rates to achieve positive real rates, and expanding loans agencies to include farmers and small business people, (6) reducing public sector deficits to eliminate reliance on foreign loans at banking standards without decreasing real development spending, and reforming agricultural marketing to spur farmers to sell their surplus, (7) liberalizing other imports, rationalizing the tariff structure,[28] and removing price controls and subsidies to the private sector, and (8) abandoning external capital-account controls.

The eighth step recognizes the necessity of reforming internal capital markets before liberalizing international capital movements. Critics contend that neither World Bank nor IMF recommendations or implementation bear much relationship to a sequence of reforms. Frequently, the World Bank asked for liberalizing trade early without limiting the imports that it should be applied to. For example, the foreign-exchange requirements associated with trade liberalization, the major component of the Bank's first structural adjustment loan in Kenya in 1980, became unsustainable, so liberalization had to be abandoned. Additionally, import liberalization preceded agricultural export expansion based on commodity market liberalization, price decontrol, and export promotional schemes. On the other hand, Ghana, under a World Bank sectoral adjustment loan beginning in 1983, allocated foreign exchange through an auction, and the goods eligible for entry to the auction expanded over time in line with the increased supply of foreign currency.

Moreover, recipients should implement IMF demand-reducing programs before the World Bank's supply-increasing ones. If countries begin with supply reforms which take a longer time, the lack of demand restraint will contribute to inflation and an unmanageable current-account deficit. Still, adjustment loan recipients also need to avoid excessive initial demand restraint that depresses the economy; simultaneous devaluation, as in stage 2, could avoid this contractionary effect.[29]

Public Enterprises and the Role of Public Goods

Speaking broadly, a public enterprise is a government entity that produces or supplies goods and services for the public. Even in a capitalist country like the United States, government produces **public goods** that the market fails to produce. Public goods like national defense and lighthouses are indivisible, involving large units that cannot be sold to individual buyers. Additionally, those who do not pay for the product cannot be excluded from its benefits. On the other hand, **quasi-public goods,** such as education and sewage disposal, while capable of being sold to individual buyers, entail substantial positive spillovers and would thus be underproduced by the market. Government agencies in the United States produce

---

[28]Because they control currency convertibility, state trading agencies in socialist economies could simply refuse to authorize imports. Thus, Ronald I. McKinnon, *The Order of Economic Liberalization: Financial Control in the Transition to a Market Economy* (Baltimore: Johns Hopkins University Press, 1993), pp. 7–9, 93, stresses the importance of LDCs, especially those in transition from a state-controlled economy, converting implicit quota restrictions into explicit tariffs. "Once formally codified, the highest tariffs . . . can then be reduced toward zero over a preannounced five- to ten-year adjustment period" (quotation from p. 9).

[29]Paul Mosley, Jane Harrigan, and John Toye, *Aid and Power: The World Bank and Policy-based Lending,* vol. 1 (London: Routledge, 1991), 110–16; and Food and Agriculture Organization of the U.N., *The State of Food and Agriculture, 1990* (Rome, 1991), pp. 101–03.

part or all of the following public or quasi-public goods: national defense, flood control, preventive medicine, lighthouses, parks, education, libraries, sewage disposal, postal service, water supplies, environmental protection, gas, electricity, and police and fire protection.[30] (Chapter 13 also discusses public goods.)

In most countries, however, as the discussion below implies, the government sector supplies more than public and quasi-public goods.

Importance of the Government Sector

In the early 1980s, government employment as a percentage of total nonagricultural employment was 24 percent for OECD countries and 44 percent for LDCs— 54 percent in Africa, 36 percent in Asia, and 27 percent in Latin America. In some countries, such as Benin, Ghana, and Zambia, the ratio was more than 70 percent. Government employment usually has a substantial effect on national wage determination where that employment comprises more than 20 to 25 percent of employment in the nonagricultural sector.

The LDCs have relied much less on state and local government than OECD countries. In the early 1980s, central government employment constituted about 85 percent of total government employment in LDCs and only 42 percent in OECD countries. At the same time, central government wages comprised 8 percent of LDC GDP compared to 5 percent for the OECD. Average LDC central government wages were 1.75 times the average wages in manufacturing, compared to only a 1.25 ratio in OECD countries.

Although the mean number of administrators per 100 population was rather similar for DCs and LDCs, African countries had the highest administrator ratio and Asian countries the lowest.[31]

As stated in Chapter 17, Nigeria's government spending as a share of GDP rose from the 1960s to the 1970s. However, during World Bank structural adjustment programs, 1986 to 1990, Nigeria's government expenditures fell substantially.[32] A number of other LDCs undertaking IMF or World Bank adjustment programs in the 1980s and 1990s also experienced a fall in government's share of spending.

Definition of State-Owned Enterprises

State-owned enterprises (SOEs), called **public enterprises** or **parastatals,** are common in transitional China, as well as market economies such as Taiwan, South Korea, and Brazil. Indeed the state sector's share of output is as large in each of these three countries as in India or Bangladesh, which have reputations for state intervention. Most SOEs are in large-scale manufacturing, public utilities (electricity,

---

[30]Karl E. Case and Ray C. Fair, *Principles of Economics* (Englewood Cliffs, N.J.: Prentice Hall, 1996), pp. 313–15, 417–23; and Campbell R. McConnell, *Economics: Principles, Problems, and Policies* (New York: McGraw-Hill, 1987), pp. 93–94.

[31]Peter Heller and Alan Tait, "Government Employment and Pay: Some International Comparisons," *Finance and Development* 20 (September 1983): 44–47.

[32]E. Wayne Nafziger, *Inequality in Africa: Political Elites, Proletariat, Peasants, and the Poor* (Cambridge: Cambridge University Press, 1988), p. 100; and E. Wayne Nafziger, *The Debt Crisis in Africa* (Cambridge: Cambridge University Press, 1993), p. 50.

gas, and water), plantation agriculture, mining, finance, transport, and communication.

For this chapter's discussion, a state enterprise consists of an enterprise (1) where government is the principal (not necessarily majority) owner or where the state can appoint or remove the chief executive officer (president or managing director) and (2) which produces or sells goods or services to the public or other enterprises, where revenues are to bear some relationship to cost. Public enterprises that do not maximize profitability may still qualify if they pursue profit subject to some limitation assigned by the state.[33] This narrow definition of state-owned enterprises differentiates public *enterprises* producing steel, palm products, electricity, and telephone, telegraph, banking, and bus services from public *agencies* that run schools, libraries, agricultural extension services, and police departments. The United States, with SOEs that include municipally owned public utilities, intracity transport, the post office, and the Tennessee Valley Authority, has fewer public enterprises than most DCs and LDCs.

Size of the State-Owned Sector

Given this definition, the contribution of state-owned enterprises to GDP in developing countries increased from 7 percent in 1970 to 10 percent in 1980 (the last figure the same as in DCs in 1980). The 1980 LDC figures varied from a high of 64 percent in Hungary (excluding cooperatives) and 38 percent in Ghana and Zambia to a low of 2 to 3 percent in the Philippines and Nepal, but most countries ranged from 7 to 15 percent.[34]

In 1980, 13 percent of LDC nonagricultural employment was in nonfinancial public enterprises compared to 4 percent in the OECD. Public enterprise employees were 1 percent of the total population in LDCs compared to 1.5 percent in the OECD.[35] However, in the 1980s and early 1990s, output and employment shares in LDCs' public sector fell, as IMF and World Bank lending to resolve external crises was usually linked to programs including privatization of public enterprise and reform of state-owned enterprises sector.

Arguments for Public Enterprises

Social profitability, in excess of financial profitability, provides major reasons for public enterprise. Public investment can create external economies, improve integration between sectors, produce social goods for low-income earners, and raise the capital essential for overcoming indivisibilities. Frequently, officials indicate that creating new jobs is the rationale for establishing state enterprises. Moreover, public firms can rescue bankrupt private firms in key sectors, or state initiative can substitute for private entrepreneurship when risk is high, capital markets are poor, or information is sparse. Finally, governments have noneconomic reasons

---

[33]Malcolm Gillis, Dwight H. Perkins, Michael Roemer, and Donald R. Snodgrass, *Economics of Development* (New York: Norton, 1987), p. 569.

[34]World Bank, *World Development Report, 1983* (New York: Oxford University Press, 1983), pp. 49–50.

[35]Peter Heller and Alan Tait, "Government Employment and Pay: Some International Comparisons," *Finance and Development* 20 (September 1983), 44–47.

for creating SOEs, including control of key sectors, wresting control from foreign owners or minority ethnic communities, responding to foreign donor pressure, or to serve other social and political goals, such as avoiding concentration of economic power among private oligopolists.

Performance of Private and Public Enterprises

EFFICIENCY

Impressions of the superior performance of private enterprise often originate in anecdotes and informal case studies of Western business people and aid officials. British economist Robert Millward carefully examines studies comparing economic efficiency to test these impressions. Few studies measure precisely the performance of public and private firms of the same size, type, and product mix, and adjust for factor prices across enterprises that management cannot control (for example, the higher wage rates and cheaper capital that public enterprises face).[36]

Studies comparing U.S. and British electricity and transport enterprises in private and public sectors indicate that productivity or cost effectiveness was as high in the public sector as in the private sector. Yet public firms, which charge lower prices, have lower financial profitability than private enterprises.

The following three LDC studies compare public and private firms, while statistically holding other variables equal. W. G. Tyler's analysis of the Brazilian steel industry indicates that if you control for size, whether a firm was privately or publicly owned had no significant impact on technical efficiency. K. S. Kim finds that government ownership had no significant effect on efficiency in Tanzania's food and machinery industries. H. Hill's study of automated weaving in Indonesia indicates that the higher productivity of private firms relative to state firms was explained by diseconomies of scale of the larger state firms.[37]

Thus the Millward survey concludes that the efficiency of public and private enterprises is comparable, given a certain size firm. Indeed, even the World Bank contended in 1983: "the key factor determining the efficiency of an enterprise is not whether it is publicly or privately owned, but how it is managed." If entry barriers are removed, the World Bank report states, there is no presumption that the private sector has better management.[38] However, Millward indicates that the variation in technical efficiency from best- to worst-practice firms is greater among government firms than private firms. Furthermore, public enterprises are more likely than private enterprises to choose an excessive scale of operations. Public firms have easier access to state financing to mute bankruptcy and more pressure to provide jobs and contracts to clients and relatives than private enterprises, as the case studies below on Russia and China indicate. As the IMF points

---

[36]The rest of this section is based largely on Robert Millward, "Measured Sources of Inefficiency in the Performance of Private and Public Enterprises in LDCs," in Paul Cook and Colin Kirkpatrick, eds., *Privatisation in Less-Developed Countries* (Sussex, U.K.: Wheatsheaf, 1988), pp. 143–61.

[37]Ibid.; W. G. Tyler, "Technical Efficiency in Production in a Developing Country: An Empirical Examination of the Brazilian Plastics and Steel Industries," *Oxford Economic Papers* 31 (November 1979): 477–95; and K. S. Kim, "Enterprise Performance in the Public and Private Sectors: Tanzanian Experience, 1970–5," *Journal of Developing Areas* 15 (April 1981): 471–84; H. Hill, "State Enterprises in a Competitive Industry: An Indonesian Case Study," *World Development* 10 (1982): 1015–23.

[38]World Bank, *World Development Report, 1983* (New York: Oxford University Press, 1983), p. 50.

out, "Over the years, inefficiency has flourished in many state enterprises, its overt consequences masked by the ready availability of budgetary support."[39]

EMPLOYMENT

Despite political pressures to overstaff LDC state enterprises, most SOEs are more capital-intensive than private firms, which avoid entering capital-intensive sectors because they are characterized by high risk and substantial economies of scale.[40] Also the emphasis of state ownership of the commanding heights—heavy industry, mining, transport, and banking—means high capital-labor ratios, which, as Chapter 9 indicates, are associated with high unemployment rates, as in Algeria. Brazil's and India's public enterprise sector is several times (and South Korea's nine times) more capital-intensive than the private sector.[41]

Politicians, in both LDCs and rich countries, often use employment as a rationale for initiating or rescuing projects with high capital intensity. In the United States, the "bail outs" of Lockheed, Chrysler, and Continental Illinois Bank and bids by governmental units on super accelerators or sports franchises, all capital intensive, were justified by employment effects, despite the high employment opportunity costs of these investments.

SAVINGS

Even Ghana's Nkrumah, Africa's most radical nationalist leader in the 1950s and early 1960s, thinks the SOEs should contribute capital for other public services:

> I must make it clear that these state enterprises were not set up to lose money at the expense of the taxpayers. Like all business undertakings, they are expected to maintain themselves efficiently, and to show profits. Such profits should be sufficient to build up capital for further investment as well as to finance a large proportion of the public services which it is the responsibility of the state to provide.[42]

But Table 20–1 indicates that in the late 1970s, SOEs in 33 of 34 LDCs incurred overall deficits, which means a deterioration of capital resources (or negative savings). This is despite the fact that SOEs frequently enjoy monopoly privileges, especially in mineral and energy resources.

A separate study on South Korea by Young C. Park indicates that South Korean government-invested enterprises had a 3.7-percent rate of return to capital in

---

[39]International Monetary Fund, *World Economic Outlook* (Washington, D.C., 1986), p. 16. See also Bertil Walstedt, *State Manufacturing Enterprise in a Mixed Economy* (Baltimore: Johns Hopkins University Press, 1980); and Charles Wolf, Jr., *Markets or Governments: Choosing between Imperfect Alternatives* (Cambridge, Mass.: MIT Press, 1988).

[40]Malcolm Gillis, Dwight H. Perkins, Michael Roemer, and Donald R. Snodgrass, *Economics of Development* (New York: Norton, 1987), pp. 581–82.

[41]John B. Sheahan, "Public Enterprise in Developing Countries," in W. G. Shepherd, ed., *Public Enterprise: Economic Analysis of Theory and Practice* (Lexington, Mass: Lexington Books, 1976), p. 211, on Brazil, India, and Algeria; and Leroy P. Jones, *Public Enterprise and Economic Development* (Seoul: Korea Development Institute, 1976), p. 123, on Korea.

[42]Kwame Nkrumah, *Revolutionary Path* (New York: International Publishers, 1973), p. 37, from a 1964 speech.

TABLE 20–1	Overall Deficits[a] or Surpluses of Public Enterprises as Percent of GDP		
		Surplus (+) or Deficit (−) as % of GDP	
	Latest Period of Data	Latest Period	Next Latest Period
Africa			
Botswana	1978–80	−0.6	−4.7
Guinea	1978–79	−23.4	−8.0
Ivory Coast	1978–79	−8.4	−3.5
Malawi	1978	−3.5	−2.5
Mali	1978	−2.7	−5.9
Senegal	1974	+2.2	
Tanzania	1974–75	−2.8	−2.6
Zambia	1972	−3.4	
Asia			
Burma	1978–80	−10.6	−1.2
India	1978	−6.2	−6.3
Nepal	1974–75	−2.1	−0.5
South Korea	1978–80	−5.2	−5.4
Taiwan	1978–80	−5.5	−7.3
Thailand	1978–79	−2.0	−1.1
Southern Europe			
Greece	1979	−1.6	−1.6
Portugal	1978–80	−8.1	
Turkey	1978–80	−7.5	−7.0
Latin America			
Argentina	1976–77	−3.1	
Bolivia	1974–77	−4.4	−4.5
Brazil	1980	−1.7	
Chile	1978–80	−0.4	−0.2
Colombia	1978–80	−0.1	−0.9
Costa Rica	1977–79	−4.4	
Dominican Rep.	1978–79	−1.6	−0.2
Guatemala	1978–80	−2.1	−1.8
Haiti	1978–80	−0.9	−2.0
Honduras	1978–79	−2.3	
Jamaica	1978–80	−2.3	−4.3
Mexico	1978	−3.7	−3.9
Panama	1978–79	−7.1	−7.1
Paraguay	1978–80	−0.9	−1.6
Peru	1974–77	−1.7	−4.8
Uruguay	1978–80	−0.8	
Venezuela	1978–80	−5.1	−5.2

[a]Revenue plus receipts of current and capital transfers minus (current and capital) expenditures.
Source: R. P. Short, "The Role of Public Enterprises: An International Statistical Comparison," working paper of the International Monetary Fund, Fiscal Affairs Department, Washington, D.C., May 17, 1983, pp. 30–36.

1982, lower than the 10.1 percent figure for Korean industry generally but higher than government enterprises in most other LDCs. However, the government's 1983 comprehensive public enterprise reform program, which eliminated day-to-day interferences by technical ministries, simplified and unified external audits, provided for an objectives-oriented evaluation and incentive system, and gave management greater power over procurement, budgeting, and personnel, improved subsequent performance.[43]

SOCIAL AND POLITICAL GOALS

Chapter 11 discussed investment to create integration and externalities, to overcome indivisibilities, and reduce monopolies. Some LDCs, although fewer than in the 1980s, are committed to increasing the socialization of capital and land for political reasons. But additionally the fact that DC (even U.S.) banks and aid agencies have found it convenient to hold the LDC government responsible for performance, payments, and debt has encouraged state-controlled enterprise.

Can the state subsidize public enterprises to redistribute goods to the poor? Chapters 6 and 7 indicate the difficulties of using the state to redistribute income.

An SOE should pay for itself in the long run unless the enterprise redistributes income to lower-income recipients (or fulfills some other objective discussed above, such as creating externalities). A public enterprise that does not pay for itself, where the recipient of the service is not charged an economic price, involves a subsidy to him or her. Since the alternative to a subsidy is resource allocation to another project, the burden of proof should fall on the subsidy's advocate.[44] This redistribution policy would be consistent with, for instance, subsidies to goods consumed disproportionately by the poor, such as sorghum (Bangladesh in 1978) and low-quality rice (Sri Lanka, 1968–77), but not with subsidies for fuel (Nigeria, 1980), electricity (most of Africa), or food generally (Poland and Tanzania in the early 1980s) in urban areas with above-average incomes.

Determinants of Public Enterprise Performance

Why do some public enterprises perform better than others? Why do SOEs in South Korea and Sweden generally achieve better economic results than those in Ghana? Why is India's Hindustan Machine Tools dynamic when most other Indian public enterprises are far less successful?

1. State enterprises perform better with competition; no investment licensing; no price, entry, nor exit controls; and liberal trade policies (low tariffs, no import quotas, and exchange rates close to market prices). In Pakistan the highly profitable parastatal Heavy Mechanical Complex faces competition from the privatized Ittefaq Foundry in road rollers and sugar mills' output; with imports and another public enterprise (Karachi Shipyard) in constructing cement plants; and with SOE Pakistan Engineering Company in manufacturing electrical towers, boilers, and overhead traveling cranes. Since 1969, India's Hindustan has learned much about remaining competitive from exporting, which has exposed the company to new technologies and management approaches. When economies of scale are not important, breaking up large enterprises, such as the Bolivian Mining Corporation and Sweden's Statsforetag (a holding company), can increase competition.[45]

---

[43]Young C. Park, "Evaluating the Performance of Korea's Government-invested Enterprises," *Finance and Development* 24 (June 1987): 25–27.

[44]Tariffs have an effect similar to subsidies. Government distorts prices, benefiting special interests by redistributing income from consumers or merchants to industrialists.

[45]This section is based on Mahmood A. Ayub and Sven O. Hegstad, "Determinants of Public Enterprise Performance," *Finance and Development* 24 (December 1987): 26–29.

2. Successful performing SOEs, such as those in Japan, Singapore, Sweden, Brazil, and post-1983 South Korea, have greater managerial autonomy and accountability than others do.[46] Excessive interference in investment, product mix, pricing, hiring and firing workers, setting wages, and procurement by government suffocates managerial initiative and contributes to operational inefficiencies. Government should demarcate its role (as owner), the board of directors' role (setting broad policy), and the enterprise management role (day-to-day operations). Central or local government rarely has the information or the skills essential for detailed control over parastatal operations. South Korea's 1983 reform is a good example of increasing managerial autonomy and reducing government interference.

Good management usually requires decentralizing power in favor of a professionally skilled board of directors and judging managers by enterprise viability and a limited number of performance indicators. In Sweden the cabinet (the formal owner of the limited liability SOE stock corporation) delegates ownership responsibility to a staff of eight professionals in the Ministry of Industry, which oversees 90,000 people in state industries. These professionals do not overpower the board with their ownership role except in times of crisis or when state financial support is required. Korea's reforms also increased decentralization and evaluation by enterprise performance.

Until the mid-1980s, managers of SOEs, which comprised 60 percent of Ghana's industrial output, had poor performance and little autonomy. In practice a Ministry of Finance and Economic Planning board set prices and approved wage contracts; the Ministry of Labor authorized worker dismissal; the Ministries of Trade and Finance allocated import licenses; the Bank of Ghana approved import licenses; and the Ghana Investment Center and the Ministry of Interior approved foreign staff quotas.

While many LDCs suffer from the Ghanaian problem of too much interference and unclear, fragmented lines of authority, other LDCs lack any effective control, creating uncertainty, misunderstanding, and distrust, with reactions sometimes swinging to the other pole, excessive control.

Financial autonomy is a major factor contributing to SOE managerial effectiveness. Two French steel parastatals, Usinor and Sacilor, which acquired funds for expansion from their government ministry, have had chronic losses. But public firms scrutinized by independent bankers before getting investment funds usually perform better. Excellent financial management involves specifying financial objectives, monitoring their progress, and holding managers accountable. Government should set SOE noneconomic goals clearly and evaluate whether the firm is using the most cost-effective way of achieving the goal, so that SOE managers do not use these same goals as an excuse for poor performance. In the mid-1980s, Zambia imposed price controls on refined oil and fats used for vegetable oil products and soaps. The controls resulted in large losses and poor staff morale and shifted output away from oil and fats, the opposite of the government's social priorities. Finally government should not allow substantial transfers between SOEs and government to undermine firms' ability to acquire "true" financial results.

---

[46]Harinder S. Kohli and Anil Sood, "Fostering Enterprise Development," *Finance and Development* 24 (March 1987): 34–36.

3. Government reduces (or keeps) the size of the public sector commensurate with technical and managerial skills. Beginning in 1983, South Korea privatized a number of SOEs to improve the effectiveness of government oversight.[47]

Privatization

Privatization refers to a range of policies including (1) changing at least part of an enterprise's ownership from the public to the private sector (through equity sales to the public or sale of the complete enterprise when capital markets are poorly developed), (2) liberalization of entry into activities previously restricted to the public sector, and (3) franchising or contracting public services or leasing public assets to the private sector. Government needs improved competition policy in the private sector if denationalization is to result in gains in allocative efficiency. A government selling a public enterprise faces a tradeoff between the higher sale price when a privatized firm is offered market protection and the greater economic efficiency when the firm operates under competitive market conditions.[48]

Some Pitfalls of Privatization

The transition from centrally managed state enterprises to a liberal, privatized economy is politically and technically difficult. Prices masked by controls inevitably rise. Forcing inefficient firms to close is likely to be unacceptable where labor is not mobile, as in Africa, or unions are well-organized, as in India. Skilled people are usually lacking. Moreover, government may require parastatals to achieve social objectives, such as setting quality standards, investing in infrastructure, producing social goods (especially for low-income earners), controlling sectors vital for national security, wresting control from foreign owners or minority ethnic communities, rescuing bankrupt firms in key sectors, avoiding private oligopolistic concentration, raising capital essential for overcoming indivisibilities, producing vital inputs cheaply for the domestic market, capturing gains from technological learning, and creating other external economies that private firms would overlook. To illustrate, Nigeria's abolition of the government Cocoa Marketing Board and licenses for marketing cocoa in 1987 resulted in poor quality control and fraudulent trading practices, which adversely affected the reputation of Nigeria's cocoa exports. The government subsequently incurred substantial costs reintroducing inspection procedures and marketing licenses.[49]

Moreover, the effectiveness of creating market incentives and deregulating state controls presupposes a class able and willing to respond by innovating, bearing risk, and mobilizing capital. While significant groups of indigenous entrepreneurs have emerged in South Korea, Taiwan, Brazil, Kenya, Nigeria, and the Ivory Coast, the private sector in Bangladesh, Haiti, Tanzania, and Zambia, for example, is much more limited. Additionally, some regimes have restricted the commercial and industrial enterprises of such visible minorities as the Asians in East Africa.

---

[47]Young C. Park, "Evaluating the Performance of Korea's Government-invested Enterprises," *Finance and Development* 24 (June 1987), 25–27.

[48]Paul Cook and Colin Kirkpatrick, eds., *Privatisation in Less Developed Countries* (Sussex, U.K.: Wheatsheaf, 1988), pp. 3–44.

[49]Paul Hackett, "Economy," in *Africa South of the Sahara* (London: Europa Publications, 1990), p. 776.

Even where privatization is desirable, government may want to proceed slowly to avoid a highly concentrated business elite being created from newly privatized firms falling into a few hands, as was true during indigenization. It would be ironic if two goals of privatization—improvements of efficiency and competition—were sabotaged because of creation of new oligopolies from a limited number of buyers. Moreover, the fact that the private sector may lack the requisite business skills and experience means that an emphasis on providing private competition to the public sector and a gradual reduction of the relative size of the public sector may be preferable to abrupt privatization. To quote a publication of the World Bank/International Monetary Fund: "The rationale for privatization is most straightforward and least controversial where a public enterprise is engaged in a purely commercial activity and is already subject to competition."[50]

While Ghana's reform of state-owned enterprises (SOEs) in the 1980s was to enhance their competitiveness and management responsibility, restructuring failed to modify management or corporate boards, criteria for management promotion and pay, or rules for allocating capital between SOEs. Indeed, existing managers, many of whom should have been discharged, oversaw enterprise divestiture, work-force retrenchment and restructuring as unrelated activities, disproportionately laying off production workers and retaining administrative and clerical staff, and sometimes, in the absence of guidelines for work-force requirements, reporting no redundant staff.[51]

Public Enterprises and Multinational Corporations

Many LDCs, including much of Latin America as well as South Korea, Taiwan, India, and Indonesia, view SOEs as a counterbalance to the power of MNCs, especially as SOEs began moving into markets previously dominated by MNCs.[52] Yet since the 1970s, joint SOE–MNC ventures and other forms of domestic-foreign tie-ins have become more common and MNC-domestic private firm ventures much less common. At best in these ventures, the LDC government can protect its national interest better, while MNCs can reduce political risks. But for some LDCs, especially in Africa, expanding public enterprises frequently did not reduce dependence much on MNCs, as indicated by our discussion of Nigeria in Chapters 13 and 14. Multinational corporate ownership was replaced by MNC-state joint enterprises, which enriched private middlemen and women and enlarged the patronage base for state officials, but did little to develop Nigerian administrative and technological skills for subsequent industrialization. Kenya, Tanzania, Zäire, Malawi, and the Ivory Coast made even less progress than Nigeria in using public enterprises to reduce dependence on MNCs.[53] Tropical African countries have

[50]World Bank and International Monetary Fund, Joint Ministerial Committee of the Boards of Governors, *Problems and Issues in Structural Adjustment* (Washington, D.C., 1989), p. 83.

[51]J. Tait Davis, "Institutional Impediments to Workforce Retrenchment and Restructuring in Ghana's State Enterprises," *World Development* 19 (August 1991): 987–1005.

[52]Malcolm Gillis, Dwight H. Perkins, Michael Roemer, and Donald R. Snodgrass, *Economics of Development* (New York: Norton, 1987), p. 584; and Raymond Vernon, "The State-Owned Enterprise in Latin American Export," in Werner Baer and Malcolm Gillis, eds., *Trade Prospects among the Americas* (Urbana: National Bureau of Economic Research and University of Illinois Press, 1981), pp. 98–114.

[53]E. Wayne Nafziger, *Inequality in Africa: Political Elites, Proletariat, Peasants, and the Poor* (Cambridge: Cambridge University Press, 1988), p. 53.

been less successful than Argentina, Brazil, Mexico, Peru, Venezuela, South Korea, Taiwan, India, and Indonesia in using MNC technology transfer to improve their own industrial capabilities.

Adjustment and Liberalization in Eastern Europe, the Former Soviet Union, and China

This model of internal and external balances clarifies the need for: macroeconomic stabilization to adjust to external deficits and debts and stagnation or collapse of the domestic economy, and structural (or supply-side) adjustments, including economic liberalization and reform, for long-term remediation of LDCs. From the perspective of the International Monetary Fund, World Bank, and the **European Bank for Reconstruction and Development (EBRD)**, a development bank based in London, which loans funds to governments of Eastern Europe and the former Soviet Union, virtually every developing and transitional countries needs to adjust and reform. As IMF Managing Director Jacques de Larosiere asserted in 1987: "Adjustment is now virtually universal [among LDCs]. . . . Never before has there been such an extensive yet convergent adjustment effort."[54] Since the collapse of communism, the IMF would add transitional countries to other LDCs.

The remainder of this chapter shows some concrete problems in undertaking reform and adjustment in transitional economies. This discussion focuses more attention on China, Russia, other states in the former Soviet Union, and Eastern Europe, because their experiences demonstrate in starkest fashion some of the prospects and problems from economic liberalization and reform. To be sure, the developing countries of Africa, Asia, and Latin America have undergone painful institutional and structural adjustments to reform their economies, but these changes have been less abrupt and the consequences less astounding than in Russia and Eastern Europe.

In 1960, a confident Soviet Premier Nikita Khrushchev, while at a summit meeting with President Dwight D. Eisenhower in the United States, boasted that "we will bury you" and predicted that Soviets would be more prosperous than Americans by 1980. However, the Soviet Union suffered through stagnation during the 1970s and early 1980s, so that, according to Harvard's Abram Bergson, in 1985, when Communist Party leader Mikhail Gorbachev came to power, consumption per capita in the Soviet Union was only about 29 percent of that in the United States[55] (see Chapter 3).

Socialism collapsed in Eastern Europe about 1989 and in the Soviet Union in 1991. These countries have faced painful transitions to a market economy, with substantial reductions in real GDP in the early 1990s before eventually attaining positive growth. Indeed the transition is like a valley between the two hills of communism and capitalism. The London *Economist* projects that most of Eastern Europe will have achieved its 1989 level of real GDP in the mid-1990s, except for Bulgaria, Romania, and the former Yugoslavia, which will probably not attain 1989 real output levels until the end of the twentieth century; Russia and the for-

---

[54]*IMF Survey* (February 23, 1987), p. 50.

[55]Abram Bergson, "The USSR Before the Fall: How Poor and Why," *Journal of Economic Perspectives* 5 (Fall 1991): 29–44.

mer Soviet Union are not expected to perform any better than Bulgaria and Romania in attaining 1989 levels of GDP.[56]

The 1995 real GDP in Russia, according to its State Statistics Committee (*Goskomstat*), shrunk to 48 percent of its 1989 pre-transition peak. Ukraine and Kazakstan suffered cumulative output declines of the same order of magnitude during the same period. The IMF estimates that, if you adjust for "black market" or unmeasured sales, real GDP for Russia, Ukraine, and Kazakstan may have fallen only one-third from 1989 to 1994. Still, average living standards probably decreased less than one-third during the period because of investment declines, a fall in the production of goods not desired by consumers, a reduction in searching and queuing costs due to the charging of market prices resulting from liberalization, and the cutback in waste and other inefficient resource use with the demise of central planning. Nevertheless, average living standards declined in the three former Soviet states from 1989 to 1994.[57] Among Eastern European and former Soviet states, Poland had the highest 1994 real GDP as a percentage of 1989 real GDP, 90.9 percent. Real output in Poland fell substantially, 1989 to 1991, but began recovering in 1992, after which its growth was one of the fastest in Europe. The 1994 GDP of Hungary was 81.7 percent of 1989 GDP, and its turn-around occurred in 1994. For other countries, 1994 GDP as a percentage of 1989 GDP was 71.1 in Bulgaria, 70.4 in Albania, 68.0 in Romania, and 50.7 in the former Yugoslavia.[58]

Economists debate whether the transition to the market should be gradual or abrupt. Harvard's Jeffrey Sachs, an advisor to the governments of Solidarity leader Lech Walesa in Poland and later Boris Yeltsin in Russia in their transitions to the market, argues in favor of "**shock therapy**," an abrupt transition to adjustment and the market.[59] Howard Wachtel, an evolutionist who emphasizes the gradual building of institutions, contends that shock therapy downplays the creation of a small-scale private sector, small independent banks, market reforms in agriculture, and funds for a "safety net" for social programs and full employment for the population.[60] Indeed by the mid-1990s, electorates in Poland, Russia, and Hungary, disillusioned with market reforms, voted the former Communist Party, often refashioned as social democrats or democratic socialists, to a parliamentary plurality in place of the party of economic reform. In response to critics of "shock therapy," Sachs argues correctly that production in the Soviet Union was in decline, inflation rates were surging, and the black-market value of the ruble was falling in the immediate years before Yeltsin's transitional government came into power in late 1991. Moreover, Sachs charges that United States and International Monetary Fund aid to Russia was disbursed too slowly, and that "shock therapy" could not have failed because it was never tried.[61]

[56]*Economist* (September 21, 1991): S4.

[57]International Monetary Fund, *World Economic Outlook, May 1995* (Washington, D.C., 1995), p. 57; and International Monetary Fund, *World Economic Outlook, October 1995* (Washington, D.C., 1995), p. 20.

[58]International Monetary Fund, *World Economic Outlook, October 1994* (Washington, D.C., 1994), p. 66.

[59]Jeffrey Sachs, *Poland's Jump to the Market Economy* (Cambridge, Mass.: MIT Press, 1993).

[60]Howard M. Wachtel, "Common Sense about Post-Soviet Economic Reforms," *Challenge* 38 (January-February 1992): 46–48.

[61]Jeffrey Sachs, "Betrayal: How Clinton Failed Russia," *New Republic* (January 31, 1994), pp. 14–18.

The Collapse of State Socialism and Problems with Subsequent Economic Reform in Russia

Since the late 1980s, state socialism has been falling apart before our eyes. The Soviet Union measured income as **net material product (NMP)**, that is, gross domestic product minus nonmaterial services, depreciation, and rent. From 1981 to 1990, income fell by 3 percent, after which it collapsed. Inflation, repressed under communism, was 19 percent in 1990, 93 percent in 1991, 1353 percent in 1992, 915 percent in 1993, and 336 percent in 1994, according to the International Monetary Fund.[62] Following are some of the reasons for the collapse of state socialism in Russia and its subsequent problems with liberalization, a case study that should provide insight into liberalization and adjustment in other developing countries, even though their collapses and transitions were less dramatic.

DISTORTED INCENTIVES AND PRICE SIGNALS

Under Soviet central planning, firms produced low quality output, with incorrect assortments, avoiding preshrunk fabrics or reducing the impurities of metals, as bonuses depend on the quantity of output. To maximize output, managers were tempted to reduce quality and disregard the composition of demand. If the rewards for nail output is gauged in tons, only giant nails will get produced, while if the output plan is stated in numbers of nails, firms will make only the tiniest ones.[63]

Soviet planning involved **material balance planning**, the detailed allocation by central administration of the supply and demand for basic industrial commodities. The material balance system was slow, cumbersome, lacked clarity, and distorted incentives. The Soviets used the previous year's production as the target for the next year. Enterprises work for part of the year without knowing what their targets are. Toward the end of the month or year, they may engage in "storming" to reach the target, or deliberately slow down operations so as not to increase targets too much for the subsequent period. The enterprise management's motivation is to hide the true capabilities of the plant from planners.

Administered input prices do not show where the firm can best use resources, thus providing false signals to firms. These establishments overorder and hoard labor and raw materials since they do not bear the cost of excess inputs needed to meet quotas or as insurance against future shortages.[64]

Incentive schemes reward managers for maximizing variables such as output rather than profit or efficiency. But even profits are poor guides to enterprise behavior when prices are set without reference to supply and demand. These prices give the wrong signal, spurring enterprises to produce too little of what is short and too much of what is in surplus. Moreover, the weak link between do-

---

[62]International Monetary Fund, *World Economic Outlook, October 1994* (Washington, D.C., 1994), pp. 65–67.

[63]Heinz Kohler, "Soviet Central Planning," in David Kennett and Marc Lieberman, eds., *The Road to Capitalism: Economic Transformation in Eastern Europe and the Former Soviet Union* (Fort Worth, Tex.: Dryden, 1992), pp. 5–14.

[64]Heinz Kohler, "Soviet Central Planning," in David Kennett and Marc Lieberman, eds., *The Road to Capitalism: Economic Transformation in Eastern Europe and the Former Soviet Union* (Fort Worth, Tex.: Dryden, 1992), p. 12.

mestic and international prices erodes the government's response in identifying and closing inefficient enterprises.[65]

THE PARTY AND STATE MONOPOLY

The Communist Party, with its interlocking and overlapping authority over the Soviet government, an institution with highly embedded interests, had a monopoly over political power, which also meant a monopoly over economic power. "Redness" or political correctness was a more important criterion than expertness in making decisions.

The party, as controller of the state, bore the full burden of economic management. Party leadership gained from concentration and limiting competition, as managers and workers received rewards for increased enterprise profits and revenues. Dissatisfaction with economic performance became a direct challenge to the political order. The position and authority of party leaders and enterprise managers were threatened by discussion, intellectual ferment, and technical innovation.

Even reforms that encouraged entrepreneurial activity suffered from the Communist Old Guard's advantages in obtaining permits and access to funds. Under reform, managers, bureaucrats, and party apparatchiks gained control of the more viable socialist enterprises through privatization. In other cases, government officials looted the enterprises, either controlling the newly privatized firms or leaving no assets for others. After 1988, managers (and other shareholders, including sometimes workers and local governments) gained autonomy at the expense of departments (ministries), who no longer could appoint them.[66]

The Soviet leadership fused the state with the economy, creating a built-in bias against change. State socialism had evolved after Stalin's period, and had become softer, leakier, and less oppressive over time. Decentralization meant the decay of the party and state, and their roles in the economy. More sophisticated methods of control replaced the brutal, random, and indiscriminate repression of Stalinism. However, the Soviet leadership did not match this softness with institutional changes recognizing the greater autonomy of decentralized units. Indeed as these units amassed greater control over their surpluses, they reduced the sequestering of these surpluses by the central government, eroding its system for revenue collection[67] (see Chapter 15).

Gorbachev and the reformers implementing perestroika overestimated the reformability of Soviet socialism, which after years of suppression of interest and voice, had little capacity for adaptation, redesign, or self-correction. Bartlomiej Kaminski argues that state socialism is nonreformable, as direct controls were essential for the party and state to defend its privileged position. Party officials and apparatchiks opposed, and even sabotaged, reform because it reduces their power

[65]Bartlomiej Kaminski, *The Collapse of State Socialism: The Case of Poland* (Princeton: Princeton University Press, 1992), p. 41.

[66]Bartlomiej Kaminski, *The Collapse of State Socialism: The Case of Poland* (Princeton: Princeton University Press, 1992), p. 25; Thomas E. Weisskopf, "Russia in Transition: Perils of the Fast Track to Capitalism," *Challenge* 38 (November-December 1992): 28–37; and Oliver Blanchard; Maxim Boycko; Marek Dabrowski; Rudiger Dornbusch; Richard Layard; and Andrei Shleifer, *Post-Communist Reform: Pain and Progress* (Cambridge, Mass.: MIT Press, 1993), pp. 42–44.

[67]Ronald I. McKinnon, *The Order of Economic Liberalization: Financial Control in the Transition to a Market Economy* (Baltimore: Johns Hopkins University Press, 1993), pp. 122–23.

and their ability to solicit kickbacks and other benefits. The large number of officials operating in the black market opposed the effect of market reform, which reduced the black market and officials' incomes and profits. The party monopolized policy initiatives, channeling special interests into association with the party.

Pathologies endemic to the Soviet bureaucracy included secrecy, formalism, cumbersome procedures, rigidity, and the tendency to concentrate on control rather than performance. The party controlled the state by using the **nomenklatura system**,[68] the power to recommend and approve managers in administration and enterprises, of appointments and promotions to control access to government positions. In 1994, James R. Millar argued that

> the "party" is over, but the nomenklatura lives on. The old members of the nomenklatura still occupy the top positions in Russian society: in industry, government, educational and research establishments, [and] the Duma. . . . The [educated and successful] nomenklatura . . . forms a self-aware network that knows how to protect itself. . . . Meanwhile the nomenklatura is quietly repositioning itself to control the new private economy.[69]

Decision making in the Soviet Union was highly centralized, with the Communist Party, its General Secretary (later the country's President), the Politburo (the policy-setting body appointed by the party), and **Gosplan** (the State Planning Committee, which reported directly to the Politburo) making the decisions. Centralized decision helped focus on particular sectors and provide resources for them. When Gorbachev removed Gosplan and central management, factories, cities, regions, and republics (independent states after 1991) were free to do what they thought best, resulting in new independently decision-making organizations, thus destabilizing the economy.[70]

According to Gary Krueger, Gorbachev did not sequence perestroika (economic restructuring) correctly. He decentralized decision making to the enterprise without introducing the market mechanism and price reform. While enterprises made more of their decisions and were self-financing, they still were obligated to make deliveries at set prices to state agencies; prices were not adjusted to reflect supply and demand.

State enterprise law, implemented after 1968, meant that Gosplan and **Gosagroprom**, the State Agro-Industrial Committee (replaced by **Gossnab**, the State Commission of Food and Procurement in 1989), substituted state orders for plan targets. Central intervention fell dramatically, from 1987 to 1989, with the number of centrally distributed commodities declining from 13,000 to 618. The state order system still made production decisions at the highest level but no longer disaggregated these decisions at the enterprise level. Enterprises stopped producing low-profit items, increased their barter, and concentrated on potentially high-value commodities, failing to produce the wider assortment of goods

---

[68]Bartlomiej Kaminski, *The Collapse of State Socialism: The Case of Poland* (Princeton: Princeton University Press, 1992), pp. 18–37.

[69]James R. Millar, "From Utopian Socialism to Utopian Capitalism: The Failure of Revolution and Reform in Russia," Paper presented to the Sixth International Conference on Socio-Economics, July 15–17, 1994, Paris, France, pp. 5–6.

[70]Michael Ellman and Vladimir Kontorovich, eds., *The Disintegration of the Soviet Economic System* (London: Routledge, 1992), p. 22; and James Angresano, *Comparative Economics* (Englewood Cliffs, N.J.: Prentice Hall, 1992), p. 385.

under previous planning. So while enterprises increased overall output (and light industrial and food output), they reduced the amount of machinery, metals, chemicals, and wood produced.[71] David Kotz criticizes Russian leaders for failing to create the essential capitalist institutions to replace socialist institutions that were abolished.[72]

Jan Winiecki, President of the Adam Smith Research Center in Warsaw, Poland, contends that the ruling stratum in Soviet-type economies, who control the means of production, maximize the **economic rents**, or returns to a factor of production in excess of what is required to elicit the supply of the factor, that they can extract. Thus, they favor powerful groups (Communist party officials and apparatchiks) in making decisions about wealth distribution. Party officials, from the center to the enterprise, use the principle of nomenklatura to achieve their goals. Officials make appointments on the basis of loyalty rather than managerial skill, extracting rent from side payments (access to goods in short supply) and kickbacks from firm managers.[73] Indeed an economic historian argues that after 1991, central planning and distribution agencies in Russia have changed names but not functions, namely the suppression of all market-oriented competition.[74]

CONTRADICATIONS UNDER DECONTROL

During the 1970s and early 1980s, the late period of Leonid Brezhnev's rule, when corruption and rigidity among Soviet officials increased, the central administrative authority deteriorated. From 1960 to 1988, the Soviet shadow economy grew rapidly, according to Soviet economists. The 5 billion rubles of unrecorded sales in 1960 added only 6 percent to recorded sales, while the 90 billion rubles of unrecorded activity in 1988 added 23 percent.[75]

Gorbachev diagnosed the major determinant of stagnation in the late Brezhnev period as the "relaxation of discipline," that is, less adherence to commands, such as output targets, technological rules, laws, and regulation. Instead of increasing investment and rationalizing the command system, Gorbachev undermined planning by envisaging an increase in machine building too abrupt to absorb, an antialcohol campaign that reduced turnover tax revenues and increased queues at liquor stores, a campaign against unearned income that hurt black-market activities that were essential to circumvent the rigidity of material balance planning, the reduced pressure of economic rewards and punishments, the removal of the Communist party from economic planning, and the attack on middle- and upper-level bureaucrats for their corruption. This attack, echoed by the media, demoralized the bureaucracy and increased the resistance of subordinates

---

[71]Gary Krueger, "Goszakazy and the Soviet Economic Collapse," *Comparative Economic Studies* 35 (Fall 1993): 1–18.

[72]David Kotz, "The Direction of Soviet Economic Reform: From Socialist Reform to Capitalist Transition," *Monthly Review* 45 (September 1992): 14–34.

[73]Jan Winiecki, "Privatization in East-Central Europe: Avoiding Major Mistakes," in Christopher Clague and Gordon C. Rausser, eds., *The Emergence of Market Economies in Eastern Europe* (Cambridge, Mass.: Blackwell, 1992), pp. 271–95.

[74]Yuri N. Afanasyev, "Russian Reform Is Dead: Back to Central Planning," *Foreign Affairs* 72 (March/April 1994): 21–27.

[75]Patrick Flaherty, "Privatization and the Soviet Economy," *Monthly Review* 44 (January 1992): 1–14; and Gregory Grossman, "The Underground Economy in Russia," *International Economic Insights* (November-December 1993), p. 15.

to carrying out the orders of superiors. The grip of the official ideology on the public mind was getting increasingly impotent, weakening economic incentives and the traditional command structure.[76]

Increasingly, perestroika and the collapse of socialism, accompanied by the relaxation of censorship and the emergence of independent media and political parties, contributed to a loss of legitimacy of the old social and political order. In the late 1980s and early 1990s, murders increased substantially, bribery and corruption were rampant, and other registered crime rose considerably. Jehu Eaves estimated that organized crime controlled 20 percent of new enterprises in the 1990s. In 1991, St. Petersburg mayor Anatoly Sobchak pointed out, "The country today is in fact out of control, because the old structures have been destroyed and the new ones have not emerged."[77]

Decontrol of economic activity has brought many activities out to the light of day, but has also created new opportunities shielding illegal activity through sweetheart deals with state-owned enterprises, asset stripping, and favorable buyouts under the rubric of privatization. In 1993, Yeltsin, in what sounded like an admission of defeat, said that mafia activity was destroying the economy, destabilizing the political climate, and undermining public morale. The mafia is not monolithic yet is interwoven within the fabric of Russia's bureaucracy and ruling elite. In the free-for-all struggle to grab Russia's material wealth, the 3,000–4,000 mafia gangs, with their corruption, criminality, and violence, have major advantages, not the least of which is their connections to major sections of the government bureaucracy, including senior finance ministry (or department) officials who want to undercut private commercial banking. On the other hand, party officials have used the opening of private commerce to siphon their illegal wealth accumulation. While inflation wipes out substantial wealth, the numerous mafia organizations have accumulated large wealth, much in foreign currency, to control many of the new privatized assets. The mafia, which has substantial international ties, deters entry by some legitimate businesses, increases the cost of business for others, and has dampened the interest of Western firms and subjected many Western business people to violence, and in some instances murder, for failing to comply.

Gregory Grossman thinks the Russian government, by liberalizing, can contain the mafia and shadow economy. For Stephen Handelman, however, the mafia undermines reform, spawns extraordinary violence in major cities, and helps fuel a growing ultranationalist backlash. However, the boundary between criminal and legal business activity is hazy, with police and politicians ascribing mafia connections to anyone with what seems an unreasonable amount of money. Indeed Handelman contends that Russian entrepreneurs operating by the rules find it impossible to survive in the face of official and criminal competition, and that the mafia is the only institution that benefited from the collapse of the Soviet Union. He argues that Russia needs to construct a civil society, with an independent judiciary, before the market can safely operate.[78]

---

[76]Michael Ellman and Vladimir Kontorovich, eds., *The Disintegration of the Soviet Economic System* (London: Routledge, 1992), pp. 10–22.

[77]Ibid., pp. 2–5, 14; and Jehu Eaves, "Is the Soviet Union Going Socialist?" *Dollars and Sense* (January-February 1992): pp. 16–18, 21.

[78]Gregory Grossman, "The Underground Economy in Russia," *International Economic Insights* (November-December 1993), pp. 14–17; and Stephen Handelman, "The Russian 'Mafiya'," *Foreign Affairs* 73 (March/April 1994): 83–96.

DISTORTED INFORMATION

Starting in the late 1980s and culminating in 1991, rulers no longer collected information about economic opportunities, enforced their planning preferences, or received feedback on the performance of managers and their units. Subordinates withheld and distorted information used to evaluate them. To an even greater extent than before, officials in enterprises, farms, and ministries padded and politicized data to avoid sanctions and collect rewards. The planners' system of outside evaluation broke down.[79]

ENTERPRISE MONOPOLIES

Soviet firms were monopolies, inflating prices and disrupting supply after the collapse of central planning. In 1991, planners had organized industry into 7,664 product groups, in which 77 percent were produced by single firms. Seven percent of Soviet industrial enterprises produced 65 percent of aggregate industrial output and employed more than 50 percent of the industrial labor force.

To increase their control over supply that would otherwise be unreliable and to reduce turnover (or sales) taxes, Russian firms have been highly vertically integrated and plagued by gigantimania, encompassing steps from producing inputs and materials to selling the final output. In 1992, the average Russian firm employed about 800 workers, twice as many as the average Polish firm and 10 times as much as the average firm in the West. Half of 1992 industrial output was produced by 1,000 giant enterprises that averaged 8,500 employees.

Suppliers also were monopolists. Thus, the manager of a shoe factory enjoyed a monopoly but had to deal with producers of leather, nails, rubber, and other inputs who were also monopolists. But reform replaced material balance planning with the market, reallocating resources away from their usual sectors. The reduction of suppliers' obligations to public enterprises resulted in price increases, output declines, excessive wage increases, and the deteriorating reliability of the supply system. Decentralization in input-output links meant supplies could reduce deliveries to increase their bargaining power and perhaps their prices. Firms stopped producing low-profit items and increased their barter. The result was that traders and speculators with monopolistic control over commodities have enjoyed real price increases of several-fold in less than a year in 1991–92.[80] To avoid price distortion by monopolists, a transitional economy should demonopolize (break up large industrial concentrations) before or at the same time as, not after, price decontrol. But these firms have been difficult to split up.

THE LACK OF SCARCITY PRICES

(1) The Soviets allocated resources inefficiently, disregarding scarcity prices. Without an interest rate to ration capital, planners allocated funds bureaucratically, with little relationship between net worth and capital expansion. In certain sectors,

---

[79]Bartlomiej Kaminski, *The Collapse of State Socialism: The Case of Poland* (Princeton: Princeton University Press, 1992), pp. 19–33.

[80]United Nations, *World Economic Survey 1992* (New York, 1992), p. 57; Jehu Eaves, "Is the Soviet Union Going Socialist?" *Dollars and Sense* (January-February 1992), pp. 16–18, 21; Thomas E. Weisskopf, "Russia in Transition: Perils of the Fast Track to Capitalism," *Challenge* 38 (November-December 1992): 29; Michael Ellman and Vladimir Kontorovich, eds., *The Disintegration of the Soviet Economic System* (London: Routledge, 1992), pp. 22–30; and *Economist* (September 13, 1992), p. S13.

enterprises managers over-ordered and invested while other sectors were neglected.

In the late 1980s, Russia used 15 times the steel, nine times the rubber, and six times the energy that the United States did per unit of GDP. For these inputs, industrial output is a value subtractor, meaning, for example, that factories using rubber produce tires whose world market prices are less than the value of the raw material embodied in them! Not surprisingly, Russia has not experienced a boom in manufactured exports with the breakup of the Soviet Union;[81] indeed, industrial output fell through the mid-1990s, as firms unable to compete at world market prices contracted or collapsed.

(2) Most prices have been administered. Since the late 1920s, the Soviets' goal has been to turn the terms of trade against peasants to release funds for the state to invest in industry. Farm procurement prices were usually low yet two-tiered, with higher prices for sales in excess of the quota. Yet losing farms have received subsidies.[82] Since 1991, state and collective farmers have resisted decollectivization and market pricing, with their loss of security.

(3) The Soviets, lacking an integrated price system, found it difficult to strike the "right" balance between carrot (reward) and stick (repression). Wrong wage and price signals do not motivate labor to increase productivity.[83]

State farms have paid their workers wages in a way similar to factories. However, state farms, which comprised a rising share (53 percent) of Russia's sown hectarage in the late 1980s, lacked incentives to increase productivity. Collective farms, with 44 percent of the sowings and which base income shares on labor day (*trudoden*), have provided little incentive for quality work, as there has been little immediate connection between effort and reward.[84]

Yuri Afanasyev contends that the gigantic state monopoly, Agroprom, is the major brake on agricultural output growth, private land ownership, and private farms or voluntary collectives. The powerful agricultural lobby demands incredible subsidies from the state, which go primarily to Agroprom.[85]

CONSUMER SECTORS AS BUFFERS

Under Soviet planning, food and other basic consumer goods comprised buffer sectors, which could be adjusted (usually downward) when inputs to higher priority sectors, such as steel and defense, were scarce. Prices set at less than market-clearing prices meant long lines, shortages, and low quality, dampening personal incentives and worker productivity.

DISTORTIONS FROM INFLATION

Rapid inflation in the early 1990s also created perverse incentives and numerous distortions. This strong inflationary momentum resulted from excessive credit creation, driven by credits and subsidies to state enterprises. Subsidies comprised

---

[81]*Economist* (September 16, 1992), p. S10; and *Economist* (October 14, 1992), p. 333.

[82]James Angresano, *Comparative Economics* (Englewood Cliffs, N.J.: Prentice Hall, 1992), p. 393.

[83]Bartlomiej Kaminski, *The Collapse of State Socialism: The Case of Poland* (Princeton: Princeton University Press, 1992), p. 34.

[84]Paul R. Gregory and Robert C. Stuart, *Comparative Economic Systems*, 4th ed. (Boston: Houghton Mifflin, 1994), pp. 292–94. The private sector had the remaining 3 percent of the sowings.

[85]Yuri N. Afanasyev, "Russian Reform Is Dead: Back to Central Planning," *Foreign Affairs* 72 (March/April 1994): 21–27.

24.5 percent (import subsidies 17.5 percent) of GDP in 1992. An additional 4.1–23.0 percent of GDP was directed credits by the Central Bank of Russia and the Ministry of Finance to government firms, granted at rates of about 10 percent annually, far below the real (inflation-adjusted) market rate of interest of several hundred percent.[86] Blanchard, et al. contend that before 1994 the Russian monetary authorities made no effort to stabilize prices, as they realized that the unemployment cost, especially in the military-industrial complex, would have been substantial.[87]

NEGATIVE REAL INTEREST RATES

Real interest rates in the early 1990s were wildly negative, as inflation, which often exceeded 800 percent yearly, was in excess of the cost of borrowing. Positive real rates of interest would have raised the cost of financing stocks and inventories, making roubles worth more than goods, and would have encouraged the selling of stocks.[88]

SOFT BUDGET CONSTRAINTS

During the early 1990s, firms operated under a **soft budget constraint**, an absence of financial penalties for enterprise failure. While management and worker bonuses and investment expansion were theoretically linked to performance, virtually no firm was penalized for losses. New firm entry was restricted and inefficient firms were rarely closed down; firms lacked the market's **creative destruction**, in which industry's old, high-cost producers are replaced by new, low-cost enterprises.[89] Firms did not fear bankruptcy, as banks continued to lend to losing firms, out of concern for the political power of their managers and professionals, who sometimes influenced planners through gifts and bribes. Indeed politicized lending by Russia's Central Bank to enterprises about to fail or default was the major contributor to inflation rates of about 1,000 percent yearly in 1992 and 1993. Harvard and Hungarian Academy of Sciences' economist Janos Kornai contended that in Hungary during the early 1990s, firms entered and exited in no relationship to profitability or loss![90] Russian firms were similar.

Socialism and its legacy can soften the firm's budget limitation in several ways. First, the national or local government grants soft subsidies in response to lobbying or bargaining by influential apparatchiks or officials (with virtually one rouble granted for each rouble lost). Second, the rules for taxation are not uniform, and tax payments, not rigorously enforced, can be reduced by pressure and pleading. Third, banks do not follow uniform principles, loaning to firms in trouble whose mangers complain or failing to insist on full adherence to credit contracts. Fourth, contracts between buyers and sellers are not free. Buyers bargain down administered prices or sellers persuade a ministry to authorize increased prices in response to rising costs, irrespective of production efficiency.

---

[86]James Angresano, *Comparative Economics* (Englewood Cliffs, NJ: Prentice Hall, 1992), pp. 396–98; and International Monetary Fund, *World Economic Survey, October 1993* (Washington, D.C., 1993), pp. 89–91.

[87]Oliver Blanchard, Maxim Boycko, Marek Dabrowski, Rudiger Dornbusch, Richard Layard, and Andrei Shleifer, *Post-Communist Reform: Pain and Progress* (Cambridge, MA: MIT Press, 1993), pp. 18–20.

[88]*Economist* (September 16, 1992), p. S16.

[89]Joseph A. Schumpeter, *Capitalism, Socialism, and Democracy* (New York: Harper & Row, 1947), pp. 81–86.

[90]Janos Kornai, *The Road to a Free Economy: Shifting From a Socialist System* (New York: Norton, 1990), p. 23.

Firms face hard budget constraints where authorities recognize a unit will fail and exit the industry when it incurs continuing losses and financial catastrophe. "Hardness" means serious consequences from a deficit. "Softness" arises from external help to protect the firm from the loss of jobs and the inability to compete against foreign producers, the redistribution of resources to weak and poor enterprise, and guarantees of security and survival to influential enterprises and their managers.[91]

THE TORN "SAFETY NET"

Enforcing hard budget constraints is difficult because of the Soviet legacy of the "company town." Millar maintains that many Soviet/Russian employers provide workers with apartment space, land for a house and to raise vegetables, medical care in clinics and hospitals, schools and specialized advanced education, subsidized cafeterias and buffets, recreational facilities, travel, vacation sanatoria, and food, clothing, and hardware stores, in addition to a job. Russia's welfare system is inextricably linked to the enterprise, which must divest itself of its welfare functions if it is to compete successfully in a market economy. Yet local owners are reluctant to dismiss employees. And enterprises purchased by workers are especially unlikely to divest themselves of these welfare and subsidiary functions.[92]

Adjustment and reform programs are initially likely to hurt the poorest one-third of the population. In Russia, wage earners, pensioners, and government officials without access to wealth in the newly formed private sector were hurt in the shift to the market. To secure support from the poor and working class, adjusting and reforming countries need programs to protect the income and social services of the most vulnerable. In Russia, the decline of the "company town" without replacement institutions meant that many of the poorest, especially elderly on fixed pensions, experienced food shortages, crowded living conditions, and a collapse of health and medical services. Tuberculosis, typhoid fever, and cholera, which had been virtually eliminated, reappeared in the early 1990s for the first time in decades. A transitional country cannot abolish the all-encompassing "company town" without providing replacement institutions to provide a "safety net" for the poor.

THE LACK OF MARKET INSTITUTIONS

The Russian government has neglected to concentrate on institutions to define property rights clearly. These institutions include legal and regulatory changes, administrative and judicial machinery, bankruptcy law, contracts, and clear transfers from the state or collective to private persons.

---

[91]Janos Kornai, *The Socialist System: The Political Economy of Communism* (Princeton: Princeton University Press, 1992), pp. 140–45.

[92]James R. Millar, "From Utopian Socialism to Utopian Capitalism: The Failure of Revolution and Reform in Russia," Paper presented to the Sixth International Conference on Socio-Economics, July 15–17, 1994, Paris, France, pp. 3–5.

China's state-owned enterprises (SOEs) also may serve the function of "company town." For example, 40 percent of state-owned enterprises nationwide have lost money, threatening the survival of the schools dependent on these enterprises, for which the government has not been willing to provide specific educational funds. Roughly 5 percent of primary and secondary students attend schools run by unprofitable SOEs. Tien Zhang and Jian Liu, "State Firm's Schools Struggling for Survival," *China News Digest* (online global news service) (July 31, 1995).

THE NEGLECT OF SERVICES

The Soviets, whose ideology denied that services were productive, tended to neglect services (trade, housing, and banking). After the collapse of socialism, Russia had to expand the services essential for a modern economy.

THE LACK OF TECHNOLOGICAL PROGRESS

Chapter 3 argued that Soviet growth from the late 1920s through the 1950s from increased inputs such as higher capital formation and labor participation rates were one-time gains that could not be replicated after 1970. To continue growth, the Soviets needed to raise productivity per worker through increased technological change. The Soviets' low total productivity growth was a consequence of the exhaustion of input growth. Extracting old mines was becoming more difficult, as the Soviets had exhausted many natural resources and lacked the improved technology to overcome diminishing returns.[93]

Motivating innovative activity in centrally managed economies like the Soviet Union is usually difficult. In 1959, Soviet Premier Nikita Khrushchev complained about an unsatisfactory rate of technological change. "In our country some bureaucrats are so used to the old nag that they do not want to change over to a good race horse, for he might tear away on the turn and even spill them out of the sleigh! Therefore, such people will hold on to the old nag's tail with both hands and teeth."[94]

Soviet managers resisted innovation, since effort and resources diverted to it might threaten plan fulfillment. While kinks in the new technology were being ironed out, managers lost part of their take-home pay, which was often tied to plan targets, or they may have been demoted. When evaluating managers for bonuses and promotions, party officials gave little weight to innovation. Also the tightly planned system had little latitude for servicing and spare parts for new equipment or for acquiring new resources and suppliers. Furthermore, the prices of new products usually counted for less in computing plan fulfillment than older, standard goods. Finally, introducing new models required extensive testing and negotiations with research institutes as well as approval from official agencies before production is authorized.[95] Managers are opposed to technical innovation. If potential productivity is increased, the firm's continuous production will be interrupted and its future quotas raised. The bureaucratic maze hampered innovation.

THE MILITARY-INDUSTRIAL COMPLEX

The unprecedented peacetime cost of military expenditures and the other costs of being a superpower made it difficult to maintain medical and social services and investment in civilian production. Russia's military industry contributed twice the share of GDP as the United States in the late 1980s.[96]

---

[93]Michael Ellman and Vladimir Kontorovich, eds., *The Disintegration of the Soviet Economic System* (London: Routledge, 1992), pp. 8–9.

[94]Joseph S. Berliner, "Bureaucratic Conservatism and Creativity in the Soviet Economy," in Frederich W. Riggs, ed., *Frontiers of Development Administration* (Durham, N.C.: Duke University Press, 1971), pp. 585–86, citing *Pravda*, 2 July 1959.

[95]Joseph S. Berliner, "Bureaucratic Conservatism and Creativity in the Soviet Economy," in Frederich W. Riggs, ed., *Frontiers of Development Administration* (Durham, N.C.: Duke University Press, 1971), pp. 569–97.

[96]Michael Ellman and Vladimir Kontorovich, eds., *The Disintegration of the Soviet Economic System* (London: Routledge, 1992), p. 14; and *Economist* (December 5, 1992), p. S10.

Afanasyev argues that the military-industrial complex continued to benefit from Russian political conflict after the end of the Cold War. In 1994, Yeltsin ceased funding conversion programs.[97]

ENVIRONMENTAL DEGRADATION

Environmental disruption in the Soviet Union in the 1970s and 1980s was greater than in the United States; energy cost per unit of GNP was much lower in the United States than in the Soviet Union. Damage to the environment was a major cause of the fall in life expectancy (from about 70 in 1978–92 to 64 in 1994) and increase in infant mortality rates rose in Russia in the 1970s, 1980s, and 1990s, a trend contrary to those in almost every other region of the world. Murray Feshbach and Alfred Friendly, Jr. say that the Soviet Union died by ecocide through plunder of rich natural resources and systematic neglect and poisoning of the Soviet people. In 1986, the Chernobyl nuclear power explosion resulted in 20 million people being exposed to excessive radiation. In Yerevan, Armenia, belching chemical works poisoned and deformed local children.[98] Judith Shapiro explains Russia's fall in life expectancy to increased poverty, which reduces strategies for coping with illnesses, and the deterioration of the medical and health-care system.[99]

THE COLLAPSE OF TRADE AMONG COMMUNIST COUNTRIES

The political crises in Poland, 1980–81, and other Eastern European countries in the 1980s, and the effect of Eastern European crises and reforms on Soviet politics and trade made it more difficult for the Soviet Union to survive, let alone develop economically. Russia and Eastern Europe suffered supply disruptions from the collapse of centrally planned input-output links under the Council for Mutual Economic Assistance (COMECON) trading bloc. With COMECON's trade patterns severed, Russia's trade with Eastern Europe fell by more than 50 percent from 1989 to 1990. Analogously, Gosplan's abolition reduced inter–republic trade in the former Soviet Union from 1991 to 1992 by 46 percent.[100]

The Transition from Socialism to the Market in Poland

This section alludes to the more successful transition from socialism to the market in Eastern Europe than in Russia during the early 1990s. The focus is on Poland, which will probably be the first East European transitional country to attain pre-1989 levels of average income. Poland's history under socialism, only since World War II, is shorter than that of Russia. Russia's socialism was more centralized and

---

[97]Yuri N. Afanasyev, "Russian Reform Is Dead: Back to Central Planning," *Foreign Affairs* 72 (March/April 1994): 23.

[98]Michael Ellman, "General Aspects of Transition," in P.H. Admiraal, ed., *Economic Transition in Eastern Europe: Michael Ellman, Egor T. Gaidar, and Grzegorz W. Kolodko* (Oxford: Blackwell, 1993), pp. 1–42; Murray Feshbach and Alfred Friendly, Jr. (with Lester Brown), *Ecocide in the USSR: Health and Nature Under Siege* (New York: Basic Books, 1991); *Economist* (April 25, 1992), pp. 99–100; and Michael Specter, "Russia Baffled as Life Loses Death Race," *International Herald Tribune* (August 3, 1995), pp. 1, 6.

[99]Judith Shapiro, "The Russian Mortality Crisis and Its Causes," in Anders Aslund, ed., *Russian Economic Reform at Risk* (London: Pinter, 1995), pp. 149–78.

[100]Michael Ellman and Vladimir Kontorovich, eds., *The Disintegration of the Soviet Economic System* (London: Routledge, 1992), pp. 6, 18–19; and *Economist* (December 5, 1992), p. S10.

totalitarian than Poland's was. Indeed Poland had sources of opposition to communism in the Roman Catholic Church, (and after 1980) the Solidarity labor union (led by Lech Walesa), and the intelligentsia. Furthermore, Poland had a larger private sector and greater toleration for the black market than Russia.

Reforms under communism during the 1980s failed to increase productivity and contributed to a "cataclysmic" balance-of-payments crisis, but created some market institutions that were further strengthened after 1989. Poland stabilized monetary policy and the zloty currency in 1989, achieving a convertibility which encouraged trade with Eastern Europe, the Soviet Union, and the West. Poland's opening of the market to foreign trade, together with the slashing of subsidies, improved domestic efficiency and undermined monopolies. The social safety net, which included price stabilization, unemployment benefits, job training, health care, and pension guarantees, contributed to greater mass support for reform than in Russia.[101] Beginning in 1990, as discussed in Chapter 17, the United States and Western governments, as well as commercial banks, wrote down debt, while DCs created a stabilization fund to defend the zloty, allowing Poland a fresh start, despite its external economic crises of the 1980s. The prospect of future integration into a prosperous European Union provides additional incentives for market reforms in Poland, as well as Hungary and the Czech Republic. However, the old guard's resistance is still an impediment to reform.

The Transition to a Market Economy in China

Mao Zedong, a founding member of the Chinese Communist Party, led the guerrilla war against the Chinese Nationalist government from 1927 to victory in 1949. From 1949 to 1976, Mao, the Chair of the Communist Party, was the leader of the People's Republic of China. Mao's ideology stressed prices determined by the state, state or communal ownership of the means of production, international and regional trade and technological self-sufficiency, noneconomic (moral) incentives, "politics" (not economics) in command, egalitarianism, socializing the population toward selflessness, continuing revolution (opposing an encrusted bureaucracy), and development of a holistic Communist person. From 1952 to 1966, pragmatists, primarily managers of state organizations and enterprises, bureaucrats, academics, managers, administrators, and party functionaries, vied with Maoists for control of economic decision-making. But during the **Cultural Revolution**, from 1966 to 1976, the charismatic Mao and his allies won out, purging moderates from the Central Communist Party (for example, Deng Xiaoping) to workplace committees.

After Mao's death in 1976, the Chinese, led by Deng, recognized that, despite the rapid industrial growth under Mao, imbalances remained from the Cultural Revolution, such as substantial waste in the midst of high investment, too little emphasis on consumer goods, the lack of wage incentives, insufficient technological innovation, too tight control on economic management, the taxing of enterprise profits and a full subsidy for losses, and too little international economic trade and relations. Since 1980, near the beginning of economic reform undertaken under Deng's leadership, China has had virtually the fastest growth in the world (see the World Bank figures in Table 2–1). To be sure, Penn economists

[101]Jeffrey Sachs, *Poland's Jump to the Market Economy* (Cambridge, Mass.: MIT Press, 1993).

Robert Summers and Alan Heston indicate "that Chinese growth rates are overstated as they are heavily based on growth in physical output figures rather than deflated expenditure series."[102] Moreover, managers understate capacity and overreport production to superiors to receive the greater reward received by those who meet or exceed plan fulfillment. Despite overreporting and continuing market distortions mentioned below, most economists believe China's growth under market reforms has been rapid but uneven.

During the early reform period, the Chinese leaders tried to improve economic management and make the planning system more flexible rather than replacing planning with the market. This was not a capitalist road, the Chinese insisted, but "socialism with Chinese characteristics." The meaning of Chinese characteristics only took shape after seven to eight years of experimentation rather than by following a grand blueprint. Reform proceeded step-by-step, through a process of trial and error but drawing on incremental changes from past experience. The Chinese explained their approach with a proverb: "Keep touching stones while walking across a river." The strategy of building incrementally on previous institutions contrasted with Russia's more abrupt changes in strategy in the early 1990s.[103] By the early 1990s, however, Chinese leaders no longer labeled their approach as socialism but a "socialist market economy."

AGRICULTURAL REFORMS

During the Maoist era, agricultural growth was slower than industrial growth (see Chapter 7). The state transferred surplus from agriculture to the state by underpricing agricultural products and overpricing industrial products sold to the peasants.[104] So while in the post-Mao period, foreign trade reforms came first, agricultural reforms had the greatest impact on the Chinese people, concentrated primarily in the countryside.

In reforms beginning in 1979, China decontrolled (and increased) prices for farm commodities, virtually eliminated their compulsory deliveries to the state, reduced multitiered pricing, relaxed interregional farm trade restrictions, encouraged rural markets, allowed direct sales of farm goods to urban consumers, and decollectivized agriculture, instituting individual household management of farm plots under long-term contracts with collectives and allowing farmers to choose cropping patterns and nonfarm activities. The household responsibility system, which Chinese peasants had previously used in 1956 and 1961–64, shifted production responsibility from a production team, the size of a village, to a household. From 1977 to 1984, China's growth in food output per capita, 4.6-percent yearly, was even outstripped by its growth in oilseed, livestock, and cotton output. Indeed gross agricultural output grew 9 percent yearly during the period. China reversed its pre-1979 dependence on imported grains, exporting corn, other coarse

[102]See the computer diskette that provides the expanded Penn World Table 5 version of Robert Summers and Alan Heston, "The Penn World Table (Mark 5): An Expanded Set of International Comparisons, 1950–1988," *Quarterly Journal of Economics* 106 (May 1991): 327–68.

[103]Christopher M. Clarke, "China's Transition to the Post-Deng Era," in Joint Economic Committee, Congress of the United States (Paul S. Sarbanes, Chair), *China's Economic Dilemmas in the 1990s: The Problems of Reforms, Modernization, and Interdependence* (Armonk: NY: M.E. Sharpe, 1991), pp. 1–14; Peter M. Lichtenstein, *China at the Brink: The Political Economy of Reform and Retrenchment in the Post-Mao Era* (New York: Praeger, 1991), pp. 136–37; and Hui Wang, *The Gradual Revolution: China's Economic Reform Movement* (New Brunswick, NJ: Transaction, 1994), pp. 14–15, 27, 113.

[104]Victor D. Lippit, *The Economic Development of China* (Armonk, N.Y.: M.E. Sharpe, 1987), p. 224.

grains, and soybeans (as well as raw cotton), which competed with exports from the U.S. Midwest and South, especially to Japan. These remarkable gains were achieved without increased farm inputs except for chemical fertilizer.[105]

Brown University economist Louis Putterman shows that technical efficiency in Chinese agriculture fell between 1952 and 1978, but increased from 1978 to 1984, becoming the major source of growth. Decollectivization, the household responsibility system, the increased link of reward to output, and modest price decontrol during the reform period increased resource productivity. Work monitoring and incentives improved, agriculture was diversified, and families allocated more labor to highly remunerative noncrop (or even nonagricultural) activities.[106]

After 1984, agricultural growth decelerated so much that Minister of Agriculture He Kang indicated in 1989 that the "situation in agricultural production is grim."[107] First, most rural areas had already captured onetime gains from household accountability. Second, in the late 1980s, the government reduced its massive subsidies, which had increased sixfold and expanded the expenditures of state revenues on agriculture from 5 percent in 1978 to 20 percent in 1984, straining government finances. This reduction in subsidies decreased the procurement price the state paid farmers. Third, in the mid-1980s, many farmers awoke to profitable opportunities in rural (township and village) enterprises, both in industry and trade. In 1984, reforms had allowed interprovincial trade, private ownership of capital, access to urban markets, hiring of wage labor, and subcontracting, all of which gave greater scope to private and collective nonstate rural enterprises. As employment and sown hectares in crops declined in the 1980s, farmers experienced diseconomies of small-scale production. Fourth, farmers, based on previous volatility and an uncertain future, feared a reversal in land tenure system, becoming reluctant to invest in agriculture and undertake innovation. Fifth, the rural banking infrastructure was underdeveloped. Government lending by the Agricultural Bank of China, under the control of local party officials, was politicized so that few loans were available at market interest rates for flourishing households. Sixth, since in the 1970s, government had distributed rights to communal land in fragmented plots on the basis of household size rather than farm management ability, few highly-productive farmers had the opportunity to expand.[108]

---

[105]World Bank, *World Development Report, 1986* (New York: Oxford University Press, 1986), pp. 104–6; Peter M. Lichtenstein, *China at the Brink: The Political Economy of Reform and Retrenchment in the Post-Mao Era* (New York: Praeger, 1991), pp. 60–61; E. Wayne Nafziger, "India versus China," *Dalhousie Review* 65 (Fall 1985): 366–92; U.S. Department of Agriculture, *World Indices of Agricultural and Food Production, 1950–85* (Washington, D.C., 1986); and U.S. Department of Agriculture, *World Indices of Agricultural and Food Production, 1977–86* (Washington, D.C., 1988).

[106]Louis Putterman, *Continuity and Change in China's Rural Development: Collective and Reform Eras in Perspective* (New York: Oxford University Press, 1993).

[107]Peter M. Lichtenstein, *China at the Brink: The Political Economy of Reform and Retrenchment in the Post-Mao Era* (New York: Praeger, 1991), p. 61, quoting the *Beijing Review* (May 8, 1989).

[108]Peter M. Lichtenstein, *China at the Brink: The Political Economy of Reform and Retrenchment in the Post-Mao Era* (New York: Praeger, 1991), pp. 60–64; Louis Putterman, *Continuity and Change in China's Rural Development: Collective and Reform Eras in Perspective* (New York: Oxford University Press, 1993); Joseph Fewsmith, *Dilemmas of Reform in China: Political Conflict and Economic Debate* (Armonk, N.Y.: M.E. Sharpe, 1994), 153–54; and John P. Hardt and Richard F. Kaufman, "Introduction," in Joint Economic Committee, Congress of the United States (Paul S. Sarbanes, Chair), *China's Economic Dilemmas in the 1990s: The Problems of Reforms, Modernization, and Interdependence* (Armonk: N.Y.: M.E. Sharpe, 1991), pp. ix–xiv.

THE INDIVIDUAL ECONOMY

Reform also included small entrepreneurial activity, what the Chinese call the individual economy. One precursor of these individual enterprises was the cooperatively-run enterprises, which required far less capital per worker than state-owned enterprises. After 1976, another trigger to urban reform was dealing with the urban unemployment caused by the return to cities of youths "sent down" to learn from peasants in the countryside during the Cultural Revolution. These youths could not be absorbed in state enterprises, already overstocked with underemployed workers. Therefore, especially after 1984, the state allowed these youths to set themselves up in businesses as individuals or as members of urban collective enterprises. They opened small restaurants, set up repair shops and other retail outlets, or became pedicab operators, increasing substantially the convenience of urban life.[109] The income was often higher, though the prestige and security were lower, than state-sector jobs. Furthermore, farmers coming to the city to sell their produce expanded the quantity and improved the quality of urban services, especially after 1984.[110] Overall China's privately self-employed in cities and towns (primarily in services, commerce, handicrafts, and catering) grew from 150,000 in 1978 to roughly 5–10 million in 1988, increasing industrial output and soaking up underemployed labor.[111]

INDUSTRIAL REFORMS

Earlier in this chapter, we discussed determinants of the performance of public enterprises in LDCs. State-owned enterprises rather than the informal or services sector are the key to China's urban reforms. However, the reform of public industrial enterprises has not been so successful as China's agricultural reform. Annual gross industrial output growth, 11.4 percent from 1952 to 1978 (9.4 percent, 1965–78), slowed to 7.0 percent from 1978 to 1982, with no substantial improvement in industrial efficiency after 1978.[112] Urban reform entails built-in contradictions, since increased market forces threaten the power and expertise of bureaucrats, who were trained to run a Soviet-style command system.

Mao's emphasis on self-reliance gave license to provincial protectionism. As provinces became more self-sufficient, their demand for other provinces' surpluses decreased, compelling potential surplus provinces to divert additional resources to self-reliance. After 1979, one of the post-Maoist leadership's major contributions to growth was the substantial gains to specialization from attacks on regional protectionism.[113]

The reform instituted a **management responsibility system,** in which an enterprise manager's task was to be carefully defined and performance was to de-

---

[109]Victor D. Lippit, *The Economic Development of China* (Armonk, N.Y.: M. E. Sharpe, 1987), pp. 201–19.

[110]Dwight H. Perkins, "The Prospects for China's Economic Reforms," in A. Doak Barnett and Ralph N. Clough, eds., *Modernizing China: Post-Mao Reform and Development* (Boulder, Colo.: Westview, 1986), pp. 39–61.

[111]Adi Ignatius, "Fast-growing Chinese Electronics Firm Emulates IBM," *Wall Street Journal* (June 3, 1988): 10.

[112]Carl Riskin, *China's Political Economy: The Quest for Development since 1949* (Oxford: Oxford University Press, 1987), pp. 368–72.

[113]Thomas P. Lyons, *Economic Integration and Planning in Maoist China* (New York: Columbia University Press, 1987), pp. 237, 278.

termine managers' and workers' pay. Reforms were to give enterprise management considerable autonomy to choose suppliers, hire and fire labor, set prices, raise capital, and contract with foreigners. Management was supposed to have responsibility for the success or failure of the enterprise. The initiative and decisions were to be centered in producing units rather than in government administration. Under this system, taxes on enterprise bonuses at more than a certain level replaced the profits and losses the state absorbed. But, as of the mid-1990s, only a fraction of managers of industrial enterprises opted for the responsibility system.

Economists identify several problems with China's industrial reform. Rewarding producers with higher pay for higher productivity requires an increase in consumer goods, especially food. And with reduced investment, growth must rely on technical innovation and increased efficiency. Although the early reform period emphasized worker authority in selecting managers, this selection was deemphasized when it increasingly conflicted with the professionalization and responsibility of managers.[114]

Moreover, in China's central planning system, the planning commission and the People's Bank make most decisions. The planning commission sets targets on an annual basis for the amount of output required in each industry and the inputs that will be required to achieve that output. The planners convey these targets to the planning commissions and eventually to individual enterprises, which recommend changes based on local conditions. However, in practice, large state-owned enterprises have been managed in the post-Mao period very much like they were during the Maoist period. Industrial reforms have not had much effect on this sector. When the reform decentralized decision making, it merely replaced central restrictions with local and regional restrictions.[115]

Another major problem is fragmented administrative control, numerous overlapping authorities for project approval, and multiple levels of controls at different levels of government, what the Chinese call too many mothers-in-law. The Qingdao Forging Machinery Plant, a state enterprise, is responsible to the national Ministry of the Machine Industry, the city materials board, and the county for material supplies, to the municipal machine industry office for plant production, to the county planning agency for output value, to relevant county agencies for supplies from the plant, to two separate county agencies for personnel, and to the county committee for party matters, which is immersed in implementing policies.[116]

Thus planning is not integrated nor coherent, and enterprises are not treated consistently concerning targets. Investment decisions are bureaucratized and politicized. Moreover, administrative agencies lack enough information about enterprises and commodities to make good decisions. Despite the management responsibility system, in practice management has still been centralized and rigid, with firm managers having limited control over performance. Enterprise managers

[114]Victor D. Lippit, *The Economic Development of China* (Armonk, N. Y.: M. E. Sharpe, 1987), pp. 209–16; and Peter M. Lichtenstein, *China at the Brink: The Political Economy of Reform and Retrenchment in the Post-Mao Era* (New York: Praeger, 1991), p. 48.

[115]Dwight H. Perkins, "The Prospects for China's Economic Reforms," in A. Doak Barnett and Ralph N. Clough, eds., *Modernizing China: Post-Mao Reform and Development* (Boulder, Colo.: Westview, 1986), pp. 52–53; and John P. Hardt and Richard F. Kaufman, "Introduction," in Joint Economic Committee, Congress of the United States (Paul S. Sarbanes, Chair), *China's Economic Dilemmas in the 1990s: The Problems of Reforms, Modernization, and Interdependence* (Armonk: N.Y.: M.E. Sharpe, 1991), p. xiii.

[116]Zheng Guangliang, "The Leadership System," in Gene Tidrick and Chen Jiyuan, eds., *China's Industrial Reform* (New York: Oxford University Press for the World Bank, 1987), pp. 303–4.

had few incentives, since the state gave managers production plans and designated product recipients, so there was little room for initiative or innovation.[117]

One redeeming feature is that plans are not as rigid in practice as in theory; otherwise the Chinese economy would have ground to a halt. Although bargaining and trading make the system more flexible, these arrangements require the enterprise manager to spend much of his or her time negotiating special deals with the planning bureaucracy and other managers. The system places a premium on "back door" deals, rather than organizing labor and other inputs to use more efficiently. The manager whose only skill is saving money is of little use in achieving success, because he or she can always borrow money cheaply from the People's Bank or take funds from the enterprise's net income.

The key to getting enterprise managers to respond to market signals is to compel them to pay more attention to making profits rather than simply expanding output. Managers will concentrate on profits if they can keep a larger and more predictable portion of them and use them for bonuses for them and their workers, rather than turning over profits to the state budget.[118]

If profits are to guide enterprise behavior, profits must be determined by prices reflecting true relative economic scarcity. If prices are set incorrectly, as in China, they will give the wrong signal, spurring enterprises to produce too little of what is short and too much of what is in surplus. For example, wrong market signals mean that enterprise managers try to purchase vast imports in excess of the foreign exchange available. The more foreign exchange and other inputs managers accumulate, the easier for them to meet their success targets.

For the market to have meaning, products of enterprises must be sold on the market rather than delivered to governmental authorities for a fixed price. To be sure, the government reduced the number of industrial products subject to compulsory planning from 131 in 1980 to fourteen in 1988.[119] Still, as of the early 1990s, prices of 60 products subject to mandatory control outside the market included foodstuffs, all energy sources, most metals, basic raw materials for the chemical industry, important machinery and electrical equipment, and several other items.

Prices are arbitrary and distorted and change only incrementally throughout the system. Setting multiple prices by regions does not correspond to the cost of distances traveled. Distorted prices mean that profits are not linked to supply and demand. Enterprises are spurred to produce overpriced goods regardless of the market. Scarce goods that are priced cheaply become even more scarce. Moreover the Chinese, like the Russians, restricted entry and exit of firms, also lacking creative destruction. Furthermore, the Chinese fear that price reform would lead to renewed inflation, with adverse political consequences.

---

[117]This discussion is based on Gene Tidrick and Chen Jiyuan, eds., *China's Industrial Reform* (New York: Oxford University Press, 1987), Peter Nan-shong Lee, "Enterprise Autonomy Policy in Post-Mao China: A Case Study of Policymaking, 1978–83," *China Quarterly,* no. 105 (March 1986): 45–71; Carl Riskin, *China's Political Economy: The Quest for Development since 1949* (Oxford: Oxford University Press, 1987), pp. 352–53; Victor D. Lippit, *The Economic Development of China* (Armonk, N.Y.: M. E. Sharpe, 1987), pp. 215–16; A. Doak Barnett and Ralph N. Clough, eds., *Modernizing China: Post-Mao Reform and Development* (Boulder, Colo.: Westview, 1986), pp. 54–57; and Peter M. Lichtenstein, *China at the Brink: The Political Economy of Reform and Retrenchment in the Post-Mao Era* (New York: Praeger, 1991), p. 73.

[118]Dwight H. Perkins, "The Prospects for China's Economic Reforms," in A. Doak Barnett and Ralph N. Clough, eds., *Modernizing China: Post-Mao Reform and Development* (Boulder, Colo.: Westview, 1986), p. 54.

[119]Peter M. Lichtenstein, *China at the Brink: The Political Economy of Reform and Retrenchment in the Post-Mao Era* (New York: Praeger, 1991), p. 47.

If increasing market forces are to result in higher levels of efficiency, enterprises must compete with each other rather than have monopoly control of particular markets. To be sure, enterprises have more freedom buying and selling, and collective businesses sometimes compete with state enterprises. Yet as long as central planners allocate key inputs administratively, competition is limited, at least for intermediate products.

For the market to have meaning, enterprises must be able to buy productive inputs on the market. But prices usually do not show where resources can best be put to use, thus providing false signals to enterprises. In many instances, enterprises are still not allowed to retain profits for capital; indeed much capital is still allocated administratively rather than by interest payment.

Additionally the Chinese lack a labor market, thus thwarting smooth labor adjustments to changes in demand. Traditionally, workers hired by state enterprises have had an "iron rice bowl," meaning that they could not be fired. During the Cultural Revolution, wages were effectively frozen and bonuses frowned on, so material incentives for improved performance were lacking. Moreover, since China lacked adequate safety nets, management was reluctant to fire labor, and substituted employment for productivity objectives. Management promulgating a system of freer hiring and firing threatened the morale and solidarity workers felt with the "iron rice bowl." Moreover, during the Maoist period, workers became increasingly disaffected so that the Chinese authorities had to compensate by becoming more repressive to maintain labor discipline. But during economic reform, managers were subject to substantial pressure from workers, so that managers' concern for profits was driven by efforts to increase worker benefits which affected managerial security.[120]

Enterprise managers have little control over paying or hiring labor and little in firing unproductive workers. Furthermore, the variety and amount of supplies available to a firm do not bear much relationship to output targets. Firms have little scope to search the market for the cheapest combination of input costs. Factor prices are highly distorted.

Firms have a soft budget constraint, meaning that though management and worker bonuses are nominally linked to profits and other targets, virtually no enterprise has lost bonuses for not meeting targets, since firms can negotiate during the output year to reduce quotas. Enterprises took excessive risks because of this soft constraint. Moreover, enterprise managers bargain for profit targets, which can often be changed retroactively. Furthermore, governmental authorities have failed to shift from a centrally directed finance system to a tax-based system; Beijing gives tax breaks to the more troubled and powerful enterprises.[121]

Also firms may receive inducements for production yet not be able to respond because managers do not have meaningful discretionary authority. Norms

---

[120]Peter M. Lichtenstein, *China at the Brink: The Political Economy of Reform and Retrenchment in the Post-Mao Era* (New York: Praeger, 1991), p. 73; and Dwight Perkins, "Price Reform vs. Enterprise Autonomy: Which Should Have Priority?" in Joint Economic Committee, Congress of the United States (Paul S. Sarbanes, Chair), *China's Economic Dilemmas in the 1990s: The Problems of Reforms, Modernization, and Interdependence* (Armonk, N.Y.: M.E. Sharpe, 1991), pp. 160–66.

[121]Penelope B. Prime, "Taxation Reform in China's Public Finance," in Joint Economic Committee, Congress of the United States (Paul S. Sarbanes, Chair), *China's Economic Dilemmas in the 1990s: The Problems of Reforms, Modernization, and Interdependence* (Armonk, N.Y.: M.E. Sharpe, 1991), pp. 167–85; and Julia Leung, "China Backtracks on Economic Reform and Fuels Inflation it Wants to Control," *Wall Street Journal* (April 13, 1994), p. A13.

for firms are too many, and changes too frequent, thus making planning difficult. The norms encourage output of high-value commodities that use a high proportion of materials and a delinking of production from marketing.

Industrial reform was supposed to permit bankruptcy, but in practice the state still has subsidized losses. While banking reform required investment financed by bank loans on an economic basis rather than state budgetary grants, half the new capital construction was financed by state grants in the late 1980s and early 1990s. Communist Party and local government leaders interfered with the People's Bank of China, forcing it to renegotiate loans on more favorable terms, especially to the politically influential. A typical procedure is to use the profits of successful firms to infuse with life the failing firms, which received an amount about one-third of the 1990 budget. Inflationary pressures were high during much of the late 1980s and early 1990s (about 25 percent annually in 1993–95), due to politicized lending and price monitoring and widespread wage pressures. These pressures were in response to a fear of worker unrest and agitation from being squeezed by increasing food prices and from an increased craving for consumer goods such as televisions, radios, tape recorders, bicycles, refrigerators, washing machines, furniture, jewelry, and Western-style homes.[122]

Chinese industry still suffers from the classic Soviet planning approach—using the preceding year's achievement as the minimum target for the current year, known by the Chinese as "whipping the fast ox." Near the end of the year, enterprises overfulfilling quotas deliberately slow down operations in order not to increase targets too much for the subsequent year. From 1979 to 1980, Beijing instituted profit retention and rewards for fulfilling profits and other performance indicators in several pilot firms. But the experiment was suspended, since the growth of profits and other performance indicators slowed down to keep future targets down, and local governments objected to the high administrative costs and reduced control associated with enterprise profit retention.

Moreover, most enterprises do not receive their quotas until after the beginning of the planning year. Due to dependence on administrative decisions and the cooperation of other firms in receiving inputs, enterprises keep excessive levels of inventory.

Since the state sets few variety, grade, or style targets, the enterprise has little incentive to produce the variety of goods demanded by the market. Price incentives are also lacking for quality improvement.

The emergence of a buyers' market in 1980, partly a result of substantial increases in the supply of light industry and consumer goods, had more effect, the World Bank and Chinese Academy of Social Sciences point out, than industrial reform in improving industrial performance and quality.

Other economists express optimism that over the years, private enterprises, which have bought shares of SOEs and, together with collective enterprises, have

[122]Peter M. Lichtenstein, *China at the Brink: The Political Economy of Reform and Retrenchment in the Post-Mao Era* (New York: Praeger, 1991), pp. 13–14, 48, 69; and *Beijing Review* (March 28, 1994), p. 4); Jan Prybyla, "A Systemic Analysis of Prospects for China's Economy," in Joint Economic Committee, Congress of the United States (Paul S. Sarbanes, Chair), *China's Economic Dilemmas in the 1990s: The Problems of Reforms, Modernization, and Interdependence* (Armonk, N.Y.: M.E. Sharpe, 1991), pp. 209–25; Julia Leung, "China Backtracks on Economic Reform and Fuels Inflation it Wants to Control," *Wall Street Journal* (April 13, 1994), p. A11; and Barry Naughton, "Inflation: Patterns, Causes and Cures," in Joint Economic Committee, Congress of the United States (Paul S. Sarbanes, Chair), *China's Economic Dilemmas in the 1990s: The Problems of Reforms, Modernization, and Interdependence* (Armonk, N.Y.: M.E. Sharpe, 1991), pp. 135–59.

grown faster than public enterprises, will eventually dominate the loss-ridden public enterprises. Indeed, the share of industrial output by state-owned enterprises fell from 78 percent in 1978 to 43 percent in 1994.[123]

Are the problems China faced with its SOEs inherent to public-enterprise reform? The Chinese government provided excessive credits to SOEs, constrained SOE managerial autonomy, and implemented multiple levels of control, suggesting how much politics limits "a level playing field" between public and private firms.

Still the support for reform is so pervasive in China that its rulers are not likely to reverse the industrial and other domestic reforms significantly. But China faces many problems related to the reforms, including excessive credit to SOEs, the collapse of the "iron rice bowl" for workers in firms, the increased migration of the rural poor to the cities, and potentially rising worker and peasant disaffection. Furthermore, the declining control by the state will require that the Communist Party change its management and reduce its authority or face social disorder and a threat to party leadership.

INCREASING INTERNATIONAL TRADE AND EXCHANGE

During the 1960s and early 1970s, the Chinese stressed self-sufficiency. In 1960, in the midst of an ideological dispute, the Soviets canceled contracts and pulled out materials, spare parts, and blueprints from aid projects and joint ventures in China, leaving bridges and buildings half built. In 1977, after Mao's death, the Chinese leadership, recognizing how costly technological self-reliance had been, opened the door toward the world market. To change, China would now not only stress basic studies and the development and application of science and technology, but also learn foreign technology through sending students to foreign academic institutions, absorb foreign production techniques suitable to China's conditions, and raise the skills of Chinese workers, technicians, and managers.[124]

In 1979–80, China first created **special economic zones (SEZs)**, export processing zones, for foreigners to set up enterprises, hire labor, and import duty-free goods for processing and re-exporting. Many foreign investors, in the SEZs enjoyed preferential tax rates, reduced tariffs, flexible labor and wage policies, more modern infrastructure, and less bureaucracy than elsewhere in China. Foreign investors included overseas Chinese, especially from Hong Kong, which was not integrated into China politically before 1997. Because of special inducements for foreigners, sometimes Chinese who wanted to start a new industrial venture disguised the enterprise by creating a front for Hong Kong ("foreign") investors. Still most Hong Kong and other Chinese overseas investors were legitimate investors, comprising the lion's share of foreign capital in China. In 1990, 55 percent of all realized foreign investment came from Hong Kong and Macao.[125] China, which attracted more foreign investment in the early 1990s than all other developing countries combined can thank the overseas Chinese for an important share of the impressive growth of the 1980s and early 1990s. Indeed the overseas Chinese

---

[123]"Shrinking the Chinese State," *Economist* (June 10, 1995): 33–34; and Gary H. Jefferson and Thomas G. Rawski, "Enterprise Reform in Chinese Industry," *Journal of Economic Perspectives* 8 (Spring 1994): 47–70.

[124]Beijing Review, *China Today: Economic Readjustment and Reform* (Beijing, 1982), pp. 20–21.

[125]Dwight Perkins, "Completing China's Move to the Market," *Journal of Economic Perspectives* 8 (Spring 1994): 23–46.

in China were more experienced and enterprising than overseas Indians or overseas members of other Asian nations. China also benefited from the fact that Western and Japanese investors feared being excluded from what might potentially become the largest market in the developing world. Many economists, however, doubt that this foreign-investment-fueled growth can be continued in the late 1990s and first decade of the twenty-first century.

In the 1990s, most foreign investment and industrial economic growth were concentrated in coastal areas, which included five SEZs, 14 port cities, and Hainan Island. China's State Statistical Bureau estimates that 46 percent of all foreign investment went to Guangdong Province,[126] near Hong Kong. China may be facing some of the hazards that modern sectors or enclaves within a dual economy encountered during colonialism and the post-colonial period of the 1960s and 1970s, a lack of linkages to other enterprises within the domestic economy. Moreover, SEZs, despite their apparent emphasis on export processing, contributed little export surplus and sometimes net imports because of illegal domestic transactions and widespread official exemptions to the restrictions of sales to export markets.[127]

Lessons from the Russian, Polish, and Chinese Transitions to the Market

Many third-world countries of Africa, Asia, and Latin America can learn from Russia's, Poland's, and China's efforts at liberalization and adjustment. Russia's state socialism, more developed and deep-seated than Poland's and China's, required more substantial institutional change for successful transition to the market. As Alec Nove, a student of socialist economies, put it, "To change everything at once is impossible, but partial change creates contradictions and inconsistencies."[128]

Russia's legacies of consumer-goods neglect, gigantimania and industrial concentration, resistance to technological innovation, shoddy quality, quota disincentives, and information concealment were more institutionalized than Poland's. For example, Poland had less industrial concentration, had made some progress in the 1980s toward privatization, and provided more competition to state-owned monopolies after reform than Russia. Other difficulties Russia encountered in its reform were lack of incentives, false signals from prices, nonprice capital allocation, monopoly pricing after price decontrol, a soft budget constraint for enterprises, a torn "safety net" for workers and the elderly, opposition to or capture of liberalization benefits by vested bureaucratic interests, neglect of institutional and legal changes essential to expedite a market economy, and severed trade links. Poland moved toward demonopolization before or concurrently with price con-

---

[126]Dwight Perkins, "Completing China's Move to the Market," *Journal of Economic Perspectives* 8 (Spring 1994): 34.

[127]George T. Crane, "Reform and Retrenchment in China's Special Economic Zone," in Joint Economic Committee, Congress of the United States (Paul S. Sarbanes, Chair), *China's Economic Dilemmas in the 1990s: The Problems of Reforms, Modernization, and Interdependence* (Armonk, N.Y.: M.E. Sharpe, 1991), pp. 841–57; and Erin Endean, "China's Foreign Commercial Relations," in Joint Economic Committee, Congress of the United States (Paul S. Sarbanes, Chair), *China's Economic Dilemmas in the 1990s: The Problems of Reforms, Modernization, and Interdependence* (Armonk, N.Y.: M.E. Sharpe, 1991), pp. 741–69.

[128]Alec Nove, *The Economics of Feasible Socialism* (London: George Unwin, 1983), p. 168.

trol, began organizing a capital and labor market, had less politicized lending to inefficient or failing firms, and provided more support to the economic welfare of the poor than Russia. While both countries encountered opposition from the bureaucracy, resistance in Poland was less substantial, perhaps because the material levels of living of wage earners did not decline as substantially as in Russia.

John Ross provides several rules for liberalization policy, based on the experiences of China, Russia, and Eastern Europe. First, decontrol prices, marketize, and privatize where you have competitive sectors, such as China's agricultural sector. Second, maintain controlled prices where you have monopolistic and oligopolistic sectors, as in China's industrial sector. Russia made the mistake of decontrolling prices, marketizing, and privatizing industrial products, thus increasing these prices for consumers and the competitive sectors. Russia's industrial firms reduced output and raised prices to maximize profits. Third, only decontrol industrial prices when you can provide international competition, as in the case of Poland's industry, or when government can break up existing enterprises or provide enough domestic competition so that firms will not restrict output. In Russia's case, the instability of the rouble hampered export expansion so that foreign exchange was not adequate to import from foreigners who might compete with domestic enterprise. Fourth, unlike Russia (and to a lesser extent China) in the early 1990s, use monetary and fiscal policies to set an interest rate to ration credit and to dampen inflation. Fifth, as in Poland in 1989, liberalize foreign exchange rates by ceasing to interfere in the market. However, you may need to restrict imports as their pent-up demand could create a balance of payments problem. Sixth, provide a safety net for the poor and unemployed to reduce the resistance of the population opposed to reform.[129] In the early 1990s, Poland and China had limited success, and Russia virtually no success, in achieving the sixth rule.

In agriculture, China decollectivized much more successfully than Russia, which stifled private initiative and marketization. In industry, China encountered many of the same stubborn interests opposing liberalization as Russia did. While China has suffered from its share of corruption, it has resisted the asset stripping and favorable buy-outs of state industrial enterprises for apparatchiks under the guise of privatization that Russia has faced. Still, China's path toward reform by "touching stones while walking across a river" could be imperiled by instability during the late 1990s or early decade of the twenty-first century. Third-world countries should not follow the path of Russia or China to reform, although these countries can learn lessons from Russia and China. Each developing country needs to find its own path toward adjustment and development.

Terms to Review

- adjustment
- balance of payments equilibrium
- conditionality
- internal balance
- external balance
- expenditure-reducing policies
- expenditure switching policies
- structuralists
- adjustment with a human face
- theory of the second best

---

[129]John Ross, "Economic Reform: Success in China and Failure in Eastern Europe," *Monthly Review* 46 (May 1994): 19–28.

- public goods
- quasi-public goods
- state-owned enterprises (SOEs)
- public enterprises
- parastatals
- privatization
- European Bank for Reconstruction and Development (EBRD)
- "shock therapy"
- net material product (NMP)
- material balance planning
- nomenklatura system

- Gosplan
- Gosagroprom
- Gossnab
- economic rents
- soft budget constraint
- creative destruction
- China's Cultural Revolution
- individual economy
- China's industrial reforms
- management responsibility system
- special economic zones (SEZs)

Questions to Discuss

1. Indicate and discuss the major World Bank and International Monetary Fund programs for ameliorating LDC external equilibria and debt problems. Analyze the effectiveness of World Bank and IMF approaches to the LDC external crisis. What changed roles, if any, would you recommend for the World Bank and IMF in attaining LDC adjustment and reducing the LDC debt crisis?

2. Discuss and evaluate the views of the critics of World Bank and IMF approaches to LDC adjustment.

3. Discuss the optimal sequence of adjustment and reforms by LDCs facing external crises. Is this sequence consistent with orthodox strategies advocated by the World Bank and International Monetary Fund?

4. Discuss the concepts of internal and external balances, and the adjustments LDCs should make to attain both balances.

5. Under what conditions, if any, would you advise LDCs to expand the share of their state-owned sector? Under what conditions, if any, would you advise LDCs to reduce SOEs?

6. Compare the performance of private and public sectors in LDCs.

7. Should the state use public enterprises to redistribute income?

8. What can LDCs do to improve the performance of their private sector?

9. What is privatization? How successful have attempts at privatization in LDCs been? What are some of the pitfalls of privatization?

10. Assess the efficacy of MNC–SOE joint ventures in LDCs.

11. Should LDCs put more emphasis on privatization or socialization, or should they continue the status quo?

12. What were the main reasons for the collapse of state socialism in the Soviet Union?

13. Barthlomiej Kaminski indicates that state socialism is nonreformable. Evaluate this contention.

14. Evaluate the effectiveness of the "shock therapy"/"big bang" approach and the alternative approach.

15. Jeffrey Sachs contends: "I blame Russia's problems on communist ineptitude and corruption, the utter degradation of the old administrative structure, and the thoughtless reaction of the West to the growing financial plight of the republics." Discuss and evaluate this view.

16. Economist Thomas E. Weisskopf states: "The outlook for revitalization of Russia's economy is bleak. Only an alternative to shock therapy can assure that the Russian economy will be successfully restructured and revitalized. . . . It would . . . require a much larger role for government in shaping the social and economic environment than radical free marketeers are willing to contemplate. Such an alternative approach would be more likely to obtain democratic support than shock therapy and therefore the Russian government would be more likely to implement it successfully." Discuss and evaluate this view.

17. Discuss China's urban reform, agricultural reform, and other reforms after 1978–79, including some of the problems associated with the reforms and the impact that the reforms had on economic performance.

18. Do you agree with economists who argue that Chinese economic strategies are characterized by continuity and evolution, not abrupt change, especially when compared to those in Russia and other former communist countries undertaking reforms in the 1990s?

19. Discuss the problems China has had with the reform of its SOEs.

Guide to Readings

World Bank (1988) (note 15), FAO (note 22), Mosley, Harrigan, and Toye (note 23), Cornia, Jolly, and Stewart (note 9), Commander, ed. (note 17), Adedeji, Rasheed, and Morrison, eds. (note 20), Economic Commission for Africa (note 12), Weeks, ed. (note 5), Nafziger (note 13); Lance Taylor, ed., *The Rocky Road to Reform: Adjustment, Income Distribution, and Growth in the Developing World* (Cambridge, Mass.: MIT Press, 1993); Tariq Banuri, *Economic Liberalization: No Panacea* (Oxford: Clarendon Press, 1991); Rudiger Dornbusch, *Stabilization, Debt, and Reform: Policy Analysis for Developing Countries* (Englewood Cliffs, NJ: Prentice Hall, 1993); Howard Stein, ed., *Asian Industrialization and Africa: Studies in Policy Alternatives to Structural Adjustment* (New York: St. Martin's Press, 1995); and Williamson (1994, note 34, second citation, Chapter 5) analyze adjustment, stabilization, and reform in LDCs. Susan George and Fabrizio Sabelli, *Faith and Credit: The World Bank's Secular Empire* (Boulder, CO: Westview, 1994) provide a history and critique of the World Bank, including its role in structural and sectoral adjustment lending. John Weiss, *Industry, Policy, and Evidence* (London: Croom Helm, 1988), examines the neoclassical, structuralist, and radical approaches to economic adjustment. On fiscal policies for adjusting countries, see Vito Tanzi, ed., Fiscal Policy in Open Developing Countries (Washington, D.C.: International Monetary Fund, 1990); and Vito Tanzi, ed., *Transition to Market: Studies in Fiscal Reform* (Washington, D.C.: International Monetary Fund, 1993). On the issue of economic liberalization, see Ronald I. McKinnon, *The Order of Economic Liberalization: Financial Control in the Transition to a Market Economy* (Baltimore: Johns Hopkins University Press, 1993); and Dwight H. Perkins and Michael Roemer, *Reforming Economic Systems in Developing Countries* (Cambridge, Mass.: Harvard University Press, 1991).

An entertaining book, Robert E. Klitgaard, *Tropical Gangsters* (New York: Basic Books, 1990), tells a tale of corruption among locals and indifference among foreign experts in efforts at structural adjustment in Equatorial Guinea.

Heller and Tait (note 35), the World Bank (note 34), and Gillis, Perkins, Roemer, and Snodgrass (note 33) discuss state-owned enterprises. Ayub and Hegsted (note 45), Kohli and Sood (note 46), and Park (note 43) examine the determinants of public enterprise performance.

Cook and Kirkpatrick's contributors (note 36), especially Millward (note 36), have excellent analyses of the issue of privatization. Raymond Vernon, ed., *The Promise of Privatization: a Challenge for American Foreign Policy* (New York: Council on Foreign Relations, 1988), has useful case studies on privatization.

Sources on the former Soviet Union include Ellman and Kontorovich (note 70), Angresano (note 70), and Paul R. Gregory and Robert C. Stuart, *Soviet and Post-Soviet Economic Structure and Performance* (New York: HarperCollins, 1994).

The International Monetary Fund, *World Economic Outlook* (biannual) and periodic country studies; the *Economist* (weekly); *The Economies of Transition, New Policy Studies*, and *Communist Economies and Economic Transformation* (quarterly), provide up-to-date information on Eastern Europe and the former Soviet Union. Other sources on Eastern Europe and the former Soviet Union include Blanchard et al. (note 66), Admiraal (note 98), Clague and Rausser (note 73), Anders Aslund, ed., *Economic Transformation in Russia* (New York: St. Martin's Press, 1994), and Anders Aslund, ed., *Russian Economic Reform at Risk* (London: Pinter, 1995). Kennett and Lieberman (note 63), Sachs (note 59) and Kaminski (note 65) are excellent sources on Poland. On transitional economies generally, see Kornai (notes 90 and 91); Chung H. Lee and Helmut Reisen, eds., *From Reform to Growth: China and Other Countries in Transition in Asia and Central and Eastern Europe* (Paris: Organization for Economic Cooperation and Development, 1994).

Joint Economic Committee, Congress of the United States (note 103); Lichtenstein (note 103); Wang (note 103); Putterman (note 102); Fewsmith (note 104); Barnett and Clough, and Perkins (note 110); Perkins (note 125); Jefferson and Rawski (note 123); Lippit (note 114); Tidrick and Chen (note 116), Lee (note 117); Peter N. S. Lee, *Industrial Management and Economic Reform in China, 1949–1984* (New York: Oxford University Press, 1987); Robert F. Dernberger, "Reforms in China: Implications for U. S. Policy," *American Economic Review* 79 (May 1989), 21–25; Shahid Yusuf, "China's Macroeconomic Performance and Management During Transition," *Journal of Economic Perspectives* 8 (Spring 1994): 71–92; and Carl Riskin, *China's Political Economy: the Quest for Development since 1949* (Oxford: Oxford University Press, 1987) are sources to consult on China's political economy. China periodicals in English include *China Quarterly, China Business Review*, the online *China News Digest* (note 92), and the official *Beijing Review*.

Peter Nolan, *China's Rise, Russia's Fall: Politics, Economics and Planning in the Transition from Stalinism* (New York: St. Martin's, 1995), discusses the reasons for the success of China's economic reforms since 1978 and for the failure of Russia's economic reforms under Gorbachev (1985–1991) and after the collapse of the Soviet Union. Nolan has two explanations for the superior growth performance of China: (1) its pursuit of economic reforms while avoiding political liberalization (similar to other East Asian fast-growing economies) and (2) China's step-by-step approach to economic reform, rejecting "shock therapy," especially as practiced by the International Monetary Fund and World Bank. Nolan shows how Russia's efforts at *glasnost* (openness) and democratization destroyed the old state apparatus while failing to construct an effective successor state, thus engendering an economic collapse. The author does, however, slight discussions of the banking system's contribution to inflation, the implications of Russia's comparative disadvantage in industry at world market prices, and reasons for the success of "shock therapy" in Poland.

Marshall I. Goldman, "Why Is the Mafia So Dominant in Russia?" *Challenge* (January–February 1996): pp. 20–47, estimates that the Russian Mafia, which controls 70 to 80 percent of all private business and banking, grew rapidly because of the enormous disparities between state controls and market pressures during Gorbachev's restrictions on entry to the private sector, and the abrupt collapse of the plan, the ministries, and other parts of the economic infrastructure without replacement with a consistent tax system and other market-type institutions. Moreover, because the Mafia has a strong interest in maintaining disequilibrium, it obstructs reform, maintains monopolies, and restrains markets (for example, refusing to allow newly privatized farmers access to farmers' markets). Goldman's solution is to cease requiring formal approval for new sellers and businesses, thus widening economic competition so that the Mafia will no longer be able to control outlets.

Dani Rodrik analyzes "Understanding Economic Policy Reform," in *Journal of Economic Literature* 34 (March 1996): 9–41.

Name and Author Index

Subject Index

Highlighted terms are defined or identified on pages designated in boldface.